GLENCOE

LITERATURE

The Reader's Choice

Teacher's Wraparound Edition

GLENCOE LITERATURE

The Reader's Choice

Program Consultants

Beverly Ann Chin

Denny Wolfe

Jeffrey Copeland

Mary Ann Dudzinski

William Ray

Jacqueline Jones Royster

Jeffrey Wilhelm

Course 2

Glencoe
McGraw-Hill

New York, New York   Columbus, Ohio   Woodland Hills, California   Peoria, Illinois

Acknowledgments

Grateful acknowledgment is given authors, publishers, photographers, museums, and agents for permission to reprint the following copyrighted material. Every effort has been made to determine copyright owners. In case of any omissions, the Publisher will be pleased to make suitable acknowledgments in future editions.

Acknowledgments continued on page R134.

THE PRINCETON REVIEW

The Standardized Test Practice pages in this book were written by The Princeton Review, the nation's leader in test preparation. Through its association with McGraw-Hill, The Princeton Review offers the best way to help students excel on standardized assessments.

The Princeton Review is not affiliated with Princeton University or Educational Testing Service.

Glencoe/McGraw-Hill

A Division of The McGraw·Hill Companies

Printed in the United States of America

Send all inquiries to:
Glencoe/McGraw-Hill
936 Eastwind Drive
Westerville, OH 43081

ISBN 0-02-635378-4
(Student Edition)

ISBN 0-02-635379-2
(Teacher's Wraparound Edition)

1 2 3 4 5 6 7 8 9 10 027/043 04 03 02 01 00 99

Book Overview

Table of Contents T8

To the Teacher

Student Edition Overview T28
Teacher's Wraparound Edition Overview T38
Theme Planning Guide Overview T44
Program Resources T48
Scope and Sequence Overview T52
Program Philosophy T56
Professional Articles T58

Student Edition

THEME ❧ ONE: What I Am, What I Want to Be 1

THEME ❧ TWO: Winds of Change 112

THEME ❧ THREE: Facing Challenge 216

THEME ❧ FOUR: Where the Heart Is 324

THEME ❧ FIVE: At the Crossroads 428

THEME ❧ SIX: Twists and Turns 538

THEME ❧ SEVEN: A Different Dimension 652

THEME ❧ EIGHT: A Delicate Balance 768

Reference Section

Literary Terms Handbook R1
Language Handbook R12
Writing Handbook R48
Communications Skills Handbook R60
Reading Handbook R70
Glossary R102
Spanish Glossary R111
Index of Skills R120
Index of Authors and Titles R129
Index of Art and Artists R132
Acknowledgments R134

Senior Program Consultants

Beverly Ann Chin is Professor of English, Co-Director of the English Teaching Program, former Director of the Montana Writing Project, and former Director of Composition at the University of Montana in Missoula. In 1995–1996, Dr. Chin served as President of the National Council of Teachers of English. She currently serves as a Member of the Board of Directors of the National Board for Professional Teaching Standards. Dr. Chin is a nationally recognized leader in English language arts standards, curriculum, and assessment. Formerly a high school English teacher and adult education reading teacher, Dr. Chin has taught in English language arts education at several universities and has received awards for her teaching and service.

Denny Wolfe, a former high school English teacher and department chair, is Professor of English Education, Director of the Tidewater Virginia Writing Project, and Director of the Center for Urban Education at Old Dominion University in Norfolk, Virginia. For the National Council of Teachers of English, he has served as Chairperson of the Standing Committee on Teacher Preparation, President of the International Assembly, member of the Executive Committee of the Council on English Education, and editor of the SLATE Newsletter. Author of more than seventy-five articles and books on teaching English, Dr. Wolfe is a frequent consultant to schools and colleges on the teaching of English language arts.

Program Consultants

Jeffrey S. Copeland is Professor and Head of the Department of English Language and Literature at the University of Northern Iowa, where he teaches children's and young adult literature courses and a variety of courses in English education. A former public school teacher, he has published many articles in the professional journals in the language arts. The twelve books he has written or edited include *Speaking of Poets: Interviews with Poets Who Write for Children and Young Adults* and *Young Adult Literature: A Contemporary Reader.*

Mary Ann Dudzinski is a former high school English teacher and recipient of the Ross Perot Award for Teaching Excellence. She also has served as a member of the core faculty for the National Endowments for the Humanities Summer Institute for Teachers of Secondary School English and History at the University of North Texas. After fifteen years of classroom experience in grades 9–12, she currently is a language arts consultant.

William Ray has taught English in the Boston Public Schools; at Lowell University; University of Wroclaw, Poland; and, for the last fourteen years, at Lincoln-Sudbury Regional High School in Sudbury, Massachusetts. He specializes in world literature. He has worked on a variety of educational texts, as editor, consultant, and contributing writer.

Jacqueline Jones Royster is Associate Professor of English at The Ohio State University. She is also on the faculty of the Bread Loaf School of English at Middlebury College in Middlebury, Vermont. In addition to the teaching of writing, Dr. Royster's professional interests include the rhetorical history of African American women and the social and cultural implications of literate practices.

Jeffrey Wilhelm, a former English and reading teacher, is currently an assistant professor at the University of Maine where he teaches courses in middle and secondary level literacy. Author of several books and articles on the teaching of reading and the use of technology, he also works with local schools as part of the fledgling Adolescent Literacy Project and is the director of two annual summer institutes: the Maine Writing Project and Technology as a Learning Tool.

Teacher Reviewers

Bill Beyer
General Wayne Middle School
Malvern, Pennsylvania

Sister Marian Christi
St. Matthew School
Philadelphia, Pennsylvania

Christine Ferguson
North Buncombe Middle School
Asheville, North Carolina

Elizabeth Fischer
Tower Heights Middle School
Centerville, Ohio

Diane Gerrety
Bridgetown Junior High
Cincinnati, Ohio

Susan Giddings
Marble Falls Middle School
Marble Falls, Texas

Denise Goeckel
Magsig Middle School
Centerville, Ohio

Debbie Hampton
Central Davidson Middle School
Lexington, North Carolina

Tammy Harris
Walnut Springs Middle School
Columbus, Ohio

Marlene Henry
Northwood Elementary
Troy, Ohio

Brian Hinders
Tower Heights Middle School
Centerville, Ohio

Cheryl Keffer
Fayette County Schools Gifted
Program
Oak Hill, West Virginia

Sheryl Kelso
Oldtown School
Oldtown, Maryland

Gail Kidd
Center Middle School
Azusa, California

Karen Mantia
Northmont City Schools
Clayton, Ohio

Nancy Mast
Hobart Middle School
Hobart, Indiana

Chiyo Masuda
Albany Middle School
Albany, California

Kim Mistler
Delhi Junior High School
Cincinnati, Ohio

Wilma Jean Nix
Baldwin Junior High School
Montgomery, Alabama

Joe Olague
Alder Junior High
Fontana, California

Bonita Rephann
Musselman Middle School
Bunker Hill, West Virginia

Marie Rinaudo
St. John Berchman's Cathedral
School
Shreveport, Louisiana

Carol Schowalter
El Roble Intermediate School
Claremont, California

Joan Slater
Strack Intermediate
Klein, Texas

Joyce Stakem
St. Catherine of Siena School
Wilmington, Delaware

Elizabeth Struckman
Bridgetown Junior High School
Centerville, Ohio

Debbie Trepanier
Jenkins Middle School
Chewelah, Washington

Sarah Vick
Central Davidson Middle School
Lexington, North Carolina

Erin Watts
Albright Middle School
Houston, Texas

Anne Welch
Huntsville Middle School
Huntsville, Alabama

James Zartler
Centennial Middle School
Portland, Oregon

Contents

THEME ❦ ONE

THEME ONE AT A GLANCE 1A–1D
THEME ONE SKILLS SCOPE AND SEQUENCE 1E–1F
THEME ONE RESOURCE MANAGER 1G–1H

What I Am, What I Want to Be 1

Julia Alvarez	**Names / Nombres**	Autobiography	5

Grammar Link Avoiding Sentence Fragments 12

James Berry	🌐 **One**	Poem	14
Emily Dickinson	**I'm Nobody! Who are you?**	Poem	15
Janet S. Wong	**Face It**	Poem	19
Arnold Adoff	**Almost Ready**	Poem	20

Writing Skills Using Dialogue in a Narrative 23

Erma Bombeck	**Media Connection** **Heroes**	Newspaper column	24
Benedict Cosgrove	**Strong Men Weep**	Essay	26
Doris Kearns Goodwin	*from* **Wait Till Next Year**	Memoir	35

Comparing Selections: Strong Men Weep *and*
from Wait Till Next Year 40

Neal Marlens and Carol Black	**Media Connection** *from* **The Wonder Years**	Television script	41
Gary Soto	**Broken Chain**	Short story	44

Technology Skills Word Processing: Desktop Publishing 56

Alice Walker	**Without Commercials**	Poem	59

🌐 *indicates world literature*

Genre Focus **Autobiography** 62

Active Reading Strategies **Autobiography** 64

Ernesto Galarza   Active Reading Model: *from* **Barrio Boy**. . . . . Autobiography 67

Vocabulary Skills Base Words 75

Amy Tan   **Fish Cheeks** . . . . Autobiography 77

Interdisciplinary Connection Social Studies:
    Food with Attitude 82

Reading and Thinking Skills Sequencing 83

Rosa Parks with
Jim Haskins   *from* **Rosa Parks: My Story** . . . . Autobiography 85

Writing Workshop Narrative Writing:
    Autobiographical Anecdote 104

Theme Wrap-Up 108

Standardized Test Practice 110

THEME ✿ TWO

THEME TWO AT A GLANCE 111A–111D

THEME TWO SKILLS SCOPE AND SEQUENCE 111E–111F

THEME TWO RESOURCE MANAGER 111G–111H

Winds of Change

. 112

Cherylene Lee   **Hollywood and the Pits** . . . . Short story 117

Interdisciplinary Connection Science: Radiocarbon Dating 130

Raymond Bloodworth,
Chris Welch, and
Billy Meshel   **Media Connection** **Time to Change** . . . . Song 131

CONTENTS

Jean Little   **Growing Pains** . . . . Poem 133

Steve Wulf   **Media Connection** *from* **The N.B.A.'s Sister Act** . . . . Magazine article 136

Yusef Komunyakaa   **Slam, Dunk, and Hook** . . . . Poem 138

Reading and Thinking Skills   Identifying Main Idea and
Supporting Details 142

Vocabulary Skills   Context Clues 143

Genre Focus   Short Story 144

Active Reading Strategies   Short Stories 146

Cynthia Rylant   **Active Reading Model:**   **A Crush** . . . . Short story 149

Technology Skills   Spreadsheets: Creating a Spreadsheet 160

Paul Annixter   **Last Cover** . . . . Short story 163

Jane Yolen   **Birthday Box** . . . . Short story 175

Mary TallMountain   **There Is No Word for Goodbye** . . . . Poem 179

Grammar Link   Using Adjectives and Adverbs Correctly 182

Writing Skills   Organizing Ideas for
Comparison and Contrast 183

Washington Irving   **Rip Van Winkle** . . . . Short story 185

E. E. Cummings   **old age sticks** . . . . Poem 205

Comparing Selections: Rip Van Winkle *and* old age sticks 207

Writing Workshop   Expository Writing:
Compare-and-Contrast Essay 208

Theme Wrap-Up 212

Standardized Test Practice 214

THEME ❧ THREE

THEME THREE AT A GLANCE 215A–215D

THEME THREE SKILLS SCOPE AND SEQUENCE 215E–215F

THEME THREE RESOURCE MANAGER 215G–215H

Facing Challenge

.................216

Maya Angelou	**New Directions**	Short story	.221
	Vocabulary Skills Using Homophones		.225
Henry Wadsworth Longfellow	**The Wreck of the Hesperus**	Poem	.227
Margaret Danner	**I'll Walk the Tightrope**	Poem	.231
Dorothy M. Johnson	**Too Soon a Woman**	Short story	.235
Martha Brooks	🌐🌐 **A Boy and His Dog**	Short story	.243
	Comparing Selections: Too Soon a Woman and A Boy and His Dog		.249
	Reading and Thinking Skills Visualizing		.250
Lillian Morrison	**The Women's 400 Meters**	Poem	.252
Frank Horne	**To James**	Poem	.253
	Interdisciplinary Connection Math: Measurement Systems		.257
Nikki Giovanni	**a poem (for langston hughes)**	Poem	.259
Langston Hughes	**Dreams**	Poem	.261
	Technology Skills E-mail: On-line Safety		.264
	Media Connection **Why 'Possum Has a Large Mouth**	Web site	.266
Joseph Bruchac	**Racing the Great Bear**	Legend	.268
	Listening, Speaking, and Viewing Analyzing Persuasion		.279

CONTENTS

Stacy Allison with
Peter Carlin   *from* **Beyond the Limits** . . . . Autobiography. 281

      Genre Focus **Nonfiction** 290

      Active Reading Strategies **Nonfiction** 292

J. Madeleine Nash   Active Reading Model: **The Fish Crisis** . . . . Nonfiction 295

Seaway Ocean Update   Media Connection **Americans Continue to**
      Worry About the Decline of the Oceans . . . Public opinion poll . . .304

Patricia Lauber   **Hurricanes** . . . . Nonfiction 306

      Grammar Link   Subject-Verb Agreement 315

      Writing Workshop   Persuasive Writing: Editorial 316
      Theme Wrap-Up 320
      Standardized Test Practice 322

THEME ❦ FOUR

THEME FOUR AT A GLANCE 323A–323D
THEME FOUR SKILLS SCOPE AND SEQUENCE 323E–323F
THEME FOUR RESOURCE MANAGER 323G–323H

Where the Heart Is

. 324

Sandra Cisneros   **Bums in the Attic** . . . . Short story 329

      Interdisciplinary Connection   Technology: Architecture 332

Francisco X. Alarcón   **En un Barrio de Los Angeles /**
      In a Neighborhood in Los Angeles . . . . Poem 334

      Technology Skills   Internet: Judging On-line Information 338

CONTENTS

Edna St. Vincent Millay   **The Courage That My Mother Had** . . . . Poem 341

Langston Hughes   **Mother to Son** . . . . Poem 342

Paisley Dodds   **Media Connection Kids from Chicago's**
Cabrini Green Learn Urban Farming
in Arkansas . . . . Newspaper story 345

Borden Deal   **Antaeus** . . . . Short story 347

Gwendolyn Brooks   **Home** . . . . Short story 361

Lucille Clifton   **the 1st** . . . . Poem 363

Reading and Thinking Skills Making Connections 366

Nicholas Gage   **The Teacher Who Changed My Life** . . . . Personal narrative . . .368

Gregory Djanikian   **How I Learned English** . . . . Poem 377

Comparing Selections: The Teacher Who Changed
My Life *and* How I Learned English 380

Grammar Link Using Irregular Verbs Correctly 381

Yoshiko Uchida   **Oh Broom, Get to Work** . . . . Short story 383

Edna Mason Kaula   **Anansi and His Visitor, Turtle** . . . . Myth 388

Vocabulary Skills Roots 394

Writing Skills Describing with Sensory Details 395

Genre Focus Essay 396

Active Reading Strategies Essay 397

CONTENTS

James Thurber   **Active Reading Model:** **The Night the Bed Fell** .... Humorous essay 399

Charles Schultz   **Media Connection** **Peanuts** .... Comic strip 409

Merrill Markoe   **The Dog Diaries** .... Humorous essay 411

     Writing Workshop Observation and Description:
         A Photo in Words 420
     Theme Wrap-Up 424
     Standardized Test Practice 426

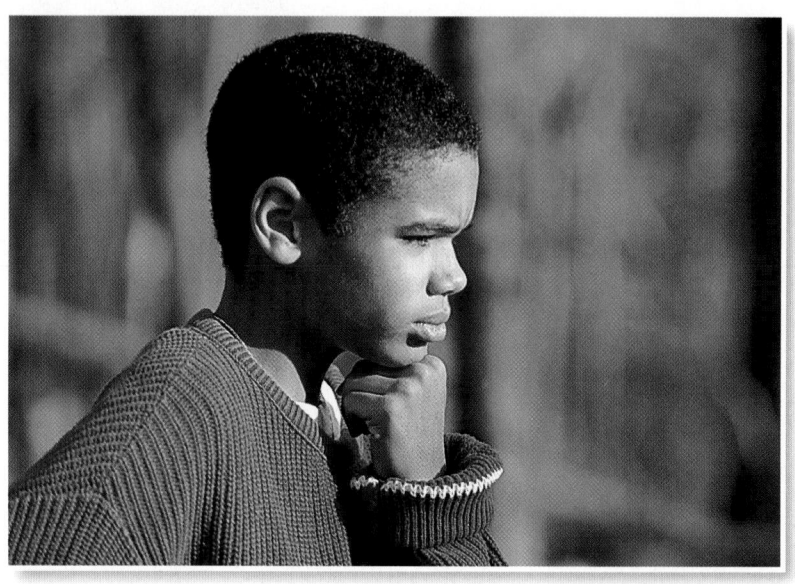

THEME ❧ FIVE

THEME FIVE AT A GLANCE 427A–427D

THEME FIVE SKILLS SCOPE AND SEQUENCE 427E–427F

THEME FIVE RESOURCE MANAGER 427G–427H

At the Crossroads
.... 428

Piri Thomas   **Amigo Brothers** .... Short story 433

Georgia Johnson   **Your World** .... Poem 445

     Comparing Selections: Amigo Brothers *and*
         Your World 447

     Interdisciplinary Connection Health: Physical Fitness 448

     Listening, Speaking, and Viewing Small-Group Discussions 449

Marta Salinas   **The Scholarship Jacket** .... Short story 451

     Media Connection **The Face of Venus** .... Web site 459

Ray Bradbury   **All Summer in a Day** .... Short story 461

Reading and Thinking Skills Drawing Conclusions 470

Carl Sandburg **Primer Lesson** . . . . Poem 472
Dorothy West **The Bird Like No Other** . . . . Short story 473

Technology Skills Becoming an Active Viewer 480

Pearl S. Buck **The Old Demon** . . . . Short story 483
Rudolfo A. Anaya **The Boy and His Grandfather** . . . . Folktale 495

Grammar Link Using Pronouns 499

Genre Focus Drama 500

Active Reading Strategies Drama 502

Rod Serling **Active Reading Model:** **The Monsters Are Due on**
Maple Street . . . . Teleplay 505

Media Connection **The Eye of the Beholder** . . . . Web site 528

Vocabulary Skills Idioms 529

Writing Workshop Expository Writing: Definition Essay 530
Theme Wrap-Up 534
Standardized Test Practice 536

CONTENTS

THEME 🐾 SIX

THEME SIX AT A GLANCE 537A–537D

THEME SIX SKILLS SCOPE AND SEQUENCE 537E–537F

THEME SIX RESOURCE MANAGER 537G–537H

Twists and Turns

Twists and Turns 538

Bill Watterson   **Media Connection**   **Calvin and Hobbes**. . . . . Comic strip 542

Shirley Jackson   **Charles** . . . . Short story 544

Connie Regan-Blake
and Barbara Freeman   **No News** . . . . Folktale 549

Grammar Link   Using Commas Correctly 553

Bud Abbott and
Lou Costello   **Who's on First?** . . . . Comedy script 555

Technology Skills   Multimedia: Using Hypertext 562

O. Henry   **After Twenty Years** . . . . Short story 565

Listening, Speaking, and Viewing   Storytelling 571

Mark Twain   **The Million-Pound Bank Note**. . . . . Drama 573

Rudolfo A. Anaya   **The Force of Luck**. . . . . Folktale 591

Comparing Selections: The Million-Pound Bank Note
and The Force of Luck 600

Interdisciplinary Connection   Social Studies: Money Matters 601

Roald Dahl   🌐🌐   **Beware of the Dog** . . . . Short story 603

Genre Focus   **Poetry** 616

Active Reading Strategies **Poetry** 618

Alfred Noyes   **Active Reading Model: The Highwayman** . . . . Poem 621

Edgar Allan Poe   **Annabel Lee** . . . . Poem 629

Vocabulary Skills Multiple-Meaning Words 633

Martha Louise Black   **Media Connection** *from* **My Ninety Years** . . . . Oral history 634

Robert Service   **The Cremation of Sam McGee** . . . . Poem 636

Reading and Thinking Skills Identifying Cause-and-Effect
Relationships 643

Writing Workshop Narrative Writing: Short Story 644

Theme Wrap-Up 648

Standardized Test Practice 650

THEME ❧ SEVEN

THEME SEVEN AT A GLANCE 651A–651D
THEME SEVEN SKILLS SCOPE AND SEQUENCE 651E–651F
THEME SEVEN RESOURCE MANAGER 651G–651H

A Different Dimension 652

Sarah Christie   **Media Connection Seizure-Alert Dog
Is Girl's Lifeline** . . . . Magazine article 656

Joan Aiken   **Lob's Girl** . . . . Short story 659

Reading and Thinking Skills Monitoring Comprehension 672

Writing Skills Using Sentence Variety 673

CONTENTS

Isaac Asimov   **Key Item** . . . . Short story 675

    Interdisciplinary Connection Communication:

      Communicating on the Net .681

Anne McCaffrey   **The Smallest Dragonboy** . . . . Short story 683

    Genre Focus Legends, Myths, and Folklore 698

    Active Reading Strategies Legends, Myths, and Folklore 699

Judith Ortiz Cofer   **Active Reading Model: Aunty Misery** . . . . Folktale 701

Gayle Ross   **Strawberries** . . . . Myth 707

    Grammar Link Capitalization 712

Rex Warner   **Atalanta's Race** . . . . Myth 714

Betty Miles   **Atalanta** . . . . Myth 718

Ed Young   **Cat and Rat: The Legend of**

    the Chinese Zodiac . . . . Legend 726

    Vocabulary Skills Analyzing Word Parts 735

Josephine Preston
Peabody   **Icarus and Daedalus** . . . . Myth 737

Bernard Evslin   **Prometheus** . . . . Myth 743

    Comparing Selections: Icarus and Daedalus *and* Prometheus 747

W. H. Auden   **Media Connection** **First Ballad Interlude from**

    Benjamin Britten's *Paul Bunyan* . . . . Opera libretto 748

Audrey Wood   **The Bunyans** . . . . Folktale 750

Julius Lester   **Brer Rabbit and Brer Lion** . . . . Folktale 755

    Writing Workshop Expository Writing: Book Review 760

    Theme Wrap-Up 764

    Standardized Test Practice 766

THEME ❧ EIGHT

THEME EIGHT AT A GLANCE 767A–767D

THEME EIGHT SKILLS SCOPE AND SEQUENCE 767E–767F

THEME EIGHT RESOURCE MANAGER 767G–767H

A Delicate Balance

A Delicate Balance 768

Lawrence Yep   **We Are All One** . . . . Folktale 773

Edie Scher   **Media Connection** *from* **See Robby Run** . . . . Journal 780

Vocabulary Skills Dictionary Skills: Pronunciation 781

Joseph Bruchac   **Birdfoot's Grampa** . . . . Poem 783

Walt Whitman   **Miracles** . . . . Poem 784

David Ansen   **Media Connection** **The Jungle Book** . . . . Movie review 787

Rudyard Kipling   **Rikki-tikki-tavi** . . . . Short story 789

Interdisciplinary Connection Science: Endangered Species 805

Leslie Marmon Silko   **Uncle Tony's Goat** . . . . Short story 807

Grammar Link Using Apostrophes to Show Possession 816

Listening, Speaking, and Viewing Critical Viewing 817

Wendy Rose   **Loo-Wit** . . . . Poem 819

Vachel Lindsay   **The Flower-Fed Buffaloes** . . . . Poem 823

Comparing Selections: Loo-Wit *and*
        The Flower-Fed Buffaloes 825

Bailey White   **Turkeys** . . . . Humorous essay 827

Reading and Thinking Skills Making Inferences 833

CONTENTS

Robert Frost **The Pasture** .... Poem .... .835

Genre Focus Short Forms of Poetry .... .838

Raymond Patterson **Glory, Glory** .... Haiku .... .841
Ann Atwood **Birds Circling at Dusk** .... Haiku .... .841
Matsuo Bashō **Bamboo Grove** .... Haiku .... .841
Myra Cohn Livingston **T-Shirt** .... Cinquain ..... .842
Anonymous **There Was a Young Fellow of Ealing** .... Limerick .... .842

Writing Workshop Expository Writing:
  Cause-and-Effect Essay .... .846
Theme Wrap-Up .... .850
Standardized Test Practice .... .852

Reference Section

Literary Terms Handbook R1

Language Handbook R12
Troubleshooter R12
Troublesome Words R22
Grammar Glossary R27
Mechanics R34
Spelling R44

Writing Handbook R48
The Writing Process R48
Writing Modes R52
Research Report Writing R54
Business Writing R58

Communications Skills Handbook R60
Using a Computer for Writing R60
Study and Test-Taking Skills R62
Listening, Speaking, and Viewing Skills ... R66

Reading Handbook R70

Glossary R102

Spanish Glossary R111

Index of Skills R120

Index of Authors and Titles R129

Index of Art and Artists R132

Acknowledgments R134

Features

MEDIA Connection

Newspaper column: Heroes. 24

Television script: *from* The Wonder Years 41

Song: Time to Change 131

Magazine article: *from* The N.B.A.'s
    Sister Act 136

Web site: Why 'Possum Has a
    Large Mouth 266

Public opinion poll: Americans Continue
    to Worry About the Decline of
    the Oceans 304

Newspaper story: Kids from Chicago's
    Cabrini Green Learn Urban Farming
    in Arkansas. 345

Comic strip: Peanuts 409

Web site: The Face of Venus 459

Web site: The Eye of the Beholder 528

Comic strip: Calvin and Hobbes 542

Oral history: *from* My Ninety Years 634

Magazine article: Seizure-Alert Dog Is
    Girl's Lifeline 656

Opera libretto: First Ballad Interlude from
    Benjamin Britten's *Paul Bunyan* 748

Journal: *from* See Robby Run 780

Movie review: The Jungle Book 787

COMPARING SELECTIONS

Strong Men Weep *and from* Wait Till
    Next Year 40

Rip Van Winkle *and* old age sticks 207

Too Soon a Woman *and* A Boy and
    His Dog 249

The Teacher Who Changed My Life *and*
    How I Learned English 380

Amigo Brothers *and* Your World 447

The Million-Pound Bank Note *and*
    The Force of Luck 600

Icarus and Daedalus *and* Prometheus 747

Loo-Wit *and* The Flower-Fed Buffaloes 825

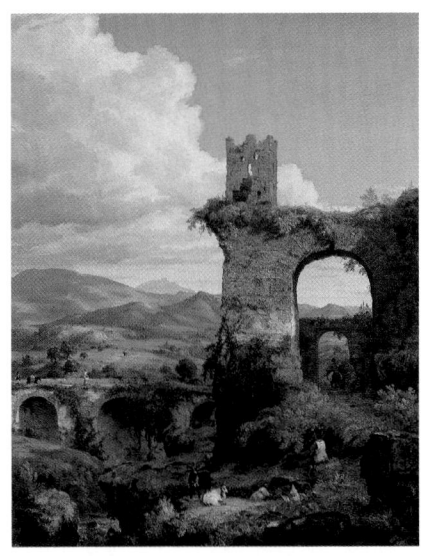

GENRE FOCUS

Autobiography 62

Short Story 144

Nonfiction 290

Essay 396

Drama 500

Poetry 616

Legends, Myths, and Folklore 698

Short Forms of Poetry 838

Active Reading Strategies

Autobiography 64

Short Stories. 146

Nonfiction 292

Essay 397

Drama. 502

Poetry 618

Legends, Myths, and Folklore 699

Interdisciplinary Connection

Social Studies: Food with Attitude 82

Science: Radiocarbon Dating 130

Math: Measurement Systems 257

Technology: Architecture 332

Health: Physical Fitness 448

Social Studies: Money Matters 601

Communication: Communicating on
     the Net 681

Science: Endangered Species 805

Writing WORKSHOP

Narrative Writing: Autobiographical
     Anecdote 104

Expository Writing:
     Compare-and-Contrast Essay. 208

Persuasive Writing: Editorial. 316

Observation and Description: A Photo
     in Words. 420

Expository Writing: Definition Essay. 530

Narrative Writing: Short Story 644

Expository Writing: Book Review 760

Expository Writing:
     Cause-and-Effect Essay. 846

Skills

Grammar Link

Avoiding Sentence Fragments 12

Using Adjectives and
    Adverbs Correctly 182

Subject-Verb Agreement. 315

Using Irregular Verbs Correctly. 381

Using Pronouns. 499

Using Commas Correctly 553

Capitalization 712

Using Apostrophes to Show Possession. . . . 816

Listening, Speaking, and Viewing

Analyzing Persuasion 279

Small-Group Discussions. 449

Storytelling. 571

Critical Viewing 817

Reading and Thinking Skills

Sequencing. 83

Identifying Main Idea and
    Supporting Details. 142

Visualizing. 250

Making Connections. 366

Drawing Conclusions. 470

Identifying Cause-and-Effect
    Relationships. 643

Monitoring Comprehension 672

Making Inferences. 833

Technology Skills

Word Processing: Desktop Publishing 56

Spreadsheets: Creating a Spreadsheet 160

E-mail: On-line Safety 264

Internet: Judging On-line Information. 338

Becoming an Active Viewer 480

Multimedia: Using Hypertext 562

Vocabulary Skills

Base Words. 75

Context Clues. 143

Using Homophones 225

Roots. 394

Idioms. 529

Multiple-Meaning Words. 633

Analyzing Word Parts 735

Dictionary Skills: Pronunciation. 781

Writing Skills

Using Dialogue in a Narrative 23

Organizing Ideas for Comparison and
    Contrast 183

Describing with Sensory Details 395

Using Sentence Variety. 673

Skill Minilessons

GRAMMAR AND LANGUAGE

Subject-Verb Agreement................55
Nouns...............................103
Italics..............................129
Vivid Verbs.........................141
Adverb Clauses......................159
Commas Used with Words in a Series.....173
Adverbs............................203
Ellipsis............................256
Possessive Pronouns.................278
Spelling Plurals....................314
Pronoun-Antecedent Agreement........331
Commas in Compound Sentences.......359
Suffixes and the Silent *e*.............393
Parentheses.........................408
Principal Parts of Verbs.............419
Using Adverbs and Adjectives.........458
Avoiding Double Negatives............469
Participles and Participial Phrases.......498
Apostrophes.........................527
Correct Pronoun Use.................552
Complex Sentences..................615
Colorful Adjectives..................627
Punctuating Poetry..................632
Apostrophes in Possessives...........671
Writing: Numbers...................697
Frequently Misspelled Words..........705
Spelling Compound Words............724
Apostrophes in Contractions..........734
Quotation Marks....................759
Sensory Language...................786
Personal Pronouns..................804
Consistent Verb Tenses..............815

Run-on Sentences....................832
Mechanics: Semicolon, Colon.........837
Prepositional Phrases................845

READING AND THINKING

Comparing and Contrasting.............17
Visualizing...........................22
Activating Prior Knowledge.............55
Cause and Effect.....................103
Cause and Effect.....................129
Sequence of Events..................135
Inference...........................159
Predicting..........................173
Evaluating..........................203
Identifying Spatial Relationships........233
Identifying Assumptions...............263
Setting a Reading Purpose.............278
Distinguishing Fact and Opinion.........314
Drawing Conclusions.................337
Visualizing.........................344
Stereotype.........................359
Problem/Solution...................393
Exaggeration.......................408
Author's Purpose...................419
Questioning/Clarifying...............458
Inference from Setting...............469
Summarizing.......................498
Visualizing.........................527
Drawing Conclusions.................552
Monitoring Comprehension...........615
Sequence of Events..................642
Scanning..........................671
Classifying.........................697

Generalizing 705

Sequence of Events 724

Using Graphic Aids 734

Paraphrasing 759

Evaluating 804

Problem/Solution 815

Elaborating 821

Cause and Effect 832

Spatial Relationships 845

VOCABULARY

Antonyms 11

Owning a Word 33

Synonyms 55

Compound Words 74

Analogies 81

Unlocking Meaning 103

Related Forms of Words 129

The Suffix -ly 159

Roots 173

Negative Prefixes 181

Synonyms and Antonyms 203

Analogies 224

Antonyms 241

Multiple-Meaning Words 278

Base Words and Suffixes 289

Suffixes 303

Prefixes That Express Number 314

Analogies: Levels of Intensity 359

Words Used in Unusual Ways 365

The Suffix -arian 375

Synonyms 393

Antonyms 408

Prefixes 419

Unlocking Meaning 443

The Prefix dis- 458

The Latin Roots vit and viv 469

Analogies: Defining Characteristics 479

The Prefix mal- 498

Base Words 527

The Prefix re- 552

Homonyms 561

The Suffix -ity 570

Etymology 589

Using Context Clues 615

Unlocking Meaning 671

Etymology 680

Synonyms: Shades of Meaning 697

Analogies 705

Synonyms: Thesaurus 711

Analogies 724

The Suffix -ful 734

Dictionary Skills: Definitions 741

Etymology 759

Synonyms 779

Dictionary Skills: Definitions 804

Unlocking Meaning 815

The Prefix de- 832

Compound Words 845

Selections by Genre

Short Story/Fiction

Broken Chain 44
Hollywood and the Pits 117
A Crush 149
Last Cover 163
Birthday Box 175
Rip Van Winkle 185
New Directions 221
Too Soon a Woman 235
A Boy and His Dog 243
Bums in the Attic 329
Antaeus 347
Home 361
Oh Broom, Get to Work 383
Amigo Brothers 433
The Scholarship Jacket 451
All Summer in a Day 461
The Bird Like No Other 473
The Old Demon 483
Charles 544
After Twenty Years 565
Beware of the Dog 603
Lob's Girl 659
Key Item 675
The Smallest Dragonboy 683
Rikki-tikki-tavi 789
Uncle Tony's Goat 807

Nonfiction

Names / Nombres 5
Heroes 24
Strong Men Weep 26
from Wait Till Next Year 35
from Barrio Boy 67
Fish Cheeks 77
from Rosa Parks: My Story 85

from The N.B.A.'s Sister Act 136
Beyond the Limits 281
The Fish Crisis 295
Americans Continue to Worry About the
    Decline of the Oceans 304
Hurricanes 306
Kids from Chicago's Cabrini Green Learn
    Urban Farming in Arkansas 345
The Teacher Who Changed My Life 368
The Night the Bed Fell 399
The Dog Diaries 411
from My Ninety Years 634
Seizure-Alert Dog Is Girl's Lifeline 656
from See Robby Run 780
The Jungle Book (movie review) 787
Turkeys 827

Poetry

One 14
I'm Nobody! Who are you? 15
Face It 19
Almost Ready 20
Without Commercials 59
Growing Pains 133
Slam, Dunk, and Hook 138
There Is No Word for Goodbye 179
old age sticks 205
The Wreck of the Hesperus 227
I'll Walk the Tightrope 231
The Women's 400 Meters 252
To James 253
a poem (for langston hughes) 259
Dreams 261
En un Barrio de Los Angeles /
    In a Neighborhood in Los Angeles 334
The Courage That My Mother Had 341
Mother to Son 342

the 1st. 363
How I Learned English 377
Your World 445
Primer Lesson 472
The Highwayman 621
Annabel Lee 629
The Cremation of Sam McGee. 636
Birdfoot's Grampa 783
Miracles. 784
Loo-Wit 819
The Flower-Fed Buffaloes 823
The Pasture. 835
Glory, Glory 841
Birds Circling at Dusk. 841
Bamboo Grove 841
T-Shirt 842
There Was a Young Fellow of Ealing. 842

Drama

from The Wonder Years. 41
The Monsters Are Due on Maple Street. . . 505
The Million-Pound Bank Note. 573

Myths, Legends, Folktales

Racing the Great Bear 268
Anansi and His Visitor, Turtle 388
The Boy and His Grandfather. 495
No News. 549
The Force of Luck. 591

Aunty Misery 701
Strawberries. 707
Atalanta's Race. 714
Atalanta 718
Cat and Rat: The Legend of the
    Chinese Zodiac. 726
Icarus and Daedalus 737
Prometheus. 743
The Bunyans. 750
Brer Rabbit and Brer Lion. 755
We Are All One 773

Electronic Media

Why 'Possum Has a Large Mouth 266
The Face of Venus. 459
The Eye of the Beholder 528

Song

Time to Change 131
First Ballad Interlude from Benjamin
    Britten's *Paul Bunyan*. 748

Comic Strip

Peanuts 409
Calvin and Hobbes 542

Comedy Script

Who's on First? 555

Book Overview

THE LITERATURE UNITS

The literature that makes up the heart of the Student Edition is organized into eight themes.
Each theme includes a wide variety of genres but also provides a focus on one particular genre.

What I Am, What I Want to Be

Girl at Mirror, 1954. Norman Rockwell. Printed by permission of the Norman Rockwell Family Trust. ©1954 the Norman Rockwell Family Trust.

66 *Only one of me and nobody can get a second one from a photocopy machine.* 99

—*James Berry, "One"*

THEME CONTENTS

Names/Nombres • autobiography by Julia Alvarez 5

One • poem by James Berry 14

I'm Nobody! Who are you? • poem by Emily Dickinson 15

Face It • poem by Janet S. Wong 19

Almost Ready • poem by Arnold Adoff 20

Strong Men Weep • essay by Benedict Cosgrove 26

from Wait Till Next Year • memoir by Doris Kearns Goodwin 35

Broken Chain • short story by Gary Soto 44

Without Commercials • poem by Alice Walker 59

GENRE FOCUS AUTOBIOGRAPHY

from Barrio Boy • autobiography by Ernesto Galarza . . . 67

Fish Cheeks • autobiography by Amy Tan 77

Rosa Parks: My Story • autobiography by Rosa Parks with Jim Haskins 85

Students explore the theme before reading the selections. Theme projects offer a wide range of learning experiences that span the whole theme.

Exploring the Theme

— What I Am, What I Want to Be —

How do other people see you? More importantly, how do you see yourself? In this theme, you will explore what makes you who you are and what it will take to become who you want to be. To begin, try one of the options below.

Starting Points

ONE AMONG MANY
What do you think makes each of these penguins stand out in a crowd?
• Write a short conversation between two of the penguins. Imagine they are introducing themselves.

YOU ARE THE ONLY YOU
You are the only you. Think about yourself for a minute, and get ready to sketch yourself in words.
• Draw a name tag. Write your name in the center of it. What are the first words that come to mind when you read your name? Around the name tag, list several words that describe what makes you unique. You may also wish to include photos or drawings on your name tag.

Theme Projects

As you read the selections in this theme, choose one of the projects below. Work on your own, with a partner, or in a group.

LEARNING FOR LIFE
Writing a Job Description
What do you dream of doing when you grow up? Do you think about being a dancer, or a veterinarian, or a designer of video games? Think about your dream job. Then write a description of your job.
1. When you have made your choice, do some library research to find out more about it. Talk to people in your community who have similar jobs. Take notes about their job descriptions.
2. Write your job description, and contribute it to a classroom Career Notebook. As you learn about other interesting careers, add new descriptions to the notebook.

MULTIMEDIA PROJECT
A Self-Portrait
Create a multimedia self-portrait.
1. Gather information about yourself. Create a summary of interesting facts about your life, perhaps using a visual format such as a time line or a graph to chart these highlights.
2. Gather photos or drawings of you and your family or friends. Try to include music, videos, and taped interviews to showcase your life.
3. Present your self-portrait to your class.

interNET CONNECTION

Check out the Web for more project ideas. Use your favorite search engine to find other job-related ideas or other topics related to the "What I Am, What I Want to Be" theme. Key words such as *jobs, employment,* and career fields like *medicine* and *aviation* can get you started.

CRITICAL LISTENING
Musical Notes
Your taste in music reflects who you are, as well as your interests.
1. Do you enjoy popular music, oldies, jazz, reggae, rap, or some other type of music? Bring in examples of different kinds of music you enjoy.
2. Talk to older family members about the kinds of music they listened to when they were your age. Research their favorite kinds of music, and bring examples, photographs, or articles about that music to class. You might even create a musical time line showing the kinds of music young people have enjoyed over time.
3. Plan a musical tour through history. Display your research and photographs. Using tapes or CDs, play examples of a wide variety of music. Invite another class or family members to your classroom to participate in your musical tour.

REFERENCE SECTION

This comprehensive set of handbooks provides a valuable resource for students. References throughout the textbook direct students to specific handbook pages for additional information and support.

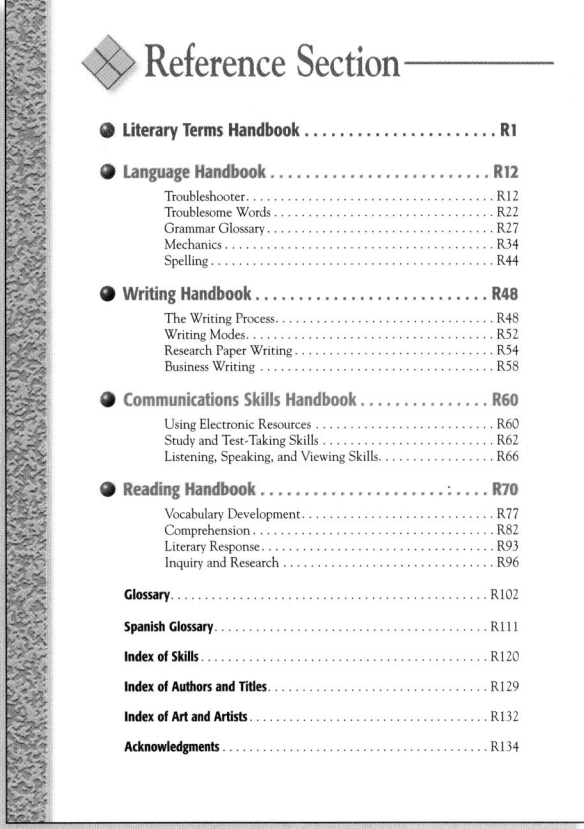

Reference Section

- **Literary Terms Handbook** **R1**
- **Language Handbook** **R12**
  - Troubleshooter R12
  - Troublesome Words R22
  - Grammar Glossary R27
  - Mechanics R34
  - Spelling R44
- **Writing Handbook** **R48**
  - The Writing Process...................... R48
  - Writing Modes........................... R52
  - Research Paper Writing R54
  - Business Writing R58
- **Communications Skills Handbook** **R60**
  - Using Electronic Resources R60
  - Study and Test-Taking Skills R62
  - Listening, Speaking, and Viewing Skills... R66
- **Reading Handbook** **R70**
  - Vocabulary Development.................. R77
  - Comprehension R82
  - Literary Response....................... R93
  - Inquiry and Research R96
- **Glossary**................................. R102
- **Spanish Glossary**......................... R111
- **Index of Skills** R120
- **Index of Authors and Titles**............... R129
- **Index of Art and Artists**.................. R132
- **Acknowledgments** R134

Literary Terms Handbook provides a glossary of all the literary terms taught with the selections in the book.

Language Handbook supplies ready reference and instructional support for grammar, usage, mechanics, and spelling.

Writing Handbook includes an overview of the writing process and the major writing modes as well as support for research paper writing.

Communications Skills Handbook addresses the use of electronic resources as well as study and test-taking skills.

Reading Handbook provides instructional support and models for a comprehensive set of reading strategies and skills.

Selection Plan

Each selection in the program is presented in a three-part format:
(1) Before You Read, (2) the selection pages, and (3) Responding to Literature.

BEFORE YOU READ

This section prepares students for reading by helping them draw upon their personal experience, build background knowledge, and set a purpose for reading.

Meet the Author motivates students to read the selection by presenting high-interest author information and quotations in an inviting format.

Background presents nuggets of relevant background information to pique students' interest and enhance their understanding of the selection.

Vocabulary Preview introduces key vocabulary that students will encounter in reading the selection.

Focus Activity creates a bridge into the selection by connecting the students' own experience to an important theme or aspect of the selection. Activities include quickwrites, journal entries, making graphic organizers, and group or whole class discussions.

Before You Read
Rip Van Winkle

MEET WASHINGTON IRVING

Washington Irving was the first American writer to win international fame. *The Sketch Book* (1820), a collection of stories admired throughout Europe, included Irving's two most famous tales, "Rip Van Winkle," and "The Legend of Sleepy Hollow." Like his famous fictional character Rip Van Winkle, Washington Irving was a born wanderer. Even as a child, he later wrote, "I began my travels, and made many tours into foreign parts and unknown regions of my native city, to the frequent alarm of my parents."

Washington Irving was born in New York City in 1783 and died in 1859.

FOCUS ACTIVITY

How has the world changed since you were born? What about since your parents were born?

Think/Pair/Share
Take a moment to jot down your responses to the questions above. Then share your thoughts and feelings with a partner.

Setting a Purpose
Read this selection for the pleasure of discovering a story that readers have enjoyed for almost two hundred years.

BACKGROUND

The Time and Place
The setting is the Hudson River valley and the Catskill Mountains, in southeastern New York State. The story takes place in the eighteenth century.

VOCABULARY PREVIEW

impunity (im pū′ nə tē) *n.* freedom from punishment, harm, or bad effects; p. 187
perseverance (pur′ sə vēr′ əns) *n.* continuation despite difficulty; determination; p. 187
incessantly (in ses′ ant lē) *adv.* endlessly; constantly; p. 188
muse (mūz) *v.* to think or reflect; p. 190
singularity (sing′ gyə lar′ ə tē) *n.* that which is remarkable or out of the ordinary; unusualness; p. 191
incomprehensible (in′ kom prē hen′ sə bəl) *adj.* not understandable; p. 191
perplexity (pər plek′ sə tē) *n.* doubt or uncertainty; puzzlement; p. 194
invariably (in vār′ ē ə blē) *adv.* without exception; p. 194
faltering (fôl′ tər ing) *adj.* shaky because of uncertainty; p. 199

184 ❧ THEME 2

SELECTION PAGES

The engaging design of the selection pages incorporates dynamic photography and fine art within a clean layout that promotes readability. A variety of carefully designed elements support and engage students as they read.

Before You Read
Rip Van Winkle

MEET WASHINGTON IRVING

FOCUS ACTIVITY

How has the world changed since you were born? What about since your parents were born?

Think/Pair/Share
Take a moment to jot down your responses to the questions above. Then share your thoughts and feelings with a partner.

Setting a Purpose
Read this selection for the pleasure of discovering a story that readers have enjoyed for almost two hundred years.

184

RIP VAN WINKLE

Whoever has made a voyage up the Hudson must remember the Kaatskill Mountains. They are a dismembered branch of the great Appalachian family, and are seen away to the west of the river, swelling up to a noble height, and lording it over the surrounding country. Every change of season, every change of weather, indeed, every hour of the day, produces some change in the magical hues and shapes of these mountains, and they are regarded by all the good wives, far and near, as perfect barometers. When the weather is fair and settled, they are clothed in blue and purple, and print their bold outlines on the clear evening sky; but sometimes, when the cloudless, they will vapors about their light up like a crown

At the foot of the voyager may have smoke curling up fro shingled roofs gleam just where the blue melt away into the nearer landscape. It great antiquity, havi some of the Dutch c times of the provinc beginning of the gov Peter Stuyvesant³ (n and there were some

original settlers standing within a few years, built of small yellow bricks brought from Holland, having latticed windows and gable fronts, surmounted with weathercocks.

In that same village and in one of these very houses (which, to tell the precise truth, was sadly timeworn and weather-

Did You Know?
A *latticed* (lat' ist) window has small panes separated by crossed strips of wood or metal. A gable is the triangular section of wall between the sides of a sloping roof.

1. The Hudson is a river in New spelled *Catskill*) Mountains a mountain range.
2. *Descried* means "caught sight
3. *Peter Stuyvesant* (stī' va sant) Dutch colony of New Netherl are now Connecticut, Delawar The narrator is poking fun at with the colonists.

186 THEME 2

Termagant Wife, 1921. N. C. Wyeth. Oil on canvas. Millpont Conservancy, Lititz, PA.
Viewing the painting: How does the painting reflect the relationship between Rip Van Winkle and his wife?

likeness, promised to inherit the habits, with the old clothes of his father. He was generally seen trooping like a colt at his mother's heels, equipped in a pair of his father's cast-off galligaskins¹¹, which he had much ado to hold up with one hand,

as a fine lady does her train in bad weather.

Rip Van Winkle, however, was one of those happy mortals, of foolish, well-oiled dispositions, who take the world easy, eat white bread or brown, whichever can be got with least thought or trouble, and would rather starve on a penny than work for a pound. If left to himself, he would have whistled life away in perfect contentment; but his wife kept continually dinning in his ears about his idleness, his carelessness, and the ruin he was bringing on his family. Morning, noon, and night, her tongue was incessantly going, and everything he said or did was sure to produce a torrent of household eloquence. Rip had but one way of replying to all lectures of the kind, and that, by frequent use, had grown into a habit. He shrugged his shoulders, shook his head, cast up his eyes, but said nothing. This, however, always provoked a fresh volley from his wife, so that he would take to the outside of the house—the only side which, in truth, belongs to a henpecked husband.

11. *Galligaskins* are the loose, baggy, knee-length trousers worn in the sixteenth and seventeenth centuries.

Vocabulary
incessantly (in ses' ant lē) *adv.* endlessly; constantly

188 THEME 2

Did You Know? notes provide illustrated definitions to help students visualize unfamiliar settings or objects mentioned in the selection.

Footnotes support comprehension by explaining unfamiliar references or clarifying difficult passages in the text. Footnotes also supply pronunciations for many names of people and places and for words from other languages.

Vocabulary words are underscored at first use in the selection; a note at the bottom of the page provides the definition, pronunciation, and part of speech.

Viewing questions prompt students to connect the fine art and photographs to the selection.

Selection Plan

(Continued)

RESPONDING TO LITERATURE

This section provides a variety of ways for students to respond to the literature through listening, speaking, and writing activities. It also provides students with an opportunity to make connections to the theme.

Personal Response questions and activities allow all students to express an immediate response to the selection. The goal here is exploration, not closure.

Analyzing Literature questions help guide students to a thorough understanding of the selection. Recall questions focus students' attention on significant details of the selection, which they will use in answering the Interpret questions. Evaluate and Connect questions often include a **Theme Connection.**

Responding to Literature

PERSONAL RESPONSE

What was your reaction to this story? Did you find it amusing, suspenseful, mysterious, or all three? Describe your impressions in your journal.

Analyzing Literature

RECALL

1. According to the narrator, what is the chief flaw in Rip's character? What is the chief flaw in his wife's character?
2. Briefly describe the strangers Rip meets in the mountains. What happens to him after he drinks their beverage?
3. What is the first change Rip notices after he wakes up? Describe one other change he notices once he returns to town.
4. According to the narrator, what is Rip's life like after his return?

INTERPRET

5. What sort of person is Rip Van Winkle? What conflict exists between him and his wife? Support your ideas with examples from the story.
6. The details used to describe the men and the atmosphere in the hollow intensify the mysterious **mood** Irving created in this part of the story. List details that helped you sense the mood of this scene.
7. In what way does Peter Vanderdonk confirm Rip's explanation of his absence?
8. In your opinion, is Rip's life better or worse after his twenty-year sleep? Explain.

EVALUATE AND CONNECT

9. Theme Connection   What historical events occurred during Rip's absence? Why do you think Irving chose that twenty-year period for Rip's long nap? Explain.
10. What is your reaction to what happens to Rip and his wife in this story? Explain.

LITERARY ELEMENTS

Setting

A **setting** is the time and place in which the events of a story, novel, or play occur. For example, the setting of "Rip Van Winkle" is the Hudson River valley in the late 1700s. Strong writers often use the setting to help create an atmosphere or mood for a story. Carefully chosen details help readers visualize the place being described.

1. Pick out details from "Rip Van Winkle" that helped you picture the setting in your mind. Explain how the details helped transport you into the time and place of the story.

2. Choose another story you've read, and describe its setting.

● See **Literary Terms Handbook,** p. R10.

Dog With Broom Thrown at Him, 1921. N. C. Wyeth. Ink on paper. Stuart Kingston Gallery, Wilmington, DE.

WINDS OF CHANGE 🐌 201

Literary Elements teach traditional literary skills and provide students with the tools necessary to analyze and interpret literature.

The panel on the left shows a Student Edition page:

RESPONDING TO LITERATURE

Literature and Writing

Writing About Literature
Thinking About a Theme   What does "Rip Van Winkle" say about the passage of time and human nature? Write a paragraph or two explaining your ideas about the theme of this well-known story.

Personal Writing
Sweet Dreams   Imagine if you were to fall asleep for the next twenty years. How do you think the world would change during that time? When you discovered these changes, how would you feel? Write a diary entry explaining what has happened, how things have changed, and how you feel.

Rip as Old Man, 1921. N. C. Wyeth. Ink on paper. Stuart Kingston Gallery, Wilmington, DE.

Extending Your Response

Literature Groups
Debating Stereotypes   A stereotype has only a few, highly exaggerated character traits. Stereotypes are never fully believable. For example, the strong, silent cowboy is a stereotype; so is the wicked villain or the innocent heroine. Stereotypes often appear in folktales, legends, and literature that is meant to teach a lesson. Are both Rip and his wife stereotypes? Why or why not? How might Irving have made these two characters more believable? Debate the issue. Support your opinions with examples and quotations from the story.

Art Activity
Social Studies: Make a Time Line   Review the notes you made for the **Focus Activity** on page 184 to help you make a personal time line starting at the year of your birth. Include important events in your own life, as well as the dates of important events and inventions in this country and around the world.

Reading Further
If you would like to read more by Washington Irving, try these works:
Diedrich Knickerbocker's History of New York
"The Legend of Sleepy Hollow" in *The Sketch Book of Geoffrey Crayon, Gent.*

Learning for Life
A Newspaper Account   Imagine that you are a journalist sent to interview Rip for the *Hudson River Valley Gazette*. Write an article about his mysterious experience. Include quotations and descriptions from Rip as well as other villagers.

■ **Save your work for your portfolio.**

202   THEME 2

Literature and Writing provides options that all students can use to respond in writing to a selection. One option is always a Writing About Literature prompt; the other option is either a Creative Writing prompt or a Personal Writing prompt.

Extending Your Response includes diverse activities that appeal to different types of learners. This section always includes Literature Groups as well as other activities chosen from the following menu: Interdisciplinary Activity, Learning for Life, Internet Connection, Listening and Speaking, Performing, and Reading Further.

Skill Minilessons provide frequent opportunities for students to practice essential language arts skills in the context of the literature they are reading.

Grammar and Language minilessons focus on skills of grammar, usage, mechanics, and style to help students improve their own writing and better appreciate literature by making a link between literature and good writing.

Reading and Thinking minilessons teach reading and critical thinking skills that students can apply not just to literature but across the curriculum.

Vocabulary minilessons teach or reinforce important vocabulary skills.

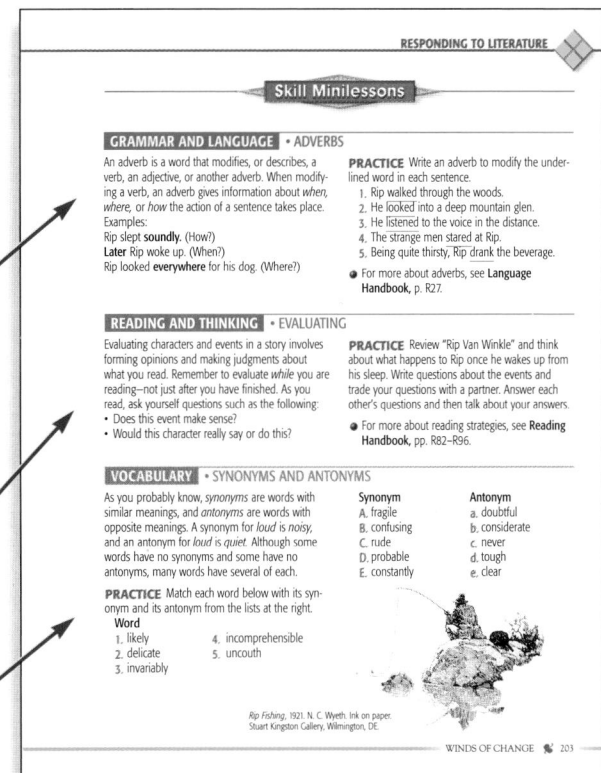

The panel on the right shows a Student Edition page:

RESPONDING TO LITERATURE

Skill Minilessons

GRAMMAR AND LANGUAGE • ADVERBS

An adverb is a word that modifies, or describes, a verb, an adjective, or another adverb. When modifying a verb, an adverb gives information about *when*, *where*, or *how* the action of a sentence takes place. Examples:
Rip slept **soundly**. (How?)
Later Rip woke up. (When?)
Rip looked **everywhere** for his dog. (Where?)

PRACTICE Write an adverb to modify the underlined word in each sentence.
1. Rip walked through the woods.
2. He looked into a deep mountain glen.
3. He listened to the voice in the distance.
4. The strange men stared at Rip.
5. Being quite thirsty, Rip drank the beverage.

● For more about adverbs, see **Language Handbook**, p. R27.

READING AND THINKING • EVALUATING

Evaluating characters and events in a story involves forming opinions and making judgments about what you read. Remember to evaluate *while* you are reading—not just after you have finished. As you read, ask yourself questions such as the following:
• Does this event make sense?
• Would this character really say or do this?

PRACTICE Review "Rip Van Winkle" and think about what happens to Rip once he wakes up from his sleep. Write questions about the events and trade your questions with a partner. Answer each other's questions and then talk about your answers.

● For more about reading strategies, see **Reading Handbook**, pp. R82–R96.

VOCABULARY • SYNONYMS AND ANTONYMS

As you probably know, *synonyms* are words with similar meanings, and *antonyms* are words with opposite meanings. A synonym for *loud* is *noisy*, and an antonym for *loud* is *quiet*. Although some words have no synonyms and some have no antonyms, many words have several of each.

Synonym	Antonym
A. fragile	a. doubtful
B. confusing	b. considerate
C. rude	c. never
D. probable	d. tough
E. constantly	e. clear

PRACTICE Match each word below with its synonym and its antonym from the lists at the right.
Word
1. likely   4. incomprehensible
2. delicate   5. uncouth
3. invariably

Rip Fishing, 1921. N. C. Wyeth. Ink on paper. Stuart Kingston Gallery, Wilmington, DE.

WINDS OF CHANGE   203

Features

A variety of special features enhance students' learning through attention to active reading, language arts skills, and connections to other literature, to other disciplines, and to technology.

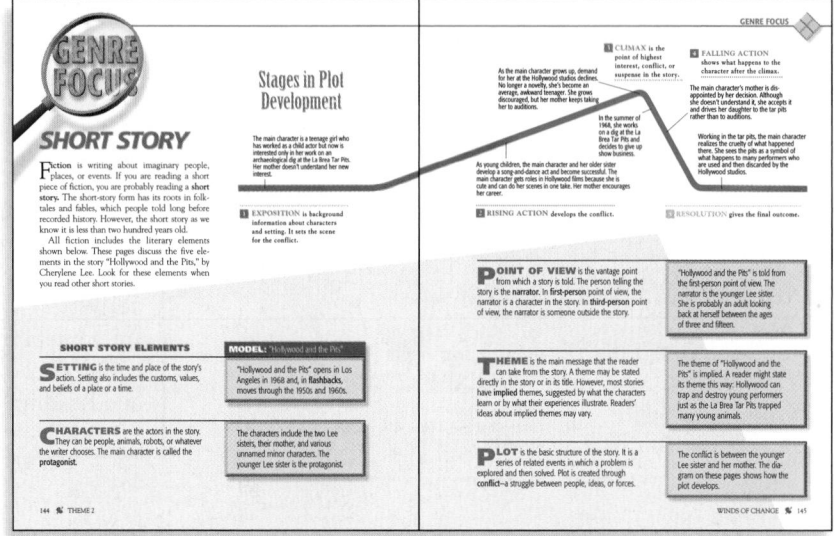

Genre Focus introduces students to the elements and characteristics of the major genres.

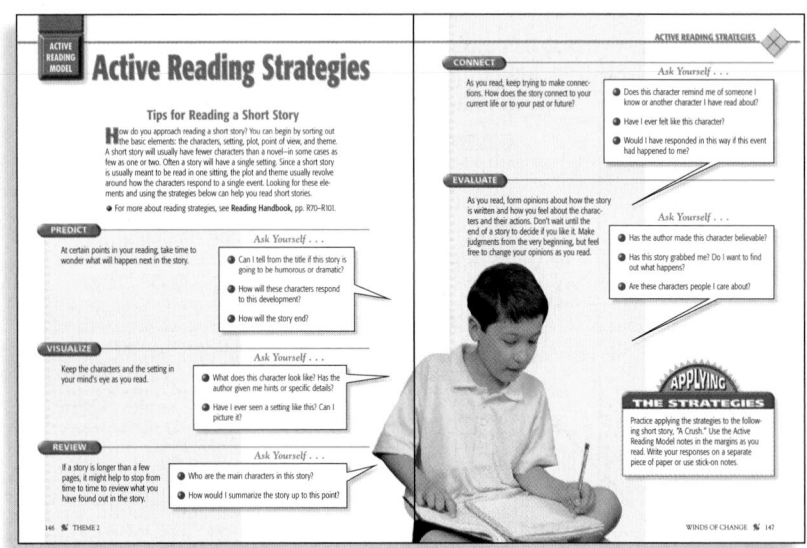

Active Reading Strategies models for students the kind of thinking and questioning that skillful readers do when reading a particular type of text.

Active Reading Model gives students the opportunity to apply active reading strategies as they read.

Media Connections provide engaging, contemporary connections to many selections through a variety of sources such as newspaper and magazine articles, Web sites, song lyrics, and screenplays.

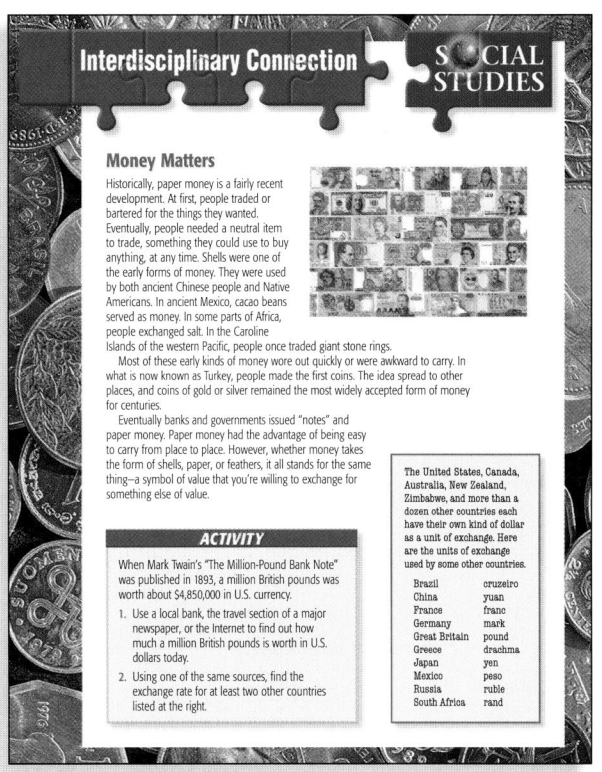

Comparing Selections Once in each theme, a Comparing Selections page presents options for comparing two selections through writing, discussions, and one of many other engaging activities.

Interdisciplinary Connections connect selections to grade-level curricular goals in disciplines such as mathematics, science, history, geography, health, and art.

Features

(Continued)

Skills Features offer students opportunities to develop key language arts skills in the context of the literature they are reading. Features include

- ❧ *Vocabulary Skills*
- ❧ *Grammar Link*
- ❧ *Reading and Thinking Skills*
- ❧ *Writing Skills*
- ❧ *Listening, Speaking, and Viewing*

Technology Skills features enrich students' experience of literature through specific applications such as word processing, multimedia, databases, E-mail, and the Internet. In Course 2, for example, students learn about such topics as desktop publishing, creating spreadsheets, and judging on-line information.

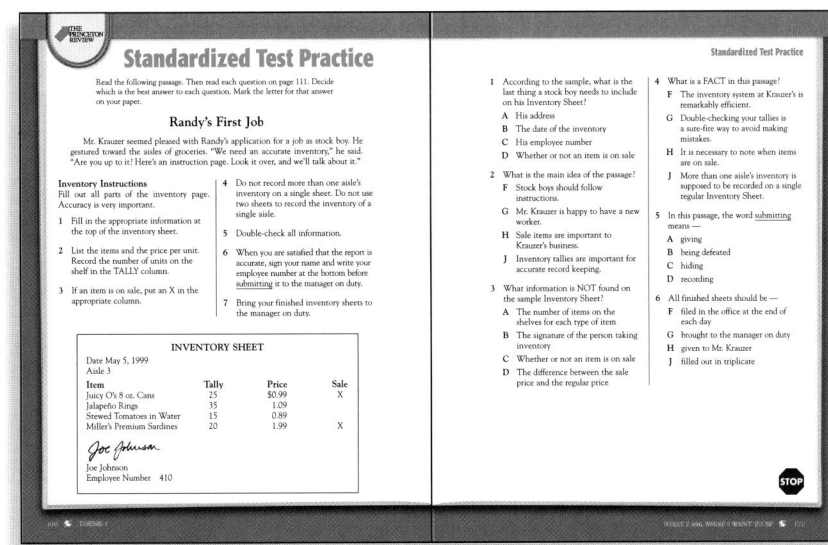

Writing Workshop at the end of each theme engages students in creating an extended piece of writing related to the theme or a specific selection within the theme. Models, strategies, and tips help students develop their writing through the stages of prewriting, drafting, revising, editing/proofreading, and publishing/presenting.

Standardized Test Practice at the end of each theme gives students practice with the types of reading and writing test formats used in many standardized tests.

Theme Support

THEME AT A GLANCE

These pages precede each theme of the Student Edition, providing a clear overview of the organization of the theme.

Theme 1 · At a Glance
What I Am, What I Want To Be

Theme 1:
WHAT I AM, WHAT I WANT TO BE

THEME OPENING

- Introducing the Theme (p. 1)
- Exploring the Theme (p. 2)
- Theme Projects (p. 3)

SELECTIONS

Names/Nombres (p. 4)
One (p. 13)
I'm Nobody! Who are you? (p. 13)
Face It (p. 18)
Almost Ready (p. 18)
Media Connection: Heroes (p. 24)
Strong Men Weep (p. 25)
from Wait Till Next Year (p. 34)

Media Connection: from The Wonder Years (pp. 41–42)
Broken Chain (p. 43)
Without Commercials (p. 58)
Active Reading Model: from Barrio Boy (p. 66)
Fish Cheeks (p. 76)
Rosa Parks: My Story (p. 84)

SKILL FEATURES

Grammar Link (p. 12)
Writing Skills (p. 23)
Technology Skills (pp. 56–57)
Genre Focus: Autobiography (pp. 62–63)
Active Reading Strategies (pp. 64–65)

Vocabulary Skills (p. 75)
Interdisciplinary Connection (p. 82)
Reading Skills (p. 83)

WRITING WORKSHOP

Narrative Writing: Autobiographical Anecdote (pp. 104–107)

1A · THEME 1

Theme 1 · At a Glance
What I Am, What I Want To Be

THEME WRAP-UP

- Responding to the Theme, Analyzing Literature, Evaluate and Set Goals (p. 108)
- Build Your Portfolio (p. 108)
- Reading on Your Own (p. 109)
  The Witch of Blackbird Pond by Elizabeth Speare George
  No-No Boy by John Okada
  Baseball in April and Other Stories by Gary Soto
  Where You Belong by Mary Ann McGuigany
- Standardized Test Practice (pp. 110–111)

KEYS TO LITERARY CONNECTIONS

Comparing Selections

The Comparing Selections feature in this theme provides opportunities for addressing diverse aspects of the reading and literature curriculum.

For example, in Comparing Selections on page 40, students compare their responses to "Strong Men Weep" and to the excerpt from Wait Till Next Year. Students also have the opportunity to discuss their feelings about sports, which will help them identify with ideas Cosgrove and Kearns Goodwin shared in these selections.

KEYS TO TEACHING OPTIONS

Block Scheduling

Activities that are particularly suited to use within a block scheduling framework are identified throughout this theme by the following designation: For detailed suggestions on block scheduling, see the Block Scheduling Guide for this grade level.

Key to Ability Levels

The Teaching Options throughout this theme have been coded for students of various abilities.

L1 BASIC activities for all students
L2 AVERAGE activities for average

Theme 1 · At a Glance
What I Am, What I Want To Be

Reading Skills in this theme

Variety of Texts
In addition to a set of autobiographical selections, this theme includes the following text types:
- poetry
- essay
- memoir
- short story
- newspaper column
- television script

Comprehension Skills
The following instructional support for comprehension skills appears in this theme of the Student Edition:
- Reading and Thinking Minilessons (pp. 17, 22, 55, 103)
- Active Reading Strategies and Model (pp. 64–74)
- Sequencing (p. 83)

See also the Reading Minilessons throughout the theme in this Teacher's Wraparound Edition.

Reading Resources

Comprehension Skills Resources

Active Reading Guides
The Active Reading Guide provides graphic organizers and study guide questions to support students' reading of each selection. (Active Reading Guide, pp. 1–10)

Reading Workbook
The Reading Workbook (pp. 1–18) includes additional instruction and reinforcement of reading strategies and skills.

Audio Library
Available both on tape and on CD, the Audio Library provides valuable comprehension support.

Resources for Reading Widely

Glencoe Literature Library
Each title in the Glencoe Literature Library includes a full-length novel or play plus related readings. A separate Study Guide is available for each title.

Literature Classics CD-ROM
The selections on this CD-ROM can be searched by author, theme, or genre.

A coproduction of Glencoe and Time, Inc., the inTime magazine includes a wealth of high interest nonfiction related to the selections in Theme One.

Assessment in this theme

Assessment Options in the Student Edition
Glencoe Literature offers a number of diverse ways to evaluate student understanding and skill proficiency. In the Student Edition, use the following:
- Responding to Literature
  Following each selection, students are asked to recall facts, interpret ideas, and evaluate concepts as they answer a variety of questions and complete activities to extend their understanding.
- Theme Wrap-Up (pp. 108–109)
  Here students respond to the selections on personal and analytical levels. They also assume ownership of their learning by setting and evaluating goals and by selecting work for their portfolios.

See also the many Assessment Resources listed on the facing page.

THE PRINCETON REVIEW

Standardized Test Practice
The Princeton Review has developed the Standardized Test Practice pages found at the end of this theme (pp. 110–111). These pages contain practice test questions that help students remain familiar with standardized test formats and content.
- ITBS Preparation and Practice
- SAT-9 Preparation and Practice
- TerraNova Preparation and Practice

1C · THEME 1

Theme 1 · At a Glance
What I Am, What I Want To Be

Writing Skills in this theme

Writing Skills
The Student Edition of Theme One offers strong instructional support for writing skills:

In Extending Your Response, which follows each selection:
- Writing About Literature
- Personal/Creative Writing

See also the Writing Minilessons throughout the theme in this Teacher's Wraparound Edition.

Writing Workshops
Theme One concludes with a Writing Workshop that guides students through the process of writing an autobiographical anecdote (pp. 104–107).

Writing Resources

Writer's Assistant CD-ROM
Each Writing Workshop is supplemented by an interactive writing guide on the Writer's Assistant CD-ROM. This easy-to-use writing guide provides prompts, templates, and other tools that lead students through the writing process.

Writing and Proofreading Practice
Blackline masters present in-depth instruction and practice on a specific step in the writing process and proofreading. (pp. 1–7, 8–14)

Writing and Proofreading Transparencies
Transparencies provide graphic organizers and proofreading exercises for whole-class instruction (pp. 1–6, 7–8, 25–26).

Research and Report Writing Guide
This resource provides extensive tips and activities to guide students in their writing projects in the literature classroom as well as in classes across the curriculum.

Style and Documentation Sourcebook for Writers
This sourcebook is a combination reference and workbook, giving students the most up-to-date information and guidance regarding traditional as well as technological research strategies and documentation.

Grammar and Composition Handbook
The Grammar and Composition Handbook provides instruction that supplements activities in the student textbook.

Assessment Resources

Selection Quick Checks
For each selection, a Quick Check of three to five short-answer questions measures students' literal comprehension.

Selection and Theme Assessment
The Selection and Theme Assessment instrument tests students' abilities to recall, interpret, and evaluate what they've read. The tests consist of multiple-choice, short answer, and essay questions.

Performance Assessment
Alternative assessment instruments and rubrics for Theme One are found in the Performance Assessment ancillary.

Writing Assessment and Portfolio Management
These notes and strategies, student models, and assessment tools assist with the task of measuring students' progress as writers and as monitors of their own writing.

Testmaker
Teachers can customize selection and Theme One tests by accessing the Testmaker database.

Mindjogger Videoquizzes
Using a popular game show format, Mindjogger Videoquizzes enable teachers to evaluate student understanding of Theme One in a quick and fun manner.

WHAT I AM, WHAT I WANT TO BE · 1D

The second spread provides a detailed look at the reading skills, writing skills, and assessment options available.

THEME SKILLS SCOPE AND SEQUENCE

For each theme, this comprehensive chart shows a selection-by-selection listing of the skill development and activities provided in the Student Edition and Teacher's Wraparound Edition.

THEME RESOURCE MANAGER

The Theme Resource Manager simplifies classroom management and planning. A tremendous resource in itself, this chart makes it easy to see what print resources, transparencies, and technology resources are available for each selection in the theme. Planning was never so easy!

Selection Support

Comprehensive point-of-use notes and strategies provide effective, inclusive instructional support to help students get into, through, and beyond their reading of the literature.

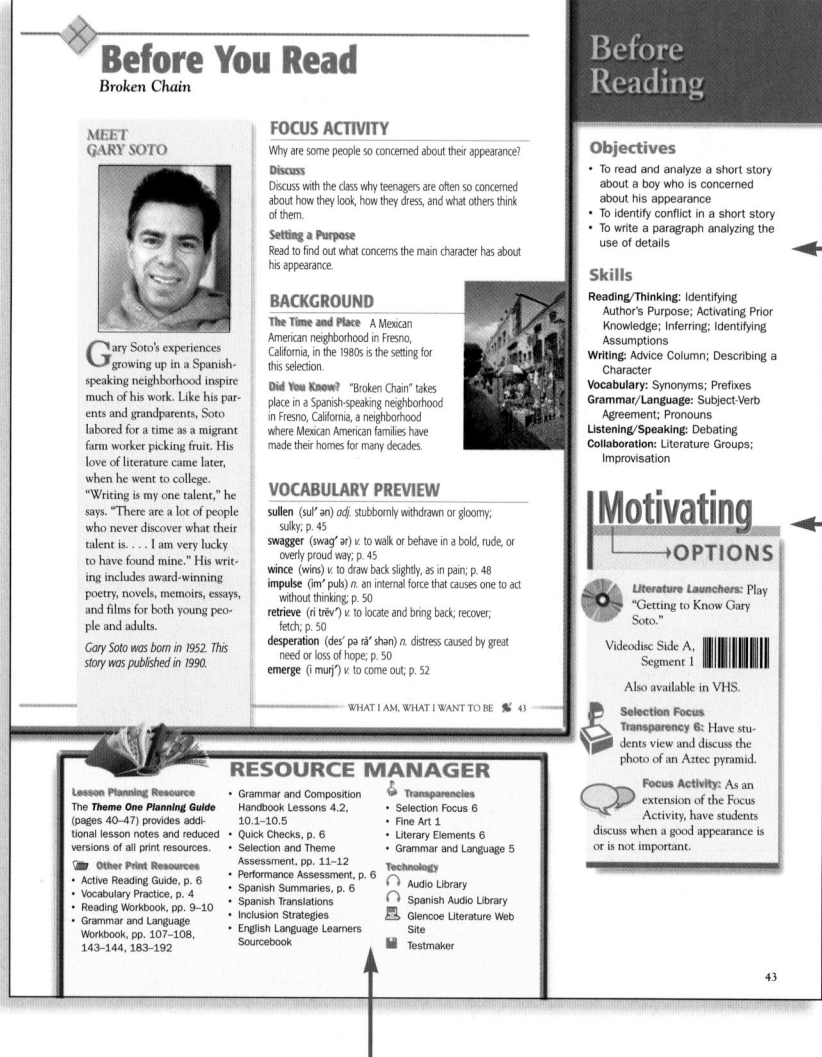

BEFORE READING

Optional activities for motivating students and a list of all program resources get each lesson off to a solid start.

Objectives and Skills Teaching objectives and skill strands help you see at a glance the skills taught in the lesson.

Motivating Options Choose from a menu of options to engage your students' interest in the selection:

- ❧ **Literature Launchers** are short, high-interest video segments, available on videodisc or VHS.
- ❧ **Selection Focus Transparencies** pique students' interest and get them thinking about ideas such as the theme, the topic, or the setting of the selection.
- ❧ **Focus Activities** offer options to expand or extend the Focus Activity in the SE.

Resource Manager This handy chart gives a complete listing of teacher's classroom resources to use to teach, reinforce, extend, and assess the lesson. These print, transparency, and technology resources allow you to customize to accommodate your own classroom needs and teaching style.

READING THE SELECTION

Core notes and teaching options offer a wealth of interactive instructional support.

Summary This note provides a brief overview of each prose selection.

Core Notes Point-of-use notes and strategies in the side columns provide instructional aid keyed to specific passages in the text. Core notes include
- ❧ *Active Reading*
- ❧ *Critical Thinking*
- ❧ *Literary Elements*
- ❧ *Author's Craft*

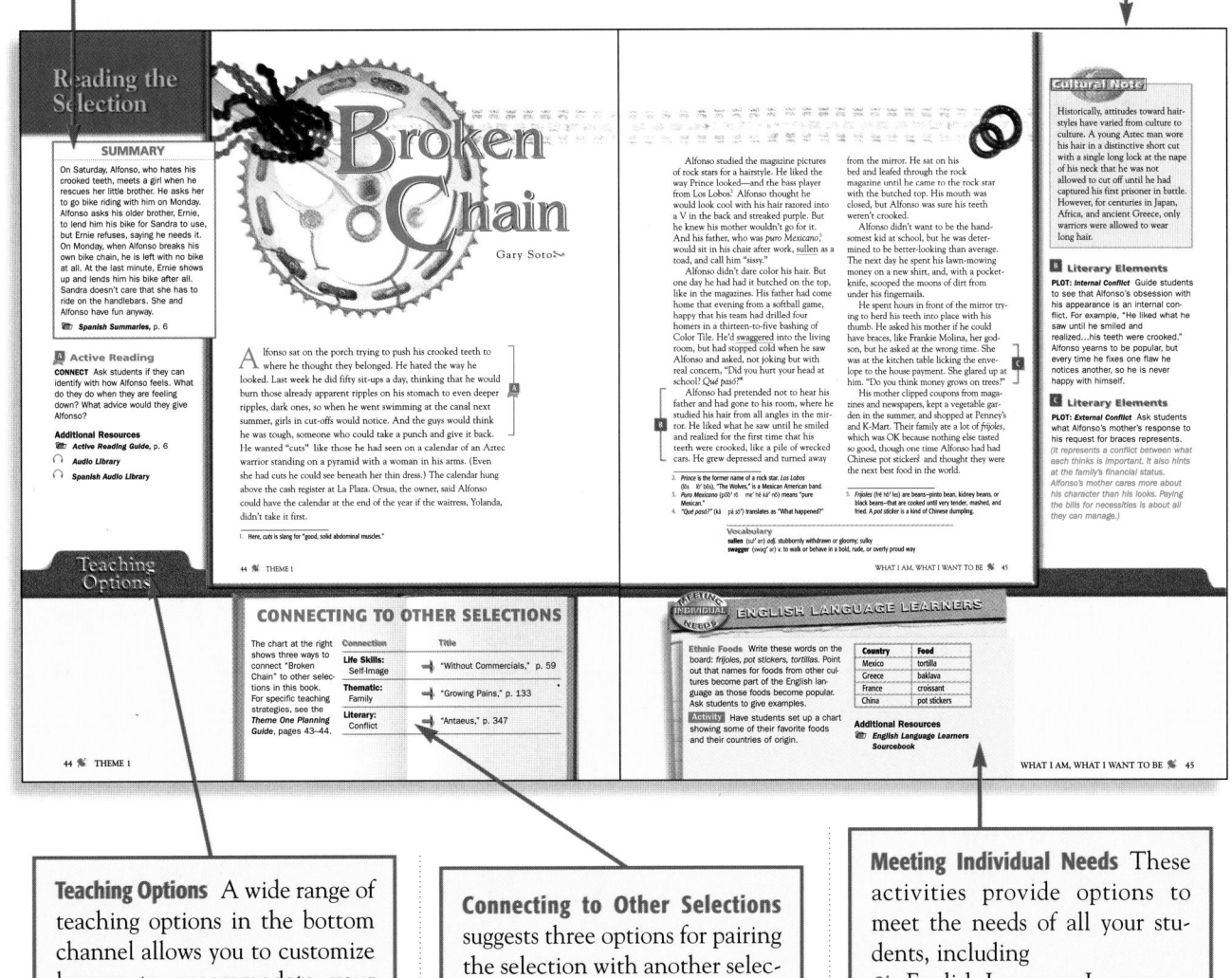

Teaching Options A wide range of teaching options in the bottom channel allows you to customize lessons to accommodate your students' individual needs and your own teaching preferences.

Connecting to Other Selections suggests three options for pairing the selection with another selection in the anthology.

Meeting Individual Needs These activities provide options to meet the needs of all your students, including
- ❧ English Language Learners
- ❧ Less-Proficient Readers
- ❧ Students with Special Needs

READING THE SELECTION (Continued)

Models that appear with many Critical Thinking and Active Reading notes serve as a tool for modeling, thinking, and reading strategies for students.

Viewing Notes provide background information about the art or artist plus an answer to the student Viewing question.

Minilessons provide regular opportunities for integrated language arts instruction in
- 🐾 Writing
- 🐾 Reading
- 🐾 Grammar and Language
- 🐾 Listening and Speaking

Connections activities relate the selection to another discipline or to the students' lives:
- 🐾 Real-World Connections
- 🐾 Interdisciplinary Connections
- 🐾 Internet Connections
- 🐾 Life Skills Connections

Point-of-Use Notes such as the following provide information and activities to broaden student understanding:
- 🐾 Thematic Focus
- 🐾 Vocabulary Skills
- 🐾 Historical/Language Notes
- 🐾 FYI

RESPONDING TO LITERATURE

Suggested answers and evaluation guidelines provide rubrics for thoughtful assessment of students' understanding of the selection.

Responding to Literature

PERSONAL RESPONSE
- What thoughts and feelings did you have at the end of the story? Describe your reactions in your journal.
- In what ways did you identify with Alfonso? Explain in detail.

Analyzing Literature

RECALL
1. What aspects of his appearance would Alfonso like to change?
2. Describe the difference between Alfonso's and Ernie's bikes.
3. How does Alfonso break his bicycle chain?
4. What is Sandra's reaction to Alfonso's appearing with just one beat-up bike?

INTERPRET
5. Why is Alfonso unhappy with the way he looks?
6. How does the author show that Alfonso cares very much about the appearance of his bike?
7. Why is Alfonso so upset when he breaks his bicycle chain? Do you think he is overreacting? Why or why not?
8. At the end of the story, Alfonso is different. How has he changed? What caused the change? Use examples to support your answers.

EVALUATE AND CONNECT
9. Alfonso is always trying to straighten his teeth. What does the **repetition** of this image show you about his state of mind throughout the story?
10. Theme Connection Does reading a story about someone your own age make you feel more connected to the character? Why or why not?

Spokes, 1983. John D. Wibberley. Acrylic on canvas, 16 x 24 in. Artist's collection.

WHAT I AM, WHAT I WANT TO BE 53

LITERARY ELEMENTS

Conflict

The struggle between two opposing forces that lie at the center of a plot in a story is called the **conflict**. An external conflict exists when a character struggles against an outside force—another person, nature, society, or fate. An **internal conflict** exists within the mind of the character who is torn between opposing feelings or goals. In "Broken Chain," Alfonso struggles with both kinds of conflicts.

1. What are the external conflicts that seem to prevent Alfonso from reaching his goal of meeting Sandra for a "date"? Find two or more examples.
2. Alfonso's desperate searching for his own style. Describe how his lack of confidence about his looks could be interpreted as an internal conflict.

• See *Literary Terms Handbook*, p. R2.

LITERARY ELEMENTS
1. The external conflicts in the story include Alfonso's fight with Ernie, Ernie's denying Alfonso the use of his bike, and the broken chain on his own bike.
2. His desire to see Sandra conflicts with

Responding to the Selection

Personal Response
- Some students may say that they were glad the story turned out happily and that Alfonso grew as a person.
- Students may say they know how it feels not to fit in, to be critical of their looks, or to fight with their siblings.

Analyzing Literature

1. Alfonso would like to change his teeth, his muscles, and his hair.
2. Alfonso's bike is so clean it gleams; Ernie's is dirty.
3. He unhooks the chain to clean it.
4. She is content to sit on the crossbar.
5. He feels insecure and is afraid girls will not like him.
6. He describes in great detail the care Alfonso takes to clean his bike.
7. He needed two bikes and now he has none, so he'll have to break his date. Most students will say he's overreacting because Sandra won't judge him by his bike (as the end of the story shows).
8. He is more confident and mature because he has overcome a crisis and learned not to worry so much: "Free of worry now," and "once he got going, it got easier."
9. It shows how obsessed he is with straightening out his teeth and, by implication, his physical appearance.
10. Most students feel more connected to characters their own age because they have similar concerns and they are easier to identify with and understand.

Answers are provided for all questions under Analyzing Literature and Literary Elements.

Assessment Options This list identifies all assessment resources available for this selection.

Evaluation Criteria supply assessment tips for activities in Literature and Writing and Extending Your Response.

Literature and Writing

Writing About Literature
Students' paragraphs should
- give appropriate examples of Soto's descriptive details.
- explain clearly how each detail helps readers understand Alfonso's life.

Creative Writing
Students' letters should
- spell out Alfonso's concerns clearly.
Students' advice columns should
- reassure Alfonso that he is normal.
- address his concerns in order.
- provide reasons for their conclusions.

Extending Your Response

Literature Groups Tell students that the chart can have as many rows as they wish, as long as they find support in the story for each item.

Interdisciplinary Activity Remind students to make sure their explanations proceed in a logical sequence and match their diagrams.

Performing Encourage students to spend time planning and rehearsing their improvisations. If possible, videotape each pair's performance and make the tapes available for viewing.

interNET CONNECTION

Bicycle Repair
Have students use a search engine to find out how to repair a broken bicycle chain. Suggest keywords, such as bicycle repair, bicycle maintenance, and biking.

54 THEME 1

RESPONDING TO LITERATURE

Literature and Writing

Writing About Literature
Details In "Broken Chain," Gary Soto includes many details about Alfonso's family and neighborhood. Write a paragraph or two about how Soto's use of details helps you understand what his life at home and at school must have been like. Choose details from the story to prove your point.

Creative Writing
Dear Advice Columnist Think back to your class discussion on the Focus Activity on page 43 about peoples' concern with their appearance. Alfonso is very self-conscious about his teeth, his hair, and his muscles. Imagine he has written a letter to an advice columnist asking about how something— anything! Still, desperation and hopelessness are synonyms, because they are close in meaning. A thesaurus, a book that lists and defines synonyms,

Extending Your Response

Literature Groups
Comparing Alfonso with Himself Together, read the first and last paragraphs in the story. Then have a discussion comparing how Alfonso feels at the beginning of the story with how he feels at the end. Make a comparison chart that shows the results of your discussion.

	AT THE BEGINNING	AT THE END
ALFONSO'S FEELINGS ABOUT HIMSELF		

Interdisciplinary Activity
Science Why does a bicycle need a chain? Can a bike work without one? With a partner, examine a bike scientifically. Write your own explanation of how a bicycle works. Use diagrams to illustrate your ideas. Check with a reference book or your science teacher to see whether your explanation is correct.

Performing
Improvisation Work with a partner to improvise a scene between Alfonso and Sandra after their bike ride at the end of the story. What would the two say to each other? Would they be nervous or shy? What would their body language look like? Perform your improvised scene in front of the class.

Reading Further
Check out these books by Gary Soto:
Poetry: *Neighborhood Odes*
Novel: *Taking Sides*
Short Stories: *Baseball in April and Other Stories*

💾 Save your work for your portfolio.

54 THEME 1

RESPONDING TO LITERATURE

Skill Minilessons

GRAMMAR AND LANGUAGE • SUBJECT-VERB AGREEMENT

A subject and a verb are basic parts of a sentence. The subject and its verb must agree in number. A singular noun used as a subject of a sentence calls for a singular form of the verb:

   Alfonso rides his bike after school.

A plural noun used as the subject calls for a plural form of the verb:

   Alfonso and Ernie ride their bikes after school.

PRACTICE For each sentence, write the subject and the correct form of the verb.

1. Gary Soto (writes, write) stories about teens.
2. The book *Baseball in April and Other Stories* (is, are) an award winner.
3. There (is, are) eleven short stories, most about Latino young people.
4. The stories, like "Broken Chain," (focuses, focus) on the difficulties of growing up.
5. The end of the book (contains, contain) a list of Spanish words and their English translations.

• For more about subject-verb agreement, see *Language Handbook*, pp. R14–R15.

READING AND THINKING • ACTIVATING PRIOR KNOWLEDGE

Things you already know can help you understand what you read. Even if you read about an adventure in another galaxy, you will understand some parts easily because of knowledge you acquired previously. All the life experiences you have had contribute to your prior knowledge.

PRACTICE What have you read or experienced that helped you better understand the characters' thoughts and feelings in "Broken Chain"? Write a paragraph describing how this prior knowledge helped you understand the story.

• For more about this and related reading strategies, see *Reading Handbook*, p. R82.

VOCABULARY • SYNONYMS

Synonyms are words that mean nearly the same thing. When you know synonyms for a word, you can decide which one best expresses the exact meaning you want. For example, *desperation* expresses a more frantic feeling than *hopelessness*. A hopeless person might just sit and do nothing. But a desperate person might try something—

can help you understand how synonyms differ in meaning.

PRACTICE Write a synonym for each word below. Then write one sentence using each word and another sentence using its synonym.
1. sullen
2. retrieve
3. swagger
4. wince
5. impulse

WHAT I AM, WHAT I WANT TO BE 55

Skill Minilessons

GRAMMAR AND LANGUAGE
SUBJECT-VERB AGREEMENT
1. Gary Soto writes
2. book is
3. are stories
4. stories focus
5. end contains

READING AND THINKING
ACTIVATING PRIOR KNOWLEDGE
Students' paragraphs should
- give examples from their own lives and their reading.
- tie the examples to the story.

VOCABULARY
SYNONYMS
Examples
1. sullen, gloomy
   The sullen clerk didn't answer.
   When it rained, he felt gloomy.
2. retrieve, fetch
   I had to retrieve the lost ring.
   My dog likes to fetch sticks.
3. strut, swagger
   The models strut down the runway.
   The winners swagger proudly.
4. wince, flinch
   The shot made him wince.
   Most people flinch from pain.
5. impulse, whim
   She had an impulse to buy it.
   He took the ride on a whim.

Additional Resources
- *Grammar and Language Workbook*, pp. 183–192
- *Grammar and Composition Handbook*, Lessons 10.1–10.5
- *Writer's Choice*, Lessons 16.1–16.5
- *Reading Workbook*, pp. 9–10
- *Vocabulary Practice*, p. 4

✓ **ASSESSMENT OPTIONS**
- *Quick Checks*, p. 6
- *Selection and Theme Assessment*, pp. 11–12
- *Performance Assessment*, p. 6
- *Testmaker*

WHAT I AM, WHAT I WANT TO BE 55

Theme Planning Guide

The Theme Planning Guides are invaluable companions to the
Teacher's Wraparound Edition. This easy-to-use sourcebook provides

- *additional background and teaching tips*
- *detailed lesson plans*
- *at-a-glance access to all print and transparency resources*

THEME OVERVIEW

This section offers additional background information and notes about
the content and structure of the
theme, including

- information about the artist whose
  work is featured on the theme
  opener in the Student Edition
- suggestions for exploring the
  theme and the genre focus

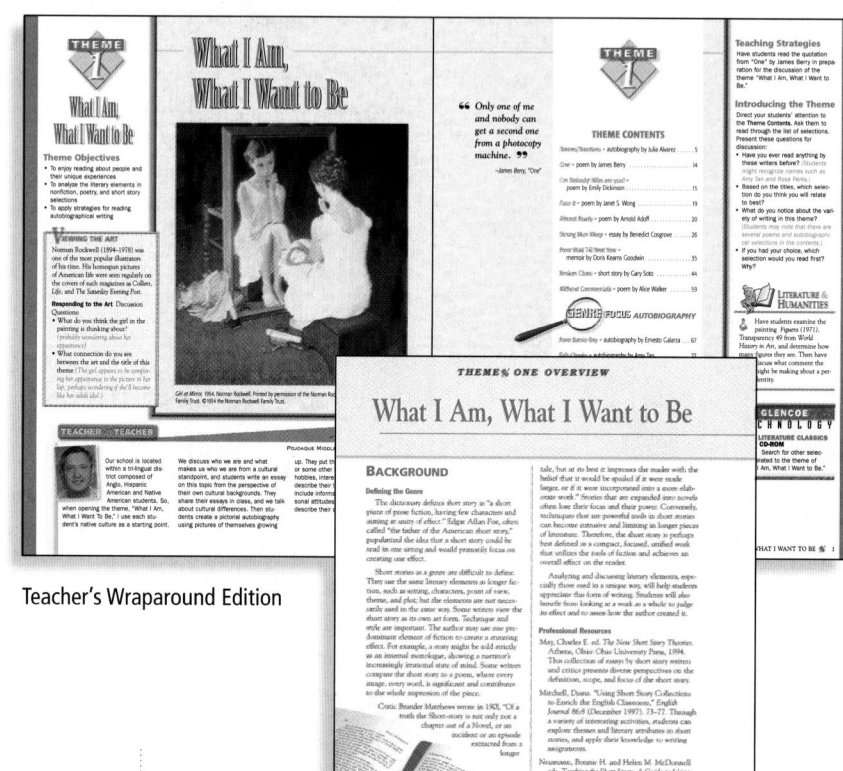

Teacher's Wraparound Edition

Theme One Planning Guide

THEME INTRODUCTION

The theme introduction elaborates on the notes in the
TWE, giving assessment rubrics for the theme projects as
well as a suggested Extra Credit Project.

Theme Resources

Reproductions of print and transparency resources show at
a glance what is available for use with this theme to make
planning that much easier.

LESSON PLAN

A detailed, reproducible lesson plan helps you organize and customize each lesson to your needs.

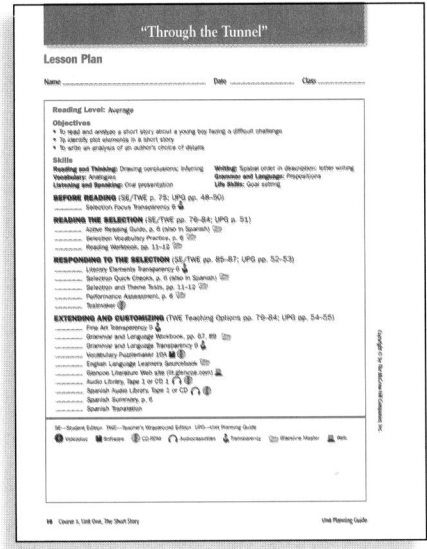

LESSON NOTES

These easy-to-use, yet comprehensive, strategies are organized to parallel the TWE plan of (1) Before Reading, (2) Reading the Selection, and (3) Responding to the Selection. Special features include

Motivating Options

These teaching tips support the use of each of the Motivating Options that appear on the Before Reading page of the TWE.

Connecting to Other Selections

Here you'll find a complete lesson plan for each of the connecting options listed in the TWE. You choose the approach—life skills, thematic, literary, or interdisciplinary.

LESSON RESOURCES

Reproductions of lesson-specific print and transparency resources allow you to see quickly what is available, saving valuable planning time.

Glencoe Literature Library

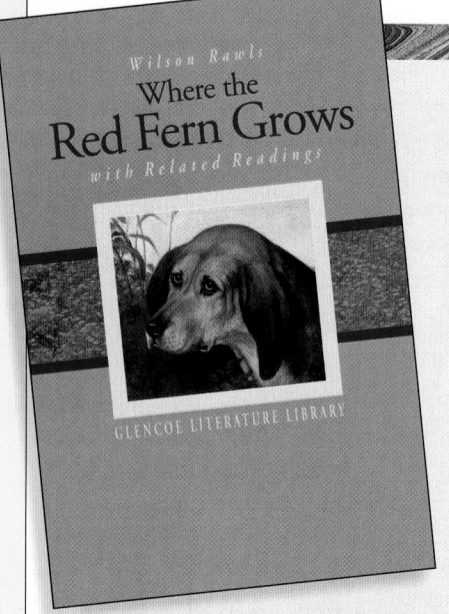

Novels and Plays ∿
with Related Readings

This collection of hardcover books allows you to extend the study of literature to your choice of full-length novels and plays. Each Literature Library book consists of a complete novel or play accompanied by several related readings, such as short stories, poems, essays, or informational articles.

The Autobiography of Miss Jane Pittman
BY ERNEST GAINES

Bearstone
BY WILL HOBBS

Bridge to Terabithia
BY KATHERINE PATERSON

The Call of the Wild
BY JACK LONDON

The Clay Marble
BY MINGFONG HO

Dragonwings
BY LAWRENCE YEP

The Glory Field
BY WALTER DEAN MYERS

Hatchet
BY GARY PAULSEN

High Elk's Treasure
BY VIRGINIA DRIVING HAWK SNEVE

House of Dies Drear
BY VIRGINIA HAMILTON

I, Juan de Pareja
BY ELIZABETH BORTON DE TREVINO

Island of the Blue Dolphins
BY SCOTT O'DELL

Johnny Tremain
BY ESTHER FORBES

Julie of the Wolves
BY JEAN CRAIGHEAD GEORGE

Missing May
BY CYNTHIA RYLANT

Number the Stars
BY LOIS LOWRY

Shiloh
BY PHYLLIS REYNOLDS NAYLOR

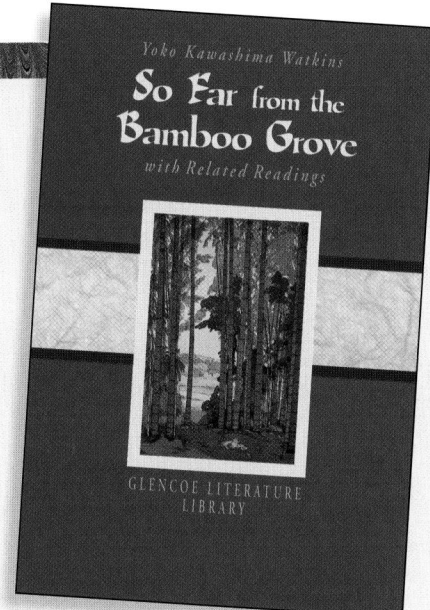

Yoko Kawashima Watkins
So Far from the Bamboo Grove
with Related Readings

GLENCOE LITERATURE LIBRARY

Study Guides ~

A separate Study Guide for each title in the Glencoe Literature Library provides teaching notes and reproducible activity pages for students.

For the Teacher
- Synopsis
- Media links
- Teaching options
- Answer key

For the Student
- Background information
- Active reading guides
- Response activities
- Test

The Slave Dancer
BY PAULA FOX

So Far from the Bamboo Grove
BY YOKO KAWASHIMA WATKINS

Tom Sawyer
BY MARK TWAIN

True Confessions of Charlotte Doyle
BY AVI

Tuck Everlasting
BY NATALIE BABBITT

The Witch of Blackbird Pond
BY ELIZABETH GEORGE SPEARE

Where the Red Fern Grows
BY WILSON RAWLS

A Wrinkle in Time
BY MADELEINE L'ENGLE

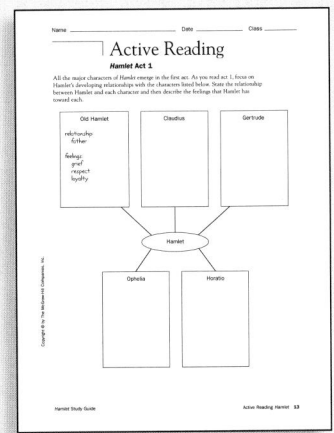

Active Reading pages include graphic organizers for students to complete as they read.

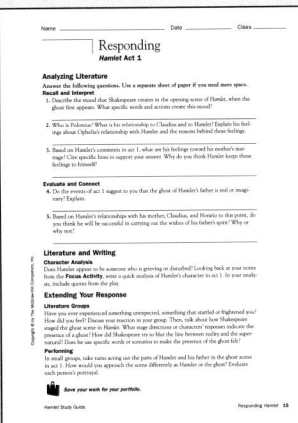

Responding pages include options for personal response, analyzing literature, and extending responses through writing and other activities.

Print Resources

Glencoe Literature has all the print resources you need to meet the needs of today's diverse classroom—and to save you valuable time.

Reading Resources
- ❧ **Active Reading Guide**
- ❧ **inTime**
- ❧ **Literature Groups Sourcebook**
- ❧ **Media Connections Activities**
- ❧ **Reading Workbook**

Language Arts Integration
- ❧ **Critical Thinking Skills**
- ❧ **Grammar and Composition Handbook**
- ❧ **Grammar and Language Workbook**
- ❧ **Interdisciplinary Activities**
- ❧ **Language Arts Guide to the Internet and Other Electronic Resources**
- ❧ **Listening and Speaking Activities**
- ❧ **Research and Report Writing**
- ❧ **Selection Vocabulary Practice**
- ❧ **Spelling Power**
- ❧ **Style and Documentation Guide for Writers**
- ❧ **Viewing and Representing Activities**
- ❧ **Vocabulary Power**
- ❧ **Writing and Proofreading Practice**

Grammar and Composition Handbook

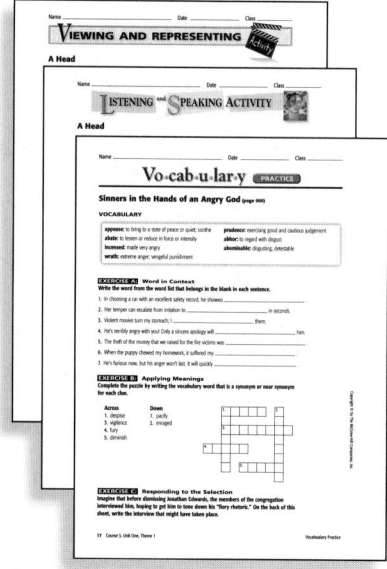

Teacher Management
- ❧ **Block Scheduling Guide**
- ❧ **Unit Planning Guide**

Meeting Individual Needs
- ❧ **English Language Learners Sourcebook**
- ❧ **Family and Community Activities**
- ❧ **Inclusion Strategies Sourcebook**

Spanish Resources
- ❧ **Spanish Summaries**
- ❧ **Spanish Translations**
- ❧ **Active Reading Guide in Spanish**
- ❧ **Selection Quick Checks in Spanish**

Assessment Resources

- ❧ Selection and Theme Assessment
- ❧ Selection Quick Checks
- ❧ Performance Assessment
- ❧ Writing Assessment and Portfolio Management

THE PRINCETON REVIEW

The Princeton Review, the nation's leading test preparation firm, has developed the following assessment resources for *Glencoe Literature*:

- • TerraNova Preparation and Practice
- • SAT-9 Preparation and Practice
- • ITBS Preparation and Practice

Name _____ Date _____ Class _____

✓ SELECTION QUICK CHECK

Score ☐

Lalla by Rosamunde Pilcher (page 000)

Name _____ Date _____ Class _____

Writing Assessment and Portfolio Management

Name _____ Date _____ Class _____

Selection Test

Score ☐

The Lady, or the Tiger? (page 000)

Recalling and Interpreting (40 points total; 8 points each)
Write the letter of the best answer.

____ 1. In the king's arena, guilt and innocence are determined by
    a. reason.   c. the on-lookers.
    b. chance.   d. the king's mood.

____ 2. The king's method of administering justice is popular with his subjects MAINLY because
    a. it promotes law and order.
    b. it involves suspense and spectacle.
    c. it usually involves a bloody slaughter.
    d. the results are always pleasing to the audience.

____ 3. According to the story, what could bring about the young man's marriage to the princess?
    a. nothing
    b. the young man's pleading guilty to his crime
    c. the young man's defeating the tiger in combat
    d. the young man's refusing to marry the lady behind the door

____ 4. The young man looks at the princess in order to
    a. defy the king.   c. prove his courage.
    b. get information.   d. try to influence her.

____ 5. In opening the door that he opens, the young man mainly displays his
    a. innocence of the charges against him.
    b. preference for the princess over the lady.
    c. preference for the lady over the princess.
    d. willingness to let the princess decide his fate.

Using Vocabulary (15 points total; 3 points each)
Write the letter of the best answer. This exercise is continued on the next page.

____ 6. What emanates from most flowers?
    a. bees   b. soil   c. scent

____ 7. A fervent feeling is one that is
    a. intense.   b. painful.   c. sympathetic.

____ 8. A person who behaves in an imperious way could be called
    a. bossy.   b. shy.   c. courageous.

Selection Tests   Course 5, Unit One, Theme 1   15

FINE ART TRANSPARENCY 3

Personal Writing

Henry Ossawa Tanner, *The Ba...*

Context for Writing You have been invited to a f... the people attending are family members you know; ot... you will meet for the very first time. You have been ask... ly member who helped to shape your life. This person... sonal attention and instruction, like the man in the pai... model. Your essay will be included in a book about the... future generations. Briefly describe a family member w... life or taught you something valuable. Then explain th... you learned.

LITERARY ELEMENTS TRANSPARENCY 12

The **plot**, or action of a story revolves around *conflict*.

- The **conflict** of the story is the problem that sets the plot in motion.
- The **climax,** or turning point, is the most exciting, interesting, or suspenseful moment in a story.
- The **resolution** of a story shows how the conflict is solved.

Analyze the plot of "Through the Tunnel."

Climax: _____

Jerry's conflicts: _____

Resolution: _____

Think of another selection you have read and identify the major conflict, the climax, and the resolution.

Transparencies

Choose from a number of overhead transparencies to engage students and to reinforce and extend understanding.

- ❧ Selection Focus Transparencies
- ❧ Literary Elements Transparencies
- ❧ Grammar and Language Transparencies
- ❧ Writing and Proofreading Transparencies
- ❧ Fine Art Transparencies

Technology Resources

With *Glencoe Literature*, you can draw upon a wealth of audio, video, software, and Internet resources to help engage students' interest and enhance their experience of literature.

VIDEO RESOURCES

❧ **Literature Launchers** Short video segments that are motivating and engaging; available on videodisc or VHS tape

❧ **MindJogger Videoquizzes** One video quiz per theme, available on videodisc or VHS tape

❧ **Video Library** Collection of documentary and performance videos available on VHS tape

AUDIO RESOURCES

❧ **Audio Library** Literature selections available on audiotape or CD

❧ **Spanish Audio Library** Readings of many selections in Spanish available on audiotape or CD

Glencoe Literature Web Site lit.glencoe.com

On-line resources for you as well as for students and parents

Features include
❧ appropriate Web site links
❧ games and activities for lessons in the Student Edition
❧ state literary sites
❧ teacher-to-teacher exchange
❧ professional articles
❧ and much more!

Literature Classics CD-ROM

Writer's Assistant

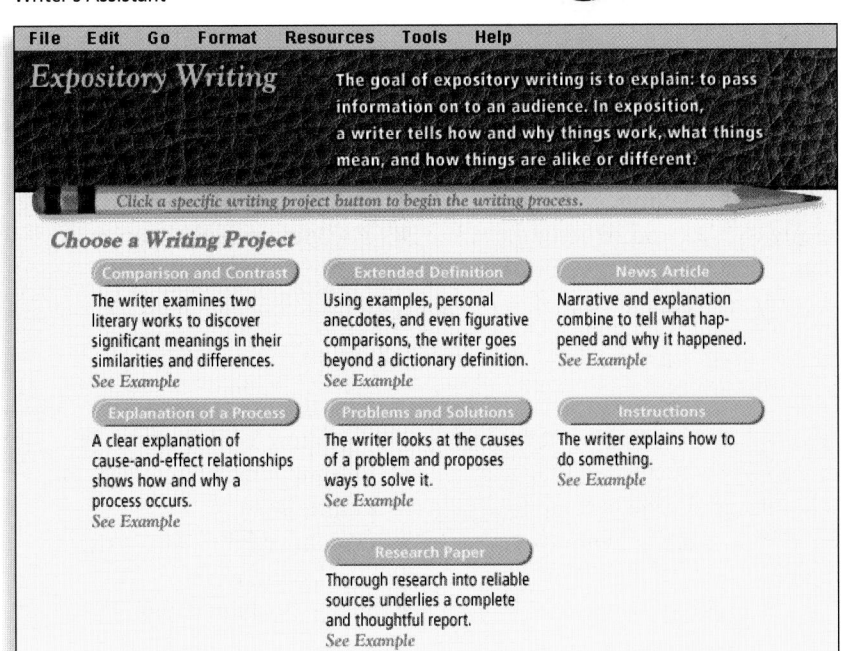

SOFTWARE

🖋 **Literature Classics CD-ROM** More than 900 additional literature selections accessible by author, title, genre, theme, or date

🖋 **Writer's Assistant** Easy-to-use, hands-on tools and templates to help students in all modes of writing

🖋 **Presentation Plus** Dynamic multimedia PowerPoint® presentation tool

🖋 **Testmaker** Editable electronic database of Selection and Theme Tests, with additional test items to customize your assessment to your needs

🖋 **Vocabulary Puzzlemaker** Make vocabulary study fun with word searches based on selection vocabulary.

🖋 **Language Arts Passkey™** Self-tutorial reading assistance for students

🖋 **Electronic Teacher's Classroom Resources** All ancillary print resources available on CD-ROM

🖋 **Interactive Grammar and Language Workbook**

Scope and Sequence Overview

Strand	Overview	Key Items for the Strand **Student Edition**
Literary Concepts and Techniques	Students develop knowledge of literary history and genres, analyze literary elements for their contribution to meaning in texts, and develop appreciation for aspects of writers' craft.	❧ Literary Elements ❧ Analyzing Literature ❧ Genre Focus ❧ Literary Terms Handbook
Reading and Thinking	Students develop proficiency with a full range of strategies and skills for comprehending a variety of texts and for thinking critically, creatively, and analytically.	❧ Active Reading Strategies ❧ Active Reading Models ❧ Reading and Thinking Skills ❧ Reading and Thinking Minilessons ❧ Reading Handbook
Writing	Students write in a variety of forms for various purposes and audiences, using a recursive writing process as appropriate. Students write to learn and to make personal connections to literature.	❧ Writing Workshops ❧ Writing Skills features ❧ Focus Activities ❧ Literature and Writing ❧ Extending Your Response ❧ Theme Projects ❧ Writing Handbook
Vocabulary and Spelling	Students build vocabulary through wide reading, attention to context clues and structural analysis, and use of dictionaries and other reference tools.	❧ Vocabulary Preview ❧ Vocabulary Minilessons ❧ Vocabulary Skills features
Grammar and Language	Students develop mastery of the conventions of grammar, usage, mechanics, and style, and apply these conventions in their own writing.	❧ Grammar Link features ❧ Grammar and Language Minilessons ❧ Grammar Hints (in Writing Workshops) ❧ Language Handbook

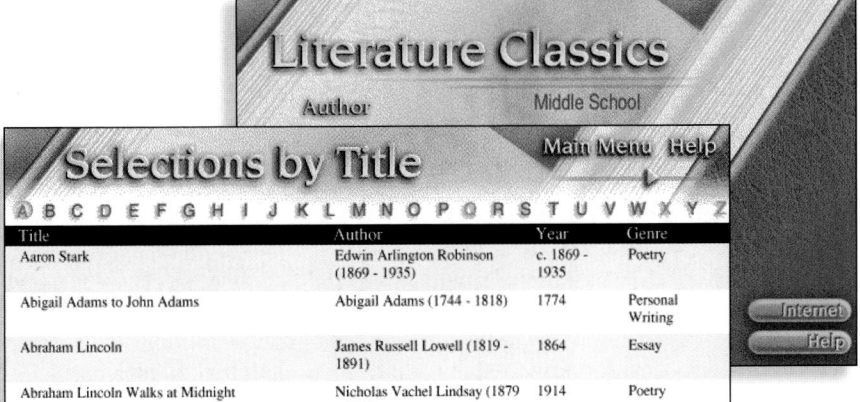

Literature Classics CD-ROM

Title	Author	Year	Genre
Aaron Stark	Edwin Arlington Robinson (1869 - 1935)	c. 1869 - 1935	Poetry
Abigail Adams to John Adams	Abigail Adams (1744 - 1818)	1774	Personal Writing
Abraham Lincoln	James Russell Lowell (1819 - 1891)	1864	Essay
Abraham Lincoln Walks at Midnight	Nicholas Vachel Lindsay (1879 - 1931)	1914	Poetry
from *Across the Plains in 1844*, Chapter 1: On the Plains in 1844	Catherine Pringle (c. 1800's)	1844	Personal Writing
Address to the Congress	Neil Armstrong (1930 -), Edwin Aldrin (1930 -), and Michael Collins (1930 -)	1969	Speech

SOFTWARE

❧ **Literature Classics CD-ROM** More than 900 additional literature selections accessible by author, title, genre, theme, or date

❧ **Writer's Assistant** Easy-to-use, hands-on tools and templates to help students in all modes of writing

❧ **Presentation Plus** Dynamic multimedia PowerPoint® presentation tool

❧ **Testmaker** Editable electronic database of Selection and Theme Tests, with additional test items to customize your assessment to your needs

❧ **Vocabulary Puzzlemaker** Make vocabulary study fun with word searches based on selection vocabulary.

❧ **Language Arts Passkey™** Self-tutorial reading assistance for students

❧ **Electronic Teacher's Classroom Resources** All ancillary print resources available on CD-ROM

❧ **Interactive Grammar and Language Workbook**

Writer's Assistant

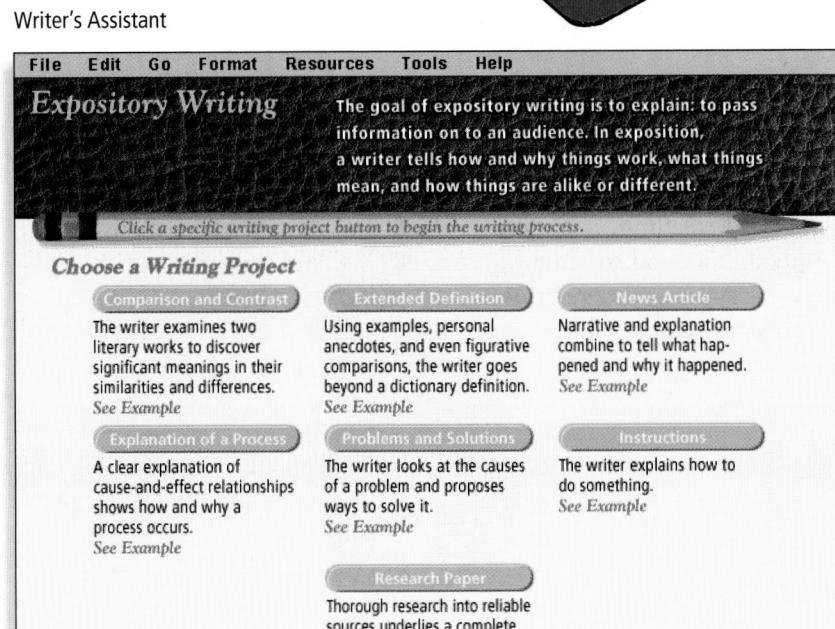

File   Edit   Go   Format   Resources   Tools   Help

Expository Writing

The goal of expository writing is to explain: to pass information on to an audience. In exposition, a writer tells how and why things work, what things mean, and how things are alike or different.

Click a specific writing project button to begin the writing process.

Choose a Writing Project

| Comparison and Contrast |
The writer examines two literary works to discover significant meanings in their similarities and differences.
See Example

| Extended Definition |
Using examples, personal anecdotes, and even figurative comparisons, the writer goes beyond a dictionary definition.
See Example

| News Article |
Narrative and explanation combine to tell what happened and why it happened.
See Example

| Explanation of a Process |
A clear explanation of cause-and-effect relationships shows how and why a process occurs.
See Example

| Problems and Solutions |
The writer looks at the causes of a problem and proposes ways to solve it.
See Example

| Instructions |
The writer explains how to do something.
See Example

| Research Paper |
Thorough research into reliable sources underlies a complete and thoughtful report.
See Example

Scope and Sequence Overview

Strand	Overview	Key Items for the Strand **Student Edition**
Literary Concepts and Techniques	Students develop knowledge of literary history and genres, analyze literary elements for their contribution to meaning in texts, and develop appreciation for aspects of writers' craft.	❧ Literary Elements ❧ Analyzing Literature ❧ Genre Focus ❧ Literary Terms Handbook
Reading and Thinking	Students develop proficiency with a full range of strategies and skills for comprehending a variety of texts and for thinking critically, creatively, and analytically.	❧ Active Reading Strategies ❧ Active Reading Models ❧ Reading and Thinking Skills ❧ Reading and Thinking Minilessons ❧ Reading Handbook
Writing	Students write in a variety of forms for various purposes and audiences, using a recursive writing process as appropriate. Students write to learn and to make personal connections to literature.	❧ Writing Workshops ❧ Writing Skills features ❧ Focus Activities ❧ Literature and Writing ❧ Extending Your Response ❧ Theme Projects ❧ Writing Handbook
Vocabulary and Spelling	Students build vocabulary through wide reading, attention to context clues and structural analysis, and use of dictionaries and other reference tools.	❧ Vocabulary Preview ❧ Vocabulary Minilessons ❧ Vocabulary Skills features
Grammar and Language	Students develop mastery of the conventions of grammar, usage, mechanics, and style, and apply these conventions in their own writing.	❧ Grammar Link features ❧ Grammar and Language Minilessons ❧ Grammar Hints (in Writing Workshops) ❧ Language Handbook

The charts on these and the following two pages provide an overview of the program scope and sequence for *Glencoe Literature*. For a detailed scope and sequence of skills for each Theme, see the Theme Skills Scope and Sequence chart that immediately follows each Theme Opener. See also the Index of Skills (pages R120–R128) for a comprehensive listing of all skills and concepts taught in this level of *Glencoe Literature*.

Key Items for the Strand **Teacher's Wraparound Edition**	Key Items for the Strand **Program Resources**
❧ Literary Elements sidenotes ❧ Author's Craft sidenotes ❧ Thematic Focus ❧ Connecting to Other Selections	❧ Literary Elements Transparencies ❧ Literature Classics CD-ROM ❧ Literature Groups Sourcebook
❧ Active Reading sidenotes ❧ Critical Thinking sidenotes ❧ Reading Minilessons ❧ Less Proficient Readers ❧ English Language Learners	❧ Active Reading Guide ❧ Reading Workbook ❧ Critical Thinking Skills ❧ Inclusion Strategies Sourcebook ❧ English Language Learners Sourcebook ❧ Language Arts Passkey
❧ Writing Minilessons ❧ Meeting Individual Needs ❧ Reading Journals	❧ Writing and Proofreading Activities ❧ Writing and Proofreading Transparencies ❧ Grammar and Composition Handbook ❧ Writer's Assistant CD-ROM ❧ Style and Documentation Sourcebook for Writers
❧ Vocabulary Skills sidenotes ❧ English Language Learners	❧ Selection Vocabulary Practice ❧ Vocabulary Power ❧ Spelling Power ❧ Vocabulary Puzzlemaker
❧ Grammar and Language Minilessons ❧ Language Notes	❧ Grammar and Language Transparencies ❧ Grammar and Language Workbook ❧ Inclusion Strategies Sourcebook ❧ Interactive Grammar and Language Workbook ❧ Grammar and Composition Handbook

Continued on T54–T55

Scope and Sequence Overview

Strand	Overview	Key Items for the Strand **Student Edition**
Listening, Speaking, and Viewing	Students develop proficiency with skills of oral communication and visual literacy and apply them in a variety of contexts.	❧ Extending Your Response ❧ Theme Projects ❧ Focus Activities ❧ Literature Groups ❧ Image captions (for Viewing)
Life Skills	Within the context of literature study, students develop skills of problem solving, decision making, and collaboration. They also perform a variety of real-world reading and writing tasks.	❧ Learning for Life Activities (Extending Your Response) ❧ Theme Projects
Research and Study Skills	Students use reading and writing for inquiry and research and develop a variety of study and test-taking skills.	❧ Extending Your Response ❧ Reading Handbook ❧ Communications Skills Handbook ❧ Theme Projects ❧ Standardized Test Practice
Media and Technology	Students enhance their study of literature through the use of the Internet and other computer and media technologies.	❧ Internet Connections (Extending Your Response) ❧ Theme Projects ❧ Technology Skills
Interdisciplinary Studies	Students make frequent conceptual and thematic connections between literature and other fields of study.	❧ Interdisciplinary Connections ❧ Interdisciplinary Activities (Extending Your Response) ❧ Theme Projects

Key Items for the Strand **Teacher's Wraparound Edition**	Key Items for the Strand **Program Resources**
❧ Viewing the Art sidenotes ❧ Listening and Speaking Minilessons	❧ Fine Art Transparencies ❧ Listening and Speaking Activities ❧ Viewing and Representing Activities ❧ Audio Library ❧ Video Library ❧ Literature Launchers
❧ Life Skills Connections ❧ Critical Thinking sidenotes ❧ Real-World Connections	❧ Critical Thinking Skills ❧ Theme Planning Guide (Life Skills Connections) ❧ Family and Community Activities
❧ Test-Taking Tips ❧ Multiple Learning Styles	❧ Research and Report Writing Guide ❧ Style and Documentation Sourcebook for Writers
❧ Technology Options ❧ Internet Connections ❧ Technology Tips	❧ Media Connections Activities ❧ Guide to Using the Internet and Other Electronic Resources ❧ Web Site (lit.glencoe.com) ❧ Writer's Assistant CD-ROM
❧ Interdisciplinary Connections ❧ Cultural Notes ❧ Historical Notes	❧ Interdisciplinary Activities ❧ Theme Planning Guide (Interdisciplinary Connections)

Program Philosophy

What are the goals of *Glencoe Literature?*

by Denny Wolfe

The impetus for *Glencoe Literature: The Reader's Choice* was the need for contemporary anthologies that would appeal to today's media-savvy students. A rich mix of classic and modern selections unites new and old voices chosen to represent our diverse communities. Each book's pages reflect a youthful energy, with color, images, media connections, interdisciplinary links, and quotations to enhance the featured literary works. The collection of poems and plays, stories and songs, letters and essays, myths and folklore enables teachers and students to explore together the literary legacies of many voices and many lands.

Glencoe Literature is particularly committed to supporting classroom teachers as they work
- to develop students' abilities as readers, writers, listeners, speakers, viewers, and critical and creative thinkers
- to guide students in developing interpretive skills that transcend specific literary voices, cultures, or times toward an understanding of the larger human experience
- to help students become life-long learners and responsible citizens for democracy in the twenty-first century

Through its varied and active instructional strategies, *Glencoe Literature* invites students to experience the entertaining and restorative powers of literature. Within this context students have frequent opportunities to
- engage in responsive reading, interpretation, and literary analysis through encounters with texts arranged by both theme and genre
- explore writing as a purposeful and flexible means of expression, reflection, and critical and creative thought
- use current and emerging technologies as tools for learning and extending the language arts
- participate in an approach to literacy development that integrates all the language arts
- experience multiple forms of assessment that are responsive to local, state, and national standards of achievement

Glencoe Literature prepares students for their literary encounters through prereading activities rooted in the experiences that students bring to texts. During and after the reading of a work, students respond personally to it; they share their responses with others; and they learn to probe ever more deeply into elements of the literary craft. This sequence enables students and teachers to create interpretive communities in their classrooms, to realize the highest standards of literary inquiry, and to participate vigorously in the cultural conversation of the twenty-first century.

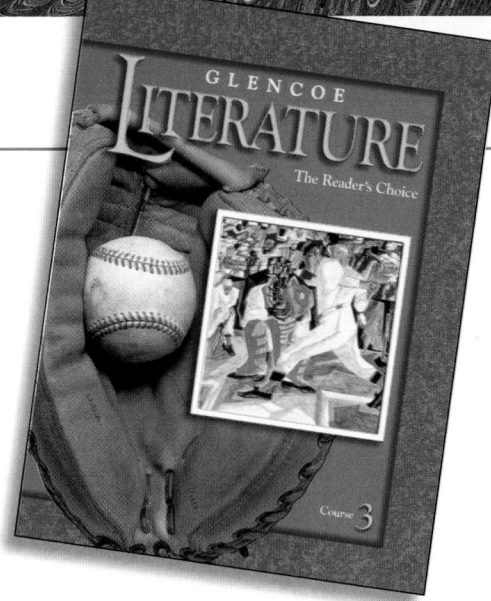

How do we honor diverse voices in the classroom?

by William Ray

The classroom in which a diverse group of students meets a diverse curriculum is perhaps happiest of all, but all students need to be exposed to a culturally diverse literature program. Even in the most homogeneous school, hearing a rich mixture of literary voices is crucial not only to a democratic society, but also to a literary education. In the following statement, Sandra Cisneros describes her participation in a discussion of "the house of the imagination" at the University of Iowa; reading these words to students can be a lesson in both democracy and metaphor:

> Everyone seemed to have some communal knowledge which I did not have—and then I realized that the metaphor of house was totally wrong for me. Suddenly I was homeless. There were no attics and cellars and crannies. I had no such house in my memories. As a child I had read of such things in books, and my family had promised such a house, but the best they could do was offer the miserable bungalow I was embarrassed with all my life. This caused me to question myself, to become defensive. What did I, Sandra Cisneros, know? My classmates were from the best schools in the country. They had been bred as fine hothouse flowers. I was a yellow weed among the city's cracks.

Many of us are fortunate enough to teach students of diverse backgrounds and so have witnessed some of our students experiencing special moments of recognition when they see their culture reflected in a piece of literature. As a student of mine, some years ago, put it, "I like this book—it feels like home." For those who teach in more homogeneous classrooms, the importance of a multicultural curriculum is not diminished.

Using literature of many cultures not only can be a revelation for students who are not of the dominant culture, but also it can provide a jumping off point for students to share their experience. I recall one of my urban, African American students, during a discussion of Sandra Cisneros' *House on Mango Street*, educating her white, suburban classmates out of their stereotypical views of urban life. On another occasion a student of Nigerian descent explained to his classmates how Igbo customs have been maintained or changed since the time of Chinua Achebe's novel *Things Fall Apart*.

Democracy demands that the voices of everyone be heard. *Glencoe Literature*, then, includes representative voices from many corners of the world and from many cultures. For students to develop their own voices, views, and values—grounded in families and communities that schools serve—they must hear and consider the voices of others. Through their own responses and the responses of classmates to literature contained in these pages, students extend their own world views and take important steps toward becoming responsible thinkers and citizens. ❧

Reading

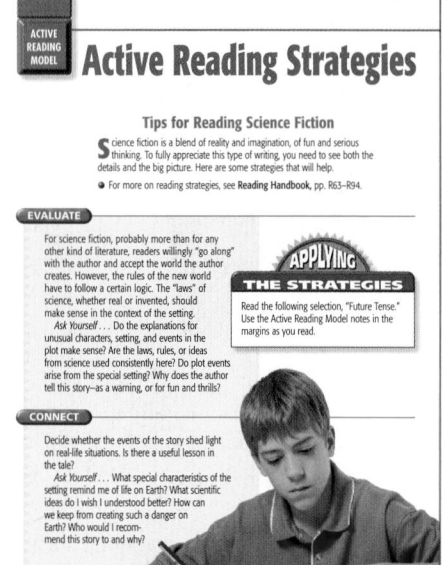

Active Reading Strategies

ACTIVE READING MODEL

Tips for Reading Science Fiction

Science fiction is a blend of reality and imagination, of fun and serious thinking. To fully appreciate this type of writing, you need to see both the details and the big picture. Here are some strategies that will help.

● For more on reading strategies, see **Reading Handbook**, pp. R63–R94.

EVALUATE

For science fiction, probably more than for any other kind of literature, readers willingly "go along" with the author and accept the world the author creates. However, the rules of the new world have to follow a certain logic. The "laws" of science, whether real or invented, should make sense in the context of the setting.

Ask Yourself . . . Do the explanations for unusual characters, setting, and events in the plot make sense? Are the laws, rules, or ideas from science used consistently here? Do plot events arise from the special setting? Why does the author tell this story—as a warning, or for fun and thrills?

APPLYING THE STRATEGIES

Read the following selection, "Future Tense." Use the Active Reading Model notes in the margins as you read.

CONNECT

Decide whether the events of the story shed light on real-life situations. Is there a useful lesson in the tale?

Ask Yourself . . . What special characteristics of the setting remind me of life on Earth? What scientific ideas do I wish I understood better? How can we keep from creating such a danger on Earth? Who would I recommend this story to and why?

*Active Reading Strategies and Models **provide prompts to help readers engage in conversations with text.***

Personal Writing
New Thoughts About Myself Return to the notes you wrote in the **Focus Activity** on page 13. Would you change the qualities you listed after reading these two poems? Write a short self-portrait that ... racter ... nce.

Art Activity
Story Map Leslie Marmon Silko uses foreshadowing when she offers her readers clues about what will occur next in the story. If you recognize these clues, you can predict what will happen. Reexamine the story. As a group, use chart paper to create a large story map that illustrates and charts the evidence foreshadowing the goat's attack on the narrator. Present ...

Performing
Words Set to Music Work with a small group to find instrumental music that evokes the mood of "Growing Pains." Then make a tape of the music to use as background during a group reading of the poem. Try various effects—for example, by grouping low and high voices or single and group voices.

*Journals, drama, **and** art support students as engaged readers who relate to characters and other story elements.*

How do we engage students through critical and creative reading?

by Jeffrey Wilhelm

Reading is a very complex act, and its complexity is largely invisible. When I studied the engagement or meaning-making strategies of young readers, I found that proficient readers regularly operated on ten different dimensions of response as they constructed meaning. Yet less proficient readers did not make any of the same response moves as their more capable peers—in fact, they did not understand that readers were supposed to "do" anything at all beyond decoding words. When I asked one student what he saw when he read, he replied, "Words, man. I see nothing but words!" Proficient readers, on the other hand, could richly describe characters, settings, and situations—often including details that went far beyond the implied meanings of the text.

Less proficient readers have an impoverished notion of reading, and they are usually not helped much by classroom materials that do not reflect a deep understanding of engagement. In *Glencoe Literature*, we base instructional activities on the notion that reading is "transactional"—that is, a conversation between a reader and a text that results in the creation of meaning. We also base our activities on knowledge of engagement—that is, that readers deploy a wide range of creative and critical strategies to evoke a "story world," to connect personally to it, and to critically reflect upon their reading experience.

A key research finding is that readers who do not first visualize a textual world and take on a relationship to characters or ideas will not do anything else. After all, they have nothing to connect to and reflect upon. So the first order of business in assisting reading performance is to support students in "seeing" and "relating" to characters, forces, and ideas. We use response journals, art, drama, and other creative activities to support this level of reading.

Once students have visualized and related, they can then begin to make inferences and elaborate on the story world. Far from being extras, inferencing and elaborating are essentials of reading. Roland Barthes writes that "elaboration is the surest sign of engagement in reading. . . . The reader does not decode, he overcodes." This is why some students who can decode words still remain poor readers—they do not know how to use sophisticated creative strategies of engagement, of bringing their own prior experience to a text, and of creating and representing textual meaning. Many of the questions and activities in *Glencoe Literature* are designed to support students in personally connecting to their readings, and in making inferences and elaborations.

Finally, there is critical reading. Because students cannot reflect upon nor critique what they have not experienced, we introduce critical reading after a rich experiential reading has been supported. At this point students may consider how texts are constructed, the use of literary conventions, and an evaluation of their own reading experience.

Crucial to teaching readers is the notion of reading as a constructive act. In this series, students have many opportunities to practice and develop specific reading skills and strategies. They are also assisted to read in both creative and critical ways and through a variety of response dimensions. Our goal is to help them not only to develop a powerful repertoire of reading strategies, but also to reconceive of reading as a personally powerful and meaningful social pursuit. 🐦

Focus Activities and Personal Response questions help students connect reading to their own experience.

Analyzing Literature allows students to interpret and evaluate and to look critically at literary elements.

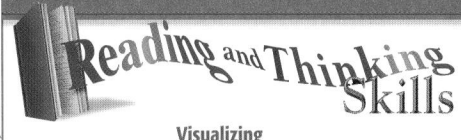

Skills pages, minilessons, and a reading handbook are valuable tools for developing reading and thinking skills.

Writing

Personal Writing
Childhood Memories Look back at your QuickWrite list from the **Focus Activity** on page 826. Use the details on the list to write a journal entry about that humorous event in your life. Be sure to explain why that event has stayed in your memory. You may share your entry with your friends or family if you wish.

Focus Activities and Personal Writing activities help students make personal connections to literature.

Writing About Literature
Point of View "Turkeys" tells of an experience Bailey White had when she was six years old. The story is told from her point of view. Imagine how one of the ornithologists might remember the incident. Then write a brief summary of the story from the ornithologist's point of view.

Learning for Life
Incident Report Imagine you are Uncle Tony. Write a report for the police about your missing goat. Summarize the events that lead to the goat's escape. Also describe the goat and your nephew. Read your report to the class.

Writing About Literature and Learning for Life activities let student writers try out many roles and points of view.

How does writing enhance the study of literature?

by Jacqueline Jones Royster

We think of the literature classroom as a language-rich environment, made all the richer by the collection of texts and activities in *Glencoe Literature*. As both art and artifact, writing is a flexible tool that can work dynamically with other elements of instruction as teachers help students to enhance both learning and performance. From this point of view, writing activities are generously incorporated throughout each unit for a variety of purposes.

Writing to understand and make personal connections with literature Through reading response journals and other writing activities, students have a mechanism for noticing the details in a text and making sense of them. Writing can help students to

- make personal connections with ideas, images, and experiences;
- see ways to go beyond their own connections toward broader implications; and
- sometimes see critical distinctions between their own lives and experiences and what they are reading.

Writing to experiment as critical and creative thinkers Through writing, students can assume many different roles and points of view as they think about what a text is saying, what it is doing, and whether it is successful. They can sort through ideas, weigh the impact and consequences of language choices, and use these assessments to make informed judgments about what works in written expression and why. They can write themselves into the text, take on characters in different times and places, or imagine on paper different scenarios as they think seriously about what it means to produce literature. As students respond to literature, writing enables them to stand back from a text to think about concepts such as "aesthetic value," "eloquence," or even "elegance"—in other words, to determine in more systematic ways what appeals to them as readers and how authors achieve those effects on readers.

Writing to discover one's own voice Teachers accomplish an important cultural task when we help students move from viewing themselves as just consumers of other people's writing to seeing themselves also as producers of writing. Literature as an expressive tradition is an ongoing enterprise, and the creative writing activities in *Glencoe Literature* encourage students to write in many genres, including fiction and nonfiction, and to compose and present their work through various media. In our view, the study of literature and the writing of literature go hand in hand as we help students to know both concretely and abstractly the power and joy of words.

Writing to understand form and function Through the Writing Workshops in *Glencoe Literature*, students can gain direct experiences with producing various forms and genres of writing. They learn to use genre options with a more creative and critical eye and to develop a more sophisticated vocabulary for talking about their writing choices. In this way the genre knowledge that they build as readers and writers helps them to see writing—like language use in general—as purposeful and capable of both consequence and reward.

Approaching writing in this way, as part and parcel of a language-rich environment, helps teachers extend students' definitions of writing to include

- writing to understand and connect with reading;
- writing to reflect on experiences (in the texts as well as in real life);
- writing to represent thoughts and ideas in multiple ways through various media for many purposes and audiences; and
- writing to display talent, ability, and understanding and thereby to demonstrate what they know and can do.

With such varied experience in using writing in the company of the other language arts, we believe that students will be well prepared to perform at high levels of quality and excellence.

Creative Writing
Epilogue   What do you think happens to T. J. after the final scene in the story? An **epilogue** is a brief concluding section to a novel, a story, or a poem. Write an epilogue to "Antaeus." Your epilogue might take place weeks, months, or many years after the end of the story.

Creative Writing activities encourage students to write in many genres and for various audiences.

Writing Skills

Using Dialogue in a Narrative

Dialogue, or conversation quoting the exact words of characters, is an effective narrative technique. It can rivet the reader's attention. And no wonder. Dialogue can bring characters to life and dramatically show them reacting to one another.

When you use dialogue in your writing, try to weave it in smoothly. Dialogue may be introduced in several ways—at the beginning, middle, or end of a sentence. Sometimes a block of conversation can continue for several lines. Following are some examples of how dialogue can be used. As you read, notice how the writer has used capitalization and punctuation marks.

Writing WORKSHOP

Narrative Writing: Autobiographical Anecdote

A story of your own experiences—an **autobiographical anecdote**—can speak to readers in a way that nothing else can. It can also speak to you. When you write an autobiographical anecdote, you may begin to see your experiences in a new light.

Assignment: Write an autobiographical anecdote. Use the process shown in this Workshop to create a piece of writing that will be memorable for your readers.

● As you write your autobiographical anecdote, see **Writing Handbook,** pp. R48–R53.

The Writing Process

PREWRITING

PREWRITING TIP
A small experience that you recall clearly will work better than a big experience that you can only vaguely remember.

● **Gather Ideas**
Which experiences have meant the most to you? Rosa Parks wrote about her involvement in a historic event; Amy Tan and Ernesto Galarza selected more personal experiences to write about. Try the following to get your ideas flowing:

Writing Workshops and Writing Skills pages help students become proficient with many forms of writing.

Technology & Media Literacy

How can we use technology to enhance the teaching of literature?

by Jeffrey Wilhelm

A technology can be defined as any tool that extends our human abilities—that helps us to do our work more easily. Literacy has always meant the ability to use the most powerful available tools to exchange information and to communicate, which humans do in a variety of deep and complex ways. Video and computer technologies, now melded through multimedia applications, currently constitute our culture's most sophisticated tools of communication. Technology offers us new and exciting ways to be literate, but of course there is also a downside. Neil Postman states that we must learn why and how to use technology for our higher human purposes or we will be doomed to be used by the technology. Many critics of computers in schools argue that this is exactly what happens: computers are often used as expensive ways to implement old and sometimes ineffective ways of teaching. Further, students often learn to use computers or particular applications in decontextualized situations—losing sight of the nature of technology as a tool, using it instead for its own sake.

However, there is an alternative, and this is the kind of technology use offered in *Glencoe Literature: The Reader's Choice*. We use technological applications in the context of sustained study to find information, organize data, and as a way to design and represent new understandings. The rewards of this kind of technological instruction are great. Students learn to use the Internet, hypermedia, and other applications in a meaningful context. They pool technological knowledge and information gleaned from electronic searches to form a community of use. Technology supports traditional ways of reading and composing as students use video and computers to construct knowledge documents that can be posted on the Internet and shared through other electronic means. Research shows that this kind of curriculum, called "learning by design," has many positive effects, particularly for students who are often considered to be reluctant or "at risk."

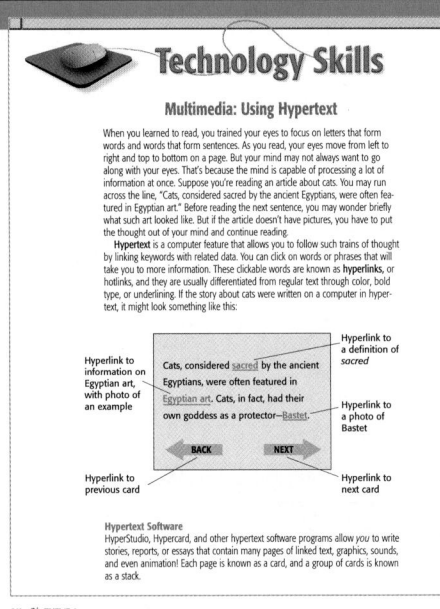

*Technology Skills **features provide opportunities for students to learn about and use a variety of technologies in the context of their study of literature.***

Seymour Papert, one of the foremost authorities on computers and learning, writes that "the computer is the world's greatest construction kit." He concurs that literacy is intimately involved in technology and its critical use. Critical use, he tells us, can only occur if students find and design knowledge with technology. This kind of work is what Papert calls "hard fun," and it leads to powerful and exciting forms of learning. We have provided the context and support for this kind of learning in the text you hold in your hands. Buckle your seatbelts and get ready for some "hard fun" of your own.

How can we help students become media literate?

by Jeffrey Wilhelm

Media literacy is closely related to technology literacy, but it casts a wider net by considering how different technologies organize and represent information in different ways and with different effects. When my own students tell me that they "know" something because they read it on a Web site or saw it on MTV, I become very concerned that they have a critical understanding and standards for how knowledge is produced and represented. In response to these and similar needs, the National Communication Association created national standards for media literacy in 1996, and various states are now embedding similar standards into their curriculum and testing guidelines.

Because of the importance of media literacy, *Glencoe Literature* deals with media use and representation in a variety of ways. Students are asked to use and critique various media, often vis-à-vis literary texts so that they can compare the strengths and weaknesses of representing knowledge through different textual forms. Students are also asked to create media responses to literature they have read, and sometimes to create stories, arguments or presentations of their own using different media possibilities. Always, we have in mind to expand the notion of what it means to be literate to include an understanding of the nature of mass media, the techniques used by them, and the ability to both produce and critique meanings using various media. 🖋

Internet Connections **engage students in on-line research and in building databases of shared knowledge in the classroom.**

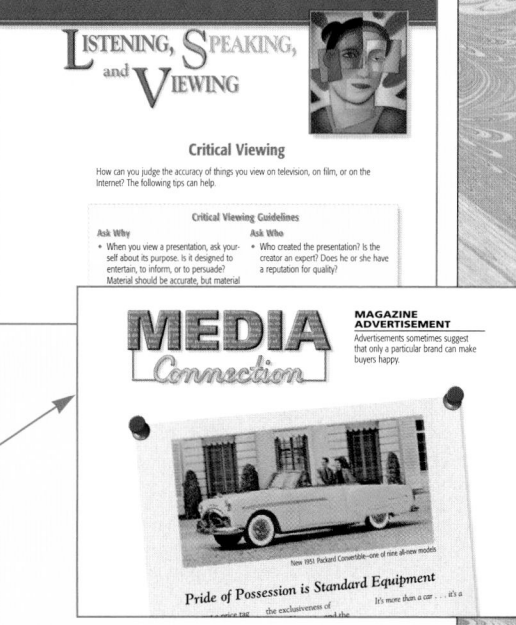

Media Connections **and** *Listening, Speaking, and Viewing* **features help students become critical readers and viewers of media.**

Integrated Language Arts

LISTENING, SPEAKING, and VIEWING

Small-Group Discussions

In "Amigo Brothers," Antonio and Felix need to talk before their bout, but it's difficult. They make the discussion work by helping each other. They listen carefully, suggest phrases, and check their understanding. When you join a small-group discussion, you can use the same strategies to help make the discussion work. Try these tips.

Group Discussion Tips
- Take turns talking. Help everyone have a chance to be heard. If there is a leader, follow his or her direction.
- Listen carefully. Try repeating other points in your own words to be sure

Literature Groups

Keeping Promises Discuss what it means to keep a promise. What promise in the story is broken? What message does a student, such as Marta, receive when a promise is broken? Which characters in the story understand what it means to keep a promise? Together, write a statement explaining why it is important to keep a promise. Share your statement with the other literature groups.

*Skill features **help students develop key listening and speaking abilities, and Literature Groups** activities provide opportunities for small group discussions with each selection.*

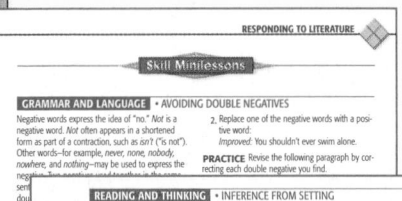

RESPONDING TO LITERATURE

Skill Minilessons

GRAMMAR AND LANGUAGE • AVOIDING DOUBLE NEGATIVES

Negative words express the idea of "no." *Not* is a negative word. *Not* often appears in a shortened form as part of a contraction, such as *isn't* ("is not"). Other words—for example, *never, none, nobody, nowhere,* and *nothing*—may be used to express the negative. Two negatives used together in the same sentence cause confusion and are considered incorrect.

Not...

2. Replace one of the negative words with a positive word:
Improved: You shouldn't ever swim alone.

PRACTICE Revise the following paragraph by correcting each double negative you find.

READING AND THINKING • INFERENCE FROM SETTING

You can use what you know about the setting to help you infer other details about life for the characters in this story. For example, since you know from the setting that it rains all the time, you can infer that most aspects of life take place indoors.

PRACTICE Reread "All Summer in a Day" and think about what you can infer about the kinds of activities and games the children in this story enjoy. Write a paragraph explaining your conclusions and how you arrived at them.

● For more about making inferences, see **Reading Handbook,** p. R89.

VOCABULARY • THE LATIN ROOTS *vit* AND *viv*

The root of *vital* is *vit,* which comes from a Latin word meaning "life." People must meet their *vital* needs, such as their needs for air, food, and water. Vitamins have that name because they are necessary for life. Over time, *vit* has come to have the somewhat broader meaning of "extremely important; absolutely necessary." Something of *vital* concern should receive immediate attention. The root *viv* is similar to *vit;* it means "live."

PRACTICE Use what you know about the roots *vit* and *viv* to answer each question.

1. Would someone show *vivacity* by leaping, coughing, or stumbling?
2. Does a *vivid* description of something make it seem frightening, boring, or real?
3. If there is a *revival* of an old-fashioned style, does it die out or become popular again?
4. What is the best synonym for *vitality*—energy, hunger, or luck?
5. Do people tend to feel *revitalized* after doing hard work, hearing a lullaby, or getting a good night's sleep?

*Skill Minilessons **provide frequent opportunities for students to develop reading and vocabulary skills in the context of their literature study.***

How can we integrate the language arts through our teaching of literature?

by Beverly Ann Chin

Integrating the English language arts into our teaching of literature is an effective way to help students improve their communication and thinking skills. Today, the English language arts include speaking, listening, reading, writing, viewing, and visually representing. We can use each of the language arts to engage our students in the study and appreciation of literature.

Listening and Speaking We integrate listening and speaking skills whenever students participate in class discussions and literature groups. Students orally share their understandings of literature, and they listen to other people's ideas and opinions. We teach speaking and listening skills when our students work in cooperative learning groups and collaborate on literature projects. Speaking and listening skills are basic components in creative drama activities, such as role playing, readers theater, improvisation, and choral reading. As students interpret literature through creative drama and oral interpretation, they discover how language and nonverbal communication affect the audience's understanding of the story. Whether students are responding to literature through a small group conversation, listening to someone read a selection aloud, or participating in a dramatic performance, they are using and improving their speaking and listening abilities.

Reading When we teach literature, we help our students develop important reading strategies. For example, before students read a literature selection, we invite students to draw upon their prior knowledge and experiences to help them make connections with the literature. During the reading process, we encourage students to make inferences about the characters' motivations and to use context clues to determine the meaning of unfamiliar vocabulary. After reading the selection, students discuss their responses and extend their comprehension. By encouraging students to respond to and reflect on literature, we help students develop their critical and creative reading abilities.

Writing Writing enhances students' understanding and enjoyment of literature. We help students grow as writers when we invite them to write in their reading response journals, to create their own literary pieces, or to write expository essays. By keeping response journals, students record their questions, discover insights, and reflect on their meaning-making processes. When students write in the literary forms and styles they are reading, they share their understanding of literary genres. At the end of a unit, we often ask students to write an essay that shows their understanding of the theme, genre, or literary style. All of these writing activities also provide an authentic and meaningful context within which students can develop control of the conventions of grammar, usage, and mechanics as well as of important elements of style. As we encourage students to use writing to learn about themselves and literature, we help students improve their abilities to write clearly, creatively, and effectively.

Viewing and Visually Representing The newest emphases in teaching English language arts are viewing and visually representing. We integrate viewing and representing in our literature curriculum when we help students see the similarities and differences between the stories they read and the films they view. For example, students can analyze how the narrator's point of view in a story is comparable to camera angles; how the story's tone and mood are conveyed through the sound track, color, and lighting; and how a story's dialogue and setting are interpreted by screen writers, location scouts, and film editors. By showing different film versions of the same work, we help students become aware of the parallel roles of authors and film directors.

We also help students become critical viewers when we encourage students to look at paintings and posters to discover how artists use color, texture, movement, shape, and form to create an effect on the audience. Many students convey their understanding and interpretation of literature by drawing character portraits, taking photographs of settings, creating story maps of the plot, illustrating book jackets, designing thematic collages, or creating multimedia projects. By encouraging students to visualize and graphically represent their ideas, we help them make connections between their lives and literature. ❧

Writing Skills
Using Sentence Variety

What do these sentences from "Lob's Girl" have in common?

He must have walked.
He was a very tired dog.
Bert Pengelly rang up Liverpool again.

If you guessed that they are all fairly short sentences, you're right. There's nothing

Skill Minilesson

GRAMMAR AND LANGUAGE • PRONOUN-ANTECEDENT AGREEMENT

A **pronoun** is a word used in place of a noun or noun phrase. An **antecedent** is the word or words the pronoun refers to. A pronoun and its antecedent must agree in number and gender.

Mario brought his mother flowers. *She* was pleased with *them.*

She, a singular feminine pronoun, refers to *mother. Them,* a plural neuter (neither masculine nor feminine) pronoun, refers to *flowers.*

PRACTICE Write the appropriate pronoun for each numbered blank. After the pronoun, write its antecedent.

Sandra Cisneros wrote *The House on Mango Street* when (1) _____ was in her twenties. "Bums in the Attic" is from (2) _____ book. (3) _____ is one of a number of short pieces that make up the book. Each of these brief vignettes can stand on (4) _____ own, but together, Cisneros says, (5) _____ "tell one big story."

Skill Minilessons

GRAMMAR AND LANGUAGE • CONSISTENT VERB TENSES

It is important to keep the verb tenses consistent in your writing. If you jump from one tense to another, readers will be confused about when events take place.

CONFUSING: Uncle Tony **works** hard on the farm. The narrator **worked** on the farm too.

BETTER: Uncle Tony **works** hard on the farm. The narrator **works** on the farm too.

PRACTICE Write a paragraph summarizing the events in "Uncle Tony's Goat." Keep your verbs in the same tense unless you have a strong reason to change them. Exchange paragraphs with a partner and check for consistent verb tenses.

◉ For more about verb tense, see **Language Handbook,** pp. R15–R16.

Minilessons and features help students develop proficiency with key elements of writing, including grammar and style.

EXPLORING THE THEME

Theme Projects

As you read the selections in this theme, choose one of the projects below. Work on your own, with a partner, or in a group.

LEARNING FOR LIFE
Writing a Job Description
What do you dream of doing when you grow up? Do you think about being a dancer, or a veterinarian, or a designer of video games? Think about your dream job. Then write a description of your job.

1. When you have made your choice, do some library research to find out more about it. Talk to people in your community who have similar jobs. Take notes about their job descriptions.
2. Write your job description, and contribute it to a classroom Career Notebook. As you learn about other interesting careers, add new descriptions to the notebook.

MULTIMEDIA PROJECT
A Self-Portrait
Create a multimedia self-portrait.
1. Gather information about yourself. Create a summary of interesting facts about your life, perhaps using a visual format such as a time line or a graph to chart these highlights.
2. Gather photos or drawings of you and your family or friends. Try to include music, videos, and taped interviews to showcase your life.
3. Present your self-portrait to your class.

interNET CONNECTION
Check out the Web for more project ideas. Use your favorite search engine to find other job-related ideas or other topics related to the "What I Am, What I Want to Be" theme. Key words such as jobs, employment, and career fields like medicine and aviation can get you started.

CRITICAL LISTENING
Musical Notes
Your taste in music reflects who you are, as well as your interests.
1. Do you enjoy popular music, oldies, jazz, reggae, rap, or some other type of music? Bring in examples of different kinds of music you enjoy.
2. Talk to older family members about the kinds of music they listened to when they were your age. Research their favorite kinds of music, and bring examples, photographs, or articles about that music to class. You might even create a musical time line showing the kinds of music young people have enjoyed over time.
3. Plan a musical tour through history. Display your research and photographs. Using tapes or CDs, play examples of a wide variety of music. Invite another class or family members to your classroom to participate.

WHAT I A

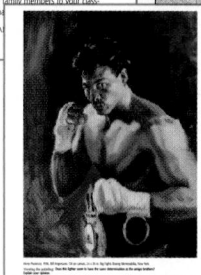

Art projects and viewing questions assist students in becoming skilled producers and viewers of visual media.

Assessment

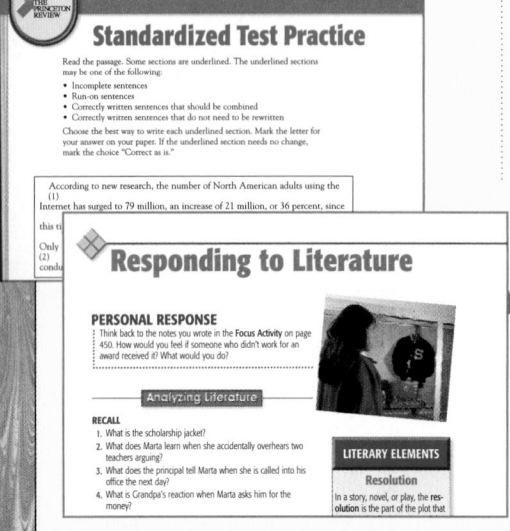

Options for formal assessment include Analyzing Literature and Standardized Test Practice as well as the Selection and Theme Assessment booklet.

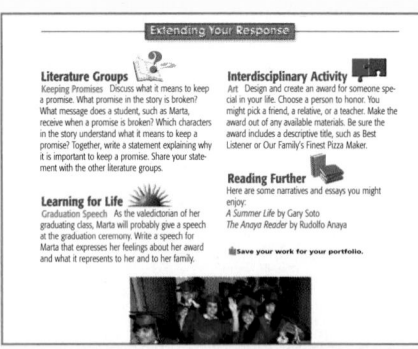

Extending Your Response activities can be used for performance assessment. In addition, the Performance Assessment booklet provides a performance task and rubric for each selection.

How can we use assessment and portfolios in our teaching of literature?

by Beverly Ann Chin

When we think about assessment in literature, we need to consider our purposes for teaching literature and our literature curriculum. Assessment in literature is authentic if it reflects what, how, and why we teach. For example, if we emphasize personal responses to literature, our assessment should evaluate students' ability to make connections with the texts and authors they read. If we emphasize critical analysis of literature, our assessment should evaluate students' ability to understand the elements of an author's craft and the structure of the text. If we emphasize the development of the full range of language arts skills through the study of literature, assessment should include activities that require students to demonstrate their understanding of literature through writing, speaking, and visual representation. If we want students to take more responsibility and ownership of their own learning, students should have regular opportunities to assess their own and their peers' accomplishments.

Formal Assessment Formal assessment focuses on measuring what students know. A variety of traditional paper-and-pencil test formats can be effective tools for assessing students' comprehension of selections and their ability to analyze and interpret what they have read. By incorporating experiences with standardized test formats into classroom assessment, teachers can also help prepare students for their participation in state and national assessments.

Performance Assessment Performance assessments in literature enable students to demonstrate their understandings of literature. For example, if your students keep reader response journals, you can ask students to select several entries and write a personal reflection paper that shows how their responses to the theme evolved during the literature unit. Creative drama activities can also serve as performance assessment; for example, students can identify and perform important events in a story to demonstrate their understanding of plot. Students can also demonstrate their interpretation of the theme by writing in a different genre or by creating interdisciplinary, multimedia projects that extend the theme.

Portfolios Portfolios can be a powerful assessment tool in the literature classroom. A portfolio is a purposeful collection of work that shows a student's accomplishments, growth, and learning processes. Many teachers who use portfolios in their literature classes encourage students to keep and review their work at the end of each unit. As teachers discuss with students the purposes of the literature portfolio, they help students develop criteria for selecting and organizing the works (entries) to be included in their portfolios.

To guide students in selecting items to include in the portfolio, teachers can ask questions such as

- Which works show your accomplishments in this course?
- Which works demonstrate your growth as a reader and writer?
- Which works reveal your abilities to think critically and creatively?
- Which works did you most enjoy?

Teachers also encourage students to reflect on each of their portfolio entries by considering these questions:

- What did you like best about this work?
- What did you learn from doing this work?
- What might you do differently if you were to do this work again?

Many students create portfolios that contain a table of contents, a preface to the portfolio, and an introduction (or reflection paragraph) for each selection. The process of creating and sharing portfolios provides students with ongoing opportunities to set goals and evaluate their own knowledge, skills, and attitudes.

Through portfolios and other forms of assessment, English language arts teachers gain important information about students' understanding and enjoyment of literature. By creating assessments that align with the literature curriculum and instruction, we enable our students to demonstrate their accomplishments, apply their knowledge, and reflect on their growth as learners.

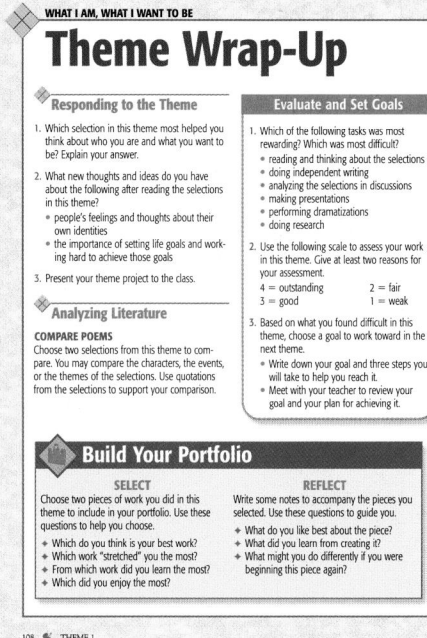

Each Theme Wrap-Up *supports students as they build their portfolios and assess their own performance. Portfolio resources for teachers appear in the* Writing Assessment and Portfolio Management *booklet.*

THEME OPENING

➤ **Theme 1:**
WHAT I AM, WHAT I WANT TO BE

- **Introducing the Theme**
  (p. 1)
- **Exploring the Theme**
  (p. 2)
- **Theme Projects**
  (p. 3)

SELECTIONS

Names/Nombres (p. 4)

One (p. 13)

I'm Nobody! Who are you? (p. 13)

Face It (p. 18)

Almost Ready (p. 18)

Media Connection: Heroes
(p. 24)

Strong Men Weep (p. 25)

from Wait Till Next Year (p. 34)

Media Connection: *from* The Wonder
Years (pp. 41–42)

Broken Chain (p. 43)

Without Commercials (p. 58)

Active Reading Model: *from* Barrio Boy
(p. 66)

Fish Cheeks (p. 76)

Rosa Parks: My Story (p. 84)

SKILL FEATURES

Grammar Link (p. 12)

Writing Skills (p. 23)

Technology Skills (pp. 56–57)

Genre Focus: Autobiography
(pp. 62–63)

Active reading Strategies
(pp. 64–65)

Vocabulary Skills (p. 75)

Interdisciplinary Connection (p. 82)

Reading Skills (p. 83)

WRITING WORKSHOP

Narrative Writing: Autobiographical Anecdote (pp. 104–107)

THEME WRAP-UP

- **Responding to the Theme, Analyzing Literature, Evaluate and Set Goals** (p. 108)
- **Build Your Portfolio** (p. 108)
- **Reading on Your Own** (p. 109)

  The Witch of Blackbird Pond by Elizabeth Speare George

  No-No Boy by John Okada

  Baseball in April and Other Stories by Gary Soto

  Where You Belong by Mary Ann McGuigan
- **Standardized Test Practice** (pp. 110–111)

KEYS TO LITERARY CONNECTIONS

 Comparing Selections

The **Comparing Selections** feature in this theme provides opportunities for addressing diverse aspects of the reading and literature curriculum.

For example, in Comparing Selections on page 40, students compare their responses to "Strong Men Weep" and to the excerpt from *Wait Till Next Year*. Students also have the opportunity to discuss their feelings about sports, which will help them identify with ideas Cosgrove and Kearns Goodwin shared in these selections.

KEYS TO TEACHING OPTIONS

 Block Scheduling

Activities that are particularly suited to use within a block scheduling framework are identified throughout this theme by the following designation: For detailed suggestions on block scheduling, see the **Block Scheduling Guide** for this grade level.

Key to Ability Levels

The Teaching Options throughout this theme have been coded for students of various abilities.

L1 BASIC activities for all students

L2 AVERAGE activities for average to above-average students

L3 CHALLENGING activities for above-average students

Reading Skills in this theme

Variety of Texts

In addition to autobiographical selections, this theme includes the following text types:

- poetry
- essay
- memoir
- short story
- newspaper column
- television script

Comprehension Skills

The following instructional support for comprehension skills appears in this theme of the Student Edition:

- **Reading and Thinking Minilessons** (pp. 17, 22, 55, 103)
- **Active Reading Strategies and Model** (pp. 64–74)
- **Sequencing** (p. 83)

See also the **Reading Minilessons** throughout the theme in this Teacher's Wraparound Edition.

Reading Resources

Comprehension Skills Resources

Active Reading Guides

The **Active Reading Guide** provides graphic organizers and study guide questions to support students' reading of each selection. (**Active Reading Guide**, pp. 1–10)

Reading Workbook

The **Reading Workbook** (pp. 1–18) includes additional instruction and reinforcement of reading strategies and skills.

Audio Library

Available both on tape and on CD, the **Audio Library** provides valuable comprehension support.

Resources for Reading Widely

Glencoe Literature Library

Each title in the *Glencoe Literature Library* includes a full-length novel or play plus related readings. A separate Study Guide is available for each title.

Literature Classics CD-ROM

The selections on this CD-ROM can be searched by author, theme, or genre.

A coproduction of Glencoe and Time, Inc., the *inTime* magazine includes a wealth of high interest nonfiction related to the selections in Theme One.

Assessment in this theme

Assessment Options in the Student Edition

Glencoe Literature offers a number of diverse ways to evaluate student understanding and skill proficiency. In the Student Edition, use the following:

- **Responding to Literature**
  Following each selection, students are asked to recall facts, interpret ideas, and evaluate concepts as they answer a variety of questions and complete activities to extend their understanding.

- **Theme Wrap-Up (pp. 108–109)**
  Here students respond to the selections on personal and analytical levels. They also assume ownership of their learning by setting and evaluating goals and by selecting work for their portfolios.

See also the many **Assessment Resources** listed on the facing page.

THE PRINCETON REVIEW

Standardized Test Practice

The Princeton Review has developed the Standardized Test Practice pages found at the end of this theme (pp. 110–111). These pages contain practice test questions that help students remain familiar with standardized test formats and content.

- ITBS Preparation and Practice
- SAT-9 Preparation and Practice
- TerraNova Preparation and Practice

Writing Skills in this theme

Writing Skills

The Student Edition of Theme One offers strong instructional support for writing skills:

In **Extending Your Response**, which follows each selection:
- **Writing About Literature**
- **Personal/Creative Writing**

See also the **Writing Minilessons** throughout the theme in this Teacher's Wraparound Edition.

Writing Workshops

Theme One concludes with a **Writing Workshop** that guides students through the process of writing an autobiographical anecdote (pp. 104–107).

Writing Resources

Writer's Assistant CD-ROM
Each Writing Workshop is supplemented by an interactive writing guide on the Writer's Assistant CD-ROM. This easy-to-use writing guide provides prompts, templates, and other tools that lead students through the writing process.

Writing and Proofreading Practice
Blackline masters present in-depth instruction and practice on a specific step in the writing process and proofreading (pp. 1–7, 8–14).

Writing and Proofreading Transparencies
Transparencies provide graphic organizers and proofreading exercises for whole-class instruction (pp. 1–6, 7–8, 25–26).

Research and Report Writing Guide
This resource provides extensive tips and activities to guide students in their writing projects in the literature classroom as well as in classes across the curriculum.

Style and Documentation Sourcebook for Writers
This sourcebook is a combination reference and workbook, giving students the most up-to-date information and guidance regarding traditional as well as technological research strategies and documentation.

Grammar and Composition Handbook
The Grammar and Composition Handbook provides instruction that supplements activities in the student textbook.

Assessment Resources

Selection Quick Checks
For each selection, a Quick Check of three to five short-answer questions measures students' literal comprehension.

Selection and Theme Assessment
The Selection and Theme Assessment instrument tests students' abilities to recall, interpret, and evaluate what they've read. The tests consist of multiple-choice, short answer, and essay questions.

Performance Assessment
Alternative assessment instruments and rubrics for Theme One are found in the Performance Assessment ancillary.

Writing Assessment and Portfolio Management
These notes and strategies, student models, and assessment tools assist with the task of measuring students' progress as writers and as monitors of their own writing.

Testmaker
Teachers can customize selection and Theme One tests by accessing the Testmaker database.

Mindjogger Videoquizzes
Using a popular game show format, Mindjogger Videoquizzes enable teachers to evaluate student understanding of Theme One in a quick and fun manner.

SELECTIONS	Literary Elements	Reading and Thinking	Writing	Vocabulary and Spelling	
Names/Nombres JULIA ALVAREZ	Theme, SE p. 10 *Theme, TWE pp. 6, 8* *Plot: Internal Conflict,* *TWE p. 7* *Mood, TWE p. 9*	*Inferring, TWE p. 6* *Classifying, TWE p. 7* *Evaluating, TWE p. 7*	Sensory Imagery, SE p. 11 Journal Entry, SE p. 11	Antonyms, SE p. 11	

One JAMES BERRY
I'm Nobody!
Who are you? EMILY DICKINSON
	Visual Imagery, SE p. 16
	Visual Imagery,
	  TWE pp. 14, 15
		Comparing and Contrasting,
		  SE p. 17
		Logical Reasoning, TWE p. 14
		Drawing Conclusions, TWE p. 15
		Summarizing, TWE p. 15
			Paragraph About Theme,
			  SE p. 17
			Self–Portrait, SE p. 17		

FACE IT JANET S. WONG ALMOST READY ARNOLD ADOFF	Irony, SE p. 21 *Repetition, TWE p. 19* *Irony, TWE p. 20* *Free Verse, TWE p. 20*	Visualizing, SE p. 22 *Generalizing, TWE p. 20* *Paraphrasing, TWE p. 20*	Poem's Speaker, SE p. 22 Short Poem, SE p. 22		

Strong Men Weep
BENEDICT COSGROVE
	Author's Purpose, SE p. 32;
	  TWE pp. 27, 29
	Genre: TWE p. 27
	Irony, TWE p. 31
		Comparing and Contrasting,
		  TWE p. 28
		Distinguishing Fact from
		  Opinion, TWE pp. 29, 30
			Critical Review, SE p. 33
			Persuasive Paragraph,
			  SE p. 33
				Owning a Word, SE p. 33
				Root Words, TWE p. 27	

from Wait Till Next Year DORIS KEARNS GOODWIN	Memoir, SE p. 39; *TWE p. 37* *Narrator, TWE p. 36* *Concrete Lang., TWE p. 37* *Memior, TWE p. 37*	*Elaborating, TWE p. 37* *Monitoring Comprehension,* *TWE p. 37* *Supporting Details, TWE p. 37*		*Etymology, TWE p. 36*	

Broken Chain
GARY SOTO
	Conflict, SE p. 53; *TWE pp.*
	  45, 47, 48, 49, 50
	Character, TWE pp. 46, 51
	Plot, TWE pp. 50, 52
		Activating Prior Knowledge,
		  SE p. 55
		Identifying Author's Purpose,
		  TWE p. 46
			Paragraph (Details), SE p. 54
			Advice Column, SE p. 54
			Explanation, SE p. 54
			Writing to Show, TWE p. 47
				Synonyms, SE p. 55
				Prefixes, TWE p. 47	

Without Commercials ALICE WALKER	Speaker, SE p. 61 *Point of View, TWE p. 60*	Drawing Conclusions, TWE p. 59 *Summarizing, TWE p. 59* *Evaluating, TWE p. 60*			

from Barrio Boy
ERNESTO GALARZA
	Description, SE p. 73
	Description, TWE pp. 68, 69,
	  70, 72
		Distinguishing Fact from
		  Opinion, TWE p. 69
		Inferring, TWE p. 71
			Paragraph (Setting), SE p. 74
			Personal Letter, SE p. 74
				Compound Words, SE p. 74
				Word Meanings, TWE p. 70	

Fish Cheeks AMY TAN	Sensory Imagery, SE p. 80 *Sensory Imagery, TWE p. 79*	*Evaluating, TWE p. 79*	Summary, SE p. 81 Story, SE p. 81	Analogies, SE p. 81 *Etymology, TWE p. 79*	

from Rosa Parks: MY STORY
ROSA PARKS
	Sequence, SE p. 101; *TWE*
	  pp. 86, 87, 89, 90, 94, 96
	Dialogue, TWE p. 89
	Setting, TWE p. 89
	Tone, TWE p. 96
	Mood, TWE p. 100
		Cause and Effect, SE p. 103
		Judging a Source, TWE p. 88
		Analyzing Arguments, TWE p. 91
		Propoganda Tech., TWE p. 91
		Logical Reasoning, TWE p. 92
		Generalizing, TWE p. 99
			Summary, SE p. 102
			Text for Children's Picture
			  Book, SE p. 102
			Maintaining Consistency in
			  Verb Tenses, TWE p. 93
				Unlocking Meaning, SE p. 103
				Jargon, TWE p. 93
				Etymology, TWE p. 97
				Antonyms, TWE p. 100	

Key: Student material is in roman. Teacher material is in italic.   Technology   **COLLAB. LEARN.** Collaboration

Grammar and Language	Listening, Speaking, and Viewing	Life Skills	Study, Research, and Technology
Proper Nouns and Proper Adjectives, *TWE p. 8*	**COLLAB. LEARN.** Literature Groups, SE p. 11 **COLLAB. LEARN.** Interviewing, SE p. 11 Readers' Theater, SE p. 11		🖥 *Foreign Names*, *TWE p. 9* *Family Tree*, *TWE p. 9*
	COLLAB. LEARN. Literature Groups, SE p. 17 Musical Brochure, SE p. 17		
	COLLAB. LEARN. Literature Groups, SE p. 22 Listening to Poetry, SE p. 22		
Main Verbs and Helping Verbs, *TWE p. 30*	**COLLAB. LEARN.** Literature Groups, SE p. 33 **COLLAB. LEARN.** *Announcing*, *TWE p. 29* *Videotape*, *TWE p. 31*		**COLLAB. LEARN.** *Perspectives on the Hero*, *TWE p. 31*
Prepositional Phrases, *TWE p. 38*	*Videotape*, *TWE p. 37*		
Subject-Verb Agreement, SE p. 55 *Pronouns Used as Objects*, *TWE p. 52*	**COLLAB. LEARN.** Literature Groups, SE p. 54 **COLLAB. LEARN.** *Improv.*, SE p. 54 *Debating*, *TWE p. 49*		
Subject-Verb Agreement, *TWE p. 72*			**COLLAB. LEARN.** *Immigration and Citizenship*, *TWE p. 71*
COLLAB. LEARN. *Adjectives*, *TWE p. 79*	**COLLAB. LEARN.** Literature Groups, SE p. 81		🖥 *Traditional Chinese Cooking*, SE p. 81
Nouns, SE p. 103 *Quotation Marks*, *TWE p. 89* *Commas*, *TWE p. 91* **COLLAB. LEARN.** *Capitalization of Proper Nouns*, *TWE p. 100*	**COLLAB. LEARN.** Literature Groups, SE p. 102; Skit, SE p. 102 **COLLAB. LEARN.** *Effective List.*, *TWE p. 95* *Video*, *TWE p. 97* *Documentary*, *TWE p. 99*	**COLLAB. LEARN.** *Supporting and Contributing*, *TWE pp. 90, 96*	🖥 *Boycott*, *TWE p. 92* **COLLAB. LEARN.** *Key Events*, *TWE p. 92* **COLLAB. LEARN.** *Working For a Cause*, *TWE p. 97* 🖥 *Rosa Parks*, *TWE p. 98* 🖥 *Civil Rights Movement*, *TWE p. 98*

SELECTIONS	📁 Print Resources		
Names/Nombres JULIA ALVAREZ	Theme 1 Planning Guide, 　pp. 6–13 * Active Reading Guide, p. 1 Vocabulary Practice, p. 1	Gr. & Comp. Hdbk., Lessons 2.1, 5.1, 　12.4 Gr.& Lang. Wkbk., pp. 61–62, 119–120 Reading Workbook, pp. 1–2	* Qk. Chks., p. 1; Perf. Assess. p. 1 Sel. and Theme Assess., pp. 1–2 Spanish Summaries, p. 1 Spanish Translations
One JAMES BERRY I'm Nobody! Who are you? EMILY DICKENSON	Theme 1 Planning Guide, 　pp. 14–18 * Active Reading Guide, p. 2	Reading Workbook, pp. 3–4	* Qk. Chks., p. 2; Perf. Assess. p. 2 Sel. and Theme Assess., pp. 3–4 Spanish Summaries, p. 2
FACE IT JANET S. WONG ALMOST READY ARNOLD ADOFF	Theme 1 Planning Guide, 　pp. 19–23 * Active Reading Guide, p. 3		* Qk. Chks., p. 3; Perf. Assess. p. 3 Sel. and Theme Assess., pp. 5–6 Spanish Summaries, p. 3
Strong Men Weep BENEDICT COSGROVE	Theme 1 Planning Guide, 　pp. 24–31 * Active Reading Guide, p. 4 Vocabulary Practice, p. 2	Gr. & Comp. Hdbk., Lesson 3.6 Gr. & Lang. Wkbk., pp. 85–86, 87–88 Reading Workbook, pp. 5–6	* Qk. Chks., p. 4; Perf. Assess. p. 4 Sel. and Theme Assess., pp. 7–8 Spanish Summaries, p. 4 Spanish Translations
from **Wait Till Next Year** DORIS KEARNS GOODWIN	Theme 1 Planning Guide, 　pp. 32–39 * Active Reading Guide, p. 5 Vocabulary Practice, p. 3	Gr. & Comp. Hdbk., Lesson 7.1 Gr. & Lang. Wkbk., pp. 141–142 Reading Workbook, pp. 7–8	* Qk. Chks., p. 5; Perf. Assess. p. 5 Sel. and Theme Assess., pp. 9–10 Spanish Summaries, p. 5 Spanish Translations
Broken Chain GARY SOTO	Theme 1 Planning Guide, 　pp. 40–47 * Active Reading Guide, p. 6 Vocabulary Practice, p. 4	Gr. & Comp. Hdbk., Lessons 4.2, 　10.1–10.5 Gr. & Lang. Wkbk., pp. 35, 107–108 Reading Workbook, pp. 9–10	* Qk. Chks., p. 6; Perf. Assess. p. 6 Sel. and Theme Assess., pp. 11–12 Spanish Summaries, p. 6 Spanish Translations
Without Commercials ALICE WALKER	Theme 1 Planning Guide, 　pp. 48–52 * Active Reading Guide, p. 7	Reading Workbook, pp. 11–12	* Qk. Chks., p. 7; Perf. Assess. p. 7 Sel. and Theme Assess., pp. 13–14 Spanish Summaries, p. 7
from **Barrio Boy** ERNESTO GALARZA	Theme 1 Planning Guide, 　pp. 53–60 * Active Reading Guide, p. 8 Vocabulary Practice, p. 5	Gr. & Comp. Hdbk., Lesson, 10.1 Gr. & Lang. Wkbk, pp. 183–184 Reading Workbook, pp. 13–14	* Qk. Chks., p. 8; Perf. Assess. p. 8 Sel. and Theme Assess., pp. 15–16 Spanish Summaries, p. 8; Spanish Translations
Fish Cheeks AMY TAN	Theme 1 Planning Guide, 　pp. 60–68 * Active Reading Guide, p. 9 Vocabulary Practice, p. 6	Gr. & Comp. Hdbk., Lesson 5.1 Gr. & Lang. Wkbk., pp. 7–8, 117–118 Reading Workbook, pp. 15–16	* Qk. Chks., p. 9; Perf. Assess. p. 9 Sel. and Theme Assess., pp. 17–18 Spanish Summaries, p. 9
from Rosa Parks: **MY STORY** ROSA PARKS	Theme 1 Planning Guide, pp. 69–76 * Active Reading Guide, p. 10 Vocabulary Practice, p. 7	Gr. & Comp. Hdbk, 2.1, 12.2–12.4, 　13.2,–13.4, 13.6; Gr & Lang, Wkbk, 　pp. 259–260, 237–238, 267–270 Reading Workbook, pp. 17–18	* Quick Checks, p. 10; Perf. Assess. p. 10 Sel. and Theme Assess., pp. 19–20 Spanish Summaries, p. 10; Spanish Translations

*Also available in Spanish

Transparencies	Technology Resources
Selection Focus Transparency 1 Grammar and Language Transparency 1 Literary Elements Transparency 1 Fine Art Transparency 4	Audio Library Spanish Audio Library Vocabulary Puzzlemaker Web Site: lit.glencoe.com
Selection Focus Transparency 2 Literary Elements Transparency 2	Audio Library Spanish Audio Library Vocabulary Puzzlemaker Web Site: lit.glencoe.com
Selection Focus Transparency 3 Literary Elements Transparency 3 Fine Art Transparency 31	Audio Library Spanish Audio Library Vocabulary Puzzlemaker Web Site: lit.glencoe.com
Selection Focus Transparency 4 Grammar and Language Transparency 3 Literary Elements Transparency 4	Literature Launchers Audio Library Spanish Audio Library Vocabulary Puzzlemaker Web Site: lit.glencoe.com
Selection Focus Transparency 5 Grammar and Language Transparency 4 Literary Elements Transparency 5	Audio Library Spanish Audio Library Vocabulary Puzzlemaker Web Site: lit.glencoe.com
Selection Focus Transparency 6 Grammar and Language Transparency 5 Literary Elements Transparency 6 Fine Art Transparency 1	Audio Library Spanish Audio Library Vocabulary Puzzlemaker Web Site: lit.glencoe.com
Selection Focus Transparency 7 Literary Elements Transparency 7	Audio/Spanish Audio Library Vocabulary Puzzlemaker Web Site: lit.glencoe.com
Selection Focus Transparency 8 Grammar and Language Transparency 6 Literary Elements Transparency 8 Fine Art Transparency 32	Audio Library Spanish Audio Library Vocabulary Puzzlemaker Web Site: lit.glencoe.com
Selection Focus Transparency 9 Grammar and Language Transparency 7 Literary Elements Transparency 9	Audio Library Spanish Audio Library Vocabulary Puzzlemaker Web Site: lit.glencoe.com
Selection Focus Transparency 10 Grammar and Language Transparencies 8, 9, 10 Literary Elements Transparency 10	Literature Launchers Audio/Spanish Audio Library Web Site: lit.glencoe.com

Theme RESOURCES

- Listening and Speaking Activities (pp. 1–3)
- Viewing and Representing Activities (pp. 1–6, 7–9)
- Critical Thinking Skills (pp. 2–4)
- Media Connection Activities, (pp. 1–2)
- Interdisciplinary Activities (pp. 2–5)
- Family and Community Activities (p. 11)
- Selection and Theme Assessment (pp. 125–126)

See also these additional planning resources:
- English Language Learners Sourcebook
- Inclusion Strategies Sourcebook
- Literature Groups Sourcebook

Use Glencoe's *Presentation Plus!* This multi-media teaching tool lets you present dynamic lessons that will engage your students. Using Microsoft PowerPoint®, you can customize the presentation to create your own personalized lessons.

THEME 1

What I Am, What I Want to Be

Theme Objectives

- To enjoy reading about people and their unique experiences
- To analyze the literary elements in nonfiction, poetry, and short story selections
- To apply strategies for reading autobiographical writing

VIEWING THE ART

Norman Rockwell (1894–1978) was one of the most popular illustrators of his time. His homespun pictures of American life were seen regularly on the covers of such magazines as *Colliers*, *Life*, and *The Saturday Evening Post*.

Responding to the Art Discussion Questions:

- What do you think the girl in the painting is thinking about? *(probably wondering about her appearance)*
- What connection do you see between the art and the title of this theme *(The girl appears to be comparing her appearance to the picture in her lap, perhaps wondering if she'll become like her adult idol.)*

What I Am, What I Want to Be

Girl at Mirror, 1954. Norman Rockwell. Printed by permission of the Norman Rockwell Family Trust. ©1954 the Norman Rockwell Family Trust.

TEACHER to TEACHER

POJOAQUE MIDDLE SCHOOL • NEW MEXICO

Our school is located within a tri-lingual district composed of Anglo, Hispanic American and Native American students. So, when opening the theme, "What I Am, What I Want To Be," I use each student's native culture as a starting point. We discuss who we are and what makes us who we are from a cultural standpoint, and students write an essay on this topic from the perspective of their own cultural backgrounds. They share their essays in class, and we talk about cultural differences. Then students create a pictorial autobiography using pictures of themselves growing up. They put these pictures on a poster or some other background; list all their hobbies, interests, and activities; and describe their likes and dislikes. They include information about various personal attitudes and use adjectives to describe their qualities.

GERALD J. ROMERO

THEME 1

> **66** *Only one of me and nobody can get a second one from a photocopy machine.* **99**
>
> –James Berry, "One"

THEME CONTENTS

Names/Nombres • autobiography by Julia Alvarez 5

One • poem by James Berry 14

I'm Nobody! Who are you? •
poem by Emily Dickinson 15

Face It • poem by Janet S. Wong 19

Almost Ready • poem by Arnold Adoff 20

Strong Men Weep • essay by Benedict Cosgrove 26

from Wait Till Next Year •
memoir by Doris Kearns Goodwin 35

Broken Chain • short story by Gary Soto 44

Without Commercials • poem by Alice Walker 59

 GENRE FOCUS *AUTOBIOGRAPHY*

from Barrio Boy • autobiography by Ernesto Galarza . . . 67

Fish Cheeks • autobiography by Amy Tan 77

Rosa Parks: My Story •
autobiography by Rosa Parks with Jim Haskins 85

WHAT I AM, WHAT I WANT TO BE 1

RESOURCE MANAGER

See the *Theme One Planning Guide* (pp. 1–5) for additional teaching notes, strategies, and resources for introducing the theme "What I Am, What I Want to Be."

Teaching Strategies

Have students read the quotation from "One" by James Berry in preparation for the discussion of the theme "What I Am, What I Want to Be."

Introducing the Theme

Direct your students' attention to the **Theme Contents.** Ask them to read through the list of selections. Present these questions for discussion:

- Have you ever read anything by these writers before? *(Students might recognize names such as Amy Tan and Rosa Parks.)*
- Based on the titles, which selection do you think you will relate to best?
- What do you notice about the variety of writing in this theme? *(Students may note that there are several poems and autobiographical selections in the contents.)*
- If you had your choice, which selection would you read first? Why?

LITERATURE & HUMANITIES

Have students examine the painting *Figuera (1971),* Transparency 49 from *World History in Art,* and determine how many figures they see. Then have them discuss what comment the artist might be making about a person's identity.

Exploring the Theme

What I Am, What I Want to Be

- Students may place themselves in their age, cultural, gender, and socioeconomic groups in describing how others see them.
- Students may see themselves very differently than how they feel they are perceived. Some may think that outward appearances are not reliable clues when it comes to discovering who a person really is.

Have students write two-sentence responses to these questions: *Who are you? Who do you want to be?*

Starting Points

One Among Many

Write the word *conformity* on the board and ask students to give examples of what the word means to them. Mention that for many animals, like the penguins pictured here, conforming to a group helps ensure their safety and survival.

(Students may feel that each penguin thinks it is unique, yet likes belonging to a crowd.)

- Find out if students think conformity is necessary for humans to survive.
- Prompt with questions such as: What are the advantages and disadvantages of *conforming to society's norms?*

You Are the Only You

Invite students to write as many words as they can think of. Encourage them to be generous with themselves and to remember that, while other students may have similar adjectives in their word-sketch, it is the combination of these words that will reveal individual uniqueness. No two students will have exactly the same self-portrait.

FINE ART
TRANSPARENCY 15

You may wish to use **Fine Art Transparency 15** to help students think about their self-portraits.

Exploring the Theme

What I Am, What I Want to Be

How do other people see you? More importantly, how do you see yourself? In this theme, you will explore what makes you who you are and what it will take to become who you want to be. To begin, try one of the options below.

Starting Points

ONE AMONG MANY
What do you think makes each of these penguins stand out in a crowd?
- Write a short conversation between two of the penguins. Imagine they are introducing themselves.

YOU ARE THE ONLY YOU
You are the only you. Think about yourself for a minute, and get ready to sketch yourself in words.
- Draw a name tag. Write your name in the center of it. What are the first words that come to mind when you read your name? Around the name tag, list several words that describe what makes you unique. You may also wish to include photos or drawings on your name tag.

Drawing by Chas. Addams; ©1977. The New Yorker Magazine, Inc.

---

interNET CONNECTION

Personality Suggest that students use *temperament, character,* or *identity* as keywords on a search engine to find out more about what makes a person unique, what makes a person an individual. Once connected to a site, they might do a search using *personality* as a keyword. Have them share their results with the class.

Theme Projects

Theme Projects

As you read the selections in this theme, choose one of the projects below. Work on your own, with a partner, or in a group.

LEARNING FOR LIFE
Writing a Job Description
What do you dream of doing when you grow up? Do you think about being a dancer, or a veterinarian, or a designer of video games? Think about your dream job. Then write a description of your job.

1. When you have made your choice, do some library research to find out more about it. Talk to people in your community who have similar jobs. Take notes about their job descriptions.
2. Write your job description, and contribute it to a classroom Career Notebook. As you learn about other interesting careers, add new descriptions to the notebook.

MULTIMEDIA PROJECT
A Self-Portrait
Create a multimedia self-portrait.

1. Gather information about yourself. Create a summary of interesting facts about your life, perhaps using a visual format such as a time line or a graph to chart these highlights.
2. Gather photos or drawings of you and your family or friends. Try to include music, videos, and taped interviews to showcase your life.
3. Present your self-portrait to your class.

interNET CONNECTION

Check out the Web for more project ideas. Use your favorite search engine to find other job-related ideas or other topics related to the "What I Am, What I Want to Be" theme. Key words such as *jobs, employment,* and career fields like *medicine* and *aviation* can get you started.

CRITICAL LISTENING
Musical Notes
Your taste in music reflects who you are, as well as your interests.

1. Do you enjoy popular music, oldies, jazz, reggae, rap, or some other type of music? Bring in examples of different kinds of music you enjoy.
2. Talk to older family members about the kinds of music they listened to when they were your age. Research their favorite kinds of music, and bring examples, photographs, or articles about that music to class. You might even create a musical time line showing the kinds of music young people have enjoyed over time.
3. Plan a musical tour through history. Display your research and photographs. Using tapes or CDs, play examples of a wide variety of music. Invite another class or family members to your classroom to participate in your musical tour.

WHAT I AM, WHAT I WANT TO BE 3

Theme Projects

Teaching Strategies
The following suggestions may help your students plan and carry out their theme projects.

Learning for Life
- Before they write, ask students to close their eyes and think of what they are happiest doing.
- Ask students to help one another identify jobs and professions connected to what they enjoy doing.
- Encourage students to ask people in the community which hobbies would be good preparation for careers in their chosen fields.

Multimedia Project
- Encourage students to create a self-portrait that reflects their present thoughts and feelings as well as dreams and plans for the future.
- You may wish to set a time limit for the final presentations.

Critical Listening
- Encourage students to seek out partners who are interested in the same kind of music.
- Invite student musicians to perform and to talk about songwriters or composers they admire.

Additional Resources
- *Interdisciplinary Activities,* pp. 2–5
- *Viewing and Representing Activities,* pp. 7–9
- *Listening and Speaking Activities,* pp. 1–3
- *Critical Thinking Skills,* pp. 2–4
- *Selection and Theme Assessment,* pp. 125–126
- *Performance Assessment,* p. 69

Family and Community Activity

Living Treasures Explain that in many countries, people who have contributed a great deal to society are considered living treasures because of their wealth of knowledge. Have students identify someone in the family or circle of family friends who could be considered a living treasure and create a short documentary film or report about this person. Encourage students to conduct interviews, research information on their subjects' contributions or on the events their subjects experienced, and gather photographs and other relevant memorabilia. Allow time for students to share their "living treasures" with classmates.

Additional Resources
- *Family and Community Activities,* p. 11

Before Reading

Objectives

- To read and analyze a short story about a girl torn between her Dominican and American identities
- To recognize and state an implied theme in a short story
- To identify and discuss sensory details in a story

Skills

Reading/Thinking: Inferring; Evaluating; Classifying
Writing: Journal Entry
Vocabulary: Antonyms
Grammar/Language: Proper Nouns and Proper Adjectives
Listening/Speaking: Interviewing
Collaboration: Literature Groups; Readers' Theater

Motivating →OPTIONS

Selection Focus Transparency 1: Encourage students to discuss how they might feel if someone changed their name for convenience.

Focus Activity: As an extension of the Focus Activity, have small groups of students discuss times when a nickname can make a person feel proud or uncomfortable.

Before You Read
Names/Nombres

MEET JULIA ALVAREZ

Asked where she finds the ideas for her richly detailed stories, Julia Alvarez says, "I think when I write, I write out of who I am and the questions I need to figure out. A lot of what I have worked through has to do with coming to this country and losing a homeland and a culture, as a way of making sense." Alvarez has written two novels, *How the Garcia Girls Lost Their Accents* and *In the Time of the Butterflies*.

Julia Alvarez was born in 1950. This selection was published in 1985.

4 🦋 THEME 1

FOCUS ACTIVITY

Have you ever stopped to think about your name? What does your name tell others about you?

Sharing Ideas
In small groups, talk about what names mean to you. Does your own name seem to capture any of the real you?

Setting a Purpose
Read the selection to find out what names mean to Julia Alvarez.

BACKGROUND

The Time and Place
This selection is set in the early 1960s in New York City. Julia Alvarez was born in New York, but she lived in the Dominican Republic until the age of ten.

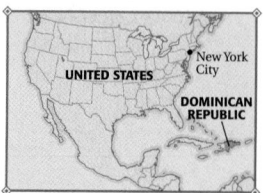

VOCABULARY PREVIEW

ironically (ī ron′ i kəl ē) *adv.* in a way that is different from what would be expected; p. 6
initial (i nish′ əl) *adj.* at the beginning; first; p. 7
merge (murj) *v.* to join together so as to become one; unite; p. 7
inevitably (i nev′ ə tə blē) *adv.* in a way that cannot be avoided or prevented; p. 7
vaguely (vāg′ lē) *adv.* in a way that is not clear, exact, or definite; p. 7
specify (spes′ ə fī′) *v.* to state or describe in detail; p. 7
exotic (ig zot′ ik) *adj.* strangely attractive; foreign; p. 8
chaotic (kā ot′ ik) *adj.* confused and disorganized; in great disorder; p. 8
commencement (kə mens′ mənt) *n.* a beginning; start; graduation ceremonies; p. 9

RESOURCE MANAGER

Lesson Planning Resource
The **Theme One Planning Guide** (pp. 6–13) provides additional lesson notes and reduced versions of all print resources.

📁 **Other Print Resources**
- Active Reading Guide, p. 1
- Vocabulary Practice, p. 1
- Reading Workbook, pp. 1–2
- Grammar and Language Workbook, pp. 61–62, 119–120

- Grammar and Composition Handbook, Lessons 2.1, 5.1, 12.4
- Quick Checks, p. 1
- Selection and Theme Assessment, pp. 1–2
- Performance Assessment, p. 1
- Spanish Summaries, p. 1
- Spanish Translations
- Inclusion Strategies
- English Language Learners Sourcebook

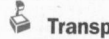 **Transparencies**
- Selection Focus 1
- Fine Art 4
- Literary Elements 1
- Grammar and Language 1

Technology
 Audio Library
 Spanish Audio Library
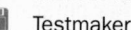 Glencoe Literature Web Site
💾 Testmaker

4 🦋 THEME 1

Names/Nombres

Julia Alvarez

When we arrived in New York City, our names changed almost immediately. At Immigration, the officer asked my father, *Mister Elbures*, if he had anything to declare. My father shook his head, "No," and we were waved through. I was too afraid we wouldn't be let in if I corrected the man's pronunciation, but I said our name to myself, opening my mouth wide for the organ blast of the *a*, trilling my tongue for the drumroll of the *r*, *All-vah-rrr-es!* How could anyone get *Elbures* out of that orchestra of sound?

Portrait of Virginia, 1929. Frida Kahlo. Fundacion Dolores Olmedo, Mexico City, D.F., Mexico.

Nombres is a Spanish word for "names."

SUMMARY

In this short autobiographical work, Julia Alvarez discusses the many names—family names, nicknames, school names, American names, and Spanish names—she has had and how her feelings about her names changed at different periods in her life.

📁 *Spanish Summaries,* p. 1

A **Active Reading**

CONNECT Ask students how they feel when their names are mispronounced. Are they proud of their names? Would they change their names if possible?

Additional Resources
📁 *Active Reading Guide,* p. 1
🎧 *Audio Library*
🎧 *Spanish Audio Library*

Teaching Options

CONNECTING TO OTHER SELECTIONS

The chart at the right shows three ways to connect "Names/Nombres" to other selections in this book.

For specific teaching strategies, see the *Theme One Planning Guide,* pages 9–10.

Connection	Title
Life Skills: Adapting	→ "Fish Cheeks," p. 77
Thematic: Changing Identity	→ "Bums in the Attic," p. 329
Literary: Theme	→ "One," p. 14

B Literary Elements

THEME Julia's teachers and friends mispronounce her name, and Julia wonders if she should correct them. Ask students what point they think Alvarez might be making about her identity. *(She suggests that because people are having a difficult time with an unfamiliar name, she feels more like an outsider.)*

C Critical Thinking

INFERRING Have students suggest what they think Julia's mother means when she responds, "A rose by any other name would smell as sweet?" *(Julia's mother means that no matter what Julia's friends call her, she is the same person.)*

D Literary Elements

THEME Here Alvarez creates an alternate identity for herself. Ask students what they think Alvarez is saying about the connection between one's name and one's identity. *(It seems the author believes that even a fake name cannot change one's true identity.)*

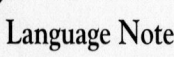

Language Note

Rich Noisy Name Ask students what they think the speaker means by *rich noisy name*. *(It has interesting sounds that stand out.)* Have students think of people or places that have rich noisy names.

Teaching Options

Names/Nombres

At the hotel my mother was *Missus Alburest*, and I was *little girl*, as in, "Hey, little girl, stop riding the elevator up and down. It's *not* a toy!"

When we moved into our new apartment building, the super called my father *Mister Alberase*, and the neighbors who became mother's friends pronounced her name *Jew-lee-ah* instead of *Hoo-lee-ah*. I, her namesake, was known as *Hoo-lee-tah* at home. But at school, I was *Judy* or *Judith*, and once an English teacher mistook me for *Juliet*.

B It took awhile to get used to my new names. I wondered if I shouldn't correct my teachers and new friends. But my mother argued that it didn't matter. "You know what your friend Shakespeare said, **C** '*A rose by any other name would smell as sweet.*'[1] My family had gotten into the habit of calling any literary figure "my friend" because I had begun to write poems and stories in English class.

By the time I was in high school, I was a popular kid, and it showed in my name. Friends called me *Jules* or *Hey Jude*, and once a group of troublemaking friends my mother forbid me to hang out with called me *Alcatraz*.[2] I was *Hoo-lee-tah* only to Mami and Papi and uncles and aunts who came over to eat *sancocho*[3] on Sunday **D** afternoons—old world folk whom I just as soon would go back to where they came from and leave me to pursue whatever mischief I wanted to in America. *JUDY*

---

1. This line is from William Shakespeare's play *Romeo and Juliet*.
2. *Alcatraz* is an island in San Francisco Bay that once was the home of a very tough federal prison.
3. *Sancocho* (sän kō′ chō) is a meat stew.

ALCATRAZ: the name on the Wanted Poster would read. Who would ever trace her to me?

My older sister had the hardest time getting an American name for herself because Mauricia did not translate into English. Ironically, although she had the most foreign-sounding name, she and I were the Americans in the family. We had been born in New York City when our parents had first tried immigration and then gone back "home," too homesick to stay. My mother often told the story of how she had almost changed my sister's name in the hospital.

After the delivery, Mami and some other new mothers were cooing over their new baby sons and daughters and exchanging names and weights and delivery stories. My mother was embarrassed among the Sallys and Janes and Georges and Johns to reveal the rich, noisy name of *Mauricia*, so when her turn came to brag, she gave her baby's name as *Maureen*.

"Why'd ya give her an Irish name with so many pretty Spanish names to choose from?" one of the women asked her.

My mother blushed and admitted her baby's real name to the group. Her mother-in-law had recently died, she apologized,

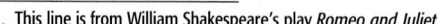

Vocabulary
ironically (ī ron′ i kəl ē) *adv.* in a way that is different from what would be expected

6 ❦ THEME 1

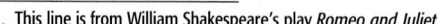

MEETING INDIVIDUAL NEEDS — ENGLISH LANGUAGE LEARNERS

Naming a Child At the top of page 7 is an explanation of how Mauricia got her name. This provides an opportunity to share customs or traditions relating to naming a child.

Activity Have English language learners gather in small groups to share how they got their names and tell about some of the naming customs of their cultures. Invite students to share their information with other groups and with the class. After students read page 8, ask those students with Hispanic surnames to share their complete names with the class.

Additional Resources
📁 *English Language Learners Sourcebook*

and her husband had insisted that the first daughter be named after his mother, *Mauran*. My mother thought it the ugliest name she had ever heard, and she talked my father into what she believed was an improvement, a combination of *Mauran* and her own mother's name *Felicia*.

"Her name is *Mao-ree-chee-ah*," my mother said to the group.

"Why that's a beautiful name," the new mothers cried. "*Moor-ee-sha, Moor-ee-sha*," they cooed into the pink blanket.

Moor-ee-sha it was when we returned to the States eleven years later. Sometimes, American tongues found even that mispronunciation tough to say and called her *Maria* or *Marsha* or *Maudy* from her nickname *Maury*. I pitied her. What an awful name to have to transport across borders!

My little sister, Ana, had the easiest time of all. She was plain *Anne*—that is, only her name was plain, for she turned out to be the pale, blond "American beauty" in the family. The only Hispanic-seeming thing about her was the affectionate nickname her boyfriends sometimes gave her, *Anita*, or as one goofy guy used to sing to her to the tune of the Chiquita Banana advertisement, *Anita Banana*.

Later, during her college years in the late '60s, there was a push to pronounce Third World[4] names correctly. I remember calling her long distance at her group house and a roommate answering.

---

4. **Third World** refers to poorer, less developed countries, mainly in Latin America, Africa, and Asia.

"Can I speak to Ana?" I asked, pronouncing her name the American way.

"Ana?" The man's voice hesitated. "Oh! you mean *Ah-nah!*"

Our first few years in the States, though, ethnicity[5] was not yet "in." Those were the blond, blue-eyed, bobby socks years of junior high and high school before the '60s ushered in peasant blouses, hoop earrings, serapes. My initial desire to be known by my correct Dominican name faded. I just wanted to be Judy and merge with the Sallys and Janes in my class. But inevitably, my accent and coloring gave me away. "So where are you from, Judy?"

"New York," I told my classmates. After all, I had been born blocks away at Columbia Presbyterian Hospital.

"I mean, *originally*."

"From the Caribbean," I answered vaguely, for if I specified, no one was quite sure what continent our island was on.

Did You Know?
A *serape* (sə rä′ pä) is a blanketlike outer garment similar to a shawl. It is often woven with bright colors and patterns and is worn chiefly by men in Latin American countries.

---

5. **Ethnicity** is a word for certain things that a group of people share, such as language, culture, history, race, and national origin. U.S. citizens come from many different ethnic backgrounds.

Vocabulary
initial (i nish′ əl) *adj.* at the beginning; first
merge (murj) *v.* to join together so as to become one; unite
inevitably (i nev′ ə tə blē) *adv.* in a way that cannot be avoided or prevented
vaguely (vāg′ lē) *adv.* in a way that is not clear, exact, or definite
specify (spes′ ə fī′) *v.* to state or describe in detail

Reading *Minilesson*

VIEWING THE PAINTING

Fernando Botero is a contemporary artist from Colombia. He often paints cheerful, balloon-shaped, not quite true-to-life people.

Viewing Response *Students may suggest that musicians like these would be appropriate for the birthday party scene, but Botero's satiric style would fit almost any part of the story.*

H Active Reading

EVALUATE Help students identify the proper spelling of Puerto Rico. Ask them why they think this spelling is given, considering the pronunciations are the same. *(Help students understand that the author seems to be poking fun at Americans' knowledge of the language and geography of the Caribbean.)*

I Literary Elements

THEME Point out to students the connection between the story's title and theme and this passage. *(The author reveals her entire name—all of her "official" names.)* Ask students how a name this long could define one's identity. *(Students should realize that by including all middle names and family surnames for four generations back, one would have a greater sense of familial identity.)*

The Musicians, 1979. Fernando Botero. Oil on canvas, 85¾ x 74¾ in. Private collection.

Viewing the painting: Which scene from the story would you like to see painted in the style of Botero?

H "Really? I've been to Bermuda. We went last April for spring vacation. I got the worst sunburn! So, are you from Portoriko?"

"No," I shook my head. "From the Dominican Republic."

"Where's that?"

"South of Bermuda."

I They were just being curious, I knew, but I burned with shame whenever they singled me out as a "foreigner," a rare, <u>exotic</u> friend.

"Say your name in Spanish, oh please say it!" I had made mouths drop one day by rattling off my full name, which according to Dominican custom, included my middle names, mother's and father's surnames for four generations back.

"Julia Altagracia Maria Teresa Alvarez Tavares Perello Espaillat Julia Pérez Rochet González," I pronounced it slowly, a name as <u>chaotic</u> with sounds as a Middle Eastern bazaar or market day in a South American village.

I suffered most whenever my extended family attended school occasions. For my graduation, they all came, the whole noisy, foreign-looking lot of old, fat aunts in their dark mourning dresses and hair nets, uncles with full, droopy mustaches and baby-blue or salmon-colored suits and white pointy shoes and fedora[6] hats, the many little cousins who

---

6. A *fedora* is a soft felt hat with a curved brim and a crease along the top.

Vocabulary
exotic (ig zot′ ik) *adj.* strangely attractive; foreign
chaotic (kā ot′ ik) *adj.* confused and disorganized; in great disorder

8 �ських THEME 1

Teaching Options

Grammar and Language *Minilesson*

Proper Nouns and Proper Adjectives
Remind students that proper nouns name a specific person, place, thing, or idea, such as *Bill, Utah, Ford,* or *June.* Proper adjectives are formed from proper nouns, such as *Texas chili.* Both proper nouns and proper adjectives begin with capital letters. Encourage students to look over pages 8–9 and list the proper nouns and proper adjectives they see.

Activity Have students change all of the listed words so that they relate to them. If they once went to Florida on vacation, they would change *Bermuda* to *Florida.* Then have each student use several of the words they have listed to write a brief paragraph about a trip, the family, or an important event. **L2**

Additional Resources

Grammar and Language Transparency 1

Grammar and Language Workbook, pp. 61–62, 119–120

Grammar and Composition Handbook, Lessons 2.1, 5.1, 12.4

Writer's Choice, Lessons 9.1, 12.2

snuck in without tickets. They sat in the first row in order to better understand the Americans' fast-spoken English. But how could they listen when they were constantly speaking among themselves in florid-sounding phrases, rococo[7] consonants, rich, rhyming vowels. Their loud voices carried . . .

How could I introduce them to my friends? These relatives had such complicated names and there were so many of them, and their relationships to myself were so convoluted. There was my Tía Josefina, who was not really an aunt but a much older cousin. And her daughter, Aída Margarita, who was adopted, *una hija de crianza*. My uncle of affection, Tío José, brought my *madrina* Tía Amelia and her *comadre* Tía Pilar.[8] My friends rarely had more than their nuclear family[9] to introduce.

After the commencement ceremony my family waited outside in the parking lot while my friends and I signed yearbooks with nicknames which recalled our high school good times: "Beans" and "Pepperoni" and "Alcatraz." We hugged and cried and promised to keep in touch.

Our good-byes went on too long. I heard my father's voice calling out across the parking lot, *"Hoo-lee-tah! Vámonos!"*[10]

Back home, my *tíos* and *tías* and *primas*, Mami and Papi, and *mis hermanas* had a party for me with *sancocho* and a storebought *pudín*,[11] inscribed with *Happy Graduation, Julie*. There were many gifts—that was a plus to a large family! I got several wallets and a suitcase with my initials and a graduation charm from my godmother and money from my uncles. The biggest gift was a portable typewriter from my parents for writing my stories and poems.

Someday, the family predicted, my name would be well-known throughout the United States. I laughed to myself, wondering which one I would go by.

---

7. *Florid* and *rococo* both mean "very showy, highly decorated, or flowery."
8. Something that is *convoluted* is all twisted, coiled, and wound around. The rest of this paragraph identifies some of the writer's convoluted family relationships. *Tía* (tē′ ə) and *Tío* (tē′ ō) mean "Aunt" and "Uncle." *Una hija de crianza* (ōō′ nə ē′ hə dä krē än′ zə) is an adopted daughter. *Madrina* (mə drē′ nə) and *comadre* (kō mä′ drā) both mean "godmother." Later, the writer mentions *primas* (prē′ məs) and *hermanas* (ār män′ əs), her female cousins and sisters.
9. Parents and their children make up what is called a *nuclear family*. An *extended family* includes other close relatives, such as grandparents, aunts, uncles, and cousins.

---

10. *"Vámonos!"* (vä′ mə nōs) means "Let's go!"
11. A *pudín* (pōō dēn′) is a pudding.

❖

Vocabulary
commencement (kə mens′ mənt) *n.* a beginning; start; graduation ceremonies

---

Author's Craft

MOOD Ask students to describe the mood or atmosphere of this scene and explain how the author helps readers picture the scene. *(The scene is noisy and filled with anticipation. She uses vivid descriptions: "florid-sounding phrases," "rococo consonants," "rich, rhyming vowels," and "loud voices carried.")*

Active Reading

EVALUATE Have students discuss this question: Although this selection is autobiographical, do you think it is entirely believable? Explain why you think so. *(Some students will say yes, because it is what could possibly have happened. Others will say no, because she did not include some of the strong negative feelings she might have had.)*

Thematic Focus

What I Am, What I Want to Be
Have students compare Julia's feelings of not wanting to be a "foreigner" or a "rare, exotic friend" with how they would feel in a similar situation. Are Julia's feelings typical of someone her age? Have students provide examples to support their ideas. You may wish to display **Fine Art Transparency 4** to enrich the discussion.

✓ ASSESSMENT OPTIONS

📁 *Quick Checks*, p. 1

REAL-WORLD CONNECTION

Names Students can use a search engine to find out more about names in different countries. They can use such keywords as *names, pronunciations, Spanish, English.*

Family Tree A student can gain a better understanding of the author's concerns by researching the names in his or her family's history or the history of a family friend.

Activity Have each student interview a grandparent or an older relative to create a family tree. Encourage them to note whether a family name was changed or modified in any way. **L2**

Responding to the Selection

Personal Response

Students may question her protected feelings, feel a strong connection to some of her experiences, or raise issues they wished she had addressed.

Analyzing Literature

1. The immigration officer cannot pronounce *Alvarez*. He pronounces it *Elbures*.
2. As a teenager, Julia wants to be called Judy because she wants to fit in and be like other American teens.
3. Julia suffers most when her extended family attends school functions. Julia describes her relatives as a noisy, foreign-looking bunch.
4. The Alvarez family predicts that Julia's name will be well-known throughout the United States.
5. Julia doesn't like the immigration officer's pronunciation, but she doesn't say anything for fear he won't let the family into the United States.
6. A passage that shows Alvarez's desire to be like her classmates: *I just wanted to be Judy and merge with the Sallys and Janes in my class.* As Julia grows up, she seems to become proud of her Spanish heritage.
7. Alvarez is embarrassed by her relatives because they are so different from those of her American friends. They dress differently, act differently, and have different manners and customs. Alvarez would prefer them to be quiet and unobtrusive.
8. Alvarez's professional name is Julia Alvarez. It signifies her pride in her Dominican heritage.
9. The title represents the importance to her of both English and Spanish names.

Responding to Literature

PERSONAL RESPONSE

Describe your impressions as you read about the writer's problems and triumphs living in two very different cultures.

Analyzing Literature

RECALL

1. How is the Alvarez family name changed when they go through immigration?
2. Why, do you think, does the teenage Alvarez just want to be called Judy?
3. Which occasions make Alvarez suffer the most? Find a **description** from the story to help explain your answer.
4. What does the Alvarez family predict about Julia's future career?

INTERPRET

5. How do you think Julia Alvarez feels about the change made to her family's name at the immigration office? Support your opinion.
6. Find a passage showing Alvarez's wish to be just like her classmates. How do you think her attitude changes as she grows up?
7. Why does Alvarez feel the way she does when her relatives appear at school functions? How would you feel?
8. Which of Alvarez's many names does she choose to use as a professional writer? In your opinion, why does she choose that one?

EVALUATE AND CONNECT

9. Why, do you think, does Alvarez give this story the title of "Names/Nombres"?
10. Theme Connection   What different cultures or groups do you belong to? When do you choose to identify with one group versus another?

LITERARY ELEMENTS

Theme

The main idea of a written work is usually expressed as a general statement called a **theme**. Sometimes a piece of writing has a **stated theme**—one that is expressed directly. More often, a piece of writing has an **implied theme**, which is not stated directly but is revealed gradually as the piece unfolds.

1. What do you think is the theme of "Names/Nombres"? Is the theme stated directly, or is it implied? Support your opinion with examples and quotations from the story.

2. How does the title of the story relate to its theme?

● See **Literary Terms Handbook,** p. R11.

---

10. Students should correctly identify the ethnic or cultural group or groups they belong to. They should also tell whether and when they identify with one group or another. You might identify your own background to get them started.

LITERARY ELEMENTS

1. The implied theme has to do with the importance of names to personal identity. One example occurs when Julia thinks that if she were to become a criminal named Judy Alcatraz, surely no one could trace that name to her.
2. The title represents Julia's conflicting feelings about her different names.

Additional Resources

Literary Elements Transparency 1

Extending Your Response

Writing About Literature

Sensory Imagery Julia Alvarez uses imagery that appeals to the senses. You can hear "the drumroll of the *r*," taste *sancocho,* and see "uncles with full, droopy mustaches." Find other sensory imagery in the selection. Name the senses they appeal to.

Literature Groups

Debating Shakespeare Julia's mother quotes Shakespeare—"a rose by any other name would smell as sweet." Do names affect how people are treated in this story? in your life? Is this fair? Share your ideas with your group.

Performing

Readers Theater Work with two or three other students to prepare a readers' theater presentation of a scene from "Names/Nombres." Choose a scene that relates to the theme of the selection.

Personal Writing

What's in a Name? Use the ideas in the **Focus Activity** on page 4 to write a journal entry about what names, including your own, mean to you and what names tell others.

Listening and Speaking

Conducting an Interview Pick three people to interview about their names. Be sure to ask people to explain how they got these names. Record their answers, and share your results.

Reading Further

For more about living in two cultures, try these:

In the Year of the Boar and Jackie Robinson by Bette Bao Lord

Going Home by Nicholasa Mohr

 Save your work for your portfolio.

Skill Minilesson

VOCABULARY • ANTONYMS

Many words have antonyms—words that mean the opposite. For example, antonyms for *happy* include *sad, miserable, gloomy,* and *unhappy.* Choosing among antonyms helps you think about the exact meaning of a word.

PRACTICE Match each word with its antonym.
1. ironically   a. final
2. chaotic   b. clearly
3. merge   c. separate
4. initial   d. predictably
5. vaguely   e. orderly

Writing About Literature
Students' lists should
• include details that clearly appeal to the senses.
• indicate which senses the details appeal to.

Personal Writing
Students' journal entries should
• express clear opinions about what their own names mean to them.
• explain what names tell other people and support their ideas with logical reasons.

Extending Your Response

Literature Groups Encourage students to give each group member time to express an idea about the meaning of the quotation before they agree or disagree. Then have students review the ideas and possibly add to their original thoughts. **COLLAB. LEARN.**

Performing Encourage students to act with their voices by using changes in volume, pitch, rhythm, stress patterns, and speed to express anger, fear, excitement, exhaustion, uncertainty, or other emotions. 📦

Listening and Speaking Remind students to ask questions that require the person being interviewed to think and give detailed answers. **COLLAB. LEARN.**

Skill Minilesson

VOCABULARY • ANTONYMS
1. d	3. c	5. b
2. e	4. a	

Additional Resources
📁 *Vocabulary Practice,* p. 1

✔️ **ASSESSMENT OPTIONS**

📁 *Quick Checks,* p. 1
📁 *Selection and Theme Assessment,* pp. 1–2
📁 *Performance Assessment,* p. 1
💾 *Testmaker*

Objective

- To recognize and correct sentence fragments

Teaching Strategies

Explain that a sentence fragment is a group of words that does not contain both a subject and a predicate. *Wrote stories and poems* leaves one wondering who wrote them. Ask each student to write a sentence about something that happened yesterday. Write a few of the sentences on the board and have volunteers identify the subject and the predicate in each.

Activity

One acceptable solution: At school, Julia's friends called her Judy, Judith, Jules, Jude, or Alcatraz. The nicknames did not bother her because they meant she was popular.

Students should
- write in complete sentences.
- use correct punctuation.

Additional Resources

📁 ***Grammar and Language Workbook,*** p. 55

📁 ***Grammar and Composition Handbook,*** Lesson 1.2

📘 ***Writer's Choice,*** Lessons 7.1, 8.9

Teaching Options

Avoiding Sentence Fragments

A complete sentence contains both a subject and a predicate. The **subject** tells who or what the sentence is about. The **predicate** tells what is happening or being done. The predicate always includes a **verb**.

> Morris sniffed.

In this complete sentence, *Morris* is the subject, and *sniffed* is the verb. A **sentence fragment** is incomplete. It leaves out the subject or the verb or both.

Problem 1 The subject is missing.
> Wrote stories and poems.

  Solution Add a subject.
  > Julia Alvarez wrote stories and poems.

Problem 2 The verb is missing.
> Julia's obvious talent as a writer.

  Solution Add a verb to the fragment.
  > Julia's obvious talent as a writer soon became apparent to her parents.

Problem 3 The subject and verb are missing.
> Her parents bought her a portable typewriter. As a graduation gift.

  Solution Combine the fragment with another sentence.
  > Her parents bought her a portable typewriter as a graduation gift.

● For more about sentence fragments, see **Language Handbook,** p. R12.

ACTIVITY

Rewrite the following paragraph, correcting any sentence fragments you find. You may be able to combine a fragment with another sentence, or you may need to add a subject or a verb.

> At school, Julia's friends called her Judy. Or sometimes Judith or Jules or Jude. Some troublemaking friends. They called her Alcatraz. These nicknames didn't bother her. Just showed her popularity with other kids.

Writing *Minilesson*

Writing Descriptive Detail Encourage each student to draw or paint a picture of a favorite relative that includes as many details about the person as possible.

Activity Suggest that students work in pairs or in small groups to write character sketches that are based on their drawings and paintings. Sketches should be written in complete sentences, not in the fragments sometimes used in dialogue. Brainstorm to develop a list of descriptive words and phrases on the board first, if necessary. **L2 COLLAB. LEARN.**

Additional Resources

📘 ***Writer's Choice,*** Lessons 3.1–3.3

Before You Read
One and I'm Nobody! Who are you?

Before Reading

MEET
JAMES BERRY

When James Berry looked around the British classroom where he was teaching and saw no books about African and Caribbean children, he began to write about his Caribbean homeland. He describes his poems as "scooped bits of the times I've lived in."

James Berry was born in Jamaica in 1925. "One" is from When I Dance: Poems, *published in 1988.*

MEET
EMILY DICKINSON

Emily Dickinson has been called a private poetic genius. Of the 1,775 poems she wrote, only seven were published during her lifetime, and none with her consent.

Emily Dickinson was born in 1830 and died in 1886. "I'm Nobody! Who are you?" was first published in 1891.

FOCUS ACTIVITY

What is it that makes you unique, or special, in this world?

QuickWrite
Reflect on your unique qualities. Then jot down these qualities, and tell how they set you apart from all others.

Setting a Purpose
Read to find out what these two poems have in common.

BACKGROUND

James Berry and Emily Dickinson lived in different centuries and on different continents. Although their paths never crossed, these two poets shared a sense of "otherness," of what it is like to be a unique individual. In his writing, James Berry often explores what it means to be part of a racial minority, something he experienced firsthand when he immigrated to Great Britain from Jamaica in 1948 at the age of 23.

A shy woman, Emily Dickinson seldom left her home in Amherst, Massachusetts. On the surface, her life seemed uneventful. She lived a quiet life, seeing few people outside of her own family. Dickinson's poetry, however, reveals a lively, sensitive, and original human being, committed to writing about the world from her own unique perspective.

Emily Dickinson's home in Amherst.

Objectives

- To read and compare two poems that express each poet's sense of self
- To identify and appreciate visual imagery in poetry
- To write a comparison of poetic themes

Skills

Reading/Thinking: Logical Reasoning; Drawing Conclusions; Summarizing; Comparing and Contrasting
Writing: Self-Portrait
Collaboration: Literature Groups

Motivating
→OPTIONS

Selection Focus Transparency 2: Have students view and discuss Andy Warhol's *Marilyn*.

Focus Activity: To extend the Focus Activity, you may want to pair each student with a friend and ask the partners to list each other's special qualities.

RESOURCE MANAGER

Lesson Planning Resource
The *Unit One Planning Guide* (pp. 14–18) provides additional lesson notes and reduced versions of all print resources.

📁 Other Print Resources
- Active Reading Guide, p. 2
- Reading Workbook, pp. 3–4
- Quick Checks, p. 2
- Selection and Theme Assessment, pp. 3–4

- Performance Assessment, p. 2
- Spanish Summaries, p. 2
- Inclusion Strategies
- English Language Learners Sourcebook

 Transparencies
- Selection Focus 2
- Literary Elements 2

Technology
- 🎧 Audio Library
- 🎧 Spanish Audio Library
- 💻 Glencoe Literature Web Site
- 💾 Testmaker

A Active Reading

Help students notice the great number of images in the poem. Ask them which are the most vivid. Then ask students to describe how the images add up to a picture of the speaker.

B Critical Thinking

LOGICAL REASONING Do students agree that they are originals? Ask those who disagree to explain. *(Most students will agree based on the examples Berry provides. Others may cite clones or twins as examples of people who are not originals.)*

C Literary Elements

VISUAL IMAGERY Read these lines aloud "*and mirrors can show me multiplied many times, say, dressed up in green, or dressed up in blue.*" Ask students to describe what they see and to discuss how the image helps readers understand that the speaker is only "One."

Additional Resources

📁 *Active Reading Guide*, p. 2

🎧 *Audio Library*

🎧 *Spanish Audio Library*

📁 *Spanish Summaries*, p. 2

One

James Berry ∾

Only one of me
and nobody can get a second one
from a photocopy machine.

> 5   Nobody has the fingerprints I have.
> Nobody can cry my tears, or laugh my laugh
> or have my expectancy° when I wait.

A

> But anybody can mimic° my dance with my dog.
> Anybody can howl how I sing out of tune.
> And mirrors can show me multiplied
> 10   many times, say, dressed up in red
> or dressed up in grey.

Nobody can get into my clothes for me
or feel my fall for me, or do my running.
Nobody hears my music for me, either.

> 15   I am just this one.
> Nobody else makes the words
> I shape with sound, when I talk.

B

But anybody can act how I stutter in a rage.
Anybody can copy echoes I make.
20   And mirrors can show me multiplied
many times, say, dressed up in green
or dressed up in blue.

C

---

6 An *expectancy* is the feeling one has while expecting something.
7 To *mimic* is to copy, or imitate.

CONNECTING TO OTHER SELECTIONS
For a teaching strategy that connects "One" to "Names/Nombres," turn to page 10 in the *Theme One Planning Guide*.

MEETING INDIVIDUAL NEEDS — ENGLISH LANGUAGE LEARNERS

Compound Words On the board write *somebody, photocopy* and *fingerprints*. Explain that often the meaning of a compound word can be figured out by combining the meanings of the words that form it. For example:

somebody = some + body (a person who exists; someone who is famous)
photocopy = photo + copy (a copy created by a photographic process)

fingerprints = finger + prints (unique impressions made by the fingertips)

Activity Have students look for other examples of compound words. You may wish to have them list and define them in their vocabulary notebooks.

Additional Resources

📁 *English Language Learners Sourcebook*

I'm Nobody! Who are you?

Emily Dickinson

I'm Nobody! Who are you?
Are you—Nobody—Too?
Then there's a pair of us!
Don't tell! they'd advertise—you know!

5   How dreary°—to be—Somebody!
How public—like a Frog—
To tell one's name—the livelong June°—
To an admiring Bog!°

_____

5 *Dreary* means "sad; depressing; dull; uninteresting."
7 The *livelong June* would be the whole month.
8 A *bog* is the swampy sort of ground where frogs live.

"Sun Shower," 1995. Diana Ong. Computer graphic, 5 x 4 in. Chrome.

D Active Reading

CONNECT Ask students what they think Emily Dickinson might say to James Berry about being "One." *(If everyone is "one," she would like to be "one" in a quiet and private way.)*

E Critical Thinking

DRAWING CONCLUSIONS Ask students why Dickinson chooses a frog to make her point. *(A frog's croaking is monotonous, and nobody cares to hear it.)*

F Literary Elements

VISUAL IMAGERY Have students describe the picture Dickinson paints using *the livelong June—To an admiring Bog!* *(These words create images of water, mud, reeds, nice weather, and a lone frog.)*

LITERATURE & HUMANITIES

Display *Green Coca Cola Bottles,* in *American Art History and Culture,* page 574. Have students examine how the images, though repeated, still reinforce the idea of individuality.

Thematic Focus

What I Am, What I Want to Be
The speakers in both poems make strong statements about who they are and who they want to be.

✔ ASSESSMENT OPTIONS

📁 *Quick Checks,* p. 2

Reading *Minilesson*

Summarizing Remind students that the purpose of summarizing is to provide a brief, easily understood restatement of the most important ideas of a text.

Activity Ask students to work individually to summarize "I'm Nobody! Who are you?" by completing the graphic organizer. Invite a few volunteers to share their work with the class and discuss whether their summaries have included the right information. **L2**

Additional Resources
📁 *Reading Workbook,* pp. 3–4

Question Used to Discover Important Facts	Answer
What does the speaker say about himself/herself?	*He or she is "nobody."*
Whom does the speaker meet?	*He or she meets another "nobody."*
What does the speaker think about his/her situation?	*It is better to be "nobody" than "somebody."*
Summary:	
The speaker, who calls him-, or herself "nobody," meets another "nobody" and says that it is better to be "nobody" than "somebody."	

Responding to the Selection

Personal Response

Student responses should indicate how the poems helped them reflect on what they are and what they want to be. Writing should include supporting passages and ideas from the poems.

Analyzing Literature

1. The author mentions fingerprints, feelings, experiences, actions, perceptions, and his way of thinking and speaking.
2. In the category of Nobodies, people are private and quiet. In the category of Somebodies, people are public and talk about themselves to anyone who will listen.
3. It lists the many things that make any person unique.
4. The speaker is a private person and feels that telling one's name in public would be dull and repetitive.
5. The speaker most values his private feelings and experiences. He finds the things that people can see him do—dress up, act angry, or show off—less valuable.
6. Students can express personal preferences for being Nobody or Somebody. Some may think that being Nobody is what makes you Somebody.
7. He would want to be appreciated for his words and for simply being who he is.
8. Some students may choose "One" because it is a confident poem that celebrates the poet's belief in his individuality. Other students may choose "I'm Nobody! Who are You?" because in it the poet asserts that she is more comfortable with herself than with others.
9. There would be no politicians, actors, musicians, or other public figures.

Responding to Literature

PERSONAL RESPONSE

What did you realize about yourself while reading these poems? What do the poems say about promoting yourself?

Analyzing Literature

RECALL

1. In what ways does the speaker in James Berry's poem feel unique? In what ways is he not unique?
2. Into what two categories does the speaker in Emily Dickinson's poem divide people, including herself? Describe each category.

INTERPRET

3. How does "One" celebrate the uniqueness of individuals?
4. Why does the speaker in Emily Dickinson's poem feel that being "Nobody" is preferable to being "Somebody"?

EVALUATE AND CONNECT

5. Which aspects of being human do you think the speaker in "One" values most? Which aspects are less valuable?
6. If you had to decide to be Dickinson's Nobody or Somebody, which would you choose? Explain.
7. What lasting impression do you imagine the speaker in "One" would want to leave on people he has known?
8. Theme Connection Which of these poems better expresses how you feel about yourself? Explain.
9. How would the world change if everyone decided to be a "Nobody"?
10. What is it about Emily Dickinson's writing **style** that makes you feel as if she is actually talking to you?

---

10. She writes in a conversational tone, addressing the reader as "you," and asking direct questions.

Extending Your Response

Writing About Literature

Theme   The **theme** of a poem is its central idea or message. Write a paragraph identifying the message of each of these two poems.

Personal Writing

New Thoughts About Myself   Return to the notes you wrote in the **Focus Activity** on page 13. Would you change the qualities you listed after reading these two poems? Write a short self-portrait that shows who you are. Explore your unique character traits and personality more than your appearance.

Interdisciplinary Activity

Music   In his poem, Berry writes "Nobody hears my music for me." What does that mean? Put together a listening brochure that reflects the real you. Illustrate your brochure, keeping it "in tune" with your musical tastes.

Literature Groups

Present Yourself!   Read each poem line by line. Identify the line that is the most thought provoking. How does the line challenge or confirm your own thoughts about yourself? Does it make you reconsider what makes a person unique? Does it give you a strong visual image? With your group, choose the line that provokes the most interest. Write the line on a banner to present to the class. Be ready to defend your choice in a larger group discussion.

Reading Further

If you enjoyed the work of these poets, you might like to check out these other works:

Short Stories: *A Thief in the Village and Other Stories* by James Berry

Biography: *Emily Dickinson* by Victoria Olsen

 Save your work for your portfolio.

Skill Minilesson

READING AND THINKING • COMPARING AND CONTRASTING

In the poems "One" and "I'm Nobody! Who are you?" the speakers share private thoughts and feelings about their own identities with you, the reader. In some ways the poems are similar. In other ways they are very different.

PRACTICE Try your hand at comparing and contrasting.
1. Write one paragraph that compares the poems, describing how they are alike.

2. Write a second paragraph that contrasts the poems, showing how they are different. Think about the structure, rhyme, rhythm, and punctuation in each poem. Pay special attention to imagery, meaning, and word choice. You might begin by examining how each poet uses the word *nobody*. They both use the word several times, but the intended meaning is quite different.

● For more about comparing and contrasting, see **Reading Handbook,** pp. R85–R86.

Extending Your Response

Writing About Literature

Students' paragraphs should
- clearly state the theme of each poem.
- list the similarities and differences in the poems' themes.

Personal Writing

Students' self-portraits should
- describe their unique character traits and personality.
- include personal details from the QuickWrite activity on page 13.

Interdisciplinary Activity   You may want to invite students to bring in a few sample recordings of the music listed on their brochures to play for the class.

Literature Groups   Encourage students to begin by deciding upon a method of coming to an agreement.
COLLAB. LEARN.

Skill Minilesson

READING AND THINKING
• COMPARING AND CONTRASTING
1. Each expresses thoughts about the poet's sense of self.
2. "One" is longer, has no rhyme, uses repetition, expresses ideas in complete sentences. The speaker's main idea is that no matter who or what mimics him, he will remain one of a kind. "I'm Nobody! Who Are You?" is shorter, uses rhyme and invented capital-ization. The speaker says she would rather remain anonymous than bear the burden of fame.

Additional Resources
Reading Workbook, pp. 3–4

✓ ASSESSMENT OPTIONS

📁 *Quick Checks,* p. 2

📁 *Selection and Theme Assessment,* pp. 3–4

📁 *Performance Assessment,* p. 2

💾 *Testmaker*

Before Reading

Objectives

- To read and analyze two poems about personal characteristics and self-confidence
- To identify and understand irony in poetry
- To write a description of the speaker in a poem

Skills

Reading/Thinking: Generalizing; Paraphrasing; Visualizing
Writing: Short Descriptive Poem
Listening/Speaking: Reading and Listening to Poetry
Collaboration: Literature Groups; Partner Reading

Before You Read
Face It and *Almost Ready*

MEET JANET S. WONG

Janet Wong's mother is Korean, her father Chinese. "Growing up, I never felt very Korean," Wong says. "Lately I have been wanting to know more about my mother, and for the first time I find myself craving Korean beef bone soup and kimchi, which I used to hate."

"Face It" is from an anthology called A Suitcase of Seaweed and Other Poems, *published in 1996.*

MEET ARNOLD ADOFF

Arnold Adoff believes that "writing a poem is making music with words and space." The award-winning poet, teacher, and lecturer is married to writer Virginia Hamilton.

"Almost Ready" is from an anthology, Slow Dance Heart Break Blues, *published in 1995.*

18   THEME 1

FOCUS ACTIVITY

What is the real *you* like? Do you have your father's chin or your grandmother's sense of humor? Think about your physical characteristics and your personality traits. Do you know which ones are family traits?

Chart It!
Make a chart showing some of your personality traits and physical characteristics. Label the ones you think are family traits and those that are unique to you.

Setting a Purpose
Read to find out what the speakers in these poems think about how they look.

BACKGROUND

Our cultural and ethnic heritage is also part of what makes each of us unique. Janet S. Wong writes: "Sometimes the first question a stranger will ask me, even before learning my name, is 'What are you?' or 'Where are you from?' These kinds of people usually stare hard at my face, as if they are testing themselves on how well they can tell the difference between Chinese and Korean and Japanese."

PEANUTS reprinted by permission of United Feature Syndicate, Inc.

FACE IT

Janet S. Wong ∾

My nose belongs
to Guangdong, China—
short and round, a Jang family nose.

My eyes belong
to Alsace, France—
wide like Grandmother Hemmerling's.

But my mouth, my big-talking mouth, belongs
to me, alone.

A Active Reading

EVALUATE The first part of this statement is not literally true. Have students explain what larger idea it implies. *(Her nose looks just like the noses of her Chinese ancestors.)*

B Literary Elements

REPETITION Ask students to point out examples of repetition that lend rhythm to the poem. *(The word belong occurs in all three stanzas, and the word mouth is repeated in the last stanza.)*

C Active Reading

EVALUATE Ask students why the speaker feels she is responsible for her mouth. *(What she says with her mouth is not hereditary like the shape of her nose and her eyes.)*

Additional Resources

📁 *Active Reading Guide,* p. 3
🎧 *Audio Library*
🎧 *Spanish Audio Library*
📁 *Spanish Summaries,* p. 3

Teaching Options

MEETING INDIVIDUAL NEEDS — ENGLISH LANGUAGE LEARNERS

Dramatic Reading Performing "Almost Ready" with its repeated language pattern gives English language learners a rewarding experience in English pronunciation, inflection, and phrasing.

Activity Read the poem aloud as students follow. Then have students read aloud with you at least twice. Concentrate on phrasing and emphasize the rhythmic lines. Then have them read the poem aloud. Coach them on pronunciation and phrasing until their delivery is fluent. After students have mastered reading the poem, invite them to give a dramatic reading for the class.

Additional Resources

📁 *English Language Learners Sourcebook*

D Literary Elements

IRONY Ask students whether the speaker in "Almost Ready" sounds self-assured. Invite a discussion of what the phrase "I am going to her birthday party as..." brings to mind. *(Students may be reminded of going to a costume party, which suggests not showing one's real self.)*

E Critical Thinking

GENERALIZING Have students consider whether they think people in real life who act hip and cool are as self-confident as they appear.

F Literary Elements

FREE VERSE Ask students to take a close look at the way the lines are arranged on the page and how the physical arrangement of lines might help deliver the poem's main idea. *(Possibly, the lines are like a list of things to do. This shows how many people think about one thing at a time and helps readers understand the speaker's growing panic.)*

Thematic Focus

What I Am, What I Want To Be In "Face It" and "Almost Ready," the speakers focus on particular, personal traits. Ask students to consider how a person's vulnerability, shyness, or talkativeness is an important part of who they are, whether it is obvious or hidden.

Teaching Options

CONNECTING TO OTHER SELECTIONS
For a teaching strategy that connects "Almost Ready" to "The Dog Diaries," turn to page 67 in the *Theme Four Planning Guide.*

FINE ART
TRANSPARENCY 31

You may wish to use *Fine Art Transparency 31* to enrich the discussion.

ALMOST READY

Arnold Adoff ∾

I	as	
am	this	
going	cool	
to	and	
her	in-	**D**
birth-	control	
day	young	
party	dude:	

as	as	as	as
soon	soon	soon	soon
as	as	as	as
I	I	I	I
find	find	find	find
my	my	my	my
new	hip	deep	right
shirt,	shoes,	voice,	mask.

E

Reading *Minilesson*

Paraphrasing Help students recall that paraphrasing something is saying it again in your own words. Remind students that a summary should contain only the most important ideas in a source, whereas a *paraphrase* should include virtually the same information as the original, including the author's opinion.

Activity Help students paraphrase "Almost Ready" by telling what the poem's speaker really means. If necessary, model the first one or two items for your students. **L2**

Additional Resources
📁 *Reading Workbook*

Responding to Literature

PERSONAL RESPONSE

What is your response to these two poems? Which lines from each poem did you find most memorable? Why?

Analyzing Literature

RECALL

1. What images does the poem "Face It" focus on?
2. Summarize what happens in "Almost Ready."

INTERPRET

3. How do you think the images and the title of the poem "Face It" relate to the poem's **theme?**
4. What inner **conflict** is the speaker of "Almost Ready" feeling? How does the conflict relate to the poem's title? Explain.

EVALUATE AND CONNECT

5. Do you agree with the speaker of "Face It" that people are a combination of their ancestors' characteristics and their own unique traits? Why or why not?
6. Do you agree that young people often show an exterior that is "cool and in-control," while their inner feelings are quite different? Explain.
7. How does the arrangement of the lines of "Almost Ready" relate to the meaning of the poem? How does this special structure affect the actual reading of the poem?
8. How do *you* prepare to go to a birthday party? In what ways are you like the speaker in "Almost Ready"? In what ways are you different?
9. Theme Connection   What did you discover or realize about yourself as you read these poems? Explain.
10. Did you find these poems humorous, serious, or both? Explain.

LITERARY ELEMENTS

Irony

When something awful happens and you say "Oh, great!" you are being ironic. In literature, **verbal irony** exists when the writer, or a character the writer creates, says the opposite of what he or she really means. Similarly, **situational irony** exists when what actually happens in a situation is the opposite of what we expect.

Irony may be used for humorous purposes, as when someone says "Nice weather" during a blizzard. It also can be used in a serious, or even bitter, way. For example, you might mutter "Nice guy" after someone has done something rude.

Watch for irony in literature. If you don't see when a writer is using irony, you may misunderstand what that author is trying to say.

1. Find and explain an example of irony in either poem.

2. Is the title of one of these poems an example of irony? Why or why not?

● See **Literary Terms Handbook,** p. R5.

Personal Response

Students may say that they know how the speakers in these poems feel because they have felt similarly.

Analyzing Literature

1. It focuses on the speaker's facial features, especially the nose, the eyes, and the mouth.
2. A boy likes a girl and wants to impress her, but he feels he has to change everything about himself to do so. At first the reader thinks the speaker is self-confident but soon realizes that he is really insecure.
3. "Face It" is a pun. It refers to the speakers' face, which is described in the poem, and it refers to being honest with oneself.
4. The speaker is in conflict about his identity. He does not have the confidence to go as himself.
5. Most students will agree and will cite examples of relatives who look like them. Students will also agree that everyone's face is unique.
6. Most students will agree and say that they often feel they need to hide strong feelings.
7. The lines are written like lists of things to do to get ready. This arrangement makes the rhythm of the poem and the repetitions more obvious.
8. Student responses should include some comparisons to the poem.
9. Students will express varied thoughts about their appearance and self-confidence.

LITERARY ELEMENTS

1. In "Almost Ready," there is irony in the speaker's view of himself.
2. "Almost Ready" is an example of irony. The speaker in the poem is clearly not ready.

Additional Resources

📖 *Literary Elements Transparency 3*

10. Most students will find serious ideas and possibly humor in both poems. Both speakers are expressing serious thoughts and feelings. The reference to the "big-talking mouth" in "Face It" and to the incongruity between the overconfidence and the dissolving self-confidence in "Almost Ready" are humorous.

Extending Your Response

Writing About Literature

Students' paragraphs should
- describe the character and personality of one of the speakers.
- use lines from the poem to support their conclusions.

Creative Writing

Students' poems should
- describe themselves or people they know.
- use exact words.

Literature Groups
Encourage students to recognize the honesty in each poem and ask them to discuss how honesty in poetry is an important element. **COLLAB. LEARN.**

Listening and Speaking
Suggest that readers practice reading the poem several times before sharing it with their partners. Remind students to speak slowly and clearly, paying attention to the musical quality of the words.

Skill Minilesson

READING AND THINKING
- **VISUALIZING**

Students' paragraphs should contain accurate descriptions of the images in the two poems.

Additional Resources
📁 *Reading Workbook*

Extending Your Response

Writing About Literature
Character The speakers in both poems reveal a great deal about themselves in very few words. Write a paragraph describing the speaker from either poem as you picture that person.

Literature Groups
Poet's Corner Both of these poems offer surprise endings. In "Almost Ready," the speaker says "as soon as I find my right mask." What does this line mean? Do you agree or disagree that clothing and "put-on" airs such as a "deep voice" can be a mask? The poem "Face It" also ends with a surprise. When the speaker refers to her "big-talking mouth," what is she revealing about herself?

Girl with a Red Hat, 1940. Raphael Soyer. Oil on canvas, 76.8 x 43.2 cm. Fundacion Coleccion Thyssen-Bornemisza, Madrid.

Creative Writing
Who Am I? Write a short poem that describes you or a person you know, such as a friend or a relative. Try to include as much information as possible, using exact words. If you are writing about yourself, review your chart from the **Focus Activity** on page 18 before you begin.

Listening and Speaking
Listening to Poetry To be fully enjoyed, a poem is best read aloud. Listeners can close their eyes and picture the images as they hear the rhythm of the lines. With a partner, take turns reading these poems to each other.

Reading Further
If you would like to read more by these poets, try these books:
All the Colors of the Race by Arnold Adoff
Good Luck Gold and Other Poems by Janet S. Wong

📖 **Save your work for your portfolio.**

Skill Minilesson

READING AND THINKING • VISUALIZING

Visualizing a story or a poem is a skill that can help you enjoy and understand that piece of writing better. As you read or listen, try to re-create images or scenes in your mind. Pay close attention to the details the writer chooses. Ask yourself: what does this image or scene look like, smell like, feel like? What is going on here?

PRACTICE Reread each of the poems. As you do, try to visualize the images in each poem.

Write a paragraph describing some of the images that come to mind as you read or listen to each poem. You might want to sketch some of the images to accompany your paragraph.

● For more about visualizing, see **Reading Handbook,** p. R84.

✔ ASSESSMENT OPTIONS

📁 *Quick Checks,* p. 3
📁 *Selection and Theme Assessment,* pp. 5–6
📁 *Performance Assessment,* p. 3
💾 *Testmaker*

Writing Skills

Using Dialogue in a Narrative

Dialogue, or conversation quoting the exact words of characters, is an effective narrative technique. It can rivet the reader's attention. And no wonder. Dialogue can bring characters to life and dramatically show them reacting to one another.

When you use dialogue in your writing, try to weave it in smoothly. Dialogue may be introduced in several ways—at the beginning, middle, or end of a sentence. Sometimes a block of conversation can continue for several lines. Following are some examples of how dialogue can be used. As you read, notice how the writer has used capitalization and punctuation marks.

How Dialogue Can Be Used in Writing	
At the beginning of a sentence: "It's a polite Chinese custom to show you are satisfied," explained my father to our astonished guests. —Amy Tan, "Fish Cheeks" **In the middle of a sentence:** He said, "Let me have those front seats," because they were the front seats of the black section. —Rosa Parks, from *Rosa Parks: My Story* **At the end of a sentence:** Ernie groaned and said, "Ah, man." —Gary Soto, "Broken Chain"	**As a block of conversation:** . . . inevitably, my accent and coloring gave me away. "So where are you from, Judy?" "New York," I told my classmates. After all, I had been born blocks away at Columbia Presbyterian Hospital. "I mean, *originally.*" "From the Caribbean," I answered vaguely, for if I specified, no one was quite sure what continent our island was on. —Julia Alvarez, "Names/Nombres" **Mechanics Tip:** Indent each time the speaker changes. **An interrupted quotation:** "Children," Miss Ryan called for attention. "Ernesto has learned how to pronounce butterfly!" —Ernesto Galarza, from *Barrio Boy*

ACTIVITIES

1. Write at least three sentences of dialogue about a childhood memory. Use dialogue to begin one sentence, to form the middle of another, and to end a third.

2. Write a paragraph in which one friend tells a joke to another. Include a block of dialogue, and indent correctly.

Objective

- To recognize and use dialogue in narrative writing

Teaching Strategies

To dramatize the difference between indirect speech and dialogue, read the following passage aloud to the class.

Kim told her sister she didn't want to paint their bedroom yellow because it would be too bright and sunny and she'd feel like she had to be happy all the time. The thought of a yellow bedroom made her feel tired. Kim's sister, Maria, said that yellow was also the color of the moon, and it could be a soothing color to paint the walls. Kim couldn't imagine who'd want to live on the moon. She certainly didn't.

Ask students to take the parts of Kim and Maria and role-play this simple conversation between sisters. Encourage them to improvise and shade the dialogue with emotion. Explain that dialogue lets the characters speak for themselves.

Activities

1. Students' sentences should adhere to the punctuation guidelines in their books.
2. Students may want to include an interrupted quotation in their blocks of dialogue.

Additional Resources

 Writer's Choice, Lessons 4.4, 20.6

Teaching Options

Grammar and Language *Minilesson*

Punctuating Dialogue Have students find a paragraph in "Names/Nombres" that includes dialogue. Ask a few volunteers to read dialogue from the story aloud, including punctuation and capitalization, as if they were dictating it to a typist.

Activity Have small groups of students conduct an informal meeting of the "Young Poets Society" to discuss one of the four poems in this Theme. They should tape-record five minutes of the discussion and transcribe a small portion, using the sample dialogue on page 23 as a model for punctuating it. Have them check for accuracy of content and punctuation. **L3**
COLLAB. LEARN.

Additional Resources

 Grammar and Language Transparency 2

 Grammar and Language Workbook, pp. 267–270

Grammar and Composition Handbook, Lesson 13.6

 Writer's Choice, Lessons 4.4, 20.6

23

MEDIA Connection

Objective

• To read and understand a newspaper column

Literature LINK

Strong Men Weep This newspaper column connects to the literature selection that immediately follows this lesson. Point out the connection: Like the disabled but victorious mountain climbers, Lou Gehrig of the New York Yankees faced one of life's great challenges with courage, determination, and grace.

Respond

1. Some students may say that the author writes short paragraphs because people skim for information when they read newspapers. Others may say that the short paragraphs make the article move along quickly and keep the reader interested.

2. Responses may include stories of popular figures who have accomplished great feats but have behaved poorly in their personal lives.

Additional Resources

📁 *Media Connections*, p. 1

Teaching Options

MEDIA Connection

NEWSPAPER COLUMN

This column was written in 1981, after John McEnroe won the tennis championship at Wimbledon, England. The young McEnroe had a reputation for behaving badly on the tennis court. Do you think Erma Bombeck's comments are relevant today?

Heroes

by Erma Bombeck—Syndicated Newspaper Column, August 2, 1981

On the first Saturday of last month, a 22-year-old U.S. tennis player hoisted a silver bowl over his head at Centre Court at Wimbledon.

The day before, five blind mountain climbers, a man with an artificial leg, an epileptic, and two deaf adventurers stood atop the snowcapped summit of Mount Rainier.

It was a noisy victory for the tennis player, who shared it with thousands of fans, some of whom had slept on the sidewalks outside the club for six nights waiting for tickets.

It was a quiet victory for the climbers, who led their own cheering, punctuated by a shout from one of them that echoed on the winds: "There's one for the epileptics!"

There was a lot of rhetoric exchanged at Wimbledon regarding "bad calls."

At Mount Rainier they learned to live with life's bad calls a long time ago. The first man to reach the mountaintop tore up his artificial leg to get there.

Somehow, I see a parallel here that all Americans are going to have to come to grips with. In our search for heroes and heroines, we often lose our perspective.

We applaud beauty pageant winners; we ignore the woman without arms who paints pictures with a brush in her teeth. We extol the courage of a man who will sail over 10 cars on a motorcycle; we give no thought (or parking place) to the man who threads his way though life in a world of darkness or silence.

The care and feeding of heroes is solely in the hands of the public. Not all winners are heroes. Not all people with disabilities are heroes. "Hero" is a term that should be awarded to those who, given a set of circumstances, will react with courage, dignity,

decency, and compassion—people who make us feel better for having seen or touched them.

I think the crowds went to the wrong summit and cheered the wrong champion.

Respond

1. The author writes mostly very short paragraphs. Why do you suppose she does so?

2. Do you agree that we cheer the wrong heroes? Give examples to support your opinion.

Reading *Minilesson*

Comparing and Contrasting In this section, Bombeck contrasts an often-rude athlete with a group of handicapped achievers—to persuade readers that society often cheers for the wrong heroes.

Activity Have the class complete this Venn diagram that will show the two types of heroes compared and contrasted.

Tennis Champ watched by thousands of fans | Both Types of Heroes achieve great things | Handicapped Mountain Climber ignored

Additional Resources

📘 *Reading Workbook*

Before You Read

Strong Men Weep

MEET BENEDICT COSGROVE

A lifetime sports fan, journalist, and writer, Benedict Cosgrove is also the co-editor of *Gluttony*, an anthology of short stories and essays. Cosgrove's most recent book, *Covering the Bases*, from which this selection is taken, is a collection of sports writing, radio transcripts, and photographs of the most unforgettable moments in baseball, as recorded by the writers and broadcasters who were there.

Benedict Cosgrove lives in San Francisco, California. This work was published in 1996.

FOCUS ACTIVITY

Do you have a hero? Why do you consider this person a hero?

Sharing Ideas
In small groups, discuss the qualities you think heroes share. Then make a list of people you think are heroes, and explain why each person is on the list. Do heroes have to be famous?

Setting a Purpose
Read to find out why Lou Gehrig is considered a hero.

BACKGROUND

This essay is about an event that took place at Yankee Stadium, New York City, in 1939. The author sets the scene for Shirley Povich's account.

Shirley Povich (1905–1998) was, at age twenty, the youngest sports reporter in the U.S. Consid-ered the *Washington Post*'s "most revered sports columnist," he wrote for that paper for 75 years. His approach to writing was simply stated: "I write what I like to read."

Shirley Povich

VOCABULARY PREVIEW

consecutive (kən sek′ yə tiv) *adj.* following one after another in order without interruption; p. 26

discrepancy (dis krep′ ən sē) *n.* a lack of agreement, as between facts; p. 27

eloquent (el′ ə kwənt) *adj.* expressive, effective, and stirring in speech or writing; p. 29

esteem (es tēm′) *n.* favorable opinion; high regard; p. 29

elicit (i lis′ it) *v.* to draw forth or bring out; p. 29

hindrance (hin′ drəns) *n.* something that holds back progress or movement; obstacle; p. 30

WHAT I AM, WHAT I WANT TO BE 25

RESOURCE MANAGER

Lesson Planning Resource
The *Theme One Planning Guide* (pp. 24–31) provides additional lesson notes and reduced versions of all print resources.

📁 **Other Print Resources**
- Active Reading Guide, p. 4
- Vocabulary Practice, p. 2
- Reading Workbook, pp. 5–6
- Grammar and Language Workbook, pp. 85–86, 87–88
- Grammar and Composition Handbook, Lesson 3.6

- Quick Checks, p. 4
- Selection and Theme Assessment, pp. 7–8
- Performance Assessment, p. 4
- Spanish Summaries, p. 4
- Spanish Translations
- Inclusion Strategies
- English Language Learners Sourcebook

🖊 **Transparencies**
- Selection Focus 4
- Literary Elements 4
- Grammar and Language 3

Technology
 Literature Launchers
 Audio Library
 Spanish Audio Library
 Testmaker

Before Reading

Objectives
- To read and analyze an article
- To identify the author's purpose in writing an article
- To write a critical review

Skills

Reading/Thinking: Comparing and Contrasting; Distinguishing Fact from Opinion

Writing: Review; Persuasive Paragraph

Vocabulary: Root Words; Owning a Word

Grammar/Language: Main Verbs and Helping Verbs

Listening/Speaking: Announcing a Game

Collaboration: Literature Groups

Motivating
→ OPTIONS

 Literature Launchers: "The Story of Lou Gehrig"

Videodisc Side A, Segment 2

Also available in VHS.

 Selection Focus Transparency 4: Have students discuss the graph of attendance at baseball games from 1900 to 1994.

 Focus Activity: As an extension of the Focus Activity, have students tell the class what heroes they think are overpraised.

Reading the Selection

SUMMARY

In 1995, Cal Ripken of the Baltimore Orioles broke the record for consecutive games played, a record set by Lou Gehrig 56 years earlier. Many fans said Ripken was a more skilled player, but Gehrig showed a heroism beyond the sport when he said goodbye at Yankee Stadium on July 4, 1939. Strong men wept because Gehrig, still at the top of his game, had developed a fatal illness. His speech was eloquent, touching, and filled with appreciation for his fans and colleagues.

📁 *Spanish Summaries,* p. 4

A **Active Reading**

PREDICT Ask students to predict what the "disturbing thread" in the discussions about The Streak might be. *(Students may guess that the "disturbing thread" might be an unkind rumor about one of the two players or about the record itself.)*

Additional Resources

📁 *Active Reading Guide,* p. 4

🎧 *Audio Library*

🎧 *Spanish Audio Library*

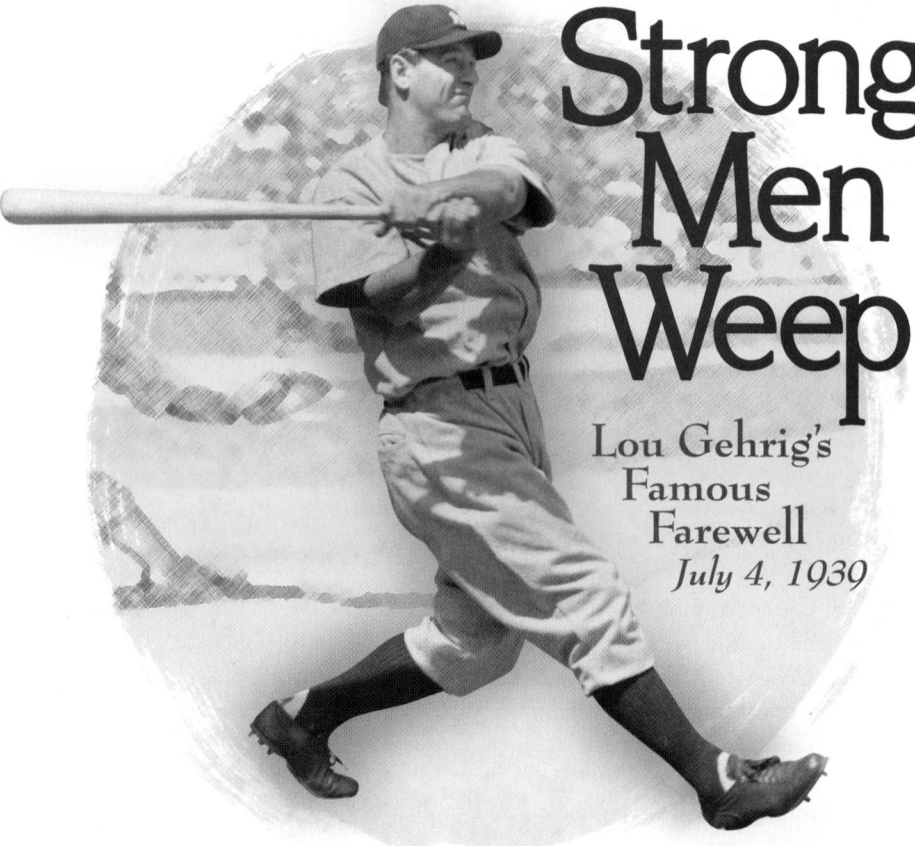

Strong Men Weep

Lou Gehrig's Famous Farewell
July 4, 1939

Benedict Cosgrove ∾

Cal Ripken breaking Lou Gehrig's streak

A of 2,130 <u>consecutive</u> games might have been the best thing that could have happened to the old Yankee captain's reputation.

For months and weeks leading up to that great night in September 1995, when Ripken finally passed Gehrig, a disturbing thread began to weave through the endless discussions surrounding The Streak.

Vocabulary
consecutive (kən sek′ yə tiv) *adj.* following one after another in order without interruption

Teaching Options

CONNECTING TO OTHER SELECTIONS

COMPARING selections

This selection is compared with "Wait Till Next Year" on page 35. A lesson for teaching a comparison of the two selections appears on page 40.

The chart at the right shows three ways to connect "Strong Men Weep" to other selections in this book.

For specific teaching strategies, see the *Theme One Planning Guide,* pages 27–28.

Connection	Title
Life Skills: Supporting and Contributing	→ "Too Soon a Woman," p. 235
Thematic: Farewells	→ "There Is No Word for Goodbye," p. 179
Literary: Sequence of Events	→ "A Crush," p. 149

Among all the factions[1] that had formed as it became clear that Ripken was going to just keep on going (factions that seemed to dissolve—along with everyone else who cared at all about the record—into a mass, warm embrace of the man the moment he began his spontaneous, lump-in-the-throat jog around the field at Camden Yards),[2] there was, it seemed, a small but nonetheless significant group of voices that appeared bent on pointing out the questionable discrepancies in Gehrig's original record.

B Gehrig played first base, as opposed to Cal, who played a far more demanding shortstop. Gehrig often played only an inning or two when he wasn't feeling 100 percent—or when he was on the road, in order to keep the streak going—while Ripken played in something insane, like eight and two-thirds of every nine innings during his streak. Gehrig never had to deal with coast-to-coast airplane travel or Astroturf or blah blah blah. The point, it seemed, was that Gehrig's legendary streak, while kind of impressive, was really nothing compared to Ripken's *more genuine* streak.

And I'll buy that. Ripken's is the more amazing streak. By far. Hands down. No question.

C With his streak broken, though, perhaps Gehrig can be fully

C appreciated as the great, great ballplayer that he was, the ballplayer whose career was cut short when he still had some good years left in him, rather than as the guy whose tainted consecutive-game streak Cal Ripken finally obliterated.[3]

But no matter how Gehrig is remembered as a player, no matter how fine or fearsome a hitter the man was (a .340 lifetime average; a .632 slugging percentage; the career mark for grand slams; 1,990 RBIs), or how loyal a teammate, or how worthy a leader as the captain of the awesome Yankee teams of the 1920s, he

---

3. *Tainted* means "spoiled or made inferior." To *obliterate* something is to destroy it completely.

Lou Gehrig poses with another baseball legend, his teammate Babe Ruth.

---

1. *Factions* are small groups of people, within a larger group, who disagree on an issue or set of issues.
2. The home field of Ripken's team, the Baltimore Orioles, is named *Camden Yards*.

Vocabulary
discrepancy (dis krep′ ən sē) *n.* a lack of agreement, as between facts

VIEWING THE POSTER

This art was created in a style called photomontage in which separate photographs are combined into one. In this photomontage, the man who broke Lou Gehrig's streak, Cal Ripken, is superimposed over Gehrig.

Viewing Response *Some students may point out that baseball (or other sports) statistics exist in order to allow such comparisons. Others might argue that later players probably are healthier and better trained and the equipment they use has been improved (metal bats, for example), making comparisons less valid.*

LITERATURE & HUMANITIES

Display *Night Baseball* from *Introducing Art*, page 206. Have students write a short sports commentary that begins just prior to the moment that this scene takes place. Have students try to create suspense in their commentaries.

Viewing the poster: Can you fairly compare athletes who lived more than fifty years apart? Why or why not?

Teaching Options

Reading *Minilesson*

Comparing and Contrasting Comparing looks at likenesses; contrasting looks at differences. Comparing and contrasting two historical figures can be a way of understanding each person better.

Activity As a class, complete a Venn diagram comparing and contrasting Gehrig and Ripkin. Have small groups discuss these questions: What makes a ballplayer "great"? Are there different kinds of greatness? How do they apply to Ripkin and Gehrig? Groups can share their answers and tell how comparing and contrasting the two men helped them understand and appreciate each athlete. **L2**

Additional Resources
📁 *Reading Workbook,* pp. 5–6

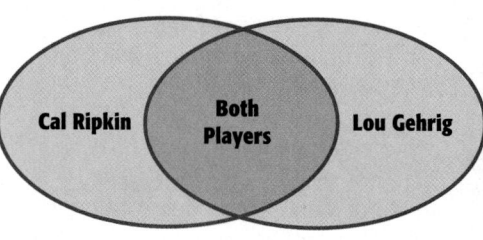

will always be most-readily associated with July 4, 1939, when 60,000 fans, old teammates, and Gehrig's own words filled Yankee Stadium for the game's most famous farewell: "Today I consider myself the luckiest man on the face of the earth."

Gehrig didn't speak for long, but not too many baseball fans are unfamiliar with what he said. No words ever uttered by another athlete have resonated[4] for so many years in the hearts and minds of so many fans, most of whom weren't even born at the time the words themselves were echoing around the far reaches of the park.

Gesturing to the "grand men," his teammates and friends, standing beside him, Gehrig asked: "Which of you wouldn't consider it the highlight of his career just to associate with them for even one day?" He went on to thank the fans, his managers, the groundskeepers, his father and mother, and his wife, in an <u>eloquent</u> and tremendously moving few minutes that ended with Gehrig breaking down and Babe Ruth stepping forward to lend his old teammate support.

Gehrig's words that day might not have been recorded verbatim[5] by Shirley Povich in his memorable *Washington Post* piece on the tribute, but no writer present when Gehrig walked to the mike better captured the <u>esteem</u> and affection Gehrig seemed to <u>elicit</u> from all who knew him—esteem and affection which, on that Tuesday afternoon, was finally given full voice.

---

4. Here, *resonated* means "echoed."
5. *Verbatim* (vər bā′ tim) means "word for word; in exactly the same words."

SHIRLEY POVICH

WASHINGTON POST, JULY 4, 1939
I saw strong men weep this afternoon, expressionless umpires swallow hard, and emotion pump the hearts and glaze the eyes of 61,000 baseball fans in Yankee Stadium. Yes, and hard-boiled news photographers clicked their shutters with fingers that trembled a bit.

It was Lou Gehrig Day at the stadium, and the first 100 years of baseball saw nothing quite like it. It was Lou Gehrig, tributes, honors, gifts heaped upon him, getting an overabundance of the thing he wanted least—sympathy. But it wasn't maudlin.[6] His friends were just letting their hair down in their earnestness to pay him honor. And they stopped just short of a good, mass cry.

They had Lou out there at home plate between games of a double-header, with the 60,000 massed in the triple tiers that rimmed the field, microphones and cameras trained on him, and he couldn't take it that way. Tears streamed down his face, circuiting the most famous pair of dimples in baseball, and he looked chiefly at the ground.

Seventy-year-old Ed Barrow, president of the Yankees, who had said to newspapermen, "Boys, I have bad news for you," when Gehrig's ailment was diagnosed as infantile paralysis[7] two weeks

---

6. If something is *maudlin,* it is overly or tearfully sentimental.
7. *Infantile paralysis* is a name for polio, a highly contagious disease that occurs mainly in children and can cause total paralysis. Gehrig's actual illness was not polio but a similar disease called amyotrophic lateral sclerosis, or ALS. It causes weakness, paralysis, and, in the end, death.

Vocabulary
eloquent (el′ ə kwənt) *adj.* expressive, effective, and stirring in speech or writing
esteem (es tēm′) *n.* favorable opinion; high regard
elicit (i lis′ it) *v.* to draw forth or bring out

The Physics of Hitting
A power hitter like Gehrig can crush a baseball with 8,000 pounds of force. This actually compresses the ball to about half of its original diameter.

D **Literary Elements**

AUTHOR'S PURPOSE Discuss the mood Povich creates with his description of the events at Lou Gehrig Day. *(He creates a very emotional mood by describing the reactions of fans, umpires, photographers, and Gehrig himself. This helps readers sympathize with Gehrig.)*

E **Critical Thinking**

DISTINGUISHING FACT FROM OPINION Encourage students to share what they know about fact and opinion. *(A fact can be proven; an opinion cannot.)* What opinions does Povich include in his article? *(Emotion pumped the hearts of fans; Gehrig didn't want sympathy.)*

F **Literary Elements**

AUTHOR'S PURPOSE Ask students what Cosgrove's and Povich's purposes were for writing about Gehrig's farewell. *(Povich wanted to make readers feel the emotions of the day. Cosgrove wanted to persuade readers that Gehrig was not only a great ballplayer but also a great man.)*

Listening and Speaking *Minilesson*

Announcing a Game A game announcer must know his or her sport and be able to think fast, speak clearly, and keep listeners interested. Point out that a good announcer can bring a game to life, even on the radio, by giving the information and sensory details that help listeners visualize exactly what is happening.

Activity To prepare for announcing a game, have students listen to professional TV or radio announcers and make notes on technique. Each should choose a real game to tape, if possible. Have students work with partners or small groups to practice several times. Then have one student from each group announce his or her game to the class. **L2** **COLLAB. LEARN.**

DISTINGUISHING FACT FROM OPINION
Some of Povich's statements are opinions, not facts. You may wish to share the following model to illustrate the thinking process involved in distinguishing facts from opinions.

Model: As I read, I noticed that the sportswriter makes statements that may be true but can't be proved. For instance, unless he could read Gehrig's mind, he couldn't be sure Gehrig was grateful for Barrow's supporting arm or know for sure that Gehrig was choking back emotions that threatened to silence him. I think he was using his opinions to make the story more dramatic.

H Active Reading

VISUALIZE Ask students to choose a moving scene on this page, visualize it, and describe it or draw a picture of it. *(They might choose the star athlete leaning on his 70-year-old boss or his tough-as-nails manager crying at the microphone.)*

Have students find out more about the disease that killed Lou Gehrig. Tell them to use *Lou Gehrig's disease* or *ALS* as keywords on a search engine.

---

ago, stepped out of the background halfway through the presentation ceremonies, and draped his arm across Gehrig's shoulder. But he was doing more than that. He was holding Gehrig up, for Big Lou needed support.

As he leaned on Barrow, Gehrig said, "Thanks, Ed." He bit his lip hard, was grateful for the supporting arm, as the Yankees of 1927 stepped to the microphone after being introduced. Babe Ruth, Bob Meusel, Waite Hoyt, Herb Pennock, Benny Bengough, Bob Shawkey, Mark Koenig, Tony Lazzeri, all of the class of '27 were there. And Gehrig had been one of them, too. He had been the only one among them to bestride both eras.

Still leaning on Barrow, Gehrig acknowledged gifts from his Yankee mates, from the Yankee Stadium ground crew, and the hot dog butchers, from fans as far as Denver, and from his New York rivals, the Giants. There was a smile through his tears, but he wasn't up to words. He could only shake the hands of the small army of officials who made the presentations.

He stood there twisting his doffed baseball cap into a braid in his fingers as Manager Joe McCarthy followed Mayor La Guardia and Postmaster General Farley in tribute to "the finest example of ball player, sportsman, and citizen that baseball has ever known," but Joe McCarthy couldn't take it that way, either. The man who has driven the highest-salaried prima donnas[8] of baseball into action, who has baited a thousand umpires, broke down.

McCarthy openly sobbed as he stood in front of the microphone and said, "Lou, what else can I say except that it was a sad day in the life of everybody who knew you when you came to my hotel room that day in Detroit and told me you were quitting as a ball player because you felt yourself a <u>hindrance</u> to the team. My God, man, you were never that."

And as if to emphasize the esteem in which he held Gehrig though his usefulness to the Yankees as a player was ended, McCarthy, too, stepped out of the fringe full into the circle where Gehrig stood and half embraced the big fellow.

Now it was Gehrig's turn to talk into the microphone, to acknowledge his gifts. The 60,000 at intervals had set up the shout, "We want Lou!" even as they used to shout "We want Ruth"— yells that they reserved for the only two men at Yankee Stadium for which the crowd ever organized a cheering section.

But Master of Ceremonies Sid Mercer was anticipating Gehrig. He saw the big fellow choked up. Infinitesimally[9] Gehrig shook his head, and Mercer announced: "I shall not ask Lou Gehrig to make a speech. I do not believe that I should."

They started to haul away the microphones. Gehrig half turned toward the dugout, with the ceremonies apparently at an end. And then he wheeled suddenly, strode back to the loud-speaking apparatus, held up his hand for attention, gulped, managed a smile, and then spoke.

---

8. Originally, a *prima donna* was the leading female singer of an opera company. Now, the term is applied to any "star" who is overly proud or demanding.

9. *Infinitesimally* means "in such a small way as to be almost unnoticeable."

Vocabulary
hindrance (hin′ drəns) *n.* something that holds back progress or movement; obstacle

---

Teaching Options

Grammar and Language *Minilesson*

Main Verbs and Helping Verbs Write on the board the four principal parts that are used to form a verb's tenses.
base form: *break*
present participle: *breaking*
past form: *broke*
past participle: *broken*
Explain that a principal part of a verb is often combined with a helping verb to form a verb phrase. In the verb phrase *are*

breaking, the helping verb is *are* and the main verb is *breaking.* The most common helping verbs are *be, have,* and *do.*

Activity Have students list verb phrases from page 30 and identify the main and helping verbs in each. Examples:

he *was doing*
Gehrig *had been* one of them

Additional Resources

📠 *Grammar and Language Transparency 3*

📖 *Grammar and Language Workbook,* pp. 85–86, 87–88

📖 *Writer's Choice,* Lesson 10.6

📖 *Grammar and Composition Handbook,* Lesson 3.6

Gehrig is overcome with emotion at his final appearance in Yankee Stadium.

Active Reading

EVALUATE What words would describe Lou Gehrig's character and how fans feel about him? *(He is brave, shy, and emotional. He seems to be loved and admired by his fans.)*

Literary Elements

IRONY Explain that situational irony exists when the outcome of a situation is the opposite of one's expectations. Point out that Gehrig's saying, "I've lots to live for, honest" is ironic because he's just been diagnosed with a terminal illness. Challenge students to find other ironies in the selection.

Thematic Focus

What I Am, What I Want to Be Encourage students to extend their discussion of what it means to be a hero. Why is Lou Gehrig considered a hero? Is Cal Ripken a hero? Ask students for examples.

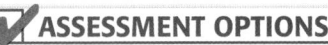

- *Pride of the Yankees* (1942, 128 minutes, NR), a Hollywood biography of Lou Gehrig recreates the tribute to Gehrig at Yankee Stadium. Preview the video to decide whether it is appropriate for your class.

"For weeks," said Gehrig, "I have been reading in the newspapers that I am a lucky fellow who got a tough break. I don't believe it. I have been a lucky guy. For 16 years, into every ballpark in which I have ever walked, I received nothing but kindness and encouragement. Mine has been a full life."

He went on, fidgeting with his cap, pawing the ground with his spikes as he spoke, choking back emotions that threatened to silence him, summoning courage from somewhere. He thanked everybody. He didn't forget the ballpark help; he told of his gratitude to newspapermen who had publicized him. He didn't forget the late Miller Huggins, or his six years with him; or Manager Joe McCarthy, or the late Col. Ruppert,[10] or Babe Ruth, or "my roommate, Bill Dickey."

And he thanked the Giants— "The fellows from across the river, who we would give our right arm to beat"—he was more at ease in front of the mike now, and he had a word for Mrs. Gehrig and for the immigrant father and mother who had made his education, his career, possible. And he denied again that he had been the victim of a bad break in life. He said, "I've lots to live for, honest."

And thousands cheered.

---

10. When Gehrig first joined the Yankees, *Huggins* managed the team and helped Gehrig develop his baseball skills. *McCarthy* became manager after Huggins. Jacob *Ruppert* was the owner or co-owner of the Yankees from 1914 to 1939.

REAL-WORLD CONNECTION

Heroes To help students gain perspective on the word *hero*, they can compare stories of different kinds of heroes.

Activity Have each student find a magazine or newspaper article about a true hero who reacts with courage, dignity, and compassion to a difficult personal or social challenge. Students in small groups should share and discuss their articles and pose and answer questions like *What challenges did this person face? How did he or she handle those challenges?* Then ask a member of each group to share the story of his or her hero with the class. **L2** **COLLAB. LEARN.**

ASSESSMENT OPTIONS

Quick Checks, p. 4

Responding to the Selection

Personal Response

- Students may say they wondered why good people die young or how Gehrig found the courage to remain optimistic and focus on others.
- Most students will probably agree that Gehrig was a hero because of his selflessness and courage in the face of death.

Analyzing Literature

1. Cal Ripken. The discussions focused on the ways in which Ripken's feat was more impressive than Gehrig's.
2. He will be most associated with his farewell speech on July 4, 1939.
3. He was referring to baseball fans, umpires, photographers, and everyone else who heard Gehrig's speech.
4. They cheered throughout his speech, especially when he said, "I've lots to live for, honest."
5. Ripken "played a far more demanding shortstop," "Gehrig often played only an inning or two when he wasn't feeling 100 percent," and "Gehrig never had to deal with coast-to-coast airplane travel or Astroturf."
6. It is ironic that Gehrig, who has just been diagnosed with a terminal disease, considers himself lucky. He shows dignity and class by being so grateful for the chance to play baseball.
7. He wanted to grab readers' emotions immediately and to emphasize that this was not a usual day at the stadium.
8. Gehrig was brave, upbeat, humble, and appreciative of others.
9. Students may say it has more impact because it's true. It is more impressive to find such an admirable man in real life than in fiction.

Responding to Literature

PERSONAL RESPONSE

- What thoughts and feelings did you have at the end of this selection?
- Think back to the discussion in the **Focus Activity** on page 25. Do you think that Lou Gehrig was a hero? Why or why not?

Analyzing Literature

RECALL

1. What player broke Lou Gehrig's streak of 2,130 consecutive games? What was the focus of the "endless discussions surrounding The Streak"?
2. With what event does Cosgrove believe Gehrig will always be most associated?
3. To whom was the journalist Shirley Povich referring when he wrote, "I saw strong men weep this afternoon"?
4. What did Gehrig say that July day that made people cheer?

INTERPRET

5. According to Cosgrove, what were the main points of discussion concerning the differences between the streaks of Cal Ripken and Lou Gehrig? Support your ideas with quotations from the selection.
6. "Today I consider myself the luckiest man on the face of the earth." Explain the significance of this statement.
7. The opening image in Povich's piece is emotional and powerful. Why do you think Povich chose this image? Explain.
8. What did you learn about Lou Gehrig's character from reading some of his farewell words?

EVALUATE AND CONNECT

9. "Strong Men Weep" is an example of **nonfiction**. It is about real events and a real person. Does knowing that this is a true story affect your experience of this man's character? Explain.
10. In your opinion, was Gehrig "the luckiest man on the face of the earth"? Explain.

LITERARY ELEMENTS

Author's Purpose

All writers have a purpose or goal they want to achieve in their writing. To **entertain** is one purpose for writing. To **describe** something is another purpose. Sometimes writers want to **inform** the reader or to **explain** something. Sometimes writers want to **persuade** their readers to believe something. A strong piece of writing often combines purposes: A persuasive essay, for example, may include description and information.

1. What was Shirley Povich's purpose in writing his memorable piece in the *Washington Post*? Support your opinion with examples from the account.
2. How would Povich's piece have been different if his purpose had been to describe Gehrig's batting statistics?

- See **Literary Terms Handbook**, p. R1.

---

10. Students will probably say no, because he was dying young. Some may agree with his perception that he had already had a wonderful life.

LITERARY ELEMENTS

1. He wanted readers to understand the esteem and affection everyone had for Gehrig.
2. He would have focused on facts and numbers only; leaving out the emotional details.

Additional Resources

Literary Elements Transparency 4

Extending Your Response

Writing About Literature

Critical Review   Write a paragraph reviewing "Strong Men Weep." Consider these questions: What did you learn from this selection? What kinds of details did Cosgrove and Povich include? How did these details affect your opinion of Gehrig?

Personal Writing

My Hero   "Strong Men Weep" recounts the famous farewell of a legendary sports hero. Who is one of your heroes? Think about the people you listed in the **Focus Activity** on page 25. Write a paragraph using effective details to convince your reader that the person you chose is a true hero.

Literature Groups

A Sporting Debate   Benedict Cosgrove and Shirley Povich wrote about a good and courageous man who happened to be a great baseball player. Does a reader have to love the game of baseball to be affected by this account of Lou Gehrig? Why or why not? Support your opinion with examples from the selection and other stories about heroes.

Reading Further

For more about sports, try these:

Dreams into Deeds: Nine Women Who Dared by Linda Peavy and Ursula Smith

The Random House Book of Sports Stories by L. M. Schulman

 Save your work for your portfolio.

Skill Minilesson

VOCABULARY • OWNING A WORD

Reading the definition of a word doesn't make the word yours, but it's a first step. Words become truly part of your vocabulary when you understand how they're used and you start using them yourself.

PRACTICE   Use what you know about the meanings of the underlined words to complete the sentences.

1. Tainted meat is likely to contain
   a. fat   c. germs
   b. ice crystals

2. The response to an eloquent speech would be
   a. applause   c. yawns
   b. boos

3. You would obliterate an answer by
   a. choosing it   c. erasing it
   b. repeating it

4. A _____ could be a hindrance to a driver.
   a. seat belt   c. store
   b. traffic jam

5. Two consecutive days are Saturday and
   a. Sunday   c. the next Saturday
   b. Monday

Extending Your Response

Writing About Literature

Students' reviews should
- tell what they learned in terms of both facts and opinions.
- give appropriate examples of Cosgrove's and Povich's details and explain how they differ.
- explain clearly how each detail affects their opinions of Gehrig.

Personal Writing

Students' paragraphs should
- name one of their heroes.
- explain why he or she is a hero.
- use details to persuade readers of the subject's heroism.

Literature Groups   Point out to students that they should think about Lou Gehrig separately from his role as a baseball player. Remind them to use examples from both the selection and their own knowledge.
COLLAB. LEARN.

Skill Minilesson

VOCABULARY • OWNING A WORD

1. c	**3.** c	**5.** a
2. a	**4.** b	

Additional Resources
📁 *Vocabulary Practice,* p. 2

✔ ASSESSMENT OPTIONS

📁 *Quick Checks,* p. 4

📁 *Selection and Theme Assessment,* pp. 7–8

📁 *Performance Assessment,* p. 4

💾 *Testmaker*

Motivating
→OPTIONS

Selection Focus Transparency 5: Have students view and discuss the Jacques Barzun quote about baseball.

Focus Activity: As an extension of the Focus Activity, have pairs of students share their past enthusiasm for a celebrity and tell how it affected them.

Before You Read
from *Wait Till Next Year*

MEET DORIS KEARNS GOODWIN

Doris Kearns Goodwin became a baseball fan at the age of six, when her father taught her to keep score as she listened to the Brooklyn Dodgers games. This early training in summarizing baseball games for her father helped her develop the storytelling skills she continues to use as an adult. In addition to *No Ordinary Time*, her Pulitzer Prize–winning book about Franklin and Eleanor Roosevelt, she has written books about other American presidents, taught at Harvard University, and appeared frequently on TV news programs.

Wait Till Next Year, *Doris Kearns Goodwin's memories of growing up in the 1950s, was published in 1997.*

FOCUS ACTIVITY

Sports heroes need not always be a single person. They can be an entire team. You can also find a hero closer to home, as young Doris Kearns Goodwin did.

Sharing Ideas
Have you ever become very enthusiastic about a group, such as a sports team or a musical group? What effect did that enthusiasm have on you? How do you feel about it now?

Setting a Purpose
As you read, think about why the young Doris became such a loyal fan of the Dodgers.

BACKGROUND

The Time and Place This selection is set in a Long Island, New York, suburb in 1949. This was ten years after Lou Gehrig said his farewell to the New York Yankees.

Did You Know? The period 1949–1956 was a glorious period for New York baseball fans. Each year, one or two of the city's three baseball teams—the Yankees, the Giants, and the Brooklyn Dodgers—competed in the World Series. The Yankees won the championship in six of those years.

VOCABULARY PREVIEW

juncture (jungk′ chər) *n.* a critical point of time; p. 36
agitated (aj′ ə tāt′ ed) *adj.* upset; disturbed; p. 36
narrative (nar′ ə tiv) *n.* story; storytelling; p. 37
ritual (rich′ o͞o əl) *n.* an established form of doing something; ceremony; p. 37
naive (nä ēv′) *adj.* simple in nature; childlike; p. 37
divulge (di vulj′) *v.* to make known; give away; p. 38
staple (stā′ pəl) *adj.* important; main; p. 38

from
Wait Till Next Year

Doris Kearns Goodwin ~

WHEN I WAS SIX, my father gave me a bright-red scorebook that opened my heart to the game of baseball. After dinner on long summer nights, he would sit beside me in our small enclosed porch to hear my account of that day's Brooklyn Dodger[1] game.

A

---

1. Until 1958, when they moved to Los Angeles, the *Dodgers* were based in Brooklyn, a part of New York City.

SUMMARY

Doris's father introduces her to baseball when she is six years old. He teaches her to keep score. She listens to every Dodger game on the radio while he is at work and gives him a play-by-play account after dinner. She learns how to build suspenseful, dramatic stories that keep his attention. Doris thinks her narratives are the only way her father can follow the games; she doesn't know he reads the box scores in the daily paper.

📁 *Spanish Summaries,* p. 5

A Active Reading

PREDICT Ask students to use clues in this paragraph to predict whether Doris will enjoy listening to baseball games and reporting them to her father. *("Opened my heart to the game of baseball," suggests that this is something Doris will enjoy.)*

Additional Resources

📁 *Active Reading Guide,* p. 5

🎧 *Audio Library*

🎧 *Spanish Audio Library*

Teaching Options

CONNECTING TO OTHER SELECTIONS

COMPARING selections

This selection is paired with "Strong Men Weep" on page 26. A lesson for teaching a comparison of the two selections appears on page 40.

The chart at the right shows three other ways to connect "Wait Till Next Year" to selections in this book.

For specific teaching strategies, see the *Theme One Planning Guide,* pages 35–36.

Connection	Title
Life Skills: Setting Reasonable Expectations	→ "A Crush," p. 149
Thematic: Home	→ "How I Learned English," p. 377
Literary: Character	→ "The Women's 400 Meters," p. 252

Vo•cab•u•lar•y Skills

Etymology Explain to students that the word *fan* is short for *fanatic*, a person who is excessively enthusiastic about something, in this case sports. Ask them if they know the meaning (specific to baseball) of the verb *fan*. (*A pitcher who fans a batter strikes the batter out.*)

Historical Note

Women in Baseball In 1963, Nancy Lotsey of New Jersey became the first girl to play in an organized baseball competition with boys. In 1974, Little League was officially opened to girls. In 1980, Crystal Fields of Maryland became the first girl to win the national Pitch, Hit, and Run Championship. In 1989, Julie Croteau was the first woman to play on a men's college varsity baseball team.

C Literary Elements

NARRATOR Who is telling the story? *(The author, Doris Kearns Goodwin, looks back on her childhood.)*

Teaching Options

---

from
Wait Till Next Year

Night after night he taught me the odd collection of symbols, numbers, and letters that enable a baseball lover to record every action of the game. Our score sheets had blank boxes in which we could draw our own slanted lines in the form of a diamond as we followed players around the bases. Wherever the baserunner's progress stopped, the line stopped. He instructed me to fill in the unused boxes at the end of each

Duke Snider

inning with an elaborate checkerboard design which made it absolutely clear who had been the last to bat and who would lead off the next inning. By the time I had mastered the art of scorekeeping, a lasting bond had been forged among my father, baseball, and me.

All through the summer of 1949, my first summer as a fan,

I spent my afternoons sitting cross-legged before the squat Philco radio which stood as a permanent fixture on our porch in Rockville Centre, on the South Shore of Long Island, New York. With my score-book spread before me, I attended Dodger games through the courtly voice of Dodger announcer Red Barber. As he announced the lineup, I carefully printed each player's name in a column on the left side of my sheet. Then, using the standard system my father had taught me, . . . I recorded every play. I found it difficult at times to sit still. As the Dodgers came to bat, I would walk around the room, talking to the players as if they were standing in front of me. At critical junctures, I tried to make a bargain, whispering and cajoling while Pee Wee Reese or Duke Snider[2] stepped into the batter's box: "Please, please, get a hit. If you get a hit now, I'll make my bed every day for a week." Sometimes, when the score was close and the opposing team at bat with men on base, I was too agitated to listen. Asking my mother to keep notes, I left the house for a walk around the block, hoping that when I returned the enemy threat would be over, and once again we'd be up at bat. Mostly, however, I stayed at my post, diligently recording each inning so that, when my father returned from his

---

2. *Pee Wee Reese* and *Duke Snider* were two of the star players on the Dodgers team during the 1950s.

Vocabulary
juncture (jungk' chər) *n.* a critical point of time
agitated (aj' ə tāt' ed) *adj.* upset; disturbed

The Art of Storytelling Goodwin's impulse to tell stories is rooted in human nature. Every culture tells stories and myths, from the German fairy tale "The Goose Girl" to the Norse story of the Tree of Life to the Nigerian myth of how the god Obatala created humans.

Activity Pair native and nonnative speakers. Have them tell each other fairy tales or myths from their own cultures. If they can't think of any, they should research the mythology of their native cultures at the library. Remind students to explain unfamiliar terms to their listeners. **COLLAB. LEARN.**

Additional Resources
📁 *English Language Learners Sourcebook*

job as bank examiner for the State of New York, I could re-create for him the game he had missed.

When my father came home from the city, he would change from his three-piece suit into long pants and a short-sleeved sport shirt. . . . Then my parents would summon me for dinner from my play on the street outside our house. All through dinner I had to restrain myself from telling him about the day's game, waiting for the special time to come when we would sit together on the couch, my scorebook on my lap.

"Well, did anything interesting happen today?" he would begin. And even before the daily question was completed I had eagerly launched into my narrative

Pee Wee Reese

of every play, and almost every pitch, of that afternoon's contest. It never crossed my mind to wonder if, at the close of a day's work, he might find my lengthy account the least bit tedious. For there was mastery as well as pleasure in our nightly ritual. Through my knowledge, I commanded my father's undivided attention, the sign of his love. It would instill in me an early awareness of the power of narrative, which would introduce a lifetime of storytelling, fueled by the naive confidence that others would find me as entertaining as my father did. . . .

These nightly recountings of the Dodgers' progress provided my first lessons in the narrative art. From the scorebook, with its tight squares of neatly arranged symbols, I could unfold the tale of an entire game and tell a story that seemed to last almost as long as the game itself. At first, I was unable to resist the temptation to skip ahead to an important play in later innings. At times, I grew so excited about a Dodger victory that I blurted out the final score before I had hardly begun. But as I became more experienced in my storytelling, I learned to build a dramatic story with a beginning, middle, and end. Slowly, I learned that if I could recount the game, one batter at a time, inning by inning, without

Vocabulary
narrative (nar′ ə tiv) *n.* story; storytelling
ritual (rich′ o͞o əl) *n.* an established form of doing something; ceremony
naive (nä ēv′) *adj.* simple in nature; childlike

WHAT I AM, WHAT I WANT TO BE 🐾 37

Reading *Minilesson*

Monitoring Comprehension When students have trouble understanding what they read, they can use a "fix-up" strategy, such as asking themselves questions to check their comprehension.

Activity Work as a class to complete the graphic organizer. Ask students to suggest self-monitoring questions about the content of page 37. *(Some samples are provided.)*

Finally, ask students to explain why Goodwin's father's reaction was important to her. **L2**

Additional Resources

📁 *Reading Workbook,* pp. 7–8

DID I UNDERSTAND WHAT I JUST READ?
What questions can I ask to check myself?
Why is Goodwin so eager to tell her father about the game?
Why doesn't she wonder whether she is being tedious?
Personal experience that can help me answer:
When you are listened to, you feel interesting.
When you want urgently to tell something, you may not notice that you are boring the listener.

Active Reading

VISUALIZE Help students visualize how commuters followed baseball games. You may wish to model process:

Model: The author says that the daily papers carried box scores that were the first thing her father and the other commuters read on the train in the morning. I can see a bunch of businessmen, all reading newspapers as they ride the train. The men are talking about the game, perhaps making jokes about the losing team.

FYI

Jackie Robinson, Trailblazer Jackie Robinson, the player shown in this photo, broke the color barrier in baseball in 1947. Signed by the Brooklyn Dodgers, he was the first African American player in the major leagues.

Thematic Focus

What I Am, What I Want to Be Doris masters the science of baseball scorekeeping and the art of storytelling. Encourage students to discuss the ways Doris learns these skills and the rewards they bring her throughout her life.

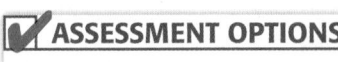

ASSESSMENT OPTIONS

📁 *Quick Checks,* p. 5

Teaching Options

Jackie Robinson

divulging the outcome, I could keep the suspense and my father's interest alive until the very last pitch. . . .

All through that summer, my father kept from me the knowledge that running box scores appeared in the daily newspapers. He never mentioned that these abbreviated histories had been a staple feature of the sports pages since the nineteenth century and were generally the first thing he and his fellow commuters turned to when they opened the *Daily News* and the *Herald Tribune* in the morning. I believed that, if I did not recount the games he had missed, my father would never have been able to follow our Dodgers the proper way, day by day, play by play, inning by inning. In other words, without me, his love of baseball would be forever unfulfilled.

Vocabulary
divulge (di vulj´) *v.* to make known; give away
staple (stā´ pəl) *adj.* important; main

Grammar and Language *Minilesson*

Prepositional Phrases Have students list some phrases such as "sitting on the floor" to describe where they are when they talk on the phone. Review *preposition,* a word that relates a noun or a pronoun to some other word in a sentence. Prepositional phrases usually answer the questions where? when? or how?

Activity Have students make a list of prepositions, choose three, and write a

sentence using each one. **L2**

Additional Resources

✏️ *Grammar and Language Transparency 5*

📕 *Grammar and Language Workbook,* pp. 141–142

📙 *Grammar and Composition Handbook,* Lesson 7.1

📗 *Writer's Choice,* Lesson 13.1

Responding to Literature

PERSONAL RESPONSE

Think back to the group discussion in the **Focus Activity** on page 34. Do you think the kind of devoted team loyalty the author describes is a good thing? Why or why not?

Analyzing Literature

RECALL

1. What triggers Doris Kearns Goodwin's interest in baseball?
2. How does Doris learn about the games she describes to her father?
3. What does Doris learn from her experience in re-creating games for her father?
4. From what other source could Doris's father have gotten the information?

INTERPRET

5. Why do you think Doris's father never tells her that he could have read about the games in the daily newspaper?
6. Why do you suppose her father never complains about her lengthy accounts of the games? Use details from the story to support your opinion.
7. In what ways did her experience in describing baseball games help Doris develop her writing skills? Explain.
8. What did you learn about the relationship between Doris and her father from the selection? Use references to the selection to back up your answer.

EVALUATE AND CONNECT

9. On the basis of this selection, who do you think was Doris's greatest childhood hero? Explain why you think so.
10. Doris Kearns Goodwin writes, "I learned to build a dramatic story with a beginning, middle, and end." Do you think that's a good idea for a young writer? Is it the only way to tell a story? Is it the best way? Explain.

LITERARY ELEMENTS

Memoir

Goodwin's *Wait Till Next Year* is a personal **memoir**—a record of her own experiences, related from her own memories. In a memoir, the author describes events for us as he or she recalls them. It usually expresses the author's opinions about events and people. In this selection, Goodwin writes from the point of view of an adult author looking back at herself as a child.

1. How do you think Doris Kearns Goodwin feels about her younger self? Use examples from the selection to support your answer.

2. How would this selection differ if it had been written in the late 1950s by a teenaged Doris rather than in the 1990s by the adult author? How would it differ if it had been written by Doris's father? Explain your answers with examples from the selection.

● See **Literary Terms Handbook,** p. R6.

Responding to the Selection

Personal Response

Some students may say that team loyalty is good because it brings people together and gives them something to care about. Others may disagree because they do not think baseball is very important.

Analyzing Literature

1. Her father gave her a scorebook when she was six years old.
2. She listened to Red Barber announce them on the radio on summer afternoons.
3. She learned how to tell a story and how to get his undivided attention.
4. He could have read the box scores in the newspapers.
5. He wanted her to feel important and needed—to think he was relying on her.
6. He loved her and enjoyed spending time with her: "I commanded my father's undivided attention," and "others would find me as entertaining as my father did."
7. It taught her to build suspense and craft a narrative with a beginning, middle, and end.
8. They love and respect each other: "a lasting bond had been forged among my father, baseball, and me," "waiting for the special time to come when we would sit together on the couch," and "I believed . . . without me, his love of baseball would be forever unfulfilled."
9. Her greatest hero was her father. He inspired her lifelong hobby and her career. As an adult, she appreciates the time he took to teach her the game and hear her stories.
10. It is often the best way to tell a story, and writers should know the rules before they break them.

LITERARY ELEMENTS

1. She looks back fondly. She may be amused by her innocence at that time.
2. Teenaged Doris may not have appreciated the extent of her father's love and patience/nor realized that storytelling could turn into a career. Her father would probably have explained what the game and their ritual meant to him.

Additional Resources

🖎 *Literary Elements Transparency 5*

✔ ASSESSMENT OPTIONS

🗀 *Quick Checks,* p. 5
🗀 *Selection and Theme Assessment,* pp. 9–10
🗀 *Performance Assessment,* p. 5
💾 *Testmaker*

COMPARING selections

Objective

- To compare two nonfiction selections that deal with heroes and the sport of baseball

COMPARE RESPONSES

- **Alike:** Both are true stories about baseball. The authors love baseball. Cosgrove/Povich: "an eloquent and tremendously moving few minutes." Goodwin: "I was too agitated to listen." **Different:** Povich's was written right after the event, Goodwin's years later.
- Some students may prefer the immediacy or the raw emotion of the first selection; others may like the nostalgia of the second.
- Students may say they learned more facts from the first selection and more about relationships from the second.

COMPARE EXPERIENCES

Groups' responses should
- give pros and cons of each sport.
- indicate favorites chosen on the basis of group discussion and evaluation. **COLLAB. LEARN.**

Additional Resources
📁 *Literature Groups Sourcebook*

COMPARE CREATIONS

Students' ads should
- be lively and appealing.
- keep their audience in mind.
- reveal knowledge about the team and the sport.

Teaching Options

COMPARING SELECTIONS

Strong Men Weep and *from* Wait Till Next Year

COMPARE RESPONSES

Both "Strong Men Weep" and the selection from *Wait Till Next Year* deal with the topic of baseball.

- How are the selections alike? How are they different? Support your responses with examples from the selections.
- Which selection did you prefer? Why?
- Which piece did you learn more from, and which challenged you more as a reader? Explain.

COMPARE EXPERIENCES

Think about your own experiences with sports and games. Do you prefer participating, like Lou Gehrig, or are you happy to be just an observer, like the young Doris Kearns Goodwin? Do you like solitary sports such as running, or do you prefer team sports? Do you prefer to be a spectator or to read about the events?

- Consider your feelings about sports and games. What is it that you really enjoy about different games? Is it the team effort of soccer or the individual positions in baseball or softball? Do you like a challenge on your own, as in chess, or do you prefer close interaction, as in volleyball? Try to figure out exactly what it is you enjoy most about your favorite sports and games.
- In small groups, take turns discussing your favorite sports and games. Respond to questions and comments from your group members.
- In your group, take a poll of favorite sporting events. Share a graph of the results of your polls in a class discussion.

COMPARE CREATIONS

Write a radio, television, or newspaper advertisement for a school or local baseball or softball team. The team may be an imaginary one or an actual team you know about. Use language and sensory details in your ad that will excite the public about the team's upcoming season.

💼 PORTFOLIO OPTIONS

Select and Reflect Have students ask themselves the following questions as they reflect on the ads they wrote:

- Does my ad include sensory details that convey the experience of being at a baseball game?
- How will my ad motivate people to come to the game? Students should clip their reflections to their ads and place them in their portfolios. Later, they may consider

using the comments to revise their ads as portfolio showcase pieces.

Additional Resources
📁 *Writing Assessment and Portfolio Management,* pp. 17–19

TELEVISION SCRIPT

These scenes from the first episode of the TV series *The Wonder Years* first aired January 31, 1988. In this episode, it is fall 1968 and the first day of junior high for Kevin, his best friend Paul, and Winnie. Wayne is Kevin's older brother, who likes to torment Kevin. The Narrator is the adult Kevin, looking back on his "wonder years."

MEDIA
Connection

Objective

• To read and understand a television script

from *The Wonder Years*
Episode 1: "The Wonder Years"

—by Neal Marlens and Carol Black

[*Exterior. Day. Bus stop.*
Kevin and Paul stand beside one another at the bus stop. Wayne and others are there.]

KEVIN
[*To Paul.*] Don't worry about it, you look fine.

PAUL
Let me see our class schedule one more time.

KEVIN
No.

NARRATOR
He was gonna have to get a grip on himself. This was the junior high bus stop and if we were gonna hold our own with the older kids we were gonna have to act mature. We seemed to have something of a height disadvantage, but we did our best to fit in.
[*Kevin and Paul stick their tongues out, mimicking the older kids. They spot Winnie who is walking toward the bus stop.*]

NARRATOR
What an incredible stroke of luck, a new kid. A helpless waif would be even more lost than we were, a helpless waif in fishnet tights and gogo boots.

WINNIE
Hi Kevin. Hi Paul.

PAUL
[*Amazed.*] Winnie Cooper?

WINNIE
Gwendolyn. I don't want to be called Winnie anymore, my real name is Gwendolyn.

NARRATOR
Well, there was no question now, we were entering uncharted territory. Even the familiar was cloaked in the vestments of the devil. Junior high school was a whole new ball of wax.

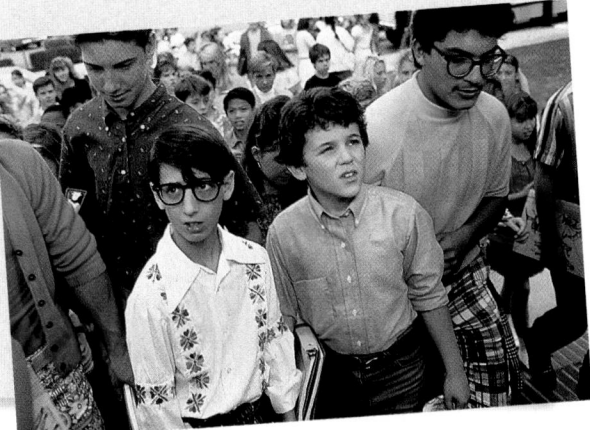

Literature LINK

Broken Chain This television script connects to "Broken Chain," the short story that immediately follows this lesson. Point out the connection by telling students that Kevin feels vulnerable on his first day of junior high and tries hard to be "cool." Alfonso, the main character in "Broken Chain," also wants very much to make a good impression while everything—including his teeth and his bicycle chain—work against him.

Historical Note

In 1968, both Martin Luther King, Jr., and Robert F. Kennedy were assassinated, American troops were fighting in Vietnam, and police and anti-war demonstrators clashed at the Democratic National Convention in Chicago.

Teaching Options

Reading *Minilesson*

Sequence of Events Because a drama usually does not include narration or explanation, a reader or viewer must pay close attention to the sequence of events to understand cause-effect relationships and characters' motives. Why Kevin behaves one way toward Winnie when she first approaches him and quite differently when Wayne and his friends come over is revealed by the sequence of events.

Activity Have students complete the graphic organizer to track the sequence of events on pp. 41–42. Then discuss how Kevin feels about his first day of school. **L2**

Additional Resources

📙 *Reading Workbook*

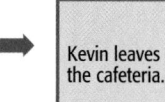

Kevin and Paul are nervous about their first day of junior high.

Kevin leaves the cafeteria.

MEDIA Connection

Pop Culture

Who's Who in 1968
- *Sgt. Pepper's Lonely Hearts Club* by the Beatles won the Grammy Award for best album.
- Peggy Fleming won the only U.S. gold medal in the Olympics in Grenoble, France.
- The Green Bay Packers won the Super Bowl; the Boston Celtics won the NBA championship; and the Detroit Tigers won the World Series.

Respond

1. Kevin exits the cafeteria quickly because his brother has embarrassed and infuriated him.
2. Some students may have felt nervous, others not. Responses may include students' stories about how they overcame nervousness or how someone else put them at ease in a new setting.

Additional Resources
📁 *Media Connections,* p. 2

Teaching Options

[*Later that day.*
Interior. Day. Cafeteria.
Kevin and Paul carry their trays and look for a table to sit at in the cafeteria.]

NARRATOR
Lunch, at last, something I figured even I couldn't screw up.

PAUL
Where do you want to sit?

KEVIN
Anywhere. Let's just sit here.
[*Kevin and Paul sit down at a table.*]

NARRATOR
A suburban junior high school cafeteria is like a microcosm of the world. The goal is to protect yourself, and safety comes in groups. You have your cool kids, you have your smart kids, you have your greasers, and in those days, of course, you had your hippies. In fact, in junior high school, who you are is defined less by who you are than by who's the person sitting next to you—a sobering thought.

KEVIN
[*To Paul.*] Try to look like you're having fun.
[*Winnie approaches the table at which Kevin and Paul are sitting.*]

WINNIE
Hi. Do you guys mind if I sit with you?

KEVIN
Sure, Winnie.

NARRATOR
We were on our way. Our group was forming. And Winnie, I mean, Gwendolyn, was not chopped liver. Who knows, maybe we even had an outside chance to become the cool seventh grade group, if we could just remain inconspicuous until we picked up a few more members.
[*Wayne, at another table with friend Steve, spots Kevin, Paul and Winnie and approaches them.*]

WAYNE
Hey Steve, it looks like my baby brother and his girlfriend have found each other.

KEVIN
She's not my girlfriend.

WAYNE
[*To Winnie.*] He thinks you are so cute.

KEVIN
I don't think she's cute.

WAYNE
He wants to give you a big wet kiss.
[*Wayne makes a sucking noise.*]

WAYNE
He told me.

KEVIN
You liar, I never said that! I don't want to kiss her, I don't even like her!
[*Kevin picks up his apple and walks briskly to exit the cafeteria.*]

Respond

1. Why do you think Kevin exits the cafeteria so quickly?

2. Did you ever have a nervous first day at a new school or in a new grade? What do you think about it now?

Before You Read
Broken Chain

MEET GARY SOTO

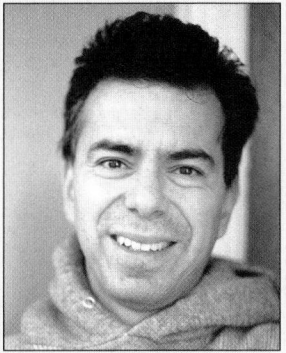

Gary Soto's experiences growing up in a Spanish-speaking neighborhood inspire much of his work. Like his parents and grandparents, Soto labored for a time as a migrant farm worker picking fruit. His love of literature came later, when he went to college. "Writing is my one talent," he says. "There are a lot of people who never discover what their talent is. . . . I am very lucky to have found mine." His writing includes award-winning poetry, novels, memoirs, essays, and films for both young people and adults.

Gary Soto was born in 1952. This story was published in 1990.

FOCUS ACTIVITY

Why are some people so concerned about their appearance?

Discuss
Discuss with the class why teenagers are often so concerned about how they look, how they dress, and what others think of them.

Setting a Purpose
Read to find out what concerns the main character has about his appearance.

BACKGROUND

The Time and Place A Mexican American neighborhood in Fresno, California, in the 1980s is the setting for this selection.

Did You Know? "Broken Chain" takes place in a Spanish-speaking neighborhood in Fresno, California, a neighborhood where Mexican American families have made their homes for many decades.

VOCABULARY PREVIEW

sullen (sul′ ən) *adj.* stubbornly withdrawn or gloomy; sulky; p. 45

swagger (swag′ ər) *v.* to walk or behave in a bold, rude, or overly proud way; p. 45

wince (wins) *v.* to draw back slightly, as in pain; p. 48

impulse (im′ puls) *n.* an internal force that causes one to act without thinking; p. 50

retrieve (ri trēv′) *v.* to locate and bring back; recover; fetch; p. 50

desperation (des′ pə rā′ shən) *n.* distress caused by great need or loss of hope; p. 50

emerge (i murj′) *v.* to come out; p. 52

Objectives
- To read and analyze a short story about a boy who is concerned about his appearance
- To identify conflict in a short story
- To write a paragraph analyzing the use of details

Skills
Reading/Thinking: Identifying Author's Purpose; Activating Prior Knowledge; Inferring; Identifying Assumptions
Writing: Advice Column; Describing a Character
Vocabulary: Synonyms; Prefixes
Grammar/Language: Subject-Verb Agreement; Pronouns
Listening/Speaking: Debating
Collaboration: Literature Groups; Improvisation

Motivating
→OPTIONS

 Literature Launchers: Play "Getting to Know Gary Soto."

Videodisc Side A, Segment 1

Also available in VHS.

 Selection Focus Transparency 6: Have students view and discuss the photo of an Aztec pyramid.

 Focus Activity: As an extension of the Focus Activity, have students discuss when a good appearance is or is not important.

RESOURCE MANAGER

Lesson Planning Resource
The *Theme One Planning Guide* (pages 40–47) provides additional lesson notes and reduced versions of all print resources.

📁 **Other Print Resources**
- Active Reading Guide, p. 6
- Vocabulary Practice, p. 4
- Reading Workbook, pp. 9–10
- Grammar and Language Workbook, pp. 107–108, 143–144, 183–192

- Grammar and Composition Handbook Lessons 4.2, 10.1–10.5
- Quick Checks, p. 6
- Selection and Theme Assessment, pp. 11–12
- Performance Assessment, p. 6
- Spanish Summaries, p. 6
- Spanish Translations
- Inclusion Strategies
- English Language Learners Sourcebook

📋 **Transparencies**
- Selection Focus 6
- Fine Art 1
- Literary Elements 6
- Grammar and Language 5

Technology
- 🎧 Audio Library
- 🎧 Spanish Audio Library
- 💻 Glencoe Literature Web Site
- 💾 Testmaker

43

Broken Chain

Gary Soto ❧

SUMMARY

On Saturday, Alfonso, who hates his crooked teeth, meets a girl when he rescues her little brother. He asks her to go bike riding with him on Monday. Alfonso asks his older brother, Ernie, to lend him his bike for Sandra to use, but Ernie refuses, saying he needs it. On Monday, when Alfonso breaks his own bike chain, he is left with no bike at all. At the last minute, Ernie shows up and lends him his bike after all. Sandra doesn't care that she has to ride on the handlebars. She and Alfonso have fun anyway.

📁 **Spanish Summaries,** p. 6

A Active Reading

CONNECT Ask students if they can identify with how Alfonso feels. What do they do when they are feeling down? What advice would they give Alfonso?

Additional Resources
📁 *Active Reading Guide,* p. 6
🎧 *Audio Library*
🎧 *Spanish Audio Library*

Teaching Options

A lfonso sat on the porch trying to push his crooked teeth to where he thought they belonged. He hated the way he looked. Last week he did fifty sit-ups a day, thinking that he would burn those already apparent ripples on his stomach to even deeper ripples, dark ones, so when he went swimming at the canal next summer, girls in cut-offs would notice. And the guys would think he was tough, someone who could take a punch and give it back. He wanted "cuts"[1] like those he had seen on a calendar of an Aztec warrior standing on a pyramid with a woman in his arms. (Even she had cuts he could see beneath her thin dress.) The calendar hung above the cash register at La Plaza. Orsua, the owner, said Alfonso could have the calendar at the end of the year if the waitress, Yolanda, didn't take it first.

A

---

1. Here, *cuts* is slang for "good, solid abdominal muscles."

CONNECTING TO OTHER SELECTIONS

The chart at the right shows three ways to connect "Broken Chain" to other selections in this book. For specific teaching strategies, see the *Theme One Planning Guide*, pages 43–44.

Connection	Title
Life Skills: Self-Image	→ "Without Commercials," p. 59
Thematic: Family	→ "Growing Pains," p. 133
Literary: Conflict	→ "Antaeus," p. 347

Alfonso studied the magazine pictures of rock stars for a hairstyle. He liked the way Prince looked—and the bass player from Los Lobos.[2] Alfonso thought he would look cool with his hair razored into a V in the back and streaked purple. But he knew his mother wouldn't go for it. And his father, who was *puro Mexicano*,[3] would sit in his chair after work, <u>sullen</u> as a toad, and call him "sissy."

Alfonso didn't dare color his hair. But one day he had had it butched on the top, like in the magazines. His father had come home that evening from a softball game, happy that his team had drilled four homers in a thirteen-to-five bashing of Color Tile. He'd <u>swaggered</u> into the living room, but had stopped cold when he saw Alfonso and asked, not joking but with real concern, "Did you hurt your head at school? *Qué pasó?*"[4]

Alfonso had pretended not to hear his father and had gone to his room, where he studied his hair from all angles in the mirror. He liked what he saw until he smiled and realized for the first time that his teeth were crooked, like a pile of wrecked cars. He grew depressed and turned away

from the mirror. He sat on his bed and leafed through the rock magazine until he came to the rock star with the butched top. His mouth was closed, but Alfonso was sure his teeth weren't crooked.

Alfonso didn't want to be the handsomest kid at school, but he was determined to be better-looking than average. The next day he spent his lawn-mowing money on a new shirt, and, with a pocketknife, scooped the moons of dirt from under his fingernails.

He spent hours in front of the mirror trying to herd his teeth into place with his thumb. He asked his mother if he could have braces, like Frankie Molina, her godson, but he asked at the wrong time. She was at the kitchen table licking the envelope to the house payment. She glared up at him. "Do you think money grows on trees?"

His mother clipped coupons from magazines and newspapers, kept a vegetable garden in the summer, and shopped at Penney's and K-Mart. Their family ate a lot of *frijoles*, which was OK because nothing else tasted so good, though one time Alfonso had had Chinese pot stickers[5] and thought they were the next best food in the world.

---

2. *Prince* is the former name of a rock star. *Los Lobos* (lōs lō′ bōs), "The Wolves," is a Mexican American band.
3. *Puro Mexicano* (pōō′ rō me′ hē kä′ nō) means "pure Mexican."
4. *"Qué pasó?"* (kā pä sō′) translates as "What happened?"

5. *Frijoles* (frē hō′ les) are beans—pinto bean, kidney beans, or black beans—that are cooked until very tender, mashed, and fried. A *pot sticker* is a kind of Chinese dumpling.

Vocabulary
sullen (sul′ ən) *adj.* stubbornly withdrawn or gloomy; sulky
swagger (swag′ ər) *v.* to walk or behave in a bold, rude, or overly proud way

Historically, attitudes toward hairstyles have varied from culture to culture. A young Aztec man wore his hair in a distinctive short cut with a single long lock at the nape of his neck that he was not allowed to cut off until he had captured his first prisoner in battle. However, for centuries in Japan, Africa, and ancient Greece, only warriors were allowed to wear long hair.

B Literary Elements

PLOT: *Internal Conflict* Guide students to see that Alfonso's obsession with his appearance is an internal conflict. For example, "He liked what he saw until he smiled and realized…his teeth were crooked." Alfonso yearns to be popular, but every time he fixes one flaw he notices another, so he is never happy with himself.

C Literary Elements

PLOT: *External Conflict* Ask students what Alfonso's mother's response to his request for braces represents. *(It represents a conflict between what each thinks is important. It also hints at the family's financial status. Alfonso's mother cares more about his character than his looks. Paying the bills for necessities is about all they can manage.)*

MEETING INDIVIDUAL NEEDS ENGLISH LANGUAGE LEARNERS

Ethnic Foods Write these words on the board: *frijoles, pot stickers, tortillas.* Point out that names for foods from other cultures become part of the English language as those foods become popular. Ask students to give examples.

Activity Have students set up a chart showing some of their favorite foods and their countries of origin.

Country	Food
Mexico	tortilla
Greece	baklava
France	croissant
China	pot stickers

Additional Resources
📁 *English Language Learners Sourcebook*

D Active Reading

PREDICT Tell students to combine clues in the text with what they already know to make predictions about what will happen next. Ask whether they think Alfonso will be able to straighten his teeth. Will he become handsome? Will he become popular?

E Literary Elements

CHARACTER Ask students what they think Alfonso's efforts to straighten his teeth reveal about his personality. Is there a more effective approach he could take? *(Alfonso's lengthy bouts of pushing show that he has determination. He is not easily discouraged, and he is trying to solve the problem himself. If he were to spend the time at his lawn-mowing job instead of pushing on his teeth, he could save the money he earns to pay for braces.)*

 You might use one or more parts of this video to connect the previous theme of heroes with this story about an self-conscious Hispanic teenager. The videotape is available from Glencoe. Be sure to preview it for appropriateness for your class.

- **Time Machine: Heroes Hispanos***

  *Also available in the Glencoe Video Library.

Viewing the photograph: What might a bike like this one symbolize, or stand for?

He didn't ask his mother for braces again, even when she was in a better mood. He decided to fix his teeth by pushing on them with his thumbs. After breakfast that Saturday he went to his room, closed the door quietly, turned the radio on, and pushed for three hours straight.

He pushed for ten minutes, rested for five, and every half hour, during a radio commercial, checked to see if his smile had improved. It hadn't.

Eventually he grew bored and went outside with an old gym sock to wipe down his bike, a ten-speed from Montgomery Ward. His thumbs were tired and wrinkled

46 ❧ THEME 1

Reading *Minilesson*

Identifying Author's Purpose Review some of the common purposes for writing: *to inform, to entertain,* and *to persuade.* For example, Gary Soto wants to entertain readers with "Broken Chain," and the information he gives us is for this purpose.

Activity Work with students to answer the following questions. Then discuss what Soto's main purpose is and talk

about how that affects the way students might read this story. **L2**

Q. Why is the author telling me about Alfonso's wish for braces?

A. *He wants me to understand how Alfonso sees himself and how poor his family is.*

Q. What does the author want me to think of Alfonso?

A. *He wants me to realize that Alfonso is lonely, dissatisfied, and frustrated.*

Q. What is the author's purpose for writing?

A. *The author wants to entertain me with a story about a dissatisfied, frustrated boy.*

Additional Resources

Reading Workbook, pp. 9–10

Gary Soto ~

and pink, the way they got when he stayed in the bathtub too long.

Alfonso's older brother, Ernie, rode up on *his* Montgomery Ward bicycle looking depressed. He parked his bike against the peach tree and sat on the back steps, keeping his head down and stepping on ants that came too close.

Alfonso knew better than to say anything when Ernie looked mad. He turned his bike over, balancing it on the handlebars and seat, and flossed the spokes with the sock. When he was finished, he pressed a knuckle to his teeth until they tingled.

Ernie groaned and said, "Ah, man."

Alfonso waited a few minutes before asking, "What's the matter?" He pretended not to be too interested. He picked up a wad of steel wool and continued cleaning the spokes.

Ernie hesitated, not sure if Alfonso would laugh. But it came out. "Those girls didn't show up. And you better not laugh."

"What girls?"

Then Alfonso remembered his brother bragging about how he and Frostie met two girls from Kings Canyon Junior High last week on Halloween night. They were dressed as gypsies, the costume for all poor Chicanas—they just had to borrow scarves and gaudy red lipstick from their *abuelitas*.[6]

Alfonso walked over to his brother. He compared their two bikes: his gleamed like a handful of dimes, while Ernie's looked dirty.

"They said we were supposed to wait at the corner. But they didn't show up. Me

---

6. Young Mexican American women are called *Chicanas* (chi kä′ nəs); *abuelitas* (ä′ bwə lē′ təs) are old women, or "grannies."

and Frostie waited and waited like fools. They were playing games with us."

Alfonso thought that was a pretty dirty trick but sort of funny too. He would have to try that some day.

"Were they cute?" Alfonso asked.

"I guess so."

"Do you think you could recognize them?"

"If they were wearing red lipstick, maybe."

Alfonso sat with his brother in silence, both of them smearing ants with their floppy high tops. Girls could sure act weird, especially the ones you meet on Halloween.

Later that day, Alfonso sat on the porch pressing on his teeth. Press, relax; press, relax. His portable radio was on, but not loud enough to make Mr. Rojas come down the steps and wave his cane at him.

Alfonso's father drove up. Alfonso could tell by the way he sat in his truck, a Datsun with a different-colored front fender, that his team had lost their softball game. Alfonso got off the porch in a hurry because he knew his father would be in a bad mood. He went to the backyard, where he unlocked his bike, sat on it with the kickstand down, and pressed on his teeth. He punched himself in the stomach, and growled, "Cuts." Then he patted his butch and whispered, "Fresh."

After a while Alfonso pedaled up the street, hands in his pockets, toward Foster's Freeze, where he was chased by a ratlike Chihuahua. At his old school, John Burroughs

Did You Know?
The *Chihuahua*, the world's smallest breed of dog, grows to about five inches tall at the shoulder. It was originally native to Mexico and is named for a city there.

WHAT I AM, WHAT I WANT TO BE 🐾 47

Vo•cab•u•lar•y Skills

Prefixes Understanding the meaning of *bicycle* can help students understand how prefixes change the meaning of a word. Write these prefixes on the board: *uni-, bi-, tri-*. You might ask them, "If a *bicycle* has two wheels and a *tricycle* has three wheels, how many wheels does a *unicycle* have?" Have students use prefixes to guess the definitions of the following words: *bifocals, bilingual, tricolor, unicellular*.

F Critical Thinking

INFERRING Ask students what Alfonso infers about his brother when Ernie comes home. What facts does he use to make this inference? *(He infers that Ernie is in a bad mood, partly because he looks depressed and partly because he keeps his head down, squishes ants that come too close, and groans.)*

G Literary Elements

CONFLICT Point out that Ernie's letdown by the girls he met on Halloween will probably lead to more conflicts later. Ask students what this event makes them curious about. *(It may make them wonder whether Ernie will get together with the girl, or whether Alfonso will.)*

H Active Reading

EVALUATE Ask students what they think about the girls' trick. Do they agree with Ernie's and Alfonso's reactions to the situation? *(Some students may think Ernie is overreacting. Some may think it is mean of Alfonso to be amused.)*

Writing *Minilesson*

Writing to Show, Not Tell Explain that writers of fiction try to avoid telling readers what to think. Instead, they show what a character is like by what the character does and says. Soto doesn't say, *"Alfonso was under the mistaken impression that looks are the only thing people care about."* Instead, through dialogue and narration, he shows that this is Alfonso's impression, which turns out not to be true.

Activity Have each student write a paragraph about either a known or invented character. Remind them to develop that character through the person's speech and actions, not by making a statement about the person. **L2**

Additional Resources

📓 *Writer's Choice,* Lesson 3.5

WHAT I AM, WHAT I WANT TO BE 🐾 47

Active Reading

QUESTION What do you think Alfonso's actions reflect about his real character. *(His actions show that he is caring and not just self-centered.)*

Literary Elements

CONFLICT Ask students how meeting Sandra increases Alfonso's conflict. How does her bike's flat tire contribute to conflict? *(Meeting her increases his internal conflict because now he has to worry about whether she will like him despite his crooked teeth. It increases his external conflict because now his brother may be jealous. Sandra's flat tire creates conflict because Alfonso will have to ask to borrow Ernie's bike.)*

Teaching Options

Broken Chain

Elementary, he found a kid hanging upside down on the top of a barbed-wire fence with a girl looking up at him. Alfonso skidded to a stop and helped the kid untangle his pants from the barbed wire. The kid was grateful. He had been afraid he would have to stay up there all night. His sister, who was Alfonso's age, was also grateful. If she had to go home and tell her mother that Frankie was stuck on a fence and couldn't get down, she would get scolded.

"Thanks," she said. "What's your name?"

Alfonso remembered her from his school and noticed that she was kind of cute, with ponytails and straight teeth. "Alfonso. You go to my school, huh?"

"Yeah. I've seen you around. You live nearby?"

"Over on Madison."

"My uncle used to live on that street, but he moved to Stockton."

"Stockton's near Sacramento, isn't it?"

"You been there?"

"No." Alfonso looked down at his shoes. He wanted to say something clever the way people do on TV. But the only thing he could think to say was that the governor lived in Sacramento. As soon as he shared this observation, he <u>winced</u> inside.

Alfonso walked with the girl and the boy as they started for home. They didn't talk much. Every few steps, the girl, whose name was Sandra, would look at him out of the corner of her eye, and Alfonso would look away. He learned that she was in seventh grade, just like him, and that she had a pet terrier named Queenie. Her father was a mechanic at Rudy's Speedy

Repair, and her mother was a teacher's aide at Jefferson Elementary.

When they came to the street, Alfonso and Sandra stopped at her corner, but her brother ran home. Alfonso watched him stop in the front yard to talk to a lady he guessed was their mother. She was raking leaves into a pile.

"I live over there," she said, pointing.

Alfonso looked over her shoulder for a long time, trying to muster enough nerve to ask her if she'd like to go bike riding tomorrow.

Shyly, he asked, "You wanna go bike riding?"

"Maybe." She played with a ponytail and crossed one leg in front of the other. "But my bike has a flat."

"I can get my brother's bike. He won't mind."

She thought for a moment before she said, "OK. But not tomorrow. I have to go to my aunt's."

"How about after school on Monday?"

"I have to take care of my brother until my mom comes home from work. How 'bout four-thirty?"

"OK," he said. "Four-thirty." Instead of parting immediately, they talked for a while, asking questions like, "Who's your favorite group?" "Have you ever been on the Big Dipper at Santa Cruz?" and "Have you ever tasted pot stickers?" But the question-and-answer period ended when Sandra's mother called her home.

Alfonso took off as fast as he could on his bike, jumped the curb, and, cool as he could be, raced away with his hands stuffed in his pockets. But when he looked back

---

Vocabulary

wince (wins) *v.* to draw back slightly, as in pain

MEETING INDIVIDUAL NEEDS — MULTIPLE LEARNING STYLES

Interpersonal Students with strong interpersonal abilities respond well to brainstorming in a group. Their classmates can benefit from these students' ability to connect with other people.

Activity Divide the class into small groups to brainstorm and develop a dialogue for Alfonso and Sandra. Tell students to imagine that Alfonso and Sandra are both too nervous to think

of anything clever to say during their first conversation, so they need help. Then have the groups write down some of the best dialogue from the brainstorming sessions so that two students from each group can perform it for the class. **L2 COLLAB. LEARN.**

over his shoulder, the wind raking through his butch, Sandra wasn't even looking. She was already on her lawn, heading for the porch.

> *Alfonso felt his stomach knot up. "She's going to be my girlfriend, not yours!"*

That night he took a bath, pampered his hair into place, and did more than his usual set of exercises. In bed, in between the push-and-rest on his teeth, he pestered his brother to let him borrow his bike.

"Come on, Ernie," he whined. "Just for an hour."

"*Chale*,[7] I might want to use it."

"Come on, man, I'll let you have my trick-or-treat candy."

"What you got?"

"Three baby Milky Ways and some Skittles."

"Who's going to use it?"

Alfonso hesitated, then risked the truth. "I met this girl. She doesn't live too far."

Ernie rolled over on his stomach and stared at the outline of his brother, whose head was resting on his elbow. "*You* got a girlfriend?"

"She ain't my girlfriend, just a girl."

"What does she look like?"

"Like a girl."

"Come on, what does she look like?"

"She's got ponytails and a little brother."

"Ponytails! Those girls who messed with Frostie and me had ponytails. Is she cool?"

"I think so."

Ernie sat up in bed. "I bet you that's her."

Alfonso felt his stomach knot up. "She's going to be my girlfriend, not yours!"

"I'm going to get even with her!"

"You better not touch her," Alfonso snarled, throwing a wadded Kleenex at him. "I'll run you over with my bike."

For the next hour, until their mother threatened them from the living room to be quiet or else, they argued whether it was the same girl who had stood Ernie up. Alfonso said over and over that she was too nice to pull a stunt like that. But Ernie argued that she lived only two blocks from where those girls had told them to wait, that she was in the same grade, and, the clincher, that she had ponytails. Secretly, however, Ernie was jealous that his brother, two years younger than himself, might have found a girlfriend.

Sunday morning, Ernie and Alfonso stayed away from each other, though over breakfast they fought over the last tortilla.[8] Their mother, sewing at the kitchen table, warned them to knock it off. At church they made faces at one another when the priest, Father Jerry,

---

7. If you want someone to "cool it" or "knock it off," say *"Chale"* (chä' lä).

8. A *tortilla* (tôr tē' yə) is made from cornmeal or flour and baked on a griddle so that it resembles a thin pancake.

K Literary Elements

CONFLICT: *Foreshadowing* Ask students to recall the story of the girls standing Ernie up. Ask them to evaluate how the author used this detail from early in the story to foreshadow the conflict now. *(The author probably had this conflict in mind when he explained earlier about Ernie's situation with the girls. Using details from earlier in the story makes this conflict between Ernie and Alfonso more believable.)*

L Critical Thinking

IDENTIFYING ASSUMPTIONS Ernie knows very few facts about Sandra. Ask students what they think he assumes about her and what reasons he gives for those assumptions. *(Ernie assumes that she is one of the girls who stood him up because she lives two blocks from where the girls told him to wait, she is in the same grade, and she has ponytails.)*

Listening and Speaking *Minilesson*

Debating Suggest that students use the following guidelines for debating:
- Let everyone have a turn speaking. Don't interrupt when someone else is talking.
- Listen to what everyone says. Jot down notes on points you want to respond to.
- When it is your turn to talk, look at your opposition. State your opinions and the reasons for them.
- Help the group stay on the topic. Make

sure your comments relate directly to it.

Activity Divide students into two teams to debate the merits of Alfonso's and Ernie's positions in their argument about Sandra. Is either character being unfair? Jumping to conclusions? Can either prove his point? Students should be persuasive in defending the brother they represent. **L2**
COLLAB. LEARN.

M Critical Thinking

INFERRING Ask students whether Alfonso's family has money. How do they know? You may wish to share the following model to illustrate the thinking process involved in making inferences.

Model: I remember that Alfonso's mother said they could not afford braces. She clips coupons, grows her own vegetables, and feeds the family beans to save money. Alfonso's and Ernie's bikes are both cheap. Their father's truck has an unmatched fender. These things lead me to infer that Alfonso's family does not have a lot of money.

N Literary Elements

FIGURES OF SPEECH A simile compares two different things by using *like* or *as*, and a metaphor compares by saying one thing *is* another thing. "The chain lay in his hand like a dead snake" is a simile. Ask students to find another simile and a metaphor on page 50. (*Simile:* slicing his hand like a snake's fang. *Metaphor:* a paper boy with dollar signs in his eyes.)

O Literary Elements

PLOT: *Climax* Ask students why Alfonso's breaking his bike chain brings the story to a climax. (*Now he doesn't even have one bike for his date. His brother is angry with him, he doesn't know what to say to Sandra, and he has no idea how to achieve his goal of going out with her.*)

Teaching Options

---

wasn't looking. Ernie punched Alfonso in the arm, and Alfonso, his eyes wide with anger, punched back.

Monday morning they hurried to school on their bikes, neither saying a word, though they rode side by side. In first period, Alfonso worried himself sick. How would he borrow a bike for her? He considered asking his best friend, Raul, for his bike. But Alfonso knew Raul, a paper boy with dollar signs in his eyes, would charge him, and he had less than sixty cents, counting the soda bottles he could cash.

Between history and math, Alfonso saw Sandra and her girlfriend huddling at their lockers. He hurried by without being seen.

During lunch Alfonso hid in metal shop[9] so he wouldn't run into Sandra. What would he say to her? If he weren't mad at his brother, he could ask Ernie what girls and guys talk about. But he *was* mad, and anyway, Ernie was pitching nickels with his friends.

Alfonso hurried home after school. He did the morning dishes as his mother had asked and raked the leaves. After finishing his chores, he did a hundred sit-ups, pushed on his teeth until they hurt, showered, and combed his hair into a perfect butch. He then stepped out to the patio to clean his bike. On an impulse, he removed the chain to wipe off the gritty oil. But while he was unhooking it from the back

---

9. The *metal shop* is a room where students learn the skills of working with metals. Schools often also have wood shops and car shops to teach similar skills.

---

sprocket, it snapped. The chain lay in his hand like a dead snake.

Alfonso couldn't believe his luck. Now, not only did he not have an extra bike for Sandra, he had no bike for himself. Frustrated, and on the verge of tears, he flung the chain as far as he could. It landed with a hard slap against the back fence and spooked his sleeping cat, Benny. Benny looked around, blinking his soft gray eyes, and went back to sleep.

Alfonso retrieved the chain, which was hopelessly broken. He cursed himself for being stupid, yelled at his bike for being cheap, and slammed the chain onto the cement. The chain snapped in another place and hit him when it popped up, slicing his hand like a snake's fang.

"Ow!" he cried, his mouth immediately going to his hand to suck on the wound.

After a dab of iodine, which only made his cut hurt more, and a lot of thought, he went to the bedroom to plead with Ernie, who was changing to his after-school clothes.

"Come on, man, let me use it," Alfonso pleaded. "Please, Ernie, I'll do anything."

Although Ernie could see Alfonso's desperation, he had plans with his friend Raymundo. They were going to catch frogs at the Mayfair canal. He felt sorry for

Did You Know?

A *sprocket* is a wheel that has teeth around its edge to grab the links of a chain. A bicycle has a small sprocket on the rear wheel and a larger one between the two wheels.

Vocabulary

impulse (im' puls) *n.* an internal force that causes one to act without thinking
retrieve (ri trēv') *v.* to locate and bring back; recover; fetch
desperation (des' pə rā' shən) *n.* distress caused by great need or loss of hope

---

MEETING INDIVIDUAL NEEDS — INCLUSION STRATEGIES

Special Needs Ask students whether they can relate to how upset Alfonso gets when his bike chain breaks—and then, in addition, he cuts his hand. Discuss what Alfonso does to handle his frustration. Point out that throwing the chain doesn't work, but talking to Ernie does (ultimately).

Activity Have students complete a chart about Alphonso's two ways of dealing with frustration, with *Ways That Work* in one column and *Ways That Don't Work* in the other. **L2**

Additional Resources
📁 *Inclusion Strategies*

Gary Soto ~

his brother, and gave him a stick of gum to make him feel better, but there was nothing he could do. The canal was three miles away, and the frogs were waiting.

Alfonso took the stick of gum, placed it in his shirt pocket, and left the bedroom with his head down. He went outside, slamming the screen door behind him, and sat in the alley behind his house. A sparrow landed in the weeds, and when it tried to come close, Alfonso screamed for it to scram. The sparrow responded with a squeaky chirp and flew away.

At four he decided to get it over with and started walking to Sandra's house, trudging slowly, as if he were waist-deep in water. Shame colored his face. How could he disappoint his first date? She would probably laugh. She might even call him *menso*.[10]

He stopped at the corner where they were supposed to meet and watched her house. But there was no one outside, only a rake leaning against the steps.

_____

10. *Menso* (men' sō) means "ignorant or foolish."

Sibling Rivals, 1989. Phoebe Beasley. Collage, 32 x 41 in. Stella Jones Gallery, New Orleans.
Viewing the collage: What does this collage say to you about rivalry? Could these figures be Alfonso and Ernie? Why or why not?

WHAT I AM, WHAT I WANT TO BE 🐿 51

Active Reading

PREDICT Ask students if they can predict whether Ernie will somehow help his brother. *(Some students may think he will. He feels sorry for Alfonso and gives him a stick of gum to make him feel better.)*

Literary Elements

CONFLICT: *Character* Ask students to think about the way Alfonso handles this conflict. What do his thoughts and actions say about his character? *(At first Alfonso is angry and frustrated, but he calms down and decides to face an embarrassing situation. This shows that Alfonso needs to learn effective ways to deal with his anger, but that he is mature enough to face Sandra and explain the situation.)*

VIEWING THE COLLAGE

While teaching art in a high school, Phoebe Beasley ran out of supplies and had her students work on collages with whatever materials were available. She became fascinated with the medium and soon became widely known as a collage artist herself. The family is one of her favorite themes.

Viewing Response *Students will bring a variety of personal interpretations to the collage, most likely noting more differences than similarities between the collage siblings and Alfonso and Ernie, whose rivalry doesn't seem to be very serious.*

REAL-WORLD CONNECTION

Create a TV Show Students may benefit from drawing upon their own experiences and knowledge to help each of them create an episode about the life of someone like Alfonso. This will help them connect to the selection and to Alfonso's concerns and frustrations.

Activity Have the class work in groups to develop ideas for a TV show based on the life of someone like Alfonso. The show should be set in the present in an average urban neighborhood. Students should answer questions like these: *Is the show a situation comedy or a drama? What will the title be? Who are the characters, both main and secondary? What is the series about in general? What will be the plot of a particular episode?* **L2 COLLAB. LEARN.**

WHAT I AM, WHAT I WANT TO BE 🐿 51

R Literary Elements

PLOT: Falling Action Remind students that falling action presents the results of the climax. Ask them what events here result from the climax. *(Ernie is no longer angry; he lends Alfonso his bike.)*

S Literary Elements

PLOT: Conflict Resolution Help students realize that Alfonso achieves his goal in the last paragraph of the story. Ask them how this paragraph resolves the tension. *(Alfonso gets together with Sandra, who seems to like him and not mind his crooked teeth. He feels comfortable with her.)*

FINE ART
TRANSPARENCY 1

You may wish to use *Fine Art Transparency 1* before students discuss the story's theme.

Thematic Focus

What I Am, What I Want to Be
Have students compare Alfonso with themselves and others their age. Are his thoughts, feelings, words, and actions typical of people his age? Ask for examples.

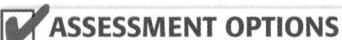

ASSESSMENT OPTIONS

📁 **Quick Checks,** p. 6

Why did he have to take the chain off? he scolded himself. He always messed things up when he tried to take them apart, like the time he tried to repad his baseball mitt. He had unlaced the mitt and filled the pocket with cotton balls. But when he tried to put it back together, he had forgotten how it laced up. Everything became tangled like kite string. When he showed the mess to his mother, who was at the stove cooking dinner, she scolded him but put it back together and didn't tell his father what a dumb thing he had done.

Now he had to face Sandra and say, "I broke my bike, and my stingy brother took off on his."

He waited at the corner for a few minutes, hiding behind a hedge for what seemed like forever. Just as he was starting to think about going home, he heard footsteps and knew it was too late. His hands, moist from worry, hung at his sides, and a thread of sweat raced down his armpit.

He peeked through the hedge. She was wearing a sweater with a checkerboard pattern. A red purse was slung over her shoulder. He could see her looking for him, standing on tiptoe to see if he was coming around the corner.

What have I done? Alfonso thought. He bit his lip, called himself *menso,* and pounded his palm against his forehead. Someone slapped the back of his head. He turned around and saw Ernie.

"We got the frogs, Alfonso," he said, holding up a wiggling plastic bag. "I'll show you later."

Ernie looked through the hedge, with one eye closed, at the girl. "She's not the one who messed with Frostie and me," he said finally. "You still wanna borrow my bike?"

Alfonso couldn't believe his luck. What a brother! What a pal! He promised to take Ernie's turn next time it was his turn to do the dishes. Ernie hopped on Raymundo's handlebars and said he would remember that promise. Then he was gone as they took off without looking back.

Free of worry now that his brother had come through, Alfonso emerged from behind the hedge with Ernie's bike, which was mud-splashed but better than nothing. Sandra waved.

"Hi," she said.

"Hi," he said back.

She looked cheerful. Alfonso told her his bike was broken and asked if she wanted to ride with him.

"Sounds good," she said, and jumped on the crossbar.

It took all of Alfonso's strength to steady the bike. He started off slowly, gritting his teeth, because she was heavier than he thought. But once he got going, it got easier. He pedaled smoothly, sometimes with only one hand on the handlebars, as they sped up one street and down another. Whenever he ran over a pothole, which was often, she screamed with delight, and once, when it looked like they were going to crash, she placed her hand over his, and it felt like love.

❖

Vocabulary
emerge (i murj´) *v.* to come out

R

S

Grammar and Language *Minilesson*

Pronouns Used as Objects Write the following on the board: Personal pronouns used as objects: (singular) *me, you, him, her, it,* (plural) *us, you, them*
Remind students that personal pronouns are used to replace nouns that refer to people or things. The sentence will still mean the same thing.
Alfonso borrowed a bike from <u>Ernesto</u>.
Alfonso borrowed a bike from *him*.

Activity Have students substitute the correct pronoun for the underlined word(s).
1. Alfonso met Sandra at four-thirty. Since he only had one bike, he asked <u>Sandra</u> to sit on the crossbar. *(her)*
2. My mother kept our baby pictures in a small, blue box. Yesterday she gave those pictures to <u>my brother and me</u>. *(us)*
3. Alfonso was angry because the chain broke when he removed <u>the chain</u>. *(it)* **L2**

Additional Resources

🖥 **Grammar and Language Transparency 5**

📁 **Grammar and Language Workbook,** pp. 107–108, 143–144

📁 **Grammar and Composition Handbook,** Lesson 4.2

📓 **Writer's Choice,** Lessons 11.1, 13.2

Teaching Options

Responding to Literature

PERSONAL RESPONSE

- ◆ What thoughts and feelings did you have at the end of the story? Describe your reactions in your journal.
- ◆ In what ways did you identify with Alfonso? Explain in detail.

Analyzing Literature

RECALL

1. What aspects of his appearance would Alfonso like to change?
2. Describe the difference between Alfonso's and Ernie's bikes.
3. How does Alfonso break his bicycle chain?
4. What is Sandra's reaction to Alfonso's appearing with just one beat-up bike?

INTERPRET

5. Why is Alfonso unhappy with the way he looks?
6. How does the author show that Alfonso cares very much about the appearance of his bike?
7. Why is Alfonso so upset when he breaks his bicycle chain? Do you think he is overreacting? Why or why not?
8. At the end of the story, Alfonso is different. How has he changed? What caused the change? Use examples to support your answers.

EVALUATE AND CONNECT

9. Alfonso is always trying to straighten his teeth. What does the **repetition** of this image show you about his state of mind throughout the story?
10. Theme Connection Does reading a story about someone your own age make you feel more connected to the character? Why or why not?

Spokes, 1983. John D. Wibberley. Acrylic on canvas, 16 x 24 in. Artist's collection.

LITERARY ELEMENTS

Conflict

The struggle between two opposing forces that lie at the center of a plot in a story is called the **conflict.** An **external conflict** exists when a character struggles against an outside force—another person, nature, society, or fate. An **internal conflict** exists within the mind of the character who is torn between opposing feelings or goals. In "Broken Chain" Alfonso struggles with both kinds of conflicts.

1. What are the external conflicts that seem to prevent Alfonso from reaching his goal of meeting Sandra for a "date"? Find two or more examples.

2. Alfonso is desperately searching for his own style. Describe how his lack of confidence about his looks could be interpreted as an internal conflict.

● See **Literary Terms Handbook,** p. R2.

Responding to the Selection

Personal Response

- Some students may say that they were glad the story turned out happily and that Alfonso grew as a person.
- Students may say they know how it feels not to fit in, to be critical of their looks, or to fight with their siblings.

Analyzing Literature

1. Alfonso would like to change his teeth, his muscles, and his hair.
2. Alfonso's bike is so clean it gleams; Ernie's is dirty.
3. He unhooks the chain to clean it.
4. She is content to sit on the crossbar.
5. He feels insecure and is afraid girls will not like him.
6. He describes in great detail the care Alfonso takes to clean his bike.
7. He needed two bikes and now he has none, so he'll have to break his date. Most students will say he's overreacting because Sandra won't judge him by his bike (as the end of the story shows).
8. He is more confident and mature because he has overcome a crisis and learned not to worry so much: "Free of worry now," and "once he got going, it got easier."
9. It shows how obsessed he is with straightening out his teeth and, by implication, his physical appearance.
10. Most students feel more connected to characters their own age because they have similar concerns and they are easier to identify with and understand.

LITERARY ELEMENTS

1. The external conflicts in the story include Alfonso's fight with Ernie, Ernie's denying Alfonso the use of his bike, and the broken chain on his own bike.
2. His desire to see Sandra conflicts with his fear that she will think he is ugly.

Additional Resources

Literary Elements Transparency 6

Writing About Literature

Students' paragraphs should

- give appropriate examples of Soto's descriptive details.
- explain clearly how each detail helps readers understand Alfonso's life.

Creative Writing

Students' letters should

- spell out Alfonso's concerns clearly.

Students' advice columns should

- reassure Alfonso that he is normal.
- address his concerns in order.
- provide reasons for their conclusions.

Extending Your Response

Literature Groups Tell students that the chart can have as many rows as they wish, as long as they find support in the story for each item. **COLLAB. LEARN.**

Interdisciplinary Activity Remind students to make sure their explanations proceed in a logical sequence and match their diagrams.

Performing Encourage students to spend time planning and rehearsing their improvisations. If possible, videotape each pair's performance and make the tapes available for viewing.

Literature and Writing

Writing About Literature

Details In "Broken Chain," Gary Soto includes many details about Alfonso's family and neighborhood. Write a paragraph or two about how Soto's use of details helps you understand what his life at home and at school must have been like. Choose details from the story to prove your point.

Creative Writing

Dear Advice Columnist Think back to your class discussion in the **Focus Activity** on page 43 about peoples' concern with their appearance. Alfonso is very self-conscious about his teeth, his hair, and his muscles. Imagine he has written a letter to an advice column for teens. What questions might Alfonso ask? What advice might a helpful person give him? Write the letter and the response.

Extending Your Response

Literature Groups

Comparing Alfonso with Himself Together, read the first and last paragraphs in the story. Then have a discussion comparing how Alfonso feels at the beginning of the story with how he feels at the end. Make a comparison chart that shows the results of your discussion.

	AT THE BEGINNING	AT THE END
ALFONSO'S FEELINGS ABOUT HIMSELF		

Interdisciplinary Activity

Science Why does a bicycle need a chain? Can a bike work without one? With a partner, examine a bike scientifically. Write your own explanation of how a bicycle works. Use diagrams to illustrate your ideas. Check with a reference book or your science teacher to see whether your explanation is correct.

Performing

Improvisation Work with a partner to improvise a scene between Alfonso and Sandra after their bike ride at the end of the story. What would the two say to each other? Would they be nervous or shy? What would their body language look like? Perform your improvised scene in front of the class.

Reading Further

Check out these books by Gary Soto:

Poetry: *Neighborhood Odes*

Novel: *Taking Sides*

Short Stories: *Baseball in April and Other Stories*

📕 **Save your work for your portfolio.**

---

interNET CONNECTION

Bicycle Repair

Have students use a search engine to find out how to repair a broken bicycle chain. Suggest keywords, such as *bicycle repair, bicycle maintenance,* and *biking.*

Skill Minilessons

GRAMMAR AND LANGUAGE • SUBJECT-VERB AGREEMENT

A subject and a verb are basic parts of a sentence. The subject and its verb must agree in number. A singular noun used as a subject of a sentence calls for a singular form of the verb:

   Alfonso rides his bike after school.

   A plural noun used as the subject calls for a plural form of the verb:

   Alfonso and Ernie ride their bikes after school.

PRACTICE For each sentence, write the subject and the correct form of the verb.

1. Gary Soto (writes, write) stories about teens.
2. The book *Baseball in April and Other Stories* (is, are) an award winner.
3. There (is, are) eleven short stories, most about Latino young people.
4. The stories, like "Broken Chain," (focuses, focus) on the difficulties of growing up.
5. The end of the book (contains, contain) a list of Spanish words and their English translations.

● For more about subject-verb agreement, see **Language Handbook,** pp. R14–R15.

READING AND THINKING • ACTIVATING PRIOR KNOWLEDGE

Things you already know can help you understand what you read. Even if you read about an adventure in another galaxy, you will understand some parts easily because of knowledge you acquired previously. All the life experiences you have had contribute to your prior knowledge.

PRACTICE What have you read or experienced that helped you better understand the characters' thoughts and feelings in "Broken Chain"? Write a paragraph describing how this prior knowledge helped you understand the story.

● For more about this and related reading strategies, see **Reading Handbook,** p. R82.

VOCABULARY • SYNONYMS

Synonyms are words that mean nearly the same thing. When you know synonyms for a word, you can decide which one best expresses the exact meaning you want. For example, *desperation* expresses a more frantic feeling than *hopelessness*. A hopeless person might just sit and do nothing. But a desperate person would try something—anything! Still, *desperation* and *hopelessness* are synonyms, because they are close in meaning. A **thesaurus,** a book that lists and defines synonyms,

can help you understand how synonyms differ in meaning.

PRACTICE Write a synonym for each word below. Then write one sentence using each word and another sentence using its synonym.

1. sullen
2. retrieve
3. swagger
4. wince
5. impulse

Skill Minilessons

GRAMMAR AND LANGUAGE
SUBJECT-VERB AGREEMENT

1. Gary Soto writes
2. book is
3. are stories
4. stories focus
5. end contains

READING AND THINKING
ACTIVATING PRIOR KNOWLEDGE

Students' paragraphs should
• give examples from their own lives and their reading.
• tie the examples to the story.

VOCABULARY
SYNONYMS

Examples
1. sullen, *gloomy*
   The *sullen* clerk didn't answer.
   When it rained, he felt *gloomy*.
2. retrieve, *fetch*
   I had to *retrieve* the lost ring.
   My dog likes to *fetch* sticks.
3. strut, *swagger*
   The models *strut* down the runway.
   The winners *swagger* proudly.
4. wince, *flinch*
   The shot made him *wince*.
   Most people *flinch* from pain.
5. impulse, *whim*
   She had an *impulse* to buy it.
   He took the ride on a *whim*.

Additional Resources

Grammar and Language Workbook, pp. 183–192

Grammar and Composition Handbook, Lessons 10.1–10.5

Writer's Choice, Lessons 16.1–16.5

Reading Workbook, pp. 9–10

Vocabulary Practice, p. 4

✓ ASSESSMENT OPTIONS

📁 *Quick Checks,* p. 6
📁 *Selection and Theme Assessment,* pp. 11–12
📁 *Performance Assessment,* p. 6
📁 *Testmaker*

Technology Skills

Objectives

- To use desktop publishing software to publish an autobiographical anecdote
- To investigate how desktop publishing techniques are used to produce the school newspaper

Teaching Strategies

Help students learn about the possibilities of desktop publishing by demonstrating the kinds of design and layout they can create on their computers. Show students how to do the following:

- set up a multiple-column page
- format text in various ways
- use such design features as drop caps and shading
- number pages automatically and create headers and footers
- create banner headlines
- create a table of contents
- use different fonts
- resize and position photos and artwork

Adapting to Available Technology

All word processing programs can be used to create newsletters, fliers, brochures, posters, and the like. They easily integrate images with text, and their text prints at a high resolution. You may wish to bring in an outside expert to demonstrate techniques.

Teaching Options

Technology Skills

Word Processing: Desktop Publishing

With a small group, examine several books, magazines, and newspapers. Notice how text and illustrations are arranged on the page. Can you tell who the intended readers are just by the way a page is designed? How do book, magazine, and newspaper pages differ? Summarize what your examination tells you about page design.

Menu bar — Toolbars — Ruler

Getting Oriented

Get to know some important features of your word processing software. Start with a document that has some text in it. Experiment with each feature by selecting a portion of text before choosing a menu command or clicking an icon.

1. Pull down the **View** menu, and select **Page Layout.** Use this view for the remaining items in this list.
2. Pull down the **Format** menu, and select **Columns.** Locate the columns icon in the toolbar.
3. Find the **Font Box** in the toolbar. Locate the **Font** feature in the **Format** menu. Experiment with some fonts. (See the **TYPOGRAPHY** chart on the next page for more information about fonts, or typefaces.)
4. Find the **Font Size** box in the toolbar. Select **Font** in the **Format** menu.
5. On the toolbar, find the buttons for align left, align right, center, and align left and right (also called justification).
6. Look under **Tools** to find the feature **Hyphenation.** (It may be in a Tools submenu under **Language.**)
7. Find the buttons that automatically create numbered and bulleted lists.
8. Locate the buttons that will decrease or increase indentations.
9. On the ruler, find the button that controls tab stops, or locate its feature in the **Format** menu.
10. Experiment with the margin markers on the ruler.

Sample Typefaces
(all in 12 pt. size)

Serif Faces
Bookman Old Style
Courier New
Garamond
Times New Roman

Sans-Serif Faces
Ariel
Avant Garde Book
Helvetica Condensed Light

MEETING INDIVIDUAL NEEDS INCLUSION STRATEGIES

Special Needs If students are not proficient keyboarders or have muscular difficulties they may want to investigate using voice-activation software. Such software is easy to set up and use, but each student must spend about thirty minutes training the program to recognize his or her particular speech patterns.

Activity Invite students who are interested in voice-activation technology to do research into how it works and where it is available.

Additional Resources
📁 *Inclusion Strategies*

TYPOGRAPHY

Typeface	Type size
Many different typefaces—each with unique roman, *italic,* and **bold** styles—are available on computers. A few are illustrated on page 56.	Type size is measured in points. One point equals about $1/72$ inch. The main text in most publications is between ten and twelve points.
Serif type	**Sans-serif type**
On serif type, the main strokes of letters are embellished with little strokes, or "feet," that are thought to make words more readable.	Sans-serif type lacks "feet." Traditionally used only for headings, sans-serif type is also used for the main text in many contemporary designs.
Headings	**Display typefaces**
Headings are often bold and usually larger than the main text. Different levels of heading may have different "weights," or sizes.	Display typefaces are typically large and eye-catching and often quite unusual. This book uses display type for its selection and feature titles.

Creating an Autobiographical Sketch

1. In the selection from *Wait Till Next Year,* Doris Kearns Goodwin tells how her relationship with her father led to a lifelong fascination with baseball. Think about the major events in your own life. Was there a particular person or incident that had a strong or lasting effect on you? Focus on a particular experience that you can describe. Try to recall the experience and the feelings you had at the time.

2. Use your computer and word processing software to plan, draft, revise, and edit a brief autobiographical sketch relating that experience.

3. Before presenting your sketch, prepare a design for it that will be appropriate to your subject. Share your designed sketch with a partner, and ask for suggestions for improvement.

4. Prepare a final version, and print your document.

ACTIVITIES

1. Use the word processing features you learned about to complete the **Writing Workshop** in this theme.

2. In a group, interview your school's newspaper sponsor (if there is one) to determine how word processing is used in the production of the school newspaper.

Activities

Create a buddy system, pairing proficient and less-proficient students. Before beginning, invite the class as a whole to create a list of suggestions that might make the publishing process easier. Encourage students to suggest solutions and alternate approaches to each other, both in class discussion and separately. After the assignment is complete, come together one last time for students to discuss what they learned, what problems they faced, and how they might solve those problems next time.

Student anecdotes should

- demonstrate an ability to lay out text in a pleasing page design.
- contain graphic elements, such as rules, banner headlines, clip art, photos, or other illustrations.
- use more than one font and type size.

Invite groups of students to share what they found out about how the school newspaper is produced.

INTERDISCIPLINARY CONNECTION

Journalism Students may want to use their desktop publishing skills to create a newsletter, magazine article, brochure, or poster about a science or social studies topic.

Activity Invite students to choose a topic, conduct research (possibly over the Internet), write an article or essay, scan photos and illustrations or create graphics, and lay out a page about their chosen topic. Students may also want to include "Did You Know?" lists or sidebars to highlight interesting tidbits they discover. If a color printer is available, students may want to experiment with colorful heads and illustrations.

Objectives

- To read and analyze a poem about human diversity and acceptance
- To think about point of view in relation to a poem

Skills

Reading/Thinking: Drawing Conclusions; Summarizing; Evaluating
Collaboration: Summarizing

Motivating

→OPTIONS

Selection Focus Transparency 7: Have students view and discuss the quotation by Dr. Martin Luther King.

Focus Activity: To extend the Focus Activity, invite students to look at photographs of people in books and magazines. Have them compare images presented in books about world cultures with images presented in current magazine advertisements.

Before You Read

Without Commercials

MEET
ALICE WALKER

From the time she was eight, Alice Walker kept a notebook of poetry. Today her writings include novels, poems, short stories, and essays. As the youngest of eight children in a Georgia sharecropping family, Walker says, "I always seemed to need more peace and quiet than anybody else. . . . Books became my world, because the world I was in was very hard." Walker is the first African American woman to win the Pulitzer Prize for a novel. Much of her writing focuses on the difficult lives of poor, heroic, African American women.

Alice Walker was born in 1944. This poem was published in 1984.

FOCUS ACTIVITY

How many different kinds of people are there in the world? Think about the variety of faces you see in a large crowd at a parade or a sports event.

Sharing Ideas
With a small group, discuss the variety of people you see in advertisements. Do ads reflect the broad diversity of human beings in the world?

Setting a Purpose
Read the poem to find out what the speaker thinks about ads.

BACKGROUND

Alice Walker grew up attending all-black schools that "gave us a feeling that they really belonged to us. There was a lot of self-help and community." Even in this supportive environment, however, Walker felt like an outcast after an older brother accidentally shot her in the eye with a BB gun. Her blinded eye was covered with scar tissue. "I used to pray every night that I would wake up and somehow it would be gone. I couldn't look people in the eye because I thought I was ugly." It was this experience that first inspired Walker to record her observations and feelings. Later, surgery repaired much of the scar tissue. This change helped improve her self-image considerably.

Walker is considered one of the major American writers of this century. She is active in both the Civil Rights and women's rights movements. She helped reintroduce readers to the author Zora Neale Hurston, another important African American writer.

RESOURCE MANAGER

Lesson Planning Resource
The *Theme One Planning Guide* (pages 48–52) provides additional lesson notes and reduced versions of all print resources.

Other Print Resources
- Active Reading Guide, p. 7
- Reading Workbook, pp. 11–12
- Quick Checks, p. 7
- Selection and Theme Assessment, pp. 13–14

- Performance Assessment, p. 7
- Spanish Summaries, p. 7
- Inclusion Strategies
- English Language Learners Sourcebook

 Transparencies
- Selection Focus 7
- Literary Elements 7

Technology
- Audio Library
- Spanish Audio Library
- Glencoe Literature Web Site
- Testmaker

Without Commercials

Alice Walker

Listen,
stop tanning yourself
and talking about
fishbelly
5   white.
The color white
is not bad at all.
There are white mornings
that bring us days.
10   Or, if you must,
tan only because
it makes you happy
to be brown,
to be able to see
15   for a summer
the whole world's
darker
face
reflected
20   in your own.

    ❖

Stop unfolding
your eyes.
Your eyes are
beautiful.
25   Sometimes
seeing you in the street
the fold zany°

and unexpected
I want to kiss
30   them
and usually
it is only
old
gorgeous
35   black people's eyes
I want
to kiss.

    ❖   ❖

Stop trimming
your nose.
40   When you
diminish°
your nose
your songs
become little
45   tinny, muted°
and snub.
Better you should
have a nose
impertinent°
50   as a flower,
sensitive

---

27 A thing that's *zany* is odd or crazy in a comical way.

41 To *diminish* means "to make smaller in size."
45 In this context, *muted* means "muffled, softened, or less strong."
49 Something *impertinent* is improperly bold or rude.

Reading the Selection

A Active Reading

QUESTION The poet uses words such as *listen, stop, must, and should.* Ask students to discuss the poet's feelings toward the topic. *(The poet feels that people should stop trying to change their appearances. She feels that a natural look is beautiful.)*

B Critical Thinking

DRAWING CONCLUSIONS Ask students to think about what these lines say about Walker's attitude toward race? *(Since Walker compares these eyes to "black people's eyes," we can assume that the people are not black people. By saying that she wants to kiss these eyes, we can conclude that Walker sees beauty in other races.)*

C Active Reading

QUESTION The speaker says that all colors, eyes, and noses are wonderful. Ask students what underlying belief this opinion expresses.

Additional Resources
📁 *Active Reading Guide,* p. 7
🎧 *Audio Library*
🎧 *Spanish Audio Library*
📁 *Spanish Summaries,* p. 7

Teaching Options

CONNECTING TO OTHER SELECTIONS
For a teaching strategy that connects "Without Commercials" to "Broken Chain," turn to page 43 in the *Theme One Planning Guide.*

Reading *Minilesson*

Summarizing Write the following summary of the first stanza on the board: *It's fine to tan yourself if it makes you happy and tanning helps you get a different perspective on life. But don't do it because you think it's bad to be white. White is a good color.*

Activity Have students work in pairs to reread the poem and create summaries of each stanza using the following checklist:

• Does the summary cover the main idea of the stanza?
• Does it consider all supporting details?
• Are the details and main idea combined so that the summary is clear but brief?
L2 **COLLAB. LEARN.**

Additional Resources
📁 *Reading Workbook,* pp. 11–12

EVALUATING Point out to students the parallels between this stanza and the first stanza. Ask them to evaluate the point Walker makes by showing opposite approaches to changing one's skin color. *(It seems Walker is saying that no matter what one's skin color, there are always reasons for wanting to change it. She illustrates the dissatisfaction common to every race.)*

E Literary Elements

POINT OF VIEW Explain that the word *Original* may refer to the story that Eve was created from one of Adam's ribs. How might this have affected the author's point of view? *(Walker, the first African American to win a Pulitzer Prize for a novel, sees herself, and us, as being as original as Eve.)*

F Active Reading

SUMMARIZE Ask a volunteer to summarize the speaker's point of view in one or two sentences. *(Possible example: We should accept ourselves and be proud of the way we look.)*

Thematic Focus

What I Am, What I Want to Be Ask students if the ideas expressed in "Without Commercials" have changed their thinking. Have the poet's ideas reinforced their feelings?

☑ ASSESSMENT OPTIONS

📁 *Quick Checks,* p. 7

Teaching Options

---

as a root;
wise, elegant,
serious and deep.
55 A nose that
sniffs
the essence°
of Earth. And knows
the message
60 of every
leaf.

     ❖   ❖   ❖

Stop bleaching
your skin
and talking
65 about
so much black
is not beautiful
The color black
is not bad
70 at all.
There are black nights
that rock
us
in dreams.
75 Or, if you must,
bleach only
because it pleases you
to be brown,
to be able to see
80 for as long
as you can bear it
the whole world's

lighter face
reflected
85 in your own.

   ❖   ❖   ❖   ❖

As for me,
I have learned
to worship
the sun
90 again.
To affirm°
the adventures
of hair.

For we are all
95 *splendid*
descendants
of Wilderness,
Eden:
needing only
100 to see
each other
without
commercials
to believe.

105 Copied skillfully
as Adam.

Original

as Eve.

---

57 Here, *essence* means "perfume."

91 To *affirm* is to state firmly and positively.

ENGLISH LANGUAGE LEARNERS

MEETING INDIVIDUAL NEEDS

Cultural Concepts of Beauty It may help students who are less familiar with American culture if you explain that in the United States, some Caucasian people spend hours in the sun or in expensive tanning salons. Americans of all backgrounds undergo cosmetic surgery to change the shape of their noses; some Asian Americans remove the fold from their eyelids; some African Americans bleach their skin; and many people straighten or dye their hair.

Activity Invite students to discuss what people from their cultures do to try to change the way they look.

Additional Resources
📁 *English Language Learners Sourcebook*

Responding to Literature

PERSONAL RESPONSE

Do you recognize yourself or anyone you know in any of the descriptions in "Without Commercials"? Explain.

Analyzing Literature

RECALL

1. Whom does the speaker address in the first stanza of the poem?
2. What message is expressed about people's differences?

INTERPRET

3. According to the poem, what effect do commercials have on people? Why is the poem called "Without Commercials"?
4. What does the speaker suggest that people of every race have in common?

EVALUATE AND CONNECT

5. Does this poem make you think twice about how you or people you know feel about their physical features? Explain.
6. Choose your favorite example of **visual imagery** in the poem, and explain why it appeals to you.
7. In your opinion, why does the poem end with a reference to Adam and Eve?
8. Think about the diversity of people you discussed in the **Focus Activity** on page 58. Choose a few lines from the poem that talk about diverse groups of people.
9. Why might people feel they should look like the people in commercials? If there were no commercials, do you think that people would change their attitudes about how they look?
10. Knowing what you do about the poet Alice Walker, what do you think she would say about her own features?

LITERARY ELEMENTS

Speaker

In talking about "Without Commercials," you might be tempted to say something like "According to her poem, Alice Walker believes that . . ." You identify the thoughts, ideas, or events in the poem with the person who wrote it. This may be true in many cases. Poets *do* use their poems to express their ideas. However, poets do so through a **speaker** that they create to express these ideas. The ideas expressed by a speaker could be the opposite of what the poet really believes. When you discuss or write about a poem, don't confuse the speaker with the poet.

1. In your opinion, are the ideas expressed in "Without Commercials" Alice Walker's ideas? Why or why not?
2. Read another poem anywhere in this book. Tell why you think the speaker can or cannot be closely identified with the poet.

● See **Literary Terms Handbook,** p. R10.

Responding to the Selection

Personal Response

Students may recognize their own efforts to change the way they look. Responses should show an understanding of American concepts of beauty that are promoted by the media.

Analyzing Literature

1. White people who think they look better with a tan are addressed in the first stanza.
2. The poem's message is that all people and all differences are beautiful.
3. Commercials convince people to believe in an unrealistic and unnatural standard of beauty. The speaker encourages us to look at others and see their beauty without using the concepts of beauty put forth by commercials.
4. People of every race think they need to change the way they look to be beautiful.
5. The poem may force students to question the concepts of beauty promoted by the media.
6. Answers may include: seeing the whole world's darker or lighter face reflected; white mornings; an impertinent nose; and black nights that rock us in dreams.
7. The reference to Adam and Eve may be meant to force the reader to think about how simple beauty was in the beginning, before we began to define it.
8. Some examples include: The whole world's darker face; gorgeous black people's eyes; and the whole world's lighter face.
9. Students may say that because they see people in commercials doing exciting things, they think their lives would change if they looked like them.
10. Students' answers should imply that Alice Walker is proud of the way she looks.

LITERARY ELEMENTS

1. The passionate appeals would seem to confirm that the poet is expressing her own ideas.
2. Answers should demonstrate an ability to distinguish between a poet's words and those of a persona, or speaker, created by the poet.

Additional Resources

📖 *Literary Elements Transparency 7*

ASSESSMENT OPTIONS

📁 *Quick Checks,* p. 7
📁 *Selection and Theme Assessment,* pp. 13–14
📁 *Performance Assessment,* p. 7
💾 *Testmaker*

Objective

- To understand the elements of an autobiography

Teaching Strategies

Explain that reading a person's autobiography is like peeking into his or her secret diary. We are given access to the innermost thoughts, joys, and fears of the writer.

Characters Suggest that students make a list of people, either famous or not, whose life stories they would most like to read. Prompt a discussion on what it is about these people that interests students. Ask which character traits inspire or intrigue them in real life: kindness, courage, intelligence?

Time and Place, or Setting Have students use the list of characters whose autobiographies they would most like to read to create a list of settings. This will help them discover particular times in history or places in the world to which they are drawn.

Events Point out the techniques of flashback and flash-forward used in "Fish Cheeks." Then encourage students to write similar anecdotes from their own experience using these techniques.

AUTOBIOGRAPHY

Are you a fan of autobiography? An **autobiography** is a person's story of his or her own life. This form of nonfiction has been popular since the days of the ancient Egyptians. More than any other form of writing, autobiography offers readers a direct, personal connection with the author.

Most autobiographies are book-length. However, there are many shorter kinds of autobiographical writing. Here are some of them:

- **diary entries**
- **travel journals**
- **memoirs**—stories of important people or periods in the author's life
- **eyewitness accounts**—stories of memorable events, written by people who were there
- **anecdotes**—brief stories of small, simple incidents

Although autobiography is a form of **nonfiction,** it shares some of the elements of fiction. For example, autobiography is usually written as a story—with characters and action or events. The main difference between autobiographical writing and fiction is that autobiography is a factual account of real events of a person's life, written by that person.

All autobiographies share the same literary elements.

CHARACTERS In autobiography, the author is almost always the main character. To make themselves believable as characters, authors of autobiography reveal their weaknesses as well as their strengths. They also show the feelings and reasons behind the things they do.

TIME AND PLACE, OR SETTING In autobiography, the author draws on real places, times, and political or social situations. The setting is portrayed in accurate detail, with enough background to let readers "put themselves there," but not so much background that it slows the story.

EVENTS As in fiction, events in autobiographies unfold in chronological (time) order. Authors may use **flashback** to show what led up to events or **flash-forward** to show outcomes or offer views of events still to come.

POINT OF VIEW Point of view is the viewpoint from which a story is told. In an autobiography, the point of view is almost always the author's, who describes his or her life, using pronouns such as *I* and *me*.

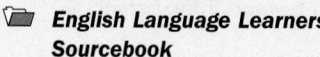

MEETING INDIVIDUAL NEEDS — ENGLISH LANGUAGE LEARNERS

Elements of Autobiography Bring in pictures of famous people from magazines. Choose one and post it on the board. Ask students to suggest ideas for an autobiography of the person in the picture. Have the class decide on a title for the story and determine its characters, setting, focus, events, and theme.

Activity Have students work in groups that include English language learners

as well as English-proficient students. Ask each group to choose a picture and repeat the class activity for that picture. Suggest that they present their work to the class in poster form—as an ad for an autobiographical book or movie.

Additional Resources
📂 *English Language Learners Sourcebook*

	Ask Yourself	Model
CHARACTER	How does the author help readers identify with a character?	Rosa Parks, in *Rosa Parks: My Story,* recalls her feelings during her historic refusal to give up her bus seat. Readers can identify with her sense of being pushed too far.
SETTING	How does the author help readers understand the time and/or place?	In *Barrio Boy,* Ernesto Galarza specifies the exact place and name of his school. He describes the furniture and layout of the principal's office, so that readers can picture it in their minds.
EVENTS	How does the author make the order of events clear to readers?	In "Fish Cheeks," Amy Tan describes, in chronological order, the preparation, celebration, and aftermath of a Christmas Eve dinner. She uses flash-forward to show readers what she later realizes about that night.
POINT OF VIEW	How does the author help readers see things through his or her eyes?	In *Barrio Boy,* Ernesto Galarza describes his feelings as a child. He shows how tall and foreign his teacher and principal looked to him and how strange the English language seemed.
THEME	What main message(s) about life or human nature might the author's experiences illustrate?	"Names/Nombres" is about more than names. When Julia Alvarez moves to the United States, the changes in her name illustrate the culture clashes that she faces.

Point of View Suggest that students describe a recent gathering of friends or family where something unusual happened. Have them think about what is special and unique in their own point of view—Do they tend to see the humor in situations? Are they critical? Accepting?

Theme Ask students to think of the stories they have read so far in this theme. Have them choose one of the stories and jot down a sentence or two about what they learned by reading it and what they think the theme of the story is. Ask students to determine whether the themes in these stories were directly stated or implied.

In the previous stories, as well as in the autobiographical writing that follows, writers describe events that illuminate one of the many themes of their lives. Ask students to think of something significant that has happened to them in their own lives and to write down what they learned by going through the experience. If they were to describe the event as part of an autobiography, what would the theme be?

THEME A **theme** is a message that readers can take from the story. A theme can be stated directly, or it can be implied. Authors of autobiographies don't tell everything that's happened in their lives. They choose events and details that add up to the theme or themes they want to convey.

When you read autobiographical writing, look for the elements discussed on these pages. Ask yourself what the author does with each element. The chart at the top of this page shows questions you might use. It also shows how you might analyze the elements of autobiographical writings that you read.

WHAT I AM, WHAT I WANT TO BE ❧ 63

Technology Option

Autobiography Table

Students can use word processing software to create a table of the five elements of autobiography. Have each student open a new document and insert a five-column table with the following headings: *Characters, Setting, Events, Point of View, and Theme.*

Characters	Setting	Events	Point of View	Theme

For each new autobiographical selection that students read, have them add a new row and complete it with information about each of the work's five elements. Students can use their tables to review the various autobiographies they read or to help them compare and contrast the various texts. **L2**

Active Reading Strategies

Objective

• To understand and apply strategies for reading and comprehending autobiographical writing

Teach the Strategies

Ask students to think of events they would include in their autobiographies. As they share their examples, classmates can practice visualizing details of the event. Point out that forming pictures in our minds helps us relate to stories we hear and read.

Preview

Explain to students that previewing a selection is like walking by a new school the day before classes start. Previewing is a way of forming a first impression, checking out a situation, and preparing for what is to come.

Predict

Ask students to identify the clues that help them make predictions:
• the title of the story
• the illustrations that accompany the selection
• qualities or characteristics of the author or main character

Teaching Options

Active Reading Strategies

Tips for Reading Autobiographical Writing

How do you get the most out of your reading? One way to become an effective reader is to become an active reader. Active readers use strategies to better understand a selection. They ask themselves questions as they read. Use the strategies below to help you read autobiographical writing.

● For more about reading strategies, see **Reading Handbook,** pp. R71–R101.

PREVIEW

Previewing a selection will help prepare you before you actually read. Look at the title and pictures, and skim through the pages to find hints about the author.

Ask Yourself . . .

● How can I tell that this selection is autobiographical?

● Has this author written anything that I've previously read?

● What do the photographs or illustrations tell me?

PREDICT

Combine clues in the text with what you already know to make predictions about what will come next.

Ask Yourself . . .

● What does the title mean?

● How will the author be affected by this event?

● My first prediction was wrong. Now I think _____ .

QUESTION

Questioning helps you clarify your understanding of the text as you go along.

Ask Yourself . . .

● Why did the author choose to write about this particular event?

● Do I understand what the author is saying here?

● Why does the author reveal this detail? Is this an unbiased view of the situation?

● I wonder why _____ .

64 ❧ THEME 1

Reading Journal

Coping with Change In "Barrio Boy," the author Ernesto Galarza presents details about his first days in a new school in a new country. Invite students to discuss events that have occurred and feelings they have had on the first day of a new school year.

Activity As they read, ask students to list in their reading journals instances when the selection reminds them of their own experiences. After reading, encourage students to write a question or comment the author should hear.

VISUALIZE

Form pictures in your mind. Pay attention to the autobiographical details writers share about their lives.

Ask Yourself . . .

- How does this scene look?

- Can I picture the author and the circle of family and friends in the author's life story?

RESPOND

Respond while you are reading. Think about what the autobiography means to you.

Ask Yourself . . .

- How is the writer's life like my own life?

- I'd like to ask the writer why _____ .

- If I wrote an autobiography like this, I would include _____ .

APPLYING THE STRATEGIES

Read the following selection from the book *Barrio Boy*. Use the Active Reading Model in the margins as you read. Write your responses on a separate piece of paper or use stick-on notes.

Question

Point out to students that good readers make a habit of asking themselves questions as they read. A questioning attitude helps them find the information they need about a story and develop insight into the writer's point of view.

Visualize

Have students compare ideas on what a character from one of the selections looks like. Suggest that when reading poetry, students practice visualizing a favorite image with their eyes closed.

Respond

Remind students that one of the main reasons writers write is to inspire certain feelings in their readers. There is seldom one "correct" response to a piece of literature. Ask students whether they have ever read a story that changed the way they felt about something in their own lives.

65

Before Reading

Objectives

- To read and analyze a story about a boy entering a new school and a new culture
- To recognize descriptions and explain why they are effective
- To write an analysis of how the setting contributes to the story

Skills

Reading/Thinking: Distinguishing Fact from Opinion; Inferring
Writing: Description; Letter
Vocabulary: Word Meanings; Compound Words
Grammar/Language: Subject-Verb Agreement

Motivating
→ OPTIONS

Selection Focus Transparency 8: Have students view the cartoon and discuss the questions. Ask volunteers to share stories about something funny that happened to them on their first day at school.

Focus Activity: As an extension of the Focus Activity, encourage students to remember small details about an experience and to describe how their first impressions changed over time.

ACTIVE READING MODEL

Before You Read
from *Barrio Boy*

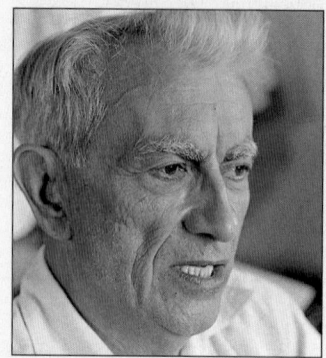

MEET ERNESTO GALARZA

Ernesto Galarza (är nes′ tō gä lär′ zä), a Mexican American union leader and writer, spent most of his life fighting for the rights of farm workers. He used his writing to expose the abuses they suffered. According to Galarza, "*Barrio Boy* is the story of a Mexican family, uprooted from its home in a mountain village. . . . The episodes of the journey were typical of those of hundreds of thousands of refugees. They settled permanently in California and other border states. The barrio of this tale is that of Sacramento, California."

Ernesto Galarza was born in 1905. He died in 1984. This selection is from Barrio Boy, *published in 1971.*

FOCUS ACTIVITY

How did you feel the first time you walked into your school as a new student? What were your first impressions of the building, the teachers, and your new classmates?

Sharing Ideas
Take a moment to jot down your responses to these questions. Then share your thoughts and feelings with a partner.

Setting a Purpose
Read the selection to learn how the author, as a young boy, faced starting at a new school.

BACKGROUND

The Time and Place The setting is the Lincoln School, an elementary school in Sacramento, California, in the early 1900s. The author has moved from Mazatlán, Mexico, to California.

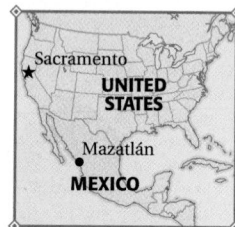

VOCABULARY PREVIEW

wholeheartedly (hōl′ här′ tid lē) *adv.* completely; sincerely; enthusiastically; p. 68
maneuver (mə noo′ vər) *v.* to move or handle skillfully, as into a position or toward a goal; p. 68
menace (men′ əs) *n.* a threat or danger; p. 68
formidable (for′ mi də bəl) *adj.* causing fear or dread by reason of size, strength, or power; p. 69
obnoxious (ob nok′ shəs) *adj.* annoying and disagreeable; p. 69
persistently (pər sis′ tənt lē) *adv.* repeatedly; p. 70

RESOURCE MANAGER

Lesson Planning Resource
The **Theme One Planning Guide** (pp. 53–60) provides additional lesson notes and reduced versions of all print resources.

📁 **Other Print Resources**
- Active Reading Guide, p. 8
- Vocabulary Practice, p. 5
- Reading Workbook, pp. 13–14
- Grammar and Language Workbook, pp. 183–184

- Grammar and Composition Handbook, Lesson 10.1
- Quick Checks, p. 8
- Selection and Theme Assessment, pp. 15–16
- Performance Assessment, p. 8
- Spanish Summaries, p. 8
- Spanish Translations
- Inclusion Strategies
- English Language Learners Sourcebook

 Transparencies
- Selection Focus 8
- Fine Art 32
- Literary Elements 8
- Grammar and Language 6

Technology
 Audio Library
 Spanish Audio Library
 Glencoe Literature Web Site
 Testmaker

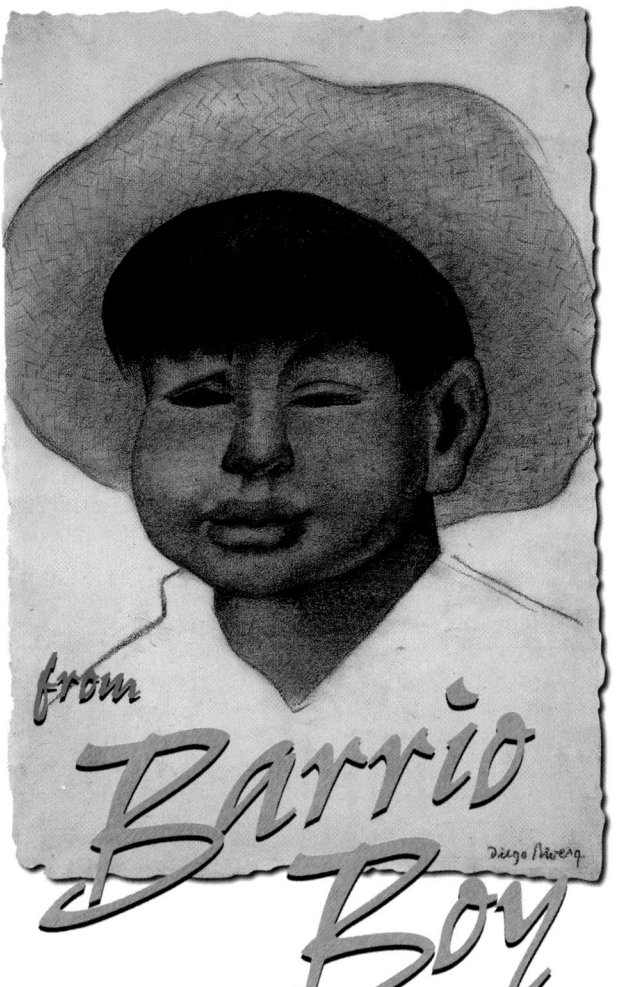

Cabeza de Nino, 1921–1929. Diego Rivera. Dibujo a la sanguina, 38 x 27.5 cm.

from Barrio Boy

Ernesto Galarza ✌

The two of us walked south on Fifth Street one morning to the corner of Q Street and turned right. Half of the block was occupied by the Lincoln School. It was a three-story wooden building, with two wings that gave it the shape of a double-T connected by a central hall. It was a new building, painted yellow, with a shingled roof that was not like the red tile of the school in Mazatlán.[1] I noticed other differences, none of them very reassuring.

---

1. *Mazatlán* (mäz' at län') is a city on Mexico's central Pacific coast.

CONNECTING TO OTHER SELECTIONS

The chart at the right shows three ways to connect the excerpt from *Barrio Boy* to other selections in this book.

For specific teaching strategies, see the **Theme One Planning Guide,** pages 56–57.

Connection	Title
Life Skills: Learning	→ "How I Learned English," p. 377
Thematic: Role Models	→ "The Scholarship Jacket," p. 451
Literary: First-Person Narrative	→ "Turkeys," p. 827

C Active Reading

RESPOND *(Most students will admit that they would be nervous because they would feel lonely without their friends and afraid of making embarrassing mistakes.)*

D Literary Elements

DESCRIPTION In this paragraph, the author uses descriptive details that help the reader picture each scene vividly. Have students find more examples of the author's use of descriptive details. *(For example, the author uses great detail when describing the layout and color of the school, the staircase and door Ernesto and his mother entered, and the principal's pinch glasses.)*

E Active Reading

PREDICT *(Students may say he will because of the phrases in this paragraph that suggest Miss Hopley's sympathetic character: "a warm welcome," "she smiled wholeheartedly," "the friendliness of her voice," and "the sparkle in her eyes.")*

FINE ART
TRANSPARENCY 32

You may wish to use *Fine Art Transparency 32* in connection with the definition of *barrio* in footnote 2.

ACTIVE READING MODEL

RESPOND

C Would you be anxious if you were entering a new school for the first time? Why or why not?

D

PREDICT

E Do you think the narrator will like Miss Hopley? Why do you think so?

We walked up the wide staircase hand in hand and through the door, which closed by itself. A mechanical contraption screwed to the top shut it behind us quietly.

Up to this point the adventure of enrolling me in the school had been carefully rehearsed. Mrs. Dodson had told us how to find it and we had circled it several times on our walks. Friends in the *barrio*[2] explained that the director was called a principal, and that it was a lady and not a man. They assured us that there was always a person at the school who could speak Spanish.

Exactly as we had been told, there was a sign on the door in both Spanish and English: "Principal." We crossed the hall and entered the office of Miss Nettie Hopley.

Miss Hopley was at a roll-top desk[3] to one side, sitting in a swivel chair that moved on wheels. There was a sofa against the opposite wall, flanked by two windows and a door that opened on a small balcony. Chairs were set around a table and framed pictures hung on the walls of a man with long white hair and another with a sad face and a black beard.

The principal half turned in the swivel chair to look at us over the pinch glasses crossed on the ridge of her nose. To do this she had to duck her head slightly as if she were about to step through a low doorway.

What Miss Hopley said to us we did not know but we saw in her eyes a warm welcome and when she took off her glasses and straightened up she smiled <u>wholeheartedly</u>, like Mrs. Dodson. We were, of course, saying nothing, only catching the friendliness of her voice and the sparkle in her eyes while she said words we did not understand. She signaled us to the table. Almost tiptoeing across the office, I <u>maneuvered</u> myself to keep my mother between me and the gringo[4] lady. In a matter of seconds I had to decide whether she was a possible friend or a <u>menace</u>. We sat down.

Did You Know?
Pinch glasses are eyeglasses clipped to the nose. Often, they're called by their French name, *pince-nez* (päns' nāz').

---

2. In the United States, *barrio* (bä' rē ō) refers to a Hispanic neighborhood.
3. A *roll-top desk* is a writing desk with a slatted, movable top.
4. *Gringo* is a sometimes scornful term for a non-Hispanic, white, North American male.

Vocabulary
wholeheartedly (hōl' härt' tid lē) *adv.* completely; sincerely; enthusiastically
maneuver (mə nōō' vər) *v.* to move or handle skillfully, as toward a goal
menace (men' əs) *n.* a threat or danger

Teaching Options

MEETING INDIVIDUAL NEEDS — ENGLISH LANGUAGE LEARNERS

Description Some of the items mentioned by the author were found in schools long ago. English language learners may need to have them described so that they can visualize them.
roll-top desk: a wooden writing desk with a slatted top that rolls down over the writing surface
swivel chair: a desk chair with wheels and a seat that turns on its base

Activity Have small groups create descriptions of objects and places in their present school, such as the staircase, the hallway, and the principal's office. **COLLAB. LEARN.**

Additional Resources
📁 *English Language Learners Sourcebook*

Ernesto Galarza

Then Miss Hopley did a <u>formidable</u> thing. She stood up. Had she been standing when we entered she would have seemed tall. But rising from her chair she soared. And what she carried up and up with her was a buxom superstructure, firm shoulders, a straight sharp nose, full cheeks slightly molded by a curved line along the nostrils, thin lips that moved like steel springs, and a high forehead topped by hair gathered in a bun. Miss Hopley was not a giant in body but when she mobilized it to a standing position she seemed a match for giants. I decided I liked her.

She strode to a door in the far corner of the office, opened it and called a name. A boy of about ten years appeared in the doorway. He sat down at one end of the table. He was brown like us, a plump kid with shiny black hair combed straight back, neat, cool, and faintly <u>obnoxious</u>.

ACTIVE READING MODEL

F

G

This class photo was taken in the early 1900s, around the time Ernesto Galarza attended the Lincoln School. What can you learn about the school and the students from studying the photo?

Vocabulary
formidable (for′ mi də bəl) *adj.* causing fear or dread by reason of size, strength, or power
obnoxious (ob nok′ shəs) *adj.* annoying and disagreeable

F **Literary Elements**

DESCRIPTION Discuss with students the author's detailed description of Miss Hopley. Ask students whether they think they know what Miss Hopley looks like. Ask students to compare Galarza's description with this one: "Miss Hopley seemed very tall and powerful when she stood up." Have them identify the details they would be missing if this were the way Galarza wrote his description of Miss Hopley.

G **Critical Thinking**

DISTINGUISHING FACT FROM OPINION Ernesto's impression of the interpreter contains both fact and opinion. Have students read the last paragraph and tell which is which. *(The facts are that the boy was "brown like us" and "a plump kid with shiny black hair combed straight back." The opinions are that he was "neat, cool, and faintly obnoxious.")*

VIEWING THE PHOTO

Viewing Response *Some of the things students may notice are that the Lincoln School had students from a variety of racial and ethnic backgrounds, that their clothing varied considerably (probably according to background and economic status), that patriotism was probably an important part of the teaching (note the flag), and that the children posed for the camera much more stiffly than would students of later generations.*

MULTIPLE LEARNING STYLES

MEETING INDIVIDUAL NEEDS

Spatial Students with strong spatial abilities will benefit from focusing on the author's abundant use of detail.

Activity Ask students each to choose a scene from the story to use as the basis for a quick sketch. Encourage them to take the time to visualize the scenes clearly and to jot down their important elements. As they create their drawings, remind them to see things from the perspective of Ernesto, a first-grader. Finally, ask students how the scenes in their drawings relate to the story and how they might affect Ernesto's feelings about his first day of school. **L2**

H Active Reading

RESPOND *(Students may say that they would feel scared, anxious, nervous, or embarrassed. Others may say that they do not mind new situations, so they would feel confident.)*

I Active Reading

PREDICT *(Students may draw on clues in the description of Miss Ryan to guess that she will be patient, understanding, helpful, and kind.)*

Vo•cab•u•lar•y Skills

Word Meanings Explain to students that the word *ado* in the expression "without further ado" means "something that wastes time, particularly with small details." Point out that *ado* can also mean "a confusing or noisy activity" or "something that is troubling," as in Shakespeare's *Much Ado About Nothing*.

J Literary Elements

DESCRIPTION All the impressions of the class come through Ernesto's eyes. Ask students to imagine how these descriptions would be different if the story were told in the third person. *(The descriptions might include Miss Ryan's and the students' impressions of Ernesto and a general picture of the classroom.)*

Teaching Options

ACTIVE READING MODEL

from **Barrio Boy**

RESPOND

H If you were the narrator, how would you feel walking into Miss Ryan's class?

PREDICT

I How will Miss Ryan help Ernesto overcome his fears?

J

Miss Hopley joined us with a large book and some papers in her hand. She, too, sat down and the questions and answers began by way of our interpreter. My name was Ernesto. My mother's name was Henriqueta. My birth certificate was in San Blas. Here was my last report card from the Escuela Municipal Numero 3 para Varones[5] of Mazatlán, and so forth. Miss Hopley put things down in the book and my mother signed a card.

As long as the questions continued, Doña[6] Henriqueta could stay and I was secure. Now that they were over, Miss Hopley saw her to the door, dismissed our interpreter and without further ado took me by the hand and strode down the hall to Miss Ryan's first grade.

Miss Ryan took me to a seat at the front of the room, into which I shrank—the better to survey her. She was, to skinny, somewhat runty me, of a withering height when she patrolled the class. And when I least expected it, there she was, crouching by my desk, her blond radiant face level with mine, her voice patiently maneuvering me over the awful idiocies of the English language.

During the next few weeks Miss Ryan overcame my fears of tall, energetic teachers as she bent over my desk to help me with a word in the pre-primer. Step by step, she loosened me and my classmates from the safe anchorage of the desks for recitations at the blackboard and consultations at her desk. Frequently she burst into happy announcements to the whole class. "Ito can read a sentence," and small Japanese Ito, squint-eyed and shy, slowly read aloud while the class listened in wonder: "Come, Skipper, come. Come and run." The Korean, Portuguese, Italian, and Polish first graders had similar moments of glory, no less shining than mine the day I conquered "butterfly," which I had been persistently

---

5. That is, her first name is *Henriqueta* (en' ri kā' tə). *San Blas* is a small city down the coast from Mazatlán but in a different state. In Mazatlán, the writer attended a public school for boys, *Escuela Municipal para Varones* (es kwā' lə   mōō ni' si päl' pär' ə   vä rō' nəs).
6. *Doña* (dōn' yə) is a form of respectful address for a married woman, like the English words *lady* and *madam*. For a man, one says *Don* (dōn), meaning "sir."

Vocabulary
persistently (pər sis' tənt lē) *adv.* repeatedly

70 THEME 1

INCLUSION STRATEGIES

Less-Proficient Readers A knowledge of prefixes can help readers understand more words as they read. Write these words on the board: *pre + pay = prepay; pre + test = pretest; pre + view = preview.*
Ask students what they think *pre-* means. ("*before in time or position*" or "*in front of*") Help students understand

that adding this prefix to a word does not change that word's spelling.

Activity Ask students to list three other words with the prefix *pre-* and write a sentence for each. **L1**

Additional Resources
📁 *Inclusion Strategies*

Ernesto Galarza ✵

pronouncing in standard Spanish as boo-ter-flee. "Children," Miss Ryan called for attention. "Ernesto has learned how to pronounce *butterfly!*" And I proved it with a perfect imitation of Miss Ryan. From that celebrated success, I was soon able to match Ito's progress as a sentence reader with "Come, butterfly, come fly with me."

Like Ito and several other first graders who did not know English, I received private lessons from Miss Ryan in the closet, a narrow hall off the classroom with a door at each end. Next to one of these doors Miss Ryan placed a large chair for herself and a small one for me. Keeping an eye on the class through the open door she read with me about sheep in the meadow and a frightened chicken going to see the king, coaching me out of my phonetic[7] ruts in words like *pasture, bow-wow-wow, hay,* and *pretty,* which to my Mexican ear and eye had so many unnecessary sounds and letters. She made me watch her lips and then close my eyes as she repeated words I found hard to read. When we came to know each other better, I tried interrupting to tell Miss Ryan how we said it in Spanish. It didn't work. She only said "oh" and went on with *pasture, bow-wow-wow,* and *pretty.* It was as if in that closet we were both discovering together the secrets of the English language and grieving together over the tragedies of Bo-Peep. The main reason I was graduated with honors from the first grade was that I had fallen in love with Miss Ryan. Her radiant, no-nonsense character made us either afraid not to love her or love her so we would not be afraid, I am not sure which. It was not only that we sensed she was with it, but also that she was with us.

> *The Korean, Portuguese, Italian, and Polish first graders had similar moments of glory, no less shining than mine the day I conquered "butterfly . . ."*

Like the first grade, the rest of the Lincoln School was a sampling of the lower part of town where many races made their home. My pals in the second grade were Kazushi, whose parents spoke only Japanese; Matti, a skinny Italian boy; and Manuel, a fat Portuguese who would never get into a fight but wrestled you to the ground and just sat on you. Our assortment of nationalities included Koreans, Yugoslavs, Poles, Irish, and home-grown Americans.

----

7. *Phonetic* (fə net′ ik) means "having to do with speech sounds."

N Active Reading

QUESTION *(The narrator means this figuratively, not literally. Unlike a melting pot, in which individual foods blend to become a new thing, the school was like a griddle, where foods are cooked side-by-side but retain their original qualities.)*

O Literary Elements

DESCRIPTION Direct students' attention to the last paragraph on this page. Have them discuss how Ernesto lets them know a bit about his life in Mexico. *(By mentioning a stagecoach, he gives them a picture of a rural place from an older time: dirt roads, probably no railroad, and only a few modern items.)*

P Active Reading

RESPOND *(Students will probably say that this is a happy ending. Ernesto does well in school; he learns to become a proud American but remains a proud Mexican.)*

Thematic Focus

What I Am, What I Want to Be
Have students compare Ernesto's experiences with their own. Is the way Ernesto adjusted to his new school familiar? How is it similar for anyone entering a new situation?

☑ ASSESSMENT OPTIONS

📁 *Quick Checks,* p. 8

Teaching Options

ACTIVE READING MODEL

QUESTION

N What does the narrator mean when he calls the school a "griddle"?

RESPOND

P What do you like about this concluding paragraph? Why?

Miss Hopley and her teachers never let us forget why we were at Lincoln: for those who were alien,[8] to become good Americans; for those who were so born, to accept the rest of us. Off the school grounds we traded the same insults we heard from our elders. On the playground we were sure to be marched up to the principal's office for calling someone a wop, a chink, a dago, or a greaser. The school was not so much a melting pot[9] as a griddle where Miss Hopley and her helpers warmed knowledge into us and roasted racial hatreds out of us.

At Lincoln, making us into Americans did not mean scrubbing away what made us originally foreign. The teachers called us as our parents did, or as close as they could pronounce our names in Spanish or Japanese. No one was ever scolded or punished for speaking in his native tongue on the playground. Matti told the class about his mother's down quilt, which she had made in Italy with the fine feathers of a thousand geese. Encarnación[10] acted out how boys learned to fish in the Philippines. I astounded the third grade with the story of my travels on a stagecoach, which nobody else in the class had seen except in the museum at Sutter's Fort. After a visit to the Crocker Art Gallery and its collection of heroic paintings of the golden age of California, someone showed a silk scroll with a Chinese painting. Miss Hopley herself had a way of expressing wonder over these matters before a class, her eyes wide open until they popped slightly. It was easy for me to feel that becoming a proud American, as she said we should, did not mean feeling ashamed of being a Mexican.

---

8. Here, *alien* refers to those who are foreign born.
9. *[wop . . . greaser]* These are all offensive names for people of various nationalities or lifestyles. Here, *melting pot* refers to the idea of a place where people of all races and cultures blend smoothly into a single society.
10. *Encarnación* (en kär nä sē ōn′)

❖

Grammar and Language *Minilesson*

Subject-Verb Agreement Write the following sentences on the board:
Ernesto is reading the book.
The students are reading the book.
Remind students that a subject must agree with its verb.

Activity Ask students to write a sentence using a singular noun subject with a singular form of the verb and a sentence using a plural noun subject with the plural form of the verb.

Additional Resources

🔊 *Grammar and Language Transparency 6*

📖 *Grammar and Language Workbook,* pp. 183–184

📖 *Grammar and Composition Handbook,* Lesson 10.1

📖 *Writer's Choice,* Lesson 16.1

Responding to Literature

Responding to the Selection

PERSONAL RESPONSE

Describe your thoughts as you followed the writer from his first day at school to his success in mastering English.

Active Reading Response
Look back at the strategies described in the **Active Reading Strategies** on pages 64–65. Choose one of the strategies, and find two places in the selection where you could apply it.

Analyzing Literature

RECALL

1. Where were Ernesto and his mother going as they walked down Fifth Street?
2. What was Ernesto's first impression of Miss Hopley?
3. What did Ernesto think of Miss Ryan as he surveyed her from his seat in the class?
4. What happened to students at the school when they traded insults on the playground?

INTERPRET

5. How do you think Ernesto felt as he walked into the Lincoln School for the first time? Support your opinion.
6. How do details from the selection show Ernesto's attitude toward the "gringo lady"?
7. How did Ernesto's feelings about Miss Ryan change over the course of the year? Support your opinions with examples.
8. What helped make it easier for Ernesto to feel that "becoming a proud American . . . did not mean feeling ashamed of being Mexican"?

EVALUATE AND CONNECT

9. From whose **point of view** is this selection told? How would it be different if it were told from Miss Ryan's point of view?
10. What lessons, beyond the academic ones, did Ernesto learn at the Lincoln School? Why were those lessons important?

LITERARY ELEMENTS

Description

A detailed portrayal of a person, a place, a thing, or an event is called a **description**. While description is the writer's primary purpose in descriptive writing, description is used widely in all kinds of fiction and nonfiction writing. Strong writers select details carefully so their readers can see, hear, smell, taste, and feel what is being described. The excerpt from *Barrio Boy* is filled with colorful descriptions of life in the Lincoln School that enable readers to feel as if they are attending school with Ernesto.

1. Pick out a description of a person or a place in the selection that helps you picture it clearly. Explain which details help you "see" the person as the writer did.

2. Choose your favorite description in this work, and explain why you chose it.

● See **Literary Terms Handbook**, p. R3.

Personal Response

Individual students will have different reactions to Ernesto's experience. Many will probably share his feelings and recognize their own similar experiences.

Active Reading Response

Students should choose one of the strategies—preview, predict, question, visualize, or respond—and apply it to two different places in the selection.

Analyzing Literature

1. Ernesto and his mother are going to enroll him in his first school in the United States.
2. His first impression was that she was warm and friendly.
3. He thought that she was very tall and intimidating.
4. When the children traded insults on the playground, they were taken to the principal's office.
5. He was nervous and fearful. The differences between this school and his school in Mexico were not reassuring.
6. At first, he is afraid of her. He keeps his mother between him and Miss Hopley. Once she stands up, he decides that he likes her and describes her as a "match for giants."
7. At first Ernesto is afraid of Miss Ryan. He describes her height as "withering," and she seems to surprise him easily. In a few weeks, he overcomes his fear. Later on he says that he has fallen in love with her.
8. The teachers called foreign students by their names in their

LITERARY ELEMENTS

1. Students will choose different passages. For example, they may choose the page 69 description of Miss Hopley standing up.
2. *Possible answer:* The description on pages 70–71 of how Miss Ryan and the class respond to the successes of Ito, Ernesto, and other first-graders

Additional Resources

📖 *Literary Elements Transparency 8*

own languages, encouraged them to share their unique experiences, did not punish them for speaking their native languages, and made it clear that becoming an American meant accepting people from every nation.

Extending Your Response

Writing About Literature

Students' paragraphs should
- give appropriate examples that show how the setting of the story affects the characters and events.
- give specific details that help visualize the place.

Creative Writing

Students' letters should
- describe the Lincoln school from Ernesto's point of view.
- describe one or two experiences that Ernesto has while at Lincoln school.
- describe how Ernesto feels and how his feelings change over time.

Art Activity Remind students that their sketches should include both interior and exterior views of the school, and that they will find appropriate descriptions in the story. The photo on page 69 will give them a hint of the exterior.

Skill Minilesson

VOCABULARY
- COMPOUND WORDS

1. d	3. c	5. a
2. e	4. b	

Additional Resources
📁 *Vocabulary Practice,* p. 5

Extending Your Response

Writing About Literature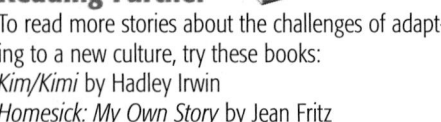

Setting   Write a paragraph or two explaining how the time and place of the excerpt from *Barrio Boy* contribute to the story. Think about how time and place affect events in the story. What details help you visualize the place?

Creative Writing

A Letter Home   Imagine that you are Ernesto. Write a letter to a relative in Mexico, describing the Lincoln School and your feelings about your experiences there. Before you write, review your notes from the **Focus Activity** on page 66.

Art Activity

Create a School   Draw pictures of the Lincoln School based on Ernesto's point of view. Use details from the selection as well as your imagination to help you sketch the school, both inside and out.

Reading Further

To read more stories about the challenges of adapting to a new culture, try these books:
Kim/Kimi by Hadley Irwin
Homesick: My Own Story by Jean Fritz

📖 **Save your work for your portfolio.**

Skill Minilesson

VOCABULARY • COMPOUND WORDS

Compound words are formed by putting two words together. The meaning of the new word combines the meanings of the words in some way. If you see an unfamiliar word that is made from words you know, think about the meanings of the individual words. There is a good chance you can figure out the meaning of the new word.

Let your imagination help. For example, a *spitfire* is a hot-tempered person, and *hogwash* is nonsense. If *heart* can mean "the center of emotion," then it's easy to see why saying that Miss Hopley smiled *wholeheartedly* indicates her sincere enthusiasm.

PRACTICE Think about the words that form the compounds in the left column. Then match each one with its definition.

1. broadcast   a. to exaggerate
2. blockhead   b. sincere
3. aftereffect   c. a later result
4. heartfelt   d. to scatter widely
5. overstate   e. a foolish person

✔ ASSESSMENT OPTIONS

📁 *Quick Checks,* p. 8
📁 *Selection and Theme Assessment,* pp. 15–16
📁 *Performance Assessment,* p. 8
💾 *Testmaker*

Vo·cab·u·lar·y *Skills*

Base Words

The words *trusting, trusty, mistrust,* and *distrustful* are formed by attaching prefixes or suffixes (or both) to *trust*. A **base word** serves as the "base" for any number of other words. Base words are whole words, not just parts of words, as roots can be.

Adding a prefix or suffix to a base word changes the meaning of the word. Sometimes the change is small. A *trusty* friend is one you can *trust*. Other times the change is major. To *distrust* someone means that you have no *trust* in that person.

Base Words	Words Formed from Base Words
happy	**happi**ness, un**happy**, **happi**ly
change	**change**s, un**chang**ing, **change**able
forget	**forget**ful, **forget**ting, un**forget**table

As you can see, small spelling changes may occur at the ends of base words when suffixes are added.

When you come across a word you don't know, check to see whether it has a base word that you *do* know. If it does, you can often figure out the meaning of the unfamiliar word, especially if the prefix or suffix is familiar to you.

EXERCISES

◆ Write the base word contained in the following words:
   1. laughter   3. capitalize   5. previewing
   2. unrecognizable   4. joylessness

◆ Use your knowledge of the base word in the underlined word to complete the statement that follows.
   6. The immigration officer's pronunciation was <u>indicative</u> of future problems. This means it
      a. created them.   **b.** stopped them.   **c.** pointed to them.
   7. It was <u>habitual</u> for Julia's mother to call any writer Julia's "friend." This means she did it
      a. rarely.   **b.** often.   **c.** never.
   8. When Julia's friends <u>sportively</u> called her "Alcatraz," they were being
      a. foolish.   **b.** mean.   **c.** playful.
   9. Julia thought that having the name Ana was <u>advantageous</u> to her sister, because it did **not** cause
      a. help.   **b.** problems.   **c.** admiration.
   10. Once Julia had <u>familiarized</u> herself with her new names, she was
      a. used to them.   **b.** annoyed by them.   **c.** confused by them.

WHAT I AM, WHAT I WANT TO BE 🦋 75

Vo·cab·u·lar·y *Skills*

Objective
• To recognize base words and to use them to figure out the meanings of unfamiliar words

Teaching Strategies

Create three columns on the board. In the first column, have students list common prefixes, such as *un-, dis-, re-, im-* and, *pre-*. In the second column, make a list of base words that can be combined with the prefixes, such as *happy, respect, think, prove, view*. In the third column, list suffixes such as *-ly, -ily, -ment, -ful,* and *-ness*. Ask students to form as many words as they can by choosing from at least two of the columns. Encourage them to use the new words in sentences that demonstrate their meanings.

Exercises
   1. laugh
   2. recognize
   3. capital
   4. joy
   5. view
   6. c
   7. b
   8. c
   9. b
  10. a

Additional Resources

📁 ***Vocabulary Power: Weekly Lessons and Activities***

Teaching Options

MEETING INDIVIDUAL NEEDS — ENGLISH LANGUAGE LEARNERS

Using Prefixes Tell students that a prefix is added to the beginning of a word to change the word's meaning. Demonstrate by writing *happy* and *fair* on the board and then adding the prefix *un-* to each word.

Activity Write the prefixes *un-, non-* and *il-* on the board. Explain that each prefix has the meaning of "not" or "opposite of." Then write *conscious,* *legal, logical, natural,* and *violent* on the board and discuss their meanings. Tell students to add one of the prefixes to each word to change its meaning. (*unconscious, illegal or nonlegal, illogical, unnatural, nonviolent*).

Additional Resources

📖 ***English Language Learners Sourcebook***

Objectives

- To read and analyze a short story about a teenage girl embarrassed by her Chinese family
- To recognize and locate sensory images in a short story
- To retell a story from a different point of view

Skills

Reading/Thinking: Evaluating
Writing: Summary; Personal Experience
Vocabulary: Etymology; Analogies
Grammar/Language: Adjectives
Collaboration: Literature Groups

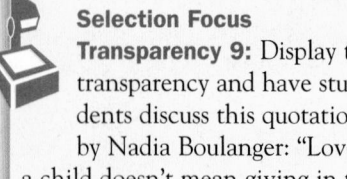

Motivating OPTIONS

**Selection Focus
Transparency 9:** Display the transparency and have students discuss this quotation by Nadia Boulanger: "Loving a child doesn't mean giving in to all his whims."

Focus Activity: As an extension of the Focus Activity, have small groups of students discuss why teenagers often find being different from others a problem instead of something to be proud of.

Before You Read

Fish Cheeks

MEET AMY TAN

Amy Tan did not always embrace her Chinese heritage. "When I was a teenager, I rejected everything Chinese. . . . I once felt ashamed to eat 'horrible' Chinese meals. I thought I'd grow up to look more American if I ate more 'American' foods." Only after her mother shared stories about the family's life in China did Tan become determined to learn all she could about her culture. Her novel *The Joy Luck Club* focuses on relationships between Chinese mothers and their American-born daughters.

Amy Tan was born in 1952. This piece was first published in a magazine in 1987.

76 🐾 THEME 1

FOCUS ACTIVITY

Think about a situation in your life that was extremely embarrassing for you. Why did you feel the way you did?

Journal Writing

Write in your journal about an embarrassing situation and your feelings about it. Would you be willing to tell a classmate about the experience? Why or why not?

Setting a Purpose

Read to find out about an embarrassing event in the life of the author, Amy Tan.

BACKGROUND

The Time and Place   It is 1966 in Oakland, California, when Amy Tan was fourteen years old.

Did You Know?

Chinese food is known the world over as one of the most sophisticated, complex, and delicious of cuisines. Meals served in Chinese homes and restaurants are most often eaten family style. Large bowls containing rice and a wide variety of dishes are placed in the middle of the table. Using chopsticks and spoons, diners share the food.

VOCABULARY PREVIEW

appalling (ə pô′ ling) *adj.* shocking; horrifying; p. 79
clamor (klam′ ər) *n.* a loud, continuous noise; uproar; p. 79
grimace (grim′ əs) *v.* to twist the face, as in pain or displeasure; p. 79

RESOURCE MANAGER

Lesson Planning Resource
The ***Theme One Planning Guide*** (pp. 60–68) provides additional lesson notes and reduced versions of all print resources.

📁 **Other Print Resources**
- Active Reading Guide. p. 9
- Vocabulary Practice, p. 6
- Reading Workbook, pp. 15–16
- Grammar and Language Workbook, pp. 7–8, 117–118

- Grammar and Composition Handbook, Lesson 5.1
- Quick Checks, p. 9
- Selection and Theme Assessment, pp. 17–18
- Performance Assessment, p. 9
- Spanish Summaries, p. 9
- Inclusion Strategies
- English Language Learners Sourcebook

 Transparencies
- Selection Focus 9
- Literary Elements 9
- Grammar and Language 7

Technology
🎧 Audio Library
🎧 Spanish Audio Library
💻 Glencoe Literature Web Site
💾 Testmaker

Fish Cheeks

Amy Tan ∿

I fell in love with the minister's son the winter I turned fourteen. He was not Chinese, but as white as Mary in the manger. For Christmas I prayed for this blond-haired boy, Robert, and a slim new American nose.

When I found out that my parents had invited the minister's family over for Christmas Eve dinner, I cried. What would Robert think of our shabby *Chinese* Christmas? What would he think of our noisy *Chinese* relatives who

SUMMARY

In this autobiographical short story, Amy Tan tells about an event that occurred when she was fourteen years old and in love with a minister's son. Amy's mother invites the minister's family over for Christmas Eve dinner. Amy is humiliated and embarrassed by the Chinese food served and her relatives' table manners.

📁 *Spanish Summaries,* p. 9

🅰 Active Reading

PREDICT Ask students to use clues in the first paragraph to predict what the narrator's conflict will be. *(Students may guess that the narrator's conflict will deal with the cultural differences between her Chinese heritage and Robert's American background.)*

Additional Resources

📁 *Active Reading Guide,* p. 9

🎧 *Audio Library*

🎧 *Spanish Audio Library*

Teaching Options

CONNECTING TO OTHER SELECTIONS

The chart at the right shows three ways to connect "Fish Cheeks" to other selections in this book.

For specific teaching strategies, see the **Theme One Planning Guide,** pages 64–65.

Connection	Title
Life Skills: Lifelong Learning	→ "Primer Lesson," p. 472
Thematic: Family	→ "Hollywood and the Pits," p. 117
Literary: Autobiography	→ "The Teacher Who Changed My Life," p. 368

77

Qui Ti (c. 1906–1958) was the only female member of the "Storm Society," a group in Shanghai that promoted modern oil painting in the 1930s. Only a few of her works are known to have survived.

Viewing Response *Examples:* com-posed, thoughtful, confident. *Most students will recognize that none of these qualities were shared by the young Amy, but all, or at least the last two, are traits of the mature narrator, who recognizes her earlier faults.*

Portrait of Pang Tao, 1944. Qui Ti. Oil. Collection of Dr. Michael Sullivan. St. Catherine's College, Oxford, England.

Viewing the painting: Choose three words to describe the mood of the girl in this paint-ing. Would the same words describe the story's narrator? Explain.

78

Teaching Options

ENGLISH LANGUAGE LEARNERS

Comparing Customs Amy is unhappy because her family does not use American table manners. Have students read the story to figure out what American table manners include, according to the author. *(Examples: wait-ing for platters to be passed and not belching at the table.)*

Activity Encourage students to observe table manners, ways that people greet each other, and conversa-tional style with friends, parents, and older people. Have partners describe customary American manners in various social situations and how they differ from those of other cultures with which students are familiar.

Additional Resources

📁 *English Language Learners Sourcebook*

lacked proper American manners? What terrible disappointment would he feel upon seeing not a roasted turkey and sweet potatoes but *Chinese* food?

On Christmas Eve I saw that my mother had outdone herself in creating a strange menu. She was pulling black veins out of the backs of fleshy prawns. The kitchen was littered with <u>appalling</u> mounds of raw food: A slimy rock cod with bulging fish eyes that pleaded not to be thrown into a pan of hot oil. Tofu,[1] which looked like stacked wedges of rubbery white sponges. A bowl soaking dried fungus back to life. A plate of squid, their backs crisscrossed with knife markings so they resembled bicycle tires.

And then they arrived—the minister's family and all my relatives in a <u>clamor</u> of doorbells and rumpled Christmas packages. Robert grunted hello, and I pretended he was not worthy of existence.

Dinner threw me deeper into despair. My relatives licked the ends of their chopsticks and reached across the table, dipping them into the dozen or so plates of food. Robert and his family waited patiently for platters to be passed to them. My relatives murmured with pleasure when my mother

---

1. *Tofu* (tō′ fōō) is a protein-rich food made from soybeans and used in soups, salads, and stir fries.

brought out the whole steamed fish. Robert <u>grimaced</u>. Then my father poked his chopsticks just below the fish eye and plucked out the soft meat. "Amy, your favorite," he said, offering me the tender fish cheek. I wanted to disappear.

At the end of the meal my father leaned back and belched loudly, thanking my mother for her fine cooking. "It's a polite Chinese custom to show you are satisfied," explained my father to our astonished guests. Robert was looking down at his plate with a reddened face. The minister managed to muster up a quiet burp. I was stunned into silence for the rest of the night.

After everyone had gone, my mother said to me, "You want to be the same as American girls on the outside." She handed me an early gift. It was a miniskirt in beige tweed. "But inside you must always be Chinese. You must be proud you are different. Your only shame is to have shame."

And even though I didn't agree with her then, I knew that she understood how much I had suffered during the evening's dinner. It wasn't until many years later— long after I had gotten over my crush on Robert—that I was able to fully appreciate her lesson and the true purpose behind our particular menu. For Christmas Eve that year, she had chosen all my favorite foods.

Vocabulary
appalling (ə pô′ ling) *adj.* shocking; horrifying
clamor (klam′ ər) *n.* a loud, continuous noise; uproar
grimace (grim′ əs) *v.* to twist the face, as in pain or displeasure

79

B Literary Elements

SENSORY IMAGERY Writers often describe something unfamiliar to their readers by comparing it to something readers are likely to know. Ask students what tofu and sponges have in common. *(They are both rubbery in texture.)*

Vo•cab•u•lar•y Skills

Etymology To *muster* originally meant "to assemble military troops for inspection or roll call." Today, *to muster up* means "to round up or collect, often with difficulty." Ask students what *mustering up a quiet burp* says about the minister? *(It was not easy or comfortable for him to observe this custom.)*

C Critical Thinking

EVALUATING Ask students why they think Amy pretended that Robert "was not worthy of existence." *(Amy did not want Robert to know that she had a crush on him. To prove it, she went to the opposite extreme and pretended she did not like him at all.)*

Thematic Focus

What I Am, What I Want to Be
Have students compare Amy's feelings with what theirs would be in a similar situation. Are Amy's feelings typical of someone her age? Have students provide examples.

☑ **ASSESSMENT OPTIONS**

📁 *Quick Checks,* p. 9

Grammar and Language *Minilesson*

Adjectives Remind students that using lively descriptive words called adjectives creates images that appeal to the five senses. One of the questions adjectives answer is *What kind?* Have students look through the story and note the adjectives Tan uses, such as *fleshy, appalling, slimy, bulging, rubbery, white,* and *quiet.*

Activity Invite students to work with partners or in small groups. Have each group write a short descriptive paragraph about food preparation for a holiday meal. Suggest that they use adjectives that appeal to each of the senses: sight, hearing, touch, smell, and taste. **L2**
COLLAB. LEARN.

Additional Resources

🖌 *Grammar and Language Transparency 7*

📕 *Grammar and Language Workbook,* pp. 7–8, 117–118

📕 *Grammar and Composition Handbook,* Lesson 5.1

📕 *Writer's Choice,* Lesson 12.1

Responding to Literature

PERSONAL RESPONSE

There is no single response to a situation like the one Amy encounters, but students may describe comparable embarrassing moments in their own lives.

PERSONAL RESPONSE

What images from this story linger in your mind? Do they cause you to recall similar experiences from your own life?

Analyzing Literature

1. Amy's family invites several Chinese relatives and an American minister and his family, who are not familiar with Chinese culture.
2. Amy thinks Robert will be disappointed with the food because it is not what most Americans eat on Christmas Eve.
3. Robert's family notices that Amy's relatives lick the ends of their chopsticks and reach across the table. When Amy's mother serves a whole steamed fish, Amy's father pokes his chopsticks into it below its eyes to pull out the cheek meat, Amy's favorite.
4. Amy's mother gives Amy a beige tweed miniskirt, a very American fashion item.
5. She thinks they will not like Chinese food and manners, especially on a traditional holiday.
6. Amy uses words that make the food sound unpleasant: *appalling, slimy, bulging fish eyes, rubbery white sponges, dried fungus,* and *they* (the squid) *resembled bicycle tires.*
7. The minister and his family wait for food to be passed to them instead of reaching for it. Robert grimaces at the sight of a whole steamed fish, and his face gets red after Amy's father belches loudly.
8. The miniskirt is a good gift because Amy wants to be like other girls her age. But Amy's mother makes it clear to her that although she adopts some American ways, she is still Chinese—a difference to be proud of.

Analyzing Literature

RECALL

1. What guests are invited to the Tans' Christmas Eve dinner?
2. Why does Amy assume that Robert will be disappointed by the food served at the meal?
3. What are some of the cultural differences Robert and his family notice about how food is eaten in a Chinese meal?
4. What does Amy's mother give her for an early Christmas present?

INTERPRET

5. Why is Amy so upset by the thought of entertaining the minister's family?
6. How does Amy's **description** of food preparation in the kitchen show how she feels about the food?
7. In what ways does the author make clear that the minister and his family are not used to eating in a traditional Chinese style?
8. Do you think Mrs. Tan's gift for Amy is a wise choice? Why or why not?

EVALUATE AND CONNECT

9. What do you think is the purpose of the final paragraph of this story?
10. Theme Connection   Amy Tan, as narrator and author, is able to stand back from this early experience and learn something about her mother and about herself. What have you learned from a similarly difficult experience in your own life?

LITERARY ELEMENTS

Sensory Imagery

Sensory imagery is language that appeals to a reader's five senses: hearing, sight, touch, taste, and smell. Imagery is used not only in poetry, but also in prose. Even if you have never seen or tasted tofu, you can picture it after reading Tan's description: "Tofu, which looked like stacked wedges of rubbery white sponges." "Fish Cheeks" is full of vivid images of a Chinese dinner being prepared and served.

1. Which two senses does the phrase "a slimy rock cod with bulging fish eyes" appeal to? Find another phrase that appeals to more than one sense.

2. Reread the paragraph about belching. How does Tan bring the scene to life for readers? Support your opinion with examples of sensory imagery from this scene.

● See **Literary Terms Handbook,** p. R9.

9. The final paragraph shows that Amy finally understands her mother and is proud of her Chinese identity. Amy's embarrassment in front of an American family had prevented her from seeing how special her traditions are.
10. Students may respond that although they were uncomfortable at the time, they learned something from an embarrassing experience.

LITERARY ELEMENTS

1. The phrase appeals to the senses of touch and sight. Another phrase is *stacked wedges of rubbery white sponges.*
2. Tan brings the scene to life by evoking sound and visual imagery. Examples of sensory imagery include *belched loudly, reddened face,* and *quiet burp.*

Additional Resources

 Literary Elements Transparency 9

Extending Your Response

Writing About Literature

Point of View The dinner in "Fish Cheeks" is described from young Amy's point of view. What do you think might be Robert's opinion about the foods served? Write a brief summary of the meal from Robert's point of view.

interNET CONNECTION

Use the Internet to find out more about traditional Chinese cooking. Look up the names and menu offerings of Chinese restaurants. You can also find recipes for Chinese food at various cooking Web sites.

Personal Writing

A Learning Experience Recall your **Focus Activity** (page 76) discussion about embarrassing experiences. Write a short piece about the incident you described and what you learned from it. Using "Fish Cheeks" as an example, try to include some humor.

Literature Groups

What to Cook? Did Mrs. Tan make the right decision about the meal? According to her daughter, she did not. But what do you think? Be prepared to share your group's opinion with the class.

Reading Further

If you enjoyed reading "Fish Cheeks," check out these books by Amy Tan:
The Moon Lady
The Chinese Siamese Cat

💼 **Save your work for your portfolio.**

Skill Minilesson

VOCABULARY • ANALOGIES

Analogies compare the relationships between things or ideas. Here is an example of an analogy:

> big : small :: happy : sad

You can read this analogy as: "*Big* is the opposite of *small* just as *happy* is the opposite of *sad*."

PRACTICE Choose the pair of words that best completes each analogy.

1. appalling : pleasing ::
   a. cheerful : lucky
   b. lazy : sleepy
   c. interesting : boring
   d. furry : cold

2. silence : clamor ::
   a. roar : zoo
   b. year : month
   c. breakfast : lunch
   d. frown : smile

● For more about analogies, see **Communications Skills Handbook,** p. R65.

Extending Your Response

Writing About Literature

Students' descriptions should
• be clearly written from Robert's point of view.
• provide sensory details relating to Robert's feelings about the food and table manners of his hosts.

Personal Writing

Students' writing should
• describe an embarrassing personal experience or event.
• emulate Tan's use of humorous details.

Literature Groups

Point out to students that they should consider how the experience would have been different for Amy if Mrs. Tan had cooked a traditional American Christmas Eve dinner. Students should discuss whether the lesson Amy learned about being proud of her heritage was worth the temporary embarrassment. **COLLAB. LEARN.**

Skill Minilesson

VOCABULARY • ANALOGIES

1. c
2. d

Additional Resources
📁 *Vocabulary Practice,* p. 6

✓ ASSESSMENT OPTIONS

📁 *Quick Checks,* p. 9
📁 *Selection and Theme Assessment,* pp. 17–18
📁 *Performance Assessment,* p. 9
💾 *Testmaker*

Objective

• To gain insight into culturally linked attitudes toward foods

Teaching Strategies

As you work through the connection activities with students, emphasize how important it is for social scientists to remain open-minded. Though foods from other cultures may be distasteful to them, they should strive not to be judgmental. Ask students to talk about foods they like that may taste strange to those who are unfamiliar with them.

Activity

Students may describe food or meal traditions that are specific to their families but which may or may not be traced to their cultural heritage. A paragraph summarizing an interview with a family member might resemble the following: *On Sundays, my whole family gets together for dinner. According to my grandmother, we have been doing this for as long as she can remember. She comes from northern Italy and is a good cook. When I was a child, I used to love the escarole soup she made, but I'd leave the rice at the bottom of the bowl. Now, I eat it all.*

Teaching Options

Food with Attitude

The young Amy Tan had a tense Christmas Eve dinner. Her mother had prepared all of her favorite foods—tofu, squid, dried mushrooms, and fish cheeks—but Amy was too embarrassed to enjoy them. She worried that these foods and her family's meal customs would be strange and unappetizing to her non-Chinese guests.

Today, a young Amy Tan might not have to worry as much. Americans have become much more sophisticated in their dining habits. You'll probably find tofu, squid, and many other once-exotic items in almost any large supermarket. Still, some dishes popular elsewhere have not yet made it into the American mainstream, and maybe never will. Here are a few of them.

Insects (including termites, ants, and grasshoppers) have been, and still are, eaten by people all over the world. They are an excellent source of protein—even better than beef. Depending on the insect and the location, insects may be eaten raw, cooked, or ground up and used as a spice or a medicine.

Headcheese is not really a cheese, but it is made from a head—a calf's head, including the brain. You can find the recipe in many cookbooks.

Haggis is a Scottish dish containing the chopped heart, liver, and lungs of a sheep mixed with suet (hard fat), oatmeal, onions, and spices. All this is stuffed into a cleaned sheep's stomach and boiled.

Fugu is a dish of puffer fish, or blowfish, so-called because the fish pumps itself full of air or water to appear larger when in danger. Highly prized in Japan, fugu must be cleaned and prepared by specially trained chefs because the fish's internal organs contain a very powerful poison. The danger seems to add to its popularity.

ACTIVITY

Pretend you are a social scientist trying to understand your family's eating customs. Interview family members, especially older ones, about foods. Ask questions such as:

• What food or meal traditions do we have in our family?
• Where did these traditions come from?
• What dishes from other countries or from other parts of our country do you enjoy?
• What foods did you enjoy as a child?
• How have your food likes and dislikes changed over the years?

Write a paragraph summarizing the results of your survey.

MEETING INDIVIDUAL NEEDS — MULTIPLE LEARNING STYLES

Intrapersonal Encourage students to share their experiences of interviewing, being interviewed, and watching interviews on TV news programs and talk shows. What do they think makes a good interviewer? List students' answers on the board. You may want to offer a few of these suggestions:
• Ask questions that get the other person talking.

• Listen closely to all answers.
• Ask follow-up questions based on what the person says.
• Query what you do not understand.

Activity Have small groups prepare lists of questions they think will get people talking. Ask the groups to give each other feedback on their interviewing techniques. **L2 COLLAB. LEARN.**

Sequencing

Sequencing is organizing things into some kind of order, or sequence. Writers often use chronological order, or time order, to sequence their stories. Events take place one after another in time order. A skillful reader looks for clues that tell the order in which events actually occurred. Consider these passages from "Fish Cheeks."

> On Christmas Eve I found out that my mother had outdone herself in creating a strange menu. . . .
>
> And then they arrived—the minister's family and all my relatives in a clamor of doorbells and rumpled Christmas packages. . . .
>
> Dinner threw me deeper into despair. . . .
>
> At the end of the meal my father leaned back and belched loudly, thanking my mother for her fine cooking. . . .
>
> After everyone had gone, my mother said to me, "You want to be the same as American girls on the outside."

As you can see, each new paragraph moves the story a little further along in time. Author Amy Tan lets you know when each event happened. She makes use of words and phrases such as *on Christmas Eve, at the end of the meal, then,* and *after.* Not all stories contain clues as specific as these. Sometimes a story moves backward as well as forward in time. Still, you can usually figure out the order in which events occur. Watch especially for words and phrases such as *meanwhile, before, after, first, second, last, eventually, then, next, earlier,* and *later.*

● For more about sequencing, see **Reading Handbook,** p. R87.

ACTIVITY

Look through a short story of your choice. List all the words you find that provide clues to the time order of the events in the story. Then make a chart sequencing at least five events from the story in their correct time order.

Teaching Strategies

Encourage students to use the events of the day before as the basis for stories they would like to write. Help them list sentences they could use to start their stories, such as:
• It all began when my alarm didn't go off.
• Things started off as usual.
• The first thing I did when I got to school yesterday was...

Have students create a personal sequence of events using sequencing words suggested in their books.

Activity

Students' responses should:
• list the words that provide clues to the sequence of events.
• list five events in their proper sequence.

Additional Resources

📖 *Reading Workbook*

Teaching Options

INCLUSION STRATEGIES

Less-Proficient Readers Help students sequence by asking them to arrange the events in proper order.

Activity Write the following event summaries on the board:
1. While Alfonso was cleaning his bike, the chain broke.
2. Sandra hopped on the crossbar and off they went.
3. The kid's sister, Sandra, agreed to go bike riding with Alfonso.

Encourage them to check the selection as a way of verifying the sequence. **L1**

Additional Resources

📁 *Inclusion Strategies*

SUMMARY

In 1955, Rosa Parks refused to give her seat on a bus to a white person. She was taken to jail and found guilty of violating a segregation law in Montgomery, Alabama. The black community boycotted the buses while a legal team and Mrs. Parks fought the segregated bus laws in court. After an eventful year, the Supreme Court's ruling that segregation on the Montgomery buses was unconstitutional marked the beginning of the Civil Rights movement.

📁 *Spanish Summaries,* p. 10

Objectives

- To read and analyze an autobiographical excerpt
- To identify a sequence of events
- To write a summary of key events

Skills

Reading/Thinking: Inferring; Identifying Cause and Effect Relationships; Drawing Conclusions; Judging the Credibility of a Source; Evaluating; Analyzing Arguments; Identifying Propaganda Techniques; Logical Reasoning; Synthesizing; Generalizing

Writing: Consistency in Verb Tenses; Summary; Script; Narrative

Vocabulary: Jargon; Etymology; Antonyms; Unlocking Meaning

Grammar/Language: Quotation Marks; Commas; Capitalization of Proper Nouns; Nouns

Listening/Speaking: Effective Listening Techniques; Skit

Life Skills: Supporting and Contributing

Collaboration: Literature Groups; Performance

Before You Read
from *Rosa Parks: My Story*

MEET ROSA PARKS

Rosa Parks experienced the injustice of segregation on a daily basis growing up in Alabama. In the 1930s, she became active in Civil Rights, focusing on voter registration. Despite much effort, little had changed for African Americans in the South. Then one day in the 1950s, Rosa Parks refused to give up her bus seat. Without planning it, she became "the mother of the Civil Rights movement."

Rosa Parks was born in 1913. This story is part of her autobiography, first published in 1992.

FOCUS ACTIVITY

When something in the world seems unjust, what can an ordinary person do about it?

List Ideas

Work with a partner and think of a situation that seems to affect people unfairly. Then make a list of actions that ordinary people might take to improve the situation.

Setting a Purpose

Find out what Rosa Parks did to improve a situation.

BACKGROUND

The Time and Place This selection begins on December 1, 1955, in racially segregated Montgomery, Alabama.

Did You Know? Until the 1960s, Southern states had laws to separate the races. African Americans fought in the courts and through organized protests to end such discrimintation.

VOCABULARY PREVIEW

comply (kəm plī′) *v.* to go along with a request; p. 86
resigned (ri zīnd′) *adj.* giving in without resistance; p. 88
boycott (boi′ kot) *n.* an organized protest in which the participants refuse to buy, sell, or use a product or service; p. 90
mobilize (mō′ bə līz′) *v.* to become prepared, as for war or an emergency; p. 91
inconvenience (in′ kən vēn′ yəns) *v.* to cause someone difficulty, bother, or hassle; p. 93
indignity (in dig′ nə tē) *n.* an offense against one's pride or dignity; humiliation; p. 94
oppression (ə presh′ ən) *n.* the act of controlling or governing by the cruel and unjust use of force or authority; p. 95
negotiate (ni gō′ shē āt′) *v.* to discuss in order to bring about an agreement; p. 97
impose (im pōz′) *v.* to apply legally; enforce; p. 100

RESOURCE MANAGER

Lesson Planning Resource
The ***Theme One Planning Guide*** (pp. 69–76) provides additional lesson notes and reduced versions of all print resources.

📁 **Other Print Resources**
- Active Reading Guide, p. 10
- Vocabulary Practice, p. 7
- Reading Workbook, pp. 17–18
- Grammar and Language Workbook, pp. 237–248, 259–260, 267–270

- Grammar and Composition Handbook, Lessons 2.1, 12.2–12.4, 13.2–13.4, 13.6
- Quick Checks, p. 10
- Selection and Theme Assessment, pp. 19–20
- Performance Assessment, p. 10
- Spanish Summaries, p. 10
- Spanish Translations
- Inclusion Strategies
- English Language Learners Sourcebook

 Transparencies
- Selection Focus 10
- Literary Elements 10
- Grammar and Language 8–10

Technology
 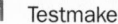
🔘 Literature Launchers
🎧 Audio Library
🎧 Spanish Audio Library
💻 Glencoe Literature Web Site
💾 Testmaker

"You're Under Arrest"

When I got off from work that evening of December 1, I went to Court Square as usual to catch the Cleveland Avenue bus home. I didn't look to see who was driving when I got on, and by the time I recognized him, I had already paid my fare. It was the same driver who had put me off the bus back in 1943, twelve years earlier. He was still tall and heavy, with red, rough-looking skin. And he was still mean-looking. I didn't know if he had been on that route before—they switched the drivers around sometimes. I do know that most of the time if I saw him on a bus, I wouldn't get on it.

from

Rosa Parks: MY STORY

Rosa Parks ∽
with Jim Haskins

Reading the Selection

Motivating → OPTIONS

Literature Launchers: "Taking a Seat, Making a Stand"

Videodisc Side A, Segment 3

Also available in VHS.

Selection Focus Transparency 10: Ask students for their interpretations of the quotation by Dr. Martin Luther King, Jr.

Focus Activity: Have students discuss ways of righting unfair social situations.

A Active Reading

PREDICT Ask students to think about the relationship between Rosa Parks and the bus driver. Have them predict what role he may play in the predicament she will describe. *(Because the driver has given Parks trouble before, students might assume that he will do it again.)*

Teaching Options

CONNECTING TO OTHER SELECTIONS

The chart at the right shows three ways to connect "Rosa Parks: My Story" to other selections in this book.

For specific teaching strategies, see the **Theme One Planning Guide,** pages 72–73.

Connection	Title
Life Skills: Taking Action	→ "New Directions," p. 222
Thematic: At the Crossroads	→ "Atalanta's Race," p. 714
Literary: Tone	→ "We Are All One," p. 773

 LITERATURE & HUMANITIES

We Shall Not Be Moved
Play "We Shall Not Be Moved," on volume 2, track 18 of the CD *American Music: Cultural Traditions.* Have students discuss the role such songs can play in social and political change.

85

B Literary Elements

SEQUENCE This passage describes the first step of Rosa Parks' ordeal. Ask students how Parks uses sequencing within this passage to bring the events to life. *(The minute-by-minute description helps readers picture the events as they happened.)*

Additional Resources

📁 *Active Reading Guide,* p. 10

🎧 *Audio Library*

🎧 *Spanish Audio Library*

📁 *Spanish Summaries,* p. 10

I saw a vacant seat in the middle section of the bus and took it. I didn't even question why there was a vacant seat even though there were quite a few people standing in the back. If I had thought about it at all, I would probably have figured maybe someone saw me get on and did not take the seat but left it vacant for me. There was a man sitting next to the window and two women across the aisle.

The next stop was the Empire Theater, and some whites got on. They filled up the white seats, and one man was left standing. The driver looked back and noticed the man standing. Then he looked back at us.

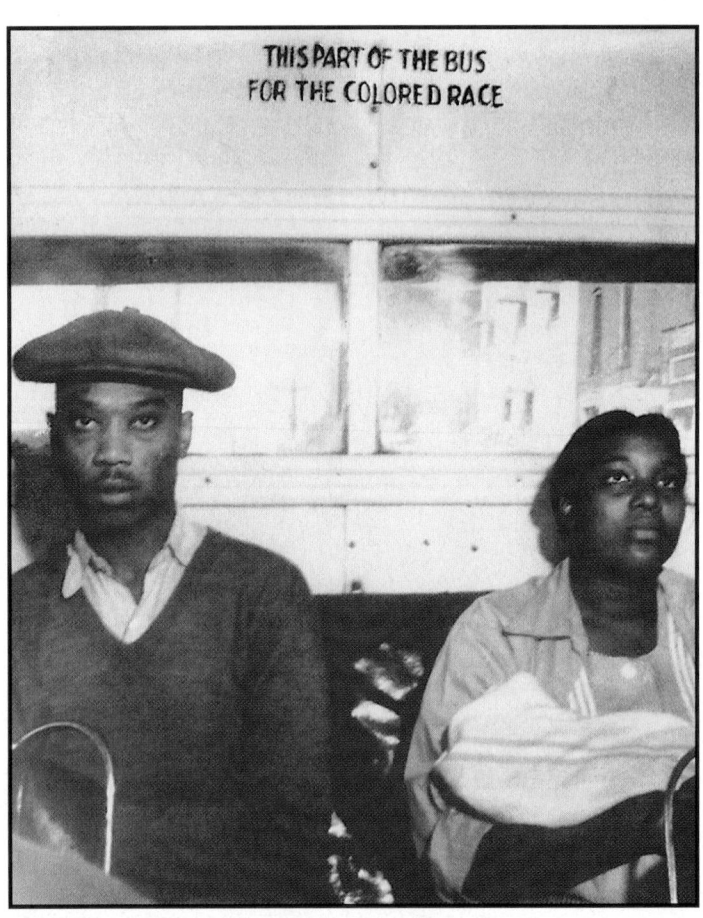

THIS PART OF THE BUS FOR THE COLORED RACE

African Americans usually had to sit in the back of the bus in the segregated South.

He said, "Let me have those front seats," because they were the front seats of the black section. Didn't anybody move. We just sat right where we were, the four of us. Then he spoke a second time: "Y'all better make it light on yourselves and let me have those seats."

The man in the window seat next to me stood up, and I moved to let him pass by me, and then I looked across the aisle and saw that the two women were also standing. I moved over to the window seat. I could not see how standing up was going to "make it light" for me. The more we gave in and complied, the worse they treated us.

I thought back to the time when I used to sit up all night and

B

Vocabulary
comply (kəm plī′) *v.* to go along with a request

Teaching Options

MEETING INDIVIDUAL NEEDS — ENGLISH LANGUAGE LEARNERS

Figures of Speech Write *make it light on yourselves* on the board. Ask English language learners what they think these words mean. Explain that *light* in this context is not the opposite of *dark* but means "easy" and that in English, words can take on meanings other than their literal ones. Offer other examples, such as *It's raining cats and dogs* and *running water.*

Activity Have students look for other examples of idioms in the selection, or have students volunteer other examples they may have come across.

Additional Resources

📁 *English Language Learners Sourcebook*

didn't sleep, and my grandfather would have his gun right by the fireplace, or if he had his one-horse wagon going anywhere, he always had his gun in the back of the wagon. People always say that I didn't give up my seat because I was tired, but that isn't true. I was not tired physically, or no more tired than I usually was at the end of a working day. I was not old, although some people have an image of me as being old then. I was forty-two. No, the only tired I was, was tired of giving in.

The driver of the bus saw me still sitting there, and he asked was I going to stand up. I said, "No." He said, "Well, I'm going to have you arrested." Then I said, "You may do that." These were the only words we said to each other. I didn't even know his name, which was James Blake, until we were in court together. He got out of the bus and stayed outside for a few minutes, waiting for the police.

As I sat there, I tried not to think about what might happen. I knew that anything was possible. I could be manhandled or beaten. I could be arrested. People have asked me if it occurred to me then that I could be the test case the NAACP[1] had been looking for. I did not think about that at all. In fact if I had let myself think too deeply about what might happen to me, I might have gotten off the bus. But I chose to remain.

Meanwhile there were people getting off the bus and asking for transfers, so that began to loosen up the crowd, especially in the back of the bus. Not everyone got off,

---

1. *NAACP* stands for National Association for the Advancement of Colored People. It wanted an opportunity to test *segregation* laws in federal court. Such laws required *discrimination* against, or unfair treatment of, African Americans.

but everybody was very quiet. What conversation there was, was in low tones; no one was talking out loud. It would have been quite interesting to have seen the whole bus empty out. Or if the other three had stayed where they were, because if they'd had to arrest four of us instead of one, then that would have given me a little support. But it didn't matter. I never thought hard of them at all and never even bothered to criticize them.

Eventually two policemen came. They got on the bus, and one of them asked me why I didn't stand up. I asked him, "Why do you all push us around?" He said to me, and I quote him exactly, "I don't know, but the law is the law and you're under arrest." One policeman picked up my purse, and the second one picked up my shopping bag and escorted me to the squad car. In the squad car they returned my personal belongings to me. They did not put their hands on me or force me into the car. After I was seated in the car, they went back to the driver and asked him if he wanted to swear out a warrant. He answered that he would finish his route and then come straight back to swear out the warrant. I was only in custody, not legally arrested, until the warrant was signed.

As they were driving me to the city desk, at City Hall, near Court Street, one of them asked me again, "Why didn't you stand up when the driver spoke to you?" I did not answer. I remained silent all the way to City Hall.

As we entered the building, I asked if I could have a drink of water, because my throat was real dry. There was a fountain, and I was standing right next to it. One of the policemen said yes, but by the time

---

Reading *Minilesson*

G **Critical Thinking**

DRAWING CONCLUSIONS Rosa Parks does not always explain why she does or does not do certain things or how she feels. Readers must draw their own conclusions. Ask students for their thoughts on why she did not respond to being denied water even though she was angry. *(Perhaps it was because she was afraid or just didn't want the situation to get worse or strain her emotions any further.)*

H **Critical Thinking**

JUDGING THE CREDIBILITY OF A SOURCE An autobiography is an author's own story, which the reader is expected to accept as completely true. Ask students what Rosa Parks does to make her story as truthful and authentic as possible. *(She keeps to the facts and even reveals some that seem complimentary to her captors. For example: "They didn't search me or handcuff me.")*

Language Note

Roots In this context, *matron* refers to a female prison guard. In other contexts, *matron* refers to a woman mature in age, character, or bearing. The word comes from the Latin word *mater*, meaning "mother." The words *mother*, *maternity*, and *maternal* come from this root.

Teaching Options

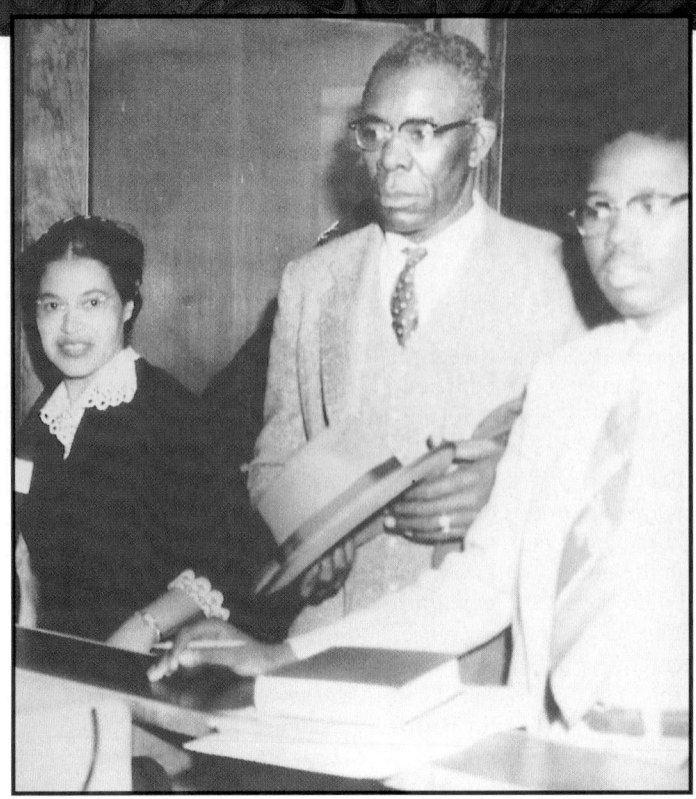

Rosa Parks, civil rights leader Edgar Daniel Nixon (center), and her attorney, Fred Gray (right), photographed after Rosa was fined $10 for breaking Montgomery's segregation laws.

as what my name was and where I lived. I asked if I could make a telephone call and they said, "No." Since that was my first arrest, I didn't know if that was more discrimination because I was black or if it was standard practice. But it seemed to me to be more discrimination. Then they escorted me back to the squad car, and we went to the city jail on North Ripley Street.

I wasn't frightened at the jail. I was more resigned than anything else. I don't recall being real angry, not enough to have an argument. I was just prepared to accept whatever I had to face. I asked again if I could make a telephone call. I was ignored.

They told me to put my purse on the counter and to empty my pockets of personal items. The only thing I had in my pocket was a tissue. I took that out. They didn't search me or handcuff me.

I was then taken to an area where I was fingerprinted and where mug shots were taken. A white matron[2] came to escort me to my jail cell, and I asked again if I might

G I bent down to drink, another policeman said, "No, you can't drink no water. You have to wait until you get to the jail." So I was denied the chance to drink a sip of water. I was not going to do anything but wet my throat. I wasn't going to drink a whole lot of water, even though I was quite thirsty. That made me angry, but I did not respond.

At the city desk they filled out the necessary forms as I answered questions such

_____

2. A *matron* is a female guard who supervises female prisoners.

_____

Vocabulary
resigned (ri zīnd') *adj.* giving in without resistance

88 ❧ THEME 1

 INCLUSION STRATEGIES

MEETING INDIVIDUAL NEEDS

Less-Proficient Readers Have students share with the class what they know of English slang words and expressions that are not formal language. For example, the word *mugshot* refers to a police photo taken of a prisoner's face. The word is derived from *mug*, a slang word for *face*.

Activity Have each student make a list of other slang expressions that appear in the selection. Then have partners work together to define the expressions. **L1** **COLLAB. LEARN.**

Additional Resources
📁 *Inclusion Strategies*

use the telephone. She told me that she would find out.

She took me up a flight of stairs (the cells were on the second level), through a door covered with iron mesh, and along a dimly lighted corridor. She placed me in an empty dark cell and slammed the door closed. She walked a few steps away, but then she turned around and came back.

She said, "There are two girls around the other side, and if you want to go over there with them instead of being in a cell by yourself, I will take you over there." I told her that it didn't matter, but she said, "Let's go around there, and then you won't have to be in a cell alone." It was her way of being nice. It didn't make me feel any better.

As we walked to the other cell, I asked her again, "May I use the telephone?" She answered that she would check.

There were two black women in the cell that the matron took me to, as she had said. One of them spoke to me and the other didn't. One just acted as if I wasn't there. The one who spoke to me asked me what had happened to me. I told her that I was arrested on the bus.

She said, "Some of those bus drivers sure are mean. You married?"

I said, "Yes," and she said, "Your husband ain't going to let you stay in here."

She wanted to know if there was anything she could do, and I said, "If you have a cup, I could drink a little water." She had a dark metal mug hanging above the toilet, and she caught a little water from the tap, and I took two swallows of that. She then started telling me about her problems. I became interested in her story and wondered how I could assist her. . . .

When the matron returned she told me to come out of the cell. I did not know where I was going until we reached the telephone booth. She gave me a card and told me to write down who I was calling and the telephone number. She placed a dime in the slot, dialed the number, and stayed close by to hear what I was saying.

I called home. My husband and mother were both there. She answered the telephone. I said, "I'm in jail. See if Parks will come down here and get me out."

She wanted to know, "Did they beat you?"

I said, "No, I wasn't beaten, but I am in jail."

She handed him the telephone, and I said, "Parks, will you come get me out of jail?"

He said, "I'll be there in a few minutes." He didn't have a car, so I knew it would be longer. But while we were still on the phone, a friend came by in his car. He'd heard about my being in jail and had driven to our place on Cleveland Court to see if he could help. He said he'd drive Parks to the jail.

The matron then took me back to the cell.

As Parks' friend had indicated, the word was already out about my arrest. Mr. [E. D.] Nixon [of the Montgomery NAACP] had been notified by his wife, who was told by a neighbor, Bertha Butler, who had seen me escorted off the bus. Mr. Nixon called the jail to find out what the charge was, but they wouldn't tell him. Then he had tried to reach Fred Gray, one of the two black lawyers in Montgomery, but he wasn't home. So finally Mr. Nixon called Clifford Durr, the white lawyer who was Mrs. Virginia Durr's husband. Mr. Durr called the jail and found out that I'd

Author's Craft

SETTING Ask students to find some sensory details the author uses to help readers visualize the setting. *("dimly lighted corridor," "empty dark cell," "slammed the door.")*

Critical Thinking

EVALUATING The matron refers to the other two prisoners as "two girls." Rosa Parks refers to them as "two black women." Ask students what this reveals about the speakers. *(Students may say that the matron does not look upon the women as social peers. Rosa Parks does.)*

Literary Elements

SEQUENCE Review the sequence of events that enables Parks to get to the jail quickly. *(Parks's friend hears about Rosa's trouble, stops by her house to see if he can help, and drives Parks to the jail.)*

What Is the NAACP?
The National Association for the Advancement of Colored People is an organization founded in 1909. It uses legal channels to alleviate untenable conditions under which African Americans live.

Grammar and Language *Minilesson*

Quotation Marks In stories, quotation marks signal a person's exact words, distinguishing dialogue from narrative. Write the following sentence on the board:
She handed him the telephone, and I said, "Parks, will you come get me out of jail?"
Point out to students that the quotation marks signal a break between the narrative and Rosa Parks's exact words to her husband.

Activity Ask students to insert quotation marks properly in the following sentences:
1. As we walked to the other cell, I asked her again, May I use the telephone?
2. I said, Yes, and she said, Your husband ain't going to let you stay in here.
3. I said, No, I wasn't beaten, but I am in jail. **L2** **COLLAB. LEARN.**

Additional Resources
- *Grammar and Language Transparency 8*
- *Grammar and Language Workbook,* pp. 267–270
- *Grammar and Composition Handbook,* Lesson 13.6
- *Writer's Choice,* Lesson 20.6

Literary Elements

SEQUENCE Ask students to identify the many different actions described in this short passage. *(Some examples include the matron's coming; Rosa Parks being released; and Mrs. Durr hugging her.)* Have students identify the words used to signal a movement from one action to another, such as *"As soon as they released me"* and *"By the time I got home"* (Another transitional phrase is *"As we were going down the stairs."*)

Active Reading

EVALUATE Ask students to suggest words that describe Rosa Parks's attitude at this point in her experience. *(She is anxious but determined.)*

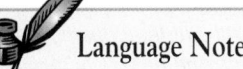

Language Note

The word *boycott* comes from Captain Charles C. Boycott (1832-1897), an English land agent in Ireland whose tenants and neighbors boycotted him (refused to associate with him) when he refused to lower rents. The Pullman, or sleeping car, gets its name from its inventor, George M. Pullman.

Teaching Options

---

been arrested under the segregation laws. He also found out what the bail was.

Meanwhile Parks had called a white man he knew who could raise the bail. His friend took him over to the man's house to pick him up. I don't remember how much the bail was. . . .

The matron came to let me know that I was being released. Mrs. Durr was the first person I saw as I came through the iron mesh door with matrons on either side of me. There were tears in her eyes, and she seemed shaken, probably wondering what they had done to me. As soon as they released me, she put her arms around me, and hugged and kissed me as if we were sisters.

I was real glad to see Mr. Nixon and Attorney Durr too. We went to the desk, where I picked up my personal belongings and was given a trial date. Mr. Nixon asked that the date be the following Monday, December 5, 1955, explaining that he was a Pullman[3] porter and would be out of Montgomery until then. We left without very much conversation, but it was an emotional moment. I didn't realize how much being in jail had upset me until I got out.

As we were going down the stairs, Parks and his friends were driving up, so I got in the car with them, and Mr. Nixon followed us home.

By the time I got home, it was about nine-thirty or ten at night. My mother was glad to have me home and wanted to know what she could do to make me comfortable.

I told her I was hungry (for some reason I had missed lunch that day), and she prepared some food for me. Mrs. Durr and my friend Bertha Butler were there, and they helped my mother. I was thinking about having to go to work the next day, but I knew I would not get to bed anytime soon.

Everyone was angry about what had happened to me and talking about how it should never happen again. I knew that I would never, never ride another segregated bus, even if I had to walk to work. But it still had not occurred to me that mine could be a test case against the segregated buses.

Then Mr. Nixon asked if I would be willing to make my case a test case against segregation. I told him I'd have to talk with my mother and husband. Parks was pretty angry. He thought it would be difficult to get people to support me as a test case. We discussed and debated the question for a while. In the end Parks and my mother supported the idea. They were against segregation and were willing to fight it. And I had worked on enough cases to know that a ruling could not be made without a plaintiff.[4] So I agreed to be the plaintiff.

"They've Messed with the Wrong One Now"

Meanwhile Fred Gray, the black attorney, had called Jo Ann Robinson and told her about my arrest. She got in touch with other leaders of the Women's Political Council, and they agreed to call for a boycott of the

---

3. Mr. Nixon was an attendant on a passenger train. The *Pullman* Company was a major manufacturer of railroad cars.

4. The *plaintiff* is the "injured party" who brings a case to court. If no one claims to have been harmed by a *defendant's* actions, a judge is not likely to allow a trial.

Vocabulary
boycott (boi′ kot) *n.* an organized protest in which the participants refuse to buy, sell, or use a product or service

---

LIFE SKILLS CONNECTION

Supporting and Contributing
Encourage students to discuss the fact that people deal with difficult situations more effectively when they have input and support from people they know, love, and trust, just as Rosa Parks did.

Activity Have small groups each create a three-column table to outline plans for dealing with a situation or decision they

may have to face, such as moving to a new town or helping a friend in trouble. The table should include the situations or decisions, the issues to be resolved, and the people to be consulted.

L2 COLLAB. LEARN.

Situation	Issues	Consultants
1.		
2.		
3.		

buses starting Monday, December 5, the day of my trial. So on the Thursday night I was arrested, they met at midnight at Alabama State, cut a mimeograph stencil,[5] and ran off 35,000 handbills. The next morning she and some of her students loaded the handbills into her car, and she drove to all the local black elementary and junior high and high schools to drop them off so the students could take them home to their parents.

This is what the handbill said:

This is for Monday, December 5, 1955.

Another Negro woman has been arrested and thrown into jail because she refused to get up out of her seat on the bus and give it to a white person.

It is the second time since the Claudette Colvin case that a Negro woman has been arrested for the same thing. This has to be stopped.

Negroes have rights, too, for if Negroes did not ride the buses, they could not operate. Three-fourths of the riders are Negroes, yet we are arrested, or have to stand over empty seats. If we do not do something to stop these arrests, they will continue. The next time it may be you, or your daughter, or mother.

This woman's case will come up on Monday. We are, therefore, asking every Negro to stay off the buses Monday in protest of the arrest and trial. Don't ride the buses to work, to town, to school, or anywhere on Monday.

You can afford to stay out of school for one day. If you work, take a cab, or walk. But please, children and grown-ups, don't ride the bus at all on Monday. Please stay off all buses Monday.

Early that Friday morning, Mr. Nixon called the Reverend Ralph David Abernathy, minister of the First Baptist Church. Mr. Nixon had decided that black ministers could do more to mobilize support in the community than anyone else. He also called eighteen other ministers and arranged a meeting for that evening. Mr. Nixon had to work as a porter on the Montgomery–Atlanta–New York route, so he would be unable to attend, but he talked to them all about what he wanted them to do.

Then he called a white reporter for the *Montgomery Advertiser* named Joe Azbell and arranged a meeting down at Union Station to show him one of the handbills. Mr. Nixon wanted the story on the front page. Joe Azbell said he would see what he could do. Meanwhile, the story of my arrest was reported in a small article in that day's paper.

On the morning of Friday, December 2, I called Felix Thomas, who operated a cab company, and took a cab to work. I was not going to ride the bus anymore. Mr. John Ball, who was in charge of men's alterations[6] at Montgomery Fair, was surprised to see me. He said, "I didn't think you would be here. I thought you would be a nervous wreck." I said, "Why should going to jail make a nervous wreck out of

---

5. Before the photocopier, a *mimeograph* machine could be used to print copies from an original called a *stencil.*

6. Mr. Ball supervises the *alterations,* or changes necessary for proper fit, of men's clothes at a local store.

Vocabulary
mobilize (mō′ bə līz′) *v.* to become prepared, as for war or an emergency

Critical Thinking sidebar

N Critical Thinking

DRAWING CONCLUSIONS The people in this story moved into action quickly. Ask students what the speed of their action suggests about their feelings on the issue of bus segregation. *(People were tired of bus segregation and were ready to protest.)*

O Critical Thinking

ANALYZING ARGUMENTS Ask students whether they think it is logical to say that if African Americans did not ride the buses, the bus lines could not operate. You may wish to share the following model to illustrate the thinking process in analyzing arguments.

Model: We have learned that African Americans rode the buses. The bus companies, therefore, made most of their money from their African American customers. No company could operate without making money.

P Critical Thinking

IDENTIFYING PROPAGANDA TECHNIQUES The purpose of the handbill was to persuade people to boycott the buses. Ask students to explain the impact of personalizing the appeal by saying "The next time it may be you, or your daughter, or mother." *(Personalizing the message reminded people they had a personal stake in the issue.)*

Grammar and Language *Minilesson*

Commas Explain that commas are used before and after the year when it is used with the month and the day and to separate the day of the week from the date. They are not used when only the month and year are given. Write the following on the board:
On May 24, 1992, we moved to Alabama.
Thursday, February 16, is my birthday.
My dad bought a new car in July 1998.

Activity Write these sentences on the board:
Rosa's ordeal began in December 1956.
On December 1 1956 she was arrested.
On the morning of Friday December 2 she called Felix Thomas.

Ask volunteers to add the commas and have others explain whether the sentences are punctuated properly. **L2**
COLLAB. LEARN.

Additional Resources

Grammar and Language Transparency 9

Grammar and Language Workbook, pp. 259–260

Grammar and Composition Handbook, Lessons 13.2–13.4

Writer's Choice, Lesson 20.4

Language Note

Discuss Rosa Parks's comparison of an office and a beehive. In what ways the two are alike? Help students understand why the author would use this figure of speech. *(Parks probably uses it to help readers picture the situation without using a lot of words.)*

Q Critical Thinking

LOGICAL REASONING Rosa explains the overwhelming support of the boycott with this sentence: "Most people had finally had enough of segregation on the buses." Ask students if this is a logical explanation for why so many stayed off the buses. Could there have been other reasons? *(Some people may have been afraid of what other African Americans would think of them if they rode the buses.)*

Teaching Options

me?" And then as soon as I got off for lunch, I went to Fred Gray's office.

Ever since Fred had opened his law practice in Montgomery, I had often done that. I'd pick up something from the store for my lunch. He usually brought his lunch. We would eat lunch together, and then sometimes I would answer the telephone while he ran out and did an errand or something, and then it was time for me to go back to work. Fred didn't have a secretary, and I often helped him out. The day after I was arrested, Fred Gray's office was like a beehive. People were calling and dropping by to ask about the boycott and the meeting the ministers had called for that night.

After work, I went to that meeting at the Dexter Avenue Baptist Church. I explained how I had been arrested, and then there were long discussions about what to do. Some of the ministers wanted to talk about

how to support the protest, but others wanted to talk about whether or not to have a protest. Many of them left the meeting before any decisions were made. But most of those who stayed agreed to talk about the protest in their Sunday sermons and to hold another meeting on Monday evening to decide if the protest should continue.

On Sunday the *Montgomery Advertiser* ran a copy of Jo Ann Robinson's handbill on the front page, and that helped spread the word to people who might have missed the leaflets or didn't go to church. But no one could be sure if the protest would be successful. Just because they read a leaflet or heard about it in church, it didn't mean that people would stay away from the buses. All eighteen black-owned cab companies in Montgomery had agreed to make stops at all the bus stops and charge only ten cents, the same fare as on the buses.

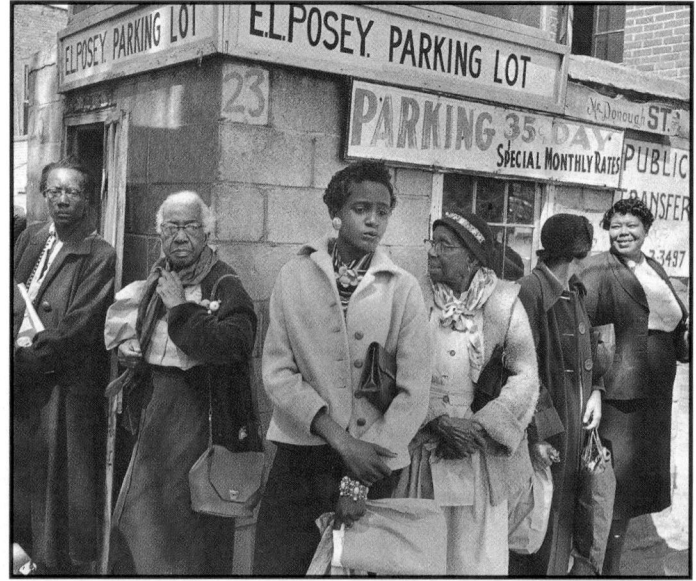

But people would have to wait for a cab that had room for them. To make matters worse, it looked like rain for Monday.

The sky was dark on Monday morning, but that didn't make any difference. Most black people had finally had enough of segregation on the buses. They stayed off those buses. They waited at the bus stops for the black-owned cabs to come along. Or they

Bus boycotters wait at one of the volunteer cab stops.

Q walked or got a ride. As a result, the Montgomery city buses were practically empty. Oh, a few black people took the buses, but they were mostly people who had not heard about the protest. Some of them were scared away from the buses. The city police had vowed to protect anyone who wanted to ride, and each bus had two motorcycle escorts. But some of the people who didn't know what was going on thought the police were there to arrest them for riding the buses, not to protect them. And

R then there were those few who didn't want to be inconvenienced. When the bus they were on passed a bus stop full of black people waiting for cabs, they ducked down low so nobody would see them.

That day I had no idea what the result was going to be, but I think everybody was quite amazed at that demonstration of people staying off the buses. It was a surprise to everybody, I think. As Mr. Nixon said, "We surprised ourselves." Never before had black people demonstrated so clearly how much those city buses depended on their business.

S More important, never before had the black community of Montgomery united in protest against segregation on the buses.

I didn't go to work that Monday. Instead that morning I went down to the courthouse for my trial. Parks went with me. I did not spend a lot of time planning what to wear, but I remember very clearly that I wore a straight, long-sleeved black dress with a white collar and cuffs, a small black velvet hat with pearls across the top, and a charcoal-gray coat. I carried a black purse and wore white gloves. I was not especially nervous. I knew what I had to do.

A lot of folks were down at the courthouse. Some people couldn't get in. Parks was almost prohibited from entering the courthouse. But when he said he was my husband, he was permitted to enter. You could hardly see the street for the crowds. Many members of the NAACP Youth Council were there, and they were all shouting their support.

There was a girl in the crowd named Mary Frances. She had a high-pitched voice, and it just came through the air: "Oh, she's so sweet. They've messed with the wrong one now." She said it like a little chant, "They've messed with the wrong one now."

It wasn't a long trial. The bus driver [James Blake] was the main prosecution witness.

I was not called to testify in my own behalf. Although my lawyers, Charles Langford and Fred Gray, entered a plea of "Not Guilty" for me, they did not intend to try to defend me against the charges. The point of making mine a test case was to allow me to be found guilty and then to appeal the conviction to a higher court. Only in higher courts could the segregation laws actually be changed, because the judges in the local courts were not going to do anything to change the way things were. So I was found guilty of violating the segregation laws and given a suspended sentence.[7] I was fined $10.00, plus $4.00 in court costs. The

---

7. In giving a *suspended sentence,* the judge has ordered Mrs. Parks to serve time in jail but, at least temporarily, will not actually require her to do so.

Vocabulary
inconvenience (ĭn′ kən vēn′ yəns) *v.* to cause someone difficulty, bother, or hassle

R Active Reading
EVALUATE The author says that people on the buses ducked down to avoid being seen by those waiting for cabs. Ask students what they think of the African Americans who rode the buses during the boycott.

S Active Reading
PREDICT Have students consider the significance of this great show of support. Ask what effect they think it had on the community. *(This show of support sent a message that the African American community could work together and be a powerful force.)*

Vocabulary Skills
Jargon Have students share with the class what they know about jargon, the specialized language used in a specific field like medicine, sports, computer science, and law. Note the various legal terms in this passage—*prosecution, witness, testify, plea, test case, appeal, conviction.* Ask students to volunteer other legal terms they know.

Writing *Minilesson*

Maintaining Consistency in Verb Tenses Work with students to identify the use of past tense in this selection. Explain that when writing about events that occurred in the past, writers must be sure that all the verbs they use are in the past tense. Students should understand that there is no shift in tense unless there is a shift in the time of the story's action.

Activity Have students each write a paragraph recording something interesting he or she did yesterday. Have them be consistent in their use of the past tense for all verbs that describe past actions. After writing, partners can check each other's paragraphs for consistency in verb tense. **L2 COLLAB. LEARN.**

Additional Resources
Writer's Choice, Lesson 10.5

Critical Thinking

INFERRING Call attention to the fact that Rosa Parks did not tell callers who she was. What does that fact say about her? *(It shows Parks was not interested in being a celebrity.)*

Literary Elements

SEQUENCE Point out that Parks uses transitional words and phrases like *"Earlier that day"* and *"that afternoon"* to help readers follow the story's sequence of events. Ask students to find other examples. *(They include* then, that night, *and* first.*)*

Martin Luther King, Jr.
Reverend King was ordained a Baptist minister at the age of 17. In college he studied the works of Indian nationalist Mohandas K. Gandhi, whose ideas became the core of King's own philosophy of nonviolent protest. The bus boycott is an example of nonviolent protest.

Active Reading

EVALUATE Have students evaluate the importance of the points raised regarding the continuation of the boycott. *(These points have merit. If the boycott failed, the African American community would be worse off than before. As bad as things had been, the white community could make them worse.)*

Teaching Options

---

crowd reacted angrily, but there was no organized protest.

I didn't go home after my trial was over. Instead I stayed downtown. I wanted to know what I could do. Fred Gray said he would appreciate it if I would stay in his office and answer the telephone, so I did. As soon as I got there, the telephone started ringing, because people had heard the news. I never did tell anybody who called that I was the one they were calling about. I just answered the phone and took messages. When Fred came back, Mr. Nixon took me home. It was getting pretty close to night, and I had to go home to get ready for the meeting at the Holt Street Baptist Church that evening.

Earlier that day Reverend Abernathy, who was about twenty-nine years old at the time, and some other ministers had met and decided to form the Montgomery Improvement Association (MIA). Mr. Nixon was there, and so was Fred Gray. The reason they wanted to form a brand-new organization was that they thought it would be better than just leaving the organizing to an established group like the NAACP. The NAACP was a relatively weak organization in Alabama; it was not a mass organization. Membership was kind of small, and you could hardly get people to join. They also wanted to rule out the NAACP so that the powers that be could not charge that this demonstration, this show of strength, was being led by outside agitators.

So they met that afternoon, and then they decided they should elect a president, and they elected the Reverend Martin Luther King, Jr., pastor of the Dexter Avenue Baptist Church. . . .

That night they had the meeting at the Holt Street Baptist Church, which was right in the black community so people wouldn't be afraid to attend. They didn't know how many people to expect, and they were not prepared for how many showed up. People filled that church, and hundreds more stood outside, so they set up a loudspeaker system so those people outside could hear what was going on inside. The meeting was already on when I got there, and I had a hard time getting into the church because there were so many people, inside and outside. I made it to the platform, and they gave me a seat.

The main thing they wanted to decide at that meeting was whether to continue the boycott. Some people thought we should quit while we were still ahead. And hardly anybody thought the boycott could go longer than the end of the week, which was four more days. If it did, it could be very dangerous, because everyone knew the whites wouldn't stand for it.

Mr. Nixon spoke first, as I recall. He was probably worried that people wouldn't really support a long boycott. He remembered all those years when it had been impossible to get black people to stand together. He said, "You who are afraid, you better get your hat and coat and go home. This is going to be a long-drawn-out affair. I want to tell you something: For years and years I've been talking about how I didn't want the children who came along behind me to have to suffer the indignities that I've suffered all these years. Well, I've

---

Vocabulary
indignity (in dig' nə tē) *n.* an offense against one's pride or dignity; humiliation

---

MEETING INDIVIDUAL NEEDS — INCLUSION STRATEGIES

Special Needs Visually impaired students may benefit from having a vivid description read aloud to them.

Activity Pair visually impaired students with students who can read with expression for a reading of the description of the ministers' meeting at the Holt Street Baptist Church. Have students begin with the paragraph starting, "So they met that afternoon,..." and end with "He received loud cheers and *Amens*..." on page 95. **L2 COLLAB. LEARN.**

Additional Resources
📁 *Inclusion Strategies*

The Reverend Martin Luther King Jr. addresses supporters of the bus boycott at the Holt Street Baptist Church, December 5, 1955.

changed my mind—I want to enjoy some of that freedom myself."

Dr. King was introduced to the audience as the president of the new Montgomery Improvement Association. He was a fine speaker, and he gave a speech that really got the crowd excited. This is part of what he said:

W

There comes a time that people get tired. We are here this evening to say to those who have mistreated us so long that we are tired—tired of being segregated and humiliated; tired of being kicked about by the brutal feet of oppression. . . . For many years we have shown amazing patience. We have sometimes given our white brothers the feeling that we like the way we are being treated. But we come here tonight to be saved from that patience that makes us patient with anything less than freedom and justice. One of the great glories of democracy is the right to protest for right. . . . [I]f you will protest courageously and yet with dignity and Christian love, when the history books are written in future generations the historians will pause and say, "There lived a great people—a black people—who injected new meaning and dignity

into the veins of civilization." That is our challenge and our overwhelming responsibility.
(*Eyes on the Prize: America's Civil Rights Years 1954–1965*, page 76)

He received loud cheers and applause and Amens. . . .

After that the Reverend Ralph Abernathy read the list of demands that the Montgomery Improvement Association was going to present to the bus company and the city's white leaders. There were three demands: 1) Courteous treatment on the buses; 2) First-come, first-served seating, with whites in front and blacks in back; 3) Hiring of black drivers for the black bus routes. Then he asked the audience to vote on these demands by standing

X

Vocabulary

oppression (ə presh′ ən) *n.* the act of controlling or governing by the cruel and unjust use of force or authority

W **Literary Elements**

FIGURES OF SPEECH: Personification
This figure of speech speaks of an inanimate object or an idea in terms of a person. In the phrase "*brutal feet of oppression*," the idea of oppression is given *feet,* a human characteristic. Challenge students to find another example of personification in King's talk. *(King speaks of "the veins of civilization.")*

X **Active Reading**

EVALUATE On this page there is a contrast of leadership styles. Each is valuable in a different way. Guide students to recognize the merits of both. Encourage students to review the roles of King and of Abernathy in this event and examine their leadership styles. You may wish to model the thinking process involved in evaluating.

Model: In this event, I see King motivating the audience with his eloquent words. He drives the emotions of the audience with phrases like *"tired of being kicked about"* and *"there lived a great people."* I see that Abernathy, on the other hand, works on the practical side, explaining the demands and asking people to vote on them. One man leads by exciting emotions; the other leads by organizing a plan of action.

Listening and Speaking *Minilesson*

Effective Listening Techniques Play a recording of a speech by Martin Luther King. Have students listen for the eloquence, the use of figurative language, and the appeal to people's emotions.

Activity Have students listen in small groups with these questions in mind.
• Which words of phrases stirred them most?

• Did they notice the rise and fall of the speaker's voice?
• Which part of the speech won them over to the speaker's point of view?

Ask them to discuss their emotional response to the speech. Students who enjoy public speaking may wish to present a portion of the speech to the class. **L2** **COLLAB. LEARN.**

Literary Elements

TONE Discuss Rosa Parks's tone—her attitude about what she is describing. Point out that though the bus company and city officials were being totally unreasonable and unfair, Rosa's tone is not complaining or bitter. Instead it is matter-of-fact, or reportorial. With very little comment, she simply tells what happened. Ask students to comment on the impact such a tone has on them as readers. *(They may say that this reportorial tone makes the account more believable because they sense that it is being told by a person whose emotions are in check.)*

Active Reading

QUESTION Have students discuss Rosa Parks's and the African American community's attitude toward attempts to thwart the boycott. *(They kept their focus and worked together to find ways to move forward.)*

Literary Elements

SEQUENCE Ask students to scan the page and list the words and phrases that signal time order. *(Examples include the following: Thursday, through that week, then through the next, how long, after that, then, and when.)*

Teaching Options

---

if they wanted to continue the boycott and make the demands. People started getting up, one or two at a time at first, and then more and more, until every single person in that church was standing, and outside the crowd was cheering "Yes!"

Stride Toward Freedom

The following Thursday, December 8, Dr. King and Attorney Fred Gray and others met with the three Montgomery city commissioners and representatives of the bus company. They presented the three demands. The bus company people denied that the drivers were discourteous to black riders and would not hear of hiring any black drivers on the predominantly[8] black routes. They also said the first-come, first-served seating arrangement was in violation of the city's segregation laws. Fred Gray said that wasn't true and that the same bus company allowed that type of arrangement in the city of Mobile, Alabama. But they wouldn't change their minds.

The city commissioners wouldn't go along with any of the demands either. They didn't want to give an inch, not even to reasonable demands. They were afraid of compromising in any way with black people.

The boycott lasted through that week, and then through the next. No one had any idea how long it would last. Some people said it couldn't last, but it seemed like those who said that were the white people and not us. The whites did everything they could do to stop it.

The police started getting after the groups of blacks who were waiting at the

---

8. Here, *predominantly* means "chiefly; for the most part."

bus stops for the black-owned cabs to pick them up. Then they threatened to arrest the cab drivers if they did not charge their regular fare, which I think was forty-five cents, to go downtown instead of ten cents like the buses charged. White private citizens resisted the boycott too.

A lot of people lost their jobs because they supported the boycott. Both Parks and I lost our jobs. . . .

After that I worked at home, taking in sewing. I started traveling quite a bit, making appearances because of my arrest and the boycott. And then I did work for the MIA.

I was on the executive board of directors of the MIA and I did whatever was needed. I dispensed clothing and shoes to people who needed them. We had an abundance of clothing and shoes sent to us from all parts of the country. Many people needed those things because they were out of work and unable to buy clothing. Those who had jobs wore out many pairs of shoes walking to and from work. I also worked for a short while as a dispatcher for the MIA Transportation Committee.

When the police started arresting cab drivers for not charging full fare, the MIA asked for volunteer drivers. Jo Ann Robinson was one. The churches collected money and bought several station wagons. Ordinary black people contributed, and so did some important white people in Montgomery, like the Durrs. As a dispatcher, I was responsible for taking calls from people who needed rides and then making calls to the drivers of private cars and the church station wagons to see that the people were picked up wherever they were.

LIFE SKILLS CONNECTION

Supporting and Contributing Parks reveals that she lost her job because of the boycott. In 1968 Martin Luther King was gunned down because of his role in the Civil Rights movement. Help students understand that a protest is more than speeches, rallies, and TV cameras. Protesters often have to make sacrifices, sometimes major ones for the cause.

Activity Have students work in small groups to list causes, such as those affecting their families, friends, town, and country for which they would be willing to make major sacrifices. Have them identify the sacrifices they would be willing to make and those they would not. **L2**
COLLAB. LEARN.

After a while quite a sophisticated[9] system was developed. There were twenty private cars and fourteen station wagons. There were thirty-two pickup and transfer sites, and scheduled service from five-thirty in the morning until twelve-thirty at night. About 30,000 people were transported to and from work every day. . . .

The Montgomery Improvement Association held regular meetings, every Monday and Thursday night, to keep the people inspired and to talk about the latest problems and what to do about them. January came. The white people were getting angrier and angrier. . . .

Now Mayor Gayle announced that he would no longer negotiate with the boycotters, although we didn't see that he'd been doing much negotiating anyhow. He called the leaders of the boycott a bunch of Negro radicals.[10] There was real violence against the people by this time. Dr. King's home was bombed at the end of January. Two days later Mr. Nixon's home was bombed. Nobody tried to bomb my home, but I did get a lot of threatening telephone calls. They'd say things like, "You're the cause of all this. You should be killed." It was frightening to get those calls, and it really bothered me when Mama answered the telephone and it was one of those calls.

In early February Fred Gray filed suit in U.S. District Court saying that bus

segregation was unconstitutional. By that time the appeal of my case had been thrown out on a technicality,[11] meaning my conviction was upheld. The new suit was our way of getting tough. The City Commission and the bus company and the mayor wouldn't even agree that bus drivers were not polite. Fred Gray wanted to challenge the whole bus-segregation system and go all the way to the Supreme Court. Clifford Durr offered to assist him. The suit was filed on behalf of five women who had been mistreated on the buses.

Meanwhile, the boycott was costing the bus company money. Every day bus after bus would go by with only one or two white riders. Then they stopped running the buses altogether. The boycott was also hurting downtown businesses, and so a group of white businessmen calling themselves Men of Montgomery decided to try to negotiate with the MIA themselves. But nothing came of those meetings.

Around the middle of February a group of white attorneys came up with an old law that prohibited boycotts, and on February 21 a grand jury handed down eighty-nine indictments[12] against Dr. King, more than twenty other ministers, leaders of the MIA, and other citizens. I was reindicted.

We were all fingerprinted. News photographers had heard about the indictments and were there to photograph us being fingerprinted. The picture of me

---

9. A *sophisticated* system is one that is developed to a high degree.
10. A *radical* is someone who supports or demands extreme change.

11. In legal terms, a *technicality* is a very small detail.
12. A *grand jury* is a special jury that hears accusations in criminal cases. If its members decide that there is enough evidence for a trial, they issue an *indictment*, which is the formal legal charge against the accused.

Vocabulary
negotiate (ni gō′ shē āt′) *v.* to discuss in order to bring about an agreement

---

Vo•cab•u•lar•y Skills

Etymology Explain that the word *inspire* means "to fill with a thought or feeling." The word is derived from the Latin *inspirare*, "to breathe into." When a speaker inspires an audience, he or she breathes not air but a thought or feeling into its members. Have students try to figure out the meaning of the word *expire*, which is built on the same root. If they need help, remind them that the prefix *ex-* means "out of," as in *exclude*. (Expire means *"to breathe out, die"*)

BB Critical Thinking

DRAWING CONCLUSIONS Ask students why they think this old law suddenly turned up. What does the unearthing of this law suggest about the attitude of the white attorneys at this point? *(The old law probably came up because the white attorneys were desperately searching for something they could use against the black community.)*

At the MOVIES

The following video puts the events of Rosa Parks's story into a larger context. Be sure to preview the video for appropriateness for your class.

- *The Fateful Decade: From Little Rock to the Civil Rights Bill**

* Also available in the Glencoe Literature *Video Library*

REAL-WORLD CONNECTION

Causes Students may have a better understanding of Rosa Parks's fight in the 1950s if they learn about someone who is working for a cause today.

Activity Have each student locate a magazine or newspaper article about an individual who shows unusual determination in working for a cause. Students may choose current civil rights activists, environmentalists, consumer advocates, or defenders of other causes. Have them consider these questions: What cause is the person working for? What challenges have to be faced? How does the person demonstrate determination in working for the cause? Have the class work in small groups to share their findings. **L2**
COLLAB. LEARN.

Teaching Options

being fingerprinted was carried on the front page of *The New York Times.* In later years people would use that picture thinking it was from my first arrest. The MIA paid everybody's bail, and we were released and went home until the trials started.

The trials began in March, and Dr. King was the first to be tried. It was March 19 and I went down to the courthouse. People crowded around and tried to get inside, but they weren't letting in anyone unless they had a seat. They wouldn't let anyone sit on the floor or stand in the aisle. There were a lot of witnesses in his defense, testifying about conditions on the buses. . . . People were not reluctant to speak out.

They found Dr. King guilty. He was sentenced to pay a $500 fine or serve a year at hard labor. He never did either, because the conviction was appealed successfully. He was the only one they actually tried. But of course he was more determined than ever to continue the boycott, because of the way the city of Montgomery had treated us. The people were willing. All through the spring we walked and carpooled.

Rosa Parks is fingerprinted after she and eighty-eight others were indicted on February 21, 1956 for boycotting the Montgomery buses.

98 🦢 THEME 1

There was a lot of interest in the boy-cott from outside Montgomery now, because of all the attention from the press. I was invited to tell about what had happened to me at various churches, schools, and organizations. I did whatever I could—accepting expense money but no speaking fees—and this helped raise money for station wagons and other expenses. I spent most of the spring making appearances and speeches. Parks was concerned for my safety, but I had no unpleas-ant experiences.

In June a special three-judge federal District Court ruled two to one in favor of our suit against segregation on the buses. But the city commissioners appealed the decision to the U.S. Supreme Court. We knew it would take several months for the Supreme Court to decide.

Summer came and I was back in Mont-gomery. We still stayed off the buses. The white people tried to break the boycott by not giving the church cars any insurance. All the churches operated the station wagons, and had their names on the sides. Without insurance, the cars could not operate legally. Every time they got insurance from a new company, the pol-icy would suddenly be canceled. But Dr. King got in touch with a black insurance agent in Atlanta named T. M. Alexander, and T. M. Alexander got Lloyd's of London, the big insurance company in England, to write a policy for the church-operated cars.

E. D. Nixon escorts Parks up the courtroom steps for the boycott trial in March 1956.

Next, Mayor Gayle went to court to try to get an order preventing black people from gathering on street corners while waiting for the church cars. Mayor Gayle said they were a "public nuisance" because they sang loudly and bothered other peo-ple. He got a court to issue such an order, but that order came on the very same day that the U.S. Supreme Court ruled in our favor, that segregation on the Montgomery buses was unconstitutional.

That was on November 13, 1956. Dr. King called a mass meeting to tell us the news, and everybody was overjoyed. But the MIA did not tell the people to go back on the buses. The written order from the

Literary Elements

MOOD At this point in the story, the boycott has been a success and Rosa is enjoying it. How does Rosa convey that mood? *(She uses the word* honors *sarcastically.)*

Vo•cab•u•lar•y Skills

Antonyms Write the words *segregate* and *integrate* on the board. Explain that *segregate* means "apart from the flock" from the Latin *se* (apart) and *grex* (flock). *Integrate* comes from the Latin *integrare*, meaning "made whole." Have students define the words *segregate* and *integrate* in English, using a dictionary if necessary.

VIEWING THE ART

Viewing Response *Students should recognize that the artist is portraying Parks sympathetically. She is the central figure, dressed in bright red, white, and blue, while the figures of authority beside her appear weaker because of their drab colors, their flatness, and the odd perspective that seems to diminish them in spite of their greater height.*

Thematic Focus

What I Am, What I Want to Be
Every person must face challenges. Some involve doing what is right, even when it is difficult.

☑ ASSESSMENT OPTIONS

📁 **Quick Checks,** p. 10

Teaching Options

Supreme Court would not arrive for another month or so. We stayed off the buses until it was official.

The written order from the U.S. Supreme Court arrived on December 20, and the following day we returned to the buses. The boycott had lasted more than a year. Dr. King, the Reverend Abernathy, Mr. Nixon, and Glen Smiley, one of the few white people in Montgomery who had supported the boycott, made a great show of riding the first integrated bus in Montgomery. . . . Three reporters from *Look* magazine . . . had me get on and off buses so they could take pictures.

James Blake, the driver who'd had me arrested, was the driver of one of the buses I got on. He didn't want to take any honors, and I wasn't too happy about being there myself. I really could have done without that. I got on two different buses, I guess, and each time they took pictures until they were satisfied. The reporter sat behind me each time while the photographer took pictures. . . .

Integrating the Montgomery buses did not go smoothly. Snipers[13] fired at buses, and the city <u>imposed</u> curfews on the buses, not letting them run after five P.M., which meant that people who worked from nine to five couldn't ride the buses home. A group of whites tried to form a whites-only bus line, but that didn't work. The homes and churches of some ministers were bombed, as I mentioned. But eventually most of the violence died down. Black people were not going to be scared off the buses any more than they were going to be scared onto them when they refused to ride.

African Americans in other cities, like Birmingham, Alabama, and Tallahassee, Florida, started their own boycotts of the segregated buses.

The direct-action civil-rights movement had begun.

Civil Rights Activist, 1983. Marshall D. Rumbaugh. Painted limewood, height: 33 in. National Portrait Gallery, Washington, DC. Gift of Barry Bingham.

Viewing the sculpture: How do you think the artist feels about what the sculpture shows? How can you tell?

---

13. *Snipers* are people who shoot at others from concealed places.

❖

Vocabulary
impose (im pōz′) *v.* to apply legally; enforce

Grammar and Language *Minilesson*

Capitalization of Proper Nouns Call students' attention to the capitalized words on this page. Remind them that the first letter of a proper noun is capitalized; for example, months, proper names, and specific organizations, such as *U.S. Supreme Court* and *City Commission*. Nouns that are generic are not capitalized; for example, *bus company* and *mayor*.

Activity Write the following on the board, omitting capitalization. Ask students to tell which words should be capitalized and why they should be.
1. montgomery improvement association *(name of a particular group)*
2. dr. king *(name of person)*
3. attorneys *(generic noun)*
4. december 20 *(name of the month)*
5. boycotts *(generic noun)* **L2** **COLLAB. LEARN.**

Additional Resources
📖 *Grammar and Language Transparency 10*

📘 *Grammar and Language Workbook,* pp. 237–248

📘 *Grammar and Composition Handbook,* Lessons 12.2–12.4

📘 *Writer's Choice,* Lesson 19.2–19.4

Responding to Literature

PERSONAL RESPONSE

- ◆ What questions would you like to ask Rosa Parks about the courage she showed? Record your questions in your journal.
- ◆ Which part of Rosa Parks's experience affected you more as a reader? What details about historic events did you find most surprising? Write your response in your journal.

Analyzing Literature

RECALL

1. Why did Rosa Parks decide not to give up her seat on the bus?
2. Who did Rosa Parks consult before deciding to become a test case for desegregation of buses?
3. How did Dr. Martin Luther King Jr. contribute to the success of the bus boycott?
4. How did the bus boycott make life difficult for local African Americans?

INTERPRET

5. Why, do you think, did Rosa Parks choose to include so many details about the incident on the bus?
6. Why did Parks agree to become a test case and support the boycott? Was she right to be concerned about the results? Explain your answer.
7. Why was Dr. King a good leader for the boycott?
8. In what ways did the African American community show its courage during the boycott?

EVALUATE AND CONNECT

9. Rosa Parks does not reveal very much about her emotions during the difficult year that began with her arrest. Why do you think she chose to use this factual **tone** in her autobiography?
10. If you were living in Alabama during the time of segregation, what do you imagine you would have thought about segregated buses?

LITERARY ELEMENTS

Sequence of Events

In nonfiction, when the writer is describing actual events, **sequence** is extremely important. If the article or book is about important moments in history, having the correct sequence is essential. Rosa Parks helps the reader keep track of sequence by using dates and words that indicate time, such as *then, earlier, eventually, meanwhile,* and *after.*

1. How well does Rosa Parks help the reader keep track of the events during the Montgomery bus boycott? Support your opinion with examples.
2. Find three examples of the use of sequence words in the selection.

● See **Literary Terms Handbook,** p. R10.

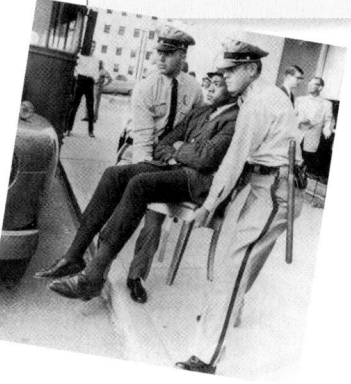

Responding to the Selection

Personal Response

- Among the questions students might ask are: Did Rosa Parks ever feel like giving up the struggle? What sustained her?
- Some students might have been affected most by Parks's determination and courage.

Analyzing Literature

1. She was "tired" of bus segregation and would not put up with it any more.
2. She consulted her husband and mother.
3. Dr. Martin Luther King, Jr. contributed to the success of the boycott by inspiring the people to support it, by enlisting the aid of others who could challenge the issue in court, and by helping to bring national attention to it.
4. Unwilling to use buses, local African Americans had to find other means of transportation. They had to walk, carpool, or wait for cabs.
5. By including so many details about the incident on the bus, Rosa enables the readers to see exactly what happened.
6. Rosa Parks agreed to become a test case because she was tired of bus segregation. Her concern was justified because if they failed, things would be worse than before.
7. Dr. King was a good leader because of his belief in nonviolent protest and his ability to persuade the community to keep fighting nonviolently.
8. The African American community supported the boycott, resisted the pressures to go back to riding the buses, and stood behind Rosa publicly.

LITERARY ELEMENTS

1. Parks does a good job by using such phrases as *next* and *in the morning,* giving dates, and mentioning the seasons, as in *"Summer came and went."*
2. Examples include *"By the time I got home it was nine-thirty,"* *"On the morning of Friday, December 2..."* and *"In June."*

Additional Resources

 Literary Elements Transparency 10

9. The factual tone makes the telling more believable and generates more sympathy from the reader than an emotional outpouring might.
10. Students may focus on the unfairness and injustice of bus segregation, the strength of the leaders and the community, and the restraint they showed in keeping the fight nonviolent.

Extending Your Response

Writing About Literature

Students' summaries should:

- touch upon the major events, but with minimal detail.
- mention those events listed in their Focus Activity that reflect in a general way the actions taken by the civil rights leaders.

Creative Writing

Students' texts should:

- explain the main events.
- recreate those events in short sentences and language children can understand.
- omit complicated issues.

Literature Groups
Remind students that the sketches should require little or no explanation. Viewers should be able to understand the entire incident and message just by looking at the pictures and the few words on the posters. **COLLAB. LEARN.**

Interdisciplinary Activity
Remind students to include only the major events in their time lines.

Performing
Suggest that students use script format for a play, stating each character's name, followed by the words the character is to speak.

Extending Your Response

Writing About Literature
Summarizing A **summary** briefly tells the main ideas, important events, or key points in a piece of writing. The excerpt from *Rosa Parks: My Story* tells about one year in Montgomery, Alabama. Summarize the main events that took place during that year, beginning with Rosa Parks's arrest. Use your list from the **Focus Activity** on page 84 to consider the actions Civil Rights leaders decided would make a difference. Did you think of similar acts?

Creative Writing
Writing the Story of Rosa Parks Using what you know about Rosa Parks's role in the bus boycott, write the text for a children's picture book about this Civil Rights movement heroine. You might want to illustrate your story and present it in a book format.

Literature Groups
Picture It! Imagine that your group has been asked to design a poster to celebrate the anniversary of the Montgomery bus boycott. Discuss a memorable scene from the selection. As a group, assign roles to plan and create a sketch that best represents the boycott. Label the poster and present it to the other groups.

Interdisciplinary Activity
Social Studies—Time Line Study the selection, and take notes on every important date mentioned. Plot out the dates on a time line, and label the major events of the bus boycott. If you can't tell the exact date on which an event occurred, try to figure out which dates the event would fit between and note it in that place on the line. Use your time line to retell the story of the bus boycott to a classmate.

Performing
Create a Skit Rosa Parks has given the reader a minute-by-minute description of the bus ride that led to her arrest. Use her words to write a script to be performed as a short skit. Choose actors for the speaking and nonspeaking parts. Line up desk chairs with an aisle between them to represent the bus.

Reading Further
If you would like to read more about the Civil Rights movement, try these books:
They Had a Dream by Jules Archer
We Shall Overcome by Fred Powledge

📖 **Save your work for your portfolio.**

✓ ASSESSMENT OPTIONS

- 📁 *Quick Checks,* p. 10
- 📁 *Selection and Theme Assessment,* pp. 19–20
- 📁 *Performance Assessment,* p. 10
- 💾 *Testmaker*

Skill Minilessons

GRAMMAR AND LANGUAGE • NOUNS

A *common noun* names any person, place, thing, or idea. A *proper noun* names a specific person, place, thing, or idea. Proper nouns are capitalized.

PRACTICE Write each noun in the sentences below in one of two lists: proper nouns and common nouns. Capitalize any proper nouns.

1. The story of rosa parks is inspiring.
2. Rosa parks showed courage in a simple act.
3. The results of her arrest in montgomery, alabama, still affect life in the united states.
4. No state can make a law that discriminates against individuals.
5. The rights of all people are guaranteed under the federal law of the united states.

● For more about nouns, see **Language Handbook,** p. R29.

READING AND THINKING • CAUSE AND EFFECT

When historians study historic events, they often think in terms of **cause and effect**. Each event was caused by other events. For example, during the Montgomery bus boycott, Rosa Parks refused to give up her seat. The effect was that she was arrested. Her arrest caused people in the Civil Rights movement to start the bus boycott.

PRACTICE Answer these questions about other causes and effects in *Rosa Parks: My Story.*

1. What caused African American cab drivers to stop at all the bus stops?
2. What effect did the availability of inexpensive cab rides have on the African Americans trying to get to work?
3. What effect did Dr. King's speech about the boycott have on the people listening?
4. What action did the city commissioners take because the federal district court ruled against segregation on the buses?
5. What finally caused Montgomery city officials to integrate the city's buses?

● For more about cause and effect, see **Reading Handbook,** p. R85.

VOCABULARY • UNLOCKING MEANING

Sometimes a new word is just a word you know with a prefix or suffix attached. Sometimes it shares a root with a familiar word. Use what you know. For example, now that you know what the verb *mobilize* means, you can guess that the noun *mobilization* means an effort to organize or prepare people and resources for action.

PRACTICE Match each word with its meaning.

1. compliance
2. resignation
3. renegotiate
4. demobilize
5. oppressive

a. to try to reach a new, modified agreement
b. harsh; cruel and unfair
c. a patient, but not happy, acceptance
d. a yielding to authority
e. to return to a normal condition after preparing for an emergency

---

Skill Minilessons

GRAMMAR AND LANGUAGE
NOUNS

Proper Nouns	Common
1. Rosa Parks	story
2. Rosa Parks	courage, act,
3. Montgomery, Alabama, United States	results, arrest, life,
4.	state, law, individuals
5. United States	rights, people, law

READING AND THINKING
CAUSE AND EFFECT

1. People who normally took the buses were boycotting them and needed a ride.
2. They could get there while continuing the boycott indefinitely.
3. Dr. King's speech inspired the people to continue the boycott in non-violent protest.
4. The city commissioners appealed the case to the Supreme Court.
5. The Supreme Court ruled that bus segregation was unconstitutional.

VOCABULARY
UNLOCKING MEANING

1. d	3. a	5. b
2. c	4. e	

Additional Resources

Grammar and Language Workbook, pp. 241–248

Grammar and Composition Handbook, Lesson 2.1

Writer's Choice, Lessons 19.2–19.4

Vocabulary Practice, p. 7

Reading Workbook, pp. 17–18

Writing WORKSHOP

Objectives

- To create a personal connection to literature
- To plan, draft, revise, edit, and present an autobiographical anecdote
- To reflect on and assess the anecdote

GLENCOE
TECHNOLOGY

WRITER'S ASSISTANT
CD-ROM
Students can use Glencoe's templates and guidelines software for narrative writing to aid them in working through the steps in the writing process.

Teaching Strategies

PREWRITING

Gather ideas Have students work in pairs or small groups to talk about significant events from their lives.

Teaching Options

Writing WORKSHOP

Narrative Writing: Autobiographical Anecdote

A story of your own experiences—an **autobiographical anecdote**—can speak to readers in a way that nothing else can. It can also speak to you. When you write an autobiographical anecdote, you may begin to see your experiences in a new light.

Assignment: Write an autobiographical anecdote. Use the process shown in this Workshop to create a piece of writing that will be memorable for your readers.

● As you write your autobiographical anecdote, see **Writing Handbook**, pp. R48–R53.

The Writing Process

PREWRITING

PREWRITING TIP
A small experience that you recall clearly will work better than a big experience that you can only vaguely remember.

● **Gather Ideas**

Which experiences have meant the most to you? Rosa Parks wrote about her involvement in a historic event; Amy Tan and Ernesto Galarza selected more personal experiences to write about. Try the following to get your ideas flowing:

- Brainstorm a list of events in your life, big and small.

- List your experiences by category, such as *funniest, hardest, saddest, most mysterious, most surprising,* or *most rewarding.*

    Choose one event as your topic. To gather the details you'll need, try filling in a chart like the one below.

Event: when my friend Ray fell into the canal				
Sight	**Sound**	**Touch**	**Smell**	**Taste**
brown, surging water	swoosh and churn of water	Ray's slippery hands	musty flood smell	
Ray's frightened eyes	big splash	pull of current		
		knot of fear inside		

MEETING INDIVIDUAL NEEDS — ENGLISH LANGUAGE LEARNERS

An Autobiographical Anecdote
English language learners may find it helpful to have an extended period of discussion and conversation before writing. Make sure that they understand what an anecdote is by offering examples and pointing them out in the selections they have read in class.

Activity Have students work in pairs or small groups to practice telling anecdotes using various forms of communication: illustrations, first language translations, or pantomime. Groups should include fluent English speakers. If writing is too difficult, students may deliver their anecdotes orally. 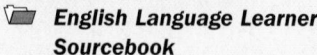 **COLLAB. LEARN.**

Additional Resources
📁 *English Language Learners Sourcebook*

● Know Your Audience and Purpose

Will you write to share an insight? Or will you write simply to entertain? Decide on a purpose. Then consider your audience—probably this will be your classmates and teacher. What information can help them relive your experience? Think of specifics about the time and place and about the people involved—including you. You might jot notes on a story map, as shown below.

● Map It Out

Like a good story, your anecdote will have a beginning, a middle, and an end. Filling in a story map can help you organize all the elements of your anecdote.

Setting by the canal after a storm **People** my friend Ray, age 9, always joking; me, age 9, no confidence	**Beginning** Ray fell in. The current caught him. I grabbed his hand.	**Middle**	**End**

Know Your Audience and Purpose
Help students decide on the purpose of the anecdote and the effect they would like it to have on readers. Would they like to make their readers laugh? think? take action?

Map It Out Model the use of a story map by having students pretend they are Rosa Parks. What would the story map for "Rosa Parks: My Story" look like? For example:
- Setting: *1955, Montgomery, Alabama*
- People: *Rosa, a bus driver, Rosa's lawyer, citizens of Montgomery*
- Beginning: *Rosa refuses to give up her seat on the bus. The driver has her arrested.*
- Middle: *Her lawyer defends Rosa's rights. Rosa's supporters organize a bus boycott. The case goes all the way to the U.S. Supreme Court.*
- End: *U.S. Supreme Court rules in Rosa's favor. Segregation on the Montgomery buses ends.*

Additional Resources

🔖 ***Writing and Proofreading Practice,*** pp. 1–7, 8–14

🔖 ***Writing and Proofreading Transparency*** 1–6, 7–8, 25–26

🔖 ***Writer's Choice,*** Lessons 4.1–4.6

MEETING INDIVIDUAL NEEDS — MULTIPLE LEARNING STYLES

Intrapersonal Students who are self-aware and find it easy to express themselves by probing their own feelings may want to write anecdotes about experiences that taught them something or led to a new insight. For these students, the story maps may be expanded or adapted to include their perceptions before, during, and after the events or experiences.

Activity Have students create new headings for their story maps, such as *How I Felt, What Happened,* and *How This Changed Me.* Encourage them not to become overly concerned with the form of their maps but to concentrate on the content of their experiences. **L2**

Start with Action and Dialogue
Have students recall or guess which selection the following lines are from:

1. The two of us walked south on Fifth Street one morning to the corner of Q Street and turned right. *("Barrio Boy")*
2. When I got off from work that evening of Dec.1, I went to Court Square as usual to catch the Cleveland Avenue bus home. *("Rosa Parks: My Story")*

Have students discuss how each action relates to the rest of the story.

Use Chronological Order Review the sequencing activity students did for page 83. List on the board the words and phrases that indicate time sequence, such as *at first, then, when, the next day,* and *finally.*

REVISING

Consider Changes The revised draft should reflect a more thoughtful perspective. The answer to the last question in "Questions for Revising" could be restated as the theme of the story. As students work in pairs, have each state the other's theme in one sentence.

TECHNOLOGY TIP

Encourage students to use computer spellcheck features to check their work.

Teaching Options

Writing **WORKSHOP**

DRAFTING TIP
Transitions, such as *at first, then, soon, in a few hours, that night,* or *finally,* will help you keep the order of events clear for your readers.

● Start with Action and Dialogue

Action in your first sentence will catch the attention of your readers. Then, set the scene and describe the people involved. Add details from your prewriting notes. Use dialogue to show more about personalities and feelings.

> **MODEL · DRAFTING**
>
> Muddy water surged past our feet. A storm had turned our irrigation canal into a rushing river. Ray struck a goofy pose. "Look!" he laughed. "I'm a surfer!" Then there was a slip and a splash.

● Use Chronological Order

With your story map as a guide, write what happened first, next, and last. You might start a new paragraph whenever the scene or action shifts. At the end, don't just stop. Sum up what the experience meant to you or how it changed you.

REVISING

REVISING TIP
Be sure that your conclusion fits your purpose. To entertain, close with a striking comment or scene. To share an insight, state it clearly at the end.

● Consider Changes

Use the **Questions for Revising** to find ways to strengthen your draft. Plan where you could add details or smooth out rough parts.

Next, ask a classmate to read your anecdote and to retell it. If your reader is confused, you may need to work on the organization of your anecdote. Try rearranging paragraphs or adding transitions.

QUESTIONS FOR REVISING
☑ Do I open with action?
☑ What specific details have I included to help my readers feel the experience?
☑ How have I used dialogue and sensory detail to bring my anecdote to life?
☑ Do I move in chronological order? What transitions have I used to help the reader follow what happens?
☑ Do I show what the experience means to me or how it changed me?

Writing *Minilesson*

Logical Sequence As students revise their work, have them confer with a partner to determine whether their anecdotes follow a logical sequence of events. Remind them that clear order in a story adds to the reader's enjoyment.

Activity Have students work in pairs to help each other outline the events in their anecdotes through illustrations. Ask stu-dents to illustrate each other's anecdote in three or four story panels. Illustrations can be elaborate or simple. Students may use these illustrations in the final presentation of their work. **L2** **COLLAB. LEARN.**

Additional Resources
Writer's Choice, Lesson 4.3

Writing WORKSHOP

EDITING/PROOFREADING

The **Proofreading Checklist** here and on the inside back cover can help you spot errors. To check your sentences for sentence fragments, use information from the **Grammar Link** on page 12.

Grammar Hint

When you review your sentences, check verb tenses. Avoid accidental shifts from past to present tense. Keep tenses consistent.

My hand ached so much, I just gave up. I relaxed my grip, and Ray was gone.

PROOFREADING CHECKLIST
- ☑ Each sentence has a subject and predicate.
- ☑ Verb tenses are consistent.
- ☑ Dialogue is punctuated correctly.
- ☑ End marks and commas are used correctly.
- ☑ Capital letters are used correctly.
- ☑ Spelling is correct.

MODEL · EDITING/PROOFREADING

Ray crawled onto the bank, shivering. "Why did you let go?" he asks. ^ed

PUBLISHING/PRESENTING

Make a neat final copy of your anecdote. You might read it aloud to a small group. Ask group members to write you notes telling you which parts they found most memorable and why.

PRESENTING TIP
When reading aloud, don't rush. Pause for commas, periods, and paragraph breaks.

Reflecting

Write a page exploring your response to these questions:

- Which part of this Workshop did you enjoy most?

- Would you like to write more autobiographical anecdotes? Why or why not?

 Save your work for your portfolio.

Remind students that it is sometimes difficult to see one's own mistakes. The checklist should help them focus on one area at a time while editing and proofreading their work. You may wish to have students exchange papers to help them hone their proofreading skills and collaborate during this part of the process.

Additional Resources
📁 *Grammar and Composition Handbook,* Lesson 16

PUBLISHING/PRESENTING

Students may wish to compile their anecdotes after they read them aloud to the class or a small group. The autobiographical selections in Theme One reflect a variety of experiences, as will the selections written by students. A copy of the student collection could be kept in the classroom to be read by visitors.

Reflecting

💼 **Portfolio** Encourage students to ask themselves these questions as they review their work:

Does my autobiographical anecdote
- express the event clearly?
- have the desired effect on my audience?
- teach me something about myself I did not know before?

 ASSESSMENT OPTIONS

📁 *Writing Assessment and Portfolio Management*
- Writing Assessment, pp. 1–16, 20–22
- Portfolio Management, pp. 17–19

Theme Wrap-Up

Objectives

- To offer a personal response to the selections in this theme
- To write a comparison of two poems
- To complete a self-evaluation, set a goal, and devise a plan for achieving the goal

Responding to the Theme

1. Students should draw on selection content for their explanations.
2. Help students distinguish between ideas they have always had about identity and new ideas based on their reading.
3. Allow time for students to share their job descriptions, self-portraits, or music displays.

Analyzing Literature

Students' writing should

- include a paragraph introducing the two poems.
- compare similarities or differences in imagery, poetic detail, and/or theme.
- use language taken directly from the poems.

Evaluate and Set Goals

Evaluate

Students may wish to discuss their work. You might suggest they develop a class rubric to determine criteria for *outstanding, good, fair,* and *weak* performance ratings.

Set Goals

Students can create a flow chart for setting and meeting goals. Meet with individual students to discuss their plans.

 WHAT I AM, WHAT I WANT TO BE

Theme Wrap-Up

Responding to the Theme

1. Which selection in this theme most helped you think about who you are and what you want to be? Explain your answer.

2. What new thoughts and ideas do you have about the following after reading the selections in this theme?
   - people's feelings and thoughts about their own identities
   - the importance of setting life goals and working hard to achieve those goals

3. Present your theme project to the class.

Analyzing Literature

COMPARE POEMS

Choose two selections from this theme to compare. You may compare the characters, the events, or the themes of the selections. Use quotations from the selections to support your comparison.

Evaluate and Set Goals

1. Which of the following tasks was most rewarding? Which was most difficult?
   - reading and thinking about the selections
   - doing independent writing
   - analyzing the selections in discussions
   - making presentations
   - performing dramatizations
   - doing research

2. Use the following scale to assess your work in this theme. Give at least two reasons for your assessment.
   4 = outstanding   2 = fair
   3 = good   1 = weak

3. Based on what you found difficult in this theme, choose a goal to work toward in the next theme.
   - Write down your goal and three steps you will take to help you reach it.
   - Meet with your teacher to review your goal and your plan for achieving it.

 Build Your Portfolio

SELECT

Choose two pieces of work you did in this theme to include in your portfolio. Use these questions to help you choose.

- Which do you think is your best work?
- Which work "stretched" you the most?
- From which work did you learn the most?
- Which did you enjoy the most?

REFLECT

Write some notes to accompany the pieces you selected. Use these questions to guide you.

- What do you like best about the piece?
- What did you learn from creating it?
- What might you do differently if you were beginning this piece again?

 ASSESSMENT OPTIONS

📁 ***Writing Assessment and Portfolio Management***
- Writing Assessment, pp. 1–16
- Portfolio Management, pp. 17–19

 GLENCOE
TECHNOLOGY

 MINDJOGGER VIDEOQUIZZES
VIDEODISC

Use *MindJogger* to review the Theme 1 content.

 Theme 1
Side A

📼 Also available in VHS.

Reading on Your Own

Have you enjoyed reading the stories and poems in this
theme? If you have, you might try reading the following books.

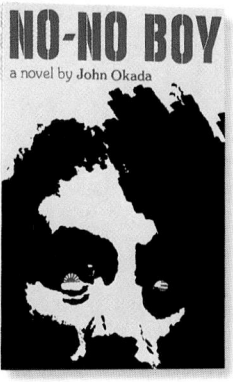

The Witch of Blackbird Pond
by Elizabeth George Speare
In Puritan New England in 1687, a
high-spirited teenager befriends
an old woman known as the
Witch of Blackbird Pond and finds
herself accused of witchcraft.

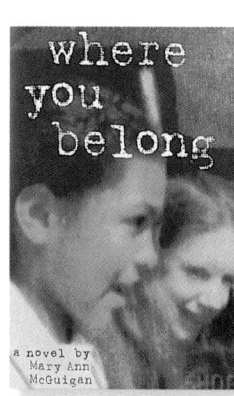

Baseball in April and Other Stories
by Gary Soto Soto's own life while
growing up poor in California's
Central Valley inspired these stories
about Mexican American teenagers
facing the kinds of experiences most
teens face.

No-No Boy
by John Okada Kenji and
Ichiro, two young men sent to
a "relocation camp" when the
United States was fighting
Japan in World War II, take
different routes as they struggle with their identity as
Japanese Americans.

Where You Belong
by Mary Ann McGuigan
Fiona, her mother, and three
siblings are evicted from their
home. After an abusive father
seems to provide no refuge
for her, the thirteen-year-old
Fiona tries to discover where
she belongs.

109

Reading on Your Own

Glencoe Literature Library

Witch of Blackbird Pond by
Elizabeth George Speare is one of
the titles available in the *Glencoe
Library*. For a complete listing, see
pages T46–T47 in this book.

The *Glencoe Literature Library:
Study Guide* provides instructional
support and student activities for
works in the *Glencoe Literature
Library*.

MEETING INDIVIDUAL NEEDS — INCLUSION STRATEGIES

You may wish to suggest to less-proficient students that they read one or
more of the short stories in Gary
Soto's *Baseball in April and Other
Stories*. Soto's stories are written in
simple, straightforward prose and are of
high interest to adolescent readers. **L1**

The following books are rated L2 for
average readers or L3 for students who
need more challenging material
• *The Witch of Blackbird Pond* **L2**
• *No-No Boy* **L2**
• *Where You Belong* **L3**

Additional Resource
📁 *Inclusion Strategies*

Standardized Test Practice

Standardized Test Practice

Read the following passage. Then read each question on page 111. Decide which is the best answer to each question. Mark the letter for that answer on your paper.

Randy's First Job

Mr. Krauzer seemed pleased with Randy's application for a job as stock boy. He gestured toward the aisles of groceries. "We need an accurate inventory," he said. "Are you up to it? Here's an instruction page. Look it over, and we'll talk about it."

Inventory Instructions
Fill out all parts of the inventory page. Accuracy is very important.

1   Fill in the appropriate information at the top of the inventory sheet.

2   List the items and the price per unit. Record the number of units on the shelf in the TALLY column.

3   If an item is on sale, put an X in the appropriate column.

4   Do not record more than one aisle's inventory on a single sheet. Do not use two sheets to record the inventory of a single aisle.

5   Double-check all information.

6   When you are satisfied that the report is accurate, sign your name and write your employee number at the bottom before submitting it to the manager on duty.

7   Bring your finished inventory sheets to the manager on duty.

INVENTORY SHEET

Date May 5, 1999
Aisle 3

Item	Tally	Price	Sale
Juicy O's 8 oz. Cans	25	$0.99	X
Jalapeño Rings	35	1.09	
Stewed Tomatoes in Water	15	0.89	
Miller's Premium Sardines	20	1.99	X

Joe Johnson

Joe Johnson
Employee Number   410

1 According to the sample, what is the last thing a stock boy needs to include on his Inventory Sheet?

  A His address

  B The date of the inventory

  C His employee number

  D Whether or not an item is on sale

2 What is the main idea of the passage?

  F Stock boys should follow instructions.

  G Mr. Krauzer is happy to have a new worker.

  H Sale items are important to Krauzer's business.

  J Inventory tallies are important for accurate record keeping.

3 What information is NOT found on the sample Inventory Sheet?

  A The number of items on the shelves for each type of item

  B The signature of the person taking inventory

  C Whether or not an item is on sale

  D The difference between the sale price and the regular price

4 What is a FACT in this passage?

  F The inventory system at Krauzer's is remarkably efficient.

  G Double-checking your tallies is a sure-fire way to avoid making mistakes.

  H It is necessary to note when items are on sale.

  J More than one aisle's inventory is supposed to be recorded on a single regular Inventory Sheet.

5 In this passage, the word submitting means —

  A giving

  B being defeated

  C hiding

  D recording

6 All finished sheets should be —

  F filed in the office at the end of each day

  G brought to the manager on duty

  H given to Mr. Krauzer

  J filled out in triplicate

Answers and Analyses

1. **C** Remind students to read the question carefully. The question asks for the *last* thing to be included. According to point 6 of the instructions, he should write his *employee number* at the bottom before submitting the sheet. Therefore the correct answer is C.

2. **J** Although choice F and H may be true, neither is mentioned in the passage itself. Choice G may be tempting, but that Mr. Krauzer *seemed pleased* is just a fact mentioned and not the main idea. In the opening paragraph, Mr. Krauzer says *We need an accurate inventory,* then he gives Randy instructions on how to do just that. Therefore the most reasonable choice is J.

3. **D** Choice A is to be found on the sheet, under the column *Tally.* Choice B is to be found on the sheet, at the bottom. Choice C is to be found on the sheet, under the column *Sale.* Only choice D is not to be found, and is therefore the answer.

4. **H** Choices F and G are not stated in the passage, and choice J is contradicted by information in the passage. Point 3 of the instructions supports choice H.

5. **A** Students should consider the context of the word *submitting* to help figure out its meaning. Instruction point 6 says that Randy should *submit* his sheet to the manager on duty; in point 7, this is re-stated as *bring* the sheet to the manager on duty. The word, *submit,* must therefore mean something like *bring.* The closest choice is A.

6. **G** According to point 7 of the instructions, finished inventory sheets should be brought to the manager on duty.

Tested Objectives

Questions	Reading Objective
1, 3	Analyze information to make inferences and generalizations
2	Summarize a variety of written texts
4	Recognize points of view, propaganda, and/or statements of fact and nonfact
5	Determine the meaning of words
6	Perceive relationships and recognize outcomes

MORE PRACTICE

For additional practice, assign practice pages from one of the following standardized test resources available as part of Glencoe Literature.

Additional Resources
ITBS Preparation and Practice
SAT-9 Preparation and Practice
Terra Nova Preparation and Practice

THEME OPENING → Theme 2: WINDS OF CHANGE

- **Introducing the Theme** (p. 113)
- **Exploring the Theme** (p. 114)
- **Theme Projects** (p. 115)

SELECTIONS

Hollywood and the Pits (p. 116)

Media Connection: Time to Change (p. 131)

Growing Pains (p. 132)

Media Connection: *from* **The N.B.A.'s Sister Act** (p. 136)

Slam, Dunk, and Hook (p. 137)

Active Reading Model: A Crush (p. 148)

Last Cover (p. 162)

Birthday Box (p. 174)

There Is No Word for Goodbye (p. 174)

Rip Van Winkle (p. 184)
old age sticks (p. 204)

SKILL FEATURES

Interdisciplinary Connection (p. 130)

Reading and Thinking Skills (p. 142)

Vocabulary Skills (p. 143)

Genre Focus: Short Story (pp. 144–145)

Active Reading Strategies (pp. 146-147)

Technology Skills (pp. 160–161)

Grammar Link (p. 182)

Writing Skills (p. 183)

WRITING WORKSHOP

Exposition: Compare-and-Contrast Essay (pp. 208–211)

THEME WRAP-UP

- **Responding to the Theme, Analyzing Literature, Evaluate and Set Goals** (p. 212)
- **Build Your Portfolio** (p. 212)
- **Reading on Your Own** (p. 213)
  So Far from the Bamboo Grove by Yoko Kawashima Watkins
  Come Sing, Jimmy Jo by Katherine Paterson
  Things Change by Troy Aikman
  The Autobiography of Miss Jane Pittman by Ernest J. Gaines
- **Standardized Test Practice** (pp. 214–215)

KEYS TO LITERARY CONNECTIONS

 Comparing Selections

The **Comparing Selections** feature in this theme provides opportunities for addressing diverse aspects of the reading and literature curriculum.

For example, in Comparing Selections on page 207, students look closely at the journeys from youth to old age in Washington Irving's "Rip Van Winkle" and E. E. Cummings's "old age sticks." Through this comparison, students can gain insight attitudes toward aging.

KEYS TO TEACHING OPTIONS

 Block Scheduling

Activities that are particularly suited to use within a block scheduling framework are identified throughout this theme by the following designation: For detailed suggestions on block scheduling, see the **Block Scheduling Guide** for this grade level.

Key to Ability Levels

The Teaching Options throughout this theme have been coded for students of various abilities.

L1 BASIC activities for all students

L2 AVERAGE activities for average to above-average students

L3 CHALLENGING activities for above-average students

Reading Skills in this theme

Variety of Texts

In addition to a group of short stories, this theme includes the following text types:
- autobiographical story
- poetry
- cartoon
- song
- magazine article

Comprehension Skills

The following instructional support for comprehension skills appears in this theme of the Student Edition:
- **Reading and Thinking Minilessons** (pp. 129, 135, 159, 173, 203)
- **Main Idea and Supporting Details** (p. 142)
- **Active Reading Strategies and Model** (pp. 146–159)

See also the **Reading Minilessons** throughout the theme in this Teacher's Wraparound Edition.

Reading Resources

Comprehension Skills Resources

Active Reading Guides

The **Active Reading Guide** provides graphic organizers and study guide questions to support students' reading of each selection. (**Active Reading Guide**, pp. 11–18)

Reading Workbook

The **Reading Workbook** (pp. 19–30) includes additional instruction and reinforcement of reading strategies and skills.

Audio Library

Available both on tape and on CD, the **Audio Library** provides valuable comprehension support.

Resources for Reading Widely

Glencoe Literature Library

Each title in the *Glencoe Literature Library* includes a full-length novel or play plus related readings. A separate Study Guide is available for each title.

Literature Classics CD-ROM

The selections on this CD-ROM can be searched by author, theme, or genre.

A coproduction of Glencoe and Time, Inc., the *inTime* magazine includes a wealth of high interest nonfiction related to the selections in Theme Two.

Assessment in this theme

Assessment Options in the Student Edition

Glencoe Literature offers a number of diverse ways to evaluate student understanding and skill proficiency. In the Student Edition, use the following:

- **Responding to Literature**

  Following each selection, students are asked to recall facts, interpret ideas, and evaluate concepts as they answer a variety of questions and complete activities to extend their understanding.

- **Theme Wrap-Up (pp. 212–213)**

  Here students respond to the selections on personal and analytical levels. They also assume ownership of their learning by setting and evaluating goals and by selecting work for their portfolios.

See also the many **Assessment Resources** listed on the facing page.

THE PRINCETON REVIEW

Standardized Test Practice

The Princeton Review has developed the Standardized Test Practice pages found at the end of this theme (pp. 214–215). These pages contain practice test questions that help students remain familiar with standardized test formats and content.
- ITBS Preparation and Practice
- SAT-9 Preparation and Practice
- TerraNova Preparation and Practice

Writing Skills in this theme

Writing Skills

The Student Edition of Theme Two offers strong instructional support for writing skills:

In **Extending Your Response**, which follows each selection:
- **Writing About Literature**
- **Personal/Creative Writing**

See also the **Writing Minilessons** throughout the theme in this Teacher's Wraparound Edition.

Writing Workshops

Theme Two concludes with a **Writing Workshop** that guides students through the process of writing a compare-and-contrast essay (pp. 208–211).

Writing Resources

Writer's Assistant CD-ROM

Each Writing Workshop is supplemented by an interactive writing guide on the Writer's Assistant CD-ROM. This easy-to-use writing guide provides prompts, templates, and other tools that lead students through the writing process.

Writing and Proofreading Practice

Blackline masters present in-depth instruction and practice on a specific step in the writing process and proofreading (pp. 1–7, 15–21).

Writing and Proofreading Transparencies

Transparencies provide graphic organizers and proofreading exercises for whole-class instruction (pp. 1–6, 9–10, 27–28).

Research and Report Writing Guide

This resource provides extensive tips and activities to guide students in their writing projects in the literature classroom as well as in classes across the curriculum.

Style and Documentation Sourcebook for Writers

This sourcebook is a combination reference and workbook, giving students the most up-to-date information and guidance regarding traditional as well as technological research strategies and documentation.

Grammar and Composition Handbook

The Grammar and Composition Handbook provides instruction that supplements activities in the student textbook.

Assessment Resources

Selection Quick Checks

For each selection, a Quick Check of three to five short-answer questions measures students' literal comprehension.

Selection and Theme Assessment

The Selection and Theme Assessment instrument tests students' abilities to recall, interpret, and evaluate what they've read. The tests consist of multiple-choice, short answer, and essay questions.

Performance Assessment

Alternative assessment instruments and rubrics for Theme Two are found in the Performance Assessment ancillary.

Writing Assessment and Portfolio Management

These notes and strategies, student models, and assessment tools assist with the task of measuring students' progress as writers and as monitors of their own writing.

Testmaker

Teachers can customize selection and Theme Two tests by accessing the Testmaker database.

Mindjogger Videoquizzes

Using a popular game show format, Mindjogger Videoquizzes enable teachers to evaluate student understanding of Theme Two in a quick and fun manner.

Theme 2 SKILLS SCOPE AND SEQUENCE

SELECTIONS	Literary Elements	Reading and Thinking	Writing	Vocabulary and Spelling	
Hollywood and the Pits CHERYLENE LEE	Symbol, SE p. 127 *Flashback, TWE p. 118* *Character, TWE pp. 118, 124* *Symbol, TWE pp. 119, 121, 122, 125* *Point of View, TWE p. 119* *Figures of Speech, TWE p. 121*	Cause and Effect, SE p. 129 *Inferring, TWE pp. 119, 124* *Evaluating, TWE pp. 120, 122* *Identifying Author's Purpose, TWE p. 121* *Drawing Conclusions, TWE pp. 125, 126*	Point of View, SE p. 128 Letter, SE p. 128 *Compare and Contrast Paragraph, TWE p. 119*	Related Forms of Words, SE p. 129	
Growing Pains JEAN LITTLE	Mood, SE p. 134 *Mood, TWE p. 133*	Sequence of Events, SE p. 135	Rhythm in Poetry, SE p. 135 Poetry, SE p. 135		
Slam, Dunk, & Hook YUSEF KOMUNYAKAA	Alliteration, SE p. 140 *Alliteration, TWE p. 138*	*Inferring, TWE p. 138* **COLLAB. LEARN.** *Monitoring Comprehension, TWE p. 139*	Paragraph: Sensory Imagery, SE p. 141 Poem or Paragraph: Opinion, SE p. 141		
A Crush CYNTHIA RYLANT	First- and Third-Person Point of View, SE p. 157 *Third-Person Point of View, TWE pp. 150, 151, 154*	Inference, SE p. 159 *Activating Prior Knowledge, TWE p. 151* *Drawing Conclusions, TWE p. 152* *Inferring, TWE p. 153*	Paragraph: Character Description, SE p. 158 Letter of Advice, SE p. 158	The Suffix *-ly*, SE p. 159	
Last Cover PAUL ANNIXTER	Plot, SE p. 171; *TWE pp. 164, 167, 168, 170* *Foreshadowing, TWE p. 164* *Character, TWE p. 166* *Flashback, TWE p. 166* *Mood, TWE p. 170*	Predicting, SE p. 173 *Identifying Cause-Effect Relationships, TWE p. 165* *Drawing Conclusions, TWE p. 167* *Inferring, TWE pp. 168, 170* *Sequencing, TWE p. 169*	Paragraph: Characterization, SE p. 172 Journal Entry, SE p. 172 *Descriptive Details, TWE p. 169*	Roots, SE p. 173 *Word Meanings, TWE p. 164*	
Birthday Box JANE YOLEN **There Is No Word for Goodbye** MARY TALLMOUNTAIN	Character, SE p. 181 *Character, TWE pp. 176, 178* *Description, TWE p. 177* *Symbol, TWE p. 177* *Metaphor, TWE p. 179*	*Verifying Predictions, TWE p. 177* *Monitoring Comp., TWE p. 177* *Focusing on a Question, TWE p. 179*	Paragraph: Setting, SE p. 181 Symbolic Gift, SE p. 181	Negative Prefixes, SE p. 181	
RIP VAN WINKLE WASHINGTON IRVING	Setting, SE p. 201; *TWE pp. 186, 189, 191, 194, 195* *Style, TWE pp. 186, 200* *Tone, TWE pp. 187, 193, 200* *Characterization, TWE pp. 187, 198* *Setting, TWE p. 190* *Author's Purpose, TWE p. 193* *Dialogue, TWE p. 198*	Evaluating, SE p. 203 *Making Critical Judgments, TWE p. 187* *Identifying Bias, TWE p. 189* *Inferring, TWE pp. 192, 199* *Drawing Conclusions, TWE pp. 194, 199* *Logical Reasoning, TWE p. 197* *Identifying Assumptions, TWE p. 199*	Paragraph: Theme, SE p. 202 Diary Entry, SE p. 202 **COLLAB. LEARN.** *Describing a Person, TWE p. 187* *Setting a Mood, TWE p. 193* *Describing with Detail, TWE p. 195*	Synonyms and Antonyms, SE p. 203 *Prefixes, TWE p. 187* *Context Clues, TWE p. 191* *Synonyms, TWE p. 196* *Word Meanings, TWE p. 198*	
old age sticks E. E. CUMMINGS	Style, SE p. 206 *Free Verse, TWE p. 205*		Advice Column, SE p. 206		

Key: Student material is in roman. Teacher material is in italic.   🖳 Technology   **COLLAB. LEARN.** Collaboration

Grammar and Language	Listening, Speaking, and Viewing	Life Skills	Study, Research, and Technology
Italics, SE p. 129 *Intensifiers, TWE p. 126*	**COLLAB. LEARN.** Literature Groups, SE p. 128 **COLLAB. LEARN.** *Music, TWE p. 125*	News Broadcast, SE p. 128	💻 Internet Connection, SE p. 128 **COLLAB. LEARN.** *Geologic Era, TWE p. 122* 💻 *Music, TWE p. 125*
	COLLAB. LEARN. Literature Groups, SE p. 135 **COLLAB. LEARN.** Set Words to Music, SE p. 135		
Vivid Verbs, SE p. 141	**COLLAB. LEARN.** Lit. Grp., SE p. 141 **COLLAB. LEARN.** Group Dramatization, SE p. 141 *Viewing, TWE p. 139*		
Adverb Clauses, SE p. 159 *Capitalization, TWE p. 156*	**COLLAB. LEARN.** Literature Groups, SE p.158 **COLLAB. LEARN.** *Role-Playing a Conversation, TWE p. 154*	Letter Writing: Job Description, SE p. 158	Community Services, SE p. 158 **COLLAB. LEARN.** *Human Interest Articles, TWE p. 155*
Commas Used with Words in a Series, SE p. 173 *Commas and Conjunctions, TWE p. 168*	**COLLAB. LEARN.** Literature Groups, SE p. 172 Dramatizing a Scene, SE p. 172		**COLLAB. LEARN.** *Foxes, TWE p. 167*
Appositives, TWE p. 178	**COLLAB. LEARN.** Literature Groups, SE p. 181	Speech for Support Group, SE p. 181	
Adverbs, SE p. 203 *Semicolons, TWE p. 190* *Hyphens, TWE p. 192* *Capitalizing Proper Nouns, TWE p. 200*	**COLLAB. LEARN.** Literature Groups, SE p. 202 *Interviewing, TWE p. 198*	Writing a Newspaper Article, SE p. 202	**COLLAB. LEARN.** *Hudson River, TWE p. 199*
	COLLAB. LEARN. Literature Groups, SE p. 206		

SELECTIONS	📂 Print Resources		

Hollywood and the Pits
CHERYLENE LEE
	Theme Two Planning Guide,
	  pp. 6–13
	* Active Reading Guide, p. 11
	Vocabulary Practice, p. 8
		Grammar & Comp. Handbook,
		  Lessons 6.2, 13.6
		Grammar & Language Workbook,
		  pp. 129–130, 271–272
		Reading Workbook, pp. 19–20
			* Quick Checks, p. 11
			Selection and Theme Assessment,
			  pp. 21–22
			Performance Assessment, p. 11
			Spanish Summaries, p. 11
			Spanish Translations

Growing Pains
JEAN LITTLE
	Theme Two Planning Guide,
	  pp. 14–18
	* Active Reading Guide, p. 12
			* Quick Checks, p. 12
			Selection and Theme Assessment,
			  p. 23
			Performance Assessment, p. 12
			Spanish Summaries, p. 12
			Spanish Translations

Slam, Dunk, & Hook
YUSEF KOMUNYAKAA
	Theme Two Planning Guide,
	  pp. 19–23
	* Active Reading Guide, p. 13
		Grammar & Comp. Handbook,
		  Lesson 3.1
		Grammar & Language Workbook,
		  pp. 73–74
		Reading Workbook, pp. 21–22
			* Quick Checks, p. 13
			Selection and Theme Assessment,
			  p. 24
			Performance Assessment, p. 13
			Spanish Summaries, p. 13
			Spanish Translations

A Crush
CYNTHIA RYLANT
	Theme Two Planning Guide,
	  pp. 24–31
	* Active Reading Guide, p. 14
	Vocabulary Practice, p. 9
		Grammar & Comp. Handbook,
		  Lessons 8.5, 12.1–12.4
		Grammar & Language Workbook,
		  pp. 159–160, 235–246
		Reading Workbook, pp. 23–24
			* Quick Checks, p. 14
			Selection and Theme Assessment,
			  pp. 25–26
			Performance Assessment, p. 14
			Spanish Summaries, p. 14
			Spanish Translations

Last Cover
PAUL ANNIXTER
	Theme Two Planning Guide,
	  pp. 32–39
	* Active Reading Guide, p. 15
	Vocabulary Practice, p. 10
		Grammar & Comp. Handbook,
		  Lessons 13.2, 13.3
		Grammar & Language Workbook,
		  pp. 255–258
		Reading Workbook, pp. 25–26
			* Quick Checks, p. 15
			Selection and Theme Assessment,
			  pp. 27–28
			Performance Assessment, p. 15
			Spanish Summaries, p. 15

Birthday Box   JANE YOLEN
There Is No Word for Goodbye   MARY TALLMOUNTAIN
	Theme Two Planning Guide,
	  pp. 40–45
	* Active Reading Guide, p. 16
	Vocabulary Practice, p. 11
		Grammar & Comp. Handbook,
		  Lesson 2.5
		Grammar & Language Workbook,
		  pp. 69–70
		Reading Workbook, pp. 27–28
			* Quick Checks, p. 16
			Selection and Theme Assessment,
			  pp. 29–30
			Performance Assessment, p. 16
			Spanish Summaries, p. 16

RIP VAN WINKLE
WASHINGTON IRVING
	Theme Two Planning Guide,
	  pp. 46–53
	* Active Reading Guide, p. 17
	Vocabulary Practice, p. 12
		Grammar & Comp. Handbook, Lessons
		  6.1, 6.2, 12.1–12.4, 13.5, 13.8
		Grammar & Language Workbook,
		  pp. 127–128, 235–246, 265–266,
		  275–276
		Reading Workbook, pp. 29–30
			* Quick Checks, p. 17
			Selection and Theme Assessment,
			  pp. 31–32
			Performance Assessment, p. 17
			Spanish Summaries, p. 17
			Spanish Translations

old age sticks
E. E. CUMMINGS
	Theme Two Planning Guide,
	  pp. 54–58
	* Active Reading Guide, p. 18
			* Quick Checks, p. 18
			Selection and Theme Assessment,
			  pp. 31–32
			Performance Assessment, p. 17
			Spanish Summaries, p. 18

*Also available in Spanish

Transparencies	Technology Resources
Selection Focus Transparency 11 Grammar and Language Transparency 11 Literary Elements Transparency 11 Fine Art Transparency 17	Literature Launchers Audio Library Spanish Audio Library Vocabulary Puzzlemaker Web Site: lit.glencoe.com
Selection Focus Transparency 12 Literary Elements Transparency 12	Audio Library Spanish Audio Library Vocabulary Puzzlemaker Web Site: lit.glencoe.com
Selection Focus Transparency 13 Literary Elements Transparency 13	Literature Launchers Audio Library Spanish Audio Library Vocabulary Puzzlemaker Web Site: lit.glencoe.com
Selection Focus Transparency 14 Grammar and Language Transparency 12 Literary Elements Transparency 14	Audio Library Spanish Audio Library Vocabulary Puzzlemaker Web Site: lit.glencoe.com
Selection Focus Transparency 15 Grammar and Language Transparency 13 Literary Elements Transparency 15	Audio Library Spanish Audio Library Vocabulary Puzzlemaker Web Site: lit.glencoe.com
Selection Focus Transparency 16 Grammar and Language Transparency 14 Literary Elements Transparency 16 Fine Art Transparency 30	Audio Library Spanish Audio Library Vocabulary Puzzlemaker Web Site: lit.glencoe.com
Selection Focus Transparency 17 Grammar and Language Transparencies 16–18 Literary Elements Transparency 17 Fine Art Transparency 14	Literature Launchers Audio Library Spanish Audio Library Vocabulary Puzzlemaker Web Site: lit.glencoe.com
Selection Focus Transparency 18 Literary Elements Transparency 18	Audio Library Spanish Audio Library Vocabulary Puzzlemaker Web Site: lit.glencoe.com

Theme RESOURCES

- Listening and Speaking Activities (pp. 4–6)
- Viewing and Representing Activities (pp. 1–6, 10–12)
- Critical Thinking Skills (pp. 5–6)
- Media Connection Activities (pp. 3–4)
- Interdisciplinary Activities (pp. 6–9)
- Family and Community Activities (p. 12)
- Selection and Theme Assessment (pp. 127–128)

See also these additional planning resources:
- English Language Learners Sourcebook
- Inclusion Strategies Sourcebook
- Literature Groups Sourcebook

Use Glencoe's *Presentation Plus!* This multimedia teaching tool lets you present dynamic lessons that will engage your students. Using Microsoft PowerPoint®, you can customize the presentation to create your own personalized lessons.

THEME 2

Winds of Change

Theme Objectives

- To enjoy reading about the excitement, growth, and wisdom brought about by change
- To analyze the literary elements in poetry and short story selections
- To apply strategies for reading short stories

Teaching Strategies

Have students read the quotation from "I Know Why the Caged Bird Sings," by Maya Angelou in preparation for the discussion questions below.

VIEWING THE ART

Diane Griffiths is a British artist, printmaker, and ceramicist.

Responding to the Art
Discussion questions:
- How does this piece of art reflect the theme? (*It illustrates a wind that will bring a change.*)
- What kind of change does it illustrate? (*It seems to illustrate a change of seasons.*)

Winds of Change

> ❝ *The need for change bulldozed a road down the center of my mind.* ❞
>
> —Maya Angelou, *I Know Why the Caged Bird Sings*

Hawthorne Dusk, 1996. Diane Griffiths. Watercolor and crayon, 60 x 75 cm. The Grand Design Gallery, Leeds, England.

112

TEACHER to TEACHER

TIOSPAYE TOPA CHEYENNE RIVER AGENCY • EAGLE BUTTE, SOUTH DAKOTA

Our school is located in an isolated region, and for my students, the theme "Winds of Change" is often represented by changes in technology, which they have little exposure to. However, cultural heritage and traditions play an important role in their lives, so it is natural for me to talk about Native American history and the changes that occurred in Native American cultures over the past 200 years. The concept of directions has significance in our way of thinking, so using North, South, East and West, I talk about how things were long ago, how they were not so long ago, how they are today and where we are headed in the future. I use a circle and point out that things in our lives have a way of going around, but we never return to the beginning and the circle never ends, so there is constant change.

BRANDI THOMAS

THEME 2

THEME CONTENTS

Hollywood and the Pits •
    short story by Cherylene Lee 117

Growing Pains • poem by Jean Little 133

Slam, Dunk, & Hook •
    poem by Yusef Komunyakaa 138

 GENRE FOCUS *SHORT STORY*

A Crush • by Cynthia Rylant 149

Last Cover • by Paul Annixter 163

Birthday Box • by Jane Yolen 175

There Is No Word for Goodbye •
    poem by Mary TallMountain 179

Rip Van Winkle • by Washington Irving 185

old age sticks • poem by E. E. Cummings 205

RESOURCE MANAGER

See the *Theme Two Planning Guide* (pp. 1–5) for additional teaching notes, strategies, and resources for introducing the theme "Winds of Change."

Introducing the Theme

Direct your students' attention to the **Theme Contents.** Ask them to read through the list of selections. Present these questions for discussion:

- Considering the titles, what do you think this theme will focus on? *(Students may say age or growing up.)*
- Does any one title catch your interest? Which one, and why? *(Students who are interested in sports may point out "Slam, Dunk, & Hook," a title that consists of basketball terms.)*
- Have you ever read the story of Rip Van Winkle before? If so, how might it relate to other titles in the theme's contents? *(Students might note that many changes occur while Rip Van Winkle is asleep and that some of the other titles also suggest growth, change, and transition.)*

LITERATURE & HUMANITIES

Have students examine *The Red Stairway* from *U. S. History and Art,* Transparency 2, a painting of an area that has been devastated by a disaster. Then have them discuss whether the actions of the figure on the stairs are hopeful or hopeless.

GLENCOE TECHNOLOGY

 LITERATURE CLASSICS CD-ROM
Search for other short selections related to the theme "Winds of Change."

Exploring the Theme

Winds of Change

Ask students to think of quotations, sayings, song lyrics, proverbs, or phrases they have heard that express people's attitudes toward change. You may wish to offer examples, such as

- *Change is gonna do you good; Don't go changing.* (song lyrics)
- *The more things change, the more they stay the same.* (French proverb)
- *Fear No Change.* (popular expression)
- *Everything changes. Nothing stays the same. That's life.* (Buddhist teaching)

  Or, you may wish to offer Fine Art Transparency 18 as an example of a visual expression.

Have each student make up a saying or proverb that expresses his or her attitude toward change.

Starting Points

Times Change

Students might mention things Calvin's father may have done as a child, such as playing sports, hiking and swimming, or riding his bike.

- Activities could include Rollerblading (in-line skating), video and computer games, or going to the mall.
- Encourage students to name the specific time periods to which they traveled in their time machines.
- Suggest that teenagers from their parents' generations would not be as shocked by television, video, and computer activities as would teenagers living a few hundred years ago or in prehistoric times.

Change Is in the Air

Students may note changes in their school activities, family life, attitudes, and friendships. Students might like to change aspects of themselves or their situations that are problems for them, and might like to have the most positive parts of their lives and the people they love stay the same.

Exploring the Theme

Winds of Change

Life never stays the same. The world is constantly changing. In this theme, you will meet people who learn to deal with changes within themselves and in their lives. Try one of the options below to start thinking about the theme of change.

Starting Points

TIMES CHANGE

Think of several things Calvin's father may have done as a child on a nice day. Then think about an invention, a game, or another activity you enjoy that did not exist when your parents were your age.

- Work with a partner. Role-play a trip in a time machine. Introduce your invention, game, or activity to a teenager from the past.

CHANGE IS IN THE AIR

Think about the changes in your own life. Write a few notes to answer these questions.

- What has changed in your life in the last few years? What effect have these changes had?
- What would you like to change about your life? What would you like to always stay the same?

Calvin and Hobbes

114 🐛 THEME 2

Ask students to list three strategies for changing something they would like to change and another three strategies for preserving something they want to stay the same. Have them discuss their strategies with partners.

Changing Times Students can use a search engine to find out more about change over the centuries. They might use keywords such as *history, music, dress,* or any other point of interest.

Theme Projects

As you read the selections in this theme, try out one of these projects. Work on your own, with a partner, or with a group.

LEARNING FOR LIFE
Writing a Proposal
How can your school be improved? Develop a proposal addressed to the board of education. Think about improvements that could be made without spending a huge amount of time or money. Suggest ideas for ways to accomplish your goals. Draft your proposal and share it with your class.

CRITICAL VIEWING
Picturing Myself in the Future
What will you be doing ten years from now? Where will you live? How will your life be different?

1. List changes you think might happen to you in the next ten years. Will you go to college? Have a job? Travel? Have a family?
2. Draw a picture or make a collage showing how your life may change in the future.

inter**NET** CONNECTION

Search the Web for more project ideas. Also, find out what other students think about selections in this theme. Use this address: lit.glencoe.com

MULTIMEDIA PROJECT
Create a Visual History Exhibit
Use collected photographs and objects to create a history exhibit of your city, town, or neighborhood that shows how it has changed over the years.

1. Find and copy pictures that show the oldest buildings and the people who lived or worked in them. Gather objects from your local historical society, historians, neighbors, and your local government.
2. Design an exhibit that compares then and now. Include photographs, documents, and objects from the past and present.

WINDS OF CHANGE 115

Theme Projects

Teaching Strategies

These ideas may help students carry out their theme projects.

Learning for Life
- Help students develop a list of realistic improvements.
- Suggest students poll other students to find out whether the change would be popular.
- Invite students to attend a school board meeting and observe how issues and proposals are handled.

Critical Viewing
- When creating their portraits of the future, students should include many aspects of their lives: work, home, school, friends, and family.
- As an alternative to drawing pictures or making collages, students could paint murals for their portraits of the future.

Multimedia Project
- Suggest that students interview longtime residents of the towns or cities they live in to gather reminiscences for their project.
- Encourage students to locate old family-owned businesses and find out how changing economic times have affected them.
- You may wish to have students do this project as a class, with different groups focusing on different parts of the project.

Additional Resources
- 📁 *Interdisciplinary Activities,* pp. 6–9
- 📁 *Viewing and Representing Activities,* pp. 10–12
- 📁 *Listening and Speaking Activities,* pp. 4–6
- 📁 *Critical Thinking Skills,* pp. 5–6
- 📁 *Selection and Theme Assessment,* pp. 127–128
- 📁 *Performance Assessment,* p. 70

Family and Community Activity

Ask students to identify places in their school they would like to beautify. For example, a dry patch of grass could become an herb garden, or a bare hallway could be transformed into a gallery featuring rotating parent, teacher, or student art exhibitions. Have the class agree on one place and create a specific plan and time frame for its beautification program. If they need materials, encourage them to have a fund-raiser or seek donations of the materials from their community. Take pictures before, during, and after the beautification program. Invite students to chronicle the change in a class journal.

Additional Resources
- 📁 *Family and Community Activities,* p. 12

Objectives

- To read and analyze an autobio-graphical story of a young girl
- To explain a story's symbols
- To write an explanation of effective use of first-person point of view

Skills

Reading/Thinking: Inferring Evaluating; Drawing Conclusions; Identifying Author's Purpose; Cause and Effect
Writing: Compare and Contrast Paragraph; Letter
Vocabulary: Related Words
Grammar/Language: Intensifiers; Italics
Collaboration: Literature Groups

Motivating

→OPTIONS

Literature Launchers: "Something Different in L.A."

Videodisc Side A, Segment 6

Also available in VHS.

Selection Focus Transparency 11: Have students read and discuss the quote about Hollywood.

Focus Activity: As an extension of the Focus Activity, have partners discuss how and why their interests may change in five years.

Before You Read

Hollywood and the Pits

MEET CHERYLENE LEE

It's hard to imagine a successful stage, movie, and TV performer becoming a paleontologist, but that's just what Cherylene Lee did. Like the narrator in "Hollywood and the Pits," Lee was a child performer in her hometown of Los Angeles. After earning degrees in paleontology and geology, she began writing stories, poetry, and plays.

"Hollywood and the Pits" appears in the collection American Dragons: Twenty-Five Asian American Voices, *edited by Laurence Yep and published in 1995.*

FOCUS ACTIVITY

Are there parts of your childhood self that you have left behind in the past few years?

Journal
Describe how your interests and hobbies have—or have not—changed in the last year or two. Write about how becoming a teenager has affected your childhood interests.

Setting a Purpose
Read to discover one teen's view on change.

BACKGROUND

The Time and Place It is 1968 in Los Angeles, California. In the middle of the city, close to the glamour of Hollywood, is an archeological site filled with the skeletons of prehistoric creatures.

VOCABULARY PREVIEW

obsessed (əb sesd′) *adj.* overly concentrated or focused on a single emotion or idea; p. 118
bewildered (bi wil′ dərd) *adj.* very confused; p. 118
barrage (bə räzh′) *n.* a heavy concentration or great outpouring, as of words; p. 119
excavated (eks′ kə vāt′ əd) *adj.* uncovered or removed by digging; unearthed; p. 119
immobilize (i mō′ bə līz′) *v.* to make unable to move; fix in place; p. 119
painstaking (pānz′ tā′ king) *adj.* requiring close, careful labor or attention; p. 123
predator (pred′ ə tər) *n.* an animal, such as a lion or hawk, that kills other animals for food; p. 125
deception (di sep′ shən) *n.* that which fools or misleads; p. 125
scavenger (skav′ in jər) *n.* an animal, such as a hyena or vulture, that feeds on dead, decaying animals; p. 125

RESOURCE MANAGER

Lesson Planning Resource
The ***Theme Two Planning Guide*** (pp. 6–13) provides additional lesson notes and reduced versions of all print resources.

📁 **Other Print Resources**
- Active Reading Guide, p. 11
- Vocabulary Practice, p. 8
- Reading Workbook, pp. 19–20
- Grammar and Language Workbook, pp. 129–130, 271–272

- Grammar and Composition Handbook, Lessons 6.2, 13.6
- Quick Checks, p. 11
- Selection and Theme Assessment, pp. 21–22
- Performance Assessment, p. 11
- Spanish Summaries, p. 11
- Spanish Translations
- Inclusion Strategies
- English Language Learners Sourcebook

 Transparencies
- Selection Focus 11
- Fine Art 17
- Literary Elements 11
- Grammar and Language 11

Technology
 Literature Launchers
 Audio Library
 Spanish Audio Library
 Glencoe Literature Web Site
Testmaker

HOLLYWOOD AND THE PITS

Cherylene Lee

I n 1968 when I was fifteen, the pit opened its secret to me. I
breathed, ate, slept, dreamed about the La Brea[1] Tar Pits. I spent
summer days working the archaeological dig[2] and in dreams saw the
bones glistening, the broken pelvises, the skulls, the vertebrae looped
like a woman's pearls hanging on an invisible cord. I welcomed those
dreams. I wanted to know where the next skeleton was, identify it,
record its position, discover whether it was whole or not. I wanted to
know where to dig in the coarse, black, gooey sand. I lost myself there
and found something else.

---

1. *La Brea* (lə brā′ ə)
2. An *archaeological* (är′ kē ə loj′ i kəl) *dig* is a place where objects such as ancient
   bones are dug up for study.

SUMMARY

The narrator, a childhood star in television and on stage, discovers at age 15 that she no longer "has what it takes." When she can no longer get parts to perform, she discovers a new reality by working at the La Brea tar pits. She is attracted by this oily, messy place where she is accepted simply for her interest and willingness to work. It teaches her about the survival of the fittest and life in Hollywood.

📁 *Spanish Summaries,* p. 11

A **Active Reading**

PREDICT Encourage students to think about the story title and the last line on this page. Considering the title and the narrator's statement, what do students think the story will be about?

Additional Resources
📁 *Active Reading Guide,* p. 11
🎧 *Audio Library*
🎧 *Spanish Audio Library*

Teaching Options

CONNECTING TO OTHER SELECTIONS

The chart at the right shows three ways to connect "Hollywood and the Pits" to other selections in this book.

For specific teaching strategies, see the *Theme Two Planning Guide,* pages 9–10.

Connection	Title
Life Skills: Lifelong Learning	→ "Bums in the Attic," p. 329
Thematic: Growing Up	→ "The Teacher Who Changed My Life," p. 368
Literary: Irony	→ "Names/Nombres," p. 5

Hollywood and the Pits

My mother thought something was wrong with me. Was it good for a teenager to be fascinated by death? Especially animal death in the Pleistocene?[3] Was it normal to be so obsessed by a sticky brown hole in the ground in the center of Los Angeles? I don't know if it was normal or not, but it seemed perfectly logical to me. After all, I grew up in Hollywood, a place where dreams and nightmares can often take the same shape. What else would a child actor do?

"Thank you very much, dear. We'll be letting you know."

I knew what that meant. It meant I would never hear from them again. I didn't get the job. I heard that phrase a lot that year.

I walked out of the plush office, leaving behind the casting director, producer, director, writer, and whoever else came to listen to my reading for a semiregular role on a family sit-com.[4] The carpet made no sound when I opened and shut the door.

I passed the other girls waiting in the reception room, each poring over her script. The mothers were waiting in a separate room, chattering about their daughters' latest commercials, interviews, callbacks, jobs. It sounded like every Oriental[5] kid in Hollywood was working except me.

My mother used to have a lot to say in those waiting rooms. Ever since I was three, when I started at the Meglin Kiddie Dance Studio, I was dubbed "The Chinese Shirley Temple"—always the one to be picked at auditions and interviews, always the one to get the speaking lines, always called "the one-shot kid," because I could do my scenes in one take—even tight close-ups. My mother would only talk about me behind my back because she didn't want me to hear her brag, but I knew that she was proud. In a way I was proud too, though I never dared admit it. I didn't want to be called a show-off. But I didn't exactly know what I did to be proud of either. I only knew that at fifteen I was now being passed over at all these interviews when before I would be chosen.

My mother looked at my face hopefully when I came into the room. I gave her a quick shake of the head. She looked bewildered. I felt bad for my mother then. How could I explain it to her? I didn't understand it myself. We left saying polite good-byes to all the other mothers.

We didn't say anything until the studio parking lot, where we had to search for our old blue Chevy among rows and rows of parked cars baking in the Hollywood heat.

"How did it go? Did you read clearly? Did you tell them you're available?"

"I don't think they care if I'm available or not, Ma."

"Didn't you read well? Did you remember to look up so they could see your eyes? Did they ask you if you could play the piano? Did you tell them you could learn?"

3. *Pleistocene* (plīs′ tə sēn′) is the name of the period that began about two million years ago, when glaciers covered much of North America and Europe.
4. *Sit-com* is short for "situation comedy," the most common type of TV comedy series.
5. People of eastern Asia and their descendants are sometimes referred to as being *Oriental*, which means "of the East."

Vocabulary
obsessed (əb sesd′) *adj.* overly concentrated or focused on a single emotion or idea
bewildered (bi wil′ dərd) *adj.* very confused

The barrage of questions stopped when we finally spotted our car. I didn't answer her. My mother asked about the piano because I lost out in an audition once to a Chinese girl who already knew how to play.

My mother took off the towel that shielded the steering wheel from the heat. "You're getting to be such a big girl," she said, starting the car in neutral. "But don't worry, there's always next time. You have what it takes. That's special." She put the car into forward and we drove through a parking lot that had an endless number of identical cars all facing the same direction. We drove back home in silence.

In the La Brea Tar Pits many of the excavated bones belong to juvenile mammals. Thousands of years ago thirsty young animals in the area were drawn to watering holes, not knowing they were traps. Those inviting pools had false bottoms made of sticky tar, which immobilized its victims and preserved their bones when they died. Innocence trapped by ignorance. The tar pits record that well.

I suppose a lot of my getting into show business in the first place was a matter of luck—being in the right place at the right time. My sister, seven years older than me, was a member of the Meglin Kiddie Dance Studio long before I started lessons. Once during the annual recital held at the Shrine Auditorium, she was spotted by a Hollywood agent who handled only Oriental performers. The agent sent my sister out for a role in the CBS *Playhouse 90* television show *The Family*

Nobody Wanted. The producer said she was too tall for the part. But true to my mother's training of always having a positive reply, my sister said to the producer, "But I have a younger sister . . ." which started my show-biz career at the tender age of three.

My sister and I were lucky. We enjoyed singing and dancing, we were natural hams, and our parents never discouraged us. In fact they were our biggest fans. My mother chauffeured us to all our dance lessons, lessons we begged to take. She drove us to interviews, took us to studios, went on location with us, drilled us on our lines, made sure we kept up our schoolwork and didn't sass back the tutors hired by studios to teach us for three hours a day. She never complained about being a stage mother. She said that we made her proud.

My father must have felt pride too, because he paid for a choreographer[6] to put together our sister act: "The World Famous Lee Sisters," fifteen minutes of song and dance, real vaudeville stuff. We joked about that a

───────────

6. A *choreographer* creates or directs dance movements.

Vocabulary
barrage (bə räzh′) *n.* a heavy concentration or great outpouring, as of words
excavated (eks′ kə vāt′ əd) *adj.* uncovered or removed by digging; unearthed
immobilize (i mō′ bə līz′) *v.* to make unable to move; fix in place

---

Writing *Minilesson*

Compare and Contrast Writing a short compare-and-contrast paragraph can help students understand and evaluate the different bits of information they receive when reading a story.

Activity Review the information the narrator has provided about herself. Have each student write a short paragraph about a personal experience at a younger age and how that experience compares with his or her interests now. Review some important compare-and-contrast words, such as *same as, different from, although, still, then,* and *now.* **L2**

Additional Resources

📖 *Writer's Choice,* Lesson 5.3

H Critical Thinking

EVALUATING Ask students to think about the long, difficult hours that Cherylene and her sister work. Encourage them to consider how the Lee sisters' lives are different from those of most children. *(Students might question whether it was fair for Cherylene and her sister to work so hard at such young ages. They live in a hotel and may not have a lot of friends their age or time to play.)*

I Active Reading

PREDICT Have students read the last paragraph on this page and then predict what they think might happen when the girls grow. *(Some students may say that when Cherylene grows she will no longer be as cute as she was at seven. She may lose her audience appeal.)*

Teaching Options

As a child, Cherylene Lee performed with some of the great Hollywood entertainers. Here, she's seen with dancer Gene Kelly (above) and with singer and TV-show host Dinah Shore (right).

lot, "Yeah, the Lee Sisters—Ug-Lee and Home-Lee," but we definitely had a good time. So did our parents. Our father especially liked our getting booked into Las Vegas at the New Frontier Hotel on the Strip. He liked to gamble there, though he said the craps tables in that hotel were "cold," not like the casinos in downtown Las Vegas, where all the "hot" action took place.

In Las Vegas our sister act was part of a show called "Oriental Holiday." The show was about a Hollywood producer going to the Far East, finding undiscovered talent, and bringing it back to the U.S. We did two shows a night in the main showroom, one at eight and one at twelve, and on weekends a third show at

120 THEME 2

two in the morning. It ran the entire summer often to standing-room-only audiences—a thousand people a show.

Our sister act worked because of the age and height difference. My sister then was fourteen and nearly five foot two; I was seven and very small for my age—people thought we were cute. We had song-and-dance routines to old tunes like

Cherylene Lee ∾

"Ma, He's Making Eyes at Me," "Together," and "I'm Following You," and my father hired a writer to adapt the lyrics to "I Enjoy Being a Girl," which came out "We Enjoy Being Chinese." We also told corny jokes, but the Las Vegas audience seemed to enjoy it. Here we were, two kids, staying up late and jumping around, and getting paid besides. To me the applause sometimes sounded like static, sometimes like distant waves. It always amazed me when people applauded. The owner of the hotel liked us so much, he invited us back to perform in shows for three summers in a row. That was before I grew too tall and the sister act didn't seem so cute anymore.

Many of the skeletons in the tar pits are found incomplete—particularly the skeletons of the young, which have only soft cartilage connecting the bones. In life the soft tissue allows for growth, but in death it dissolves quickly. Thus the skeletons of young animals are more apt to be scattered, especially the vertebrae protecting the spinal cord. In the tar pits, the central ends of many vertebrae are found unconnected to any skeleton. Such bone fragments are shaped like valentines, disks that are slightly lobed—heart-shaped shields that have lost their connection to what they were meant to protect.

I never felt my mother pushed me to do something I didn't want to do. But I always knew if something I did pleased her. She was generous with her praise, and I was sensitive when she withheld it. I didn't like to disappoint her.

I took to performing easily, and since I had started out so young, making movies or doing shows didn't feel like anything special. It was part of my childhood—like

going to the dentist one morning or going to school the next. I didn't wonder if I wanted a particular role or wanted to be in a show or how I would feel if I didn't get in. Until I was fifteen, it never occurred to me that one day I wouldn't get parts or that I might not "have what it takes."

When I was younger, I got a lot of roles because I was so small for my age. When I was nine years old, I could pass for five or six. I was really short. I was always teased about it when I was in elementary school, but I didn't mind because my height got me movie jobs. I could read and memorize lines that actual five-year-olds couldn't. My mother told people she made me sleep in a drawer so I wouldn't grow any bigger.

But when I turned fifteen, it was as if my body, which hadn't grown for so many years, suddenly made up for lost time. I grew five inches in seven months. My mother was amazed. Even I couldn't get used to it. I kept knocking into things, my clothes didn't fit right, I felt awkward and clumsy when I moved. Dumb things that I had gotten away with, like paying children's prices at the movies instead of junior admission, I couldn't do anymore. I wasn't a shrimp or a small fry any longer. I was suddenly normal.

Before that summer my mother had always claimed she wanted me to be normal. She didn't want me to become spoiled by the attention I received when I was working at the studios. I still had chores to do at home, went to public school when I wasn't working, was punished severely when I behaved badly. She didn't want me to feel I was different just because I was in the movies. When I was eight, I was interviewed by a reporter who wanted to know if I thought I had a big head.

J Literary Elements

FIGURES OF SPEECH Draw students' attention to how Lee compares the applause to static and distant waves. Remind them that this is called a *simile,* a comparison using the words *like* or *as.* Encourage students to find other examples of similes in this story or to make up their own.

K Literary Elements

SYMBOL Discuss how the description of scattered young skeletons and disconnected bone fragments relates to Cherylene's story. *(The image presents a picture of the young as vulnerable and unprotected.)*

L Active Reading

CONNECT Ask students if they have ever felt clumsy and uncomfortable with the way they look. Ask them to think of examples of things they did when they were younger but can no longer get away with. *(Students might say they can no longer pay children's prices at certain events, go on children's rides at a fair, or be excused from certain activities and responsibilities because they are too young.)*

Reading *Minilesson*

Identifying Author's Purpose
Understanding why the author included the italicized sections in this piece can help students understand it as a whole.

Activity Work with students to make a list of questions that can help determine Lee's reasons for including the italicized paragraph on page 121. For example:
Q. Why is the author telling me about the

La Brea Tar Pits? *A. She wants me to compare the Tar Pits to the life of a child star.*
Q. How is the information on the skeletons similar to the information about Hollywood? *A. In both cases, young creatures are tempted to places that are traps.* **L2**

Additional Resources
📁 ***Reading Workbook,*** pp. 19–20

Critical Thinking

EVALUATING Ask students to state whether they think Cherylene's mother is completely accurate when she tells the reporter "I don't do that—I'm not that way." *(Some students may think that she is "that way"; others may point out that she seems to be very emotionally involved in the situation and just wants the best for her daughters.)*

Literary Elements

SYMBOL Discuss how the image of the churning tar pits relates to or is symbolic of the confusion Cherylene is experiencing about her life. *(The tar pits create a situation in which the normal order of things is skewed. This is how Cherylene feels as she faces rejection where she once had success.)*

Teaching Options

"Sure," I said.

"No you don't," my mother interrupted, which was really unusual, because she generally never said anything. She wanted me to speak for myself.

I didn't understand the question. My sister had always made fun of my head. She said my body was too tiny for the weight—I looked like a walking Tootsie Pop. I thought the reporter was making the same observation.

"She better not get that way," my mother said fiercely. "She's not any different from anyone else. She's just lucky and small for her age."

The reporter turned to my mother, "Some parents push their children to act. The kids feel like they're used."

"I don't do that—I'm not that way," my mother told the reporter.

But when she was sitting silently in all those waiting rooms while I was being turned down for one job after another, I could almost feel her wanting to shout, "Use her. Use her. What is wrong with her? Doesn't she have it anymore?" I didn't know what I had had that I didn't seem to have anymore. My mother had told the reporter that I was like everyone else. But when my life was like everyone else's, why was she disappointed?

The churning action of the La Brea Tar Pits makes interpreting the record of past events extremely difficult. The usual order of deposition—the oldest on the bottom, the youngest on the top—loses all meaning when some of the oldest fossils can be brought to the surface by the movement of natural gas. One must look for an undisturbed spot, a place untouched by the action of underground springs or natural gas or human interference. Complete skeletons

become important, because they indicate areas of least disturbance. But such spots of calm are rare. Whole blocks of the tar pit can become displaced, making false sequences of the past, skewing the interpretation[7] for what is the true order of nature.

That year before my sixteenth birthday, my mother seemed to spend a lot of time looking through my old scrapbooks, staring at all the eight-by-ten glossies of the shows that I had done. In the summer we visited with my grandmother often, since I wasn't working and had lots of free time. I would go out to the garden to read or sunbathe, but I could hear my mother and grandmother talking.

"She was so cute back then. She worked with Gene Kelly when she was five years old. She was so smart for her age. I don't know what's wrong with her."

"She's fifteen."

"She's too young to be an ingenue[8] and too old to be cute. The studios forget so quickly. By the time she's old enough to play an ingenue, they won't remember her."

"Does she have to work in the movies? Hand me the scissors."

My grandmother was making false eyelashes using the hair from her hairbrush. When she was young she had incredible hair. I saw an old photograph of her when it flowed beyond her waist like a cascading black waterfall. At seventy, her hair was still black as night, which made her few strands of silver look like shooting stars. But her hair had thinned greatly with age. It sometimes fell out in clumps.

---

7. *Skewing* (skū′ ing) *the interpretation* is twisting it so that it is wrong or off the mark.
8. An *ingenue* (än′ jə nōō′) is an actress who plays innocent, inexperienced young women.

INTERDISCIPLINARY CONNECTION

Science Scientists learn a great deal about the natural history of an area by carefully digging up and preserving animal and plant fossils. In a typical archeological site, the deeper one digs, the older the fossils will be.

Activity There are names for the geologic eras spanning millions of years of Earth's history. Ask students to work in pairs or small groups to research information about geologic eras and to create time lines that show their names and dates. They may wish to list each era's distinct life forms and climate. **L2**

COLLAB. LEARN.

Oil seeping up through the earth's surface evaporated, leaving soft tar that trapped Ice Age animals in the area now called the La Brea Tar Pits.

FYI

The La Brea Tar Pits
This site lies within an area designated as Hancock Park in Los Angeles, California. These pits are an important archaeological site for information about the Pleistocene epoch.

Historical Note

The Pleistocene epoch, or Ice Age, was the time during which glaciers advanced and receded over North and South America, Europe, and Asia and during which human beings appeared. This epoch lasted from about 1.8 million to 10,000 years ago.

0 Active Reading

RESPOND Discuss how Cherylene's grandmother changes her reasons for feeling proud of her hair. *(At one time she was proud of the way it looked; now she is proud because it makes her feel useful.)* Ask students how this kind of change relates to Cherylene. *(Cherylene once succeeded because of her looks; now she must make herself useful.)*

She wore it brushed back in a bun with a hairpiece for added fullness. My grandmother had always been proud of her hair, but once she started making false eyelashes from it, she wasn't proud of the way it looked anymore. She said she was proud of it now because it made her useful.

It was <u>painstaking</u> work—tying knots into strands of hair, then tying them together to form feathery little crescents.

Vocabulary
painstaking (pānz' tā' king) *adj.* requiring close, careful labor or attention

---

MEETING INDIVIDUAL NEEDS MULTIPLE LEARNING STYLES

Spatial Some students may benefit from creating a sketch that illustrates the sequence of an elephant's sinking into the tar. Their classmates may gain a better understanding of the process by looking carefully at these drawings.

Activity Have students make six drawings that show the elephant in the photograph approaching, stepping into, sinking, and disappearing into the tar. When students have finished their drawings, have them share them with the class or display them on posters. **L2**

Q Critical Thinking

INFERRING Ask students to state how Cherylene feels as she listens to her mother. Have them tell what words or phrases helped them infer their answers. You may wish to use the following model to guide students in the process of inferring.

Model: I've read that Cherylene is very confused about the changes going on in her life. I think Cherylene is uncomfortable listening to her mother talk about how cute she once was. The words *going on and on* make me think that Cherylene has heard enough about this topic.

R Literary Elements

CHARACTER Have students compare the mother's and the grandmother's reactions to the changes taking place in Cherylene's life. *(The grandmother seems to be accepting the changes, while the mother is unable to do so.)*

Teaching Options

Hollywood and the Pits

Her glamorous false eyelashes were much sought after. Theatrical make-up artists waited months for her work. But my grandmother said what she liked was that she was doing something, making a contribution, and besides it didn't cost her anything. No overhead. "Till I go bald," she often joked.

She tried to teach me her art that summer, but for some reason strands of my hair wouldn't stay tied in knots.

"Too springy," my grandmother said. "Your hair is still too young." And because I was frustrated[9] then, frustrated with everything about my life, she added,

"You have to wait until your hair falls out, like mine. Something to look forward to, eh?" She had laughed and patted my hand.

My mother was going on and on about my lack of work, what might be wrong, that something she couldn't quite put her finger on. I heard my grandmother reply, but I didn't catch it all: "Movies are just make-believe, not real life. Like what I make with my hair that falls out—false. False eyelashes. Not meant to last."

The remains in the La Brea Tar Pits are mostly of carnivorous animals. Very few herbivores are found—the

---

9. To be *frustrated* is to be kept from doing something or achieving some goal.

MEETING INDIVIDUAL NEEDS — INCLUSION STRATEGIES

Less-Proficient Readers Write *carnivore* and *herbivore* on the board. Explain that the ending *-vore* comes from a Latin word that means "to devour or eat," *carni-* from a Latin word that means "flesh or meat," and *herbi-* from a Latin word that means "a flowering plant."

Activity Suggest that students create

charts to help them identify word roots in the future. **L1**

carni (meat) + vore (eat) = meat eater
herbi (plant) + vore (eat) = plant eater

Additional Resources
📁 *Inclusion Strategies*

Cherylene Lee ∾

ratio is five to one, a perversion of the natural food chain. The ratio is easy to explain. Thousands of years ago a thirsty animal sought a drink from the pools of water only to find itself trapped by the bottom, gooey with subterranean[10] oil. A shriek of agony from the trapped victim drew flesh-eating <u>predators</u>, *which were then trapped themselves by the very same ooze which provided the bait. The cycle repeated itself countless times. The number of victims grew, lured by the image of easy food, the* <u>deception</u> *of an easy kill. The animals piled on top of one another. For over ten thousand years the promise of the place drew animals of all sorts, mostly predators and* <u>scavengers</u>—*dire wolves, panthers, coyotes, vultures—all hungry for their chance. Most were sucked down against their will in those watering holes destined to be called the La Brea Tar Pits in a place to be named the City of Angels, home of Hollywood movie stars.*

I spent a lot of time by myself that summer, wondering what it was that I didn't have anymore. Could I get it back? How could I if I didn't know what it was?

That's when I discovered the La Brea Tar Pits. Hidden behind the County Art Museum on trendy[11] Wilshire Boulevard, I found a job that didn't require me to be small or cute for my age. I didn't have to audition. No one said, "Thank you very much, we'll call you." Or if they did, they meant it. I volunteered my time one afternoon, and my fascination stuck—like tar on the bones of a saber-toothed tiger.

My mother didn't understand what had changed me. I didn't understand it myself. But I liked going to the La Brea Tar Pits. It meant I could get really messy and I was doing it with a purpose. I didn't feel awkward there. I could wear old stained pants. I could wear T-shirts with holes in them. I could wear disgustingly filthy sneakers and it was all perfectly justified. It wasn't a costume for a role in a film or a part in a TV sit-com. My mother didn't mind my dressing like that when she knew I was off to the pits. That was okay so long as I didn't track tar back into the house. I started going to the pits every day, and my mother wondered why. She couldn't believe I would rather be groveling[12] in tar than going on auditions or interviews.

While my mother wasn't proud of the La Brea Tar Pits (she didn't know or care what a fossil was), she didn't discourage me either. She drove me there, the same way she used to drive me to the studios.

"Wouldn't you rather be doing a show in Las Vegas than scrambling around in a pit?" she asked.

"I'm not in a show in Las Vegas, Ma. The Lee Sisters are retired." My older sister

---

10. *Carnivorous* (kär niv′ ər əs) animals eat meat; *herbivores* (hur′ bə vôrz′) eat mainly plants. So, the remains in the pits are a *perversion* because they give a false picture of reality. *Subterranean* means "underground."
11. *Trendy* describes what is currently popular, and Wilshire Boulevard is loaded with trendy shops, stores, and restaurants.
12. *Groveling* is lying or crawling facedown in a demeaning manner.

Vocabulary
predator (pred′ ə tər) *n.* an animal, such as a lion or hawk, that kills other animals for food
deception (di sep′ shən) *n.* that which fools or misleads
scavenger (skav′ in jər) *n.* an animal, such as a hyena or vulture, that feeds on dead, decaying animals

---

S Literary Elements

SYMBOL Discuss with students how this description symbolizes the dark side of show business and particularly the movie-making industry in Hollywood. Encourage them to see how both the tar pits and Hollywood have attracted many who were doomed to failure, "sucked down against their will."

T Active Reading

EVALUATE Ask students why they think Cherylene decides to work at the tar pits. *(The job does not require her to be small or cute, and she finds the pits very interesting.)*

U Critical Thinking

DRAWING CONCLUSIONS Although Cherylene's mother would prefer to have her go to auditions instead of the tar pits, she drives Cherylene to work every day. Discuss with students what her mother is telling Cherylene through her actions. *(Students may understand that Cherylene's mother is giving the same support and approval now that she gave when Cherylene was acting, even though she is not saying it aloud.)*

REAL-WORLD CONNECTION

Music of the Times Throughout the years, music has chronicled not only the changes occurring in the world but also the more personal changes that occur in people's lives. Initiate a discussion with students about songs that deal with the theme of change.

Activity Students can work in pairs or small groups and write songs about change in their own or other people's lives. The lyrics, or words, should tell a story. Encourage students to create their own melodies or, if necessary, use a melody all group members know. When each group has written a song and practiced it, invite the groups to perform for the class. **L2** **COLLAB. LEARN.**

Music Students can search with the keywords *classical, broadway,* and *movies* to find more information about music.

V Active Reading

EVALUATE Ask students which character, Cherylene or her mother, has the more realistic outlook on what is happening. Why? *(Cherylene does because she accepts the fact that her career in show business is over. Her mother is still hoping that somehow things will return to the way they had been.)*

W Critical Thinking

DRAWING CONCLUSIONS Discuss with students how Cherylene's feelings about the changes in her life might be affected by what she is learning at the pits. *(She is gaining a mature perspective of time and gaining a better understanding of Hollywood.)*

Thematic Focus

Winds of Change Cherylene Lee faced a major change in her life when she was no longer chosen for acting, singing, or dancing parts.

FINE ART
TRANSPARENCY 17

You may want to use *Fine Art Transparency 17* to enrich a discussion of how Cherylene Lee adjusts to the change in her life and uses it to grow.

ASSESSMENT OPTIONS

 Quick Checks, p. 11

Hollywood and the Pits

had married and was starting a family of her own.

"But if you could choose between . . ."

"There isn't a choice."

"You really like this tar-pit stuff, or are you just waiting until you can get real work in the movies?"

I didn't answer.

My mother sighed. "You could do it if you wanted, if you really wanted. You still have what it takes."

I didn't know about that. But then, I couldn't explain what drew me to the tar pits either. Maybe it was the bones, finding out what they were, which animal they belonged to, imagining how they got there, how they fell into the trap. I wondered about that a lot.

At the La Brea Tar Pits, everything dug out of the pit is saved—including the sticky sand that covered the bones through the ages. Each bucket of sand is washed, sieved, and examined for pollen grains, insect remains, any evidence of past life. Even the grain size is recorded—the percentage of silt to sand to gravel that reveals the history of deposition, erosion, and disturbance. No single fossil, no one observation, is significant enough to tell the entire story. All the evidence must be weighed before a semblance[13] of truth emerges.

The tar pits had its lessons. I was learning I had to work slowly, become observant, to concentrate. I learned about time in a way that I would never experience—not in hours, days, and months, but in thousands

---

13. A *semblance* of truth would be the slightest likeness of truth.

and thousands of years. I imagined what the past must have been like, envisioned Los Angeles as a sweeping basin, perhaps slightly colder and more humid, a time before people and studios arrived. The tar pits recorded a warming trend; the kinds of animals found there reflected the changing climate. The ones unadapted disappeared. No trace of their kind was found in the area. The ones adapted to warmer weather left a record of bones in the pit. Amid that collection of ancient skeletons, surrounded by evidence of death, I was finding a secret preserved over thousands and thousands of years. There was something cruel about natural selection and the survival of the fittest.[14] Even those successful individuals that "had what it took" for adaptation still wound up in the pits.

I never found out if I had what it took, not the way my mother meant. But I did adapt to the truth: I wasn't a Chinese Shirley Temple any longer, cute and short for my age. I had grown up. Maybe not on a Hollywood movie set, but in the La Brea Tar Pits.

---

14. *[Natural . . . fittest]* refers to natural selection, the theory that the plants and animals best suited to their environment tend to survive and pass on their characteristics to their offspring.

❖

Grammar and Language *Minilesson*

Intensifiers Write the following words on the chalkboard: *almost, extremely, just, nearly, practically, quite, rather, really, so, somewhat, too,* and *very.* Explain to students that these words are called *intensifiers,* adverbs that emphasize or intensify an adjective or another adverb.

Activity Write the following sentences on the board; then have students identify the intensifiers in each sentence.

1. I remember the child performer Cherylene Lee. *(none)*
2. She was very small and extremely cute. *(very; extremely)*
3. Cherylene and her sister were a rather successful act. *(rather)*
4. Cherylene became quite frustrated when she was too old to get parts. *(quite; too)* **L2**

Additional Resources

Grammar and Language Transparency 11

Grammar and Language Workbook, pp. 129–130

Grammar and Composition Handbook, Lesson 6.2

Writer's Choice, Lesson 12.7

Responding to Literature

PERSONAL RESPONSE

If you were the main character, would you have continued to pursue your career as a performer? Discuss your opinions with a partner.

Analyzing Literature

RECALL

1. Describe the narrator's career as a successful child star.
2. What begins to happen to the narrator's success after she turns fifteen?
3. What does the narrator do in the tar pits?
4. How does the narrator's mother react to her daughter's lack of jobs as she becomes a teenager and her newfound interest in the tar pits?

INTERPRET

5. In your opinion, why was "The World Famous Lee Sisters" act so successful?
6. In your opinion, how does the narrator feel about the slump in her Hollywood career?
7. In your opinion, why does the narrator find working in the tar pits so rewarding?
8. How does the narrator's relationship with her mother change over the course of the story?

EVALUATE AND CONNECT

9. Why is the story of the narrator's life interrupted from time to time with factual material about the tar pits? What connection do you think the author is making between Hollywood and the La Brea Tar Pits?
10. Theme Connection   "Hollywood and the Pits" describes the changes in one person's life from childhood to adolescence. Does the story remind you about changes in your own life? Add these ideas to your journal entry from the **Focus Activity**.

LITERARY ELEMENTS

Symbol

A **symbol** is any object, person, place, or experience that stands for more than what it is. In "Hollywood and the Pits," the narrator uses the animals trapped in the La Brea Tar Pits to symbolize her experience as a child actor.

1. On page 119, find the statement "Innocence trapped by ignorance." How does this phrase help you understand Lee's use of symbolism in the story?

2. Find and explain another example of symbolism from a section of the selection printed in slanted, or italic, type.

● See **Literary Terms Handbook**, p. R10.

Personal Response

Most students will probably feel that Cherylene made the right choice to quit acting. Others may say that she should have persisted.

Analyzing Literature

1. At age three, she began working in television and on the stage, even in Las Vegas. She and her sister told jokes, sang, and danced.
2. She is no longer able to get acting parts.
3. She works to help recover and classify the animal bones that are found there.
4. She doesn't really understand how her daughter has changed and wants her to keep pursuing her acting career.
5. People thought they were very cute because of their age and height difference. They sang old, familiar songs and told corny jokes.
6. She seems to be confused. She wonders whether she can get back whatever she has lost; yet, she seems to be able to accept the change.
7. She doesn't have to worry about auditioning for the job, she can be as messy as she likes, and most importantly, she feels that the work has a real purpose.
8. In the beginning, they are close and share a purpose. When Cherylene begins to work at the tar pits, her mother drives her there but really wants Cherylene to stay in show business.
9. The information about the tar pits reflects what is happening to the narrator. The tar pits are a strong reminder that all living things must die and that Holly-

---

LITERARY ELEMENTS

1. She is pointing out how she was trapped in her acting career.
2. The passage on page 121 states that the heart-shaped bone fragments were disconnected from any skeleton. This image suggests that Hollywood can "tear the heart out" of a young, innocent person.

Additional Resources

 Literary Elements Transparency 11

wood is insignificant compared to millions of years of time.

10. Students should identify aspects of change in their own lives and show how the story reminded them of these.

Extending Your Response

Writing About Literature

Students' explanations should

- state clearly whether the story's point of view was the most effective possible.
- explain why they think this or another point of view would be the most effective.

Personal Writing

Students' letters should

- reflect a clear understanding of the narrator's experience.
- compare the narrator's experience with events from their own lives.
- follow the format and tone of a friendly letter.

Internet Connection Students can find more information on the La Brea Tar Pits and the Pleistocene Epoch on the Web by entering these words as search terms on a search engine.

Literature Groups Point out to students that they should use the text to create and answer the questions and that they should include answers for both Cherylene and her mother. **COLLAB. LEARN.**

Learning for Life Encourage students to choose animals about which they know little or nothing. Be sure that students write their news reports in an appropriate style.

Extending Your Response

Writing About Literature

Point of View Most fiction is written from one of two points of view. The events are described from the point of view of either a character in the story or an unknown, all-seeing narrator. In "Hollywood and the Pits," Cherylene Lee uses the point of view of her main character. The reader sees the events as the main character saw them. Do you think this was the most effective point of view to use for this story? Explain your opinion.

Personal Writing

Moving On Look back at your journal entry for the **Focus Activity** on page 116. Write a letter to Cherylene Lee, comparing the narrator's experience of becoming a teenager and abandoning her childhood interests with your own experience.

interNET CONNECTION

You can find out more about prehistoric animals at many sites on the World Wide Web. Just type *"prehistoric animals"* in the subject window of your browser or search engine. Don't forget the quotation marks. They help to narrow the number of choices.

Literature Groups

Follow-up Interview The narrator tells about being interviewed when she was in the movies at age eight. Imagine that the reporter has come back ten years later to interview the narrator, again in the presence of her mother. What questions might the reporter ask, and how might the narrator's responses differ from her mother's? Devise questions and answers using details from the story.

Learning for Life

News Broadcast Imagine that you are a science news reporter, and a complete skeleton of a prehistoric animal has just been discovered at the La Brea Tar Pits. First, research animals that have been found at the pits during the last ninety years. Then choose one animal, research its characteristics, and write a news story about the finding of its skeleton. Add illustrations to your story.

Reading Further

If you would like to read more about life as a child actor or about the La Brea Tar Pits, try these books:

Shirley Temple Black by James Haskins

Death Trap: The Story of the La Brea Tar Pits by Sharon Elaine Thompson

📖 **Save your work for your portfolio.**

Skill Minilessons

GRAMMAR AND LANGUAGE • ITALICS

Italic type is a special *slanted* type used to set off titles of books, plays, movies, CDs, magazines, newspapers, and other long works. Italic type is also used to call out a foreign word or a word used as a word. In handwritten work, underline the words you want read as italic.

PRACTICE Write each sentence, underlining for italics where needed.

1. I read an article about fossils in National Geographic.

2. My teacher said that I overused terrifying in my review of the movie Jurassic Park.
3. Ed learned that the book Dinosaur Defeat was made into a play called The End of Their World.
4. I can't believe that the Times misspelled the word riot as rot in this morning's headline.
5. I learned from the local newspaper, Our Town, about the future filming of a movie in our city.

● For more about using italics, see **Language Handbook,** p. R39.

READING AND THINKING • CAUSE AND EFFECT

A **cause** is a condition or event that makes something happen. What happens as the result of a cause is an **effect.** Many events in stories are connected by cause-and-effect relationships. In "Hollywood and the Pits," when the narrator's older sister is too tall for a part in a TV show, the narrator gets the part. This begins her acting career.

Cause		Effect
Older sister is too tall	→	Younger sister gets part

PRACTICE Answer these questions about other causes and effects in "Hollywood and the Pits."
1. What causes the narrator's mother to worry that her daughter is fascinated by death?
2. What is a possible cause of the narrator's lack of acting work?
3. What led prehistoric mammals to become trapped in the tar pits?
4. What effect did the screaming of trapped animals in the pits have on predators in the area?

● For more about cause and effect, see **Reading Handbook,** p. R85.

VOCABULARY • RELATED FORMS OF WORDS

If you know the meaning of *happy* (an adjective), you probably also know the meaning of *happiness* (a noun) and *happily* (an adverb). If you know the meaning of one form of a word, you can usually figure out the meanings of its other forms. For example, if you know that a *predator* hunts its food, you can figure out what *predatory* behavior is.

PRACTICE Use what you know about the vocabulary words in "Hollywood and the Pits" to write definitions of the underlined words below.
1. to have an obsession
2. the child's bewilderment
3. the car's immobilization
4. to work painstakingly
5. a deceptive statement

Skill Minilessons

GRAMMAR AND LANGUAGE
ITALICS

1. *National Geographic*
2. *terrifying, Jurassic Park*
3. *Dinosaur Defeat; The End of Their World*
4. *Times; riot; rot*
5. *Our Town*

READING AND THINKING
CAUSE AND EFFECT

1. The daughter begins spending every day at the tar pits where they study the skeletons of ancient dead animals.
2. She has grown and is no longer cute.
3. Predators came to drink and were trapped by the gooey, sticky tar and oil.
4. They came to feed on the trapped animals, only to become trapped themselves.

VOCABULARY
RELATED FORMS OF WORDS

1. something that draws a great deal of one's attention or focus
2. confusion
3. state of being unable to move
4. with great care and attention to detail
5. misleading

Additional Resources

▌ *Grammar and Language Workbook,* pp. 271–272

▌ *Grammar and Composition Handbook,* Lesson 13.6

▌ *Writer's Choice,* Lesson 20.6

▌ *Reading Workbook,* pp. 19–20

📁 *Vocabulary Practice,* p. 8

✔ ASSESSMENT OPTIONS

📁 *Quick Checks,* p. 11
📁 *Selection and Theme Assessment,* pp. 21–22
📁 *Performance Assessment,* p. 11
💾 *Testmaker*

Objective

- To understand the process and purpose of radiocarbon dating

Teaching Strategies

Ask students to brainstorm a list of items that might be unearthed in an archaeological dig. Have them categorize the list into items that would contain carbon-14 and items that wouldn't. Help students create a time line that traces a now-extinct animal's journey from life to fossilization to a museum of natural history.

Activity

Other state fossils:
Alabama—Basilosaurus
Alaska—Woolly Mammoth
Connecticut—Eubrontes Giganteus
Idaho—Hagerman Horse
Maine—Pertica Quadrifaria
Maryland—Ecphora Gardnerae
Mississippi—Prehistoric Whale
Nebraska—Mammoth
Nevada—Ichthyosaur
New Jersey—Hadrosaurus Foulkii
New Mexico—Coelophysis
North Dakota—Teredo Petrified Wood
Utah—Allosaurus
Wisconsin—Trilobite

Encourage students to use the Internet as a way of beginning their research.

Additional Resources
Interdisciplinary Activities, pp. 6–9

Teaching Options

Radiocarbon Dating

If you're a scientist who wants to know the age of a fossil you dug up, radiocarbon dating might help you. This type of dating tells us that the bone and plant fossils found in the La Brea Tar Pits range from 8,000 to 40,000 years old.

Only a small sample of a fossil, as little as a few grams, is needed for radiocarbon dating. Before dating the sample, a scientist cleans it by placing the sample in a jar filled with a chemical solution. Every tool the scientist uses to handle the fossil must also be clean and dry to prevent inaccurate results. Data about where the object was found can help confirm a dating.

Radiocarbon dating works by measuring the level of a radioactive form of carbon called carbon-14 inside a fossil. All living things contain carbon-14. Plants constantly absorb this element from the atmosphere. Human beings and other animals absorb it mainly through food provided by plants. Once an organism dies, however, it stops absorbing carbon-14. The carbon-14 remaining in its body begins to decay, or break down. Scientists know that carbon-14 decays at a particular rate, or speed. It takes 5,730 years for carbon-14 to reach what scientists call a half-life. By measuring the amount of carbon-14 left in an object, scientists can get an accurate idea of its age.

Radiocarbon dating doesn't work with every found object. Metal objects, such as ancient coins, tools, or weapons, were never alive, so scientists must use other methods to date them. Objects less than 50,000 years old qualify best for radiocarbon dating. That's pretty young for a fossil when you consider that scientists have uncovered the skeletal remains of sea animals that lived more than 500 million years ago!

ACTIVITY

Some states have an official state fossil or dinosaur. Smilodon, the most famous of the saber-toothed cats, is California's state fossil. Find out which fossil or dinosaur, if any, represents your state. Locate a picture of the creature or its fossilized remains. During which time period was it alive? Share what you learn with your class.

If your state doesn't have an official state fossil, you might plan a campaign to have one adopted. Begin by finding out what fossils have been found in your state. Then choose the one you think would best represent the state.

MEETING INDIVIDUAL NEEDS **MULTIPLE LEARNING STYLES**

Spatial A time line can help students understand where the La Brea fossils fit into Earth's history.

Activity Have students work in small groups to create a prehistory time line. Suggest that they begin 500 million years ago—the time of the fossilized sea creatures—and end 8,000 years ago—the last period "recorded" by the La Brea Tar Pits. Encourage students to make their time lines proportional. *(Time line: 5,370 years = half-life of carbon-14; 8,000 years ago = latest La Brea Tar Pit remains; 40,000 years ago = earliest tar pit remains; 50,000 years ago = outer limit of radiocarbon dating; and 500 million years ago = time when fossilized sea creatures lived)* **L2** **COLLAB. LEARN.**

SONG

This song was written for the January 14, 1972, episode of the TV show *The Brady Bunch.* In the episode, the oldest brother, Greg, writes the song for the Brady Six to record after Peter's voice unexpectedly starts to change.

Time to Change

Words and Music by Raymond Bloodworth, Chris Welch, and Billy Meshel

Sha na na na na na na na na
Sha na na na na
Sha na na na na na na na na
Sha na na na na

Autumn turns to winter,
and then winter turns
to spring.
It's not just the seasons,
you know; it goes for
everything.
It's even true for voices as
boys begin to grow.
You gotta take a lesson
from Mother Nature,
and if you do you'll
know
When it's time to change,
then it's time to change.

Don't fight the tide, come
along for the ride.
Don't you see?
When it's time to change,
you've got to rearrange
Who you are into what
you're going to be.
Sha na na na . . . [repeat]

Day by day it's hard to see
the changes you've
been through.
A little bit of livin', a little
bit of growin' all adds
up to you.

Every boy's a man inside,
a girl's a woman too.
And if you want to reach
your destiny, here's
what you've got to do.
When it's time to change,
then it's time to change.
Don't fight the tide, come
along for the ride.
Don't you see?
When it's time to change,
you've got to rearrange
Who you are into what
you're going to be.

Sha na na na . . .
[repeat]

©1971 Famous Music Corporation

Respond

1. What does the song mean by "you've got to rearrange / Who you are into what you're going to be"? Explain in your own words.

2. Describe a time when you've had to rearrange yourself into "what you're going to be" or a time when you expect you'll need to.

WINDS OF CHANGE 🦢 131

Objective

- To read and understand song lyrics

Respond

1. Some students may say that the lyric means that we shouldn't be afraid of change. Others may say it means we need to be flexible and "go with the flow."
2. Responses may refer to school- or home-related situations in which students were called upon to face up to challenges or were confronted by something new.

Additional Resources

📁 *Media Connections* p. 3

Teaching Options

Reading *Minilesson*

Varying Reading Rate Reading a poem or a song often requires readers to slow down enough to appreciate the rhythm and rhyme or even to sing the song aloud or in their heads. The "feel" of a song—the way that the music, rhythm, and rhyme interact—is often as important as, or even more important than, the actual words.

Activity Have small groups create rhythmic, dramatic readings of the song. Encourage them to take turns with different lines, clapping along to the rhythm or chanting the "Sha na na" chorus. Have each group perform its rendition. **L2**
COLLAB. LEARN.

Additional Resources

📕 *Reading Workbook*

interNET CONNECTION

Brady Bunch Have students use a search engine to look for additional information about *The Brady Bunch.*

Objectives

- To read and analyze a poem about a young girl and her relationship with her mother
- To identify the mood of a poem and describe how it changes
- To write about rhythm's contribution to the effect of a poem

Skills

Reading/Thinking: Sequence of Events
Writing: Short Poem
Listening/Speaking: Group Poetry Reading
Collaboration: Literature Groups

Motivating
→ OPTIONS

Selection Focus Transparency 12: Have students view and discuss *Beth and Kate*, a photograph by Tamarra Kaida. Tell students that the photograph is of a mother and daughter.

Focus Activity: As an extension of the Focus Activity, have students discuss in small groups what they do when they are angry and how they resolve their anger.

Before You Read
Growing Pains

MEET JEAN LITTLE

Jean Little was born with seriously impaired eyesight. As she grew, however, her sight improved enough so that she could learn to read on her own. "Reading," she says, "became my greatest joy." As Little went through school, she showed enthusiasm for writing. When she was eighteen, a magazine published two of her poems. She remembers her father reading them aloud. "I listened, and [when] his voice broke, I knew why I wanted to be a writer."

Jean Little was born in 1932 in Taiwan. "Growing Pains" was first published in 1986.

FOCUS ACTIVITY

Think about how you feel when someone is angry with you. When you get angry with someone, do you keep your anger inside or do you express it? How do you feel after the person who expressed anger with you apologizes?

Think/Pair/Share
After you have jotted down your responses to these questions, share your thoughts with a partner.

Setting a Purpose
Read to discover one person's feelings about anger—and growing up.

RESOURCE MANAGER

Lesson Planning Resource
The *Theme Two Planning Guide* (pp. 14–18) provides additional lesson notes and reduced versions of all print resources.

📁 **Other Print Resources**
- Active Reading Guide, p. 12
- Quick Checks, p. 12
- Selection and Theme Assessment, p. 23
- Performance Assessment, p. 12

- Spanish Summaries, p. 12
- Spanish Translations
- Inclusion Strategies
- English Language Learners Sourcebook

🔖 **Transparencies**
- Selection Focus 12
- Literary Elements 12

Technology
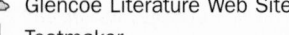
🎧 Audio Library
🎧 Spanish Audio Library
💻 Glencoe Literature Web Site
💾 Testmaker

Growing Pains

Jean Little

Mother got mad at me tonight and bawled me out.
She said I was lazy and self-centered.
She said my room was a pigsty.
She said she was sick and tired of forever nagging but I gave her no choice.
5 She went on and on until I began to cry.
I hate crying in front of people. It was horrible.

I got away, though, and went to bed and it was over.
I knew things would be okay in the morning;
Stiff with being sorry, too polite, but okay.
10 I was glad to be by myself.

Then she came to my room and apologized.
She explained, too.
Things had gone wrong all day at the store.
She hadn't had a letter from my sister and she was worried.
15 Dad had also done something to hurt her.
She even told me about that.
Then *she* cried.
I kept saying, "It's all right. Don't worry."
And wishing she'd stop.

20 I'm just a kid.
I can forgive her getting mad at me. That's easy.
But her sadness . . .
I don't know what to do with her sadness.
I yell at her often, "You don't understand me!"
25 But I don't want to have to understand her.
That's expecting too much.

A **Active Reading**

CONNECT Ask students how they feel when a parent is angry with them?

B **Literary Elements**

MOOD Ask students to write how the poem makes them feel and how the speaker might feel. *(They may say they feel sad, lonely, and hurt.)*

C **Active Reading**

EVALUATE Ask students what the speaker is feeling at the end of the poem. *(She is not prepared to understand her mother's feelings. She is burdened with the knowledge that her mother has problems, too.)*

Thematic Focus

Winds of Change The speaker is not ready to understand her mother's sadness, but she is changed by knowing it exists.

Additional Resources

📁 *Active Reading Guide,* p. 12

🎧 *Audio Library*

🎧 *Spanish Audio Library*

📁 *Spanish Summaries,* p. 12

✔ASSESSMENT OPTIONS

📁 *Quick Checks,* p. 12

Teaching Options

CONNECTING TO OTHER SELECTIONS
For a teaching strategy that connects "Growing Pains" to "Broken Chain," turn to page 43 in the *Theme One Planning Guide.*

MEETING INDIVIDUAL NEEDS — ENGLISH LANGUAGE LEARNERS

Relationships American children and their parents relate in many different ways. This poem shows one example. Call on volunteers to explain *bawled me out, pigsty, sick and tired,* and *nagging.* What do these expressions suggest about the relationship between this mother and daughter?

Activity Explore with students some of the different ways children relate to their parents. You might like to initiate the discussion with these questions: Can they express their anger in a discussion? Are there certain chores they are expected to do, or is everything done for them?

Additional Resources
📁 *English Language Learners Sourcebook*

Responding to the Selection

Personal Response

Many students will probably identify with the speaker, relating the poem to their own experiences. Some students may suggest ways to comfort the mother.

Analyzing Literature

1. The speaker is a young person, probably a girl, who is upset because she and her mother are fighting.
2. She cries and asks for understanding.
3. The title suggests that growing up can sometimes be painful.
4. She feels embarrassed about it, and watching her mother cry makes her feel uncomfortable.
5. No, because her mother apologizes, saying that she had had a very bad day.
6. The speaker has mixed feelings and seems very human. She is upset but understands that her mother's anger will pass. She hates to see her mother cry and does not want to have to take care of her.
7. No, the poem is written from the daughter's point of view. We hear the mother's side only through the daughter's words.
8. When people are hurt or upset, they are more likely to lose their tempers.
9. The speaker is probably twelve or thirteen. Her mother may suddenly confide in her because she is becoming a teenager and seems grown up.
10. Teenagers may not enjoy being expected to behave like adults. Even though they are growing up, they are not adults yet.

Responding to Literature

PERSONAL RESPONSE

What went through your mind as you read this poem? What, if anything, would you have done differently?

Analyzing Literature

RECALL

1. Who is the **speaker** in the poem and what is she feeling?
2. What does the main character do that she wishes her mother would not do?

INTERPRET

3. Why do you think the author chose "Growing Pains" as the title for this poem?
4. How do you think the speaker's feelings about her own crying in front of people affect how she feels about her mother's crying?

EVALUATE AND CONNECT

5. Does the speaker think she deserved to be "bawled out"? How can you tell?
6. How do the main character's feelings about her mother's behavior seem true to life? Support your opinion with examples.
7. Do you think the poet showed both sides of the conflict between the mother and the daughter? Why or why not?
8. What does the poem tell you is one common reason that people often lose their tempers?
9. **Theme Connection** About how old do you think the speaker might be? Why do you think her mother suddenly confides in her?
10. How does the poem express feelings about the new responsibilities that come with growing up?

LITERARY ELEMENTS

Mood

The emotional atmosphere, or feeling, of a story or poem is called the **mood**. Writers choose details to create a mood or feeling that brings a scene to life. Descriptive words, setting, dialogue, and characters' actions can all contribute to the mood of a piece of writing. In "Growing Pains," the poet uses such lines as, "It was horrible" and "I was glad to be by myself" to express the mood of the poem.

1. Reread "Growing Pains." How would you describe the mood of the poem?
2. Find two other examples of details that express the mood of the poem.
3. Compare the mood of the first two stanzas with the mood of the last stanza.

● See **Literary Terms Handbook,** p. R6.

LITERARY ELEMENTS

1. Some words to describe the mood of the poem are *tense, angry,* and *sad.*
2. Possible answers: "She went on and on until I began to cry." and "Dad had done something to hurt her."
3. The mood in the first two stanzas is self-assured and angry; in the last stanza it is one of sadness and confusion.

Additional Resources

📖 *Literary Elements Transparency 12*

Extending Your Response

Writing About Literature

Appreciating Rhythm "Growing Pains" is an example of a poem that does not rhyme but that has a rhythm most easily grasped if you read the poem aloud. Working with a partner, read the poem aloud to each other, and then write about how the rhythm affects the listener or contributes to the effect of the poem.

Creative Writing

Expressing Yourself Return to your notes from the **Focus Activity** on page 132. Write a short poem telling about a time when you were angry or confused because someone had hurt your feelings. Use details that describe why you were angry or confused.

Performing

Words Set to Music Work with a small group to find instrumental music that evokes the mood of "Growing Pains." Then make a tape of the music to use as background during a group reading of the poem. Try various effects—for example, by grouping low and high voices or single and group voices.

Literature Groups

Problem Solving The speaker in the poem is having trouble communicating with her mother. Find examples from the poem that describe how the two characters are not getting along. Then work together to come up with a list of recommendations to help them better understand each other. Write a plan with suggestions for both characters, and share it with the class.

Reading Further

If you enjoyed this poem, try these other books by Jean Little:
Mama's Going to Buy You a Mockingbird
Little by Little: A Writer's Education

📖 **Save your work for your portfolio.**

Skill Minilesson

READING AND THINKING • SEQUENCE OF EVENTS

Jean Little divided "Growing Pains" into four stanzas. The first three tell a story that is a sequence of events. The events appear in the order they happened. Paying attention to the sequence of events in a story or poem helps you better understand the piece of literature. How would "Growing Pains" be different if the poem began with the mother crying?

PRACTICE Reread "Growing Pains," paying special attention to the events that happen in each stanza. Then write one paragraph that explains the sequence of events in the poem.

• For more about sequencing, see **Reading Handbook**, p. R87.

Extending Your Response

Writing About Literature

Students' explanations should
- tell ways that the rhythm of the poem affects the listener.
- explain how they think the poem's rhythm contributes to its meaning.

Creative Writing

Students' poems should
- describe a time when they were angry because someone hurt their feelings.
- include details that clearly show why they were angry or confused.

Performing Encourage students to try several different pieces of music and choose the one that works best. When students perform, be sure that the music never obscures the spoken text.

Literature Groups Have students carefully reread the poem, looking for examples. Then encourage students to use their own experience to brainstorm recommendations. **COLLAB. LEARN.**

Skill Minilesson

READING AND THINKING
• SEQUENCE OF EVENTS

Possible answer:
A mother got mad at her daughter and bawled her out. Then the daughter left and went to her room. The mother went to the daughter's room and apologized and cried. This made the daughter uncomfortable. She is still not an adult and doesn't want to have to understand her mother or handle her sadness.

Additional Resources

 Reading Workbook

✓ ASSESSMENT OPTIONS

📁 *Quick Checks,* p. 12
📁 *Selection and Theme Assessment,* p. 23
📁 *Performance Assessment,* p. 12
💾 *Testmaker*

MEDIA
Connection

Objective

- To read and understand a magazine article

Literature LINK

Slam, Dunk, and Hook This magazine article connects to "Slam, Dunk, and Hook," the literature selection that immediately follows it. Point out the connection by telling students that women's basketball, the subject of the article, has reached new heights of success in the world of professional sports. The article focuses on the early excitement generated by the W.N.B.A. In "Slam, Dunk, and Hook," we see the game from a poet's point of view.

Respond

1. Students may mention the exciting pace of the game, the finesse and skill of the players, or the competition between teams.
2. For the first time in American history, there is a national women's basketball league. This represents a significant change in a male-dominated sport.

Additional Resources
📁 *Media Connections*, p. 4

Teaching Options

MEDIA
Connection

MEDIA
Connection

MAGAZINE ARTICLE
This article comes from the business section of a weekly newsmagazine. Why, do you think, did it appear in the business section?

from "The N.B.A.'s Sister Act"
by Steve Wulf—*Time*, August 4, 1997

An hour and a half before the tip-off last Wednesday, the doors of the Charlotte Coliseum swung open, and America came pouring in. Charlotte was about to play New York, and the excitement was as palpable as it would be before any game between the Hornets and the Knicks.

Except this was July, the teams were called the Sting and the Liberty, and the players that the fans were beseeching for autographs were not Ewing and Rice but Lobo and Bullett. One of the hottest items at the souvenir stands was a T-shirt that read

INVENTED BY MAN,
PERFECTED BY WOMAN.

"This is phenomenal," said a woman who drove 65 miles from South Carolina to bring her daughter to the game. "My daughter thinks I'm the best mama in the world." Following the laser lights and loud music required of every N.B.A. pregame show, the announcer thundered, "O.K., Charlotte, We Got Next!"

Welcome to the W.N.B.A., the Women's National Basketball Association, or the N.B.A.'s baby sister. On the court, the sneakers squeak with the same urgency as they do in the N.B.A., the coaches yell, "Why isn't that a foul?" at the refs, and the players get fined for roughhousing—though

the $500 recently assessed Nancy Lieberman-Cline of the Phoenix Mercury for holding Jamila Wideman of the Los Angeles Sparks by the neck equals what Dennis Rodman spends in a year for eyeliner.

Backed by the N.B.A., the W.N.B.A. has exceeded all expectations midway through its two-month inaugural season, averaging 8,766 in attendance, and occasionally eclipsing Major League Soccer and P.G.A. golf in television ratings. W.N.B.A. games are televised nationally. Viewers watching the N.B.A. playoffs in June were besieged with the W.N.B.A. slogan, "We Got Next." The phrase is commonly used on playgrounds to reserve the next game, but in light of the early success of the league, it takes on a new meaning. "We are building a first-class operation that appeals to fans, players, television, corporate sponsors," says Val Ackerman, W.N.B.A.'s president. "Our dream is to become the fifth major league."

Respond

1. What, do you think, makes basketball such a popular sport?
2. How is the W.N.B.A. a sign of the "winds of change" during our time?

Reading Minilesson

Setting a Purpose for Reading Remind students that a good reader usually reads to answer a specific question and may, while reading, revise his or her purpose for reading.

Activity Have students read the headline and the blurb about the article at the top of the page. Then have each student write down a question that can be answered by reading the article. Remind students to

ask another question, or set a new purpose, as soon as they have found the answer to the first one, and so forth. After they have read the article, discuss the process. Did it make it easier for them to understand the article? More interesting? Easier to remember? **L2**

Additional Resources
📁 *Reading Workbook*

Before You Read
Slam, Dunk, & Hook

MEET YUSEF KOMUNYAKAA

The poet and educator Yusef Komunyakaa (ū' sef   kō mun yä' kä) uses his Louisiana childhood and his time in Vietnam as an Army correspondent as resources for the material in his poetry. A winner of the Pulitzer Prize for Poetry in 1994, Komunyakaa writes poems on a wide variety of subjects, including jazz, racial prejudice, and war.

Yusef Komunyakaa was born in 1947. "Slam, Dunk, & Hook" was published in 1992 in a collection of his poetry called Magic City.

FOCUS ACTIVITY

What do you like about sports? Which games do you prefer, and why?

QuickWrite
Make a quick list of your feelings about sports. Tell which games you love and which games you hate. Then explain your own role in sports: do you prefer to play or to watch? Which do you value more—fierce competition between teams or intense loyalty among team members? Describe your feelings.

Setting a Purpose
Read this poem to appreciate the speaker's love of basketball.

BACKGROUND

Did You Know?   Basketball was invented in 1891 by James Naismith, an instructor in physical education who lived in Springfield, Massachusetts. In need of an indoor game for the winter months, Naismith used a soccer ball and two peach baskets, one hung at each end of a gym. The rules Naismith made up for that game form the basis of today's game.

RESOURCE MANAGER

Lesson Planning Resource
The *Theme Two Planning Guide* (pp. 19–23) provides additional lesson notes and reduced versions of all print resources.

📁 **Other Print Resources**
• Active Reading Guide, p. 13
• Reading Workbook, pp. 21–22
• Grammar and Language Workbook, pp. 73–74

• Grammar and Composition Handbook, Lesson 3.1
• Quick Checks, p. 13
• Selection and Theme Assessment, p. 24
• Performance Assessment, p. 13
• Spanish Summaries, p. 13
• Spanish Translations
• Inclusion Strategies
• English Language Learners Sourcebook

🖐 **Transparencies**
• Selection Focus 13
• Literary Elements 13

Technology
🔊 Literature Launchers
🎧 Audio Library
🎧 Spanish Audio Library
💻 Glencoe Literature Web Site
💾 Testmaker

Before Reading

Objectives
• To read and analyze a poem about playing basketball
• To recognize and identify examples of alliteration in a poem and write a short poem using alliteration
• To write about sensory imagery

Skills
Reading/Thinking: Inferring
Writing: Short Poem
Grammar/Language: Vivid Verbs
Listening/Speaking: Debate; Dramatic Reading
Collaboration: Literature Groups; Listening and Speaking

Motivating
→OPTIONS

Literature Launchers: "Playing Basketball"

Videodisc Side A, Segment 5

Also available in VHS.

Selection Focus Transparency 13: Have students look at the photos and discuss what they notice about the physical intensity of basketball.

Focus Activity: As an extension of the Focus Activity, encourage students to discuss how people have very different reactions to sports—there is no one right way to feel.

A **Active Reading**

PREDICT Have students read the first four lines of the poem and predict what the speaker's attitude toward basketball is. *(The speaker is a player who loves the sport.)*

Additional Resources
📁 *Active Reading Guide*, p. 13
🎧 *Audio Library*
🎧 *Spanish Audio Library*
📁 *Spanish Summaries*, p. 13

B **Literary Elements**

ALLITERATION Ask students to identify the sound device in lines 5 and 10. *(It is alliteration created by the repetition of the s sound.)*

C **Critical Thinking**

INFERRING What is the speaker saying about the power of the sport? *(Basketball can be used to impress young girls [lines 18–19], comfort someone [lines 24–26], and help kids stay out of trouble [lines 29–31].)*

D **Active Reading**

VISUALIZE Ask students to visualize a basketball game and imagine some sounds one could hear. *(One could hear whistles, squeaking tennis shoes, and a ball being dribbled.)*

Teaching Options

Slam, Dunk, & Hook

Yusef Komunyakaa

Fast breaks. Lay ups. With Mercury's°
Insignia on our sneakers,
We outmaneuvered the footwork
Of bad angels. Nothing but a hot
5   Swish of strings like silk
Ten feet out. In the roundhouse°
Labyrinth° our bodies
Created, we could almost
Last forever, poised in midair
10 Like storybook sea monsters.
A high note hung there
A long second. Off
The rim. We'd corkscrew
Up & dunk balls that exploded
15 The skullcap of hope & good
Intention. Bug-eyed, lanky,
All hands & feet . . . sprung rhythm.
We were metaphysical° when girls
Cheered on the sidelines.

20 Tangled up in a falling,
Muscles were a bright motor
Double-flashing to the metal hoop
Nailed to our oak.
When Sonny Boy's mama died
25 He played nonstop all day, so hard
Our backboard splintered.
Glistening with sweat, we jibed°
& rolled the ball off our
Fingertips. Trouble
30 Was there slapping a blackjack°
Against an open palm.
Dribble, drive to the inside, feint,°
& glide like a sparrow hawk.
Lay ups. Fast breaks.
35 We had moves we didn't know
We had. Our bodies spun
On swivels of bone & faith,
Through a lyric slipknot
Of joy, & we knew we were
40 Beautiful & dangerous.

---

1 In ancient Roman mythology, *Mercury* was the swift messenger of the gods. He was often portrayed wearing winged sandals.
6–7 *Roundhouse* is a slang term for a sweeping movement—in this case, wide, swinging arm movements. A *labyrinth* is any confusing, complicated arrangement.
18 Here, *metaphysical* means that the players seemed to go beyond the limits of the physical world.

---

27 To *jibe* is to be in harmony with one another.
30 A *blackjack* is a weighted, flexible, leather-covered weapon.
32 A *feint* is a movement intended to "fake out" an opponent.

MEETING INDIVIDUAL NEEDS — ENGLISH LANGUAGE LEARNERS

Basketball Slang English language learners may be familiar with the game but not with its American slang.

Activity Have English language learners work in small groups with English-proficient students. Ask a student from each group to read a few lines of "Slam, Dunk, and Hook." Then invite the group to paraphrase them. Model by reading aloud and paraphrasing lines 1–4: *We made fast breaks and lay ups. Our cool shoes made us feel as fast as the messenger of the gods. We played more skillfully than our super-powerful opponents.* Have volunteers identify and demonstrate some of the moves. **L2** **COLLAB. LEARN.**

Additional Resources
📁 *English Language Learners Sourcebook*

Reading *Minilesson*

Monitoring Comprehension This poem uses many sensory images to convey the fast-paced excitement of a basketball game and what it means to the players. Encourage students to be sure they understand these sensory images by comparing them with actual basketball terms they are familiar with.

Activity Have students work in small groups. Ask them to reread the poem in sections and prepare graphic organizers for comparing the sensory images from the poem to commonly used terms. **L2**
COLLAB. LEARN.

Additional Resources
📁 *Reading Workbook,* pp. 21–22

Images from the Poem	Commonly Used Terms
the footwork of bad angels	the opposite team
roundhouse labyrinth	A complicated sweeping movement

139

Responding to the Selection

Personal Response

Some students will identify strongly with the poem, while others may not. Most should connect the rhythm and feeling of the poem to the fast-paced action of basketball. Students should explain their choice of lines.

Analyzing Literature

1. These terms include *fast breaks, lay ups, footwork, swish, ten feet out, roundhouse, off the rim, dunk, metal hoop, backboard, ball, dribble, drive to the inside, feint,* and *moves.*

2. People are playing basketball. They move quickly, running, jumping, and shooting the ball. A shot just misses off the rim, and someone dunks the ball. The narrator describes Sonny, who played a whole day through when his mother died. The players keep going, sweating, making moves, and feeling joyful.

3. These are all basketball terms, and they convey the dramatic, fast pace of the poem.

4. They are strenuous and joyful, a way to connect with other people and a way to work off emotions.

5. Students should speak from their own experience and explain their responses.

6. The poem is presented, like a basketball game, in two halves. The language contains short words and phrases, which give the poem a very fast rhythm. It also shifts quickly, almost stopping and starting up again, the way basketball players move.

7. Students should describe a personal experience and explain how it reminds them of the poem.

8. The game connects the players to one another.

Responding to Literature

PERSONAL RESPONSE

What is your response to this poem? Which line from the poem did you find most memorable? Why?

 Analyzing Literature

RECALL

1. What are some of the terms in "Slam, Dunk, & Hook" that are directly related to the game of basketball? Make a list of terms.

2. Summarize the action in "Slam, Dunk, & Hook."

INTERPRET

3. Why is "Slam, Dunk, & Hook" a good title for this poem?

4. What message about team sports does "Slam, Dunk, & Hook" express?

EVALUATE AND CONNECT

5. According to "Slam, Dunk, & Hook," team sports are dramatic, emotional, and exhilarating. Do you agree or disagree? Explain.

6. How do the structure and the rhythm of the poem help to create the feel of an actual game of basketball? Explain.

7. Does this poem remind you of an experience of your own? Explain.

8. What is Komunyakaa saying about the connection between participation in basketball and friendship? Do you agree or disagree? Explain.

9. What did you learn about basketball, or about the attitude of the players, from reading this poem? Explain.

10. **Theme Connection** How do you think playing basketball might have changed the speaker of the poem? Has participation in sports or other activities changed you? How?

Alliteration

Alliteration is the repetition of sounds, most often consonant sounds, at the beginnings of words. Writers often use alliteration in their poetry to enhance the sounds of the lines as a poem is read aloud. Consider the example of alliteration in these lines from "Slam, Dunk, & Hook":

> **Our bodies spun**
>
> **On swivels of bone & faith**

The words *bodies* and *bone* both begin with *b;* the words *spun* and *swivels* both begin with *s.*

1. Find another example of alliteration in this poem or in another poem in this book. Read the example aloud and point out the alliteration.

2. Write your own short poem or paragraph about a real or imaginary sports event. Use images to help your readers see, hear, and feel what you describe in your writing. Try to use alliteration appropriate to your subject.

● See **Literary Terms Handbook,** p. R1.

---

9. Students should understand that basketball is a fast-paced, strenuous, exciting sport that demands a lot of strength, stamina, and physical coordination. It is also a way for players to work together and connect with each other.

10. Through the game he becomes aware of his own strength, power, and beauty. Some students may say that sports have helped them become strong, learn to cooperate with others, and learn to keep going even when they are fatigued.

LITERARY ELEMENTS

1. Other examples of alliteration are *A high note hung there; Dribble, drive to the inside; We were metaphysical when girls/Cheered.*

2. Students' poems should describe a sports event, use clear, strong images, and contain examples of alliteration.

Additional Resources

🖐 *Literary Elements Transparency 13*

Extending Your Response

Writing About Literature
Sensory Imagery   "Slam, Dunk, & Hook" is filled with **sensory imagery,** or words that appeal to our senses. Pick out your favorite image, and write a paragraph explaining why it is memorable.

Creative Writing
Sports: Up Close and Personal   What do you like best about sports in general? What specific sport do you like best? Do you prefer to play or to watch? Review your response to the **Focus Activity** on page 137. Then write a short poem or a paragraph or two that describes your feelings about sports.

Literature Groups
Hooray for Sports!   "Slam, Dunk, & Hook" strongly endorses participation in team sports. What about the win-at-all-costs attitude that sometimes comes with competition? Should amateur teams feel and act differently than professional teams? Debate the issue. Support your opinions with examples from the poem and from your own experience.

Listening and Speaking
Appreciating Poetry   In small groups, choose the most dramatic and exhilarating images from the poem. One group member should read the lines aloud while the remaining members dramatize the scene. Share your dramatization with your classmates.

Reading Further
If you would like to read more poems about basketball or other sports, try these books:

Slam Dunk, compiled by Lillian Morrison

American Sports Poems, edited by R. R. Knudson and May Swenson

📖 **Save your work for your portfolio.**

Skill Minilesson

GRAMMAR AND LANGUAGE • VIVID VERBS

"Slam, Dunk, & Hook" is filled with colorful, **vivid verbs** that help readers visualize the quick action taking place on the basketball court. For example, think about this description:

> *We'd corkscrew*
> *Up & dunk balls that exploded*

The vivid verbs help you visualize the scene. The image is much more effective than just saying, "We'd jump up and throw balls that went into the basket." A **thesaurus,** a book of synonyms, can help you find vivid verbs.

PRACTICE Reread the poem. As you do, pick out some of the vivid verbs that helped you visualize the images in the poem. Keep a list of vivid verbs in your journal, and add verbs to the list as you find them in your reading.

● For more about verbs, see **Language Handbook,** p. R33.

Extending Your Response

Writing About Literature
Students' paragraphs should
- describe an image from the poem.
- explain why it is memorable.

Creative Writing
Students' writing should
- describe their feelings about all sports and their favorites.
- focus on whether they prefer to play or watch.

Literature Groups   Have students prepare for the debate by making notes about their own experiences and those of people they know.
COLLAB. LEARN.

Listening and Speaking
Have students rehearse a scene several times, working to create an effective dramatization.

Skill Minilesson

GRAMMAR AND LANGUAGE
• VIVID VERBS

Examples of vivid verbs from the poem include *outmaneuvered, poised, hung, corkscrew, exploded, cheered, tangled, double-flashing, nailed, splintered, jibed, rolled, slapping, dribble, drive, feint, glide,* and *spun.*

Additional Resources

📘 ***Grammar and Language Workbook,*** pp. 73–74

📘 ***Grammar and Composition Handbook,*** Lesson 3.1

📘 ***Writer's Choice,*** Lesson 10.1

✓ ASSESSMENT OPTIONS

📁 ***Quick Checks,*** p. 13
📁 ***Selection and Theme Assessment,*** p. 24
📁 ***Performance Assessment,*** p. 13
💾 ***Testmaker***

Objective

- To recognize the main idea in a paragraph and apply strategies to identify supporting details

Teaching Strategies

Help students recognize the main idea in a paragraph by having them listen to the paragraph before they read it. Read the paragraph aloud and have students discuss what they thought was most important about what they heard. Then, ask them to read the paragraph to themselves and identify the topic sentence.

Exercise

1. The narrator did not get the part.
2. These are some supporting details: the mother looked at her daughter's face hopefully; the narrator shook her head; her mother then looked bewildered; and the narrator felt sad and confused.

Additional Resources

 Reading Workbook

Reading and Thinking Skills

Identifying Main Idea and Supporting Details

Skillful readers know to look for the **main idea** in a paragraph. In many paragraphs, a topic sentence states the main idea. The other sentences add **supporting details**.

> In the La Brea Tar Pits many of the excavated bones belong to juvenile mammals. Thousands of years ago thirsty young animals in the area were drawn to watering holes, not knowing they were traps. Those inviting pools had false bottoms made of sticky tar, which immobilized its victims and preserved their bones when they died. Innocence trapped by ignorance. The tar pits record that well.

In this passage, the main idea is stated in a topic sentence. That sentence, the first one, tells us that many of the bones found in the tar pits are those of young animals. The other sentences further explain the main idea by adding supporting details.

Often, the main idea is implied, not stated directly. Without a topic sentence, the reader needs to figure out the main idea that connects the supporting details. If you can't find a topic sentence, try to state the implied main idea in your own words.

● For more about main idea and details, see **Reading Handbook,** p. R86.

EXERCISE

Read the following excerpt from "Hollywood and the Pits." Then answer the questions.

> My mother looked at my face hopefully when I came into the room. I gave her a quick shake of the head. She looked bewildered. I felt bad for my mother then. How could I explain it to her? I didn't understand it myself. We left saying polite good-byes to all the other mothers.

1. What is the implied main idea of the paragraph?
2. List three details that support the main idea.

Teaching Options

MEETING INDIVIDUAL NEEDS INCLUSION STRATEGIES

Less-Proficient Readers To reinforce students' ability to identify the main idea of a paragraph, create two short paragraphs based on their opinions.

Activity Ask students to state an opinion on whether becoming a child actor is a good idea. Write a positive and a negative opinion on the board.

Then ask for reasons that support those opinions and write them in sentence form beneath the opinion they support. Ask students to circle the topic sentences and underline the supporting sentences in the paragraphs they have created. **L1**

Vo·cab·u·lar·y Skills

Context Clues

She gave me an *imperious* smile.   He makes *imperious* remarks.

These sentences are no help to you in figuring out what *imperious* means because they provide no useful **context clues.** Context is the sentence or group of sentences in which a word appears. The context often provides clues as to what an unfamiliar word means. Following are some kinds of context clues:

Definition: *She gave me an imperious—overbearing and arrogant—smile.*

The writer provides a definition: imperious means "overbearing and arrogant."

Example: *He makes imperious remarks, such as, "You will immediately do as I say."*

Here an example is provided. You can tell what an *imperious* person is like by the kind of remark such a person would make.

Restatement: *I don't know how to react to imperious people. I don't know what to say or do around those who are so bossy and sure of themselves.*

The writer has used other words to restate the idea.

Contrast: *She's humble and unassuming—not at all imperious like her brother.*

Here, the reader can tell that an *imperious* person must be the opposite of the type of person described.

EXERCISE

Use context clues to figure out what the underlined words mean. Write a synonym or a short definition for each.

1. Lee interrupts her story to interpose descriptions of the tar pits.
2. These pits were lethal to every animal that stepped into them, for death was certain.
3. The sticky mud precluded the animals' escape, trapping them forever.
4. Is Lee intimating that Hollywood is also a trap, suggesting without actually saying it?
5. She makes it clear that child actors are not at all safe. Instead, child actors are in peril of failure when they outgrow their childish cuteness.

Objective

• To recognize and use context clues to comprehend unfamiliar words

Teaching Strategies

To demonstrate how context clues can help in deciphering the meaning of an unfamiliar word, offer an example using a non-English word: *Yesterday, I went to the store and bought a chapeau (pronounced sha pō´).* Ask students to guess what you bought. Begin giving clues: *Normally, I don't like to cover my head, but this time I had to make an exception.*

Exercise

1. interpose: interject, insert
2. lethal: fatal, something that causes death
3. precluded: prevented, hindered
4. intimating: hinting, insinuating
5. peril: danger

Additional Resources
📁 *Vocabulary Power: Weekly Lessons and Activities*

Teaching Options

ENGLISH LANGUAGE LEARNERS

Creating Context The imagery and figurative language in poetry can be challenging for English language learners. They will often depend on context clues to get at meaning.

Activity Divide the poem "Slam, Dunk, and Hook" into segments of four or five lines and distribute them to small groups that include proficient speakers. Each student should take one line of the poem, draw a picture to convey its content and mood, and add it to a bucher-paper mural. The class can then try to locate the line in the poem each picture represents. **COLLAB. LEARN.**

Additional Resources
📁 *English Language Learners Sourcebook*

Objective

- To understand the elements of a short story

Teaching Strategies

Ask each student to think of his or her favorite childhood story. Prompt a discussion about what the stories were, whether they were told or read to them, who passed the stories along, and what students liked about them.

Setting Since most students are familiar with Hollywood through the movies, ask them to call out the first word that comes to mind when they hear the word *Hollywood*. Create a word collage of student responses on the board. Explain that these ideas, images, and perceptions could all be included in the setting of a short story about Hollywood.

Characters Ask students to use their imaginations to come up with a list of characters for a short story about Hollywood. These could be movie stars or other people they would expect to find in Hollywood. Encourage a discussion about how we often learn something unexpected about human nature through a short story.

Teaching Options

SHORT STORY

Fiction is writing about imaginary people, places, or events. If you are reading a short piece of fiction, you are probably reading a **short story.** The short-story form has its roots in folktales and fables, which people told long before recorded history. However, the short story as we know it is less than two hundred years old.

All fiction includes the literary elements shown below. These pages discuss the five elements in the story "Hollywood and the Pits," by Cherylene Lee. Look for these elements when you read other short stories.

Stages in Plot Development

The main character is a teenage girl who has worked as a child actor but now is interested only in her work on an archaeological dig at the La Brea Tar Pits. Her mother doesn't understand her new interest.

1 **EXPOSITION** is background information about characters and setting. It sets the scene for the conflict.

SHORT STORY ELEMENTS

MODEL: "Hollywood and the Pits"

SETTING is the time and place of the story's action. Setting also includes the customs, values, and beliefs of a place or a time.

"Hollywood and the Pits" opens in Los Angeles in 1968 and, in **flashbacks,** moves through the 1950s and 1960s.

CHARACTERS are the actors in the story. They can be people, animals, robots, or whatever the writer chooses. The main character is called the **protagonist.**

The characters include the two Lee sisters, their mother, and various unnamed minor characters. The younger Lee sister is the protagonist.

144 ❧ THEME 2

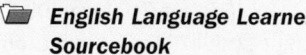

MEETING INDIVIDUAL NEEDS — ENGLISH LANGUAGE LEARNERS

Multicultural Stories Storytelling is a wonderful way to expose all students to the richness of other cultures.

Activity Ask each English language learner to prepare to tell a legend that is popular in his or her native culture and involves an interesting protagonist. Create a storytelling atmosphere by having students sit in small circles to tell one another their stories.

Make sure students give their stories titles. Have them join different story circles during the week. At the end of the week, you may wish to play a game of charades. Write the story titles on slips of paper and have students pick one to act out for classmates to guess.

Additional Resources
📁 *English Language Learners Sourcebook*

3 CLIMAX is the point of highest interest, conflict, or suspense in the story.

As the main character grows up, demand for her at the Hollywood studios declines. No longer a novelty, she's become an average, awkward teenager. She grows discouraged, but her mother keeps taking her to auditions.

In the summer of 1968, she works on a dig at the La Brea Tar Pits and decides to give up show business.

4 FALLING ACTION shows what happens to the character after the climax.

The main character's mother is disappointed by her decision. Although she doesn't understand it, she accepts it and drives her daughter to the tar pits rather than to auditions.

Working in the tar pits, the main character realizes the cruelty of what happened there. She sees the pits as a symbol of what happens to many performers who are used and then discarded by the Hollywood studios.

As young children, the main character and her older sister develop a song-and-dance act and become successful. The main character gets roles in Hollywood films because she is cute and can do her scenes in one take. Her mother encourages her career.

2 RISING ACTION develops the conflict.

5 RESOLUTION gives the final outcome.

POINT OF VIEW is the vantage point from which a story is told. The person telling the story is the **narrator**. In **first-person** point of view, the narrator is a character in the story. In **third-person** point of view, the narrator is someone outside the story.

"Hollywood and the Pits" is told from the first-person point of view. The narrator is the younger Lee sister. She is probably an adult looking back at herself between the ages of three and fifteen.

THEME is the main message that the reader can take from the story. A theme may be stated directly in the story or in its title. However, most stories have **implied** themes, suggested by what the characters learn or by what their experiences illustrate. Readers' ideas about implied themes may vary.

The theme of "Hollywood and the Pits" is implied. A reader might state its theme this way: Hollywood can trap and destroy young performers just as the La Brea Tar Pits trapped many young animals.

PLOT is the basic structure of the story. It is a series of related events in which a problem is explored and then solved. Plot is created through **conflict**—a struggle between people, ideas, or forces.

The conflict is between the younger Lee sister and her mother. The diagram on these pages shows how the plot develops.

WINDS OF CHANGE 145

Point of View Encourage a discussion of how students feel about the point of view in "Hollywood and the Pits." Ask if they can relate to the feelings the narrator expresses. Invite them to share their own points of view on the situation of child actors and parents who want their children to be stars.

Theme Explain to students that the writer has used italics to help her express the theme of the story. She interjects italicized information about the tar pits to give the reader deeper insight into how she is feeling about herself as a performer. Suggest that students locate passages in italics and describe what the passages tell them about the theme.

Plot Students may associate plot with the action of the story. In this case, the plot centers around the conflicting ambitions of a mother and her daughter.

Technology Option

Short Story Table

Students can use word-processing software to create a table of the five elements of a short story. Have each student open a new document and insert a five-column table with the following headings: *Setting, Characters, Point of View, Theme,* and *Plot.*

Setting	Characters	Point of View	Theme	Plot

For each new short story that students read, have them add a new row and complete the table with information about each of the work's five elements. Students can use their tables to review the various short stories they read, or to help them compare and contrast the various texts. **L2**

Active Reading Strategies

Objective

- To understand and apply strategies for reading and comprehending short stories

Teach the Strategies

Ask students to think of their favorite jokes. Encourage each of them to jot down a joke—preferably one with characters and a setting. Have students work in small groups to tell their jokes. Apply active reading strategies: Could students predict the outcome? Visualize the setting? Connect the joke to their own experience?

Predict

Remind students that a skillful reader pays attention to the details of a story when predicting its outcome. Writers often use "trivial" details to foreshadow greater events.

Visualize

Point out that visualizing can help students remember what they have read.

Review

Reviewing the sequence of events can sometimes interfere with a reader's pace, but it can help prevent confusion and frustration.

Teaching Options

Active Reading Strategies

Tips for Reading a Short Story

How do you approach reading a short story? You can begin by sorting out the basic elements: the characters, setting, plot, point of view, and theme. A short story will usually have fewer characters than a novel—in some cases as few as one or two. Often a story will have a single setting. Since a short story is usually meant to be read in one sitting, the plot and theme usually revolve around how the characters respond to a single event. Looking for these elements and using the strategies below can help you read short stories.

● For more about reading strategies, see **Reading Handbook,** pp. R70–R101.

PREDICT

At certain points in your reading, take time to wonder what will happen next in the story.

Ask Yourself . . .

● Can I tell from the title if this story is going to be humorous or dramatic?

● How will these characters respond to this development?

● How will the story end?

VISUALIZE

Keep the characters and the setting in your mind's eye as you read.

Ask Yourself . . .

● What does this character look like? Has the author given me hints or specific details?

● Have I ever seen a setting like this? Can I picture it?

REVIEW

If a story is longer than a few pages, it might help to stop from time to time to review what you have found out in the story.

Ask Yourself . . .

● Who are the main characters in this story?

● How would I summarize the story up to this point?

146 ❦ THEME 2

Reading Journal

Quirky Characters

Cynthia Rylant in "The Crush" tells the story of two unique, interesting characters. Invite students to describe physical features and personality traits of unusual characters they have read about.

Activity As they read, invite students to create two webs, one for Ernie and one for Dolores. Around each web have students record details about each character. After reading, have students review their webs and then write a brief epilogue to the story telling what the lives of Ernie and Dolores are like one, five, or ten years in the future.

CONNECT

As you read, keep trying to make connections. How does the story connect to your current life or to your past or future?

Ask Yourself . . .

- Does this character remind me of someone I know or another character I have read about?

- Have I ever felt like this character?

- Would I have responded in this way if this event had happened to me?

EVALUATE

As you read, form opinions about how the story is written and how you feel about the characters and their actions. Don't wait until the end of a story to decide if you like it. Make judgments from the very beginning, but feel free to change your opinions as you read.

Ask Yourself . . .

- Has the author made this character believable?

- Has this story grabbed me? Do I want to find out what happens?

- Are these characters people I care about?

APPLYING THE STRATEGIES

Practice applying the strategies to the following short story, "A Crush." Use the Active Reading Model notes in the margins as you read. Write your responses on a separate piece of paper or use stick-on notes.

Connect

Remind students that most authors write in order to connect with their readers. As characters develop and the plot unfolds, the students should be aware of how they are feeling about a story and whether it is relevant to their lives. Challenge students to find something or someone in each story they read that makes them feel connected to the selection.

Evaluate

Encourage students to think of reading a short story as making a new friend. There will be things they like and things they don't like. Aspects of the story may seem strange, exciting, dull, or even confusing. It is important for students to realize that their own opinions are important and will help determine the kinds of literature they may be drawn to later in their lives. Remind them that judging a work should enhance, not interfere with, the experience of reading.

Objectives

- To read and analyze a short story about a change in feelings
- To identify point of view in a short story
- To write a character description

Skills

Reading/Thinking: Activating Prior Knowledge; Drawing Conclusions; Inferring
Writing: Letter of Advice
Vocabulary: Suffix *-ly*
Grammar/Language: Capitalization; Adverb Clauses
Listening/Speaking: Role Playing a Conversation
Life Skills: Writing a Job Description
Collaboration: Literature Groups

Motivating
→OPTIONS

Selection Focus Transparency 14: Have students view and discuss the quote about love from Dr. Karl Menninger.

Focus Activity: As an extension of the Focus Activity, have pairs of students share their ways of meeting people and tell how new friends have changed them.

ACTIVE READING MODEL

Before You Read
A Crush

MEET CYNTHIA RYLANT

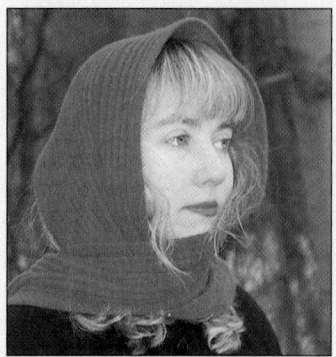

Cynthia Rylant (rī′ lənt) grew up poor in the Appalachian Mountains of West Virginia in a home without electricity or running water. In her early writings, she drew on this experience to describe ordinary characters in difficult situations. "I get a lot of personal gratification," says Rylant, "thinking of those people who don't get any attention in the world and making them really valuable in my fiction—making them absolutely shine with their beauty. . . . I want to deal with people who don't have what they want."

Cynthia Rylant was born in 1954. This story was first published in 1990.

FOCUS ACTIVITY

Think about someone your age you wish you knew better. How could you let that person know you are interested?

List Ideas
List ways you might quietly let someone know you'd like to get to know him or her better.

Setting a Purpose
Read "A Crush" to discover how one person decides to show interest in another.

BACKGROUND

The Time and Place It is the late 1900s in a small town in the United States.

VOCABULARY PREVIEW

excess (ek′ ses) *adj.* more than usual or necessary; p. 149
speculation (spek′ yə lā′ shən) *n.* the act of forming an opinion or conclusion based on guesswork; p. 150
taut (tôt) *adj.* stretched tight; p. 150
improbable (im prob′ ə bəl) *adj.* not likely; p. 151
illuminated (i lōō′ mə nāt id) *adj.* lit up; p. 152
venture (ven′ chər) *v.* to do something in spite of possible risk or danger; p. 152
eventually (i ven′ chōō ə lē) *adv.* in the end; finally; p. 153
intently (in tent′ lē) *adv.* in a firmly focused way; with concentration; p. 154
discreetly (dis krēt′ lē) *adv.* in a manner showing good judgment; cautiously; p. 155
hardy (här′ dē) *adj.* able to endure hardship; strong and healthy; p. 155

RESOURCE MANAGER

Lesson Planning Resource
The ***Theme Two Planning Guide*** (pp. 24–31) provides additional lesson notes and reduced versions of all print resources.

📁 **Other Print Resources**
- Active Reading Guide, p. 14
- Vocabulary Practice, p. 9
- Reading Workbook, p. 23–24
- Grammar and Language Workbook, pp. 159–160, 235–246

- Grammar and Composition Handbook, Lessons 8.5, 12.1–12.4
- Quick Checks, p. 14
- Selection and Theme Assessment, pp. 25–26
- Performance Assessment, p. 14
- Spanish Summaries, p. 14
- Spanish Translations
- Inclusion Strategies
- English Language Learners Sourcebook

 Transparencies
- Selection Focus 14
- Literary Elements 14
- Grammar and Language 12

Technology
 Audio Library
 Spanish Audio Library
- Glencoe Literature Web Site
- Testmaker

A Crush

Cynthia Rylant

When the windows of Stan's

Hardware started filling up with flowers, everyone in town knew something had happened. Excess flowers usually mean death, but since these were all real flowers bearing the aroma of nature instead of floral preservative,[1] and since they stood bunched in clear mason jars instead of impaled on styrofoam crosses, everyone knew nobody had died. So they all figured somebody had a crush and kept quiet.

---

1. *Floral preservative* is a chemical that helps cut flowers stay fresh looking.

Vocabulary
excess (ek′ ses) *adj.* more than usual or necessary

ACTIVE READING MODEL

QUESTION

What is the author telling us about the size of the town?

SUMMARY

Ernie is a shy, mentally disabled man who moves to a group home when his mother dies. Jack becomes his friend and teaches him to garden. Jack also begins taking Ernie to breakfast at a restaurant across the street from a hardware store. When Ernie sees Dolores, the tough manager of the store, he falls in love with her. He begins leaving flowers in front of the store before it opens. Although she doesn't find out who is giving her the flowers, they make her happy.

📁 *Spanish Summaries,* p. 14

A Active Reading

QUESTION *(Students can infer that this is a small town. The phrase everyone in town is a clue that the town must be very small if everyone pays attention to the hardware store.)*

Additional Resources
📁 *Active Reading Guide,* p. 14
🎧 *Audio Library*
🎧 *Spanish Audio Library*

Teaching Options

CONNECTING TO OTHER SELECTIONS

The chart at the right shows three ways to connect "A Crush" to other selections in this book.

For specific teaching strategies, see the *Theme Two Planning Guide,* pages 27–28.

Connection		Title
Life Skills: Teaching and Mentoring	→	"The Scholarship Jacket," p. 451
Thematic: At the Crossroads	→	"The Boy and His Grandfather," p. 495
Literary: Plot	→	"Charles," p. 544

B Literary Elements

THIRD-PERSON POINT OF VIEW Ask students to evaluate the narrator's viewpoint. Who is telling the story? *(Students might suggest that the narrator is someone outside the story; that is, he or she is not a named character.)* Explain to students that this story is told from the third-person point of view. The words *he, she,* and *they* signal a third-person narrator.

C Active Reading

PREDICT *(Students may guess that the tattoo is an ordinary object, such as a rose, or an object that is unique and personal.)*

D Active Reading

VISUALIZE Ask students to describe their images aloud, or encourage them to draw sketches of Dolores's tattoo.

Teaching Options

ACTIVE READING MODEL

B

PREDICT

C

What do you think the tattoo might be?

VISUALIZE

D

Can you picture what this tattoo would look like?

There wasn't really a Stan of Stan's Hardware. Dick Wilcox was the owner, and since he'd never liked his own name, he gave his store half the name of his childhood hero, Stan Laurel in the movies. Dick had been married for twenty-seven years. Once, his wife Helen had dropped a German chocolate cake on his head at a Lion's Club dance, so Dick and Helen were not likely candidates for the honest expression of the flowers in those clear mason jars lining the windows of Stan's Hardware, and speculation had to move on to Dolores.

Dolores was the assistant manager at Stan's and had worked there for twenty years, since high school. She knew the store like a mother knows her baby, so Dick—who had trouble keeping up with things like prices and new brands of drywall compound[2]—tried to keep himself busy in the back and give Dolores the run of the floor. This worked fine because the carpenters and plumbers and painters in town trusted Dolores and took her advice to heart. They also liked her tattoo.

Dolores was the only woman in town with a tattoo. On the days she went sleeveless, one could see it on the taut brown skin of her upper arm: "Howl at the Moon." The picture was of a baying coyote which must have been a dark gray in its early days but which had faded to the color of the spackling paste Dolores stocked in the third aisle. Nobody had gotten out of Dolores the true story behind the tattoo. Some of the men who came in liked to show off their own, and they'd roll up their sleeves or pull open their shirts, exhibiting bald eagles and rattlesnakes, and they'd try to coax out of Dolores the history of her coyote. All of the men had gotten their tattoos when they were in the service, drunk on weekend leave and full of the spitfire[3] of young soldiers. Dolores had never been in the service and she'd never seen weekend leave and there wasn't a tattoo parlor anywhere near. They couldn't figure why or where

Did You Know?
Stan Laurel was the thin man with the long face; Oliver Hardy was his not-so-thin partner. The popular comedy team of Laurel and Hardy made movies together from the late 1920s to 1951.

---

2. *Drywall compound* and *spackling paste* (mentioned in the next paragraph) are used to prepare walls before painting.
3. When soldiers are off duty and allowed to go off base, they're on *leave.* When they're full of *spitfire,* they're quick-tempered and ready to fight.

Vocabulary
speculation (spek´ yə lā´ shən) *n.* the act of forming an opinion or conclusion based on guesswork
taut (tôt) *adj.* stretched tight

MEETING INDIVIDUAL NEEDS

ENGLISH LANGUAGE LEARNERS

Rites of Passage Point out to English language learners that getting a tattoo is a rite of passage to adulthood in some cultures. The combination of withstanding physical pain and making a permanent decision implies commitment. Brainstorm to develop a list of rites of passage common to the American culture: learning to drive, getting a job, and so on.

Activity Have students make lists of rites of passage from their cultures. Do their communities still use these rituals? Do they follow some American traditions as well?

Additional Resources
📁 *English Language Learners Sourcebook*

Cynthia Rylant ⌁

any half-sober woman would have a howling coyote ground into the soft skin of her upper arm. But Dolores wasn't telling.

That the flowers in Stan's front window had anything to do with Dolores seemed completely <u>improbable</u>. As far as anyone knew, Dolores had never been in love nor had anyone ever been in love with her. Some believed it was the tattoo, of course, or the fine dark hair coating Dolores's upper lip which kept suitors away. Some felt it was because Dolores was just more of a man than most of the men in town, and fellows couldn't figure out how to court someone who knew more about the carburetor of a car or the back side of a washing machine than they did. Others thought Dolores simply didn't want love. This was a popular theory among the women in town who sold Avon and Mary Kay cosmetics. Whenever one of them ran into the hardware for a package of light bulbs or some batteries, she would mentally pluck every one of the black hairs above Dolores's lip. Then she'd wash that grease out of Dolores's hair, give her a good blunt cut, dress her in a decent silk-blend blouse with a nice Liz Claiborne skirt from the Sports line, and, finally, tone down that swarthy, longshoreman[4] look of Dolores's with a concealing beige foundation, some frosted peach lipstick, and a good gray liner for the eyes.

Dolores simply didn't want love, the Avon lady would think as she walked back to her car carrying her little bag of batteries. If she did, she'd fix herself up.

The man who was in love with Dolores and who brought her zinnias and cornflowers and nasturtiums[5] and marigolds and asters and four-o'clocks in clear mason jars did not know any of this. He did not know that men showed Dolores their tattoos. He did not know that Dolores understood how to use and to sell a belt sander. He did not know that Dolores needed some concealing beige foundation so she could get someone to love her. The man who brought flowers to Dolores on Wednesdays when the hardware opened its doors at 7:00 A.M. didn't care who Dolores had ever been or what anyone had ever thought of her. He loved her and he wanted to bring her flowers.

Ernie had lived in this town all of his life and had never before met Dolores. He was thirty-three years old, and for thirty-one of those years he had lived at home with his mother in a small, dark house on the edge of town near Beckwith's Orchards. Ernie had been a beautiful baby, with

---

4. A *swarthy longshoreman* is a dark or sunburned dockworker.
5. *nasturtiums* (nä stur′ shəms)

Vocabulary
improbable (im prob′ ə bəl) *adj.* not likely

E **Active Reading**
EVALUATE Ask students which of these details paints the most vivid picture of Dolores. *(Students might choose the description of her facial hair or her knowledge of machines.)*

F **Active Reading**
RESPOND *(Students might respond negatively because these ladies seem too judgmental and concerned with people's looks.)*

G **Active Reading**
QUESTION Encourage students to think about the nature of a crush when answering this question.

FYI

Bachelor's Button
The cornflower is also known as the bachelor's button. This is partly because rural bachelors used to carry this flower in their pockets. If it stayed fresh, it meant the girlfriend still cared. If it shriveled up, it meant "she loves me not."

H **Literary Elements**
THIRD-PERSON POINT OF VIEW Ask students to list some of the characters' thoughts revealed on this page by the narrator. *(People think Dolores hasn't had a suitor because of her tattoo or facial hair; the Avon lady believes Dolores doesn't want love; Ernie loves Dolores no matter what people think about her.)*

Reading *Minilesson*

Activating Prior Knowledge Readers often have to draw on knowledge from previous reading or from their own experience. For example, in order to understand the townspeople's perception of Dolores, readers need to be aware of common stereotypes concerning men and women.

Activity Draw the following chart on the board, and work with students to create a list of common male and female stereotypes. Discuss with students why Dolores, as the narrator describes her, does not match many of the ideas about women on your list. Finally, ask students how their own prior knowledge of male and female stereotypes helped them understand this part of the story. **L2**

Men	Women
have facial hair	wear makeup
work with their hands fixing and building things	are homemakers—caring for their homes and families
have tattoos	do not have tattoos

Additional Resources
📁 *Reading Workbook,* pp. 23–24

Historical Note

W. Atlee Burpee & Co. is the world's largest mail-order seed company. It was founded in Pennsylvania more than one hundred years ago by eighteen-year-old W. Atlee Burpee, who borrowed $1,000 from his mother to start the business.

A Crush

ACTIVE READING MODEL

CONNECT

Do you know of any children or adults whose mental development happened this slowly?

REVIEW

Who are the major characters you have met so far?

VISUALIZE

How does the author help you picture this scene in your mind?

a shock of shining black hair and large blue eyes and a round, wise face. But as he had grown, it had become clearer and clearer that though he was indeed a perfectly beautiful child, his mind had not developed with the same perfection. Ernie would not be able to speak in sentences until he was six years old. He would not be able to count the apples in a bowl until he was eight. By the time he was ten, he could sing a simple song. At age twelve, he understood what a joke was. And when he was twenty, something he saw on television made him cry.

Ernie's mother kept him in the house with her because it was easier, so Ernie knew nothing of the world except this house. They lived, the two of them, in tiny dark rooms always illuminated by the glow of a television set, Ernie's bags of Oreos and Nutter Butters littering the floor, his baseball cards scattered across the sofa, his heavy winter coat thrown over the arm of a chair so he could wear it whenever he wanted, and his box of Burpee seed packages sitting in the middle of the kitchen table.

These Ernie cherished. The seeds had been delivered to his home by mistake. One day a woman wearing a brown uniform had pulled up in a brown truck, walked quickly to the front porch of Ernie's house, set a box down, and with a couple of toots of her horn, driven off again. Ernie had watched her through the curtains, and when she was gone, had ventured onto the porch and shyly, cautiously, picked up the box. His mother checked it when he carried it inside. The box didn't have their name on it but the brown truck was gone, so whatever was in the box was theirs to keep. Ernie pulled off the heavy tape, his fingers trembling, and found inside the box more little packages of seeds than he could count. He lifted them out, one by one, and examined the beautiful photographs of flowers on each. His mother was not interested, had returned to the television, but Ernie sat down at the kitchen table and quietly looked at each package for a long time, his fingers running across the slick paper and outlining the shapes of zinnias and cornflowers and nasturtiums and marigolds and asters and four-o'clocks, his eyes drawing up their colors.

Vocabulary
illuminated (i lōō′ mə nāt id) *adj.* lit up
venture (ven′ chər) *v.* to do something in spite of possible risk or danger

Cynthia Rylant

Two months later Ernie's mother died. A neighbor found her at the mailbox beside the road. People from the county courthouse came out to get Ernie, and as they ushered him from the home he would never see again, he picked up the box of seed packages from his kitchen table and passed through the doorway.

Eventually Ernie was moved to a large white house near the main street of town. This house was called a group home, because in it lived a group of people who, like Ernie, could not live on their own. There were six of them. Each had his own room. When Ernie was shown the room that would be his, he put the box of Burpee seeds—which he had kept with him since his mother's death—on the little table beside the bed and then he sat down on the bed and cried.

Ernie cried every day for nearly a month. And then he stopped. He dried his tears and he learned how to bake refrigerator biscuits and how to dust mop and what to do if the indoor plants looked brown.

Ernie loved watering the indoor plants and it was this pleasure which finally drew him outside. One of the young men who worked at the group home—a college student named Jack—grew a large garden in the back of the house. It was full of tomato vines and the large yellow blossoms of healthy squash. During his first summer at the house, Ernie would stand at the kitchen window, watching Jack and sometimes a resident of the home move among the vegetables. Ernie was curious, but too afraid to go into the garden.

Then one day when Ernie was watching through the window, he noticed that Jack was ripping open several slick little packages and emptying them into the ground. Ernie panicked and ran to his room. But the box of Burpee seeds was still there on his table, untouched. He grabbed it, slid it under his bed, then went back through the house and out into the garden as if he had done this every day of his life.

He stood beside Jack, watching him empty seed packages into the soft black soil, and as the packages were emptied, Ernie asked for them, holding out his hand, his eyes on the photographs of red radishes and purple eggplant. Jack handed the empty packages over with a smile and with that gesture became Ernie's first friend.

Jack tried to explain to Ernie that the seeds would grow into vegetables but Ernie could not believe this until he saw it come true. And when it did, he looked all the more

Vocabulary
eventually (i ven′ chōō ə lē) *adv.* in the end; finally

ACTIVE READING MODEL

PREDICT

Do you think someone like Ernie could live alone?

M

PREDICT

How long do you think it will take Ernie to go outdoors?

N

QUESTION

Do you think Ernie usually talks much to Jack or the other people in the group home?

P

M Active Reading

PREDICT *(Students should recognize that Ernie could probably not live alone because he is mentally handicapped and has spent most of his life inside his mother's house.)*

N Active Reading

PREDICT *(Students might suggest that Ernie will go outside when he makes a connection between the garden and the pictures on his most prized possessions—the Burpee seeds.)*

O Critical Thinking

INFERRING Ask students what Ernie thinks when he first sees Jack ripping open seed packages. What good effect does this misunderstanding have? *(He thinks Jack has taken his flower seeds and is planting them. It gives him the courage to go out to the garden for the first time.)*

P Active Reading

QUESTION *(It seems that Ernie is extremely shy, probably because the only person he's talked to has been his mother. Also, the narrator tells us that Jack is Ernie's first friend.)*

INTERDISCIPLINARY CONNECTION

Science Explain to students how seeds grow into vegetables and flowers. Tell them that a seed is the embryo of a plant and carries the genetic information it needs to grow into that kind of plant. The seed also contains the nutrients the plant needs to begin to grow. All the gardener must add is light, water, and soil.

Activity Have students plant seeds (indoors or out, depending on the time of year and climate). Suggest that they try growing different batches of seeds under different conditions: some with fertilizer and others without, some with six hours of light per day and others with twelve, and so on. Have them record which plants grow best under which conditions.

VIEWING THE PAINTING

Suggest that students take note not only of the diner but also the neighborhood around it as they study the painting.

Viewing Response *Students may suggest that young people or working-class people would probably be the customers at a diner like this.*

Q **Active Reading**

EVALUATE Encourage students to explain their opinions using examples from the story. *(Students might suggest that the use of transitional words and phrases, such as* Wednesday morning *and* the first time, *help readers follow the passage of time.)*

R **Active Reading**

CONNECT Explain to students that although going to breakfast might seem easy to them, it is very scary for Ernie. Encourage them to write about scary first experiences in their journals.

S **Literary Elements**

THIRD-PERSON POINT OF VIEW
Discuss with students how and what readers learn about Jack's personality from the narrator. *(Because we learn Jack's thoughts from the narrator, we know that he is a kind and patient person. When Jack takes Ernie to breakfast, he leaves very early to avoid the crowds that frighten Ernie.)*

Teaching Options

Boulevard Diner–Worcester, MA, 1992. John Baeder. Oil on canvas, 30¼ x 48¼ in. O. K. Harris Works of Art, New York.

Viewing the painting: While Ernie was eating breakfast at the Big Boy restaurant, his life was changed. Whose life might be changed at the diner in this painting?

EVALUATE

Q Do you think the author has done a good job of showing the passage of time?

CONNECT

R Have you ever been really frightened to try a new experience?

intently at the packages of zinnias and cornflowers and the rest hidden beneath his bed. He thought more deeply about them but he could not carry them to the garden. He could not let the garden have his seeds.

That was the first year in the large white house.

The second year, Ernie saw Dolores, and after that he thought of nothing else but her and of the photographs of flowers beneath his bed.

Jack had decided to take Ernie downtown for breakfast every Wednesday morning to ease him into the world outside that of the group home. They left very early, at 5:45 A.M., so there would be few people and almost no traffic to frighten Ernie and make him beg for his room. Jack and Ernie drove to the Big Boy restaurant which sat across the street from Stan's Hardware. There they ate eggs and bacon and French toast among those whose work demanded rising before the sun: bus drivers, policemen, nurses, mill workers. Their first time in the Big Boy, Ernie was too nervous to eat. The second time, he could eat but he couldn't look up. The third time, he not only ate everything on his

S

Vocabulary
intently (in tent′ lē) *adv.* in a firmly focused way; with concentration

154 🐾 THEME 2

Listening and Speaking *Minilesson*

Role-Playing a Conversation Post these guidelines for role-playing:
- Discuss with your partner what the characters are like and what situation they are in.
- Be spontaneous. React as you think your character would react.
- Use facial expressions and gestures to reinforce what you say.

Activity Have students work with partners to role-play a conversation between Ernie and Jack the first time they go to breakfast together. Remind them that Ernie is shy, has a small vocabulary, and usually speaks slowly, while Jack is self-confident and friendly. After students practice, have them perform their conversations for the class. **L2** **COLLAB. LEARN.**

Cynthia Rylant ~

plate, but he lifted his head and he looked out the window of the Big Boy restaurant toward Stan's Hardware across the street. There he saw a dark-haired woman in jeans and a black T-shirt unlocking the front door of the building, and that was the moment Ernie started loving Dolores and thinking about giving up his seeds to the soft black soil of Jack's garden.

Love is such a mystery, and when it strikes the heart of one as mysterious as Ernie himself, it can hardly be spoken of. Ernie could not explain to Jack why he went directly to his room later that morning, pulled the box of Burpee seeds from under his bed, then grabbed Jack's hand in the kitchen and walked with him to the garden where Ernie had come to believe things would grow. Ernie handed the packets of seeds one by one to Jack, who stood in silent admiration of the lovely photographs before asking Ernie several times, "Are you sure you want to plant these?" Ernie was sure. It didn't take him very long, and when the seeds all lay under the moist black earth, Ernie carried his empty packages inside the house and spent the rest of the day spreading them across his bed in different arrangements.

That was in June. For the next several Wednesdays at 7:00 A.M. Ernie watched every movement of the dark-haired woman behind the lighted windows of Stan's Hardware. Jack watched Ernie watch Dolores, and discreetly said nothing.

When Ernie's flowers began growing in July, Ernie spent most of his time in the garden. He would watch the garden for hours, as if he expected it suddenly to move or to impress him with a quick trick. The fragile green stems of his flowers stood uncertainly in the soil, like baby colts on their first legs, but the young plants performed no magic for Ernie's eyes. They saved their shows for the middle of the night and next day surprised Ernie with tender small blooms in all the colors the photographs had promised.

The flowers grew fast and hardy, and one early Wednesday morning when they looked as big and bright as their pictures on the empty packages, Ernie pulled a glass canning jar off a dusty shelf in the basement of his house. He washed the jar, half filled it with water, then carried it to the garden where he placed in it one of every kind of flower he had grown. He met Jack at the car and rode off to the Big Boy with the jar of flowers held tight between his small hands. Jack told him it was a beautiful bouquet.

Vocabulary
discreetly (dis krēt′ lē) *adv.* in a manner showing good judgment; cautiously
hardy (här′ dē) *adj.* able to endure hardship; strong and healthy

---

ACTIVE READING MODEL

REVIEW
Go over in your mind what has happened so far in the story.

RESPOND
What would you like to ask the writer about this scene? Do you imagine that she knows someone like Ernie?

EVALUATE
Does Jack's behavior in the restaurant reflect what you know about him so far?

T Active Reading

REVIEW Encourage students to list not only events but also character descriptions. Prompt students with questions if they omit an important event or description.

U Active Reading

RESPOND *(Students might suggest that the author knows someone like Ernie because she captures his personality so well.)*

V Active Reading

EVALUATE You may wish to share the following model to guide students in the process of evaluating.

Model: From what I've read so far, I know that Jack seems to care about Ernie's well-being. He takes Ernie to breakfast once a week to help Ernie develop social skills. I think Jack knows Ernie has a crush on Dolores, but doesn't say anything because he has patience. He knows that Ernie does things carefully. That's why he doesn't say anything to Ernie about Dolores.

REAL-WORLD CONNECTION

Love Stories Students might enjoy reading and discussing real-life stories about love. Have each student find a magazine or newspaper article about love. It can be about romantic love or about love of family, friends, pets, an activity, an idea, or a place.

Activity Have the class work in groups to discuss their articles. Students should answer such questions as *Who is the sub-ject of the article? Who or what does this person love? What has he or she learned from this experience? How does the person describe his or her feelings?*
L2 COLLAB. LEARN.

Active Reading

W **Active Reading**

VISUALIZE Encourage students to draw quick sketches of this scene to help them visualize it.

X **Active Reading**

PREDICT *(Ernie may gather the courage to give Dolores the flowers directly, as he eventually gathered the courage to visit Jack in the garden for the first time.)*

Y **Active Reading**

QUESTION Encourage students to think about what the flowers mean to Dolores and Dick and how they change their attitudes about themselves.

Z **Active Reading**

PREDICT *(Students can then infer that Jack and Ernie will grow flowers indoors during the winter.)*

AA **Active Reading**

RESPOND *(The ending of the story offers the hope that this nice Wednesday morning routine will continue.)*

Thematic Focus

Winds of Change Lead students to discuss how things change in Ernie's life from the beginning of the story to the end.

☑ ASSESSMENT OPTIONS

📁 *Quick Checks,* p. 14

VISUALIZE

W Can you picture this scene in a movie or television drama?

PREDICT

X Do you think Ernie will have the courage to give the bouquet to Dolores?

QUESTION

Y Do you think bunches of flowers could actually change people's lives?

PREDICT

Z Can you guess the purpose for this light?

RESPOND

AA How do you feel about the ending of the story?

A Crush

When they reached the door of the Big Boy, Ernie stopped and pulled at Jack's arm, pointing to the building across the street. "OK," Jack said, and he led Ernie to the front door of Stan's Hardware. It was 6:00 A.M. and the building was still dark. Ernie set the clear mason jar full of flowers under the sign that read "Closed," then he smiled at Jack and followed him back across the street to get breakfast.

When Dolores arrived at seven and picked up the jar of zinnias and cornflowers and nasturtiums and marigolds and asters and four-o'clocks, Ernie and Jack were watching her from a booth in the Big Boy. Each had a wide smile on his face as Dolores put her nose to the flowers. Ernie giggled. They watched the lights of the hardware store come up and saw Dolores place the clear mason jar on the ledge of the front window. They drove home still smiling.

All the rest of that summer Ernie left a jar of flowers every Wednesday morning at the front door of Stan's Hardware. Neither Dick Wilcox nor Dolores could figure out why the flowers kept coming, and each of them assumed somebody had a crush on the other. But the flowers had an effect on them anyway. Dick started spending more time out on the floor making conversation with the customers, while Dolores stopped wearing T-shirts to work and instead wore crisp white blouses with the sleeves rolled back off her wrists. Occasionally she put on a bracelet.

By summer's end Jack and Ernie had become very good friends, and when the flowers in the garden behind their house began to wither, and Ernie's face began to grow gray as he watched them, Jack brought home one bright day in late September a great long box. Ernie followed Jack as he carried it down to the basement and watched as Jack pulled a long glass tube from the box and attached this tube to the wall above a table. When Jack plugged in the tube's electric cord, a soft lavender light washed the room.

"Sunshine," said Jack.

Then he went back to his car for a smaller box. He carried this down to the basement where Ernie still stood staring at the strange light. Jack handed Ernie the small box, and when Ernie opened it he found more little packages of seeds than he could count, with new kinds of photographs on the slick paper.

"Violets," Jack said, pointing to one of them.

Then he and Ernie went outside to get some dirt.

Teaching Options

Grammar and Language *Minilesson*

Capitalization Write the following words on the board:

1. ernie
2. Big Boy
3. Dolores
4. wednesday
5. Stan's hardware
6. a Hardware Store
7. zinnia
8. seeds

Remind students that proper nouns—people's names, place names, company names, days of the week, and months of the year—should be capitalized. Likewise,

the beginning of a sentence and the beginning of a quotation should be capitalized.

Activity Ask students to correct the words on the board. If the word is correct as it is, have them write *correct.* **L2**

1. Ernie
2. correct
3. correct
4. Wednesday
5. Stan's hardware
6. a hardware store
7. correct
8. correct

Additional Resources

📖 *Grammar and Language Transparency 12*

📕 *Grammar and Language Workbook,* pp. 235–246

📕 *Grammar and Composition Handbook,* Lesson 12.1–12.4

📕 *Writer's Choice,* Lessons 19.1–19.4

Responding to Literature

PERSONAL RESPONSE

What are your thoughts about the ending? Did you expect that Dolores would eventually find out who had a crush on her?

Active Reading Response
Look back at the **Active Reading Strategies** on pages 146–147. Choose one of the strategies and find three places in the story where you could apply it.

Analyzing Literature

RECALL

1. What makes Dolores different from the other women in town?
2. What are Ernie's most prized possessions?
3. Whom do Dolores and Dick Wilcox think the flowers are for?
4. What does Jack buy to help Ernie deal with the end of summer and the gardening season?

INTERPRET

5. In your opinion, why do the women in town judge Dolores the way they do?
6. Why does Ernie love his seed packages so much?
7. In your opinion, why did the bouquets affect the behavior of Dick and Dolores at the store?
8. What makes Jack a good caretaker and friend for Ernie?

EVALUATE AND CONNECT

9. Why do you think Cynthia Rylant chose to write a story about a character like Ernie?
10. Theme Connection   How did Ernie's crush change his life and the lives of the other three characters in the story?

LITERARY ELEMENTS

First- and Third-Person Point of View

Before Cynthia Rylant began to write "A Crush," she had to decide from which point of view to tell the story. In the **first-person point of view**, the narrator is one of the characters. He or she speaks to the reader and uses the pronouns *I, me,* and *we.* In a third-person narrative, the story is told by an unnamed person who may seem to know what every character is thinking. When the story is told from the **third-person point of view**, the narrator uses the pronouns *he, she,* and *they.*

1. Which point of view did Rylant choose for writing "A Crush"?

2. Choose one paragraph from the story and rewrite it from a different point of view.

● See **Literary Terms Handbook,** p. R8.

Personal Response

Students might say they enjoyed the ending because it was uplifting. Most students probably did expect Dolores to find out about Ernie.

Active Reading Response
Examples for *Connect: How would I feel if I started receiving flowers anonymously?* (p. 149); and *If I named my store after my favorite actor, who would it be?* (p. 150).

Analyzing Literature

1. She knows more about fixing things than most men, she doesn't wear makeup, and she has a tattoo.
2. His prized possessions are his flower seeds.
3. Each thinks the flowers are for the other.
4. He buys him a grow light so they can continue to grow flowers indoors in the winter.
5. They don't like the fact that her values are different from theirs. Maybe they envy her a little for her knowledge and self-sufficiency.
6. They're the only thing he has left from when he lived with his mother, and the pictures on them are beautiful.
7. The flowers make both of them wonder if someone likes them, so both become happier.
8. He's patient, thoughtful, and friendly.
9. Maybe she wanted the challenge of writing about someone who had trouble communicating or of moving the action forward without much dialogue.

LITERARY ELEMENTS

1. She chose the third-person point of view, using *he, she,* and *they* to tell the story.
2. If Ernie were to tell the story, the last paragraph on page 153 might read: *Jack said the seeds would grow, but I didn't believe him until I saw it happen. I want to grow my flower seeds, but I'm still afraid of wasting them.*

Additional Resources
🖎 *Literary Elements Transparency 14*

10. It pushed Ernie to reach out to Jack and to learn to garden. It gave Jack a way to connect to Ernie. It made both Dolores and Dick feel special.

Literature and Writing

Writing About Literature

Students' descriptions should
- illustrate Dolores's physical appearance.
- describe Dolores's skills and attitudes.

Creative Writing

Students' letters should
- spell out clearly what steps they think their friend should take.
- give reasons why they think theirs is the best strategy.
- follow the format and tone of a friendly letter.

Extending Your Response

Literature Groups Point out to students that a short story does not need to answer all questions. Some questions may be left for the reader to answer. Encourage them to consider what they know of the characters' personalities as they answer these questions. **COLLAB. LEARN.**

Learning for Life Encourage students to present Ernie in a way that will make an employer want to hire him. Remind them to revise and proofread their letters.

Interdisciplinary Activity Remind students to use the facts they learn, along with an appeal to emotions, to persuade people who see their posters to volunteer.

Literature and Writing

Writing About Literature

Detailed Description In the beginning of "A Crush," Cynthia Rylant describes how the other men and women in town see Dolores. Write a paragraph describing Dolores in your own words.

Creative Writing

A Crush Revealed Review your ideas from the **Focus Activity** on page 148. Then write a letter to an imaginary friend your age who has a secret crush on someone. Advise your friend on how to deal with the crush.

Extending Your Response

Literature Groups

Asking Questions There are a number of unanswered questions in "A Crush." For example, why didn't Dick Wilcox or Dolores try to find out who sent the flowers? Why didn't someone from the restaurant see Ernie and Jack leaving the flowers? Discuss possible answers to these questions and share them with the class.

Learning for Life

Job Description Residents of group homes for the mentally handicapped often have jobs. If Jack thought Ernie was ready to have a job, he might try to find employment for him at a plant nursery. Write a job description for the kind of gardening work Ernie might do. Include the description in a letter to a local plant nursery, explaining Jack's connection to Ernie and Ernie's experience and potential.

Interdisciplinary Activity

Social Studies Find out what kinds of services for the mentally handicapped your community offers. Research the opportunities for volunteering at a group home, for a school program, or for the Special Olympics. The Special Olympics sponsors local, state, and national sports events for mentally and physically challenged people. Use the information you find to create a persuasive poster encouraging young people to help the mentally handicapped in their community. Present your poster to the class.

Reading Further

If you would like to read more of Cynthia Rylant's writings, try these books:

Short Stories: *A Couple of Kooks, and Other Stories About Love*

Poetry: *Waiting to Waltz*

Save your work for your portfolio.

Skill Minilessons

Skill Minilessons

GRAMMAR AND LANGUAGE • ADVERB CLAUSES

An **adverb clause** is a subordinate clause that modifies, or describes, the verb in the main clause of a complex sentence. An adverb clause tells *how, when, where, why,* or *under what conditions* the action occurs.

"*When the windows of Stan's Hardware started filling up with flowers,* everyone in town knew something had happened." In this sentence from the story, the italicized adverb clause modifies the verb *knew.* The adverb clause tells when everyone knew. Adverb clauses are introduced by subordinating conjunctions such as *after, although, as, because, before, if, since, than, though, unless, until, when,* and *where.*

PRACTICE Review "A Crush" to find two other examples of sentences with adverb clauses. Copy each sentence. Then underline the adverb clause and double underline the verb it modifies.

● For more about adverb clauses, see **Language Handbook,** p. R37.

READING AND THINKING • INFERENCE

Clues in a piece of writing can help the reader infer, or figure out, information that is not stated directly. For example, in "A Crush," the writer never states that Ernie is mentally handicapped. The reader makes this inference from the description of Ernie's difficulty in learning to speak, his dependence on his mother, and his moving to a group home.

PRACTICE Does Dolores have any friends or boyfriends in town? Write a paragraph about what you can infer from the story about Dolores's social life. Refer to clues from the selection to support your inference.

● For more about inference, see **Reading Handbook,** p. R89.

VOCABULARY • THE SUFFIX -ly

A *quick* answer is given *quickly*. If you react *sadly*, it's because you are *sad*. The pattern you see in those words is one of the easy features of English. Adding -*ly* to the end of an adjective changes it to an adverb. Removing -*ly* from the end of an adverb changes it to an adjective. Not all adverbs end in -*ly,* and some words that end in -*ly* aren't adverbs, but if an adverb ends in -*ly,* you can usually make the adjective form of it by taking the -*ly* off. So, when you learn a new adverb, chances are you will also understand the adjective form of it, and vice versa.

The only tricky part about changing adjectives to adverbs involves spelling. If an adjective ends with *y,* you change the *y* to an *i* before adding -*ly. Creepy* becomes *creepily,* not *creepyly.* If an adjective ends with *le,* you just change the *e* to *y. Loveable* becomes *lovably,* not *loveably.*

PRACTICE Expand your vocabulary. If an adverb is given, write the adjective form of it. If an adjective is given, write the adverb form of it. Then use each word you've written in a sentence.

Adjectives	Adverbs
1. hardy	_____
2. _____	discreetly
3. taut	_____
4. _____	eventually
5. improbable	_____

Skill Minilessons

GRAMMAR AND LANGUAGE
ADVERB CLAUSES

Possible choices:
1. Page 152: "At age twelve, he understood what a joke was."
2. Page 155: "When Ernie's flowers began growing in July, Ernie spent most of his time in the garden."

READING AND THINKING
INFERENCE

Students' paragraphs should
- cite specific phrases in the story from which they can infer the information.
- avoid making assumptions that are not supported by the text.

VOCABULARY
THE SUFFIX -ly

1. hardily
2. discreet
3. tautly
4. eventual
5. improbably

Additional Resources

📗 *Grammar and Language Workbook,* pp. 159–160

📗 *Grammar and Composition Handbook,* Lesson 8.5

📗 *Writer's Choice,* Lesson 14.4

📗 *Reading Workbook,* pp. 23–24

📁 *Vocabulary Practice,* p. 9

✔ ASSESSMENT OPTIONS

📁 *Quick Checks,* p. 14
📁 *Selection and Theme Assessment,* pp. 25–26
📁 *Performance Assessment,* p. 14
💾 *Testmaker*

Technology Skills

Objectives

- To create a simple spreadsheet
- To calculate averages using a spreadsheet
- To create a bar graph from spreadsheet data

Teaching Strategies

Demonstrate how to do some or all of the following spreadsheet tasks:
- edit column and row headings
- change column widths
- add and delete columns and rows
- enter data into cells
- create formulas using functions
- copy formulas across rows or down columns
- print a spreadsheet
- create bar, pie, and line graphs from spreadsheet data

Adapting to Available Technology

Many computers come with a spreadsheet program already installed. Some common spreadsheet programs are
- Microsoft Excel
- Lotus 1-2-3
- Quatro Pro
- ClarisWorks

While there are minor differences between programs, they can all be used to perform complex calculations using formulas and functions. Data in these spreadsheets can easily be converted into graphs.

Teaching Options

Technology Skills

Spreadsheets: Creating a Spreadsheet

Accountants use spreadsheet software for budgets and other kinds of financial planning and record keeping. You can use one to help with your own financial planning and for other purposes. The terrific thing about electronic spreadsheets is that the mathematical work is all done by the computer.

When you open a new spreadsheet document, you'll see a worksheet and menus and toolbars similar to those on a word-processing document. Some of the icons, however, are found only on spreadsheet programs. Data is entered into small cells that make up rows and columns on the worksheet. A cell carries one piece of information. A column contains a category of data—for example, persons' names. A row contains a complete record for one person or thing. For example, a row might contain one person's name, address, job title, weekly salary, and other data.

You can also convert spreadsheet data into various kinds of graphs. (Spreadsheet software programs usually refer to graphs as charts.) The example on page 161 shows a bar graph that compares the estimated costs of the gifts listed on the left with their actual costs.

	A	B	C
1	Gift List	Estimated Cost	Actual Cost
2	New CD	$ 15.00	$ 12.95
3	Mall gift certificate	$ 25.00	$ 25.00
4	Scarf	$ 25.00	$ 27.50
5	Book	$ 10.00	$ 12.50
6	Movie gift certificate	$ 20.00	$ 20.00
7			
8	Totals	$ 95.00	$ 97.95

This shows a simple example of a spreadsheet. After the data was typed in, the computer found the total (or sum) of the costs. With a spreadsheet, you can do even difficult calculations quickly and easily.

TECHNOLOGY TIP

Be sure you check with your teacher or lab instructor about the spreadsheet program you are using. You may need to change these directions somewhat. In one popular spreadsheet program, for example, the formula for adding a group of cells uses two periods in place of a colon: =SUM(B2..B6).

Practice

1. Open your spreadsheet software.
2. Select **New** from the **File** menu. This will open a blank worksheet.
3. Without clicking, move your cursor over each item on the toolbars to get an idea of what functions are available. Use the program's Help if you want additional information about any of the tools.
4. Enter the gifts and estimated prices shown in the first spreadsheet example.
5. To get the computer to figure the sum, click in the cell where you want the sum to appear, but don't enter a figure into the cell.
6. Look at the top of your screen, and find the formula bar (look for an equal sign). Click on the = to begin the formula. An equal sign will appear in the space to the right of the formula bar. Without leaving any spaces, complete the

MEETING INDIVIDUAL NEEDS — MULTIPLE LEARNING STYLES

Logical/Mathematical These learners may find the Activities on page 161 relatively easy, whereas other students may find them more challenging.

Activity Have students work in groups whose members have various learning styles. Invite each student to identify something he or she is good at that might help the group complete the activities on page 161. Before the groups begin their tasks, have them discuss how each student's particular talent can contribute to the group's work. Invite groups to discuss this again about halfway through the assignment, and then to evaluate their group's process after the assignment has been completed. **L2**

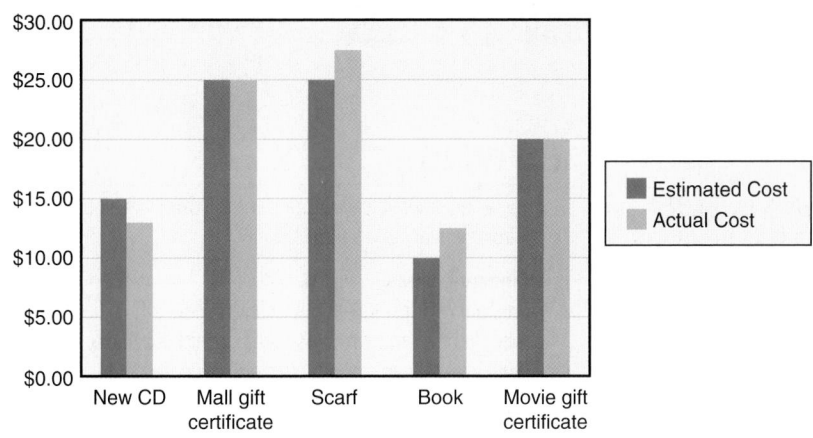

formula so that it looks like this: **=SUM(B2:B6)**. This tells the program that you want to add all the cells from B2 to B6. Hit the **Enter** key on your keyboard (the **Return** key on a Mac) when you finish your formula. The sum of the figures will appear in the highlighted cell.

ACTIVITIES

1. Working with a small group, find out how many hours per week each member spends: (a) studying for school and (b) watching television. Record the figures on a spreadsheet that looks something like this:

	A	B	C
1	**Student**	**Hours Studying**	**Hours Watching TV**
2	name		
3	name		
4	name		
5	name		
6			
7	**Averages**		

2. Have the spreadsheet figure the group's average time spent on studying for school and the average time spent watching television. The formula for computing an average is =SUM followed by the range of cells to be added, followed by a slash mark and the total number of students—for example, (B2:B5)/4.

3. Open a new worksheet. Add your data with the data of all the other groups in class. Have the computer calculate the class averages. Then make a bar graph to compare the averages for your class. Most programs will walk you through the steps in creating a chart. Use the Help feature if you need more help.

Invite students to identify questions and concerns they have as they read the directions for the three activities on this page. Encourage students to offer one another suggestions and answers to their questions.

Each group's first spreadsheet should
• properly list all the students in the group and the amount of time they study and watch TV per week.
• use formulas to calculate the group's average studying time and TV-watching time per week.

Each group's second spreadsheet should list and sum up each group's average times to find the average times for the class. Student bar graphs should accurately show the data from the group's second spreadsheet.

Language Note

Old and New Cells The English word *cell* was first used in the 1100s to mean a "small religious house." It came from the Latin word *cella*, meaning "small room." The word evolved over time to mean a "small compartment" or "bounded space." Invite students to explain how modern uses for the word *cell* still fit in with its original meaning. (*A prison cell is a small room; a cell in biology is a small organism bounded by a membrane; a cell in a spreadsheet is a small unit bounded by row and column edges.*)

REAL-WORLD CONNECTION

Budget Help Spreadsheets can be used to keep track of all kinds of financial information, including stock portfolios.

Activity Have each student use a set amount of imaginary money (say $50,000) to buy shares of several stocks and then use a spreadsheet to track the stocks' performance over several weeks. One column can be for the price paid, another for each day's closing price. They can find closing prices in newspapers and on many Internet sites. Encourage students to create formulas to calculate the profit or loss for each stock based on the day's closing price. Also have students calculate their percent profit or loss for each stock. Finally, let students calculate the total profit/loss and percent profit/loss for their portfolios.

Objectives

- To read and analyze a short story about trust between two brothers and a pet fox
- To understand and restate the plot of a short story
- To write a critical review

Skills

Reading/Thinking: Identifying Cause-Effect Relationships; Drawing Conclusions; Inferring; Logical Reasoning; Analyzing; Predicting; Sequencing

Writing: Another Point of View; Descriptive Details

Vocabulary: Roots

Grammar/Language: Commas and Conjunctions; Commas Used with Words in a Series

Listening/Speaking: Debate; Performing a Scene

Collaboration: Literature Groups

Motivating
→ OPTIONS

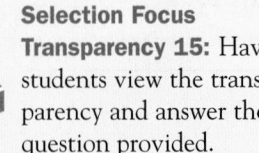

Selection Focus Transparency 15: Have students view the transparency and answer the question provided.

Focus Activity: As an extension of the Focus Activity, have students discuss how differences of opinion can lead to tension in a family or among friends. Ask them to recall a time when they have changed an opinion about something and what caused them to change.

Before You Read
Last Cover

MEET PAUL ANNIXTER

Paul Annixter (a niks′ tər) is the pseudonym, or pen name, of Howard Sturtzel. Best known for his stories about nature and animal life, Sturtzel has been writing since the age of nineteen. Asked why he became a writer, Sturtzel responded, "As a very young man I took up a timber claim in northern Minnesota. It was while proving up on the land that I began writing, mostly nature stories about the animals and elements I was up against." By 1950 he had written more than five hundred short stories.

Paul Annixter was born in 1894 in Minneapolis, Minnesota. He died in 1985.

FOCUS ACTIVITY

What relationships are important to you? Have you ever felt strongly attached to a pet?

Sharing Ideas
In small groups, talk about different kinds of relationships people have and why close relationships—with people and animals—play an important role in everyone's life.

Setting a Purpose
Read to discover the relationships shared by the characters in this story.

BACKGROUND

Did You Know? Stories and fables have long portrayed the red fox as a clever and sly creature, always ready to trick an unsuspecting animal out of its food—or its life. Red foxes hunt small prey and do not hunt in packs. They are quick, solitary hunters.

VOCABULARY PREVIEW

bleak (blēk) *adj.* cheerless; depressing; p. 164
surly (sur′ lē) *adj.* rude and bad tempered; gruff; p. 164
invalid (in′ və lid) *n.* one who is disabled by disease or injury; p. 165
passive (pas′ iv) *adj.* not participating or active; p. 166
instinct (in′ stingkt) *n.* a way of knowing, behaving, or reacting that comes naturally rather than through learning; p. 167
sanction (sangk′ shən) *v.* to give support or encouragement to; approve; p. 168
wily (wī′ lē) *adj.* full of tricks; crafty; sly; p. 170
sanctuary (sangk′ chōō er′ ē) *n.* a place of safety or protection; p. 170
incredulous (in krej′ ə ləs) *adj.* unwilling or unable to believe something; p. 170

RESOURCE MANAGER

Lesson Planning Resource
The *Theme Two Planning Guide* (pp. 32–39) provides additional lesson notes and reduced versions of all print resources.

📁 **Other Print Resources**
- Active Reading Guide, p. 15
- Vocabulary Practice, p. 10
- Reading Workbook, pp. 25–26
- Grammar and Language Workbook, pp. 255–258

- Grammar and Composition Handbook, Lessons 13.2, 13.3
- Quick Checks, p. 15
- Selection and Theme Assessment, pp. 27–28
- Performance Assessment, p. 15
- Spanish Summaries, p. 15
- Spanish Translations
- Inclusion Strategies
- English Language Learners Sourcebook

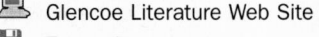 **Transparencies**
- Selection Focus 15
- Literary Elements 15
- Grammar and Language 13

Technology
🎧 Audio Library
🎧 Spanish Audio Library
💻 Glencoe Literature Web Site
💾 Testmaker

Last Cover

Paul Annixter ∿

I'm not sure I can tell you what you want to know about my brother; but everything about the pet fox is important, so I'll tell all that from the beginning.

It goes back to a winter afternoon after I'd hunted the woods all day for a sign of our lost pet. I remember the way my mother looked up as I came into the kitchen. Without my speaking, she knew what had happened. For six hours I had walked, reading signs, looking for a delicate print in the damp soil or even a hair that might have told of a red fox passing that way—but I had found nothing.

"Did you go up in the foothills?" Mom asked.

I nodded. My face was stiff from held-back tears. My brother, Colin, who was going on twelve, got it all from one look at me and went into a heartbroken, almost silent, crying.

Three weeks before, Bandit, the pet fox Colin and I had raised from a tiny kit,[1] had disappeared, and not even a rumor had been heard of him since.

"He'd have had to go off soon anyway," Mom comforted. "A big, lolloping fellow like him, he's got to live his life same as us. But he may come back. That fox set a lot of store by[2] you boys in spite of his wild ways."

---

1. Although it's a shortened form of kitten, *kit* refers to any young, fur-bearing animal, especially one that's smaller than normal.
2. *Lolloping* means "leaping or bounding," and *to set store by* means to "have trust or confidence in."

Reading the Selection

SUMMARY

In this short story, Stan and his brother Colin rescue and raise a baby fox. When the fox matures, it leaves the boys. Because it is familiar with humans and their ways, the fox kills chickens belonging to area farmers. Colin often observes the fox in the wild and knows of a special hiding place the fox favors. The fox hides in this spot when local farmers band together to hunt it down.

📁 *Spanish Summaries,* p. 15

A **Active Reading**

PREDICT Ask students to predict whether the brothers will find the missing pet. Which brother seems more attached to the pet? Why? *(Some students may say both brothers; some may say Stan, because he looks for the fox; and some may say Colin, because he cries when Stan has no news.)*

Additional Resources
📁 *Active Reading Guide,* p. 15
🎧 *Audio Library*
🎧 *Spanish Audio Library*

Teaching Options

CONNECTING TO OTHER SELECTIONS

The chart at the right shows three ways to connect "Last Cover" to other selections in this book.

For specific teaching strategies, see the *Theme Two Planning Guide,* pages 35–36.

Connection	Title
Life Skills: Teaching and Mentoring	→ "The Birthday Box," p. 175
Thematic: Animal Nature	→ "Uncle Tony's Goat," p. 807
Literary: Short Story	→ "Broken Chain," p. 44

B **Literary Elements**

PLOT: *Conflict* Have students describe in their own words how the father and the brothers feel about the fox. *(The father thinks of the fox as an egg thief and chicken killer; the boys think of the fox as their pet.)*

C **Active Reading**

PREDICT Have students discuss whether they think the fox will attack the chickens. You may wish to use the following model to guide students in the process of predicting.

Model: I know that it's the middle of winter, and most animals are hibernating. There may not be much food for the fox. Since the fox knows where the chickens are and has killed at least one chicken already, I think the fox will return to his old ways and steal chickens.

D **Author's Craft**

FORESHADOWING Have students list things the father says that hint at what the fox may do in the future. *(The father says, "We'll be seeing a lot more of that fellow," "That fox learned to…not likely to forget that." "Late winter's a high time…they're out deviling.")*

Vo•cab•u•lar•y Skills

Word Meanings Draw students' attention to the phrase *the seven sleepers are under cover.* Explain that *under cover* means that these seven animals are "sheltered, hidden, or covered over for protection."

Teaching Options

Last Cover

"He set a lot of store by our food, anyway," Father said. He sat in a chair by the kitchen window mending a piece of harness. "We'll be seeing a lot more of that fellow, never fear. That fox learned to pine for table scraps and young chickens. He was getting to be an egg thief, too, and he's not likely to forget that."

"That was only pranking[3] when he was little," Colin said desperately.

From the first, the tame fox had made tension in the family. It was Father who said we'd better name him Bandit, after he'd made away with his first young chicken.

"Maybe you know," Father said shortly. "But when an animal turns to egg sucking he's usually incurable. He'd better not come pranking around my chicken run again."

It was late February, and I remember the bleak, dead cold that had set in, cold that was a rare thing for our Carolina hills. Flocks of sparrows and snowbirds had appeared to peck hungrily at all that the pigs and chickens didn't eat.

"This one's a killer," Father would say of a morning, looking out at the whitened barn roof. "This one will make the shoats[4] squeal."

A fire snapped all day in our cookstove and another in the stone fireplace in the living room, but still the farmhouse was never warm. The leafless woods were bleak and empty, and I spoke of that to Father when I came back from my search.

"It's always a sad time in the woods when the seven sleepers are under cover," he said.

---

3. Here, *pranking* means "playfulness; mischief."
4. The *shoats* are young pigs.

Vocabulary
bleak (blēk) *adj.* cheerless; depressing
surly (sur′ lē) *adj.* rude and bad tempered; gruff

164 ❧ THEME 2

"What sleepers are they?" I asked. Father was full of woods lore.[5]

"Why, all the animals that have got sense enough to hole up and stay hid in weather like this. Let's see, how was it the old rhyme named them?

> *Surly* bear and sooty bat,
> Brown chuck and masked coon,
> Chippy-munk and sly skunk,
> And all the mouses
> 'Cept in men's houses.

"And man would have joined them and made it eight, Granther Yeary always said, if he'd had a little more sense."

"I was wondering if the red fox mightn't make it eight," Mom said.

Father shook his head. "Late winter's a high time for foxes. Time when they're out deviling, not sleeping."

My chest felt hollow. I wanted to cry like Colin over our lost fox, but at fourteen a boy doesn't cry. Colin had squatted down on the floor and got out his small hammer and nails to start another new frame for a new picture. Maybe then he'd make a drawing for the frame and be able to forget his misery. It had been that way with him since he was five.

I thought of the new dress Mom had brought home a few days before in a heavy cardboard box. That box cover would be fine for Colin to draw on. I spoke of it, and Mom's glance thanked me as she went to

---

5. The accumulated stories and beliefs about a subject are called *lore*.

MEETING INDIVIDUAL NEEDS

ENGLISH LANGUAGE LEARNERS

Animal Characteristics Draw English language learners' attention to the different animals named on this page. As they read about each animal, have them write down the animal's name. *(chickens, fox, shoats, sparrows, snowbirds, pigs, bear, bat, chuck, coon, skunk, chippy munk, mouses)* Explain that *coon* is short for *raccoon, chuck* is short for *woodchuck, chippy-munk* refers to a chipmunk, and the normal plural for *mouses* is *mice.*

Activity Have students create posters or dictionaries that list each animal name. Next to each name have students draw a picture to illustrate it.

Additional Resources
📁 *English Language Learners Sourcebook*

get it. She and I worried a lot about Colin. He was small for his age, delicate and blond, his hair much lighter and softer than mine, his eyes deep and wide and blue. He was often sick, and I knew the fear Mom had that he might be predestined.[6] I'm just ordinary, like Father. I'm the sort of stuff that can take it—tough and strong—but Colin was always sort of special.

Mom lighted the lamp. Colin began cutting his white cardboard carefully, fitting it into his frame. Father's sharp glance turned on him now and again.

---

6. Mom fears that Colin has been chosen by God to die at a very young age.

"There goes the boy making another frame before there's a picture for it," he said. "It's too much like cutting out a man's suit for a fellow that's, say, twelve years old. Who knows whether he'll grow into it?"

Mom was into him then, quick. "Not a single frame of Colin's has ever gone to waste. The boy has real talent, Sumter, and it's time you realized it."

"Of course he has," Father said. "All kids have 'em. But they get over 'em."

"It isn't the pox we're talking of," Mom sniffed.

"In a way it is. Ever since you started talking up Colin's art, I've had an <u>invalid</u> for help around the place."

Vocabulary
invalid (in′ və lid) *n.* one who is disabled by disease or injury

Fox Hunt, 1893. Winslow Homer. Oil on canvas, 38 x 68½ in. Museum of American Art, Pennsylvania Academy of Fine Art.

Viewing the painting: Do you think the painting captures Father's explanation that "winter's a high time for foxes"? Explain.

Reading *Minilesson*

Last Cover

CHARACTER Have students describe the father's character. Invite them to explain why the father doesn't like "white-livered" interpretations of nature or soft ways. *(The father has to be tough to survive on the land. He is also a protector—of his animals and his family. He can't let foxes kill his animals or the family won't eat.)*

FLASHBACK Remind students that flashbacks take readers back to events that happened earlier. Ask students to explain how they think readers can tell when these flashbacks have ended. *(The time shifts back to the present with the phrase "at supper that night." When the second flashback ends, there is a line space on the page—top of the left column, p. 167.)*

CONNECT Guide students to realize that the father understands the realities and harshness of nature. Ask students why they think the father doesn't want the boys to become too attached to the fox. *(The father knows the fox will leave the boys one day. He doesn't want the boys to feel hurt when that day comes.)* Ask students if they have experienced this kind of protectiveness in their families.

Father wasn't as hard as he made out, I knew, but he had to hold a balance against all Mom's frothing. For him the thing was the land and all that pertained to it. I was following in Father's footsteps, true to form, but Colin threatened to break the family tradition with his leaning toward art, with Mom "aiding and abetting[7] him," as Father liked to put it. For the past two years she had had dreams of my brother becoming a real artist and going away to the city to study.

It wasn't that Father had no understanding of such things. I could remember, through the years, Colin lying on his stomach in the front room making pencil sketches, and how a good drawing would catch Father's eye halfway across the room, and how he would sometimes gather up two or three of them to study, frowning and muttering, one hand in his beard, while a great pride rose in Colin, and in me too. Most of Colin's drawings were of the woods and wild things, and there Father was a master critic. He made out to scorn what seemed to him a passive "white-livered" interpretation of nature through brush and pencil instead of rod and rifle.

At supper that night Colin could scarcely eat. Ever since he'd been able to walk, my brother had had a growing love of wild things, but Bandit had been like his very own, a gift of the woods. One afternoon a year and half before, Father and Laban Small had been running a vixen through the hills with their dogs. With the

last of her strength the she-fox had made for her den, not far from our house. The dogs had overtaken her and killed her just before she reached it. When Father and Laban came up, they'd found Colin crouched nearby holding her cub in his arms.

Father had been for killing the cub, which was still too young to shift for itself, but Colin's grief had brought Mom into it. We'd taken the young fox into the kitchen, all of us, except Father, gone a bit silly over the little thing. Colin had held it in his arms and fed it warm milk from a spoon.

"Watch out with all your soft ways," Father had warned, standing in the doorway. "You'll make too much of him. Remember, you can't make a dog out of a fox. Half of that little critter has to love, but the other half is a wild hunter. You boys will mean a whole lot to him while he's a kit, but there'll come a day when you won't mean a thing to him and he'll leave you shorn."[8]

For two weeks after that Colin had nursed the cub, weaning it from milk to bits of meat. For a year they were always together. The cub grew fast. It was soon following Colin and me about the barnyard. It turned out to be a patch fox, with a saddle of darker fur across its shoulders.

I haven't the words to tell you what the fox meant to us. It was far more wonderful owning him than owning any dog. There was something rare and secret like the spirit of the woods about him, and back of his calm, straw-gold eyes was the sense

---

7. *Abetting* means "encouraging."

8. To be left *shorn* is to be cut off, like hair, and left alone.

Vocabulary
passive (pas′ iv) *adj.* not participating or active

MEETING INDIVIDUAL NEEDS — INCLUSION STRATEGIES

Less-Proficient Readers Explain that the characters in this story use a regional dialect when they speak.

Activity Write the following phrases and sentence on the board:

- *pine for table scraps*
- *that was only pranking*
- *animals that have got the sense to hole up and stay hid in weather like this*

- *out deviling*
- *Late winter's a high time for foxes.*

Have students offer simpler, more modern ways of saying them. **L1**

Additional Resources
📁 *Inclusion Strategies*

of a brain the equal of a man's. The fox became Colin's whole life.

Each day, going and coming from school, Colin and I took long side trips through the woods, looking for Bandit. Wild things' memories were short, we knew; we'd have to find him soon or the old bond would be broken.

Ever since I was ten I'd been allowed to hunt with Father, so I was good at reading signs. But, in a way, Colin knew more about the woods and wild things than Father or me. What came to me from long observation, Colin seemed to know by instinct.

It was Colin who felt out, like an Indian, the stretch of woods where Bandit had his den, who found the first slim, small fox-print in the damp earth. And then, on an afternoon in March, we saw him. I remember the day well, the racing clouds, the wind rattling the tops of the pine trees and swaying the Spanish moss. Bandit had just come out of a clump of laurel; in the maze of leaves behind him we caught a glimpse of a slim red vixen, so we knew he had found a mate. She melted from sight like a shadow, but Bandit turned to watch us, his mouth open, his tongue lolling as he smiled his old foxy smile. On his thin chops, I saw a telltale chicken feather.

Colin moved silently forward, his movements so quiet and casual he seemed to be standing still. He called Bandit's name, and the fox held his ground, drawn to us with all his senses. For a few moments he let Colin actually put an arm about him. It was then I knew that he loved us still, for all of Father's warnings. He really loved us back, with a fierce, secret love no tame thing ever gave. But the urge of his life just then was toward his new mate. Suddenly, he whirled about and disappeared in the laurels.

Colin looked at me with glowing eyes. "We haven't really lost him, Stan. When he gets through with his spring sparking[9] he may come back. But we've got to show ourselves to him a lot, so he won't forget."

"It's a go," I said.

"Promise not to say a word to Father," Colin said, and I agreed. For I knew by the chicken feather that Bandit had been up to no good.

A week later the woods were budding and the thickets were rustling with all manner of wild things scurrying on the love scent. Colin managed to get a glimpse of Bandit every few days. He couldn't get close though, for the spring running was a lot more important to a fox than any human beings were.

Every now and then Colin got out his framed box cover and looked at it, but he never drew anything on it; he never even picked up his pencil. I remember wondering if what Father had said about framing a picture before you had one had spoiled something for him.

I was helping Father with the planting now, but Colin managed to be in the woods every day. By degrees he learned Bandit's range, where he drank and rested and where he was likely to be according to the time of day. One day he told me how

_____

9. *Spring sparking* refers to the mating season.

Vocabulary
instinct (in' stingkt) *n.* a way of knowing, behaving, or reacting that comes naturally rather than through learning

I **Literary Elements**

PLOT: *Rising Action* Point out to students that the events that occur and the information readers receive here all add to the rising action, or building, of the story. Ask students to identify the events and information. *(The boys see Bandit, they learn that Bandit has a mate, and Colin touches Bandit.)*

J **Active Reading**

EVALUATE Ask students to explain why the boys don't want to tell their father they have seen Bandit. *(Bandit has a chicken feather on his mouth. He has been stealing chickens. The boys know their father would not approve of their continuing to see Bandit.)*

K **Critical Thinking**

DRAWING CONCLUSIONS Every once in a while, Colin looks at his framed blank page. Have students explain why he doesn't draw anything on it. You may wish to use the following model to guide students in the process of drawing conclusions.

Model: I know Colin draws the woods and wild things, and I know he is observant and sensitive. Maybe Colin doesn't draw anything yet because he is hoping for Bandit's return after the spring running. Or maybe Colin is waiting for inspiration or a more powerful feeling before he draws.

INTERDISCIPLINARY CONNECTION

Science Explain that foxes frequently live near farms because they eat rodents, which are easy to hunt in fields. When foxes are killed off in an area, rodent populations can grow out of control. Even though foxes often live near humans, they are rarely seen because their sharp hearing, sight, and sense of smell alert them to humans before humans are aware of them.

Activity Have students work in groups to conduct research and use what they find to write reports about foxes. They might want to investigate the red fox or other types of foxes, fox territories or ranges, or how parents care for fox cubs. They can also research the differences between foxes and their relatives, such as wolves, coyotes, jackals, and dogs. **L2**
COLLAB. LEARN.

L **Literary Elements**

PLOT: *Rising Action* Have students identify the important events that build the story's tension and suspense. *(Bandit has been raiding barns and hen runs, so the farmers are banding together to hunt him down with dogs— or to shoot him on sight.)*

M **Critical Thinking**

INFERRING Even though the father has made threats against Bandit, he doesn't join the fox hunt. Later, he smiles with satisfaction when the dogs lose Bandit's trail. Have students explain what this shows about Father. *(Father likes Bandit, too, and does not want to see him killed. On the other hand, the father and the boys both know they can't stop the farmers from protecting their poultry.)*

he had petted Bandit again, and how they had walked together a long way in the woods. All this time we had kept his secret from Father.

As summer came on, Bandit began to live up to the prediction Father had made. Accustomed to human beings he moved without fear about the scattered farms of the region, raiding barns and hen runs that other foxes wouldn't have dared go near. And he taught his wild mate to do the same. Almost every night they got into some poultry house, and by late June Bandit was not only killing chickens and ducks but feeding on eggs and young chicks whenever he got the chance.

Stories of his doings came to us from many sources, for he was still easily recognized by the dark patch on his shoulders. Many a farmer took a shot at him as he fled and some of them set out on his trail with dogs, but they always returned home

without even sighting him. Bandit was familiar with all the dogs in the region, and he knew a hundred tricks to confound[10] them. He got a reputation that year beyond that of any fox our hills had known. His confidence grew, and he gave up wild hunting altogether and lived entirely off the poultry farmers. By September the hill farmers banded together to hunt him down.

It was Father who brought home that news one night. All time-honored rules of the fox chase were to be broken in this hunt; if the dogs couldn't bring Bandit down, he was to be shot on sight. I was stricken and furious. I remember the misery of Colin's face in the lamplight. Father, who took pride in all the ritual of the hunt, had refused to be a party to such an affair, though in justice he could do nothing but sanction any sort of hunt, for

---

10. Here, *confound* means "confuse."

Vocabulary

sanction (sangk′ shən) *v.* to give support or encouragement to; approve

168   THEME 2

Teaching Options

Grammar and Language *Minilesson*

Commas and Conjunctions Write these sentences on the board, underlining the subjects once and the verbs twice:

1. <u>He</u> <u>called</u> Bandit's name, and the <u>fox</u> <u>held</u> his ground.
2. <u>Colin</u> <u>got</u> out his framed box cover and <u>looked</u> at it.

Explain that a clause has both a subject and a verb and can stand alone as a sentence. Commas are used when *and, or,* or

but join more than one main clause. In the second sentence there is only one main clause, so a comma is not used.

Activity Have students find other story sentences that use commas before conjunctions. Students should copy each sentence, underlining each subject once and each verb twice. **L2**

Additional Resources

Grammar and Language Transparency 13

Grammar and Language Workbook, pp. 257–258

Grammar and Composition Handbook, Lesson 13.3

Writer's Choice, Lesson 20.3

Bandit, as old Sam Wetherwax put it, had been "purely getting in the Lord's hair."

The hunt began next morning, and it was the biggest turnout our hills had known. There were at least twenty mounted men in the party and as many dogs. Father and I were working in the lower field as they passed along the river road. Most of the hunters carried rifles, and they looked ugly.

Twice during the morning I went up to the house to find Colin, but he was nowhere around. As we worked, Father and I could follow the progress of the hunt by the distant hound music on the breeze. We could tell just where the hunters first caught sight of the fox and where Bandit was leading the dogs during the first hour. We knew as well as if we'd seen it how Bandit roused another fox along Turkey Branch and forced it to run for him, and how the dogs swept after it for twenty minutes before they sensed their mistake.

Noon came, and Colin had not come in to eat. After dinner Father didn't go back to the field. He moped about, listening to the hound talk. He didn't like what was going on any more than I did, and now and again I caught his smile of satisfaction when we heard the broken, angry notes of the hunting horn, telling that the dogs had lost the trail or had run another fox.

I was restless, and I went up into the hills in midafternoon. I ranged the woods for miles, thinking all the time of Colin. Time lost all meaning for me, and the short day was nearing an end, when I heard the horn talking again, telling that the fox had put over another trick. All day he had deviled the dogs and mocked the hunters. This new trick and the coming night would work to save him. I was wildly

glad, as I moved down toward Turkey Branch and stood listening for a time by the deep, shaded pool where for years we boys had gone swimming, sailed boats, and dreamed summer dreams.

Suddenly, out of the corner of my eye, I saw the sharp ears and thin, pointed mask of a fox—in the water almost beneath me. It was Bandit, craftily submerged there, all but his head, resting in the cool water of the pool and the shadow of the two big beeches that spread above it. He must have run forty miles or more since morning. And he must have hidden in this place before. His knowing, crafty mask blended perfectly with the shadows and a mass of drift and branches that had collected by the bank of the pool. He was so still a pair of thrushes flew up from the spot as I came up, not knowing he was there.

Bandit's bright, harried[11] eyes were looking right at me. But I did not look at him direct. Some woods instinct, swifter than thought, kept me from it. So he and I met as in another world, indirectly, with feeling but without sign or greeting.

Suddenly I saw that Colin was standing almost beside me. Silently as a water snake, he had come out of the bushes and stood there. Our eyes met, and a quick and secret smile passed between us. It was a rare moment in which I really "met" my brother, when something of his essence[12] flowed into me and I knew all of him. I've never lost it since.

My eyes still turned from the fox, my heart pounding. I moved quietly away, and Colin moved with me. We whistled softly

---

11. Bandit's eyes show that he is troubled (*harried*).
12. Colin's *essence* is his most basic nature or spirit.

N Critical Thinking

SEQUENCING Have students state in what order the fox hunt events take place and what words in the passage indicate this. *(Events are ordered by time. The writer uses words such as* morning, first hour, twenty minutes, noon, after dinner, midafternoon, *and* day was nearing an end.*)*

O Active Reading

VISUALIZE Ask students to use the descriptive details in this passage to visualize Bandit's hiding place. Ask them to describe what they see and what they imagine about smells and sounds.

P Active Reading

EVALUATE Ask students what they think about the relationship between Stan and Colin and what this hunt does to their understanding of each other. *(Stan is protective of Colin. The boys are close, but the hunt makes them grow closer. It helps them understand each other better—a bond that is never broken.)*

Writing *Minilesson*

Descriptive Details Guide students to understand that when writing descriptive passages, writers organize descriptive details in different ways, including *placement* (describing a scene from left to right or top to bottom), *time* (describing events in the order they occur), or *importance* (describing the most important details first or last).

Activity Have each student write a short descriptive paragraph using one method of ordering the details—by placement, by time, or by importance. **L2**

Additional Resources

📖 ***Writer's Choice,*** Lesson 2.4

Literary Elements

MOOD Ask students how they feel about the way the boys protect Bandit. Encourage them to describe the emotional quality of the story. *(There is a feeling of magic, warmth, and caring.)*

Critical Thinking

INFERRING Have students suggest ideas about why Colin finally makes his drawing. *(Colin feels compelled to share the secret of how Bandit fooled them all.)*

Literary Elements

PLOT: Resolution Ask students to describe how Bandit helps Colin and his father resolve their conflict over Colin's artwork. *(Colin draws a picture of Bandit in his final hiding place. The father realizes that Colin knew where the fox was all along. He finally accepts and approves of Colin's artwork.)*

Thematic Focus

Winds of Change Discuss the changes that took place in the boys, their parents, the community, and Bandit himself as the baby fox matured.

✔ ASSESSMENT OPTIONS

📁 **Quick Checks,** p. 15

---

as we went, pretending to busy ourselves along the bank of the stream. There was magic to it, as if by will we wove a web of protection about the fox, a ring-pass-not that none might penetrate. It was so, too, we felt, in the brain of Bandit, and that doubled the charm. To us he was still our little pet that we had carried in our arms on countless summer afternoons.

Two hundred yards upstream, we stopped beside slim, fresh tracks in the mud where Bandit had entered the branch. The tracks angled upstream. But in the water the wily creature had turned down.

We climbed the far bank to wait, and Colin told me how Bandit's secret had been his secret ever since an afternoon three months before, when he'd watched the fox swim downstream to hide in the deep pool. Today he'd waited on the bank, feeling that Bandit, hard pressed by the dogs, might again seek the pool for sanctuary.

We looked back once we turned homeward. He still had not moved. We didn't know until later that he was killed that same night by a chance hunter, as he crept out from his hiding place.

That evening Colin worked a long time on his framed box cover that had lain about the house untouched all summer. He kept at it all the next day too. I had never seen him work so hard. I seemed to sense in the air the feeling he was putting into it, how

he was *believing* his picture into being. It was evening before he finished it. Without a word he handed it to Father. Mom and I went and looked over his shoulder.

It was a delicate and intricate pencil drawing of the deep branch pool, and there was Bandit's head and watching, fear-filled eyes hiding there amid the leaves and shadows, woven craftily into the maze of twigs and branches, as if by nature's art itself. Hardly a fox there at all, but the place where he was—or should have been. I recognized it instantly, but Mom gave a sort of incredulous sniff.

"I'll declare," she said, "It's mazy as a puzzle. It just looks like a lot of sticks and leaves to me."

Long minutes of study passed before Father's eye picked out the picture's secret, as few men's could have done. I laid that to Father's being a born hunter. That was a picture that might have been done especially for him. In fact, I guess it was.

Finally he turned to Colin with his deep, slow smile. "So that's how Bandit fooled them all," he said. He sat holding the picture with a sort of tenderness for a long time, while we glowed in the warmth of the shared secret. That was Colin's moment. Colin's art stopped being a pox to Father right there. And later, when the time came for Colin to go to art school, it was Father who was his solid backer.

❖

Vocabulary
wily (wī′ lē) *adj.* full of tricks; crafty; sly
sanctuary (sangk′ chōō er′ ē) *n.* a place of safety or protection
incredulous (in krej′ ə ləs) *adj.* unwilling or unable to believe something

MEETING INDIVIDUAL NEEDS — MULTIPLE LEARNING STYLES

Spatial Some students respond well to text that describes spatial relationships. Other learners can benefit from observing these students' depictions of spatial relationships. Work with students to outline the locations of the events in the fox hunt.

Activity Have students work in pairs. Have them use the outline of the locations and the description of the fox hunt to draw diagrams or maps of Bandit's escape during the hunt. Encourage students to use arrows or numbers to show the sequence of events. **L2**

Responding to Literature

PERSONAL RESPONSE

- Were you surprised by the outcome of the story? Explain.
- Think back to the group discussion in the **Focus Activity** on page 162. What, if any, new ideas did the story give you about relationships? Record your thoughts in your journal.

Analyzing Literature

RECALL

1. Who named Bandit? What does the name tell about this person's attitude toward the fox?
2. What is Colin's talent? At the beginning of the story, what is his father's attitude toward this talent?
3. According to the narrator, what are some differences between the two brothers?
4. Why does the hunt take place and what happens to Bandit?

INTERPRET

5. At the beginning, what effect does the fox have on the relationship between family members? Explain.
6. Why does Colin's father feel threatened by his son's talent? What tradition is Colin threatening? Explain.
7. What do the narrator's feelings about his brother and about the pet fox reveal about the narrator? Use details from the story to support your ideas.
8. Why does the father's attitude about Bandit change during the course of the story?

EVALUATE AND CONNECT

9. Trust is one of the **themes** of "Last Cover." What role do you think trust plays in the story? Explain.
10. Theme Connection   How does the relationship between Colin and his father change over the course of the story? How does the relationship between the brothers change? Explain.

LITERARY ELEMENTS

Plot

The sequence of events in a story, novel, or play is called a **plot.** A good writer uses each event in a plot to cause or lead to the next event. The plot begins by introducing the story's characters, setting, and situation. This is called the **exposition.** It captures the reader's attention with a strong **conflict** between opposing forces. **Rising action** in the plot adds complications to the conflict that lead to a **climax,** or point when the reader's interest is at its highest. A **resolution** reveals the final outcome of the plot.

1. Briefly outline the plot of "Last Cover."

2. Use examples from the plot to show how Bandit at first causes tensions in the family but finally helps bring the family together.

● See **Literary Terms Handbook,** p. R8.

Responding to the Selection

Personal Response

Even though students may feel sad that Bandit is killed at the end of the story, they might have predicted that "his bad habits would get him into trouble." Students' journal entries might describe an awareness that relationships grow and change over time.

Analyzing Literature

1. Father named Bandit. The name tells readers that Father thinks Bandit is up to no good.
2. Colin is artistic and likes to draw. The father thinks Colin's drawing is just a passing fancy that keeps him from more useful farm chores.
3. Colin is small, delicate, sickly, and artistic. Stan is tough and strong, more like their father.
4. The hunt takes place because Bandit and his mate have been raiding the chicken coops of local farmers. Bandit gets killed, but not by the members of the hunt.
5. The fox creates tension in the family because the boys think of him as a pet, but the father knows he is wild and will, in time, act like a wild animal.
6. Colin's father feels threatened by Colin's talent because he thinks Colin will not learn to be a farmer like his brother Stan.
7. Stan, the narrator, feels protective and supportive of Colin. This is shown when he suggests Colin draw on a cardboard box cover. Stan cares strongly for the fox. He shows this when he looks for it for six hours.
8. The father's attitude toward Bandit changes as Bandit cleverly raids farms all summer but skillfully avoids being killed by farmers or their dogs. The father respects Bandit's skill and knowledge of the land.

LITERARY ELEMENTS

1. Two boys raise a fox. It grows up, it leaves them, and kills chickens to live. It evades farmers who hunt it but is killed by a chance hunter.
2. Bandit's chicken-killing causes tension in the family, but Colin's skill at drawing Bandit's hiding place reconciles them.

Additional Resources

 Literary Elements Transparency 15

9. Bandit learns to trust the boys when he is a kit. On the day the farmers hunt him, the boys do not give away Bandit's secret hiding place.
10. Colin and his father come to understand each other better. Stan and Colin become closer, too, especially as they both observe Bandit hiding from the hunters and share the secret.

Extending Your Response

Writing About Literature

Students' reviews should

- include details from the story to support their opinions.
- use appropriate quotations and examples from the story to show how the characters change.
- flow logically from one thought to another and have a clear conclusion.

Creative Writing

Students' journal entries should

- clearly present Colin's thoughts, ideas, and viewpoints.
- interpret the actions of Stan, Bandit, and the father through Colin's eyes.
- relate some events in the story from Colin's perspective.

Literature Groups Point out to students that they should list arguments to support Colin's ideas and arguments to support the farmers' ideas. Then they should consider counterarguments to both points of view. COLLAB. LEARN.

Performing Once students understand each character's motivation, have them convey the characters vocally by changing the volume, pitch, and tone of their voices and the rate at which they speak.

Extending Your Response

Writing About Literature

Characterization   The manner in which a writer develops the characters in a story is called **characterization.** Write a paragraph or two reviewing the characters Annixter created in "Last Cover." In your opinion, do these characters seem true to life? Why or why not? How do the characters change during the story? Which character do you like the most? Why? Use examples and quotations from the story to support your opinions.

Creative Writing

Changing Point of View   How would this story be different if Colin had narrated it? Imagine that you are Colin. Write a journal entry about Bandit's life, what happens to him, and your feelings about the whole situation. Be sure to include your attitude toward the other members of your family.

Literature Groups

Problem Solving   Imagine that Colin, his brother, his father, and several local farmers are sitting down to discuss the problems Bandit has caused. What are the problems? Are there solutions other than the hunt? Debate the issue. From Colin's point of view, offer suggestions to resolve the problems. Support your ideas with details from the story.

Performing

With a small group, choose an important scene from the story and dramatize it for your classmates. Reread the section of the story several times and discuss each character's actions and feelings so that you understand what motivates each character in that scene.

Reading Further

If you would like to read more stories by Paul Annixter, try these books:
Pride of Lions, and Other Stories
The Best Nature Stories of Paul Annixter

📖 **Save your work for your portfolio.**

GRAMMAR AND LANGUAGE • COMMAS USED WITH WORDS IN A SERIES

Commas make sentences easier to understand by signaling a pause or separation between parts of a sentence. Use commas to separate three or more words, phrases, or clauses in a series.

Example: Colin carried his pens, his pencils, and his paper to his desk.

PRACTICE Review "Last Cover" to find an example of a sentence that uses commas to separate three or more words or phrases in a series. Write this sentence in your journal, and then make up one of your own.

● For more about using commas in a series, see **Language Handbook,** p. R37.

READING AND THINKING • PREDICTING

Good readers make many types of inferences as they read. One type involves predicting outcomes. Readers may use details to predict the outcomes of conversations, actions, or events within a story. In other words, you may be able to figure out what will happen next in a story. Then, as you read, you can check your predictions by finding out what actually happened.

PRACTICE Reread "Last Cover" and find two examples of details that could help a reader predict what will happen next in the story. Share your findings with your classmates and see how many different details were found.

● For more about predicting, see **Reading Handbook,** pp. R82–R83.

VOCABULARY • ROOTS

The root of a word is the word part that is used as the base in making other words. Knowing the meaning of a root helps you understand other words with the same root. For example, *invalid* contains the root *val,* meaning "strong or well." An *invalid* is not strong or well. A *valid* argument is one that's well supported. *Valor* is the kind of bravery that comes from inner strength.

The word *incredulous* contains the root *cred,* which comes from a Latin word meaning "to believe." *Credit* can mean "approval or acknowledgment," but it can also mean "belief or trust." If you *credit* someone's statement, you believe it. By combining your understanding of the root *cred*

with any context clues that may exist, you can probably figure out the meaning of words in which this root appears.

PRACTICE Briefly state what you'd guess is the meaning of each underlined word.
1. I doubted his credibility.
2. She told an incredible story.
3. Don't give credence to such a ridiculous statement.
4. It's not fair to lie to an innocent, credulous child.
5. His lawyer tried to discredit the witnesses for the other side.

GRAMMAR AND LANGUAGE
COMMAS USED WITH WORDS IN A SERIES

Sentences should show that students understand how to use commas with words in a series correctly.

READING AND THINKING
PREDICTING

Students should be able to state their predictions and give examples of details that support them.

VOCABULARY
ROOTS
1. believability
2. unbelievable
3. trust
4. believing
5. destroy trust in

Additional Resources

Grammar and Language Workbook, pp. 255–256

Grammar and Composition Handbook, Lesson 13.2

Writer's Choice, Lesson 20.2

Reading Workbook, pp. 25–26

Vocabulary Practice, p. 10

✔ ASSESSMENT OPTIONS

Quick Checks, p. 15
Selection and Theme Assessment, pp. 27–28
Performance Assessment, p. 15
Testmaker

Objectives

- To read and analyze a story and a poem about characters dealing with separation
- To identify and explore major and minor characters in a story or poem
- To explain how the setting of the story contributes to its effect

Skills

Reading/Thinking: Verifying Predictions; Monitoring Comprehension; Drawing Conclusions; Focusing on a Question
Writing: Short Story; Speech
Vocabulary: Negative Prefixes
Grammar/Language: Appositives
Life Skills: Speech for Support Group
Collaboration: Literature Groups

Motivating OPTIONS

Selection Focus Transparency 16: Have students read the quote from Jane Yolen and discuss the ways in which readers can make a story their own.

Focus Activity: As an extension of the Focus Activity, have students make a list of their favorite presents and then discuss the ones that cannot be held in one's hands.

Before You Read
Birthday Box and There Is No Word for Goodbye

MEET JANE YOLEN

Jane Yolen wrote her first two books before she was in high school. One was about pirates and the other about the pioneer west. Since then she has written more than 150 books.

Jane Yolen was born in 1939. This story was first published in 1995.

MEET MARY TALLMOUNTAIN

Mary Tall-Mountain was born into the Koykon-Athabascan tribe in Nulato, Alaska. It wasn't until she was in her fifties that TallMountain began to write poetry, sometimes for sixteen hours a day! Her poems recapture her Athabascan childhood.

Mary TallMountain was born in 1918. "There Is No Word for Goodbye" was published in Continuum: Poems by Mary TallMountain in 1988.

174 🐦 THEME 2

FOCUS ACTIVITY

What's the most memorable gift you ever unwrapped? Have you ever thought about the gifts you have been given that you can't hold in your hands—gifts like time, friendship, or love?

QuickWrite
Make a quick list of your favorite gifts—the kind you can and cannot hold in your hands.

Setting a Purpose
Read these selections to discover two views on love and separation.

BACKGROUND

Sometimes writers don't have to spend days and weeks coming up with an idea for a story. In 1995 an editor named Johanna Hurwitz decided to invite ten writers, including Jane Yolen, to write about a child who receives a beautifully wrapped empty box for a birthday present. The writers were inspired to write fairy tales, fantasy, poetry, and realistic stories. Each writer's imagination was sparked by the same idea, and each writer wrote a completely original piece of literature.

VOCABULARY PREVIEW

insistent (in sis′ tənt) *adj.* demanding attention or notice; p. 176
stark (stärk) *adv.* completely; harshly or grimly; p. 177
infinite (in′ fə nit) *adj.* boundless; limitless; extremely great; p. 177
subtle (sut′ əl) *adj.* not open or direct; not obvious; p. 178

RESOURCE MANAGER

Lesson Planning Resource
The *Theme Two Planning Guide* (pp. 40–45) provides additional lesson notes and reduced versions of all print resources.

📁 **Other Print Resources**
- Active Reading Guide, p. 16
- Vocabulary Practice, p. 11
- Reading Workbook, pp. 27–28
- Grammar and Language Workbook, pp. 69–70

- Grammar and Composition Handbook, Lesson 2.5
- Quick Checks, p. 16
- Selection and Theme Assessment, pp. 29–30
- Performance Assessment, p. 16
- Spanish Summaries, p. 16
- Spanish Translations
- Inclusion Strategies
- English Language Learners Sourcebook

 Transparencies
- Selection Focus 16
- Fine Art 30
- Literary Elements 16
- Grammar and Language 14

Technology

🎧 Audio Library
🎧 Spanish Audio Library
💻 Glencoe Literature Web Site
💾 Testmaker

BIRTHDAY Box

Jane Yolen

I was ten years old when my mother died. Ten years old on that very day. Still she gave me a party of sorts. Sick as she was, Mama had seen to it, organizing it at the hospital. She made sure the doctors and nurses all brought me presents. We were good friends with them all by that time, because Mama had been in the hospital for so long.

The head nurse, V. Louise Higgins (I never did know what that V stood for), gave me a little box, which was sort of funny because she was the biggest of all the nurses there. I mean she was tremendous. And she was the only one who insisted on wearing all white. Mama had called her the great white shark when she was first admitted, only not to V. Louise's face. "All those needles," Mama had said. "Like teeth." But V. Louise was sweet, not sharklike at all, and she'd been so gentle with Mama.

Literary Elements

CHARACTER Ask students what they have learned about Katie up to this point. *(Katie is ten years old; her mother is very sick; her parents are separated; her father is not very involved in her life; she is very responsive to her mother; she's polite—her Mama was "real big on politeness.")*

Active Reading

PREDICT Ask students to evaluate Katie's interests. What seems to be her favorite thing to do? Encourage them to support their ideas with examples. *(Katie loves paperback books, writing paper, and pens. These details help us recognize that she is creative and likes to write.)*

Literary Elements

SETTING Remind students to use the descriptions of the setting to help them gather information about the characters. Discuss with students the significance of the breathing machine. *(It shows that Katie's mother is very sick. She cannot even breathe by herself.)*

Teaching Options

I opened the little present first. It was a fountain pen, a real one, not a fake one like you get at Kmart.

"Now you can write beautiful stories, Katie," V. Louise said to me.

I didn't say that stories come out of your head, not out of a pen. That wouldn't have been polite, and Mama—even sick—was real big on politeness.

"Thanks, V. Louise," I said.

The Stardust Twins—which is what Mama called Patty and Tracey-Lynn because they reminded her of dancers in an old-fashioned ballroom—gave me a present together. It was a diary and had a picture of a little girl in pink, reading in a garden swing. A little young for me, a little too cute. I mean, I read Stephen King[1] and want to write like him. But as Mama always reminded me whenever Dad finally remembered to send me something, it was the thought that counted, not the actual gift.

"It's great," I told them. "I'll write in it with my new pen." And I wrote my name on the first page just to show them I meant it.

They hugged me and winked at Mama. She tried to wink back but was just too tired and shut both her eyes instead.

Lily, who is from Jamaica, had baked me some sweet bread. Mary Margaret gave me a gold cross blessed by the pope, which I put on even though Mama and I weren't churchgoers. That was Dad's thing.

Then Dr. Dann, the intern[2] who was on days, and Dr. Pucci, the oncologist (which

is the fancy name for a cancer doctor), gave me a big box filled to the top with little presents, each wrapped up individually. All things they knew I'd love—paperback books and writing paper and erasers with funny animal heads and colored paper clips and a rubber stamp that printed FROM KATIE'S DESK and other stuff. They must have raided a stationery store.

There was one box, though, they held out till the end. It was about the size of a large top hat. The paper was deep blue and covered with stars; not fake stars but real stars, I mean, like a map of the night sky. The ribbon was two shades of blue with silver threads running through. There was no name on the card.

"Who's it from?" I asked.

None of the nurses answered, and the doctors both suddenly were studying the ceiling tiles with the kind of intensity they usually saved for X rays. No one spoke. In fact the only sound for the longest time was Mama's breathing machine going in and out and in and out. It was a harsh, horrible, insistent sound, and usually I talked and talked to cover up the noise. But I was waiting for someone to tell me.

At last V. Louise said, "It's from your mama, Katie. She told us what she wanted. And where to get it."

I turned and looked at Mama then, and her eyes were open again. Funny, but sickness had made her even more beautiful than good health had. Her skin was like that old paper, the kind they used to write on with quill pens, and stretched out over her bones so she looked like a model. Her

---

1. An extremely popular novelist, *Stephen King* writes mainly tales of horror and the supernatural.
2. An *intern* is a recent medical school graduate who works under the supervision of experienced doctors.

Vocabulary
insistent (in sis' tənt) *adj.* demanding attention or notice

---

REAL-WORLD CONNECTION

Life-Changing Incidents Ask students how they would cope with a life-changing incident. How might such an event change their day-to-day lives?

Activity Ask students to work in small groups to discuss how they would feel if they lost someone they know, or someone they loved. If some students have experienced such a loss, they may wish to

share their personal experiences and how they came to terms with the loss. You may wish to have a school counselor address the class and discuss constructive ways to manage the anger, the frustration, and the sense of helplessness a person feels when faced by such circumstances. **L2** **COLLAB. LEARN.**

Jane Yolen

eyes, which had been a deep, brilliant blue, were now like the fall sky, bleached and softened. She was like a faded photograph of herself. She smiled a very small smile at me. I knew it was an effort.

"It's you," she mouthed. I read her lips. I had gotten real good at that. I thought she meant it was a present for me.

"Of course it is," I said cheerfully. I had gotten good at that, too, being cheerful when I didn't feel like it. "Of course it is."

I took the paper off the box carefully, not tearing it but folding it into a tidy packet. I twisted the ribbons around my hand and then put them on the pillow by her hand. It made the stark white hospital bed look almost festive.

Under the wrapping, the box was beautiful itself. It was made of a heavy cardboard and covered with a linen material that had a pattern of cloud-filled skies.

I opened the box slowly and . . .

"It's empty," I said. "Is this a joke?" I turned to ask Mama, but she was gone. I mean, her body was there, but she wasn't. It was as if she was as empty as the box.

Dr. Pucci leaned over her and listened with a stethoscope,[3] then almost absently patted Mama's head. Then, with infinite care, V. Louise closed Mama's eyes, ran her hand across Mama's cheek, and turned off the breathing machine.

---

3. A *stethoscope* (steth′ ə skōp′) is an instrument used to listen to sounds made by the internal organs of the body, especially the lungs and heart. The French doctor who invented the stethoscope in 1817 got the idea after seeing children making sounds through a hollow log.

"Mama!" I cried. And to the nurses and doctors, I screamed, "Do something!" And because the room had suddenly become so silent, my voice echoed back at me. "Mama, do something."

❈ ❈ ❈ ❈ ❈

I cried steadily for, I think, a week. Then I cried at night for a couple of months. And then for about a year I cried at anniversaries, like Mama's birthday or mine, at Thanksgiving, on Mother's Day. I stopped writing. I stopped reading except for school assignments. I was pretty mean to my half brothers and totally rotten to my stepmother and Dad. I felt empty and angry, and they all left me pretty much alone.

And then one night, right after my first birthday without Mama, I woke up remembering how she had said, "It's you." Not, "It's for you," just "It's you." Now Mama had been a high school English teacher and a writer herself. She'd had poems published in little magazines. She didn't use words carelessly. In the end she could hardly use any words at all. So—I asked myself in that dark room—why had she said, "It's you"? Why were they the very last words she had ever said to me, forced out with her last breath?

I turned on the bedside light and got out of bed. The room was full of shadows, not all of them real.

Pulling the desk chair over to my closet, I climbed up and felt along the top shelf, and against the back wall, there was the birthday box, just where I had thrown it the day I had moved in with my dad.

Vocabulary

stark (stärk) *adv.* completely; harshly or grimly
infinite (in′ fə nit) *adj.* boundless; limitless; extremely great

---

DESCRIPTION Point out to students the way the author describes Katie's mother. Then ask students how each of these images relates to her situation. *(Old paper conveys the look of her skin; fall sky refers to the fall season, a time of dying; and faded photograph suggests someone who is very old, sick, or dead.)*

SYMBOL Ask students to think about why Katie's mother gives her an empty box. Encourage them to keep their hunches in mind as they read to the end of the selection. *(Some students may understand that it has a meaning that Katie must discover.)*

VERIFYING PREDICTIONS Ask students what they think Mama means when she says, "It's you," to Katie. Remind them to keep in mind the title of the story. You might share the following model to guide students in the thinking process involved in drawing conclusions.

Model: The story shows that Katie's mother is very caring and thoughtful. If she wants to give Katie a beautiful empty box, it must be for a reason. She knows Katie well enough to understand how "empty" she will feel without her. By saying "It's you," she is telling Katie that she, like the box, is beautiful on the outside and needs to fill herself with her writings, her thoughts, and her memories.

Reading *Minilesson*

Monitoring Comprehension Students might have trouble understanding the significance the narrator finds in the few words her mother uses on page 177.

Activity To monitor their comprehension and relate that part of the story to their own experience, have groups answer the following questions as they read: Did I understand what I just read? What questions can I ask to check myself? Why does the narrator wake up suddenly? What is the difference between saying "It's for you" and "It's you"? What does Mama's being an English teacher and a writer have to do with anything? **L2**
COLLAB. LEARN.

Additional Resources
📁 *Reading Workbook,* pp. 27–28

VIEWING THE PAINTING

A professional artist for more than thirty years, John S. Bunker is also director of the Jacksonville (Florida) Art Museum.

Viewing Response *Like the angel, who is a spirit, Katie's spirit is just beginning to emerge and manifest itself in her writing.*

H Critical Thinking

DRAWING CONCLUSIONS Have students explain why Katie stops crying. *(She realizes that her mother wanted her to write and fill the box with her work. She knows that it is time to stop crying and begin writing.)*

I Literary Elements

CHARACTER Ask students what the last two lines of the story emphasize about Katie. What change in her character might this point out? *(After she begins writing, Katie is very aware of her feelings, her energies, and her abilities.)*

LITERATURE & HUMANITIES

● Use the painting *Eggs* from **The National Museum of Women in the Arts** CD, and have students compare the way the themes of life and death are represented in the story and the painting.

Teaching Options

Emerging Angel. John S. Bunker. Mixed media, 8 x 11 in.

Viewing the painting: How is the subject of the painting like Katie? How is it like her writing?

I pulled it down and opened it. It was as empty as the day I had put it away.

"It's you," I whispered to the box.

And then suddenly I knew.

Mama had meant *I* was the box, solid and sturdy, maybe even beautiful or at least interesting on the outside. But I had to fill up the box to make it all it could be. And I had to fill me up as well. She had guessed what might happen to me, had told me in a <u>subtle</u> way. In the two words she could manage.

I stopped crying and got some paper out of the desk drawer. I got out my fountain pen. I started writing, and I haven't stopped since. The first thing I wrote was about that birthday. I put it in the box, and pretty soon that box was overflowing with stories. And poems. And memories.

And so was I.

And so was I.

Vocabulary
subtle (sut′ əl) *adj.* not open or direct; not obvious

178 ❧ THEME 2

Grammar and Language *Minilesson*

Appositives Write the following on the board: *The doctor used a stethoscope, a device for listening.* Point out that the underlined phrase is an appositive, a word or phrase, usually after a noun, that gives additional information about the noun. Appositives identify, define, or rename nouns and are set off by commas.

Activity Ask students to rewrite the fol-

lowing sentences using the phrases in parentheses as appositives.
1. Katie had a difficult birthday. (a ten-year-old girl) *(Katie, a ten-year-old girl, had …)*
2. V. Louise's gift was Katie's favorite. (a fountain pen) *(V. Louise's gift, a fountain pen, was Katie's favorite.)*
3. I put the letters into a special box. (all handwritten) *(I put the letters, all handwritten, into a special box.)* **L2**

Additional Resources

📠 *Grammar and Language Transparency 14*

📖 *Grammar and Language Workbook,* pp. 69–70

📖 *Grammar and Composition Handbook,* Lesson 2.5

📖 *Writer's Choice,* Lesson 9.6

178

There Is No Word for Goodbye

Mary TallMountain ∾

Sokoya,° I said, looking through
    the net of wrinkles into
    wise black pools
    of her eyes.

5 What do you say in Athabaskan
    when you leave each other?
    What is the word
    for goodbye?

A shade of feeling rippled
10   the wind-tanned skin.
    Ah, nothing, she said,
    watching the river flash.

She looked at me close.
    We just say, Tlaa. That means,
15   See you.
    We never leave each other.
    When does your mouth
    say goodbye to your heart?

She touched me light
20   as a bluebell.
    You forget when you leave us,
    You're so small then.
    We don't use that word.

We always think you're coming back,
25   but if you don't,
    we'll see you some place else.
    You understand.
    There is no word for goodbye.

---

1 *Sokoya* means "aunt."

Female Figure, 1830. Haida, Queen Charlotte Islands, British Columbia. Hardwood (possibly crab apple), wool, red and black paint, 11 x 5 x 2⅞ in. The Thaw Collection, Fenimore House Museum, Cooperstown, NY.

J **Literary Elements**

FIGURES OF SPEECH: *Metaphor* Help students identify two metaphors for Sokoya's face. *(Tall Mountain uses the metaphors* net of wrinkles *and* wise black pools of her eyes.*)*

K **Critical Thinking**

FOCUSING ON A QUESTION Ask students to compare the meanings of *goodbye* and *see you. (They may say that* goodbye *implies a permanent parting, while* see you *suggests another meeting.)*

LITERATURE & HUMANITIES

💿 Have students listen to "Rain Dance" from the CD *American Music and Cultural Traditions,* " Vol. 1, Track 1. The selection is based on a Native American creation myth.

Thematic Focus

Winds of Change Coping with the loss of someone important is a difficult lesson to learn.

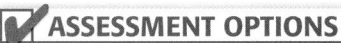

☑ **ASSESSMENT OPTIONS**

📁 *Quick Checks,* p. 16

FINE ART
TRANSPARENCY 30

You may want to use *Fine Art Transparency 30* to enrich a discussion on trying to find something positive in the loss of a loved one.

INCLUSION STRATEGIES
MEETING INDIVIDUAL NEEDS

Less-Proficient Readers Explain to students that poets often use relatively few words to say a lot. The fun of reading a poem is discovering the poet's message and how it is delivered. Often, poets use figures of speech, including metaphors, to express their ideas and feelings.

Activity Have small groups decide on two or three metaphors that create vivid images. Then have students make titled posters that illustrate them. **L1**
COLLAB. LEARN.

Additional Resources
📁 *Inclusion Strategies*

CONNECTING TO OTHER SELECTIONS
For a teaching strategy that connects "There Is No Word For Goodbye" to "Strong Men Weep," turn to page 27 in the *Theme One Planning Guide.*

Responding to the Selection

Personal Response

Have students share with the class their ideas about gifts. Be sure they understand that Sokoya lovingly gives the gift of wisdom.

Analyzing Literature

1. She explained to the nurses what she wanted and had them get it for her.
2. Katie goes to live with her father and stepmother.
3. She asks what the Athabaskan word for *goodbye* is.
4. She was a very caring person who thought a lot about the needs of other people, especially her daughter.
5. She doesn't ever say goodbye because she feels that people never really leave each other.
6. By telling the reader what happens, she sets the mood right at the beginning. The reader knows that this is going to be a serious story.
7. Writing her thoughts and feelings helps her better understand and express her emotions. Expressing her feelings will allow Katie eventually to move beyond her angry and empty feelings.
8. Students may say that it would depend on the situation. If they received an empty box as a joke, they might be angry.
9. Encourage students to talk about their own experiences or to think of a specific person each may have to say goodbye to in the future.
10. Both selections say that family members have a great deal to give each other. Also, the selections show that there is a strong bond between family members—a bond that remains even if people are separated.

Responding to Literature

PERSONAL RESPONSE

- ◆ Recall the list of gifts you made for the **Focus Activity** on page 174. Before reading the story did you imagine a gift that you both can and cannot hold?
- ◆ What kind of gift did the aunt in "There Is No Word for Goodbye" give the speaker of the poem?

Analyzing Literature

RECALL

1. How did Katie's mother manage to buy her the birthday box?
2. What happens to the family after Katie's mother dies?
3. What question does the speaker in "There Is No Word for Goodbye" ask the aunt in the beginning of the poem?

INTERPRET

4. What can you **infer** about the character of Katie's mother when you realize that, in spite of her serious illness, she had planned a party and presents for Katie?
5. How does the aunt in TallMountain's poem feel about saying goodbye to the people she loves?

EVALUATE AND CONNECT

6. Why do you think Jane Yolen tells the reader what happens to Katie's mother in the first sentence?
7. How does filling the box with her writing help Katie deal with her grief?
8. How would you react if someone you loved gave you an empty box? Explain your answer.
9. Think about a relationship you have with an older friend or relative. How would you feel if you had to say goodbye to each other?
10. Theme Connection   What do both "Birthday Box" and "There Is No Word for Goodbye" have to say about love between family members?

LITERARY ELEMENTS

Character

Characters are the actors in a work of literature. They can be people, animals, or whatever the writer chooses. In "Birthday Box," Katie and her mother are the main characters. The minor characters are the nurses and doctors in the hospital. In "There Is No Word for Goodbye," the characters are the speaker and the speaker's aunt.

1. Katie's mother hardly speaks in "Birthday Box." In what other ways does the author tell the reader about this character?

2. What do the aunt in "There Is No Word for Goodbye" and Katie's mother have in common?

● See **Literary Terms Handbook**, p. R2.

LITERARY ELEMENTS

1. She describes how she looks; she tells about her through Katie's thoughts and through her own actions.
2. They both care about a younger person and help her grow; they both give valuable gifts of the spirit.

Additional Resources

Literary Elements Transparency 16

Extending Your Response

Writing About Literature

Setting   Most of the action in "Birthday Box" takes place in a hospital room. What details can you visualize about the hospital room from Yolen's description? Write a paragraph explaining how the hospital setting contributes to the effect of the story.

Creative Writing

Symbolic Gifts   Katie's box is a symbol of Katie herself and of her mother's love. The language lesson received by the speaker in "There Is No Word for Goodbye," is also a symbol of love. Write a short story about a character who receives a symbolic gift.

Literature Groups

The Empty Box   When Katie receives the empty box she thinks it is a joke. It takes her a year to understand what her mother meant by this gift. Do you think Katie's mother should have made sure Katie understood the meaning of the box from the beginning? Discuss your ideas and draw a conclusion. Be prepared to share your group's opinion with the whole class.

Learning for Life

Writing a Speech   Sometimes people who have lived through a painful experience want to help others in a similar situation. Imagine that five years after her mother has died, Katie is asked to speak to a group of children who have lost a parent. Write a speech for Katie that expresses what she has learned about overcoming grief and finding meaning in life after such a loss.

Art Activity

Wrap It!   Design your own wrapping paper. Decide what special occasion your paper will be used for. Then design a paper to suit that occasion. Draw your design at a smaller scale on regular 8½ x 11-inch paper, and share it with your class.

Reading Further

Check out these other books by Jane Yolen:
The Devil's Arithmetic
Here There Be Dragons

📖 **Save your work for your portfolio.**

Skill Minilesson

VOCABULARY • NEGATIVE PREFIXES

How do you change *active, moral, regular,* and *legal* into words that mean the exact opposite? Add a prefix to each one, making *inactive, immoral, irregular,* and *illegal.* The basic prefix is *in-,* but its spelling changes to *im-, ir-,* or *il-* before certain letters. Be careful, though, because these prefixes have other meanings, and they don't always change a word into its opposite. When in doubt, use a dictionary for help.

PRACTICE   Write the five words from this list in which you think *in-, im-, ir-,* or *il-* is a negative prefix.

impress	income	inconsiderate
impure	injustice	impractical
irritate	indeed	irresponsible
	illustrate	

Extending Your Response

Writing About Literature

Students' paragraphs should
- explain how they think the setting of the story contributes to its effect.
- include details from the story that support their ideas about the effect of the setting.

Creative Writing

Students' stories should
- include a character who receives a symbolic gift.
- reflect an understanding of how the gifts in these two pieces are symbolic.

Literature Groups   Encourage students to express their ideas and to listen to those of other people. Be sure they understand that there is no single "right" answer in this kind of situation. COLLAB. LEARN.

Learning for Life   Encourage students to prepare by first putting themselves in Katie's place. Then have them write down how she eventually begins to deal with her loss. 🗂

Art Activity   Encourage students to sketch several possible designs and then choose the one they think best suits the occasion. 🗂

Skill Minilesson

VOCABULARY
• NEGATIVE PREFIXES
1. impure   4. impractical
2. injustice   5. irresponsible
3. inconsiderate

Additional Resources
🗂 *Vocabulary Practice,* p. 11

✔ ASSESSMENT OPTIONS

🗂 *Quick Checks,* p. 16
🗂 *Selection and Theme Assessment,* pp. 29–30
🗂 *Performance Assessment,* p. 16
💾 *Testmaker*

Objective

• To recognize comparative and superlative forms of adjectives and adverbs and apply strategies for using the forms correctly

Teaching Strategies

Begin by making sure that students are able to distinguish between adjectives and adverbs. Ask them to think of a list of descriptive words. Write them on the board. Categorize the words into adjectives and adverbs. Ask students to use the words in sentences. Create situations in which comparative and/or superlative forms come naturally. For example, you might wish to ask students to compare sixth grade with seventh.

Exercise

1. more slowly
2. better/more
3. most fond, fondest
4. more strongly
5. most curious

Additional Resources

Grammar and Language Workbook, pp. 133–134

Grammar and Composition Handbook, Lesson 6.4

Writer's Choice, Lesson 12.9

Teaching Options

Using Adjectives and Adverbs Correctly

Adjectives describe nouns or pronouns. The **comparative** form of an adjective compares two nouns or pronouns; the **superlative** form compares more than two.

Comparative: Maria is <u>younger</u> than Ricardo.

Superlative: Maria is her parents' <u>youngest</u> child.

Adverbs describe verbs, adjectives, or other adverbs. The comparative form of an adverb compares two actions; the superlative form compares more than two.

Comparative: Susan runs <u>faster</u> than Jeff.

Superlative: Of all the runners on the team, Susan runs the <u>fastest</u>.

The endings *-er* and *-est* are used to form the comparative and superlative forms of most short adjectives and adverbs. For longer adjectives and adverbs, the words *more* and *most* are usually used.

Adjectives: <u>dark</u> hair, <u>darker</u> hair, <u>darkest</u> hair

   <u>curious</u> student, <u>more curious</u> student, <u>most curious</u> student

Adverbs: works <u>hard</u>, works <u>harder</u>, works <u>hardest</u>

   smiles <u>happily</u>, smiles <u>more happily</u>, smiles <u>most happily</u>

Some adjectives and adverbs are *irregular.* Irregular adjectives and adverbs do not follow the same rules for forming comparatives and superlatives. Examples: good, better, best; badly, worse, worst.

● For more about using adjectives and adverbs, see **Language Handbook,** p. R27.

EXERCISE

Write the correct comparative or superlative form of the modifier shown in parentheses.

1. Ernie learned (slowly) than an average child.
2. Jack knew him (well) than anyone else and helped him (much) than anyone.
3. Of all the things in the world, Ernie was (fond) of his seed packets.
4. Ernie started feeling (strongly) about Dolores than he felt about his seeds.
5. Who was (curious) about the flowers—Dolores, Dick, or the Avon lady?

Writing Minilesson

Writing a Poem Encourage students to talk about some of the older people in their lives. What are some of the differences between youth and old age? Create a list of ideas using the comparative form. (For example: *Elderly people often have more experience but less energy than young people.*)

Activity Have each student write a short poem to an elderly person who has influenced him or her and imagine reading it to the person for whom it was written. How might that person react? **L2**

Additional Resources

Writer's Choice, Lesson 1.1

Organizing Ideas for Comparison and Contrast

When you write to explore likenesses and differences, you are using **comparison and contrast**. As you plan an essay of comparison and contrast, diagrams can help you organize details.

Venn Diagram The Venn diagram below organizes details about Alfonso and his brother Ernie, from "Broken Chain" in Theme 1, pages 44–52. Each oval shows traits of one character. Traits shared by both characters appear where the ovals overlap.

Alfonso
seventh grade
smaller, with crooked teeth
wants to look good
considers others' feelings
keeps his things neat

Both
have bikes
want to impress girls
are easily embarrassed

Ernie
ninth grade
bigger and tougher
wants to be in charge
puts himself first
lets his things get messy

Comparison Chart A comparison chart helps when you know which features you will compare. List features as headings along the left side. List subjects as headings across the top. In the example, the features are literary elements of the Theme 1 stories "Broken Chain" and "Fish Cheeks."

	BROKEN CHAIN	**FISH CHEEKS**
SETTING	Fresno, California, in the 1980s	Oakland, California, in 1966
MAIN CHARACTERS	Alfonso, his brother Ernie, Sandra	Amy, her parents, Robert, and his parents

EXERCISES

1. Choose two characters from a story in this theme. Make your own Venn diagram to show how the characters are alike and how they are different.

2. Make a comparison chart for two of your favorite movies.

WINDS OF CHANGE 🐦 183

Objective

- To organize ideas for exploring likenesses and differences

Teaching Strategies

Have students review the use of the Venn diagrams and create their own. Encourage students to compare their looks, feelings, and actions in sixth grade and now. Headings for their diagrams might be *Sixth Grade; Seventh Grade; Both Grades.*

Discuss the differences between the Venn diagram and the comparison chart. Ask students what other kinds of information could be organized on a comparison chart.

Exercises

1. Examples might include Dolores and Ernie from "A Crush":

Dolores
woman
works in a hardware store
seems experienced in life

Both
live in the same town
are seen as outsiders
are unmarried

Ernie
man
lives in a group home has led a sheltered life

2. Headings may include *Title, Actors, Setting, Genre, Favorite Scene, and Rating.*

Additional Resources

Writer's Choice, Lessons 5.3, 5.11

Teaching Options

Grammar and Language *Minilesson*

The Superlative Form This form of an adjective or adverb is used to compare three or more people, things, or events.

Activity Have students list things for which someone might hold a record. Have each student use at least three superlatives in writing a short paragraph describing a record holder and explaining why that person holds the record. **L2**

Additional Resources

Grammar and Language Workbook pp. 121–124, 131–132

Grammar and Composition Handbook, Lessons 5.3, 5.4, 6.3

Writer's Choice, Lessons 12.3, 12.4, 12.8

Objectives

- To read and enjoy a short story
- To visualize the setting
- To write about the story's theme

Skills

Reading/Thinking: Making Critical Judgments; Identifying Main Idea; Identifying Bias; Drawing Conclusions; Logical Reasoning; Inferring; Evaluating; Identifying Assumptions

Writing: Describing a Person; Setting a Mood; Diary Entry

Vocabulary: Prefixes; Context Clues; Synonyms and Antonyms

Grammar/Language: Semicolons; Hyphens; Capitalizing; Adverbs

Listening/Speaking: Interviewing; Debating Stereotypes

Motivating
→OPTIONS

Literature Launchers: "Washington Irving's New York"

Videodisc Side A, Segment 4

Also available in VHS.

Selection Focus Transparency 17: Have the class discuss communication changes in their lifetime.

Focus Activity: Have groups list things that have come into being since they were born.

Before You Read
Rip Van Winkle

Washington Irving was the first American writer to win international fame. *The Sketch Book* (1820), a collection of stories admired throughout Europe, included Irving's two most famous tales, "Rip Van Winkle," and "The Legend of Sleepy Hollow." Like his famous fictional character Rip Van Winkle, Washington Irving was a born wanderer. Even as a child, he later wrote, "I began my travels, and made many tours into foreign parts and unknown regions of my native city, to the frequent alarm of my parents."

Washington Irving was born in New York City in 1783 and died in 1859.

FOCUS ACTIVITY

How has the world changed since you were born? What about since your parents were born?

Think/Pair/Share
Take a moment to jot down your responses to the questions above. Then share your thoughts and feelings with a partner.

Setting a Purpose
Read this selection for the pleasure of discovering a story that readers have enjoyed for almost two hundred years.

BACKGROUND

The Time and Place
The setting is the Hudson River valley and the Catskill Mountains, in southeastern New York State. The story takes place in the eighteenth century.

VOCABULARY PREVIEW

impunity (im pū′ nə tē) *n.* freedom from punishment, harm, or bad effects; p. 187

perseverance (pur′ sə vēr′ əns) *n.* continuation despite difficulty; determination; p. 187

incessantly (in ses′ ənt lē) *adv.* endlessly; constantly; p. 188

muse (mūz) *v.* to think or reflect; p. 190

singularity (sing′ gyə lar′ ə tē) *n.* that which is remarkable or out of the ordinary; unusualness; p. 191

incomprehensible (in′ kom prē hen′ sə bəl) *adj.* not understandable; p. 191

perplexity (pər plek′ sə tē) *n.* doubt or uncertainty; puzzlement; p. 194

invariably (in vār′ ē ə blē) *adv.* without exception; p. 194

faltering (fôl′ tər ing) *adj.* shaky because of uncertainty; p. 199

RESOURCE MANAGER

Lesson Planning Resource
The **Theme Two Planning Guide** (pp. 46–53) provides additional lesson notes and reduced versions of all print resources.

📁 **Other Print Resources**
- Active Reading Guide, p. 17
- Vocabulary Practice, p. 12
- Reading Workbook, pp. 29–30
- Grammar and Language Workbook, pp. 127–128, 235–246, 265–266, 275–276

- Grammar and Composition Handbook, Lessons 6.1, 6.2, 12.1–12.4, 13.5, 13.8
- Quick Checks, p. 17
- Selection and Theme Assessment, pp. 31–32
- Performance Assessment, p. 17
- Spanish Summaries, p. 17
- Spanish Translations
- Inclusion Strategies
- English Language Learners Sourcebook

 Transparencies
- Selection Focus 17
- Fine Art 14
- Literary Elements 17
- Grammar and Language 16–18

Technology
 Literature Launchers
 Audio Library
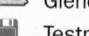 Spanish Audio Library
Glencoe Literature Web Site
 Testmaker

Title page from *Rip Van Winkle*, 1921. N. C. Wyeth.
Oil on canvas. Millport Conservancy, Lititz, PA.

Washington Irving

SUMMARY

The story is set in the peaceful Kaatskill (Catskill) Mountains overlooking the Hudson River. Rip Van Winkle is a likable man who is always willing to help children in their play and neighbors in their chores, but who does not do much work on his own farm or in his own home. One day he ventures into the woods, falls asleep, and awakens to a number of strange occurrences. When he returns to the village, he finds he has been asleep for twenty years, and many changes have taken place.

📁 *Spanish Summaries,* p. 17

A Active Reading

PREDICT Ask students to use the story's title and this illustration to make some predictions about the setting of the story. *(Because of the odd title and the fairy tale quality of the illustration, students may suggest that the story will take place in a time and place very different from this one.)*

Additional Resources
📁 *Active Reading Guide,* p. 17
🎧 *Audio Library*
🎧 *Spanish Audio Library*

Teaching Options

CONNECTING TO OTHER SELECTIONS

COMPARING *selections*

This selection is paired with "old age sticks" on page 205. A lesson for teaching a comparison of the two selections is on page 207.

The chart at the right shows three ways to connect "Rip Van Winkle" to other selections in this book.

For specific teaching strategies, see the *Theme Two Planning Guide,* pages 49–50.

Connection	Title
Life Skills: Lifelong Learning	→ "The Old Demon," p. 483
Thematic: Family	→ "The Boy and His Grandfather," p. 495
Literary: Plot Twist	→ "After Twenty Years," p. 565

B Literary Elements

SETTING After reading the first paragraph, ask students to point out passages that help the reader visualize the setting. *(The students may provide the following suggestions:* every hour of the day, produces some change in the magical hues and shapes of these mountains; they are clothed in blue and purple, and print their bold outlines on the clear evening sky; they will gather a hood of gray vapors about their summits, which, in the last rays of the setting sun, will glow and light up like a crown of glory.*)*

Historical Note

The colony of New Netherland was founded by the Dutch West India Company in 1624. Fort Orange (now Albany, NY) was the colony's first permanent settlement.

C Author's Craft

STYLE Ask students to observe how Washington Irving makes the reader think well of Rip Van Winkle.

(Washington Irving presents all the character's good qualities while downplaying his weaknesses. He is setting the stage for the reader to be sympathetic to Rip's character.)

Teaching Options

B

Whoever has made a voyage up the Hudson must remember the Kaatskill Mountains. They are a dismembered branch of the great Appalachian[1] family, and are seen away to the west of the river, swelling up to a noble height, and lording it over the surrounding country. Every change of season, every change of weather, indeed, every hour of the day, produces some change in the magical hues and shapes of these mountains, and they are regarded by all the good wives, far and near, as perfect barometers. When the weather is fair and settled, they are clothed in blue and purple, and print their bold outlines on the clear evening sky; but sometimes, when the rest of the landscape is cloudless, they will gather a hood of gray vapors about their summits, which, in the last rays of the setting sun, will glow and light up like a crown of glory.

At the foot of these fairy mountains, the voyager may have descried[2] the light smoke curling up from a village, whose shingled roofs gleam among the trees, just where the blue tints of the upland melt away into the fresh green of the nearer landscape. It is a little village, of great antiquity, having been founded by some of the Dutch colonists, in the early times of the province, just about the beginning of the government of the good Peter Stuyvesant[3] (may he rest in peace!) and there were some of the houses of the original settlers standing within a few years, built of small yellow bricks brought from Holland, having latticed windows and gable fronts, surmounted with weathercocks.

In that same village and in one of these very houses (which, to tell the precise truth, was sadly timeworn and weather-beaten), there lived many years since, while the country was yet a province of Great Britain, a simple good-natured fellow, of the name of Rip Van Winkle. He was a descendant of the Van Winkles who figured so gallantly in the chivalrous[4] days of Peter Stuyvesant. He inherited, however, but little of the martial[5] character of his ancestors. I have observed that he was a simple good-natured man; he was, moreover, a kind neighbor, and an obedient henpecked husband. Indeed, to the latter circumstance might be owing that meekness of spirit which gained him such universal popularity; for those men are most apt to be obsequious and conciliating abroad, who are under the discipline of shrews at home. Their tempers, doubtless, are rendered pliant and malleable in the fiery furnace of domestic tribulation, which

Did You Know?

A *latticed* (lat′ ist) window has small panes separated by crossed strips of wood or metal. A gable is the triangular section of wall between the sides of a sloping roof.

C

---

1. The Hudson is a river in New York, and the *Kaatskill* (now spelled *Catskill*) Mountains are part of the *Appalachian* mountain range.
2. *Descried* means "caught sight of."
3. *Peter Stuyvesant* (stī′ və sənt) was the last governor of the Dutch colony of New Netherland, which included parts of what are now Connecticut, Delaware, New Jersey, and New York. The narrator is poking fun at Stuyvesant, who was unpopular with the colonists.

4. A *chivalrous* (shiv′ əl rəs) person has the qualities of a knight, such as honor, courage, and skill in battle. The narrator again mocks Stuyvesant, who surrendered New Netherland to England in 1664, allowing it to become the British colony of New York.
5. *Martial* (mär′ shəl) means "warlike."

MEETING INDIVIDUAL NEEDS — ENGLISH LANGUAGE LEARNERS

Cultural Changes Cultural references change over time as well as from place to place, country to country. Explain that the author wrote this story in the early 1800s, so many of its phrases are outdated or are culturally different from today's. For example:

1. Women were called *good wives.*
2. The houses resembled those in Holland with yellow brick, *latticed* windows, and *gable* fronts.
3. Rip's gun is called a *fowling piece.*

Activity Have pairs of students list cultural changes they have experienced in their communities and share their lists with the class.

Additional Resources

📁 *English Language Learners Sourcebook*

Washington Irving

is worth all the sermons in the world for teaching the virtues of patience and long-suffering. A nagging wife may, therefore, in some respects, be considered a tolerable blessing; and if so, Rip Van Winkle was thrice blessed.[6]

D

Certain it is that he was a great favorite among all the good wives of the village, who took his part in all family squabbles; and never failed, whenever they talked those matters over in their evening gossipings, to lay all the blame on Dame[7] Van Winkle. The children of the village, too, would shout with joy whenever he approached. He assisted at their sports, made their playthings, taught them to fly kites and shoot marbles, and told them long stories of ghosts, witches, and Indians. Whenever he went dodging about the village, he was surrounded by a troop of them hanging on his coat skirts, clambering on his back, and playing a thousand tricks on him with <u>impunity</u>; and not a dog would bark at him throughout the neighborhood.

E

The great error in Rip's composition was an insuperable aversion[8] to all kinds of profitable labor. It could not be from the want of <u>perseverance</u>; for he would sit on a wet rock, with a rod as long and heavy as a Tartar's lance,[9] and fish all day without a

murmur, even though he should not be encouraged by a single nibble. He would carry a fowling piece[10] on his shoulder for hours together, trudging through woods and swamps, and up hill and down dale, to shoot a few squirrels or wild pigeons. He would never refuse to assist a neighbor even in the roughest toil, and was a foremost man at all country frolics for husking Indian corn, or building stone fences. The women of the village, too, used to employ him to run their errands, and to do such little odds jobs as their less obliging husbands would not do for them. In a word, Rip was ready to attend to anybody's business but his own; but as to doing family duty, and keeping his farm in order, he found it impossible.

F

In fact, he declared it was of no use to work on his farm; it was the most pestilent little piece of ground in the whole country. Everything about it went wrong, and would go wrong, in spite of him. His fences were continually falling to pieces; his cow would either go astray or get among the cabbages; weeds were sure to grow quicker in his fields than anywhere else; the rain always made a point of setting in just as he had some outdoor work to do; so that though his estate had dwindled away under his management, acre by acre, until there was little more left than a mere patch of Indian corn and potatoes, yet it was the worst conditioned farm in the neighborhood.

His children, too, were as ragged and wild as if they belonged to nobody. His son Rip, an urchin begotten in his own

---

6. *[Indeed, to the latter . . . blessed]* The narrator suggests that dealing with nagging, bad-tempered wives makes men become better, more popular people. Rip, then, is especially blessed.
7. *Dame* is a title formerly used for the woman in charge of a household.
8. An *insuperable aversion* is a great dislike that cannot be overcome.
9. A *Tartar's lance* was a twelve-foot spear carried by thirteenth-century warriors in what is now Turkey.

10. A *fowling piece* is a shotgun used to hunt wild birds.

Vocabulary

impunity (im pū′ nə tē) *n.* freedom from punishment, harm, or bad effects
perseverance (pur′ sə vēr′ əns) *n.* continuation despite difficulty; determination

---

Sidebar

D Literary Elements

TONE Ask students if they catch the playful tone in Irving's writing. Explain that even when he criticizes Dame Van Winkle's nagging, he does so in a playful way, saying Rip is "thrice blessed."

E Literary Elements

CHARACTERIZATION Explain that one way an author can delineate a character is by showing how other characters act toward him or her. Elicit from students that the favorable attitude that the children, women, and animals show toward Rip suggests that he is a likable person, despite his wife's opinion to the contrary.

F Critical Thinking

MAKING CRITICAL JUDGMENTS Ask students whether they think Rip is a good man or a deadbeat. *(Students might have a difficult time deciding how they feel about Rip, since he is helpful to everyone in town but does not take good care of his family.)*

Vo•cab•u•lar•y Skills

Prefixes Call attention to the word *insuperable* and discuss its meaning. Explain that the prefix *in-* often means "not," as in *insufficient, inattentive,* and *inaccurate.* Ask students for other examples of words using this prefix. *(Other examples include: insincere, inseparable, insane,* and *ineffective.)*

Writing *Minilesson*

Describing a Person Throughout the story, the author uses vivid sensory details to describe Rip Van Winkle and to help the reader visualize him. Sensory details involve all the senses—taste, hearing, touch, smell, and sight.

Activity Have students work in small groups. Each group should think of a well-known person to use as the subject of a descriptive paragraph. Have them brainstorm to develop a list of sensory details about that person, and then write a paragraph about him or her, that includes the sensory details they like best. **L2**

COLLAB. LEARN.

Additional Resources
Writer's Choice, Lesson 3.5

Call attention to the look on Dame Van Winkle's face, her arm bent at the elbow, her hand in a fist, the broom in her other hand. Call attention, also, to Rip's face. Ask students to identify other aspects that might reflect ideas already presented in the story. For example, the window shutter is hanging from one hinge.

Viewing Response *From her stance and facial expression, it appears that the woman is angry with the man. The woman holds a broom and seems to be working hard, but the house is falling apart and the man is walking away.*

G Literary Elements

FIGURES OF SPEECH: Simile Explain that a comparison of two unlike things using the words *like* or *as* is called a simile. Ask students to identify a simile in this paragraph. *(The simile is "He was...trooping like a colt.")* Ask students how Rip's son is "like a colt." *(He follows his mother closely, as a colt would his mare.)*

H Active Reading

EVALUATE Ask students to explain in their own words Rip and Dame Van Winkle's relationship. *(Although Rip seems to be a good man, he is lazy and makes life difficult for Dame Van Winkle. She constantly yells at him, hoping to motivate him, but to no avail.)*

Teaching Options

Termagant Wife, 1921. N. C. Wyeth. Oil on canvas. Millport Conservancy, Lititz, PA.
Viewing the painting: How does the painting reflect the relationship between Rip Van Winkle and his wife?

G likeness, promised to inherit the habits, with the old clothes of his father. He was generally seen trooping like a colt at his mother's heels, equipped in a pair of his father's cast-off galligaskins[11], which he had much ado to hold up with one hand,

11. *Galligaskins* are the loose, baggy, knee-length trousers worn in the sixteenth and seventeenth centuries.

as a fine lady does her train in bad weather.

Rip Van Winkle, however, was one of those happy mortals, of foolish, well-oiled dispositions, who take the world easy, eat white bread or brown, whichever can be got with least thought or trouble, and would rather starve on a penny than work for a pound. If left to himself, he would have whistled life away in perfect contentment; but his wife kept continually dinning in his ears about his idleness, his carelessness, and the ruin he was bringing on his family. Morning, noon, and night, her tongue was incessantly going, and everything he said or did was sure to produce a torrent of household eloquence. Rip had but one way of replying to all lectures of the kind, and that, by frequent use, had grown into a habit. He shrugged his shoulders, shook his head, cast up his eyes, but said nothing. This, however, always provoked a fresh volley from his wife; so that he would take to the outside of the house—the only side which, in truth, belongs to a henpecked husband.

H

Vocabulary
incessantly (in ses' ənt lē) *adv.* endlessly; constantly

188 THEME 2

Reading Minilesson

Identifying Main Idea and Supporting Details A main idea is the most important idea given about a topic, while supporting details are words, phrases, or sentences that tell something about the main idea.

Activity Work with the class to fill in the following chart about the character of Rip Van Winkle and his relationship with his wife. **L2**

Main Idea about Rip:
He is lazy and easy-going.

Supporting Details:
• "foolish, well-oiled disposition"
• "takes the world easy"
• "eats white bread or brown," whichever is the least trouble
• "would rather starve on a penny than work for a pound"

Main Idea About Rip's Relationship with His Wife:
She nags him all the time, and he avoids her.

Supporting Details:
• her tongue goes "incessantly"
• he shrugs but says nothing
• he retreats from the house

Additional Resources
📕 ***Reading Workbook,*** pp. 29–30

Rip's sole domestic adherent[12] was his dog Wolf, who was as much henpecked as his master; for Dame Van Winkle regarded them as companions in idleness, and even looked upon Wolf with an evil eye, as the cause of his master's going so often astray. True it is, in all points of spirit befitting an honorable dog, he was as courageous an animal as ever scoured the woods—but what courage can withstand the ever-during and all-besetting terrors of a woman's tongue? The moment Wolf entered the house, his crest fell, his tail drooped to the ground, or curled between his legs, he sneaked about with a gallows air,[13] casting many a sidelong glance at Dame Van Winkle, and at the least flourish of a broomstick or ladle, he would fly to the door, yelping.

Times grew worse and worse with Rip Van Winkle as years of matrimony rolled on; a tart temper never mellows with age, and a sharp tongue is the only edged tool that grows keener with constant use. For a long while he used to console himself, when driven from home, by frequenting a kind of perpetual club of the sages, philosophers, and other idle personages[14] of the village; which held its sessions on a bench before a small inn, designated by a rubicund portrait of his Majesty George the Third. Here they used to sit in the shade through a long lazy summer's day, talking listlessly over village gossip, or telling endless sleepy stories about nothing. But it would have been worth any stateman's money to have heard the profound discussions that sometimes took place, when by

chance an old newspaper fell into their hands from some passing traveler. How solemnly they would listen to the contents, as drawled out by Derrick Van Bummel, the schoolmaster, a dapper learned little man, who was not to be daunted by the most gigantic word in the dictionary; and how sagely they would deliberate upon public events some months after they had taken place.

The opinions of this junto[15] were completely controlled by Nicholas Vedder, a patriarch of the village, and landlord of the inn, at the door of which he took his seat from morning till night, just moving sufficiently to avoid the sun and keep in the shade of a large tree; so that the neighbors could tell the hour by his movements as accurately as by a sundial. It is true he was rarely heard to speak, but smoked his pipe incessantly. His adherents, however (for every great man has his adherents), perfectly understood him, and knew how to gather his opinions. When anything that was read or related displeased him, he was observed to smoke his pipe vehemently, and to send forth short, frequent, and angry puffs, but when pleased he would inhale the smoke slowly and tranquilly, and emit it in light and placid clouds. Sometimes, taking the pipe from his mouth, and letting the fragrant vapor curl about his nose, he would gravely nod his head in token of perfect approbation.[16]

From even this stronghold the unlucky Rip was at length routed by his wife, who would suddenly break in upon the tranquillity of the assemblage and call the members

---

12. An *adherent* is a firm supporter.
13. Having a *gallows air* is looking like one who is about to be hanged.
14. *Idle personages* are lazy persons.

---

15. A *junto* (jun′ tō) is a group with a common purpose.
16. *Approbation* means approval.

Margin notes

I Critical Thinking

IDENTIFYING BIAS Ask students to evaluate Irving's writing style. Do they think his representation of Dame Van Winkle is biased? Ask students to offer opinions as to why he speaks of her so harshly. *(Students might suggest that Irving speaks of her this way because he is trying to build sympathy for Rip. This, indeed, indicates bias toward Rip.)*

J Active Reading

EVALUATE Ask students if they think the people in this "perpetual club" are actually "sages and philosophers," or if Irving is just being playful again. *(Help students recognize that Irving is being playful.)*

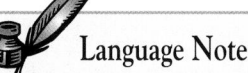

Language Note

In this context, the word *patriarch* refers to the leader of the village. The word comes from the Latin *pater*, which means "father." *Patriarch* can refer to the father or head of a family, the founder of an organization, or sometimes to a bishop. *Paternal* is an adjective based on the same root.

K Literary Elements

SETTING Carefully chosen details can help readers visualize a person. Have students describe how they picture Vedder, adding details not in the story.

INCLUSION STRATEGIES

Less-Proficient Readers To help readers understand Irving's use of exaggeration and humor, explain that people often exaggerate for emphasis; for example, "I'm so hungry I could eat a horse."

Activity Help students understand the author's actual intent in these lines: *could tell the hour by his movements as* *accurately as by a sundial* and *would rather starve on a penny than work for a pound.* **L1**

Additional Resources
📁 *Inclusion Strategies*

Have students consider the "interaction" taking place between the man and dog in the picture. Ask them to study particular aspects of the subjects, such as their posture and their steady gaze at one another.

Viewing Response *The sketch here shows Rip and his dog resting atop "a green knoll," as described on this page. Their titles describe where each of the later sketches fits into the story.*

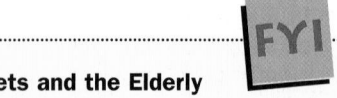

Pets and the Elderly
Studies have shown the positive effects pets have on people who live alone, particularly older people. Discuss why having a pet to care for and to talk to can keep older people healthier and happier.

L Literary Elements

SETTING: *Detail* Call attention to the details Irving uses to convey this peaceful scene. Have students identify words and phrases that emphasize the tranquillity of the scene. (*Some examples include* silent, reflection of a purple cloud, lagging bark, *and* sleeping on its glassy bosom.)

Rip With Dog Under Tree, 1921. N. C. Wyeth. Ink on paper. Stuart Kingston Gallery, Wilmington, DE.

Viewing the art: This drawing and those on pages 201–203 and 207 come from N. C. Wyeth's sketch books. They are early studies for the artist's Rip Van Winkle paintings. What parts of the story do they illustrate?

all to naught; nor was that august personage, Nicholas Vedder himself, sacred from the daring tongue of this terrible virago,[17] who charged him outright with encouraging her husband in habits of idleness.

Poor Rip was at last reduced almost to despair; and his only alternative, to escape from the labor of the farm and clamor of his wife, was to take gun in hand and stroll away into the woods. Here he would sometimes seat himself at the foot of a tree, and share the contents of his wallet[18] with Wolf, with whom he sympathized as a fellow sufferer in persecution. "Poor Wolf," he would say, "thy mistress leads thee a dog's life of it; but never mind, my lad, whilst I live thou shalt never want a friend to stand by thee!" Wolf would wag his tail, look wistfully in

his master's face, and if dogs can feel pity, I verily believe he returned the sentiment with all his heart.

In a long ramble of the kind on a fine autumnal day, Rip had unconsciously scrambled to one of the highest parts of the Kaatskill Mountains. He was after his favorite sport of squirrel shooting, and the still solitudes had echoed and reechoed with the reports of his gun. Panting and fatigued, he threw himself, late in the afternoon, on a green knoll, covered with mountain herbage, that crowned the brow of a precipice.[19] From an opening between the trees he could overlook all the lower country for many a mile of rich woodland. He saw at a distance the lordly Hudson, far, far below him, moving on its silent but majestic course, with the reflection of a purple cloud, or the sail of a lagging bark,[20] here and there sleeping on its glassy bosom, and at last losing itself in the blue highlands.

On the other side he looked down into a deep mountain glen, wild, lonely, and shagged, the bottom filled with fragments from the impending[21] cliffs, and scarcely lighted by the reflected rays of the setting sun. For some time Rip lay <u>musing</u> on this

---

17. A *virago* (və rä′ gō) is a scolding woman.
18. In Rip's time, *wallet* referred to a knapsack.

19. A *green knoll . . . precipice* (pres′ ə pis) refers to a high, steep cliff topped with a grassy hill.
20. A *lagging bark* is a slow-moving sailboat.
21. In this context, *impending* means overhanging.

Vocabulary
muse (mūz) *v.* to think or reflect

190 THEME 2

Teaching Options

Grammar and Language *Minilesson*

Semicolons Point out that Irving is fond of writing long sentences, many of them being a collection of shorter statements joined by semicolons. Guide students to understand that the semicolon is used in this way to join two or more independent clauses. Each clause could stand on its own as a separate sentence. The author combines them into one because the thoughts are closely related.

Activity Call attention to the paragraph that begins on page 189 and continues to page 190. Ask how many sentences comprise this paragraph. Have students explain why each clause in the sentence is an independent clause. (*Each clause has a subject and a verb.*) Then have each student write a sentence joining two independent clauses with a semicolon. **L2**

Additional Resources

Grammar and Language Transparency 16–18

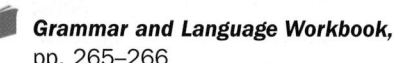
Grammar and Language Workbook, pp. 265–266

Grammar and Composition Handbook, Lesson 13.5

Writer's Choice, Lesson 20.5

scene; evening was gradually advancing; the mountains began to throw their long blue shadows over the valleys; he saw that it would be dark long before he could reach the village, and he heaved a heavy sigh when he thought of encountering the terrors of Dame Van Winkle.

As he was about to descend, he heard a voice from a distance, hallooing, "Rip Van Winkle! Rip Van Winkle!" He looked round, but could see nothing but a crow winging its solitary flight across the mountain. He thought his fancy must have deceived him, and turned again to descend, when he heard the same cry ring through the still evening air: "Rip Van Winkle! Rip Van Winkle!"—at the same time Wolf bristled up his back, and, giving a loud growl, skulked to his master's side, looking fearfully down into the glen. Rip now felt a vague apprehension stealing over him; he looked anxiously in the same direction, and perceived a strange figure slowly toiling up the rocks, and bending under the weight of something he carried on his back. He was surprised to see any human being in this lonely and unfrequented place; but supposing it to be some one of the neighborhood in need of his assistance, he hastened down to yield it.

On nearer approach he was still more surprised at the singularity of the stranger's appearance. He was a short, square-built old fellow, with thick bushy hair and a grizzled beard. His dress was of the antique Dutch fashion—a cloth jerkin, strapped round the waist—several pair of breeches, the outer one of ample volume, decorated

with rows of buttons down the sides, and bunches at the knees. He bore on his shoulder a stout keg, that seemed full of liquor, and made signs for Rip to approach and assist him with the load. Though rather shy and distrustful of this new acquaintance, Rip complied with his usual alacrity;[22] and mutually relieving each other, they clambered up a narrow gully, apparently the dry bed of a mountain torrent. As they ascended, Rip every now and then heard long rolling peals, like distant thunder, that seemed to issue out of a deep ravine, or rather cleft,[23] between lofty rocks, toward which their rugged path conducted. He paused for an instant, but supposing it to be the muttering of one of those transient thundershowers which often take place in mountain heights, he proceeded. Passing through the ravine, they came to a hollow, like a small amphitheater,[24] surrounded by perpendicular precipices, over the brinks of which impending trees shot their branches, so that you only caught glimpses of the azure sky and the bright evening cloud. During the whole time Rip and his companion had labored on in silence, for though the former marvelled greatly what could be the object of carrying a keg of liquor up this wild mountain; yet there was something strange and incomprehensible about the unknown, that inspired awe and checked familiarity.

---

22. *Alacrity* (ə lak′ rə tē) means "eager willingness."
23. A *cleft* is a wide crack or opening, as in a rock.
24. An *amphitheater* is a circular structure with rising rows of seats around a central open space.

Vocabulary
singularity (sing′ gyə lar′ ə tē) *n.* that which is remarkable or out of the ordinary; unusualness
incomprehensible (in′ kom prē hen′ sə bəl) *adj.* not understandable

M **Active Reading**

CONNECT Ask students whether they would have gone to the stranger if they were in Rip's place. *(Most students will say they would not because he startled both Rip and Wolf.)*

N **Literary Elements**

SETTING Draw students' attention to this description of the hollow. Point out how this description contrasts with the descriptions of more pleasant settings in the story. Ask students to identify a few words or phrases that make the hollow seem eerie. *(Examples include* long rolling peals, like distant thunder; deep ravine; rugged path; *and* impending trees.*)*

N

Vo•cab•u•lar•y Skills

Context Clues Remind students that when they come across a word they do not know, they should try to figure out the meaning from the context—the surrounding words and sentences. For example, to understand the meaning of *apprehension*, ask students to look at the sentences immediately preceding and following. Does the dog's looking down *fearfully* suggest a meaning for apprehension? What about the following sentence: "He looked anxiously in the same direction"? *(Both suggest a sense of fear and caution, approximate meanings for* apprehension.*)*

MEETING INDIVIDUAL NEEDS **ENGLISH LANGUAGE LEARNERS**

Former and Latter Write this on the board: *My sister and my friend each gave me an opinion: the former agreed with me, but the latter did not.* Explain that *former* refers to the first person mentioned, *My sister,* and *latter* refers to the last, *my friend.*

Activity Ask students to identify who in the following example sentences agreed with the speaker.

1. John and Mr. Stone disagreed. The *former* thought he should play soccer; the *latter* thought he should not.
2. Susan and Pat want to see the play. The *former* has band practice. The *latter* is free. **L2**

Additional Resources
📁 *English Language Learners Sourcebook*

VISUALIZE You might want to have students examine closely the description of each of the three personages presented. Ask students to close their eyes and try to visualize them. Do they remind them of some other characters they know in literature? *(One possible example is the seven dwarfs in Snow White.)*

Language Note

The word *Flemish* refers to the area of Flanders, its people, and their language. Flanders is a historic region comprised of parts of Belgium, France, and the Netherlands.

P Critical Thinking

INFERRING Ask students to determine the author's purpose in describing these men as being extremely solemn and grave as they are playing a game. *(Perhaps the solemnity and gravity contribute to the strangeness of the entire scene.)*

On entering the amphitheater, new objects of wonder presented themselves. On a level spot in the center was a company of odd-looking personages playing at ninepins.[25] They were dressed in a quaint outlandish fashion; some wore short doublets, others jerkins,[26] with long knives in their belts, and most of them had enormous breeches, of similar style with that of the guide's. Their visages, too, were peculiar; one had a large head, broad face, and small piggish eyes; the face of another seemed to consist entirely of nose, and was surmounted by a white sugar-loaf hat, set off with a little red cock's tail. They all had beards, of various shapes and colors. There was one who seemed to be the commander. He was a stout old gentleman, with a weather-beaten countenance; he wore a laced doublet, broad belt and hanger, high-crowned hat and feather, red stockings, and high-heeled shoes, with roses in them. The whole group reminded Rip of the figures in an old Flemish painting, in the parlor of the village parson, which had been brought over from Holland at the time of the settlement.

What seemed particularly odd to Rip was, that though these folks were evidently amusing themselves, yet they maintained the gravest faces, the most mysterious silence, and were the most melancholy party of pleasure he had ever witnessed. Nothing interrupted the stillness of the scene but the noise of the balls, which, whenever they were rolled, echoed along the mountains like rumbling peals of thunder.

As Rip and his companion approached them, they suddenly desisted from their

---

25. *Ninepins* is a bowling game.
26. A *jerkin* is the close-fitting, hip-length jacket, usually sleeveless and collarless, worn by men in the sixteenth and seventeenth centuries. It was often worn over a *doublet,* a close-fitting, waist-length jacket, with or without sleeves.

Grammar and Language *Minilesson*

Hyphens On the board, write the following hyphenated phrases:
   odd-looking personages
   sugar-loaf hat
   high-heeled shoes
Explain that when two words are combined to form an adjective and the adjective precedes the noun it modifies, the words are usually separated by a hyphen.

Activity Provide students with the following phrases and have them add hyphens if needed.
• wind blown hair *(wind-blown hair)*
• wide eyed reaction *(wide-eyed reaction)*
• large head *(correct)*
• moth eaten clothes *(moth-eaten clothes)*
L2

Additional Resources

📖 *Grammar and Language Transparency 16–18*

📓 *Grammar and Language Workbook,* pp. 275–276

📓 *Grammar and Composition Handbook,* Lesson 13.8

📓 *Writer's Choice,* Lesson 20.8

Gnomes Bowling, 1921. N. C. Wyeth. Oil on canvas.
Millport Conservancy, Lititz, PA.

Viewing the painting: How does the mood of the
painting relate to the mood of Rip's night on the
mountain?

they quaffed the liquor in profound
silence, and then returned to their
game.

By degrees Rip's awe and
apprehension subsided. He even
ventured, when no eye was fixed
upon him, to taste the beverage,
which he found had much of the
flavor of excellent Holland ale.
He was naturally a thirsty soul,
and was soon tempted to repeat
the draft. One taste provoked
another; and he repeated his visits to the flagon so often, that at
length his senses were overpowered, his eyes swam in his head,
his head gradually declined, and
he fell into a deep sleep.

On waking, he found himself
on the green knoll whence he had
first seen the old man of the glen.
He rubbed his eyes—it was a
bright sunny morning. The birds
were hopping and twittering
among the bushes, and the eagle
was wheeling aloft, and breasting the pure
mountain breeze. "Surely," thought Rip, "I
have not slept here all night." He recalled
the occurrences before he fell asleep. The
strange man with a keg of liquor—the
mountain ravine—the wild retreat among
the rocks—the woebegone[29] party at
ninepins—the flagon—"Oh! that flagon!
that wicked flagon!" thought Rip; "what
excuse shall I make to Dame Van Winkle?"

play, and stared at him with such fixed,
statue-like gaze, and such strange, uncouth,
lackluster countenances,[27] that his heart
turned within him, and his knees smote
together. His companion now emptied the
contents of the keg into large flagons,[28] and
made signs to him to wait upon the company. He obeyed with fear and trembling;

---

27. *Uncouth, lackluster countenances* means "crude and dull
    faces."
28. *Flagons* are containers with handles and spouts, used to hold
    liquids.

---

29. *Woebegone* means "sorrowful or mournful."

Q Author's Craft

AUTHOR'S PURPOSE Ask students to
think about the "odd-looking personages." How does their silence affect
both Rip and the reader? How would
the effect be different if they did
speak? *(Their silence makes them
and the event seem even more
mysterious. If they spoke, Rip would
probably ask who they are, and a
response would end the mystery
and suspense of this scene.)*

R Literary Elements

TONE Remind students of Irving's
playful tone. Ask students what
these words "he repeated his visits
to the flagon so often" actually
mean. *(They imply that he kept going
back to drink more and more ale.)*

Writing *Minilesson*

Setting a Mood Review a passage in
which the author provides much detail to
set a mood. For example, on page 193,
"The birds were hopping and twittering
among the bushes, and the eagle was
wheeling aloft, and breasting the pure
mountain breeze." Remind students that
though other details could be seen, the
writer omitted them because they would
have upset the mood.

Activity Have each student write a
description of a favorite place at a specific time of the day or year using details
that contribute to a particular mood they
wish to create. Have them read their work
aloud or post it for the class to enjoy. **L2**

Additional Resources

📘 *Writer's Choice,* Lesson 3.3

Literary Elements

S Literary Elements

MOOD Ask students to note the difference in the details used to describe Rip when he wakes up. Have students carefully reread the paragraph and discover the phrases and words pointing to a shift in the atmosphere of the story. (*Possible words or phrases include* suspected; robbed him of his gun; Wolf, too, had disappeared; *and* all in vain.)

T Literary Elements

SETTING Ask students to consider how the description of the mountains has changed. Why do they think the mountains are now described as difficult to travel? (*Students may suggest that the mountains represent Rip's state of mind—confused and entangled.*)

U Critical Thinking

DRAWING CONCLUSIONS Ask students to think about why the amphitheater has disappeared. Does it relate to Rip's discovery of a stream where the dry gully had been? (*Students should begin to conclude that things around Rip have been changing while he slept.*)

He looked round for his gun, but in place of the clean well-oiled fowling piece, he found an old firelock[30] lying by him, the barrel incrusted with rust, the lock falling off, and the stock worm-eaten. He now suspected that the grave roisters[31] of the mountain had put a trick upon him, and, having dosed him with liquor, had robbed him of his gun. Wolf, too, had disappeared, but he might have strayed away after a squirrel or partridge. He whistled after him, and shouted his name, but all in vain; the echoes repeated his whistle and shout, but no dog was to be seen.

He determined to revisit the scene of the last evening's gambol, and, if he met with any of the party, to demand his dog and gun. As he rose to walk he found himself stiff in the joints. "These mountain beds do not agree with me," thought Rip; "and if this frolic should lay me up with a fit of the rheumatism, I shall have a blessed time with Dame Van Winkle." With some difficulty he got down into the glen. He found the gully up which he and his companion had ascended the preceding evening; but to his astonishment, a mountain stream was now foaming down it—leaping from rock to rock, and filling the glen with babbling murmurs. He, however, made shift to scramble up its sides, working his toilsome way through thickets of birch, sassafras, and witch hazel, and sometimes tripped up or entangled by the wild grapevines that twisted their coils or tendrils from tree to tree, and spread a kind of network in his path.

At length he reached to where the ravine had opened through the cliffs to the amphitheater; but no traces of such opening remained. The rocks presented a high wall, over which the torrent came tumbling in a sheet of feathery foam, and fell into a broad, deep basin, black from the shadows of the surrounding forest. Here, then, poor Rip was brought to a stand. He again called and whistled after his dog; he was only answered by the cawing of a flock of idle crows, who seemed to look down and scoff at the poor man's perplexities. What was to be done? The morning was passing away, and Rip felt famished for want of his breakfast. He grieved to give up his dog and his gun; he dreaded to meet his wife; but it would not do to starve among the mountains. He shook his head, shouldered the rusty firelock, and, with a heart full of trouble and anxiety, turned his steps homeward.

As he approached the village he met a number of people, but none whom he knew, which somewhat surprised him, for he had thought himself acquainted with everyone in the country round. Their dress, too, was of a different fashion from that to which he was accustomed. They all stared at him with equal marks of surprise, and, whenever they cast their eyes upon him, invariably stroked their chins. The recurrence of this gesture induced[32] Rip,

---

30. A *firelock* is an early type of gun.
31. *Grave roisters* refers to the humorless partygoers of the previous night.
32. *[The recurrence . . . induced]* In other words, Rip repeated the gesture made by each of the people he met.

Vocabulary
perplexity (pər plek′ sə tē) *n.* doubt or uncertainty; puzzlement
invariably (in vār′ ē ə blē) *adv.* without exception

Teaching Options

MEETING INDIVIDUAL NEEDS — INCLUSION STRATEGIES

Less-Proficient Readers Write *preceding* on the board. Explain that it is composed of a root word, *cede,* and a prefix, *pre-. Pre-* generally means "before."

Activity Pair students and have them determine the meanings of the following words: *prearranged (arranged in advance); prerecorded (recorded earlier);* *prepay (pay in advance); preschool (before school);* and *precook (cook in advance).* Have partners write sentences with these words. **L1**
COLLAB. LEARN.

Additional Resources
Inclusion Strategies

involuntarily, to do the same—when, to his astonishment, he found his beard had grown a foot long!

He had now entered the outskirts of the village. A troop of strange children ran at his heels, hooting after him, and pointing at his gray beard. The dogs, too, not one of which he recognized for an old acquaintance, barked at him as he passed. The very village was altered; it was larger and more populous. There were rows of houses which he had never seen before, and those which had been his familiar haunts[33] had disappeared. Strange names were over the doors—strange faces at the windows—everything was strange. His mind now misgave him; he began to doubt whether both he and the world around him were not bewitched. Surely this was his native village, which he had left but the day before. There stood the Kaatskill Mountains—there ran the silver Hudson at a distance—there was every hill and dale precisely as it had always been. Rip was sorely perplexed. "That flagon last night," thought he, "has addled my poor head sadly!"

<hr>

33. *Haunts* are places often visited, or hangouts.

Rip Van Winkle Returns Home, 1921 (detail). N. C. Wyeth. Oil on canvas. Millport Conservancy, Lititz, PA.
Viewing the painting: How does Wyeth's interpretation add to your understanding of the story?

Active Reading

REVIEW Ask students to recall events earlier in the story and contrast them to the current ones. For example, students may compare how the children acted toward Rip earlier and contrast it with how they treat him now. Encourage students to give other examples from the text. *(For example, none of the villagers knew him, and he didn't recognize names and faces.)*

Literary Elements

SETTING Point out to students that these details of setting are presented more as facts than as description. Ask students why Irving might have chosen to write the new description of the village this way. *(Students may suggest that Irving wants the reader to focus more on Rip's confusion. This makes the details of setting important, but secondary.)*

VIEWING THE PAINTING

Ask students to compare this Rip with the one on page 188 and list the differences between them.

Viewing Response *Wyeth adds his own details to the setting of the story and to Rip's character to help the reader visualize Rip Van Winkle in his setting.*

Writing Minilesson

Describing with Detail Have students review how the town has changed—the rows of houses that weren't there before, the strange names over doors, and the strange faces in the windows. Explain how critical it is for a writer to do more than tell readers that "things had changed." The writer must show them with details related to the setting.

Activity Have each student write a description of a place that is familiar, such as home, neighborhood, or school and describe that place as it is today and as it might be in 20 years. **L2**

Additional Resources

Writer's Choice, Lesson 3.4

Vo•cab•u•lar•y Skills

Synonyms Point out that in describing the condition of the house Rip returns to, Irving uses a number of words that are close in meaning—*empty, forlorn,* and *abandoned.* You might want to have students use a dictionary to see the similarities and differences in meanings.

X Author's Craft

IMAGERY Ask how Irving's word choice in this passage helps the reader see and feel the scenes described. *(He uses words that have negative connotations.)*

Y Active Reading

RESPOND Ask students to discuss their reactions to this passage and their feelings for Rip. *(Some students may sympathize with Rip's plight. Others may feel he deserves it.)*

VIEWING THE PAINTING

John Quidor (1801–1881) rejected the conventions of realism common in the art of his time, using exaggeration and distortion to heighten the mood of his paintings. Washington Irving's fantastic tales inspired many of Quidor's best works.

Viewing Response *Many people appear to be shocked or surprised. The man in front of Rip seems skeptical. The man leaning against the tree (who will turn out to be Rip's son) appears to be drunkenly amused.*

Teaching Options

It was with some difficulty that he found the way to his own house, which he approached with silent awe, expecting every moment to hear the shrill voice of Dame Van Winkle. He found the house gone to decay—the roof fallen in, the windows shattered, and the doors off the hinges. A half-starved dog that looked like Wolf, was skulking about it. Rip called him by name, but the cur snarled, showed his teeth, and passed on. This was an unkind cut indeed—"My very dog," sighed poor Rip, "has forgotten me!"

He entered the house, which to tell the truth, Dame Van Winkle had always kept in neat order. It was empty, forlorn, and apparently abandoned. The desolateness overcame all his fears—he called loudly for his wife and children—the lonely chambers rang for a moment with his voice, and then all again was silence.

The Return of Rip Van Winkle, 1829. John Quidor. Oil on canvas, 39¼ x 49¾ in. Mellon Collection, National Gallery of Art, Washington, DC.

Viewing the painting: Look at the details in the painting. How are people responding to Rip's sudden appearance?

196 THEME 2

MEETING INDIVIDUAL NEEDS — MULTIPLE LEARNING STYLES

Logical and Mathematical These students are likely to consider the ages of the characters and the logical changes in the surroundings after twenty years.

Activity Have small groups create charts showing the changes in the story after twenty years have passed. **L2**
COLLAB. LEARN.

Original	After 20 Years
Rip's wife is alive.	*Rip's wife is dead.*
King George is on the sign	*General Washington is on the sign.*
Rip's home is neat and lived in.	*His home is empty and forlorn.*
Rip has young children.	*Rip's children have families.*

Washington Irving

He now hurried forth, and hastened to his old resort, the village inn—but it too was gone. A large, rickety, wooden building stood in its place, with great gaping windows, some of them broken and mended with old hats and petticoats, and over the door was painted, "The Union Hotel, by Jonathan Doolittle." Instead of the great tree that used to shelter the quiet little Dutch inn of yore, there was now reared a tall naked pole, with something on the top that looked like a red nightcap,[34] and from it was fluttering a flag, on which was a singular assemblage of stars and stripes—all this was strange and incomprehensible. He recognized on the sign, however, the ruby face of King George, under which he had smoked so many a peaceful pipe; but even this was singularly changed. The red coat was changed for one of blue and buff, a sword was held in the hand instead of a scepter, the head was decorated with a cocked hat, and underneath was painted in large characters, GENERAL WASHINGTON.

There was, as usual, a crowd of folks about the door, but none that Rip recollected. The very character of the people seemed changed. There was a busy, bustling tone about it, instead of the accustomed drowsy tranquillity. He looked in vain for the sage Nicholas Vedder, with his broad face, double chin, and fair long pipe, uttering clouds of tobacco smoke instead of idle speeches; or Van Bummel, the schoolmaster, doling forth the contents of an ancient newspaper. In place of these, a lean, bilious-looking fellow, with his pockets full of handbills, was haranguing[35] vehemently about the rights of citizens—elections—members of Congress—liberty—Bunker's Hill—heroes of seventy-six—and other words, which were a perfect Babylonish jargon[36] to the bewildered Van Winkle.

The appearance of Rip, with his long grizzled beard, his rusty fowling piece, his uncouth dress, and an army of women and children at his heels, soon attracted the attention of the tavern politicians. They crowded round him, eyeing him from head to foot with great curiosity. The orator bustled up to him, and, drawing him partly aside, inquired "on which side he voted?" Rip stared in vacant stupidity. Another short but busy little fellow pulled him by the arm, and, rising on tiptoe, inquired in his ear, "Whether he was Federal or Democrat?"[37] Rip was equally at a loss to comprehend the question; when a knowing, self-important old gentleman, in a sharp cocked hat, made his way through the crowd, putting them to the right and left with his elbows as he passed, and planting himself before Van Winkle, with one arm akimbo, the other resting on his cane, his keen eyes and sharp hat penetrating, as it were, into his very soul, demanded in an austere tone, "What brought him to the election with a gun on his shoulder, and a mob at his heels, and whether he meant to breed a riot in the village?"—"Alas! gentlemen," cried Rip, somewhat dismayed, "I am a poor quiet man, a native of the place, and a loyal subject of the king, God bless him!"

---

34. A *red nightcap* is a "liberty cap," often worn as a symbol of independence during the American Revolution.
35. To be *bilious* is to be cross or bad-tempered; *haranguing* (ha rang′ ing) is making a long, noisy speech.

36. *Babylonish jargon* is confusing language.
37. *Federal or Democrat* refers to U.S. political parties following the Revolution.

WINDS OF CHANGE 197

Z Critical Thinking

LOGICAL REASONING Guide students to think about what they know about American history and help them use that knowledge in understanding events. Have students discuss the historical background for the changes that Rip cannot understand. *(For example, students should recognize that the Revolutionary War has taken place and that George Washington, not King George, is now leading the country.)*

AA Critical Thinking

EVALUATING Ask students how they would characterize these changes in the country. Do they see these changes as positive or negative? *(Some students may see these changes as trading the old easy-going atmosphere for a "busy, bustling" one. Others, in contrast, may see that change has ultimately enabled the country to grow and prosper.)*

BB Literary Elements

CLIMAX Ask students if this is the point of greatest interest in the story. Remind students that, until now, Rip has not spoken with anyone, though the children have been hooting at him. In this scene, the people of the town confront him and he them, which begins to bring the mystery to a head. *(This scene, in effect, is the beginning of the story's climax, the turning point in the story's conflict.)*

REAL-WORLD CONNECTION

Out with the Old Students might benefit from looking at today's world closely and evaluating the changes that are taking place around them.

Activity Ask students to work in small groups and discuss the kinds of changes they see in the world around them. Are old trees being cut down? Are farmlands being used as sites for homes, factories, shopping malls, and parking lots? Have them list the changes they have observed in their schools, homes, or communities. They may wish to create posters titled "Then and Now." **L2 COLLAB. LEARN.**

WINDS OF CHANGE 197

CC Literary Elements

DIALOGUE Call attention to the dialogue in this passage. Explain to students that writers try to make dialogue sound authentic—much like the language spoken by real people similar to the characters in the story. Have students identify conversational aspects of the dialogue here. *(Students may point to the broken sentences:* Well—who are they?—Name them. *Students may also mention the rambling sentence:* He went off to the wars too, was a great militia general.*)*

Vo•cab•u•lar•y Skills

Word Meanings Point to Irving's use of two adverbs, *apparently* and *certainly.* Ask students how Rip would be able to see that *certainly* the man was just as ragged as he, while he would only be able to guess that *apparently* the man was just as lazy. If necessary, have students look up the meanings of the words in a dictionary.

DD Literary Elements

CHARACTERIZATION Ask students what Rip's words reveal about his personality and state of mind. What does Rip's rambling suggests about his mental state at the moment? *(They should see his rambling as a sign of his nervousness and confusion.)*

Teaching Options

Here a general shout burst from the bystanders—"A Tory! a Tory! a spy! a refugee![38] hustle him! away with him!" It was with great difficulty that the self-important man in the cocked hat restored order; and demanded again of the unknown culprit, what he came there for, and whom he was seeking? The poor man humbly assured him that he meant no harm, but merely came there in search of some of his neighbors, who used to keep about the tavern.

"Well—who are they?—name them."

Rip bethought himself a moment, and inquired, "Where's Nicholas Vedder?"

There was a silence for a little while, when an old man replied in a thin piping voice, "Nicholas Vedder! why, he is dead and gone these eighteen years! There was a wooden tombstone in the churchyard that used to tell all about him, but that's rotten and gone too."

"Where's Brom Dutcher?"

"Oh, he went off to the army in the beginning of the war; some say he was killed at the storming of Stony Point— others say he was drowned in a squall at the foot of Antony's Nose.[39] I don't know—he never came back again."

"Where's Van Bummel, the schoolmaster?"

"He went off to the wars too, was a great militia general, and is now in Congress."

Rip's heart died away at hearing of these sad changes in his home and friends, and finding himself thus alone in the world. Every answer puzzled him too, by treating of such enormous lapses of time, and of matters which he could not understand; war—Congress—Stony Point;—he had no courage to ask after any more friends, but cried out in despair, "Does nobody here know Rip Van Winkle?"

"Oh, Rip Van Winkle!" exclaimed two or three. "Oh, to be sure! that's Rip Van Winkle yonder, leaning against the tree."

Rip looked, and beheld a precise counterpart[40] of himself, as he went up the mountain: apparently as lazy, and certainly as ragged. The poor fellow was now completely confounded. He doubted his own identity, and whether he was himself or another man. In the midst of his bewilderment, the man in the cocked hat demanded who he was, and what was his name?

"God knows," exclaimed he, at his wits' end; "I'm not myself—I'm somebody else— that's me yonder—no—that's somebody else got into my shoes—I was myself last night, but I fell asleep on the mountain, and they've changed my gun, and everything's changed, and I'm changed, and I can't tell what's my name, or who I am!"

The bystanders began now to look at each other, nod, wink significantly, and tap their fingers against their foreheads. There was a whisper, also, about securing the gun, and keeping the old fellow from doing mischief, at the very suggestion of which the self-important man in the cocked hat retired quickly. At this critical moment a fresh, comely woman pressed through the throng to get a peep at the gray-bearded man. She had a chubby child in her arms, which, frightened at his looks, began to

---

38. A *Tory* was a person who supported the British during the Revolution. A *refugee* was a member of a group of British supporters who attacked the American revolutionaries.

39. *Stony Point* is a small bay on the Hudson River, and *Antony's Nose* is a mountain. Both are in southeastern New York.

40. A *precise counterpart* is a person who looks exactly like another.

Listening and Speaking Minilesson

Interviewing Have students interview an older person about some event, historical or personal, that he or she recalls. Suggest events that involved some kind of change, such as the introduction of the computer or television. They might ask such questions as What is one of the most memorable changes or periods of change you recall? What were the circumstances of the change? What brought it about? How did the change affect society or you personally?

Activity Have students take notes during the interviews or capture them on tape. Then have each of them present a short oral report to the class, playing portions of the tape or reading excerpts from the interview. **L2 COLLAB. LEARN.**

Washington Irving

cry. "Hush, Rip," cried she, "hush you little fool; the old man won't hurt you." The name of the child, the air of the mother, the tone of her voice, all awakened a train of recollections in his mind.

"What is your name, my good woman?" asked he.

"Judith Gardenier."

"And your father's name?"

"Ah, poor man, Rip Van Winkle was his name, but it's twenty years since he went away from home with his gun, and never has been heard of since—his dog came home without him; but whether he shot himself, or was carried away by the Indians, nobody can tell. I was then but a little girl."

Rip had but one question more to ask; but he put it with a faltering voice,—

"Where's your mother?"

"Oh, she too had died but a short time since; she broke a blood vessel in a fit of passion at a New England peddler."

There was a drop of comfort, at least, in this intelligence. The honest man could contain himself no longer. He caught his daughter and her child in his arms. "I am your father!" cried he—"Young Rip Van Winkle once—old Rip Van Winkle now!—Does nobody know poor Rip Van Winkle?"

All stood amazed, until an old woman, tottering out from among the crowd, put her hand to her brow, and peering under it in his face for a moment, exclaimed, "Sure enough! it is Rip Van Winkle—it is himself! Welcome home again, old neighbor—Why, where have you been these twenty long years?"

Rip's story was soon told, for the whole twenty years had been to him but as one night. The neighbors stared when they heard it; some were seen to wink at each other, and put their tongues in their cheeks; and the self-important man in the cocked hat, who, when the alarm was over, had returned to the field, screwed down the corners of his mouth, and shook his head—upon which there was a general shaking of the head throughout the assemblage.

It was determined, however, to take the opinion of old Peter Vanderdonk, who was seen slowly advancing up the road. He was a descendant of the historian of that name, who wrote one of the earliest accounts of the province. Peter was the most ancient inhabitant of the village, and well versed in all the wonderful events and traditions of the neighborhood. He recollected Rip at once, and corroborated[41] his story in the most satisfactory manner. He assured the company that it was a fact, handed down from his ancestor the historian, that the Kaatskill Mountains had always been haunted by strange beings. That it was affirmed that the great Henry Hudson, the first discoverer of the river and country, kept a kind of vigil there every twenty years, with his crew of the *Half-Moon*; being permitted in this way to revisit the scenes of his enterprise and keep a guardian eye upon the river and the great city called by his name. That his father had once seen them in their old Dutch dresses playing at ninepins in a hollow of the mountain; and that he himself

---

41. Something *corroborated* (kə rob′ ə rāt əd) is supported, or confirmed.

Vocabulary
faltering (fôl′ tər ing) *adj.* shaky because of uncertainty

EE **Critical Thinking**

IDENTIFYING ASSUMPTIONS Ask students to discuss how the "air of the mother, the tone of her voice" struck a chord with Rip. *(Students may realize that this woman's voice and manner reminded Rip of someone in his family, perhaps his wife.)*

FF **Critical Thinking**

DRAWING CONCLUSIONS Discuss with students the meaning of the word *faltering*. Then ask why Rip might have asked about his wife in a "faltering voice." You may wish to share the following model to illustrate the thinking process involved in drawing conclusions.

Model: From what I've read so far, I know that Rip fears his wife and that one of his first thoughts upon waking was what his wife's reaction to his absence would be. So his voice may be faltering, or wavering, because he is dreading the reunion with her that might be coming. It is also possible that he assumes she is dead, and for that reason his voice is unsteady.

GG **Critical Thinking**

INFERRING Ask students to think about the townspeople's reaction to Rip. What do the winks and other gestures suggest about the people's reaction to Rip's story? *(Students should see that these people don't believe Rip. They may think he is an old man who has "lost it.")*

INTERDISCIPLINARY CONNECTION

Social Studies Students may be interested in learning more about the Hudson River, the setting of this story. Researching this geographical area can give students deeper insight into the story of Rip Van Winkle.

Activity Have students work in pairs or small groups to research the Hudson River, particularly from its discovery to the years around the Revolutionary War. Students may write or deliver oral reports on the flow of the river, its role in the economic growth of the region, or its role in the war. Students may want to concentrate their study on the person for whom the river is named, Henry Hudson. **L2**
COLLAB. LEARN.

Author's Craft

STYLE Help students understand that Irving modifies his storytelling style here by presenting all these facts in summarized form.

Critical Thinking

INFERRING Ask students why they think Rip prefers the younger generation to his older cronies. *(Rip has lost 20 years.)*

Author's Craft

TONE Point out that the terms Irving uses in speaking of Rip's wife deal with forms of government: *despotism, petticoat government, tyranny.* Have students look up the meanings of these words and explain why they are funny when used in connection with Rip's wife.

Thematic Focus

Winds of Change Many changes took place as Rip slept through an important period in our history.

FINE ART
TRANSPARENCY 30

You may want to use *Fine Art Transparency 30* to discuss the kinds of changes that might take place in our country in the next 20 years.

☑ ASSESSMENT OPTIONS

📂 *Quick Checks,* p. 17

---

had heard, one summer afternoon, the sound of their balls, like distant peals of thunder.

To make a long story short, the company broke up, and returned to the more important concerns of the election. Rip's daughter took him home to live with her; she had a snug, well-furnished house, and a stout cheery farmer for her husband, whom Rip recollected for one of the urchins that used to climb upon his back. As to Rip's son and heir, who was the ditto of himself, seen leaning against the tree, he was employed to work on the farm; but showed an hereditary disposition to attend to anything else but his business.

Rip now resumed his old walks and habits; he soon found many of his former cronies, though all rather the worse for the wear and tear of time; and preferred making friends among the rising generation, with whom he soon grew into great favor.

Having nothing to do at home, and being arrived at that happy age when a man can be idle with impunity, he took his place once more on the bench at the inn door, and was reverenced as one of the patriarchs of the village, and a chronicle of the old times "before the war." It was some time before he could get into the regular track of gossip, or could be made to comprehend the strange events that had taken place during his sleep. How that there had been a Revolutionary War—that the country had thrown off the yoke of Old England—and that, instead of being a subject of His Majesty George the Third, he was now a free citizen of the United States. Rip, in fact, was no politician; the changes of states and empires made but

little impression on him; but there was one species of despotism[42] under which he had long groaned, and that was—petticoat government. Happily that was at an end; he had got his neck out of the yoke of matrimony, and could go in and out whenever he pleased without dreading the tyranny of Dame Van Winkle. Whenever her name was mentioned, however, he shook his head, shrugged his shoulders, and cast up his eyes; which might pass either for an expression of resignation to his fate, or joy at his deliverance.

He used to tell his story to every stranger that arrived at Mr. Doolittle's hotel. He was observed at first to vary on some points every time he told it, which was, doubtless, owing to his having so recently awaked. It at last settled down precisely to the tale I have related, and not a man, woman, or child in the neighborhood but knew it by heart. Some always pretended to doubt the reality of it, and insisted that Rip had been out of his head, and that this was one point on which he always remained flighty. The old Dutch inhabitants, however, almost universally gave it full credit. Even to this day they never hear a thunderstorm of a summer afternoon about the Kaatskills, but they say Henry Hudson and his crew are at their game of ninepins; and it is a common wish of all henpecked husbands in the neighborhood, when life hangs heavy on their hands, that they might have a quieting draft out of Rip Van Winkle's flagon.

---

42. A *despotism* (des′ pə tiz′ əm) is a government under a ruler who has unlimited authority.

Teaching Options

Grammar and Language *Minilesson*

Capitalizing Proper Nouns Review that proper nouns are names of particular persons, places or things. Proper nouns are capitalized.

Activity Have students capitalize proper nouns in the following list as needed. If a word should not be capitalized, have them write *correct.* **L2**

1. atlantic ocean *(Atlantic Ocean)*
2. cellular phone *(correct)*
3. amusement park *(correct)*
4. general washington *(General Washington)*
5. paris, france *(Paris, France)*
6. dame van winkle *(Dame Van Winkle)*
7. dutch inhabitants *(Dutch inhabitants)*
8. revolutionary war *(Revolutionary War)*

Additional Resources

Grammar and Language Transparency 16–18

Grammar and Language Workbook, p. 235–236

Grammar and Composition Handbook, Lesson 12.1–12.4

Writer's Choice, Lesson 19.1–19.4

Responding to Literature

PERSONAL RESPONSE

What was your reaction to this story? Did you find it amusing, suspenseful, mysterious, or all three? Describe your impressions in your journal.

Analyzing Literature

RECALL

1. According to the narrator, what is the chief flaw in Rip's character? What is the chief flaw in his wife's character?
2. Briefly describe the strangers Rip meets in the mountains. What happens to him after he drinks their beverage?
3. What is the first change Rip notices after he wakes up? Describe one other change he notices once he returns to town.
4. According to the narrator, what is Rip's life like after his return?

INTERPRET

5. What sort of person is Rip Van Winkle? What conflict exists between him and his wife? Support your ideas with examples from the story.
6. The details used to describe the men and the atmosphere in the hollow intensify the mysterious **mood** Irving created in this part of the story. List details that helped you sense the mood of this scene.
7. In what way does Peter Vanderdonk confirm Rip's explanation of his absence?
8. In your opinion, is Rip's life better or worse after his twenty-year sleep? Explain.

EVALUATE AND CONNECT

9. Theme Connection   What historical events occurred during Rip's absence? Why do you think Irving chose that twenty-year period for Rip's long nap? Explain.
10. What is your reaction to what happens to Rip and his wife in this story? Explain.

LITERARY ELEMENTS

Setting

A **setting** is the time and place in which the events of a story, novel, or play occur. For example, the setting of "Rip Van Winkle" is the Hudson River valley in the late 1700s. Strong writers often use the setting to help create an atmosphere or mood for a story. Carefully chosen details help readers visualize the place being described.

1. Pick out details from "Rip Van Winkle" that helped you picture the setting in your mind. Explain how the details helped transport you into the time and place of the story.
2. Choose another story you've read, and describe its setting.

● See **Literary Terms Handbook**, p. R10.

Dog With Broom Thrown at Him, 1921. N. C. Wyeth. Ink on paper. Stuart Kingston Gallery, Wilmington, DE.

Personal Response

Some students may have found humor in the way Irving describes Rip and his overbearing wife. Others may have enjoyed trying to figure out the meaning of the changes.

Analyzing Literature

1. Rip's chief flaw is his reluctance to work on his own property. His wife's is her nagging.
2. The strangers are short older men who seem very serious though they are playing a game. After he drinks their beverage, Rip falls asleep.
3. Rip notices that his rifle is rusty, the town's buildings and people are different, and the tree at the inn has been replaced by a flagpole.
4. Life after Rip's return is like it was before except that he is no longer being nagged.
5. Rip is a happy-go-lucky man. His wife nags him constantly about his aversion to work.
6. The details include the men's strange clothes, peculiar faces, and beards of various shapes and colors and the long knives in their belts.
7. Vanderdonk says that his ancestor the historian told of the vigil of Henry Hudson and his crew in the Kaatskills every 20 years.
8. Rip's life may be better because he can enjoy his life of leisure without being nagged. He is, however, 20 years older.

LITERARY ELEMENTS

1. The writer's descriptive details about the village and its river valley help readers visualize a quiet way of life long ago, before modern conveniences, transportation, and communication.
2. Descriptions should include vivid details about the story's setting.

Additional Resources

📖 *Literary Elements Transparency 17*

9. The American colonies have declared their independence from England and fought the Revolutionary War. George Washington is now president, and the people are living under a democratic form of government. Irving probably chose this period because it contains so many important historical events.
10. Some students may feel everything works out well for Rip and be content with Dame Van Winkle's demise. Others may feel she was not as bad as she was made out to be.

Literature and Writing

Writing About Literature

Students' paragraphs should
- have a clear theme statement.
- support that theme with references to the text.

Personal Writing

Students' diary entries should
- consider specific aspects of their world, such as communication, transportation, and food.
- give details about the changes.
- show that the writer is coming upon these changes suddenly, not gradually.

Extending Your Response

Literature Groups Remind students there are basically two questions. One is whether the characters are stereotypes. The other is whether Irving could have made the characters more believable. Remind students that each answer must be supported by details from the story. **COLLAB. LEARN.**

Learning for Life Remind students to probe for details and to move from surface issues to feelings and emotions. Students should have some questions prepared to ask others in response to what they say.

Art Activity Suggest that, in addition to important political events, students might include important cultural events and entertainment milestones.

Literature and Writing

Writing About Literature
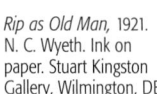
Thinking About a Theme   What does "Rip Van Winkle" say about the passage of time and human nature? Write a paragraph or two explaining your ideas about the theme of this well-known story.

Personal Writing

Sweet Dreams   Imagine if you were to fall asleep for the next twenty years. How do you think the world would change during that time? When you discovered these changes, how would you feel? Write a diary entry explaining what has happened, how things have changed, and how you feel.

Rip as Old Man, 1921. N. C. Wyeth. Ink on paper. Stuart Kingston Gallery, Wilmington, DE.

Extending Your Response

Literature Groups

Debating Stereotypes   A stereotype has only a few, highly exaggerated character traits. Stereotypes are never fully believable. For example, the strong, silent cowboy is a stereotype; so is the wicked villain or the innocent heroine. Stereotypes often appear in folktales, legends, and literature that is meant to teach a lesson. Are both Rip and his wife stereotypes? Why or why not? How might Irving have made these two characters more believable? Debate the issue. Support your opinions with examples and quotations from the story.

Learning for Life

A Newspaper Account   Imagine that you are a journalist sent to interview Rip for the *Hudson River Valley Gazette.* Write an article about his mysterious experience. Include quotations and descriptions from Rip as well as other villagers.

Art Activity

Social Studies: Make a Time Line   Review the notes you made for the **Focus Activity** on page 184 to help you make a personal time line starting at the year of your birth. Include important events in your own life, as well as the dates of important events and inventions in this country and around the world.

Reading Further

If you would like to read more by Washington Irving, try these works:

Diedrich Knickerbocker's History of New York

"The Legend of Sleepy Hollow" in *The Sketch Book of Geoffrey Crayon, Gent.*

📖 **Save your work for your portfolio.**

Skill Minilessons

GRAMMAR AND LANGUAGE • ADVERBS

An adverb is a word that modifies, or describes, a verb, an adjective, or another adverb. When modifying a verb, an adverb gives information about *when, where,* or *how* the action of a sentence takes place.
Examples:
Rip slept **soundly.** (How?)
Later Rip woke up. (When?)
Rip looked **everywhere** for his dog. (Where?)

PRACTICE Write an adverb to modify the underlined word in each sentence.
1. Rip walked through the woods.
2. He looked into a deep mountain glen.
3. He listened to the voice in the distance.
4. The strange men stared at Rip.
5. Being quite thirsty, Rip drank the beverage.

● For more about adverbs, see **Language Handbook,** p. R27.

READING AND THINKING • EVALUATING

Evaluating characters and events in a story involves forming opinions and making judgments about what you read. Remember to evaluate *while* you are reading—not just after you have finished. As you read, ask yourself questions such as the following:
• Does this event make sense?
• Would this character really say or do this?

PRACTICE Review "Rip Van Winkle" and think about what happens to Rip once he wakes up from his sleep. Write questions about the events and trade your questions with a partner. Answer each other's questions and then talk about your answers.

● For more about reading strategies, see **Reading Handbook,** pp. R82–R96.

VOCABULARY • SYNONYMS AND ANTONYMS

As you probably know, *synonyms* are words with similar meanings, and *antonyms* are words with opposite meanings. A synonym for *loud* is *noisy,* and an antonym for *loud* is *quiet.* Although some words have no synonyms and some have no antonyms, many words have several of each.

PRACTICE Match each word below with its synonym and its antonym from the lists at the right.

Word
1. likely
2. delicate
3. invariably
4. incomprehensible
5. uncouth

Synonym	Antonym
A. fragile	a. doubtful
B. confusing	b. considerate
C. rude	c. never
D. probable	d. tough
E. constantly	e. clear

Rip Fishing, 1921. N. C. Wyeth. Ink on paper.
Stuart Kingston Gallery, Wilmington, DE.

Skill Minilessons

GRAMMAR AND LANGUAGE
ADVERBS

Possible answers:
1. slowly; happily; nervously; casually
2. *steadily; longingly; intently*
3. *eagerly; anxiously; closely*
4. *bewilderingly; intently*
5. *quickly; sloppily; shockingly*

READING AND THINKING
EVALUATING

Suggest that students ask these questions as if they did not know the outcome. Questions might include Why didn't he notice his long beard or the changes in the skin on his hands and arms?

VOCABULARY
SYNONYMS AND ANTONYMS

1. D, a   3. E, c   5. C, b
2. A, d   4. B, e

Additional Resources

Grammar and Language Workbook, pp. 127–128

Grammar and Composition Handbook, Lessons 6.1, 6.2

Writer's Choice, Lesson 12.6

Reading Workbook, pp. 29–30

Vocabulary Practice, p. 12

✔ ASSESSMENT OPTIONS

Quick Checks, p. 17

Selection and Theme Assessment, pp. 31–32

Performance Assessment, p. 17

Testmaker

Before You Read

old age sticks

Objectives
- To read a free-verse poem about the differences between the young and the old
- To recognize the characteristics of free verse
- To write an advice column

Skills

Writing: Advice Column
Listening/Speaking: Dramatization
Collaboration: Literature Groups

Motivating
→ OPTIONS

Selection Focus Transparency 18: Have students discuss whether they agree or disagree with the quotations on the transparency.

Focus Activity: As an extension of the Focus Activity, have students talk about personal experiences with older people and stories they have read that show young people interacting with older people. Have them describe those relationships.

MEET E. E. CUMMINGS

Edward Estlin Cummings (who often wrote his name as e. e. cummings) knew while still a child that he would become a poet. In fact, between the ages of eight and twenty-two he wrote a poem a day. By the time his first collection of poetry was published in 1923, his quirky use of grammar, capitalization, and punctuation was well established.

E. E. Cummings was born in Cambridge, Massachusetts in 1894, and he died in 1962. This poem is from his Complete Poems.

FOCUS ACTIVITY

Do most people take advice from people who are older than they are? Should they? Why or why not?

QuickWrite

What do you think older people can teach younger people? How about the reverse? Are there things younger people can teach their elders? Take a moment to jot down your thoughts and feelings about these questions.

Setting a Purpose

Read the poem to find out what the poet has to say about youth and old age.

BACKGROUND

A famous French writer once defined poetry as "the music of the soul." Do you agree? Yet, no matter how much you enjoy poetry, a poem may sometimes be hard to read, especially when its format or punctuation is unusual. The following poem, "old age sticks," is just such a poem. Here are some tips on how to read it:

- Read the poem aloud, all the way through. Keep going, even if you come to a word or phrase you don't understand, or if the lack of punctuation confuses you.
- Don't feel that you need to pause at the end of a line, or even a stanza.
- Don't try to analyze the meaning of each line. Just think about your reactions to the whole poem.
- Read the poem again . . . and then again. Concentrate on the parts of the poem that seem confusing. Listen to how the poem sounds.
- Finally, think about the poem's meaning for you. Remember: reading a poem is a personal experience.

CONNECTING TO OTHER SELECTIONS
For a teaching strategy that connects "old age sticks" to "Too Soon a Woman," turn to page 20 in the *Theme Three Planning Guide.*

RESOURCE MANAGER

Lesson Planning Resource
The *Theme Two Planning Guide* (pp. 54–58) provides additional lesson notes and reduced versions of all print resources.

📁 **Other Print Resources**
- Active Reading Guide, p. 18
- Quick Checks, p. 18
- Selection and Theme Assessment, pp. 31–32

- Performance Assessment, p. 17
- Spanish Summaries, p. 18
- Spanish Translations
- English Language Learners Sourcebook

 Transparencies
- Selection Focus 18
- Literary Elements 18

Technology
- 🎧 Audio Library
- 🎧 Spanish Audio Library
- 💻 Glencoe Literature Web Site
- 📠 Testmaker

old age sticks

E. E. Cummings

Old Man Walking in a Rye Field. Lauris Anderson Ring.

old age sticks
up Keep
Off
signs)&

5   youth yanks them
down(old
age
cries No

Tres)&(pas)
10 youth laughs
(sing
old age

scolds Forbid
den Stop
15 Must
n't Don't

&)youth goes
right on
gr
20 owing old

A   Active Reading

EVALUATE Ask students to count the syllables in each line. What pattern do they notice? *(It is 3-2-1-2.)*

Additional Resources

📁 *Active Reading Guide,* p. 18

🎧 *Audio Library*

🎧 *Spanish Audio Library*

📁 *Spanish Summaries, p. 18*

B   Literary Elements

FREE VERSE What do students notice about the poem? *(four-line stanzas; a 3-2-1-2 pattern; no rhyme)*

Thematic Focus

Winds of Change Discuss the differences in the theme's treatment in the compared selections.

LITERATURE & HUMANITIES

Have groups examine how *The Truant Gamblers* in *American Art History and Culture,* page 23, captures the poem's theme.

✓ ASSESSMENT OPTIONS

📁 *Quick Checks,* p. 18

Teaching Options

COMPARING selections

This selection is compared with "Rip Van Winkle" on page 185. A lesson for teaching a comparison of the two selections is on page 207.

MEETING INDIVIDUAL NEEDS   ENGLISH LANGUAGE LEARNERS

Sentences Without Punctuation
Explain to English language learners that free verse, particularly that of Cummings, often has little or no punctuation. Readers may have difficulty determining where one sentence ends and the next begins.

Activity Have pairs of students read the poem aloud to each other. Ask them to listen for the stops that might nor-mally require a period. Then ask them to write two versions of an original poem—one with punctuation and one without punctuation. Ask each group to share their poems with the class. **L2**
COLLAB. LEARN.

Additional Resources

📁 *English Language Learners Sourcebook*

Responding to Literature

Personal Response

Students may consider the last stanza the most memorable. They may want to ask the poet's age when he wrote the poem, his inspiration for it, or his reason for writing in this form.

Analyzing Literature

1. Main images are the *Keep Off* signs, youth yanking them down and laughing, and old age scolding. *Yanks, laughs,* and *scolds* help the reader visualize the images.
2. *Keep Off* is used for grass; *No Trespassing,* for property. These signs represent old age's cautious, protective attitude.
3. Youth laughs in response to old age and ignores its advice.
4. When young, people have few worries and fears. As they get older, they become more cautious, fearful, and protective.
5. Answers may include an older relative or friend or perhaps a young friend who takes a negative attitude toward older people.
6. The poem says that the young who scoff at the warnings of old age will one day be old and have "old" attitudes.

Extending Your Response

Literature Groups Suggest that students work out speech patterns and gestures to reinforce the words spoken by each group. Props for old age are the signs mentioned in the poem. Youth can create its own props, such as T-shirts with youth-oriented messages on them.
COLLAB. LEARN.

Creative Writing
Students' advice columns should
- treat specific issues or attitudes.
- detail the issues or attitudes and make recommendations.
- be sympathetic to and encouraging about readers' dilemmas.

PERSONAL RESPONSE

- ◆ Which lines from the poem did you find most memorable, powerful, or surprising? Why?
- ◆ What questions would you like to ask the poet if you could meet him?

Analyzing Literature

RECALL AND INTERPRET

1. What are the main images in this poem? Pick out the words and details that help you visualize the images.
2. What signs does Cummings include in this poem? Explain what each one means. Why do you think he uses signs?
3. According to the speaker of the poem, how does "youth" respond to the advice of "old age"?

EVALUATE AND CONNECT

4. What thoughts about life do you think Cummings is communicating in this poem? Explain.
5. Do you know someone who would enjoy reading this poem? Why would the poem appeal to that person?
6. Theme Connection   How does this poem focus on the theme of change as a natural part of life?

Extending Your Response

Literature Groups
Readers Theater   In small groups, practice a reader's theater dramatization of "old age sticks." You might divide your group into two parts—one half dramatizing "old age" and the other half "youth." Then think about the images that you want to portray from the poem. Use props such as signs to help your audience understand the main images.

Creative Writing
Writing an Advice Column   Do you feel there are topics about which you can give advice? For example, can you offer advice to younger students about what they should do on their first day at the middle school or junior high school? Write an advice column. Make up some questions, and then answer them with your best advice.

LITERARY ELEMENTS

Style

Style includes the qualities that make a writer's work unlike the work of all other writers. Word choice, sentence length, sentence patterns, degree of formality, and use of imagery are a few of many factors that make up a style.

1. Suggest two characteristics that you think are part of E. E. Cummings's style.

2. Choose another poet from this book. Tell how that poet's style differs from Cummings's. Support your comparison with examples.

● See **Literary Terms Handbook,** p. R10.

ASSESSMENT OPTIONS

- 📁 *Quick Checks,* p. 18
- 📁 *Selection and Theme Assessment,* pp. 31–32
- 📁 *Performance Assessment,* p. 17
- 💾 *Testmaker*

LITERARY ELEMENTS

1. The appearance (no capitals or punctuation) and odd line breaks are part of his style.
2. *Example:* Edgar Allan Poe's structured rhythm and meter are the opposite of Cummings' free verse style.

Additional Resources

📖 *Literary Elements Transparency 18*

COMPARING SELECTIONS

RIP VAN WINKLE and old age sticks

COMPARE THEME CONNECTIONS

"Rip Van Winkle" and "old age sticks" focus on special kinds of journeys vividly described by two very different writers. The theme of change plays an important role in both of these selections.

- On what kind of journey does Rip Van Winkle go? By the end of the story, how has Rip changed?
- What is the special journey depicted in "old age sticks"? Who or what has changed by the end of the poem?
- How are these two journeys alike? How are they different?

COMPARE IDEAS

Plan a panel discussion about life and the problems of aging.

- With your group, brainstorm topics for the panel discussion. Review your **QuickWrite** from page 204 for ideas.
- Select a moderator to lead the discussion, and have group members take the roles of Rip, his wife, and people representing "old age" and "youth."
- Hold your panel discussion before your class. Encourage your classmates to ask the panel members questions.

COMPARE ENDINGS

Compare the endings of these two pieces of writing. How are they alike? How are they different? How else might each of these selections have ended?

- What else might have happened to Rip Van Winkle after he woke up from his sleep? Consider different possibilities.
- How else might the poem "old age sticks" end? In what other ways might "youth" respond to the advice of "old age"? Think about ideas for an alternative last stanza.
- Use your imagination to write an alternative ending to either the story or the poem. If you choose the poem, remember to use vivid verbs and colorful details to create strong images that communicate your ideas.

Rip Hunting, 1921. N. C. Wyeth. Ink on paper. Stuart Kingston Gallery, Wilmington, DE.

Objective

- To compare a short story and a poem that deal with change

COMPARE THEME CONNECTIONS

- Rip goes on a physical journey into the mountains and a "mystical" trip through time. Only his age changes.
- The journey is from youth to old age. Youth's ideas have changed.
- Time passes by in both. Rip does not change after 20 years, but youth is always growing old.

COMPARE IDEAS

Topics might include health problems or living alone. Questions can move from the selections to life today.

Additional Resources
Literature Groups Sourcebook

COMPARE ENDINGS

Youth grows older in each selection. Conflict seems to be over for Rip, but in the poem, it continues for youth.

- Rip might have had difficulty adjusting to new ideas and customs.
- It could end with youth recognizing old age's wisdom.
- Students' endings should try to maintain the style and tone of the original.

Teaching Options

PORTFOLIO OPTIONS

Select and Reflect Have students reflect on the alternative endings they wrote for the poem by asking themselves these questions:

- Does my ending include colorful details that make my writing more descriptive?
- Is my ending believable?

Students should clip their reflections to their alternative endings and place them in their portfolios. Later, they may consider using the comments to revise their ads as portfolio showcase pieces.

Additional Resources
Writing Assessment and Portfolio Management, pp. 17–19

Writing WORKSHOP

Objectives

- To create a personal response to literature
- To plan, draft, revise, edit, and present a compare-and-contrast essay
- To reflect on and assess the essay

GLENCOE
TECHNOLOGY

WRITER'S ASSISTANT
CD-ROM

Students can use Glencoe's templates and guidelines software for essay writing to aid them in working through the steps in the writing process in this lesson.

PREWRITING

Teaching Strategies

Choose Your Characters Encourage students to choose characters who interest or intrigue them. Suggest that they consider pairing characters whom they would like to meet in real life or whose conversations they would most like to hear.

Teaching Options

Writing WORKSHOP

Expository Writing: Compare-and-Contrast Essay

Think about a good friend. Why is he or she important to you? Then think about how the two of you are alike and how you are different. Thinking about your similarities and differences can give you insight into your friendship. Similarly, comparing and contrasting characters in literature can help you understand them better.

Assignment: Use the process shown in this Workshop to write a compare-and-contrast essay about two characters from stories in this theme.

● As you write your essay, refer to the **Writing Handbook,** pp. R48–R53.

The Writing Process

PREWRITING

PREWRITING TIP
Choose characters who share at least one important quality. If they are completely different, your essay will fall flat.

● **Choose Your Characters**

You can compare two characters from the same selection or from two different selections. Try these strategies:

● Look through your reading journal for mention of characters who interest you.

● Scan the selections again. Then fill in your own choice of characters in sentences such as those below.

The character I know the least about is Dick Wilcox from "A Crush."

If Rip Van Winkle and Ernie ever met, they would probably understand each other.

Dolores and Rip's wife probably would dislike each other.

My favorite character from this theme is Dolores.

Two characters who might like each other are Colin and Ernie.

Two characters who appear to be different but are really similar are Colin and his father.

208 ❧ THEME 2

MEETING INDIVIDUAL NEEDS
ENGLISH LANGUAGE LEARNERS

Speaking Before Writing Before students begin to write their essays, have them form small groups that include English language learners as well as students who are more proficient speakers to discuss the characters they have just read about.

Activity Have each student choose a character. Using butcher paper, cardboard, or poster board taped to a ruler, have each make a mask depicting the character. Have students hold the masks in front of them and pretend they are the characters, telling as much as they can about their experiences.

Additional Resources
📁 *English Language Learners Sourcebook*

● Explore Details

Use a Venn diagram, as in the **Writing Skills** activity on page 183, to gather details about your characters. List qualities you *can't* see as well as those you can.

● Find Your Thesis

Think about how your details support your ideas about the two characters. What main point do they add up to? Write this point, your **thesis,** as a sentence.

> **MODEL · PREWRITING**
>
> Thesis sentence: In many ways, Alfonso is a more responsible person than his older brother Ernie is.

● Consider Your Audience and Purpose

Your teacher and classmates will probably be the main audience for this essay. Do you want to amuse them, or will your essay have a more serious purpose? Keep your audience and purpose in mind as you plan your comparison.

● Make a Plan

Your essay needs an introduction, a body, and a conclusion. To organize the body, you might choose one of the two patterns shown below. (Both compare brothers in Gary Soto's story "Broken Chain," from Theme 1.) Fill in your own graphic to compare the two characters you have chosen. Choose details that support your thesis.

Subject-by-subject	Feature-by-feature
With this plan, you begin by describing the qualities of one character. Then you go on to describe the same qualities of the other character in the same order.	With this plan, you write one paragraph for each feature you have selected. Within each paragraph, you describe a single feature in both of the characters you are comparing.

Subject-by-subject

Paragraph 1: Describe Alfonso
> What are his physical traits, his wishes or motivations, his inner weaknesses, and his inner strengths?

Paragraph 2: Describe Ernie
> What are his physical traits, his wishes or motivations, his inner weaknesses, and his inner strengths?

Feature-by-feature

Paragraph	Feature
1 ⟶	physical traits (Alfonso's, then Ernie's)
2 ⟶	motivations or wishes (Alfonso's, then Ernie's)
3 ⟶	inner weaknesses (Alfonso's, then Ernie's)
4 ⟶	inner strengths (Alfonso's, then Ernie's)

WINDS OF CHANGE 🦋 209

Explore Details Have students compare notes on what they have discovered or remembered about characters from the selections.

Find Your Thesis Suggest a freewrite as a way of getting all the information they have accumulated onto a page. From this, a thesis statement can be constructed. The thesis statement should be about aspects of the characters that interest them personally. This will make their essays easier to write and more interesting to read.

Consider Your Audience and Purpose Encourage students to put a "face" on their audience as they write. Picturing those for whom they are writing for may help keep them on track and assist them in choosing the most relevant details for their essays.

Make a Plan Have students follow the pattern described and create their own graphic organizers. Suggest that they keep the organizers visible when they begin to write.

Additional Resources

📁 *Writing and Proofreading Practice,* pp. 1–7, 15–21

🖌 *Writing and Proofreading Transparencies* 1–4, 9–10, 27–28

📔 *Writer's Choice,* Lesson 5.3

MEETING INDIVIDUAL NEEDS — MULTIPLE LEARNING STYLES

Linguistic Students may want to expand their compare-and-contrast skills by scripting dialogues between two characters.

Activity Have each student write a dialogue between the two characters to be compared and contrasted. The dialogue should contain hints about their similarities and differences. Encourage students to use situations that would prompt the characters to have to work together, such as painting a room or helping at a school carnival, and write in script format with stage directions. Working with partners, students should rehearse the dialogues and then present them to the class. **L2 COLLAB. LEARN.**

Start with the Basics Remind students that a clear framework begins with a well-written thesis statement. Supporting details should clarify and expand the idea put forth in the topic sentence.

Draft Your Essay Have students begin their drafts by following their thesis statements with logical supporting details. Encourage them to use the graphic organizers they created. Details that don't serve the overall purpose of an essay can be edited out during the revising process.

Improve Your Draft Encourage students to read their essays aloud when they finish writing—and then again the next day. They may do this alone or with partners. Hearing the flow of the essays can help students revise and refine their ideas.

TECHNOLOGY TIP

Encourage students to explore the basic formatting options available in most word processing programs, such as italics, boldface, and underlining.

Teaching Options

Writing **WORKSHOP**

DRAFTING TIP
Cite details from the selection(s) to support each statement you make about a character. If you call a character kind, cite an action showing kindness.

DRAFTING TIP
Transition words such as *like, unlike, in the same way,* and *similarly* will help readers understand your comparisons.

● **Start with the Basics**

Use your first paragraph to build a clear framework for your readers.

● Name the *characters* you will compare, the *selection(s)* in which they appear, and the *author(s)* of the story or stories.

● State your thesis so readers know what to expect from your essay.

● **Draft Your Essay**

Compare and contrast your characters, using your prewriting notes to guide you. Use transitions to help readers follow your ideas. To end your essay, restate your thesis. You might add a final thought from a slightly different perspective.

MODEL · DRAFTING

In the short story "Broken Chain" by Gary Soto, Alfonso is like his big brother Ernie in many ways. Yet Alfonso, the younger brother, is the more mature and responsible of the two.

REVISING TIP
Give your essay a title that reflects your thesis. For example, "The Bigger Brother" is a stronger title than "Comparing and Contrasting Alfonso and Ernie."

● **Improve Your Draft**

Let your draft sit for a few hours, or even overnight. Then come back to it with fresh eyes. As you read, mark the places where you could make improvements. Use the **Questions for Revising** as a guide.

Now read your essay aloud to a friend. Have your friend answer the **Questions for Revising**.

QUESTIONS FOR REVISING
☑ How does the opening identify the characters and selections for readers?
☑ Where is the thesis stated?
☑ How is the essay organized?
☑ Where does the essay cover likenesses? Where does it cover differences?
☑ Where might more details make a character's traits clearer?

Writing ℳ*inilesson*

Paragraph Development Since students are comparing two characters, you might suggest that they develop their paragraphs line by line, focusing first on one character and then on the other.

Activity Using a few pieces of paper cut in sentence-length strips, students should write sentences about their characters. Have students work individually or in small groups to arrange the sentences into logical paragraphs and then copy their paragraphs on paper, adding transition words and conjunctions as necessary. **L2 COLLAB. LEARN.**

Additional Resources

📖 *Writer's Choice,* Lesson 2.7

EDITING/PROOFREADING

When you are satisfied with the content of your essay, use the **Proofreading Checklist** to help you look for errors in grammar, usage, mechanics, and spelling. Be sure to use the correct comparative forms of modifiers, as shown in the **Grammar Link** on page 182.

TECHNOLOGY TIP
On a computer, you can use italics rather than underlining for titles of books, plays, and other long works.

Grammar Hint

Underline titles of books, plays, and longer literary works. Use quotation marks to set off titles of short stories, poems, and essays.

I found the short story "Circles" in Jane Yolen's book Here There Be Witches.

PROOFREADING CHECKLIST
☑ Comparative forms of adjectives and adverbs are used correctly.
☑ Each sentence has a complete subject and predicate.
☑ Titles of selections are set off with quotation marks, italics, or underlining, as appropriate.
☑ Commas, end marks, and other punctuation marks are used correctly.
☑ Spelling is correct.

MODEL · EDITING/PROOFREADING

In Broken Chain, Ernie may be ~~more~~ bigger and tougher, but I vote Alfonso more likely to succeed.

PUBLISHING/PRESENTING

Share your essay with classmates. You might work in a small group to gather and bind your essays as models for future students. Essays might be grouped by subject or alphabetically by author or title.

PRESENTING TIP
People who have chosen the same characters can compare interpretations.

Reflecting

Consider the following question. Then write your response.

● How has comparing and contrasting your characters deepened your understanding of them? (If it has not, explain why.)

 Save your work for your portfolio.

Have students use the Proofreading Checklist to review their work. They may want to use colored pencils to edit their essays, using one color for each item on the list.

Additional Resources

📖 *Grammar and Composition Handbook*

Students who have chosen one or both of the same characters may want to read their work to one another in a group and share their points of view. Encourage them to discuss the topic sentences they wrote when comparing the characters.

Reflecting

Portfolio Encourage students to ask themselves as they review their writing, does my essay
● adequately compare and contrast two fictional characters?
● have a clear topic sentence?
● contain several supporting details?

✓ ASSESSMENT OPTIONS

📁 *Writing Assessment and Portfolio Management*
● Writing Assessment, pp. 1–16, 23–25
● Portfolio Management, pp. 17–19

Theme Wrap-Up

Objectives

- To offer a personal response to the selections in this theme and the importance of change
- To write a comparison of two short stories
- To complete a self-evaluation, set a goal, and devise a plan for achieving the goal

---

Responding to the Theme

1. Students should explain how change altered a situation by describing what happened before and after the change took place.
2. Encourage students to relate their answers to changes in their own lives.
3. Allow time for students to share their proposals, future self-portraits, and visual history exhibits with classmates.

Analyzing Literature

Students' writing should

- include a paragraph introducing the two short stories and the literary element they have chosen to compare.
- use examples and quotations from the stories to support their conclusions.

Evaluate and Set Goals

Evaluate

Have students review their work in this theme by listing the activities they have completed for each task. They may wish to include other tasks, such as participation in discussion groups.

Have students use the class rubric they developed in their last theme's evaluation to assess their work.

Have each student create a bar graph with the tasks listed along the bottom line and the ratings along the side.

Theme Wrap-Up

Responding to the Theme

1. Which story or poem in this theme most helped you think about how change, though often difficult, can be a powerful learning tool? Explain.

2. What new thoughts do you have about the following as a result of reading the stories and poems in this theme?
   - people's reactions to change in their lives
   - the importance of seeing change as a vital and powerful part of the journey of life

3. Present your theme project to the class.

Analyzing Literature

COMPARE SHORT STORIES

Compare two short stories from this theme. You may compare the stories in terms of characters, details chosen by the writers, or themes. Use examples and quotations from the stories to support your opinions.

Evaluate and Set Goals

1. Which of the following tasks was most rewarding for you? Which was most difficult?
   - reading and thinking about the stories and poems
   - writing independently
   - analyzing the stories and poems in discussions
   - making presentations
   - performing dramatizations
   - doing research

2. Using the following scale, how would you assess your work for this theme? Give at least two reasons for your assessment.
   4 = outstanding   2 = fair
   3 = good   1 = weak

Build Your Portfolio

SELECT

Look for the best pieces of work you did for this theme and add them to your portfolio. Ask yourself the following questions to help you decide:

- Is this my best work?
- Did I learn something from doing this?
- Did working on this piece stretch me?
- Did I enjoy doing this?

REFLECT

Write some notes to accompany the work you selected. Use the following questions to guide you:

- What do you like best about the piece?
- What did you learn from creating it?
- How would you revise the piece to make it even better?

ASSESSMENT OPTIONS

📁 ***Writing Assessment and Portfolio Management***
- Writing Assessment, pp. 1–16
- Portfolio Management, pp. 17–19

GLENCOE TECHNOLOGY

 MINDJOGGER VIDEOQUIZZES
VIDEODISC

Use *MindJogger* to review the Theme 2 content.

 Theme 2
Side A

 Also available in VHS.

Reading on Your Own

Have you enjoyed the stories and poems in this theme? If so, here are some other books you might enjoy.

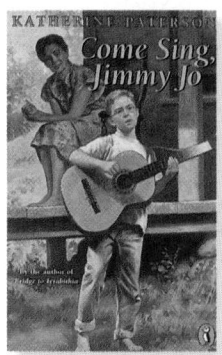

So Far from the Bamboo Grove

by Yoko Kawashima Watkins In this novel based on the author's experience, Yoko and her family must leave their home in North Korea and go through many hardships to get to Japan.

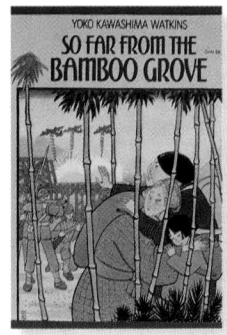

Come Sing, Jimmy Jo

by Katherine Paterson This novel tells the story of young James Johnson, who is discovered by a country music agent and thrust into a life on the road with his musical family.

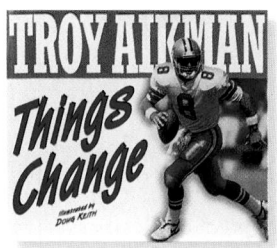

Things Change

by Troy Aikman The Dallas Cowboys quarterback describes his life from childhood to Superbowl champ, using his own experiences to show that change can provide an opportunity to grow.

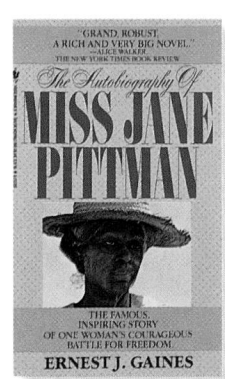

The Autobiography of Miss Jane Pittman

by Ernest J. Gaines In this novel about a 110-year-old African American woman, Miss Jane Pittman recollects events in her life in the South from the Civil War to the Civil Rights movement of the 1960s.

Reading on Your Own

Glencoe Literature Library

So Far from the Bamboo Grove is one of the titles available in the *Glencoe Literature Library*. For a complete listing, see pp. 46–47 in this book.

The *Glencoe Literature Library: Study Guide* provides instructional support and student activities for works in the *Glencoe Literature Library*.

MEETING INDIVIDUAL NEEDS
INCLUSION STRATEGIES

Less-proficient readers may enjoy *Things Change* by Troy Aikman. The simple, informal style and many photos make this book appealing to and appropriate for these students.

The following books are rated for average readers (**L2**) or for students who need more challenging reading (**L3**):

- *So Far from the Bamboo Grove* by Yoko Kawashima Watkins **L2**
- *Come Sing, Jimmy Jo* by Katherine Paterson **L2**
- *The Autobiography of Miss Jane Pittman* by Ernest J. Gaines **L3**

Additional Resources
📁 *Inclusion Strategies*

Standardized Test Practice

Read the following passage. Then read each question on page 215. Decide which is the best answer to each question. Mark the letter for that answer on your paper.

RealBaby is all Wrong

You may have bought a product at one time with which you were dissatisfied. What can you do when that happens? Here is a letter one student has written to the company that made a product he bought.

> 2342 North High St.
> Montville, MS 02541
> August 10, 1999
>
> Mr. Ronald Wesson
> Director of Customer Service
> ToyCo
> 4532 Main St.
> Lake Prima, NC 23687
>
> Dear Mr. Wesson:
>
> I am writing to you to express my dissatisfaction with your product, RealBaby. I bought the doll for my little sister because your commercial said that it was lifelike and acted like a real baby. I really liked your commercial because I saw the children playing with RealBaby, and they looked like they were having fun.
>
> However, when my sister opened the box to play with the RealBaby, I was surprised to see that the doll looked nothing like the doll on television. It was not lifelike at all. The arms and legs are supposed to move and the eyes are supposed to open and close. On the doll, only one eye opens and closes and one leg does not bend at all.
>
> In addition, the doll does not make any sounds, even though in the commercial it seems to cry and say words. If you follow the directions and fill it with water, instead of small tears coming out of its eyes, the water pours out in a steady stream.

Answers and Analyses

1. **C** Have students point out the lines that indicate the author's mood or attitude. The opening line of the letter states *I am writing to you to express my dissatisfaction.* Therefore the best choice is C.

2. **F** Students should look back to the story to find the reason that the writer does not want another doll. In the last line of the letter, Robert says *I am not interested in receiving another doll, since I know that it is not a doll that lives up to its advertisement.* The choice that paraphrases this idea is F.

3. **B** This is an excellent opportunity to review process of elimination. Choice A is an opinion, and therefore can be eliminated right away. Choices C and D can be eliminated, because the letter never states that Robert broke the doll or that it is popular. Choice B is supported by the last line of the second paragraph that states *one leg does not bend at all.*

My sister was very disappointed with the toy, and I am too. I paid $19.99 for the doll with my own money, and I would like a full refund. I feel that it is a fair request. I am not interested in receiving another doll, since I know that it is not a doll that lives up to its advertisement.

Please send my refund to the above address. Thank you.

Sincerely,

Robert Jones

1   The writer of the letter can best be described as —

A   joyful

B   confused

C   displeased

D   rude

2   Based on what the letter states, the reason the writer doesn't want a replacement doll is because —

F   RealBaby doesn't do what the commercial said it would do

G   he wants the money to give back to his mother

H   all of the dolls' eyes are probably broken

J   his sister already has too many dolls

3   Which of these sentences expresses a FACT about the letter?

A   I feel that this a fair request.

B   The arms and legs on the doll Robert bought do not all bend.

C   Robert broke his sister's doll and is trying to get a refund.

D   RealBaby is very popular.

4   Which of these things did Robert do last in his letter?

F   give the reason he bought the doll

G   state his address

H   ask for a full refund

J   list what was wrong with the doll

5   According to Robert, he was interested in RealBaby because —

A   it looked like his sister

B   it was popular with others

C   it looked real on television

D   it would add to a doll collection

6   How does Robert show that the doll does not do what the commercial said it would do?

F   by referring to it as defective

G   by saying that he never received it

H   by complaining about how it was wrapped

J   by describing the things that are wrong with it

STOP

Answers and Analyses

4. H   Robert's address appears at the top of the letter, his reason for buying the doll is stated in the first paragraph, and he lists the problems with the doll in the second and third paragraphs. He asks for a refund at the end of the fourth paragraph, so this is the last thing that he does. Therefore answer choice H is correct.

5. C   Remind students to look back to the text to find evidence for their answer. We can eliminate choices A and C, because there is no evidence in the text to support either choice. Answer choice B may be tempting, but simply because the doll looked like fun on television does not mean it is popular. The end of the first paragraph states *I bought the doll for my little sister because your commercial said that it was lifelike and acted like a real baby.* The choice that best paraphrases this idea is C.

6. J   There is no evidence to support choices G or H, which can be eliminated right away. Choosing between F and J is difficult, but remind students that one of the choices will always be better than the other. Robert never actually states that the doll is defective; he only describes the problems with the doll. He says that one eye does not open, one leg does not bend, and it does not make any sounds. Therefore the best choice is J.

THEME OPENING ➡

- **Introducing the Theme** (p. 217)
- **Exploring the Theme** (p. 218)
- **Theme Projects** (p. 219)

Theme 3:
FACING CHALLENGE

SELECTIONS

New Directions (p. 220)

The Wreck of Hesperus (p. 226)

I'll Walk the Tightrope (p. 226)

Too Soon a Woman (p. 234)

A Boy and His Dog (p. 242)

The Women's 400 Meters (p. 251)

To James (p. 251)

a poem (for langston hughes) (p. 258)

Dreams (p. 258)

Media Connection: Why 'Possum Has a Large Mouth (p. 266)

Racing the Great Bear (p. 267)

Beyond the Limits (p. 280)

Active Reading Model: The Fish Crisis (p. 294)

Media Connection: Americans Continue to Worry About the Decline of the Oceans (p. 304)

Hurricanes (p. 305)

SKILL FEATURES

Vocabulary Skills (p. 225)

Reading and Thinking Skills (p. 250)

Interdisciplinary Connection (p. 257)

Technology Skills (pp. 264–265)

Listening, Speaking, and Viewing (p. 279)

Genre Focus: Nonfiction (pp. 290–291)

Active Reading Strategies (pp. 292–293)

Grammar Link (p. 315)

WRITING WORKSHOP

Persuasive Writing: Editorial (pp. 316–319)

THEME WRAP–UP

- **Responding to the Theme, Analyzing Literature, Evaluate and Set Goals** (p. 320)

- **Build Your Portfolio** (p. 320)

- **Reading on Your Own** (p. 321)

    Where the Red Fern Grows by Wilson Rawls

    Hostage by Edward P. Myers

    Reach Higher by Scottie Pippen

    The Outsiders by S. E. Hinton

- **Standardized Test Practice** (pp. 322–323)

KEYS TO LITERARY CONNECTIONS

 Comparing Selections

The **Comparing Selections** feature in this theme provides opportunities for addressing diverse aspects of the reading and literature curriculum.

For example, in Comparing Selections on page 249, students are asked to examine the way the characters in "Too Soon a Woman" and "A Boy and His Dog" were affected by loss.

KEYS TO TEACHING OPTIONS

 Block Scheduling

Activities that are particularly suited to use within a block scheduling framework are identified throughout this theme by the following designation: 🔳 For detailed suggestions on block scheduling, see the **Block Scheduling Guide** for this grade level.

Key to Ability Levels

The Teaching Options throughout this theme have been coded for students of various abilities.

L1 BASIC activities for all students

L2 AVERAGE activities for average to above-average students

L3 CHALLENGING activities for above-average students

Reading Skills in this theme

Variety of Texts

In addition to a variety of nonfiction selections, this theme includes the following text types:

- narrative essay
- poetry
- short story
- legend
- cartoon
- Web site
- public opinion poll

Comprehension Skills

The following instructional support for comprehension skills appears in this theme of the Student Edition:

- **Reading and Thinking Minilessons** (pp. 233, 263, 278, 314)
- **Visualizing** (p. 250)
- **Active Reading Strategies and Model** (pp. 292–303)

See also the **Reading Minilessons** throughout the theme in this Teacher's Wraparound Edition.

Reading Resources

Comprehension Skills Resources

📁 **Active Reading Guides**

The **Active Reading Guide** provides graphic organizers and study guide questions to support students' reading of each selection. (**Active Reading Guide**, pp. 19–28)

📁 **Reading Workbook**

The **Reading Workbook** (pp. 31–48) includes additional instruction and reinforcement of reading strategies and skills.

🎧 **Audio Library**

Available both on tape and on CD, the **Audio Library** provides valuable comprehension support.

Resources for Reading Widely

🦉 **Glencoe Literature Library**

Each title in the *Glencoe Literature Library* includes a full-length novel or play plus related readings. A separate Study Guide is available for each title.

💿 **Literature Classics CD-ROM**

The selections on this CD-ROM can be searched by author, theme, or genre.

*in*TIME

A coproduction of Glencoe and Time, Inc., the *inTime* magazine includes a wealth of high interest nonfiction related to the selections in Theme Three.

✔ Assessment in this theme

Assessment Options in the Student Edition

Glencoe Literature offers a number of diverse ways to evaluate student understanding and skill proficiency. In the Student Edition, use the following:

- **Responding to Literature**

  Following each selection, students are asked to recall facts, interpret ideas, and evaluate concepts as they answer a variety of questions and complete activities to extend their understanding.

- **Theme Wrap-Up (pp. 320–321)**

  Here students respond to the selections on personal and analytical levels. They also assume ownership of their learning by setting and evaluating goals and by selecting work for their portfolios.

See also the many **Assessment Resources** listed on the facing page.

THE PRINCETON REVIEW

Standardized Test Practice

The Princeton Review has developed the Standardized Test Practice pages found at the end of this theme (pp. 322–323). These pages contain practice test questions that help students remain familiar with standardized test formats and content.

- ITBS Preparation and Practice
- SAT-9 Preparation and Practice
- TerraNova Preparation and Practice

Writing Skills in this theme

Writing Skills

The Student Edition of Theme Three offers strong instructional support for writing skills:

In **Extending Your Response**, which follows each selection:
- **Writing About Literature**
- **Personal/Creative Writing**

See also the **Writing Minilessons** throughout the theme in this Teacher's Wraparound Edition.

Writing Workshops

Theme Three concludes with a **Writing Workshop** that guides students through the process of writing an editorial (pp. 316–319).

Writing Resources

Writer's Assistant CD-ROM
Each Writing Workshop is supplemented by an interactive writing guide on the Writer's Assistant CD-ROM. This easy-to-use writing guide provides prompts, templates, and other tools that lead students through the writing process.

Writing and Proofreading Practice
Blackline masters present in-depth instruction and practice on a specific step in the writing process and proofreading (pp. 1–7, 22—28).

Writing and Proofreading Transparencies
Transparencies provide graphic organizers and proofreading exercises for whole-class instruction (pp. 1–6, 11-14, 29–30).

Research and Report Writing Guide
This resource provides extensive tips and activities to guide students in their writing projects in the literature classroom as well as in classes across the curriculum.

Style and Documentation Sourcebook for Writers
This sourcebook is a combination reference and workbook, giving students the most up-to-date information and guidance regarding traditional as well as technological research strategies and documentation.

Grammar and Composition Handbook
The Grammar and Composition Handbook provides instruction that supplements activities in the student textbook.

Assessment Resources

Selection Quick Checks
For each selection, a Quick Check of three to five short-answer questions measures students' literal comprehension.

Selection and Theme Assessment
The Selection and Theme Assessment instrument tests students' abilities to recall, interpret, and evaluate what they've read. The tests consist of multiple-choice, short answer, and essay questions.

Performance Assessment
Alternative assessment instruments and rubrics for Theme Three are found in the Performance Assessment ancillary.

Writing Assessment and Portfolio Management
These notes and strategies, student models, and assessment tools assist with the task of measuring students' progress as writers and as monitors of their own writing.

Testmaker
Teachers can customize selection and Theme Three tests by accessing the Testmaker database.

Mindjogger Videoquizzes
Using a popular game show format, Mindjogger Videoquizzes enable teachers to evaluate student understanding of Theme Three in a quick and fun manner.

SELECTIONS	Literary Elements	Reading and Thinking	Writing	Vocabulary and Spelling	
New Directions MAYA ANGELOU	Biography, SE p. 223 *Biography, TWE p. 222* *Imagery, TWE p. 222*	*Distinguishing Fact from Opinion, TWE p. 222* *Problem and Solution, TWE p. 222*	Finding Solutions, SE 224 Journal Entry, SE p. 224	Analogies, SE p. 224	
The Wreck of the Hesperus HENRY WADSWORTH LONGFELLOW **I'll Walk the Tightrope** MARGARET DANNER	Narrative Poetry, SE p. 232 *Character, TWE p. 227* *Setting, TWE p. 228* *Dialogue, TWE p. 228* *Narrative Poetry, TWE pp. 229, 230, 231* *Plot, TWE p. 230*	Identifying Spatial Relationships, SE p. 233 *Sequence of Events, TWE p. 228* *Inferring, TWE p. 229*	Describing Imagery, SE p. 233 Writing an Article, SE p. 233 *Personal Poems, TWE p. 231*	*Etymology, TWE p. 229*	
Too Soon a Woman DOROTHY M. JOHNSON	Dialect, SE p. 240 *Setting, TWE p. 236* *Dialect, TWE pp. 236–238* *Character, TWE pp. 236, 239*	*Inferring, TWE p. 237* *Cause and Effect, TWE p. 237* *Draw. Conclusions, TWE pp. 238, 239*	Surprise Ending, SE p. 241 An Introduction, SE p. 241	Antonyms, SE p. 241 *Homophones, TWE p. 237*	
A Boy and His Dog MARTHA BROOKS	Foreshadowing, SE p. 248; *TWE p. 247* *Point of View, TWE p. 244* *Tone, TWE p. 244*	*Sequence of Events, TWE p. 245* *Inferring, TWE p. 247* *Draw. Conclusions, TWE p. 247*			
The Women's 400 Meters LILLIAN MORRISON **To James** FRANK HORNE	Free Verse, SE p. 255 *Alliteration, TWE p. 252* *Free Verse, TWE pp. 252, 253, 254*	*Evaluating, TWE p. 252* *Inferring, TWE p. 254* *Drawing Conclusions, TWE p. 254*	Theme, SE p. 256 Journal Entry, SE p. 256	*Prefixes, TWE p. 253*	
a poem (for langston hughes) NIKKI GIOVANNI **DREAMS** LANGSTON HUGHES	Rhyme Scheme, SE p. 262 *Rhyme Scheme, TWE p. 259* *Rhythm, TWE p. 259* *Repetition, TWE p. 261*	Identifying Assumptions, SE p. 263 *Analyzing Arguments, TWE p. 260*	Sensory Images, SE p. 263 Short Poem, SE p. 263		
Racing the Great Bear JOSEPH BRUCHAC	Oral Tradition, SE p. 276; *TWE pp. 269, 270, 271, 272, 273, 274, 275* *Char., TWE pp. 270, 272, 274*	Setting a Purpose, SE p. 278 *Focusing on a Question, TWE p. 269* *Monitoring Comp., TWE p. 271*	Dialogue, SE p. 277 Journal Entry, SE p. 277	Multiple-Meaning Words, SE p. 278	
from Beyond the Limits STACY ALLISON	Autobiography, SE p. 288; *TWE pp. 282–284* *Description, TWE p. 282, 287*	Setting a Purpose, SE p. 278 *Generalizing, TWE p. 285* *Crit. Judgment, TWE p. 287*	Challenges, SE p. 289 Journal Entry, SE p. 289 *Using Detail, TWE p. 284*	Base Words and Suffixes, SE p. 289	
The Fish Crisis J. MADELEINE NASH	Essay, SE p. 302; *TWE p. 298* *Author's Purpose, TWE p. 300*	*Using Text Structures, TWE p. 297* *Identifying Propaganda Techniques, TWE p. 299*	Evaluating Sources, SE p. 303 Letter to the Editor, SE p. 303 *Interview, TWE p. 298*	Suffixes, SE p. 303 *Prefixes, TWE p. 296*	
Hurricanes PATRICIA LAUBER	Informational Text, SE p. 312; *TWE pp. 307, 308, 309* *Suspense, TWE p. 308* *Concrete Language, TWE pp. 308, 310* *Repetition, TWE pp. 309*	Distinguishing Fact and Opinion, SE p. 314 *Summarizing, TWE p. 308* *Evaluating, TWE p. 310*	Summary, SE p. 313 Postcard, SE p. 313	Prefixes that Express Number, SE p. 314 *Word Origins, TWE p. 309*	

Key: Student material is in roman. Teacher material is in italic. 💻 Technology **COLLAB. LEARN.** Collaboration

Grammar and Language	Listening, Speaking, and Viewing	Life Skills	Study, Research, and Technology
	COLLAB. LEARN. Literature Groups, SE p. 224		
Identifying Adjectives, TWE p. 230	**COLLAB. LEARN.** Literature Groups, SE p. 233 Reading Aloud, SE p. 233		
Punctuating Dialogue, TWE p. 238	**COLLAB. LEARN.** Literature Groups, SE p. 241	Learning for Life: Report, SE p. 241	Research: Report, SE p. 241 Internet Connection, SE p. 241 **COLLAB. LEARN.** *Mushrooms, TWE p. 239*
Usage: Lie *and* Lay, *TWE p. 246*	**COLLAB. LEARN.** Literature Groups, SE p. 248 Invited Speaker, SE p. 248		Interview, SE p. 248
Ellipsis, SE p. 256 *Present and Past Participles, TWE p. 253*	**COLLAB. LEARN.** Literature Groups, SE p. 256 Interview, SE p. 256 *Sports Broadcast, TWE p. 254*		
Prepositional Phrases, TWE p. 260	**COLLAB. LEARN.** Literature Groups, SE p. 263 Appreciating Poetry, SE p. 263		
Possessive Pronouns, SE p. 278 *Comparative and Superlative Adjectives, TWE p. 274*	**COLLAB. LEARN.** Literature Groups, SE p. 277 *Radio Play, TWE p. 270*		Internet Connection, SE p. 277 Iroquois Longhouse, SE p. 277 **COLLAB. LEARN.** *Bears, TWE p. 275*
Apostrophe, TWE p. 286	**COLLAB. LEARN.** Literature Groups, SE p. 289 *Documentary, TWE p. 286*	**COLLAB. LEARN.** *Planning and Designing, TWE p. 285*	Internet Connection, SE p. 289 Create a Map, SE p. 289
Using Quotation Marks, TWE p. 300	**COLLAB. LEARN.** Literature Groups, SE p. 303		Interdisciplinary Activity: Diagram, SE p. 303
Spelling Plurals, SE p. 314 *Compound Predicates, TWE p. 310*	**COLLAB. LEARN.** Literature Groups, SE p. 313 **COLLAB. LEARN.** News Broadcast, SE p. 313 *Video, TWE p. 311*	News Broadcast, SE p. 313	Mural, SE p. 313

SELECTIONS	📁 Print Resources		
New Directions MAYA ANGELOU	Theme 3 Plan. Guide, pp. 6–10 * Active Reading Guide, p. 19 Vocabulary Practice, p. 13	Reading Workbook, pp. 31–32	* Qk. Chks., p. 19; Perf. Assess., p. 18 Sel. and Theme Assess., pp. 33–34 Spanish Summaries, p. 19 Spanish Translations
The Wreck of the Hesperus HENRY WADSWORTH LONGFELLOW **I'll Walk the Tightrope** MARGARET DANNER	Theme 3 Plan. Guide, pp. 11–15 * Active Reading Guide, p. 20	Gr. & Comp. Hdbk., Lesson 5.1 Gr. & Lang. Wkbk., pp. 117–119 Reading Workbook, pp. 33–34	* Qk. Chks., p. 20; Perf. Assess., p. 19 Sel. and Theme Assess., pp. 35–36 Spanish Summaries, p. 20
Too Soon a Woman DOROTHY M. JOHNSON	Theme 3 Plan. Guide, pp. 17–24 * Active Reading Guide, p. 21 Vocabulary Practice, p. 14	Gr. & Comp. Hdbk., Lesson 13.6 Gr. & Lang. Wkbk., pp. 267–270 Reading Workbook, pp. 35–36	* Qk. Chks., p. 21; Perf. Assess., p. 20 Sel. and Theme Assess., pp. 37–38 Spanish Summaries, p. 21 Spanish Translations
A Boy and His Dog MARTHA BROOKS	Theme 3 Plan. Guide, pp. 25–32 * Active Reading Guide, p. 22 Vocabulary Practice, p. 15	Gr. & Comp. Hdbk., Lessons 3.11, 3.12 Gr. & Lang. Wkbk., pp. 223–224 Reading Workbook, pp. 37–38	* Qk. Chks., p. 22; Perf. Assess., p. 21 Sel. and Theme Assess., pp. 39–40 Spanish Summaries, p. 22 Spanish Translations
The Women's 400 Meters LILLIAN MORRISON **To James** FRANK HORNE	Theme 3 Plan. Guide, pp. 33–38 * Active Reading Guide, p. 23	Gr. & Comp. Hdbk., Lesson 9.1 Gr. & Lang. Wkbk., pp. 167–168	* Qk. Chks., p. 23; Perf. Assess., p. 22 Sel. and Theme Assess., pp. 41–42 Spanish Summaries, p. 23 Spanish Translations
a poem (for langston hughes) NIKKI GIOVANNI **DREAMS** LANGSTON HUGHES	Theme 3 Plan. Guide, pp. 39–44 * Active Reading Guide, p. 24	Gr. & Comp. Hdbk., Lesson 7.1 Gr. & Lang. Wkbk., pp. 141–142 Reading Workbook, pp. 39–40	* Qk. Chks., p. 24; Perf. Assess., p. 23 Sel. and Theme Assess., pp. 43–44 Spanish Summaries, p. 24
Racing the Great Bear JOSEPH BRUCHAC	Theme 3 Plan. Guide, pp. 45–52 * Active Reading Guide, p. 25 Vocabulary Practice, p. 16	Gr. & Comp. Hdbk., Lsns. 4.4, 5.3, 5.4 Gr. & Lang. Wkbk., pp. 109–110 Reading Workbook, pp. 41–42	* Qk. Chks., p. 25; Perf. Assess., p. 23 Sel. and Theme Assess., pp. 45–46 Sp. Sum., p. 25; Sp. Trans.
from Beyond the Limits STACY ALLISON	Theme 3 Plan. Guide, pp. 53–60 * Active Reading Guide, p. 26 Vocabulary Practice, p. 17	Gr. & Comp. Hdbk., Lesson 13.7 Gr. & Lang. Wkbk., pp. 273–274 Reading Workbook, pp. 43–44	* Qk. Chks., p. 26; Perf. Assess., p. 25 Sel. and Theme Assess., pp. 47–48 Sp. Sum., p. 26; Sp. Trans.
The Fish Crisis J. MADELEINE NASH	Theme 3 Plan. Guide, pp. 61–68 * Active Reading Guide, p. 27 Vocabulary Practice, p. 18	Gr. & Comp. Hdbk., Lesson 13.6 Gr. & Lang. Wkbk., pp. 267–270 Reading Workbook, pp. 45–46	* Qk. Chks., p. 27; Perf. Assess., p. 26 Sel. and Theme Assess., pp. 49–50 Sp. Sum., p. 27; Sp. Trans.
Hurricanes PATRICIA LAUBER	Theme 3 Plan. Guide, pp. 69–76 * Active Reading Guide, p. 28 Vocabulary Practice, p. 19	Gr. & Comp. Hdbk., Lessons 1.5, 15.1 Gr. & Lang. Wkbk., pp. 53–54, 297–300; Rdg. Wkbk., pp. 47–48	* Qk. Chks., p. 28; Perf. Assess., p. 27 Sel. and Theme Assess., pp. 51–52 Spanish Summaries, p. 28

*Also available in Spanish

Transparencies	Technology Resources
Selection Focus Transparency 19 Literary Elements Transparency 19 Fine Art Transparency 8	Audio/Spanish Audio Library Vocabulary Puzzlemaker Web Site: lit.glencoe.com
Selection Focus Transparency 20 Grammar and Language Transparency 19 Literary Elements Transparency 20	Literature Launchers Audio/Spanish Audio Library Vocabulary Puzzlemaker Web Site: lit.glencoe.com
Selection Focus Transparency 21 Grammar and Language Transparency 20 Literary Elements Transparency 21 Fine Art Transparency 21	Audio/Spanish Audio Library Vocabulary Puzzlemaker Web Site: lit.glencoe.com
Selection Focus Transparency 22 Grammar and Language Transparency 21 Literary Elements Transparency 22	Audio/Spanish Audio Library Vocabulary Puzzlemaker Web Site: lit.glencoe.com
Selection Focus Transparency 23 Grammar and Language Transparency 22 Literary Elements Transparency 23	Audio/Spanish Audio Library Vocabulary Puzzlemaker Web Site: lit.glencoe.com
Selection Focus Transparency 24 Grammar and Language Transparency 23 Literary Elements Transparency 24	Literature Launchers Audio/Spanish Audio Library Vocabulary Puzzlemaker Web Site: lit.glencoe.com
Selection Focus Transparency 25 Grammar and Language Transparency 24 Literary Elements Transparency 25	Audio/Spanish Audio Library Vocabulary Puzzlemaker Web Site: lit.glencoe.com
Selection Focus Transparency 26 Grammar and Language Transparency 25 Literary Elements Transparency 26 Fine Art Transparency 7	Audio/Spanish Audio Library Vocabulary Puzzlemaker Web Site: lit.glencoe.com
Selection Focus Transparency 27 Grammar and Language Transparency 26 Literary Elements Transparency 27	Audio/Spanish Audio Library Vocabulary Puzzlemaker Web Site: lit.glencoe.com
Selection Focus Transparency 28 Grammar and Language Transparency 27 Literary Elements Transparency 28	Literature Launchers Audio/Spanish Audio Library Web Site: lit.glencoe.com

Theme RESOURCES

- Listening and Speaking Activities (pp. 7–9)
- Viewing and Representing Activities (pp. 1–6, 13–15)
- Critical Thinking Skills (pp. 7–8)
- Media Connection Activities (pp. 5–6)
- Interdisciplinary Activities (pp. 10–13)
- Family and Community Activities (p. 13)
- Selection and Theme Assessment (pp. 129–130)

See also these additional planning resources:
- English Language Learners Sourcebook
- Inclusion Strategies Sourcebook
- Literature Groups Sourcebook

Use Glencoe's *Presentation Plus!* This multimedia teaching tool lets you present dynamic lessons that will engage your students. Using Microsoft PowerPoint®, you can customize the presentation to create your own personalized lessons.

THEME 3

Facing Challenge

Theme Objectives

- To enjoy reading about ways in which people cope with and prevail over difficult circumstances
- To analyze the literary elements in nonfiction, legends, poetry, and short story selections
- To apply strategies for reading informative nonfiction

Teaching Strategies

Have students read the quotation by Joseph Bruchac in preparation for the discussion questions below.

VIEWING THE ART

Responding to the Art Discussion questions:

- What challenge is the woman in the photograph facing? (*the challenge of doing her best in a soccer game*)
- How does the photo relate to the Bruchac quotation? (*Both deal with challenges people must face.*)
- What does Bruchac mean by "monsters"? (*problems, demands, or trials people must face*)

Facing Challenge

> **"** *Sooner or later, each of us must . . . challenge our own monsters, with our survival in the balance.* **"**
>
> —Joseph Bruchac, *Flying with the Eagle, Racing the Great Bear*

216

The newspaper is a valuable instrument in the classroom because there is a reality to newspapers that forces students to confront possibilities in their own lives that they may think they can ignore in fiction. When introducing the theme "Facing Challenge" I bring in a number of newspaper articles and let students each select one that personally represents a challenge. We discuss how students might face these challenges, focusing on both the positive and negative aspects of reality. I like to include inspirational stories of real people who have faced and overcome challenges and apply these real-life stories to students. I ask, "What would you do if you were the person in this newspaper story?" We discuss what students may have to face and overcome one day in order to become the people they want to be.

WEIS MIDDLE SCHOOL TEXAS CITY, TEXAS

LINDA I. RODRIGUEZ

THEME 3

THEME CONTENTS

New Directions • narrative essay by Maya Angelou ... 221

The Wreck of the Hesperus •
   poem by H. W. Longfellow 227

I'll Walk the Tightrope • poem by Margaret Danner ... 231

Too Soon a Woman •
   short story by Dorothy M. Johnson 235

A Boy and His Dog • short story by Martha Brooks .. 243

The Women's 400 Meters •
   poem by Lillian Morrison 252

To James • poem by Frank Horne 253

a poem (for langston hughes) •
   poem by Nikki Giovanni 259

Dreams • poem by Langston Hughes 261

Racing the Great Bear • legend by Joseph Bruchac .. 268

from Beyond the Limits • by Stacy Allison 281

GENRE FOCUS NONFICTION

The Fish Crisis • by J. Madeleine Nash 295

Hurricanes • by Patricia Lauber 306

FACING CHALLENGE ✤ 217

RESOURCE MANAGER

See the **Theme Three Planning Guide** (pp. 1–5) for additional teaching notes, strategies, and resources for introducing the theme "Facing Challenge."

Introducing the Theme

Direct your students' attention to the **Theme Contents.** Ask them to read through the list of selections. Present these questions for discussion:

• What does the title of the first selection, by Maya Angelou, tell you about the theme of facing challenge? *(A challenging situation prompts a change in direction for a character in the story.)*

• Which titles seem to have something in common? *(Among other similarities, students may suggest that two of the titles mention women, three mention athletic feats, two are related to Langston Hughes, and three mention animals.)*

• Which titles interest you most among the poems? among the short stories?

LITERATURE & HUMANITIES

⊙ Have students examine the painting *Fair Weather* on the *National Museum of Women in the Arts* CD and discuss why a mountain is often used as a metaphor for a challenge. Have them discuss ways people might get to the other side of this mountain in relation to ways people might deal with a problem.

GLENCOE
TECHNOLOGY

LITERATURE CLASSICS CD-ROM
   Search for other selections related to the theme "Facing Challenge."

Exploring the Theme

Facing Challenge

Ask that each student first write a few sentences about a challenging situation he or she has faced, and then a few sentences about a challenge from within.

Starting Points

Facing the Monster

Have students explain what is happening in the Gary Larson cartoon and what they find humorous about it. *(Students may think that George Miller's normal response to the absurd situation is funny and that the humor comes from the fact that the Millers have found themselves in the middle of* The Three Little Pigs *story and need to find a way out.)*

- Encourage students to role-play the story of *The Three Little Pigs* from the wolf's point of view. Challenge them to make the wolf a sympathetic character.
- In addition to role-playing what may happen next in the cartoon, have students improvise the conversation between the Millers and the pigs before the wolf arrived.
- Encourage students to role-play other well-known stories in which humans and animals interact, such as *Little Red Riding Hood* and *Goldilocks and the Three Bears.*

Personal Challenges

On the board, list a few of the common challenges students could face in daily life. Create another list of major challenges in life, such as losing a loved one or experiencing a serious health problem.

- Discuss with students which of these problems are within our ability to control and which are not. Direct their responses with questions. For example, ask *How do people face problems that are not within their power to solve, such as the death of a loved one?*
- Before students write their journal entries, encourage them each to focus on a personal problem, either large or small, that was successfully solved or faced. *(Students may write journal entries that include advice for others who face similar problems.)*

Exploring the Theme

— Facing Challenge —

We face challenges every day. Sometimes, outside forces put us in challenging situations. Sometimes, the challenges are inside ourselves. In this theme, you will meet real and imaginary characters who face a wide range of challenges. Try one of the options below to start your own thinking about the theme.

Starting Points

FACING THE MONSTER

If you remember the story of *The Three Little Pigs,* you'll appreciate Gary Larson's cartoon about the pigs' unlucky visitors.

- Role-play the situation in the cartoon, showing what happens next. Then expand your performance by role-playing a parody of another well-known story in which the characters face a challenge.

PERSONAL CHALLENGES

Think about a problem you faced in the past year and about how you prepared yourself for the challenge.

- Write a journal entry about a challenge you faced and what you learned from the experience.

The Far Side

1982

"Listen out there! We're George and Harriet Miller! We just dropped in on the pigs for coffee! We're coming out!... We don't want trouble!"

FINE ART
TRANSPARENCY 24

You may wish to display **Fine Art Transparency 24** to help students think about facing challenge.

Challenges Students can use a search engine to find out more about challenging issues they are interested in. They might use such keywords as *health, environment,* and *global warming.*

Theme Projects

As you read the selections in this theme, try your hand at one of these projects. Work on your own, with a partner, or with a group.

CRITICAL READING
Challenges in Fiction

1. Think about the main characters in your favorite books. Choose one character who faced a big challenge. You will pretend you are that character.

2. Plan how to portray your character. Take notes about the character's life and the special challenge that he or she faced.

3. Meet with four or five classmates for a chat. Stay in character as you talk about the ups and downs of your fictional life.

4. Compare your character's challenges and outcomes with those of your classmates. What similarities and differences did you notice?

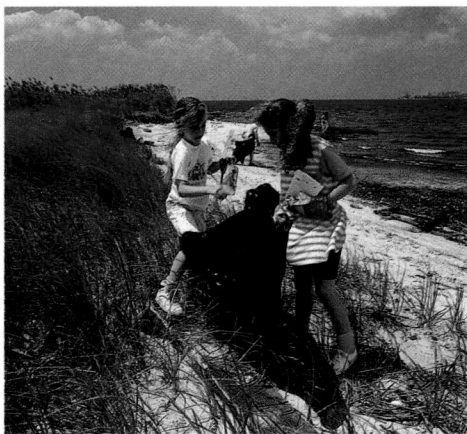

*inter*NET
CONNECTION

Check out the Web for more project ideas. Brainstorm some keywords about facing challenges that you can enter in your search engine to locate suitable sites. You can also check out the Glencoe Literature site at: lit.glencoe.com

LEARNING FOR LIFE
Writing a Persuasive Memo

What are some challenges your community faces? Is there a park that needs repair, a river that is polluted, or a dangerous intersection that needs a stop sign?

1. Choose one problem that you feel strongly about solving, and brainstorm ways to involve the community in the solution.

2. Draft a memo to your town or city government that will persuade officials to help organize community volunteers to solve the problem.

MULTIMEDIA PROJECT
Newsmakers Facing Challenges

1. Read magazines and newspapers, browse the Web, listen to the radio, and watch television news to learn about people facing challenges.

2. Choose one person and write a make-believe interview with her or him about life's challenges.

3. With a small group, produce a news video or a radio news show using the interview as the basis for a presentation to the class.

FACING CHALLENGE 219

Theme Projects
Teaching Strategies

The following suggestions may help your students plan and carry out their theme projects.

Critical Reading

- Suggest that students bring the books in to share with classmates and explain to them why they chose their characters.
- Invite students to become the characters by wearing costumes, speaking in the characters' voices, and imagining the characters' thoughts.

Learning for Life

- Direct students' attention to potential challenges to the school community.
- Write the names of local officials on the board and make a local telephone book available.
- Encourage students to focus on solutions in their memos.

Multimedia Project

- Have students use real news or radio shows as models for theirs. Encourage them to credit group members at the end of the show for their contributions.
- During the presentation, have students write questions they might ask if they could interview this person.

Additional Resources

- 📁 *Interdisciplinary Activities,* pp. 10–13
- 📁 *Viewing and Representing Activities,* pp. 13–15
- 📁 *Listening and Speaking Activities,* pp. 7–9
- 📁 *Critical Thinking Skills,* pp. 7–8
- 📁 *Selection and Theme Assessment,* pp. 129–130
- 📁 *Performance Assessment,* p. 71

Family and Community Activity

Have students choose a community organization or agency that helps people cope with challenges. Have them work in groups and ask each group to prepare a pamphlet for the class that includes

- the name, address, and phone number of the organization.
- who the organization helps or serves.
- a list of services the organization provides.
- the price of the services.
- statements from agency workers about the help they offer.
- statements from people who have benefited from the services. **COLLAB. LEARN.**

Additional Resources
- 📁 *Family and Community Activities,* p. 13

Objectives

- To read and analyze a biography about facing and overcoming a challenge
- To recognize characteristics of biographies
- To write a problem-solution paragraph

Skills

Reading/Thinking: Distinguishing Fact from Opinion; Problem and Solution
Writing: Journal Entry
Vocabulary: Analogies
Collaboration: Literature Groups

Motivating
→OPTIONS

Selection Focus Transparency 19: Have students read the quote by Gilbert Ware. Encourage them to discuss how overcoming small challenges can eventually lead to great accomplishment.

Focus Activity: As an extension of the Focus Activity, have small groups of students discuss how they can arrive at creative solutions to a problem.

Before You Read
New Directions

MEET MAYA ANGELOU

Author, poet, playwright, editor, educator, professional stage and screen performer, and singer—each of these words describes Maya Angelou (mī yə an′ jel ō). Angelou's extraor-dinary career has taken her to many places around the world, including Egypt and Ghana. She read her poem "On the Pulse of Morning," commissioned by President Clinton, at the 1993 inauguration.

Maya Angelou was born in 1928. "New Directions" was published in Wouldn't Take Nothing for My Journey Now *in 1993.*

FOCUS ACTIVITY

Each person has his or her own method of problem solving. How do you go about solving a problem?

Think/Pair/Share
Think about a problem you recently solved. Share your problem-solving method with a partner. With your partner, put together a list of three to five words that describe an approach to solving a problem.

Setting a Purpose
As you read the selection, try to discover a problem and its solution.

BACKGROUND

The Time and Place   This selection is set in Arkansas in the early 1900s.

Did You Know?   Many of Maya Angelou's most famous books are autobiographical. Although Angelou spent some of her childhood with her mother in large cities, she was raised mainly by her grandmother in the small town of Stamps, Arkansas. "New Directions" is based on the life of Angelou's grandmother, a determined woman who had a vision and then worked hard to reach her goal.

VOCABULARY PREVIEW

concede (kən sēd′) *v.* to admit to be true or proper; p. 221
meticulously (mi tik′ yə ləs lē) *adv.* in a way that shows careful attention to details; p. 221
balmy (bä′ mē) *adj.* mild; soothing; p. 222
assess (ə ses′) *v.* to determine the meaning or importance of; analyze; p. 222
loom (lo͞om) *v.* to appear to the mind as threatening; p. 222
ominous (om′ ə nəs) *adj.* threatening harm or evil; p. 222
unpalatable (un pal′ ə tə bəl) *adj.* not agreeable to the taste, mind, or feelings; unacceptable; p. 222

RESOURCE MANAGER

Lesson Planning Resource
The *Theme Three Planning Guide* (pp. 6–10) provides additional lesson notes and reduced versions of all print resources.

 Other Print Resources
- Active Reading Guide, p. 19
- Vocabulary Practice, p. 13
- Reading Workbook, pp. 31–32
- Quick Checks, p. 19

- Selection and Theme Assessment, pp. 33–34
- Performance Assessment, p. 18
- Spanish Summaries, p. 19
- Spanish Translations
- Inclusion Strategies
- English Language Learners Sourcebook

 Transparencies
- Selection Focus 19
- Fine Art 8
- Literary Elements 19

Technology
🎧 Audio Library
🎧 Spanish Audio Library
💻 Glencoe Literature Web Site
💾 Testmaker

New Directions

Maya Angelou

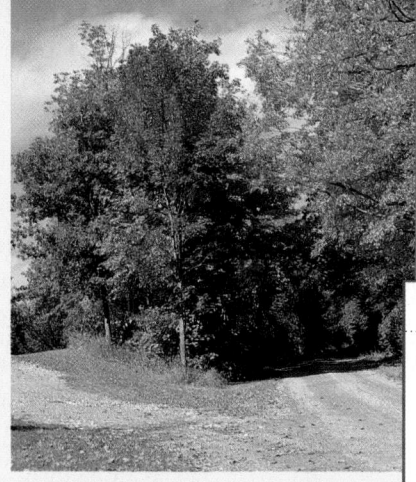

In 1903 the late Mrs. Annie Johnson of Arkansas found herself with two toddling sons, very little money, a slight ability to read and add simple numbers. To this picture add a disastrous marriage and the burdensome fact that Mrs. Johnson was a Negro.

When she told her husband, Mr. William Johnson, of her dissatisfaction with their marriage, he conceded that he too found it to be less than he expected, and had been secretly hoping to leave and study religion. He added that he thought God was calling him not only to preach but to do so in Enid, Oklahoma. He did not tell her that he knew a minister in Enid with whom he could study and who had a friendly, unmarried daughter. They parted amicably,[1] Annie keeping the one-room house and William taking most of the cash to carry himself to Oklahoma.

Annie, over six feet tall, big-boned, decided that she would not go to work as a domestic[2] and leave her "precious babes" to anyone else's care. There was no possibility of being hired at the town's cotton gin or lumber mill, but maybe there was a way to make the two factories work for her. In her words, "I looked up the road I was going and back the way I come, and since I wasn't satisfied, I decided to step off the road and cut me a new path." She told herself that she wasn't a fancy cook but that she could "mix groceries well enough to scare hungry away and from starving a man."

She made her plans meticulously and in secret. One early evening to see if she was ready, she placed stones in two five-gallon pails and carried them three miles to the cotton gin. She rested a little, and then, discarding some rocks, she walked in the darkness to the saw mill five miles farther along the dirt road. On her way back to her little house and her babies, she dumped the remaining rocks along the path.

That same night she worked into the early hours boiling chicken and frying ham. She made dough and filled the rolled-out pastry with meat. At last she went to sleep.

---

1. Mr. and Mrs. Johnson parted on friendly terms *(amicably)*.
2. A *domestic* (də mes′ tik) is a household servant.

Vocabulary
concede (kən sēd′) *v.* to admit to be true or proper
meticulously (mi tik′ yə ləs lē) *adv.* in a way that shows careful attention to details

SUMMARY

In this brief essay, Annie Johnson, a single mother in Arkansas in 1903, decides to build a better life for herself and her two sons. Annie doesn't like the job options available to her, so she decides to create her own opportunity. Annie begins a small business selling meat pies to factory workers. Annie eventually builds a permanent stall, which she later turns into a successful store.
📁 *Spanish Summaries,* p. 19

A **Active Reading**

PREDICT Ask students to think about Annie's options at this point in her life. What "new path" might Annie take? *(Students might suggest that Annie will evaluate her talents and create a job for herself instead of choosing one that already exists.)*

Additional Resources
📁 *Active Reading Guide,* p. 19
🎧 *Audio Library*
🎧 *Spanish Audio Library*

Teaching Options

CONNECTING TO OTHER SELECTIONS
For a teaching strategy that connects "New Directions" to "The Fish Crisis," turn to page 64 in the *Theme Three Planning Guide*.

LITERATURE & HUMANITIES

💿 Have students listen to volume 2, track 7, of the CD *American Music: Cultural Traditions* to hear "The Downhearted Blues," which might have been sung around the time Maya Angelou's story takes place.

B Literary Elements

BIOGRAPHY Ask students what a biography is. *(It is a true story about a person that conveys information about the subject's personality, attitudes, and surroundings.)*

C Author's Craft

IMAGERY Have students list images that help readers visualize rural Arkansas. *(Some vivid images include dirt road, blistering summer noons, and cold, wet, and wintry middays.)*

D Critical Thinking

DISTINGUISHING FACT FROM OPINION Ask students to review the difference between fact and opinion and give examples of both in this passage. *(Fact is verifiable; opinion is what a person or group believes or feels. The details about Annie are presented as fact. The last paragraph of the essay presents Angelou's opinions.)*

Thematic Focus

Facing Challenge Have students think about how they would respond to Annie's challenges.

FINE ART
TRANSPARENCY 8

Use *Fine Art Transparency 8* to enrich students' thinking.

✔ **ASSESSMENT OPTIONS**

📁 *Quick Checks,* p. 19

Teaching Options

New Directions

Did You Know?
A *brazier* (brā′ zhər) is a metal container that holds burning coals. It is used for cooking food.

The next morning she left her house carrying the meat pies, lard, an iron brazier, and coals for a fire. Just before lunch she appeared in an empty lot behind the cotton gin. As the dinner noon bell rang, she dropped the savors into boiling fat and the aroma rose and floated over to the workers who spilled out of the gin, covered with white lint, looking like specters.[3]

Most workers had brought their lunches of pinto beans and biscuits or crackers, onions and cans of sardines, but they were tempted by the hot meat pies which Annie ladled out of the fat. She wrapped them in newspapers, which soaked up the grease, and offered them for sale at a nickel each. Although business was slow, those first days Annie was determined. She balanced her appearances between the two hours of activity.

So, on Monday if she offered hot fresh pies at the cotton gin and sold the remaining cooled-down pies at the lumber mill for three cents, then on Tuesday she went first to the lumber mill presenting fresh,

---

3. A *specter* (spek′ tər) is a ghost.

---

just-cooked pies as the lumbermen covered in sawdust emerged from the mill.

For the next few years, on balmy spring days, blistering summer noons, and cold, wet, and wintry middays, Annie never disappointed her customers, who could count on seeing the tall, brown-skin woman bent over her brazier, carefully turning the meat pies. When she felt certain that the workers had become dependent on her, she built a stall between the two hives of industry and let the men run to her for their lunchtime provisions.

She had indeed stepped from the road which seemed to have been chosen for her and cut herself a brand-new path. In years that stall became a store where customers could buy cheese, meal, syrup, cookies, candy, writing tablets, pickles, canned goods, fresh fruit, soft drinks, coal, oil, and leather soles for worn-out shoes.

Each of us has the right and the responsibility to assess the roads which lie ahead, and those over which we have traveled, and if the future road looms ominous or unpromising, and the roads back uninviting, then we need to gather our resolve and, carrying only the necessary baggage, step off that road into another direction. If the new choice is also unpalatable, without embarrassment, we must be ready to change that as well.

Vocabulary

balmy (bä′ mē) *adj.* mild; soothing
assess (ə ses′) *v.* to determine the meaning or importance of; analyze
loom (lo̅o̅m) *v.* to appear to the mind as threatening
ominous (om′ ə nəs) *adj.* threatening harm or evil
unpalatable (un pal′ ə tə bəl) *adj.* not agreeable to the taste, mind, or feelings; unacceptable

222 🐾 THEME 3

Reading *Minilesson*

Problem and Solution In the story, Annie is faced with the problem of supporting her children while caring for them herself. To reach the solution, she has to take several intermediate steps.

Activity Have small groups of students review story details and record their information in a two-column chart with the

headings *Action* and *Result*. **L2**
COLLAB. LEARN.

Action	Result

Additional Resources
📁 *Reading Workbook,* pp. 31–32

Responding to Literature

PERSONAL RESPONSE

- ◆ What went through your mind as you finished reading this selection?
- ◆ Think back to the **Focus Activity** on page 220. What words would you use to describe Mrs. Annie Johnson's method of problem solving? How does your method of problem solving compare with hers? Record your responses in a journal.

The Storyteller, 1995. Christian Pierre (b. 1962). Acrylic on Masonite, 48 x 52 in. Private collection.

Analyzing Literature

RECALL

1. What is the problem facing Mrs. Annie Johnson at the beginning of the narrative?
2. According to the narrator, what were Johnson's options for employment?
3. List the steps Johnson took to start her own business.
4. What became of Annie Johnson's stall?

INTERPRET

5. What is Johnson's attitude toward her problem? Explain.
6. Explain what Johnson means by the statement "I looked up the road I was going and back the way I come, and since I wasn't satisfied, I decided to step off the road and cut me a new path."
7. What does the title of the selection mean? How does it relate to Johnson's new career? Use quotations from the selection to support your ideas.
8. How did Annie Johnson's original vision become a thriving business?

EVALUATE AND CONNECT

9. The **theme** of a piece of writing is the message the writer hopes to communicate. What is the theme of this selection? Explain.
10. **Theme Connection** Think of someone you know who faced a challenge and set out boldly in a new direction. Tell about the result of that person's action.

LITERARY ELEMENTS

Biography

A **biography** is a true story written by an author about the life of another person. The writer researches the person's life by conducting interviews and by reading letters, books, and diaries. A good biography tells more than what the subject said or did. A good biography makes its subject come alive for readers. A biography may cover a person's entire life, or it may focus on one period of time.

1. What details did you learn about Annie Johnson's life from reading this biographical essay?

2. What else would you like to learn about Annie Johnson's life?

● See **Literary Terms Handbook**, p. R2.

Responding to the Selection

Personal Response

Students might have thought about their road, or life path, as they read this selection. Students should explain how their problem-solving methods are similar to, or different from, Mrs. Annie Johnson's.

Analyzing Literature

1. Mrs. Johnson needs a job to support herself and her two young sons.
2. Mrs. Johnson's options were to work as a household servant, while leaving her sons in someone else's care, or to make the local factories work for her.
3. First, Mrs. Johnson practiced walking and carrying her two pails of stones eight miles. Next, she cooked the meat pies. Then she walked to one factory and sold hot pies. After that, she walked to the other factory and sold the remaining cooled-down pies.
4. Over time, Mrs. Johnson's stall became a store.
5. Mrs. Johnson is quite determined. She doesn't give up, even though her business is not greatly successful at first. Over time, she builds a customer base.
6. Mrs. Johnson's future didn't look promising and she didn't want to continue what she had been doing, so she decided to try something completely different.
7. The title refers to the new direction Mrs. Johnson took. She was a single mother supporting two sons. She didn't like the direction in which she was headed, so she stepped "off the road" in a new direction.
8. Mrs. Johnson's original vision was bringing meat pies to factory workers. Once she had enough steady customers, she built a stall from which to sell the pies. Over time it grew into a store.

LITERARY ELEMENTS

1. To support herself and her two sons after her husband leaves, Annie walks to and from the factories to sell meat pies. As her business improves, she builds a stall and then a store.
2. Students may want to know more about how the stall becomes a store or about the narrator's connection to Annie.

Additional Resources

 Literary Elements Transparency 19

9. One of the themes of this essay is that we should not be afraid to take risks and to try new things. Another theme is that persistence can take you far in life.
10. Answers should clearly state what the challenge was and how the person responded to it.

Extending Your Response

Writing About Literature

Students' paragraphs should

- explain how to approach and solve a problem step by step.
- include relevant examples from the selection to support ideas about how to solve a problem.

Literature Groups
Groups should create their lists of five important qualities only after all ideas have been discussed. Students may want to assign roles, such as a leader who keeps the discussion on the topic, a clarifier who makes sure everyone understands, and a recorder who writes down the main points covered. **COLLAB. LEARN.**

Creative Writing

Students' journal entries should

- present Annie's feelings, thoughts, and fears about what could happen the next day.
- be clearly written from Annie's perspective.

Art Activity
If students want to design a menu on a computer, have them use a font they like in a size that will show up well from a distance. They may want to use clip art to add visual appeal to the menu. Students may want to try several different layouts before completing a final menu.

Skill Minilesson

VOCABULARY • ANALOGIES

1. a   2. b   3. c

Additional Resources
📁 *Vocabulary Practice,* p. 13

Extending Your Response

Writing About Literature
Finding Solutions "New Directions" focuses on one woman's imaginative solution to a difficult problem. Use the story and ideas you came up with in the **Focus Activity** on page 220 to write a paragraph about how to deal with a personal problem. Use examples from "New Directions" to support your ideas.

Literature Groups
A Vision of Success An entrepreneur is someone who has a vision for a business and then succeeds in creating that business. Many entrepreneurs are people like Annie Johnson, who follow their own unique paths to success. What personal qualities do you think Johnson had that enabled her to take charge of her life and start a successful business? In a small group, brainstorm a list of five important qualities necessary for achieving personal success. Support your ideas with details from the selection.

Creative Writing
A Journal Entry Imagine that you are Mrs. Annie Johnson the night before your first day selling food to the workers. How might you feel? What might you think? Describe your thoughts and feelings in a journal entry.

Art Activity
Design a Menu Design a menu for Mrs. Annie Johnson to hang on her food stall. Make your own drawings or cut out photographs of food from old magazines. Be sure to make up a catchy name for Johnson's food business.

📂 **Save your work for your portfolio.**

Skill Minilesson

VOCABULARY • ANALOGIES

Analogies compare relationships. Analogies are usually written in this form:

    balmy : mild :: ominous : threatening

This analogy is read:

    balmy is to *mild* as *ominous* is to *threatening*.

In this example, the words in each pair are synonyms, words that are similar in meaning. Analogies can state other kinds of relationships, such as antonyms (cold : hot); cause and effect (determination : success); or part and a whole (wheel : automobile). The relationship between the second pair of words must be the same as the relationship between the first pair.

PRACTICE Decide on the relationship of the first two words. Then apply that relationship to the second set of words.

1. smile : friendly :: frown : _____
   a. hostile   b. balmy   c. frighten
2. grumble : complain :: concede : _____
   a. refuse   b. acknowledge   c. assess
3. delicious : unpalatable :: meticulous : _____
   a. tasty   b. attentive   c. careless

✔ ASSESSMENT OPTIONS

📁 *Quick Checks,* p. 19
📁 *Selection and Theme Assessment,* pp. 33–34
📁 *Performance Assessment,* p. 18
💾 *Testmaker*

Vo·cab·u·lar·y Skills

Using Homophones

Words that sound the same but have different meanings and spellings are called **homophones.** There are hundreds of homophones in the English language. A bad bird is a foul fowl. Rabbit fur might be called hare hair. A forbidden musical group is a banned band. A string that won't stay tied will not knot.

You have to be careful to write the right word. Even if you work on a computer that can check your spelling, you need to watch for homophone mistakes. If you type *brake* when you mean *break,* no computer spell-check program can fix your mistake because both *brake* and *break* are correctly spelled words.

EXERCISES

A. Read the passage below. If the underlined word is the correct one to use, write *Correct.* If it is a homophone for the correct word, write the correct word.

> When Annie Johnson's husband left her, she needed to <u>billed</u> a <u>new</u>
>   1   2
> life. She did not have a job, but she did have <u>two</u> children to take
>   3
> care of. Instead of feeling trapped by the <u>passed</u>, she moved with
>   4
> energy toward the future. With little education, she wondered if
> anyone <u>wood</u> <u>higher</u> her, so she created her own business. Every
>   5   6   7
> day, Annie <u>maid</u> food to <u>cell</u> to workers at nearby factories. The
>   8   9
> <u>scent</u> of the cooking pies guaranteed her success.
>   10

B. Complete each sentence by using two homophones. An example is provided.

Example: The bigger, better grinder could be called the *greater grater.*

1. A king's tossed chair is a _____.
2. If people take metal without paying for it, they _____.
3. If you chewed up seven grapes and then one more, you _____.
4. What the group of cows listened to is what the _____.
5. Buttons, snaps, and zippers are used to _____.

Vo·cab·u·lar·y Skills

Objective

- To recognize homophones and apply strategies for using them correctly

Teaching Strategies

After students read the explanation in their books, have them help create a list of homophones on the board. Ask students to work individually or in small groups to create definitions for each pair of homophones by following the examples given in their books. Additional homophones might include *stair/stare; boar/bore;* and *wait/weight.* Have students read their definitions aloud. Classmates can guess the answers.

Exercises

A.
1. build	6. hire
2. correct	7. correct
3. correct	8. made
4. past	9. sell
5. would	10. correct

B.
1. thrown throne	4. herd heard
2. steal steel	5. close clothes
3. ate eight	

Additional Resources
📁 ***Vocabulary Power: Weekly Lessons and Activities***

Teaching Options

MEETING INDIVIDUAL NEEDS — ENGLISH LANGUAGE LEARNERS

Pair Pictures Write the following words on the board: *tail/tale; wait/weight;* and *flower/flour.* Use each word in the pairs in a sentence. Explain to English language learners that they can tell which meaning is intended by thinking about how the word is used.

Activity Have students work in small groups to illustrate three pairs of homo-phones. Help each group choose their words, and then ask the students to illustrate them on posterboard or large sheets of paper. Post the illustrations so students can look at classmates' work.

Additional Resources
📁 *English Language Learners Sourcebook*

Objectives

- To read and analyze two poems about facing challenge
- To identify elements of narrative poetry
- To write a description of how images convey a poem's message

Skills

Reading/Thinking: Sequence of Events; Inferring; Identifying Spatial Relationships
Writing: Personal Poems; Newspaper Article
Vocabulary: Etymology
Grammar/Language: Identifying Adjectives
Listening/Speaking: Performing and Listening to Poems
Collaboration: Literature Groups

Motivating
→ OPTIONS

Literature Launchers: "Storms at Sea"

Videodisc Side A, Segment 7

Also available in VHS.

Selection Focus Transparency 20: Have students view and discuss the quote from Helen Keller.

Focus Activity: As an extension of the Focus Activity, have pairs of students share descriptions of the adventures they have had or would like to have.

Before You Read
The Wreck of the Hesperus and I'll Walk the Tightrope

MEET HENRY WADSWORTH LONGFELLOW

Henry Wadsworth Longfellow was one of the first American writers to use the traditions of European writing to create a distinctly American form of literature.

Henry Wadsworth Longfellow was born in 1807 and died in 1882.

MEET MARGARET DANNER

Margaret Danner began writing poetry in junior high school. After college, Danner became the first African American assistant editor of *Poetry* magazine. In 1960 she published her first collection of poetry. Later, Danner became poet-in-residence at Wayne State University in Detroit.

Margaret Danner was born in 1915 and died in 1984.

FOCUS ACTIVITY

Do you like to have adventures, or do you prefer to read about them?

Sharing Ideas
An adventure can be any experience or activity that is exciting for you, from traveling through a storm to learning to swim. In a small group, talk about adventures you have had or have read about. What did you learn from these adventures?

Setting a Purpose
Read to discover the adventure in each of these poems.

Shipwreck, 1833 (detail). Thomas Birch. Oil on canvas, 20 x 30 in.

BACKGROUND

In December 1839, a series of winter storms swept New England. Two shipwrecks caused by the storms became the inspiration for Longfellow's "The Wreck of the Hesperus." Longfellow commented on the poem in a diary entry dated December 30, 1839.

> ". . . I sat till twelve o'clock by my fire . . . , when suddenly it came into my mind. . . . Then I went to bed, but could not sleep. New thoughts were running in my mind, and I got up to add them to the ballad. It was three by the clock. I then went to bed and fell asleep. . . . It did not come into my mind by lines, but by stanzas."

RESOURCE MANAGER

Lesson Planning Resource
The ***Theme Three Planning Guide*** (pp. 11–15) provides additional lesson notes and reduced versions of all print resources.

📁 **Other Print Resources**
- Active Reading Guide, p. 20
- Reading Workbook, pp. 33–34
- Grammar and Language Workbook, pp. 117–119

- Grammar and Composition Handbook, Lesson 5.1
- Quick Checks, p. 20
- Selection and Theme Assessment, pp. 35–36
- Performance Assessment, p. 19
- Spanish Summaries, p. 20
- Spanish Translations
- Inclusion Strategies
- English Language Learners Sourcebook

Transparencies
- Selection Focus 20
- Literary Elements 20
- Grammar and Language 19

Technology
- Literature Launchers
- Audio Library
- Spanish Audio Library
- 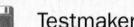 Glencoe Literature Web Site
- Testmaker

The Wreck of the Hesperus

Henry Wadsworth Longfellow

It was the schooner° Hesperus,
    That sailed the wintry sea;
And the skipper had taken his little daughter,
    To bear him company.

5   Blue were her eyes as the fairy-flax,
    Her cheeks like the dawn of day,
And her bosom white as the hawthorn buds,
    That ope° in the month of May.

The skipper he stood beside the helm,
10   His pipe was in his mouth,
And he watched how the veering flaw° did blow
    The smoke now West, now South.

Then up and spake an old Sailor,
    Had sailed to the Spanish Main,°
15 "I pray thee, put into yonder port,
    For I fear a hurricane.

"Last night, the moon had a golden ring,
    And tonight no moon we see!"
The skipper, he blew a whiff from his pipe,
20   And a scornful laugh laughed he.

---

1 A *schooner* is a ship with two or more masts. Masts are the tall, strong poles
   used to support the sails.
8 *Ope* (ōp) is an old, poetic form of *open*.
11 Here, *veering flaw* (vēr′ ing   flô) means "shifting, or changing, gusts of wind."
14 The *Spanish Main* refers to the Caribbean Sea along the coast of South
   America, where Spanish trading ships traveled in colonial times.

Reading the Selection

A Active Reading

PREDICT Ask students to predict what might happen to the skipper and his daughter on this "wintry sea." Remind them to consider the poem's title. *(There could be a winter storm that will wreck the ship.)*

B Literary Elements

NARRATIVE POETRY Narrative poetry spins a tale, using such story elements as character and setting. Ask students to identify these elements in the poem. *(The characters are the skipper, his daughter, and an old sailor. The setting is a ship at sea during a winter storm.)*

C Literary Elements

NARRATIVE POETRY: *Character* Ask students to describe the skipper's personality and use lines from this opening page to support their opinions. *(The skipper enjoys the company of his little daughter, lines 3–4. He is arrogant and overconfident; he laughs at the experienced sailor's warning, lines 13–20.)*

Additional Resources
📁 *Active Reading Guide,* p. 20
🎧 *Audio Library*
🎧 *Spanish Audio Library*
📁 *Spanish Summaries,* p. 20

Teaching Options

CONNECTING TO OTHER SELECTIONS
For a teaching strategy that connects "The Wreck of the Hesperus" to "Icarus and Daedalus," turn to page 61 in the *Theme Seven Planning Guide*.

D Literary Elements

NARRATIVE POETRY: *Setting* Remind students that a simile is a comparison of two unlike things, using the words *like* or *as*. Ask them to find the two similes on this page that describe the setting. *(They are* The billows frothed like yeast, *and* She shuddered and paused, like a frightened steed.)*

FYI

Hurricanes are actually tropical cyclones. Three or four tropical storms a year become hurricanes. They generally span a five-hundred-mile area and can last up to thirty days.

E Active Reading

VISUALIZE Ask students to visualize where the characters are in relation to one another and how they must feel. *(The daughter is tied to a mast near the father, who is steering the ship. She is fearful; he is confident.)*

F Author's Craft

NARRATIVE POETRY: *Dialogue* Ask students what they notice about the exchange between the skipper and his daughter and why the poet set it up this way. *(It consists of questions and answers that show the contrasting emotions of the characters.)*

The Wreck of the Hesperus

Colder and louder blew the wind,
　　A gale from the Northeast,
The snow fell hissing in the brine,
　　And the billows frothed like yeast.

25　Down came the storm, and smote° amain°
　　The vessel in its strength;
She shuddered and paused, like a frighted steed,
　　Then leaped her cable's length.°

"Come hither! come hither! my little daughter,
30　And do not tremble so;
For I can weather the roughest gale
　　That ever wind did blow."

He wrapped her warm in his seaman's coat
　　Against the stinging blast;
35　He cut a rope from a broken spar,°
　　And bound her to the mast.

"O father! I hear the church bells ring,
　　Oh say, what may it be?"
"'Tis a fog bell on a rock-bound coast!"—
40　And he steered for the open sea.

"O father! I hear the sound of guns,
　　Oh say, what may it be?"
"Some ship in distress, that cannot live
　　In such an angry sea!"

45　"O father! I see a gleaming light,
　　Oh say, what may it be?"
But the father answered never a word,
　　A frozen corpse was he.

---

25 The storm struck *(smote)* with full force *(amain)*.
28 In sailing, *cable's length* is a unit of measurement equal to 720 feet (219.5 meters).
35 A *spar* is any of the strong poles used to support a ship's rigging (the ropes, cables, etc., that hold and control the sails).

228 🐦 THEME 3

Teaching Options

Reading *Minilesson*

Sequence of Events Put the following general frame for sequencing on the board. Guide students in summarizing events up to this point in the narrative, and point out that the order of events is straightforward. Ask a volunteer to record the events as students provide them.

Activity After students finish reading the poem, have them complete the graphic organizer. You might wish to have them work in small groups to discuss the results. **L2 COLLAB. LEARN.**

Additional Resources
📁 *Reading Workbook,* pp. 33–34

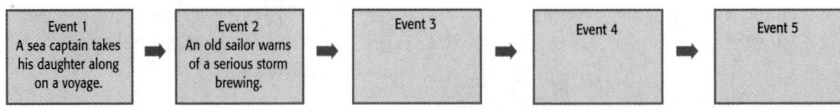

| Event 1 | Event 2 | Event 3 | Event 4 | Event 5 |
| A sea captain takes his daughter along on a voyage. | An old sailor warns of a serious storm brewing. | | | |

Northeaster, 1895. Winslow Homer. Oil on canvas. Metropolitan Museum of Art, New York.

Viewing the painting: How is the mood of the painting similar to the mood of "The Wreck of the Hesperus"?

Lashed to the helm, all stiff and stark,
50   With his face turned to the skies,
The lantern gleamed through the gleaming snow
    On his fixed and glassy eyes.

Then the maiden clasped her hands and prayed
    That saved she might be;
55   And she thought of Christ, who stilled the wave,
    On the Lake of Galilee.

And fast through the midnight dark and drear,
    Through the whistling sleet and snow,
Like a sheeted ghost, the vessel swept
60   Tow'rds the reef of Norman's Woe.

FACING CHALLENGE 229

Winslow Homer (1836–1910), an almost entirely self-taught naturalist painter, is considered one of the greatest American nineteenth-century artists. His best-known works portray the beauty of nature, its awesome power, and human struggle with its forces. This painting captures the mood of a northeaster, a potentially deadly winter storm that occurs on the eastern coast of the United States.

Viewing Response *Students may say that the mood of the painting is identical to that of the poem in its fury and power.*

G Literary Elements

ALLITERATION The repeated *st* sound in *stiff* and *stark* is an example of alliteration. Ask students to find at least two more examples of alliteration on this page. *(Other examples include* sailed to the Spanish Main *and* dark and drear.*)*

H Critical Thinking

INFERRING Ask students to infer how the little girl feels after her father dies. What does she hope? *(Alone in the storm, she's terrified and prays that the waters will be stilled.)*

Vo•cab•u•lar•y Skills

Etymology Point out the words *ghost* in line 59 and *aghast* in line 78. Both come from the Middle English word *gasten*, meaning "to frighten."

Learning Disabled Hearing a poem read aloud helps learning-disabled students gain a better understanding of it.

Activity Have students take turns reading one of the poem's 22 stanzas. Tell them to relax and picture the story unfolding in their mind's eye like a movie. Remind readers to pause only where they see punctuation, not at the end of every line, and to express the appropriate emotions in their voices. **L2**

Additional Resources
📁 *Inclusion Strategies*

I Literary Elements

PERSONIFICATION Longfellow personifies the rocks by calling them "cruel," giving them human qualities. Challenge students to find another example of personification on this page. *(Another example of personification is the repeated use of the word* she *when referring to the ship.)*

J Active Reading

QUESTION Encourage students to ask questions about the events of the poem and the characters' reactions to them. You may wish to share the following model to illustrate the thinking process involved in formulating questions.

Model: I know that the storm is terrible and the father is dead. How does the ship look as it sinks? What scene does the sun reveal as it rises? How must the fisherman feel when he sees the dead girl still lashed to the mast? How would I feel in his place?

K Literary Elements

NARRATIVE POETRY: *Plot* Ask students to review the key moments in the story. *(The exposition includes the introduction of the skipper, the daughter, and the setting. The rising action includes the sailor's warning, the storm's onset, and the father's death. The climax is the daughter's confrontation with death. The falling action is the wreck of the ship, and the resolution is the fisherman's discovery of the girl's body.)*

Teaching Options

And ever the fitful gusts between
    A sound came from the land;
It was the sound of the trampling surf
    On the rocks and the hard sea sand.

65 The breakers were right beneath her bows,
    She drifted a dreary wreck,
And a whooping billow swept the crew
    Like icicles from her deck.

    She struck where the white and fleecy waves
70   Looked soft as carded wool,°
But the cruel rocks, they gored her side
    Like the horns of an angry bull.

Her rattling shrouds,° all sheathed° in ice,
    With the masts went by the board;°
75 Like a vessel of glass, she stove° and sank,
    Ho! ho! the breakers roared!

At daybreak, on the bleak sea beach,
    A fisherman stood aghast,°
To see the form of a maiden fair,
80   Lashed close to a drifting mast.

The salt sea was frozen on her breast,
    The salt tears in her eyes;
And he saw her hair, like the brown seaweed,
    On the billows fall and rise.

85 Such was the wreck of the Hesperus,
    In the midnight and the snow!
Christ save us all from a death like this,
    On the reef of Norman's Woe!

---

70 *Carded wool* has been cleaned and combed to prepare it for spinning.

73–75 The ropes that support the masts *(shrouds)* were encased *(sheathed)* in heavy ice. After the shrouds and masts were torn away *(went by the board)*, the ship itself was smashed *(stove)* on the rocks.

78 Being *aghast* (ə gast′) means to be filled with horror and amazement.

230 🐚 THEME 3

Grammar and Language *Minilesson*

Identifying Adjectives Write the following phrases on the board: *fitful gusts, trampling surf,* and *hard sea sand.* Remind students that an adjective describes a person, place, thing, or idea. It provides information about the size, shape, color, texture, feeling, sound, smell, number, or condition of a noun or pronoun. Point to the first phrase and ask *What kind of* *gusts?* Invite volunteers to suggest other adjectives from this poem.

Activity On the board, list the sentences below. Have students identify the adjective in each one, as underlined here.
1. She drifted a <u>dreary</u> wreck.
2. A <u>forceful</u> billow swept the crew.
3. The waves looked soft as <u>fleecy</u> wool.
L2 **COLLAB. LEARN.**

Additional Resources

📋 ***Grammar and Language Transparency 19***

📕 ***Grammar and Language Workbook,*** pp. 117–119

📕 ***Grammar and Composition Handbook,*** Lesson 5.1

📕 ***Writer's Choice,*** Lesson 12.1

230

I'll Walk the Tightrope

Fatima, 1994. Elizabeth Barakah Hodges. Acrylic, 23 x 18 in.

Margaret Danner ∾

I'll walk the tightrope that's been stretched for me,
and though a wrinkled forehead, perplexed why,
will accompany me, I'll delicately
step along. For if I stop to sigh
at the earth-propped stride
of others, I will fall. I must balance high
without a parasol° to tide°
a faltering step, without a net below,
without a balance stick to guide.

Historical Note

The oldest wire walker on record was William Ivy Baldwin, who walked 320 feet across South Boulder Canyon, Colorado, on his 82nd birthday in 1948.

L Active Reading

PREDICT Ask students to predict what the tightrope might represent. *(Some students might predict that the tightrope represents life.)*

M Active Reading

CONNECT Help students draw parallels between the speaker and themselves or people they know.

N Literary Elements

RHYME This poem employs several different kinds of rhyme, including end rhyme and internal rhyme. Ask students to find examples of each. *(end rhyme:* me *and* delicately; why, sigh, *and* high; stride, tide, *and* guide: internal rhyme:* stop *and* propped; fall *and* parasol)

Thematic Focus

Facing Challenge Have students think about the girl in "The Wreck of the *Hesperus*" and the speaker in "I'll Walk the Tightrope." How do their challenges and their responses to them differ?

☑ ASSESSMENT OPTIONS

🗀 *Quick Checks,* p. 20

Writing *Minilesson*

Personal Poems Personal poetry can be about something as simple as a trip to the grocery store or as complicated as a conversation that makes one see a close friend or family member in a whole new light. Sometimes people write poems to figure out how they feel about something.

Activity Have each student write a short poem about a personal event. To help them get started, suggest a few possible titles:

- The Girl Who Talked to Cats
- Why Isn't Chocolate a Vegetable?
- Earth to Mom—Where Are You? **L2**

Additional Resources

📕 *Writer's Choice,* Lesson 1.1

CONNECTING TO OTHER SELECTIONS
For a teaching strategy that connects "I'll Walk the Tightrope" with "Antacus," turn to page 25 in the *Theme Four Planning Guide*.

Responding to the Selection

Personal Response

Students may find any of several images in *"Hesperus"* most striking: perhaps when the skipper wraps his daughter in his coat and ties her to the mast, or when he dies, or when the sun rises on the sight of her body. From "Tightrope," they'll likely choose the image of the tightrope walker high above the ground.

Analyzing Literature

1. The ship sank and both the skipper and his daughter died.
2. She says she'll walk the tightrope without any help and without envying other people's easier paths.
3. The central conflict is humans versus nature. It's resolved when nature wins: the storm kills both the captain and the girl and wrecks their ship.
4. The central metaphor is the speaker as high-wire walker. The tightrope represents the challenges she must face in her life.
5. The skipper feels superior to nature ("I can weather the roughest gale."). The old sailor respects nature's power.
6. Many students will say the skipper is selfish to risk his daughter's life. Some may say it's nice they are so close, and it isn't his fault that the storm came up.
7. She'll do whatever it takes to meet life's challenges. Some students will agree with her high-achieving attitude. Others may think that people like her burn out early and don't have enough fun along the way.
8. She's trying hard and is troubled by demands from all sides. The main contrasting image is "the earth-propped stride of others." Not only must she walk on the tightrope instead of the ground, but she must do it without help or protection—no parasol, net, or balance stick.

9. Some may say they like the story or adventure or third-person point of view of *"Hesperus."* Others may prefer the personal tone, emotional subject, and first-person point of view of *"Tightrope."*
10. *"Hesperus"* is about the challenge of facing a physical danger. *"Tightrope"* is about the challenge of balancing all the many demands of one's life.

Responding to Literature

PERSONAL RESPONSE

Which image from each poem did you find the most dramatic or striking? Why?

Analyzing Literature

RECALL AND INTERPRET

1. According to the speaker of "The Wreck of the Hesperus," what happened to the ship, the skipper, and the skipper's young daughter?
2. Summarize what the speaker tells you in "I'll Walk the Tightrope."
3. What is the central **conflict** in the plot of "The Wreck of the Hesperus"? How is the conflict resolved?
4. What is the central **metaphor** in the poem "I'll Walk the Tightrope"? What do you think the tightrope represents?

EVALUATE AND CONNECT

5. What attitude toward nature does the skipper express in "The Wreck of the Hesperus"? How does his attitude contrast with that of the old sailor? Explain.
6. Describe the relationship between the skipper and his daughter in "The Wreck of the Hesperus." Do you think the skipper should have taken his daughter on the voyage? Explain.
7. In "I'll Walk the Tightrope," what is the speaker's attitude about facing the challenges of life? Do you agree with that point of view? Explain.
8. How do you think the speaker in "I'll Walk the Tightrope" sees herself? What images are used to compare or contrast the speaker with other people?
9. Which poem do you prefer? Why?
10. Theme Connection How is each of these poems related to the theme of facing challenges? Explain.

First Rate Man of War Foundering in a Gale, late 19th century. George Philip Reinagle. Oil on canvas. Royal Albert Memorial Museum, Exeter, England.

LITERARY ELEMENTS

Narrative Poetry

Narrative poetry is poetry that tells a story. "The Wreck of the Hesperus" is an example of a narrative poem. Like a short story or a novel, a narrative poem usually includes a setting, some characters, and a plot. The events in a narrative poem are often told in chronological order, the order in which they happen. In a narrative poem, the theme unfolds as the story is told.

1. Describe the setting, the plot, and the main characters of "The Wreck of the Hesperus."
2. Find another example of a narrative poem in this book or in another book. Tell why the poem is an example of narrative poetry.

● See **Literary Terms Handbook**, p. R7.

LITERARY ELEMENTS

1. The setting is the coast of New England on a cold winter night; the plot is the tale of a shipwreck; and the characters include the ship's skipper, his daughter, his crew, an old sailor, and a fisherman.
2. The poems in Theme 6 are examples of narrative poetry.

Additional Resources

Literary Elements Transparency 20

Extending Your Response

Writing About Literature

Looking at Imagery   Both poems contain strong images that help readers "see" what is happening in the poems and understand the themes of the poems. Pick out an image from each poem. Then, describe how each image helps you understand the poem's message.

Creative Writing

News Flash   Turn the plot of "The Wreck of the Hesperus" into a newspaper article. Add any details you need, including eyewitness interviews with other sailors and weather reports about the storm.

Literature Groups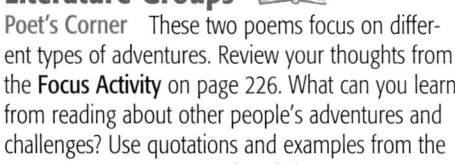

Poet's Corner   These two poems focus on different types of adventures. Review your thoughts from the **Focus Activity** on page 226. What can you learn from reading about other people's adventures and challenges? Use quotations and examples from the poems to support your point of view.

Listening and Speaking

The Drama of Poetry   Poetry should be read aloud to be fully appreciated. As a poem is read, listeners may close their eyes, picture the images, and hear the natural rhythm of the lines. With a partner or in a small group, choose one of the poems to read aloud. Perform your reading for the class.

Reading Further

If you would like to read more by these poets, try these books:

Selected Poems by Henry Wadsworth Longfellow, edited by Laurance Buell (many other editions available)

To Flower: Poems by Margaret Danner

📖 **Save your work for your portfolio.**

Skill Minilesson

READING AND THINKING • IDENTIFYING SPATIAL RELATIONSHIPS

One way to organize details is to use **spatial order**—that is, showing where things are located. When you read a poem, try to visualize where things are in relation to other things. For example, in the first scene of "The Wreck of the Hesperus," the skipper is standing by the helm. As you read, ask:
• What does this scene or image look like?
• Where is each thing in relation to the other things in the scene?

PRACTICE   Reread each of the poems. As you do, try to think about the spatial order in the different scenes and images in each poem. For each poem, make a simple diagram (with labels) to illustrate one important scene or image. Show where each thing is in relation to the other things mentioned.

● For more about spatial order, see **Reading Handbook,** p. R87.

Extending Your Response

Writing About Literature

Students' descriptions should
• describe the image clearly.
• explain the image's relation to the poem's meaning.

Creative Writing

Students' articles should
• explain the most important facts first.
• include direct quotes from eyewitnesses and family members.
• describe the extent of the storm's damage.

Literature Groups   Point out to students that both external, life-threatening events and internal thoughts can be adventures.
COLLAB. LEARN.

Listening and Speaking

Encourage students to spend time rehearsing their poetry readings. If possible, videotape readers' performances and make the tapes available to the class. 📦

Skill Minilesson

READING AND THINKING
• **IDENTIFYING SPATIAL RELATIONSHIPS**
Students' diagrams should
• include the level of detail needed for clarity (more for "*Hesperus*").
• estimate the sizes and distances of things in the poems.

Additional Resources
📁 *Reading Workbook,* pp. 33–34

✔ ASSESSMENT OPTIONS

📁 *Quick Checks,* p. 20
📁 *Selection and Theme Assessment,* pp. 35–36
📁 *Performance Assessment,* p. 19
💾 *Testmaker*

Before Reading

Objectives

- To read and analyze a short story about the challenges of a pioneer family
- To understand dialect and recognize how dialect reflects periods and cultures
- To write a paragraph that analyzes the story's surprise ending

Skills

Reading/Thinking: Inferring; Cause and Effect; Drawing Conclusions
Writing: Introduction
Vocabulary: Homophones; Antonyms
Grammar/Language: Punctuating Dialogue
Collaboration: Literature Groups

Motivating
→OPTIONS

Selection Focus Transparency 21: Have students discuss the quote by Depression-era photographer Dorothea Lange.

Focus Activity: As an extension of the Focus Activity, have small groups of students discuss what they would need to bring with them if they were starting a new life in a different location.

Before You Read
Too Soon a Woman

MEET
DOROTHY M.
JOHNSON

Dorothy M. Johnson was born in Iowa, but her experiences at the University of Montana inspired a lifelong love of the scenery and history of the American West. An honorary member of the Blackfoot Tribe, Johnson wrote vividly about Native Americans and cowboys, sheriffs and outlaws. Three of her short stories—"The Hanging Tree," "The Man Who Shot Liberty Valance," and "A Man Called Horse"—were made into classic Western movies.

Dorothy M. Johnson was born in 1905 and died in 1984.

234 🐿 THEME 3

FOCUS ACTIVITY

What traits do you think pioneers needed to survive?

Think/Pair/Share
With a partner, list survival characteristics for a pioneer family traveling west 150 years ago.

Setting a Purpose
Read this story to discover what one family learns about survival.

BACKGROUND

The Time and Place This story takes place sometime in the 1800s, on the way west across the American prairie.

Did You Know?
Pioneers traveled west on overland routes such as the Oregon Trail. Pioneer wagon trains began traveling the Oregon Trail in the 1840s. The difficult trip lasted four to six months.

VOCABULARY PREVIEW

skimpy (skim′ pē) *adj.* lacking in quantity, fullness, or size; barely enough or not quite enough; p. 236
grudging (gruj′ ing) *adj.* given or allowed unwillingly or resentfully; p. 236
gaunt (gônt) *adj.* looking like skin and bones; p. 237
grim (grim) *adj.* fierce; severe; stern; forbidding; p. 237
endure (en door′) *v.* to put up with; undergo, as pain, stress, or other hardship; p. 238
savor (sā′ vər) *v.* to take great delight in; p. 239
gruffly (gruf′ lē) *adv.* in a rough, stern manner; p. 239
sedately (si dāt′ lē) *adv.* in a quiet, restrained style or manner; calmly; p. 239

RESOURCE MANAGER

Lesson Planning Resource
The *Theme Three Planning Guide* (pp. 17–24) provides additional lesson notes and reduced versions of all print resources.

📁 **Other Print Resources**
- Active Reading Guide, p. 21
- Vocabulary Practice, p. 14
- Reading Workbook, pp. 35–36
- Grammar and Language Workbook, pp. 267–270

- Grammar and Composition Handbook, Lesson 13.6
- Quick Checks, p. 21
- Selection and Theme Assessment, pp. 37–38
- Performance Assessment, p. 20
- Spanish Summaries, p. 21
- Spanish Translations
- Inclusion Strategies
- English Language Learners Sourcebook

 Transparencies
- Selection Focus 21
- Fine Art 21
- Literary Elements 21
- Grammar and Language 20

Technology
🎧 Audio Library
🎧 Spanish Audio Library
💻 Glencoe Literature Web Site
💾 Testmaker

234 🐿 THEME 3

Too Soon a Woman

Dorothy M. Johnson ⁓

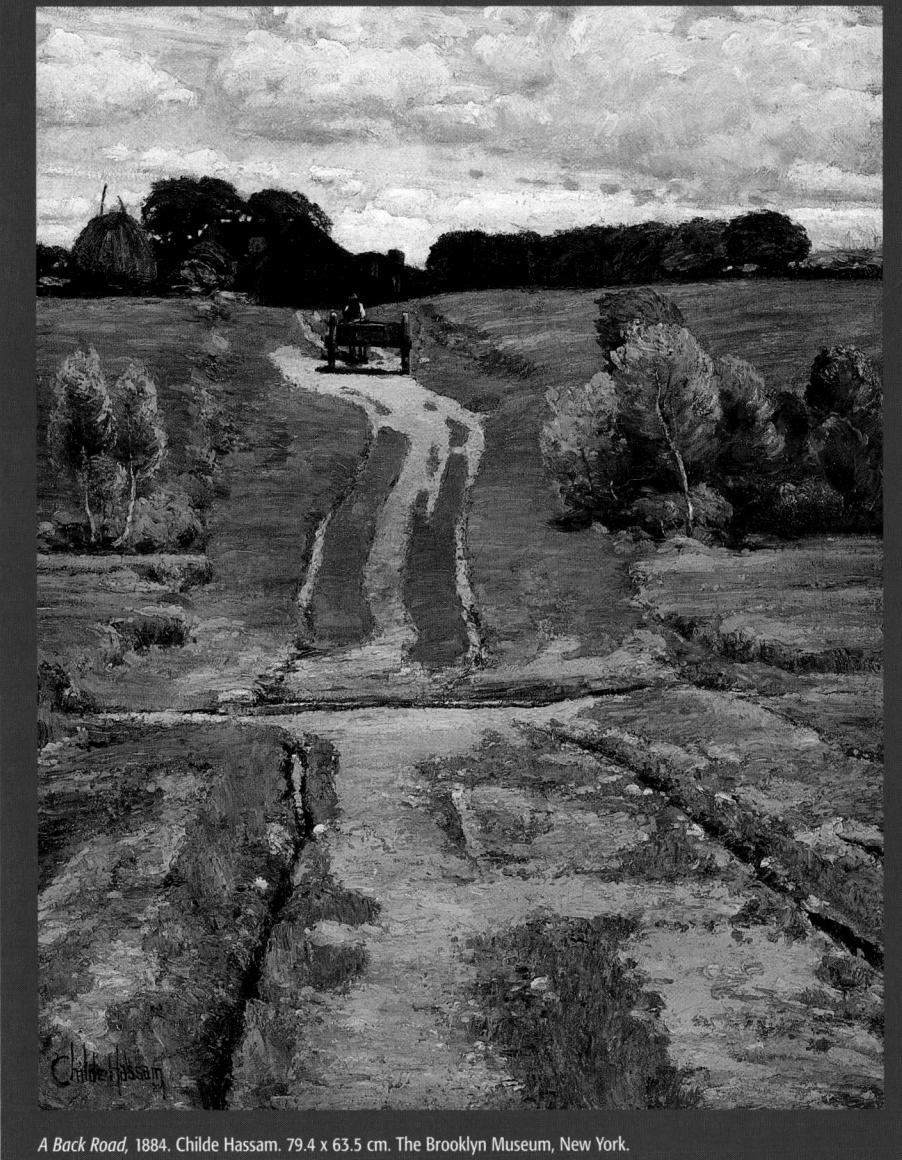

A Back Road, 1884. Childe Hassam. 79.4 x 63.5 cm. The Brooklyn Museum, New York.

SUMMARY

In this short story, an eleven-year-old boy, his younger sisters, and their father head west in the 1800s. The family meets an eighteen-year-old woman whom the father grudgingly allows to travel with them. Eventually the father must leave his family to find food. While he is gone the food runs out, but the young woman finds a giant mushroom. Not sure whether it is poisonous, she eats a portion herself. When she doesn't get sick, she feeds the rest of it to the children.

📁 *Spanish Summaries,* p. 21

A Active Reading

PREDICT Ask students to consider the painting by Childe Hassam and the title of the story to predict what the subject of the story might be. *(Students might suggest that the story will be about a young woman who must act like an adult while on a difficult journey through the wilderness.)*

Additional Resources
📁 *Active Reading Guide,* p. 21

🎧 *Audio Library*

🎧 *Spanish Audio Library*

Teaching Options

CONNECTING TO OTHER SELECTIONS

COMPARING *selections*

This selection is paired with "A Boy and His Dog" on page 243. A lesson for teaching a comparison of the two selections appears on page 249.

The chart at the right shows three ways to connect "Too Soon a Woman" to other selections in this book.

For specific teaching strategies, see the *Theme Three Planning Guide,* pages 20–21.

Connection	Title
Life Skills: Problem Solving →	"Rosa Parks: My Story," p. 85
Thematic: Growing Up →	"Old Age Sticks," p. 205
Literary: Dialogue →	"Broken Chain," p. 44

B Author's Craft

SETTING Ask students what phrases the author uses to describe the setting. *(She uses such phrases as old farm wagon, skimpy load, one weary horse, and two-bit sawmill to tell us that times are hard.)*

C Literary Elements

DIALECT Call students' attention to the use of dialect in the selection. Encourage students to locate an example and restate it in modern English. *("We're prid'near out of grub," becomes "We're almost out of food." "We're clean out of money" becomes "We have no money at all.")*

Historical Note

To encourage westward expansion, the U.S. Congress passed the Homestead Act in 1862. It gave citizens, applicants for citizenship, or veterans who were twenty one years old or heads of households up to 160 acres of public land if they paid $10, put a dwelling on it, grew crops on it, and lived on it for five years.

D Literary Elements

CHARACTER Encourage students to describe the father, using what they know so far. *(He's caring and capable, but also scared and desperate.)*

Teaching Options

Too Soon a Woman

We left the home place behind, mile by slow mile, heading for the mountains, across the prairie where the wind blew forever.

At first there were four of us with the one-horse wagon and its skimpy load. Pa and I walked, because I was a big boy of eleven. My two little sisters romped and trotted until they got tired and had to be boosted up into the wagon bed.

That was no covered Conestoga, like Pa's folks came west in, but just an old farm wagon, drawn by one weary horse, creaking and rumbling westward to the mountains, toward the little woods town where Pa thought he had an old uncle who owned a little two-bit sawmill.

Did You Know?
A *Conestoga* (kon′ is tō′gə) is a covered wagon with a canvas top and large wheels.

Two weeks we had been moving when we picked up Mary, who had run away from somewhere that she wouldn't tell. Pa didn't want her along, but she stood up to him with no fear in her voice.

"I'd rather go with a family and look after the kids," she said, "but I ain't going back. If you won't take me, I'll travel with any wagon that will."

Pa scowled at her, and her wide blue eyes stared back.

"How old are you?" he demanded.

"Eighteen," she said. "There's teamsters[1] come this way sometimes. I'd rather go with you folks. But I won't go back."

"We're prid'near out of grub," my father told her. "We're clean out of money. I got all I can handle without taking anybody else." He turned away as if he hated the sight of her. "You'll have to walk," he said.

So she went along with us and looked after the little girls, but Pa wouldn't talk to her.

On the prairie, the wind blew. But in the mountains, there was rain. When we stopped at little timber claims along the way, the homesteaders said it had rained all summer. Crops among the blackened stumps were rotted and spoiled. There was no cheer anywhere and little hospitality. The people we talked to were past worrying. They were scared and desperate.

So was Pa. He traveled twice as far each day as the wagon. He ranged through the woods with his rifle, but he never saw game. He had been depending on venison, but we never got any except as a grudging gift from the homesteaders.

He brought in a porcupine once; that was fat meat and good. Mary roasted it in chunks over the fire, half crying with the smoke. Pa and I rigged up the tarp sheet for a shelter to keep the rain from putting the fire clean out.

---

1. *Teamsters* are people who drive teams of horses or oxen.

Vocabulary
skimpy (skim′ pē) *adj.* lacking in quantity, fullness, or size; barely enough or not quite enough
grudging (gruj′ ing) *adj.* given or allowed unwillingly or resentfully

236 ❦ THEME 3

MEETING INDIVIDUAL NEEDS ENGLISH LANGUAGE LEARNERS

Past Perfect Verbs Write on the board: *We picked up Mary. Mary had run away.* Have English language learners tell you which event happened first. Explain that, though both events happened in the past, the helping word *had* in the past perfect tense shows that one happened further in the past than the other.

Activity Ask students which event came first in these sentences:

1. *We had been moving.* We picked up Mary.
2. We cooked mushroom slices. *Mary had saved the porcupine fat.*
3. I searched for hours. *The horse had run away.*

Additional Resources
📁 *English Language Learners Sourcebook*

E

The porcupine was long gone, except for some of the tried-out[2] fat that Mary had saved, when we came to an old, empty cabin. Pa said we'd have to stop. The horse was wore out, couldn't pull anymore up those grades on the deep-rutted roads in the mountains.

At the cabin, at least there was shelter. We had a few potatoes left and some corn meal. There was a creek that probably had fish in it, if a person could catch them. Pa tried it for half a day before he gave up. To this day I don't care for fishing. I remember my father's sunken eyes in his gaunt, grim face.

He took Mary and me outside the cabin to talk. Rain dripped on us from branches overhead.

F

"I think I know where we are," he said. "I calculate to get to old John's and back in about four days. There'll be grub in the town, and they'll let me have some whether old John's still there or not."

He looked at me. "You do like she tells you," he warned. It was the first time he had admitted Mary was on earth since we picked her up two weeks before.

"You're my pardner," he said to me, "but it might be she's got more brains. You mind what she says."

He burst out with bitterness, "There ain't anything good left in the world, or people to care if you live or die. But I'll get grub in the town and come back with it."

2. Here, *tried-out* refers to the melted fat from the roasted porcupine.

He took a deep breath and added, "If you get too all-fired hungry, butcher the horse. It'll be better than starvin'."

He kissed the little girls good-bye and plodded off through the woods with one blanket and the rifle.

The cabin was moldy and had no floor. We kept a fire going under a hole in the roof, so it was full of blinding smoke, but we had to keep the fire so as to dry out the wood.

The third night, we lost the horse. A bear scared him. We heard the racket, and Mary and I ran out, but we couldn't see anything in the pitch dark.

In gray daylight I went looking for him, and I must have walked fifteen miles. It seemed like I had to have that horse at the cabin when Pa came or he'd whip me. I got plumb lost two or three times and thought maybe I was going to die there alone and nobody would ever know it, but I found the way back to the clearing.

That was the fourth day, and Pa didn't come. That was the day we ate up the last of the grub.

The fifth day, Mary went looking for the horse. My sisters whimpered, huddled in a quilt by the fire, because they were scared and hungry.

I never did get dried out, always having to bring in more damp wood and going out to yell to see if Mary would hear me and not get lost. But I couldn't cry like the little girls did, because I was a big boy, eleven years old.

G

It was near dark when there was an answer to my yelling, and Mary came into the clearing.

Vocabulary
gaunt (gônt) *adj.* looking like skin and bones
grim (grim) *adj.* fierce; severe; stern; forbidding

E **Critical Thinking**

INFERRING Point out to students that besides cooking with it, pioneers often used animal fat for waterproofing, making candles, and making soap. Have students infer which of these uses other than cooking would have been most important to these travelers. *(The travelers were most in need of protection from the rain; therefore, using the fat as waterproofing would have been most important to them.)*

Vo•cab•u•lar•y Skills

Homophones Ask students what definition they think of first for the word *pitch*. *(Some will say throwing a baseball or a sales talk.)* Direct their attention to the phrase *pitch dark* on this page. Have them define the word *pitch* as it is used here. *(Pitch is a dark substance made from the distillation of coal; it can also be a dark pine resin.)*

F **Literary Elements**

DIALECT Continue developing the concept of dialect. (A detailed discussion is located on page 240.) Encourage students to think about the reasons the author used it in this story. *(It adds local color and atmosphere.)*

G **Critical Thinking**

INFERRING Ask students how the boy feels when his calls to Mary go unanswered, and then when Mary returns. *(He is afraid that he and his sisters are alone. He must feel great relief when Mary returns.)*

Reading *Minilesson*

Cause and Effect Story plots are most often a series of cause-and-effect connections. In this story, these connections lead to a surprising conclusion. Discuss what happens first in the story, and the effects of that action.

Activity Have students work in small groups to complete the diagram. Sample answers are in italics. **L2** **COLLAB. LEARN.**

Additional Resources
📁 ***Reading Workbook,*** pp. 35–36

Cause	Effect	Effect	Surprising Conclusion:
A family sets out to find a new home.	*The family meets Mary.*		*Mary becomes the children's stepmother.*

H ◼ Literary Elements

PLOT: *Conflict* Have students describe Mary's problem and how she feels about it. (*She doesn't know whether this mushroom is poisonous, but the children need food. She could either save them or hurt them with the mushroom. She needs time to find out whether it's poisonous.*)

I ◼ Literary Elements

DIALECT Remind students that they can sometimes figure out the meaning of dialect by substituting more familiar phrases, then checking them for sense. (*For example: It hefts ten pounds means "It weighs ten pounds"; I don't set up to know all about everything means "I don't pretend to know all about everything."*)

J 📖 Active Reading

EVALUATE Why does the narrator use the word *cruel* here, when readers already know that Mary is testing the mushroom. (*It reflects how the children feel about Mary's keeping the food from them. They don't know that she is protecting them.*)

K ◼ Critical Thinking

DRAWING CONCLUSIONS Have students explain what Mary means when she says, "By tomorrow morning, I guess you can tell whether you want any." (*By tomorrow morning, it should be clear whether the mushroom is poisonous or safe to eat.*)

Mary didn't have the horse—we never saw hide nor hair of that old horse again—but she was carrying something big and white that looked like a pumpkin with no color to it.

She didn't say anything, just looked around and saw Pa wasn't there yet, at the end of the fifth day.

"What's that thing?" my sister Elizabeth demanded.

"Mushroom," Mary answered. "I bet it hefts ten pounds."

"What are you going to do with it now?" I sneered. "Play football here?"

"Eat it—maybe," she said, putting it in a corner. Her wet hair hung over her shoulders. She huddled by the fire.

My sister Sarah began to whimper again. "I'm hungry!" she kept saying.

"Mushrooms ain't good eating," I said. "They can kill you."

"Maybe," Mary answered. "Maybe they can. I don't set up to know all about everything, like some people."

"What's that mark on your shoulder?" I asked her. "You tore your dress on the brush."

"What do you think it is?" she said, her head bowed in the smoke.

"Looks like scars," I guessed.

"'Tis scars. They whipped me. Now mind your own business. I want to think."

Elizabeth whimpered, "Why don't Pa come back?"

"He's coming," Mary promised. "Can't come in the dark. Your pa'll take care of you soon's he can."

She got up and rummaged around in the grub box.

"Nothing there but empty dishes," I growled. "If there was anything, we'd know it."

Mary stood up. She was holding the can with the porcupine grease.

"I'm going to have something to eat," she said coolly. "You kids can't have any yet. And I don't want any squalling,[3] mind."

It was a cruel thing, what she did then. She sliced that big, solid mushroom and heated grease in a pan.

The smell of it brought the little girls out of their quilt, but she told them to go back in so fierce a voice that they obeyed. They cried to break your heart.

I didn't cry. I watched, hating her.

I endured the smell of the mushroom frying as long as I could. Then I said, "Give me some."

"Tomorrow," Mary answered. "Tomorrow, maybe. But not tonight." She turned to me with a sharp command: "Don't bother me! Just leave me be."

She knelt there by the fire and finished frying the slice of mushroom.

If I'd had Pa's rifle, I'd have been willing to kill her right then and there.

She didn't eat right away. She looked at the brown, fried slice for a while and said, "By tomorrow morning, I guess you can tell whether you want any."

---

3. *Squalling* is the screaming cries of complaint Mary expects from the hungry little girls.

Vocabulary
endure (en door′) *v.* to put up with; undergo, as pain, stress, or other hardship

Teaching Options

Grammar and Language *Minilesson*

Punctuating Dialogue Review with students some basic rules to follow when punctuating dialogue:

- Quotation marks enclose the exact words a speaker says.
- Commas separate a phrase, such as *he said,* from the speaker's actual words.
- Periods go inside quotation marks.
- Question marks go inside quotation marks if the dialogue is a question.

Activity Have students punctuate the following quotations from page 238 without referring to the story.

1. What's that thing my sister Elizabeth demanded

2. Elizabeth whimpered Why don't Pa come back

3. Mushroom Mary answered I bet it hefts ten pounds. **L2** **COLLAB. LEARN.**

Additional Resources

✍ ***Grammar and Language Transparency 20***

📖 ***Grammar and Language Workbook,*** pp. 267–270

📖 ***Grammar and Composition Handbook,*** Lesson 13.6

📖 ***Writer's Choice,*** Lesson 20.6

Dorothy M. Johnson :~

The little girls stared at her as she ate. Sarah was chewing an old leather glove.

When Mary crawled into the quilts with them, they moved away as far as they could get.

I was so scared that my stomach heaved, empty as it was.

Mary didn't stay in the quilts long. She took a drink out of the water bucket and sat down by the fire and looked through the smoke at me.

She said in a low voice, "I don't know how it will be if it's poison. Just do the best you can with the girls. Because your pa will come back, you know. . . . You better go to bed, I'm going to sit up."

And so would you sit up. If it might be your last night on earth and the pain of death might seize you at any moment, you would sit up by the smoky fire, wide-awake, remembering whatever you had to remember, <u>savoring</u> life.

We sat in silence after the girls had gone to sleep. Once I asked, "How long does it take?"

"I never heard," she answered. "Don't think about it."

I slept after a while, with my chin on my chest. Maybe Peter dozed that way at Gethsemane[4] as the Lord knelt praying.

Mary's moving around brought me wide-awake. The black of night was fading.

"I guess it's all right," Mary said. "I'd be able to tell by now, wouldn't I?"

I answered <u>gruffly</u>, "I don't know."

Mary stood in the doorway for a while, looking out at the dripping world as if she found it beautiful. Then she fried slices of the mushroom while the little girls danced with anxiety.

We feasted, we three, my sisters and I, until Mary ruled, "That'll hold you," and would not cook any more. She didn't touch any of the mushroom herself.

That was a strange day in the moldy cabin. Mary laughed and was gay; she told stories, and we played "Who's Got the Thimble?" with a pine cone.

In the afternoon we heard a shout, and my sisters screamed, and I ran ahead of them across the clearing.

The rain had stopped. My father came plunging out of the woods leading a packhorse—and well I remember the treasures of food in that pack.

He glanced at us anxiously as he tore at the ropes that bound the pack.

"Where's the other one?" he demanded.

Mary came out of the cabin then, walking <u>sedately</u>. As she came toward us, the sun began to shine.

My stepmother was a wonderful woman.

❖

---

4. The New Testament of the Christian Bible says that Jesus, knowing his death was near, went to the Garden of *Gethsemane* (geth sem′ə nē) to pray. Although *Peter* and other disciples had come to pray with him, they all fell asleep.

Vocabulary
savor (sā′ vər) *v.* to take great delight in
gruffly (gruf′ lē) *adv.* in a rough, stern manner
sedately (si dāt′ lē) *adv.* in a quiet, restrained style or manner; calmly

FACING CHALLENGE 🐾 239

L Active Reading

EVALUATE Ask students to explain why they think the narrator is so frightened. *(He knows the mushroom Mary ate could be poisonous.)*

M Literary Elements

CHARACTER Ask students why they think Mary would risk her life for people she hardly knows. *(They are the only family Mary has. They've treated her better than she has been treated.)*

N Critical Thinking

DRAWING CONCLUSIONS The father is gruff with Mary. Yet he puts her in charge of the family. What does this say about his true feelings?

Model: The father acts tough, but he must value her, or he wouldn't trust his children to her or ask where she is when he returns.

O Active Reading

REVIEW Have students describe the surprise ending in their own words. *(Pa eventually marries Mary, so she becomes the narrator's stepmother.*

Thematic Focus

Facing Challenge Have students discuss how the characters's challenge changes them and what prompts the change.

FINE ART
TRANSPARENCY 21

Fine Art Transparency 21 may help students pull their thoughts together on why the family now thinks highly of Mary.

REAL-WORLD CONNECTION

Poisonous Mushrooms Explain to students that, even today, people must be very careful when choosing wild mushrooms to eat. Students might better understand Mary's sacrifice if they do some research on poisonous mushrooms.

Activity Have students use the library or the Internet to research mushrooms. Ask them to gather information concerning how many types of poisonous mushrooms there are, what some of their names are, what they look like, and where they grow. Students can share their results with the class. To extend this activity, ask students to choose one type of poisonous mushroom to use as the subject of a thorough report. **L2**

COLLAB. LEARN.

ASSESSMENT OPTIONS

 Quick Checks, p. 21

Responding to the Selection

Personal Response

Students' drawings should represent the anticipation of the scene—the girls dancing "with anxiety" while Mary fries the mushroom strips.

Analyzing Literature

1. The original group was a father, his eleven-year-old son, and his two little girls.
2. The most pressing problem is getting food to eat.
3. Mary finds a large, white mushroom.
4. After the story ends, Mary becomes the narrator's stepmother.
5. The mother must be dead because she isn't traveling with the family, and the father marries Mary.
6. Crops have failed, so local homesteaders have already killed most of the game.
7. Mary makes the children wait to eat until she sees whether the mushroom makes her sick. Mary's actions reveal that she is willing to take great risks to save the children.
8. The last line of the story makes readers realize that good times lie ahead. Even though events seemed hopeless in the beginning, if these events hadn't occurred, the family would not have met Mary.
9. Mary is only eighteen, but she takes responsibility and risks her life for the children. This is a very adult course of action—one that a teenager shouldn't have to take.
10. Students might crave the excitement of the pioneer journey. Students might respond that technology has made today's challenges different, but no less challenging.

Responding to Literature

PERSONAL RESPONSE

Draw a picture that shows your interpretation of the situation in the cabin before the children eat the mushroom.

Analyzing Literature

RECALL

1. Who were the members of the original group who left the "home place"?
2. What is the most pressing problem the family and Mary have to solve?
3. What does Mary finally find to feed the children?
4. What do you find out about Mary at the very end of the story?

INTERPRET

5. What can you infer about the mother of the family?
6. In your opinion, why does Pa have such a hard time providing food for the family?
7. Why does Mary make the children wait so long before she lets them eat the mushroom? What does Mary's way of testing the mushroom reveal about her?
8. How does the last line of the story make you rethink the beginning?

EVALUATE AND CONNECT

9. Why, do you think, did Johnson choose "Too Soon a Woman" for her title?
10. Theme Connection   Would you have liked to experience a trek across the prairie? Does this story change the way you think about the challenges in your own life? Explain your answer.

● See Literary Terms Handbook, p. R3.

LITERARY ELEMENTS

Dialect

In certain regions of America, particular groups speak variations of English called **dialects**. Dialects differ from Standard English because they contain different pronunciations, word forms, and meanings. The conversational language in "Too Soon a Woman" represents the author's idea of the dialect of Midwestern pioneers in the mid-1800s.

1. What do the phrases "We're prid'near out of grub" and "Just leave me be" mean?
2. Does the author's use of dialect add to the story? Why or why not?

LITERARY ELEMENTS

1. They mean "We're almost out of food" or "We're pretty near out of food" and "Just leave me alone."
2. The author's use of dialect adds to the story because it makes the story seem more realistic and true to the period.

Additional Resources

 Literary Elements Transparency 21

Extending Your Response

Writing About Literature

Surprise Ending The last sentence in "Too Soon a Woman" comes as a surprise to the reader. Mary is a recent and, at first, unwelcome addition to the family. Then, suddenly, the narrator tells us she became his stepmother. Write a paragraph analyzing the effectiveness of the ending of the story.

Creative Writing

A Learning Experience Recall the list you made for the **Focus Activity** on page 234. Using your list and what you learned from the story, write an introduction that explains the courage and survival techniques pioneers needed.

Literature Groups

A Caretaker's Responsibility When Mary cooked the mushroom, she had no idea if she would survive eating it. Did she take too great a risk? What would have happened to the children if she became sick or died? Would you have eaten the mushroom? Discuss these questions, and be prepared to share your group's opinions with the whole class.

interNET CONNECTION

Use the Web to learn more about pioneer life. Try typing words and phrases such as *Oregon Trail* and *Conestoga* into a search engine.

Learning for Life

Poison or Not Write a report about mushrooms. In an encyclopedia or science book, look up mushrooms. Then choose an edible mushroom and draw a picture of it. List its characteristics, and form a conclusion about its nutritional value.

💾 **Save your work for your portfolio.**

Skill Minilesson

VOCABULARY • ANTONYMS

Antonyms are words with opposite, or nearly opposite, meanings.

PRACTICE In each blank, write an antonym for the underlined word.

1. She had been <u>plump</u> before her illness, but afterwards she was quite _____.
2. The losers looked _____, but the winners looked <u>delighted</u>.
3. Some people react _____ to good news, while others jump up and down <u>excitedly</u>.
4. The portions that were served weren't <u>generous</u> at all; they were downright _____.
5. Successful salespeople treat customers <u>politely</u>, not _____.

Extending Your Response

Writing About Literature

Students' paragraphs should

- explain the effect of the surprise ending on readers.
- analyze the effectiveness of the ending.
- logically flow from one thought to another and have a clear conclusion.

Creative Writing

Students' introductions should

- evaluate survival techniques from their earlier lists or those they learned in the story.
- show an understanding of courageous actions.
- contain a topic sentence and a conclusion.

Literature Groups Encourage each member to list questions and ideas about the topic before coming together as a group. Have groups assign one person to take notes while the group discusses the topic. **COLLAB. LEARN.**

Learning for Life Remind students that a good report contains an introductory paragraph with a strong lead, a body (several paragraphs, each around one main idea), and a conclusion that sums up the main points of the report.

Skill Minilesson

VOCABULARY • ANTONYMS

Example antonyms:

1. gaunt   4. skimpy
2. grim   5. gruffly
3. sedately

Additional Resources

📁 *Vocabulary Practice,* p. 14

✓ ASSESSMENT OPTIONS

📁 *Quick Checks,* p. 21

📁 *Selection and Theme Assessment,* pp. 37–38

📁 *Performance Assessment,* p. 20

💾 *Testmaker*

Objectives

- To read and analyze a short story about the challenge a teenage boy must face
- To recognize how writers foreshadow coming events

Skills

Reading/Thinking: Sequence of Events; Inferring; Drawing Conclusions

Grammar/Language: Usage: *Lie* and *Lay*

Listening/Speaking: Interviewing

Collaboration: Literature Groups

Motivating
→OPTIONS

Selection Focus Transparency 22: Have students discuss the quote by American novelist Agnes Sligh Turnbull.

Focus Activity: As an extension of the Focus Activity, have students discuss what special care ill pets might need from their owners.

Before You Read
A Boy and His Dog

MEET MARTHA BROOKS

Martha Brooks writes mainly about teenagers and their joys and disappointments. Her own childhood was spent at a tuberculosis sanatorium in rural Canada, where her parents were part of the medical staff. She and her sister grew up on the grounds with just a few other children. In her writing, Brooks has said that "what is important is that I try to be true to the characters I invent—listening to them, letting them tell their stories, and respecting the lives they live on the page."

Martha Brooks was born in 1944. This story was first published in 1988.

FOCUS ACTIVITY

Human beings and their pets can become very dependent on each other. Do you have, or wish you had, a pet?

Chart It!
Choose a pet. Then create a two-column chart that shows what a pet needs from its owner and what the owner receives from the pet.

Setting a Purpose
Read this story to find out how one person feels about his dog.

BACKGROUND

Did You Know?
Veterinary medicine deals with the diseases and injuries of animals. Animals can suffer from many of the same diseases that affect people, including heart disease and cancer.

VOCABULARY PREVIEW

spasm (spaz′ əm) *n.* a sudden uncontrollable tightening of a muscle; p. 243

obligingly (ə blī′ jing lē) *adv.* helpfully; agreeably; p. 244

slither (sli<u>th</u>′ ər) *v.* to move along with a sliding or gliding motion, as a snake; p. 246

frenzy (fren′ zē) *n.* a state of intense excitement or disturbance; p. 246

vigor (vig′ ər) *n.* strength and energy; p. 246

lolling (lol′ ing) *adj.* hanging down loosely; drooping; p. 246

saunter (sôn′ tər) *v.* to walk in a relaxed way; p. 246

reluctantly (ri luk′ tənt lē) *adv.* unwillingly; p. 247

RESOURCE MANAGER

Lesson Planning Resource
The ***Theme Three Planning Guide*** (pp. 25–32) provides additional lesson notes and reduced versions of all print resources.

📁 **Other Print Resources**
- Active Reading Guide, p. 22
- Vocabulary Practice, p. 15
- Reading Workbook, pp. 37–38
- Grammar and Language Workbook, pp. 223–224

- Grammar and Composition Handbook, Lessons 3.11, 3.12
- Quick Checks, p. 22
- Selection and Theme Assessment, pp. 39–40
- Performance Assessment, p. 21
- Spanish Summaries, p. 22
- Spanish Translations
- Inclusion Strategies
- English Language Learners Sourcebook

 Transparencies
- Selection Focus 22
- Literary Elements 22
- Grammar and Language 21

Technology
🎧 Audio Library
🎧 Spanish Audio Library
💻 Glencoe Literature Web Site
📁 Testmaker

A Boy and His Dog

Martha Brooks

A My dog is old. His eyes are constantly runny on account of he's going blind. Sometimes when we go for his walk he falls down. We'll be moving right along, I'll feel an unexpected tug at his leash, and bingo! he's over. The first time it happened he cried, sort of whimpered, and looked at his leg, the back one, the one that had betrayed him. I crouched in the tall grass (we take our walks in a sky-filled prairie field near the townhouses where we live) and felt the leg, which was in a spasm. I told him if it didn't work too well to just give up for a while. He seemed to know what I was telling him because he looked at me, whimpered some more, and finally flopped his head back on my leg. That's what kills me about dogs. They figure you're in charge of everything. Like if you pointed your finger, you could make a house fall down. Or if you told them everything's going to be okay, it would be.

After a couple of minutes he stood up and took off again in that businesslike, let's-get-the-show-on-the-road manner of his, sniffing, squatting to pee (he doesn't lift his leg anymore) near every bush in sight. Later, I found out he fell over because of arthritis. "Nothing you can do, really," said the vet, patting Alphonse's broad flat head. "He's just getting old, Buddy." She gave me some red pellet-shaped arthritis pills and sent us home.

Vocabulary
spasm (spaz′ am) *n.* a sudden uncontrollable tightening of a muscle

CONNECTING TO OTHER SELECTIONS

COMPARING selections

This selection is paired with "Too Soon a Woman" on page 235. A lesson for teaching a comparison of the two selections appears on page 249.

The chart at the right shows three other ways to connect "A Boy and His Dog" to selections in this book.

For specific teaching strategies, see the **Theme Three Planning Guide,** pages 28–29.

Connection	Title
Life Skills: Lifelong Learning	→ "Last Cover," p. 163
Thematic: Loss	→ "Birthday Box," p. 175
Literary: Foreshadowing	→ "Broken Chain," p. 44

B Author's Craft

POINT OF VIEW Ask students to discuss why this piece feels so personal. *(Buddy talks directly to the reader and shares his personal thoughts and feelings.)*

C Active Reading

EVALUATE Have students explain the meaning of this sentence: *Around our house, nobody put their hands over my ears.* *(Family members allow Buddy to hear whatever they say.)*

D Literary Elements

TONE Ask students to explain how Buddy's conversational style affects the story. *(It makes the story seem as if it really is being told by a fourteen year old.)*

E Active Reading

REVIEW Ask students to review what they know about Alphonse up to this point. *(Alphonse is very old and his health is failing. He is Buddy's confidante and companion.)*

F Literary Elements

CHARACTER Ask students what Buddy reveals about himself in this speech. *(He's thoughtful, logical, and takes responsibility seriously.)*

Teaching Options

A Boy and His Dog

After that, whenever he fell, he'd look quite cheerful. He'd lick the leg a bit, hang out his tongue, pant, and patiently wait. Just before stumbling to his feet, he'd look up like he was saying thank you—when I hadn't done anything!

I couldn't let him see how bad all this made me feel. He's so smart sometimes you have to put your hands over his ears and spell things so he won't know what you're talking about. Things like cheese, cookie, walk. All his favorites.

Mom said, "He can't last forever. Everybody dies sooner or later. It's the natural course of events. And big dogs don't live as long as little dogs."

Around our house, nobody put their hands over my ears.

Alphonse was a present for my first birthday. Dad brought him home, just a scruffy little brown pup someone was giving away. No special breed. I still have a snapshot of him and me at the party. I was this goopy-looking blond kid in blue corduroy overalls and a Donald Duck T-shirt. Alphonse was all over me in the way of puppies. I'd been startled by Dad's flash and also by Alphonse, who'd chosen that exact moment to paw me down and slurp strawberry ice cream off my face and hands. Dad says I didn't cry or anything! Just lay bug-eyed on the shag rug with Alphonse wiggling and slopping all over me. We got on like a house on fire after that.

Which is why it's so unfair that I'm fourteen going on fifteen and he's thirteen going on ninety-four.

I guess I thought we'd just go on forever with Alphonse being my dog. Listening

when I tell him stuff. When he goes, who am I going to tell my secrets to? I tell him things I wouldn't even tell Herb Malken, who is my best friend now that we've been in this city a year. My dad's always getting transferred. He's in the army. When I grow up that's one thing I'm not going to be. In the army. I won't make my kids move every three years and leave all their friends behind. Which is one thing I *am* going to do: have more than one kid when I get married.

There's a big myth that only children are selfish and self-centered. I can say from personal experience that only children are more likely to feel guilty and be too eager to please. It's terrible when you are one kid having to be everything to two parents.

Which is why Alphonse is more than just a dog, you see. Mom even sometimes calls him "Baby." Like he's my brother. Which it sometimes feels like.

Last week he had bad gas. I always sleep with the windows open. Even so, it got pretty awful in my bedroom.

Alphonse doesn't make much sound when he has gas. Just a little "phhhht" like a balloon with a slow leak and there's no living with him. I swear when he gets like that it would be dangerous to light a match.

I sent him out. He went <u>obligingly</u>. He's always been a polite dog. I listened, first to his toenails clicking over the hardwood floors, then to the scratching of his dry bristly fur as he slumped against the other side of the bedroom door. When you can't be in the same room with someone who's shared your dreams for thirteen years, it's hard to get properly relaxed. It isn't the

---

Vocabulary
obligingly (ə blī′ jing lē) *adv.* helpfully; agreeably

Unusual Expressions List on the board the following expressions from the story: *hang out his tongue, goopy-looking blond kid, Alphonse was all over me, bug-eyed, we got on like a house on fire, he's thirteen going on ninety-four.* Explain to students that this story is told as if Buddy is talking to the reader. The style is informal and conversational. It uses expressions that English language learners might not be familiar with.

Activity Have students work in pairs or small groups to discuss these words and to use context to figure them out.
COLLAB. LEARN.

Additional Resources
📁 *English Language Learners Sourcebook*

Companions. James Charles (1851–1906). Oldham Art Gallery, Manchester, England.

Viewing the painting: How do you think the lives of this boy and his dog differ from the lives of the boy and dog in the story?

FYI

Dogs and people have been companions for thousands of years. In Idaho, scientists found the remains of a dog estimated to be from 10,500 years ago. Asian, African, European, and North and South American cultural groups all bred dogs to use as companions, guards, workers, hunters, or protectors. Ancient cave paintings, artifacts, and writings show people and dogs living together the world over.

FYI

Dog Years The ratio of dog years to human years is approximately seven to one. This means that dogs age seven times as quickly as humans.

Reading *Minilesson*

Sequence of Events Ask volunteers to tell briefly what they have done since they walked into school today. As they speak, record any time words they use; for example, *first, next, then, after that, while, when, now, while, during, earlier, before,* and *after.* Remind students that they can keep the order of events in a story straight by charting them.

Activity Ask students to work in small groups to compile lists of time words from the story. Then have students create charts that track the story's sequence of events. They can use their lists of time words to provide clues to the sequencing.
L2 COLLAB. LEARN.

Additional Resources
📁 *Reading Workbook,* pp. 37–38

G Active Reading

PREDICT Have students predict what the vet might say about Buddy's condition. *(The dog seems to be in a general decline; this latest event might signal that he's sicker than Buddy realizes.)*

H Literary Elements

IMAGERY Have students notice the sensory images the author uses to describe the fall day. Ask students why they think the author uses so many color words. *(This is a very strong contrast to the fact that Alphonse cannot see. It brings out the growing sense of sadness.)*

On The Lighter Side

Generally, dogs are lovable pets, so it is hard to understand why so many dog expressions have negative connotations: "You ain't nothing but a *hound dog*" (Elvis Presley) refers to a mean and contemptible person; *hound* means "nag" or "pursue"; *dog-eared* means "damaged and worn"; *in the doghouse* means "in trouble, disfavor"; and *dogged* means "plodding."

I Literary Elements

CHARACTER Ask students to describe the kind of person the vet is. *(She seems dedicated and emotionally involved in the lives of the animals, and she cares deeply for them.)*

Teaching Options

---

same when they aren't near you, breathing the same air.

G For the next few days he lay around more than usual. I thought perhaps he was just overtired (even though I hadn't been able to stand it and had begun to let him back into my room, gas and all). By Sunday, Mom cocked her head at him and said to Dad and me, "I don't like the way Alphonse looks. Better take him back to the vet, Buddy."

Mom works at the army base too. It's late when she and Dad get home and by that time the vet is closed for the day. So I always take Alphonse right after school. It isn't far—three blocks past the field.

H Monday was the kind of fall day that makes you breathe more deeply—the field all burning colors, far-off bushes little flames of magenta[1] and orange, dry wavy grass a pale yellow, and the big sky that kind of deep fire blue you see only once a year, in October. Alphonse didn't fall down once. Eyes half closed, he walked slowly, sniffing the air to take in messages.

A young ginger-colored cat <u>slithered</u> under a wooden fence and into the field. It saw Alphonse and suddenly crouched low, eyes dark, motionless. For a minute there I didn't think he would notice it. Then his ears went up and his head shot forward. Next thing, he was hauling me along at the end of his leash, barking himself into a <u>frenzy</u>. The cat parted the grass

---
1. *Magenta* is a purplish-red color.
---

like wildfire and, reaching the fence, dug its body gracelessly under at a spot where there seemed hardly an inch between wood and solid earth.

Alphonse has that effect on cats. They must think he's death on wheels the way they scatter to get out of his way. He stared proudly in the direction of the fence; his nose hadn't failed him. He walked on, a little more <u>vigor</u> in his step, his tongue <u>lolling</u> out, his ears nice and perky.

We reached the edge of the field where we usually turn around on our walks. This time, of course, we didn't. He lost some of his bounce and trailed slightly behind. I looked back. He lowered his head. "She's not going to do anything to you, you crazy dog," I told him. "She's going to shake her head again, and tell us to go home." He kept pace with me after that. Like I said, dogs believe everything you tell them.

I The vet is the kind of person whose job runs her life. One minute she's smiling over a recovering patient, or one who's come in just for shots; the next, she's blowing her nose like the place is a funeral parlor. It must be murder to become so involved with your patients. She always looks as if she needs some place to hole up for a good sleep. And her legs are magnets for strays who are forever up for adoption.

At the clinic, I sat down with Alphonse resignedly backed up between my knees. To my astonishment, a resident cat <u>sauntered</u> over and actually rubbed against him. Alphonse sniffed its head and then ignored

Vocabulary
slither (slith′ ər) *v.* to move along with a sliding or gliding motion, as a snake
frenzy (fren′ zē) *n.* a state of intense excitement or disturbance
vigor (vig′ ər) *n.* strength and energy
lolling (lol′ ing) *adj.* hanging down loosely; drooping
saunter (sôn′ tər) *v.* to walk in a relaxed way

246 THEME 3

Grammar and Language *Minilesson*

Usage: Lie and Lay Copy this chart on the board. Explain that the verb *lie* means "to recline" (I will lie down for a nap), while *lay* means "to put" or "to place," (I will lay the pen on the desk).

Present	Past	Past Participle	Present Participle
lie	lay	lain	lying
lay	laid	laid	laying

Activity Have students choose a form of *lie* or *lay* to complete the following:
1. Yesterday the cat (*lay, laid*) on my father's favorite chair all day.
2. When he came into the classroom, he (*lay, laid*) the booklets on the floor.
3. You will have to (*lie, lay*) down to reach under the car. **L2** **COLLAB. LEARN.**

Additional Resources
- *Grammar and Language Transparency 21*
- *Grammar and Language Workbook,* pp. 223–224
- *Grammar and Composition Handbook,* Lessons 3.11, 3.12
- *Writer's Choice,* Lessons 10.9, 17.2

it (he only likes cats who run). He watched the door to the examining room and trembled. I wondered if his eyesight was improving. With one hand I held his leash; the other I bit away at because of hangnails.

When the vet, smiling, summoned us, I got to my feet and Alphonse reluctantly pattered after me. Inside the examining room he pressed against the door, willing it to open. I picked him up and lugged him over to the table.

"He's lost weight," said the vet, stroking, prodding gently.

"He was too fat," I said, patting his stomach.

She laughed, continuing her way down his body. "Has he been on a diet?"

"No. I guess older dogs don't eat as much—like older people."

She looked at his rectum. "How long has this been here?" she said softly, more to herself than to me.

"This what?" I looked.

"It's quite a small lump," she said, pressing it hard.

Alphonse stood politely on the table, shaking and puffing.

"Sometimes," she said, with a reassuring smile, "older dogs get these lumps and they usually aren't anything to worry about, Buddy."

Usually? What did she mean, *usually?* My heart began to race.

"Older neutered dogs," she continued, in the same even tone, "very often get

benign[2] lumps in the anal region. But we'd better check this out, anyway. . . ."

My dog has cancer. What do I tell him now? What am I going to do? Mom and Dad have left it up to me. The vet, with strained sad eyes, says the little lump is just a symptom of what's going on inside. Why didn't I notice that he was so short of breath? That he was peeing more than usual? That he didn't eat much? That his bowels weren't working? She tells me that when dogs are old all of these things become a problem, it's the usual progress of aging. Except not in Alphonse's case. But how would I know that? I shouldn't blame myself. She says there was nothing I could have done to stop it, anyway.

So what do I tell him? Is he in pain? I couldn't stand it if he were in pain. Tonight Mom wanted to give me a sleeping pill. I refused it. Alphonse is here with me on my bed. He's going to sleep with me one last time. I'll hold him and tell him about me and what I plan to do with my life. I'll have to lie a little, fill in a few places, because I'm not *exactly* sure. But he has a right to know what he'll be missing. I'll have a good life, I know it, just like he's had. I'm going to tell him about it now, whisper it in his ear, and I won't leave out a single detail.

---

2. A *neutered* animal is one from which certain reproductive organs have been surgically removed, usually to prevent breeding. A *benign* (bi nīn´) lump is an abnormal growth that is not cancerous and, therefore, not usually dangerous.

Vocabulary
reluctantly (ri luk´ tənt lē) *adv.* unwillingly

J Active Reading

EVALUATE Ask students how they know that Buddy is more worried than he lets on. *(He bites his nails nervously as he waits for the vet.)*

K Critical Thinking

INFERRING The vet says she'd better check out Alphonse's lump. Then there is a break in the text. The next words are *My dog has cancer.* *(It means time has passed.)*

L Critical Thinking

DRAWING CONCLUSIONS Have students explain how they know that Buddy thinks of Alphonse more as a friend than a dog. *(Buddy asks, "So what do I tell him?" as if Alphonse could really understand the whole concept.)*

M Author's Craft

FORESHADOWING Have students discuss how the author has led up to this moment. *(The story details focus on Alphonse's failing stamina and the vet's inability to give any reassurance that Alphonse will recover.)*

Thematic Focus

Facing Challenge Have students discuss the challenge Buddy faces with Alphonse. Do they think he handles the situation in a mature way? Do they think Alphonse, if he could, might consider Buddy his hero?

✔ ASSESSMENT OPTIONS

📁 *Quick Checks,* p. 22

INCLUSION STRATEGIES

MEETING INDIVIDUAL NEEDS

Special Needs Selecting an appropriate word or phrase to complete a sentence helps promote understanding and effective communication.

Activity Have students work in pairs to complete the following sentences. Encourage them to reread page 247 for clues. **L1 COLLAB. LEARN.**

1. Buddy picked Alphonse up and lugged him over to the _____. *(table)*
2. The vet found that Alphonse had lost a lot of _____. *(weight)*
3. The boy told Alphonse all about his _____. *(future plans)*

Additional Resources
📁 *Inclusion Strategies*

Responding to the Selection

Personal Response

Answers should show a deeper understanding of the relationship between humans and their pets.

Analyzing Literature

1. Alphonse is arthritic and going blind. He has spasms in his leg and he stumbles.
2. The dog has become lethargic, and Buddy's mother doesn't like the way Alphonse looks.
3. Alphonse will be put to sleep.
4. They have been together almost their entire lives.
5. Buddy needs to tell Alphonse his plans because Alphonse won't be around to see them.
6. The author uses the first-person point of view to make readers feel what it is like to be Buddy.
7. Buddy will have to take Alphonse to the vet one last time. Then he will have to deal with the loss of Alphonse.

Extending Your Response

Literature Groups Encourage each group member to list several ideas. Have groups assign one person to take notes while the group discusses the topic, and another to share the group's final ideas with the rest of the class. **COLLAB. LEARN.**

Interdisciplinary Activity You may want to have several students work together to create the career-path chart. One student can show the steps a student needs to take in middle and high school; another, the steps to take in college.

 # Responding to Literature

PERSONAL RESPONSE

Think back to the chart about humans and their pets you made in the **Focus Activity** on page 242. How would you change the chart now that you have read "A Boy and His Dog"?

 Analyzing Literature

RECALL AND INTERPRET

1. What are some of the signs of old age in Alphonse?
2. Why did Buddy take Alphonse back to the vet?
3. What will happen to Alphonse after the story ends?
4. What is significant about the amount of time the boy and his dog have been together?
5. Why does the boy need to tell his dog about his future plans?

EVALUATE AND CONNECT

6. Why did the author choose the first-person point of view?
7. Theme Connection   What challenges will Buddy face after the story ends?

Extending Your Response

Literature Groups

A Last Good-bye   Have you ever lost a beloved pet–or person? How would you say good-bye to someone you loved? Discuss with your group how you think a person should act in such a situation.

Interdisciplinary Activity

Science   Invite a veterinarian or a vet student to your class. Prepare questions to ask–for example:
• Why did you choose to become a vet?
• How are vets trained?

• What subjects do they need to know before they study medicine?
Then design a career-path chart that shows the steps a person needs to take to become a vet.

Reading Further

If you would like to read other stories written by Martha Brooks, try these:
Paradise Cafe and Other Stories
Two Moons in August

💾 **Save your work for your portfolio.**

LITERARY ELEMENTS

Foreshadowing

Clues that prepare readers for events that will happen later in a story are called **foreshadowing**. Foreshadowing can build suspense. For example, a weapon found in a drawer might foreshadow a future crime.

1. Does Alphonse's first visit to the vet foreshadow a later event? Explain your answer.
2. Find the paragraph in which Alphonse's death is foreshadowed by a casual statement.

● See **Literary Terms Handbook**, p. R4.

LITERARY ELEMENTS

1. Yes. The first visit to the vet sets the stage for later visits. Readers learn that Alphonse is old and feeble; more problems may arise.
2. Buddy's mother says, "He can't last forever. Everybody dies sooner or later. It's the natural course of events."

Additional Resources

📖 **Literary Elements Transparency 22**

✓ ASSESSMENT OPTIONS

📁 *Quick Checks,* p. 22
📁 *Selection and Theme Assessment,* pp. 39–40
📁 *Performance Assessment,* p. 21
💾 *Testmaker*

COMPARING SELECTIONS

Too Soon a Woman and A Boy and His Dog

COMPARE **CHARACTERS**

The boy narrator and Mary, in "Too Soon a Woman," and Buddy, in "A Boy and His Dog," are young people who must deal with loss in their lives. Present a skit in which, through time travel, the two boys and Mary meet to talk about how life's challenges have changed them and helped them grow. Present two acts, a first act that takes place when the characters are the same ages as they are in the stories, and a second act that takes place ten years later.

COMPARE **TONE**

Both selections are written from the first-person point of view, but they differ greatly in tone. Discuss these questions in small groups.

1. Which story uses elements of humor? Why do you think one writer chose to include humor and the other didn't?

2. How would you describe the tone of each story?

3. In what ways does the tone of each story suit the events the author is describing?

COMPARE **DESCRIPTIONS**

You probably noticed that Martha Brooks tells very little about how Buddy looks, and that Dorothy M. Johnson tells almost nothing about her narrator's appearance. Can you explain why these two writers did so little to describe how their main characters look? Write a paragraph or two explaining what you think these writers were most interested in telling us about their characters.

Objective
- To compare two short stories about facing challenge

COMPARE **CHARACTERS**
Students' skits should
- show differences in how the characters feel and behave.
- be well rehearsed before they are presented.

COMPARE **TONE**
1. "A Boy and His Dog" uses humor. "Too Soon a Woman" doesn't use humor because the author wants readers to realize how serious and desperate the situation is.
2. In "Too Soon a Woman" the tone is one of quiet happiness. At the beginning of "A Boy and His Dog," the tone is lighthearted but it becomes increasingly serious after the second trip to the vet.
3. In both stories the tone is cheerful or serious to match the events being described.

Additional Resources
📁 *Literary Groups Sourcebook*

COMPARE **DESCRIPTIONS**
Students' paragraphs should
- contain a clear topic sentence and conclusion.
- present facts from the stories to support their ideas.

Teaching Options

 PORTFOLIO OPTIONS _____

Select and Reflect Have students reflect on the paragraphs they wrote for the activity above by asking themselves these questions:
- Do my paragraphs explain why the writers did not describe how the characters look?
- Do my paragraphs explain what the writers most wanted to tell?
- Do I use examples from the stories to support my ideas?
Students should clip their reflections to their

paragraphs and place them in their portfolios. At a later time, they might consider using the comments to revise their paragraphs as portfolio showcase pieces. **L2**

Additional Resources
📁 *Writing Assessment and Portfolio Management,* pp. 17–19

Objective

• To recognize details in a literary work and use strategies for visualizing a story

Teaching Strategies

Before asking students to read the passage in their books, you may wish to have them close their eyes as you read it aloud to them. Ask them to visualize the scene and then share the images that come to mind of the woman in the story. To extend the activity, encourage students to draw the scene or a detail from it.

Exercises

1. The characters are in and around a horse-drawn wagon on a prairie. Students may pick out words and details from the first paragraph to place the characters.
2. Students' responses may include details of the setting: the prairie, the mountain, the long, slow road, as well as the one-horse wagon, the father, the son, and two small daughters. Students may also jot down emotions and observations about the characters in this situation even though the words *poor, lonely,* and *homeless* are not directly stated.

Additional Resources
📁 *Reading Workbook*

Teaching Options

Reading and Thinking Skills

Visualizing

Good writers use exact, vivid words and strong, colorful details so that their readers can **visualize**, or picture, what is going on as they read. For example, consider the following passage from "New Directions." As you read the passage, notice how the exact words and the vivid details add to your ability to picture the scene.

> The next morning she left her house carrying the meat pies, lard, an iron brazier, and coals for a fire. Just before lunch she appeared in an empty lot behind the cotton gin. As the dinner noon bell rang, she dropped the savors into boiling fat and the aroma rose and floated over to the workers who spilled out of the gin, covered with white lint, looking like specters.

As a skillful reader, use your own experiences to help you understand as well as imagine the scene. For example, have you ever felt the weight of a heavy load, such as your school books as you walked to school?

● For more about visualizing, see **Reading Handbook,** p. R84.

EXERCISES

Read the opening paragraphs from "Too Soon a Woman" by Dorothy M. Johnson. Then answer the questions at the right.

> We left the home place behind, mile by slow mile, heading for the mountains, across the prairie where the wind blew forever.
> At first there were four of us with the one-horse wagon and its skimpy load. Pa and I walked, because I was a big boy of eleven. My two little sisters romped and trotted until they got tired and had to be boosted up into the wagon bed.

1. Where are the characters in relation to one another and their surroundings in this scene? Pick out the words and details that tell where they are.

2. Close your eyes and visualize this scene. Then quickly jot down the words and details that help you see this scene in your imagination.

MEETING INDIVIDUAL NEEDS **INCLUSION STRATEGIES**

Less-Proficient Readers The technique of visualization is particularly beneficial to less-proficient readers.

Activity Have students listen to and visualize the first sentence of "Too Soon a Woman." Have students describe the image brought to mind by each part of the sentence: *We left the home place behind • mile by slow mile • heading for the mountains • across the prairie where the wind blew forever.* Ask each student to write a sentence that contains at least two visual images. **L1** **COLLAB. LEARN.**

Additional Resources
📁 *Inclusion Strategies*

Before You Read

The Women's 400 Meters and To James

MEET LILLIAN MORRISON

A full-time author and poet, Lillian Morrison is an avid sports fan who has written entire collections of poems about sports. Morrison's connection to teenagers comes from her experience as coordinator of young adult services at the New York Public Library. She has also collected and published collections of folk rhymes and folk sayings.

Lillian Morrison was born in 1917.

MEET FRANK HORNE

Frank Horne's love of track began when he ran the quarter mile as a college student. Later, after becoming an optometrist, he coached a championship high school track team. "To James" was inspired by his coaching experiences.

Frank Horne was born in 1899. "To James" is from a 1963 collection of Horne's poetry titled Haverstraw.

FOCUS ACTIVITY

Have you ever tried to run as fast and as long as you could or push your body all the way to the edge in some other way? How did it feel?

Journal
Write an entry about how your body and mind feel when you test your physical endurance. If you have ever been in a race, write about that experience.

Setting a Purpose
The first time through, just read to enjoy the poems and get an idea of what they are about. Read them aloud and listen to their sounds. Then you can read the poems more carefully to see how the poets use sounds and images to express their ideas.

BACKGROUND

Track-and-field events, held since the Olympic Games in 776 B.C., are the oldest organized sports. These athletic meets include running and walking races, and jumping and throwing events. Track meets are usually held in a field or stadium built around a 400-meter (437-yard) oval track. The fastest, shortest races are dashes that range from 50 to 400 meters. The racers begin in a crouch at the starting line. When the starter fires a pistol, the runners leap into a full stride and run at top speed to the finish line. A fast start can often mean the difference between winning and losing the race.

FACING CHALLENGE 251

Objectives
- To read and analyze two poems about runners and races
- To recognize the use of free verse in a poem
- To write a short essay describing the theme "Facing Challenge"

Skills
Reading/Thinking: Evaluating; Inferring; Drawing Conclusions
Writing: Journal Entry
Vocabulary: Prefixes
Grammar/Language: Present and Past Participles; Ellipsis
Listening/Speaking: Sports Broadcast; Interview
Collaboration: Literature Groups

Motivating
→OPTIONS

Selection Focus Transparency 23: Have students comment on Samuelson's experience and compare it to their own. Encourage them to see how her statement applies to all parts of life.

Focus Activity: As an extension of the Focus Activity, have partners discuss ways that people push themselves to the limits of their endurance.

RESOURCE MANAGER

Lesson Planning Resource
The **Theme Three Planning Guide** (pp. 33–38) provides additional lesson notes and reduced versions of all print resources.

📁 **Other Print Resources**
- Active Reading Guide, p. 23
- Grammar and Language Workbook, pp. 167–168
- Grammar and Composition Handbook, Lesson 9.1

- Quick Checks, p. 23
- Selection and Theme Assessment, pp. 41–42
- Performance Assessment, p. 22
- Spanish Summaries, p. 23
- Spanish Translations
- Inclusion Strategies
- English Language Learners Sourcebook

 Transparencies
- Selection Focus 23
- Literary Elements 23
- Grammar and Language 22

Technology
🎧 Audio Library
🎧 Spanish Audio Library
💻 Glencoe Literature Web Site
💾 Testmaker

A Literary Elements

ALLITERATION Have students identify alliteration in the first stanza. (*It is the* s *sound in* skittish *and* starting.) Draw their attention also to the consequence of the final s sounds in *flex, knees,* and *heels.*

B Active Reading

VISUALIZE Have students visualize this starting scene. You might ask them to sketch it.

C Critical Thinking

EVALUATING Ask students to compare the runners in the first and third stanzas. (*At first, they are nervous; their energy is pent up, waiting for release. Later they are focused, propelling themselves at great speed, almost out of control.*)

D Literary Elements

FREE VERSE Free verse poetry has no fixed pattern of rhyme, rhythm, line length, or stanza arrangement. Ask students whether this poem is written in free verse.

Additional Resources

 Active Reading Guide, p. 23

🎧 *Audio Library*

📂 *Spanish Summaries,* p. 23

Teaching Options

CONNECTING TO OTHER SELECTIONS
For a teaching strategy that connects "The Women's 400 Meters" to "Wait Till Next Year," turn to page 36 in the *Theme One Planning Guide.*

The Women's 400 Meters

Lillian Morrison ∼

Skittish,°
they flex knees, drum heels and
shiver at the starting line

waiting the gun
to pour them over the stretch
like a breaking wave.

Bang! they're off
careening° down the lanes,
each chased by her own bright tiger.

---

1 The word *skittish* means "easily frightened or excited."
8 *Careening* is rushing along, perhaps swaying from side to side as if out of control.

MEETING INDIVIDUAL NEEDS — ENGLISH LANGUAGE LEARNERS

Track and Field Some English language learners might not be familiar with track events as they are organized in the United States. Tell students that the gun in the poem is used to signal the start of the race. When the gun goes off, the racers leave the starting line. Explain that the gun uses cartridges called blanks to provide a loud noise that all the racers can hear.

Activity If possible, show a video of a race or display photos of runners. Point out the cinders on the track and the way the runners lurch out of the starting blocks. Have students create word webs of track and field words.

Additional Resources

📂 *English Language Learners Sourcebook*

To James

Frank Horne ∿

Do you remember
how you won
that last race . . . ?
how you flung your body
5   at the start . . .
how your spikes
ripped the cinders
in the stretch . . .
how you catapulted°
10 through the tape . . .
do you remember . . . ?
Don't you think
I lurched° with you
out of those starting holes . . . ?

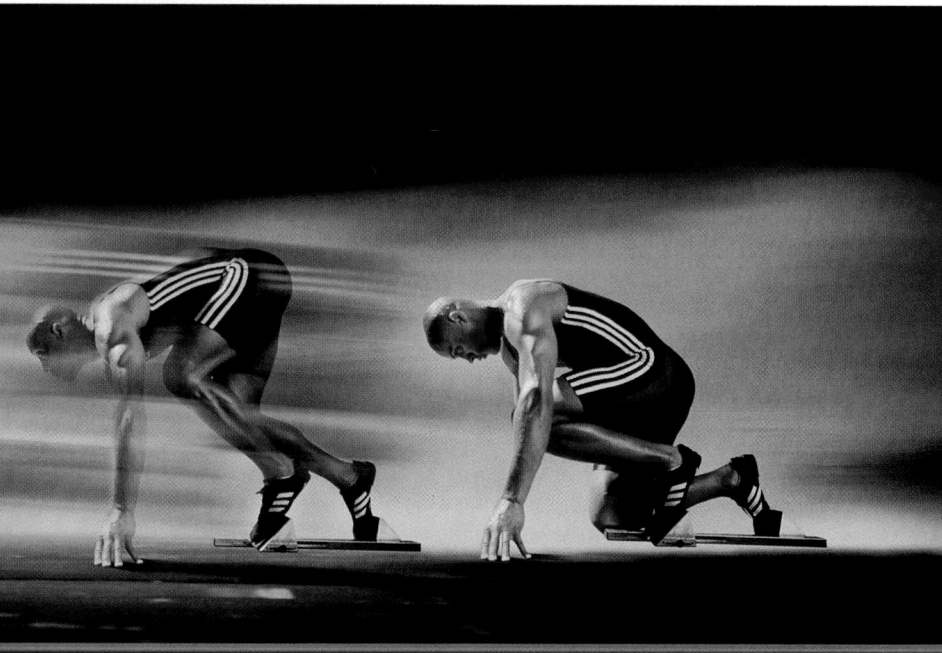

---

9 To *catapult* is to leap or hurl oneself, as if from a
giant slingshot.
13 To *lurch* is to plunge forward suddenly in a jerky
manner.

253

E Active Reading

EVALUATE Ask students whom the speaker is addressing in this poem. *(Students will probably understand that the person being spoken to is a runner; however, they might not be able to be more specific until they finish reading the poem.)*

F Literary Elements

VISUALIZE Have students take a moment to picture each detail of the race as it is described in this first stanza. *(Students might choose the image of the runner flinging his or her body forward at the start or catapulting through the tape.)*

Vo•cab•u•lar•y Skills

Prefixes Point out that the prefix *cata-* in *catapulted* comes from a Greek word that means "down." *Catapult* literally means "to throw down." Explain that other words begin with *cata-*, including *catalog* (literally "to count down"); *cata-strophe* (literally "to turn down"); and *cataclysm* (literally "to wash down").

G Literary Elements

FREE VERSE Have students read the poem, noting rhyme or other repeated patterns. Ask them if they think "To James" is written in free verse. Have them explain their reasoning. *("To James" is written in free verse. It has no fixed rhyme or other repeated patterns.)*

Grammar and Language *Minilesson*

Present and Past Participles Review with students that participles function as main verbs and as adjectives. With regular verbs, the present participle is formed by adding *–ing*. The past participle is formed by adding *-ed*. Write the following lines from "To James" on the board:

1. Dig your <u>starting</u> holes deep and firm
   (present participle, adjective)
2. finish with an ecstatic burst that car-

ries you <u>hurtling</u> through the tape to victory *(present participle, adjective)*
3. how your spikes <u>ripped</u> the cinders
   (past participle, main verb)

Activity Ask students to identify the participles in the lines on the board. Have them tell whether the participles are main verbs or adjectives and whether they are in the present or the past tense. **L2**

Additional Resources

- *Grammar and Language Transparency 22*
- *Grammar and Language Workbook*, pp. 167–168
- *Grammar and Composition Handbook*, Lessons 9.1
- *Writer's Choice*, Lesson 15.1

Literary Elements

FREE VERSE In what ways are lines 1–28 and lines 29–51 of the poem similar? How are they different? *(Neither section contains rhymes or other repeated patterns. Lines 1–28 ask a series of questions; lines 29–51 make a series of statements.)*

Ⓗ Critical Thinking

INFERRING Ask students what they think the poet means when he says "it's a short dash." *(He means that we don't have a long time to live.)*

Ⓘ Critical Thinking

DRAWING CONCLUSIONS Have students discuss the meaning of the final lines of the poem. Ask them to explain what victory means. *(The end of the race of life is death; the victory is living life to the fullest.)*

LITERATURE & HUMANITIES

📖 Have students examine the poster *Study for the Munich Olympic Games* in *Art Talk*, page 114. Encourage them to discuss the feelings expressed by each of the runners. What is the artist suggesting about the importance of races and other competitions in the lives of the competitors?

☑ **ASSESSMENT OPTIONS**

📁 **Quick Checks,** p. 23

Teaching Options

CONNECTING TO OTHER SELECTIONS
For a teaching strategy that connects "To James" to "After Twenty Years," turn to page 32 in the *Theme Six Planning Guide*.

For a teaching strategy that connects "To James" to "After Twenty Years," turn to page 32 in the *Theme Six Planning Guide*.

---

15   Don't you think
    my sinews° tightened
    at those first
    few strides . . .
    and when you flew into the stretch
20   was not all my thrill
    of a thousand races
    in your blood . . . ?
    At your final drive
    through the finish line
25   did not my shout
    tell of the
    triumphant ecstasy°
    of victory . . . ?

    Live
30   as I have taught you
    to run, Boy—
    it's a short dash.
    Dig your starting holes
    deep and firm
35   lurch out of them
    into the straightaway
    with all the power
    that is in you
    look straight ahead
40   to the finish line
    think only of the goal
    run straight
    run high
    run hard
45   save nothing
    and finish
    with an ecstatic burst
    that carries you
    hurtling
50   through the tape
    to victory . . .

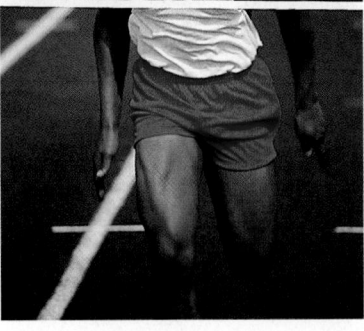

16 The cords of tissue that connect muscles to bones are called tendons or *sinews* (sin′ ūz).
27 *Ecstasy* is a state of overwhelming joy or delight.

Listening and Speaking *Minilesson*

Sports Broadcast Students might gain a deeper understanding of the track and field images presented in these two poems if they develop a sports broadcast describing those images.

Activity In small groups, have students choose one of the poems to broadcast. Have students describe the race as a sportscaster would. Encourage them to create characters, describe the setting and the crowd, and dramatize the action of the race. Finally, have groups present their broadcasts to the class. **L2**

COLLAB. LEARN.

Responding to Literature

PERSONAL RESPONSE

Choose an image from each poem that stays in your mind's eye. How did the poetry affect the way you picture a track event?

Analyzing Literature

RECALL

1. What part of a race is described in "The Women's 400 Meters"?
2. Who are the two characters in the poem "To James"?

INTERPRET

3. How does the rhythm of "The Women's 400 Meters" make you feel like you are at the start of a race?
4. How does the speaker in "To James" feel about the runner? How can you tell?

EVALUATE AND CONNECT

5. What does the first stanza of "The Women's 400 Meters" compare the racers to? Why is this an effective comparison?
6. Describe the image in the second stanza of "The Women's 400 Meters." How effective is this image?
7. In the third stanza of "The Women's 400 Meters," the poet suggests that each runner is being chased by a tiger. What does she mean by that?
8. Imagine that the speaker in "To James" had given you similar advice before a race. Would you agree or disagree? Explain.
9. Much of the advice in "To James" applies to life as well as to running. Find one line from the poem that you think people your age could use to help them succeed in school.
10. **Theme Connection** How do you think the runners in each poem could use their experience to inspire other young people?

LITERARY ELEMENTS

Free Verse

Poetry without a fixed pattern of rhyme, rhythm, line length, or stanza arrangement is called **free verse**. Both "To James" and "The Women's 400 Meters" are written in free verse. Some poets use free verse to give their poems the natural, realistic rhythms of conversation. Repetition and strong images are often the main poetic devices in free verse poetry.

1. Read the first stanza of "To James" aloud. Notice how Horne uses repetition to give some rhythm to the free verse. Write the phrases that are repeated.

2. Describe three examples of strong imagery in "The Women's 400 Meters."

● See **Literary Terms Handbook**, p. R5.

Responding to the Selection

Personal Response

Students will choose different images. Some may say that the poems gave them the feeling of being a runner or a coach. Others may now see a foot race as a metaphor for life.

Analyzing Literature

1. The moments just before the race and the beginning of the race are described.
2. The characters are a runner and either his coach or his father.
3. At first, the rhythm is short and choppy; it feels a bit tense. With the word *bang,* the rhythm shifts and becomes smoother.
4. The speaker is very close to the runner; lines 12–28 describe different ways the speaker has experienced what the racer is experiencing.
5. The word *skittish* is often used to describe horses, which behave similarly before they race.
6. The author compares the group of racers to a breaking wave. Most students should think this is effective because the racers will break forward and flood the track.
7. Students should understand that the women are racing as if their lives depend on it. Also, the idea of a "bright tiger" conveys a sense of grace, great strength, and power.
8. Most students should see the advice is sound if they want to run well.
9. Possible responses include: *Dig your starting holes deep and firm, look straight ahead to the finish line,* or *think only of the goal.*

LITERARY ELEMENTS

1. *Do you remember, how you,* and *don't you think* are repeated.
2. Possible answers: *skittish, pour them over the stretch like a breaking wave,* and *each chased by her own bright tiger.*

Additional Resources

🖳 *Literary Elements Transparency 23*

10. Runners must work hard, practice consistently and diligently, and focus on a goal. All these traits could be used by young people. The runners could talk about how they have achieved their own goals.

Extending Your Response

Writing About Literature

Students' essays should
- describe different ways that people face challenges in their lives.
- clearly explain the challenge that is involved in each example.

Personal Writing

Students' journal entries should
- compare descriptions of their own experiences with those in the poem.
- include a description that contains poetic images.

Literature Groups
Have students quickly jot down their impressions as soon as they have finished their runs and encourage them to compare their experiences to those in the poem. **COLLAB. LEARN.**

Listening and Speaking
To encourage productive interviews, suggest that students prepare questions that cannot be answered *yes* or *no*.

Skill Minilesson

GRAMMAR AND LANGUAGE • ELLIPSIS

Possible answers: "do you remember...?" This implies the speaker is waiting for the runner to remember; at those first few strides.... The ellipses indicate time between the beginning of the race and the stretch.

Extending Your Response

Writing About Literature

Theme   Consider how these poems connect to the theme of "Facing Challenge." What are some other ways in which people face challenge in their everyday lives?

Personal Writing

Journal   Recall your response to the **Focus Activity** on page 251. How does your description of pushing your body to the edge compare with the descriptions in the two poems? Write a more poetic description of your experience in your journal.

Literature Groups

Experience the Words!   Run once around the schoolyard or the sports field with your group. Then sit down and compare your experiences with the descriptions of running in each poem.

Listening and Speaking

Why Run?   Interview a student athlete about the reasons he or she chooses to run. Be sure to ask about the physical and psychological benefits and any negative aspects of running and competing.

Reading Further

If you would like to read more poems about sports, try these books by Lillian Morrison:
Sprints and Distances
At the Crack of the Bat

Save your work for your portfolio.

Skill Minilesson

GRAMMAR AND LANGUAGE • ELLIPSIS

An **ellipsis** is the omission, or leaving out, of one or more words. In writing, three spaced periods are used to show an ellipsis. These periods are called *ellipses* (the plural of *ellipsis*). For example, the sentence "The team, without a great deal of talent or effort, won the track-and-field event" could be shortened (if you were interested only in the *result* of the event) to "The team . . . won the track-and-field event." Ellipsis marks are also used to indicate a

pause in dialogue, such as: "The reason I was late for practice, Coach, is that I . . . uh . . . I needed to go home and . . . check on my sick dog."

PRACTICE   Reread "To James," and find two places where the poet has used an ellipsis. Write the examples and then explain why, in your opinion, the poet has used them.

✔ ASSESSMENT OPTIONS

 Quick Checks, p. 23

 Selection and Theme Assessment, pp. 41–42

Performance Assessment, p. 22

Testmaker

Measurement Systems

In Lillian Morrison's poem, runners anxiously wait at the starting line of a 400-meter race. The meter is the primary unit of measure for length in the metric system. However, before standardized measurements were invented, people used their bodies to measure distances and lengths.

Systems of Measure–Length

Metric Unit	U.S. Equivalent
1 kilometer = 1000 meters	0.62 mile
1 meter = 10 decimeters	39.37 inches
1 decimeter = 10 centimeters	3.94 inches
1 centimeter = 10 millimeters	0.39 inch

Kingly Feet

Hundreds and hundreds of years ago, the width of a man's thumb and the length of his foot were commonly used as standard measurements for the inch and the foot. Of course, not many thumbs or feet were of equal length, which caused great frustration between merchants and buyers in the marketplace.

In Egypt, one king attempted to set a standard for the foot by distributing official measuring sticks of his own foot length. Each new king, however, wanted to use the length of *his* foot for the official standard, so the problem continued. In the fourteenth century, an English king set the standard for the length of the yard based upon the measurement of his rather rotund waist. During Queen Elizabeth's reign, the standard for the yard was the measurement from the queen's nose to the tip of her longest finger.

All Thumbs

People still sometimes use a thumb's width to guess the equivalent of an inch. Measure the width of your desktop with your thumb. Then share your answer with a classmate. Do your estimates match? Probably not.

Although your thumb won't measure an inch very accurately, it can help you estimate distances you might not be able to judge accurately with your eyes. For instance, look at the two lines drawn below. Which line is longer? Take a guess, then measure each line in thumb widths to see if you were right.

ACTIVITY

Walking heel to toe, count the "feet" between opposite walls of your classroom. Now measure the same distance with a reliable tool for measuring feet. How do the two units of measurement— your own foot versus a standard "foot"–compare?

Objective
- To understand and calculate units of measure

Teaching Strategies

Review with students the measurement system used in the United States. This will be particularly important if some of the students are English language learners. Brainstorm a list of countries where the metric system is used (*virtually every country other than the United States*). After students have read the chart in their books, ask them to calculate their height in meters. To expand students' understanding, you might ask them to look around their homes and list items that utilize the metric system of measurement, such as measuring sticks, measuring cups, scales, car speedometers, packaged food, and beverage or soda bottles.

Activity

Students may find great variation in the number of "feet" they measure by walking, since this will depend on the size of their feet. They should not, however, find any discrepancy in the number of feet each measures using a reliable tool.

MULTIPLE LEARNING STYLES

Logical and Mathematical Students with strong logical-mathematical abilities will appreciate an opportunity to create a measurement conversion resource sheet. Begin by asking them to list the ways in which things are measured in the United States. For example: distance is measured in inches, feet, yards, and miles; temperature is measured in Fahrenheit degrees; weight is measured in pounds and ounces.

Activity Have students research and list how distance, temperature, and weight are measured in countries that use the metric system. Ask them to organize the information on a resource sheet that could be used by tourists from their town traveling to Paris. **L2**

Objectives

- To read and analyze two poems
- To identify rhyme scheme
- To write an explanatory paragraph about sensory imagery

Skills

Reading/Thinking: Analyzing Arguments; Identifying Assumptions
Writing: Poem
Grammar/Language: Prepositional Phrases
Listening/Speaking: Poetry Reading
Collaboration: Literature Groups

Motivating
→ OPTIONS

Literature Launchers: "Getting to Know Nikki Giovanni"

Videodisc Side A, Segment 8

Also available in VHS.

Selection Focus Transparency 24: Have students discuss Hughes's comparison of poems and rainbows. Ask them to which other things poems might be compared.

Focus Activity: As an extension of the Focus Activity, have students use their ideas to write poems and share them in small groups.

Before You Read

a poem (for langston hughes) and *Dreams*

MEET NIKKI GIOVANNI

In addition to being a poet, Nikki Giovanni is a professor of English at Virginia Polytechnic Institute, a recording artist, a writer, a scholar, and a political and social activist.

Nikki Giovanni was born in 1943. "a poem (for langston hughes)" is from Shimmy Shimmy Shimmy Like My Sister Kate.

MEET LANGSTON HUGHES

Called the leading African American poet of the twentieth century, Langston Hughes wrote poetry, fiction, children's books, scripts, song lyrics, and works about history and music. (For more about Langston Hughes, see page 340.)

Langston Hughes was born in 1902 and died in 1967. "Dreams" can be found in his Collected Poems.

FOCUS ACTIVITY

If you were given an assignment to write a poem, what would you write about?

Sharing Ideas
Make a quick list of topics that are special to you and that might make good subjects for poems. Share your list with your classmates.

Setting a Purpose
The Nikki Giovanni selection includes a poem and a nonfiction prose piece. Read to see how those two parts relate and how both parts relate to the Langston Hughes poem.

BACKGROUND

According to Nikki Giovanni, if you're going to do anything about poetry, you should begin with Langston Hughes. Hughes remains the most important and respected African American poet of his time. In a simple yet powerful voice alive with the rhythm of jazz, he deals with racial injustice, social issues, and the human struggle for a life with dignity.

RESOURCE MANAGER

Lesson Planning Resource
The **Theme Three Planning Guide** (pp. 39–44) provides additional lesson notes and reduced versions of all print resources.

📁 **Other Print Resources**
- Active Reading Guide, p. 24
- Reading Workbook, pp. 39–40
- Grammar and Language Workbook, pp. 141–142
- Grammar and Composition Handbook, Lesson 7.1

- Quick Checks, p. 24
- Selection and Theme Assessment, pp. 43–44
- Performance Assessment, p. 23
- Spanish Summaries, p. 24
- Spanish Translations
- Inclusion Strategies
- English Language Learners Sourcebook

 Transparencies
- Selection Focus 24
- Literary Elements 24
- Grammar and Language 23

Technology
 Literature Launchers
 Audio Library
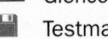 Spanish Audio Library
Glencoe Literature Web Site
Testmaker

a poem
(for langston hughes)

Nikki Giovanni ∾

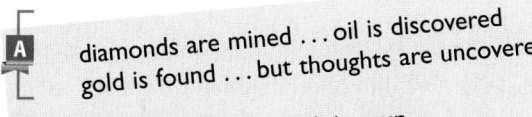

A
diamonds are mined . . . oil is discovered
gold is found . . . but thoughts are uncovered

B
wool is sheared . . . silk is spun
weaving is hard . . . but words are fun

5 highways span . . . bridges connect
country roads ramble . . . but i suspect

C
    if i took a rainbow ride
    i could be there by your side

metaphor° has its point of view
10 allusion° and illusion° . . . too

meter . . . verse . . . classical . . . free
poems are what you do to me

let's look at this one more time
since i've put this rap to rhyme

15   when i take my rainbow ride
      you'll be right there at my side

D
hey bop hey bop hey re re bop

---

9 In a *metaphor,* two unlike things are compared (without using *like* or *as*).
10 An *allusion* is a reference that is not directly identified or explained, like
the poet's reference to rap in line 14. The poet assumes the reader knows
what a rap is. An *illusion* is a false idea or a misleading appearance, like a
magician's trick.

FACING CHALLENGE 🎋 259

DIALOGUE Ask students to think about how Giovanni uses dialogue. *(The way it is written it flows like a conversation. Also, Giovanni shares her thoughts during the phone conversation.)*

F **Critical Thinking**

ANALYZING ARGUMENTS Ask students if they agree or disagree with Giovanni when she says "the fax is not your friend...." Encourage students to consider how fax machines and other tools can both save time and add pressure to people's lives. If you wish, share this model to guide students in analyzing arguments.

Model: My first idea is that fax machines are great because they are so fast. Then I realize the newspaper could not ask for the poem on such short notice if there were no fax machines. It seems that now everything is expected to be done very quickly, which adds a lot of pressure to people's lives.

G **Literary Elements**

POINT OF VIEW Point out to students that this piece is written from the first-person point of view. Have them discuss how it might be different if it were written from the point of view of the person at the newspaper. *(Readers might see the other woman's fear that Giovanni won't get the poem finished on time.)*

---

a poem (for langston hughes)

USA Today called my office one day. It was a Tuesday, a pretty day. I remember sitting there, the phone rang, I said, "Giovanni," because that's the way I answer the phone. A woman said, "I'm from *USA Today* and we're going to do a feature on poetry and we'd like to know if you could contribute to it."

I said, "Sure," thinking they want an interview or something of that nature. The woman said, "We really would like a poem from you." I said, "You'd like a poem from me?" Great. And she said, "We'd like it on Wednesday or Thursday." I said, "Wednesday and Thursday when?" "No, no," she said. "We want it within two days." I said, "You're kidding."

But I thought about it and thought, "Okay, okay, I'm not going to say I can't do it." So I said, "Well, okay, I'll do it. I'll mail it over." And she said, "No, no, I want to give you the fax number and you have to fax it over because we'll be just putting it right in the paper and we need it at once. Not only by Thursday, but by Thursday at ten o'clock in the morning." The fax is not your friend, because in the old days of the post office you could always say, "Gee, I put it in the mail yesterday, I'm surprised you don't have it," one of those kind of things. But with a fax, you fax it over at 9:00, it's supposed to be there at 9:05.

I was sitting in my office brooding. I have a small office. Actually I'm quite fortunate because at least it's mine, I don't have to share it. It overlooks Virginia Tech;[1] we have a drill field and my office overlooks the drill field. I was just sitting, looking out my window, pouting. I said to myself, and I think it's a human kind of thing, "It isn't that *I* couldn't write a poem and have it there overnight practically; nobody could." And then a little voice said, "Langston Hughes could have done it."

It's true, Langston Hughes could have done it. I was still pouting, but now it was okay, and I said, "If Langston Hughes could have done it, what would he have done it on?" By now I'm trying to think really, really hard. Langston said, "Always write a love poem no matter what you're doing. Always write a love poem." That made sense. You should always love what you're doing. That's all he meant. . . .

So I wrote *a poem (for langston hughes)*. If you're going to do anything on poetry it ought to start, in all fairness, with Langston Hughes.

---

1. *Virginia Tech* is Virginia Polytechnic Institute, the university where Giovanni teaches.

Teaching Options

Grammar and Language *Minilesson*

Prepositional Phrases Write these sentences on the board: *You'd like a poem from me? We'd like it on Wednesday or Thursday.* Remind students that a prepositional phrase begins with a preposition and ends with a noun or pronoun. The first phrase modifies *poem*, a noun, so it is acting as an adjective. The second modifies *'d like (would like)*, a verb, so it is acting as an adverb.

Activity Have students tell whether the underlined phrases act as adjectives or adverbs and which words they modify.
1. I was sitting in my office.
2. We're going to do a feature on poetry.
3. We really would like a poem from you.

(Answers: 1. adverb; *was sitting* 2. adjective; *feature* 3. adjective; *poem*) **L2**
COLLAB. LEARN.

Additional Resources

📖 ***Grammar and Language Transparency 23***

📕 ***Grammar and Language Workbook,*** pp. 141–142

📕 ***Grammar and Composition Handbook,*** Lesson 7.1

📕 ***Writer's Choice,*** Lesson 13.1

260

DREAMS

Langston Hughes

Hold fast to dreams
For if dreams die
Life is a broken-winged bird
That cannot fly.

Hold fast to dreams
For when dreams go
Life is a barren field
Frozen with snow.

Portrait of Langston Hughes, 1902–1967, Poet. Winold Reiss (1886–1953). Pastel on artist board, 76.3 x 54.9 cm. National Portrait Gallery, Washington, DC.

Responding to the Selection

Personal Response

Students should be able to understand that Giovanni's poem is speaking about her connection with Langston Hughes, with his poems, and with poetry in general.

Analyzing Literature

1. She was asked to write the poem for a newspaper.
2. He encourages his readers to keep their dreams alive.
3. When she writes poems, Langston Hughes as a person and a poet is always with her.
4. The first four words are referring to different aspects and styles of poetry; then she speaks directly to Hughes, saying his poems affect her deeply.
5. The poet uses *Life is a broken-winged bird/That cannot fly.* and *Life is a barren field/Frozen with snow.*
6. "Always write a love poem no matter what you're doing." Giovanni follows his advice by writing a poem to Hughes. Students might recognize the importance of doing all activities with care, respect, and love.
7. Some students may suggest that she is talking about any creative act, such as writing a poem.
8. Students should understand that a "broken-winged bird" cannot function—that without dreams people cannot function.
9. She had to write a poem in a very short time. At first she doubted whether she could do it, but then she looked to Langston Hughes's example, and she wrote the poem.
10. Some students may say they learned about poetic images, others may mention how poetry connects people to one another, and still others may say that poetry can contain important messages about how to live.

Responding to Literature

PERSONAL RESPONSE

Could you feel Giovanni's connection to Langston Hughes and to the subject of poetry as you read these two poems? Explain.

Analyzing Literature

RECALL

1. What circumstances led Giovanni to write her poem?
2. What advice does Langston Hughes give in "Dreams"?

INTERPRET

3. How do you think the title of Giovanni's poem relates to her poem's theme?
4. What do you think Giovanni means by these lines?

   meter . . . verse . . . classical . . . free
   poems are what you do to me

5. What two **metaphors** (figures of speech that compare two unlike things) does the poet use in "Dreams"?

EVALUATE AND CONNECT

6. What advice by Langston Hughes does Giovanni mention? Does she follow it? Do you think it is good advice? Explain.
7. What do you think Giovanni means when she uses the expression "my rainbow ride"?
8. In your opinion, what does Hughes mean by "broken-winged bird"?
9. Theme Connection   What challenge did Nikki Giovanni face? How did she respond to it?
10. What did you learn about poetry from reading the two poems?

LITERARY ELEMENTS

Rhyme Scheme

The most common type of rhyme in poetry is called end rhyme, so called because it occurs at the ends of lines. To find the **rhyme scheme,** or pattern, of a poem that uses end rhymes, mark each line according to the sound at the end. Mark the first line with an *a.* Whenever you find another line that ends with the same sound, mark that line with an *a* also. Then mark the next end-of-the-line sound with a *b* and so on.

Mary had a little lamb	*a*
Its fleece was white as snow,	*b*
And everywhere that Mary went	*c*
The lamb was sure to go.	*b*

1. Copy "a poem (for langston hughes)" and mark the end of each line as shown above. Then describe the rhyme scheme.

2. Find another poem in this book that has end rhymes. Copy it and mark its rhyme scheme.

● See **Literary Terms Handbook,** p. R9.

LITERARY ELEMENTS

1. The rhyme scheme for "a poem (for langston hughes)" is aa, bb, cc, dd, ee, ff, gg, dd, h
2. The rhyme scheme for "Dreams" is abcb, aded.

Additional Resources

Literary Elements Transparency 24

Extending Your Response

Writing About Literature

Sensory Imagery The poems by Giovanni and Hughes are filled with images that appeal to the senses. Pick out your favorite image from one of the poems. Write a paragraph explaining the image and telling why you find it particularly effective.

Literature Groups

Poet's Corner In her poem, Nikki Giovanni states, "i've put this rap to rhyme." Could this poem be performed as a rap? What do you think the last line of the poem means? In small groups, talk about the connection between music and poetry. Then decide what kind of music would best suit each of the two poems.

Creative Writing

For Whom? Think about the ideas you discussed for the **Focus Activity** on page 258. Were any of these ideas based on some special person? Write a short poem for a person in your life. Focus on one special thing that is important to this person, as Giovanni does in "a poem (for langston hughes)."

Listening and Speaking

Appreciating Poetry Take turns sharing your group's musical interpretations of the poems with your classmates. Notice how different readings and different music affect your experience of the poems.

Reading Further

To read more by Nikki Giovanni, try:

Ego-Tripping and Other Poems for Young People

For more of Langston Hughes's poetry, try:
The Dream Keeper and Other Poems

Save your work for your portfolio.

Skill Minilessons

READING AND THINKING • IDENTIFYING ASSUMPTIONS

An **assumption** is a piece of information that a writer assumes, or takes for granted, the reader knows. For example, Nikki Giovanni assumes that her readers know about Langston Hughes and his importance to the world of poetry. She also assumes that her readers know what a rap is. As you read, identify the assumptions the writer is making about your knowledge about a topic. Ask yourself: *Is there something I should know more about*

in order to understand this poem clearly? How can I learn more about this topic?

PRACTICE Reread the poem "Slam, Dunk, & Hook" in Theme 2. What assumptions does the poet make about his readers' prior knowledge? In a paragraph, identify one or two of these assumptions.

● For more about related reading strategies, see **Reading Handbook,** pp. R86–R96.

Extending Your Response

Writing About Literature

Students' paragraphs should
- focus on one image that appeals to them.
- explain the image and why it is effective.

Creative Writing

Students' poems should
- be about a person in their lives.
- focus on one thing important to this person.

Literature Groups Explain to students that musical lyrics and poetry are closely connected by rhyme, rhythm, and melody.
COLLAB. LEARN.

Listening and Speaking

Encourage students to discuss how the feeling of each poem changes with different types of music.

Skill Minilesson

READING AND THINKING
- **IDENTIFYING ASSUMPTIONS**

Students' paragraphs should identify the poet's assumption that readers know such basketball terms as *slam*, *dunk*, and *hook*.

Additional Resources
📁 *Reading Workbook,* pp. 39–46

✔ ASSESSMENT OPTIONS

📁 *Quick Checks,* p. 24

📁 *Selection and Theme Assessment,* pp. 43–44

📁 *Performance Assessment,* p. 23

💾 *Testmaker*

Technology Skills

Objectives

- To use E-mail (electronic mail) to communicate over the Internet
- To understand on-line safety rules
- To use the Internet to investigate Internet safety and Internet scams

Teaching Strategies

An excellent motivational introduction to this feature would be to show students how to use a computer in your school to send and retrieve E-mail. You may want to include some or all of the following:

- how to connect to the Internet or an on-line service
- how to send and retrieve messages electronically
- how to forward E-mail
- how to send multiple copies of messages
- how to save, print, and delete E-mail
- how to upload a text file to send as E-mail

Adapting to Available Technology

Some telephone companies, cable companies, and other companies now offer extremely high-speed Internet access. If your school relies on slower modems for Internet access, you may want to warn students not to send large graphic files electronically, as they will slow down or even make the system crash.

Teaching Options

E-Mail: On-line Safety

When you communicate via the Internet, you have the chance to talk with people from all over the world. You can learn about other cultures, get homework help, and share messages with kids your own age. But you may also run into people who do not have your best interests at heart. It's important that you follow a few simple rules to keep yourself safe as you cruise along the information superhighway.

Talk About It

In a small group, spend five minutes brainstorming some safety rules you think may apply to E-mail communication. Record each rule your group comes up with. Share your rules and the reasons behind them with your classmates. Decide as a class which rules are the most helpful. Then compare your findings with the following rules.

Rules for On-line Safety

1. Never give out personal information, such as your address, telephone number, or a parent's work address or phone number, in a public message—like a chat room, bulletin board, or message to an E-mail pal—without the permission of your parent or guardian.

2. Never share your Internet password with anyone, not even your best friend. Only you and your parents should know it.

3. Never give the name and location of your school to anyone on the Internet.

4. Never agree to a face-to-face meeting with someone you've encountered on the Internet without informing your parent or guardian. If your parent or guardian agrees to a meeting, it should be in a public place, and your parent or guardian should go with you.

5. If you receive an E-mail message that is threatening or belligerent, or if anyone sends you mail or files that make you feel uncomfortable in any way, tell a responsible adult immediately. Do not respond to such a message.

6. Never send your picture or anything else to someone on the Internet without the permission of your parent or guardian.

7. If an E-mail mentor claims to work for a certain company, verify that by logging on to the company's Web site and searching for her or his name and title. If the company doesn't have a Web site, ask an adult to call the company's personnel office to confirm her or his employment.

264   THEME 3

MEETING INDIVIDUAL NEEDS — INCLUSION STRATEGIES

Learning Disabled Some students may have trouble remembering the steps used to send electronic mail.

Activity Have one student perform the steps needed to send E-mail while another student explains each step aloud: turning on the computer, logging on, connecting to the Internet, and finally sending E-mail. You may want to

have the pair post their instructions near the computer for others to refer to as needed. **L1 COLLAB. LEARN.**

Additional Resources
📂 *Inclusion Strategies*

8. Remember that people on-line may not be who they claim to be.

9. Don't get involved in chain letters, especially those that require you to send anyone money.

10. Don't respond to spam offers that sound too good to be true. They almost certainly *are* too good to be true.

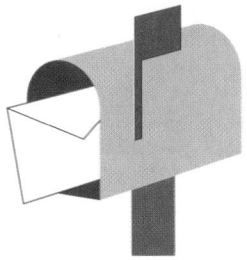

Spam

Spam is unsolicited mass mailings by way of E-mail. It's the Internet version of junk mail. If you get on a mailing list, you may end up getting spammed. One reason the rules above warn you against giving out information about yourself or your family is that it could fall into the hands of people who will send you spam. They can also sell or trade information about you to other spammers. While much of the spam that circulates on the Net is legitimate advertising, there are also scam artists out there trying to make money (maybe your money) dishonestly. Remember, you don't have to give anyone any information you don't want to share.

All these warnings do not mean that you can't trust anyone on the Net. What they do mean is that you ought to exercise caution anytime you're in contact with someone you don't know.

ACTIVITIES

1. In your journal, keep a list of the names and E-mail addresses of people with whom you communicate regularly. If you start receiving E-mail that is threatening or inappropriate, cross that person's name and address from your list and notify a responsible adult.

2. Log on to the World Wide Web and search for sites that address Internet safety. You may want to begin your search at www.safeteens.com.

3. Go to the Federal Trade Commission's Web site (www.ftc.gov) to find out more about the kinds of scams that can reach people's E-mail boxes. Look for the FTC's "Dirty Dozen" list. Share what you learn with your classmates.

4. Share your knowledge of E-mail safety with the computer club at a local elementary school.

Activities

Discuss the directions with the class to be sure everyone understands how to complete the activities and to answer any questions students might have about Internet safety or sending E-mail.

Students should

- find and share information from the World Wide Web relating to Internet safety.
- share with the class information about Internet scams they find on the Federal Trade Commission's Web Site.
- create posters for or deliver a talk to elementary school students about Internet safety.
- keep a journal listing the names and E-mail addresses of people they communicate with regularly.

TechnoTalk

The Internet and the World Wide Web The Internet, which began in 1969, is a network of interconnected computers. Its purpose was to allow scientists to communicate with each other even if part of the network were destroyed, say by a bomb or sabotage. The World Wide Web, which wasn't created until 1990, is a system for publishing information on the Internet. Web pages look much like magazine pages and include text (in many styles and sizes) and graphics. There were as many as 150 million Web pages in 1997.

INTERDISCIPLINARY CONNECTION

Internet Safety Rules Some students may want to use their artistic and computer skills to create a poster or banner that lists on-line safety rules.

Activity Invite a small group of students to work together to list what they have learned about Internet safety from the activities on these pages. Have students use this list to create a computer-generated poster or banner listing their Internet safety rules. Encourage students to think carefully about design elements, such as color schemes, layout, and typefaces, so that the text on their poster is attractive, engaging, and easy to read from a distance. **L2**

MEDIA Connection

Objectives

- To read and understand a folktale
- To understand and apply strategies for accessing a Web site

Literature ——— LINK

Racing the Great Bear This story from the Choctaw tradition connects to "Racing the Great Bear," the literature selection that immediately follows this lesson. Point out the connection by telling students that many traditional stories and tales give us insight into how ancient peoples understood the world around them. The Choctaw explain the 'possum's wide mouth with a humorous story about his mischievous nature and the trick he plays on a deer. The Iroquois story, "Racing the Great Bear," explains the perilous journey one boy makes into manhood.

Respond

1. Some students may say he is mischievous or mean. Others may think he is smart and funny.
2. Students may find such folktales as the Anansi tales, the Just-So stories, and the many Native American tales.

Additional Resources
📁 *Media Connections*, p. 5

Teaching Options

interNET CONNECTION

To gather information about the Native American nations mentioned, have students enter such keywords as *Iroquois Confederacy* or *Choctaw Nation*.

MEDIA Connection

WEB SITE

On the Internet, you'll often find something unexpected. The following Native American folktale came from a Web site devoted to information about skunks and opossums.

Why 'Possum Has a Large Mouth: A Choctaw Folktale

Address: ▼ | The Wonderful Skunk and Opossum Web Site

As Told by Bayou Lacomb

Very little food there was for Deer one dry season. He became thin and weak. One day he met 'Possum. Deer at once exclaimed, "Why, 'Possum, how fat you are! How do you keep so fat when I cannot find enough to eat?"

'Possum said, "I live on persimmons. They are very large this year, so I have all I want to eat."

"How do you get the persimmons?" asked Deer. "They grow so high!"

"That is easy," said 'Possum. "I go to the top of a high hill. Then I run down and strike a large persimmon tree so hard with my head that all the ripe persimmons

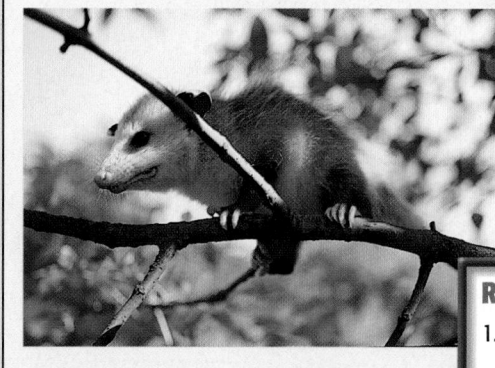

drop to the ground. Then I sit there and eat them."

"That is easily done," said Deer. "I will try it. Now watch me."

'Possum waited. Deer went to the top of a nearby hill. He ran down and struck the tree with his head. 'Possum watched him, laughing. He opened his mouth so wide while he laughed that he stretched it out. That is why 'Possum has such a large mouth.

Respond

1. What characteristic of 'Possum can you identify from his behavior in this folktale?
2. There are many folktales and myths that tell how some animal or plant got to be the way it is. Look on the Internet or in a library for another one that you can share with the class.

266 🐿 THEME 3

Reading Minilesson

Using Graphic Aids Students will see that monitoring their own comprehension is a simple task when reading the folktale on this page.

Activity Have each student create a reading handprint for the Web site "Why 'Possum Has a Large Mouth" by tracing a hand on a sheet of paper and writing the story's title on the palm. Students should write these words one per finger: *Somebody; Wanted; But; So; Then.* Students can fill in the information on the handprint as they read or later. For reading "Racing the Great Bear," have students each make at least two handprints, replacing *Then* on the second handprint with *Finally.* **L2**

Additional Resources
📁 *Reading Workbook*

Before You Read

Racing the Great Bear

MEET JOSEPH BRUCHAC

Joseph Bruchac (broo' shak) grew up in the Adirondack region of New York. As a member of the Abenaki tribe, he has drawn on his own life and Native American legends for many of his more than sixty books. He writes, "One of the reasons I have devoted so much of my own life to the understanding and the respectful telling of traditional Native stories is my strong belief that now, more than ever, these tales have much to teach us."

Joseph Bruchac was born in 1942. This story was first published in 1993.

FOCUS ACTIVITY

How do people become leaders? Is it because they are intelligent, ambitious, compassionate, or brave?

Discuss
Talk with your classmates about the traits and experiences that make some men and women stand out as leaders.

Setting a Purpose
Read to see what you can learn about how some people become leaders.

BACKGROUND

The Time and Place   This story takes place in an unknown time in the ancient past.

Did You Know?   When the early Europeans came to America, the Iroquois lived south of Lake Ontario in the area that is now New York State. The Iroquois referred to themselves with a name that means "people of the longhouse," the longhouse being their traditional dwelling.

VOCABULARY PREVIEW

clan (klan) *n.* a group of families descended from a common ancestor; p. 270
keen (kēn) *adj.* highly sensitive; sharp; p. 272
pursue (pər soo') *v.* to chase; p. 273
spare (spār) *v.* to treat with mercy; hold back from harming or injuring; p. 274
sinewy (sin'ū ē) *adj.* physically tough, or powerful; p. 274
embrace (em brās') *v.* to hug or hold in the arms, especially as a sign of love or affection; p. 275

Before Reading

Objectives

• To read and analyze a Native American story about a boy who faces a great challenge
• To recognize how the oral tradition can affect a story
• To analyze the effectiveness of dialogue in a story

Skills

Reading/Thinking: Focusing on a Question; Synthesizing; Inferring; Monitoring Comprehension; Drawing Conclusions; Setting a Reading Purpose
Writing: Journal Entry
Vocabulary: Multiple-Meaning Words
Grammar/Language: Comparative and Superlative Adjectives; Possessive Pronouns
Listening/Speaking: Radio Play; Telling a Story
Collaboration: Literature Groups

Motivating

→OPTIONS

Selection Focus Transparency 25: Have students discuss the qualities of a hero. Point out that hero stories in cultures throughout the world often contain the same or similar elements.

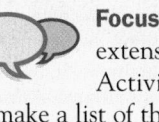

Focus Activity: As an extension of the Focus Activity, have students make a list of the traits they think a hero has. Then have them share their ideas in small groups.

RESOURCE MANAGER

Lesson Planning Resource
The *Theme Three Planning Guide* (pp. 45–52) provides additional lesson notes and reduced versions of all print resources.

📁 **Other Print Resources**
• Active Reading Guide, p. 25
• Vocabulary Practice, p. 16
• Reading Workbook, pp. 41–42
• Grammar and Language Workbook, pp. 109–110, 121–124

• Grammar and Composition Handbook, Lessons 4.4, 5.3, 5.4
• Quick Checks, p. 25
• Selection and Theme Assessment, pp. 45–46
• Performance Assessment, p. 24
• Spanish Summaries, p. 25
• Inclusion Strategies
• English Language Learners Sourcebook

🖥 **Transparencies**
• Selection Focus 25
• Literary Elements 25
• Grammar and Language 24

Technology
🎧 Audio Library
🎧 Spanish Audio Library
🖥 Glencoe Literature Web Site
💾 Testmaker

SUMMARY

When some of the Seneca go to visit the Onondaga, they do not return. The village wants a brave warrior to discover the reason. When no one volunteers, the chief chooses a boy named Swift Runner. Swift Runner discovers and defeats a monster bear, brings the lost people back to life, and grows into a strong warrior and a healer.

📁 *Spanish Summaries,* p. 25

 Active Reading

PREDICT Ask students to predict whether this messenger will be successful in establishing peace. *(Some students might say he will be because he is sent by the Creator.)*

Additional Resources
📁 *Active Reading Guide,* p. 25

🎧 *Audio Library*

🎧 *Spanish Audio Library*

Teaching Options

Racing the Great Bear

Retold by Joseph Bruchac ∾

NE ONENDJI. Hear my story, which happened long ago. For many generations, the five nations of the Haudenosaunee, the People of the Longhouse, had been at war with one another. No one could say how the wars began, but each time a man of one nation was killed, his relatives sought revenge in the blood feud,[1] and so the fighting continued. Then the Creator took pity on his people and sent a messenger of peace.

---

1. A *feud* (fūd) is a bitter, long-running quarrel or clash between two individuals or groups. A *blood feud* involves members of the same group. Here, that group is the Five Nations.

CONNECTING TO OTHER SELECTIONS

The chart at the right shows three ways to connect "Racing the Great Bear" to other selections in this book.

For specific teaching strategies, see the *Theme Three Planning Guide,* pages 48–49.

Connection	Title
Life Skills: Implementing and Performing	➡ "Atalanta," p. 718
Thematic: Heroes	➡ "Prometheus," p. 743
Literary: Oral Tradition	➡ "The Boy and His Grandfather," p. 495

Grizzly Bear in a Mountainous Landscape (detail). Carl Rungius (1869–1959). Oil on canvas, 47 x 52 in. Private collection.

FYI

The painter Carl Rungius was born in Germany and lived in Los Angeles during the 1930s. He was well known for his paintings of large American game animals.

B Critical Thinking

FOCUSING ON A QUESTION Ask students to explain why the young Seneca men decide to visit the Onondaga people. *(After generations of war, a Great Peace has been established; they think it is now safe to visit their former enemies.)*

Historical Note

The Great Peace referred to in the story is a historic fact. Around 1570, the Iroquois formed the League of Five Nations, or Iroquois Confederacy. It consisted of the Seneca, Onondega, Oneida, Mohawk, and Cayuga nations. The League was a representative organization. When the United States was founded, the Iroquois League served as a model for the country's new democracy.

C Literary Elements

ORAL TRADITION: *Narrator* Point out that most oral tradition stories are told from a third-person point of view because they are about the history and culture of an entire people.

The Peacemaker traveled from nation to nation, convincing the people of the Five Nations—the Mohawk, the Oneida, the Onondaga, the Cayuga, and the Seneca[2]—that it was wrong for brothers to kill one another. It was not easy, but finally the nations agreed and the Great Peace began. Most welcomed that peace, though there were some beings with bad hearts who wished to see the return of war.

B One day, not long after the Great Peace had been established, some young men in a Seneca village decided they would pay a visit to the Onondaga people.

2. Pronunciations: *Oneida* (ō nī′ də), *Onondaga* (on′ ən dô′ ga), *Cayuga* (kā ū′ gə), *Seneca* (sen′ ə kə)

"It is safe now to walk the trail between our nations," the young men said. "We will return after the sun has risen and set seven times."

Then they set out. They walked toward the east until they were lost from sight in the hills. But many more than seven days passed, and those young men never returned. Now another group of young men left, wanting to find out where their friends had gone. They, too, did not return. **C**

The people grew worried. Parties were sent out to look for the vanished young men, but no sign was found. And the searchers who went too far into the hills did not return, either.

ENGLISH LANGUAGE LEARNERS

Multiple-Meaning Words Explain to English language learners that the word *party* has several meanings. Students will probably be familiar with *party* as in "a gathering." In this story, *party* means "a group of people doing something together."

Activity Have students use the dictionary to find more definitions of the word *party*. Have them write a sentence for each definition they find. (Other possible definitions: "a group of people organized to gain political control," *political party;* "a person who takes part in something," *a party to a plot;* and "each of the sides in a contract," *the party of the first part.*) **COLLAB. LEARN.**

Additional Resources

📁 *English Language Learners Sourcebook*

D Critical Thinking

SYNTHESIZING Have students identify the reasons the chief calls the council meeting. *(After many groups do not return, the clan mothers advise the chief to send a warrior.)*

E Critical Thinking

INFERRING Ask students what the consequences might be if the Onondaga have captured the young Seneca men. *(The Great Peace will be broken and there will be war.)*

F Literary Elements

ORAL TRADITION Point out that in many stories from the oral tradition the main character, or hero, is often an outcast who must face a challenge of some kind.

G Literary Elements

CHARACTER Ask students what the young man's statement tells them about Swift Runner. *(The tribe shouldn't expect very much.)* What tone does the young man use when he makes this statement? *(His tone is probably sarcastic.)*

H Literary Elements

CHARACTER Ask students how they would describe Swift Runner. *(He's quiet, small, poor, shabby, unassuming, and has no experience in war, hunting, or survival away from the camp.)*

Teaching Options

The old chief of the village thought long and hard. He asked the clan mothers, those wise women whose job it was to choose the chiefs and give them good advice, what should be done.

"We must find someone brave enough to face whatever danger is out there," the clan mothers said.

So the old chief called the whole village to a council meeting. He held up a white strand of wampum beads made from quahog[3] clamshells as he spoke.

Did You Know?

Wampum is a shortened form of the Algonquian word *wampumpeag,* or *wampum-peake,* which means "a string of white shell beads." These small, polished beads were used to decorate headbands, belts, collars, or necklaces. Some Native Americans in the Northeast used wampum as a form of money, but its most significant use was in rituals of kinship and mourning and to record history. White wampum, the most precious of all, symbolizes a state of well-being and truth.

"Hear me," he said. "I am of two minds about what has happened to our people. It may be that the Onondaga have broken the peace and captured them. It may be there is something with an evil mind that wishes to destroy this new peace and so has killed our people. Now someone must go and find out. Who is brave enough? Who will come and take this wampum from my hand?"

Many men were gathered in that council. Some were known to speak of themselves as brave warriors. Still, though they muttered to one another, no man stepped forward to take the strand of wampum. The old chief began to walk about the circle, holding the wampum in front of each man in turn. But each man only lowered his eyes to the ground. No man lifted his hand to take the wampum.

Just outside the circle stood a boy who had not yet become a man. His parents were dead, and he lived with his grandmother in her old lodge at the edge of the village. His clothing was always torn and his face dirty because his grandmother was too old to care for him as a mother would. The other young men made fun of him, and as a joke they called him Swift Runner—even though no one had ever seen him run and it was thought that he was weak and lazy. All he ever seemed to do was play with his little dog or sit by the fire and listen when the old people were talking.

"Our chief has forgotten our greatest warrior," one of the young men said to another, tilting his head toward Swift Runner.

"*Nyoh,*" the other young man said, laughing. "Yes. Why does he not offer the wampum to Swift Runner?"

The chief looked around the circle of men, and the laughing stopped. He walked out of the circle to the place where the small boy in torn clothes stood. He held out the wampum and Swift Runner took it without hesitating.

"I accept this," Swift Runner said. "It is right that I be the one to face the danger.

---

3. The *quahog* (kwô′ hŏg) is a type of clam found on the Atlantic coast of North America.

Vocabulary
clan (klan) *n.* a group of families descended from a common ancestor

Listening and Speaking *Minilesson*

Radio Play Discuss with students the elements that make a radio play effective, pointing out that it must rely solely on dialogue, sound effects, and narration.

Activity Have students create a radio play about the Seneca council as it is described on this page. The play can begin with the clan mothers' advice and end with Swift Runner accepting the wampum. You might divide the class into small groups, and have each group present a different version of the event. Make sure that the students' plays include lines for the narrator, the clan mothers, the chief, the young men, and Swift Runner. **L2 COLLAB. LEARN.**

Joseph Bruchac ∾

In the eyes of the people I am worthless, so if I do not return, it will not matter. I will leave when the sun rises tomorrow."

When Swift Runner arrived home at his grandmother's lodge, the old woman was waiting for him.

"Grandson," she said, "I know what you have done. The people of this village no longer remember, but your father was a great warrior. Our family is a family that has power."

Then she reached up into the rafters and took down a heavy bow. It was blackened with smoke and seemed so thick that no man could bend it.

Iroquois Wampum Belts. Rufus Grider. Newberry Library, Chicago.

"If you can string this bow, Grandson," the old woman said, "you are ready to face whatever waits for you on the trail."

Swift Runner took the bow. It was as thick as a man's wrist, but he bent it with ease and strung it.

"Wah-hah!" said his grandmother. "You are the one I knew you would grow up to be. Now you must sleep. At dawn we will make you ready for your journey."

It was not easy for Swift Runner to sleep, but when he woke the next morning, he felt strong and clearheaded. His grandmother was sitting by the fire with a cap in her hand.

"This was your grandfather's cap," she said. "I have sewed four hummingbird feathers on it. It will make your feet more swift."

Swift Runner took the cap and placed it on his head.

His grandmother held up four pairs of moccasins.

"Carry these tied to your waist. When one pair wears out, throw them aside and put on the next pair."

Swift Runner took the moccasins and tied them to his belt.

Next his grandmother picked up a small pouch. "In this pouch is cornmeal mixed with maple sugar," she said. "It is the only food you will need as you travel. It will give you strength when you eat it each evening."

Swift Runner took the pouch and hung it from his belt by the moccasins.

"The last thing I must give you," said the old woman, "is this advice. Pay close attention to your little dog. You have treated him well and so he is your great friend. He is small, but his eyes and nose

I ⬛ Literary Elements

ORAL TRADITION Swift Runner's grandmother transfers information to him orally, as it was passed on to her. Ask students to talk about information they have received this way. *(Students might mention stories their parents have told them.)*

J ⬛ Active Reading

CONNECT Ask students to whom they think the bow belonged. *(It might have belonged to Swift Runner's father or grandfather.)*

> **Language Note**
>
> Many of the names of states in the U.S. have Native American origins; for example, *Idaho* ("Behold the sun coming down the mountains."), *Massachusetts* ("at the big hill"), *Dakota* ("allies"), *Kentucky* ("level land"), and *Oklahoma* ("the red people").

K ⬛ Critical Thinking

DRAWING CONCLUSIONS Discuss the possible reasons Swift Runner's grandmother knows all the things he will need for his journey. *(She has great power and wisdom. Also, she may have helped Swift Runner's grandfather and father prepare for long journeys.)*

L ⬛ Literary Elements

ORAL TRADITION The oral tradition of many cultures includes animals who help a hero in times of need.

FACING CHALLENGE 🐾 271

Reading *Minilesson*

Monitoring Comprehension Remind students that they need to check their comprehension as they are reading. A good "fix-it" strategy is to stop and ask themselves questions about what they just read.

Activity Work with students to create a list of questions about Swift Runner and his journey. Then ask students to answer

the questions. **L2**
- Why is Swift Runner going on a journey?
- Who asked Swift Runner to take the journey? Why?
- Who is traveling with Swift Runner?
- What things does Swift Runner's grandmother give him? Why?

Additional Resources
📁 ***Reading Workbook,*** pp. 41–42

FACING CHALLENGE 🐾 271

272 🦫 THEME 3

Teaching Options

Active Reading

M Active Reading

RESPOND Have students explain whether they are surprised by Swift Runner's reaction to the bear. How would they expect him to react? *(Most students will probably say that they would expect him to be afraid or to run away.)*

N Literary Elements

ORAL TRADITION Point out to students that stories handed down from generation to generation also provide tips for success. In this case it goes something like this: Listen to the voice of experience.

O Active Reading

QUESTION Ask students why they think such a strong and dangerous bear would run away from a boy and a small dog. *(Swift Runner uses the special words a monster bear speaks when it attacks to terrify the bear, so the bear probably sees Swift Runner as a powerful warrior to be feared.)*

P Literary Elements

CHARACTER Encourage students to identify what the storyteller reveals about Swift Runner. *(He is brave and extremely determined to finish his task.)* How does the storyteller reveal this? *(He provides details of Swift Runner's actions along with the young man's actual words.)*

---

are <u>keen</u>. Keep him always in front of you. He will warn you of danger before it can strike you."

Then Swift Runner set out on his journey. His little dog stayed ahead of him, sniffing the air and sniffing the ground. By the time the sun was in the middle of the sky, they were far from the village. The trail passed through deep woods, and it seemed to the boy as if something was following them among the trees. But he could see nothing in the thick brush.

The trail curved toward the left, and the boy felt even more the presence of something watching. Suddenly his little dog ran into the brush at the side of the trail, barking loudly. There were the sounds of tree limbs breaking and heavy feet running. Then out of the forest came a Nyagwahe, a monster bear. Its great teeth were as long as a man's arm. It was twice as tall as a moose. Close at its heels was Swift Runner's little dog.

"I see you," Swift Runner shouted. "I am after you. You cannot escape me."

Swift Runner had learned those words by listening to the stories the old people told. They were the very words a monster bear speaks when it attacks, words that terrify anyone who hears them. On hearing those words, the great bear turned and fled from the boy.

Beaded Pouch. Iroquois. Velvet, metal, beads, cloth, length: 6½ in.

"You cannot escape me," Swift Runner shouted again. Then he ran after the bear.

The Nyagwahe turned toward the east, with Swift Runner and his dog close behind. It left the trail and plowed through the thick forest, breaking down great trees and leaving a path of destruction like that of a whirlwind. It ran up the tallest hills and down through the swamps, but the boy and the dog stayed at its heels. They ran past a great cave in the rocks. All around the cave were the bones of people the bear had caught and eaten.

"My relatives," Swift Runner called as he passed the cave, "I will not forget you. I am after the one who killed you. He will not escape me."

Throughout the day, the boy and his dog chased the great bear, growing closer bit by bit. At last, as the sun began to set, Swift Runner stopped at the head of a small valley and called his small dog to him.

"We will rest here for the night," the boy said. He took off his first pair of moccasins, whose soles were worn away to nothing. He threw them aside and put on a new pair. Swift Runner made a fire and

Vocabulary
keen (kēn) *adj.* highly sensitive; sharp

272 🦫 THEME 3

MEETING INDIVIDUAL NEEDS — INCLUSION STRATEGIES

Less-Proficient Readers Point out that the word *plowed* has several meanings. The most common is "to turn up soil with a plow." Explain that in this story it means "crash with great force into something." Another meaning is "to move as a plow does." (The ship *plowed* the waves.)

Activity Have students look up the verb *plow* and then write a sentence for each of its meanings. Be sure that students distinguish between the noun *plow* and the verb *to plow*. **L1**

Additional Resources
📁 *Inclusion Strategies*

Joseph Bruchac

sat beside it with his dog. Then he took out the pouch of cornmeal and maple sugar, sharing his food with his dog.

"Nothing will harm us," Swift Runner said. "Nothing can come close to our fire." He lay down and slept.

In the middle of the night, he was awakened by the growling of his dog. He sat up with his back to the fire and looked into the darkness. There, just outside the circle of light made by the flames, stood a dark figure that looked like a tall man. Its eyes glowed green.

"I am Nyagwahe," said the figure. "This is my human shape. Why do you pursue me?"

"You cannot escape me," Swift Runner said. "I chase you because you killed my people. I will not stop until I catch you and kill you."

The figure faded back into the darkness.

"You cannot escape me," Swift Runner said again. Then he patted his small dog and went to sleep.

As soon as the first light of the new day appeared, Swift Runner rose. He and his small dog took the trail. It was easy to follow the monster's path, for trees were uprooted and the earth torn by its great paws. They ran all through the morning. When the sun was in the middle of the sky, they reached the head of another valley. At the other end they saw the great bear running toward the east. Swift Runner pulled off his second pair of moccasins, whose soles were worn away to nothing. He put on his third pair and began to run again.

All through that day, they kept the Nyagwahe in sight, drawing closer bit by bit. When the sun began to set, Swift Runner stopped to make camp. He took off the third pair of moccasins, whose soles were worn away to nothing, and put on the last pair.

"Tomorrow," he said to his small dog, "we will catch the monster and kill it." He reached for his pouch of cornmeal and maple sugar, but when he opened it, he found it filled with worms. The magic of the Nyagwahe had done this. Swift Runner poured out the pouch and said in a loud voice, "You have spoiled our food, but it will not stop me. I am on your trail. You cannot escape me."

That night, once again, he was awakened by the growling of his dog. A dark figure stood just outside the circle of light.

Eastern Woodlands Moccasins. Iroquois. Hide, dyed quills, beads, length: 10 in.

Vocabulary
pursue (pər soo′) *v.* to chase

Q Active Reading

REVIEW Ask students to recall what Swift Runner's grandmother tells him about his little dog. Explain to them that they have to pull together many seemingly small details of a story to gain a deeper understanding of events that occur later. If you wish, use this model to illustrate the thinking process involved in reviewing.

Model: I remember that Swift Runner's grandmother told him to pay attention to his little dog because he would warn him of danger. When the monster bear approaches, the little dog growls to wake Swift Runner. Because he listened to his grandmother, Swift Runner is prepared for danger.

R Literary Elements

ORAL TRADITION In many traditional stories, how something happens is not always explained. How does he know that Nyagwahe killed his relatives? Have students list other questions about things that are not explained. *(Possible questions: How can Nyagwahe, in his animal shape, understand the threat from Swift Runner? How can the bear take on a human shape?)*

S Literary Elements

CHARACTER Swift Runner finds that his food has been spoiled. Ask students how he exhibits the qualities of a hero when faced with a major setback. *(Swift Runner does not give up. In fact, he seems more determined.)*

MEETING INDIVIDUAL NEEDS MULTIPLE LEARNING STYLES

Linguistic Some students may benefit from hearing part or all of this story read aloud. You might remind students that for hundreds of years storytellers told it aloud to younger generations as part of the Iroquois oral tradition.

Activity Ask volunteers to take turns reading the story aloud to the class. You may wish to have them develop a

Readers' Theater presentation. After the reading, have the audience share any new insights they may have developed as a result of hearing the story read aloud. **L2**

Literary Elements

T ORAL TRADITION Discuss with students how it is possible for the bear to assume a human form and speak to Swift Runner. Help students understand that the story reflects a Native American worldview in which spirits inhabit all aspects of the universe.

Active Reading

U PREDICT Encourage students to predict whether Swift Runner will kill the bear or simply take the great teeth to use for healing. Ask them to use what they know about Swift Runner's character to make their predictions. *(Students may predict that Swift Runner will kill the bear because he has repeated those intentions throughout the story and seems very determined to do so. Other students might say that Swift Runner will take only the bear's teeth because he can use them to help his people.)*

Literary Elements

V CLIMAX Point out to students that the bear's collapse is the climax, or turning point, of the story.

Literary Elements

W ORAL TRADITION Ask students to explain why Swift Runner can be so sure of himself at this very tense point. *(He has paid attention to the wisdom of the tribe, and it has paid off every time so far.)*

T It looked smaller than the night before, and the glow of its eyes was weak.

"I am Nyagwahe," the dark figure said. "Why do you pursue me?"

"You cannot escape me," Swift Runner said. "I am on your trail. You killed my people. You threatened the Great Peace. I will not rest until I catch you."

U "Hear me," said the Nyagwahe. "I see your power is greater than mine. Do not kill me. When you catch me, take my great teeth. They are my power, and you can use them for healing. Spare my life and I will go far to the north and never again bother the People of the Longhouse."

"You cannot escape me," Swift Runner said. "I am on your trail."

The dark figure faded back into the darkness, and Swift Runner sat for a long time, looking into the night.

At the first light of day, the boy and his dog took the trail. They had not gone far when they saw the Nyagwahe ahead of them. Its sides puffed in and out as it ran. The trail was beside a big lake with many alder trees close to the water. As the great bear ran past, the leaves were torn from the trees. Fast as the bear went, the boy and his dog came closer, bit by bit. At last, when the sun was in the middle of the sky, the giant bear could run no longer. It fell heavily to the earth, panting so hard that it stirred up clouds of dust.

V Swift Runner unslung his grandfather's bow and notched an arrow to the sinewy string.

Bear Claw Necklace. Native American. Bear claws, metal beads, otter or fisher tail, length: 57½ in.

"Shoot for my heart," said the Nyagwahe. "Aim well. If you cannot kill me with one arrow, I will take your life."

"No," Swift Runner said. "I have listened to the stories of my elders. Your only weak spot is the sole of your foot. Hold up your foot and I will kill you."

The great bear shook with fear. "You have defeated me," it pleaded. "Spare my life and I will leave forever."

"You must give me your great teeth," Swift Runner said. "Then you must leave and never bother the People of the Longhouse again."

W

Vocabulary

spare (spãr) *v.* to treat with mercy; hold back from harming or injuring
sinewy (sin′ū ē) *adj.* physically tough, strong, or powerful

Teaching Options

Grammar and Language *Minilesson*

Comparative and Superlative Adjectives Remind students that comparative adjectives compare two things or people and that superlative adjectives compare more than two things or people. Write the following sentence from the story on the board: *He was taller than the tallest man, and his little dog was bigger than a wolf.* Ask students to identify the comparative and superlative adjectives in

this sentence. (comparative: *taller, bigger;* superlative: *tallest*)

Activity Have each student write five sentences that contain comparative and superlative adjectives using information about the characters in the story as the subject matter of their sentences. **L2**

Additional Resources

📖 *Grammar and Language Transparency 24*

📕 *Grammar and Language Workbook,* pp. 121–124

📕 *Grammar and Composition Handbook,* Lesson 5.3, 5.4

📕 *Writer's Choice,* Lessons 12.3, 12.4

"I shall do as you say," said the Nyagwahe. "Take my great teeth."

Swift Runner lowered his bow. He stepped forward and pulled out the great bear's teeth. It rose to its feet and walked to the north, growing smaller as it went. It went over the hill and was gone.

Carrying the teeth of the Nyagwahe over his shoulder, Swift Runner turned back to the west, his dog at his side. He walked for three moons before he reached the place where the bones of his people were piled in front of the monster's empty cave. He collected those bones and walked around them four times. "Now," he said, "I must do something to make my people wake up." He went to a big hickory tree and began to push it over so that it would fall on the pile of bones.

"My people," he shouted, "get up quickly or this tree will land on you."

The bones of the people who had been killed all came together and jumped up, alive again and covered with flesh. They were filled with joy and gathered around Swift Runner.

"Great one," they said, "who are you?"

Alabaster Bear with Heartline. Contemporary Zuni. Alabaster, 1⅝ x 2¾ in. Private collection.

"I am Swift Runner," he said.

"How can that be?" one of the men said. "Swift Runner is a skinny little boy. You are a tall, strong man."

Swift Runner looked at himself and saw that it was so. He was taller than the tallest man, and his little dog was bigger than a wolf.

"I am Swift Runner," he said. "I was that boy and I am the man you see before you."

Then Swift Runner led his people back to the village. He carried with him the teeth of the Nyagwahe, and those who saw what he carried rejoiced. The trails were safe again, and the Great Peace would not be broken. Swift Runner went to his grandmother's lodge and <u>embraced</u> her.

"Grandson," she said, "you are now the man I knew you would grow up to be. Remember to use your power to help the people."

So it was that Swift Runner ran with the great bear and won the race. Throughout his long life, he used the teeth of the Nyagwahe to heal the sick, and he worked always to keep the Great Peace.

Da neho. I am finished.

❖

Vocabulary
embrace (em brās′) *v.* to hug or hold in the arms, especially as a sign of love or affection

---

⊠ Active Reading

QUESTION Ask students why they think Swift Runner has not noticed how he has changed. *(He has been too focused on his task to notice.)* Discuss why it is difficult to recognize gradual personal changes.

⊠ Literary Elements

ORAL TRADITION In the oral tradition, the story ends with a word of advice (from Swift Runner's grandmother). Ask students to find another example of the oral tradition in the closing lines. *(The narrator says "I am finished." This makes it sound like the story is being told aloud.)*

Thematic Focus

Facing Challenge Swift Runner accepts a challenge for which he needs great courage, strength, and wisdom. Have students give examples of the ways Swift Runner meets his challenge, including the traits he summons to meet his goal.

LITERATURE & HUMANITIES

Have students examine the sculpture *The Bear Tamer* in *American Art History and Culture*, page 383. Considering the stance and size of the figures, do students think this is a good representation of the young warrior's triumph over the bear?

✓ ASSESSMENT OPTIONS

📁 *Quick Checks,* p. 25

REAL-WORLD CONNECTION

Bear Facts Students might be interested in finding out more about bears. There are a variety of sources of information about bears, including books, videos, Internet sites, and zoos.

Activity Encourage students to learn more about a specific type of bear, such as a grizzly or a Kodiak. Tell them to search for information on the bears' geographical locations, their most suitable habitat, whether certain species are endangered, and what steps might be taken to improve or protect the bears' lives. When students have gathered information, have them work as a class or in small groups to share what they have learned. **L2** **COLLAB. LEARN.**

Responding to Literature

Personal Response

Most students will probably say that Swift Runner is brave, physically and mentally strong, intelligent, and compassionate.

Analyzing Literature

1. Several groups of people have left the village and have not returned. The chief wants to know what happened to them.
2. He was a boy with torn clothing and a dirty face, and people made fun of him, thinking he was weak and lazy.
3. A monster bear, twice the size of a moose, with teeth as long as a man's arm was to blame.
4. He has grown from a small boy into a strong and powerful man.
5. If they had broken the peace, the tribes would have returned to war.
6. She tells him that if he can string a thick, heavy bow, he will be the right person. She also gives him gifts of special moccasins, food, and his grandfather's cap.
7. It represents the physical and mental challenge of moving from childhood into adult life.
8. It is so called because Swift Runner is a boy who faces a daunting challenge to prove he is a man.
9. Initially, he is described as "weak and lazy," but after defeating the bear, he is described as "a tall, strong man."
10. Students should draw on their own experiences and clearly explain how a story or a character has influenced them.

PERSONAL RESPONSE

Think back to the discussion you had about leaders in the **Focus Activity** on page 267. Which traits make Swift Runner a leader of his tribe?

Analyzing Literature

RECALL

1. What happened in the village that causes the chief to seek a brave person?
2. Why was Swift Runner an unlikely candidate for the journey?
3. Who did Swift Runner discover had been killing the villagers? Describe the killer.
4. How is Swift Runner changed when he returns from his journey?

INTERPRET

5. Why was it so important to find out if the Onondaga had broken the peace?
6. How does Swift Runner's grandmother reassure him that he is ready to face the danger?
7. What does the Great Bear symbolize?
8. Why is "Racing the Great Bear" called a "coming of age" story?

EVALUATE AND CONNECT

9. How does the writer show that the character of Swift Runner changes during the story?
10. A number of times in the story, Swift Runner knows what to do because he has listened well to the stories of his elders. How have the stories and legends you've heard at home and in school affected your behavior?

LITERARY ELEMENTS

Oral Tradition

Stories that are passed from generation to generation by retelling them aloud are part of an **oral tradition.** "Racing the Great Bear" is part of the Iroquois oral tradition. As Joseph Bruchac has written, "When I first began telling the traditional stories that were part of my own Native heritage, it was to share them with my own children. . . . That is how the circle of stories works, linking the generations."

1. Stories in the oral tradition are often inspired by a group's values. What are some of the values reinforced in "Racing the Great Bear"?
2. Find and explain a place in the story where the oral tradition helps Swift Runner scare away the bear.

● See **Literary Terms Handbook,** p. R7.

LITERARY ELEMENTS

1. Students may indicate bravery, strength, determination, caring for others, and listening to and learning from elders.
2. Students may choose the passage on page 272 that begins *Swift Runner had learned...*; or the passage on page 274 that begins *"No," Swift Runner said....*

Additional Resources

 Literary Elements Transparency 25

Literature and Writing

Writing About Literature

Dialogue The dialogue in this story—the words spoken by the characters—does not sound like everyday speech. That is because the words are part of an ancient legend that has been repeated from generation to generation. Analyze the effectiveness of the dialogue in the story.

Personal Writing

Journeys Swift Runner traveled from the village to the woods to find the bear. He also went on a personal journey from childhood to adulthood. Write a journal entry about a personal journey of growth you or someone you know has taken.

Extending Your Response

Literature Groups

Storytelling The story of Swift Runner is part of the oral tradition of the Iroquois. Work with your group to retell the story to another class. Discuss which parts are most important and which parts are most exciting. Choose whether to use a single narrator or several voices to tell the story.

Interdisciplinary Activity

Art Using natural materials, build a model longhouse. First, research the traditional design of an Iroquois longhouse. Then decide what materials to use that will recreate the look. Make sure your model is in the correct proportion to the actual structures.

Reading Further

If you would like to read more about the Iroquois, try these books:

Iroquois Stories: Heroes and Heroines, Monsters and Magic by Joseph Bruchac

The Iroquois by Craig and Katherine Doherty

■ **Save your work for your portfolio.**

interNET CONNECTION

Use your search engine to locate sites devoted to Native Americans. Library and bookstore sites have information about books and audio- or videotapes. Many museums have Native American collections, and most of them have their own Web sites.

Literature and Writing

Writing About Literature

Students' explanations should
- make clear how the dialogue is different from everyday speech.
- state whether this type of dialogue is effective.

Personal Writing

Students' journal entries should
- describe a personal journey of growth about themselves or someone they know.
- show the evolution of the journey, illustrating how the person changes.

Extending Your Response

Literature Groups As students work on the storytelling project, encourage them to learn the story by heart. Point out that they don't have to memorize the story word for word; they can just remember the important events and tell them in the correct order. **COLLAB. LEARN.**

Interdisciplinary Activity Help students find reference sources in the library or on the Internet. Then have them use the images they have found to create their own sketches, which should include a scale and correct proportions.

☑ **ASSESSMENT OPTIONS**

📁 ***Quick Checks,*** p. 25
📁 ***Selection and Theme Assessment,*** pp. 45–46
📁 ***Performance Assessment,*** p. 24
📁 ***Testmaker***

GRAMMAR AND LANGUAGE
POSSESSIVE PRONOUNS

1. his   3. their   5. my
2. its   4. his

READING AND THINKING
SETTING A READING PURPOSE

Students should include a clearly stated purpose and show how the purpose can help them better understand the selection.

VOCABULARY
MULTIPLE-MEANING WORDS

1. e   3. b   5. a
2. d   4. c

Additional Resources

Grammar and Language Workbook, pp. 109–110

Grammar and Composition Handbook, Lesson 4.4

Writer's Choice, Lesson 11.4

Reading Workbook, pp. 41–42

Vocabulary Practice, p. 16

Skill Minilessons

GRAMMAR AND LANGUAGE • POSSESSIVE PRONOUNS

A **possessive pronoun** shows who or what has or owns something. A possessive pronoun can be used in place of one or more possessive nouns. For example, "The brother's and sister's pets" can be replaced by "Their pets." *Their* is a plural possessive pronoun.

PRACTICE Write each sentence, replacing each underlined word or words with the correct possessive pronoun.

1. Then Swift Runner set out on <u>Swift Runner's</u> journey.
2. When the monster bear came out of the forest, <u>the monster bear's</u> teeth were as long as a man's arm.
3. The old people had told <u>the old people's</u> stories to Swift Runner.
4. The boy and <u>the boy's</u> dog chased the bear.
5. Swift Runner said, "I chase you because you killed <u>Swift Runner's</u> people."

● For more about pronouns, see **Language Handbook,** p. R31.

READING AND THINKING • SETTING A READING PURPOSE

Before you begin reading a story or an article, it often helps to set a purpose for reading. What do you want to learn from the selection? Will you have to remember ideas in order to discuss the piece or answer questions? Do you want to better understand the subject or the type of writing? Do you want to be entertained?

PRACTICE Choose a selection in this book that you haven't read. Set a purpose for reading the selection before you begin reading. The title, author, and the art may help give you an idea for a purpose. After setting a purpose, write a few sentences that explain how the purpose you set might help you better enjoy or understand the selection.

● For more about setting a reading purpose, see **Reading Handbook,** p. R82.

VOCABULARY • MULTIPLE-MEANING WORDS

Many words have more than one meaning, which usually doesn't cause a problem if both meanings are familiar. You are unlikely to mistake the bark of a tree for the bark of a dog. However, when one meaning is familiar but another one isn't, the situation can be confusing.

In "Racing the Great Bear," *spare* means "to treat with mercy." It can also have several other meanings:

  a. *v.* to treat with mercy; hold back from harming
  b. *v.* to keep from using or use only with care
  c. *adj.* not in regular use; extra
  d. *adj.* small in amount; barely enough or not enough
  e. *adj.* lean or thin

PRACTICE For each sentence, write the letter of the corresponding meaning of *spare*.

1. Abraham Lincoln was a tall, spare man.
2. After their spare meal, the soldiers were still hungry.
3. Wait for a sale and spare your bank account.
4. The company stayed in our spare room.
5. Is it wrong to tell a lie in order to spare someone's feelings?

LISTENING, SPEAKING, and VIEWING

Analyzing Persuasion

A friend talks you into sharing your lunch. A television commercial urges you to try a new shampoo. A magazine ad asks you to support a charity. A billboard warns you against smoking. In these ways, and many more, you encounter persuasion every day.

Persuasion is based on appeals to emotion and appeals to reason. Appeals to emotion involve words, sounds, or images that create strong feelings. Appeals to reason involve logic or factual evidence.

When you encounter persuasion, identify the kinds of appeals being used. Then decide whether they are used responsibly. Ask yourself questions like those below.

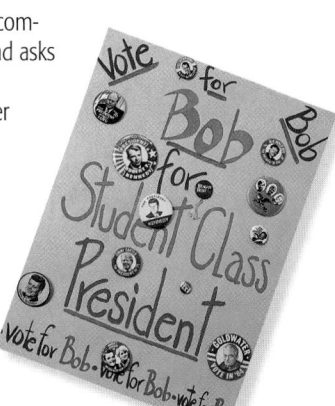

Appeals to Emotion	**Appeals to Reason**
◆ Which images catch my interest? What feelings do they create?	◆ What conclusion is the audience asked to draw? What evidence supports the conclusion?
◆ Which words suggest feelings? What feelings do they suggest?	◆ What is the general line of reasoning used here? Does it make sense?
◆ Are the appeals straightforward? Or do they reflect a "hidden agenda"—an attempt to manipulate the audience?	◆ Is the reasoning supported with facts, statistics, or other solid evidence?

EXERCISES

1. Use the questions above to analyze your favorite (or least favorite) television commercial. Look for appeals to emotion and appeals to reason.
2. Write a short persuasive essay.
   a. Ask a classmate to analyze it.
   b. List the appeals to emotion and the appeals to reason that you notice in your classmate's essay.
   c. Discuss your analyses with your classmate.

Objective

• To recognize and use strategies for analyzing persuasion

Teaching Strategies

Prompt a discussion about peer pressure with students. Ask them to think of a situation in which they were persuaded in a positive manner by a friend. Find out if the friend appealed to their emotions or to their reason. Role-play a situation in which one student tries to persuade another to help paint a fence by appealing to his or her emotions. Conduct the same role-play with the student appealing to reason.

Exercises

1. Students may wish to "act out" or describe the commercial before discussing its appeal. If students don't watch television, encourage them to choose a poster or billboard they have seen.
2. Permit students to read their essays aloud to their partners if they wish. This will give them an opportunity to practice speaking persuasively.

Teaching Options

MEETING INDIVIDUAL NEEDS — ENGLISH LANGUAGE LEARNERS

Persuading the Public Have English language learners work with proficient speakers to create interesting public service advertising campaigns.

Activity Ask each group to write a public service slogan, such as "Seat belts save lives" and develop a list of supporting arguments: one appealing to emotion and another appealing to reason. Ask each group to use its slogan and material from the list to create an eye-catching poster and a thirty-second public service radio announcement to read to classmates. Have classmates discuss whether they were persuaded and why. **COLLAB. LEARN.**

Additional Resources
📁 *English Language Learners Sourcebook*

Objectives

- To read an autobiographical account of a mountain climber who faces a great challenge
- To recognize the elements of an autobiography
- To write about the similarities and differences in challenges

Skills

Reading/Thinking: Drawing Conclusions; Identifying Main Idea and Supporting Details; Inferring; Generalizing; Making Critical Judgments
Writing: Using Detail; Journal Entry
Vocabulary: Base Words and Suffixes
Grammar/Language: Apostrophe
Listening/Speaking: Debating
Life Skills: Planning and Designing
Collaboration: Literature Groups

Motivating
→OPTIONS

Selection Focus Transparency 26: Have students discuss their interpretations of the lyrics from a song used as the theme in John F. Kennedy's presidential campaign in 1960.

Focus Activity: To extend the Focus Activity, have students identify challenges faced by people they know. Have them list some qualities one needs to meet a challenge.

Before You Read
Beyond the Limits

MEET STACY ALLISON

Stacy Allison, a gifted mountain climber, author, businessperson, and public speaker, certainly knows about challenges and dreams. In 1987 she took part in an unsuccessful attempt to reach the top of Mount Everest. The following year, she returned to the mountain and reached its peak. Allison later led a team to the top of K2, the world's second-highest mountain—and an even greater challenge than Mount Everest.

This story is part of an autobiographical account, Beyond the Limits: A Woman's Triumph on Everest, *first published in 1993.*

FOCUS ACTIVITY

Think of a time when you faced a big challenge that resulted in disappointment.

Sharing Ideas
In small groups, share stories about your own experiences in facing challenges that ended in disappointment.

Setting a Purpose
Why would anyone want to climb a mountain on which more than a hundred climbers have been killed? See if you can discover an answer as you read.

BACKGROUND

The Time and Place   It is the fall of 1987 in a small tent on the jagged North Face of Mount Everest, in the Himalayas.

Did You Know?
At 29,028 feet (about 5.5 miles) above sea level, Mount Everest is the world's highest mountain. In May 1953, Edmund Hillary and his Nepalese guide, Tenzing Norgay, became the first climbers to reach its peak.

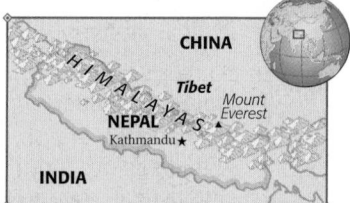

VOCABULARY PREVIEW

agility (ə jil′ ə tē) *n.* quickness and ease in motion or thought; p. 282
brink (bringk) *n.* the point at which something may begin; p. 282
charismatic (kar′ iz mat′ ik) *adj.* having personal qualities that enable one to inspire loyalty and devotion; p. 283
pinnacle (pin′ ə kəl) *n.* a high point, or peak; p. 285
distinct (dis tingkt′) *adj.* different in quality or kind; p. 285
anguished (ang′ gwisht) *adj.* having or showing extreme mental or physical suffering; p. 286

RESOURCE MANAGER

Lesson Planning Resource
The ***Theme Three Planning Guide*** (pp. 53–60) provides additional lesson notes and reduced versions of all print resources.

📁 **Other Print Resources**
- Active Reading Guide, p. 26
- Vocabulary Practice, p. 17
- Reading Workbook, pp. 43–44
- Grammar and Language Workbook, pp. 273–274

- Grammar and Composition Handbook, Lessons 13.7
- Quick Checks, p. 26
- Selection and Theme Assessment, pp. 47–48
- Performance Assessment, p. 25
- Spanish Summaries, p. 26
- Spanish Translations
- Inclusion Strategies
- English Language Learners Sourcebook

Transparencies
- Selection Focus 26
- Literary Elements 26
- Grammar and Language 25
- Fine Art 7

Technology
 Audio Library
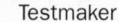 Spanish Audio Library
- Glencoe Literature Web Site
- Testmaker

from

Beyond the Limits

A Woman's Triumph on Everest

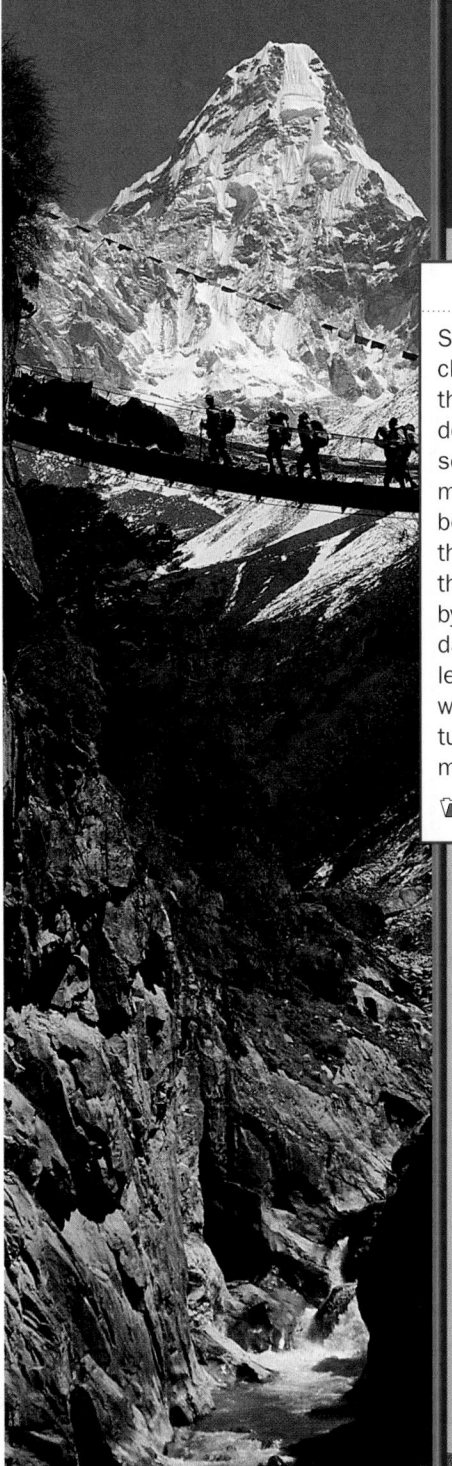

Stacy Allison ·~
with Peter Carlin

We were so close. From where we were sitting, curled in the dim light of a snow cave, the top of the world was only 3,000 feet away. Less than two days of climbing on the jagged North Face. But we weren't climbing.

We were hiding. Four American mountain climbers—Scott Fischer, Wes Krause, Samuel "Q" Belk, and me—tunneled into the side of Mount Everest, listening to the roar of the jet stream[1] wind. It was late in the climbing season and the winter winds had descended, tearing across the top of the mountain at 150 miles an hour. But for how long?

---

1. The *jet stream* is the high-speed air current several miles above the earth's surface.

SUMMARY

Stacy Allison sets out with three other climbers to climb Mount Everest, something no woman had yet succeeded in doing. After years of preparation—seeking financial support, getting permits, buying equipment—the group begins its climb. About 5000 feet from the top, less than two days' climb to the summit, the group is pinned down by fierce winds. They wait nervously for days. When the bad weather does not let up and one of the group is getting weak from the thin air at that high altitude, the group climbs back down the mountain.

📁 *Spanish Summaries,* p. 26

A Active Reading

PREDICT Have students use the title and clues from the first paragraph to predict what they think the conflict in the story might be. Suggest that students periodically revisit their predictions as they read to verify or revise them.

Additional Resources

📁 *Active Reading Guide,* p. 26

🎧 *Audio Library*

🎧 *Spanish Audio Library*

Teaching Options

CONNECTING TO OTHER SELECTIONS

The chart at the right shows three ways to connect "Beyond the Limits" to other selections in this book.

For specific teaching strategies, see the *Theme Three Planning Guide,* pages 56–57.

Connection	Title
Life Skills: Leading and Organizing ➡	"Rosa Parks: My Story," p. 85
Thematic: Testing Oneself ➡	"Amigo Brothers," p. 433
Literary: Autobiography ➡	"Wait Till Next Year," p. 35

DRAWING CONCLUSIONS Ask students what the author is trying to do when she says "I could imagine..." and "I could overlook...." *(Students may realize that the author is trying to convince herself that the weather will change and everything will be fine.)*

C Literary Elements

AUTOBIOGRAPHY Point out the use of the word *I* here. Explain that the author speaks about her own life, so the selection is written in the first person. Ask students to find other words that show the author is speaking about herself. *(Other words include* my, me, our, we, *and* us.)

D Literary Elements

DESCRIPTION Have students describe the images that are conveyed by this experience with the weather. *(Students may say that the shroud image suggests a mountain covered in a heavy shawl. "Belted by gale-force winds" might suggest an image of the mountain being punched.)*

E Active Reading

EVALUATE The writing in this passage presents factual detail. Ask students to identify a different type of writing in the selection. *(Students may recognize that this passage deals with details, as opposed to the writer's personal thoughts, as in the previous passage.)*

Teaching Options

---

from **Beyond the Limits**

B Sitting up in my sleeping bag, balancing a cup of hot chocolate in my lap, I could imagine that the hurricane outside would vanish. In the dim light of the cave, I could overlook the life-squeezing pressure of life at 25,500 feet.

C I could almost convince myself we wouldn't have to turn around when morning came. *Turn around?* Not after I had devoted years of my life to get here. Years spent dreaming of scaling this massive hill and then leaving my footprint on the crown of the earth. Now I was two-thirds of the way there—25,500 feet up the North Face of Everest. Stranded in a snow cave . . . but so close.

I was determined to get to the top.

Hunched beneath the snow, I could imagine the grace of those final steps. Beyond the limits of gravity, human strength, and mental <u>agility</u>—out to where there are no limits. Nothing but the snow-covered mountain, the sky, and me, and right then it would be hard to tell where one ended and another began. I could have it all, but only if the jet stream rose off the mountain for one more day.

D Everything depends on the weather: even the best climber in the world won't get very high on a mountain shrouded[2] in a storm or belted by gale-force winds. We'd worked so hard for so long, but on that cold night in the fall of 1987, I knew our entire expedition was on the <u>brink</u>.

E The fifteen climbers on the 1987 American Everest North Face Expedition each had more than a decade of climbing

---

2. Here, *shrouded* means "covered" or "concealed."

Vocabulary

agility (ə jil′ ə tē) *n.* quickness and ease in motion or thought
brink (bringk) *n.* the point at which something may begin

---

experience. For two years most of us had committed our lives to climbing this one mountain. We spent two years maneuvering the bureaucracies[3] of two governments, scraping for the money to cover airplane tickets, freight, climbing permits, and fees, convincing manufacturers to give us equipment and food. Two years planning and preparing and then three months on the expedition itself—the flight into Nepal, the trek from Kathmandu into Tibet and the yak-powered climb to Advance Base Camp, then the weeks of mountain-side preparation. We built Advance Base Camp at the foot of the North Face, and then set up four intermediate camps on the

Did You Know?
The *yak* is a long-haired ox, native to central Asia. Yaks are often used to carry heavy loads.

mountain. We fixed our route up the mountain using ice screws, aluminum stakes, and rope to anchor a safety line up the steep sections, then dug snow caves in the steep mountainside and hauled up loads of food and gear to stock them. Only then could we set our sights on the summit. Set our sights, and hope the mountain would be kind to us as we tried to creep up her icy shoulders.

Kindness was a lot to hope for this high in the world. More, in fact, than what we'd been able to secure for ourselves. By the time the second summit team—our

---

3. *Bureaucracies* (byoo rok′ ra sēz) refers to all of the departments, officials, rules, and paperwork that one must deal with to get government approval for a project or program.

MEETING INDIVIDUAL NEEDS **ENGLISH LANGUAGE LEARNERS**

Emphasize and Organize Explain that putting bits of text in italics is a technique an author can use to emphasize an idea or create a pattern of organization in a story. In the sentence *Turn around?* on this page and throughout this selection, Allison uses italics to emphasize her thoughts, feelings, and memories.

Activity Have small groups look for other ways the story is organized. Suggest that they make lists of all the italicized sentences and discuss what they think each conveys about how the author is feeling. **COLLAB. LEARN.**

Additional Resources
📁 *English Language Learners Sourcebook*

charismatic, blond team leader Scott Fischer, our more reserved deputy leader Wes Krause, the hyperkinetic[4] young bond trader Samuel "Q" Belk, and me—set out for the mountaintop, an ugly wind was blowing through the expedition tents at base camp. So we moved with a redoubled sense of purpose. *I just want to climb,* Scott said when we left our Advance Base Camp. *Forget everything else and climb the mountain.*

The mountain cooperated for thirty-six hours. On the first day we climbed under calm, clear skies, moving from Camp 1 at 19,500 feet to Camp 2 at 23,500 feet by midday. We spent the night in the snow cave, then headed up again the next morning, climbing halfway up the White Limbo snowfield before a gathering snowstorm sent us scurrying back to Camp 2. The blizzard ravaged[5] the mountain for four long days and nights, and when the sky finally cleared we scaled the 2,000 feet to Camp 3. But then the stubborn blasting wind descended and we were pinned down again.

We were running out of time. Climbers call the upper reaches of the world the Death Zone— above 19,000 feet the earth's atmosphere is too thin to support life. No matter how much you eat, your digestive system can't assimilate enough nourishment to keep you alive. After a few days your muscles

start to atrophy.[6] You grow weaker. Most climbers start to fade after a week, although some can hold on for two or even three weeks. Soon I'd discover how strong I was—this was our second night above 25,000 feet. It was our seventh night in the Death Zone.

A shower of loose snow tumbled in through the tunnel entry, settling onto my head, my shoulders, melting cold down my neck. As the empty hours passed I sat in silence, sharing the same thought as my three companions. *This can't be happening.* I needed success too much this year.

When the storm first pinned us down at Camp 2, we tried not to seem concerned. Snowstorms never last forever, not even in the Himalayas. We had enough food in the cave to hold out for days, and then once

> ### Climbers call the upper reaches of the world the Death Zone . . .

the sky did clear nothing would hold us back. As it turned out, that storm was the worst autumn blizzard to hit Everest in more than forty years. But it did clear one night, and by the next afternoon we were

---

4. Being *hyperkinetic,* Belk likes to be always moving about or doing something.
5. *Ravaged* (rav′ ijd) means "destroyed violently; ruined."
6. To *assimilate* food is to absorb it and use it to create living tissue. If this doesn't happen, the body will waste away, or *atrophy.*

Vocabulary
charismatic (kar′ iz mat′ ik) *adj.* having personal qualities that enable one to inspire loyalty and devotion

F Literary Elements

CHARACTER Ask students to think of phrases that best describe the author, as she has done to describe her teammates. *(Possible answers: doesn't give up easily; a determined person; not afraid to take chances; courageous; thinks deeply about what is happening.)*

G Active Reading

VISUALIZE Ask students if they can picture the climbers spending the night in the snow cave. Ask them to describe what it might look like inside and outside the cave during the blizzard. *(Students might say that they see the climbers in their sleeping bags lying awake, surrounded by their gear. They are staring at the ceiling of the cave, waiting to hear the wind stop. Outside the cave, snow is whipped against the side of the mountain.)*

H Literary Elements

SUSPENSE Explain to students that, even though this is not a work of fiction, the author injects suspense into the narrative. Ask students to point out words, phrases, and details that add to the suspense. *(Students may cite the details of how long people can survive in the Death Zone and how long this team has been there. Others may point to the line Soon I'd discover how strong I was.)*

Reading *Minilesson*

Identifying Main Idea and Supporting Details Explain to students that there are so many technical details in this narrative that it may be difficult to follow the climbers' progress toward their goal.

Activity Have small groups each create a chart with the story's main idea as its title and three columns labeled *Day; Progress;* and *Setback.* Have students read carefully for details that will help them chart the climbers' daily experiences on the world's highest mountain.

Additional Resources
📁 *Reading Workbook,* pp. 43–44

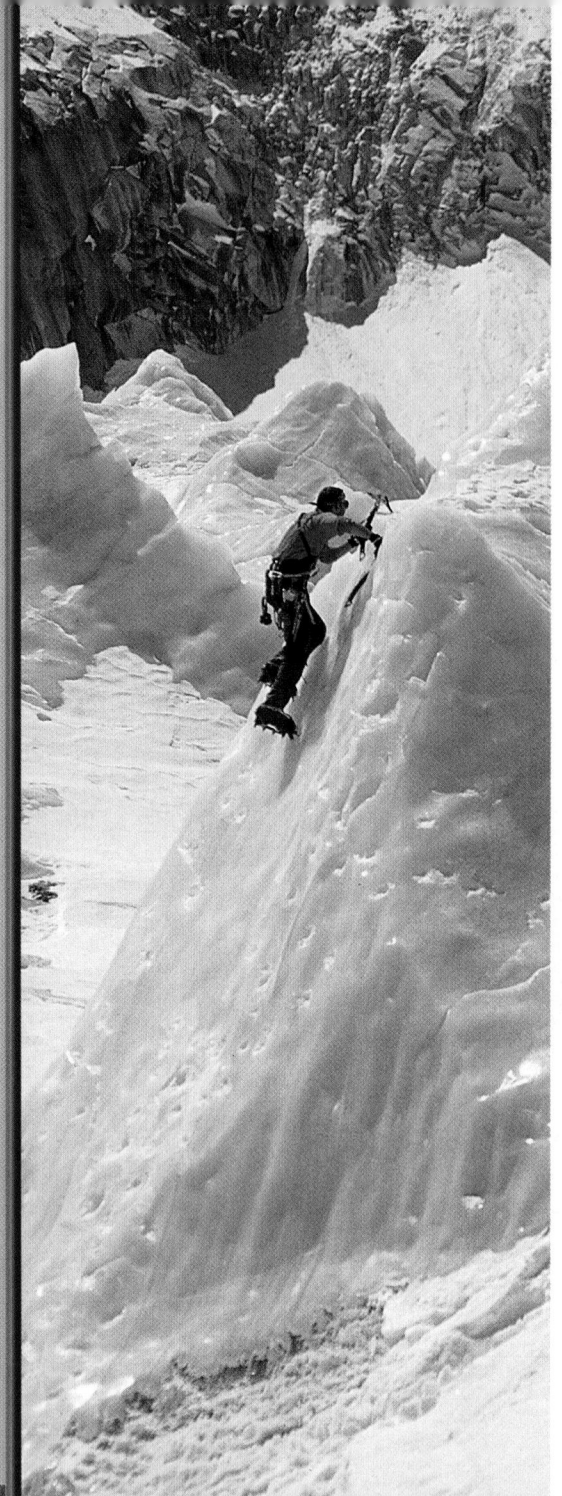

Critical Thinking

INFERRING Ask students what they think "we ran out of words" means. *(Students should realize that the statement is not to be taken literally but that the climbers were no longer able to keep up a conversation. They were probably becoming so demoralized that they could no longer "chat.")*

Literary Elements

POINT OF VIEW Explain to students that at this point the author is letting the reader know that what the climbers are facing is overwhelming. Ask students what they think her view of the situation is. *(Students will possibly say that this climb would be the last chance for a long time, if not forever, for some climbers to reach the summit. Working and training for two years preparing for the climb to the summit and then being defeated is devastating.)*

in Camp 3. By then, the summit was only two days away . . . until we woke up the next morning and saw the gale-force winds ripping across the top of the mountain. So we went back to the cave, the four of us, back to talking and waiting. Two days passed and eventually we ran out of words. The wind kept blowing.

Then there was silence—the sound of breathing, the sputtering of the stove, the dry stuttering of the spindrift[7] blowing in the tunnel. After seven days the altitude had weakened us, and it was too late in the season to retreat to base camp and wait for better weather. If we didn't get to the summit now, we couldn't try again. Unless the jet stream lifted by morning, we would have to go down. *Two years of work. A decade of training. A lifetime of hope.* Blown away.

Sleep wouldn't come. The cold air sank down through the tunnel, covering us like a dark, wet blanket. Lying closest to the entry, Q was curled into a ball, trembling under three layers of down. Scott flopped around in his bag, occasionally heaving up a great dispirited[8] sigh. Wes lay still, his eyes burning. The minutes crept past. I swam in my sleeping bag, searching for the comfortable spot. But my body had been whittled away by the months of high-altitude effort, and comfort was beyond me. I was a stick figure of a woman, fragile bones jutting against pale flesh, muscles stretched taut like rubber bands: a body pulled to the breaking point.

Come on, morning. Our last chance would come with the daylight. I tried to push the hours along, pulling up the dawn by force of willpower. *Give me this one*

---

7. Here, *spindrift* refers to light, misty, blowing snow.
8. *Dispirited* (dis pir′ ə tid) means "discouraged; depressed."

Writing *Minilesson*

Using Detail Point out to students that the author conveys the nervousness the climbers are feeling by describing in detail their most inconsequential activities. Reading details like these makes readers feel closer to the story.

Activity Have students work in small groups. Have each group think of a situation that might be tense or cause those

involved to be nervous. Suggest that students each write a short paragraph using details to describe how he or she might act while waiting impatiently for someone to arrive or for something to happen. **L2**
COLLAB. LEARN.

Additional Resources

Writer's Choice, Lessons 3.3, 3.4

 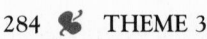

Stacy Allison ~

chance. The dawn, and calm skies. Just two more days without the jet stream. *Please, please, I need this now.*

When life gets tangled there's something so reassuring about climbing a mountain. The challenge is unambiguous.[9] Ice and snow and rock. Self-discipline. Concentration. Focus. As you push higher you work yourself into a trance. Can I reach that ledge? Are my fingers strong enough to hold on to this crack? Will this ice screw hold? Eventually the weight of the world slides away. For those moments when it's just you and the rock and the ice and the snow, life always makes sense.

Climbing has always been more than a physical pursuit for me. Each mountain I face is another <u>pinnacle</u> in an internal adventure. An exploration of myself, an expression of my spirit. For ten years I had climbed, from desert cliffs in Utah to small mountains in the Cascade Range of the Pacific Northwest. Looking higher, I reached up into the clouds, then past the clouds. To larger mountains, and more complex climbs: Mount McKinley in Alaska, Ama Dablam in Nepal, Pik Kommunizma in the Soviet Union. I reached up, step by step, until I could see myself standing on the peak of the world's tallest mountain.

Mount Everest. Chomolungma to the Tibetans. Sagamartha to the Nepali. The Mother Goddess of the Earth to everyone living in its shadow. The top of Everest is the top of the world—29,028 feet up into the empty Himalayan sky. The only spot on earth where you can't climb any higher.

I had to get up there. Usually I don't get obsessed about mountaintops—I had learned long ago that the time spent climbing in life means more than the time spent standing on a summit. But when my life turned sour, the tip of Everest gained significance. It was the top of the world! Reaching that windswept perch, I decided, would cleanse my spirit and heal my wounds. More than that, it would send me home with a title: The First American Woman to Climb Everest.

For so many years I wouldn't even allow myself to think I could get this far. Everest was for the big boys, and I was a very small woman. The climbing community has never had a lot of patience with women. It draws a <u>distinct</u> crowd—generally men equipped with a surplus of money, opinions, and muscle.

It came a step at a time, a decade of effort leading up to this one summit attempt, this journey to the top of the world. And now the world wasn't cooperating. Why did I think it would? I knew Everest wasn't like any other mountain. Only one of ten climbers who attempt the mountain stands on the summit. And for every three climbers who do scale the mountain, one dies trying. The facts aren't welcoming. But you don't plan a trip to Everest believing those facts will apply to you.

9. Something that's *unambiguous* is perfectly clear, leaving no room for doubt or confusion.

Vocabulary
pinnacle (pin′ ə kəl) *n.* a high point, or peak
distinct (dis tingkt′) *adj.* different in quality or kind

FACING CHALLENGE 🐾 285

K Active Reading
EVALUATE Explain to students that the author gives some of her reasons for climbing mountains. Ask students to give the details that explain why the author likes the challenge of climbing. *(The author likes to exercise her self-discipline and concentration. She also likes to find out how strong she is—it helps her make sense of life.)*

L Critical Thinking
GENERALIZING Ask students if they think people who climb mountains engage in a never-ending pursuit of a higher mountain. *(Some students may agree that mountain climbing brings out a desire for ever bigger challenges. Other students, however, might argue that it depends more on the person, explaining that many athletes in other sports, people in government and business, and even students will seek out another challenge once they've met one successfully.)*

M Critical Thinking
INFERRING Ask students what they think the author might mean by saying "my life turned sour." How would climbing "cleanse" her spirit and heal her "wounds"? *(Students may see the source of "sour" as family or career problems. She might feel cleansed because she must focus on this task, and that helps her forget about the "sour" part of her life. She will also feel a great sense of accomplishment when she reaches the top.)*

LIFE SKILLS CONNECTION

Planning and Designing The author knows the odds are against her. First, there are not many women who have attempted the climb, and second, only a small percentage of all climbers make it to Mt. Everest's summit. Yet she is willing to try. The passage shows, however, that she knows full well what she is getting into.

Activity Have small groups of students work together to plan a student trip to the top of Mount Everest. Encourage them to use information from the text, plus whatever they know about planning for trips. Encourage them to think about what they need for the trip as well as what they need to do physically to get themselves ready to climb. **L2 COLLAB. LEARN.**

FACING CHALLENGE 🐾 285

VIEWING THE PHOTO

N Active Reading

EVALUATE Point out the contrast between the climbers' high-tech clothing and the primitive image of *crawled out of the cave.* Ask students how this contrast helps readers learn about mountain climbing. *(Students might say that even though the climbers benefit from technology, they must perform their task in a very primitive way.)*

O Active Reading

PREDICT Ask students if they can predict what will happen from this descriptive paragraph. *(The news is probably not good because Wes's shoulders slump and the author says, "I saw it in Scott's eyes....")*

At the MOVIES

Everest (1998, 44 minutes, NR) will give students some idea of the mountain's grandeur and the difficulties faced by climbers. Preview it for suitability before showing or recommending it.

Teaching Options

Viewing the photograph: How are the conditions here similar to those faced by the climbers in the selection?

When dawn finally came we got dressed for the summit—pulling our down climbing suits over the layers of polypropylene long underwear, polypro socks, plastic climbing boots, polypro and down gloves, a heavy pile hat, a neoprene[10] face mask—then crawled out of the cave, pulled along by a fine thread of hope, and walked gingerly[11] to the side of the ice tower that stood above our cave. Above us we'd see the summit, that great crooked pyramid on top of the world, the crown for the Mother Goddess. If she rose straight into a clean blue sky, we could try to push ourselves higher. But if she sent off a tail of white, if the winds were still ripping the snow from the hillside, we had to go down.

Wes turned the corner first. I didn't have to look up. I could read it in his shoulders. Wes slumped, then turned to see Scott, coming around the corner after us. I saw it in Scott's eyes, then heard his voice, shouting above the constant roar of the wind.

"Well, that's the ballgame."

Scott stomped back toward the snow cave, anguished, shaking his head. Wes stayed, staring into the sky. I turned my face

---

10. *Polypropylene, pile,* and *neoprene* are human-made fabrics that provide insulation from cold temperatures.
11. *Gingerly* (jin' jər lē) means "with extreme caution; carefully."

Vocabulary
anguished (ang' gwisht) *adj.* having or showing extreme mental or physical suffering

286   THEME 3

Grammar and Language *Minilesson*

Apostrophe Write the following words on the board: *can not = can't; he would = he'd.* Remind students that the apostrophe has two primary functions: to signal possession and to form a contraction indicating the omission of letters when two words are combined into one.

Activity Ask students to identify other words on pages 286–287 that use an apostrophe to form a contraction. Have students list the words that make up the contraction. *(Sample answers are listed below.)* **L2**

we'd *(we had)*   I'm *(I am)*
didn't *(did not)*   we're *(we are)*
that's *(that is)*   couldn't *(could not)*
can't *(cannot)*   I'd *(I had)*
don't *(do not)*

Additional Resources

Grammar and Language Transparency 25

Grammar and Language Workbook, pp. 273–274

Grammar and Composition Handbook, Lesson 13.7

Writer's Choice, Lesson 20.7

Stacy Allison

[P] upward and saw it, too. The thick plume of spindrift sailing from the mountain-top. The jet stream had not lifted. It was slamming against the mountain at 150 miles an hour for the third day in a row. And the thin thread of hope snapped.

Back in the cave Scott's blond hair hung lank over dim eyes, his usually rosy cheeks looked pale and sunken. His chest caved in beneath his shoulders.

[Q] "If you guys want to wait another day," I said, "I can wait." Q looked up dimly and coughed. I was grasping at thin air. We had failed. It was over. Even so, Scott flashed a look at the rest of us, measuring reactions.

"One more day? Give it a shot?"

[R] Q shook his head. The Death Zone was wreaking its havoc[12] on him. He was losing wattage with every passing hour. "I can't stay up here another day," Q said. He'd been barely able to eat breakfast that morning. "If I don't go down today, I'm not going to get down."

Now just the sound of breathing, and outside the wind and then occasionally a light cloud of spindrift, floating through the tunnel and down into the cave. The cold drifted down my spine until I could feel it in my toes.

Scott picked up the walkie-talkie and called to our expedition mates waiting at base camp. *We're finished. We're coming down.* The message was received, tenderly, and we started packing. Sleeping bags,

Thinsulate[13] pads, ice screws, rope, and cook gear over here, stoves, food, fuel over there. We'd carry the fragile gear, but the really soft and really hard gear could take the fast way down the Great Couloir, the chutelike valley just to the left of our route on the North Face. Camp 1 was just below the bottom of the chute; once the gear rocketed down, the other climbers would try to collect it.

We went back to the cave entry and slung on our packs. And we stood there for a moment, not looking at each other. Just stood there in the cold and the wind before taking the first step down. And then Wes moved, and Q followed, and then we were all moving. After two long years of planning and working and hoping, we were walking away from the summit. I could barely fathom[14] the disappointment. I couldn't, not with the descent ahead of us. I still had to focus on getting down in one piece.

[S] I turned to take a last look and my eyes fell on Scott's face. Tears were sliding down his cheeks. Did he see me watching him? It was only a moment, and he was wearing reflecting shades so it was impossible to tell. I turned around again and continued down dry-eyed. Whatever anguish I felt, I'd deal with it when we got down to safe terrain.[15]

---

13. *Thinsulate* is the brand name of an insulating material.
14. Here, *fathom* (fath′ am) means "to understand fully."
15. Scott Fischer successfully reached Everest's peak in 1994. Two years later, he and seven other climbers died in another attempt to reach the top.

---

12. The expression *wreaking havoc* means "causing destruction."

FACING CHALLENGE 🐾 287

[P] Literary Elements

METAPHOR Ask students to find a metaphor in this paragraph. *(It is The thin thread of hope snapped.)*

[Q] Critical Thinking

MAKING CRITICAL JUDGMENTS Ask students how these climbers might react to the idea of failing? *(They might consider themselves failures or acknowledge that their attempt has failed.)*

[R] Literary Elements

CONNOTATION Ask students the literal meaning of *losing wattage*. *(It means "losing power.")* Ask them to explain the use of the phrase here. *(It means "losing physical strength.")*

[S] Active Reading

CONNECT Ask students each to recall a major disappointment in life. Can they understand what the author might be feeling?

Thematic Focus

Facing Challenge Discuss the fact that facing a physical challenge is as much a test of emotional strength as it is of physical endurance.

FINE ART
TRANSPARENCY 7

You may use *Fine Art Transparency 7* to develop the discussion further.

✔ **ASSESSMENT OPTIONS**

📁 *Quick Checks*, p. 26

INCLUSION STRATEGIES
MEETING INDIVIDUAL NEEDS

Less-Proficient Readers Explain that the expression *Well, that's the ballgame* is sometimes used to signal the conclusion of an event. Suggest that sports expressions are used in many situations; for example, a person who is said to have hit a *grand slam* has had great success, and one who is said to have *covered all the bases* has been thorough.

Activity Have students work with partners to find other examples of words or phrases used in an unusual way on page 287. Ask students to write the expressions down, then define them.
L2 COLLAB. LEARN.

Additional Resources
📁 *Inclusion Strategies*

FACING CHALLENGE 🐾 287

Personal Response

Some students may ask what "soured" her life and exactly how mountain climbing helped "sweeten" it. Others may ask if the small number of women in mountain climbing was a motivating factor in her choosing this hobby.

Analyzing Literature

1. The climbers faced the problems of the fierce wind and the thin air, which made breathing and digesting food difficult.
2. The writer is reassured by the fact that the objective is "unambiguous." The climber knows exactly what the objective is and there are no conflicting objectives.
3. The fierce wind and the fact that one member of the team was in a weakened condition kept the team from the top.
4. At that altitude, one should expect fierce conditions of high winds and cold.
5. The writer believes the climb is a test of her personal strength and endurance and is very disappointed when she can't finish it.
6. If the mountain is not "kind," the climbers will run out of time and have to end the expedition.
7. She uses climbing as a means of testing the extent of her courage, strength, and endurance.
8. The conflict was between waiting another day to try for the top or returning that day to ensure the safety of their weakened companion.
9. The account might have been restricted to the external part of the challenge rather than the mental and emotional aspects of the climb as well.

10. Some students may mention the challenge of getting better grades in school, winning a sports event, overcoming personal fears or limitations, or helping people in need.

Responding to Literature

PERSONAL RESPONSE

Suppose you had a chance to interview Stacy Allison. What questions would you like to ask her about the challenges she faced? Record your questions in your journal.

Analyzing Literature

RECALL

1. What problems did the climbers face as they sat stranded in their snow cave?
2. What does the writer find reassuring about climbing a mountain?
3. Why didn't the team of climbers reach the summit?

INTERPRET

4. According to the writer, "Kindness was a lot to hope for this high in the world." Explain what she means.
5. How would you describe the writer's attitude about the challenge she and the other climbers faced?
6. Why was it so important that the mountain be "kind" to the climbers?
7. According to the writer, mountain climbing was "an exploration of myself." What do you think she means?
8. What was the conflict the climbers faced on their final morning at Camp 3? How did they resolve it?

EVALUATE AND CONNECT

9. How might the account of this adventure be different if it had been written by someone who wasn't a part of the expedition? Explain.
10. **Theme Connection** What "summit" would you like to face? Why is that particular goal important to you?

LITERARY ELEMENTS

Autobiography

Have you ever written an account of your own life? If so, you have written an autobiography. The word part *auto* means "self," *bio* means "life," and *graphy* means "something written." A **biography** is the story of someone's life. An **autobiography** is the story of a person's life written by that person. An autobiography may cover a person's entire life, or it may focus on one aspect of that life, such as an important event or a childhood experience. Such works are sometimes called **memoirs**. Autobiography is almost always written from the first-person point of view.

1. What details did you learn about Stacy Allison's life from reading this autobiographical selection?
2. What else would you like to learn about her life?

● See **Literary Terms Handbook,** p. R1.

LITERARY ELEMENTS

1. Details about her life include these facts: she is physically and mentally strong; something went "sour" in her life; and she cares about opportunities for women.
2. Students might be interested in learning how her life turned out after this climb and later, after she did conquer Everest.

Additional Resources

📖 *Literary Elements Transparency 26*

Extending Your Response

Writing About Literature

Comparing Challenges *Beyond the Limits* is an account of one person's experience in facing a difficult challenge. Think about the challenges you discussed for the **Focus Activity** on page 280. Write a paragraph comparing your or your group's challenges with those of the author.

inter**NET**
CONNECTION

If you are interested in learning more about mountain climbing, use a Web browser, and type in the phrase "mountain climbing" to search for Web sites about this challenging sport.

Creative Writing

Entry from the Top of the World Imagine that you are one of the members of the 1987 North Face expedition. You are stranded in a sleeping bag in a snow cave at Camp 3. Think about how you would feel. Write a journal entry describing your thoughts and feelings.

Literature Groups

Debate It! Mountain climbing demands physical fitness, skill, self-discipline, and courage. Critics of the sport claim that climbing is costly, dangerous, and often destructive to the natural environment. Choose one point of view, and defend your position in a small group discussion.

Interdisciplinary Activity

Social Studies/Art Reread the selection, and take notes on each place in the expedition. Use a real map to give you an outline of the journey. Then draw your own map of the area and label each site. Use your map to retell the story to a family member or a friend.

 Save your work for your portfolio.

Skill Minilesson

VOCABULARY • BASE WORDS AND SUFFIXES

The suffix *-ic* means "characteristic of." The adjective *charismatic* is formed from the noun *charisma*. *Charisma* means "a special quality of leadership that inspires people." A charismatic person, therefore, has characteristics of inspirational leadership.

PRACTICE Write the base word from which each of the following words was formed. You may need to add, delete, or change other letters as you take away the suffix.
1. problematic
2. historic
3. magnetic
4. periodic
5. climatic

Extending Your Response

Writing About Literature
Students' responses should
• identify the specific challenges.
• explain similarities and differences.

Creative Writing
Students' writing should
• consider what would run through one's mind, including present matters and past memories.
• write as if speaking to a diary or a trusted friend.
• be specific in identifying feelings and give details.

Literature Groups Remind students to support their positions with specific facts and details from the selection or research sources.
COLLAB. LEARN.

Interdisciplinary Activity
Remind students that creating the map will enhance their appreciation of the autobiography.

Skill Minilesson

VOCABULARY
• BASE WORDS AND SUFFIXES
1. problem 3. magnet 5. climate
2. history 4. period

Additional Resources
Vocabulary Practice, p. 17

✔ ASSESSMENT OPTIONS

📁 *Quick Checks,* p. 26

📁 *Selection and Theme Assessment,* pp. 47–48

📁 *Performance Assessment,* p. 25

📁 *Testmaker*

Objective

- To understand the elements of nonfiction

Teaching Strategies

Explain that one of the appeals of nonfiction is that through it we learn about real life. Have students talk about the kinds of nonfiction they like to read. Ask for examples of people and events they have read about that interested them. Encourage students to think of themselves as writers and find out what aspects of their lives they would most enjoy writing about.

Thinking

Remind students to keep the intent of the nonfiction writing in mind when they read. If they feel that the writer is someone they could relate to in real life, the writing will be easier for them to connect to. In fiction, a writer might use an unreliable narrator to tell a story, knowing that the readers will recognize this and will see the story through the eyes of an unusual kind of person. In nonfiction, this shouldn't happen. The writer or narrator of a piece of nonfiction should be a reliable source of information.

Teaching Options

NONFICTION

Nonfiction is writing that tells about real-life people, places, events, and ideas. Fiction, too, can deal with real-life stories, but authors of fiction can invent characters, situations, and dialogue. Writers of nonfiction, on the other hand, deal with the truth, with reality, and with the world we live in.

When you read nonfiction, notice not only the information it offers, but also how the writer presents the information. Look for the three T's: Thinking, Technique, and Thoroughness.

THINKING

Does the writer's thinking make sense? For example, does the writer

- present specific facts and evidence?
- use careful, step-by-step reasoning?
- take all likely possibilities into account?
- make only those generalizations that the evidence supports?
- leave you with unanswered questions?

Look at the model below to see how one writer applied these techniques.

Technique: Imagery ⎯⎯⎯⎯⎯

Thoroughness: Source and date ⎯⎯⎯⎯
Technique: Statistics ⎯⎯⎯⎯

Thinking: Specific evidence ⎯⎯⎯⎯

Thinking: Generalization fits ⎯⎯⎯⎯
the evidence

> **MODEL**
>
> Forget everything you've ever heard about dumb athletes. Researchers have found that the stereotypical muscle-brained jock–the one who'd rather spend time in the gym than the classroom–is rare.
>
> In fact, studies seem to show that athletic activity actually improves most students' classroom performance.
>
> In the 1980s, the Women's Sports Foundation conducted a four-year study of more than 30,000 high-school boys and girls.
>
> After examining the students' test scores, monitoring their extracurricular activities, and conducting private interviews, researchers discovered that varsity athletes were more likely than nonathletes to "score well on achievement tests, report high popularity, stay in high school, attend college, and seek a bachelor's degree."

 ENGLISH LANGUAGE LEARNERS

Cultural Observations Have students talk in small groups or with partners about experiences that taught them something about another culture. Encourage English language learners to think of something that surprises or interests them about American culture.

Activity Pair English language learners with English-proficient students. Have students practice listening and retelling by asking them to share their cultural observations with their partners and then retell their partners' stories to the class. Finally, ask each partner whether the story has been told correctly. **COLLAB. LEARN.**

Additional Resources
📁 *English Language Learners Sourcebook*

TECHNIQUE

Effective techniques include the use of

- **Imagery** Sensory details help readers picture people, settings, and events.
- **Comparisons** Metaphors, similes, and analogies compare unfamiliar items or concepts to familiar things.
- **Examples** Examples help to show readers exactly what is meant.
- **Statistics** Numerical data—such as results from polls, surveys, or studies—present precise information.

Questionable techniques involve the use of propaganda—attempts to manipulate readers' emotions and thinking. Watch out for propaganda strategies such as

- **Transfer** "Famous people [who have no expertise in this area] believe this, so you should, too."

- **Bandwagon** "Everyone supports this [just take our word for it]. Don't be left out—get on the bandwagon!"
- **Glittering Generality** "This idea can be described in great-sounding words [they may be meaningless, but they sure sound good], so it must be valid."

THOROUGHNESS

- Does the writer offer enough information about the topic?
- Do the facts presented reflect only one approach, or does the writer explore the topic from several angles?
- Does the writer make his or her sources clear? Are they up-to-date and unbiased?

Chris Voelz, University of Minnesota women's athletic director, said that lessons learned in athletics, like being a good sport and working as part of a team, are skills that can help athletes become better students.

— Thoroughness: Source name and credentials

— Technique: Examples

"Sports hold you accountable," Voelz once said. "They teach you to take responsibility, teach you to build a safety net for failure, to work for a common goal instead of concentrating on yourself.

— Technique: Comparison (metaphor)

"Sports teach you to work under pressure. They teach you that you can compete and win."

—Andy Steiner, *A Sporting Chance: Sports and Gender*

Technique

Explain to students that it is important for them to recognize the difference between legitimate, effective techniques and questionable techniques used in nonfiction writing. Help students list examples of the use of questionable techniques. The list might include TV commercials, magazine and newspaper ads, and infomercials. Ask students how they recognize these techniques. Encourage them to read newspapers, magazines, and other sources of nonfiction writing for a week and bring in examples of both kinds of techniques.

Thoroughness

Compare short stories to magazine articles. Ask students how they feel when information is left out of a short story. They may say that a fiction writer leaves something out intentionally as a way of allowing the reader to use his or her imagination. Find out from students how they feel when they finish reading a magazine article and still have several questions in their minds. This may be an indication that the nonfiction writer has not been thorough.

Technology Option

Short Story Table

Students can use word processing software to create tables of the three Ts of analyzing nonfiction. Have each student open a new document and insert a four-column table with the following headings: Title, Thinking, Technique, and Thoroughness.

Title	Thinking	Technique	Thoroughness
1.			
2.			

For each new piece of nonfiction students read, have them add a new row and complete the tables with an analysis of the three Ts. Students can use their tables to review the nonfiction they read or to help them compare and contrast the selections. **L2**

Active Reading Strategies

Objective

- To understand and apply strategies for reading and comprehending informative nonfiction

Teach the Strategies

Ask students to name a few of the places they get their information. Find out whether they receive news by word of mouth from family members and friends or from newspapers, magazines, and television. Prompt a discussion about whether they believe everything they hear or read. Find out what they consider reliable sources of information in their lives.

Preview

Remind students to preview what they are about to read, whether it is fiction or nonfiction. Previewing helps prepare the reader to absorb information—it gives him or her a head start.

Question

The process of questioning what we read as we go along is especially important when reading informative nonfiction. Remind students that they are the guardians of their own minds and beliefs—they need to question in order to judge and discern the accuracy of what they read.

Teaching Options

ACTIVE READING MODEL

Active Reading Strategies

Strategies for Informative Nonfiction

Do you enjoy reading about real life, about factual events in the past or present? Nonfiction writing deals with real people, places, and events. Literary nonfiction includes autobiography, biography, and essays. Informative nonfiction includes encyclopedias, books on topics such as history and science, and most articles in newspapers and magazines. Informative nonfiction is written primarily to inform readers. Facts, therefore, are extremely important.

When reading informative nonfiction, active readers use strategies like those below to figure out the organization of a selection and to separate facts from opinions.

- For more about these and other reading strategies, see **Reading Handbook,** pp. R82–R101.

PREVIEW

Previewing a selection by looking at the title, headings, illustrations, and any diagrams or charts will give you an idea of what it will be about. Previewing may also help you figure out how the author has organized the work.

Ask Yourself . . .

- Does the author give the facts in chronological order or some other sequence appropriate to the subject?
- Will I need to understand this chart (graph, diagram, etc.) before I read the article?
- What do the photographs or illustrations tell me about the subject?

QUESTION

Questioning helps you clarify the facts in the text.

Ask Yourself . . .

- What do I know about this subject that will help me judge this information?
- Do I understand why the writer has included this specific information?
- Do I agree with the writer's opinion here?

ℛeading Journal

The Scary Truth

Madeleine Nash's informative nonfiction article "The Fish Crisis" presents surprising and alarming facts about the depletion of fish in the world's oceans. Invite students to discuss what they already know about fishing controversies in their region and throughout the world.

Activity As they read "The Fish Crisis," invite students to list in their reading journals information that surprises or worries them. After reading, have each student write a brief summary of the part of the selection that was most alarming or comforting and why he or she found it so.

Review

Students may want to jot down notes as they read the informative nonfiction in this unit. Keeping track of names, numbers, dates, distances, and other statistics can be challenging. In some students, however, this kind of information promotes further interest in the subject matter. Students should be encouraged to review the material in a manner that contributes to their understanding and interest.

Evaluate

Encourage students to be mindful of the evaluation process while they are reading a piece of informative nonfiction—and afterward. Their opinions and judgments are important tools for participating in the information age. Have each of them keep a note card with the four evaluation questions on the desk as a reminder when reading. As a follow-up to the questions, ask students to explain where their opinions come from. For example, if a student does not believe a writer is qualified to write on a certain topic, he or she should be able to give reasons for the opinion and to cite aspects of the essay or article that led to that conclusion.

REVIEW

Think about what you read. Summarize and rephrase the information.

Say to Yourself . . .

● In other words, the author means _____.

● So far in this work _____.

● The most important fact I have learned about this subject is _____.

EVALUATE

Form opinions and make judgments about what you have read.

Ask Yourself . . .

● Is this writer qualified to write on this topic?

● Are the sources for these facts reliable?

● Is this actually an opinion that the writer is presenting as a fact?

● If I wrote an essay on this subject, what would I include that this author hasn't included?

APPLYING THE STRATEGIES

Read "The Fish Crisis." Use the Active Reading Model notes in the margins as you read. Write your own responses on a separate piece of paper or use self-stick notes.

FACING CHALLENGE ❧ 293

Teaching Options

Objectives

- To read a work of nonfiction and understand the challenge in preserving the world's fisheries
- To recognize the persuasive techniques in an essay
- To list and evaluate the major sources used in an essay

Skills

Reading/Thinking: Using Text Structures; Evaluating; Identifying Propaganda Techniques; Distinguishing Fact from Opinion
Writing: Letter to the Editor; Interview
Vocabulary: Prefixes; Suffixes
Grammar/Language: Using Quotation Marks
Collaborating: Literature Groups

Motivating
→ OPTIONS

Selection Focus Transparency 27: Ask students how the quotation by Edward Young might relate to the title of the selection.

Focus Activity: As an extension of the Focus Activity, have students work in small groups to research in which seas tunas can be found.

ACTIVE READING MODEL

Before You Read
The Fish Crisis

MEET J. MADELEINE NASH

Starting her career in journalism in 1966 as a researcher at *Time* magazine, J. Madeleine Nash went on to become a reporter for the magazine. Nash has also used her experience as a journalist to research and write a book about parent involvement in education called *Schools Where Parents Make a Difference*.

J. Madeleine Nash was born in 1943. This article was published in the August 11, 1997, issue of Time.

FOCUS ACTIVITY

When you eat a tuna sandwich for lunch, do you ever think about where the tuna fish came from?

List Ideas
Work in a small group to list all the edible fish you have heard about or tasted. Then try to guess where the fish originate—in fresh water (lakes, rivers) or the ocean.

Setting a Purpose
Read the following article to learn about the world's supply of fish.

BACKGROUND

Did You Know? The waters where fishing takes place are called *fisheries.* The most productive fisheries are in oceans, especially areas near coastlines.

VOCABULARY PREVIEW

contemplate (kon′ təm plāt′) *v.* to give intense attention to; consider carefully; p. 296
plummet (plum′ it) *v.* to fall or drop straight downward; plunge; p. 296
depleted (di plēt′ id) *adj.* greatly reduced in amount; p. 296
undermine (un′ dər mīn′) *v.* to weaken, wear away, or destroy slowly; p. 298
exploit (iks ploit′) *v.* to use or develop for profit, often in a selfish, unjust, or unfair way; p. 299
converge (kən vurj′) *v.* to come together at a place; p. 299
amplify (am′ plə fī′) *v.* to increase; extend; p. 300
indiscriminately (in′ dis krim′ ə nit lē) *adv.* in a way that does not pay attention to differences; carelessly; p. 300
diligently (dil′ ə jənt lē) *adv.* in a way that shows great attention, care, and effort; p. 301
subsidize (sub′ sə dīz′) *v.* to aid or support with a contribution of money; p. 301

The Fish Crisis

J. Madeleine Nash

THICK SWORDFISH STEAKS. Orange roughy fillets. Great mounds of red-fleshed tuna. Judging from the seafood sections of local supermarkets, there would seem to be plenty of fish left in the oceans. But this appearance of abundance is an illusion, says Sylvia Earle, former chief scientist for the National Oceanic and Atmospheric Administration.

295

Reading the Selection

SUMMARY

Some species of fish are dying out because the fishing industry is not giving nature enough time to replenish what has been taken. Local and international officials are trying to set limits on the industry, but it is a difficult task and their efforts have not been completely successful.

Spanish Summaries, p. 27

A **Active Reading**

PREVIEW (Students might assume the article deals with an overview of various kinds of fish. The chart on page 298, however, may suggest that the article deals with some kind of problem.)

B **Active Reading**

PREDICT Point out to students that because the article has no subheads, it may be a little difficult to identify key ideas. However, the first sentence in most paragraphs seems to be a topic sentence.

Additional Resources

Active Reading Guide, p. 27

Audio Library

Spanish Audio Library

Teaching Options

CONNECTING TO OTHER SELECTIONS

The chart at the right shows three ways to connect "The Fish Crisis" to other selections in this book.

For specific teaching strategies, see the *Theme Three Planning Guide,* pages 64–65.

Connection		Title
Life Skills: Problem Solving	→	"New Directions," p. 221
Thematic: Interdependence	→	"We Are All One," p. 773
Literary: Author's Purpose	→	"The Dog Diaries," p. 411

C Active Reading

QUESTION *(The opinion seems to be not that of the author of the essay, but of the Natural Resources Defense Council. One would assume their "sobering report" has facts to back up their opinion, but we are not sure of that.)*

D Active Reading

PREDICT *(Students might suggest that a worse threat could be the deliberate elimination of a species or something unknown that causes the population of a species to plummet.)*

Vo•cab•u•lar•y Skills

PREFIXES The prefix *over-* signifies an excess or too much of something, as in *overfishing*. The meaning of the word can be understood by combining *over-* with the root word. Some examples are *overabundant, overanimated, overflow, overstuffed,* and *overmatched*.

ACTIVE READING MODEL

QUESTION

C Is the author stating a fact here, or her opinion?

PREDICT

D What could be a worse threat than this?

The Fish Crisis

Already, Earle fears, an international armada of fishing vessels is on the verge of exhausting a storehouse of protein so vast that it once appeared to be infinite. "It's a horrible thing to <u>contemplate</u>," shudders Earle. "What makes it even worse is that we know better. Yet here we go, making the same mistake over and over again."

If fishermen around the world soon start hauling back empty nets and fishing lines, it will not be for lack of warning. In the 1990s, after increasing for nearly four decades, the wild catch of marine fish leveled off worldwide and in some years actually declined. "We are reaching, and in many cases have exceeded, the oceans' limits," declare the authors of a sobering report released by the Natural Resources Defense Council earlier this year. "We are no longer living off the income but eating deeply into the capital."[1]

Fights have already started to break out over the dwindling supply. Two weeks ago, hundreds of Canadian fishermen blockaded a British Columbia port for several days to keep an Alaskan ferry from leaving. The reason for their protest? Alaskan trawlers[2] were sweeping up the salmon that spawn in Canada's rivers. Now the Canadians are threatening to do to the salmon runs of Washington State what U.S. fishermen have done to theirs.

Of course, overfishing is not the only human activity that is jeopardizing life in the oceans. Coastal pollution and habitat destruction—filling in wetlands, building dams—are contributing to the crisis. But it is overfishing, the NRDC report makes plain, that constitutes[3] the most urgent threat and demands the most immediate action.

Until now, the worst threat most creatures of the sea had faced at fishermen's hands was so-called commercial extinction.[4] Whenever local populations of a particular fish <u>plummeted</u>, boats simply targeted some other species or moved to more distant waters. The <u>depleted</u> stocks almost always recovered. But now, experts warn,

---

1. In financial terms, *capital* is wealth that is used to produce more wealth. A savings account, for example, adds to your income by earning interest. However, if you spend the savings (your capital), you earn less interest and gradually use up all your savings.
2. *Trawlers* are boats that catch fish by towing strong, bag-shaped nets across the ocean bottom.
3. Here, *constitutes* means "forms; makes up."
4. An *extinction* is the permanent elimination of something.

Vocabulary
contemplate (kon′ təm plāt′) *v.* to give intense attention to; consider carefully
plummet (plum′ it) *v.* to fall or drop straight downward; plunge
depleted (di plēt′ id) *adj.* greatly reduced in amount

Teaching Options

MEETING INDIVIDUAL NEEDS — ENGLISH LANGUAGE LEARNERS

Phrasal Verbs Point out to English language learners the following phrasal verbs in the second and third paragraphs on page 296: *leveled off, break out,* and *sweep up.* Explain that these verbs all have a particle attached that is considered part of the verb. Elicit other examples from students, such as to *look up* or *run across* a friend, to *put* someone *down,* or to *get away* with something.

Activity Have students work with partners to continue reading the selection. As they read, ask them to look for other examples of phrasal verbs to add to their vocabulary notebooks.

Additional Resources
📁 *English Language Learners Sourcebook*

FYI

The U.S. National Marine Fisheries Service is the government agency that supports the domestic and international conservation efforts of fisheries. This agency offers statistics on fisheries and related legislation.

FYI

Tunas travel in the open waters of the tropics and in the warm seas of the world. Sometimes they travel the entire Pacific Ocean from the California coast to Japan to spawn. Tunas can swim at high speed and their body temperature is a few degrees higher than the surrounding waters. There are forty species with the common name *tuna*.

Reading *Minilesson*

Using Text Structures Explain to students that when reading a nonfiction article, they can benefit from taking notes. A Who-What-Why chart can help them keep track of the facts.

Activity Have students work in small groups or in pairs. Suggest that they read or reread the text one paragraph at a time and write down the information they gather in a chart like the one below. **L2**

COLLAB. LEARN.

Who	What	Why
Fishing industry	Overfishing	Consumer demand

Additional Resources

Reading Workbook, pp. 45–46

E Literary Elements

ESSAY Explain to students that authors of essays often use many different techniques to communicate their ideas or opinions. Here, the author presents a chart displaying some fishing facts and explaining in simple terms how readers can help.

F Critical Thinking

EVALUATING Explain to students that when detailed information is presented in graphic form, their understanding will be enhanced by evaluating the way it is organized. Suggest that students start with the heading, note the larger elements, and work down to the smaller elements. Ask them if they think the chart is an effective visual aid and companion to the selection. *(Some students might feel it is simple enough to understand and provides important supporting information to the selection. Others might think the chart is confusing and poorly organized.)*

G Active Reading

PREDICT *(It is likely that the author will explain more about fishing gear because of the statement that "technological barriers that have kept overfishing within bounds" are "shaky.")*

Some Endangered Fish Species

PREDICT

Do you think the author will explain more about the kind of fishing gear that is depleting fish?

WHAT YOU CAN DO

AVOID EATING
sharks, swordfish, bluefin tuna (most canned tuna is fine), beluga sturgeon or caviar, orange roughy, grouper

O.K. TO EAT
Pacific cod; Atlantic striped bass, mackerel, and herring; farm-raised trout, catfish, shrimp, and salmon*

*Some aquaculture operations in Europe and Southeast Asia pollute marine environments.

unprecedented forces—among them, industrial-scale fishing gear and a burgeoning[5] global seafood market—are altering this age-old cycle. The economic and technological barriers that have kept overfishing within bounds appear increasingly shaky, like dikes along a river that floodwaters have underlined. Should these barriers collapse, commercial extinction could escalate into biological catastrophe.[6]

In most imminent peril[7] are the giant predators of the oceans—sharks, of course, but also marlin, sailfish, swordfish, and bluefin tuna, the magnificent swimming machines that have earned the nickname "Porsches of the sea." In the western Atlantic, the breeding population of northern bluefin, the largest tuna species, is thought to consist of perhaps 40,000

---

5. When something is *unprecedented,* there has never before been anything like it. When something is *burgeoning,* it is growing rapidly.
6. The gradual wiping out of food fish could increase by stages *(escalate)* into a sudden, terrible disaster for all sea creatures *(biological catastrophe).*
7. *In most imminent peril* could be restated as: "Likely to be in danger first."

Vocabulary
undermine (un´ dər mīn´) *v.* to weaken, wear away, or destroy slowly

---

Teaching Options

Writing *Minilesson*

Interview Explain to students that one of the best ways to obtain more information about an issue is to interview the people involved.

Activity Have students work in pairs and take the roles of interviewer and interviewee. Have them choose a role: the fisherman or the conservationist. Suggest that they use the information they gath-

ered in reading the selection to write the questions they will use. Then have students write a few paragraphs explaining what they have learned about each side of the overfishing issue. **L2 COLLAB. LEARN.**

Additional Resources

Writer's Choice, Lesson 26.2

J. Madeleine Nash :~

adults, down from some 250,000 two decades ago. Reason: the flourishing airfreight industry that allows fish brokers to deliver Atlantic Ocean bluefin overnight to Tokyo's sashimi[8] market, where a single fish can fetch $80,000 or more at auction. "To a fisherman, catching a bluefin is a lot like winning the lottery," sighs Stanford University marine biologist Barbara Block.

The crash of commercially important fisheries is not new. What is new is how quickly fisheries arise and how quickly they are <u>exploited</u>. In recent years, piked dogfish, a small spiny shark, has begun to stand in for cod in the fish and chips served by British pubs, and the Patagonian toothfish has become a popular substitute for sablefish in Japan. But environmental groups are concerned about the long-term viability of the fisheries that are serving up these quaintly named piscine[9] treats. This year, for example, ships from around the world have <u>converged</u> on the Southern Ocean, where the toothfish makes its home. "At this rate," predicts Beth Clark, a scientist with the Antarctica Project, "the entire fishery will be gone in 18 months."

Unfortunately, it takes longer to rebuild a fishery than it does to ruin one. Consider the present state of the orange roughy on New Zealand's Challenger Plateau. Discovered in 1979, this deep-water fishing hole took off in the 1980s when the mild-tasting, white-fleshed fish became popular with U.S. chefs. Happy to stoke the surging demand, fishermen are believed to have reduced the biomass of orange roughy as much as 80% before officials stepped in. Now, says Yale University ichthyologist[10] Jon Moore, it may take centuries before the fishery rebounds. As scientists have belatedly learned, orange roughy grow extremely slowly, live 100 years or more and take 25 to 30 years to reach sexual maturity.

How can a fishing fleet do so much damage so quickly? Until recently, many fish, especially deep-water fish, were too hard to find to make tempting commercial targets. But technical advances have given fishermen the power to peer beneath the waves and plot their position

---

8. This is the market where Tokyo's restaurants buy their fish. *Sashimi* is raw fish.
9. To have *viability* is to be able both to survive and to work as intended. *Piscine* (pī′ sēn) means "of or relating to fish."
10. *Biomass* is the total amount of living matter within a given environmental area. It's a term that might be used by an *ichthyologist,* a scientist who specializes in the study of fish.

Vocabulary

exploit (iks ploit′) *v.* to use or develop for profit, often in a selfish, unjust, or unfair way

converge (kən vurj′) *v.* to come together at a place

Active Reading

L Active Reading

EVALUATE *(Yes, the author describes in simple terms how the technology works and is used. She does not overexplain.)*

M Literary Elements

AUTHOR'S PURPOSE Ask students why they think the author uses such descriptions as "ships as large as football fields." Why doesn't she just say the fishermen use large ships? Challenge them to find another example of this type of description. *(The author wants the reader to visualize the overwhelming challenge the fishing industry poses to fish populations, and she can do that effectively with these kinds of images.)*

N Active Reading

QUESTION *(Yes, this is some of the industrial fishing gear mentioned above.)* Explain to students that the technological aspect of the equipment is secondary to its size, which is the key idea in this paragraph.

O Active Reading

RESPOND *(Some students may feel encouraged by the fact that something positive can be done. Others, however, may feel that the positive steps already taken are quite small in comparison to the problem.)*

ACTIVE READING MODEL

EVALUATE

L Does the author do a good job describing how these technical advances work?

QUESTION

N Is this some of the industrial fishing gear the author mentioned earlier?

RESPOND

O How did you feel when you read that something positive could be done to help solve part of the overfishing problem?

---

with unprecedented accuracy. Sonar makes it possible to locate large shoals of fish that would otherwise remain concealed beneath tens, even hundreds of feet of water. And once a fishing hot spot is pinpointed by sonar, satellite-navigation systems enable vessels to return unerringly to the same location year after year. In this fashion, fishermen from New Zealand to the Philippines have been able to home in on orange roughy and giant groupers as they gather to spawn, in some cases virtually eliminating entire generations of reproducing adults.

But what has amplified the destructive power of modern fishing more than anything else is its gargantuan[11] scale. Trawling for pollock in the Bering Sea and the Gulf of Alaska, for example, are computerized ships as large as football fields. Their nets—wide enough to swallow a dozen Boeing 747s—can gather up 130 tons of fish in a single sweep. Along with pollock and other groundfish, these nets indiscriminately draw in the creatures that swim or crawl alongside, including halibut, Pacific herring, Pacific salmon, and king crab. In similar fashion, so-called longlines—which stretch for tens of miles and bristle with thousands of hooks—snag not just tuna and swordfish but also hapless sea turtles and albatrosses, marlin and sharks.

What happens to the dead and dying animals that constitute this so-called "by-catch"? Most are simply dumped overboard, either because they are unwanted or because fishery regulations require it. In 1993, for example, shrimp trawlers in the Gulf of Mexico caught and threw away an estimated 34 million red snappers, including many juveniles. By contrast, the annual catch of red snapper from the Gulf averages only around 3 million fish. Indeed, so many snappers are being scooped up as by-catch that the productivity of the fishery has been compromised. Fortunately, there is a solution. Shrimp nets can be outfitted with devices that afford larger animals like snappers and sea turtles a trapdoor escape hatch.

To a surprising extent, solutions to the problem of overfishing also exist, at least on paper, and that's what critics of the fishing industry find so encouraging—and so frustrating. Last year, for example, Congress passed landmark legislation that requires fishery managers to crack down on overfishing in U.S. waters. Perhaps even more impressive, the

---

11. From the name of a fictional giant, Gargantua, *gargantuan* means "enormous; huge."

Vocabulary
amplify (am′ plə fī′) *v.* to increase; extend
indiscriminately (in′ dis krim′ ə nit lē) *adv.* in a way that does not pay attention to differences; carelessly

---

Teaching Options

Grammar and Language *Minilesson*

Using Quotation Marks Write the following sentence on the board: *"The number of fish is dwindling," sighed Carl. "We need to do something about it."* When a person's exact words are quoted, those words are placed within quotation marks. When the quote is interrupted, the quotation is closed and then reopened with quotation marks.

Activity Ask students to identify quotations in the following sentences and to place quotation marks where necessary.
1. We are reaching the limits, declared the official. We must end this crisis. *("We are reaching the limits," declared the official. "We must end this crisis.")*
2. Soon all the nets will be empty, warned the fisherman. *("Soon all the nets will be empty," warned the fisherman.)* **L2**

Additional Resources
📠 *Grammar and Language Transparency 26*

📘 *Grammar and Language Workbook,* pp. 267–270

📘 *Grammar and Composition Handbook,* Lesson 13.6

📘 *Writer's Choice,* Lesson 20.6

J. Madeleine Nash ∾

U.N. has produced a tough-minded treaty that promises to protect stocks of fish that straddle the coastal zones of two or more countries or migrate, as bluefin tuna and swordfish do, through international waters in the wide-open oceans. The treaty will take effect, however, only after 30 or more nations ratify[12] it—and even then, some question how <u>diligently</u> its provisions will be enforced.

What has been missing is a willingness to take action. Consumers no less than politicians bear some of the blame. Simply by refusing to buy bluefin tuna in Tokyo, grouper in Hong Kong or swordfish in Chicago, consumers could relieve the pressure on some of the world's most beleaguered[13] fisheries and allow them the time they need to recover. To help shoppers become more selective about what they put on the dinner table, the Worldwide Fund for Nature and Unilever, one of the world's largest purveyors of frozen seafood, have launched a joint venture[14] that in 1998 will start putting labels on fish and fish products caught in environmentally responsible ways.

R A sign that consumers are worried about the world's fisheries could provide the jolt political leaders need. For the past half-century, billions of dollars have been spent by maritime nations to expand their domestic fishing fleets, <u>subsidizing</u> everything from fuel costs to the construction of factory trawlers. And until countries like Canada, China, Japan, South Korea, New Zealand, Norway, Spain, and, yes, the U.S. are willing to confront this monster of their own making, attempts to control overfishing are likely to prove ineffectual.[15] The problem, as Carl Safina, director of the National Audubon Society's Living Oceans Program, observes, is this: there is just too much fishing power chasing too few fish.

---

12. To *ratify* means to approve a document and agree to obey its rules.
13. The most *beleaguered* fisheries are those in the greatest trouble.
14. These food suppliers *(purveyors)* have formed a partnership *(joint venture).*
15. If the attempts are *ineffectual,* they will fail to produce the desired result.

❖

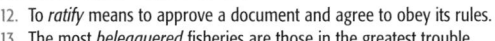

Vocabulary
diligently (dil′ ə jənt lē) *adv.* in a way that shows great attention, care, and effort
subsidize (sub′ sə dīz′) *v.* to aid or support with a contribution of money

---

P Active Reading

QUESTION *(Perhaps the author feels the treaty will not matter anyhow. Her next words might imply that: ...even then, some question how diligently its provisions will be enforced.)*

Q Active Reading

CONNECT *(Some students may feel that their families should take a stand. Others may feel that the government should step in.)*

R Critical Thinking

DISTINGUISHING FACT FROM OPINION Ask students if they accept the detail in the first sentence as fact or if they suspect that some of the information is really the author's opinion. *(Students might use the word* could *as a clue that the author is predicting what might happen in the future. This is her interpretation—her opinion.)*

S Active Reading

EVALUATE *(Some students may feel that the author should have given more information about fish, technology, and the fishing industry.)*

Thematic Focus

Facing Challenge In a sense, the author challenges students to do their part in preserving fish species. Have students discuss how they can influence fishing companies, government agencies, and consumers.

✔ **ASSESSMENT OPTIONS**

📁 *Quick Checks,* p. 27

MEETING INDIVIDUAL NEEDS — GIFTED AND TALENTED ACTIVITY

The Flip Side In this selection, the author presents one side of the overfishing problem. Some students might be interested in learning the concerns of those on the other side of the issue.

Activity Invite students to work in pairs to do further research on the topic of overfishing. Have them concentrate on the facts and opinions set forth by the fishermen, fishing companies, and fish supply companies. Ask them to write essays presenting their research. You might like to challenge students by asking them to present their own ideas for solving the problem. **L3** **COLLAB. LEARN.**

Responding to the Selection

Personal Response

Students might suggest that the author's purpose is to make the public aware of the fish crisis. Others may feel the purpose is to try to move readers to take action.

Active Reading Response

For example, students might choose Review and find three paragraphs to rephrase in their own words.

Analyzing Literature

1. The fishing industry, equipped with sophisticated and huge equipment, is depleting the supply of many types of fish to the point of interfering with the reproduction and replenishment of these species. The continuous demand for fish fuels the industry's efforts.
2. Rebuilding a fishery may take generations, whereas ruining it takes only a few years.
3. Some of the technical advances in fishing are the use of computers, sonar, and huge nets that collect not only fish but also by-catch.
4. The UN and the U.S. Congress have produced a treaty to protect stocks of fish.
5. Some may see consumer demand as the cause. Others may blame the industry's greed.
6. If they want to make money, the fish distributors must supply the most popular fish.
7. The huge scale of fishing seems to be the fundamental cause. The industry could scale back its use of the technical advances and use technology to help preserve the supply.
8. Some may feel that the industry will take action to save its own livelihood. Others may think that consumers or the government will take action once they learn about the problem.

Responding to Literature

ACTIVE READING MODEL

PERSONAL RESPONSE

Did you discover the author's purpose, as suggested in the **Focus Activity** on page 294? Were you convinced by the author's arguments about the "fish crisis"? Explain why or why not.

Active Reading Response
Look back at the strategies described in the **Active Reading Model** notes on pages 292–293. Choose one of the strategies and find three places in the article where you could apply it.

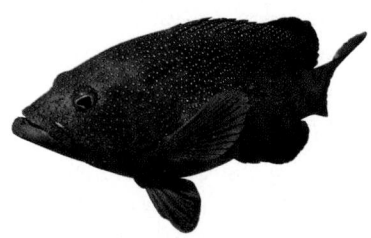

Analyzing Literature

RECALL

1. Summarize what has happened to the world's ocean fish supply in the 1990s.
2. Which takes longer, ruining a fishery or rebuilding one?
3. List the technical advances that have affected fishing.
4. What have the U.S. Congress and the United Nations done to solve the problem of overfishing?

INTERPRET

5. In your opinion, what is the leading cause of the depleted fish supply?
6. Why, do you think, do fishers converge at a fishery when a new fish becomes popular?
7. Which do you think has caused the most damage to the fish population, technical advances or the huge scale of the fishing industry? Explain your answer.
8. Do you think the fishing industry or consumers will ever take action on their own to prevent overfishing? Why or why not?

EVALUATE AND CONNECT

9. Do you think the writer presented both sides of the debate on overfishing? Use examples to support your answer.
10. How would your life be changed if the supply of ocean fish dwindled to almost nothing?

LITERARY ELEMENTS

Essay

An **essay** is a short piece of nonfiction writing on any topic. The purpose of an essay is to communicate an idea or opinion. In a **persuasive essay**, such as "The Fish Crisis," the author tries to convince the reader of an opinion. One persuasive technique essayists use is the addition of emotional words, as in this sentence from "The Fish Crisis": "[Overfishing is] a horrible thing to contemplate."

1. What is J. Madeleine Nash trying to persuade the reader to believe?

2. Give three examples in which the writer uses emotional words to persuade the reader.

● See **Literary Terms Handbook**, p. R3.

---

9. Some may say she did present both sides, first describing the problem and then the solutions. Others may feel she didn't give the industry a chance to tell its side of the story.
10. Students' answers will depend on their typical intake of fish.

LITERARY ELEMENTS

1. The author is trying to get people to see that overfishing has damaging effects and should be controlled.
2. Some possibilities are the word *crisis* in the title; *a sobering report,* page 296; and *biological catastrophe,* page 298.

Additional Resources

✦ *Literary Elements Transparency 27*

Literature and Writing

Writing About Literature

Looking at Sources   A powerful persuasive essay or article like "The Fish Crisis" should contain facts and quotations from a number of trustworthy sources. Write a list of the major sources Nash uses in her article. Does the use of these sources help convince you that the author is right?

Creative Writing

Letter to the Editor   On the editorial pages of newspapers, both professional journalists and local readers can express their opinions in print. Write a persuasive letter alerting the people in your community to the dangers of overfishing in the world's oceans.

Extending Your Response

Literature Groups
Persuade the Public!   Your group has decided that everyone needs to know about the danger to the ocean fish supply. Brainstorm a slogan, and then design a poster that includes your warning and an illustration that calls attention to your cause.

Interdisciplinary Activity

Science/Math: Diagram   Study the selection and take notes on the statistics listed in different parts of the essay. Then find a way to represent these facts in a graph or chart.

Reading Further
If you would like to read more about fish, try these:
Fish by Steve Parker
Threatened Oceans by Jenny T. Tesar

📖 **Save your work for your portfolio.**

Skill Minilesson

VOCABULARY • SUFFIXES

If you *purify* something, you make it more *pure*. If you *electrify* a car, you make it *electric*. As you can see, the suffix *-fy* means "to make or cause to be." When the *-fy* suffix is added, an *e* or a *y* at the end of the original word will change to *i*. Sometimes an *i* is inserted to make the new word easier to pronounce.

PRACTICE Complete each sentence without using a form of the underlined word.
1. You might <u>beautify</u> a room by . . .
2. You could <u>solidify</u> water by . . .
3. You might <u>simplify</u> a statement by . . .
4. You could <u>signify</u> that you were happy by . . .
5. You could <u>intensify</u> your cheering by . . .

Writing About Literature
Students' responses should
• identify the specific sources.
• explain whether the author's use of sources is effective.

Creative Writing
Students' writing should
• reflect an awareness of the need to write with brevity and directness.
• use techniques such as citing statistics and quoting authorities.

Extending Your Response

Literature Groups Remind students that the posters should be eye-catching and get their message across in a few words. **COLLAB. LEARN.**

Interdisciplinary Activity
Remind students that using a chart is an effective way of conveying detailed factual information in a relatively small space. Suggest that students group facts of a common nature in the same chart.

Skill Minilesson

VOCABULARY • SUFFIXES

Some possibilities include:
1. decorating it
2. freezing it
3. expressing the main idea without extra detail
4. smiling
5. shouting

Additional Resources
📁 *Vocabulary Practice,* p. 18

MEDIA
Connection

PUBLIC OPINION POLL

Polls are surveys done to get an idea of what a large body of people, like the American public, thinks about some topic, person, or product.

Objective

- To understand and apply strategies for reading a public opinion poll

Literature LINK

The Fish Crisis The Seaway public opinion poll report connects to "The Fish Crisis," the literature selection that immediately precedes this lesson. Point out the connection by telling students that both readings deal with humanity's relationship with nature.

Respond

1. Questions might include *Would you say that the oceans of the world are in poor condition, good condition, or excellent condition? Does the destruction of the ocean represent a serious threat, a very serious threat, or no threat to humans? Are commercial fishing and oil drilling taking too much out of the ocean? Are we allowing excessive waste, oil, and agricultural runoff to be dumped into the waters?*

2. Students may use a bar graph, chart, web, or Venn diagram.

Additional Resources
📁 *Media Connections*, p. 6

Teaching Options

interNET CONNECTION

Endangered Species To search for more information, have students enter such keywords in quotes as *endangered species, natural resource,* and *Sea Web.*

Americans Continue to Worry About the Decline of the Oceans

A Seaway Ocean Update, February 1998

As the International Year of the Ocean dawns, a new poll shows that more than half (59%) of Americans continue to view the health of the oceans today negatively, with 17% saying the oceans are in poor condition. Only one-fifth say the oceans are in good shape, while a mere 1% call the oceans' health "excellent."

The poll, conducted by the Washington, D.C.–based Mellman Group for SeaWeb, shows also that a majority (60%) believe the condition of the seas has become worse over the past few years, while only 11% say it has improved.

Nearly three-quarters (72%) agree that human beings are also in trouble as a result of the seas' problems, while 53% say that the destruction of the oceans represents a "very serious" threat to the quality of life today. Fifty percent believe we are currently taking too much out of the ocean in the form of commercial fishing and oil drilling, while 80% say we are dumping too much into the ocean in the form of waste, oil, and agricultural runoff.

"When a mere 1% call the condition of the ocean 'excellent,' it is obvious that Americans understand that we are doing more harm than good to our ocean," says Vikki Spruill, executive director of SeaWeb.

304

Respond

1. From the reported results, figure out what questions the people were asked. Then answer them yourself. Total the results for your class, and see how your class's opinions compare with those of the public.

2. Take your class's results and the statistics from the report, and put them into some graphic form—for example, a bar graph.

Reading *Minilesson*

Problem and Solution As students read this selection, they may feel that the poll focuses on problems that are caused by humans and that could be solved by changes in human behavior.

Activity Ask students to work in pairs or small groups to read the selection and keep a record of problems and solutions. Suggest that they use a two-column chart with the headings *Problems* and *Solutions.*
L2 COLLAB. LEARN.

Additional Resources
📁 *Reading Workbook*

Before You Read
Hurricanes

MEET PATRICIA LAUBER

A person who is setting out to tell a story offers a hand and says, 'Come with me and I will show you many wondrous things.'" So says award-winning writer Patricia Lauber, who has written more than ninety nonfiction books for young people. Her book, *Volcano: The Eruption and Healing of Mount St. Helens*, was named a Newbery Honor Book. Lauber was awarded the Washington Post/Children's Book Guild Award for her contribution to nonfiction for children.

Patricia Lauber was born in 1924. She lives in Connecticut, where she has experienced several hurricanes. "Hurricanes" comes from her 1996 book Hurricanes: Earth's Mightiest Storms.

FOCUS ACTIVITY

Close your eyes and imagine this scene. You are at home, in the dark. The howling wind sounds like a rushing freight train hurtling toward the walls of your house. What are you thinking? How do you feel?

QuickWrite

Jot down at least three words that describe your thoughts and feelings as the storm heads your way.

Setting a Purpose

Read to find out about one of nature's most powerful storms.

BACKGROUND

Did You Know? Hurricanes and typhoons are tropical cyclones that have steady winds of at least seventy-five miles per hour. Storms that occur in the Atlantic and Pacific oceans are called hurricanes. Storms that take place in the western Pacific are called typhoons. The main energy source for these kinds of storms is the heat released when water vapor condenses. Because only very moist air can supply the energy necessary for one of these storms, tropical cyclones can only form over oceans with water temperatures of at least 80 degrees Fahrenheit. After forming, these types of storms intensify as they pass over warmer water and weaken as they pass over colder water or land.

VOCABULARY PREVIEW

compact (kəm pakt′) *adj.* occupying a relatively small space or area; tightly packed; p. 306
evacuate (i vak′ ū āt′) *v.* to leave or clear an area; p. 307
ecology (ē kol′ ə jē) *n.* the relationship of living things to their environment and to each other; p. 309
unique (ū nēk′) *adj.* highly uncommon; rare; one-of-a-kind; p. 309

Objectives

- To read and analyze a selection about hurricanes
- To identify informational text
- To write a selection summary

Skills

Reading/Thinking: Summarizing; Evaluating; Distinguishing Fact and Opinion
Writing: Postcard
Vocabulary: Word Origins; Prefixes
Grammar/Language: Compound Predicates; Spelling Plurals
Listening/Speaking: News Broadcast
Collaboration: Literature Groups; Mural

Motivating
→ OPTIONS

Literature Launchers: "In the Wake of a Storm"

Videodisc Side A, Segment 9

Also available in VHS.

Selection Focus Transparency 28: Have students view and discuss the diagram showing a hurricane's ingredients.

Focus Activity: As an extension of the Focus Activity, have pairs of students share what their feelings would have been (or were) when severe weather hit.

RESOURCE MANAGER

Lesson Planning Resource
The *Theme Three Planning Guide* (pp. 69–76) provides additional lesson notes and reduced versions of all print resources.

📁 Other Print Resources
- Active Reading Guide, p. 28
- Vocabulary Practice, p. 19
- Reading Workbook, pp. 47–48
- Grammar and Language Workbook, pp. 53–54, 297–300

- Grammar and Composition Handbook Lessons 1.5, 15.1
- Quick Checks, p. 28
- Selection and Theme Assessment, pp. 51–52
- Performance Assessment, p. 27
- Spanish Summaries, p. 28
- Spanish Translations
- Inclusion Strategies
- English Language Learners Sourcebook

🖐 Transparencies
- Selection Focus 28
- Literary Elements 28
- Grammar and Language 27

Technology
 Literature Launchers
 Audio Library
 Spanish Audio Library
🖥 Glencoe Literature Web Site
💾 Testmaker

SUMMARY

Hurricane Andrew devastated southern Florida in August 1992. It came ashore south of Miami carrying winds of almost 200 miles per hour. It nearly destroyed two towns, Homestead and Florida City, killing 22 people. A quarter of a million people had to camp out in the ruins, homeless. The storm also ripped through Everglades National Park trashing mangrove swamps and other animal habitats. Nature has always healed itself after severe weather, but now human activities may prevent nature's healing.

📁 *Spanish Summaries,* p. 28

A Active Reading

EVALUATE Ask students if they think modern technology can protect people from the devastation of storms like hurricanes and tornadoes. *(Students should realize that technology offers forecasts, giving people a chance to protect themselves. However, technology cannot keep the storms from occurring.)*

Additional Resources

📁 *Active Reading Guide,* p. 28

🎧 *Audio Library*

🎧 *Spanish Audio Library*

Teaching Options

Hurricanes:
Big Winds and Big Damage

Patricia Lauber 〜

In mid-August of 1992, satellite pictures showed a low-pressure area of wind and rain moving west across the Atlantic. Though the storm did not seem to amount to much, the National Hurricane Center in Miami, Florida, tracked it carefully.

By August 20 the storm was about 400 miles east of Puerto Rico. Here it weakened so much that it almost disappeared. The lower part of the storm was moving northwest, but the upper part was being blown northeast by strong high-altitude winds. For a time, it seemed the storm might be torn apart. Instead, the high-altitude winds began to flow around the storm. It charged ahead, with all its parts moving in the same direction.

By then scientists at the Hurricane Center were working with computer models of storms. They were trying to predict the storm's behavior and decide whether people should be told to leave coastal areas. The scientists fed their computers all the data they had received from satellites, radar, and airplane flights into the storm.

By 4:00 A.M. of August 22, winds within the storm were blowing at more than 75 miles an hour. The storm had become a hurricane. First of the season, it was named Andrew.[1]

As its winds swirled ever faster, Andrew churned across the Bahamas. It was a furious and <u>compact</u> storm, with an eye[2] only eight miles wide and winds that reached out for 60 miles. It was heading for the east coast of Florida.

---

1. In North America, hurricanes tend to occur from June through November, with most striking in September. Each season's first storm is given a name beginning with an *A*. Male and female names are used alternately through the alphabet.
2. A hurricane's *eye,* or center, has very light winds and can be as much as several miles across. If you were caught in a hurricane as the eye passed over, you might well see clear, blue sky overhead.

Vocabulary
compact (kəm pakt') *adj.* occupying a relatively small space or area; tightly packed

306 🐚 THEME 3

CONNECTING TO OTHER SELECTIONS

The chart at the right shows three ways to connect "Hurricanes: Big Winds and Big Damage" to other selections in this book.

For specific teaching strategies, see the *Theme Three Planning Guide,* pages 72–73.

Connection	Title
Life Skills: Planning and Designing	→ "Almost Ready," p. 20
Thematic: Humans and Nature	→ "Miracles," p. 163
Literary: Nonfiction	→ "The Fish Crisis," p. 295

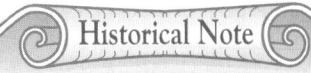

INFORMATIONAL TEXT Remind students to evaluate, as they read, the author's main purpose in this selection. Suggest that they take notes on the new facts they learn. *(The author's main purpose is to inform.)*

Historical Note

Hurricane Andrew was the most expensive natural disaster in U.S. history. Damage was estimated at $25 billion. Early warning systems kept the death toll down to 58 people in Florida and Louisiana.

C **Active Reading**

EVALUATE Ask students how the author's description of the beautiful day contrasts with what one would expect of a hurricane. *(The sky is blue, clear, and calm. Describing the day like this will make the approaching hurricane more frightening.)*

FYI

Hurricanes From 1953 through 1978, all hurricanes were given women's names. They'd say, "Hurricane Agnes flirted with the coast" or "Camille threw a temper tantrum." Starting in 1979, the names given to the big winds are alternately male and female.

B The computer models could not predict exactly where Andrew would come ashore. For 250 miles, from Fort Lauderdale to Key West, people were ordered to evacuate all low-lying areas along the coast.

Sunday, August 23, dawned clear and fair in south Florida. The sky was blue with fleecy clouds. Temperatures rose into the 90s. The air was damp and salty. Herons and frigate birds drifted over blue waters. **C**

Vocabulary
evacuate (i vak′ ū āt′) *v.* to leave or clear an area

MEETING INDIVIDUAL NEEDS — ENGLISH LANGUAGE LEARNERS

The Importance of Weather Remind English language learners of the many ways that weather conditions affect our food, shelter, and way of life.

Activity Ask students to interview adults in their lives about the weather and other natural conditions in the countries they are from. Have them ask what types of natural disasters are likely to occur there and how they affect people's lives. Then have them report to the class using illustrations if possible.

Additional Resources
📁 *English Language Learners Sourcebook*

D Author's Craft

SUSPENSE Ask students to suggest how the author builds suspense here. *(The author describes the way people fled from the storm, mentioning that "wind and sea were rising" and that "People woke in terror.")*

E Author's Craft

VIVID VERBS Point out the verbs the author uses and how they give exact shades of meaning. Have students find examples of vivid verbs. *(The roads aren't just crowded; they are* jammed. *The wind is* shrieking, growling, howling.*)*

F Literary Elements

INFORMATIONAL TEXT Explain that informational text is often organized in chronological order to make it easy to follow. Ask students to use the facts they've learned about Andrew to outline the chronology of the storm. *(For example: In mid-August, satellite photos showed a minor storm. On August 20, a storm was sighted 400 miles east of Puerto Rico. On August 22, the storm became a hurricane.)*

VIEWING THE PHOTO

Viewing Response *Students with some knowledge or experience of hurricanes will probably respond that the efforts might be effective if only the edges of a hurricane passed the area. A direct hit might level the building.*

Teaching Options

Hurricanes

It could have been any summer day, except that roads were jammed with cars as people fled inland and north.

By evening, wind and sea were rising. Shortly after midnight, in the early hours of August 24, Andrew came ashore south of Miami, with winds gusting to 195 miles an hour.

People woke in terror to dark houses, without electricity. The wind, sometimes shrieking, sometimes growling like a rushing freight train, snatched at shutters and shingles and pounded the sides of houses. Walls bulged in, then out. Howling winds toppled trees, ripped off roofs, blew in windows and doors, and knocked down houses. Where roofs or walls were gone, rain poured in. Inside their houses, people huddled together, held hands, and prayed.

The eye of the storm passed quickly through, bringing only minutes of calm and silence. Then the second half of the storm arrived, with winds howling from the opposite direction.

Moving west, Andrew cut a 25-mile-wide path through Everglades National Park, flattening trees, tearing out boardwalks, and leveling the visitors center.

The storm moved out over the Gulf of Mexico and made a second landfall, west of Baton Rouge, Louisiana, where it died out over the swamps and marshes.

The sun rose on a strange landscape. In Miami large boats, hurled ashore, now

Workers prepare for Hurricane Andrew by boarding up windows.
Viewing the photograph: How successful do you think efforts like these were against Andrew?

308 🐚 THEME 3

Reading *Minilesson*

Summarizing Remind students that in informational text, readers are often overwhelmed by facts and details as they read. Often, taking notes while reading and stopping occasionally to summarize the information already presented helps readers better understand a selection.

Activity Have students read through the article once, paying close attention to the

details they learn about Hurricane Andrew and its path of destruction. Have students reread pages 306–308, taking notes about Andrew's approach and what happened when it made landfall. Ask them to work in pairs to write one- to two-paragraph summaries of this section. They should include some of the most important facts and dates, being both thorough

and concise. To extend the activity, encourage pairs to come up with titles for their paragraphs, further summarizing the selection; for example, "Hurricane Andrew: Shy in the Beginning, Devastating in the End."
L2 **COLLAB. LEARN.**

Additional Resources

📕 *Reading Workbook,* pp. 47–48

leaned against lampposts and lay across highways. Wind had stripped the signs off posts and the fronds off palm trees. Fallen trees, telephone poles, and cables blocked streets. Traffic lights had disappeared.

But Miami had been at the edge of the hurricane. The center of the storm had hit to the south, bulldozing the towns of Homestead and Florida City. Twenty miles inland, they had been crushed not by the sea but by the wind. They looked as if they had been bombed, and 22 people had died.

The people in this area were not wealthy. Most were fishermen, small farmers, migrant workers, retired couples, people with low-paying jobs in Miami. They had just enough money to buy or rent a small home. Many lived in trailer parks. Some had no insurance. Now their houses were kindling wood. Their trailer homes looked like crushed soda cans. And with their homes had gone everything they owned, from clothes and furniture to toys and family photographs. Of the houses still standing, most had serious damage.

Shopping centers, warehouses, churches, and schools were ripped out of the ground or hammered into piles of twisted steel beams and splintered wood. Trees littered the ground. Lampposts were bent in two. Street signs were gone, and streets were buried under wreckage. Dogs and cats, horses and cows wandered about, lost.

Help was slow to arrive. The armed forces had planned ahead and were ready to move even before Andrew hit. But civilian leaders were slow to realize how great the damage was, slow to ask for help, slow to give orders.

Meanwhile, in South Florida some 250,000 people camped out in the ruins as best they could, living with rain and mosquitoes. In all, Andrew had destroyed 20,000 houses and badly damaged another 90,000.

Finally, the troops were given their orders and arrived. Tent cities sprang up. Generators hummed, bringing back electricity. Food and water were supplied. Troops patrolled against looters and directed traffic. Bulldozers and cranes began a giant cleanup. But it would be years before Homestead and Florida City looked like towns again, years before people could put their lives together again.

It would also be years before anyone could tell how plant and animal life had been affected. In the past, many hurricanes have roared across South Florida. Each time, plant and animal life recovered. But in recent years, people have made many changes in the region. Because of these changes, the effects of Andrew's pounding may pose a long-term threat to the <u>ecology</u> of Everglades National Park.

Like other national parks, Everglades is a piece of wilderness set aside to be preserved in its natural state. But in one way Everglades is <u>unique</u>. Other parks were chosen to preserve landforms. Everglades National Park was to preserve lifeforms. It is a park of birds, mammals, fish, reptiles, and amphibians, and of plants.

Andrew cut through the heart of the park, felling[3] everything in its path. Animals

---

3. To *fell* is to strike and knock down, as a lumberjack chops down a tree.

Vocabulary
ecology (ē kol′ ə jē′) *n.* the relationship of living things to their environment and to each other
unique (ū nēk′) *adj.* highly uncommon; rare; one-of-a-kind

FACING CHALLENGE 🐌 309

G **Literary Elements**

INFORMATIONAL TEXT Point out to students that the author begins to focus on the two towns most damaged by Andrew—Homestead and Florida City. Ask students why the author might focus on two of the many towns affected. *(These two towns were the hardest hit. Also, the author might want readers to concentrate on the experiences of one area to personalize the selection.)*

Vo•cab•u•lar•y Skills

Word Origins *Looters* comes from the Hindi word *lut*, which in India originally meant "goods seized in wartime." The meaning of *loot* has broadened to include any stolen goods, and a *looter* is now anyone who steals.

H **Active Reading**

VISUALIZE Ask students to choose the visual image from the article that has the most impact for them. *(Some may choose the image of crushed homes on page 307. Others may be most affected by the satellite image on page 311, which shows the great size of the storm.)*

I **Literary Elements**

REPETITION Ask students why the author uses the word *slow* four times in three sentences. *(It reinforces her point and emphasizes the frustration of waiting for help to arrive.)*

MULTIPLE LEARNING STYLES

MEETING INDIVIDUAL NEEDS

Bodily/Kinesthetic Students with strong kinesthetic abilities may respond more readily to movement to help themselves and other students visualize key events and emotions. For example, if you run away from an imaginary hurricane and your pulse begins to pound, you understand better how the people running from the real hurricane felt.

Activity As students read the article, have them stop whenever they form a strong impression of motion and act out that impression. They may choose to swoop down on a balsa-wood house like Hurricane Andrew, or they may mimic the behavior of a person fleeing or a tree being toppled. Kinesthetic learners will find this experience very useful. **L2**

Literary Elements

SIMILE Point out that the author uses similes to help paint word pictures. Ask students to find the two similes on this page. *(They are* slash pines snapped like matchsticks, *paragraph 1, and* their seeds spread like wildfire, *paragraph 3.)*

Active Reading

EVALUATE Ask students how the author's use of the word *fear* affects how they might feel about the scientists' statement of fact. *(By saying that the scientists "fear," the author makes the statement of fact seem more significant and makes the reader pay closer attention to what the scientists have to say.)*

Critical Thinking

EVALUATING Ask students to stop and evaluate whether the author has done a good job of informing readers. Have them support their opinions with examples from the text. If you wish, share the following model to illustrate the thinking process involved in evaluating.

MODEL: So far, I have learned a lot about Hurricane Andrew from this selection. The author has explained what a hurricane is and described clearly how Hurricane Andrew hit southern Florida. She has also described the aftermath of the storm. I think the author has written a very informative selection.

Hurricanes

in the park survived well. But in Andrew's winds, slash pines snapped like matchsticks. Gumbo-limbo, wild tamarind, and ancient mahogany trees were uprooted. The storm left behind a tangled mass of dead and dying plants, lying in torn-up ground.

The last hurricane that seriously damaged Everglades swept through in 1960. That time the park recovered well. Some fallen trees resprouted. Seeds from similar plants blew in on the winds or were carried in by animals.

Since then many changes have taken place in areas around the park. To the north, land has been drained and cleared for towns, ranches, and farms. The natural flow of water through the park has changed, and

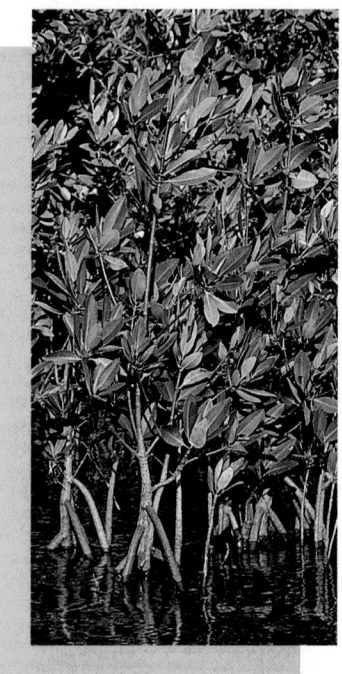

Mangrove trees have a system of exposed roots that help support the plant.

chemicals seep into the water. Housing developments have gone up right next to the park. And foreign plants have been brought in and planted just outside the park. Among these are Australian pines, Brazilian pepper shrubs, and melaleuca trees. All were brought in as ornamental plants. But they are a problem. Their seeds spread like wildfire, grow fast, and thrive in disturbed soil. Once they take hold, they are nearly impossible to get rid of.

Before Andrew, the park was under stress because of changes to the north. Now park scientists fear that foreign plants will invade the hurricane-damaged areas, take hold, and drive out native plants. This would change the park's plant life. It would also change the animal life, because animals depend on native plants for food and for places to nest and raise their young.

No one knows how big a change will take place or how it will affect the songbirds and wading birds, the raccoons, bobcats, deer, alligators, snakes, and tree frogs. Park scientists can only wait and see.

Natural scientists are also concerned about damage to mangrove swamps along southern Biscayne Bay, where Andrew came ashore.

The storm surge spent itself on a string of small barrier islands.[4] But the hurricane's winds and waves battered the shore, which was lined with swamps of mangrove trees. The raging winds shredded the mangroves. When mangroves are lost, many food chains and food webs are affected.

Mangroves are umbrella-shaped trees that can grow in salty water. There are

---

4. *Barrier islands* are long, narrow islands that lie in the shallow waters along a shore. They are made of sand and gravel piled up into ridges and dunes by waves and winds.

310   THEME 3

Teaching Options

Grammar and Language *Minilesson*

Compound Predicates Write the following sentence on the board: *Plant seeds* blew in *or* were carried in. Tell students that the underlined words are part of the compound predicate. A compound predicate has two or more simple predicates, or verbs that have the same subject. The simple predicates are usually connected by *and, but,* or *or*.

Activity Write the following sentences on the board and have students determine the simple predicates in each:
1. The storm weakened, organized, and then charged ahead.
2. The hurricane beat and battered southern Florida.
3. The scientists observe and study the effects on Everglades National Park.
4. The armed forces had planned ahead

and were ready to move. **L2**

Additional Resources

- *Grammar and Language Transparency 27*
- *Grammar and Language Workbook,* pp. 53–54
- *Grammar and Composition Handbook,* Lesson 1.5
- *Writer's Choice,* Lesson 8.5

Satellite images help scientists track hurricanes. In this image of a hurricane over the state of Florida, the land areas are outlined by computer.

three kinds—the red, the black, and the white. The red is the kind most people are familiar with, because much of its root system is above ground. The roots arch out, like the legs of a crab, around the trunk. They protect the land against ocean storms.

 Mangroves are the start of many food chains. These trees shed leaves heavily. The leaves fall in the water, where they become food for bacteria and fungi. The bacteria and fungi are grazed, or fed on, by one-celled animals. All three are eaten by tiny crabs, shrimp, worms, insect young, and small fishes. These animals are in turn eaten by bigger ones—blue crabs, sardines, anchovies, eels, sunfish. They are also eaten by young tarpon, snook, gray snapper, spotted sea

trout, and others, all of which grow up into big fishes that are at or near the head of food chains. These chains also include other fish eaters, among them alligators, herons, egrets, eagles, wood storks, white ibises, and humans.

Because of the mangroves, the shores are rich in food for many animals. They are also a nursery for the young of many fishes and other sea creatures. They are important to the lives of animals and also to the lives of humans—to those who take their living from the sea and to those who eat food from the sea.

It will be years before anyone can tell how badly Andrew damaged the mangrove swamps and the food chains that begin in them. Florida has lost many miles of mangrove swamps in the past 30 years. They have been filled, cleared, and built on. The remaining ones are precious.

Hurricanes are part of nature. They are natural events. And they have been making landfalls for a very long time. In the past, nature always healed itself after a big blow—plant and animal life came back quickly to damaged areas. Today human activities may have changed the ways in which nature can heal itself. Scientists are concerned about these changes.

They are also concerned about another kind of change: the huge number of people who have moved to coastal areas. The years ahead, scientists say, may see more and more of earth's mightiest storms roaring in from the sea and putting these people at risk.

Active Reading

VISUALIZE Guide students in visualizing the process of the food chain described here. Encourage them to picture all the details Lauber provides.

Active Reading

QUESTION Ask students why they think the author included such specific information about mangroves. *(They are a very important part of the food chain and are therefore vital to the delicate balance of nature.)*

Thematic Focus

Facing Challenge Have students put themselves in the place of the people described on page 309. How would they meet the challenge of losing their possessions to a hurricane? How would they cope with camping out in rainy, mosquito-infested ruins without electricity? How do they think most young people would handle such a situation?

A&E HOME VIDEO. ® *The following videotape program is available from Glencoe. Be sure to preview the video for appropriateness for your class.*

• **Disasters in America, Hurricanes: Deadly Wind, Deadly Rain**

✔ ASSESSMENT OPTIONS

📁 *Quick Checks,* p. 28

MEETING INDIVIDUAL NEEDS — INCLUSION STRATEGIES

Less-Proficient Readers A large amount of detailed information about the food chain is presented on this page. Work with less-proficient readers to organize the steps visually.

Activity Have students work in pairs to illustrate the steps in the food chain. Have students draw six steps on a piece of paper starting at the lower left side and write *Mangroves* on the line to the right of the lowest step. As they read the information on this page, they can fill in the names of the animals that exist on each successively higher level of the food chain. **L2**

Additional Resources
📁 *Inclusion Strategies*

Responding to the Selection

Personal Response

- Students may be worried about the human impact on the environment—especially the Everglades.
- Students will probably mention scenes of destruction (wind like a freight train, trailers crushed like soda cans, tent cities).

Analyzing Literature

1. They wanted to identify which storms would become severe and to predict where and when the hurricane would hit, so that they could warn people.
2. It hit in the very early hours of August 24, just south of Miami.
3. It nearly destroyed Homestead and Florida City. Then it headed west through Everglades National Park. It moved into the Gulf of Mexico, hit land again west of Baton Rouge, and died out over the swamps and marshes.
4. It ripped out trees, leaving space for nonnative plants to spread. It destroyed animals' habitats and damaged their food chains.
5. Winds can change speed and direction at any moment.
6. They heard the shrieking winds and woke to find themselves without electricity.
7. It gives some idea of how extensive the damage was. Many houses were demolished.
8. Many trees, especially mangroves, were killed. Chemicals seeped into the water and foreign plants spread. Food webs affecting many animals, from sardines to alligators to egrets, were damaged, perhaps permanently.
9. Students may say they'd like to know how the animals are doing and whether the pressures of human expansion can be resisted. They may wonder what's happened to the people who lost their homes.

Responding to Literature

PERSONAL RESPONSE

- ◆ What went through your mind as you finished reading "Hurricanes"?
- ◆ What images from this selection linger in your mind?

Analyzing Literature

RECALL

1. Why were scientists working with computer models of storms? What were they hoping to predict?
2. Where and when did Andrew come ashore?
3. Describe the path of destruction caused by Hurricane Andrew.
4. How was plant and animal life affected by the hurricane?

INTERPRET

5. Why is the path of a storm so difficult to predict? Explain.
6. Why did people awake in terror?
7. The writer states that the storm had "bulldozed" the towns of Homestead and Florida City. Why do you think the writer used this image?
8. Summarize the changes that have taken place around Everglades National Park since the hurricane.

EVALUATE AND CONNECT

9. What questions would you like to ask the writer of this selection?
10. **Theme Connection** What challenges would you face if a hurricane or some other severe storm hit your community?

LITERARY ELEMENTS

Informational Text

All types of writing have a main purpose, or an objective, to achieve. You know that the purpose of fiction is to tell a story. Nonfiction tells about real people, events, and places. **Informational text** is one kind of nonfiction. This type of nonfiction conveys facts and information without introducing personal opinion. The purpose of informational text is to inform readers about a topic. Few pieces of writing are confined to a single purpose. A single article may inform, persuade, and entertain—all at the same time. However, one purpose will usually be the main purpose.

1. In your opinion, what was the writer's main purpose in writing "Hurricanes"? Support your opinion with examples from the selection.

2. What secondary purpose or purposes do you observe in "Hurricanes"? Give examples.

● See **Literary Terms Handbook**, p. R5.

---

10. Students may foresee transportation challenges, loss of electric power with widespread consequences, economic depression if enough businesses are destroyed to leave a lot of people unemployed, and psychological problems among those who live through the crisis.

LITERARY ELEMENTS

1. Her main purpose was to give information, as evidenced by her description of Andrew's formation, the damage it did, and its effect on the area's ecology.
2. A secondary purpose was to alert people to the threat to the Everglades' ecology and to persuade them to do something about it.

Additional Resources

📑 *Literary Elements Transparency 28*

Literature and Writing

Writing About Literature

Summarizing   A **summary** is a brief account that contains the main ideas or main points. Write a paragraph or two summarizing what you have learned about the power of hurricanes from reading this selection.

Personal Writing

A Postcard Home   Imagine that you were visiting relatives in southern Florida when Hurricane Andrew struck. Write a postcard home, explaining what you witnessed and how you felt. Try to use the descriptive words you listed for the **Focus Activity** on page 305.

Extending Your Response

Literature Groups

A Natural Disaster   How would local officials respond to a natural disaster if one occurred in your area? In small groups, talk about the steps that should be taken to safeguard your community. Make a chart outlining the steps. If possible, invite a local representative from the Red Cross or the fire department to speak about the kinds of precautions that are already in place in preparation for a major emergency.

Interdisciplinary Activity

Art/Science: Tracking a Hurricane   Work with classmates to create a giant mural tracking the life of a hurricane. Use the information in "Hurricanes," as well as other facts you have researched, to plan and create the mural. Show the development of a hurricane from its beginnings at sea to its destructive path across land. Display your mural on a classroom wall or a hall bulletin board.

Learning for Life

News Broadcast   Imagine that you were part of the first group of reporters on the scene to witness Hurricane Andrew's destruction. Use the information in the selection as well as your imagination to create a news broadcast detailing the hurricane story. In small groups, work on different parts of the story, such as providing background information, following the progress of the hurricane, or interviewing disaster victims or a scientist in the Everglades. Share your broadcast with your classmates in a class presentation.

Reading Further

If you would like to read more books by Patricia Lauber, try these:

Fur, Feathers, and Flippers: How Animals Live Where They Do

Volcano: The Eruption and Healing of Mount St. Helens

📖 **Save your work for your portfolio.**

Literature and Writing

Writing About Literature

Students' summaries should
- include some statistics.
- give at least three specific examples of hurricanes' power.

Personal Writing

Students' postcards should
- describe what they saw.
- include details about how it made them feel.

Extending Your Response

Literature Groups Help students get an outside expert to speak to the class about disaster plans. Challenge students to think of possible problems that aren't covered by existing disaster relief plans. **COLLAB. LEARN.**

Interdisciplinary Activity Remind students that this is a chance to combine scientific rigor with artistic creativity. Encourage them to use the library or Internet to find more information on the weather.

Learning for Life Encourage students to rehearse their broadcasts. If possible, videotape each group's program and make the tapes available for viewing.

✓ ASSESSMENT OPTIONS

📁 *Quick Checks,* p. 28

📁 *Selection and Theme Assessment,* pp. 51–52

📁 *Performance Assessment,* p. 27

💾 *Testmaker*

GRAMMAR AND LANGUAGE
SPELLING: PLURALS

Sample paragraph:

Everglades National Park is home to reptiles and amphibians as well as to birds, fish, and mammals. Crabs, shrimp, worms, young insects, and small fishes feed on bacteria, fungi, and one-celled animals. At the top of the food chain, alligators, herons, egrets, eagles, wood storks, and white ibises eat many types of fish. So, of course, do humans.

READING AND THINKING
DISTINGUISHING FACT AND OPINION

Examples of facts:
- August 23 dawned clear and fair in south Florida.
- Housing developments have gone up right next to Everglades National Park.

Examples of opinions:
- A hurricane is the worst kind of natural disaster.
- Hurricanes love trailer parks.

VOCABULARY
PREFIXES THAT EXPRESS NUMBER

1. any shape (e.g. square, rectangle) with four sides
2. any animal with two feet
3. any one-syllable word
4. any animal with four feet
5. trisect it

Additional Resources

📗 *Grammar and Language Workbook,* pp. 297–300

📗 *Grammar and Composition Handbook,* Lesson 15.1

📗 *Writer's Choice,* Lesson 23.7

📁 *Reading Workbook,* pp. 47–48

📁 *Vocabulary Practice,* p. 19

GRAMMAR AND LANGUAGE • SPELLING PLURALS

The usual way to form plurals in English is to add *-s* or *-es.* However, there are some other general rules for forming plurals.

- If the noun ends in *s, sh, ch, x,* or *z,* then add *-es.* (bus/buses, tax/taxes, buzz/buzzes)
- If the noun ends in a consonant + *y,* then change *y* to *i* and add *-es.* (candy/candies)
- If the noun ends in *lf,* then change the *f* to *v* and add *-es.* (calf/calves)
- If the noun ends in *fe,* then change the *f* to *v* and add *-s.* (wife/wives)

PRACTICE Write a paragraph describing the different kinds of animals found at Everglades National Park. Underline each plural noun used in your paragraph. Check that each plural form is spelled correctly.

● For more about forming plurals, see **Language Handbook,** pp. R46–R47.

READING AND THINKING • DISTINGUISHING FACT AND OPINION

A fact is something that can be proved to be true. An opinion, on the other hand, is someone's point of view about a topic.

> **Fact:** Hurricane Andrew came ashore south of Miami, Florida, in the early hours of August 24, 1992.

> **Opinion:** Hurricanes are scary.

When you include your opinion in a piece of writing, support it with facts and examples.

PRACTICE Reread "Hurricanes," and find two examples of facts. Then write two examples of opinions about the topic of hurricanes. Share the facts and the opinions with your classmates. Write each example on the board, and ask classmates to tell whether each statement is a fact or an opinion.

● For more about distinguishing fact and opinion, see **Reading Handbook,** p. R90.

VOCABULARY • PREFIXES THAT EXPRESS NUMBER

Unique comes from a Latin word that means "one." Something unique is one-of-a-kind. *Unity, unite,* and *unit* come from that same Latin word. Many other words use *uni-* as a prefix meaning "one." For example, the word *uniform* means "one form."

Here are some prefixes that express number:

one	*uni-, mono-*
two	*bi-, di-*
three	*tri-*
four	*quadri-, tetra-*

PRACTICE Use the list of prefixes that express number to answer the questions. A few hints are provided.

1. What common shape is a quadrilateral? (Hint: The word *lateral* means "side.")
2. Name an animal that is a biped. (Hint: *Ped* means "foot.")
3. Write down a word that is a monosyllable.
4. Name an animal that is a tetrapod. (Hint: *Pod* also means "foot.")
5. To divide something into two parts, you bisect it. What do you do if you divide it into three parts?

Subject-Verb Agreement

The **subject** of a sentence tells who or what is doing something. The **verb** tells what the subject is doing. These two parts of a sentence must match or "agree."

Singular: A hurricane is a big storm.   **Plural:** Hurricanes are dangerous.

Problem 1 A subject is separated from the verb by an intervening phrase.

The hurricane, with its mighty winds, were terrifying.

Solution   Ignore a prepositional phrase between a subject and a verb.

The hurricane, with its mighty winds, was terrifying.

Problem 2 A sentence begins with *here* or *there.*

Here is a writer's impressions of a hurricane's power.

Solution   The subject is never *here* or *there.* In sentences beginning with *here* or *there,* the subject always comes after the verb.

Here are a writer's impressions of a hurricane's power.

Problem 3 A compound subject is joined by *or* or *nor.*

Neither mangrove swamps nor the food chain survive such a storm undamaged.

Solution   If a compound subject is joined by *or* or *nor,* the verb agrees with the subject closest to it.

Neither mangrove swamps nor the food chain survives such a storm undamaged.

● For more about subject-verb agreement, see **Language Handbook,** pp. R14–R15.

EXERCISES

For each sentence, write the correct form of the verb in parentheses.

1. Mountain climbers on Mount Everest (faces, face) life-and-death challenges.
2. There (is, are) frequent storms late in the climbing season.
3. Years of planning (goes, go) into such a climb.
4. Neither careful planning nor the climbers' efforts (affects, affect) the force of nature.
5. There (is, are) no choice but to give up the climb.

Objective

• To recognize subject-verb agreement problems in sentences and use strategies for correcting them

Teaching Strategies

After students read the problems-and-solutions segment of the lesson, point out that another way to identify subject-verb agreement problems is to read a sentence aloud. Present the following examples and ask students if the sentence "sounds right" to them. Ask them to correct it orally.

• *There are the bag of groceries.*
• *The student, and all her classmates, were excited about the party.*
• *Neither the cat nor the hamsters likes the food.*

Exercises

1. face
2. are
3. go
4. affect
5. is

Additional Resources

📕 *Grammar and Language Workbook,* pp. 183–192

📕 *Grammar and Composition Handbook,* Lesson 10.1–10.5

📕 *Writer's Choice,* Lesson 16.1–16.5

Teaching Options

Writing *Minilesson*

Writing a Dramatic Account Ask students to share experiences they have had in which natural dangers, such as animals or weather, played a part. Explain that an experience doesn't need to be life-threatening to be dangerous or frightening.

Activity Have each student write a short account of the experience. Encourage them to include vivid details about the setting and how they felt before, during, and after the event. Ask students to pay special attention to subject-verb agreement in their work. Have them share what they have written with classmates. You may wish to assemble the accounts into an anthology of class adventures. **L2**

Additional Resources

📕 *Writer's Choice,* Lesson 3.3

Objectives

- To create a personal response to literature
- To plan, draft, revise, edit, and present a persuasive editorial
- To reflect on and assess one's editorial piece

Teaching Strategies

PREWRITING

Gather Ideas You may wish to introduce the slogan: *Think Globally—Act Locally.* This might inspire students to recognize the wide range of topics about which they can write.

Focus Your Views In addition to the sentence completion activity in their books, have students think aloud about a few issues that concern people in their community.

Teaching Options

Writing WORKSHOP

Persuasive Writing: Editorial

You probably have strong opinions about many of the challenges that you face. When you write about your opinions, you clarify them for yourself. You may also convince others to share your opinions or spur them to take action.

Assignment: Follow the process explained in these pages to develop a persuasive editorial about one strong opinion that you hold.

● As you write your editorial, see **Writing Handbook,** pp. R48–R53.

The Writing Process

PREWRITING

PREWRITING TIP
Try working in a group, brainstorming many different ways to complete each sentence.

● **Gather Ideas**

Look through your reading journal for your views on issues raised in this unit. For example, you might favor better planning for natural disasters such as hurricanes or tornadoes. You might wish for more concern for the environment and its inhabitants, or more awareness of the struggles that young people or homeless people experience. To find other ideas, try completing the following sentences:

- I really think it's unfair that . . .
- One of the most helpful things that people today can do is . . .
- I don't think many people care enough about . . .

● **Focus Your Views**

Filling in a pro/con chart can help you see both sides of an issue. Then ask yourself what underlying issue(s) the ideas in your chart reflect or raise. You might choose to write about your original issue or about an underlying issue that you discover.

Issue: "My Kid Can Beat Up Your Honor Student" bumper stickers

Pro: • funny
• may reduce pressure kids are under

MEETING INDIVIDUAL NEEDS
ENGLISH LANGUAGE LEARNERS

Now Hear This You may wish to adapt the writing workshop for English language learners.

Activity Offer students a soapbox (a stool) on which to stand and express their opinions. You can do this as a class or in small groups. Discuss the ways in which people voice concerns throughout the world: demonstrations, newspaper columns, commercials, bill-boards, even bumper stickers. Have each English language learner create an object that expresses his or her opinion on an issue. This could include a collage, a picture or painting, a placard, a personally decorated T-shirt, or a poster. **COLLAB. LEARN.**

Additional Resources
📁 *English Language Learners Sourcebook*

Writing **WORKSHOP**

Con: • condones violence
 • puts down kids with good grades
 • encourages indifference to education

Underlying issue: Getting students to value education

● Ask Yourself About Audience and Purpose

You might choose to write your persuasive editorial as a letter to a friend, as a newspaper or magazine editorial, or even as an op-ed piece for local TV. Since your purpose is to persuade, think about your audience. Ask yourself:

● What are their ages, experiences, and concerns?

● How can I best appeal to them?

● What facts should I give them?

● What objections might my audience raise, and how can I best respond?

● Plan Your Strategy

Sum up your opinion in a sentence. This single-sentence position statement will guide your draft. Opinions need support, so plan several supporting points, backed up with evidence (facts, examples, statistics, quotations).

Position Statement: Students value education when their efforts are recognized.

Point 1: Compliments from teachers are powerful.

Evidence ⎯⎯▶ Example: our school's Awards Day
  teachers complimented every single student
  students' attitudes more upbeat

Point 2: Parents should support personal best, not competition.

Evidence ⎯⎯▶ Statistics (survey of my homeroom):
  over 80% already feel pressured about GPAs
  90% find work load heavier in higher grades

Point 3: Students need support from one another.

Evidence ⎯⎯▶ Quotes from people in my school:
  "If people hate you for getting higher grades, is it worth it?"
  "In hockey, we encourage each other. It makes us all push harder."
  "When a friend says school is a loss, I feel kind of dumb for trying."

FACING CHALLENGE 🐦 317

Ask Yourself About Audience and Purpose Have students go through the selections and try to identify who the audience might have been in the minds of the writers. Prompt a discussion about the kinds of things that would appeal to various audiences. Encourage students to try to reach as broad an audience as possible with their editorials, using the techniques described in the Genre Focus on pages 290-291.

Plan Your Strategy In addition to writing single-sentence position statements, have students jot down all the points they wish to cover in their persuasive editorials. In cases where students have "big feelings" about the topic chosen, encourage them to plan where and how they will incorporate the emotions effectively in their work.

Additional Resources

📂 *Writing and Proofreading Practice,* pp. 1–7, 22–28

🖋 *Writing and Proofreading Transparencies 1–6, 11–14*

📕 *Writer's Choice,* Lessons 6.1–6.5

MEETING INDIVIDUAL NEEDS — MULTIPLE LEARNING STYLES

Bodily/Kinesthetic Students who are inclined toward total physical response may appreciate an opportunity to act out their thoughts and opinions.

Activity Have students work in small groups with the goal of putting on a short play or skit that dramatizes a topic of concern for them, such as recycling or a local environmental issue.

Encourage them to write a script, create costumes, and make a set. Let other students be audience members and write editorials on what they have seen.
L2 COLLAB. LEARN.

FACING CHALLENGE 🐦 317

Start Your Draft Bring in a few opening sentences from newspaper or magazine editorials that you think are effective. Encourage students to start their drafts with a sentence that will grab the reader's interest.

Follow Through Remind students that while it is important to follow the organizational plans they have created, it is also important to let thoughts and images come freely to the page. This enables students to feel confident in their ability to write and think, even if the ability to organize is not one of their strengths.

Plan Improvements Encourage students to read their editorials aloud to someone at home. Have them ask for feedback, then evaluate whether they agree with what has been said. You may wish to discuss ways of handling negative feedback on a controversial opinion during the revision process.

Teaching Options

Writing **WORKSHOP**

DRAFTING

DRAFTING TIP
Don't ignore valid objections that your audience might raise. Acknowledge them. Then offer reasonable responses.

● **Start Your Draft**

Try opening with a question or description that alerts your audience to your issue. For clarity, put a version of your position statement in this first paragraph.

● **Follow Through**

With your prewriting notes for reference, write at least a paragraph about each supporting point. Include your evidence.

MODEL · DRAFTING

How can we get students who have forgotten about their education to come back to it? A good start would be something as simple as recognition. Every single kid's efforts must be recognized.

Recently, my school held an Awards Day for every student. In the hallways on that day, I actually heard compliments instead of put-downs.
—Andrew Klaber, Buffalo Grove, IL, Guest editorial, *Chicago Tribune*

REVISING

REVISING TIP
To avoid generalizing, consider adding qualifiers—words such as *often, seldom, sometimes, few, many,* or *most.*

● **Plan Improvements**

Take a break. After a few hours, reread your draft. Mark places where you could make improvements, such as clarifying a point or providing stronger evidence.

Use the **Questions for Revising** as a guide for revising your draft. If you wish, read your editorial aloud to a friend to test its persuasive power.

QUESTIONS FOR REVISING
☑ How do the opening sentences alert my audience to my issue?
☑ What facts might I add near the opening to give my audience more background?
☑ Where could I add more evidence to convince my audience?
☑ How logical is my reasoning, and how do I handle possible objections?
☑ What changes in my conclusion might strengthen its appeal?

Writing *Minilesson*

Power Words Students may find that they would like to use a powerful vocabulary for expressing strong thoughts and opinions. Point out that the reader will be jarred if a word seems too out of character for a piece, but adding colorful words and vivid phrases can go a long way in persuading an audience.

Activity Make sure students have access to a thesaurus and encourage them to use it during the writing process. Demonstrate the power of well-chosen words by distributing a persuasive piece of writing you admire, with a few key words left blank. Have students fill in the blanks with persuasive words. **L2**

Additional Resources

📖 ***Writer's Choice,*** Lesson 16.1

Writing WORKSHOP

EDITING/PROOFREADING

When you finish revising, go over your draft once more to correct errors in grammar, usage, and mechanics. Use the **Proofreading Checklist.**

Grammar Hint

One way to fix a run-on sentence is to use a semicolon between the two main clauses.

Many "funny" put-downs I hear aren't really funny; they're sad.

PROOFREADING CHECKLIST

- ☑ There are no sentence fragments or run-on sentences.
- ☑ Verb forms are correct, and verb tenses are consistent.
- ☑ Verbs agree with their subjects.
- ☑ Comparative forms of modifiers are correct.
- ☑ Commas, semicolons, and end marks are used correctly.
- ☑ All words are spelled correctly.

MODEL · EDITING/PROOFREADING

A compliment from a teacher can last throughout the week, it can even last throughout a lifetime.

PUBLISHING/PRESENTING

Consider submitting your editorial, letter to the editor, or op-ed piece to your school or local newspaper. As an alternative, you may wish to audiotape or videotape your persuasive editorial. Working with friends, prepare a taped "commentary session" that presents several opinion pieces, and play it for your class.

TECHNOLOGY TIP
With desktop publishing software, you can design, lay out, and print your opinion piece in a newspaper format.

Reflecting

- What grade would you give yourself on this piece of writing? Why does your work merit that grade?
- What other topic might you address in a persuasive piece? How might your writing process differ from the process you followed this time?

📖 **Save your work for your portfolio.**

EDITING/PROOFREADING

Have students use the Proofreading Checklist to review their work. Encourage them to check for each item on the list in a separate reading. Give them a few editorial symbols they can use for corrections.

Additional Resources

Grammar and Composition Handbook, Lesson 16.4

PUBLISHING/PRESENTING

Students may want to post their editorials on the Internet by locating Web sites dedicated to the topic they have chosen.

Reflecting

Portfolio Have students ask themselves these questions as they review their persuasive editorials:

- Would I be persuaded if someone else had written this editorial?
- What parts of the writing process are most difficult for me? What parts do I look forward to?
- Have I done my best to make my opinion clear?

☑ ASSESSMENT OPTIONS

📁 *Writing Assessment and Portfolio Management*
- Writing Assessment, pp. 1–16, 26–28
- Portfolio Management, pp. 17–19

Theme Wrap-Up

Objectives

- To offer a personal response to the selections and activities in this theme
- To write a comparison of two pieces of nonfiction
- To complete a self-evaluation, set a goal, and devise a plan for achieving the goal

---

Responding to the Theme

1. Students should cite examples from the literature in their responses.
2. Have students express their current attitudes toward facing challenge. Accept all thoughtful observations.
3. Allow time for students to share their reports, persuasive memos, and news programs with classmates.

Analyzing Literature

Students' writing should

- include an introductory paragraph that identifies the two nonfiction selections.
- demonstrate an understanding of the elements of nonfiction writing.
- contain examples and quotes from each selection.

Evaluate and Set Goals

Evaluate

Have students list some of the activities they have completed for each task. Suggest that they add other tasks as well, such as working in pairs or small groups.

Have students use the class rubric they developed in the first theme's evaluation to assess their work.

Set Goals

Have students use pitchfork graphics to chart the steps they plan to take in achieving the goals they have set.

Theme Wrap-Up

Responding to the Theme

1. Which piece of fiction, nonfiction, or poetry in this theme most helped you think about how facing challenges can be a powerful experience? Explain your answer.

2. As a result of your reading in this unit, what new thoughts do you have about the following?
   - the kinds of challenges people face in their everyday lives
   - people's feelings and thoughts about facing those challenges
   - the importance of seeing challenge as a necessary part of life

3. Present your theme project to the class.

Analyzing Literature

COMPARE NONFICTION

Compare two pieces of nonfiction writing from this theme. Use examples and quotes from the selections to support your opinions.

Evaluate and Set Goals

1. Which of the following was most rewarding to you? Which was most difficult?
   - reading and thinking about the fiction, nonfiction, and poetry
   - doing independent writing
   - analyzing the selections in discussions
   - making presentations
   - doing research

2. Using the following scale, how would you assess your work in this theme? Give at least two reasons for your assessment.

   4 = outstanding   2 = fair
   3 = good   1 = weak

3. Based on what you found difficult in this theme, choose a goal to work toward in the next theme.
   - Write down your goal and three steps you will take to reach it.
   - Meet with your teacher to review your goal and your plan for achieving it.

Build Your Portfolio

SELECT

Select two pieces of work you did during this theme to include in your portfolio. Use the following questions to help you decide.

- Which work do you think is your best work?
- From which work did you learn the most?
- Which work "stretched" you the most?
- Which work did you enjoy the most?

REFLECT

Write some notes to accompany the work you selected. Use the following questions to guide you.

- What do you like best about the piece?
- What did you learn from creating it?
- What might you do differently if you were beginning this piece again?

ASSESSMENT OPTIONS

📁 ***Writing Assessment and Portfolio Management***
- Writing Assessment, pp. 1–16
- Portfolio Management, pp. 17–19

GLENCOE
TECHNOLOGY

 MINDJOGGER VIDEOQUIZZES
VIDEODISC

Use *MindJogger* to review the Theme 3 content.

Theme 3
Side A

 Also available in VHS.

Reading on Your Own

Have you liked reading the stories and poems in this theme?
If you have, here are some other books you might enjoy.

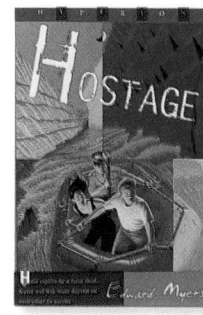

Where the Red Fern Grows
by Wilson Rawls
This story of a young boy living in the Oklahoma Ozarks and the pair of hunting dogs he trains has become a favorite with young readers.

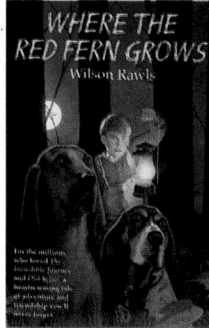

Hostage
by Edward P. Myers Alyssa and Rob must use their wits and survival techniques after a fossil thief takes them hostage on a trek through the Utah desert.

Reach Higher
by Scottie Pippen Pippen tells about his life and the challenges he faced to become an NBA champion with the Chicago Bulls. The title describes his advice to his young readers.

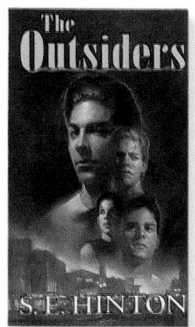

The Outsiders
by S. E. Hinton Fourteen-year-old Ponyboy is proud to be a "greaser," until a friend kills a member of a rival gang and starts a chain of events that causes him to question his outsider status.

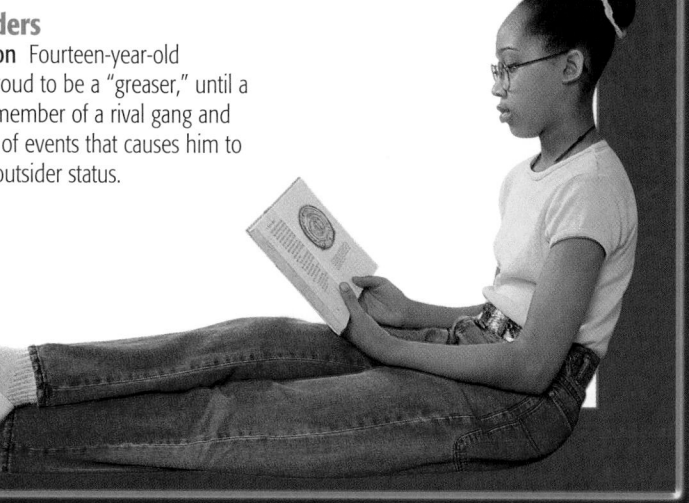

Reading on Your Own

Glencoe Literature Library

Where the Red Fern Grows by Wilson Rawls is one of the titles available in the *Glencoe Literature Library*. For a complete listing, see pages T46–T47 in this book.

The *Glencoe Literature Library: Study Guide* provides instructional support and student activities for works in the *Glencoe Literature Library*.

At the MOVIES

Students who read *Where the Red Fern Grows* might enjoy seeing the movie version (1974, 97 minutes, G). Those who haven't read the book might be encouraged to do so by the movie.

Be sure to preview the video for appropriateness for your class.

MEETING INDIVIDUAL NEEDS — INCLUSION STRATEGIES

You may wish to recommend *Reach Higher* by Scottie Pippen to your less-proficient readers. The many color photographs, large type size, attractive layout, and inviting topic make this book appealing to reluctant readers. **L1**

The following books are rated for average students (**L2**) or for students who need more challenging reading material (**L3**):

Where the Red Fern Grows by Wilson Rawls (**L2**)
Hostage by Edward P. Myers (**L2**)
The Outsiders by S. E. Hinton (**L3**)

Additional Resources
📁 *Inclusion Strategies*

Answers and Analyses

1. **C** The sentence as written is incomplete since the subordinate clause does not contain a conjugated verb. Choices A and D are incomplete sentences, and the word *or* creates an illogical construction in choice B. Therefore the best choice is C.

2. **F** The sentence as written is a run-on sentence and should be rewritten. Choice G also is a run-on sentence and can be eliminated. Choice H and J illogically insert *or* and *because,* and can also be eliminated. The remaining choice, and the best choice, is F.

 TEST-TAKING TIP

Students should look for two types of errors, the incomplete sentence and the run-on sentence. If there is no error, it may be that the sentence should be rewritten for a smoother flow of language. Students should read each answer choice carefully before deciding which is best.

 TEST-TAKING TIP

Remind students that making mistakes during test-taking practice is actually helpful. Mistakes are good indications for what can be improved, and every mistake they make in class is one they can avoid on the actual test!

 THE PRINCETON REVIEW

Standardized Test Practice

Read the passage. Some sections are underlined. The underlined sections may be one of the following:

- Incomplete sentences
- Run-on sentences
- Correctly written sentences that should be combined
- Correctly written sentences that do not need to be rewritten

Choose the best way to write each underlined section. Mark the letter for your answer on your paper. If the underlined section needs no change, mark the choice "Correct as is."

It is reported that eighteen inches of rain falling between Sunday morning and (1) Monday morning in a small river town. The rain flooded nearby creeks, swamped neighborhoods, and turned streets into swirling rivers. "It just rained for hours," said Captain John Shandy of the National Weather Service. All of the roads in the (2) area, were closed, electricity, gas, and phone service were temporarily lost.

---

1 A Eighteen inches of rain between Sunday morning and Monday morning in a small river town.

B It is reported that eighteen inches of rain fell between Sunday morning and Monday morning or in a small river town.

C It is reported that eighteen inches of rain fell between Sunday morning and Monday morning in a small river town.

D Sunday morning and Monday morning in a small river town, it is reported that eighteen inches of rain fell between.

2 F All of the roads in the area were closed, and electricity, gas, and phone service were temporarily lost.

G All of the roads closed, electricity, gas, and phone service in the area were temporarily lost.

H All of the roads in the area were closed, or electricity, gas, and phone service were temporarily lost.

J All the roads in the area were closed, because electricity, gas, and phone service were temporarily lost.

Standardized Test Practice

Read the passage and choose the word or group of words that belongs in each space. Mark the letter for your answer on your paper.

> In the book *Lost on Chimborazo*, Edel, his brother Carem, and their pet Chihuahua __(1)__ for a lost city on the highest volcano in South America. At the beginning of __(2)__ journey up the volcano, the adventurers are exposed to clear air, mild temperatures, and light winds. However, as they begin to ascend the mountain in search of the city, they __(3)__ colder temperatures and biting winds that force them to sleep in caves far from the __(4)__ path on the map. One night, as they sleep, the ground in the cave gives way. They fall into the heart of the __(5)__ volcano, and lose their bearings. After climbing out of the pit and gathering their scattered gear, the three find their way back to the trail. While they continue looking for the lost city, they __(6)__ many other dangers and even find traces of past explorers. Eventually they get to their final destination, the lost city of Chimborazo.

1 A have looked
   B look
   C is looking
   D looking

2 F their
   G our
   H his
   J its

3 A will have experienced
   B experienced
   C had experienced
   D experience

4 F mark
   G marking
   H marked
   J markings

5 A large
   B larger
   C largest
   D largely

6 F encounters
   G has encountered
   H encounter
   J is encountering

STOP

Answers and Analyses

1. **B** In the second sentence the present tense *are exposed* is used, so the first sentence should also be in the present tense. Therefore the correct answer is choice B, *look*.
2. **F** Since the subject of the sentence is *Edel, his brother Carem, and their pet chihuahua,* students should look for a plural third-person possessive pronoun.
3. **D** The sentence starts in the present tense with the verb *begin,* and so should continue in the present tense with *experience.*
4. **H** What kind of word can describe a noun? The correct answer must be the adjective *marked,* choice H.
5. **A** Students should ask themselves what kind of word the blank is describing. In this case, it describes the word *volcano.* What kind of word can describe a noun? Only an adjective. Choice D is an adverb and can be therefore eliminated. Further, since there is no comparison made in this sentence, choices B and C can also be eliminated. The best and remaining choice is A.
6. **H** The sentence begins in the present tense with the verb *continue.* So the correct answer should be in the present tense, and therefore, *encounter,* choice H, must be correct.

  TEST-TAKING TIP

Review with students the most important parts of speech: nouns, verbs, adjectives, and adverbs. Remind them how each one should be used.

THEME OPENING → Theme 4:
WHERE THE HEART IS

- **Introducing the Theme** (p. 325)
- **Exploring the Theme** (p. 326)
- **Theme Projects** (p. 327)

SELECTIONS

Bums in the Attic (p. 328)

In a Neighborhood in Los Angeles (p. 333)

The Courage That My Mother Had (p. 340)

Mother to Son (p. 340)

Media Connection: Kids from Chicago's Cabrini Green Learn Urban Farming in Arkansas (p. 345)

Antaeus (p. 346)

Home (p. 360)

The 1st (p. 360)

 The Teacher Who Changed My Life (p. 367)

How I Learned English (p. 376)

Oh Broom, Get to Work (p. 382)

Anansi and His Visitor, Turtle (p. 382)

Active Reading Model: The Night the Bed Fell (p. 398)

Media Connection: Peanuts (p. 409)

The Dog Diaries (p. 410)

SKILL FEATURES

Interdisciplinary Connection (p. 332)

Technology Skills (pp. 338–339)

Reading and Thinking Skills (p. 366)

Grammar Link (p. 381)

Vocabulary Skills (p. 394)

Writing Skills (p. 395)

Genre Focus: Essay (p. 396)

Active Reading Strategies (p. 397)

WRITING WORKSHOP

Observation and Description: A Photo in Words (pp. 420–423)

THEME WRAP-UP

- **Responding to the Theme, Analyzing Literature, Evaluate and Set Goals** (p. 424)

- **Build Your Portfolio** (p. 424)

- **Reading on Your Own** (p. 425)

  Dragonwings by Laurence Yep

  On the Way Home by Laura Ingalls Wilder and Rose Wilder Lane

  Homecoming by Cynthia Voigt

  Where Angels Glide at Dawn: New Stories from Latin America edited by Lori M. Carlson and Cythia L. Ventura

- **Standardized Test Practice** (pp. 426–427)

KEYS TO LITERARY CONNECTIONS

 Comparing Selections

The **Comparing Selections** feature in this theme provides opportunities for addressing diverse aspects of the reading and literature curriculum.

For example, in Comparing Selections— "The Teacher Who Changed My Life" and "How I Learned English"—on page 380, students look at similarities and differences in the experiences of immigrants trying to assimilate into a new culture. From this comparison, students can gain insight into the struggles and triumphs of the human spirit.

KEYS TO TEACHING OPTIONS

 Block Scheduling

Activities that are particularly suited to use within a block scheduling framework are identified throughout this theme by the following designation: For detailed suggestions on block scheduling, see the **Block Scheduling Guide** for this grade level.

Key to Ability Levels

The Teaching Options throughout this theme have been coded for students of various abilities.

L1 BASIC activities for all students

L2 AVERAGE activities for average to above-average students

L3 CHALLENGING activities for above-average students

Reading Skills in this theme

Variety of Texts

In addition to essay selections, this theme includes the following text types:

- short story
- poetry
- personal narrative
- folktale
- cartoon
- newspaper story
- comic strip

Comprehension Skills

The following instructional support for comprehension skills appears in this theme of the Student Edition:

- **Reading and Thinking Minilessons** (pp. 337, 344, 359, 393, 408, 419)
- **Making Connections** (p. 366)
- **Active Reading Strategies and Model** (pp.397–408)

See also the **Reading Minilessons** throughout the theme in this Teacher's Wraparound Edition.

Reading Resources

Comprehension Skills Resources

📁 **Active Reading Guides**

The **Active Reading Guide** provides graphic organizers and study guide questions to support students' reading of each selection (**Active Reading Guide**, pp. 29–38).

📁 **Reading Workbook**

The **Reading Workbook** (pp. 49–68) includes additional instruction and reinforcement of reading strategies and skills.

🎧 **Audio Library**

Available both on tape and on CD, the **Audio Library** provides valuable comprehension support.

Resources for Reading Widely

Glencoe Literature Library

Each title in the *Glencoe Literature Library* includes a full-length novel or play plus related readings. A separate Study Guide is available for each title.

💿 **Literature Classics CD-ROM**

The selections on this CD-ROM can be searched by author, theme, or genre.

A coproduction of Glencoe and Time, Inc., the *inTime* magazine includes a wealth of high interest nonfiction related to the selections in Theme Four.

✔ Assessment in this theme

Assessment Options in the Student Edition

Glencoe Literature offers a number of diverse ways to evaluate student understanding and skill proficiency. In the Student Edition, use the following:

- **Responding to Literature**

  Following each selection, students are asked to recall facts, interpret ideas, and evaluate concepts as they answer a variety of questions and complete activities to extend their understanding.

- **Theme Wrap-Up (pp. 424–425)**

  Here students respond to the selections on personal and analytical levels. They also assume ownership of their learning by setting and evaluating goals and by selecting work for their portfolios.

See also the many **Assessment Resources** listed on the facing page.

THE PRINCETON REVIEW

Standardized Test Practice

The Princeton Review has developed the Standardized Test Practice pages found at the end of this theme (pp. 426–427). These pages contain practice test questions that help students remain familiar with standardized test formats and content.

- **ITBS Preparation and Practice**
- **SAT-9 Preparation and Practice**
- **TerraNova Preparation and Practice**

Writing Skills in this theme

Writing Skills

The Student Edition of Theme Four offers strong instructional support for writing skills:

In **Extending Your Response**, which follows each selection:
- **Writing About Literature**
- **Personal/Creative Writing**

See also the **Writing Minilessons** throughout the theme in this Teacher's Wraparound Edition.

Writing Workshops

Theme Four concludes with a **Writing Workshop** that guides students through the process of writing a description (pp. 420–423).

Writing Resources

Writer's Assistant CD-ROM
Each Writing Workshop is supplemented by an interactive writing guide on the Writer's Assistant CD-ROM. This easy-to-use writing guide provides prompts, templates, and other tools that lead students through the writing process.

Writing and Proofreading Practice
Blackline masters present in-depth instruction and practice on a specific step in the writing process and proofreading (pp. 1–7, 29–34).

Writing and Proofreading Transparencies
Transparencies provide graphic organizers and proofreading exercises for whole-class instruction (pp. 1–6, 15–16, 31–32).

Research and Report Writing Guide
This resource provides extensive tips and activities to guide students in their writing projects in the literature classroom as well as in classes across the curriculum.

Style and Documentation Sourcebook for Writers
This sourcebook is a combination reference and workbook, giving students the most up-to-date information and guidance regarding traditional as well as technological research strategies and documentation.

Grammar and Composition Handbook
The Grammar and Composition Handbook provides instruction that supplements activities in the student textbook.

Assessment Resources

Selection Quick Checks
For each selection, a Quick Check of three to five short-answer questions measures students' literal comprehension.

Selection and Theme Assessment
The Selection and Theme Assessment instrument tests students' abilities to recall, interpret, and evaluate what they've read. The tests consist of multiple-choice, short answer, and essay questions.

Performance Assessment
Alternative assessment instruments and rubrics for Theme Four are found in the Performance Assessment ancillary.

Writing Assessment and Portfolio Management
These notes and strategies, student models, and assessment tools assist with the task of measuring students' progress as writers and as monitors of their own writing.

Testmaker
Teachers can customize selection and Theme Four tests by accessing the Testmaker database.

Mindjogger Videoquizzes
Using a popular game show format, Mindjogger Videoquizzes enable teachers to evaluate student understanding of Theme Four in a quick and fun manner.

Theme 4   SKILLS SCOPE AND SEQUENCE

SELECTIONS	Literary Elements	Reading and Thinking	Writing	Vocabulary and Spelling
Bums in the Attic SANDRA CISNEROS	First-Person Point of View, SE p. 330 *First-Person Point of View, TWE p. 329*		Analyzing Style, SE p. 331 Journal Entry, SE p. 331	
In a Neighborhood in Los Angeles / En un Barrio de Los Angeles FRANCISCO X. ALARCÓN	Imagery, SE p. 336 *Imagery, TWE pp. 334, 335* *Free Verse, TWE p. 335*	Drawing Conclusions, SE p. 337 *Inferring, TWE p. 334* *Summarizing, TWE p. 335*	Character Sketch, SE p. 337 Poem, SE p. 337	
The Courage That My Mother Had EDNA ST. VINCENT MILLAY **Mother to Son** LANGSTON HUGHES	Figurative Language, SE p. 343 *Figurative Language, TWE p. 342* *Dialect, TWE p. 342*	Visualizing, SE p. 344 *Evaluating, TWE p. 341* *Drawing Conclusions, TWE p. 342*	Paragraph (Poetry), SE p. 344 Advice Column, SE p. 344	
Antaeus BORDEN DEAL	Allusion, SE p. 357 *Dialect, TWE p. 348* *Allusion, TWE pp. 350, 351, 352, 353, 355, 356* *Plot, TWE p. 350* *Conflict, TWE p. 354*	Stereotype, SE p. 359 *Draw. Conclusions, TWE p. 351* *Main Idea/Details, TWE p. 352* *Synthesizing, TWE p. 353* *Analyzing Arguments, TWE p. 355*	Character Review, SE p. 358 Epilogue, SE p. 358 *Describing a Character, TWE p. 349*	Analogies, SE p. 359
Home GWENDOLYN BROOKS **the 1st** LUCILLE CLIFTON	Theme, SE p. 364 *Theme, TWE pp. 361, 362* *Author's Purpose, TWE p. 363*	*Evaluating, TWE p. 361* *Main Idea/Details, TWE p. 361* *Inferring, TWE p. 362* *Drawing Conclusions, TWE p. 363*	Dialogue, SE p. 365 One-Act Play, SE p. 365	Words Used in Unusual Ways, SE p. 365
The Teacher Who Changed My Life NICHOLAS GAGE	Main Idea, SE p. 374 *Characterization, TWE p. 369* *Main Idea, TWE pp. 371, 372, 373*	*Inferring, TWE pp. 370, 372* *Activating Prior Knowledge, TWE p. 370* *Conclusions, TWE p. 373*	Author's Purpose, SE p. 375 Autobiographical Essay, SE p. 375	The Suffix -arian, SE p. 375
How I Learned English GREGORY DJANIKIAN	Setting, SE p. 379 *Setting, TWE p. 377*	*Drawing Conclusions, TWE p. 378* *Sequence of Events, TWE p. 378*	Point of View, SE p. 379	*Context Clues, TWE p. 377*
Oh Broom, Get to Work YOSHIKO UCHIDA Anansi and His Visitor, Turtle EDNA MASON KAULA	Metaphors, SE p. 391 *Folktale, TWE pp. 384–390*	Problem/Solution, SE p. 393 *Classifying, TWE p. 384* *Inferring, TWE pp. 385–387*	Comparing Characters, SE p. 392 Writing a Sequel, SE p. 392	Synonyms, SE p. 393 *Etymology, TWE p. 386*
The Night the Bed Fell JAMES THURBER	Characterization, SE p. 406; TWE pp. 400, 403, 404 *Dialogue, TWE p. 404* *Figurative Lang., TWE p. 405*	Exaggeration, SE p. 408 *Making Critical Judgments, TWE p. 401* *Cause and Effect, TWE p. 403*	Paragraph (Climax), SE p. 407 Another Point of View, SE p. 407 *Characterizing, TWE p. 401*	Antonyms, SE p. 408 *Root Words, TWE p. 401*
The Dog Diaries MERRILL MARKOE	Point of View, SE p. 417; TWE pp. 413, 415 *Tone, TWE pp. 413, 415* *Absract/Concrete Lang., TWE p. 413* *Style, TWE p. 415*	Author's Purpose, SE p. 419 *Id. Spatial Rel., TWE p. 413* *Evaluating, TWE p. 414* *Drawing Conclusions, TWE pp. 415, 416* *Inferring, TWE p. 416*	Recognizing Humor, SE p. 418 Testing Theories, SE p. 418 *Diary Entry, TWE p. 414*	Prefixes, SE p. 419

Key: Student material is in roman. Teacher material is in italic.   🖳 Technology   **COLLAB. LEARN.** Collaboration

Grammar and Language	Listening, Speaking, and Viewing	Life Skills	Study, Research, and Technology
Pronoun-Antecedent Agreement, SE p. 331	**COLLAB. LEARN.** Literature Groups, SE p. 331		
	COLLAB. LEARN. Literature Groups, SE p. 337 **COLLAB. LEARN.** Tableau, SE p. 337		
Verb Tenses, TWE p. 342	**COLLAB. LEARN.** Literature Groups, SE p. 344 Appreciating Poetry, SE p. 344		
Commas in Compound Sentences, SE p. 359 *Adjectives, TWE p. 356*	**COLLAB. LEARN.** Literature Groups, SE p. 358 **COLLAB. LEARN.** *Read Aloud, TWE p. 350* **COLLAB. LEARN.** *Readers' Theater, TWE p. 354*	Learning for Life: Proposal, SE p. 358 **COLLAB. LEARN.** *Organizing a Project, TWE p. 351*	🖥 *Internet Connection, TWE p. 350* 🖥 *Enriching Enterprises, TWE p. 355*
Possessive Nouns, TWE p. 362	**COLLAB. LEARN.** Literature Groups, SE p. 365	Learning for Life: Persuasive Memo, SE p. 365	
Adverbs, TWE p. 372	**COLLAB. LEARN.** Literature Groups, SE p. 375 Storytelling, SE p. 375 *Discussion, TWE p. 373*		
	COLLAB. LEARN. Literature Groups, SE p. 379		
Suffixes and the Silent e, SE p. 393 *Capitalizing Names, TWE p. 386* *Adjectives and Adverbs, TWE p. 390*	**COLLAB. LEARN.** Literature Groups, SE p. 392 *Storytelling, TWE p. 388*	Learning for Life: Letter of Introduction, SE p. 392	**COLLAB. LEARN.** *Popular Japanese Dishes, TWE p. 387* **COLLAB. LEARN.** *Customs, TWE p. 389*
Parentheses, SE p. 408 *Consistency in Verb Tense, TWE p. 404*	**COLLAB. LEARN.** Lit. Grps., SE p. 407 Oral Reading, SE p. 407 *Film, TWE p. 402* *Interviewing, TWE p. 405*		
Principal Parts of Verbs, SE p. 419 *Subject-Verb Agreement, TWE p. 416*	**COLLAB. LEARN.** Literature Groups, SE p. 418 The Talking Dog Show, SE p. 418	*Goal Setting, TWE p. 415*	🖥 Internet Connection, SE p. 418

WHERE THE HEART IS 323F

Theme 4 RESOURCE MANAGER

SELECTIONS	📁 Print Resources		
Bums in the Attic SANDRA CISNEROS	Theme 4 Planning Guide, pp. 6-10 * Active Reading Guide, p. 29	Grammar & Comp. Handbook, Lesson 4.3 Grammar & Language Workbook, pp. 105-106 Reading Workbook, pp. 49-50	* Quick Checks, p. 29 Sel. & Th. Assess., p. 53 Performance Assessment, p. 28 Spanish Summaries, p. 29 Spanish Translations
In a Neighborhood in Los Angeles / En un Barrio de Los Angeles FRANCISCO X. ALARCÓN	Theme 4 Planning Guide, pp. 11-15 * Active Reading Guide, p. 30	Reading Workbook, pp. 51-52	* Quick Checks, p. 30 Sel. & Th. Assess., p. 54 Performance Assessment, p. 29 Spanish Summaries, p. 30 Spanish Translations
The Courage That My Mother Had EDNA ST. VINCENT MILLAY **Mother to Son** LANGSTON HUGHES	Theme 4 Planning Guide, pp. 16-21 * Active Reading Guide, p. 31	Grammar & Comp. Handbook, Lesson 3.5 Grammar & Language Workbook, pp. 83-86 Reading Workbook, pp. 53-54	* Quick Checks, p. 31 Sel. & Th. Assess., pp. 55-56 Performance Assessment, p. 30 Spanish Summaries, p. 31 Spanish Translations
Antaeus BORDEN DEAL	Theme 4 Planning Guide, pp. 22-29 * Active Reading Guide, p. 32 Vocabulary Practice, p. 20	Grammar & Comp. Handbook, Lessons 5.1, 13.3 Grammar & Language Workbook, pp. 117-118, 257-258 Reading Workbook, pp. 55-56	* Quick Checks, p. 32 Sel. & Th. Assess., pp. 57-58 Performance Assessment, p. 31 Spanish Summaries, p. 32
Home GWENDOLYN BROOKS **the 1st** LUCILLE CLIFTON	Theme 4 Planning Guide, pp. 30-35 * Active Reading Guide, p. 33 Vocabulary Practice, p. 21	Grammar & Comp. Handbook, Lesson 2.3 Grammar & Language Workbook, pp. 65-66 Reading Workbook, pp. 57-58	* Quick Checks, p. 33 Sel. & Th. Assess., pp. 59-60 Performance Assessment, p. 32 Spanish Summaries, p. 33
The Teacher Who Changed My Life NICHOLAS GAGE	Theme 4 Planning Guide, pp. 36-43 * Active Reading Guide, p. 34 Vocabulary Practice, p. 22	Grammar & Comp. Handbook, Lessons 6.1, 6.2 Grammar & Language Workbook, pp. 127-128 Reading Workbook, pp. 59-60	* Quick Checks, p. 34 Sel. & Th. Assess., pp. 61-62 Performance Assessment, p. 33 Spanish Summaries, p. 34
How I Learned English GREGORY DJANIKIAN	Theme 4 Planning Guide, pp. 44-48 * Active Reading Guide, p. 35	Reading Workbook, pp. 61-62	* Qk. Chks., p. 35; Perf. Assess., p. 33 Sel. & Th. Assess., pp. 61-62 Sp. Sum., p. 35; Sp. Trans.
Oh Broom, Get to Work YOSHIKO UCHIDA **Anansi and His Visitor, Turtle** EDNA MASON KAULA	Theme 4 Planning Guide, pp. 49-54 * Active Reading Guide, p. 36 Vocabulary Practice, p. 23	Gr. & Comp. Hdbk., Lsn. 5.1, 6.1, 6.2, 12.2, 15.4; Gr. & Lang. Wkbk., pp. 117-118, 127-128, 237-238, 291-292; Rdg. Wkbk., pp. 63-64	* Quick Checks, p. 36 Sel. & Th. Assess., pp. 63-64 Performance Assessment, p. 34 Sp. Sum., p. 36; Sp. Trans.
The Night the Bed Fell JAMES THURBER	Theme 4 Planning Guide, pp. 55-62 * Active Reading Guide, p. 37 Vocabulary Practice, p. 24	Gr. & Comp. Hdbk., Lsn., 3.5, 13.8 Grammar & Language Workbook, pp. 83-86, 275-276 Reading Workbook, pp. 65-66	* Quick Checks, p. 37 Sel. & Th. Assess., pp. 65-66 Performance Assessment, p. 35 Sp. Sum., p. 37; Sp. Trans.
The Dog Diaries MERRILL MARKOE	Theme 4 Plan. Guide, pp. 63-70 * Active Reading Guide, p. 38 Vocabulary Practice, p. 25	Gr. & Comp. Hdbk., Lsn., 3.6, 10.1 Gr. & Lang. Wkbk., pp. 87-90, 183-184; Rdg. Wkbk., pp. 67-68	* Qk. Chks., p. 38; Perf. Assess., p. 36 Sel. & Th. Assess., pp. 67-68 Spanish Summaries, p. 38

*Also available in Spanish

Transparencies	Technology Resources
Selection Focus Transparency 29 Literary Elements Transparency 29	Audio Library Spanish Audio Library Vocabulary Puzzlemaker Web Site: lit.glencoe.com
Selection Focus Transparency 30 Literary Elements Transparency 30 Fine Art Transparency 10	Audio Library Spanish Audio Library Vocabulary Puzzlemaker Web Site: lit.glencoe.com
Selection Focus Transparency 31 Grammar and Language Transparency 28 Literary Elements Transparency 31	Audio Library Spanish Audio Library Vocabulary Puzzlemaker Web Site: lit.glencoe.com
Selection Focus Transparency 32 Grammar and Language Transparency 29 Literary Elements Transparency 32 Fine Art Transparency 3	Audio Library Spanish Audio Library Vocabulary Puzzlemaker Web Site: lit.glencoe.com
Selection Focus Transparency 33 Grammar and Language Transparency 30 Literary Elements Transparency 33	Audio Library Spanish Audio Library Vocabulary Puzzlemaker Web Site: lit.glencoe.com
Selection Focus Transparency 34 Grammar and Language Transparency 31 Literary Elements Transparency 34	Literature Launchers Audio Library Spanish Audio Library Vocabulary Puzzlemaker Web Site: lit.glencoe.com
Selection Focus Transparency 35 Literary Elements Transparency 35	Audio/Sp. Audio Library Vocabulary Puzzlemaker Web Site: lit.glencoe.com
Selection Focus Transparency 36 Grammar and Language Transparencies 32, 33 Literary Elements Transparency 36	Audio Library Spanish Audio Library Vocabulary Puzzlemaker Web Site: lit.glencoe.com
Selection Focus Transparency 37 Grammar and Language Transparency 35 Literary Elements Transparency 37 Fine Art Transparency 2	Literature Launchers Audio/Spanish Audio Library Vocabulary Puzzlemaker Web Site: lit.glencoe.com
Selection Focus Transparency 38 Grammar and Language Transparency 36 Literary Elements 38; Fine Art 27	Literature Launchers Audio/Spanish Audio Library Web Site: lit.glencoe.com

Theme RESOURCES

- Listening and Speaking Activities (pp. 10–12)
- Viewing and Representing Activities (pp. 1–6, 16–18)
- Critical Thinking Skills (pp. 9–11)
- Media Connection Activities (pp. 7–8)
- Interdisciplinary Activities (pp. 14–17)
- Family and Community Activities (p. 14)
- Selection and Theme Assessment (pp. 131–132)

See also these additional planning resources:
- English Language Learners Sourcebook
- Inclusion Strategies Sourcebook
- Literature Groups Sourcebook

Use Glencoe's *Presentation Plus!* This multimedia teaching tool lets you present dynamic lessons that will engage your students. Using Microsoft PowerPoint®, you can customize the presentation to create your own personalized lessons.

THEME 4

Where the Heart Is

Theme Objectives

- To enjoy reading about how and where people feel at home
- To analyze the literary elements in nonfiction, poetry, folktale, and short story selections
- To apply strategies for reading essays

Teaching Strategies

Have students read the quotation "Home is where one starts from" by T. S. Eliot in preparation for the discussion questions on page 325.

VIEWING THE PAINTING

Hands or stylized figures with over-sized hands appear again and again in the art of Eduardo Kingman (1913–). The Ecuadorian artist has explored themes of sorrow and tenderness in paintings, murals, and book illustrations since the 1930s.

Responding to the Painting If necessary, tell students that the title of this painting translates to *Birthplace*. Ask:
- How does this painting reflect the theme? (*The hands seem to be cradling the small town, expressing loving care for the birthplace, or hometown.*)

Where the Heart Is

" *Home is where one starts from.* "

—*T. S. Eliot*

Lugar Natal, 1989. Eduardo Kingman. Oil on canvas, 40 x 53 in. Inter-American Development Bank Art Collection, Washington, D.C. Reproduced by permission of the IDB.

324

TEACHER to TEACHER

BRINKLEY MIDDLE SCHOOL, MISSISSIPPI

When opening the theme "Where the Heart Is," I give my class the following writing prompt: "You are a passenger on the Titanic along with all of your friends and family. As the ship sinks, you are seated in a lifeboat. You must choose five of your friends or family members to be in the lifeboat

too. Who will you choose and why? What factors will you consider in the decision?" Sometimes I assign vocabulary words to be used in their responses, such as nouns ending in *-ty—loyalty, responsibility, longevity,* and *honesty,* for example. This activity makes students reflect on the deeper meanings of life, and at the same time sharpens their writing and vocabulary skills. After volunteers read

their responses aloud, there is class discussion. As students challenge one another on the choices they have made or the reasons they present, the disagreements sharpen their critical thinking skills.

EMMA CLOWERS

THEME CONTENTS

Bums in the Attic •
    short story by Sandra Cisneros 329

In a Neighborhood in Los Angeles •
    poem by Francisco X. Alarcón 334

The Courage That My Mother Had •
    poem by Edna St. Vincent Millay 341

Mother to Son • poem by Langston Hughes 342

Antaeus • short story by Borden Deal 347

Home • short story by Gwendolyn Brooks 361

the 1st • poem by Lucille Clifton 363

The Teacher Who Changed My Life •
    personal narrative by Nicholas Gage 368

How I Learned English •
    poem by Gregory Djanikian 377

Oh Broom, Get to Work • story by Yoshiko Uchida . . . 383

Anansi and His Visitor, Turtle •
    Ashanti story retold by Edna Mason Kaula 388

GENRE FOCUS NONFICTION: ESSAY

The Night the Bed Fell •
    humorous essay by James Thurber 399

The Dog Diaries •
    humorous essay by Merrill Markoe 411

Introducing the Theme

Direct your students' attention to the **Theme Contents.** Ask them to read through the list of selections. Discuss these questions:

• If you did not know the theme, what would you guess it is according to these titles? *(Students may guess family, childhood, school, or significant people in one's life.)*

• What genres are represented in the theme contents? *(Poems, personal narratives, short stories, folktales, and essays are included.)*

• Do any of these titles sound like something you could have written yourself? Which ones? Why? *(English language learners may choose "How I Learned English"; other students may identify titles that are relevant to their own experiences.)*

LITERATURE & HUMANITIES

Display the painting *The Family* from *U.S. History and Art,* Transparency 28. Have students discuss the family in the painting and compare it with their own ideas about what constitutes a family.

GLENCOE TECHNOLOGY

LITERATURE CLASSICS CD-ROM

Search for other selections related to the theme "Where the Heart Is."

RESOURCE MANAGER

See the **Theme Four Planning Guide** (pp. 1–5) for additional teaching notes, strategies, and resources for introducing the theme "Where the Heart Is."

Exploring the Theme

Where the Heart Is

Ask students to draw or paint pictures of the places they think of as home. Remind students that "home" does not have to be where they live; as the theme states, it is where the heart is.

Starting Points

Home Is Where the Heart Is

Introduce the word *nesting* and discuss its meaning. *(Nesting is the process of contributing to the building and maintenance of a nest, or home.)*

- Ask students if they are "nesters." Have them imagine they are birds: Would they prefer to sit in their nests or fly and explore what might be dangerous territory?
- After they create "top ten" lists, ask students to name things they do at home that contribute to the well-being of their households.

FINE ART
TRANSPARENCY 27

You may wish to display **Fine Art Transparency 27** to enrich the concept.

Within Your Own Heart

Students may want to create postcards of the places they think of as home. Suggest that they write notes to family members and friends telling what they love most about them.

- Invite each student to refer to the notes to compose an "Ode to Home" and to think of the ode as a valentine—a poem or verse inspired by feelings about home—to send to a place he or she loves.

Quotations Suggest that students use *quotations, aphorisms,* or *proverbs* as keywords on a search engine to find other possible quotations. Once connected to a site, they can do a search using *home* as a keyword. Have them share their results with the class.

Exploring the Theme

— Where the Heart Is —

What would life be like without the love of your family and friends? How would you feel without the warmth and security of a place called home? In the stories, poems, and essays in this theme, you will meet characters who face these questions. To begin your own thinking about the theme, try one of the options below.

Starting Points

HOME IS WHERE THE HEART IS

Do you ever feel like the pair of birds in the cartoon—staying home with your family and doing something fun, like playing a game or baking something delicious?

- Brainstorm a list of things that you enjoy doing at home. Then, as a class, create a "top ten" list of favorite things to do at home.

WITHIN YOUR OWN HEART

Think about the people and places that are most important to you.

- What do you love most about your family members and friends? What makes your home special to you? Write a few notes about your feelings.

"I don't feel like going out. Why don't just the two of us stay in and open a can of worms?"

©The New Yorker Collection 1972 Edward Koren from cartoonbank.com. All rights reserved.

MEETING INDIVIDUAL NEEDS — ENGLISH LANGUAGE LEARNERS

Understanding the Theme Be sure students understand that "Where the Heart Is" is not a question. Point out that the theme title is part of an old expression "Home is where the heart is." Also explain the rules for capitalizing titles: Capitalize the first word and all other words except for coordinating conjunctions, articles, and prepositions of less than four letters.

Activity After they have read the introduction, invite students to work in small groups to think of and record three titles for this theme. **COLLAB. LEARN.**

Additional Resources
📁 *English Language Learners Sourcebook*

Theme Projects

As you read the selections in this theme, try your hand at one of the projects below. Work on your own, with a partner, or with a group.

CRITICAL VIEWING
Families in Books and on Screen

1. Keep a journal about how families are portrayed in your favorite books and on your favorite television shows. How do the average fictional families look and act? What conclusions can you draw from your observations?

2. Organize your findings in a chart. Choose headings to represent the various categories of behavior you have found. You can use drawings or pictures from old magazines and newspapers to illustrate your chart.

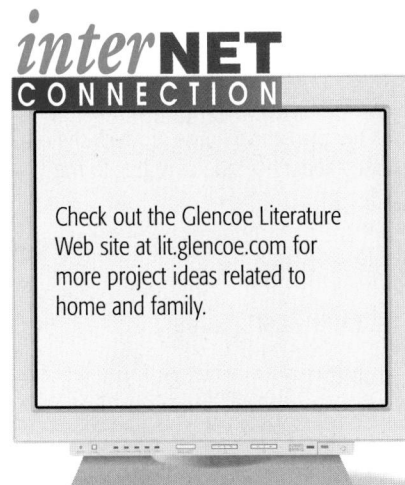

Check out the Glencoe Literature Web site at lit.glencoe.com for more project ideas related to home and family.

LEARNING FOR LIFE
Writing a Policy Statement
Some of the characters in this unit are fortunate enough to speak two languages—the language of their parents' native country and English. In today's global economy, the ability to speak more than one language has great advantages.

1. Develop a policy statement for the establishment of a school-wide second-language program that would begin in kindergarten. Start with your own ideas about why knowing more than one language is important.

2. Gather information from teachers, bilingual students, librarians, and your family. Draft your policy statement and share it with the class.

MULTIMEDIA PROJECT
Homes Around the World

1. Gather data about the different kinds of homes people live in around the world. The **Interdisciplinary Connection** on page 332 shows some examples; see what others you can find. Look for information about architecture, life in other countries, and traditional cultures on the Web and in books and magazines.

2. Choose a kind of housing that interests you. Consider how it differs from the housing you are familiar with in such matters as size, architectural style, and building materials.

3. Build a model or draw pictures and diagrams of your chosen house. Present your finished project to the class.

Kitchen	Bathroom	Second bedroom
Living room		Master bedroom

Theme Projects

Teaching Strategies
The following suggestions may help your students plan and carry out their theme projects.

Critical Viewing
- Students can compare families like *The Brady Bunch* and *The Partridge Family* to current TV families.
- Use students' charts to discuss whether TV families represent real-life families.
- Ask students who choose fictional families from books to write what they like and don't like about these families in their journals.

Learning for Life
- Encourage students to poll classmates to find out how many languages are spoken in the class.
- Suggest that students find out what other local schools offer second-language programs.
- Recommend that students write their policy statements in English, translate them into the other languages spoken in your classroom, and create multilingual posters.

Multimedia Project
- Have students include a weather-related explanation for why homes are constructed this way.
- Encourage students to present overviews of the countries or regions in which the homes are found.

Additional Resources
- 📁 *Interdisciplinary Activities,* pp. 14–17
- 📁 *Viewing and Representing Activities,* pp. 16–18
- 📁 *Listening and Speaking Activities,* pp. 10–12
- 📁 *Critical Thinking Skills,* pp. 9–11
- 📁 *Selection and Theme Assessment,* pp. 131–132
- 📁 *Performance Assessment,* p. 72

Family and Community Activity

Have student groups adopt a kindergarten or first-grade classroom. Ask students to think about their own earlier years and how important it is for young children to feel happy and secure. Encourage them to coordinate this effort with teachers from the younger grades. Have them visit the classrooms and talk to the children. Encourage your students to come up with a list of things they might do to create a home-away-from-home environment for these children at school. Ideas could include helping students hang pictures of their families on the walls, reading to students at recess one day a week, and greeting them individually each morning.

Additional Resources
- 📁 *Family and Community Activities,* p. 14

Objectives

- To read and analyze a personal narrative about a young girl's feelings about home
- To identify first-person point of view in a narrative
- To write a paragraph analyzing the author's style

Skills

Writing: Journal Entry
Grammar/Language: Pronoun-Antecedent Agreement
Collaboration: Literature Groups; Art Activity

Motivating
→OPTIONS

Selection Focus Transparency 29: Have students view and discuss the photograph of Chesterwood, the house in which sculptor Daniel Chester French lived. Compare the photograph to the houses the narrator describes.

Focus Activity: Have students give reasons for the dreams and plans they listed in the Focus Activity. Do a class tally to compare students' lifestyle choices.

Before You Read
Bums in the Attic

MEET SANDRA CISNEROS

Sandra Cisneros (sis nā′ rōs′) was born in Chicago, the only daughter in a family with seven children. Her family frequently moved between the United States and Mexico because of her father's homesickness for Mexico. As a result, Cisneros often felt lonely and unsettled. "Because we moved so much," Cisneros said, ". . . I retreated inside myself." Throughout her childhood, Cisneros spent much of her time reading and writing stories and poems.

Sandra Cisneros was born in 1954. "Bums in the Attic" is from her book The House on Mango Street, *published in 1983.*

FOCUS ACTIVITY

What are your dreams for the future? What will you do? Where will you live—in a house, in an apartment, on a farm?

QuickWrite
Describe in a few sentences how and where you imagine yourself living in the future.

Setting a Purpose
Read to find out what dream for the future is expressed in this selection.

BACKGROUND

The Time and Place This selection is set in our time in Chicago, Illinois.

Did You Know? Organized in a series of vignettes, or brief scenes, *The House on Mango Street* tells the story of Esperanza Cordero, a young girl growing up in Chicago, who longs for a room of her own and a house of which she can be proud. When asked about her style of writing in *The House on Mango Street,* Sandra Cisneros commented, "I wanted to write stories that were a cross between poetry and fiction. . . . [I] wanted to write a collection which could be read at any random point without having any knowledge of what came before or after. Or, that could be read in a series to tell one big story."

RESOURCE MANAGER

Lesson Planning Resource
The *Theme Four Planning Guide* (pp. 6–10) provides additional lesson notes and reduced versions of all print resources.

📁 **Other Print Resources**
- Active Reading Guide, p. 29
- Reading Workbook, pp. 49–50
- Grammar and Language Workbook, pp. 105–106
- Grammar and Composition Handbook, Lesson 4.3

- Quick Checks, p. 29
- Selection and Theme Assessment, p. 53
- Performance Assessment, p. 28
- Spanish Summaries, p. 29
- Spanish Translations
- Inclusion Strategies
- English Language Learners Sourcebook

 Transparencies
- Selection Focus 29
- Literary Elements 29

Technology
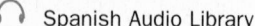 🎧 Audio Library
🎧 Spanish Audio Library
💻 Glencoe Literature Web Site
💾 Testmaker

Bums in the Attic

Sandra Cisneros

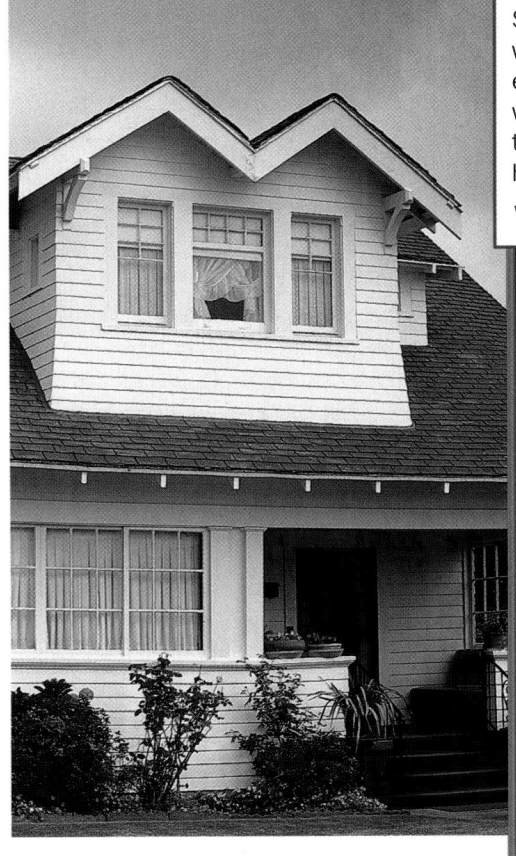

I want a house on a hill like the ones with the gardens where Papa works. We go on Sundays, Papa's day off. I used to go. I don't anymore. You don't like to go out with us, Papa says. Getting too old? Getting too stuck-up, says Nenny. I don't tell them I am ashamed—all of us staring out the window like the hungry. I am tired of looking at what we can't have. When we win the lottery . . . Mama begins, and then I stop listening.

People who live on hills sleep so close to the stars they forget those of us who live too much on earth. They don't look down at all except to be content to live on hills. They have nothing to do with last week's garbage or fear of rats. Night comes. Nothing wakes them but the wind.

One day I'll own my own house, but I won't forget who I am or where I came from. Passing bums will ask, Can I come in? I'll offer them the attic, ask them to stay, because I know how it is to be without a house.

Some days after dinner, guests and I will sit in front of a fire. Floorboards will squeak upstairs. The attic grumble.

Rats? they'll ask.

Bums, I'll say, and I'll be happy.

❖

SUMMARY

The narrator's family goes for a ride on Sundays to look at the big houses where her father works, but the girl, embarrassed by the family's staring at what they can't have, no longer joins them. She dreams of having a house of her own some day.

📁 *Spanish Summaries,* p. 29

A Active Reading

PREDICT Have students use the title to predict what the selection will be about. Suggest that students revise their prediction's as they read.

Additional Resources

📁 *Active Reading Guide,* p. 29

🎧 *Audio Library*

🎧 *Spanish Audio Library*

B Literary Elements

FIRST-PERSON POINT OF VIEW Help students identify the first-person point of view in this story. Discuss how it affects readers' knowledge of the character's thoughts and feelings.

✓ ASSESSMENT OPTIONS

📁 *Quick Checks,* p. 29

Teaching Options

CONNECTING TO OTHER SELECTIONS
For a teaching strategy that connects "Bums in the Attic" to "Hollywood and the Pits," turn to page 9 in the *Theme Two Planning Guide.*

MEETING INDIVIDUAL NEEDS — ENGLISH LANGUAGE LEARNERS

Symbolism English language learners might find it difficult to understand the symbolism Cisneros uses in the selection, for example, a bird in flight often symbolizes freedom, and the color white often symbolizes purity. In "Bums in the Attic," the fact that rich people live on the hill symbolizes their position above the less fortunate in society.

Activity Pair English language learners with English-proficient students. Have them reread the story and list symbolic phrases and their meanings in a two-column chart.

Additional Resources

📁 *English Language Learners Sourcebook*

Responding to the Selection

Personal Response

Some students may dream, as does the author, of being in a position to help the less fortunate. Some may dream of lives similar to their lives now, while others may dream of better, or simply different, lives.

Analyzing Literature

1. The narrator's family drives past the rich people's houses. She doesn't go because she is embarrassed.
2. She feels the people living high on the hill are too far removed from the people living down below to notice them.
3. She intends to own her own house.
4. Homeless people will ask if they can stay with her, and she will offer them space in her attic.
5. The narrator is embarrassed by her family because she knows they will never live in such houses.
6. She feels they live a privileged life and are unaware or unconcerned about poor people who live below them.
7. The narrator will remember when she was poor and will help those in the same situation. "I'll offer them the attic... I know how it is to be without a house."
8. The narrator will be happy and proud to tell her guests about the bums in the attic.
9. Students may suggest that the theme is knowing who you are, helping others, or having a dream.
10. Some students may think the narrator knows how it feels to be homeless. Because of her family's poor living conditions, she can understand how homeless people feel.

Responding to Literature

PERSONAL RESPONSE

- ◆ What do you think about the narrator's hopes and dreams for the future?
- ◆ Think back to your QuickWrite for the **Focus Activity** on page 328. How do your dreams for the future compare to the thoughts and feelings described in this selection? Write your response in your journal.

Analyzing Literature

RECALL

1. What does the narrator's family do on Sundays? Why doesn't the narrator go anymore?
2. According to the narrator, why do the people in the houses on the hill forget about other people?
3. What does the narrator intend to own when she grows up?
4. Describe how bums will end up in the narrator's attic.

INTERPRET

5. What is the narrator's attitude toward her family's Sunday activity? Why?
6. How does the narrator feel about the people who live on the hill? Explain.
7. What does the narrator mean when she says, "I won't forget who I am or where I came from"? Use quotations from the story to support your ideas.
8. How do you imagine the narrator will feel when she tells her guests that she has bums in the attic?

EVALUATE AND CONNECT

9. The **theme** of a piece of writing is the message that the writer hopes to communicate. What is the theme of this selection? Explain why you think so.
10. Do you think the narrator knows how it feels to be homeless, like the bums she mentions in her writing? Explain.

LITERARY ELEMENTS

First-Person Point of View

In a story, a book, or an essay, the **point of view** is the relationship of the narrator, or storyteller, to the story. In a story with **first-person point of view,** the story is always told by one of the characters, who refers to himself or herself as "I." All information about the story must come from this character. Readers can only know what this character knows and can only feel what this character feels. "Bums in the Attic" is an example of writing told from a first-person point of view.

1. Why, do you think, did Cisneros write "Bums in the Attic" from a first-person point of view?
2. How would this piece be different if it were told from a third-person point of view? (See page 157.) Explain.

● See **Literary Terms Handbook,** p. R8.

LITERATURE & HUMANITIES

Have students examine the painting *Why Not Use the "L"?* in *Art Talk,* page 284, and discuss how the characters react to homelessness. Have them compare Cisneros's and the artist's attitudes towards homeless people.

LITERARY ELEMENTS

1. Cisneros's use of first-person point of view allows the narrator to express feelings, thoughts, and ideas about real-life experiences.
2. If the piece were told from a third-person point of view, it would be less personal because the narrator would not be part of the experiences and feelings described.

Additional Resources
📖 *Literary Elements Transparency 29*

Extending Your Response

Writing About Literature

Analyzing Style   How would you describe the writer's style in this piece of writing? How does Cisneros create a response in her readers to the idea of bums in an attic? Does she use humor? Realism? Emotional situations? Write a paragraph explaining how Cisneros weaves together a style that makes her story effective. Support your conclusions with examples.

Creative Writing

Changing Point of View   How would this selection be different if another character had narrated it? Choose a different character: Papa, Nenny, Mama, or one of the bums. Write a journal entry from the point of view of that person. Tell about the character's life and dreams for the future. Make up any details you wish.

Literature Groups

Home Is Where the Heart Is   In a small group discussion, compare the details about the narrator's present life with her dreams for the future. How does the narrator hope her life will change? How does she intend to hang on to her identity? Do you think the narrator will one day live in a house on the hill? Why or why not? Support your ideas with details and quotations.

Art Activity

The House on the Hill   Work with classmates to create a large floor plan of the house on the hill. Before drawing the house, make a list of all the necessary details, such as the fireplace, the garden, and the attic. Use your imagination for details the selection does not include. Display your plan.

📔 **Save your work for your portfolio.**

Skill Minilesson

GRAMMAR AND LANGUAGE • PRONOUN-ANTECEDENT AGREEMENT

A **pronoun** is a word used in place of a noun or noun phrase. An **antecedent** is the word or words the pronoun refers to. A pronoun and its antecedent must agree in number and gender.

Mario brought his mother flowers. *She* was pleased with *them*.

She, a singular feminine pronoun, refers to *mother. Them,* a plural neuter (neither masculine nor feminine) pronoun, refers to *flowers.*

PRACTICE   Write the appropriate pronoun for each numbered blank. After the pronoun, write its antecedent.

Sandra Cisneros wrote *The House on Mango Street* when (1) _____ was in her twenties. "Bums in the Attic" is from (2) _____ book. (3) _____ is one of a number of short pieces that make up the book. Each of these brief vignettes can stand on (4) _____ own, but together, Cisneros says, (5) _____ "tell one big story."

● For more about pronoun-antecedent agreement, see **Language Handbook,** p. R17.

Extending Your Response

Writing About Literature

Students' paragraphs should
• explain how Cisneros weaves together a unique style to make her story effective.
• give examples of scenes that Cisneros describes humorously and those she relates realistically.

Creative Writing

Students' journal entries should
• express the feelings of and include details about the character's life.
• follow the style and tone of a journal entry.

Literature Groups   Encourage students to discuss the narrator's character to help them decide whether she will retain her identity and realize her dreams. COLLAB. LEARN.

Art Activity   Remind students that the narrator views the house on the hill as majestic and grand. 🔲

Skill Minilesson

GRAMMAR AND LANGUAGE
• PRONOUN-ANTECEDENT AGREEMENT

1. she   3. it   5. they
2. her   4. its

Additional Resources

📘 *Grammar and Language Workbook,* pp. 105–106

📘 *Grammar and Composition Handbook,* Lesson 4.3

📘 *Writer's Choice,* Lesson 11.2

✔ ASSESSMENT OPTIONS

📁 *Quick Checks,* p. 29
📁 *Selection and Theme Assessment,* p. 53
📁 *Performance Assessment,* p. 28
💾 *Testmaker*

Interdisciplinary Connection

TECHNOLOGY

Objectives

- To appreciate cultural differences in housing
- To understand and create a basic floor plan for a house

Teaching Strategies

It would be helpful if students could see a professionally drawn floor plan or blueprint of a house or room before they try to create their own. If you do not have a copy of a blueprint, you can find one in a home-design magazine. Bring in the sample and give students time to examine it. Explain that the blueprint contains instructions for the builders, plumbers, and electricians. Ask students to consider the floor plan they see in the blueprint and discuss whether they would change anything if they were building the house.

Activity

Floor plans may include students' homes, dream homes, or impressions of the houses described in students' books from Zimbabwe, Mexico, Japan, or Mongolia.

Architecture

No matter how similar the floor plans, no two homes are ever *exactly* the same. Throughout the world, the technology and design used in home construction varies greatly. However, all people build homes for the same reason: to feel comfortable and safe.

In Zimbabwe, villagers use wood, grass, or dried mud to construct a hut with circular walls. Inside, the hut remains cool and dry because of its thatched grass or corrugated metal roof. Zimbabweans build their huts close together to create a village.

Mexican villagers often build their own houses, too, shaping and drying clay into adobe bricks. The villagers typically whitewash their houses to deflect the hot sun. Sometimes colorful tiles add decoration to the roof or around windows and over the door frame.

Traditional Japanese houses use latticed paper walls to divide the living space into rooms. These sliding screens can be easily rearranged to add more space or to let summer breezes in. At night, the family unrolls futons onto woven grass mats (*tatami*) that cover the floor, and the rooms convert to bedrooms.

In Mongolia, nomadic families live in portable homes, similar to tents. This type of house, called a *yurt,* looks simple, but underneath its felt walls, a complex wooden frame keeps the structure from collapsing in desert winds. The family adds carpets and furniture to the single room to make it cozy.

ACTIVITY

Draw a floor plan of your home or a "dream home" you would like to have someday. Be sure to create a scale (for instance, 1 inch = 4 feet), and write each room's dimensions on the floor plan.

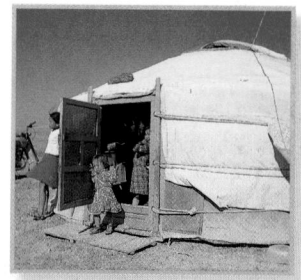

Teaching Options

MEETING INDIVIDUAL NEEDS — MULTIPLE LEARNING STYLES

Interpersonal Students who are community-oriented benefit from activities that allow them to exercise and develop such qualities as leadership, cooperation, and organization.

Activity Have students work in groups of five or six to design ideal towns for seventh-graders. Each group should decide what needs to be included, where the town will be located, and who will lead the project. They can decide what services, stores, restaurants, and recreational facilities should be part of the town they design. The towns may be drawn on butcher paper and presented to the class by group spokespersons. Have students determine in which town they would most like to live.
L3 COLLAB. LEARN.

Before You Read

En un Barrio de Los Angeles /
In a Neighborhood in Los Angeles

MEET FRANCISCO X. ALARCÓN

Francisco X. Alarcón (al är sôn') arrived in this country from Mexico with only five dollars in his pocket. After working as a dishwasher and a migrant laborer, he began taking classes in an adult-education program in Los Angeles. By the time he had completed his education, Alarcón had received three college degrees. Today, as a poet, a professor, and a performer, Alarcón's mission is to bring his poetry to the widest possible audience.

Francisco X. Alarcón was born in 1954. This poem comes from his collection of poems Body in Flames, *published in 1990.*

FOCUS ACTIVITY

Think of a family member you love. What is special about your relationship with this person?

Sharing Ideas
Jot down a list of things you love about this person. Share your list with your classmates.

Setting a Purpose
Read the poem to discover how the speaker feels about his grandmother and why he feels that way.

BACKGROUND

The Language of the Poem "In a Neighborhood in Los Angeles" was originally written in Spanish. It was then translated into English. Both versions are presented here. If you or one of your classmates can read Spanish, read "En un Barrio de Los Angeles" aloud so that you can hear how it sounds in the original language.

Spanish-Speaking Californians Francisco X. Alarcón came to Los Angeles from Mexico. Spanish-speaking people, however, have been in California for a long time. Seven years before thirteen British colonies declared themselves the United States of America, Spanish missionaries founded the first of twenty-one missions they would build in California between 1769 and 1823. One of them was located in what is now Los Angeles. The Spanish also built a number of presidios—military posts—in California. When Mexico won its independence from Spain in 1821, California became part of Mexico. California didn't belong to the United States until the middle 1800s.

Objectives

- To read and analyze a poem about the author's grandmother
- To identify imagery in a poem
- To write a character sketch

Skills

Reading/Thinking: Inferring; Summarizing; Drawing Conclusions
Writing: Poem
Listening/Speaking: Performing a Tableau
Collaboration: Literature Groups

Motivating
→ OPTIONS

Selection Focus Transparency 30: Have students view and discuss the painting by Paul Klee.

Focus Activity: As an extension of the Focus Activity, have students work in pairs to discuss their family members. Encourage partners to ask each other for specific reasons why they consider a person special.

RESOURCE MANAGER

Lesson Planning Resource
The ***Theme Four Planning Guide*** (pp. 11–15) provides additional lesson notes and reduced versions of all print resources.

📁 **Other Print Resources**
- Active Reading Guide, p. 30
- Reading Workbook, pp. 51–52
- Quick Checks, p. 30
- Selection and Theme Assessment, p. 54

- Performance Assessment, p. 29
- Spanish Summaries, p. 30
- Spanish Translations
- Inclusion Strategies
- English Language Learners Sourcebook

📖 **Transparencies**
- Selection Focus 30
- Fine Art 10
- Literary Elements 30

Technology
 Audio Library
 Spanish Audio Library
💻 Glencoe Literature Web Site
💾 Testmaker

A **Active Reading**

CONNECT Ask students to think of something special they learned from a grandparent or another older person. Have volunteers share their answers with the class.

B **Critical Thinking**

INFERRING Explain to students that they can conclude something about the grandmother's character from the speaker's description of what she says and does. Ask them how they would describe her. *(She's affectionate, [soothing him] and fun-loving [singing to and dancing with chairs].)*

C **Literary Elements**

IMAGERY Explain that imagery is language that creates vivid sensory impressions. Ask students whether the language is creating a vivid picture of the grandmother. *(Students will probably say that they can see the grandma dancing and twirling around the kitchen.)*

Additional Resources

📁 *Active Reading Guide,* p. 30

🎧 *Audio Library*

🎧 *Spanish Audio Library*

📁 *Spanish Summaries* p. 30

Teaching Options

CONNECTING TO OTHER SELECTIONS
For a teaching strategy that connects "In a Neighborhood in Los Angeles" to "The Scholarship Jacket," turn to page 22 in the **Theme Five Planning Guide.**

En un Barrio de Los Angeles

In a Neighborhood in Los Angeles

Francisco X. Alarcón
Translated by Francisco Aragon

el español	I learned
lo aprendí	Spanish
de mi abuela	from my grandma
mijito	*mijito*°
5 no llores	5 don't cry
me decía	she'd tell me
en las mañanas	on the mornings
cuando salían	my parents
mis padres	would leave
10 a trabajar	10 to work
en las canerías	at the fish
de pescado	canneries
mi abuela	my grandma
platicaba	would chat
15 con las sillas	15 with chairs
les cantaba	sing them
canciones	old
antiguas	songs
les bailaba	dance
20 valses en	20 waltzes with them
la cocina	in the kitchen

───────────────
4 *Mijito* (mē hē′ tō) means "my little child."

334 🦋 THEME 4

MEETING INDIVIDUAL NEEDS **ENGLISH LANGUAGE LEARNERS**

Shades of Meaning Write these words on the board: *talk, chat, whisper, sing.* Point out that all these words have similar but not quite identical meanings. Ask students to think of words in their first languages that have slightly different meanings.

Activity Have small groups fill in the following chart for as many languages as they know.

English	Spanish	French
talk	hablar	parler
chat	platicar	causer
whisper	susurrar	chuchoter
sing	cantar	chanter

Additional Resources

📁 *English Language Learners Sourcebook*

cuando decía
niño barrigón
se reía

25 con mi abuela
aprendí
a contar nubes

a reconocer
en las macetas
30 la yerbabuena

mi abuela
llevaba lunas
en el vestido

la montaña
35 el desierto
el mar de México

en sus ojos
yo las veía
en sus trenzas

40 yo los tocaba
con su voz
yo los olía

un día
me dijeron:
45 se fue muy lejos

pero yo aún
la siento
conmigo

diciéndome
50 quedito al oído
mijito

when she'd say
niño barrigón°
she'd laugh

25 with my grandma
I learned
to count clouds

to point out
in flowerpots
30 mint leaves

my grandma
wore moons
on her dress

Mexico's mountains
35 deserts
ocean

in her eyes
I'd see them
in her braids

40 I'd touch them
in her voice
smell them

one day
I was told:
45 she went far away

but still
I feel her
with me

whispering
50 in my ear
mijito

D

E

F

23 The grandmother was teasing the speaker by
calling him *niño barrigón* (nēn′ yō   bär′ rē gon′),
which means "big-bellied boy."

WHERE THE HEART IS   335

Reading *Minilesson*

Summarizing Explain to students that
poems achieve much of their power
through very careful word choice. Point out
that putting a poem into one's own words
is a good way to understand it better.

Activity Have students summarize four
or five stanzas of the poem with one sentence. Point out that in paragraph form,
the answers to the three following ques-

tions will summarize the events of the
poem. **L2**

1. What did the grandmother do when the
child's parents were at work? *(The
child's grandmother taught him Spanish
and entertained him by singing and
dancing.)*

2. What sensory impressions did the
speaker have of his grandmother? *(She
wore moons on her dress and he could*

*see, touch, and smell her memories of
Mexico.)*

3. What happened to the grandmother?
Where does the poet tell us she went?
*(The poet tells us that she went away—
probably died—but that he still feels her
with him.)*

Additional Resources

📁 *Reading Workbook,* pp. 51–52

Personal Response

Students may refer to one or more of the following images: the grandmother singing and dancing with chairs; counting clouds; her dress with moons on it; or seeing Mexico's mountains, deserts, and ocean in her eyes and in her braids.

Analyzing Literature

1. She took care of him while his parents were at work.
2. She called him *mijito* or *niño barrigón*. She would chat and dance with chairs. She taught him to count clouds and recognize mint leaves. She shared her memories of Mexico.
3. Yes, because he has such happy memories of his time with her, and he describes her as a loving, entertaining person.
4. He says his grandmother died, but he still carries her with him.
5. Many students will say he manages to make her seem real by describing specific things she said and did.
6. The details of this poem may or may not remind students of an older relative.
7. The message is that love stays forever, even after the person who loved you dies ("but still/I feel her/with me").
8. She took care of him every day, almost like a parent. She made him feel secure and loved. She introduced him to his heritage.
9. Many students will say the translator captured both the sentiment and the rhythm of the poem.
10. Possible answer: My mother would like it because it would remind her of her mother, who also came here from another country or who also liked to sing and dance around the house.

Responding to Literature

PERSONAL RESPONSE

What images from the poem linger in your mind?

Analyzing Literature

RECALL

1. Why did the speaker spend so much time with his grandmother as a child?
2. What are some special memories of his grandmother that the speaker shares with his readers?

INTERPRET

3. Do you think the speaker enjoyed being with his grandmother? Why or why not?
4. What does the speaker tell us in the last three stanzas of the poem?

EVALUATE AND CONNECT

5. How well does the poet succeed in making the grandmother in this poem seem real to you? Explain.
6. Do any of the details in this poem remind you of experiences you have had with a grandparent or another older relative? Explain.
7. What message about human relationships does this poem express? Use words from the poem to support your opinion.
8. Describe the special role the grandmother played in the speaker's life.
9. A good translator tries to put the style, meaning, and feeling of the original work into a different language. If you are bilingual in Spanish and English or can find someone who can translate each Spanish word of "En un Barrio de Los Angeles" for you, compare the two versions of the poem. Do both versions create the same feeling? Why or why not?
10. **Theme Connection** Think of someone you know who would enjoy reading this poem. Why would he or she enjoy it?

LITERARY ELEMENTS

Imagery

Imagery is language that creates vivid pictures and sensory impressions. Poets use words and phrases to create images that appeal to readers' senses. For example, in the poem "In a Neighborhood in Los Angeles," the poet uses several sensory images so that readers can visualize clearly the grandmother in the poem: "my grandma / would chat / with chairs / sing them / old / songs / dance / waltzes with them / in the kitchen." For readers, being able to "see" the grandmother talking, singing, and dancing with chairs leaves a wonderful sensory impression.

1. Pick out your favorite example of imagery in the poem and explain why you like it.
2. Select an especially effective image from another poem in this book and tell how details helped you to visualize the image.

● See **Literary Terms Handbook**, p. R5.

LITERARY ELEMENTS

1. Possible answer: I liked the final image of the grandmother whispering *mijito* in the poet's ear because it's comforting.
2. Possible answer: In "Slam, Dunk & Hook" images like *bug-eyed, lanky, all hands & feet* and *our bodies spun on swivels of bone & faith* helped me visualize the players.

Additional Resources

 Literary Elements Transparency 30

Extending Your Response

Writing About Literature
Character Sketch In this poem, the speaker describes his grandmother and the special relationship he shared with her. Write a paragraph describing how you picture the grandmother.

Creative Writing
Poem Write a short poem about a person who is, or was, important in your life. As a starting point, you may want to look back at the list you created in the **Focus Activity** on page 333. Use vivid images to describe the special nature of the relationship you and this person have shared together.

Performing
Tableau Select a dramatic moment from this poem. With a partner, create a tableau of that moment by getting into, freezing, and holding the exact pose of the characters in that scene. Choose a third person to tap each character one at a time. As each character is tapped, that person comes to life and speaks and acts just as that character would in the poem.

Literature Groups

Vivid Descriptions To the speaker of "In a Neighborhood in Los Angeles," time spent with his grandmother was an unforgettable part of his childhood. Pick out one or more descriptions that focus on the special nature of the speaker's relationship with his grandmother. Discuss how the descriptions explain the importance of the relationship. Then talk about why older people can be important in the lives of young people.

Reading Further
For more poetry, try these books:

Imaginary Gardens: American Poetry and Art for Young People edited by Charles Sullivan

Tortillitas Para Mamma: and Other Spanish Nursery Rhymes by Margot C. Griego

📖 **Save your work for your portfolio.**

Skill Minilesson

READING AND THINKING • DRAWING CONCLUSIONS

As a skillful reader, you should always ask questions about what you read. Evaluate the characters, actions, and events. By using the details and the information in a piece of writing, you can draw conclusions that will help you understand the story or the poem.

● For more about drawing conclusions, see **Reading Handbook,** pp. R89 and R100.

PRACTICE Reread "In a Neighborhood in Los Angeles." As you do, pay attention to the details and images that Alarcón includes about the speaker's special experiences with his grandmother. In a short paragraph, use the clues in the poem to help you draw your own conclusions about the speaker's feelings about his grandmother's death.

Extending Your Response

Writing About Literature
Students' character sketches should
- include sensory details.
- create mental pictures for readers.
- go beyond the information in the poem, adding new details they think would go with this character.

Creative Writing
Students' poems should
- make readers feel they know the person described.
- give reasons why the writer loves the person.

Performing Encourage students to spend time rehearsing their tableaux. If possible, videotape each group's performance and make tapes available for the class to view later.

Literature Groups Remind students to concentrate on the relationship between the speaker and his grandmother. **COLLAB. LEARN.**

Skill Minilesson

READING AND THINKING
- DRAWING CONCLUSIONS

Students' paragraphs should
- recognize that the speaker loved his grandmother and missed her when she died.
- cite specifics in the poem that support their conclusions.
- draw on their own experiences to support their conclusions.

Additional Resources
📁 *Reading Workbook,* pp. 51–52

✔ ASSESSMENT OPTIONS

📁 *Quick Checks,* p. 30
📁 *Selection and Theme Assessment,* p. 54
📁 *Performance Assessment,* p. 29
💾 *Testmaker*

Technology Skills

Objectives

- To recognize reliable information posted on Internet sites
- To examine a site's credibility
- To separate fact from opinion when gathering information from Internet sites

Teaching Strategies

Walk students through the process of logging onto Web sites and model your thinking as you examine each site and form a judgment of it. For example: "This site looks interesting, but everyone on it belongs to the same organization. Their opinions may be interesting—but I'm only going to get one viewpoint." You may want to visit the sites of a news organization, a government agency, and a university. You can use such leading questions as How reliable is the information on this site? and What makes you think so? to prompt students judgments.

Adapting to Available Technology

If the number of computers available is limited, have students work in small groups to perform the Practice. Each group member can select one site to visit, which all group members can then scrutinize for examples of fact and opinion.

Teaching Options

Internet: Judging On-Line Information

It's sometimes difficult to determine fact from opinion. A fact is a statement that can be supported by evidence. An opinion, on the other hand, represents a personal viewpoint, one that really can't be proved. When an opinion is stated strongly, it might be hard to recognize it for what it is: only one point of view.

Because the Internet is based on the free exchange of ideas, anyone can write and publish anything. It's up to you to decide whether a posting is fact or opinion. Remember: something isn't true just because you read about it on the Internet.

Fact or Opinion?

With a partner, decide which of the following statements are facts and which are opinions. How can you tell? Discuss your answers with the rest of the class.

1. Chickadee Net is a fun place for kids.
2. Owl Kids Online won the 1997 Internet Impact Award.
3. There will be 20.9 million kids on-line by the year 2002.
4. Kids go on-line to learn and have fun.
5. As the Internet becomes more user-friendly and accessible to the public at large, the number of schools and homes going on-line continues to grow.
6. SafeTeens.com is a site dedicated to keeping teens safe in cyberspace.
7. As of today, less than one percent of kids access the Internet from school.
8. The Internet can be viewed as one giant encyclopedia, but one important difference is obvious: the bulk of the Internet is written by unreliable sources.
9. The *Cool Site of the Day* crew selects an outstanding Web site each day of the year.
10. This slick Webzine with neon-bright, pop-art graphics dishes the best daily buzz about the alternative-music scene.

How Can You Tell?

One way to determine whether something you read on the Internet is true is to look for the name of the author. Is it someone whose name you recognize as an authority on the topic? An article about the movies written by a well-known movie reviewer, for example, is more believable than one written by someone you've never heard of. (Remember, however, that people you've never heard of may be experts in their fields.)

Another clue lies in the site's host. Information found at university or government sites can often be verified, whereas statements posted on Internet service providers may be difficult to confirm. You can tell a university sponsors a site

---

INDIVIDUAL MEETING NEEDS **INCLUSION STRATEGIES**

Less-Proficient Readers Some students need help distinguishing fact from opinion.

Activity Before students begin reading material on Web sites, help less-proficient readers learn to distinguish between facts and opinions.

Fact or Opinion?
- Statements that begin "I think" or "I feel" are statements of opinion.
- Statements that include statistics or figures are usually statements of fact (although the facts may be incorrect).
- Descriptive words—*beautiful, terrible, wonderful, impressive*—usually indicate opinions.

Additional Resources
📁 *Inclusion Strategies*

because the URL (Net address) ends with an *.edu* extension. Similarly, government sites end with *.gov.* Of course, just because something is posted from a college's Web site doesn't automatically make it true.

You can also determine the truthfulness of a posting if statements are backed up with sources. Sources may be noted directly in the text, in parentheses, or in hyperlinks. If the reference is hyperlinked, you can go to the original document to see for yourself whether the statement is a fact.

In many cases, time may be a factor in determining how accurate something is. An article about the current state of the Internet, for example, wouldn't be very reliable if it was posted three years ago. Look for information about when the document was published or last revised. (Such information, if it's given, usually comes at the beginning or the end of a site's home page.)

In many cases, you will have to rely on your own judgment. As you examine information on the Web, always ask yourself: Is this a fact or an opinion? Don't be misled because you agree totally with what an author says. Sharing an author's opinion doesn't make that opinion a fact.

On the other hand, don't think that a Web document is useless just because it contains someone's opinions. Very often, opinions are just what you want. You read editorials and essays for their authors' opinions. Reviews of books, movies, plays, and CDs can help you decide whether to spend your time and money on something. It's when opinions are based on faulty reasoning or prejudice that we need to mistrust them.

Practice

1. Log on to the World Wide Web.

2. Browse through at least five sites that interest you. Look for examples of fact and opinion.

3. For each site, determine how believable the information offered is. Write down the name and URL of the site and the criteria you use to determine whether it is trustworthy.

4. Share your findings in a class-wide discussion.

ACTIVITIES

1. Start a class list of sites divided into *Mostly Fact* and *Mostly Opinion* categories. Add to the list as you discover new sites.

2. In your journal, keep a list of questionable "facts" you find on the Internet.

3. Write a letter to the editor of your school newspaper or to a Web site that accepts student contributions. In your letter, emphasize the importance of not believing everything you read. Include examples from your own research.

 TECHNOLOGY TIP

A good way to avoid misinformation on the Internet is to keep the addresses of sites you've found trustworthy in your favorites folder (or as bookmarks if you use a Mac). Here are a few sites you might find useful. For news, try *Time* for Kids (pathfinder.com/TFK) and Yahooligans! News (www.yahooligans.com/content/news). For science topics, visit Discovery News Online (www.discovery.com/online). The National Geographic site (www.nationalgeographic.com) is useful for science and social studies topics. Yak's Corner (www.yakscorner.com) covers a variety of topics of interest to teens. Most of these sites also include some fun activities or games.

Activities

Suggest that students ask themselves these questions to recognize bias:
- Is the choice of words meant to influence my opinion?
- Is the material meant to be humorous or sarcastic?
- Is the writer trying to get me to take a particular action or buy something?

Students letters should
- clearly state an opinion.
- contain examples from Internet sites to support the opinion.
- offer a strong conclusion.

 TechnoTalk

Playful Terms Do you like to *surf the Net,* explore *cyberspace,* or play *virtual reality* games? These terms describe new activities, but each has its origin in old terms. *Surfing the Net* comes from the phrase *channel surfing*—which in turn comes from the activity of *surfing,* riding a wave. The word *cyberspace* was first used by William Gibson in his 1984 science fiction novel *Neuromancer.* The term comes from the word part *cyber-,* which refers to computers. *Virtual* is an old term that refers to anything that does not physically exist. *Virtual reality,* however, is a new term, referring to a computer world that does not exist in the physical world.

 inter*NET* CONNECTION

Research on the Net Invite students to use a search engine to locate a Web site for each different type of organization they are interested in. Internet addresses, URLs (Uniform Resource Locators), can end in *.com* (commercial), *.gov* (government), *.org* (nonprofit organization), *.net* (network), *.mil* (military), or *.edu* (educational institution).

Objectives

- To read and analyze two poems about mothers
- To identify figurative language in poetry
- To write an analysis of parents' roles

Skills

Reading/Thinking: Evaluating; Drawing Conclusions; Visualizing
Writing: Advice Column
Grammar/Language: Verb Tenses
Listening/Speaking: Reading Orally and Listening Effectively to Poetry
Collaboration: Literature Groups

Motivating

→OPTIONS

Selection Focus Transparency 31: Have students view and discuss the quote about poetry from Mark Strand.

Focus Activity: As an extension of the Focus Activity, have pairs of students share their ideas about the nonmaterial gifts parents give their children.

Before You Read
The Courage That My Mother Had and *Mother to Son*

MEET EDNA ST. VINCENT MILLAY

Edna St. Vincent Millay dreamed of becoming a pianist, but the Pulitzer Prize–winning poet focused her energies on writing. Millay wrote not only poetry, but also dramatic works, and even librettos for operas.

Edna St. Vincent Millay was born in Maine in 1892 and died in New York in 1950.

MEET LANGSTON HUGHES

During his career, Langston Hughes worked as a cook, busboy, seaman, reporter, and teacher. He produced poetry, novels, collections of short stories, works of nonfiction, plays, and nine children's books.

Langston Hughes was born in Joplin, Missouri, in 1902. He died in 1967 in New York City. "Mother to Son" appeared in his 1932 book The Dream Keeper and Other Poems.

FOCUS ACTIVITY

What important kinds of nonmaterial "gifts," such as love and confidence, do parents try to give to their children?

Sharing Ideas

In small groups, talk about the many nonmaterial gifts that parents give to their children. Put together a list of these gifts. Why are they important?

Setting a Purpose

Reading these poems might help you to discover the kinds of gifts parents can give their children.

BACKGROUND

Did You Know? Edna St. Vincent Millay and Langston Hughes shared some interesting similarities in their lives. Both came from single-parent homes. Both began writing poetry early. Millay saw her first verses published at age fourteen. Hughes had poems published in his high school's monthly magazine. Each later published one poem that made the critics take notice. Millay's breakthrough came with "Renascence," which she entered in a poetry contest at age twenty. Hughes began attracting attention after publishing "The Negro Speaks of Rivers" at age nineteen.

Each poet attended college, traveled a great deal overseas, lived for a time in Paris, and settled in New York City—Millay downtown in Greenwich Village, Hughes uptown in Harlem. Both were interested in the theater. Millay wrote a verse play and joined a theater company as an actress. Hughes wrote a play that had a successful run on Broadway. Both poets also wrote texts for operas.

In addition, the two poets worked all their adult lives for causes that were important to them—Millay for women's rights and Hughes for the rights of African Americans.

RESOURCE MANAGER

Lesson Planning Resource
The ***Theme Four Planning Guide*** (pp. 16–21) provides additional lesson notes and reduced versions of all print resources.

📁 **Other Print Resources**
- Active Reading Guide, p. 31
- Reading Workbook, pp. 53–54
- Grammar and Language Workbook, pp. 83–86
- Grammar and Composition Handbook, Lesson 3.5

- Quick Checks, p. 31
- Selection and Theme Assessment, pp. 55–56
- Performance Assessment, p. 30
- Spanish Summaries, p. 31
- Spanish Translations
- Inclusion Strategies
- English Language Learners Sourcebook

🖐 **Transparencies**
- Selection Focus 31

- Literary Elements 31
- Grammar and Language 28

Technology
🎧 Audio Library
🎧 Spanish Audio Library
💻 Glencoe Literature Web Site
💾 Testmaker

The Courage That My Mother Had

Edna St. Vincent Millay

The courage that my mother had
Went with her, and is with her still:
Rock from New England quarried;°
Now granite in a granite hill.

5   The golden brooch° my mother wore
She left behind for me to wear;
I have no thing I treasure more:
Yet, it is something I could spare.

Oh, if instead she'd left to me
10 The thing she took into the grave!—
That courage like a rock, which she
Has no more need of, and I have.

3 **quarry:** to cut or blast rock from the earth for use in construction.

5 **brooch:** a piece of jewelry fastened by a clasp; an ornamental pin worn on clothing.

The Way It Is (detail). GG Kopilak. Private collection. Do you think the artist has captured in this woman's face the quality that Millay speaks of in her poem? Why or why not?

Reading the Selection

A Active Reading

PREDICT Have students use the title to predict what the poem will reveal about the main character. Have them verify or revise their predictions after reading the poem.

VIEWING THE PAINTING

Viewing Response *The woman's face is careworn. Her gaze, although somewhat sad, is direct, and she seems resolute.*

B Critical Thinking

EVALUATING Ask students whether they agree that the speaker hasn't inherited her mother's courage. *(Students may say that by observing her mother live courageously, she may have become brave herself.)*

Additional Resources

📁 *Active Reading Guide,* p. 31

🎧 *Audio Library*

🎧 *Spanish Audio Library*

📁 *Spanish Summaries,* p. 31

Teaching Options

MEETING INDIVIDUAL NEEDS

ENGLISH LANGUAGE LEARNERS

Building Fluency Have English language learners discuss what the poem means to them. Does the speaker's mother remind them of their own mothers or grandmothers? Which kinds of courage are most valued in their native cultures? Give some examples: the courage to climb a mountain, to go through childbirth, or to be true to oneself.

Activity Pair students who need to build fluency in English with those who have strong oral language skills. Invite students to tape-record their thoughts about the poem and its relevance to their native cultures.

Additional Resources

📁 *English Language Learners Sourcebook*

342   THEME 4

C   Literary Elements

FIGURATIVE LANGUAGE: *Metaphor*
This entire poem is a metaphor. The stairway is life. Ask students where that metaphor is spelled out. *(It is spelled out in lines 2 and 20: Life for me ain't been no crystal stair.)*

D   Literary Elements

DIALECT Hughes gave this dialect to the speaker to show that she had little formal education, yet he clearly believed she had the eye and the soul of a poet.

E   Critical Thinking

DRAWING CONCLUSIONS Is the mother's advice encouraging? *(It is encouraging because she's had a hard life but has prevailed.)*

LITERATURE & HUMANITIES

Show students the photograph *Ophelia, Nashville,* from the *National Music of Women in the Arts* CD and discuss how the hardships of life are expressed in it.

Thematic Focus

Where the Heart Is Ask students what they would think and feel as either woman's child.

✓ ASSESSMENT OPTIONS

📁   *Quick Checks,* p. 31

Teaching Options

Mother to Son

Langston Hughes ～

Well, son, I'll tell you:
Life for me ain't been no crystal stair.
It's had tacks in it,
And splinters,
5   And boards torn up,
And places with no carpet on the floor—
Bare.
But all the time
I'se been a-climbin' on,
10   And reachin' landin's,
And turnin' corners,
And sometimes goin' in the dark
Where there ain't been no light.
So, boy, don't you turn back.
15   Don't you set down on the steps
'Cause you finds it kinder hard.
Don't you fall now—
For I'se still goin', honey,
I'se still climbin',
20   And life for me ain't been no crystal stair.

Survivor, 1978. Elizabeth Catlett. Linocut, 10⅞ x 9⅞ in. Armistad Research Center, Tulane University, New Orleans.

Grammar and Language *Minilesson*

Verb Tenses Write on the board *wore, wear, will wear.* Explain that these are the past, present, and future tenses of *wear.*

Activity Draw a four-column chart on the board and fill in several verbs in the first column. Have students fill in the missing tenses. **L2**

Verb	Past	Present	Future
To have	had	have/has	will have

Additional Resources

✏️   *Grammar and Language Transparency 28*

📖   *Grammar and Language Workbook,* pp. 83–86

📖   *Grammar and Composition Handbook,* Lesson 3.5

📖   *Writer's Choice,* Lesson 10.5

Responding to Literature

PERSONAL RESPONSE

Which lines from each poem did you find most memorable? Why?

Analyzing Literature

RECALL

1. In "The Courage That My Mother Had," what did the mother leave the speaker of the poem when the mother died?
2. What does the speaker of "The Courage That My Mother Had" wish she had inherited? Why?
3. What advice does the speaker give her son in "Mother to Son"?

INTERPRET

4. What two unlike things are compared in "The Courage That My Mother Had"?
5. To what does the mother in "Mother to Son" compare her life?
6. What is the **theme** of "Mother to Son"?

EVALUATE AND CONNECT

7. How can parents leave their children gifts such as courage or confidence?
8. How are the mothers in the two poems alike?

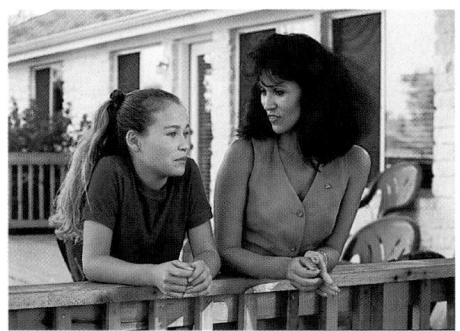

LITERARY ELEMENTS

Figurative Language

Figurative language is imaginative language used by writers for descriptive effect. Instances of figurative language are called figures of speech. A **simile** is a figure of speech that uses the words *like* or *as* to compare two seemingly unlike things. Have you ever heard someone described as being "pretty as a picture"? That's a simile. A **metaphor** is a figure of speech in which one thing is described as if it *were* another. "This test is a breeze" is a metaphor.

1. Find an example of a simile in either poem. Explain what two things are being compared and why.

2. Find an example of a metaphor in either poem. What two things are being compared? How does the metaphor enrich the poem?

● See **Literary Terms Handbook,** p. R4.

Personal Response

Example: From Millay, line 4 because the mother's courage (and the mother herself) are part of a granite hill. From Hughes, lines 18 and 19 because they show how strong this woman is and how she has never given up.

Analyzing Literature

1. She left her a golden brooch.
2. She wishes she had her mother's courage, because she needs it to get through life.
3. Don't turn back and don't fall. In other words, don't give up on life.
4. Courage (an intangible character trait) is compared to rock (very tangible, hard, unyielding granite).
5. She compares her life to a stairway that has splinters, tacks, and missing boards and is sometimes dark and uncarpeted.
6. The theme is that you have to keep trying, no matter how hard life is.
7. Parents can show their children by example how to live and thus reinforce good character traits in them.
8. Both mothers are strong, determined, and enduring.

LITERARY ELEMENTS

1. Millay: *Courage like a rock* compares the intangible quality of courage to a tangible piece of granite to emphasize the mother's bravery.
2. Hughes: Throughout the poem, life is a stairway. The metaphor shows readers how hard the mother's life has been.

Additional Resources

 Literary Elements Transparency 31

Extending Your Response

Literature Groups Remind students to discuss the reasons for any gender-specific differences.
COLLAB. LEARN.

Writing About Literature
Students' analyses should
- express a clear opinion about what parents give to children.
- connect what children hope to learn with the concept of intangible gifts.
- support their ideas with examples from the poems.

Listening and Speaking
Encourage students to practice reading the poems out loud several times before they read them to their partners. Remind them to pause when punctuation indicates it (not at the end of every line) and not to overemphasize the rhythm.

Creative Writing
Students' advice columns should
- include realistic, age-appropriate questions.
- give advice in a friendly, supportive tone that is not patronizing or judgmental.

Skill Minilesson

READING AND THINKING
- VISUALIZING

Students' sketches should
- either capture a scene the way a snapshot would or convey the scene impressionistically.
- try to hint at the experience of the other senses.

Additional Resources
📁 *Reading Workbook,* pp. 53–54

Extending Your Response

Literature Groups
Dad's Turn Suppose these two poems had been called "The Courage That My Father Had" or "Father to Son." How would these poems be similar to or different from the poems you just read? Talk about the reasons for any similarities and differences you suggest.

Writing About Literature
Poetry and Ideas Mothers play an important role in both poems. These poets believe that parents give their children many things besides shelter, food, and clothing. Do you agree or disagree? What do children hope to learn from their parents? Review your list from the **Focus Activity** on page 340. Use examples from the poems to support your ideas.

Listening and Speaking
Appreciating Poetry Most poetry should be read aloud to be fully appreciated. As a poem is read, listeners may close their eyes, picture the images, and hear the natural rhythm of the lines. With a partner, take turns reading these poems to each other.

Creative Writing
An Advice Column Has a younger brother or sister or a good friend ever asked you for advice? Do you enjoy giving people words of wisdom? Write an advice column for a school newspaper. Make up some questions that students your age might ask, and then answer the questions with advice. Your tone may be serious, humorous, or both.

Reading Further
If you would like to read more by these poets, try these books:

The Block: Poems and *Black Misery* by Langston Hughes

Collected Sonnets of Edna St. Vincent Millay

📖 **Save your work for your portfolio.**

Skill Minilesson

READING AND THINKING • VISUALIZING

When you read or listen to a poem, remember to form pictures in your mind. Pay attention to the wide range of details in the poem, and make each detail a part of your sensory experience of the poem. Keep asking yourself:
- How does this (person, place, thing) look?
- What sounds does this poem make me think of?
- How does this detail feel, smell, or taste?

PRACTICE Reread each of the poems. As you do, try to visualize the different images in each poem. Draw a sketch that shows an important image in each poem. Then write a paragraph explaining why you chose those two images.

● For more about visualizing, see **Reading Handbook,** p. R84.

✔ ASSESSMENT OPTIONS

📁 *Quick Checks,* p. 31
📁 *Selection and Theme Assessment,* pp. 55–56
📁 *Performance Assessment,* p. 30
💾 *Testmaker*

MEDIA Connection

NEWSPAPER STORY

What happens when you take a city person to the country? Sometimes, as you'll discover in this news story, the person will learn something that can be useful back in the city.

Kids from Chicago's Cabrini Green Learn Urban Farming in Arkansas

by Paisley Dodds—Associated Press, Tuesday, August 19, 1997

PERRYVILLE, Ark.—No overalls or straw hats in this crowd.

Fresh from Chicago's Cabrini Green housing complex and another development in Milwaukee, a dozen kids are visiting Arkansas to learn how to become inner-city farmers.

Growing cucumbers may keep 16-year-old Helen Marshbanks from joining a gang. Raising catfish under an apartment window sill may put more food on the table for the family of 14-year-old Darius Moore.

For 19-year-old Eric Brown, urban farming is a "cool" complement to playing basketball and watching television. "I want to be a writer when I grow up," Brown said. "But this thing, yeah, it's been real cool."

"For me, doing these kinds of projects has kept me out of trouble and out of gangs that are in my neighborhood," Marshbanks said Monday.

All are at a four-day, inner-city farming seminar at the Heifer International Project, an international grassroots organization.

The seminar, held on Heifer's 1,100-acre ranch in central Arkansas, provides some of the budding farmers their first time out of the city. They stay at the "Heifer Hilton"—a barn that sleeps about two dozen.

The seminar aims to show how to boost inner-city crops and expand into rooftop beekeeping, catfish harvesting, worm composting, goat-cheese making, and organic farming.

"We feel really good about doing this," Moore said. "There are a lot of people who can't afford things in our neighborhood. I think when people see what we're doing, they'll want to get involved too."

Learning professional techniques could help the gardening projects already running and encourage donors to keep them afloat, Marshbanks said.

"We can see what a difference it's made in our neighborhood," she said. "It makes people happy."

Respond

1. What kinds of skills will city kids learn from the Heifer International Project?

2. Suppose a similar project brought country kids to the city. What might they learn that would be helpful back on the farm?

MEDIA Connection

Objective

• To read and understand a newspaper story

Literature LINK

Antaeus This newspaper story connects to "Antaeus" (pp. 347–356). Point out to students that the urban children described in the newspaper story, who visit the Heifer ranch in Arkansas every summer, learn surprising lessons about how to farm in the city. T. J., the main character in "Antaeus," moves from the country to the city and teaches his new friends how to farm on the rooftop of a building.

Respond

1. Responses might include growing cucumbers, raising catfish under a window sill, rooftop beekeeping, worm composting, goat-cheese making, and organic farming.

2. Some students may say they would learn about different foods, cultures, and languages, which is helpful no matter where a person lives; others may think of things that are fun or interesting to learn, like street games.

Additional Resources
📁 *Media Connections*

Teaching Options

Urban Farming Have students use a search engine to find information on urban farming projects. Suggest they enter the keywords *organic farming* and *city farming*.

Reading Minilesson

Skimming Even before students read a story or text, they should be able to predict certain things about the story by observing its format.

Activity Have students look at the newspaper story in their books and practice finding information "at a glance." Ask them to list all the relevant information they can about the story by skimming it quickly, looking for specific words or phrases that will give them an overview of the story. **L2**

Additional Resources
📁 *Reading Workbook*

interNET CONNECTION

Objectives

- To read and analyze a short story about boys who create a roof garden
- To identify an allusion in a short story
- To write a character review

Skills

Reading/Thinking: Drawing Conclusions; Identifying Main Idea and Supporting Details; Synthesizing; Analyzing Arguments; Inferring; Stereotype
Writing: Character Description; Epilogue
Vocabulary: Analogies
Grammar/Language: Adjectives; Commas in Compound Sentences
Listening/Speaking: Readers' Theater
Life Skills: Organizing; Proposal
Collaboration: Literature Groups; Interdisciplinary Activity

Motivating

→OPTIONS

Selection Focus Transparency 32: Have students view and discuss *Hercules Strangling Antaeus*, a sculpture by Antonio Pollaiuolo.

Focus Activity: As an extension of the Focus Activity, have pairs of students share memorable experiences they have had outdoors.

Before You Read
Antaeus

MEET BORDEN DEAL

The son of Mississippi farmers, Borden Deal explored the places of his childhood again and again in his writings. A prize-winning author, Deal wrote several novels and over one hundred short stories. The central themes running through much of Deal's work are the search for identity as well as the need for land of one's own. His story "Antaeus" focuses on both of these themes.

Borden Deal was born in 1922 in Mississippi. He died in Florida in 1985.

FOCUS ACTIVITY

Do you feel a special bond to the world of nature? Do you enjoy hiking, gardening, or walking in the park?

Sharing Ideas
In small groups, talk about why many people need to feel connected in some way to nature. Make a list of ways that people of all ages enjoy the outdoors.

Setting a Purpose
Read to discover how some city boys learn about being connected to the land.

BACKGROUND

The Time and Place The setting of this story is a northern city in the United States, sometime during World War II.

Did You Know? The title "Antaeus" refers to the name of a mighty wrestler from Greek mythology. Antaeus was a son of Gaia (jē′ ə), the goddess of the earth. His enormous strength came from contact with the earth, and he remained unbeatable as long as his feet touched the ground. The Greek hero Hercules learned of the source of Antaeus's strength and defeated him by lifting him off the ground.

VOCABULARY PREVIEW

robust (rō bust′) *adj.* strong and full of energy; p. 348
resolute (rez′ ə lo͞ot′) *adj.* determined; stubborn; p. 348
obscure (əb skyoor′) *adj.* difficult to understand; p. 350
awe (ô) *n.* wonder combined with respect; p. 351
inert (i nurt′) *adj.* without power to move or act; p. 352
bravado (brə vä′ dō) *n.* a false show of bravery; p. 353
principle (prin′ sə pəl) *n.* a basic law, truth, or belief; rule of personal conduct; p. 354
flourishing (flur′ ish ing) *adj.* growing or developing successfully; doing very well; p. 354
nurture (nur′ chər) *v.* to care for and help grow; p. 356

RESOURCE MANAGER

Lesson Planning Resource
The *Theme Four Planning Guide* (pp. 22–29) provides additional lesson notes and reduced versions of all print resources.

📁 **Other Print Resources**
- Active Reading Guide, p. 32
- Vocabulary Practice, p. 20
- Reading Workbook, pp. 55–56
- Grammar and Language Workbook pp. 117–118, 257–258

- Grammar and Composition Handbook, Lessons 5.1, 13.3
- Quick Checks, p. 32
- Selection and Theme Assessment, pp. 57–58
- Performance Assessment, p. 31
- Spanish Summaries, p. 32
- Spanish Translations
- Inclusion Strategies
- English Language Learners Sourcebook

 Transparencies
- Selection Focus 32
- Fine Art 3
- Literary Elements 32
- Grammar and Language 29

Technology
 Audio Library
 Spanish Audio Library
 Glencoe Literature Web Site
🖥 Testmaker

Antaeus

Borden Deal ⁓

This was during the wartime, when lots of people were coming North for jobs in factories and war industries,[1] when people moved around a lot more than they do now, and sometimes kids were thrown into new groups and new lives that were completely different from anything they had ever known before. I remember this one kid, T. J. his name was, from somewhere down South, whose family moved into our building during that time. They'd come North with everything they owned piled into the back seat of an old-model sedan that you wouldn't expect could make the trip, with T. J. and his three younger sisters riding shakily on top of the load of junk.

Our building was just like all the others there, with families crowded into a few rooms, and I guess there were twenty-five or thirty kids about my age in that one building. Of course, there were a few of us who formed a gang and ran together all the time after school, and I was the one who brought T. J. in and started the whole thing.

---

1. *[war industries]* During World War II (1939–1945), many U.S. industries switched from making consumer goods to producing weapons and equipment for the military.

SUMMARY

T. J., a boy from rural Alabama, moves to a northern city with his family. He meets a boy his age who takes him to the roof of a factory where he and his friends hang out. T. J. soon convinces the boys to haul dirt to the roof and create a roof garden. When the owner of the factory discovers the garden, he orders his men to get rid of it. T. J. decides to shovel off the earth himself rather than let the men touch it, and the other boys help. T. J. then runs away. The police find him two weeks later, heading South.

📁 *Spanish Summaries,* p. 32

A Active Reading

PREDICT Have students use the title and text clues from the first paragraph to predict what they think the conflict in the story might be. Suggest that students periodically revisit their predictions as they read to verify or revise them.

Additional Resources

📁 *Active Reading Guide,* p. 32

🎧 *Audio Library*

🎧 *Spanish Audio Library*

Teaching Options

CONNECTING TO OTHER SELECTIONS

The chart at the right shows three ways to connect "Antaeus" to other selections in this book.

For specific teaching strategies, see the *Theme Four Planning Guide,* pages 25–26.

Connection	Title
Life Skills: Planning and Designing	→ "Icarus and Daedalus," p. 737
Thematic: Rebellion	→ "I'll Walk the Tightrope," p. 231
Literary: Setting	→ "Rikki-tikki-tavi," p. 789

VISUALIZE Ask students to visualize the factory building, the buildings around it, and the place where the boys meet. You might suggest that they use the author's details to draw sketches of the area.

C Active Reading

CONNECT Encourage students to remember a time they moved to a new town or school, met new friends, or simply found themselves in a new situation. Ask students whether they think T. J. feels awkward meeting the rest of the gang. *(T. J. feels confident and doesn't seem to be nervous about meeting this new bunch.)*

D Author's Craft

DIALECT Explain that dialect is a language variation spoken by a particular group, often within a particular region. Ask students why they think the author is using dialect to introduce T. J. *(The author presents dialect words and grammar to show how different T. J. is from the others and how his strength may come from his Alabama roots.)*

Teaching Options

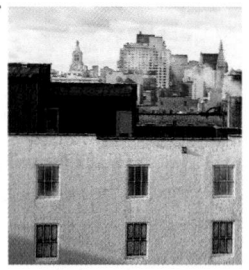

Did You Know?
A *parapet* is a low, protective wall along the edge of a roof or balcony.

The building right next door to us was a factory where they made walking dolls. It was a low building with a flat, tarred roof that had a parapet all around it about head-high, and we'd found out a long time before that no one, not even the watchman, paid any attention to the roof because it was higher than any of the other buildings around. So my gang used the roof as a headquarters. We could get up there by crossing over to the fire escape from our own roof on a plank and then going on up. It was a secret place for us, where nobody else could go without our permission.

I remember the day I first took T. J. up there to meet the gang. He was a stocky, robust kid with a shock of white hair, nothing sissy about him except his voice; he talked in this slow, gentle voice like you never heard before. He talked different from any of us and you noticed it right away. But I liked him anyway, so I told him to come on up.

We climbed up over the parapet and dropped down on the roof. The rest of the gang were already there.

"Hi," I said. I jerked my thumb at T. J. "He just moved into the building yesterday."

He just stood there, not scared or anything, just looking, like the first time you see somebody you're not sure you're going to like.

"Hi," Blackie said. "Where are you from?"

"Marion County," T. J. said.

We laughed. "Marion County?" I said. "Where's that?"

He looked at me for a moment like I was a stranger, too. "It's in Alabama," he said, like I ought to know where it was.

"What's your name?" Charley said.

"T. J.," he said, looking back at him. He had pale blue eyes that looked washed-out, but he looked directly at Charley, waiting for his reaction. He'll be all right, I thought. No sissy in him, except that voice. Who ever talked like that?

"T. J.," Blackie said. "That's just initials. What's your real name? Nobody in the world has just initials."

"I do," he said. "And they're T. J. That's all the name I got."

His voice was resolute with the knowledge of his rightness, and for a moment no one had anything to say. T. J. looked around at the rooftop and down at the black tar under his feet. "Down yonder where I come from," he said, "we played out in the woods. Don't you-all have no woods around here?"

"Naw," Blackie said. "There's the park a few blocks over, but it's full of kids and cops and old women. You can't do a thing."

T. J. kept looking at the tar under his feet. "You mean you ain't got no fields to raise nothing in? . . . no watermelons or nothing?"

Vocabulary
robust (rō bust') *adj.* strong and full of energy
resolute (rez' ə lōōt') *adj.* determined; stubborn

348

Dialogue That Mimics Speech
Write the following on the board: *"Naw," Blackie said. "There's the park a few blocks over, but it's full of kids and cops and old women. You can't do a thing."* Students may find it easier to understand dialogue that mimics speech if they hear it read aloud with expression and intonation.

Activity Pair English language learners with students proficient in English. Have partners read the dialogue aloud and substitute familiar language. Encourage students to record unfamiliar words and substitutions in their vocabulary notebooks.

Additional Resources
📁 *English Language Learners Sourcebook*

Early New York Evening, 1954. Jane Freilicher. Oil on canvas, 51½ x 31¾ in. Private collection. Courtesy Tibor de Nagy Gallery, New York.

Viewing the painting: How does putting a few flowers on a window sill compare with T. J.'s need for plant life?

349

VIEWING THE PAINTING

Born in Brooklyn in 1924, Jane Freilicher grew up, studied art, and worked in New York, remaining a realist through an era when most of her contemporaries embraced abstract expressionism. Her landscapes and cityscapes use or adapt real scenes to express personal emotion or vision.

Viewing Response *Some students might say that it expresses a similar but less intense need than T. J.'s.*

Historical Note

When men left the workforce to join the military during World War II, women were called on to enter their jobs. In 1943, Norman Rockwell created the character Rosie the Riveter in an illustration that pays tribute to the six million women who worked in the factories producing war goods and other items.

Writing *Minilesson*

Describing a Character Explain that a writer can describe a person by showing how the person looks and acts. Read aloud the physical descriptions of T. J. on page 348 and have students identify the details that help them "see" T. J. Ask students to note also phrases that describe T. J.'s actions and reactions.

Activity Invite each student to write a short description of a favorite celebrity (athlete, movie actor, or musical performer) and to use words and phrases that show how the person looks and how the person acts toward his or her fans. **L2**

Additional Resources

📗 *Writer's Choice,* Lesson 3.5

"Naw," I said scornfully. "What do you want to grow something for? The folks can buy everything they need at the store."

He looked at me again with that strange, unknowing look. "In Marion County," he said, "I had my own acre of cotton and my own acre of corn. It was mine to plant and make ever' year."

He sounded like it was something to be proud of, and in some obscure way it made the rest of us angry. Blackie said, "Who'd want to have their own acre of cotton and corn? That's just work. What can you do with an acre of cotton and corn?"

T. J. looked at him. "Well, you get part of the bale offen[2] your acre," he said seriously. "And I fed my acre of corn to my calf."

We didn't really know what he was talking about, so we were more puzzled than angry; otherwise, I guess, we'd have chased him off the roof and wouldn't let him be part of our gang. But he was strange and different, and we were all attracted by his stolid[3] sense of rightness and belonging, maybe by the strange softness of his voice contrasting our own tones of speech into harshness.

He moved his foot against the black tar. "We could make our own field right here," he said softly, thoughtfully. "Come spring we could raise us what we want to—watermelons and garden truck[4] and no telling what all."

"You'd have to be a good farmer to make these tar roofs grow any watermelons," I said. We all laughed.

But T. J. looked serious. "We could haul us some dirt up here," he said. "And spread it out even and water it, and before you know it, we'd have us a crop in here." He looked at us intently. "Wouldn't that be fun?"

"They wouldn't let us," Blackie said quickly.

"I thought you said this was you-all's roof," T. J. said to me. "That you-all could do anything you wanted to up here."

"They've never bothered us," I said. I felt the idea beginning to catch fire in me. It was a big idea, and it took a while for it to sink in; but the more I thought about it, the better I liked it. "Say," I said to the gang. "He might have something there. Just make us a regular roof garden, with flowers and grass and trees and everything. And all ours, too," I said. "We wouldn't let anybody up here except the ones we wanted to."

"It'd take a while to grow trees," T. J. said quickly, but we weren't paying any attention to him. They were all talking about it suddenly, all excited with the idea after I'd put it in a way they could catch hold of it. Only rich people had roof gardens, we knew, and the idea of our own private domain[5] excited them.

"We could bring it up in sacks and boxes," Blackie said. "We'd have to do it while the folks weren't paying any attention to us, for we'd have to come up to the

---

2. *[offen]* This is an informal way of saying *off of.* T. J. is describing the situation of a sharecropper, who farms land owned by someone else and shares the crop or the profit from its sale with the landowner.
3. *Stolid* means "firm and unemotional."
4. Here, *truck* refers to vegetables, especially those driven by truck from farms to markets.

5. A *domain* is the area under the rule or control of a person or group.

Vocabulary
obscure (ab skyoor′) *adj.* difficult to understand

roof of our building and then cross over with it."

"Where could we get the dirt?" somebody said worriedly.

"Out of those vacant lots over close to school," Blackie said. "Nobody'd notice if we scraped it up."

I slapped T. J. on the shoulder. "Man, you had a wonderful idea," I said, and everybody grinned at him, remembering that he had started it. "Our own private roof garden."

He grinned back. "It'll be ourn," he said. "All ourn." Then he looked thoughtful again. "Maybe I can lay my hands on some cotton seed, too. You think we could raise us some cotton?"

We'd started big projects before at one time or another, like any gang of kids, but they'd always petered out for lack of organization and direction. But this one didn't; somehow or other T. J. kept it going all through the winter months. He kept talking about the watermelons and the cotton we'd raise, come spring, and when even that wouldn't work, he'd switch around to my idea of flowers and grass and trees, though he was always honest enough to add that it'd take a while to get any trees started. He always had it on his mind, and he'd mention it in school, getting them lined up to carry dirt that afternoon, saying in a casual way that he reckoned a few more weeks ought to see the job through.

Our little area of private earth grew slowly. T. J. was smart enough to start in one corner of the building, heaping up the carried earth two or three feet thick so that we had an immediate result to look at, to contemplate with <u>awe</u>. Some of the evenings T. J. alone was carrying earth up to the building, the rest of the gang distracted by other enterprises[6] or interests, but T. J. kept plugging along on his own, and eventually we'd all come back to him again, and then our own little acre would grow more rapidly.

He was careful about the kind of dirt he'd let us carry up there, and more than once he dumped a sandy load over the parapet into the areaway below because it wasn't good enough. He found out the kinds of earth in all the vacant lots for blocks around. He'd pick it up and feel it and smell it, frozen though it was sometimes, and then he'd say it was good growing soil or it wasn't worth anything, and we'd have to go on somewhere else.

Thinking about it now, I don't see how he kept us at it. It was hard work, lugging paper sacks and boxes of dirt all the way up the stairs of our own building, keeping out of the way of the grown-ups so they wouldn't catch on to what we were doing. They probably wouldn't have cared, for they didn't pay much attention to us, but we wanted to keep it secret anyway. Then we had to go through the trap door to our roof, teeter over a plank to the fire escape, then climb two or three stories to the parapet, and drop them down onto the roof. All that for a small pile of earth that sometimes didn't seem worth the effort.

6. Here, *enterprises* means "projects or activities."

Vocabulary
awe (ô) wonder combined with respect

351

K Literary Elements

ALLUSION Point out to students that the author devotes this entire paragraph to describing the earth. Ask students how this reminds them of the mythical Antaeus. *(The life-giving features of the earth give T. J. the strength to continue living in the North.)*

L Active Reading

REVIEW Suggest that students pause at this point in the story to summarize what has happened so far. Ask students to tell the story in their own words.

VIEWING THE PAINTING

Antonio Berni (1905–1981) helped found a neorealist movement in his native Argentina. Much of his later work expresses a strong social awareness.

Responding to the painting *Many of the boys in the painting may be similar in age to those in "Antaeus," and they share the story's urban setting. However, they and their interest in soccer contrasts with the story's gang, who appear to have had no driving interest until T. J. inspired them to create a roof garden.*

New Chicago Athletic Club, 1937. Antonio Berni. Oil on canvas, 184.3 x 300.3 cm. Museum of Modern Art, New York.

Viewing the painting: In what ways do these boys seem similar to those in the story?

But T. J. kept the vision bright within us, his words shrewd and calculated[7] toward the fulfillment of his dream; and he worked harder than any of us. He seemed driven toward a goal that we couldn't see, a particular point in time that would be definitely marked by signs and wonders that only he could see.

The laborious[8] earth just lay there during the cold months, <u>inert</u> and lifeless, the clods lumpy and cold under our feet when we walked over it. But one day it rained, and afterward there was a softness in the air, and the earth was live and giving again with moisture and warmth.

That evening T. J. smelled the air, his nostrils dilating with the odor of the earth under his feet. "It's spring," he said, and there was a gladness rising in his voice that filled us all with the same feeling. "It's mighty late for it, but it's spring. I'd just about decided it wasn't never gonna get here at all."

We were all sniffing at the air, too, trying to smell it the way that T. J. did, and I can still remember the sweet odor of the earth under our feet. It was the first time in my life that spring and spring earth had meant anything to me. I looked at T. J. then, knowing in a faint way the hunger within

---

7. T. J.'s words are clever and practical *(shrewd)* and reasoned out beforehand *(calculated)*.
8. The earth is *laborious* in that getting it to the roof required difficulty and hard labor.

Vocabulary
inert (i nurt′) *adj.* without power to move or act

352

Teaching Options

Reading *Minilesson*

Identifying Main Idea and Supporting Details Sometimes listing the supporting details of a story in chart form can help students better understand the main idea.

Activity Draw the following chart on the board and fill in the main idea. Have students reread pages 351–353 and jot down the supporting details: *T. J. alone carried the dirt to the roof. T. J. chose the dirt carefully, feeling it and smelling it. T. J. smelled spring in the air. T. J. was a new Antaeus, preparing his own bed of strength. T. J. wanted to grow something, even if it was grass. T. J. taught the boys how to prepare the earth and sow the seeds.* **L2**

Main Idea	Details
T.J. is connected to the earth.	

Additional Resources

Reading Workbook, pp. 55–56

352

M him through the toilsome[9] winter months, knowing the dream that lay behind his plan. He was a new Antaeus, preparing his own bed of strength.

"Planting time," he said. "We'll have to find us some seed."

"What do we do?" Blackie said. "How do we do it?"

"First we'll have to break up the clods," T. J. said. "That won't be hard to do. Then we plant the seed, and after a while they come up. Then you got you a crop." He frowned. "But you ain't got it raised yet. You got to tend it and hoe it and take care of it, and all the time it's growing and growing, while you're awake and while you're asleep. Then you lay it by when it's growed and let it ripen, and then you got you a crop."

"There's these wholesale seed houses over on Sixth," I said. "We could probably swipe some grass seed over there."

T. J. looked at the earth. "You-all seem mighty set on raising some grass," he said. "I ain't never put no effort into that. I spent all my life trying not to raise grass."

"But it's pretty," Blackie said. "We could play on it and take sunbaths on it. Like having our own lawn. Lots of people got lawns."

"Well," T. J. said. He looked at the rest of us, hesitant for the first time. He kept on looking at us for a moment. "I did have it in mind to raise some corn and vegetables. But we'll plant grass."

He was smart. He knew where to give in. And I don't suppose it made any

difference to him, really. He just wanted to grow something, even if it was grass.

"Of course," he said. "I do think we ought to plant a row of watermelons. They'd be mighty nice to eat while we was a-laying on that grass."

We all laughed. "All right," I said. "We'll plant us a row of watermelons."

Things went very quickly then. Perhaps half the roof was covered with the earth, the half that wasn't broken by ventilators, and we swiped pocketfuls of grass seed from the open bins in the wholesale seed house, mingling among the buyers on Saturdays and during the school lunch hour. T. J. showed us how to prepare the earth, breaking up the clods and smoothing it and sowing the grass seed. It looked rich and black now with moisture, receiving of the seed, and it seemed that the grass sprang up overnight, pale green in the early spring.

We couldn't keep from looking at it, unable to believe that we had created this delicate growth. We looked at T. J. with understanding now, knowing the fulfillment of the plan he had carried alone within his mind. We had worked without full understanding of the task, but he had known all the time.

We found that we couldn't walk or play on the delicate blades, as we had expected to, but we didn't mind. It was enough just to look at it, to realize that it was the work of our own hands, and each evening, the whole gang was there, trying to measure the growth that had been achieved that day.

One time a foot was placed on the plot of ground, one time only, Blackie stepping onto it with sudden <u>bravado</u>. Then he

---

9. The months are *toilsome* (a synonym for *laborious*) in that they are difficult and tiresome.

Vocabulary
bravado (brə vä′ dō) *n.* a false show of bravery

353

Borden Deal ∾

M Literary Elements

ALLUSION Discuss with students why the author directly compares T. J. to Antaeus here. *(Antaeus got his physical strength from the earth, and T. J., too, feels connected to the earth through his love of growing things. At this point in the story, we know that T. J.'s connection gives him spiritual strength.)*

N Active Reading

VISUALIZE Encourage students to use the details the author gives them to visualize the roof garden. Suggest that they ask themselves *How does this scene look? What are the characters doing? What expressions might they have on their faces?*

O Critical Thinking

SYNTHESIZING Ask students whether they think the boys have changed. What does this paragraph reveal about them? *(The boys have grown to respect the earth, to understand the satisfaction of growing things, and to appreciate the work involved. This is revealed by the shame Blackie feels and the silence of the other boys.)*

MEETING INDIVIDUAL NEEDS — INCLUSION STRATEGIES

Learning Disabled Presenting a story visually often helps students comprehend what they read. Combine this strategy with partner reading by pairing learning-disabled students with proficient readers.

Activity Have partners read the paragraph in the first column on page 353 in which T. J. explains the steps for growing a crop. Ask students to draw simple pictures that illustrate these steps. **L1** **COLLAB. LEARN.**

Additional Resources
📁 *Inclusion Strategies*

WHERE THE HEART IS 🌿 353

Active Reading

CONNECT Ask students to think of a time when they sacrificed something to get something else they wanted.

Author's Craft

CONFLICT Point out to students that the author reveals the conflict of the story slowly, making readers wonder what the adults will do about the rooftop garden.

Active Reading

PREDICT Encourage students to stop at this point in the story and predict what will happen next. What do they think the men are going to do? What do they think the boys are going to do?

---

looked at the crushed blades and there was shame in his face. He did not do it again. This was his grass, too, and not to be desecrated.[10] No one said anything, for it was not necessary.

T. J. had reserved a small section for watermelons, and he was still trying to find some seed for it. The wholesale house didn't have any watermelon seed, and we didn't know where we could lay our hands on them. T. J. shaped the earth into mounds, ready to receive them, three mounds lying in a straight line along the edge of the grass plot.

We had just about decided that we'd have to buy the seed if we were to get them. It was a violation of our principles, but we were anxious to get the watermelons started. Somewhere or other, T. J. got his hands on a seed catalog and brought it one evening to our roof garden.

"We can order them now," he said, showing us the catalog. "Look!"

We all crowded around, looking at the fat, green watermelons pictured in full color on the pages. Some of them were split open, showing the red, tempting meat, making our mouths water.

"Now we got to scrape up some seed money," T. J. said, looking at us. "I got a quarter. How much you-all got?"

We made up a couple of dollars among us and T. J. nodded his head. "That'll be more than enough. Now we got to decide what kind to get. I think them Kleckley Sweets. What do you-all think?"

He was going into esoteric[11] matters beyond our reach. We hadn't even known there were different kinds of melons. So we just nodded our heads and agreed that yes, we thought the Kleckley Sweets too.

"I'll order them tonight," T. J. said. "We ought to have them in a few days."

"What are you boys doing up here?" an adult voice said behind us.

It startled us, for no one had ever come up here before, in all the time we had been using the roof of the factory. We jerked around and saw three men standing near the trap door at the other end of the roof. They weren't policemen, or night watchmen, but three men in plump business suits, looking at us. They walked toward us.

"What are you boys doing up here?" the one in the middle said again.

We stood still, guilt heavy among us, levied[12] by the tone of voice, and looked at the three strangers.

The men stared at the grass flourishing behind us. "What's this?" the man said. "How did this get up here?"

"Sure is growing good, ain't it?" T. J. said conversationally. "We planted it."

The men kept looking at the grass as if they didn't believe it. It was a thick carpet over the earth now, a patch of deep greenness startling in the sterile[13] industrial surroundings.

---

10. To treat something holy with disrespect is to *desecrate* (des′ ə krāt′) it.

11. *Esoteric* (es′ ə ter′ ik) matters are beyond the understanding or knowledge of most people. T. J.'s knowledge of melons and farming seems esoteric to the other boys.
12. Here, *levied* means "enforced."
13. Most often, *sterile* (ster′ əl) is used to mean free from bacteria—like a surgeon's instruments. Here, the meaning is "having little or no plant life."

Vocabulary

principle (prin′ sə pəl) *n.* a basic law, truth, or belief; rule of personal conduct
flourishing (flur′ ish ing) *adj.* growing or developing successfully; doing very well

354

Teaching Options

Listening and Speaking *Minilesson*

Readers' Theater The purpose of Readers' Theater is to suggest characters, action, and scenery so that listeners can interpret, imagine, and visualize a story. The narrator speaks to the audience and may read or explain what happens between sections of dialogue. All participants read with text in hand.

Activity Invite students to read "Antaeus" as Readers' Theater. Assign roles for all characters and one or more narrators. Ask students who are not performing to act as dialogue coaches to help partners practice reading expressively. Have students first perform for classmates. Later, students may wish to perform for other students of the same age. **L2** **COLLAB. LEARN.**

"Yes, sir," T. J. said proudly. "We toted that earth up here and planted that grass." He fluttered the seed catalog. "And we're just fixing to plant us some watermelon."

The man looked at him then, his eyes strange and faraway. "What do you mean, putting this on the roof of my building?" he said. "Do you want to go to jail?"

T. J. looked shaken. The rest of us were silent, frightened by the authority of his voice. We had grown up aware of adult authority, of policemen and night watchmen and teachers, and this man sounded like all the others. But it was a new thing to T. J.

"Well, you wasn't using the roof," T. J. said. He paused a moment and added shrewdly, "So we just thought to pretty it up a little bit."

"And sag it so I'd have to rebuild it," the man said sharply. He started turning away, saying to another man beside him, "See that all that junk is shoveled off by tomorrow."

"Yes, sir," the man said.

T. J. started forward. "You can't do that," he said. "We toted it up here, and it's our earth. We planted it and raised it and toted it up here."

The man stared at him coldly. "But it's my building," he said. "It's to be shoveled off tomorrow."

"It's our earth," T. J. said desperately. "You ain't got no right!"

The men walked on without listening and descended clumsily through the trap door. T. J. stood looking after them, his body tense with anger, until they had disappeared. They wouldn't even argue with him, wouldn't let him defend his earth rights.

He turned to us. "We won't let 'em do it," he said fiercely. "We'll stay up here all day tomorrow and the day after that, and we won't let 'em do it."

We just looked at him. We knew that there was no stopping it.

He saw it in our faces, and his face wavered for a moment before he gripped it into determination. "They ain't got no right," he said. "It's our earth. It's our land. Can't nobody touch a man's own land."

We kept looking at him, listening to the words but knowing that it was no use. The adult world had descended on us even in our richest dream, and we knew there was no calculating the adult world, no fighting it, no winning against it.

We started moving slowly toward the parapet and the fire escape, avoiding a last look at the green beauty of the earth that T. J. had planted for us, had planted deeply in our minds as well as in our experience. We filed slowly over the edge and down the steps to the plank, T. J. coming last, and all of us could feel the weight of his grief behind us.

"Wait a minute," he said suddenly, his voice harsh with the effort of calling.

We stopped and turned, held by the tone of his voice, and looked up at him standing above us on the fire escape.

"We can't stop them?" he said, looking down at us, his face strange in the dusky light. "There ain't no way to stop 'em?"

"No," Blackie said with finality.[14] "They own the building."

We stood still for a moment, looking up at T. J., caught into inaction by the decision working in his face. He stared back at us, and his face was pale and mean in the poor light, with a bald nakedness in his skin like cripples have sometimes.

---

14. Blackie speaks with decisiveness (*finality*); the issue is settled.

355

Antaeus

"They ain't gonna touch my earth," he said fiercely. "They ain't gonna lay a hand on it! Come on."

He turned around and started up the fire escape again, almost running against the effort of climbing. We followed more slowly, not knowing what he intended to do. By the time we reached him, he had seized a board and thrust it into the soil, scooping it up and flinging it over the parapet into the areaway below. He straightened and looked at us.

"They can't touch it," he said. "I won't let 'em lay a dirty hand on it!"

We saw it then. He stooped to his labor again, and we followed, the gusts of his anger moving in frenzied labor among us as we scattered along the edge of earth, scooping it and throwing it over the parapet, destroying with anger the growth we had <u>nurtured</u> with such tender care. The soil carried so laboriously upward to the light and the sun cascaded swiftly into the dark areaway, the green blades of grass crumpled and twisted in the falling.

It took less time than you would think; the task of destruction is infinitely easier than that of creation. We stopped at the end, leaving only a scattering of loose soil, and when it was finally over, a stillness stood among the group and over the factory building. We looked down at the bare sterility of black tar, felt the harsh texture of it under the soles of our shoes, and the anger had gone out of us, leaving only a sore aching in our minds, like over-stretched muscles.

T. J. stood for a moment, his breathing slowing from anger and effort, caught into the same contemplation of destruction as all of us. He stooped slowly, finally, and picked up a lonely blade of grass left trampled under our feet and put it between his teeth, tasting it, sucking the greenness out of it into his mouth. Then he started walking toward the fire escape, moving before any of us were ready to move, and disappeared over the edge.

We followed him, but he was already halfway down to the ground, going on past the board where we crossed over, climbing down into the areaway. We saw the last section swing down with his weight, and then he stood on the concrete below us, looking at the small pile of anonymous[15] earth scattered by our throwing. Then he walked across the place where we could see him and disappeared toward the street without glancing back, without looking up to see us watching him.

They did not find him for two weeks.

Then the Nashville police caught him just outside the Nashville freight yards. He was walking along the railroad track, still heading South, still heading home.

As for us, who had no remembered home to call us, none of us ever again climbed the escapeway to the roof.

---

15. The word *anonymous* has two main meanings: "of unknown authorship or origin" and "lacking personality or special features." Here, the scattered soil looks as though it could have come from anywhere. Without grass growing on it, it's just ordinary dirt.

❖

Vocabulary
nurture (nur′ chər) *v.* to care for and help grow

356

Responding to Literature

PERSONAL RESPONSE

◆ Were you surprised by the outcome of the story? Explain why or why not.

◆ Look back at your notes from the **Focus Activity** on page 346. Do any of the characters in the story connect to the world of nature in ways you discussed? Explain.

Analyzing Literature

RECALL

1. Where does the narrator take T. J. to meet his gang?
2. What does T. J. convince the gang to do?
3. Why does the narrator believe that the roof garden project did not fade away like other big projects the boys had started? Explain.
4. What happens after the roof garden is discovered? According to the narrator, where was T. J. going when he was found?

INTERPRET

5. At the beginning, how does the gang react to T. J.? What do readers learn about T. J. from his reaction to them?
6. Why do the boys become so excited by the thought of a roof garden? Explain.
7. What does the narrator mean when he says, "We were all sniffing at the air, too, trying to smell it the way that T. J. did"?
8. Why does T. J. react as he does to the discovery of the garden?

EVALUATE AND CONNECT

9. In your opinion, what was the most important thing T. J. taught the members of the gang? Explain.
10. Theme Connection   State the theme, or main idea, of "Antaeus" in a single sentence. Then write a paragraph telling how the theme of this story relates to the general theme of this group of selections.

LITERARY ELEMENTS

Allusion

An **allusion** is a reference to a well-known character, place, or situation from another work of literature, music, art, history, politics, or science. When readers recognize an allusion, it enriches their understanding of the piece of writing by making a connection between two characters, places, or situations.

1. Explain the connection between T. J. and the mythical Antaeus. Is T. J. a modern-day hero? Why or why not? Support your ideas with examples from the story.

2. In your opinion, in what ways is the story strengthened by the allusion to Greek mythology? Explain.

● See **Literary Terms Handbook,** p. R1.

WHERE THE HEART IS   357

WHERE THE HEART IS   357

Literature and Writing

Writing About Literature

Students' reviews should

- explain why they think the character does or does not seem true to life.
- give examples of how the character changes over the course of the story.
- give examples of obstacles the character has to overcome to reach his goals.

Creative Writing

Students' epilogues should

- describe clearly what action T. J. takes.
- tell when and where events take place.
- follow the writing style of the story.

Extending Your Response

Literature Groups After students talk about T. J. and before they debate, encourage them to discuss the narrator's way of life in the city.
COLLAB. LEARN.

Learning for Life Before students begin writing, encourage them to describe the lot and the neighborhood where it's located.

Interdisciplinary Activity
Provide garden books and magazines as well as gardening articles from local newspapers for student's research.

Literature and Writing

Writing About Literature

Character Review Write a paragraph or two reviewing either T. J. or the narrator. In your opinion, does this person seem true to life? Why or why not? How does the character change over the course of the story? What obstacles does the character have to overcome to reach his goals? Support your opinions with examples and quotations from the story.

Creative Writing

Epilogue What do you think happens to T. J. after the final scene in the story? An **epilogue** is a brief concluding section to a novel, a story, or a poem. Write an epilogue to "Antaeus." Your epilogue might take place weeks, months, or many years after the end of the story.

Extending Your Response

Literature Groups

Home Is Where the Heart Is Talk about T. J.'s connection to nature. What does the earth represent to him? Why does he need to create a garden in the city? Do you think T. J. could ever be happy living in a city? Debate the question: Can country people and city people ever be happy living in the other's environment? Support your ideas with examples from the story and details from your own experience.

Learning for Life

Community Garden Proposal Is there a vacant lot near your school or somewhere in your town or city? Write a proposal to convince public officials to allow you to transform the vacant lot into a community garden. Describe how important a garden would be to the neighborhood. Outline a plan to complete the project, using students and other volunteers to do the work.

Interdisciplinary Activity

Art/Science Work with classmates to create a community garden in honor of T. J.'s vision. Find out which flowers or vegetables will thrive in your location and decide which ones to include in the garden. Decide on the size of the garden, the location of the plants within the garden, and additional items such as paths, benches, and lights. Make a mural of the garden to display on a classroom wall.

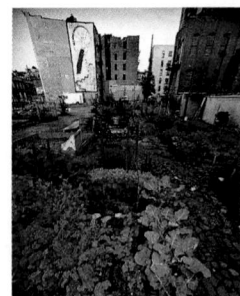

Reading Further

If you would like to read more stories about nature, try these books:
A Day No Pigs Would Die by Robert Newton Peck
The Island Keeper by Harry Mazer

💾 **Save your work for your portfolio.**

Skill Minilessons

GRAMMAR AND LANGUAGE • COMMAS IN COMPOUND SENTENCES

If the main clauses in a compound sentence are connected by a conjunction (*and, but,* or *or*), a comma should come before the conjunction.

Example: The soil was heavy, **but** the boys carried it up to the rooftop nevertheless.

PRACTICE Review "Antaeus" to find and copy two examples of compound sentences containing commas. Then write two compound sentences of your own, using commas and conjunctions correctly.

● For more about commas, see **Language Handbook,** p. R37.

READING AND THINKING • STEREOTYPE

A **stereotype** is an oversimplified or generalized opinion or prejudice about a particular group or issue. For example, someone who thinks that all Texans are either ranchers or oil drillers is using a stereotype. **Bias**—favoritism toward or against something—may lead people to use stereotypes. Stereotypes in writing can show a writer's bias. In fiction, they can show a character's bias.

PRACTICE Identify the following stereotypes from "Antaeus." Look back at the story if you need help.

1. In "Antaeus," the narrator says that there was "nothing sissy" about T. J. "except his voice." What stereotype does that comment demonstrate?
2. What stereotype do you think the man who ordered the boys off his roof had about teenagers?
3. What stereotype did the gang members probably have about grown-ups?

● For more about stereotypes, see **Literary Terms Handbook,** p. R10.

VOCABULARY • ANALOGIES: LEVELS OF INTENSITY

Analogies compare the relationships between things or ideas. One kind of analogy deals with levels of intensity. That is, the words in each pair have similar meanings, but one word is stronger, more intense, than the other.

angry : furious :: happy : overjoyed

Angry and *furious* are similar in meaning, and so are *happy* and *overjoyed.* But in each pair, the second word describes a feeling that is more intense than the first word suggests. Someone who is extremely *angry* is *furious,* just as someone who is extremely *happy* is *overjoyed.*

To finish an analogy, think of the relationship between the first pair of words. Then find another pair of words that have the same relationship.

PRACTICE Complete each analogy.
1. surviving : flourishing ::
   a. thankful : grateful
   b. sad : lonely
   c. cautious : careless
   d. large : old
   e. damp : soaked
2. well : robust ::
   a. wrong : mistaken
   b. weak : small
   c. pretty : beautiful
   d. poetic : musical
   e. muscular : healthy

● For more about analogies, see **Communications Skills Handbook,** p. R65.

Skill Minilessons

GRAMMAR AND LANGUAGE
COMMAS IN COMPOUND SENTENCES

Examples of compound sentences:
- "His voice was resolute with the knowledge of his rightness, and for a moment no one had anything to say."
- "We had worked without full understanding of the task, but he had known all the time."

READING AND THINKING
STEREOTYPE

1. The narrator assumes that all boys should be tough and that a southern accent is not tough.
2. The man probably assumed that all teenagers are troublemakers.
3. The gang members probably believed that all grown-ups exercise their authority over younger people without real cause.

VOCABULARY
ANALOGIES: LEVELS OF INTENSITY

1. e
2. c

Additional Resources

 Grammar and Language Workbook, pp. 257–258

Grammar and Composition Handbook, Lesson 13.3

Writer's Choice, Lessons 20.3

 Reading Workbook, pp. 55–56

Vocabulary Practice, p. 20

✔ ASSESSMENT OPTIONS

📁 *Quick Checks,* p. 32
📁 *Selection and Theme Assessment,* pp. 57–58
📁 *Performance Assessment,* p. 31
💾 *Testmaker*

Before Reading

Objectives
- To read and analyze a short story and a poem about home
- To identify the themes in a short story and a poem
- To write a paragraph or two explaining what the dialogue reveals about the characters

Skills

Reading/Thinking: Evaluating; Identifying Main Idea and Supporting Details; Inferring; Drawing Conclusions
Writing: One-Act Play
Vocabulary: Words Used in Unusual Ways
Grammar/Language: Possessive Nouns
Life Skills: Writing Persuasive Memos
Collaboration: Literature Groups

Motivating
→ OPTIONS

Selection Focus Transparency 33: Read aloud John Howard Payne's quotation about home and ask students to discuss what they think Payne means.

Focus Activity: As an extension of the Focus Activity, have students work with the same partners to create song lyrics about home.

Before You Read
Home and *the 1st*

MEET GWENDOLYN BROOKS

Gwendolyn Brooks's advice to young poets is "Tell your truth. Don't try to sugar it up." In 1950 Brooks became the first African American author to win the Pulitzer Prize for Poetry.

Gwendolyn Brooks was born in Kansas in 1917. Maud Martha, the novel from which "Home" is taken, was published in 1953.

MEET LUCILLE CLIFTON

Lucille Clifton now lives in Columbia, Maryland, where she is Distinguished Professor of Humanities at Saint Mary's College. Clifton is a former poet laureate of Maryland and has received numerous awards and prizes for her poetry.

Lucille Clifton was born in 1936. "the 1st" comes from Good Woman: Poems and a Memoir 1969–1980, published in 1987.

360 🐾 THEME 4

FOCUS ACTIVITY

When you hear the word *home,* what do you think about? What are some things that make a home important to the people who live there?

Think/Pair/Share
Jot down your thoughts and feelings about the word *home.* Then share your ideas with a partner.

Setting a Purpose
As you read, look for what makes their home important to the characters in these selections.

Children Dancing, 1948. Robert Gwathmey (1903–1988). Oil on canvas, 32 x 40 in. The Butler Institute of American Art, Youngstown, OH.

VOCABULARY PREVIEW

obstinate (ob′ stə nit) *adj.* stubborn; difficult to overcome or control; p. 361
emphatic (em fat′ ik) *adj.* strongly expressive; forceful; p. 361
possessively (pə zes′ iv lē) *adv.* in a way that shows ownership or control; p. 361
staccato (stə kä′ tō) *adj.* made of short, sharp sounds or movements; p. 362
casually (kazh′ o͞o əl lē) *adv.* in a relaxed, informal way; p. 362

RESOURCE MANAGER

Lesson Planning Resource
The *Theme Four Planning Guide* (pp. 30–35) provides additional lesson notes and reduced versions of all print resources.

📁 **Other Print Resources**
- Active Reading Guide, p. 33
- Vocabulary Practice, p. 21
- Reading Workbook, pp. 57–58
- Grammar and Language Workbook, pp. 65–66

- Grammar and Composition Handbook, Lesson 2.3
- Quick Checks, p. 33
- Selection and Theme Assessment, pp. 59–60
- Performance Assessment, p. 32
- Spanish Summaries, p. 33
- Spanish Translations
- Inclusion Strategies
- English Language Learners Sourcebook

📠 **Transparencies**
- Selection Focus 33
- Literary Elements 33
- Grammar and Language 30

Technology
🎧 Audio Library
🎧 Spanish Audio Library
💻 Glencoe Literature Web Site
💾 Testmaker

Home

Gwendolyn Brooks ‿

What had been wanted was this always, this always to last, the talking softly on this porch, with the snake plant in the jardiniere[1] in the southwest corner, and the obstinate slip from Aunt Eppie's magnificent Michigan fern at the left side of the friendly door. Mama, Maud Martha and Helen rocked slowly in their rocking chairs, and looked at the late afternoon light on the lawn, and at the emphatic iron of the fence and at the poplar tree. These things might soon be theirs no longer. Those shafts and pools of light, the tree, the graceful iron, might soon be viewed possessively by different eyes.

Papa was to have gone that noon, during his lunch hour, to the office of the Home Owners' Loan. If he had not succeeded in getting another extension, they would be leaving this house in which they had lived for more than fourteen years. There was little hope. The Home Owners'

Woman Holding a Jug, 1932–1933. James A. Porter. Oil on canvas. Carl Van Vechten Gallery of Fine Arts, Fisk University, Nashville, TN.

Loan was hard. They sat, making their plans.

"We'll be moving into a nice flat[2] somewhere," said Mama. "Somewhere on South Park, or Michigan, or in Washington Park Court." Those flats, as the girls and Mama knew well, were burdens on wages twice the size of Papa's. This was not mentioned now.

"They're much prettier than this old house," said Helen. "I have friends I'd just as soon not bring here. And I have other friends that wouldn't come down this far for anything, unless they were in a taxi."

Yesterday, Maud Martha would have attacked her. Tomorrow she might. Today she said nothing. She merely gazed at a little hopping robin in the tree, her tree, and tried to keep the fronts of her eyes dry.

"Well, I do know," said Mama, turning her hands over and over, "that I've been getting tireder and tireder of doing that

---

1. A *jardiniere* (järd′ ən ēr′) is an ornamental pot or plant stand.

2. Here, *flat* means "apartment."

Vocabulary
obstinate (ob′ stə nit) *adj.* stubborn; difficult to overcome or control
emphatic (em fat′ ik) *adj.* strongly expressive; forceful
possessively (pə zes′ iv lē) *adv.* in a way that shows ownership or control

---

A Active Reading

PREDICT Ask students to use the title and clues from the first paragraph to predict what this story might be about.

B Literary Elements

THEME Remind students that the theme of a story is the primary message that is conveyed by the plot, setting, and characters. Encourage students to identify the theme as they read the story.

C Critical Thinking

EVALUATING Ask students if they think Mama really believes that they'll be moving into a nice flat. Why is she saying this? *(No, she doesn't really believe it. She is trying to make everyone feel better because they are all afraid that they will have to move.)*

Additional Resources

📁 *Active Reading Guide,* p. 33

🎧 *Audio Library*

🎧 *Spanish Audio Library*

📁 *Spanish Summaries,* p. 33

Teaching Options

CONNECTING TO OTHER SELECTIONS
For a teaching strategy that connects "Home" to "Beware of the Dog," turn to page 48 in the *Theme Six Planning Guide.*

Reading *Minilesson*

Identifying Main Idea and Supporting Details Point out that in the second paragraph of "Home," the narrator explains the situation. The rest of the story is a series of conversations that show how each family member feels about what is taking place.

Activity Have students answer the following questions to identify the main idea and supporting details of this story:

- What is the main idea of the story?
- What does Mama say about moving?
- Does Helen agree or disagree?
- How does Maud Martha feel?
- What do they all really feel about the house? **L2** **COLLAB. LEARN.**

Additional Resources

📁 *Reading Workbook,* pp. 57–58

D Literary Elements

THEME What is the theme in Maud Martha's thoughts and feelings? *(Home is very important, and there is no other place like it.)*

E Literary Elements

THEME Ask students what other theme Mama expresses when she says, "And he'll have us...wherever"? *(Being together is the most important part of having a home.)*

F Critical Thinking

INFERRING Ask students to infer what Mama and the family are feeling when they see Papa coming home. You may wish to share the following model to illustrate the thinking process involved in inferring.

Model: At first the family talks about how those "flats" were much prettier than the house they live in. After reading that they want to jump over the fence to "shake the truth out of" Papa's collar, I know that they want to keep their house.

LITERATURE & HUMANITIES

Have students examine the quilt *Tar Beach*, in *Introducing Art*, page 238, and discuss how the positive aspects of home are contrasted with a sense of dissatisfaction. Ask how this contrast relates to the story.

---

firing. From October to April, there's firing to be done."

"But lately we've been helping, Harry and I," said Maud Martha. "And sometimes in March and April and in October, and even in November, we could build a little fire in the fireplace. Sometimes the weather was just right for that."

She knew, from the way they looked at her, that this had been a mistake. They did not want to cry.

But she felt that the little line of white, somewhat ridged with smoked purple, and all that cream-shot saffron,[3] would never drift across any western sky except that in back of this house. The rain would drum with as sweet a dullness nowhere but here. The birds on South Park were mechanical birds, no better than the poor caught canaries in those "rich" women's sun parlors.

"It's just going to kill Papa!" burst out Maud Martha. "He loves this house! He *lives* for this house!"

"He lives for us," said Helen. "It's us he loves. He wouldn't want the house, except for us."

"And he'll have us," added Mama, "wherever."

"You know," Helen sighed, "if you want to know the truth, this is a relief. If this hadn't come up, we would have gone on, just dragged on, hanging out here forever."

---

3. The orange-yellow color *(saffron)* is streaked or mixed *(shot)* with a cream color.

"It might," allowed Mama, "be an act of God. God may just have reached down, and picked up the reins."

"Yes," Maud Martha cracked in, "that's what you always say—that God knows best."

Her mother looked at her quickly, decided the statement was not suspect, looked away.

Helen saw Papa coming. "There's Papa," said Helen.

They could not tell a thing from the way Papa was walking. It was that same dear little <u>staccato</u> walk, one shoulder down, then the other, then repeat, and repeat. They watched his progress. He passed the Kennedys', he passed the vacant lot, he passed Mrs. Blakemore's. They wanted to hurl themselves over the fence, into the street, and shake the truth out of his collar. He opened his gate—the gate—and still his stride and face told them nothing.

"Hello," he said.

Mama got up and followed him through the front door. The girls knew better than to go in too.

Presently Mama's head emerged. Her eyes were lamps turned on.

"It's all right," she exclaimed. "He got it. It's all over. Everything is all right."

The door slammed shut. Mama's footsteps hurried away.

"I think," said Helen, rocking rapidly, "I think I'll give a party. I haven't given a party since I was eleven. I'd like some of my friends to just <u>casually</u> see that we're homeowners."

Vocabulary

staccato (stə kä′ tō) *adj.* made of short, sharp sounds or movements
casually (kazh′ oo əl lē) *adv.* in a relaxed, informal way

Teaching Options

Grammar and Language *Minilesson*

Possessive Nouns Remind students that a possessive noun names who or what owns or has something. Explain that possessive nouns can be common or proper nouns, singular or plural, and that they are formed in one of two ways. To form the possessive of most nouns, add an apostrophe and *s* (*'s*). To form the possessive of plural nouns already ending in *s*, add only an apostrophe (*'*). Direct students'

attention to the possessive nouns on page 362 (*women's; Kennedys'; Mrs. Blakemore's*).

Activity Have students choose ten nouns from "Home" and write the possessive form of each. When students have written the possessive noun forms, ask them to write each one in a sentence. **L2**
COLLAB. LEARN.

Additional Resources

- *Grammar and Language Transparency 30*
- *Grammar and Language Workbook,* pp. 65–66
- *Grammar and Composition Handbook,* Lesson 2.3
- *Writer's Choice,* Lesson 9.3

the 1st

Lucille Clifton

what i remember about that day
is boxes stacked across the walk
and couch springs curling through the air
and drawers and tables balanced on the curb
and us, hollering,
leaping up and around
happy to have a playground;

nothing about the emptied rooms
nothing about the emptied family

The Apartment, 1943. Jacob Lawrence. Gouache on paper, 21.25 x 29.25 in. The Hunter Museum of American Art, Chattanooga, TN.

G Author's Craft

AUTHOR'S PURPOSE Ask students why they think Lucille Clifton chose to call this poem "The 1st." *(The 1st refers to the first day of the month, which is the date on which many leases begin and end.)*

H Active Reading

QUESTION Ask students what playground is being referred to in the poem. *(The children are playing among the family's furniture and belongings, which are outside waiting to be moved.)*

I Critical Thinking

DRAWING CONCLUSIONS Ask students what they think the last two lines of the poem mean. *(The speaker only remembers playing, not the sadness of moving.)*

Thematic Focus

Where the Heart Is Invite students to talk about the relationship between home and family, focusing on the value of stability. At the same time, discuss how a family can provide an important home for the heart, even when people must move from place to place or be separated.

ASSESSMENT OPTIONS

📁 *Quick Checks,* p. 33

MEETING INDIVIDUAL NEEDS — ENGLISH LANGUAGE LEARNERS

Understanding Poetry Explain to English language learners that the poem "The 1st" is essentially a single sentence, even though the first word is not capitalized and there is no end punctuation.

Activity Draw the following cluster diagram on the chalkboard and help students identify the important details.

COLLAB. LEARN.

boxes stacked / couch springs / tables on the curb / **What I remember** / us (kids) hollering and leaping / happy to have a playground

Additional Resources

📁 *English Language Learners Sourcebook*

Responding to the Selection

Personal Response

Students should offer clear explanations for their responses. Most students will probably agree with the importance of home expressed in both works. Some may realize that children can play even in the midst of a difficult situation.

Analyzing Literature

1. They are not able to pay their mortgage on time. Papa gets an extension of time to pay the mortgage near the end of the story.

2. The speaker is recalling a moving day. She remembers playing, but not the sadness of leaving.

3. The family loves their home and wants to keep it. For example: "It's just going to kill Papa!"; "He loves this house! He *lives* for this house!"

4. One emotion is light and playful; the other is dark and sad. The repetition of the last two lines emphasizes the finality of the move.

5. The short story form allows a writer to include dialogue and detailed description in order to explain more about what is going on. The poem form is more concise and allows a writer the chance to say a great deal with relatively few words and images.

6. The reader realizes that the speakers are not telling the truth when they act as if they want to move.

7. It is common for people who are afraid of something to act as if they aren't. Children often play with each other, even when something is happening that is sad or difficult.

8. Most students will probably be able to relate to the hardships and fears that can accompany leaving a home.

9. In both cases, the home seems to be a strong focus for the entire family. Clifton refers to "the emptied family," implying that the family is deeply affected by moving.

10. Students should support their responses with clear explanations and examples from the story or poem.

Responding to Literature

PERSONAL RESPONSE

- ◆ What is your response to these selections? Explain.
- ◆ Review your notes from the **Focus Activity** on page 360. How do your thoughts and feelings about the word *home* compare with the thoughts and feelings of the characters in these selections?

Analyzing Literature

RECALL

1. What problem does the family in "Home" face? Near the end of the story, what news does Papa bring home?

2. In the poem "the 1st," what event is the speaker recalling from her childhood? What does she remember about her feelings? Explain.

INTERPRET

3. How does the family in "Home" feel about their home? Support your opinion with examples from the story.

4. What are the two conflicting images and emotions in the poem "the 1st"? Why, do you think, are the last two lines almost the same? Explain.

EVALUATE AND CONNECT

5. Both of these selections deal with the subject of moving and loss. How do the forms—a short story and a poem—allow the writers to deal differently with the same topic? Explain.

6. How does the dialogue between the characters in "Home" contribute to the story's suspense? Give examples.

7. In what ways do these selections seem true to life? Explain.

8. How do you feel about what happens to these families?

9. Theme Connection   Why is a place to call home important to the characters in these selections? Explain.

10. Which of these selections do you prefer? Why? Use quotations from the selections to support your ideas.

LITERARY ELEMENTS

Theme

A **theme** is the message that is expressed in a work of literature. A story, a novel, or a poem may have more than one theme, but one message will usually be the strongest. A theme may be stated directly, but more often it is revealed gradually, through the words, thoughts, and actions of the characters. Since readers usually need to *infer* the theme—that is, figure it out through reasoning—it is always open to interpretation. A strong piece of literature may mean different things to different people.

1. What, do you think, is the theme of the story "Home"? Use examples from the story to support your ideas.

2. Summarize the central theme of the poem "the 1st."

● See **Literary Terms Handbook,** p. R11.

LITERARY ELEMENTS

1. Possible answer: Having a home is very special, and it is frightening to be forced to move. "It's all right.... He got it. It's all over. Everything is all right."

2. The speaker remembers moving day as a day of play. She has forgotten about the pain of leaving her home and the effect of moving on her family.

Additional Resources

✎ *Literary Elements Transparency 33*

Extending Your Response

Writing About Literature

Dialogue   Dialogue is conversation between characters. Readers learn a great deal of information through the dialogue in a story. Write a paragraph or two explaining what you learned from the dialogue in "Home" about the thoughts and feelings of the different characters.

Creative Writing
One-Act Play   With a partner, write a one-act play based on "the 1st." Think about the poem's central images and the different emotions they create. Make up any details you wish, including dialogue. If you wish, perform your play. Use props to make the dramatization seem real.

Literature Groups
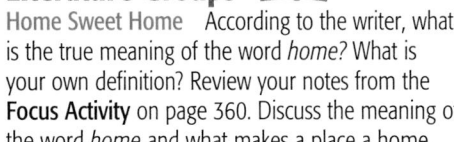

Home Sweet Home   According to the writer, what is the true meaning of the word *home*? What is your own definition? Review your notes from the **Focus Activity** on page 360. Discuss the meaning of the word *home* and what makes a place a home.

Learning for Life

A Persuasive Memo   Imagine you are Papa in the story "Home." The Home Owners' Loan Association has asked you to write them a memo explaining why you need another extension on your loan, how you intend to repay the loan, and what the house means to you and your family. Be persuasive!

 Save your work for your portfolio.

Skill Minilesson

VOCABULARY • WORDS USED IN UNUSUAL WAYS

Gwendolyn Brooks says that the iron of the fence was *emphatic*. A fence can't literally be emphatic, but by describing it that way, Brooks suggests that the iron of the fence is strong and not flexible.

PRACTICE   To complete each sentence, think about what is suggested by the underlined word.

1. A <u>tired</u> roof is probably
   a. sagging
   b. leaking
   c. flat
2. A <u>bold</u> flower probably has
   a. thorns
   b. a sweet smell
   c. bright colors
3. A <u>heavy</u> sky probably has many
   a. stars
   b. dark clouds
   c. puffy clouds
4. A <u>forgiving</u> rug doesn't
   a. look new
   b. fit the room
   c. show stains easily
5. An <u>undecided</u> path probably
   a. twists
   b. is narrow
   c. goes uphill

Extending Your Response

Writing About Literature
Students' paragraphs should
- explain what they learned from the dialogue in "Home."
- give examples to support their ideas.

Creative Writing
Students' plays should
- be about the central images, emotions, and theme of the poem.
- include made-up details and dialogue among the children.

Literature Groups
Most students will understand that the writer expresses her sense of *home* in these lines: *"He lives for us," said Helen. "It's us he loves. He wouldn't want the house, except for us."* It is the people in the family who really create a home. **COLLAB. LEARN.**

Learning for Life
As students write their memos, encourage them to focus on what the house means to them and their family. Stress that they should be both businesslike and persuasive.

Skill Minilesson

VOCABULARY
• WORDS USED IN UNUSUAL WAYS

1. a	3. b	5. a
2. c	4. c	

Additional Resources
📁 *Vocabulary Practice*, p. 21

✔ ASSESSMENT OPTIONS

📁 *Quick Checks,* p. 33
📁 *Selection and Theme Assessment,* p. 59–60
📁 *Performance Assessment,* p. 32
💾 *Testmaker*

Objective

- To make connections with characters or situations in a story

Teaching Strategies

Ask students to talk about characters from fiction, television, movies, or real life with whom they identify. Discuss the kinds of characters students look for in the books they read or programs they watch. Encourage students to focus on what they can learn about themselves by connecting with a fictitious character.

Activity

1. Students may choose a character from a short story in the theme, such as T. J. in "Antaeus." This character may be familiar to students who have felt out of place at times.
2. Students may find similarities in the experiences or emotional aspects of the character and themselves but find differences in concrete circumstances, such as where and when the character lived.
3. Responses may include learning that people tend to react in similar ways to basic human experiences, such as kindness, cruelty, happiness, and sadness.

Additional Resources
📁 *Reading Workbook*

Teaching Options

Reading and Thinking Skills

Making Connections

When you get involved in a story, you may identify with one or more of its characters. Skillful readers put themselves in a story by **making connections** between their own life experiences and the experiences of the characters. Thinking about these connections while you read makes a story more meaningful.

Read the following passage from "Home" by Gwendolyn Brooks. As you read, try to connect the situation in the story with a situation in your own life.

> "We'll be moving into a nice flat somewhere," said Mama. "Somewhere on South Park, or Michigan, or in Washington Park Court." Those flats, as the girls and Mama knew well, were burdens on wages twice the size of Papa's. This was not mentioned now.
>
> "They're much prettier than this old house," said Helen. "I have friends I'd just as soon not bring here. And I have other friends that wouldn't come down this far for anything, unless they were in a taxi."

Were you able to make a connection between your life and the characters and situation described in this excerpt? Perhaps you remembered a time when a relative or friend tried to comfort you after you did not make the team or the cast of the school play. Or, perhaps you recalled a time when you helped a friend see the brighter side of a difficult situation. Connecting your personal experiences with the actions, emotions, motivations, and situations of the characters in a story makes fiction come alive.

● For more about reading strategies, see **Reading Handbook**, pp. R70–R100.

ACTIVITY

Reread "Antaeus," by Borden Deal, or another short story of your choosing. Then answer the following questions.

1. Which character or event in the story reminded you of a person or situation in your own life?
2. How are the two characters or events alike? How are they different?
3. How did connecting the people and experiences in your own life to those in the story help you better understand the characters' emotions and motivations?

MEETING INDIVIDUAL NEEDS — INCLUSION STRATEGIES

Less-Proficient Readers Students may find it easier to make connections with characters in the stories they read if the stories are read aloud first and difficult vocabulary is previewed.

Activity Read the passage from "Home" aloud to students. Have them discuss who the characters are, where the scene is taking place, and what the circumstances seem to be. Ask students to list words or phrases that describe how the characters feel. **L2**

Additional Resources
📁 *Inclusion Strategies*

Before You Read
The Teacher Who Changed My Life

MEET NICHOLAS GAGE

When Nicholas Gage first came to America, he was nine years old and did not speak English. Thirty years later, when he left America for Greece, Gage was a top investigative reporter for *The New York Times*. He returned to Lia, the tiny remote village of his birth to find his mother's murderers. The best-selling book he wrote about his search was named after his mother, *Eleni*. This autobiographical essay begins in 1953, when the author was a fourteen-year-old refugee from war-torn Greece.

Nicholas Gage was born in 1939. This story is part of his memoir, A Place for Us, *published in 1989.*

FOCUS ACTIVITY

How can one person positively influence another's life? What people do you think of when it comes to making a difference?

Journal

Write a paragraph in your journal about a person who has been a big influence in your life.

Setting a Purpose

Read about one person who made a difference in a young man's life.

BACKGROUND

Did You Know? Between 1940 and 1949, Greeks fought in two wars–World War II and a civil war. During this time, 600,000 Greeks were killed, including Nicholas Gage's mother. The civil war was mostly fought in the northern mountain villages, where Greek Communist guerrillas, who had fought the Germans in World War II, plotted to take over the Greek government. Their policy was to abduct over twenty-eight thousand Greek children and send them to Albania, Yugoslavia, and Bulgaria to grow up as communists.

VOCABULARY PREVIEW

portly (pôrt′ lē) *adj.* having a stout but dignified appearance; p. 369
authoritarian (ə thôr′ ə tār′ ē ən) *adj.* having or expecting complete obedience to authority; p. 369
ultimately (ul′ tə mit lē) *adv.* in the end; finally; p. 369
perspective (pər spek′ tiv) *n.* point of view; p. 370
impoverished (im pov′ ər isht) *adj.* reduced to poverty; made very poor; p. 370
mortified (môr′ tə fīd′) *adj.* greatly embarrassed; p. 370
tact (takt) *n.* the ability to handle people or situations without causing displeasure or resentment; p. 370
ecstatic (ek stat′ ik) *adj.* overwhelmed with joy; p. 371
avidly (av′ id lē) *adv.* eagerly; enthusiastically; p. 372
consolation (kon sə lā′ shən) *n.* a comfort; p. 373

WHERE THE HEART IS 🐦 367

RESOURCE MANAGER

Lesson Planning Resource
The *Theme Four Planning Guide* (pp. 36–43) provides additional lesson notes and reduced versions of all print resources.

📁 **Other Print Resources**
- Active Reading Guide, p. 34
- Vocabulary Practice, p. 22
- Reading Workbook, pp. 59–60
- Grammar and Language Workbook, pp. 127–128

- Grammar and Composition Handbook, Lessons 6.1, 6.2
- Quick Checks, p. 34
- Selection and Theme Assessment, pp. 61–62
- Performance Assessment, p. 33
- Spanish Summaries, p. 34
- Spanish Translations
- Inclusion Strategies
- English Language Learners Sourcebook

📠 **Transparencies**
- Selection Focus 34
- Literary Elements 34
- Grammar and Language 31

Technology
 Literature Launchers
 Audio Library
 Spanish Audio Library
💻 Glencoe Literature Web Site
💾 Testmaker

Objectives

- To read and analyze a personal narrative about a war refugee
- To identify the main idea of an essay
- To write an analysis of an author's strategies

Skills

Reading/Thinking: Inferring; Drawing Conclusions; Activating Prior Knowledge
Writing: Autobiographical Essay
Vocabulary: The Suffix *-arian*
Grammar/Language: Adverbs
Listening/Speaking: Storyteller
Collaboration: Literature Groups

Motivating
→ OPTIONS

Literature Launchers: "Nicholas Gage and His Mentor"

Videodisc Side A, Segment 11

Also available in VHS.

Selection Focus Transparency 34: Have students view and discuss the photograph of a village in Greece.

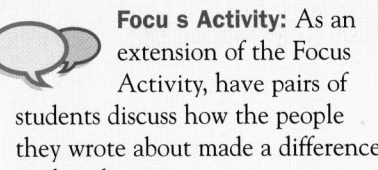
Focus Activity: As an extension of the Focus Activity, have pairs of students discuss how the people they wrote about made a difference in their lives.

SUMMARY

Nicholas Gage, a best-selling author, remembers the tough but caring teacher who introduced him to literature and the power of the written word. He describes coming to the United States as a young war refugee from Greece and meeting the teacher who instilled pride in his heritage and inspired him to write the story of his mother's tragic death in Greece.

📁 **Spanish Summaries,** p. 34

A **Active Reading**

PREDICT Ask students if, by reading the title alone, they can predict what the author will learn from the teacher. Suggest that students revisit their predictions as they read to verify or to revise them.

Additional Resources

📁 **Active Reading Guide,** p. 34

🎧 **Audio Library**

🎧 **Spanish Audio Library**

Teaching Options

The Teacher Who Changed My Life

Nicholas Gage ∾

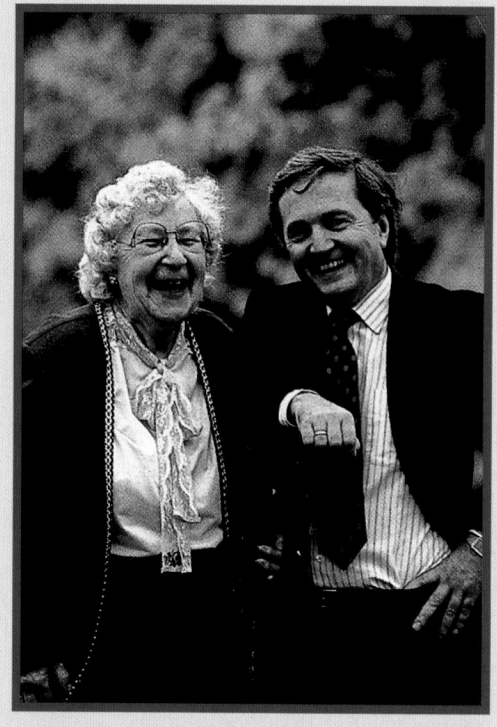

The grown-up Nicholas and his former teacher, Marjorie Hurd Rabidou.

The person who set the course of my life in the new land I entered as a young war refugee—who, in fact, nearly dragged me onto the path that would bring all the blessings I've received in America—was a salty-tongued,[1] no-nonsense schoolteacher named Marjorie Hurd. When I entered her classroom in 1953, I had been to six schools in five years, starting in the Greek village where I was born in 1939.

When I stepped off a ship in New York Harbor on a gray March day in 1949, I was an undersized 9-year-old in short pants who had lost his mother and was coming to live with the father he didn't know. My mother, Eleni Gatzoyiannis, had been imprisoned, tortured, and shot

---

1. A *salty-tongued* person speaks in a sharp, witty, and often sarcastic way.

CONNECTING TO OTHER SELECTIONS

COMPARING selections

This selection is compared with "How I Learned English" on page 377. A lesson for teaching a comparison of the two selections appears on page 380.

The chart at the right shows three ways to connect "The Teacher Who Changed My Life" to other selections in this book.

For specific teaching strategies, see the **Theme Four Planning Guide,** pages 39–40.

Connection	Title
Life Skills: Teaching and Mentoring	→ "The Bird Like No Other," p. 473
Thematic: Growing Up	→ from *Barrio Boy*, p. 67
Literary: Memoir	→ from *Beyond the Limits*, p. 281

by Communist guerrillas[2] for sending me and three of my four sisters to freedom. She died so that her children could go to their father in the United States.

The <u>portly</u>, bald, well-dressed man who met me and my sisters seemed a foreign, <u>authoritarian</u> figure. I secretly resented him for not getting the whole family out of Greece early enough to save my mother. <u>Ultimately</u>, I would grow to love him and appreciate how he dealt with becoming a single parent at the age of 56, but at first our relationship was prickly,[3] full of hostility.

As Father drove us to our new home—a tenement in Worcester,[4] Mass.—and pointed out the huge brick building that would be our first school in America, I clutched my Greek notebooks from the refugee camp, hoping that my few years of schooling would impress my teachers in this cold, crowded country. They didn't. When my father led me and my 11-year-old sister to Greendale Elementary School, the grim-faced Yankee principal put the two of us in a class for the mentally retarded. There was no facility in those days for non-English-speaking children.

By the time I met Marjorie Hurd four years later, I had learned English, been placed in a normal, graded class and had even been chosen for the college preparatory track in the Worcester public school system. I was 13 years old when our father moved us yet again, and I entered Chandler Junior High shortly after the beginning of seventh grade. I found myself surrounded by richer, smarter and better-dressed classmates who looked askance[5] at my strange clothes and heavy accent. Shortly after I arrived, we were told to select a hobby to pursue during "club hour" on Fridays. The idea of hobbies and clubs made no sense to my immigrant ears, but I decided to follow the prettiest girl in my class—the blue-eyed daughter of the local Lutheran minister. She led me through the door marked "Newspaper Club" and into the presence of Miss Hurd, the newspaper adviser and English teacher who would become my mentor and my muse.[6]

A formidable, solidly built woman with salt-and-pepper hair, a steely eye and a flat Boston accent, Miss Hurd had no patience with layabouts. "What are all you goof-offs doing here?" she bellowed at the would-be journalists. "This is the Newspaper Club! We're going to put out a *newspaper*. So if there's anybody in this room who doesn't like work, I suggest you go across to the Glee Club now, because you're going to work your tails off here!"

I was soon under Miss Hurd's spell. She did indeed teach us to put out a newspaper, skills I honed during my next 25 years as a journalist. Soon I asked the principal

---

2. *Guerrillas* (gə ril′ əz) are members of small, organized forces, usually made up of volunteers who are not soldiers in a regular army.
3. Here, *prickly* means "difficult; troublesome."
4. [*Worcester*] This city's founders brought its oddly pronounced name with them from England. It's pronounced as if it were spelled *Wooster,* with an *o* sound as in *wood.*

5. The expression *looked askance* (ə skans′) means "viewed with suspicion or disapproval."
6. A *mentor* is a wise and trusted counselor, and a *muse* is a source of artistic inspiration.

Vocabulary

portly (pôrt′ lē) *adj.* having a stout but dignified appearance
authoritarian (ə thôr′ ə târ′ ē ən) *adj.* having or expecting complete obedience to authority
ultimately (ul′ tə mit lē) *adv.* in the end; finally

E **Critical Thinking**

INFERRING Ask students to discuss why Miss Hurd asked Nick to write about what happened to his family in Greece. If you wish, share the following model to illustrate the thinking process involved in inferring.

Model: I think Miss Hurd knew that Nick had painful memories of leaving Greece. Because of the author's affection for her, I know that under her tough personality was a caring person. This makes me believe she thought writing about his painful experience would help Nick come to terms with his grief.

FYI

The Greek Civil War
started in 1946. After three years of fighting, the democratically elected government, with aid from the United States, finally defeated the Communist rebels.

F **Active Reading**

REVIEW Have students summarize the story young Nick told in his essay. *(To escape from the Communist guerrillas, Nick's family left their village in Greece. They traveled in the mountains at night, crossed minefields, and reached a refugee camp. Nick's mother could not leave with them because the guerrillas had sent her to work in distant fields.)*

**Teaching
Options**

---

to transfer me to her English class as well. There, she drilled us on grammar until I finally began to understand the logic and structure of the English language. She assigned stories for us to read and discuss; not tales of heroes, like the Greek myths I knew, but stories of underdogs—poor people, even immigrants, who seemed ordinary until a crisis drove them to do something extraordinary. She also introduced us to the literary wealth[7] of Greece—giving me a new perspective on my war-ravaged, impoverished homeland. I began to be proud of my origins.

One day, after discussing how writers should write about what they know, she assigned us to compose an essay from our own experience. Fixing me with a stern look, she added, "Nick, I want you to write about what happened to your family in Greece." I had been trying to put those painful memories behind me and left the assignment until the last moment. Then, on a warm spring afternoon, I sat in my room with a yellow pad and pencil and stared out the window at the buds on the trees. I wrote that the coming of spring always reminded me of the last time I said goodbye to my mother on a green and gold day in 1948.

I kept writing, one line after another, telling how the Communist guerrillas occupied our village, took our home and

food, how my mother started planning our escape when she learned that the children were to be sent to re-education camps behind the Iron Curtain[8] and how, at the last moment, she couldn't escape with us because the guerrillas sent her with a group of women to thresh wheat in a distant village. She promised she would try to get away on her own, she told me to be brave and hung a silver cross around my neck, and then she kissed me. I watched the line of women being led down into the ravine and up the other side, until they disappeared around the bend—my mother a tiny brown figure at the end who stopped for an instant to raise her hand in one last farewell.

I wrote about our nighttime escape down the mountain, across the minefields, and into the lines of the Nationalist soldiers, who sent us to a refugee camp. It was there that we learned of our mother's execution. I felt very lucky to have come to America, I concluded, but every year, the coming of spring made me feel sad because it reminded me of the last time I saw my mother.

I handed in the essay, hoping never to see it again, but Miss Hurd had it published in the school paper. This mortified me at first, until I saw that my classmates reacted with sympathy and tact to my family's story. Without telling me, Miss

---

7. Greece's *literary wealth,* dating from about 750 to 300 B.C., includes plays, poems, and other texts that greatly influenced the development of European and American civilization.

8. During the years following World War II, the *Iron Curtain* was an imaginary barrier separating the former Soviet Union and its allies from the non-Communist world.

Vocabulary
perspective (pər spek′ tiv) *n.* point of view
impoverished (im pov′ ər isht) *adj.* reduced to poverty; made very poor
mortified (môr′ tə fīd′) *adj.* greatly embarrassed
tact (takt) *n.* the ability to handle people or situations without causing displeasure or resentment

---

Reading *Minilesson*

Activating Prior Knowledge Write the phrase *salt-and-pepper hair* on the board. Explore the phrase's meaning by using this think-aloud model: *I know salt is white and pepper is black, so I think salt-and-pepper hair must mean black hair that has white hair in it.* Some students may find it easier to understand the meanings of certain words, phrases, and expressions if they break them into parts.

Activity Have students work in small groups to reread the selection, looking for phrases or expressions whose meanings are unclear. Suggest that they list them as they read so that they can create glossaries of the terms. **L2** **COLLAB. LEARN.**

Additional Resources
📁 *Reading Workbook,* pp. 59–60

Hurd also submitted the essay to a contest sponsored by the Freedoms Foundation at Valley Forge, Pa., and it won a medal. The Worcester paper wrote about the award and quoted my essay at length. My father, by then a "five-and-dime-store chef," as the paper described him, was <u>ecstatic</u> with pride, and the Worcester Greek community celebrated the honor to one of its own.

For the first time I began to understand the power of the written word. A secret ambition took root in me. One day, I vowed, I would go back to Greece, find out the details of my mother's death and write about her life, so her grandchildren would know of her courage. Perhaps I would even track down the men who killed her and write of their crimes. Fulfilling that ambition would take me 30 years.

Meanwhile, I followed the literary path that Miss Hurd had so forcefully set me on. After junior high, I became the editor of my school paper at Classical High School and got a part-time job at the Worcester *Telegram and Gazette*. Although my father could only give me $50 and encouragement toward a college education, I managed to finance four years at Boston University with scholarships and part-time jobs in journalism. During my last year of college, an article I wrote about a friend who had died in the Philippines—the first person to lose his life working for the Peace Corps[9]—led to my winning the Hearst Award for College

G

9. A *scholarship* is money given to help a student continue his or her education. The *Peace Corps* is a U.S. program that sends volunteers to help people in poorer countries to improve their living conditions. It was begun by President Kennedy in 1961.

Vocabulary
ecstatic (ek stat′ ik) *adj.* overwhelmed with joy

Nicholas Gage's third-grade class. Nicholas is in the back row, second from the left.
Viewing the photograph: Compare this class photo with the one on page 69. How did students change between the early 1900s and the middle 1900s? How do today's students differ from both earlier groups?

WHERE THE HEART IS 371

RESPOND Encourage students to think about the author's description of his father here. How does it make them feel about Gage's relationship with his father? What does it tell them about his father? About Nicholas Gage?

I **Critical Thinking**

INFERRING Ask students what they can infer about the author's view of his relationship with Miss Hurd, given this comparison to his mother. *(It seems that he views Miss Hurd as a mother figure—someone who shares the pride of his accomplishments with his father.)*

J **Literary Elements**

MAIN IDEA Ask students what they learn about Mrs. Rabidou in this paragraph. What is the main idea? *(She continued to make a difference in the lives of many students.)*

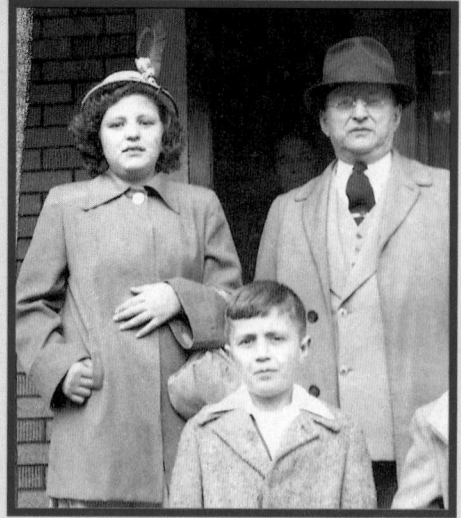
Young Nicholas with his sister and his father in 1950.

Journalism. And the plaque was given to me in the White House by President John F. Kennedy.

For a refugee who had never seen a motorized vehicle or indoor plumbing until he was 9, this was an unimaginable honor. When the Worcester paper ran a picture of me standing next to President Kennedy, my father rushed out to buy a new suit in order to be properly dressed to receive the congratulations of the Worcester Greeks. He clipped out the photograph, had it laminated in plastic and carried it in his breast pocket for the rest of his life to show everyone he met. I found the much-worn photo in his pocket on the day he died 20 years later.

In our isolated Greek village, my mother had bribed a cousin to teach her to read, for girls were not supposed to attend school beyond a certain age. She had always dreamed of her children receiving an education. She couldn't be there when I graduated from Boston University, but the person who came with my father and shared our joy was my former teacher, Marjorie Hurd. We celebrated not only my bachelor's degree but also the scholarships that paid my way to Columbia's Graduate School[10] of Journalism. There, I met the woman who would eventually become my wife. At our wedding and at the baptisms of our three children, Marjorie Hurd was always there, dancing alongside the Greeks.

By then, she was Mrs. Rabidou, for she had married a widower when she was in her early 40s. That didn't distract her from her vocation[11] of introducing young minds to English literature, however. She taught for a total of 41 years and continually would make a "project" of some balky student in whom she spied a spark of potential.[12] Often these were students from the most troubled homes, yet she would alternately bully and charm each one with her own special brand of tough love until the spark caught fire. She retired in 1981 at the age of 62 but still avidly follows the lives and careers of former students while overseeing her adult stepchildren and driving her husband on camping trips to New Hampshire.

---

10. Upon completing four years (usually) of study, college students receive an honor called a *bachelor's degree.* Some then go on to *graduate schools* for more advanced training.
11. Besides referring to an occupation, the word *vocation* can mean the particular work one feels called to do or is especially suited for.
12. A *balky* student is one who tends to stop short and refuse to go on. A student with *potential* has qualities or abilities capable of being developed.

Vocabulary
avidly (av′ id lē) *adv.* eagerly; enthusiastically

Teaching Options

Grammar and Language *Minilesson*

Adverbs Write this on the board, underlining the adverbs: *"I suggest you go across to the Glee Club now, because you're going to work your tails off here!"* Remind students that an adverb modifies a verb, an adjective, or another adverb. When it modifies a verb, it tells how, when, or where the action is done. Invite volunteers to identify the verb each adverb modifies *(across/go, now/go, off/work,*

here/work) and what it tells about the action *(across/where, now/when, off/how, here/where).*

Activity Have students find a sentence in the selection with an adverb and identify the word it modifies. If it modifies a verb, ask them to identify whether the adverb tells how, when, or where the action was done. **L2** **COLLAB. LEARN.**

Additional Resources

📠 *Grammar and Language Transparency 31*

📒 *Grammar and Language Workbook,* pp. 127–128

📒 *Grammar and Composition Handbook,* Lessons 6.1, 6.2

📒 *Writer's Choice,* Lesson 12.6

Miss Hurd was one of the first to call me on Dec. 10, 1987, when President Reagan, in his television address after the summit meeting with Gorbachev, told the nation that Eleni Gatzoyiannis' dying cry, "My children!" had helped inspire him to seek an arms agreement[13] "for all the children of the world."

"I can't imagine a better monument for your mother," Miss Hurd said with an uncharacteristic catch in her voice.

Did You Know?
Shish kebab (shish′ kə bob′) consists of chunks of meat and vegetables threaded on a long, thin skewer and broiled.

Although a bad hip makes it impossible for her to join in the Greek dancing, Marjorie Hurd Rabidou is still an honored and enthusiastic guest at all our family celebrations, including my 50th birthday picnic last summer, where the shish kebab was cooked on spits, clarinets and *bouzoukis* wailed, and costumed dancers led the guests in a serpentine[14] line around our colonial farmhouse, only 20 minutes from my first home in Worcester.

---

13. In 1987 Mikhail *Gorbachev* was the leader of the Soviet Union. An *arms agreement* is a treaty in which nations agree to limits on certain kinds of weapons.
14. A *bouzouki* (boo zōō′ kē) is a stringed instrument similar to a mandolin; a *serpentine* (sur′ pən tēn′) line winds around, like a snake's body.

My sisters and I felt an aching void because my father was not there to lead the line, balancing a glass of wine on his head while he danced, the way he did at every celebration during his 92 years. But Miss Hurd was there, surveying the scene with quiet satisfaction. Although my parents are gone, her presence was a <u>consolation</u>, because I owe her so much.

This is truly the land of opportunity, and I would have enjoyed its bounty even if I hadn't walked into Miss Hurd's classroom in 1953. But she was the one who directed my grief and pain into writing, and if it weren't for her I wouldn't have become an investigative reporter and foreign correspondent, recorded the story of my mother's life and death in *Eleni* and now my father's story in *A Place for Us*, which is also a testament to the country that took us in. She was the catalyst[15] that sent me into journalism and indirectly caused all the good things that came after. But Miss Hurd would probably deny this emphatically.

A few years ago, I answered the telephone and heard my former teacher's voice telling me, in that won't-take-no-for-an-answer tone of hers, that she had decided I was to write and deliver the eulogy[16] at her funeral. I agreed (she didn't leave me any choice), but that's one assignment I never want to do. I hope, Miss Hurd, that you'll accept this remembrance instead.

---

15. Here, the *testament* is a statement of gratitude and respect. A *catalyst* is one who stirs to action.
16. At a funeral, the *eulogy* (ū′ lə jē) is a speech praising the dead.

Vocabulary
consolation (kon′ sə lā′ shən) *n.* a comfort

WHERE THE HEART IS 373

Nicholas Gage

K **Literary Elements**

MAIN IDEA Help students recognize the main idea of this paragraph by studying the details and determining how they relate to Miss Hurd. *(Miss Hurd was responsible for directing Gage to a career as a writer, which led to many of his achievements in life.)*

L **Critical Thinking**

DRAWING CONCLUSIONS Encourage students to share their feelings about the author and his relationship with Miss Hurd. Ask students how they feel about her request and Gage's response. *(Students will feel that they have mutual respect for each other. Gage had to accept the honor of delivering her eulogy but was saddened by the thought of having to do it at all.)*

Thematic Focus

Where the Heart Is Encourage students to discuss where the heart of young Nicholas Gage was. Have students talk about why his heart was in his homeland, in his father's house, and in school. Ask students for examples from the selection to support their responses.

✓ ASSESSMENT OPTIONS

📁 *Quick Checks,* p. 34

REAL-WORLD CONNECTION

Refugees Provide students with magazine or newspaper articles about refugees who have come to the United States from a variety of countries.

Activity Arrange students in small groups and have each group discuss an article. Ask students to answer such questions as From which country did the people come? Why did they leave their homelands? How are they adjusting to life in a new country? How are the children doing in school? What provisions have the schools made for non-English-speaking students?

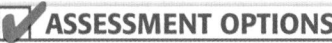

WHERE THE HEART IS 373

Responding to the Selection

Personal Response

Some students may express thoughts about a teacher who has made a difference in their lives. Some students may react to the description of young Nicholas leaving his mother with feelings of sadness and horror.

Analyzing Literature

1. Non-English speakers were put into classes for the mentally retarded.
2. The author fell under Miss Hurd's spell of tough love and became a devoted, hardworking pupil.
3. The author was trying to forget what happened to his family during the Greek civil war.
4. Miss Hurd came to family events and supported him as a parent would.
5. The author's first school experience in America prompted him to learn English, move out of the class for the mentally retarded, and qualify for college preparatory classes.
6. Writing the essay inspired Nicholas Gage to become a professional writer and to return to Greece to research a book about his mother.
7. He earned undergraduate and graduate degrees. He won awards for his writing and met the president of the United States.
8. She was an understanding and caring person when he needed one the most. She remained in his life, expressing pride in his accomplishments.
9. A *mentor* is a trusted person who offers advice and direction. A *muse* is someone who inspires. Miss Hurd directed Gage toward a literary career and inspired him to write about his life.

10. Some students may think it is easier because schools provide for non-English speakers and communities offer outreach activities for refugees. Other students may think it is harder because not all refugees will meet a teacher like Miss Hurd.

Responding to Literature

PERSONAL RESPONSE

What reactions and thoughts did you experience while reading this story?

Analyzing Literature

RECALL

1. According to the selection, how did the Worcester, Massachusetts, school system handle the education of non-English speakers in the 1950s?
2. Describe the "spell" that the author fell under as one of Miss Hurd's pupils.
3. What painful memories was the author trying to forget?
4. Give two examples of ways Miss Hurd became a part of the author's family.

INTERPRET

5. How did the author's first school experience in America shape him?
6. Miss Hurd assigned Nicholas Gage to write an essay about what happened to his family in Greece. What effect did that assignment have on the rest of his life?
7. In what ways did Gage live up to his mother's dreams for him?
8. Why, do you think, did Miss Hurd become such an important presence in Nicholas Gage's family life?

EVALUATE AND CONNECT

9. **Theme Connection**   In Gage's **narrative**, he refers to his teacher as "my mentor and my muse." What do those words mean? Why do you think Gage chose those words?
10. There are children in this country today who are war refugees like Nicholas Gage. How do you imagine they are adjusting to life in America? Do you think it would be easier or harder than it was for Gage? Give reasons for your opinions.

374   THEME 4

LITERARY ELEMENTS

Main Idea

The most important idea expressed in a paragraph or an essay is called the **main idea.** The main idea in a paragraph may or may not be directly stated in a topic sentence. Sometimes the reader has to study all the details in the paragraph and make an educated guess about its main idea. The main idea of an essay might be stated in the title or in an introductory or concluding paragraph.

1. Does the title of this selection express the main idea? Support your opinion.

2. Imagine you wanted to tell someone about the essay "The Teacher Who Changed My Life." Write one or two sentences that express the main idea of the selection.

● See **Literary Terms Handbook,** p. R6.

LITERARY ELEMENTS

1. The title expresses the main idea. Gage states in the introductory paragraph, "The person who set the course of my life...was a salty-tongued, no-nonsense schoolteacher named Marjorie Hurd."
2. The writer Nicholas Gage credits one of his schoolteachers for his literary successes.

Additional Resources

 Literary Elements Transparency 34

374   THEME 4

Extending Your Response

Writing About Literature

Author's Purpose In the midst of describing his teacher, Nicholas Gage summarizes a book he wrote about his mother's tragic death. Write a paragraph analyzing why the author chose to include this information. What emotional impact did he hope to create?

Creative Writing

Autobiographical Essay Develop your journal entry for the **Focus Activity** on page 367 into a personal narrative.

Listening and Speaking

Storyteller In ancient Greece, storytellers taught the Greek people their history and legends. Play the part of a modern storyteller and tell the story of someone who has had an influence on you or on society.

Literature Groups

Award Winner! Imagine that you and the other members of your group are among Miss Hurd's students. A national award is being presented to "The Teacher Who Changed My Life," and you have nominated Miss Hurd. Brainstorm a list of her teaching style characteristics that would convince the judges to vote for Miss Hurd. Make your presentation to the class.

Reading Further

If you would like to read more about young people and their families caught in political turmoil, try these books:
The Endless Steppe by Esther Hautzig
My Brother Sam Is Dead by James Lincoln Collier

📖 **Save your work for your portfolio.**

Skill Minilesson

VOCABULARY • THE SUFFIX -*arian*

Young Nicholas Gage's first impression of his father was of someone who seemed *authoritarian,* someone who believes in the use of *authority.* The suffix -*arian* means "one who or one that." It may mean "one who believes in," "one who supports," or "one who works in or with."

Understanding the suffix -*arian* may help you with some new words. For example, if you know that *utility* means "usefulness," you can figure out that a *utilitarian* kitchen contains things that are definitely useful.

PRACTICE Look carefully at the familiar part of each word on the left to match it to its meaning.

One who works with, believes in, or supports:
1. disciplinarian   a. people's right to be free
2. libertarian   b. system of rules and correction
3. grammarian   c. same treatment and rights for all
4. humanitarian   d. welfare of all people
5. equalitarian   e. rules for speaking and writing

Extending Your Response

Writing About Literature

Students' paragraphs should
- explain why they think Gage includes details about his mother's death.
- give examples of emotional reactions to this information, including their own.

Creative Writing

Students' personal narratives should
- characterize their subjects.
- give examples of the person's influence.
- follow the style of a personal narrative.

Listening and Speaking

Encourage students to practice telling the story with expression, varying the volume and tone of voices and using gestures.

Literature Groups

Suggest that students review the text for brainstorming ideas. Students might present a character sketch.

COLLAB. LEARN.

Skill Minilesson

VOCABULARY
• THE SUFFIX -*arian*

1. b	3. e	5. c
2. a	4. d	

Additional Resources
📁 *Vocabulary Practice,* p. 22

✔ ASSESSMENT OPTIONS

📁 *Quick Checks,* p. 34
📁 *Selection and Theme Assessment,* pp. 61–62
📁 *Performance Assessment,* p. 33
💾 *Testmaker*

Objectives

- To read and analyze a poem about a young boy's introduction to English
- To identify setting in a poem
- To write a poem or a prose paragraph from another character's point of view

Skills

Reading/Thinking: Drawing Conclusions; Sequence of Events
Vocabulary: Context Clues
Collaboration: Literature Groups

Motivating
→OPTIONS

Selection Focus Transparency 35: Explain to students as they view and discuss the photograph of a cricket game that even though cricket might seem unfamiliar to them, it remains popular in Great Britain and has become even more popular in India, which was formerly a British colony.

Focus Activity: As an extension of the Focus Activity, have students share with partners ways in which they have made friends and give details about their experiences.

Before You Read
How I Learned English

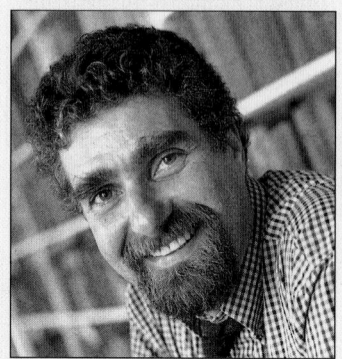

MEET GREGORY DJANIKIAN

Gregory Djanikian (jə nik′ ē ən) is an American who was born and raised in Egypt. Djanikian is an award-winning poet who has published several collections of his poems. He is currently the Director of Creative Writing at the University of Pennsylvania.

Gregory Djanikian was born in 1949. "How I Learned English" was published in 1987.

Union Prisoners at Salisbury, N.C., 1863. Otto Boetticher. Colored stone lithograph with buff and blue tints, 21 x 37½ in. Lithographer: Sarony, Major and Knapp. The Stokes Collection. The New York Public Library.

FOCUS ACTIVITY

Imagine moving to a new school in a new country. How would you meet friends?

Chart It!
Work with your classmates to make a chart that shows the different ways you have made your current friends.

At School	In Sports or Clubs	At a Friend's House

Setting a Purpose
Read this poem to discover what bonds connect people.

BACKGROUND

The Time and Place The poem is set sometime in the later half of the twentieth century in the town of Williamsport, Pennsylvania.

Did You Know? Baseball, or an English variation of the modern game called "rounders," has been around since the 1700s. In 1845 an amateur New York City player suggested a few changes in the game rules, including tagging the runner out. The new rules were adopted by many amateur New York City club teams, and the game's popularity grew. During the Civil War, soldiers from New York and New Jersey taught the game to other Americans.

RESOURCE MANAGER

Lesson Planning Resource
The *Theme Four Planning Guide* (pp. 44–48) provides additional lesson notes and reduced versions of all print resources.

📁 **Other Print Resources**
- Active Reading Guide, p. 35
- Reading Workbook, pp. 61–62
- Quick Checks, p. 35

- Selection and Theme Assessment, pp. 61–62
- Performance Assessment, p. 33
- Spanish Summaries, p. 35
- Spanish Translations
- Inclusion Strategies
- English Language Learners Sourcebook

 Transparencies
- Selection Focus 35
- Literary Elements 35

Technology
🎧 Audio Library
🎧 Spanish Audio Library
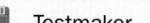 Glencoe Literature Web Site
💾 Testmaker

How I Learned English

Gregory Djanikian

It was in an empty lot
Ringed by elms and fir and honeysuckle.
Bill Corson was pitching in his buckskin jacket,
Chuck Keller, fat even as a boy, was on first,
5 His t-shirt riding up over his gut,
Ron O'Neill, Jim, Dennis, were talking it up
In the field, a blue sky above them
Tipped with cirrus.
            And there I was,
Just off the plane and plopped in the middle
10 Of Williamsport, Pa. and a neighborhood game,
Unnatural and without any moves,
My notions of baseball and America
Growing fuzzier each time I whiffed.

Reading the Selection

A Active Reading

PREDICT Have students use the illustrations on these pages to predict how the poet learns English. Suggest they revisit their predictions as they read the poem to verify or to revise them.

B Literary Elements

SETTING Ask students to identify details about the setting that help them visualize the baseball game. *(The game is being played in an empty lot that has elm trees, firs, and honeysuckle shrubs around it. It is a beautiful day with just a few clouds in the sky.)*

Additional Resources

📁 *Active Reading Guide,* p. 35

🎧 *Audio Library*

🎧 *Spanish Audio Library*

📁 *Spanish Summaries,* p. 35

Vo•cab•u•lar•y Skills

Context Clues Encourage students to picture the setting as it's described, including the sky tipped with *cirrus*. Ask students what they think *cirrus* means considering its relationship with the sky. *(white, thin clouds)*

Teaching Options

COMPARING selections

This selection is compared with "The Teacher Who Changed My Life" on page 368. A lesson for teaching a comparison of the two selections appears on page 380.

MEETING INDIVIDUAL NEEDS — ENGLISH LANGUAGE LEARNERS

How Did You Learn English? Draw English language learners' attention to the story's title and the baseball on page 377. Ask them to make some predictions about what a baseball might have to do with learning English.

Activity As students read, make sure they understand the humor in the phrase *"Oh my shin."* Ask what part of the body *shin* refers to. Invite students to discuss why the poet thought it was important to join in the laughter rather than feel embarrassed. Afterward, invite students to share with the class some of their own funny stories about learning English. **COLLAB. LEARN.**

Additional Resources

📁 *English Language Learners Sourcebook*

Active Reading

C Active Reading

CONNECT Have students recall a time when they were participating in a sport and saw a ball or another person coming toward them. Encourage students to share humorous stories about their experiences.

D Active Reading

RESPOND Encourage students to express how they feel about the boys' laughing while the speaker is in pain. Remind them of the humorous nature of the incident. Ask students to describe how they would react if they were in the speaker's situation.

E Critical Thinking

DRAWING CONCLUSIONS Have students think about the ending of the poem. Discuss whether they think it's a realistic conclusion. Do students feel that the writer's use of details and language enhances the ending? Have students give examples to support their opinions.

Thematic Focus

Where the Heart Is Have students discuss where they think the speaker's heart is. Point out that even though the speaker might daydream of another place, it is mentioned only once and is not identified.

☑ **ASSESSMENT OPTIONS**

📁 *Quick Checks,* p. 35

Teaching Options

CONNECTING TO OTHER SELECTIONS
For a teaching strategy that connects "How I Learned English" to "Wait Till Next Year," turn to page 35 in the *Theme One Planning Guide.*

How I Learned English

So it was not impossible that I,
15 Banished° to the outfield and daydreaming
    Of water, or a hotel in the mountains,
    Would suddenly find myself in the path
    Of a ball stung by Joe Barone.
    I watched it closing in
20 Clean and untouched, transfixed°
    By its easy arc before it hit
    My forehead with a thud.
                              I fell back,
    Dazed, clutching my brow,
    Groaning, "Oh my shin, oh my shin,"
25 And everybody peeled away from me
    And dropped from laughter, and there we were,
    All of us writhing on the ground for one reason
    Or another.
                  Someone said "shin" again,
    There was a wild stamping of hands on the ground,
30 A kicking of feet, and the fit
    Of laughter overtook me too,
    And that was important, as important
    As Joe Barone asking me how I was
    Through his tears, picking me up
35 And dusting me off with hands like swatters,
    And though my head felt heavy,
    I played on till dusk
    Missing flies and pop-ups and grounders
    And calling out in desperation things like
40 "Yours" and "take it," but doing all right,
    Tugging at my cap in just the right way,
    Crouching low, my feet set,
    "Hum baby" sweetly on my lips.

─────────────

15 To be *banished* is to be expelled or driven away—in this case, from the infield.
20 To be *transfixed* is to be made motionless, as from wonder or fear.

Reading *Minilesson*

Sequence of Events Explain to students that in poetry the sequence of events is not always clear. It is often helpful to pull the events from a story or a poem, paraphrase them, and then put them in the order in which they occurred. This can help readers keep straight not only the events but also the characters' involvement in those events.

Activity Reread the poem with the class and create a chart to track the sequence of events. Encourage students to include the names of the characters involved in each step. **L2** **COLLAB. LEARN.**

Additional Resources
📁 *Reading Workbook,* pp. 61–62

Responding to Literature

PERSONAL RESPONSE

Return to the **Focus Activity** on page 376. How does the speaker's experience connect with your ideas about making friends?

Analyzing Literature

RECALL AND INTERPRET

1. Why are the speaker's notions of America and baseball fuzzy?
2. Why do all the players end up on the ground when the speaker groans, "my shin, my shin"?
3. Why does the speaker mention the other players by name? Do you think they are still friends? Explain your answer.

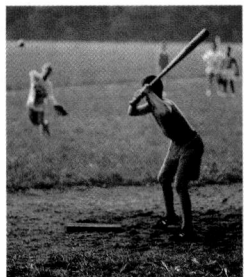

EVALUATE AND CONNECT

4. At what point in the poem do you know that the boys have become friends? How does this experience connect with your own?
5. How does the poet bring to life the experience of playing a lighthearted baseball game?
6. Have you ever attempted to play a new game with strangers, or had a stranger join your own game? Describe your experience.

LITERARY ELEMENTS

Setting

The **setting** of a story, poem, or play is the time and place in which the events take place. The setting can include the geographic location, the time period, the season of the year, and even the time of day. Sometimes the writer describes all or part of the setting. For example, the poet tells the reader that the events in "How I Learned English" take place during a baseball game in the town of Williamsport, Pennsylvania.

1. How can you tell what time of day the baseball game started?
2. Why would a newly arrived immigrant find the setting of the poem meaningful?

● See **Literary Terms Handbook,** p. R10.

Extending Your Response

Literature Groups

Changing Places Imagine that you are the speaker of "How I Learned English." Work with your group to write a series of letters about your new life in America to people in your old home town.

Writing About Literature

Point of View "How I Learned English" is told from the point of view of a young boy who has recently immigrated to the United States. Write a brief poem or a prose paragraph from another character's point of view.

LITERARY ELEMENTS

1. It was most likely late afternoon because there was a blue sky and the boys played until dusk.
2. Baseball is generally considered an American sport. Not only did the speaker learn a lesson in English from this game, he also made his first friends in America while playing.

Additional Resources

 Literary Elements Transparency 35

✓ ASSESSMENT OPTIONS

📁 *Quick Checks,* p. 35
📁 *Selection and Theme Assessment,* pp. 61–62
📁 *Performance Assessment,* p. 33
💾 *Testmaker*

Responding to the Selection

Personal Response

Students may describe experiences in which they have made friends through playing sports or humorous incidents.

Analyzing Literature

1. They are fuzzy because he has just moved to America. He seems unfamiliar with the game.
2. The other players laugh so hard they fall down because he uses the word *shin* instead of *forehead.*
3. He mentions names because they are new friends. Some students will note that the reference to "Chuck Keller, fat even as a boy," implies that the speaker knows him as an adult.
4. The friendship seems to begin when the boys laugh together and help the poet stand up. Students may relate experiences about new friends offering them help.
5. The poet uses vivid details, humor, informal language, and real-life images.
6. Students may describe experiences that were amusing, embarrassing, or enlightening.

Extending Your Response

Literature Groups Suggest that students include descriptions in the letters of the neighborhood, new activities, and new friends.
COLLAB. LEARN.

Writing About Literature

Students' writings should
- incorporate details from the poem.
- include the feelings and observations of the character who is describing the action.
- take the form of a poem or a short narrative.

COMPARING selections

Objective

- To compare a personal narrative and a poem, both about immigrants adjusting to life in the United States

COMPARE RESPONSES

1. Students should give reasons for their preferences.
2. Most students will agree that Gage includes more details about the immigrant experience. However, Djanikian offers a view of an immigrant's attempt to assimilate American culture as he makes friends.

COMPARE CHARACTERS

Students' conversations should

- describe each character's motivation to learn English.
- explain how each character learned English.
- share each character's feelings about learning English.

Additional Resources

📁 *Literature Groups Sourcebook*

COMPARE EXPERIENCES

Students should

- investigate the country's languages, customs, and activities.
- use details from their research to visualize themselves in the country.
- describe their way of communicating in a non-English-speaking country.

Teaching Options

COMPARING SELECTIONS

The Teacher Who Changed My Life and How I Learned English

COMPARE RESPONSES

Both Nicholas Gage's personal narrative and Gregory Djanikian's poem focus on the experiences of a new immigrant.

1. Which selection did you prefer—the narrative or the poem? Give reasons for your answer.
2. From which selection did you learn more about the immigrant experience? What did you learn?

COMPARE CHARACTERS

In both selections, the narrator or speaker tells of his experience in learning English. If Nicholas Gage and the speaker in "How I Learned English" could meet, what do you think they might tell each other? Write an imaginary conversation between the two characters as they compare their experiences of learning English.

COMPARE EXPERIENCES

The essay and the poem each give the reader a different sense of how it feels to be a new immigrant in this country.

- Think of a non-English-speaking country you would like to visit someday. Find pictures of the places that interest you. Try to find out a bit about the language and the customs.
- Close your eyes and imagine traveling to this country and meeting students your age. What would be a typical activity for them? Think about how you would communicate with your new friends.
- Share your ideas with a partner or a small group.

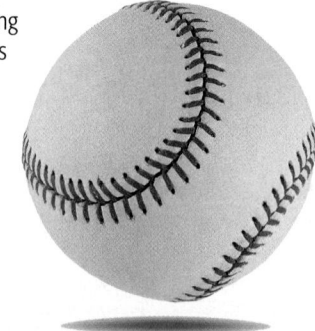

380 THEME 4

PORTFOLIO OPTIONS

Select and Reflect Encourage students to reflect on conversations they wrote for the activity above by asking themselves these questions:

- Is my dialogue believable?
- Did I include questions that these two characters might want to ask each other?

 Activity Have students attach their reflections to their conversations and place them in their portfolios. At a later time, they might consider using the comments to revise their conversations as portfolio showcase pieces. **L2**

Additional Resources
📁 *Writing Assessment and Portfolio Management*, pp. 17–19

Using Irregular Verbs Correctly

For **regular verbs,** the past form is made by adding -ed to the base. The past participle form is the same as the past form, but with a "helping" verb such as *has.*

Base form: I *like* poems. **Past form:** I *liked* the poem by Lucille Clifton.
Past participle form: I *have liked* most of the poems in this book.

Many **irregular verbs** use the same form for the past and the past participle.

Base form: *catch* **Past form:** *caught*
Past participle form: *has caught*

Some irregular verbs, however, have two different forms—one for use without a helping verb and another for use with a helping verb.

Base form: *grows* **Past form:** *grew*
Past participle form: *had grown*

Problem 1 an improperly formed irregular verb

*The player **standed** in the outfield.*

Solution *The player **stood** in the outfield.*

Problem 2 use of the past form when the past participle is needed

*He **seen** the ball before it hit him.*

Solution *He **had seen** the ball before it hit him.*

Here are the base form, past form, and past participle form of some irregular verbs.

begin, began, begun do, did, done know, knew, known
give, gave, given tell, told, told write, wrote, written

● For more about irregular verbs, see **Language Handbook,** p. R16.

EXERCISE

Write the correct form of each verb in parentheses.

1. Marjorie Hurd (give) Nicholas Gage an assignment.
2. He (write) the first essay he had ever (write).
3. He (tell) about how his journey had (begin) in a nighttime escape.
4. His classmates had not (knew) the difficulties Gage had (go) through.

Objective
• To recognize and use correctly past forms of regular and irregular verbs

Teaching Strategies
Ask students to draw a quick picture of one thing they did yesterday. Have them present their pictures and write a sentence on the board describing the activity. For example, *Yesterday, I baby-sat my sister; I rode my bike; I watched TV.* Go through the sentences on the board and ask students to determine which verbs are regular and which are irregular. List the verbs in two columns.

Exercise
1. gave
2. wrote/written
3. told/begun
4. known/gone

Additional Resources

■ *Grammar and Language Workbook,* pp. 95–100

■ *Grammar and Composition Handbook,* Lessons 3.11, 3.12

■ *Writer's Choice,* Lesson 10.10

Teaching Options

Writing *Minilesson*

A Memoir Using "The Teacher Who Changed My Life" as an example, explain to students that a memoir is usually written in the past tense, since it focuses on the personal recollections of the writer. Ask students whether they think the poem, "How I Learned English," by Gregory Djanikian could be considered a memoir.

Activity Have each student choose a form in which to write: poem, essay, short story, article, or play. Then ask each to write a memoir about something or someone that changed his or her life. Have students read their memoirs aloud to the class or in small groups. **L2**

Additional Resources

■ *Writer's Choice,* Lesson 1.4

Objectives

- To read and analyze two stories about the relationship between guest and host
- To recognize similes and metaphors and to understand what they compare
- To write a paragraph that compares how characters in two stories deal with unwanted guests

Skills

Reading/Thinking: Inferring; Drawing Conclusions; Classifying; Problem/Solution
Writing: Sequel to a Folktale
Vocabulary: Synonyms; Etymology
Grammar/Language: Capitalizing Names; Adjectives and Adverbs; Suffixes and the Silent e
Listening/Speaking: Storytelling
Life Skills: Letter of Introduction
Collaboration: Literature Groups

Motivating
→OPTIONS

Selection Focus Transparency 36: Have students view and discuss the superstition about dealing with unwanted guests. Invite them to share any superstitions they know.

Focus Activity: As an extension of the Focus Activity, have pairs talk about misunderstandings that can arise between guests and hosts from different cultures.

Before You Read
Oh Broom, Get to Work and *Anansi and His Visitor, Turtle*

MEET
YOSHIKO UCHIDA

Yoshiko Uchida (yō shē′ kō ū′ chē dä) was born in California to Japanese parents. As a child and young adult, she did not feel accepted as an American. She expressed her thoughts in journals in which she "was trying to . . . preserve the . . . joy and sadness of certain moments."

Yoshiko Uchida was born in 1921 and died in 1992. This story was first published in 1977.

MEET
EDNA MASON KAULA

Born in Australia, Edna Mason Kaula (kä ōō′ lä) has lived in several countries. Kaula has written and illustrated books for children and adults, based on her travels around the world.

Edna Mason Kaula was born in 1906. The story about Anansi and Turtle comes from her book African Village Folktales, *published in 1968.*

FOCUS ACTIVITY

How should hosts and their guests behave toward each other?

QuickWrite
List ways to deal with guests who don't behave properly.

Setting a Purpose
Read these two stories to discover ways to deal with an awkward guest-host situation.

BACKGROUND

Did You Know? The traditional tales of West Africa include a trickster named Anansi. Anansi is often a spider who is a smart and funny mischief-maker. His tricks can be nasty, but his victims usually get even in the end.

VOCABULARY PREVIEW

intrusion (in trōō′ zhən) *n.* a sudden interruption; p. 384
devise (di vīz′) *v.* to think out; invent; plan; p. 384
pious (pī′ əs) *adj.* having either genuine or pretended religious devotion; p. 385
pompous (pom′ pəs) *adj.* showing an exaggerated sense of self-importance; p. 385
dispense (dis pens′) *v.* to give out in portions; p. 385
indifferent (in dif′ ər ənt) *adj.* having or showing a lack of feeling, concern, or care; p. 385
laden (lād′ ən) *adj.* loaded; weighed down; burdened; p. 386
meek (mēk) *adj.* patient and mild in manner; gentle; p. 389
delectable (di lek′ tə bəl) *adj.* highly pleasing or delightful, especially to the taste; delicious; p. 389
ravenous (rav′ ə nəs) *adj.* extremely hungry; p. 390
cunning (kun′ ing) *adj.* crafty; sly; p. 390
anticipation (an tis′ ə pā′ shən) *n.* a feeling of excited expectation; p. 390

RESOURCE MANAGER

Lesson Planning Resource
The *Theme Four Planning Guide* (pp. 49–54) provides additional lesson notes and reduced versions of all print resources.

📁 **Other Print Resources**
- Active Reading Guide, p. 36
- Vocabulary Practice, p. 23
- Reading Workbook, pp. 63–64
- Grammar and Language Workbook, pp. 117–118, 127–128, 237–238, 291–292

- Grammar and Composition Handbook, Lessons 5.1, 6.1, 6.2, 12.2, 15.4
- Quick Checks, p. 36
- Selection and Theme Assessment, pp. 63–64
- Performance Assessment, p. 34
- Spanish Summaries, p. 36
- Spanish Translations
- Inclusion Strategies
- English Language Learners Sourcebook

 Transparencies
- Selection Focus 36
- Literary Elements 36
- Grammar and Language 32, 33

Technology
🎧 Audio Library
🎧 Spanish Audio Library
💻 Glencoe Literature Web Site
💾 Testmaker

Oh Broom, Get to Work

Yoshiko Uchida

Fuji from Lava Beach. Lilla Cabot Perry (1848–1933). Oil on canvas, 7 x 21¾ in. Collection of Mrs. Lilla Cabot Levitt.

I was on my way home from school when I found it. A little dead sparrow. It lay still and stiff, its legs thrust in the air like two sticks. It was the first dead creature I had seen close up, and it filled me with both dread and fascination.

I knew what I would do. I would give the bird a nice funeral. Mama would find a piece of soft red silk for me from her bag of sewing scraps. I would wrap the bird in a silken shroud,[1] put it in a candy box, and bury it beneath the peach tree. Maybe I would have Mama say a prayer for it, like the minister did at real funerals.

---

1. Here, *shroud* means "a cloth used to wrap a body for burial."

SUMMARY

In the first story, "Oh Broom, Get to Work," Yo Chan puts up with her parents' many pompous guests—until one day she gets even. In the second story, Anansi invites Turtle in for dinner—but only after Turtle washes his paws. By the time Turtle finishes washing, Anansi has finished the meal. Turtle, too, figures out how to get even.

📁 *Spanish Summaries,* p. 36

A Active Reading

PREDICT Ask students to read the title "Oh Broom, Get to Work" and the first paragraph. Have them predict what the rest of the story might be about. Suggest that they periodically revisit their predictions as they read to verify or to revise them.

Additional Resources

📁 *Active Reading Guide,* p. 36

🎧 *Audio Library*

🎧 *Spanish Audio Library*

Teaching Options

CONNECTING TO OTHER SELECTIONS
For a teaching strategy that connects "Oh Broom, Get to Work" to "Turkeys," turn to page 48 in the *Theme Eight Planning Guide.*

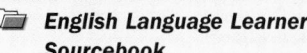

ENGLISH LANGUAGE LEARNERS

Behavior of Hosts and Guests
Some of Yo Chan's visitors have customs that are strange to her, such as leaving water in the bathtub. How does this unfamiliar custom differ from the American custom?

Activity Have students observe how American hosts and their guests behave in real life and on television. Then have English language learners and English-proficient students work together to list "proper" guest and host behavior. Pairs may want to share with the class differences between how Americans and people from their native cultures behave.
COLLAB. LEARN.

Additional Resources

📁 *English Language Learners Sourcebook*

B **Literary Elements**

NARRATOR What words let readers know the story is being told through the eyes of a first-person narrator? *(When talking about herself, the narrator uses I, my, and myself; about others, she uses she or he.)*

C **Literary Elements**

FIGURATIVE LANGUAGE: *Simile* Point out the phrase *a squat blob of a man...as silent as a mushroom.* Remind students that comparisons between two things that use the words *like* or *as* are similes. Have students explain what image this simile creates in their minds.

D **Active Reading**

EVALUATE Have students discuss what the problem or conflict in this story appears to be. The following model illustrates the thinking process involved in evaluating.

Model: The narrator needs her mother's help, but an uninvited visitor is taking up her mother's time. It sounds as if this has happened before because the narrator says this visitor was one of "countless visitors, who came to see my parents." I think the conflict has to do with all these unwanted visitors.

E **Literary Elements**

CHARACTER Have students explain what type of person the mother is. *(She is patient and polite because she tolerates uninvited visitors even if they are boring.)*

Oh Broom, Get to Work

B I picked up the bird carefully, cupping it in both hands, and ran home. I rushed through the kitchen and flung open the swinging door to the dining room.

"Look, Mama! I found a dead sparrow!"

C But Mama was busy. She was sitting in the easy chair, knitting quietly. Sitting across from her on the sofa was a squat blob of a man—balding and gray—as silent as a mushroom.

The only sound was the soft ticking of the Chelsea clock on the mantel above the fireplace. I could see dust motes floating in the shaft of late afternoon sun that filtered in from the small west window.

Poor Mama was stuck with company again. She and the guest had both run out of things to say, but the visitor didn't want to leave.

"Hello, Yo Chan," my mother called. She seemed happy for the intrusion. "How was school today?"

D But all I thought was, company again! It wasn't the first time a visitor had deprived me of my mother's time and attention, and I was tired of having them intrude into our lives uninvited. I stomped out of the living room without even a word of greeting to our guest, and knew I would have to bury the sparrow by myself.

Mama might have sung a Japanese hymn for me in her high, slightly off-key voice, and she certainly would have offered a better prayer than I could devise. But I did the best I could.

"Dear Heavenly Father," I began. "Please bless this little bird. It never hurt anybody. Thank you. Amen."

I buried the box beneath a mound of soft, loose dirt, picked a few nasturtiums to lay on top, and made a cross out of two small twigs.

The gray-blob mushroom was just another of the countless visitors, usually from Japan, who came to see my parents. They were both graduates of Doshisha, one of Japan's leading Christian universities, and had close ties with many of its professors. This meant that many of our visitors were ministers or young men studying to become ministers at the Pacific School of Religion in Berkeley.[2]

Once in a while, one of the visitors would be a pleasant surprise. Like the Reverend Kimura, who sang the books of the Bible to the tune of an old folk song.

"*Mah-tai, Mah-ko, Luka, Yoha-neh-deh-un* . . ." he sang out in a loud, clear voice. "*Shito, Roma, Corinto, Zen-ko-sho* . . ." He clapped in time as he sang.

I saw Mama's eyes light up as she listened, and soon she joined in, clapping and singing and laughing at the pure joy of it.

E Mama surprised me sometimes. She could be a lot of fun depending on whom she was with. It was too bad, I thought, that so much of the time she had to be

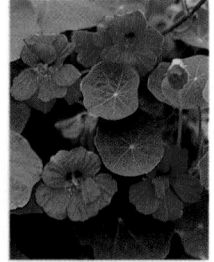

Did You Know?
The *nasturtium* is a common, funnel-shaped flower that grows in a variety of colors.

2. This school is in *Berkeley,* California.

Vocabulary
intrusion (in trōō′ zhən) *n.* a sudden interruption
devise (di vīz′) *v.* to think out; invent; plan

384 🦢 THEME 4

Reading *Minilesson*

Classifying Write on the board: *Sitting on the sofa was a squat blob of a man—balding and gray—as silent as a mushroom.* Explain to students that the author, Yoshiko Uchida, uses many sensory images to describe story events. Have them suggest which senses the underlined words in the sentence appeal to. *(blob: vision; balding: vision; gray: vision; as silent as a mushroom: hearing)*

Activity Have students work in small groups to identify other sensory images in the story. Ask each group to prepare a chart, like the one at right, that shows to which senses the images appeal.

L2 **COLLAB. LEARN.**

Additional Resources

📁 *Reading Workbook,* pp. 63–64

Vision	Touch	Hearing
blob		as silent as a mushroom
stomped		stomped
		off-key voice
soft, loose dirt		soft, loose dirt
clapping	clapping	clapping
singing		singing
laughing		laughing

Yoshiko Uchida ❧

E serious and proper, while visiting ministers smothered her with their <u>pious</u> attitudes.

To me they were all achingly and endlessly boring. It was only once in a great while that a Reverend Kimura turned up, **F** like a bright red jelly bean in a jar full of black licorice.

One <u>pompous</u> minister from Japan not only stayed overnight, which was bad enough, but left his dirty bathwater in the tub for Mama to wash out.

"What nerve!" Keiko fumed.[3]

"I'll say!" I echoed.

But Mama explained that in Japan everyone washed and rinsed outside the tub and got in just to soak. "That way the water in the tub stays clean, and you leave it for the next person."

Mama got down on her knees to wash out the tub, saying, "We're lucky he didn't try to wash himself outside the tub and flood the bathroom."

Some kind of luck, I thought.

I didn't feel at all lucky about the seminary[4] students who often dropped in, plunked themselves down on our sofa, and stayed until they were invited to have supper with us.

"Poor boys, they're lonely and homesick," Mama would say.

"They just need some of Mama's kind heart and good cooking," Papa would add. And if they needed some fatherly advice,

he was more than willing to <u>dispense</u> plenty of that as well.

Both my parents had grown up poor, and they also knew what it was to be lonely. They cared deeply about other people and were always ready to lend a helping hand to anyone. Mama couldn't bear to think of her children ever being less than kind and caring.

"Don't ever be <u>indifferent</u>," she would say to Keiko and me. "That is the worst fault of all." **G**

It was a fault she certainly never had. She would even send vitamins or herbs to some ailing person she had just met in the dentist's waiting room.

On holidays all the Japanese students from the Pacific School of Religion— sometimes as many as five or six—were invited to dinner. Keiko and I always complained shamelessly when they came. **H**

"Aw, Mama . . . do you *have* to invite them?"

But we knew what we were expected to do. We flicked the dust cloth over the furniture, added extra boards to the dining room table so it filled up the entire room, and set it with Mama's good linen tablecloth and the company china.

If it was to be a turkey dinner, we put out the large plates and good silverware. If it was a sukiyaki dinner, we put out the rice bowls, smaller dishes, and black lacquer chopsticks.

The men came in their best clothes, their squeaky shoes shined, their hair smelling of camellia hair oil. Papa didn't

---

3. Here, *fume* means "to be filled with or show anger or irritation."
4. A *seminary* is a school that trains ministers, priests, or rabbis.

Vocabulary

pious (pī′ əs) *adj.* having either genuine or pretended religious devotion
pompous (pom′ pəs) *adj.* showing an exaggerated sense of self-importance
dispense (dis pens′) *v.* to give out in portions
indifferent (in dif′ ər ənt) *adj.* having or showing a lack of feeling, concern, or care

---

INCLUSION STRATEGIES

Learning Disabled Some students may have difficulty connecting the visual images on these pages to what these images say about a character.

Activity Have students draw one of the visual images Uchida uses on this page, such as *a bright red jelly bean in a jar full of black licorice.* Then have stu-

dents create a list of visual images telling what each image and its related character have in common. **L1**

Additional Resources
📁 *Inclusion Strategies*

Vo·cab·u·lar·y Skills

Etymology In Japanese, *suki* means "slices of" and *yaki* means "roast." *Sukiyaki*, therefore, refers to slices of cooked meat and vegetables. In Japanese, *sukiyaki* is pronounced "ski-ya-kee," but most Americans pronounce it "su-kee-ya-kee."

I **Active Reading**

CONNECT How do your students imagine a sukiyaki dinner makes the guests feel? *(They probably enjoy it. Sukiyaki is a familiar meal in a strange country, so the guests probably feel comforted.)*

J **Active Reading**

EVALUATE Ask your students why Yo Chan at first thinks Mr. Okada is heading in the wrong direction when he goes into the kitchen. *(Yo Chan probably thinks Mr. Okada wants to visit the restroom.)*

K **Critical Thinking**

INFERRING Keiko and Yo Chan start laughing at the dinner table. Ask students how they think this laughter makes the guests feel? *(It may make them uncomfortable, but it might not bother them because it comes from a pair of young girls.)*

---

cook much else, but he was an expert when it came to making sukiyaki,[5] and he cooked it right at the table with gas piped in from the kitchen stove. As the men arrived, he would start the fat sizzling in the small iron pan.

Soon Mama would bring out huge platters <u>laden</u> with thin slivers of beef, slices of bean curd cake, scallions, bamboo shoots, spinach, celery, and yam noodle threads. Then Papa would combine a little of everything in broth flavored with soy sauce,[6] sugar, and wine, and the mouth-watering smells would drift through the entire house.

One evening in the middle of a sukiyaki dinner, one of the guests, Mr. Okada, suddenly rose from the table and hurried into the kitchen. We all stopped eating as the scholarly Mr. Okada vanished without explanation.

"Mama," I began, "he's going the wrong way if he has to . . ."

Mama stopped me with a firm hand on my knee. My sister and I looked at each other. What did he want in the kitchen anyway? More rice? Water? What?

It seemed a half hour before Mr. Okada finally reappeared. But he was smiling and seemed much happier.

"I'm sorry," he murmured, "but it was so warm I had to remove my winter undershirt." He wiped his face with a big

handkerchief and added, "I feel much better now."

I knew if I looked at Keiko we would both explode. But I did. And we did. We laughed so hard we had to leave the table and rush into the kitchen holding our sides. Keiko and I often got the giggles at company dinners, and the harder we tried to stop, the harder we laughed. The only solution was for us not ever to glance at each other if we felt the giggles coming on.

In spite of all our grumbling, Keiko and I often enjoyed ourselves at these dinners. Sometimes it was Papa who provided the laughs. He loved to talk, and everyone always liked listening to his stories. Sometimes he would tell a joke he had heard at the office:

A visitor from Japan looked up at the sky. "Beautiful pigeons!" he says to a native San Franciscan.

"No, no," answers the native. "Those aren't pigeons, they're gulls."

---

5. This Japanese dish consists of thin strips of meat, vegetables, and other ingredients cooked together, usually at the dining table.

6. *Bean curd,* also known as tofu (tō´ foo), is a food made from soybeans. *Scallions* are young green onions. *Soy sauce,* another soybean product, is a salty, dark-brown sauce used in Japanese and Chinese cooking.

Vocabulary
laden (lād´ ən) *adj.* loaded; weighed down; burdened

Teaching Options

Grammar and Language *Minilesson*

Capitalizing Names Write the following two pairs of sentences on the board:
1. *I asked Dad if I could go.*
   I asked my dad if I could go.
2. *We enjoy Aunt Maria's visits.*
   My aunt is a nurse.
Remind students to capitalize a title that describes a family relationship when it is used with or in place of a proper name.

Activity Ask students to decide which relationship titles should be capitalized in these sentences.
1. My grandfather is a jazz musician. *(correct)*
2. I invited uncle James to dinner. *(Uncle)*
3. When will mom be home? *(Mom)*
4. His aunt lives in England. *(correct)*
L2

Additional Resources

🖌 *Grammar and Language Transparency 32*

📕 *Grammar and Language Workbook,* pp. 237–238

📕 *Grammar and Composition Handbook,* Lesson 12.2

📕 *Writer's Choice,* Lesson 19.2

The visitor replies, smiling, "Well, gulls or boys, they're beautiful pigeons!"

Much laughter all around.

After dinner Papa liked to gather everyone around the piano. He had a good baritone voice, often sang solos at church, and even organized the church choir. Keiko played the piano, and we sang everything from "Old Black Joe" to "In the Good Old Summertime."

 Sometimes Keiko and I added to the entertainment by playing duets for our guests—a fairly audacious[7] act since most of the time I hadn't practiced all week. It never occurred to me then, but I suppose we were just as boring to them as they so often seemed to us.

I once thought I'd found the perfect solution for getting rid of unwanted guests. Mrs. Wasa, who was like an adopted grandmother, told me one day of an old Japanese superstition.

"If you want someone to leave," she said, "just drape a cloth over the bristles of a broom and stand it upside down. It always works!"

 I filed that wonderful bit of information inside my head, and the very next time Mama was trapped in the living room with another silent mushroom, I gave it a try. I did just as Mrs. Wasa instructed and stood the broom at the crack of a swinging door leading to the dining and living rooms.

"Oh broom," I murmured. "Get to work!"

I kept a watchful eye on our visitor, and before too long, he actually got up and left.

---

7. An *audacious* (ô dā′ shəs) act is recklessly or shamelessly bold and daring.

"Mama, it worked! It worked!" I shouted, dancing into the living room with the broom. "He left! I got him to leave!"

But Mama was horrified.

"*Mah,* Yo Chan," she said. "You put the broom at the doorway where he could see?"

I nodded. "I didn't think he'd notice."

Only then did I realize that our visitor had not only seen the broom, but had probably left because he knew a few Japanese superstitions himself.

I'd always thought the seminary on the hill was bent on endlessly churning out dull ministers to try my soul. But that afternoon I felt as though I'd evened the score just a little.

❖

---

0 **Literary Elements**

FOLKTALE Ask students what a folk-tale is and if they can name the different types of folktales. *(A folktale is a traditional story passed along orally long before it was written down. The author is usually unknown. The following are different types of folktales: fairy tales, myths, legends, tall tales, trickster stories, and animal stories.)*

⌾ Historical Note ⌾

This story is an Ashanti tale. The Ashanti people live in the West African nation of Ghana. They are well known for their skills in making pottery and gold and silver ornaments. Beginning in medieval days, Ghana was an important gold trading center. The Ashanti people traded gold from the south for products (especially salt) from North Africa. Later they traded with Europeans.

Anansi and His Visitor, Turtle
A Story from the Ashanti People

Retold by Edna Mason Kaula ∿

Teaching Options

CONNECTING TO OTHER SELECTIONS
For a teaching strategy that connects "Anansi and His Visitor, Turtle," to "The Force of Luck," turn to page 40 in the *Theme Six Planning Guide.*

Listening and Speaking *Minilesson*

Storytelling "Anansi and His Visitor, Turtle" is part of the oral tradition of the Ashanti culture. Invite interested students to try their hands at this ancient art.

Activity Have students choose folktales they enjoy that are relatively short and have an engaging plot. Some may want to memorize their tales, while others may just want to memorize key points or impor-

tant dialogue. Have students practice using their voices to engage listeners. Let them practice using different voices for different characters and varying the pitch, tone, and loudness of their voices. Pausing while telling a story can also have a dramatic effect. When students are ready, have them perform their stories for a small group. **L2** **COLLAB. LEARN.**

It was almost time for Sun to sink to his resting place when Turtle, tired and dusty from hours of wandering, came to Anansi's house in the middle of a clearing in the woods. Turtle was hungry and the appetizing aroma of freshly cooked fish and yams drew him to approach Anansi's door and to knock. Anansi jerked the door open. When he saw the tired stranger he was inwardly annoyed, but it was an unwritten law of his country that one must never, no never, refuse hospitality to a passer-by.

P Anansi smiled grimly and said, "Come in, come in, and share my dinner, Mr. Turtle."

As Turtle stretched out one paw to help himself from the steaming platter Anansi almost choked on a mouthful of food. In a shocked voice he said, "Turtle, I must remind you that in my country it is ill-mannered to come to the table without first washing. Please go to the stream at the foot of the hill and wash your dusty paws."

Turtle waddled down the hill and waded in the water for a while. He even washed his face. By the time he had trudged back up the trail to Anansi's house, the platter of fish was half empty. Anansi was eating at a furious rate.

Turtle stretched out one paw to help himself to food, but again Anansi stopped him. "Turtle, your paws are still dusty. Please, go wash them."

"It is the dust from the long trail up the hill," Turtle explained in a meek voice. Clearly, it was not Turtle's place to argue if he expected to share the delectable meal,

Q

Viewing the painting: How does the artist combine animal and human characteristics in artwork here and on page 388? Why does he do so?

Vocabulary
meek (mēk) *adj.* patient and mild in manner; gentle
delectable (di lek′ tə bəl) *adj.* highly pleasing or delightful, especially to the taste; delicious

P ## Literary Elements

FIGURATIVE LANGUAGE: *Personification*
Remind students that personification occurs when an animal or an object is given human characteristics. What human things do the characters do in the first few paragraphs of this tale? *(Sun rests at day's end. Turtle knocks on a door. Anansi cooks his food and invites Turtle in to be hospitable.)*

Q ## Literary Elements

CONFLICT Discuss the conflict of the story. *(The unwritten rule is that Anansi must invite Turtle in, but Anansi doesn't want to share his meal. To get around the rule, he tricks Turtle, who misses the meal.)*

VIEWING THE PAINTING

The illustrations on these two pages are by Andrew Glass, who has illustrated a number of books—his own as well as those of other authors—for young readers.

Viewing Response *The artist portrays animal features, such as the turtle's shell and the spider's eight legs, but he gives the animals human expressions and behaviors, shows them wearing human garments, and provides Anansi with a very human-looking table full of food. These details help make the characters accessible to readers and add to the story's humor.*

INTERDISCIPLINARY CONNECTION

Social Studies Meals play an important role in both "Oh Broom, Get to Work" and "Anansi and His Visitor, Turtle," one, a story based on Japanese traditions, and the other, an African folktale. This presents an opportunity for learning about festive meals and customs in different cultures.

Activity Have small groups do research and plan short reports for the class on foods, festivals, or other interesting customs in cultures other than the one they now share with their classmates. Students who grew up in different cultures can draw on their own experience; others can do research, using personal interviews as well as books, magazines, and the Internet as sources. **L2**

Active Reading

PREDICT Ask students what might happen to Anansi. *(In trickster tales, like this one, characters usually get back at the one who played the trick. Therefore, Turtle will probably get even with Anansi.)*

Literary Elements

IRONY Verbal irony occurs when a character says one thing but means another. Turtle says, "Thank you for your wonderful hospitality, Anansi." Ask students why this statement is ironic. *(Turtle didn't get anything to eat, and he goes home "in a huff.")*

Literary Elements

REPETITION Turtle says, "I must remind you that in my country…" What does this sentence remind readers of? Have students explain what effect this repetition has. *(Anansi made an almost identical statement. Turtle's repetition makes it obvious that he is repaying Anansi for his earlier inhospitality.)*

Thematic Focus

Where the Heart Is Ask students to discuss how this story relates to the theme. Where is Anansi's heart when he goes through the motions of acting hospitable?

✓ ASSESSMENT OPTIONS

📁 *Quick Checks,* p. 36

Teaching Options

---

so he crawled down the hill a second time and rewashed his paws. Turtle was careful to walk on the grass beside the dusty trail on the climb back to Anansi's house. He hurried, for by now he was <u>ravenous</u>.

But, oh dear! Anansi had scraped the platter bare of fish and yams. "My, that was a good dinner," he said, wiping the last drop of gravy from his chin.

"Thank you for your wonderful hospitality, Anansi. Some day you must visit me." And Turtle, in a huff, went on home.

Some months later Anansi visited Turtle. After creepy-crawling all day from one tall grass stem to the next, he found Turtle snoozing beside the river.

"Well, well," exclaimed Turtle. "So you have come to share my dinner. Make yourself comfortable, my dear Anansi, while I go below and prepare the food." He plunged into the river with a splash. Anansi was hungry. He paced the shore line and watched for Turtle's reappearance.

At last Turtle's head popped above the water. "Dinner is ready," he called as he bit into a huge clam. "Come on down." Then he disappeared from sight.

Anansi dived head first into the water, sank a few inches, then floated to the surface. His spindly legs and tiny body prevented him from sinking. He flipped and flapped his puny[1] arms, tried swallow dives

---

1. *Puny* (pyōō′ nē) means "small and weak."

---

and belly flops, but he could not reach the bed of the river.

Then that <u>cunning</u> spider schemed. He filled the pockets of his jacket with small round pebbles, dived into the river, and sank with a bump that landed him right at the dinner table. Before him was spread the most delicious meal he had ever seen. There were oysters and clams, mussels, slices of eel, and crabs. As a centerpiece, sprays of watercress rested against large pink shrimp. Anansi's eyes widened with pleasure, his stomach rumbled in <u>anticipation</u>.

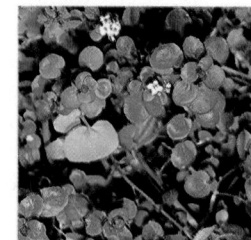

Did You Know?
Watercress is a floating water plant bearing long clusters of small white flowers. Its leaves are eaten as salad greens.

Turtle, already seated at the table, swallowed a piece of eel, looked at Anansi and said, "Oh, Anansi, I must remind you that in my country it is ill-mannered to come to the table wearing a jacket. Please take it off."

Very slowly Anansi removed his jacket. Very slowly Anansi left the table. Without the weight of the pebbles to hold him down, he floated straight up through the green water and out of sight.

When you set out to outsmart another person to your own advantage, there is usually someone who can outsmart you.

Vocabulary
ravenous (rav′ ə nəs) *adj.* extremely hungry
cunning (kun′ ing) *adj.* crafty; sly
anticipation (an tis′ ə pā′ shən) *n.* a feeling of excited expectation

---

Grammar and Language *Minilesson*

Adjectives and Adverbs Remind students that an adjective is a word that modifies, or describes, a noun. An adverb, however, is a word that describes a verb, an adjective, or another adverb.

Activity Work with students to help them identify the adjectives and adverbs in the following sentences.

1. His <u>spindly</u> legs and <u>tiny</u> body prevented him from sinking. *(adjectives)*
2. <u>Very slowly</u> Anansi removed his jacket. *(adverbs)*
3. Turtle bit into a <u>huge</u> clam. *(adjective)*

Ask students to write three sentences about the story that include an adjective or an adverb. Finally, challenge them to write one sentence that includes both an adjective and an adverb. **L2**

Additional Resources

📖 *Grammar and Language Transparency 33*

📕 *Grammar and Language Workbook,* pp. 117–118, 127–128

📗 *Grammar and Composition Handbook,* Lessons 5.1, 6.1, 6.2

📘 *Writer's Choice,* Lessons 12.1, 12.6

Responding to Literature

Oh Broom, Get to Work and *Anansi and His Visitor, Turtle*

PERSONAL RESPONSE

Take another look at your list of ways to deal with guests from the **Focus Activity** on page 382. How do your ideas compare with the methods of the narrator in "Oh Broom, Get to Work" or Anansi in "Anansi and His Visitor, Turtle"?

Analyzing Literature

RECALL

1. What is Yo Chan's opinion about most of the visiting students?
2. What are the two meals served on holidays at Yo Chan's house?
3. What is the Japanese superstition about getting rid of guests who stay too long?
4. How does Anansi get rid of Turtle? What does Turtle do to Anansi to get even?

INTERPRET

5. Do you think Yo Chan appreciates her mother's hospitality to the young men? How can you tell?
6. From the description of cooking sukiyaki, what can you **infer** about Yo Chan's feelings toward her father and her heritage?
7. Does Yo Chan or Anansi feel guilty for sending their guests away? Support your opinion with evidence from the stories.
8. Why, do you think, does the storyteller end "Anansi and His Visitor, Turtle" with a moral?

EVALUATE AND CONNECT

9. The characters in "Anansi and His Visitor, Turtle" talk and act like people. How would your response to the story change if the characters were real human beings?
10. Do you think Yo Chan's reaction to her parents' guests is hospitable? How would you have behaved in her situation?

LITERARY ELEMENTS

Metaphors

Think about what you have learned about **figurative language**. A **metaphor** compares two seemingly different things by saying one thing is the other thing. A **simile** uses the words *like* or *as* to compare two things. In "Oh Broom, Get to Work," Yo Chan uses a metaphor when she calls the first uninvited guest "the gray-blob mushroom." He isn't actually a mushroom, but Yo Chan thinks he looks and acts like one.

1. Reread or skim "Oh Broom, Get to Work" to find another example of a metaphor and one of a simile. Write a sentence explaining what two things are being compared in each example.

2. Find and copy an example of a metaphor or a simile from any other selection in this theme. Tell what two things are being compared in it.

● See **Literary Terms Handbook,** p. R6.

Literature and Writing

Writing About Literature

Students' paragraphs should

- describe similarities and differences in how the guests are treated in each of the stories.
- compare these similarities and differences.
- use smooth transitions to move from one example to the next.

Creative Writing

Students' sequels should

- contain dialogue and behaviors in keeping with the characters' traits.
- show reasonable motivation.
- conclude logically.

Extending Your Response

Literature Groups Encourage students on each side of this issue to list their main arguments. Then have them develop ways to counter what they imagine will be the other team's main arguments. **COLLAB. LEARN.**

Interdisciplinary Activity Remind students that humor often arises when characters do the wrong thing with unexpected or surprising results. Encourage students to think of funny situations before they begin drawing their comic books. They may want to include a moral after each situation they show.

Learning for Life Letters should be written in proper letter format. They should introduce the student and explain why the student wants to stay with the Uchidas. Above all, the letters should be polite and respectful.

Literature and Writing

Writing About Literature

Comparing Characters Write a paragraph or two comparing the way the narrator in "Oh Broom, Get to Work" deals with uninvited guests with the way Anansi and Turtle treat each other in "Anansi and His Visitor, Turtle."

Creative Writing

The Next Meal What happened to the jacket that Anansi left at the bottom of the river with Turtle? Write a sequel to "Anansi and His Visitor, Turtle" in which Turtle returns the jacket and manages to drop in during another delicious meal at Anansi's house.

Extending Your Response

Literature Groups

Debating Indifference In the story, Yo Chan's mother says, "Don't ever be indifferent. That's the worst fault of all." Do you agree with this philosophy? Choose to be for or against this belief and hold a group debate.

Interdisciplinary Activity

Art The characters of Yo Chan and Anansi have been taught by their families and community that polite people (or animals) invite guests into their homes and treat them well. Yet both characters have trouble being kind hosts. Using the character of Yo Chan or Anansi as a narrator, create a comic book for younger children about the proper way to be a host. Include humorous drawings or cartoons to illustrate your rules.

Learning for Life

Letter of Introduction Imagine you are a Japanese student planning to study in Berkeley, California. You have heard from another student that the Uchidas are wonderful hosts who might let you stay at their home until you find a place of your own. Write a letter to the Uchidas introducing yourself and explaining your needs.

Reading Further

To read more by these two writers, try:
A Jar of Dreams by Yoshiko Uchida
African Village Folktales by Edna Mason Kaula

 Save your work for your portfolio.

Skill Minilessons

Skill Minilessons

GRAMMAR AND LANGUAGE • SUFFIXES AND THE SILENT *e*

For words ending with a silent *e,* remember to drop the final *e* when you add a suffix. For example, in the sentence: "The dead bird continued to *fascinate* Yo Chan," the word *fascinate* is a verb. The suffix -*ion* is added to *fascinate* to create the noun form in this sentence: "The dead sparrow filled me with dread and *fascination.*"

● For more about suffixes and spelling, see **Language Handbook,** p. R44.

PRACTICE Tell if each word in the list is the noun form or the verb form. Then use the other form of each word in a sentence.
1. confuse
2. invention
3. narrate
4. correction
5. protection

READING AND THINKING • PROBLEM/SOLUTION

The plots in most short stories contain one or more problems that the characters try to solve. In many stories, character development is revealed in the way characters respond to problems in their lives. In "Oh, Broom, Get to Work," the narrator tries to solve her major problem (too many guests) in a variety of ways until she comes upon the solution of the broom.

PRACTICE Reread "Anansi and His Visitor, Turtle," and find two problems that are solved by the end of the story.

● For more about helpful reading strategies, see **Reading Handbook,** pp. R70–R100.

VOCABULARY • SYNONYMS

Synonyms are words with similar meanings. That does not mean that they have the *same* meaning. For example, *neutral* and *indifferent* are synonyms. However, a judge, an umpire, or a referee should be neutral but not indifferent. *Neutral* suggests not taking sides, while *indifferent* suggests not caring.

PRACTICE Think about what the underlined word means in each sentence. Then choose the better synonym for that word *as it is used in the sentence.*

1. A friend who telephones during dinner might apologize for the intrusion.
   a. invasion   b. interruption
2. There's no excuse for being pompous about your school or family.
   a. proud   b. conceited
3. The pickup truck pulled into the parking lot, laden with gifts for the children.
   a. loaded   b. burdened

GRAMMAR AND LANGUAGE
SUFFIXES AND THE SILENT *e*

Example sentences:
1. Verb; *Confusion ensued during the fire.*
2. Noun; *He will invent solutions for new problems.*
3. Verb; *The narration was long but exciting.*
4. Noun; *I correct my spelling mistakes when I proofread my work.*
5. Noun; *The dog will protect his owner.*

READING AND THINKING
PROBLEM/SOLUTION

1. Anansi solves the problem of how to get to the bottom of the river by putting stones in his jacket pocket.
2. Turtle solves the problem of how to get even by not allowing Anansi to wear his jacket at the dinner table.

VOCABULARY
SYNONYMS

1. b   2. b   3. a

Additional Resources
- *Grammar and Language Workbook,* pp. 291–292
- *Grammar and Composition Handbook,* Lesson 15.4
- *Writer's Choice,* Lesson 23.3
- *Reading Workbook,* pp. 63–64
- *Vocabulary Practice,* p. 23

ASSESSMENT OPTIONS

- *Quick Checks,* p. 36
- *Selection and Theme Assessment,* pp. 63–64
- *Performance Assessment,* p. 34
- *Testmaker*

Vo•cab•u•lar•y Skills

Objective

• To recognize the root of a word and to use it in understanding unfamiliar words

Teaching Strategies

After students have previewed the chart in their books, ask them to come up with other words derived from the same roots. You may wish to conduct a game in which small groups of students are given a root from the chart. Tell students they have ten minutes to write down as many words as they can that contain the root. Encourage them to use resources such as you, one another, and a dictionary. Allow students to use various forms and tenses of the same word, such as *dictate, dictation, dictator,* and *dictatorship.* This will increase the number of word possibilities and elevate the drama of the game.

Exercises

A. 1. c   2. a   3. c   4. b   5. a
B. 1. b   2. e   3. d   4. a   5. c

Additional Resources

📁 *Vocabulary Power: Weekly Lessons and Activities*

Vo•cab•u•lar•y Skills

Roots

A **root** is a word part that is the base of many words. A root may be a whole word, such as *place.* A root that is a whole word is also called a "base word." When prefixes or suffixes are attached to a root, new words are formed, for example *placement, replace,* and *displaced.*

Many roots are difficult to recognize because they are not whole words in English. For example, the root of *memory* is *mem,* which comes from Latin and means "to bring to mind" or "mindful." Adding prefixes or suffixes creates such words as *memorable, remember,* and *memorial.*

The chart shows some common roots.

If you recognize the root in an unfamiliar word, you may have at least some idea of what the word means.

Root	Meaning	Examples
dic, dict	say	predict
fac, fact	make, do	factory
mort	die	mortal
port	carry	portable
rupt	break	interrupt
sol	alone	sole
terr	land	territory
tort	twist, turn	torture
var	different	variety
viv	live	survive

EXERCISES

A. Use the list of roots above to figure out the answer that completes each sentence.
1. If Anansi preferred <u>solitude</u>, then he would probably prefer to eat
    a. quickly   **b.** with company   **c.** alone
2. If Turtle followed a <u>tortuous</u> path to get to Anansi's house, the path was
    a. twisting   **b.** low   **c.** narrow
3. Anansi's <u>edict</u> to Turtle is something that he
    a. offers him   **b.** shows him   **c.** says to him
4. If Turtle needed some dinner in order to feel <u>vivacious</u>, food would make him
    a. happy   **b.** lively   **c.** grateful
5. Anansi's problems with the <u>terrain</u> in Turtle's country were problems with the
    a. land   **b.** language   **c.** rules

B. Use the list of roots to match each word on the left with its definition.
1. facsimile   a. burst
2. mortal   b. a copy
3. invariable   c. lonely
4. ruptured   d. unchanging
5. desolate   e. causing death

ENGLISH LANGUAGE LEARNERS

MEETING INDIVIDUAL NEEDS

Searching for Our Roots Use this activity to expose English language learners to a variety of new root words.

Activity Prepare two sets of note-cards with the total equaling the number of students. On one set, write one root per card. On the other set, write a list of three or four words per card that contain the same root. Give each student a card. Have students circulate, searching for the matching card. Ask students to sit or stand together until all the matches have been made. Then have students read their cards aloud.

Additional Resources

📁 *English Language Learners Sourcebook*

Writing Skills

Describing with Sensory Details

Do you remember this description from Yoshiko Uchida's story "Oh Broom, Get to Work"?

> "... on the sofa was a squat blob of a man—balding and gray—silent as a mushroom."

Suppose Uchida had written only, "On the sofa sat a very boring man." You would have understood what she meant, but you would not have been able to picture the man or hear his silence. Uchida uses **sensory details**—details appealing to the senses—to bring her description to life.

When you write descriptions, rely on sensory details. They fill your writing with vivid, memorable images. The chart below shows some sensory details from "Oh, Broom, Get to Work." Use a similar chart to list sensory details for your own descriptive writing.

Chris's Apartment

Start:	Front Door
Details:	sticks
	slams
	good smells come out

⬇

Straight ahead:	Living Room
Details:	TV
	window to street
	comfy sofa

⬇

To Left:	Kitchen
Details:	Chris's dad
	bright light
	always hot

ACTIVITY

1. Create and fill in a sensory detail chart about a place where you like to be. Include at least two details for each of as many of the five senses as you can.

2. Using details from your chart, write a paragraph describing this place.

Objective

- To recognize and use sensory details in writing

Teaching Strategies

Write a few "dull" sentences on the board, such as *The woman looked sad; It rained;* and *An eagle flew up the river.* Encourage students to come up with comparisons of their own for a sad-faced woman, rain, and an eagle in flight. Have students work in groups to add sensory detail to these sentences.

Activity

1. Students' charts should include two details about how a place looked, sounded, felt, smelled, and even tasted. For example: *My grandmother's kitchen looks like a beauty parlor/waiting room; smells like a spice market on a hot day/curry; sounds like a resort/a pool with kids splashing; tastes like a sweet dessert/the sea.*

2. Paragraphs based on the charts may rely on similes to create sensory images, such as *My grandmother's kitchen smells like freshly baked bread.*

Additional Resources

Writer's Choice, Lessons 3.1–3.5

Teaching Options

Grammar and Language *Minilesson*

Apostrophe Write the following sentences on the board without the apostrophes: *One of the places I've always loved going to is a house that belongs to my father's family. It's actually my father's twin brothers' house. Their children's friends often spend vacations there, as do we.*

Activity Ask students to copy the sentence and add the apostrophes in the appropriate places. **L2**

Additional Resources

Grammar and Language Transparency 34

Grammar and Language Workbook, pp. 273–274

Grammar and Composition Handbook, Lesson 13.7

Writer's Choice, Lesson 20.7

Objective

• To understand the elements of an essay

Teaching Strategies

Explain that when beginning an essay, a writer is often not certain of what the outcome will be. Refer students to the idea expressed in their books that writing an essay is a way of "trying out" one's ideas.

Theme Explain to students that the theme of an essay is often the essential point of interest that motivates the writer to start writing about a topic in the first place.

Purpose Ask students to pay attention to the purpose of the essays they read in this theme and to think about what the writer's intentions are in each selection.

Style It can be an interesting exercise for students to try to imitate the style of a famous writer or a piece of writing they admire. Stress, however, the importance of developing one's own style.

Tone Explain that a writer often uses different tones to express particular points and to explain how he or she views certain topics.

Teaching Options

ESSAY

The word *essay* comes from a French verb meaning "to try." The noun *essay* refers to a particular kind of writing. In an **essay,** an author "tries out" an idea in a short work of nonfiction focusing on a single subject. All essays contain the basic elements described on this page.

MODEL

THEME refers to the main point or message of the essay. The theme of an essay may be stated directly in a thesis statement that appears in the introduction. The **thesis statement**—usually a single sentence—gives the main idea of the essay.

> "Bums in the Attic" begins with a clear, direct thesis statement: "I want a house on a hill like the ones with the gardens where Papa works."

PURPOSE refers to an author's reason for writing an essay. An essayist usually has one or more purposes in mind—to inform, to entertain, to persuade, or to tell about real people, places, and events.

> The purpose of Nicholas Gage's "The Teacher Who Changed My Life" is to tell you about a remarkable person, ". . . a salty-tongued, no-nonsense school teacher named Marjorie Hurd."

STYLE is an author's personal way of using language. You can see an essayist's style in his or her word choice, sentence patterns, and ways of moving from idea to idea.

> In "The Night the Bed Fell," Thurber's style comes through in his lively, surprising language, ". . . it is almost necessary to throw furniture around, shake doors, and bark like a dog, to lend the proper atmosphere . . . to what is admittedly a somewhat incredible tale."

TONE is the author's attitude toward his or her subject. An essayist's tone may be witty or serious, sad or upbeat, scholarly or sarcastic, admiring or angry.

> In "The Dog Diaries," Markoe describes her dogs with humor and honesty, "I pick dogs that remind me of myself—scrappy, mutt-faced, with a hint of mange."

396 ❦ THEME 4

INCLUSION STRATEGIES

Learning Disabled Review with students the difference between fiction and nonfiction. Remind students that in fiction, the characters are invented by the writer, while in nonfiction the writer deals with real people and real experiences.

Activity Have students suggest at least one question relating to each of the basic elements described on this page; for example, What is the main point or message of this selection? Then show students how to use such questions to analyze a selection and determine what type of writing it is.

Additional Resources
📁 *Inclusion Strategies*

Active Reading Strategies

Tips for Reading an Essay

When reading an essay, active readers use strategies like the ones below to build on their understanding of the essay and to evaluate what they have read.

- For more about these and other reading strategies, see **Reading Handbook**, pp. R70–R100.

PREDICT

While reading, ask yourself questions such as, "What does the title mean?" or "How will the author respond?" Combine clues in the text with what you already know to predict what will happen next.

QUESTION

Questioning helps you separate facts from opinions. Facts are statements that can be proved. Opinions express a person's beliefs and cannot be proved. Writers sometimes present strong opinions as if they were facts. Questioning will help you recognize the difference.

VISUALIZE

Use the details the essayist gives you to form pictures in your mind. As you read a descriptive passage in an essay, ask yourself, "What does this person look like?" or "Can I picture the scene the writer is describing?"

EVALUATE

After you finish reading an essay, think about what it means to you. Discuss it with your classmates. Listening to the observations of others will give you a deeper understanding of the essay.

APPLYING THE STRATEGIES

Read the following essay, "The Night the Bed Fell." Use the **Active Reading Model** notes in the margins as you read. Write your responses on a separate piece of paper or use self-stick notes.

Active Reading Strategies

Objective

- To understand and apply strategies for reading essays

Teach the Strategies

Mention to students that the essay writer poses questions to him- or herself as he or she writes. The reader should do the same as he or she reads.

Predict

To help students keep track of their predictions, you may wish to have each of them make a learning chart with two headings:
- *What I know about the essay*
- *What I might learn by reading it*

Question

Point out to students that questioning the writer is just as important as questioning oneself during essay reading.

Visualize

The descriptive, sensory details included in the essays in this theme will provide students with plenty of opportunity for visualization.

Evaluate

Ask students to use the chart described in the prediction process to evaluate what they have learned.

Teaching Options

Before Reading

Objectives

- To read and analyze an essay about a family's hectic night
- To identify techniques of characterization in an essay
- To write an analysis of the story's climax

Skills

Reading/Thinking: Making Critical Judgments; Exaggeration; Cause and Effect

Writing: Characterizing; Different Point of View

Vocabulary: Antonyms; Root Words

Grammar/Language: Consistency in Verb Tense; Parentheses

Listening/Speaking: Oral Reading; Interviewing

Collaboration: Literature Groups

Motivating

→ OPTIONS

Literature Launchers: "James Thurber's World"

Videodisc Side A, Segment 12

Also available in VHS.

Selection Focus Transparency 37: Have students discuss the sense of humor of an artist who would draw a sketch like this.

Focus Activity: As an extension of the Focus Activity, have students share how they felt right after the incident and how they feel about it now.

Before You Read
The Night the Bed Fell

MEET JAMES THURBER

James Thurber is considered one of America's greatest humorists. He was born in Columbus, Ohio, the middle child in an eccentric family of three boys. He wrote hilarious-but-true stories about his unusual childhood home, but, as he explained, "all truths in that house were peculiar." He also used his wit and his artistic talent to create well-loved cartoons that were published in magazines and collected in books.

James Thurber was born in 1894 and died in 1961. This story was first published in 1933.

FOCUS ACTIVITY

What stories about unusual relatives or humorous situations are retold again and again in your family?

QuickWrite

Write about a funny family incident—for example, a holiday meal that didn't turn out right, or a visit from a relative.

Setting a Purpose

Some titles tease your imagination. You might want to read this essay to find out what happened the night the bed fell.

BACKGROUND

Did You Know? James Thurber was successful in nearly every category of writing. He was a newspaper reporter, magazine writer and editor, cartoonist, children's book writer, essayist, humorist, novelist, playwright, and screenwriter for movies and television!

VOCABULARY PREVIEW

premonition (prē′ mə nish′ ən) *n.* a feeling that something is about to happen; warning or sign; p. 400

destine (des′ tin) *v.* to determine beforehand; p. 400

avert (ə vurt′) *v.* to keep from happening; prevent; p. 401

fortitude (fôr tə tōōd′) *n.* firm courage or strength of mind in the face of pain or danger; p. 401

perilous (per′ə ləs) *adj.* dangerous; risky; p. 403

uncanny (un kan′ ē) *adj.* so strange as to cause fear or wonder; weird; p. 404

endeavor (en dev′ ər) *n.* a serious attempt to accomplish something; undertaking; p. 404

extricate (eks′ trə kāt′) *v.* to release from entanglement or difficulty; set free; p. 404

culprit (kul′ prit) *n.* one guilty of some offense; p. 405

RESOURCE MANAGER

Lesson Planning Resource
The *Theme Four Planning Guide* (pp. 55–62) provides additional lesson notes and reduced versions of all print resources.

📁 **Other Print Resources**
- Active Reading Guide, p. 37
- Vocabulary Practice, p. 24
- Reading Workbook, pp. 65–66
- Grammar and Language Workbook, pp. 83–86, 275–276

- Grammar and Composition Handbook, Lessons 3.5, 13.8
- Quick Checks, p. 37
- Selection and Theme Assessment, pp. 65–66
- Performance Assessment, p. 35
- Spanish Summaries, p. 37
- Spanish Translations
- Inclusion Strategies
- English Language Learners Sourcebook

 Transparencies
- Selection Focus 37
- Fine Art 2
- Literary Elements 37
- Grammar and Language 35

Technology
 Literature Launchers
 Audio Library
 Spanish Audio Library
 Glencoe Literature Web Site
 Testmaker

The Night the Bed Fell

James Thurber

I suppose that the high-water mark of my youth in Columbus, Ohio, was the night the bed fell on my father. It makes a better recitation (unless, as some friends of mine have said, one has heard it five or six times) than it does a piece of writing, for it is almost necessary to throw furniture around, shake doors, and bark like a dog, to lend the proper atmosphere and verisimilitude[1] to what is admittedly a somewhat incredible tale. Still, it did take place.

---

1. If something has *verisimilitude* (ver′ ə si mil′ ə tōōd′), it has the appearance of being true.

ACTIVE READING MODEL

QUESTION

What details suggest that the tale might be humorous?

A

SUMMARY

The narrator tells of an incident that occurred in his home when he was young. He describes the peculiar ideas of members of his extended family—parents, grandfather, cousin, brother, and aunts. In the middle of the night, the narrator tips over his own cot. Each household member thinks the noise is created by something else, sending everyone into a loud, chaotic state. Ultimately, they all discover that their fears are unfounded.

📁 *Spanish Summaries,* p. 37

A Active Reading

QUESTION Have students look at Thurber's choice of words and the images they bring to mind. *(Students might focus on the picture of someone throwing furniture around, shaking doors, and barking like a dog while telling a story as an indicator that the story will be humorous.)*

Additional Resources

📁 *Active Reading Guide,* p. 37

🎧 *Audio Library*

🎧 *Spanish Audio Library*

Teaching Options

CONNECTING TO OTHER SELECTIONS

The chart at the right shows three ways to connect "The Night the Bed Fell" to other selections in this book.

For specific teaching strategies, see the *Theme Four Planning Guide,* pages 58–59.

Connection	Title
Life Skills: Problem Solving	"Icarus and Daedalus," p. 737
Thematic: Growing Pains	"A Crush," p. 149
Literary: Characterization	"Birthday Box," p. 175

Active Reading

QUESTION *(Students should gather that Grandfather is not completely stable mentally.)*

Literary Elements

CHARACTERIZATION Have students identify what the grandfather and cousin have in common. *(Both are somewhat strange in their behavior and thinking.)*

FYI

Breathing Unless there is illness or trauma, or a person purposely controls it, human breathing is automatic. The control center is located in the base of the human brain. Rate of breathing averages fourteen times per minute, and average lung capacity is three pints of air.

Active Reading

PREDICT *(He's going to sniff the camphor.)* Help students see that since Thurber is announcing its place in the story, camphor will make an appearance later on.

Author's Craft

CHARACTERIZATION Sometimes a narrator will make a direct comment about a character. What is the narrator saying here about his family members? *(The statement says that Briggs, as well as others, exhibits some peculiar behavior.)*

Teaching Options

ACTIVE READING MODEL

QUESTION

B What do these details tell you about Grandfather's character?

C

PREDICT

D What might happen to Briggs Beall later in the essay?

The Night the Bed Fell

It happened, then, that my father had decided to sleep in the attic one night, to be away where he could think. My mother opposed the notion strongly because, she said, the old wooden bed up there was unsafe: it was wobbly and the heavy headboard would crash down on father's head in case the bed fell, and kill him. There was no dissuading[2] him, however, and at a quarter past ten he closed the attic door behind him and went up the narrow twisting stairs. We later heard ominous creakings as he crawled into bed. Grandfather, who usually slept in the attic bed when he was with us, had disappeared some days before. (On these occasions he was usually gone six or eight days and returned growling and out of temper, with the news that the federal Union was run by a passel of blockheads and that the Army of the Potomac[3] didn't have a chance.)

We had visiting us at this time a nervous first cousin of mine named Briggs Beall, who believed that he was likely to cease breathing when he was asleep. It was his feeling that if he were not awakened every hour during the night, he might die of suffocation. He had been accustomed to setting an alarm clock to ring at intervals until morning, but I persuaded him to abandon this. He slept in my room and I told him that I was such a light sleeper that if anybody quit breathing in the same room with me, I would wake instantly. He tested me the first night—which I had suspected he would—by holding his breath after my regular breathing had convinced him I was asleep. I was not asleep, however, and called to him. This seemed to allay his fears a little, but he took the precaution of putting a glass of spirits of camphor[4] on a little table at the head of his bed. In case I didn't arouse him until he was almost gone, he said, he would sniff the camphor, a powerful reviver. Briggs was not the only member of his family who had his crotchets.[5] Old Aunt Melissa Beall (who could whistle like a man, with two fingers in her mouth) suffered under the premonition that she was destined to die on South High Street, because she had been born on South High Street and married on South High Street. Then there was Aunt Sarah

E

---

2. To *dissuade* is to argue or advise against an action or belief.
3. The *Army of the Potomac* was the eastern branch of the Union army during the Civil War.
4. To *allay* is to calm or relieve. *Spirits of camphor* is a strong-smelling, distilled mixture that is used to soothe aches.
5. The family members' *crotchets* are their peculiar ideas or beliefs.

Vocabulary
premonition (prē′ mə nish′ ən) *n.* a feeling that something is about to happen; warning or sign
destine (des′ tin) *v.* to determine beforehand

Idiomatic Expression Begin by making sure English language learners are aware that this is a humorous essay. Point out the clues on page 400 (paragraphs 1 and 2) where the author uses the idiomatic expression *in case.* The expression, in context, means "if," or "if something should happen."

Activity Have students use *in case* to replace the italicized words in these

sentences:
1. I have an extra pen *if* this one runs dry.
2. Take the umbrella *in the event* it should rain.
Then have each student write a sentence or two using *in case.*

Additional Resources
📁 *English Language Learners Sourcebook*

Shoaf, who never went to bed at night without the fear that a burglar was going to get in and blow chloroform under her door though a tube. To avert this calamity—for she was in greater dread of anesthetics[6] than of losing her household goods—she always piled her money, silverware, and other valuables in a neat stack just outside her bedroom, with a note reading: "This is all I have. Please take it and do not use your chloroform, as this is all I have." Aunt Gracie Shoaf also had a burglar phobia,[7] but she met it with more fortitude. She was confident that burglars had been getting into her house every night for forty years. The fact that she never missed anything was to her no proof to the contrary. She always claimed that she scared them off before they could take anything, by throwing shoes down the hallway. When she went to bed she piled, where she could get at them handily, all the shoes there were about her house. Five minutes after she had turned off the light, she would sit up in bed and say "Hark!" Her husband, who had learned

F

G

---

6. The sweet-smelling fumes of *chloroform* used to be a common *anesthetic*—a substance used to put patients to sleep before surgery.

7. A *phobia* is a strong, continuing, and unreasonable fear.

Vocabulary

avert (ə vurt′) *v.* to keep from happening; prevent

fortitude (fôr′ tə tōōd′) *n.* firm courage or strength of mind in the face of pain or danger

CONNECT

How does the description of Aunt Gracie Shoaf's actions connect to the first paragraph, where the narrator says that to tell the story "it is almost necessary to throw furniture"?

H

F Critical Thinking

MAKING CRITICAL JUDGMENTS Fear of being burglarized is a serious matter. Ask students to judge what makes Aunt Sarah's and Aunt Gracie's fears funny. You may wish to share the following model to illustrate the thinking process involved in making critical judgments.

Model: While being concerned about burglars is natural, the peculiarities of Sarah's and Gracie's fears make them funny. Sarah ties up her valuables and leaves a note for the burglars; Gracie throws shoes down the hall and thinks this strategy has worked for forty years.

Vo•cab•u•lar•y Skills

Root Words The word *fortitude* comes from the Latin *fortis*, meaning "strong." It can also mean "pluck," "grit," or "having backbone." Ask students to think of other words that share the same root.

G Active Reading

QUESTION Why does the author single out only their crotchets dealing with nighttime behavior? *(This is the behavior that comes into play in this incident. The author does not want to divert the reader's attention from this incident.)*

H Active Reading

CONNECT *(The narrator's live reenactment of throwing shoes would be funny to see. It would enhance the drama of the retelling.)*

Writing *Minilesson*

Characterizing Students might enjoy taking the characters from this story and including them in their own writing.

Activity Ask students to create character traits these family members might have during the day. Encourage each student to write one paragraph to describe each character: Grandfather, Briggs, Aunt Melissa, Aunt Sarah, and Aunt Gracie.

Encourage students to think of normal behavior and then take it to an extreme; for example, Briggs might think it is necessary to wear a snorkel in the shower. **L2**

Additional Resources

📖 *Writer's Choice,* Lesson 3.5

The family's bull terrier, Rex, is lucky to have a name. James Thurber owned more than forty dogs in his lifetime. In the short essay "How to Name a Dog," Thurber explains that most of those dogs were litters of puppies that he didn't keep long enough to name anything but Hey, You! and Cut That Out! and Let Go!

FYI

Strong Women

Thurber had little difficulty depicting strong women in his sketches and writing. In fact, much of his work shows women as being domineering in their relationships with men. "The Secret Life of Walter Mitty" is a good example of a Thurber story depicting that kind of woman.

At the MOVIES

• *The Secret Life of Walter Mitty* (1947, 110 minutes, not rated) James Thurber's famous short story was the source for this hilarious Danny Kaye movie. Preview it to decide whether it would be suitable for your students.

Teaching Options

INTERDISCIPLINARY CONNECTION

Art Explain to students that drawings do not need to be literal renderings of reality to be effective. Many cartoons, comic strips, and other works use rather simple, even primitive, drawing. The key seems to be in capturing a particular physical or character trait, or capturing a moment in a person's behavior that viewers recognize and that prompts a response.

Activity Ask each student to create a simple pencil sketch of a person doing something unusual or atypical. Remind them not to worry about realistic accuracy but to strive more for capturing the moment. **L2**

James Thurber

to ignore the whole situation as long ago as 1903, would either be sound asleep or pretend to be sound asleep. In either case he would not respond to her tugging and pulling, so that presently she would arise, tiptoe to the door, open it slightly and heave a shoe down the hall in one direction, and its mate down the hall in the other direction. Some nights she threw them all, some nights only a couple of pair.

J   But I am straying from the remarkable incidents that took place during the night that the bed fell on father. By midnight we were all in bed. The layout of the rooms and the disposition of their occupants is important to an understanding of what later occurred. In the front room upstairs (just under father's attic bedroom) were my mother and my brother Herman, who sometimes sang in his sleep, usually "Marching Through Georgia" or "Onward, Christian Soldiers." Briggs Beall and myself were in a room adjoining this one. My brother Roy was in a room across the hall from ours. Our bull terrier, Rex, slept in the hall.

My bed was an army cot, one of those affairs which are made wide enough to sleep on comfortably only by putting up, flat with the middle section, the two sides which ordinarily hang down like the sideboards of a drop-leaf table. When these sides are up, it is <u>perilous</u> to roll too far toward the edge, for then the cot is likely to tip completely over, bringing the whole bed down on top of one, with a tremendous banging crash. This, in fact, is precisely what happened, about two o'clock in the morning. (It was my mother who, in recalling the scene later, first referred to it as "the night the bed fell on your father.")

Did You Know?
A *canopy* is an overhanging covering, such as on a bed, throne, or building entrance.

Always a deep sleeper, slow to arouse (I had lied to Briggs), I was at first unconscious of what had happened when the iron cot rolled me onto the floor and toppled over on me. It left me still warmly bundled up and unhurt, for the bed rested above me like a canopy. Hence I did not wake up, only reached the edge of consciousness and went back. The racket, however, instantly awakened my mother, in the next room, who came to the immediate conclusion that her worst dread was realized: the big wooden bed upstairs had fallen on father. She therefore screamed, "Let's go to your poor father!" It was this shout, rather than the noise of my cot falling, that awakened Herman, in the same room with her. He thought that mother had become, for no apparent reason, hysterical.

Vocabulary
perilous (per'ə ləs) *adj.* dangerous; risky

WHERE THE HEART IS 403

ACTIVE READING MODEL

REVIEW | I
What does each of the narrator's relatives fear?

PREDICT | K
Thurber is very precise about the layout of the rooms. Why do you think he wants you to know this information?

VISUALIZE | L
How does Thurber help you visualize this kind of bed?

RESPOND | M
Do you know anyone who sleeps this soundly? Is Thurber exaggerating? Why or why not?

I Active Reading

REVIEW *(Mother fears the bed will fall on father and kill him; Briggs fears suffocation; Aunt Melissa fears dying on South High Street; Aunt Sarah fears being killed by chloroform; Aunt Gracie fears burglars.)*

J Author's Craft

CHARACTERIZATION The narrator admits a weakness when he says he is "straying from" the story. Ask students what this says about him. *(He wants to make telling the story feel more personal.)*

K Active Reading

PREDICT *(Knowing this information will probably enable the reader to appreciate what follows.)* If students have a difficult time answering this question, revisit it again after they have finished reading page 405.

L Active Reading

VISUALIZE *(Thurber helps the reader visualize the bed by comparing it to a drop-leaf table, something readers may be more familiar with than a cot.)* If some students have a problem picturing this, have volunteers sketch both items on the board.

M Active Reading

RESPOND *(Some students may be sound sleepers or have experience with people who are. Some students may say that Thurber exaggerates to increase the drama.)*

Reading *Minilesson*

Cause and Effect This story is based on a series of quirky situations and comical outcomes. The actual narrative involves two story threads: father and the wobbly bed in the attic and Briggs and James sharing the same room. Draw the diagram at the right on the board.

Activity Have pairs of students select one of the two threads, complete the dia- gram, and present it to a small group. Have students use these questions to identify implied cause and effect:
1. What happened?
2. Why did it happen?
3. What is the outcome of this event? **L2**

Additional Resources
📁 *Reading Workbook,* pp. 65–66

Event That Starts the Actions
Father decides to sleep in the attic

Effect	Effect
Final Outcome	Final Outcome

403

Literary Elements

N **Literary Elements**

CHARACTERIZATION Ask students how Thurber prepared readers to believe the behavior being shown here. *(Earlier, Thurber described the characters' crotchets, thus preparing readers to accept this bizarre behavior.)*

O **Active Reading**

PREDICT *(Briggs may knock over the camphor and add to the confusion.)* Remind students of Briggs' last concern before falling asleep.

P **Active Reading**

QUESTION *(Camphor is a strong-smelling liquid that can make people cough.)*

Q **Literary Elements**

DIALOGUE Ask students to read the direct speech aloud. Discuss why the author gives these exact quotes. *(This dialogue is funny—Ugf, ahfg. To have written "Briggs was choking" would not have been funny.)*

R **Active Reading**

CONNECT *(If students are reluctant to speak of personal situations, ask about movie or other story plots revolving around misunderstandings.)*

S **Active Reading**

EVALUATE *(If the father were a sound sleeper and the battering were loud, it is quite possible he would react in this way.)*

ACTIVE READING MODEL

N

PREDICT

O What do you think will happen to Briggs in all the confusion?

QUESTION

P What do you learn about camphor from this description?

Q

CONNECT

R Have you ever been in a situation where simple misunderstandings caused comic complications?

EVALUATE

S Take a minute to ask yourself if you think the father would really respond this way to the battering on the door.

The Night the Bed Fell

"You're all right, Mamma!" he shouted, trying to calm her. They exchanged shout for shout for perhaps ten seconds: "Let's go to your poor father!" and "You're all right!" That woke up Briggs. By this time I was conscious of what was going on, in a vague way, but did not yet realize that I was under my bed instead of on it. Briggs, awakening in the midst of loud shouts of fear and apprehension, came to the quick conclusion that he was suffocating and that we were all trying to "bring him out." With a low moan, he grasped the glass of camphor at the head of his bed and instead of sniffing it poured it over himself. The room reeked of camphor. "Ugf, ahfg," choked Briggs, like a drowning man, for he had almost succeeded in stopping his breath under the deluge of pungent[8] spirits. He leaped out of bed and groped toward the open window, but he came up against one that was closed. With his hand, he beat out the glass, and I could hear it crash and tinkle on the alleyway below. It was at this juncture that I, in trying to get up, had the uncanny sensation of feeling my bed above me! Foggy with sleep, I now suspected, in my turn, that the whole uproar was being made in a frantic endeavor to extricate me from what must be an unheard-of and perilous situation. "Get me out of this!" I bawled. "Get me out!" I think I had the nightmarish belief that I was entombed in a mine. "Gugh," gasped Briggs, floundering in his camphor.

By this time my mother, still shouting, pursued by Herman, still shouting, was trying to open the door to the attic, in order to go up and get my father's body out of the wreckage. The door was stuck, however, and wouldn't yield. Her frantic pulls on it only added to the general banging and confusion. Roy and the dog were now up, the one shouting questions, the other barking.

Father, farthest away and soundest sleeper of all, had by this time been awakened by the battering on the attic door. He decided that the house was on fire. "I'm coming, I'm coming!" he wailed in a slow, sleepy voice—it took him many minutes to regain full consciousness. My mother, still believing he was caught under the bed, detected in his "I'm coming!" the mournful, resigned note of one who is preparing to meet his Maker. "He's dying!" she shouted.

---

8. Briggs is overwhelmed by a flood *(deluge)* of strong-smelling, sharp-tasting *(pungent)* fumes.

Vocabulary
uncanny (un kan′ ē) *adj.* so strange as to cause fear or wonder; weird
endeavor (en dev′ ər) *n.* a serious attempt to accomplish something; undertaking
extricate (eks′ trə kāt′) *v.* to release from entanglement or difficulty; set free

---

Grammar and Language *Minilesson*

Consistency in Verb Tense Point out that Thurber is consistent in his use of verb tenses. Explain to students that all of the verbs are in the past tense because all of the actions took place at the same time in the past: *yelled, believed, found, unlocked,* etc.

Activity Read the following passage and have students identify the inconsistencies in verb tense. Have them tell what form of the verbs should be used.
Last night, people gathered for the rally. The candidate stands at the podium and waved to the crowd. Delegates danced on chairs and throw flowers. (Stands should be stood; throw should be threw) **L1**

Additional Resources

📖 ***Grammar and Language Transparency 35***

📘 ***Grammar and Language Workbook,*** pp. 83–86

📘 ***Grammar and Composition Handbook,*** Lesson 3.5

📙 ***Writer's Choice,*** Lesson 10.5

"I'm all right!" Briggs yelled to reassure her. "I'm all right!" He still believed that it was his own closeness to death that was worrying mother. I found at last the light switch in my room, unlocked the door, and Briggs and I joined the others at the attic door. The dog, who never did like Briggs, jumped for him—assuming that he was the <u>culprit</u> in whatever was going on—and Roy had to throw Rex and hold him. We could hear father crawling out of bed upstairs. Roy pulled the attic door open, with a mighty jerk, and father came down the stairs, sleepy and irritable but safe and sound. My mother began to weep when she saw him. Rex began to howl. "What in the name of God is going on here?" asked father.

The situation was finally put together like a gigantic jigsaw puzzle. Father caught a cold from prowling around in his bare feet but there were no other bad results. "I'm glad," said mother, who always looked on the bright side of things, "that your grandfather wasn't here."

❖

Vocabulary
culprit (kul′ prit) *n.* one guilty of some offense

ACTIVE READING MODEL

VISUALIZE

What would a video-tape or photograph of this scene look like?

RESPOND

Do you agree with Thurber that this story would make "a better recitation than it does a piece of writing"? Why or why not?

T Active Reading

VISUALIZE *(There would be a small hall crowded with people dressed for bed, rushing about and shouting. The dog is barking and jumping on Briggs.)*

U Literary Elements

FIGURATIVE LANGUAGE: *Simile* A simile compares two unlike things using the words *like* or *as*. Similes compare the less familiar to something more familiar. What do this situation and a jigsaw puzzle have in common? *(Both have many pieces to put together; both start out scrambled.)*

V Active Reading

RESPOND *(Students may agree that the confusion and noise in the story make it suitable for a recitation.)*

Thematic Focus

Where the Heart Is What is Thurber's attitude toward his family? Is he mean-spirited or mocking in any way? Ask students to support their responses with details from the essay. *(The author is not mocking his relatives. He is never caustic or biting in talking about them.)*

FINE ART
TRANSPARENCY 2

You may wish to use ***Fine Art Transparency 2*** to extend theme concepts.

✔ ASSESSMENT OPTIONS

🗂 ***Quick Checks,*** p. 37

Listening and Speaking *Minilesson*

Interviewing Review the important aspects of interviewing:

• Prepare: Set a purpose. Develop a thorough list of questions to ask the interviewee.
• Interview: Listen carefully. Take notes. Get clarification on any important but muddy points. Ask for examples that support the person's statements.
• Conclude: Thank the person for taking the time to be interviewed.

Activity Have pairs of students role-play interviews with Thurber's family about the night the bed fell. Ask one student to identify his or her character while the partner prepares the interview accordingly. The class can take notes and discuss the strong points of the interviews, developing a list of effective interviewing techniques.
L2 COLLAB. LEARN.

Responding to the Selection

Personal Response

- Possibilities include humorous stories or those about a similarly chaotic experience.
- If students choose the Visualize strategy, they might describe father's bed in the attic, Aunt Gracie throwing shoes, and Rex attacking Briggs.

Analyzing Literature

1. The night the bed fell on the narrator is what Thurber referred to as "the high-water mark of his youth."
2. Thurber describes his grandfather, cousin Briggs, Aunts Melissa, Sarah, and Gracie, and his brother Herman.
3. The narrator tips his cot over, causing a loud noise.
4. Mrs. Thurber thinks the bed in the attic fell on her husband.
5. Father thinks the house is on fire.
6. The first paragraph shows that Thurber's purpose is to entertain readers.
7. Because these people are somewhat strange, readers can believe that they would react as they do later in the story.
8. Her conclusion is consistent with her pessimistic personality.
9. The narrator admits at the beginning that the tale is "incredible," preparing us for what might seem like an exaggeration.
10. Students might choose a family situation that is already humorous or one that challenges them to create humor.

Responding to Literature

PERSONAL RESPONSE

Take a look at your responses to the **Focus Activity** on page 398. Which of your family stories do you think Thurber would have most enjoyed hearing? Why?

Active Reading Response
Look back at the **Active Reading Strategies** described on page 397. Choose one of the strategies and find three places in the selection where you could apply it.

Analyzing Literature

RECALL

1. What did Thurber call "the high-water mark" of his youth?
2. Which relatives with "crotchets" or strange ideas does Thurber describe?
3. What starts the chain of events that Thurber narrates?
4. What does Mrs. Thurber think happened?
5. What does Father think is happening when he is awakened by all the noise?

INTERPRET

6. What can you tell from the first paragraph about Thurber's purpose for this essay?
7. How does the introduction of Thurber's strange relatives prepare you for the rest of the essay?
8. In what way is Mother's conclusion that Father is dying characteristic of her personality?

EVALUATE AND CONNECT

9. How does Thurber prepare readers that this essay, though based on fact, is going to be exaggerated and humorous?
10. Theme Connection   How has this selection changed the way you think about your own family stories? What parts of your own family history might you use to write a humorous essay?

LITERARY ELEMENTS

Characterization

The methods a writer uses to develop the personality of a character are called **characterization**. In direct characterization, a writer makes direct statements about a character's personality, as in this description: "We had visiting us at this time a nervous first cousin of mine named Briggs Beall, who believed that he was likely to cease breathing when he was asleep." Characterization can also be indirect. Thurber does not directly state that his grandfather was eccentric. Rather, he describes the man's strange behavior to give readers that impression. Writers often characterize through a character's words, actions, and interactions with other characters.

1. Choose one of the characters in the essay. Then find and list all of the descriptions Thurber uses to characterize that person.
2. Write a sentence or two of your own describing that character's personality.

● See **Literary Terms Handbook,** p. R2.

LITERARY ELEMENTS

1. Students might choose Grandfather, who disappears for days at a time and returns with news of the Civil War.
2. Grandfather might be described as an interesting man who has lost touch with reality.

Additional Resources

 Literary Elements Transparency 37

Literature and Writing

Writing About Literature

Recognizing Climax   The **climax** is a story's point of highest interest, or turning point. Ask yourself, at what point is the conflict of the evening at Thurber's house resolved? When does the outcome of the essay become clear? Write a paragraph that describes the story's climax.

Creative Writing

Another Point of View   Choose one of the characters in the essay. Retell the events from that character's point of view. Remember to begin this version from the moment in the evening where your character would have been aware of the strange happenings.

Extending Your Response

Literature Groups

Diagramming the Confusion   The sequence of events in "The Night the Bed Fell" is quite elaborate. One way to help recall all the "remarkable incidents" is to make a chain-of-events diagram showing how each event caused the next event. Share your group's diagram with those of the other groups.

Interdisciplinary Activity

Art: A Cartoonist at Heart   James Thurber is well known as a cartoonist. His cartoons were published for many years in magazines and books. Look at some examples of his cartoons. Then, in either his style or your own style, draw a series of cartoons about some of the events or characters in "The Night the Bed Fell."

Listening and Speaking

Oral Reading   Take turns reading the essay aloud to the rest of the class. Pay attention to how your voice can reflect the selection's humorous events.

Reading Further

If you would like to read more humorous stories by James Thurber, try these books:
Fables for Our Time and Famous Poems
The 13 Clocks

 Save your work for your portfolio.

Literature and Writing

Writing About Literature

Students' explanations should
- identify the climax as the point at which Father exits the attic, safe and sound.
- indicate that the outcome becomes clear in the last paragraph when the family members understand what's happened and that no one is hurt.
- make specific references to the text.

Creative Writing

Students' narratives should
- record events one after the other, as the original does.
- keep with the personality of the character.
- include the original narrator in the telling of the event.

Extending Your Response

Literature Groups Suggest that students use boxes to encapsulate events and draw arrows from one to the other to indicate cause-and-effect relationships. **COLLAB. LEARN.**

Interdisciplinary Activity Suggest that students choose characters and events not captured in the drawings in the selection.

Listening and Speaking Remind students that Thurber says the incident is ideal for being told aloud. Encourage students to have fun with different voices and sound effects.

Skill Minilessons

Skill Minilessons

GRAMMAR AND LANGUAGE
PARENTHESES

Parentheses within sentences:
- p. 399: *(unless, as some friends...five or six times)*
- p. 403: *(just under father's attic bedroom)*
- p. 403: *(I had lied to Briggs)*

Complete sentences within parentheses:
- p. 400 *(On these occasions... didn't have a chance.)*
- p. 403: *(It was my mother..."the night the bed fell on your father.")*

READING AND THINKING
EXAGGERATION

Suggest that students exaggerate amounts, heights, and sounds as well as actions and reactions.

VOCABULARY
ANTONYMS

1. a	**3.** a	**5.** b
2. c	**4.** c	

Additional Resources

- 📙 ***Grammar and Language Workbook,*** pp. 275–276
- 📙 ***Grammar and Composition Handbook,*** Lesson 13.8
- 📙 ***Writer's Choice,*** Lesson 20.8
- 📙 ***Reading Workbook,*** pp. 65–66
- 📁 ***Vocabulary Practice,*** p. 24

GRAMMAR AND LANGUAGE • PARENTHESES

Writers use parentheses to set off words that define, add information, or helpfully explain a word in the sentence. For example, in "The Night the Bed Fell," Thurber uses parentheses to set off a description: "Old Aunt Melissa Beall (who could whistle like a man, with two fingers in her mouth) suffered under the premonition that she was destined to die on South High Street." Parentheses can also be used around an entire sentence that adds extra information to a paragraph.

PRACTICE Skim "The Night the Bed Fell" to find three other examples of parentheses within sentences and two complete sentences that are enclosed in parentheses. Choose one of the examples and write about why you think Thurber chose to include the information within parentheses.

● For more about parentheses, see **Language Handbook,** pp. R41–R42.

READING AND THINKING • EXAGGERATION

Much of the humor in "The Night the Bed Fell" comes from Thurber's exaggeration of his characters' actions. He stretches the truth until his essay is much funnier than everyday life.

PRACTICE Think of something from your own life that you can tell as an **anecdote,** a short account of an interesting event or incident. First write your anecdote in a straightforward way, without humor. Then write it a second time, using exaggeration to make it humorous.

VOCABULARY • ANTONYMS

Finding synonyms is usually easier than finding **antonyms,** or opposites. You often have to think about what a word really means before you can figure out a good antonym for it. When you need to choose an antonym for a given word, don't give up just because the answer is not obvious right away. You might have to think about it.

PRACTICE Choose the word that is most closely opposite in meaning to the first word in each item.

1. **avert**
   a. cause b. discourage c. attempt
2. **uncanny**
   a. lovely b. pleasant c. normal
3. **perilous**
   a. safe b. boring c. fortunate
4. **fortitude**
   a. sadness b. playfulness c. weakness
5. **extricate**
   a. search b. trap c. irritate

✔ ASSESSMENT OPTIONS

- 📁 ***Quick Checks,*** p. 37
- 📁 ***Selection and Theme Assessment,*** pp. 65–66
- 📁 ***Performance Assessment,*** p. 35
- 💾 ***Testmaker***

MEDIA Connection

COMIC STRIP

Cartoon strips, or comic strips, are among the most popular newspaper features. Few comic strips have been as well liked or as long lasting as Charles Schulz's *Peanuts,* which began in 1950.

Peanuts   by Charles Schulz

WELL, TIME FOR SCHOOL AGAIN..

I GUESS THAT DOESN'T MEAN MUCH TO YOU..YOUR LIFE IS MORE SIMPLE..

3-23

EDUCATION ISN'T THAT IMPORTANT..

ANYWAY, I'LL SEE YOU LATER..

AU REVOIR

© 1998 United Feature Syndicate, Inc.

PEANUTS reprinted by permission of United Feature Syndicate, Inc.

Respond

1. Why does the cartoonist have Snoopy respond with "Au revoir," the French words for "See you later"? How does that response contrast with what Charlie Brown has been saying to his dog?

2. Snoopy and many other animal characters used in cartoon strips speak and often do the same kinds of things humans do. How does this add to the humor of the strip?

MEDIA Connection

Objective

- To understand and apply strategies for reading a cartoon strip

Respond

1. Some students may recognize the irony of the dog's speaking French to a boy who has just commented on the dog's lack of education; others may think Snoopy is just bored with Charlie Brown's chatter.

2. Students may say that it is the inappropriateness of having the animals say, think, and do things we attribute only to humans that creates humor.

Additional Resources
📁 *Media Connections,* p. 8

Teaching Options

Reading *Minilesson*

Sequence of Events Point out to students the importance of the sequence of events in the *Peanuts* cartoon.

Activity Ask students to look through newspapers, magazines, or the Internet for comic strips that are organized in separate boxes, like the *Peanuts* cartoon on this page. Have students bring their cartoons to class and share them with partners.

Then have students cut out each box of their cartoons and rearrange the boxes, jumbling the cartoon's sequence of events. Have partners reassemble the cartoons in the proper order. Discuss how important sequence of events is in making the humor clear. **L2**

Additional Resources
📁 *Reading Workbook*

interNET CONNECTION

Comical Animals Have students use a search engine to look for information and/or Web sites that focus on other animals featured in cartoon strips.

Objectives

- To read and enjoy a humorous essay about the behavior of dogs
- To recognize the role of point of view in a work of nonfiction
- To write a humorous piece in the style of the selection's author

Skills

Reading/Thinking: Identifying Spatial Relationships; Evaluating; Drawing Conclusions; Identifying Author's Purpose; Inferring
Writing: Diary Entry
Vocabulary: Prefixes
Grammar/Language: Subject-Verb Agreement; Principal Parts of Verbs
Listening/Speaking: Performing Self-Written Script
Life Skills: Goal Setting
Collaboration: Literature Groups; Television Script

Motivating
→OPTIONS

Selection Launchers: "A Visit with Merrill Markoe"

Videodisc Side A, Segment 10

Also available in VHS.

Selection Focus Transparency 38: Have students view the transparency and encourage them to speculate about why the cartoonist decided on dogs to deliver the idea.

Focus Activity: Have small groups share ideas about why dogs are so popular all over the world.

Before You Read
The Dog Diaries

MEET MERRILL MARKOE

When Merrill Markoe's neighbors see her outside with Lewis and Beau, her two dogs, they must wonder if she is about to start barking. The Emmy-award-winning comedy writer has been known to imitate her dogs in an effort to understand them. Markoe has written humor for *Late Night with David Letterman*, a number of television specials, and popular magazines.

Merrill Markoe was born in 1949. This essay was first published in 1992.

FOCUS ACTIVITY

Have you ever wondered why dogs chase their tails or why cats claw couches?

Think/Pair/Share
What is your personal theory about pet behavior? With a partner, discuss your thoughts on why pets do the strange things they do. Use examples from pets you know.

Setting a Purpose
Read this essay to find out what one dog owner discovers about the behavior of her dogs.

BACKGROUND

Did You Know? The dog family includes wolves, foxes, jackals, and wild and domestic dogs. All members of the dog family have teeth adapted to kill their prey, chew meat, and gnaw bones. Whether they live in packs in the wild or alone in a home, they rely upon their alert ears and sensitive noses for survival.

VOCABULARY PREVIEW

infantile (in′ fən tīl′) *adj.* like an infant; childish; p. 413
comprehend (kom′ pri hend′) *v.* to grasp mentally; understand fully; p. 413
ascertain (as′ ər tān′) *v.* to find out with certainty; determine; p. 413
obsession (əb sesh′ ən) *n.* a single emotion or idea that occupies or troubles the mind; p. 414
murky (mur′ kē) *adj.* dark; not clear; p. 414
etiquette (et′ i kit) *n.* the rules of good manners and polite behavior; p. 414
collaborator (kə lab′ ə rā′ tər) *n.* one who works or cooperates with another; p. 415
confront (kən frunt′) *v.* to come face to face with; stand facing; p. 416

RESOURCE MANAGER

Lesson Planning Resource
The *Theme Four Planning Guide* (pp. 63–70) provides additional lesson notes and reduced versions of all print resources.

📂 **Other Print Resources**
- Active Reading Guide, p. 38
- Vocabulary Practice, p. 25
- Reading Workbook, pp. 67–68
- Grammar and Language Workbook, pp. 87–90, 183–184

- Grammar and Composition Handbook, Lessons 3.6, 10.1
- Quick Checks, p. 38
- Selection and Theme Assessment, pp. 67–68
- Performance Assessment, p. 36
- Spanish Summaries, p. 38
- Spanish Translations
- Inclusion Strategies
- English Language Learners Sourcebook

 Transparencies
- Selection Focus 38
- Fine Art 27
- Literary Elements 38
- Grammar and Language 36

Technology
 Literature Launchers
 Audio Library
 Spanish Audio Library
 Glencoe Literature Web Site
 Testmaker

The Dog Diaries

Merrill Markoe ∿

SUMMARY

In an attempt to understand her two dogs better, the owner decides to live as one of them. She spends the day "acting like a dog," recording their activities in a diary. In a clever and humorous account, she writes from the point of view of a dog, narrating adventures throughout the house and outdoors. Sometimes the narrator reverts to her human point of view and offers human comments. The man of the house gets angry over the mess in the kitchen; but this has no effect on the narrator. In a last person-as-dog gesture, she uses her teeth to take his sandwich.

📁 *Spanish Summaries,* p. 38

🅐 Active Reading

CONNECT Encourage students to think about dogs they know and their owners. Have them discuss whether they think the author's generalization is valid.

Additional Resources

📁 *Active Reading Guide,* p. 38

🎧 *Audio Library*

🎧 *Spanish Audio Library*

I pick dogs that remind me of myself—scrappy, mutt-faced, with a hint of mange.[1] People look for a reflection of their own personalities or the person they dream of being in the eyes of an animal companion. That is the reason I sometimes look into the face of my dog Stan and see wistful sadness and existential angst,[2] when all he is actually doing is slowly scanning the ceiling for flies.

1. *Mange* (mānj) is a disease that produces scaly skin and loss of hair in domestic animals.
2. *Existential angst* (eg′ zis ten′ shəl ängst) involves feelings of depression or worry over the value and meaning of one's life.

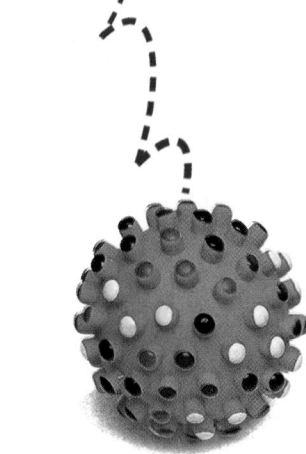

Teaching Options

CONNECTING TO OTHER SELECTIONS

The chart at the right shows three ways to connect "The Dog Diaries" to other selections in this book.

For specific teaching strategies, see the *Theme Four Planning Guide,* pages 66–67.

Connection	Title
Life Skills: Implementing and Performing →	"Fish Cheeks," p.77
Thematic: Facing Challenge →	"A Boy and His Dog," p. 243
Literary: Point of View →	"Almost Ready," p. 20

George Rodrigue, born in 1944 in New Iberia, Louisiana, is best known for his Cajun landscapes, his portraits, and his blue dog paintings. The dog's name is Tiffany.

Viewing Response *There are many possible answers. In fact, Rodrigue's first blue dog was a loup-garou, or Cajun ghost dog, that looked blue in the moonlight.*

Historical Note

Wild canines learned to follow early hunters for meat scraps left at campsites. Humans may have begun keeping them around because they warned of threatening animals. Gradually, an interdependent relationship developed.

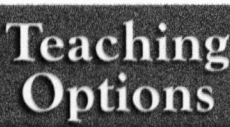

On the Lighter Side

"The probable view of the fox terrier or dachshund which lies upon our hearthrug is that he is one of a pack, the other members of which are the human inhabitants of the house… From the dog's point of view, his master is an elongated and abnormally cunning dog."
—Louise Robinson

Teaching Options

My Favorite Part of Town, 1990. George Rodrigue. Oil on canvas, 30 x 24 in. Private collection.
Viewing the painting: Why do you think the artist painted the dog blue?

MEETING INDIVIDUAL NEEDS ENGLISH LANGUAGE LEARNERS

Pets Across Cultures People in almost every culture have pets. Pets are enjoyed by city-dwellers, suburbanites, and those who live in rural areas. In different countries and different types of locations, however, people may have different kinds of pets. Ask students to discuss pets in various cultures or in different locations.

Activity Have students plan and conduct a survey on pets in different cultures. Help students develop a set of questions to use for the survey. Then have students interview people from a variety of cultures or locations and compare their results.

Additional Resources
📁 *English Language Learners Sourcebook*

We pet owners demand a great deal from our pets. When we give them the job, it's a career position. Pets are required to listen to us blithely,[3] even if we talk to them in infantile and goofy tones of voice that we'd never dare use around another human being for fear of being forced into psychiatric observation. On top of that, we make them wear little sweaters or jackets, and not just the cool kind with the push-up sleeves, either, but weird little felt ones that say, *It's raining cats and dogs.*

We are pretty sure that we and our pets share the same reality, until one day we come home to find that our wistful, intelligent friend who reminds us of our better self has decided a good way to spend the day is to open a box of Brillo pads, unravel a few, distribute some throughout the house, and eat or wear all the rest. And we shake our heads in an inability to comprehend what went wrong here.

Is he bored or is he just out for revenge? He certainly can't be as stupid as this would indicate. In order to answer these questions more fully, I felt I needed some kind of new perspective, a perspective that comes from really knowing both sides of the story.

Thus, I made up my mind to live with my pets as one of them: to share their hopes, their fears, their squeaking vinyl lamb chops, their drinking space at the toilet.

What follows is the revealing, sometimes shocking, sometimes terrifying, sometimes really stupid diary that resulted.

8:45 A.M. We have been lying on our sides in the kitchen for almost an hour now. We started out in the bedroom with just our heads under the bed. But then one of us heard something, and we all ran to the back door. I think our quick response was rather effective because, although I never ascertained exactly what we heard to begin with, I also can't say I recall ever hearing it again.

9:00 A.M. We carefully inspected the molding in the hallway, which led us straight to the heating duct by the bedroom. Just a coincidence? None of us was really sure. So we watched it suspiciously for a while. Then we watched it for a little while longer.

Then, never letting it out of our sight, we all took a nap.

10:00 A.M. I don't really know whose idea it was to yank back the edge of the carpet and pull apart the carpet pad, but talk about a rousing good time! How strange that I could have lived in this house for all these years, and never before felt the fur of a carpet between my teeth. Or actually bit into a moist, chewy chunk of carpet padding. I will never again think of the carpet as simply a covering for the floor.

11:15 A.M. When we all wound up in the kitchen, the other two began to stare at me eagerly. Their meaning was clear. The pressure was on for me to produce snacks. They remembered the old me—the one with the prehensile[4] thumb, the one who could

---

3. To listen *blithely* is to do so in a lighthearted and carefree way.

4. A thumb that can grasp something by folding around it is *prehensile* (prē hen′ sil). Some monkeys have prehensile fingers and tails.

Vocabulary
infantile (in′ fən tīl′) *adj.* like an infant; childish
comprehend (kom′ pri hend′) *v.* to grasp mentally; understand fully
ascertain (as′ ər tān′) *v.* to find out with certainty; determine

---

B Literary Elements
POINT OF VIEW The author is poking fun at pet owners. Ask students how her point of view makes "poking fun" acceptable. (*The author includes herself in the group and sees some of her group's behaviors and attitudes as humorous.*)

C Author's Craft
TONE: *Humor* One way of achieving humor is through contrast. Ask students to identify the contrast in this passage and explain why it is funny. (*The author puts in the same list the human qualities of "hopes" and "fears" along with the very animal-like "vinyl lamb chops" and "drinking space at the toilet."*)

D Literary Elements
POINT OF VIEW Though still in the first person, the narrator switches to plural. Ask students who else is included in the "we"? (*She includes her two dogs.*)

E Literary Elements
ABSTRACT VS. CONCRETE LANGUAGE To make the experiment humorous yet factual, the author includes concrete details of dog behavior. Ask students to list dog behaviors in this sequence and comment on the accuracy of the details. (*Actions include inspecting the molding, following it, staring at the heating duct, and losing interest in it. The details seem to capture a dog's real behavior very accurately.*)

Reading *Minilesson*

Identifying Spatial Relationships
This strategy helps readers use distance, shape, and location descriptors to understand setting, plot events, character's actions, or causality. Some spatial signal words that answer the "where" question include *between, below, left, near, in,* and *beside.* Encourage students to look for signal words as they read the story.

Activity Have students work in groups. Have each group choose one scene from the story and create a diagram or sketch of the scene. Ask each group to create a customized title for it that includes a spatial signal word. **L2 COLLAB. LEARN.**

Additional Resources
📁 *Reading Workbook,* pp. 67–68

Viewing Response *For a dog-lover, the photograph will be closer to a dream than a nightmare.*

F Critical Thinking

EVALUATING The author says the dogs are obsessed with the garbage can. Ask if *obsession* accurately describes the behavior of dogs. You may wish to share the following model to illustrate the thinking process involved in evaluating.

Model: When someone is obsessed with something, the person keeps thinking about or focusing on that one thing. Nothing can distract the person from the obsession. I once saw a dog chase a rabbit into a garden. The dog was obsessed with that rabbit and searched for a long time. So I think *obsession* does accurately describe some animal behavior.

G Author's Craft

CHARACTERIZATION Ask students to name the actions the author describes to characterize herself as a dog. *(She mentions diving headfirst into the can, putting her head in the garbage, and seizing upon the hair-coated clump of chewing gum.)*

Teaching Options

Viewing the photograph: Is it a dream or a nightmare? Evaluate the photograph from the viewpoint of a dog-lover.

open refrigerators and cabinets. I saw they didn't yet realize that today, I intended to live as their equal. But as they continued their staring, I soon became caught up in their <u>obsession</u>. That is the only explanation I have as to why I helped them topple over the garbage. At first I was nervous, watching the <u>murky</u> fluids soak into the floor. But the heady sense of acceptance

I felt when we all dove headfirst into the can more than made up for my compromised sense of right and wrong. Pack <u>etiquette</u> demanded that I be the last in line. By the time I really got my head in there, the really good stuff was gone. But wait! I spied a tiny piece of tinfoil hidden in a giant clump of hair, and inside, a wad of previously chewed gum, lightly coated with

Vocabulary
obsession (əb sesh′ ən) *n.* a single emotion or idea that occupies or troubles the mind
murky (mur′ kē) *adj.* dark; not clear
etiquette (et′ i kit) *n.* the rules of good manners and polite behavior

Writing *Minilesson*

Diary Entry A diarist usually records things that happen in his or her daily life, including sights, sounds, and thoughts about these and other things.

Activity Have each student write two short diary entries for a pet, another animal, or an object. Set the two entries for ten minutes apart at any time, day or night. For example, they could write from

the point of view of a picture frame in a home just before and after the family returns home. Remind students to maintain the point of view of the characters they choose. **L2**

Additional Resources

Writer's Choice, Lesson 1.2

sugar or salt. I was settling down to my treasure when I had the sense that I was being watched. Raising my head just slightly, I looked into the noses of my companions. Their eyes were glued to that hard rubber mass. Their drools were long and elastic, and so, succumbing to peer[5] pressure, I split up my gum wad three ways. But I am not sure that I did the right thing. As is so often the case with wanting popularity, I may have gained their short-term acceptance. But I think that in the long run, I lost their real respect. No dog of reasonable intelligence would ever divide up something that could still be chewed.

11:50 A.M. Someone spotted a fly, and all three of us decided to catch him in our teeth. I was greatly relieved when one of the others got to him first.

12:20 P.M. Someone heard something, and in a flash, we were all in the backyard, running back and forth by the fence, periodically hooting. Then one of us spotted a larger-than-usual space between two of the fence boards, and using both teeth and nails, began to make the space larger. Pretty soon, all three of us were doing everything in our power to help. This was a case where the old prehensile thumb really came in handy. Grabbing hold of one of the splinters, I was able to enlarge the hole immediately. Ironically, I alone was unable to squeeze through to freedom, and so I watched with envy as the others ran in pointless circles in the lot next door. What was I going to do? All of my

choices were difficult. Sure, I could go back into the house and get a hacksaw, or I could simply let myself out the back gate, but if I did that, did I not betray my companions? And would I not then be obligated to round us all up and punish us? No, I was a collaborator, and I had the lip splinters to prove it. So I went back to the hole and continued chewing. Only a few hundred dollars' worth of fence damage later, I was able to squeeze through that darn hole myself.

1:30 P.M. The extra time I took was just enough for me to lose sight of my two companions. And so, for the first time, I had to rely on my keen, new animal instincts. Like the wild creature I had become, I was able to spot their tracks immediately. They led me in a series of ever-widening circles, then across the lot at a forty-five-degree angle, then into a series of zigzags, then back to the hole again. Finally, I decided to abandon the tracking and head out to the sidewalk. Seconds later, I spotted them both across the street, where they were racing up and back in front of the neighbor's house. They seemed glad to see me, and so I eagerly joined them in their project. The three of us had only been running and hooting for less than an hour when the apparent owner of the house came to the front door. And while I admit this may not have been the best of circumstances for a first introduction, nevertheless I still feel the manner in which he threatened to turn the hose on us was both excessively violent and unnecessarily vulgar.

---

5. To *succumb* (sə kum′) is to give in or yield. One's *peers* are those who are equal in age, social status, ability, and so on.

Vocabulary
collaborator (kə lab′ ə rā′ tər) *n.* one who works or cooperates with another

---

H **Critical Thinking**
DRAWING CONCLUSIONS After they have read this description, ask students to comment on the level of intelligence of the dogs. *(The dogs drool over a clump of chewed gum, they are easily distracted by a fly, and they run around in pointless circles. These actions don't seem to reflect great intelligence.)*

I **Literary Elements**
POINT OF VIEW Call students' attention to how the dual first-person point of view (author as owner and author as pet) makes for humor. Ask students to explain the humor. *(The sentence implies that the pet owner would have to punish the dogs— including herself—for their behavior.)*

J **Author's Craft**
STYLE Often writers use transition words and phrases, such as *then*, to convey a sense of order to the readers. Ask students to identify other transition words or phrases in this passage. *(Other examples include* then, finally, *and* seconds later.*)*

K **Literary Elements**
TONE Have students discuss the tone of this passage by identifying the author's attitude toward what is happening and the language she uses to describe events. *(Though the narrator is being threatened angrily by the man, her attitude is one of complete calm, almost indifference. Her language is very restrained, showing no excitement, fear, or anger.)*

LIFE SKILLS CONNECTION

Goal Setting The dogs' obsession with the garbage can earlier in the selection could be described as "dogged persistence" in achieving a goal. They worked at this activity until they were satisfied.

Activity Have students set goals for themselves. Encourage them to work out plans that include what they have to do, what help they might need, and a time frame. Each may wish to develop a chart such as the one that follows. **L2**

Goal		
Help Needed:		
Steps	**Start Date**	**Finish Date**
1.		
2		
3.		
4		
5		
6.		
7.		
8		
9.		
Notes:		

QUESTION How do the author's interjections in the dog's narration affect the story's impact? *(They make it humorous and entertaining.)*

M **Critical Thinking**

INFERRING What is the author implying when she notes that the man is "irritated by the fact that no one offers any explanation"? *(Pet owners ask questions of their pets when they have misbehaved as if they expect the pets to answer.)*

N **Critical Thinking**

DRAWING CONCLUSIONS Ask students what conclusions they draw from the statement "...garbage someone has strewn all over the house." *(Though the dogs are responsible for the garbage mess, they do not recall any involvement.)*

Thematic Focus

Where the Heart Is What are the author's feelings for her pets? *(The author loves her dogs who shouldn't be expected to act like humans.)*

FINE ART
TRANSPARENCY 27

To enrich this discussion, you may wish to display *Fine Art Transparency 27.*

☑ ASSESSMENT OPTIONS

📁 *Quick Checks,* p. 38

Teaching Options

The Dog Diaries

Clearly, it was up to me to encourage our group to relocate, and I was shocked at how easily I could still take command of our unit. A simple "Let's go, boys," and everyone was willing to follow me home. (It's such a power-packed phrase. That's how I met my last boyfriend!)

3:00 P.M. By the time we had moved our running and hooting activities into our own front yard, we were all getting a little tired. So we lay down on our sides on the porch.

4:10 P.M. We all changed sides.

4:45 P.M. We all changed sides again.

5:20 P.M. We all lay on our backs. (What a nice change of pace!)

6:00 P.M. Everyone was starting to grow restless. Occasionally, one of us would get up, scratch the front door, and moan. I wrestled silently with the temptation simply to let us all in. But then I realized I didn't have any keys on me. Of course, it occurred to me that we could all go back through the new hole in the fence, but everyone else seemed to have forgotten about the entire fence incident by this time. As they say, "a word to the wise." And so, taking a hint from my friends, I began to forget about the whole thing myself.

6:30 P.M. The sound of an approaching car as it pulls into the driveway. The man who shares this house with us is coming home. He is both surprised and perplexed to see us all out in the front yard running in circles. He is also quickly irritated by the fact that no one offers any explanations. And once he opens the front door, he unleashes a furious string of harsh words as he confronts the mounds of garbage someone has strewn all over the house. We have nothing but sympathy for him in his tragic misfortune. But since none of us knows anything about it, we all retire to the coat closet until the whole thing blows over. And later, as he eats his dinner, I sit quietly under the table. As I watch him, a pleasant feeling of calm overtakes me as I realize just how much I have grown as a person. Perhaps that is why the cruel things he says to me seem to have no effect. And so, when he gets up to pour himself another beverage, I raise my head up to his plate, and, with my teeth, I lift off his sandwich.

Vocabulary
confront (kən frunt′) *v.* to come face to face with; stand facing

---

Grammar and Language *Minilesson*

Subject-Verb Agreement Remind students that a singular subject takes a singular verb, as in *The dog barks at the mailman.* A plural subject takes a plural verb, as in *The dogs bark at the mailman.* Point out that some subjects that look plural take a singular verb. For example, *Everyone works well together.*

Activity Have students use the correct form of the verb to complete the following sentences. **L2**

1. As he (eat, <u>eats</u>) dinner, I sit under the table.
2. When he (get up, <u>gets up</u>), I raise my head.
3. Everybody (<u>is</u>, are) confused.
4. Lianne and Niko (has, <u>have</u>) a dog.
5. Peter and I (am, <u>are</u>) going to walk the dogs.

Additional Resources

📠 *Grammar and Language Transparency 36*

📕 *Grammar and Language Workbook,* pp. 183–184

📗 *Grammar and Composition Handbook,* Lesson 10.1

📘 *Writer's Choice,* Lesson 16.1

Responding to Literature

PERSONAL RESPONSE

Can you imagine spending your day acting like a dog? What do you think the author has actually learned about dog behavior?

Analyzing Literature

RECALL

1. According to the author, what kinds of demands do pet owners put on their pets?
2. What does the author decide to do to gain a new perspective on dog behavior?
3. What choices did the author have to make about getting through the fence?
4. How did the man of the house react to the actions of "all" the dogs?

INTERPRET

5. What can you tell from the first two paragraphs about the author's opinion of dogs?
6. Why, do you think, does the author decide to "live with my pets as one of them"?
7. How does the author use exaggeration to add humor to the episode about chewing through the fence?
8. How, do you think, will the man react to his sandwich being stolen by the narrator?

EVALUATE AND CONNECT

9. Why did Merrill Markoe choose a diary format for this story? Do you think she actually did any of the things she described?
10. Theme Connection   Scientists have proved that having pets is good for your health because pets are such loving companions. How do you think a pet can improve a family's life?

LITERARY ELEMENTS

Point of View

When an author uses the pronouns *I, we, me,* and *us,* the reader knows the story is told from the first-person **point of view.** In "The Dog Diaries," Merrill Markoe does something unusual; she uses a first-person point of view throughout the essay, but the antecedent of *we* and *us* changes.

1. Reread "The Dog Diaries" with point of view in mind. In the introduction, to whom does *we* refer? To whom does *he* refer?

2. Once the actual diary begins, when the author writes, "We have been lying on our sides," to whom is she referring? Who is the *he* in this section of the essay? How does Markoe's point of view in the diary section add to the humor of the essay?

● See **Literary Terms Handbook,** p. R8.

Responding to the Selection

Personal Response

Some students may say the author has learned that the dog's existence is basically without direction. Others may say dogs don't understand as much as some people think they do.

Analyzing Literature

1. Pet owners expect their pets to listen blithely and wear sweaters.
2. The author decides to live with her pets as one of them to gain a new perspective.
3. The author's choices were to act as a human and get a hacksaw or act as a dog and chew a hole through the fence.
4. The man is surprised and perplexed to see "all" the dogs. He yells about the garbage strewn on the floor.
5. The author seems to like dogs, and she thinks they are not as "human" as people sometimes think they are.
6. Perhaps the author really wants to learn more about a typical day in the life of a dog, or she sees this idea as a promising topic for a funny essay.
7. She exaggerates her "oneness" with the dogs, referring to herself as a collaborator with them.
8. The man will probably react as he did when he saw the garbage on the floor. He will be angry and yell.
9. The diary format lends itself to a first-person point of view, emphasizing that she is part of the action. She probably didn't do these things.
10. Students might answer that young people learn responsibility by caring for pets. The funny things pets do make people laugh.

LITERARY ELEMENTS

1. In the introduction, *we* refers to pet owners, the author included. *He* refers the author's dog Stan.
2. In the diary, *we* refers to the dogs and the author. *He* refers to the man of the house. Commenting intelligently on some of the things dogs do is funny.

Additional Resources

📖 *Literary Elements Transparency 38*

Literature and Writing

Writing About Literature

Students' essays should

- analyze the situation playfully.
- be written in the first person.
- use vocabulary that is loftier than the situation would normally call for.

Personal Writing

Students' paragraphs should

- take a semi-scientific approach to testing the theory.
- be more concerned with humor than with a realistic experiment.
- include an exaggeration or two.

Extending Your Response

Literature Groups Individuals may differ on what is most humorous, so students may have to convince one another and compromise. **COLLAB. LEARN.**

Performing Encourage students not to worry about setting down every word in the script. Leave room for spontaneous improvisation.

Literature and Writing

Writing About Literature

Recognizing Humor One reason "The Dog Diaries" is funny is that the author describes very silly behavior in a serious way. Imagine that you are the writer's husband returning from work on the day the author is acting like a dog. In the same humorous tone as the essay, write about what you saw and felt when the sandwich was stolen from your plate.

Personal Writing

A Learning Experience Recall your discussion about pet behavior in the **Focus Activity** on page 410. Write a paragraph about how to test your theories the way Merrill Markoe wrote about testing her ideas. Try to include humor and exaggeration in your writing.

Extending Your Response

Literature Groups

Now *That's* Funny! Discuss with your group members which image from the story is the most humorous. Work together to draw a sketch of that scene and share it with the rest of the class.

inter*NET* CONNECTION

There is a wealth of information about dogs on the Web. You can find descriptions of different breeds, questions about health and training, and funny stories about people's beloved pets! Check it out.

Performing

The Talking Dog Talk Show Imagine that the two dogs from the story are guests on a dog talk show. They are complaining to the host about the strange day they spent with their eccentric owner. For some reason she followed them wherever they went. Have the dogs discuss their reactions to her nonhuman-like behavior. Write a television script with a partner, and then act it out for the class.

Reading Further

Check out these other books about animals and their behaviors:
All Things Bright and Beautiful by James Herriot
The Gorilla Signs Love by Barbara Brenner

📖 **Save your work for your portfolio.**

Skill Minilessons

GRAMMAR AND LANGUAGE • PRINCIPAL PARTS OF VERBS

Verbs have four principal parts that are used to form all tenses. The chart below shows how the principal parts of most verbs are formed.

Principal Parts of the Verb *bark*
Base Form: bark
Present Participle: barking
Past Form: barked
Past Participle: (has or have) barked

The principal parts of a verb are often combined with helping verbs such as *be, have,* and *do* to form verb phrases. Look at this sentence:

My dogs **are barking** at the neighbors.

In this sentence the word *are* is the helping verb and the present participle *barking* is the main verb. Together they form a verb phrase.

PRACTICE Copy the "Principal Parts" chart. Then fill in the four principal parts for these verbs from "The Dog Diaries."

1. demand
2. require
3. remember
4. chew
5. punish

● For more about verbs, see **Language Handbook,** p. R33.

READING AND THINKING • AUTHOR'S PURPOSE

Before authors choose what to write about, they need to decide their purpose. Do they want to inform the reader about a certain subject? Do they want to persuade the reader to do or believe something? Do they want to entertain the reader?

PRACTICE Write a paragraph stating what you think Markoe's purpose was in "The Dog Diaries." Use examples from the essay to support your opinion. Conclude your thoughts by explaining how well you think the author achieved her purpose.

● For more about author's purpose, see **Reading Handbook,** p. R95.

VOCABULARY • PREFIXES

Co-, com-, con-, and *col-* are different spellings of the same prefix, which means "together" or "with." The spelling depends on what letter follows the prefix. *Comprehend, collaborator,* and *confront* are words with this prefix in "The Dog Diaries."

Even if you understand the prefix, *comprehend* is not clear unless you know that the Latin word *prehendere* means "to grasp." *Confront* is easier. If you confront someone, you come face to face (or "front to front") with the person or a situation. *Collaborator* is quite clear if you see *labor* in the word. A *collaborator* "labors with," or works with, someone else.

PRACTICE Think about the prefixes *co-, com-, con-,* and *col-* and the base words they are attached to in the list of words. Then match each word to its definition.

1. context
2. coexist
3. colleague
4. commingle
5. composition

a. to blend or mix together
b. a member of the same group; fellow worker
c. an organized arrangement
d. the words that occur with or near another word
e. to live together at the same time or in the same place

Skill Minilessons

GRAMMAR AND LANGUAGE
PRINCIPAL PARTS OF VERBS

1. demand, demanding, demanded, (has or have) demanded
2. require, requiring, required, (has or have) required
3. remember, remembering, remembered, (has or have) remembered
4. chew, chewing, chewed, (has or have) chewed
5. punish, punishing, punished, (has or have) punished

READING AND THINKING
AUTHOR'S PURPOSE

Remind students that their purpose in this assignment is to explain. To do that well, they should state clearly their idea about Markoe's purpose and support that idea with details and examples from the selection.

VOCABULARY
PREFIXES

1. d 3. b 5. c
2. e 4. a

Additional Resources

📕 *Grammar and Language Workbook,* pp. 87–90

📕 *Grammar and Composition Handbook,* Lesson 3.6

📕 *Writer's Choice,* Lesson 10.6

📕 *Reading Workbook,* pp. 67–68

📁 *Vocabulary Practice,* p. 25

✔ASSESSMENT OPTIONS

📁 *Quick Checks,* p. 38

📁 *Selection and Theme Assessment,* pp. 67–68

📁 *Performance Assessment,* p. 36

💾 *Testmaker*

Writing WORKSHOP

Objectives

- To write a description of a person or place
- To plan, draft, edit, and present a descriptive passage
- To reflect on and assess the descriptive passage

Teaching Strategies

PREWRITING

Find a Topic Talk about the way a photographer searches for a subject. Have students experiment with visualizing the people and places in their lives the way a photographer scans a landscape.

Zoom in on Details Remind students that the more personal a recollection or description is, the more universal it is.

Teaching Options

Writing WORKSHOP

Observation and Description: A Photo in Words

What says "home" to you? Picture a place where you feel truly at home. Now imagine taking a photo of it—a photo that shows what makes it special. What angle would you use? What things would you include? Writing a description is like taking a photo. You observe carefully, choose an angle, and decide which details to include.

Assignment: Write a description of an important place or person in your life. Follow the process on these pages to create a description as striking as a sharp photograph.

● As you write your description, refer to the **Writing Handbook,** pp. R48–R53.

The Writing Process

PREWRITING

PREWRITING TIP
Close your eyes to mentally "observe" the person or place you choose. Recall obvious things as well as small details that only you may have noticed.

● Find a Topic

Think of people and places described in this unit: Miss Hurd, who changed Nicholas Gage's life; James Thurber's wacky family; T. J.'s rooftop garden; Maud Martha's home. For your own description, try brainstorming two lists. Title them "My Most Unforgettable People" and "My Most Unforgettable Places."

● Zoom In on Details

A cluster can help you remember details about a person or place. For a person, cluster physical traits as well as inner qualities. For a place, cluster physical details as well as details about how you feel there. Search your memory for sensory images, as shown in the **Writing Skills** activity on page 395.

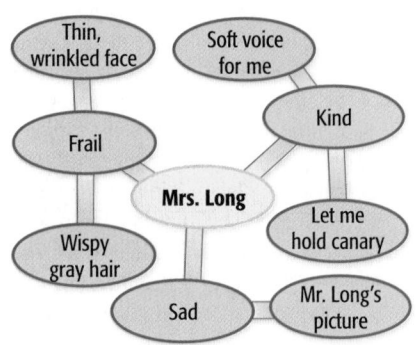

MEETING INDIVIDUAL NEEDS — ENGLISH LANGUAGE LEARNERS

Describing the Topic English language learners may wish to make illustrations of the people or places they have chosen to describe.

Activity Have students work in small groups to discuss their topics. Encourage students to make the illustrations of their topics as detailed as they can. They can then use their draw-ings to develop descriptive vocabulary in preparation for writing. Using both the illustration and the cluster, students can proceed to the next step in the Writing Workshop process. **COLLAB. LEARN.**

Additional Resources
📁 *English Language Learners Sourcebook*

Writing WORKSHOP

● Choose Your Angle: Audience and Purpose

Some of your readers may already know the person or place you are describing. However, no one sees exactly as you do, so plan to show your unique view. Decide on your purpose. Do you want readers to chuckle with you, to appreciate a special place or person, or perhaps to wonder at someone or someplace mysterious?

● Focus and Frame

To focus your description, choose one main impression that you want to convey. Write your main impression as a phrase or sentence. For example: *Chris's apartment is my second home.* Then try using a graphic to frame your organization, as shown below. Fill in details that will illustrate your main impression.

My House, Woodstock, 1924. George Bellows. Oil on panel, 17¾ x 22 in. Sid and Diana Avery Trust.

Spatial Order

To describe a place, you might use **spatial order**—the order in which things exist in space. Start at a given point. From there, describe things in order, moving from closest to farthest, from right or left, or from top to bottom.

Chris's Apartment

Start:	Front Door
Details:	sticks
	slams
	good smells come out

↓

Straight ahead:	Living Room
Details:	TV
	window to street
	comfy sofa

↓

To Left:	Kitchen
Details:	Chris's dad
	bright light
	always hot

Order of Importance

To describe a person, you might discuss the person's traits in **order of importance.** You can either begin with the traits that mean the most to you or begin with less important traits and gradually work up to the most important ones.

Mrs. Long

Trait:	Frailty
Details:	thin, wrinkled face
	wispy gray hair
	shaky hands

↓

Trait:	Sadness
Details:	Mr. Long's picture
	faraway look

↓

Trait:	Kindness
Details:	soft voice for me
	let me hold canary
	fed blue jays

Choose Your Angle: Audience and Purpose Explain to students that if they write about a topic honestly and from their own unique points of view, they may find that their descriptions serve more than one purpose: they might make people laugh in one place, feel sad or curious in another. Likewise, one reader may find something humorous, while another finds it mysterious.

Focus and Frame Before students begin to organize their descriptions on graphic frames, you may wish to have them free-write descriptions, observations, and impressions randomly on notebook or drawing paper. A "freeing" activity can help students expand their ways of thinking about their topics. Encourage them to write whatever comes into their minds and not to worry about whether the ideas form complete sentences. Give them time when they have finished to look at what they have written to determine whether "photos" of their topics are emerging.

Additional Resources

📁 *Writing and Proofreading Practice,* pp. 1–7, 29–34

🖌 *Writing and Proofreading Transparencies* 1–6, 15–16, 31–32

📘 *Writer's Choice,* Lesson 3.2

MEETING INDIVIDUAL NEEDS · MULTIPLE LEARNING STYLES

Spatial Students who enjoy drawing, designing, and building may wish to complement their descriptive passages with something visual.

Activity Discuss the ways in which a person or place could be visually represented by an artist. The list might include drawing, sculpting, building, or painting. Give students an opportunity to create "monuments" of their own to the people or places they have chosen to describe. Set up an exhibition of their paintings, sculptures, blueprints, and models alongside the descriptive passages they have written. Invite other classes to come and see the exhibit. **L2**

Catch Your Reader's Eye Remind students that the first sentence written is not necessarily the best first sentence for a passage. Encourage them to look over their first paragraphs so that each can a find favorite sentence or image and try starting with that one instead.

Work with Details In addition to following their prewriting plans, students may wish to use the pages of random details and images they created during the prewriting process.

Take Another Look If students exchange papers with partners, they can have the partners read their passages aloud. Hearing their work read by someone else can be a valuable part of the revising process. If the partner stumbles over certain words or phrases, the writer might want to go back and make sure the syntax is clear. In addition, the writer may form new impressions while listening to the work and can revise it accordingly.

Teaching Options

Writing **WORKSHOP**

DRAFTING

DRAFTING TIP

If you get a new idea while drafting, go ahead and try it. If it leads you off track, your prewriting notes can bring you back.

TECHNOLOGY TIP

On a computer, copy your draft before you revise. By saving the original, you are free to experiment. If an experiment doesn't turn out well, you can return to your original draft and try again.

● Catch Your Reader's Eye

Try beginning with a single, vivid image. Show the person in a characteristic pose. Show the place at one specific time. You might go on to state your main impression near the end of this first paragraph.

> **MODEL · DRAFTING**
>
> Rattle, rattle, thunk! The front door sticks, then opens. The smell of macaroni and cheese floats out. Chris's dad yells, "Don't slam the door!" and I know I'm welcome. This is my best friend's apartment and my second home.

● Work with Details

Follow your prewriting plan, using sensory details to illustrate your statements. Include details that show your feelings, so readers can tell what the place or person means to you. To conclude, you might refer again to your main impression and reflect on the role that this place or person plays in your life.

REVISING

REVISING TIP

If you reword your main impression, adjust your paragraphs to illustrate the revised version.

● Take Another Look

Read over your description. Did your main impression change as you drafted? If so, reword it now to reflect your new insights. Use the **Questions for Revising** to plan other changes.

Try trading papers with a partner. You can go over the **Questions for Revising** with each other. Keep changing your description until it is as good as you can make it.

QUESTIONS FOR REVISING

- ☑ How does my introduction catch the readers' attention?
- ☑ Where do I state my main impression?
- ☑ How does each paragraph illustrate my main impression?
- ☑ Where might I add details or rearrange parts to make my description clearer?
- ☑ Where do I show readers what this place or person means to me?

Writing *Minilesson*

Descriptive Images In revising and refining their passages, students may benefit from hearing which of their descriptions and images classmates enjoyed most.

Activity Set up small writing workshop groups around the classroom. Give students time to read their passages aloud to their groups. Ask listeners to jot down notes on the descriptions, images, or impressions they liked best. When a student has finished reading, the other writers in the workshop group can let him or her know which details left an impression on them. **L2**

Additional Resources

📖 **Writer's Choice,** Lesson 3.2

EDITING/PROOFREADING

Before you make a final copy of your description, use the **Proofreading Checklist** to spot errors. Correct any that you find.

Grammar Hint

In a compound sentence, you can use *however* to join two clauses. Put a semicolon before *however* and a comma after it.

Thurber fell out of bed; however, the fall didn't waken him.

PROOFREADING CHECKLIST

☑ Each sentence has at least one complete subject and predicate.

☑ Compound sentences are structured correctly. (Double-check sentences joined with *however.*)

☑ Punctuation is correct. (Double-check compound sentences.)

☑ Capitalization and spelling are correct.

MODEL · EDITING/PROOFREADING

The apartment can get pretty noisy, however, it's my favorite kind of noise.

PUBLISHING/PRESENTING

Consider submitting your description to a magazine that publishes young people's writing. Your teacher or a librarian can suggest magazines, show you how to find their addresses, and help you prepare your manuscript for submission.

PRESENTING TIP
Some magazines have Web sites that tell you how to submit manuscripts.

Reflecting

Take time to think about the following questions; then write your responses.

- Did your view of your subject change as you worked on this description? If so, explain how. If not, offer some ideas about why it did not.

- Which aspects of your subject come through best in your description? Which aspects come through only faintly or are left out?

💼 **Save your work for your portfolio.**

Have students use the Proofreading Checklist to review their work. Encourage them to check for each item on the list in separate readings, paying special attention to compound sentences.

Additional Resources

📖 *Grammar and Composition Handbook,* Lesson 16.4

PUBLISHING/PRESENTING

Have students read through a few magazines that publish writing for young readers to determine which publication might be most receptive to the passage they have written.

Reflecting

Portfolio Have students ask themselves these questions as they review their descriptive passages:

- Would the person I have written about recognize himself or herself?

- If someone were to draw a picture of the place I have described, what would it look like?

- What parts of descriptive writing are most difficult for me? What parts do I like best?

✔ ASSESSMENT OPTIONS

📁 *Writing Assessment and Portfolio Management*
- Writing Assessment, pp. 1–16, 29–31
- Portfolio Management, pp. 17–19

Theme Wrap-Up

Objectives

- To offer a personal response to the selections and activities in this theme
- To write a comparison of two essays
- To complete a self-evaluation, set a goal, and devise a plan for achieving the goal

---

Responding to the Theme

1. Students should cite examples from selections in their responses.
2. Have students explain what they learned by relating the selections to their own experiences with home and family.
3. Allow time for students to share their charts, policy statements, and home projects with the class.

Analyzing Literature

Students' writing should

- include an introductory paragraph that identifies the two essays and the element being compared.
- contain examples and quotes taken directly from the essays.

Evaluate and Set Goals

Evaluate

Have students review the work they have done in Theme 4 and compile a list of activities they have completed for each task. Suggest that they add other tasks as well, such as viewing and discussing artwork.

Set Goals

Have students create goal pyramids. The goal should be written at the top of the pyramid and the three steps needed to achieve it in three tiers beneath the goal. Suggest that students also make detailed notes to use for each step. Discuss students' plans in individual conferences.

 WHERE THE HEART IS

Theme Wrap-Up

Responding to the Theme

1. Which story, poem, or essay in this theme most helped you think about what home and family mean to you? Explain your answer.

2. What new ideas do you have about the following as a result of reading the literature in this theme?
   - How the people and places you love affect your life
   - The importance of seeing warmth and humor in family situations

3. Present your theme project to the class.

Analyzing Literature

COMPARE ESSAYS

Compare two essays from this theme. You may compare them in terms of point of view, use of humor, vividness of characters, or the author's purpose. Remember to support your opinions with quotations from the essays.

Evaluate and Set Goals

1. Which of the following tasks was most rewarding to you? Which was most difficult?
   - reading and thinking about the stories, poems, and essays
   - doing independent writing
   - analyzing the stories, poems, and essays in discussions
   - performing dramatizations
   - doing research

2. Using the following scale, how would you assess your work in this theme? Give at least two reasons for your assessment.
   4 = outstanding   2 = fair
   3 = good   1 = weak

3. Based on what you found difficult in this theme, choose a goal to work toward in the next theme.
   - Write down your goal and three steps you will need to take to help you reach it.
   - Meet with your teacher to review your goal and your plan for achieving it.

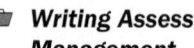 **Build Your Portfolio**

SELECT

Select two pieces of work you did during this theme to include in your portfolio. Use the following questions to help you decide.

- Which work do you consider your best?
- From which work did you learn the most?
- Which work did you enjoy the most?

REFLECT

Write some notes to accompany the work you selected. Use these questions to guide you.

- What do you like best about the piece?
- What did you learn from creating it?
- What might you do differently if you were beginning this piece again?

✓ ASSESSMENT OPTIONS

📁 ***Writing Assessment and Portfolio Management***
   - Writing Assessment, pp. 1–16
   - Portfolio Management, pp. 17–19

 GLENCOE
TECHNOLOGY

 MINDJOGGER VIDEOQUIZZES
VIDEODISC

Use *MindJogger* to review the Theme Four content.

Theme 4
Side A

 Also available in VHS.

Reading on Your Own

Have you enjoyed reading the essays, stories, and poems in this theme? Here are some other books you might like.

Dragonwings

by **Laurence Yep** A Chinese immigrant father and son build a flying machine in the era of the Wright brothers and the San Francisco earthquake.

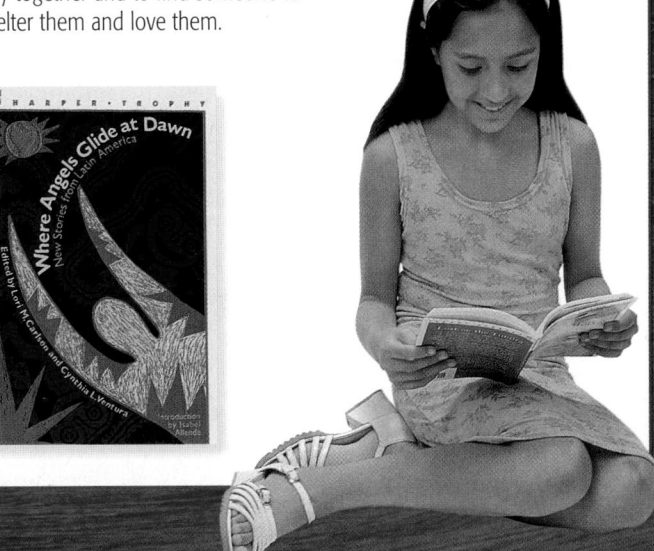

On the Way Home

by **Laura Ingalls Wilder** and **Rose Wilder Lane** The diary of the author of *Little House on the Prairie* describes her family's exciting 1894 journey from South Dakota to a new home in the Missouri Ozarks. Her daughter adds her own memories of the trip.

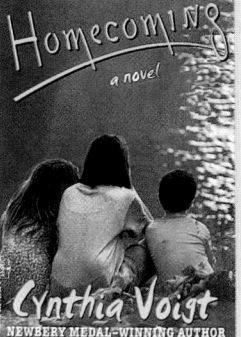

Homecoming

by **Cynthia Voigt** This poignant story focuses on the four Tillerman kids, left parentless when they are abandoned by their mother. They must struggle to stay together and to find someone to shelter them and love them.

Where Angels Glide at Dawn: New Stories from Latin America

edited by **Lori M. Carlson and Cynthia L. Ventura** Homes and families provide a background in several of these ten stories from Latin America. The stories display a variety of cultures and writing styles.

Reading on Your Own

Glencoe Literature Library

For a complete listing of titles available in the *Glencoe Literature Library*, see pages T46–T47 in this book.

The *Glencoe Literature Library: Study Guide* provides instructional support and student activities for works in the *Glencoe Literature Library*.

At the MOVIES

Be sure to preview the following video for appropriateness for your class.

• *ET: The Extra-Terrestrial* (1982, 115 minutes, PG) The Steven Spielberg classic brings a new twist to the "Where the Heart Is" theme.

MEETING INDIVIDUAL NEEDS   INCLUSION STRATEGIES

You may wish to recommend *Dragonwings*, by Laurence Yep, to your less-proficient readers and English language learners. Language is a challenge faced by one of the characters in this exciting story. **L1**

The following books are rated for average readers (L2) or for students who need more challenging reading (L3):

• *Homecoming* by Cynthia Voigt **L2**
• *On the Way Home* by Laura Ingalls Wilder and Rose Wilder Lane **L2**
• *Where Angels Glide at Dawn: New Stories from Latin America* edited by Lori M. Carlson and Cynthia L. Ventura **L3**

Additional Resources
📁 *Inclusion Strategies*

Standardized Test Practice

 TEST-TAKING TIP

Sometimes the "best" answer is simply the "least bad." Advise students that sometimes none of the answer choices will seem right. In these cases, they should eliminate the worst choices. The one they have left, the "least bad" is the one they should choose.

 TEST-TAKING TIP

Every once in a while a student will hit a question that will seem extremely difficult. Students should eliminate, guess, and then move on. If there is no penalty for wrong answers on the test, students should answer every question. In this case, even if the student isn't able to eliminate any of the answer choices, it's still to his or her advantage to guess.

Standardized Test Practice

Read the following passage. Then read each question on page 427. Decide which is the best answer to each question. Mark the letter for that answer on your paper.

Learning the Game

Rita stared ahead at the green grass curving out before her. She could make out the fluttering orange tongue of the flag 250 yards away. She was on the shortest hole at the Shady Views Golf Course, but Rita knew that she was no expert at the first swing off the tee.

Her father sensed her apprehension and gave her a little smile. "It's OK," he said. "I've got a feeling this one is going to work out for you just fine."

"I just can't use this driver," Rita complained, holding up the club in question as if it were a poisonous snake. "I'm pretty good when I'm close to the hole. I can hit pretty well with the shorter clubs. I need more practice with the drivers, though."

"Nothing to it," her father shrugged. "You've got the basics down. Take a wide stance, relax your shoulders, and breathe through the swing. I've seen you do it before. Stop worrying about it and just try it. Golf is not a game for people who think too much."

"All right," Rita sighed, planting her feet. She limbered her knees and loosely shook her head back and forth. "Talk me through it, okay?"

Her father moved around her and studied her form with a practiced eye. He remembered the first time he had taken Rita golfing after she had expressed interest in the sport—she had been ten years old, but she hadn't been

all that bad! She had a natural talent for swinging the clubs. True, she needed more work with the bigger clubs, especially the drivers. But he was certain that once she crossed that hurdle, she could be a great player.

"Take a few practice swings . . . very nice. A little wider in your stance . . ."

Rita adjusted her feet accordingly.

"Good!" her father said. "No, no. Straighten the left elbow."

Rita made the correction.

"Yes! Now remember to keep your head tucked. Don't look up until after you've swung through."

"OK. You've helped," Rita mumbled. "Now let me swing."

There was silence for a moment while Rita and her golf ball held quiet commerce with each other. Rita's father knew that golf might not be a game for folks who thought too much, but it surely was a game for those who could concentrate. He knew that Rita could focus with amazing intensity.

Rita took in a sharp breath and slowly released it. Her arms drew back the golf club like a ballet dancer moving through heavy water, graceful and poised. The head of the club rose like a new moon until it crested over her ear. Then the swing came down, rocketing the club around like a whipcord, slicing through the air with a sizzling *huwuuuff!* The ball exploded forward like a rifle shot, bolting through the air. Rita and her father watched it fly straight as an arrow toward the flag pin so many yards away.

"That's a keeper—" Rita's father started to say, but then he cut himself off. Suddenly he spun on his heel and dove for his golf bag, digging through a pocket until he found his field glasses. Holding the binoculars up to his eyes for a brief moment, he held his breath before letting out a huge shout.

"What? What is it?" Rita demanded.

"See for yourself," her father laughed, pressing the glasses into her hand.

Rita held the binoculars up to her own eyes and scanned the distant putting green for a sign of her ball. She couldn't find it anywhere. "Did I sink it in the water trap?" she asked. "Why can't I see it?"

Her father's grin was so huge it nearly fell off his face. "Because it's in the cup, Rita," he laughed. "Congratulations! That's your first hole in one!"

---

1 The word <u>tucked</u> in this story probably means —

   A straight up

   B backward

   C tilted down

   D looking around

2 The main point of the story is that —

   F sometimes it's best to try something rather than think too much about it

   G golf can be a great sport for fathers and daughters to play together

   H a hole in one is one of the rarest events in all sports

   J hitting with a driver in golf is a difficult skill to master

3 What does the author mean by the phrase "Rita and her golf ball held quiet commerce with each other"?

   A Rita likes to talk to her sporting equipment.

   B Rita took a moment to be still and concentrate on hitting the ball.

   C Rita silently pictured buying the golf ball in her mind.

   D Rita didn't want her father disturbing her, so she stared at her ball.

4 Rita wanted her father to talk her through the swing with the driver because —

   F she knew that she was good

   G she had been playing since she was ten

   H she was uncertain of her own ability to swing the driver

   J she wanted to hit a hole in one

5 At the beginning of the story, Rita felt —

   A apprehensive

   B angry

   C elated

   D confident

Answers and Analyses

1. **C** Students should consider the context of the word *tucked* to help figure out its meaning. Just after the mention of the word *tucked*, Rita's father says that she should not *look up*. Therefore tuck must mean the opposite of *looking up*. The best choice is C.

2. **F** Ask the students to summarize the story in their own words. At the beginning, Rita is self-conscious and unable to relax. Her father tells her *Golf is not a game for people who think too much.* Rita then concentrates and hits a hole-in-one. The best re-statement of this idea is choice F. Remind students that though choices G, H, and J may all be true, choice J is just a detail in the story, choice H is not mentioned in the story at all, and though choice G may be tempting, it is not the main point in the story.

3. **B** Students should consider the context of the phrase in question. The story says *There was silence for a moment while Rita and her golf ball held quiet commerce.* On this basis, *quiet commerce* must mean a silent time in which Rita concentrates solely on the ball, so choice A can be eliminated. Choice C can also be eliminated since buying golf balls is irrelevant to the story. Since Rita was preparing herself to hit the ball, choice B seems more reasonable than choice D.

4. **H** Rita claims that she can't use this driver. Her father then reassures her, and she asks him to talk her through the swing. The most reasonable choice is therefore H.

5. **A** The beginning of the second paragraph states *Her father sensed her apprehension.* The best paraphrase is choice A.

THEME OPENING	→	Theme 5: AT THE CROSSROADS

THEME OPENING

- **Introducing the Theme** (p. 429)
- **Exploring the Theme** (p. 430)
- **Theme Projects** (p. 431)

SELECTIONS

Amigo Brothers (p. 432)

Your World (p. 444)

The Scholarship Jacket (p. 450)

Media Connection: The Face of Venus (p. 459)

All Summer in a Day (p. 460)

Primer Lesson (p. 471)

The Bird Like No Other (p. 471)

The Old Demon (p. 482)

The Boy and His Grandfather (p. 482)

Active Reading Model: The Monsters Are Due on Maple Street (p. 504)

Media Connection: The Eye of the Beholder (p. 528)

SKILL FEATURES

Interdisciplinary Connection (p. 448)

Listening, Speaking, and Viewing (p. 449)

Reading and Thinking Skills (p. 470)

Technology Skills (pp. 480–481)

Grammar Link (p. 499)

Genre Focus: Drama (pp. 500–501)

Active Reading Strategies (pp. 502–503)

Vocabulary Skills (p. 529)

WRITING WORKSHOP

Expository Writing: Definition Essay (pp. 530–533)

THEME WRAP-UP

- **Responding to the Theme, Analyzing Literature, Evaluate and Set Goals** (p. 534)
- **Build Your Portfolio** (p. 534)
- **Reading on Your Own** (p. 535)
  The Slave Dancer by Paula Fox
  Sounder by William Armstrong
  Father Figure by Richard Peck
  Running Out of Time by Margaret Peterson Haddix
- **Standardized Test Practice** (pp. 536–537)

KEYS TO LITERARY CONNECTIONS

 Comparing Selections

The **Comparing Selections** feature in this theme provides opportunities for addressing diverse aspects of the reading and literature curriculum.

For example, in Comparing Selections on page 447, students look closely at the messages and life choices of the young men in "Amigo Brothers" by Piri Thomas and the speaker in "Your World" by Georgia Johnson.

KEYS TO TEACHING OPTIONS

 Block Scheduling

Activities that are particularly suited to use within a block scheduling framework are identified throughout this theme by the following designation: 🔲 For detailed suggestions on block scheduling, see the **Block Scheduling Guide** for this grade level.

Key to Ability Levels

The Teaching Options throughout this theme have been coded for students of various abilities.

L1 BASIC activities for all students

L2 AVERAGE activities for average to above-average students

L3 CHALLENGING activities for above-average students

Reading Skills in this theme

Variety of Texts

In addition to a full-length drama, this theme includes the following text types:

- short story
- poem
- cartoon
- folktale
- Web site

Comprehension Skills

The following instructional support for comprehension skills appears in this theme of the Student Edition:

- **Reading and Thinking Minilessons** (pp. 458, 469, 498, 527)
- **Drawing Conclusions** (p. 470)
- **Active Reading Strategies and Model** (pp. 502–527)

See also the **Reading Minilessons** throughout the theme in this Teacher's Wraparound Edition.

Reading Resources

Comprehension Skills Resources

📁 **Active Reading Guides**

The **Active Reading Guide** provides graphic organizers and study guide questions to support students' reading of each selection (**Active Reading Guide**, pp. 39–45).

📁 **Reading Workbook**

The **Reading Workbook** (pp. 69–80) includes additional instruction and reinforcement of reading strategies and skills.

🎧 **Audio Library**

Available both on tape and on CD, the **Audio Library** provides valuable comprehension support.

Resources for Reading Widely

Glencoe Literature Library

Each title in the *Glencoe Literature Library* includes a full-length novel or play plus related readings. A separate Study Guide is available for each title.

💿 **Literature Classics CD-ROM**

The selections on this CD-ROM can be searched by author, theme, or genre.

 *in*TIME

A coproduction of Glencoe and Time, Inc., the *inTime* magazine includes a wealth of high interest nonfiction related to the selections in Theme Five.

✓ Assessment in this theme

GLENCOE'S ASSESSMENT ADVANTAGE

Assessment Options in the Student Edition

Glencoe Literature offers a number of diverse ways to evaluate student understanding and skill proficiency. In the Student Edition, use the following:

- **Responding to Literature**

  Following each selection, students are asked to recall facts, interpret ideas, and evaluate concepts as they answer a variety of questions and complete activities to extend their understanding.

- **Theme Wrap-Up (pp. 534–535)**

  Here students respond to the selections on personal and analytical levels. They also assume ownership of their learning by setting and evaluating goals and by selecting work for their portfolios.

See also the many **Assessment Resources** listed on the facing page.

THE PRINCETON REVIEW

Standardized Test Practice

The Princeton Review has developed the Standardized Test Practice pages found at the end of this theme (pp. 536–537). These pages contain practice test questions that help students remain familiar with standardized test formats and content.

- ITBS Preparation and Practice
- SAT-9 Preparation and Practice
- TerraNova Preparation and Practice

Writing Skills in this theme

Writing Skills

The Student Edition of Theme Five offers strong instructional support for writing skills:

In **Extending Your Response**, which follows each selection:
- **Writing About Literature**
- **Personal/Creative Writing**

See also the **Writing Minilessons** throughout the theme in this Teacher's Wraparound Edition.

Writing Workshops

Theme Five concludes with a **Writing Workshop** that guides students through the process of writing a definition essay (pp. 530–533).

Writing Resources

Writer's Assistant CD-ROM
Each Writing Workshop is supplemented by an interactive writing guide on the Writer's Assistant CD-ROM. This easy-to-use writing guide provides prompts, templates, and other tools that lead students through the writing process.

Writing and Proofreading Practice
Blackline masters present in-depth instruction and practice on a specific step in the writing process and proofreading (pp. 1–7, 35–42).

Writing and Proofreading Transparencies
Transparencies provide graphic organizers and proofreading exercises for whole-class instruction (pp. 1–6, 17–18, 33–34).

Research and Report Writing Guide
This resource provides extensive tips and activities to guide students in their writing projects in the literature classroom as well as in classes across the curriculum.

Style and Documentation Sourcebook for Writers
This sourcebook is a combination reference and workbook, giving students the most up-to-date information and guidance regarding traditional as well as technological research strategies and documentation.

Grammar and Composition Handbook
The Grammar and Composition Handbook provides instruction that supplements activities in the student textbook.

Assessment Resources

Selection Quick Checks
For each selection, a Quick Check of three to five short-answer questions measures students' literal comprehension.

Selection and Theme Assessment
The Selection and Theme Assessment instrument tests students' abilities to recall, interpret, and evaluate what they've read. The tests consist of multiple-choice, short answer, and essay questions.

Performance Assessment
Alternative assessment instruments and rubrics for Theme Five are found in the Performance Assessment ancillary.

Writing Assessment and Portfolio Management
These notes and strategies, student models, and assessment tools assist with the task of measuring students' progress as writers and as monitors of their own writing.

Testmaker
Teachers can customize selection and Theme Five tests by accessing the Testmaker database.

Mindjogger Videoquizzes
Using a popular game show format, Mindjogger Videoquizzes enable teachers to evaluate student understanding of Theme Five in a quick and fun manner.

SELECTIONS	Literary Elements	Reading and Thinking	Writing	Vocabulary and Spelling	
Amigo Brothers PIRI THOMAS	Internal/External Conflict, SE p. 442; *TWE pp. 434, 437, 438, 440* *Setting, TWE p. 434* *Imagery, TWE p. 440* *Character, TWE p. 441* *Plot, TWE p. 441*	*Evaluating, TWE pp. 434, 436* *Comparing/Contrasting, TWE p. 435* *Logical Reasoning, TWE p. 436* *Drawing Conclusions, TWE p. 439*	Analyzing an Ending, SE p. 443 Newspaper Article, SE p. 443 *Using Realistic Language, TWE p. 437*	Unlocking Meaning, SE 443 *Context Clues, TWE p. 434* *Etymology, TWE pp. 437, 440*	
Your World GEORGIA JOHNSON	Symbol, SE p. 446 *Symbol, TWE p. 445*		Analyze Theme, SE p. 446		
The Scholarship Jacket MARTA SALINAS	Resolution, SE p. 456; *TWE p. 455* *Character, TWE p. 452*	Questioning/Clarifying, SE p. 458 *Inferring, TWE pp. 452, 454* *Drawing Conclusions, TWE pp. 452, 453, 455* *Sequence of Events, TWE p. 453*	Critical Review of Story, SE p. 457 Journal Entry, SE p. 457	The Prefix: *-dis*, SE p. 458 *Word Meanings, TWE p. 453*	
All Summer in a Day RAY BRADBURY	Science Fiction, SE p. 467 *Figures of Speech, TWE p. 462* *Science Fiction, TWE pp. 462, 464, 465, 466* *Character, TWE p. 463*	Inference, SE p. 469 *Inferring, TWE pp. 462, 463* *Monitor Comp., TWE p. 463* *Draw Conclusions, TWE p. 464, 466* *Crit. Judg., TWE p. 466*	Paragraph (Setting), SE p. 468 Sequel to Science Fiction, SE p. 468	Latin Roots: *vit* and *viv*, SE p. 469	
PRIMER LESSON CARL SANDBURG **THE BIRD LIKE NO OTHER** DOROTHY WEST	Descriptive Details, SE p. 478 *Personification, TWE p. 472* *Repetition, TWE p. 472* *Details, TWE pp. 473, 476, 477* *Character, TWE p. 473* *Literary Language, TWE p. 474*	*Inferring, TWE p. 473* *Synthesizing, TWE p. 473* *Sequencing, TWE p. 473* *Drawing Conclusions, TWE p. 476*	Paragraph (Poem's Theme), SE p. 479 Personal Letter (Different Point of View), SE p. 479	Analogies, SE p. 479 *Word Mappings, TWE p. 472* *Multiple Suffixes, TWE p. 474*	
The Old Demon PEARL S. BUCK **The Boy and His Grandfather** RUDOLFO A. ANAYA	Theme, SE p. 496 *Simile, TWE p. 484* *Implied Theme, TWE pp. 484, 485, 488, 489, 491* *Narrator, TWE p. 485* *Characterization, TWE p. 492* *Plot, TWE pp. 493, 494* *Allegory, TWE p. 495*	Summarizing, SE p. 498 *Drawing Conclusions, TWE pp. 484, 487, 489, 493* *Cause and Effect, TWE p. 484* *Inferring, TWE p. 486* *Evaluating, TWE pp. 487, 490* *Synthesizing, TWE p. 489* *Logical Reasoning, TWE p. 491*	Paragraph (Analyzing Descriptions), SE p. 497 Essay (Personal Courage), SE p. 497 *Narrating Action, TWE p. 487*	The Prefix *mal-*, SE p. 498 *Etymology, TWE p. 486* *Suffixes, TWE p. 488*	
The Monsters Are Due on Maple Street ROD SERLING	Teleplay, SE p. 525; *TWE pp. 506, 508, 509, 510, 512, 513, 523* *Mood, TWE p. 506* *Characterization, TWE pp. 508, 509, 510, 513* *Foreshadowing, TWE p. 511* *Irony, TWE p. 517* *Symbol, TWE p. 519*	Visualizing, SE p. 527 *Evaluating, TWE pp. 510, 512, 515, 517, 518* *Source Credibility, TWE p. 511* *Purpose for Rdg., TWE p. 511* *Compare/Contrast, TWE p. 516* *Synthesizing, TWE p. 521* *Generalizing, TWE p. 522*	Paragraph (Conflict), SE p. 526 Description from Another Point of View, SE p. 526 *Narrative, TWE p. 514* *Narrating Action with Verbs, TWE p. 522* *Analytical Writing, TWE p. 524*	Base Words, SE p. 527 *Root Meanings, TWE p. 507* *Idioms, TWE p. 512* *Roots, TWE p. 515* *Synonyms, TWE p. 518*	

Key: Student material is in roman. Teacher material is in italic.   💻 Technology   **COLLAB. LEARN.** Collaboration

Grammar and Language	Listening, Speaking, and Viewing	Life Skills	Study, Research, and Technology
Action Verbs, TWE p. 440	**COLLAB. LEARN.** Literature Groups, SE p. 443 Radio Script, SE p. 443 *Describing a Match, TWE p. 438*		🖥 *Internet Connection, TWE p. 441* 🖥 *Tournament, TWE p. 441*
Comparative and Superlative Adjectives, TWE p. 445	**COLLAB. LEARN.** Literature Groups, SE p. 446		
Using Adverbs and Adjectives, SE p. 458 *Subject-Verb Agreement, TWE p. 454*	**COLLAB. LEARN.** Literature Groups, SE p. 457	Learning For Life: Graduation Speech, SE p. 457	🖥 *Real-World Connection: Awards, TWE p. 445*
Avoiding Double Negatives, SE p. 469 *Commas to Set Off Interrupters, TWE p. 466*	**COLLAB. LEARN.** Literature Groups, SE p. 468	Creating a Travel Brochure, SE p. 468	🖥 *Job Search, TWE p. 465*
Using Troublesome Words: Its and It's, TWE p. 476	**COLLAB. LEARN.** Literature Groups, SE p. 479		🖥 *Extraordinary People, TWE p. 477*
Participles and Participial Phrases, SE p. 498 *Verbs in the Past Tense, TWE p. 488*	**COLLAB. LEARN.** Literature Groups, SE p. 497 Prepare and Present a Story Orally, SE p. 497 *Video, TWE p. 493* *Film, TWE p. 494* *Create and Enact a Dialogue, TWE p. 486*	**COLLAB. LEARN.** *Decision Making, TWE p. 492*	🖥 *Methods of Flood Control, TWE p. 485* 🖥 *Political Conflict, TWE p. 491*
Apostrophes, SE p. 527 *Using End Marks, TWE p. 509* *Complete Sentences, TWE p. 520*	**COLLAB. LEARN.** Literature Groups, SE p. 526 *Film, TWE p. 506* *Music, TWE p. 515* **COLLAB. LEARN.** *Oral Reading: Teleplay, TWE p. 518*	News Broadcast, SE p. 526 *Lifelong Learning, TWE p. 513* **COLLAB. LEARN.** *Discussion on Crowd Behavior, TWE p. 517*	🖥 Internet Connection, SE p. 526 🖥 *Screenwriters, TWE p. 523* *Real-World Connection: Riots, TWE p. 523*

SELECTIONS	📁 Print Resources		
Amigo Brothers PIRI THOMAS	Theme Five Planning Guide, pp. 6–13 * Active Reading Guide, p. 39 Vocabulary Practice, p. 26	Grammar & Comp. Handbook, Lesson 3.1 Grammar & Language Workbook, pp. 73–74 Reading Workbook, pp. 69–70	* Quick Checks, p. 39 Selection and Theme Assessment, pp. 69–70 Performance Assessment, p. 37 Spanish Summaries, p. 39 Spanish Translations
Your World GEORGIA JOHNSON	Theme Five Planning Guide, pp. 14–18 * Active Reading Guide, p. 40	Grammar & Comp. Handbook, Lessons 5.3, 5.4 Grammar & Language Workbook, pp. 121–124	* Quick Checks, p. 40 Selection and Theme Assessment, pp. 69–70 Performance Assessment, p. 37 Spanish Summaries, p. 40
The Scholarship Jacket MARTA SALINAS	Theme Five Planning Guide, pp. 19–26 * Active Reading Guide, p. 41 Vocabulary Practice, p. 27	Grammar & Comp. Handbook, Lessons 5.1, 6.1, 6.2, 10.1 Grammar & Language Workbook, pp. 117–118, 127–128, 183–184 Reading Workbook, pp. 71–72	* Quick Checks, p. 41 Selection and Theme Assessment, pp. 71–72 Performance Assessment, p. 38 Spanish Summaries, p. 41 Spanish Translations
All Summer in a Day RAY BRADBURY	Theme Five Planning Guide, pp. 27–34 * Active Reading Guide, p. 42 Vocabulary Practice, p. 28	Grammar & Comp. Handbook, Lessons 6.5, 13.2 Grammar & Language Workbook, pp. 135–136, 255–256 Reading Workbook, pp. 73–74	* Quick Checks, p. 42 Selection and Theme Assessment, pp. 73–74 Performance Assessment, p. 39 Spanish Summaries, p. 42 Spanish Translations
PRIMER LESSON CARL SANDBURG THE BIRD LIKE NO OTHER DOROTHY WEST	Theme Five Planning Guide, pp. 35–40 * Active Reading Guide, p. 43 Vocabulary Practice, p. 29	Grammar & Language Workbook, pp. 223–224 Reading Workbook, pp. 75–76	* Quick Checks, p. 43 Selection and Theme Assessment, pp. 75–76 Performance Assessment, p. 40 Spanish Summaries, p. 43
The Old Demon PEARL S. BUCK The Boy and His Grandfather RUDOLFO A. ANAYA	Theme Five Planning Guide, pp. 41–46 * Active Reading Guide, p. 44 Vocabulary Practice, p. 30	Grammar & Comp. Handbook, Lessons 3.5, 9.1 Grammar & Language Workbook, pp. 83–86, 167–170 Reading Workbook, pp. 77–78	* Quick Checks, p. 44 Selection and Theme Assessment, pp. 77–78 Performance Assessment, p. 41 Spanish Summaries, p. 44 Spanish Translations
The Monsters Are Due on Maple Street ROD SERLING	Theme Five Planning Guide, pp. 47–54 * Active Reading Guide, p. 45 Vocabulary Practice, p. 31	Grammar & Comp. Handbook, Lessons 1.2, 13.1, 13.7 Grammar & Language Workbook, pp. 55–56, 253–254, 273–274 Reading Workbook, pp. 79–80	* Quick Checks, p. 45 Selection and Theme Assessment, pp. 79–80 Performance Assessment, p. 42 Spanish Summaries, p. 45 Spanish Translations

*Also available in Spanish

📝 **Transparencies**	**Technology Resources**
Selection Focus Transparency 39 Grammar and Language Transparency 37 Literary Elements Transparency 39	💿 Literature Launchers 🎧 💿 Audio Library 🎧 💿 Spanish Audio Library 💾 💿 Vocabulary Puzzlemaker 💻 Web Site: lit.glencoe.com
Selection Focus Transparency 40 Grammar and Language Transparency 38 Literary Elements Transparency 40	🎧 💿 Audio Library 🎧 💿 Spanish Audio Library 💾 💿 Vocabulary Puzzlemaker 💻 Web Site: lit.glencoe.com
Selection Focus Transparency 41 Grammar and Language Transparency 39 Literary Elements Transparency 41 Fine Art Transparency 5	🎧 💿 Audio Library 🎧 💿 Spanish Audio Library 💾 💿 Vocabulary Puzzlemaker 💻 Web Site: lit.glencoe.com
Selection Focus Transparency 42 Grammar and Language Transparency 40 Literary Elements Transparency 42	💿 Literature Launchers 🎧 💿 Audio Library 🎧 💿 Spanish Audio Library 💾 💿 Vocabulary Puzzlemaker 💻 Web Site: lit.glencoe.com
Selection Focus Transparency 43 Grammar and Language Transparency 41 Literary Elements Transparency 43	🎧 💿 Audio Library 🎧 💿 Spanish Audio Library 💾 💿 Vocabulary Puzzlemaker 💻 Web Site: lit.glencoe.com
Selection Focus Transparency 44 Grammar and Language Transparency 42 Literary Elements Transparency 44	💿 Literature Launchers 🎧 💿 Audio Library 🎧 💿 Spanish Audio Library 💾 💿 Vocabulary Puzzlemaker 💻 Web Site: lit.glencoe.com
Selection Focus Transparency 45 Grammar and Language Transparencies 43–44 Literary Elements Transparency 45	🎧 💿 Audio Library 🎧 💿 Spanish Audio Library 💾 💿 Vocabulary Puzzlemaker 💻 Web Site: lit.glencoe.com

📁 *Theme* RESOURCES

- Listening and Speaking Activities (pp. 13–15)
- Viewing and Representing Activities (pp. 1–6, 19–21)
- Critical Thinking Skills (pp. 12–14)
- Media Connection Activities (pp. 9–10)
- Interdisciplinary Activities (pp. 18–21)
- Family and Community Activities (p. 15)
- Selection and Theme Assessment (pp. 133–134)

See also these additional planning resources:
- English Language Learners Sourcebook
- Inclusion Strategies Sourcebook
- Literature Groups Sourcebook

Use Glencoe's *Presentation Plus!* This multimedia teaching tool lets you present dynamic lessons that will engage your students. Using Microsoft PowerPoint®, you can customize the presentation to create your own personalized lessons.

THEME 5

At the Crossroads

At the Crossroads

Theme Objectives

- To enjoy reading about people who confront tough decisions with courage and ingenuity
- To analyze the literary elements in poetry, folktale, short story, and drama selections
- To apply strategies for reading drama

Teaching Strategies

Have students read the quotation from "The Road Not Taken" by Robert Frost in preparation for the discussion questions below.

VIEWING THE PHOTOGRAPH

Responding to the Photograph

- What might the roads in the quote represent? (*They could represent life's journey.*)
- What difference might taking the less-traveled road make? (*It could provide experiences most other travelers would never have and great satisfaction in having accomplished something special.*)

TEACHER to TEACHER

HARWOOD MIDDLE SCHOOL • EVANSVILLE, IN.

When opening the theme "At The Crossroads," I have students write "Live and Learn" sentences. I say, "From birth to death, our entire lives are journeys on which we live and learn. Along the way we encounter many crossroads. What have you lived and learned?" I give a few examples: "I've learned that going out with pretty girls is not all that it's cracked up to be. I've learned that two heads are better than one, provided one of those heads isn't two-faced. I've learned the best way to shut out trouble is to have an open mind, open heart, and open arms." First, each student writes ten sentences, and then in groups they decide on the ten best sentences and refine them. We pick the best thirty or forty as a class and display them in the hall.

DAVE BARCLAY

THEME 5

> 66 *Two roads diverged in a wood, and I— I took the one less traveled by, And that has made all the difference.* 99

—*Robert Frost*
"The Road Not Taken"

THEME CONTENTS

Amigo Brothers • short story by Piri Thomas 433

Your World • poem by Georgia Johnson 445

The Scholarship Jacket •
    short story by Marta Salinas 451

All Summer in a Day •
    short story by Ray Bradbury 461

Primer Lesson • poem by Carl Sandburg 472

The Bird Like No Other •
    short story by Dorothy West 473

The Old Demon • short story by Pearl S. Buck 483

The Boy and His Grandfather •
    folktale retold by Rudolfo A. Anaya 495

 GENRE **FOCUS** DRAMA

The Monsters Are Due on Maple Street •
    teleplay by Rod Serling 505

Introducing the Theme

Direct your students' attention to the **Theme Contents.** Ask them to read through the list of selections. Present these questions for discussion:

• Another word for *crossroads* is *intersection.* Which titles in the Contents indicate stories about intersections where the natural and supernatural worlds meet? *(Students may say "All Summer in a Day," "The Old Demon," and "The Monsters Are Due on Maple Street.")*

• What might the characters in these diverse genres (stories, poems, folktales, and a teleplay) have in common? *(Students may speculate that the characters are confronted with challenging decisions to make or problems to solve.)*

• Do any of the titles give you a clue as to what the crossroads in the story might be? *(Students may think that family decisions are being considered in selections such as "Amigo Brothers" and "The Boy and his Grandfather.")*

 # FINE ART
TRANSPARENCY 20

You may wish to use *Fine Art Transparency 20* to enrich students' thinking about the theme.

GLENCOE
T E C H N O L O G Y

LITERATURE CLASSICS CD-ROM
    Search for other selections related to the theme "At the Crossroads."

RESOURCE MANAGER

See the ***Theme Five Planning Guide*** (pp. 1–5) for additional teaching notes, strategies, and resources for introducing the theme "At the Crossroads."

Exploring the Theme

At the Crossroads

Students may offer situations such as how to handle moving to a new school, getting caught up in arguments between friends, and deciding on the appropriate strategy in an ambiguous situation.

Have students draw portraits of themselves standing at a crossroads in their lives. Ask them to give the viewer a sense of the dilemma by including street names for each road they could choose or by labeling the elements of the conflict in some other way. For example, students might draw themselves looking confused by two choices marked: *Join in gossip* and *Be loyal to my friend.*

Starting Points

A Tough Decision
Have students think of a time they or someone they know used humor to extricate themselves from a sticky situation, as Charlie Brown does in the comic strip.

- Introduce the word *diplomat.* Explain that a *diplomat* is a government representative who is skilled in dealing with people tactfully. Ask students if they think Charlie Brown offered a *diplomatic* answer to Peppermint Pattie's question. Have them try to include at least one other diplomatic response in their dialogues.
- Invite students to write and dramatize their dialogues, using other well-known characters from the *Peanuts* cartoon in addition to the three pictured here.

Which Way to Turn
Have students rate themselves as decision makers using these questions: *Do I make decisions quickly and easily? Do I worry over every little decision I have to make? Do I think things through? Do I often look back and regret my decisions—or do I chalk up bad decisions to experience and move on?* After students have made up their lists of decisions, ask them to draw a star next to the decisions they are happy with.

Exploring the Theme

At the Crossroads

Have you ever been at a point in your life where you had a difficult problem to solve or a decision to make? In this theme's stories, poems, and play, you will meet characters who confront their problems by making courageous or difficult decisions. Begin thinking about the theme by trying one of the activities below.

Starting Points

A TOUGH DECISION
Can you identify with Charlie Brown's difficult situation?

- What other decisions could Charlie Brown have made? With a partner or in a small group, write and then dramatize a dialogue between Charlie Brown and his friends, discussing the different decisions he might have made.

WHICH WAY TO TURN
You have to make choices and decisions every day of your life. Sometimes the decision is easy. Which movie should you see next Saturday? Other times the decision is more difficult. Should you stand up for an unpopular cause in which you believe strongly?

- Write a list of some decisions you have made today. Explain which decisions were more difficult for you to make and why.

PEANUTS
by Charles M. Schulz

PEANUTS reprinted by permission of United Features Syndicate, Inc.

Interviewing Tools Students can use a search engine to find out more about technical tools they can use to interview people. They might use such keywords as *audio, video,* or *photos.*

Theme Projects

As you read the selections in this theme, complete one of the projects below. Work on your own, with a partner, or with a group.

LEARNING FOR LIFE
Interview Questions
People make personal decisions every day about many small and large problems. Some people make decisions that affect many other people. Think about doctors, school principals, mayors, presidents of corporations, and the president of the United States.

1. Develop a list of questions to ask a local decision maker about how she or he solves problems.
2. Interview the person—on the phone, by E-mail, by regular mail, or in person. Share the information with your class.

MULTIMEDIA PROJECT
A Decision Maker
Select a person who has come to a crossroads in his or her life and has made a difficult or important decision.

1. Find people through biographies, magazine articles, other library research, or through people you know.
2. Using a tape recorder or video camera, interview the person you have chosen to report on or other people who can comment on that person's decision.
3. Gather information from a variety of sources to add to your presentation—for example, photos, newspaper clippings, or objects that are connected to the person's decision. Use these objects along with your audio or video interviews to create a multimedia presentation for the class.

interNET CONNECTION

For more project ideas take a look at the Glencoe Web site. While you are there, you can also find out more about the selections in this theme. Here's the address: lit.glencoe.com

CRITICAL THINKING
Personal Problem-Solving Techniques
1. Think about a problem you have had and about how you tried to solve it.
2. Create a flow chart that illustrates your problem-solving process. On the chart, indicate the steps you took to solve the problem, the point where you had to make an important decision, and the end solution.

AT THE CROSSROADS 🐚 431

Theme Projects

Teaching Strategies
These suggestions may help students carry out their theme projects.

Learning For Life
- Help students start a list of topics entitled *What I want to know.* Help them change each topic into a question or series of questions.
- Students can compile their findings in a booklet.

Multimedia Project
- Suggest that students conduct initial interviews to gather background information and explain the project to the people being interviewed. Questions for follow-up interviews can then be written, using information gathered in the initial interviews.
- Before preparing the final presentation, each student should decide his or her purpose by asking: Do I hope to inform, persuade, or entertain my audience?

Critical Thinking
- Students may want to talk about the problems, how they solved them, and who helped them before creating the flowcharts.
- Allow time for students to share their completed flowcharts with partners and to note any comments or feedback partners offer.

Additional Resources
- 📁 *Interdisciplinary Activities,* pp. 18–21
- 📁 *Viewing and Representing Activities,* pp. 19–21
- 📁 *Listening and Speaking Activities,* pp. 13–15
- 📁 *Critical Thinking Skills,* pp. 12–14
- 📁 *Selection and Theme Assessment,* pp. 133–134
- 📁 *Performance Assessment,* p. 73

Family and Community Activity

Decision Making Have each student investigate a decision made at the community level within the last year by reading past issues of the local newspaper and talking to parents and other members of the community. Then each can create a visual representation of how this decision was made, such as steps in a staircase or a journey from one point to another.

Suggest that they include information on
- what the issue was.
- why it was brought to the forefront.
- who made the decision and why.
- what the outcome was.

Additional Resources
📁 *Family and Community Activities,* p. 15

Before Reading

Objectives

- To read and analyze a short story
- To recognize and describe external and internal conflict in a story
- To write an analysis of an ending

Skills

Reading/Thinking: Evaluating; Logical Reasoning; Drawing Conclusions; Comparing and Contrasting
Writing: Using Realistic Language; Newspaper Article
Vocabulary: Etymology; Context Clues; Unlocking Meaning
Grammar/Language: Action Verbs
Listening/Speaking: Broadcast
Collaboration: Literature Groups

◆ **Before You Read**
Amigo Brothers

MEET PIRI THOMAS

Piri Thomas first began writing while serving a prison term for attempted armed robbery. For Thomas, creative writing was a way to escape his prison surroundings, break down stereotypes used to judge people of African American and Puerto Rican descent, and change his life. After his release from prison, Thomas began working in drug rehabilitation centers. His autobiography and novels are known for their use of the Spanish Harlem dialect and for the tough reality they portray.

Piri Thomas was born in 1928. This story was first published in 1978 in the collection Stories from El Barrio.

FOCUS ACTIVITY

Think about your closest friend. What qualities make that person such a good friend?

Chart It!
Create a chart that shows the character traits that you feel make a good friend.

Setting a Purpose
Read to find out how two friends respond to a test of their friendship.

BACKGROUND

In the ancient Greek Olympic games, boxers were not classified in different weight divisions. The strongest and largest boxers held the greatest advantage in competition. Today, professional boxers compete in eight different weight divisions, so that they are evenly matched in size. The divisions range from flyweight, 112 pounds or less, to heavyweight, 195 pounds and over.

VOCABULARY PREVIEW

devastating (dev′ əs tāt′ ing) *adj.* causing great pain, damage, or destruction; overwhelming; p. 434
wary (wār′ ē) *adj.* cautious; on the alert; p. 437
perpetual (pər pech′ o͞o əl) *adj.* constant; unceasing; p. 437
improvise (im′ prə vīz′) *v.* to invent, compose, or do without much preparation; p. 438
nimble (nim′ bəl) *adj.* light and quick in movement; p. 439
flail (flāl) *v.* to wave or swing, especially swiftly or violently; p. 440
evading (i vād′ ing) *adj.* escaping or avoiding; p. 440
surge (surj) *v.* to rise or increase suddenly; move with a violent swelling motion, as waves; p. 441

RESOURCE MANAGER

Lesson Planning Resource
The *Theme Five Planning Guide* (pp. 6–13) provides additional lesson notes and reduced versions of all print resources.

📁 **Other Print Resources**
- Active Reading Guide, p. 39
- Vocabulary Practice, p. 26
- Reading Workbook, pp. 69–70
- Grammar and Language Workbook, pp. 73–74

- Grammar and Composition Handbook, Lesson 3.1
- Quick Checks, p. 39
- Selection and Theme Assessment, pp. 69–70
- Performance Assessment, p. 37
- Spanish Summaries, p. 39
- Spanish Translations
- Inclusion Strategies
- English Language Learners Sourcebook

 Transparencies
- Selection Focus 39
- Literary Elements 39
- Grammar and Language 37

Technology
 Literature Launchers
 Audio Library
 Spanish Audio Library
 Glencoe Literature Web Site
📘 Testmaker

Amigo Brothers

Piri Thomas ~

A

Antonio Cruz and Felix Varga were both seventeen years old. They were so together in friendship that they felt themselves to be brothers. They had known each other since childhood, growing up on the lower east side of Manhattan in the same tenement building on Fifth Street between Avenue A and Avenue B.

Antonio was fair, lean, and lanky, while Felix was dark, short, and husky. Antonio's hair was always falling over his eyes, while Felix wore his black hair in a natural Afro style.

Each youngster had a dream of someday becoming lightweight[1] champion of the world. Every chance they had the boys worked out, sometimes at the Boys Club on 10th Street and Avenue A and sometimes at the pro's gym on 14th Street. Early morning sunrises would find them running along the East River Drive, wrapped in sweat shirts, short towels around their necks, and handkerchiefs Apache style around their foreheads.

While some youngsters were into street negatives, Antonio and Felix slept, ate, rapped, and dreamt positive. Between them, they had a collection of *Fight* magazines second to none, plus a scrapbook filled with torn tickets to every boxing match they had ever attended, and some clippings of their own. If asked a question about any given fighter, they would immediately zip out from their memory banks divisions, weights, records of fights, knock-outs, technical knock-outs,[2] and draws or losses.

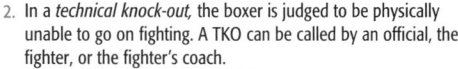

Each had fought many bouts representing their community and had won two gold-plated medals plus a silver and bronze medallion. The difference was in their style. Antonio's lean form and long reach made him the better boxer, while Felix's short and muscular frame made him the better slugger. Whenever they had met in the ring for sparring sessions,[3] it had always been hot and heavy.

---

1. Boxers compete in classes, or divisions, based on their weight. In professional boxing, the *lightweight* division is 131–135 pounds.
2. In a *technical knock-out,* the boxer is judged to be physically unable to go on fighting. A TKO can be called by an official, the fighter, or the fighter's coach.
3. *Sparring sessions* are practice fights.

SUMMARY

Antonio and Felix are great friends and amateur boxers. They each dream of one day being lightweight champion of the world. But there is a problem. The two best buddies must fight each other in the division finals and the winner will represent the Boys Club in the Golden Gloves Championship Tournament. A wall rises between them. Can their friendship survive this test?

📁 *Spanish Summaries,* p. 39

A Active Reading

PREDICT Invite students to look at the title of this story and the photograph of the boxing gloves. Then let a volunteer read aloud the first paragraph. Who do your students think the Amigo Brothers are? What do they think the Amigo Brothers like to do, and what do they imagine the conflict will be? Suggest that students periodically revisit their predictions as they read to verify or revise them.

Additional Resources

📁 *Active Reading Guide,* p. 39

🎧 *Audio Library*

🎧 *Spanish Audio Library*

Teaching Options

CONNECTING TO OTHER SELECTIONS

COMPARING *selections*

This selection is paired with "Your World" on page 445. A lesson for teaching a comparison of the two selections appears on page 447.

The chart at the right shows three ways to connect "Amigo Brothers" to other selections in this book.

For specific teaching strategies, see the *Theme Five Planning Guide,* pages 9–10.

Connection	Title
Life Skills: Problem Solving	→ "Too Soon a Woman," p. 235
Thematic: Challenge	→ "Strong Men Weep," p. 26
Literary: Short Story	→ "Lob's Girl," p. 659

Teaching Options

B Literary Elements

PLOT: *External Conflict* Have students explain the conflict between Antonio and Felix. How does it affect the boys' relationship? *(They must fight each other in the division finals. The winner will represent the Boys Club in the Golden Gloves championship. It causes a wall to rise between them.)*

C Literary Elements

SETTING Encourage students to think about the story's setting. Ask them to list clues from the story and explain their importance. *(The story takes place in New York City. Descriptions of the city include: dirty East River's edge and shores of Brooklyn. The names make the story seem authentic, as if the author were familiar with the area.)*

D Critical Thinking

EVALUATING Have students list examples of English and Spanish slang and explain the effect the slang has on the story. *(The narrator uses words like* ace-boon buddies, bro, panin, *and* cheverote. *The use of these slang words makes the boys' dialogue seem real.)*

Vo•cab•u•lar•y Skills

Context Clues A welterweight boxer is a fairly lightweight boxer. Therefore, a welterweight tugboat is a boat that is small in comparison to what it is pulling.

Amigo Brothers

Now, after a series of elimination bouts,[4] they had been informed that they were to meet each other in the division finals that were scheduled for the seventh of August, two weeks away—the winner to represent the Boys Club in the Golden Gloves Championship Tournament.

The two boys continued to run together along the East River Drive. But even when joking with each other, they both sensed a wall rising between them.

One morning less than a week before their bout, they met as usual for their daily work-out. They fooled around with a few jabs at the air, slapped skin, and then took off, running lightly along the dirty East River's edge.

Antonio glanced at Felix who kept his eyes purposely straight ahead, pausing from time to time to do some fancy leg work while throwing one-twos followed by upper cuts to an imaginary jaw. Antonio then beat the air with a barrage of body blows and short <u>devastating</u> lefts with an over-hand jaw-breaking right.

After a mile or so, Felix puffed and said, "Let's stop a while, bro. I think we both got something to say to each other."

Antonio nodded. It was not natural to be acting as though nothing unusual was happening when two ace-boon buddies[5] were going to be blasting each other within a few short days.

They rested their elbows on the railing separating them from the river. Antonio wiped his face with his short towel. The sunrise was now creating day.

Felix leaned heavily on the river's railing and stared across to the shores of Brooklyn. Finally, he broke the silence.

"Man, I don't know how to come out with it."

Antonio helped. "It's about our fight, right?"

"Yeah, right." Felix's eyes squinted at the rising orange sun.

"I've been thinking about it too, *panin*. In fact, since we found out it was going to be me and you, I've been awake at night, pulling punches[6] on you, trying not to hurt you."

"Same here. It ain't natural not to think about the fight. I mean, we both are *cheverote*[7] fighters and we both want to win. But only one of us can win. There ain't no draws in the eliminations."

Felix tapped Antonio gently on the shoulder. "I don't mean to sound like I'm bragging, bro. But I wanna win, fair and square."

Antonio nodded quietly. "Yeah. We both know that in the ring the better man wins. Friend or no friend, brother or no . . ."

Felix finished it for him. "Brother. Tony, let's promise something right here. Okay?"

"If it's fair, *hermano*, I'm for it." Antonio admired the courage of a tug boat pulling a barge five times its welterweight[8] size.

---

4. *[elimination bouts]* These are fights in a tournament; the winners advance to fight again, but the losers are eliminated from competition.
5. Here, *ace* means "best" and *boon* means "merry," so *ace-boon buddies* are best friends who share fun and good times.

6. In American Spanish slang, *panin* (pä' nēn) means "pal; buddy." *Pulling punches* is holding back from delivering full-strength blows.
7. *Cheverote* (che ve rô' tä) is American Spanish slang for "really cool; fine."
8. *Hermano* (är män' ō) means "brother." A professional *welterweight* boxer weighs between 141 and 147 pounds.

Vocabulary
devastating (dev' as tāt' ing) *adj.* causing great pain, damage, or destruction; overwhelming

434 THEME 5

MEETING INDIVIDUAL NEEDS — ENGLISH LANGUAGE LEARNERS

Spanish Words Have English language learners look at the words on page 434 in italic type. Let students explain what these words have in common. *(They are Spanish words.)*

Activity Have students begin a chart listing the Spanish words used in this story in the first column. In a second column, have students write an English definition for each word. If students speak Spanish, have them explain to other students several ways in which these words might be used.

Spanish Word	English Meaning
panin	buddy
cheverote	very fine

Additional Resources

📁 *English Language Learners Sourcebook*

Vinny Pazienza, 1996. Bill Angresano. Oil on canvas, 24 x 20 in. Big Fights Boxing Memorabilia, New York.

Viewing the painting: Does this fighter seem to have the same determination as the *amigo* brothers? Explain your opinion.

Artist Bill Angresano was himself a New Jersey Golden Gloves semi-finalist in the 1970s. This painting is probably of Rhode Islander Vinnie Pazienza at a match fought against Dana Rosenblatt in 1996. Rosenblatt led the entire fight until Pazienza landed a punch that knocked Rosenblatt out. Said Pazienza of the match, "The war is over only when you quit, and I don't quit." Pazienza said about boxing, "It's not just the fight that counts; it's everything. It's what happens between the rounds, and it's the intensity."

Viewing Response *Pazienza looks determined and focused. He seems to be fighting with the intensity of the amigo brothers.*

Historical Note

Boxing In ancient Greece, boxing was a popular sport and an Olympic event. Roman boxers wore metal-studded gloves that could kill their opponents. In the 1700s, boxing became popular in London. Fighters did not wear gloves and were allowed to pull hair or hit opponents who were down. By the late 1800s, boxers began wearing gloves, and the sport began emphasizing skill and strength.

Reading *Minilesson*

Comparing and Contrasting Antonio Cruz and Felix Varga share a dream. Yet the two boxers are different from each other in many ways. On the board, draw a Venn diagram.

Activity Encourage students to list ways that Antonio and Felix are alike and ways they are different. **L2**

Differences
Antonio
fair
lean
lanky

Likenesses
• want to be world light-weight champ
• work out every chance

Differences
Felix
dark
husky
short

Additional Resources
📁 *Reading Workbook,* pp. 69–70

E Active Reading

PREDICT Have students predict how the two boys will treat each other when they meet in the ring. The following model illustrates the thinking process involved in predicting.

Model: I know the boys are serious boxers with big dreams. Although they are friends and do not want to hurt each other, I think they will fight as hard as they can. Only then will the fight be fair and show who is the better boxer.

F Critical Thinking

EVALUATING Have students explain why the boys decide to separate before the fight. *(They think they can prepare better mentally if they don't see each other before the fight.)*

G Critical Thinking

LOGICAL REASONING Ask students if they think the boys could get together again "like nothing ever happened" after the fight? *(The boys may not feel as if they are equals anymore, and it could affect their relationship. They might see a new side of each other in the ring—one they don't like.)*

H Active Reading

CONNECT Have students explain why Antonio thinks knocking Felix out early will spare him. How would they feel? *(A first-round knockout is less painful than being pummeled for the complete match. However, a quick knockout might be humiliating.)*

Teaching Options

"It's fair, Tony. When we get into the ring, it's gotta be like we never met. We gotta be like two heavy strangers that want the same thing and only one can have it. You understand, don'tcha?"

"*Si*, I know." Tony smiled. "No pulling punches. We go all the way."

"Yeah, that's right. Listen, Tony. Don't you think it's a good idea if we don't see each other until the day of the fight? I'm going to stay with my Aunt Lucy in the Bronx. I can use Gleason's Gym for working out. My manager says he got some sparring partners with more or less your style."

Tony scratched his nose pensively.[9] "Yeah, it would be better for our heads." He held out his hand, palm upward. "Deal?"

"Deal." Felix lightly slapped open skin.

"Ready for some more running?" Tony asked lamely.

"Naw, bro. Let's cut it here. You go on. I kinda like to get things together in my head."

"You ain't worried, are you?" Tony asked.

"No way, man." Felix laughed out loud. "I got too much smarts for that. I just think it's cooler if we split right here. After the fight, we can get it together again like nothing ever happened."

The amigo brothers were not ashamed to hug each other tightly.

"Guess you're right. Watch yourself, Felix. I hear there's some pretty heavy dudes up in the Bronx. *Sauvecito*,[10] okay?"

"Okay. You watch yourself too, *sabe?*"[11]

Tony jogged away. Felix watched his friend disappear from view, throwing

rights and lefts. Both fighters had a lot of psyching[12] up to do before the big fight.

The days in training passed much too slowly. Although they kept out of each other's way, they were aware of each other's progress via the ghetto grapevine.

The evening before the big fight, Tony made his way to the roof of his tenement. In the quiet early dark, he peered over the ledge. Six stories below the lights of the city blinked and the sounds of cars mingled with the curses and the laughter of children in the street. He tried not to think of Felix, feeling he had succeeded in psyching his mind. But only in the ring would he really know. To spare Felix hurt, he would have to knock him out, early and quick.

Up in the South Bronx, Felix decided to take in a movie in an effort to keep Antonio's face away from his fists. The flick was *The Champion* with Kirk Douglas, the third time Felix was seeing it.

The champion was getting the daylights beat out of him. He was saved only by the sound of the bell.

Felix became the champ and Tony the challenger.

The movie audience was going out of its head. The champ hunched his shoulders grunting and sniffing red blood back into his broken nose. The challenger, confident that he had the championship in the bag, threw a left. The champ countered with a dynamite right.

Felix's right arm felt the shock. Antonio's face, superimposed on the screen, was hit by the awesome force of the blow. Felix saw himself in the ring, blasting

---

9. Doing a thing *pensively* is doing it in a deeply thoughtful and, perhaps, sad way.
10. This American Spanish slang expression translates as "Take it easy" or "Be cool." Pronunciation: *sauvecito* (sä′ vä sē′ tō)
11. *Sabe?* (sä′ bā) means "You know?"

12. *Psyching* (sī′ king) *up* is getting into the right mental or emotional state.

MEETING INDIVIDUAL NEEDS · INCLUSION STRATEGIES

Special Needs Help students realize that while boxing is a dangerous sport, the emphasis in modern boxing is on athletic skill and strength, rather than on brawling and maiming. In Golden Gloves boxing, the contestants wear helmets and thickly padded gloves to minimize injury.

Activity Have students work in pairs and compare how Felix and Antonio train with the way athletes in another sport prepare. Ask students to share their comparisons with the class. **L1**
COLLAB. LEARN.

Additional Resources
📁 *Inclusion Strategies*

Antonio against the ropes. The champ had to be forcibly restrained. The challenger fell slowly to the canvas.

When Felix finally left the theatre, he had figured out how to psyche himself for tomorrow's fight. It was Felix the Champion vs. Antonio the Challenger.

He walked up some dark streets, deserted except for small pockets of wary-looking kids wearing gang colors. Despite the fact that he was Puerto Rican like them, they eyed him as a stranger to their turf. Felix did a fast shuffle, bobbing and weaving, while letting loose a torrent of blows that would demolish whatever got in its way. It seemed to impress the brothers, who went about their own business.

Finding no takers, Felix decided to split to his aunt's. Walking the streets had not relaxed him, neither had the fight flick. All it had done was to stir him up. He let himself quietly into his Aunt Lucy's apartment and went straight to bed, falling into a fitful sleep with sounds of the gong for Round One.

Antonio was passing some heavy time on his rooftop. How would the fight tomorrow affect his relationship with Felix? After all, fighting was like any other profession. Friendship had nothing to do with it. A gnawing doubt crept in. He cut negative thinking real quick by doing some speedy fancy dance steps, bobbing and weaving like mercury.[13] The night air was blurred with perpetual motions of left hooks and right crosses. Felix, his *amigo*

brother, was not going to be Felix at all in the ring. Just an opponent with another face. Antonio went to sleep, hearing the opening bell for the first round. Like his friend in the South Bronx, he prayed for victory, via a quick clean knock-out in the first round.

Large posters plastered all over the walls of local shops announced the fight between Antonio Cruz and Felix Vargas as the main bout.

The fight had created great interest in the neighborhood. Antonio and Felix were well liked and respected. Each had his own loyal following.

Antonio's fans had unbridled[14] faith in his boxing skills. On the other side, Felix's admirers trusted in his dynamite-packed fists.

Felix had returned to his apartment early in the morning of August 7th and stayed there, hoping to avoid seeing Antonio. He turned the radio on to *salsa*[15] music sounds and then tried to read while waiting for word from his manager.

The fight was scheduled to take place in Tompkins Square Park. It had been decided that the gymnasium of the Boys Club was not large enough to hold all the people who were sure to attend. In Tompkins Square Park, everyone who wanted could view the fight, whether from ringside or window fire escapes or tenement rooftops.

The morning of the fight Tompkins Square was a beehive of activity with

---

13. *Mercury* is a metal that is liquid at room temperature and moves about as if it were alive.

14. Here, *unbridled* means "uncontrolled."

15. *Salsa* is lively Latin American dance music that uses elements of rhythm and blues, jazz, and rock.

Vocabulary
wary (wār′ ē) *adj.* cautious; on the alert
perpetual (pər pech′ ōō əl) *adj.* constant; unceasing

I Literary Elements

PLOT: *External Conflict* Ask students to describe the external conflict Felix faces after leaving the theater. Have students explain how Felix defuses the situation. *(Felix encounters gang members who distrust him. To diffuse the situation, he shows off his boxing moves. The group leaves him alone.)*

J Literary Elements

PLOT: *Internal Conflict* Have students identify the internal conflict Antonio struggles with on his rooftop. *(Antonio worries about how the fight will affect his relationship with Felix.)*

Vo•cab•u•lar•y Skills

Etymology In ancient Greece, each city had a gymnasium where young men exercised, played sports, and studied philosophy, music, and literature. Because it is hot in Greece, the men exercised in the nude. The word *gymnasium* means "school for naked exercise." In English, *gymnasium* has come to mean "a place for physical activity." In Germany, a gymnasium is a high school.

Writing *Minilesson*

Using Realistic Language Write on the board:
1. *Felix decided to split.*
2. *The fight flick had not relaxed him.*
3. *It had stirred him up.*

Explain to students that this informal language makes the story seem authentic. Have students restate the sentences without slang. *(Felix decided to leave. The fight movie had not relaxed him. It had upset him.)*

Activity Have students write a paragraph or story about an activity they engage in. Encourage students to use realistic, informal speech patterns to lend an air of authenticity to their work. **L2**

numerous workers setting up the ring, the seats, and the guest speakers' stand. The scheduled bouts began shortly after noon and the park had begun filling up even earlier.

The local junior high school across from Tompkins Square Park served as the dressing room for all the fighters. Each was given a separate classroom with desk tops, covered with mats, serving as resting tables. Antonio thought he caught a glimpse of Felix waving to him from a room at the far end of the corridor. He waved back just in case it had been him.

The fighters changed from their street clothes into fighting gear. Antonio wore white trunks, black socks, and black shoes. Felix wore sky blue trunks, red socks, and white boxing shoes. Each had dressing gowns to match their fighting trunks with their names neatly stitched on the back.

The loudspeakers blared into the open windows of the school. There were speeches by dignitaries, community leaders, and great boxers of yesteryear. Some were well prepared, some improvised on the spot. They all carried the same message of great pleasure and honor at being part of such a historic event. This great day was in the tradition of champions emerging from the streets of the lower east side.

Interwoven with the speeches were the sounds of the other boxing events. After the sixth bout, Felix was much relieved when his trainer Charlie said, "Time change. Quick knock-out. This is it. We're on."

Waiting time was over. Felix was escorted from the classroom by a dozen fans in white T-shirts with the word FELIX across their fronts.

Antonio was escorted down a different stairwell and guided through a roped-off path.

As the two climbed into the ring, the crowd exploded with a roar. Antonio and Felix both bowed gracefully and then raised their arms in acknowledgment.

Antonio tried to be cool, but even as the roar was in its first birth, he turned slowly to meet Felix's eyes looking directly into his. Felix nodded his head and Antonio responded. And both as one, just as quickly, turned away to face his own corner.

Bong—bong—bong. The roar turned to stillness.

"Ladies and Gentlemen, *Señores y Señoras.*"[16]

The announcer spoke slowly, pleased at his bilingual[17] efforts.

"Now the moment we have all been waiting for—the main event between two fine young Puerto Rican fighters, products of our lower east side.

"In this corner, weighing 134 pounds, Felix Vargas. And in this corner, weighing 133 pounds, Antonio Cruz. The winner will represent the Boys Club in the tournament of champions, the Golden Gloves. There will be no draw. May the best man win."

The cheering of the crowd shook the window panes of the old buildings surrounding Tompkins Square Park. At the center of the ring, the referee was giving instructions to the youngsters.

"Keep your punches up. No low blows. No punching on the back of the head. Keep your heads up. Understand. Let's

16. Pronunciation: *Señores y Señoras* (sen yôr′ ās   ē   sen yôr′ əs)
17. A *bilingual* person can use two languages.

Vocabulary
improvise (im′ prə vīz′) *v.* to invent, compose, or do without much preparation

Listening and Speaking *Minilesson*

Describing a Match Explain to students that real boxers use fighting strategies much like those of Felix and Antonio.

Activity Have interested students watch a boxing match on TV. Encourage them to take notes to keep track of who is leading each round and what strategies each boxer uses. Then have students describe the highlights of the match to the class.

Have students try to recreate the suspense and excitement of the fight by varying the pitch, tone, and loudness of their voices. Remind students that pausing while speaking can have a dramatic effect, too. **L2**

Boxing. G. Cominetti. 75.3 x 92 cm. Private collection.

Viewing the painting: Is the artist's style of painting appropriate to the subject? Why or why not?

have a clean fight. Now shake hands and come out fighting."

Both youngsters touched gloves and nodded. They turned and danced quickly to their corners. Their head towels and dressing gowns were lifted neatly from their shoulders by their trainers' nimble fingers. Antonio crossed himself. Felix did the same.

BONG! BONG! ROUND ONE. Felix and Antonio turned and faced each other squarely in a fighting pose. Felix wasted no time. He came in fast, head low, half hunched toward his right shoulder, and lashed out with a straight left. He missed a right cross as Antonio slipped the punch and countered with one-two-three lefts that snapped Felix's head back, sending a mild shock coursing through him. If Felix had any small doubt about their friendship

affecting their fight, it was being neatly dispelled.[18]

Antonio danced, a joy to behold. His left hand was like a piston pumping jabs one right after another with seeming ease. Felix bobbed and weaved and never stopped boring in. He knew that at long range he was at a disadvantage. Antonio had too much reach on him. Only by coming in close could Felix hope to achieve the dreamed-of knockout.

Antonio knew the dynamite that was stored in his *amigo* brother's fist. He ducked a short right and missed a left hook. Felix trapped him against the ropes just long enough to pour some punishing rights and lefts to Antonio's hard midsection. Antonio slipped away from Felix, crashing two lefts to his head, which set Felix's right ear to ringing.

Bong! Both *amigos* froze a punch well on its way, sending up a roar of approval for good sportsmanship.

Felix walked briskly back to his corner. His right ear had not stopped ringing. Antonio gracefully danced his way toward his stool none the worse, except for glowing glove burns, showing angry red against the whiteness of his midribs.

"Watch that right, Tony." His trainer talked into his ear. "Remember Felix

---

18. To *dispel* something is to make it go away or disappear.

Vocabulary
nimble (nim′ bəl) *adj.* light and quick in movement

Vo•cab•u•lar•y Skills

Etymology St. Mary of Bethlehem Hospital opened in England in 1330 to care for the mentally ill. People referred to the hospital as *Bedlam*, short for *Bethlehem*. Since medications to treat the mentally ill did not exist then, such a hospital was often a place of uproar and confusion, which is what *bedlam* now connotes.

---

always goes to the body. He'll want you to drop your hands for his overhand left or right. Got it?"

P Antonio nodded, spraying water out between his teeth. He felt better as his sore midsection was being firmly rubbed.

Felix's corner was also busy.

"You gotta get in there, fella." Felix's trainer poured water over his curly Afro locks. "Get in there or he's gonna chop you up from way back."

Bong! Bong! Round two. Felix was off his stool and rushed Antonio like a bull, sending a hard right to his head. Beads of water exploded from Antonio's long hair.

Antonio, hurt, sent back a blurring barrage of lefts and rights that only meant pain to Felix, who returned with a short left to the head followed by a looping right to the body. Antonio countered with his own flurry, forcing Felix to give ground. But not for long.

Felix bobbed and weaved, bobbed and weaved, occasionally punching his two gloves together.

Antonio waited for the rush that was sure to come. Felix closed in and feinted[19] with his left shoulder and threw his right instead. Lights suddenly exploded inside Felix's head as Antonio slipped the blow and hit him with a pistonlike left, catching him flush on the point of his chin.

Bedlam[20] broke loose as Felix's legs momentarily buckled. He fought off a

---

19. To *feint* is to make a movement intended to fool an opponent.
20. Noisy uproar and confusion is *bedlam*.

---

series of rights and lefts and came back with a strong right that taught Antonio respect.

Antonio danced in carefully. He knew Felix had the habit of playing possum when hurt, to sucker an opponent within reach of the powerful bombs he carried in each fist. **Q**

A right to the head slowed Antonio's pretty dancing. He answered with his own left at Felix's right eye that began puffing up within three seconds.

Antonio, a bit too eager, moved in too close and Felix had him entangled into a rip-roaring, punching toe-to-toe slugfest that brought the whole Tompkins Square Park screaming to its feet.

Rights to the body. Lefts to the head. Neither fighter was giving an inch. Suddenly a short right caught Antonio squarely on the chin. His long legs turned to jelly and his arms flailed out desperately. Felix, grunting like a bull, threw wild punches from every direction. Antonio, groggy, bobbed and weaved, evading most of the blows. Suddenly his head cleared. His left flashed out hard and straight catching Felix on the bridge of his nose.

Felix lashed back with a haymaker, right off the ghetto streets. At the same instant, his eye caught another left hook from Antonio. Felix swung out trying to clear the pain. Only the frenzied screaming of those along ringside let him know that he had dropped Antonio. Fighting off the growing haze, Antonio struggled to his feet, got up, ducked, and threw a smashing right that dropped Felix flat on his back. **R**

Vocabulary
flail (flāl) *v.* to wave or swing, especially swiftly or violently
evading (i vād' ing) *adj.* escaping or avoiding

Grammar and Language *Minilesson*

Action Verbs Write the following on the board: *Felix tapped his gloves. What did Felix do? He tapped.* Remind students that action verbs describe mental actions *(think, prefer, regard)* as well as physical actions. Students can tell if a word is an action word by changing a sentence into a "do" question. The answer, *tapped,* indicates an action. Explain that since sporting events are games of fast action,

writers often use vivid action words to make events come alive for readers.

Activity Have students write sentences using each of the following action verbs: *block, tackle, catch, charge,* and *attack.* **L2**

Additional Resources

- *Grammar and Language Transparency 37*
- *Grammar and Language Workbook,* pp. 73–74
- *Grammar and Composition Handbook,* Lesson 3.1
- *Writer's Choice,* Lesson 10.1

440

Piri Thomas ~

Felix got up as fast as he could in his own corner, groggy but still game. He didn't even hear the count. In a fog, he heard the roaring of the crowd, who seemed to have gone insane. His head cleared to hear the bell sound at the end of the round. He was very glad. His trainer sat him down on the stool.

S In his corner, Antonio was doing what all fighters do when they are hurt. They sit and smile at everyone.

The referee signaled the ring doctor to check the fighters out. He did so and then gave his okay. The cold water sponges brought clarity to both *amigo* brothers. They were rubbed until their circulation ran free.

T *Bong!* Round three—the final round. Up to now it had been tic-tac-toe, pretty much even. But everyone knew there could be no draw and that this round would decide the winner.

This time, to Felix's surprise, it was Antonio who came out fast, charging across the ring. Felix braced himself but couldn't ward off the barrage of punches. Antonio drove Felix hard against the ropes.

The crowd ate it up. Thus far the two had fought with *mucho corazón.*[21] Felix tapped his gloves and commenced his attack anew. Antonio, throwing boxer's caution to the winds, jumped in to meet him.

Both pounded away. Neither gave an inch and neither fell to the canvas. Felix's left eye was tightly closed. Claret[22] red blood poured from Antonio's nose. They fought toe-to-toe.

The sounds of their blows were loud in contrast to the silence of a crowd gone completely mute.

Bong! Bong! Bong! The bell sounded over and over again. Felix and Antonio were past hearing. Their blows continued to pound on each other like hailstones.

U Finally the referee and the two trainers pried Felix and Antonio apart. Cold water was poured over them to bring them back to their senses.

They looked around and then rushed toward each other. A cry of alarm <u>surged</u> through Tompkins Square Park. Was this a fight to the death instead of a boxing match?

The fear soon gave way to wave upon wave of cheering as the two *amigos* embraced.

No matter what the decision, they knew they would always be champions to each other.

BONG! BONG! BONG! "Ladies and Gentlemen. *Señores* and *Señoras.* The winner and representative to the Golden Gloves Tournament of Champions is . . ."

The announcer turned to point to the winner and found himself alone. Arm in arm the champions had already left the ring.

---

21. They fought with "great heart." Pronunciation: *mucho corazón* (mōō′ chō   kō′ rə zōn′)

22. *Claret* (klar′ it) is a dark, purplish-red color.

❖❖

Vocabulary
surge (surj) *v.* to rise or increase suddenly; move with a violent swelling motion, as waves

---

Literary Elements

S **CHARACTER** Ask students how the author reveals Antonio's personality by having him smile when he is actually in pain. (*The author reveals how much self-pride Antonio has by not showing the pain he feels.*)

Literary Elements

T **PLOT:** *Rising Action* Have students describe how the author increases reader interest when Round three begins. (*Readers know that the fight is even and that this round will decide the outcome. Antonio changes strategy and charges Felix.*)

Active Reading

U **REVIEW** Have students review how Round three ends. How does this compare with the end of Round one? (*After Round three, the two don't stop punching when the bell rings. They don't even hear the bell. In Round one, they both stopped their punches in midair.*)

Thematic Focus

At the Crossroads Ask students to explain how this story relates to the theme "At the Crossroads." At what crossroads are Felix and Antonio? (*Throughout the story, their friendship is threatened.*)

✔ ASSESSMENT OPTIONS

📁 *Quick Checks,* p. 39

---

 interNET CONNECTION

Boxing Students can use a search engine to find out more about boxing. They might use such keywords as *champions, rounds,* and *heavyweight.*

REAL-WORLD CONNECTION

In This Corner Invite students to use research from the Internet, the school library, or from the U.S. Olympic Committee to create posters announcing a tournament.

Activity Have students work in small groups. Ask each group to review the information they have gathered and to decide which part they will use to illustrate their poster. **L2**

Responding to the Selection

Personal Response

Students should compare qualities that Felix and Antonio possess with qualities they listed in the Focus Activity.

Analyzing Literature

1. They each want to become light-weight boxing champion of the world.
2. They have to fight each other in the division finals to represent the Boys Club at the Golden Gloves Championship.
3. Antonio goes up to the roof to think. Felix goes to a movie and then to bed.
4. The fighters leave the ring together before the winner is announced.
5. Antonio and Felix are both determined, hardworking, focused, and ambitious.
6. Felix moves to his aunt's house so he can prepare for the fight without being distracted by his friendship with Antonio.
7. The fighters were evenly matched because they knocked each other down the same number of times and inflicted similar injuries on each other.
8. The two embrace because they know each has done his absolute best. Also, their competition is finally over.
9. The author didn't tell who won because winning wasn't what was important. What was important was how the match affected the boys' friendship. When the two embrace, readers know the friendship has survived.
10. Someone won. The results may change the relationship a bit, but probably not in a devastating way. The story's ending suggests that the boys' friendship will survive their competition.

Responding to Literature

PERSONAL RESPONSE

Do the characters in the story have any of the qualities you charted in the **Focus Activity** on page 432? Which ones?

Analyzing Literature

RECALL

1. What dream do Antonio and Felix share?
2. What causes the wall between the two friends?
3. How does each boxer prepare the night before for the fight?
4. How does the fight end?

INTERPRET

5. What do the efforts of Antonio and Felix to achieve their dream tell you about them?
6. Why do you think Felix moves to his aunt's house before the fight?
7. Do you think the fighters were evenly matched? Explain your opinion.
8. Why do you think the two friends embrace before they hear the results of the match?

Bokszolok. Sandor Botnyik (1893–1976). Gouache on paper, 9¼ x 11½ in. Private collection.

EVALUATE AND CONNECT

9. In your opinion, why did the author choose not to reveal the result of the fight? How does this affect the ending of the story?
10. **Theme Connection** If you were one of the characters, do you think the fight would change your relationship with your friend? Explain your answer.

LITERARY ELEMENTS

Internal/External Conflict

A struggle between two opposing forces is usually at the center of a plot. This struggle is called the **conflict.** There are two basic kinds of conflict, and a plot may include either one or both. An **external conflict** exists when a character struggles against some outside force, such as another person, nature, society, or fate. An **internal conflict** takes place within a character's mind when the character is torn between opposing feelings or goals—for example, loyalty vs. pride.

1. What is the external conflict that drives the plot of "Amigo Brothers"?
2. Write two or three sentences explaining the internal conflicts with which Felix and Antonio struggle.

● See **Literary Terms Handbook,** p. R2.

LITERARY ELEMENTS

1. The two boys fight each other in the division finals.
2. Felix and Antonio do not want to harm their friendship, yet each wants to win. They struggle mentally with the best way to accomplish this goal.

Additional Resources

🖎 *Literary Elements Transparency 39*

Extending Your Response

Writing About Literature

Analysis   Do you agree with the author's decision to end "Amigo Brothers" as he did? Explain with examples from the story.

Creative Writing

Sports Pages   Write a newspaper article about the upcoming battle of two "amigos" and the fighting styles of the opponents. Choose a headline for your article.

Literature Groups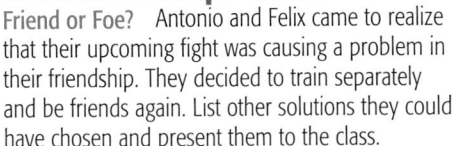

Friend or Foe?   Antonio and Felix came to realize that their upcoming fight was causing a problem in their friendship. They decided to train separately and be friends again. List other solutions they could have chosen and present them to the class.

Performing

Sportscaster   Using the description of the fight as an aid, write a script for a radio announcer at the fight in "Amigo Brothers." Remember that a radio audience can see none of the action, so every detail needs to be described. Perform your radio script for the class.

Reading Further

Check out these other books about boxing:
Muhammad Ali by Norman Macht
Shadow Boxer by Chris Lynch

 Save your work for your portfolio.

Skill Minilesson

VOCABULARY • UNLOCKING MEANING

If you know what *nimble* means, you can guess that *nimbleness* is the quality of being light and quick in movement. *Nimbleness* is the noun form of the adjective *nimble*.

PRACTICE   Use what you know about the *italicized* words to complete the statements.

1. *improvise* A group that does improvisational theater performs without
   a. an audience
   b. any rehearsal
   c. getting paid

2. *surge* If your hopes are resurgent, they are
   a. foolish
   b. brand new
   c. increasing again

3. *perpetual* An agreement that lasts in perpetuity lasts
   a. forever
   b. a short time
   c. for a few years

4. *devastate* The devastation of a house could result from
   a. fire
   b. painting it
   c. mowing the lawn

5. *wary* A person shows his or her wariness by being very
   a. brave
   b. polite
   c. careful

Extending Your Response

Writing About Literature

Students' analyses should
- critically explore the effects of the ending.
- clearly state whether they agree with the way the author ended the story.
- contain examples from the story to support their reasons.

Creative Writing

Students' articles should
- answer the questions *who? what? where? when?* and *how?*
- describe the upcoming match, the fighting styles of Felix and Antonio, and the neighborhood aspects of the battle.
- interest and entertain readers.

Literature Groups Before students meet as groups, encourage them to jot down some ideas. Then have the groups discuss the ideas and further develop and modify the ones they like best. **COLLAB. LEARN.**

Performing Students may want to intersperse visual details from the story with the action of the fight. Radio announcers should speak in a confident voice, although they may get excited during an intense match.

Skill Minilesson

VOCABULARY • UNLOCKING MEANING

1. b	3. a	5. c
2. c	4. a	

Additional Resources
📁 *Vocabulary Practice,* p. 26

✓ ASSESSMENT OPTIONS

📁 *Quick Checks,* p. 39
📁 *Selection and Theme Assessment,* pp. 69–70
📁 *Performance Assessment,* p. 37
💾 *Testmaker*

Objectives

- To read and appreciate a poem about a speaker at a turning point
- To recognize symbolism in poetry
- To write a paragraph that analyzes how imagery supports the theme of a poem

Skills

Writing: Imagery and Theme
Grammar/Language: Comparative and Superlative Adjectives
Collaboration: Literature Groups

Motivating → OPTIONS

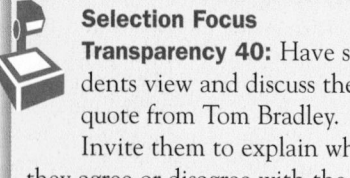

Selection Focus Transparency 40: Have students view and discuss the quote from Tom Bradley. Invite them to explain why they agree or disagree with the quotation.

Focus Activity: As an extension of the Focus Activity, have pairs of students share and compare their dreams. Encourage students to list things they can do to ensure that they reach their goals.

Before You Read
Your World

MEET GEORGIA DOUGLAS JOHNSON

Georgia Douglas Johnson inspired younger African American writers in the early 1900s. From her home in Washington, D.C., she hosted weekly meetings with Harlem Renaissance writers such as Countee Cullen and Langston Hughes. Johnson was one of the first African American female poets to gain wide recognition. Born in Georgia, she studied at Atlanta University and Oberlin Conservatory in Ohio. Johnson's works often advocated greater rights for women and minorities.

Georgia Douglas Johnson was born in 1877 and died in 1966.

FOCUS ACTIVITY

Think of a challenge you face now or will face in the near future. Does it seem a bit scary, or even overwhelming?

Journal
Describe the challenge and what makes it seem frightening or overwhelming.

Setting a Purpose
Read to discover what one poet has to say about meeting new challenges.

BACKGROUND

Did You Know? From 1920 to 1930, in Harlem, a mostly African American part of New York City, a group of writers, artists, and composers took part in a cultural movement that came to be known as the Harlem Renaissance. In their poems, novels, plays, and music, these men and women expressed a renewed pride in their heritage and their community.

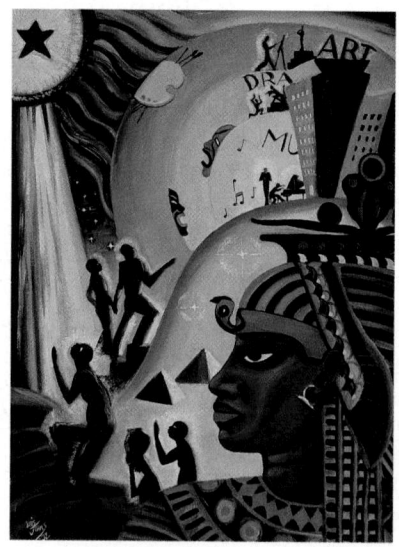

The Ascent of Ethiopia, 1932. Loïs Mailou Jones. Oil on canvas, 23½ x 17¼ in. Milwaukee Art Museum, Purchase, African-American Acquisition Fund, matching funds from Suzanne and Richard Pieper, with additional funds from Arthur and Dorothy Nelle Sanders.

RESOURCE MANAGER

Lesson Planning Resource
The *Theme Five Planning Guide* (pp. 14–18) provides additional lesson notes and reduced versions of all print resources.

📁 **Other Print Resources**
- Active Reading Guide, p. 40
- Grammar and Language Workbook, pp. 121–124
- Grammar and Composition Handbook, Lessons 5.3, 5.4

- Quick Checks, p. 40
- Selection and Theme Assessment, pp. 69–70
- Performance Assessment, p. 37
- Spanish Summaries, p. 40
- Spanish Translations
- Inclusion Strategies
- English Language Learners Sourcebook

📚 **Transparencies**
- Selection Focus 40
- Literary Elements 40
- Grammar and Language 38

Technology
🎧 Audio Library
🎧 Spanish Audio Library
💻 Glencoe Literature Web Site
💾 Testmaker

Your World

Georgia Douglas Johnson ～

Your world is as big as you make it.
I know, for I used to abide
In the narrowest nest in a corner,
My wings pressing close to my side.

5   But I sighted the distant horizon
Where the sky line encircled the sea
And I throbbed with a burning desire
To travel this immensity.

I battered the cordons around me
10   And cradled my wings on the breeze
Then soared to the uttermost reaches
With rapture, with power, with ease!

---

2 Here, *abide* may mean either "dwell" or "remain."
8 Anything of great size or extent is an *immensity.*
9 *Cordons* are barriers.
12 *Rapture* is the condition of being carried away
   by strong emotion, such as joy or love.

Reading the Selection

A Active Reading

PREDICT Ask students to read only the first line of the poem and predict what the poet might mean by it. *(Students might say that they have the power to take advantage of the many opportunities they might discover.)*

B Literary Elements

SYMBOL Explain to students that a symbol is something that means more than just what it is. Ask students what the nest and wings might symbolize in lines 3–4. *(The nest symbolizes her small world. The wings symbolize a willingness to try new things; however, she was afraid of the unknown.)*

C Literary Elements

SYMBOL Ask students to explain what the soaring bird in the last stanza symbolizes. *(It symbolizes a person who has set a lofty goal and achieved it.)*

Additional Resources

📁 *Active Reading Guide,* p. 40

🎧 *Audio Library*

🎧 *Spanish Audio Library*

📁 *Spanish Summaries,* p. 40

Teaching Options

Grammar and Language *Minilesson*

Comparative and Superlative Adjectives Comparative adjectives compare two items. Superlative adjectives compare more than two and add emphasis.

Activity Ask students to identify the adjectives in these sentences.
1. It's the chef's best dish. *(superlative)*
2. He was taller than she. *(comparative)*

Additional Resources

✎ *Grammar and Language Transparency 38*

📕 *Grammar and Language Workbook,* pp. 121–124

📕 *Grammar and Composition Handbook,* Lessons 5.3, 5.4

📕 *Writer's Choice,* Lessons 12.3, 12.4

COMPARING *selections*

This selection is compared with "Amigo Brothers" on page 433. A lesson for teaching a comparison of the two selections appears on page 447.

Responding to the Selection

Personal Response

Students might feel more motivated to face their challenges after reading this poem.

Analyzing Literature

1. The speaker is compared to a bird. The metaphor works because the speaker overcomes a challenge and soars to new heights, much like a bird.
2. *Narrowest nest* uses alliteration. The repeated beginning consonant sound gives emphasis to the image.
3. The speaker sees the horizon and wants to travel there.
4. Yes. People can overcome obstacles on the path to success.
5. In the beginning, the speaker is afraid to try. By the end, the speaker is not afraid to try, and soars.
6. The rhythm emphasizes the words *rapture, power,* and *ease.* It instills in the reader a sense that anything is possible.

Extending Your Response

Literature Groups Before students begin writing the poem, encourage them to think of a symbol that works for their group. They may want to ask how they see themselves: as birds, as fish, as automobiles, as jets, and so on. **COLLAB. LEARN.**

Writing About Literature

Students' paragraphs should
- clearly state a theme found in "My World."
- use images from the poem to support their ideas.
- contain a concluding or summarizing sentence.

Responding to Literature

PERSONAL RESPONSE

How might this poem inspire you to face the challenge you described for the **Focus Activity** on page 444?

Analyzing Literature

RECALL AND INTERPRET

1. To what creature does the speaker compare himself or herself? Do you think the **metaphor** works in the poem? Why or why not?
2. **Alliteration** is the repetition of the consonant sounds at the beginnings of words. Find an example of alliteration in the first stanza of "Your World." How does it contribute to the poem's effect?
3. What does the speaker see in the second stanza? How does this change the direction of his or her life?

EVALUATE AND CONNECT

4. Do you agree with the speaker's belief that "Your world is as big as you make it"? Explain your answer.
5. How does the speaker change during the poem? Summarize the differences in the speaker at the beginning and end of the poem.
6. Read the last two lines of the poem aloud. How does the rhythm contribute to the poem's emotional effect?

Extending Your Response

Literature Groups

Classroom Changes Discuss "Your World" with your group. How does the poet's use of symbol add emphasis to her ideas? Then, using the poem as a model, work together to compose a new short poem, "Our World."

Writing About Literature

Imagery and Theme What is the **theme**—the poet's main idea or message—of "Your World"? Write a paragraph analyzing how the poet's use of imagery supports the poem's theme.

LITERARY ELEMENTS

Symbol

In literature, when a person, a place, an object, or an action stands for something else, it becomes a **symbol**. For example, a dove is a symbol for peace. Writers use symbols in stories and poems to add meaning and to emphasize the theme. In "Your World," the poet uses a bird's nest as a symbol of a life with no room to grow.

1. What do the speaker's wings symbolize in the first and third stanzas?
2. What does "battered the cordons" mean? How does the poet use this image as a symbol?

● See **Literary Terms Handbook,** p. R10.

✔ ASSESSMENT OPTIONS

📁 *Quick Checks,* p. 40

📁 *Selection and Theme Assessment,* pp. 69-70

📁 *Performance Assessment,* p. 37

💾 *Testmaker*

LITERARY ELEMENTS

1. The wings symbolize the speaker's willingness to try. In the first stanza the speaker didn't try—wings pressed close to the side. In the third, the speaker did try—and soared.
2. It means "smashed the barriers." This is a symbol for overcoming obstacles.

Additional Resources

✍ *Literary Elements Transparency 40*

COMPARING SELECTIONS

Amigo Brothers and *Your World*

COMPARE **THEMES**

In "Amigo Brothers" and "Your World," people arrive at crossroads in their lives. Think about the decisions or changes they make to open up new directions and possibilities.

1. At what crossroads do Antonio and Felix find themselves? What decisions do they each make?
2. What advice does the speaker of "Your World" have for others who stand at the crossroads?
3. The speaker in "Your World" was inspired to leave "the narrowest nest" and soar "to the uttermost reaches." What dreams are calling Antonio and Felix away from their current lives toward a larger world?

COMPARE **RESPONSES**

"Amigo Brothers" and "Your World" offer inspiring messages in different forms— one a short story, the other a poem.

1. Which selection do you find more inspiring? Why?
2. What life lesson is reinforced in "Amigo Brothers"?
3. The speaker in "Your World" believes that people must break through certain barriers in order to change. What barriers do the characters in "Amigo Brothers" break through?

COMPARE **ACTIONS**

The poem "Your World" is a call to action. The speaker breaks the bonds of a narrow life and finds opportunities in the larger world. It is a poem that could inspire young people to think differently about their own lives.

• What do you think would happen to Antonio or Felix if they read "Your World" and took it to heart?
• Write a letter from one *amigo* brother to the other about what the poem meant to him, and how he thinks the philosophy in the poem could benefit each of their lives.

Objective

• To compare a short story and a poem, both of which relate to the theme "At the Crossroads"

COMPARE **THEMES**

1. Antonio and Felix have to decide if a boxing match is more important than their friendship. They preserve their friendship by fighting their best fight.
2. The speaker's advice is to try.
3. Each dreams of being lightweight boxing champion of the world.

COMPARE **RESPONSES**

1. Answers should explain why students feel the way they do.
2. Friendships are important. A good one can weather adversity.
3. The friends in "Amigo Brothers" must break through the barrier created by their having to fight each other.

COMPARE **ACTIONS**

• They would be inspired by the poem to work toward their goal.
• Students' letters should be written in proper format from the point of view of either Antonio or Felix.

Additional Resources
📁 *Literature Groups Sourcebook*

Teaching Options

 PORTFOLIO OPTIONS

Select and Reflect Have students reflect on the letters they wrote by asking themselves these questions:

• Does my letter explain what the poem means to the character in his life?
• Do I use examples from the story or events that could have happened in the character's life to support my ideas?

• Do I clearly explain how the message of the poem can help the two friends? Students should clip their reflections to their letters and place them in their portfolios. **L2**

Additional Resources
📁 *Writing Assessment and Portfolio Management,* pp. 17–19

Objectives

• To understand and express the benefits of physical fitness

Teaching Strategies

Ask students to pantomime a household chore they are required to do, such as sweeping the floor, making a bed, washing dishes, emptying trash, or hanging laundry. Encourage classmates to pantomime the same activity in a way that transforms it into an exercise, creating a series of "household aerobic exercises." Remind students that the muscles and endurance they build pushing a vacuum cleaner can help them train for a marathon.

Activity

Students may write this letter in the form of a journal or diary in order to track how their bodies feel from day to day. Letters could include descriptions of how and where the exercise takes place as well as whether or not finding the time to exercise becomes easier as the week progresses.

Teaching Options

Interdisciplinary Connection

HEAL H

Physical Fitness

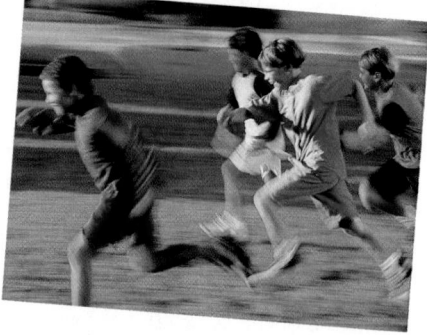

In the short story "Amigo Brothers," Antonio and Felix keep themselves physically fit by working out at the gym and by running. However, you don't need to be a sports pro or have special training to enjoy being physically active and fit. In fact, you don't even need to be particularly athletic to have fun that's good for your body.

One family, the Kuntzelmans, planned a unique "walk across America" to see how far they could travel as a team. They totaled the miles they walked near home, then marked those distances across a United States map each week. After walking enough miles to reach Mexico, the whole family celebrated by eating at a local Mexican restaurant.

At a middle school in Naperville, Illinois, students discovered a way everyone could track his or her personal best. Rather than competing against each other, each student individually decided how far to run, then recorded the distance, using a heart monitor to watch for an improved heart rate.

Changing everyday habits can get your body moving and increase your fitness, too. Here are a few tips:

• Ride your bike or walk when you visit a friend or go on an errand.

• Whenever possible, take the stairs instead of an elevator or escalator.

• Dance to your favorite CD, jump rope, swim, build a snow fort, or just stretch your muscles after sitting through a movie or TV show—or an English class.

• Go outside for a game of kickball, baseball, basketball, soccer, or even a walk around the block.

ACTIVITY

Choose a physical activity to include in your life for the next two weeks. You might start with fifteen minutes of an activity such as dancing, or with a few sit-ups, push-ups, stretches, or laps. Chart your daily progress and heart rate. Then let "your body" write you a letter describing how it feels to be physically active.

MEETING INDIVIDUAL NEEDS — MULTIPLE LEARNING STYLES

Musical/Bodily/Kinesthetic
Encourage musically inclined students to team up with kinesthetic learners to develop a dance routine promoting physical fitness among middle school students.

Activity In small groups, students can work together to come up with a dance or exercise routine simple enough for anyone, including students with disabili-

ties. Musical students should find or make up a song or rap/jazz chant to accompany the short exercise routine developed by kinesthetic learners. Have students teach the routine to the class. You may wish to videotape the exercise routine and song to show other classes. **L2**

LISTENING, SPEAKING, and VIEWING

Small-Group Discussions

In "Amigo Brothers," Antonio and Felix need to talk before their bout, but it's difficult. They make the discussion work by helping each other. They listen carefully, suggest phrases, and check their understanding. When you join a small-group discussion, you can use the same strategies to help make the discussion work. Try these tips.

Group Discussion Tips

- Take turns talking. Help everyone get a chance to be heard. If there is a group leader, follow his or her directions.
- Listen carefully. Try repeating others' points in your own words to be sure you understand them.
- To keep the discussion on track, make only comments that deal directly with the topic.
- Avoid interrupting or raising your voice. If you are interrupted, resume in an even tone after the interruption ends.
- Disagree with ideas, not with people. Avoid personal comments or put-downs.
- When someone criticizes your ideas, listen quietly. Give the criticism careful thought before you respond.

ACTIVITIES

1. Watch a group discussion on television, in a film or video, or in real life. Note how group members follow (or ignore) the tips listed above. Then share your observations with classmates.

2. Join a small-group discussion of ideas that group members have written about. Afterwards, rate your own performance on each tip listed above.

Objective

- To recognize and practice strategies for participating in small group discussions

Teaching Strategies

Ask students to describe how it feels when someone interrupts them, raises his or her voice, or doesn't listen. Go through the tips in the student edition and discuss with students why and how communication suffers when people don't respect these basic guidelines. Students might create humorous role-plays to dramatize each of the tips.

Activities

1. Students can keep a list of discussion participants' names and a list in numerical order of the Group Discussion Tips. They may chart their observations using these lists.

2. Students may wish to rate their performance of the Group Discussion Tips on a scale of 1 to 10. If so, they can create graphs that represent their strengths and weaknesses as discussion participants.

Teaching Options

MEETING INDIVIDUAL NEEDS — ENGLISH LANGUAGE LEARNERS

Group Discussion Tips Have English language learners as well as students who are proficient in English work in small groups to create posters that describe and illustrate the Group Discussion Tips.

Activity Assign each group one of the tips. Have them copy it onto posterboard or butcher paper and think of an imaginative way to illustrate it. They can use collage, paintings, drawings, magazine or newspaper pictures, cartoons, or photographs. Finally, have them hang their posters in class and encourage English language learners to ask questions about any tips they still don't understand.

Additional Resources

📁 *English Language Learners Sourcebook*

Objectives

- To read and analyze a short story about a girl and a prize
- To state the final outcome, or resolution, of a story
- To write a critical review of a short story

Skills

Reading/Thinking: Inferring; Drawing Conclusions; Sequence of Events; Questioning/Clarifying

Writing: Critical Review; Journal Entry

Vocabulary: Word Meanings; The Prefix *dis-*

Grammar/Language: Subject-Verb Agreement; Adverbs and Adjectives

Life Skills: Graduation Speech

Collaboration: Literature Groups

Motivating
→OPTIONS

Selection Focus Transparency 41: Encourage students to discuss how allowing a small injustice or unfairness can lead to allowing greater injustices.

Focus Activity: As an extension of the Focus Activity, have students in small groups describe awards they have received. Ask each student how he or she would have felt if the award had gone to someone else.

Before You Read
The Scholarship Jacket

MEET MARTA SALINAS

Marta Salinas is the author of many short stories. Her short story "The Scholarship Jacket" was first published in *Cuentos Chicanos: A Short Story Anthology.* Her work has also appeared in the *Los Angeles Herald Examiner* and in *California Living* magazine.

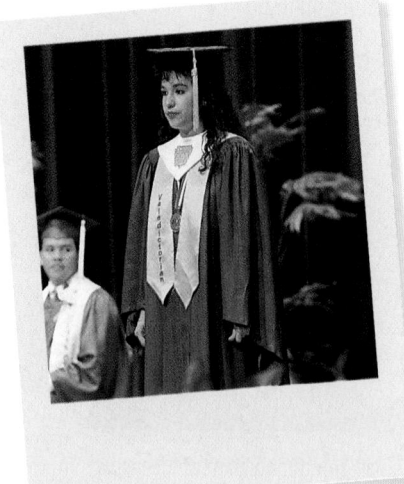

FOCUS ACTIVITY

Think about an award you have earned or would like to earn.

Think/Pair/Share

For what did you receive an award? What did you do to prepare for it? Or, what award would you be pleased to get? What would you have to do to earn it? Describe what receiving it was like (or would be like) for you.

Setting a Purpose

Read the story to find out what a school award means to a young girl.

BACKGROUND

The Time and Place   This story takes place in recent time in a small town in Texas.

Did You Know?   Have you ever heard of the word *valedictorian?* The word comes from the Latin word *valedicere,* which means "to say farewell." A valedictorian is the student who has achieved the highest grades in a graduating class during all his or her years at school. This person is usually given the honor of giving the farewell address at the graduation ceremony.

VOCABULARY PREVIEW

coincidence (kō in′ si dəns) *n.* an accidental occurrence of events, ideas, or circumstances at the same time, without one causing the other; p. 452

dismay (dis mā′) *n.* a feeling of alarm or uneasiness; p. 453

muster (mus′ tər) *v.* to find and gather together; collect; p. 453

withdrawn (with drôn′) *adj.* shy, reserved, or unsociable; p. 454

vile (vīl) *adj.* very bad; unpleasant; foul; p. 455

RESOURCE MANAGER

Lesson Planning Resource
The *Theme Five Planning Guide* (pp. 19–26) provides additional lesson notes and reduced versions of all print resources.

Other Print Resources
- Active Reading Guide, p. 41
- Vocabulary Practice, p. 27
- Reading Workbook, pp. 71–72
- Grammar and Language Workbook, pp. 117–118, 127–128, 183–184

- Grammar and Composition Handbook, Lessons 5.1, 6.1, 6.2, 10.1
- Quick Checks, p. 41
- Selection and Theme Assessment, pp. 71–72
- Performance Assessment, p. 38
- Spanish Summaries, p. 41
- Spanish Translations
- Inclusion Strategies
- English Language Learners Sourcebook

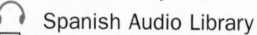 **Transparencies**
- Selection Focus 41
- Fine Art 5
- Literary Elements 41
- Grammar and Language 39

Technology
 Audio Library
 Spanish Audio Library
Glencoe Literature Web Site
Testmaker

The Scholarship Jacket

Marta Salinas :~

The small Texas school that I attended carried out a tradition every year during the eighth grade graduation; a beautiful gold and green jacket, the school colors, was awarded to the class valedictorian, the student who had maintained the highest grades for eight years. The scholarship jacket had a big gold S on the left front side and the winner's name was written in gold letters on the pocket.

My oldest sister Rosie had won the jacket a few years back and I fully expected to win also. I was fourteen and in the eighth grade. I had been a straight A student since the first grade, and the last year I had looked forward to owning that jacket. My father was a farm laborer who couldn't earn enough money to feed eight children, so when I was six I was given to my grandparents to raise. We couldn't participate in sports at school because there were registration fees, uniform costs, and trips out of town; so even though we were quite agile and athletic, there would never be a sports school jacket for us. This one, the scholarship jacket, was our only chance.

In May, close to graduation, spring fever struck, and no one paid any attention in class; instead we stared out the windows and at each other, wanting to speed up the last few weeks of school. I despaired every time I looked in the mirror. Pencil thin, not a curve anywhere, I was called "Beanpole" and "String Bean" and I knew that's what I looked like.

SUMMARY

Marta has the highest grade point average in her school. In years past, the school has awarded a scholarship jacket to the valedictorian. This year, however, the jacket may go to a student with an influential father rather than to the real winner.

📁 *Spanish Summaries,* p. 41

A Active Reading

PREDICT Invite students to read the title "The Scholarship Jacket" and the first two paragraphs of the story aloud. Have students predict whether the narrator will win the scholarship jacket like her oldest sister. Suggest that students revisit their predictions as they read to verify or to revise them.

Additional Resources
📁 *Active Reading Guide,* p. 41
🎧 *Audio Library*
🎧 *Spanish Audio Library*

Teaching Options

CONNECTING TO OTHER SELECTIONS

The chart at the right shows three ways to connect "The Scholarship Jacket" to other selections in this book.

For specific teaching strategies, see the *Theme Five Planning Guide,* pages 22–23.

Connection	Title
Life Skills: Setting Goals	→ "The Smallest Dragonboy," p. 683
Thematic: Family	→ "In a Neighborhood in Los Angeles," p. 334
Literary: Conflict	→ "The Old Demon," p. 483

CHARACTER Ask students what we learn about Marta's personality from this description. *(Marta is unhappy with the way she looks, but she knows she is smart.)*

C **Critical Thinking**

INFERRING Ask students what the conflict is between Mr. Boone and Mr. Schmidt. *(Mr. Boone wants Mr. Schmidt to lie so that another student will get Marta's scholarship jacket.)*

D **Active Reading**

REVIEW Have students tell what they have learned so far about Joann and her father. *(Joann's grades are not as good as Marta's; Joann's father is on the school board and owns the only store in town.)*

E **Critical Thinking**

DRAWING CONCLUSIONS Ask students why they think the school board changed its policy. Use the following model to illustrate the thinking process involved in drawing conclusions.

Model: Joann's father owns the only store in town, meaning he is probably wealthy and influential. I think he used his position on the board to influence the others.

Teaching Options

The Scholarship Jacket

A flat chest, no hips, and a brain, that's what I had. That really isn't much for a fourteen-year-old to work with, I thought, as I absentmindedly wandered from my history class to the gym. Another hour of sweating in basketball and displaying my toothpick legs was coming up. Then I remembered my P.E. shorts were still in a bag under my desk where I'd forgotten them. I had to walk all the way back and get them. Coach Thompson was a real bear if anyone wasn't dressed for P.E. She had said I was a good forward and once she even tried to talk Grandma into letting me join the team. Grandma, of course, said no.

I was almost back at my classroom's door when I heard angry voices and arguing. I stopped. I didn't mean to eavesdrop; I just hesitated, not knowing what to do. I needed those shorts and I was going to be late, but I didn't want to interrupt an argument between my teachers. I recognized the voices: Mr. Schmidt, my history teacher, and Mr. Boone, my math teacher. They seemed to be arguing about me. I couldn't believe it. I still remember the shock that rooted me flat against the wall as if I were trying to blend in with the graffiti written there.

"I refuse to do it! I don't care who her father is, her grades don't even begin to compare to Martha's. I won't lie or falsify records. Martha[1] has a straight A plus average and you know it." That was Mr. Schmidt

and he sounded very angry. Mr. Boone's voice sounded calm and quiet.

"Look, Joann's father is not only on the Board, he owns the only store in town; we could say it was a close tie and—"

The pounding in my ears drowned out the rest of the words, only a word here and there filtered through. ". . . Martha is Mexican. . . . resign. . . . won't do it. . . ." Mr. Schmidt came rushing out, and luckily for me went down the opposite way toward the auditorium, so he didn't see me. Shaking, I waited a few minutes and then went in and grabbed my bag and fled from the room. Mr. Boone looked up when I came in but didn't say anything. To this day I don't remember if I got in trouble in P.E. for being late or how I made it through the rest of the afternoon. I went home very sad and cried into my pillow that night so grandmother wouldn't hear me. It seemed a cruel <u>coincidence</u> that I had overheard that conversation.

The next day when the principal called me into his office, I knew what it would be about. He looked uncomfortable and unhappy. I decided I wasn't going to make it any easier for him so I looked him straight in the eye. He looked away and fidgeted with the papers on his desk.

"Martha," he said, "there's been a change in policy this year regarding the scholarship jacket. As you know, it has always been free." He cleared his throat and continued. "This year the Board decided to charge fifteen dollars—which still won't cover the complete cost of the jacket."

---

1. The main character is called "Martha" at school and "Marta" at home. Martha is an English version of the main character's Spanish name.

Vocabulary
coincidence (kō in′ si dəns) *n.* an accidental occurrence of events, ideas, or circumstances at the same time, without one causing the other

MEETING INDIVIDUAL NEEDS — ENGLISH LANGUAGE LEARNERS

Visualizing Words Explain that writers often choose words to create images in readers' minds. For example, *toothpick legs* helps us visualize legs as skinny as toothpicks.

Activity Have pairs or small groups of students examine these sentences:
Coach Thompson was a real <u>bear</u>.
The music <u>drowned</u> what he said.

Only a word or two <u>filtered</u> through.
Have each student draw a picture of an image created by one of the underlined words in these sentences. **COLLAB. LEARN.**

Additional Resources
📁 *English Language Learners Sourcebook*

I stared at him in shock and a small sound of dismay escaped my throat. I hadn't expected this. He still avoided looking in my eyes.

"So if you are unable to pay the fifteen dollars for the jacket, it will be given to the next one in line."

Standing with all the dignity I could muster, I said, "I'll speak to my grandfather about it, sir, and let you know tomorrow." I cried on the walk home from the bus stop. The dirt road was a quarter of a mile from the highway, so by the time I got home, my eyes were red and puffy.

"Where's Grandpa?" I asked Grandma, looking down at the floor so she wouldn't ask me why I'd been crying. She was sewing on a quilt and didn't look up.

"I think he's out back working in the bean field."

I went outside and looked out at the fields. There he was. I could see him walking between the rows, his body bent over the little plants, hoe in hand. I walked slowly out to him, trying to think how I could best ask him for the money. There was a cool breeze blowing and a sweet smell of mesquite in the air, but I didn't appreciate it. I kicked at a dirt clod. I wanted that jacket so much. It

Did You Know?
Mesquite (mes kēt′) is a small thorny tree. Its pleasant-smelling wood is a favored barbecue fuel in the Southwest.

was more than just being a valedictorian and giving a little thank you speech for the jacket on graduation night. It represented eight years of hard work and expectation. I knew I had to be honest with Grandpa; it was my only chance. He saw me and looked up.

He waited for me to speak. I cleared my throat nervously and clasped my hands behind my back so he wouldn't see them shaking. "Grandpa, I have a big favor to ask you," I said in Spanish, the only language he knew. He still waited silently. I tried again. "Grandpa, this year the principal said the scholarship jacket is not going to be free. It's going to cost fifteen dollars and I have to take the money in tomorrow, otherwise it'll be given to someone else." The last words came out in an eager rush. Grandpa straightened up tiredly and leaned his chin on the hoe handle. He looked out over the field that was filled with the tiny green bean plants. I waited, desperately hoping he'd say I could have the money.

He turned to me and asked quietly, "What does a scholarship jacket mean?"

I answered quickly; maybe there was a chance. "It means you've earned it by having the highest grades for eight years and that's why they're giving it to you." Too late I realized the significance of my words. Grandpa knew that I understood it was not a matter of money. It wasn't that. He went back to hoeing the weeds that sprang up between the delicate little bean plants. It was a time consuming job; sometimes the small shoots were right

Vocabulary
dismay (dis mā′) *n.* a feeling of alarm or uneasiness
muster (mus′ tər) *v.* to find and gather together; collect

F Active Reading

CONNECT Have students explain what it means when another person won't look them in the eye when talking. What do they think it means when the principal won't look Marta in the eye? *(Not looking someone in the eye can mean you are intimidated or shy or uneasy. The principal is uncomfortable with what he is doing.)*

Vo•cab•u•lar•y Skills

Word Meanings People often confuse *principal* and *principle*. Explain to students that one way to keep the words straight is to remember that *principal* always means "chief." For example, the *principal* of a school is the chief of the school and the *principal* reason is the chief reason. *Principle* always means "rule or law," as in a fundamental *principle* of human nature.

G Active Reading

EVALUATE Have students think about this scene. What impression do they get of Marta's grandfather? *(He is a hardworking farmer who cares about his land.)*

H Critical Thinking

DRAWING CONCLUSIONS Have students explain what having to pay for the jacket means. *(Paying for the jacket means that the jacket is no longer about achievement; it is only about who is most willing or able to pay for it.)*

Reading *Minilesson*

Sequence of Events One thing that makes a story engaging to readers is the way its characters change over time.

Activity Invite students to create a chart, illustrating how Marta, the principal, and the grandfather change as they respond to events in the story. When the chart is complete, have students discuss the changes. **L2**

Character	Event	What Happens
Principal	School board changes rules	Tells Marta she must buy jacket
Marta	Learns jacket cost $15	Asks grandfather for the money
Grandfather	Learns Marta needs $15	Tells her if she pays it won't be a scholarship jacket

Additional Resources
📁 *Reading Workbook,* pp. 71–72

Ernest L. Blumenschein, born in Pittsburgh, Pennsylvania, in 1874, studied art in Cincinnati, New York, and Paris, France. He settled permanently in Taos, New Mexico, in 1919, where he was a founding member of the Taos Society of Artists.

Viewing Response *The laborer in the painting is reminiscent of Marta's grandfather, who was a farmer in Texas.*

I Active Reading

CONNECT Have students ever been mad at a parent even though they knew the parent was right? Have students explain what they would feel and do if they were in Marta's position.

J Critical Thinking

INFERRING Have students explain how the principal's behavior is different during this second meeting. *(He looks Marta in the eyes.)* What do students think this means? *(The principal has changed and he feels good about himself.)*

K Active Reading

PREDICT Have students explain what they think will happen next. *(They may think that he is going to make a fair decision and not be pushed around by Joann's father.)*

Teaching Options

New Mexico Peon, 1942. Ernest L. Blumenschein. Oil on canvas, 40 x 25 in. Gerald Peters Gallery, Sante Fe.
Viewing the painting: Does the person in the painting remind you of any character in the story? Explain.

next to each other. Finally he spoke again.

"Then if you pay for it, Marta, it's not a scholarship jacket, is it? Tell your principal I will not pay the fifteen dollars."

I walked back to the house and locked myself in the bathroom for a long time. I was angry with grandfather even though I knew he was right, and I was angry with the Board, whoever they were. Why did they have to change the rules just when it was my turn to win the jacket?

It was a very sad and <u>withdrawn</u> girl who dragged into the principal's office the next day. This time he did look me in the eyes.

"What did your grandfather say?"

I sat very straight in my chair.

"He said to tell you he won't pay the fifteen dollars."

The principal muttered something I couldn't understand under his breath, and walked over to the window. He stood looking out at something outside. He looked bigger than usual when he stood up; he was a tall gaunt[2]

_____

2. A *gaunt* person is thin and bony.

Vocabulary

withdrawn (with drôn') *adj.* shy, reserved, or unsociable

Grammar and Language *Minilesson*

Subject-Verb Agreement Explain to students that writers must be careful to make subjects and verbs agree. For example, in this story the author writes:

I waited for him to speak.
Your grandfather has the money.
He looked at me.
I'll tell the board.
I spoke in a rush.
Your grandmother needs help.

Activity Have pairs of students decide whether the verb in each of these sentences tells about something that has happened, is happening now, or will happen. Then have students take turns changing the tense of the verbs or making the subjects plural in these sentences. Students should make sure subjects and verbs agree. **L2** **COLLAB. LEARN.**

Additional Resources

📙 *Grammar and Language Transparency 39*

📕 *Grammar and Language Workbook,* pp. 183–184

📕 *Grammar and Composition Handbook,* Lesson 10.1

📕 *Writer's Choice,* Lesson 16.1

Marta Salinas :~

man with gray hair, and I watched the back of his head while I waited for him to speak.

"Why?" he finally asked. "Your grandfather has the money. Doesn't he own a small bean farm?"

I looked at him, forcing my eyes to stay dry. "He said if I had to pay for it, then it wouldn't be a scholarship jacket," I said and stood up to leave. "I guess you'll just have to give it to Joann." I hadn't meant to say that; it had just slipped out. I was almost to the door when he stopped me.

"Martha—wait."

I turned and looked at him, waiting. What did he want now? I could feel my heart pounding. Something bitter and vile tasting was coming up in my mouth; I was afraid I was going to be sick. I didn't need any sympathy speeches. He sighed loudly and went back to his big desk. He looked at me, biting his lip, as if thinking.

"Okay, damn it. We'll make an exception in your case. I'll tell the Board, you'll get your jacket."

I could hardly believe it. I spoke in a trembling rush. "Oh, thank you sir!" Suddenly I felt great. I didn't know about adrenalin[3] in those days, but I knew something was pumping through me, making me feel as tall as the sky. I wanted to yell, jump, run the mile, do something. I ran out so I

could cry in the hall where there was no one to see me. At the end of the day, Mr. Schmidt winked at me and said, "I hear you're getting a scholarship jacket this year."

His face looked as happy and innocent as a baby's, but I knew better. Without answering I gave him a quick hug and ran to the bus. I cried on the walk home again, but this time because I was so happy. I couldn't wait to tell Grandpa and ran straight to the field. I joined him in the row where he was working and without saying anything I crouched down and started pulling up the weeds with my hands. Grandpa worked alongside me for a few minutes, but he didn't ask what had happened. After I had a little pile of weeds between the rows, I stood up and faced him.

"The principal said he's making an exception for me, Grandpa, and I'm getting the jacket after all. That's after I told him what you said."

Grandpa didn't say anything, he just gave me a pat on the shoulder and a smile. He pulled out the crumpled red handkerchief that he always carried in his back pocket and wiped the sweat off his forehead.

"Better go see if your grandmother needs any help with supper."

I gave him a big grin. He didn't fool me. I skipped and ran back to the house whistling some silly tune.

❖

---

3. A chemical released into the blood in times of stress or excitement, *adrenalin* (ə dren' əl in) increases the body's energy.

Vocabulary
vile (vīl) *adj.* very bad; unpleasant; foul

Responding to the Selection

Personal Response

Encourage students to describe an emotion they would feel and what they would do.

Analyzing Literature

1. It's a jacket given to the student who has earned the highest grades for eight years.
2. She learns that she might not receive the scholarship jacket even though she has the highest grades.
3. He tells her that the jacket will cost fifteen dollars this year.
4. Grandpa says he will not pay the fifteen dollars.
5. Marta expects to receive the jacket because she has the highest grades in the school. The jacket is important because Marta has worked hard for it.
6. Mr. Schmidt and Mr. Boone are arguing about who should receive the scholarship jacket. Mr. Schmidt is angry because Mr. Boone wants him to lie or falsify records.
7. Joann's father wants his daughter to receive it. He is a powerful man on the school board. The other members of the school board do not want to make him angry, so they go along with his proposal.
8. Grandpa decides not to pay the fifteen dollars. Grandpa means that if the jacket must be bought, it is not an award.
9. The principal is at first influenced by Joann's father. Then he learns that Marta's grandfather believes that paying for the jacket compromises its meaning. The principal agrees.
10. The jacket should be important to Marta because she has worked hard for it for eight years.

Responding to Literature

PERSONAL RESPONSE

Think back to the notes you wrote in the **Focus Activity** on page 450. How would you feel if someone who didn't work for an award received it? What would you do?

Analyzing Literature

RECALL

1. What is the scholarship jacket?
2. What does Marta learn when she accidentally overhears two teachers arguing?
3. What does the principal tell Marta when she is called into his office the next day?
4. What is Grandpa's reaction when Marta asks him for the money?

INTERPRET

5. As the story begins, why does Marta expect to receive the jacket? Why is the jacket so important to her?
6. Why are Mr. Schmidt and Mr. Boone arguing? Why might Mr. Schmidt have sounded so angry?
7. In your opinion, why was the policy regarding the scholarship jacket changed? Explain.
8. Theme Connection   What was Grandpa's decision concerning the jacket? What does Grandpa mean when he says, "If you pay for it, Marta, it's not a scholarship jacket, is it?"

EVALUATE AND CONNECT

9. A conclusion based on known information is called an **inference**. What can you infer about the character of the principal in this story? How does his attitude about the jacket change? Explain.
10. Should the jacket be so important to Marta? Why or why not?

LITERARY ELEMENTS

Resolution

In a story, novel, or play, the **resolution** is the part of the plot that presents the final outcome of the story. At that time, the plot's conflicts are resolved and the story ends. For example, in "Amigo Brothers" the resolution occurs once the final bell sounds and the two champions leave the ring, arm in arm.

1. What happens at the resolution of "The Scholarship Jacket"? What problem is solved? How do the main characters feel?
2. Think about one of your favorite stories from this book. What happens at the resolution of the story?

● See **Literary Terms Handbook,** p. R9.

LITERARY ELEMENTS

1. Marta gets the scholarship jacket. The principal stands up to the school board to make sure Marta gets the jacket. All the main characters feel pleased and happy.
2. Answers should describe what happens at the end to solve the problem in the story.

Additional Resources

✑ *Literary Elements Transparency 41*

Literature and Writing

Writing About Literature

Critical Review   A **critical review** of a story evaluates it. Is the story good, bad, or somewhere in between? The review supports its opinions with examples or quotations from the work. Write a critical review of "The Scholarship Jacket," concentrating on its plot, characters, and theme.

Creative Writing

Journal   Imagine you are Marta. You have just learned that you will be given the scholarship jacket after all. At this moment, how do you, as Marta, feel? In your journal, describe the events of the last few days and your feelings about those events.

Extending Your Response

Literature Groups

Keeping Promises   Discuss what it means to keep a promise. What promise in the story is broken? What message does a student, such as Marta, receive when a promise is broken? Which characters in the story understand what it means to keep a promise? Together, write a statement explaining why it is important to keep a promise. Share your statement with the other literature groups.

Learning for Life

Graduation Speech   As the valedictorian of her graduating class, Marta will probably give a speech at the graduation ceremony. Write a speech for Marta that expresses her feelings about her award and what it represents to her and to her family.

Interdisciplinary Activity

Art   Design and create an award for someone special in your life. Choose a person to honor. You might pick a friend, a relative, or a teacher. Make the award out of any available materials. Be sure the award includes a descriptive title, such as Best Listener or Our Family's Finest Pizza Maker.

Reading Further

Here are some narratives and essays you might enjoy:
A Summer Life by Gary Soto
The Anaya Reader by Rudolfo Anaya

📖 **Save your work for your portfolio.**

Literature and Writing

Writing About Literature
Students' reviews should
- briefly summarize the story.
- clearly explain why they would or would not recommend the story to others.
- contain examples from the story to support their ideas.

Creative Writing
Students' journal entries should
- be written from Marta's point of view.
- describe how Marta feels about the events of the last few days.
- describe how Marta feels at the moment she learns that she will receive the jacket after all.

Extending Your Response

Literature Groups Before students meet as groups, encourage them to answer the listed questions briefly. Then, in groups, have students share their ideas. The groups can then discuss why it is important to keep a promise. **COLLAB. LEARN.**

Learning for Life Invite volunteers to present their speeches to the class. Encourage class members to listen attentively.

Interdisciplinary Activity Encourage each student to first make a miniature sketch of the award, so he or she can see what it will look like. Students may want to use a computer graphics program to design the awards.

GRAMMAR AND LANGUAGE
USING ADVERBS AND ADJECTIVES

Students' paragraphs should
- use *good* and *bad* as adjectives.
- use *well* and *badly* as adverbs.
- use *well* to describe someone's health.

READING AND THINKING
QUESTIONING/CLARIFYING

Students' questions should
- investigate confusing parts of the story.
- help them clear up the meaning of confusing parts of the story.
- help to enhance understanding of the story's characters and events.

VOCABULARY
THE PREFIX: *dis-*

1. d	**3.** b	**5.** c
2. e	**4.** a	

Additional Resources

- *Grammar and Language Workbook,* pp. 117–118, 127–128
- *Grammar and Composition Handbook,* Lessons 5.1, 6.1, 6.2
- *Writer's Choice,* Lessons 12.1, 12.6
- *Reading Workbook,* pp. 71–72
- *Vocabulary Practice,* p. 27

Skill Minilessons

GRAMMAR AND LANGUAGE • USING ADVERBS AND ADJECTIVES

Good and *bad* are adjectives. Use them after linking verbs. *Well* and *badly* are adverbs. Use them to describe action verbs. *Well* may also be used as an adjective when describing someone's health. In this case it will follow a linking verb. Here are some examples.

The Sanchez sisters were **good** dancers. (adjective)
The rainy weather was **bad** for a picnic. (predicate adjective)
Rain **badly** damaged the crops. (adverb)

My grandmother sings **well**. (adverb)
After a long illness, Grandpa is finally **well**. (adjective)

PRACTICE Write a paragraph reviewing one of the stories you have read in this book. In the paragraph, include the words *good, bad, badly,* and *well.* Trade paragraphs with a partner and edit each other's work.

- For more about adverbs and adjectives, see **Language Handbook,** p. R18.

READING AND THINKING • QUESTIONING/CLARIFYING

Questioning what you are reading helps you understand more clearly the characters and events in a short story or a novel. As you read, ask yourself questions such as these:
- What's really going on here?
- Why did she or he say that?
- Why is the writer describing this?

PRACTICE Reread "The Scholarship Jacket." Write two or three questions about the story that help clarify what is happening. Trade questions with a partner and answer each other's questions.

- For more about these and other reading strategies, see **Reading Handbook,** p. R83.

VOCABULARY • THE PREFIX: *dis-*

Like the prefix *un-,* the prefix *dis-* often adds a negative meaning to a word. Something that *discourages* you takes away your courage. To *disarm* an enemy is to take away his or her "arms," or weapons.

PRACTICE Use what you know about *dis-* to match each underlined word on the left with its synonym or meaning on the right.

1. a house in <u>disrepair</u>	a. ineligible
2. do a <u>disservice</u> to me	b. lack of care
3. to show <u>disinterest</u>	c. reveal
4. <u>disqualified</u> runner	d. bad condition
5. to <u>disclose</u> the facts	e. injury or harm

✓ ASSESSMENT OPTIONS

- *Quick Checks,* p. 41
- *Selection and Theme Assessment,* pp. 71–72
- *Performance Assessment,* p. 38
- *Testmaker*

MEDIA Connection

The Face of Venus

Address: www.hawastsoc.org/solar/eng/homepage.htm

Astronomers refer to Venus as Earth's sister planet. Both are similar in size, mass, density and volume. Both formed about the same time and condensed out of the same nebula. However, during the last few years scientists have found that the kinship ends here. Venus is very different from the Earth. It has no oceans and is surrounded by a heavy atmosphere composed mainly of carbon dioxide with virtually no water vapor. Its clouds are composed of sulfuric acid droplets. At the surface, the atmospheric pressure is 92 times that of Earth at sea level.

Venus is scorched with a surface temperature of about 482°C (900°F). This high temperature is primarily due to a runaway greenhouse effect caused by the heavy atmosphere of carbon dioxide. Sunlight passes through the atmosphere to heat the surface of the planet. Heat is radiated out, but is trapped by the dense atmosphere and not allowed to escape into space. This makes Venus hotter than Mercury.

A Venusian day is 243 Earth days and is longer than its year of 225 days. Oddly, Venus rotates from east to west. To an observer on Venus, the Sun would rise in the west and set in the east.

Until just recently, Venus's dense cloud cover has prevented scientists from uncovering the geological nature of the surface. Developments in radar telescopes and radar imaging systems orbiting the planet have made it possible to see through the cloud deck to the surface below. As spacecraft began mapping the planet, a new picture of Venus emerged.

Respond
1. Use information from the article to make a chart comparing Earth and Venus.
2. What conditions would make it difficult for us to live on Venus? Do you think it will ever happen? Explain your answer.

MEDIA Connection

Objective
- To read and understand a Web site

Literature LINK

All Summer in a Day This Web site connects to "All Summer in a Day" (pp. 461–466). Point out to students that the Face of Venus Web site explains scientific information that has been gathered about the cloud-covered planet Venus. "All Summer in a Day" is a science fiction story about a group of children who live on Venus and spend their lives waiting for the sun.

Respond
1. Charts might include comparisons of oceans, cloud composition, atmospheric pressure, surface temperature, length of days and years, and planetary rotation.
2. Students may cite the heavy sulfuric cloud cover of Venus, extreme heat and lack of water, and the inability to grow food in these conditions. Some students may believe that life on Venus will be possible in the future with advanced technology.

Additional Resources
📁 *Media Connections,* p. 9

Teaching Options

Reading Minilesson

Activating Prior Knowledge Students can create a time capsule of information about the planets in our solar system today.

[Activity] Divide the class into nine groups. Have each group choose one planet. List questions such as *What is the weather like on this planet? What is it made of? How many moons does it have? What color is it?* Encourage each group to write everything they can about their planet, including myths, lore, or folk stories, and draw a picture of it. Groups can then share their reports and discuss where to bury them in hopes of having them discovered in 100 years. **L2**

Additional Resources
📁 *Reading Workbook,* pp. 73–74

Web Site Have students locate other Web sites to research missions sent to Venus. Keywords could be *NASA, space program, Venus missions, Venera,* and *Magellan.*

Objectives

- To read and analyze a science-fiction story
- To identify elements common to science fiction literature
- To write a paragraph that explains the importance of setting

Skills

Reading/Thinking: Inferring; Drawing Conclusions; Making Critical Judgments; Monitoring Comprehension; Inference from Setting
Writing: Sequel
Vocabulary: Latin Roots: *vit* and *viv*
Grammar/Language: Commas; Avoiding Double Negatives
Collaboration: Literature Groups

Motivating

→OPTIONS

Literature Launchers: "All About Ray Bradbury"

Videodisc
Side B, Segment 13

Also available in VHS.

Selection Focus Transparency 42: Share the quote and discuss the questions that follow.

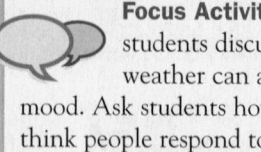

Focus Activity: Have students discuss how the weather can affect one's mood. Ask students how they think people respond to living in very cold and dark climates.

Before You Read

All Summer in a Day

MEET RAY BRADBURY

Ray Bradbury has been writing since he was a boy. "My parents had given me a toy typewriter for Christmas," Bradbury wrote, "and I stormed it with words. Anytime I liked I could turn a faucet on each finger and let the miracles out, yes, into machines and onto paper where I might freeze and control them forever. I haven't stopped writing since." Besides his novels and short stories, Bradbury has written poetry and plays for stage, screen, and television.

Ray Bradbury was born in Waukegan, Illinois, in 1920. This story was first published in 1954.

FOCUS ACTIVITY

Imagine living where it rains continuously and the sun shines only once every seven years.

Think/Pair/Share

Take a moment to jot down how life would be different. How would nonstop rain make you feel? Share your thoughts and feelings with a partner.

Setting a Purpose

Read the story to discover one version of life on another planet.

BACKGROUND

The Time and Place The story takes place at a school on the planet Venus, sometime in the future.

Did You Know? Some science-fiction writers try to be as scientifically correct as they can. Ray Bradbury is not one of those writers. Character, style, and theme are far more important to him than scientific accuracy. Today, we know much more about Venus than anyone knew when Bradbury wrote this story. Still, the story remains fascinating in spite of its outdated science.

VOCABULARY PREVIEW

frail (frāl) *adj.* lacking in strength; weak; p. 463
vital (vīt′ əl) *adj.* of primary importance; essential; p. 464
consequence (kon′ sə kwens′) *n.* importance; significance; p. 464
apparatus (ap′ ə rat′ əs) *n.* something created or invented for a particular purpose; p. 465
tumultuously (too mul′ choo əs lē) *adv.* in a wildly excited, confused, or disturbed way; p. 465
resilient (ri zil′ yənt) *adj.* capable of springing back into shape or position after being bent, stretched, or compressed; p. 465

RESOURCE MANAGER

Lesson Planning Resource
The *Theme Five Planning Guide* (pp. 27–34) provides additional lesson notes and reduced versions of all print resources.

 Other Print Resources
- Active Reading Guide, p. 42
- Vocabulary Practice, p. 28
- Reading Workbook, pp. 73–74
- Grammar and Language Workbook, pp. 135–136, 255–256

- Grammar and Composition Handbook, Lessons 6.5, 13.2
- Quick Checks, p. 42
- Selection and Theme Assessment, pp. 73–74
- Performance Assessment, p. 39
- Spanish Summaries, p. 42
- Spanish Translations
- Inclusion Strategies
- English Language Learners Sourcebook

 Transparencies
- Selection Focus 42
- Literary Elements 42
- Grammar and Language 40

Technology
- Literature Launchers
- 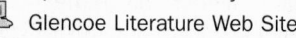 Audio Library
- Spanish Audio Library
- Glencoe Literature Web Site
- Testmaker

All Summer in a Day

Ray Bradbury ❧

"READY?"

"Ready."

"Now?"

"Soon."

"Do the scientists really know? Will it happen today, will it?"

"Look, look; see for yourself!"

The children pressed to each other like so many roses, so many weeds, intermixed, peering out for a look at the hidden sun.

It rained.

It had been raining for seven years; thousand upon thousands of days compounded and filled from one end to the other with rain, with the drum and gush of water, with the sweet crystal fall of showers and the concussion[1] of storms so heavy they were tidal waves come over the islands. A thousand forests had been crushed under the rain and grown up a thousand times to be crushed again. And this was the way life was forever on the planet Venus, and this was the schoolroom of the children of the rocket men and women who had come to a raining world to set up civilization and live out their lives.

---

1. Here, *concussion* refers to a violent shaking or pounding.

SUMMARY

Margot goes to school underground on the planet Venus, where outside, lightning flashes, the wind howls, and the rain pours all the time. Once every seven years, the sun briefly shines. Margot alone among her peers has seen the sun, for she arrived from Earth only five years earlier. Margot longs for the sun, but her peers do not understand, and this makes Margot an outcast. The day the sun comes out, Margot's classmates lock her in a closet.

📁 *Spanish Summaries,* p. 42

A Active Reading

PREDICT Ask students what the title "All Summer in a Day" might mean. Read the first nine lines and ask them if they can predict what the conflict in the story may be. Suggest that students periodically revisit their predictions as they read to verify or revise them.

Additional Resources

📁 *Active Reading Guide,* p. 42

🎧 *Audio Library*

🎧 *Spanish Audio Library*

Teaching Options

CONNECTING TO OTHER SELECTIONS

The chart at the right shows three ways to connect "All Summer in a Day" to other selections in this book.

For specific teaching strategies, see the *Theme Five Planning Guide,* pages 30–31.

Connection		Title
Life Skills: Assimilating	→	from *Barrio Boy,* p. 67
Thematic: The Different	→	"Antaeus," p. 347
Literary: Science Fiction	→	"Key Item," p. 675

INFERRING Ask students why they think Margot stands apart from the group. The following model illustrates the thinking process involved in inferring.

Model: Margot must not feel connected to the group since she is the only one who remembers the warmth of the sun on Earth. She must feel like a stranger.

C **Literary Elements**

FIGURES OF SPEECH: *Simile* Remind students that a simile uses *like* or *as* to compare seemingly unlike things. What similes are used here to describe the sun? *(It is like a blushing in the face and a lemon.)*

D **Literary Elements**

SCIENCE FICTION: *Mood* Ask students what they feel when reading Margot's poem and the description of her "quiet voice." *(Students might say that they feel her sadness and her longing for the sun.)*

E **Active Reading**

QUESTION Invite students to explain why William is critical of Margot. *(William doesn't understand Margot. He doesn't seem to like her because she keeps to herself.)*

Teaching Options

"It's stopping, it's stopping!"
"Yes, yes!"

B Margot stood apart from them, from these children who could never remember a time when there wasn't rain and rain and rain. They were all nine years old, and if there had been a day, seven years ago, when the sun came out for an hour and showed its face to the stunned world, they could not recall. Sometimes, at night, she heard them stir, in remembrance, and she knew they were dreaming and remembering gold or a yellow crayon or a coin large enough to buy the world with. She knew they thought they remembered a warmness, like a blushing in the face, in the body, in the arms and legs and trembling hands. But then they always awoke to the tatting drum, **C** the endless shaking down of clear bead necklaces upon the roof, the walk, the gardens, the forests, and their dreams were gone.

All day yesterday they had read in class about the sun. About how like a lemon it was, and how hot. And they had written small stories or essays or poems about it:

> *I think the sun is a flower,*
> *That blooms for just one hour.*

D That was Margot's poem, read in a quiet voice in the still classroom while the rain was falling outside.

"Aw, you didn't write that!" protested **E** one of the boys.

"I did," said Margot. "I *did*."

"William!" said the teacher.

But that was yesterday. Now the rain was slackening, and the children were crushed in the great thick windows.

"Where's teacher?"
"She'll be back."
"She'd better hurry, we'll miss it!"
They turned on themselves, like a feverish wheel, all tumbling spokes.

MEETING INDIVIDUAL NEEDS **ENGLISH LANGUAGE LEARNERS**

Sunny Day and Rainy Day Activities This story presents a good opportunity for exploring activities related to the weather.

Activity Have students work in small groups. On one half of a piece of poster board, students can list and draw activities related to sunny weather. On the other half, they can do the same for rainy weather. Encourage volunteers to explain the activities. **COLLAB. LEARN.**

Sunny Weather Activities	Rainy Weather Activities
Swim outdoors	Play indoors
Play baseball	Walk in the rain

Additional Resources
📁 *English Language Learners Sourcebook*

Midnight Sun, Lofoten, 1937 (detail). William H. Johnson. Oil on burlap, 41½ x 59⅛ in. National Museum of American Art, Washington, DC.
Viewing the painting: In what way does this painting reflect the emotions in this story?

VIEWING THE PAINTING

Encourage students to locate Norway on a map and to find Lofoten. (*An island group off the northwest coast.*) In the summer, in far northern regions like Lofoten, the sun never drops below the horizon, so it is daylight all night long.

Viewing Response *The painting is appropriate because the sun in Lofoten doesn't set in the summer. This is exactly the opposite of what happens in the story, where the sun rarely shines. Both conditions create an unusual landscape.*

hair. She was an old photograph dusted from an album, whitened away, and if she spoke at all her voice would be a ghost. Now she stood, separate, staring at the rain and the loud wet world beyond the huge glass.

"What're *you* looking at?" said William.

Margot said nothing.

"Speak when you're spoken to." He gave her a shove. But she did not move; rather she let herself be moved only by him and nothing else.

They edged away from her, they would not look at her. She felt them go away. And this was because she would play no games with them in the echoing tunnels of the underground city. If they tagged her and ran, she stood blinking after them and did not follow. When the class sang songs about happiness and life and games her lips barely moved. Only when they sang about the sun and the summer did her lips move as she watched the drenched windows.

And then, of course, the biggest crime of all was that she had come here only five

Margot stood alone. She was a very frail girl who looked as if she had been lost in the rain for years and the rain had washed out the blue from her eyes and the red from her mouth and the yellow from her

F Literary Elements
CHARACTER Have students describe what Margot looks like and what her appearance says about her. (*Margot looks pale. This is a reflection of how she truly feels about the rain...washed out and lifeless.*)

G Active Reading
CONNECT Have students explain how they would feel about someone who would not participate in their games or activities. (*Students will probably say that they would avoid that student.*)

H Critical Thinking
INFERRING Have students describe the one thing that seems to make Margot happy. (*The sun or singing about the sun makes Margot happy.*)

Vocabulary
frail (frāl) *adj.* lacking in strength; weak

Reading *Minilesson*

Monitoring Comprehension Bradbury uses many sensory images to describe story events. Write the following on the board:

1. They always awoke to the <u>tatting drum</u>, the <u>endless shaking down</u> of clear <u>bead necklaces</u> upon the roof.
2. She would play no games with them in the <u>echoing tunnels</u> of the <u>underground city</u>.

Activity Have students work in small groups to prepare charts that list the images in the sentences and what senses they appeal to. **L2** **COLLAB. LEARN.**

Sight	Touch	Hearing
photograph	bead necklaces	tatting drum

Additional Resources
📁 *Reading Workbook,* pp. 73–74

Literary Elements

SCIENCE FICTION: Description Ask students which descriptions in this paragraph indicate that this is a science fiction story. *(Statements such as "she had come here only five years ago from Earth" and "they had been on Venus all their lives")*

Critical Thinking

DRAWING CONCLUSIONS Have students explain what Margot's behavior shows about her attitude toward rain. *(Margot refuses to take a shower so water won't touch her. This shows she despises the rain.)*

Active Reading

EVALUATE Bradbury describes Margot's "waiting silence." Encourage students to explain what Margot is waiting for. *(Margot is waiting for the sun. It is supposed to come out that day.)*

Active Reading

PREDICT Have students explain what they think will happen to Margot after the other children put her in the closet. *(They may think that she will miss seeing the sun, since that is the only thing she really cares about.)*

---

years ago from Earth, and she remembered the sun and the way the sun was and the sky was when she was four in Ohio. And they, they had been on Venus all their lives, and they had been only two years old when last the sun came out and had long since forgotten the color and heat of it and the way it really was. But Margot remembered.

"It's like a penny," she said once, eyes closed.

"No it's not!" the children cried.

"It's like a fire," she said, "in the stove."

"You're lying, you don't remember!" cried the children.

But she remembered and stood quietly apart from all of them and watched the patterning windows. And once, a month ago, she had refused to shower in the school shower rooms, had clutched her hands to her ears and over her head, screaming the water mustn't touch her head. So after that, dimly, dimly, she sensed it, she was different and they knew her difference and kept away.

There was talk that her father and mother were taking her back to Earth next year; it seemed vital to her that they do so, though it would mean the loss of thousands of dollars to her family. And so, the children hated her for all these reasons of big and little consequence. They hated her pale snow face, her waiting silence, her thinness, and her possible future.

"Get away!" The boy gave her another push. "What're you waiting for?"

Then, for the first time, she turned and looked at him. And what she was waiting for was in her eyes.

"Well, don't wait around here!" cried the boy savagely. "You won't see nothing!"

Her lips moved.

"Nothing!" he cried. "It was all a joke, wasn't it?" He turned to the other children. "Nothing's happening today. *Is* it?"

They all blinked at him and then, understanding, laughed and shook their heads.

"Nothing, nothing!"

"Oh, but," Margot whispered, her eyes helpless. "But this is the day, the scientists predict, they say, they *know*, the sun . . ."

"All a joke!" said the boy, and seized her roughly. "Hey, everyone, let's put her in a closet before teacher comes!"

"No," said Margot, falling back.

They surged about her, caught her up and bore her, protesting, and then pleading, and then crying, back into a tunnel, a room, a closet, where they slammed and locked the door. They stood looking at the door and saw it tremble from her beating and throwing herself against it. They heard her muffled cries. Then, smiling, they turned and went out and back down the tunnel, just as the teacher arrived.

Vocabulary
vital (vīt′ əl) *adj.* of primary importance; essential
consequence (kon′ sə kwens′) *n.* importance; significance

Teaching Options

LITERATURE & HUMANITIES

To help students better understand what the world would look like without the sun, show them the photograph "The Lightening Field" from the book *American Art History and Culture*, page 610. Students can write in their journals about a world with no sun.

MEETING INDIVIDUAL NEEDS · MULTIPLE LEARNING STYLES

Spatial Some students may have special visual and spatial skills. Encourage these students to notice the striking visual images Bradbury creates in this story.

Activity Have students work in pairs or small groups to create a mural showing life on Venus. Encourage students to incorporate details from the story — when it is rainy or sunny— as well as the colors and images that Bradbury so vividly describes. Have them discuss with each other what they will illustrate in order to decide which area each pair or group will work on and to coordinate the design and area of the mural.
L2 COLLAB. LEARN.

Ray Bradbury ~

"Ready, children?" She glanced at her watch.

"Yes!" said everyone.

"Are we all here?"

"Yes!"

The rain slackened still more.

They crowded to the huge door.

The rain stopped.

It was as if, in the midst of a film concerning an avalanche, a tornado, a hurricane, a volcanic eruption, something had, first, gone wrong with the sound apparatus, thus muffling and finally cutting off all noise, all of the blasts and repercussions[2] and thunders, and then, second, ripped the film from the projector and inserted in its place a peaceful tropical slide which did not move or tremor. The world ground to a standstill. The silence was so immense and unbelievable that you felt your ears had been stuffed or you had lost your hearing altogether. The children put their hands to their ears. They stood apart. The door slid back and the smell of the silent, waiting world came in to them.

The sun came out.

It was the color of flaming bronze and it was very large. And the sky around it was a blazing blue tile color. And the jungle burned with sunlight as the children, released from their spell, rushed out, yelling, into the springtime.

"Now, don't go too far," called the teacher after them. "You've only two hours, you know. You wouldn't want to get caught out!"

_____
2. As used here, the *repercussions* are echoes or vibrations.

But they were running and turning their faces up to the sky and feeling the sun on their cheeks like a warm iron; they were taking off their jackets and letting the sun burn their arms.

"Oh, it's better than the sun lamps, isn't it?"

"Much, much better!"

They stopped running and stood in the great jungle that covered Venus, that grew and never stopped growing, tumultuously, even as you watched it. It was a nest of octopi, clustering up great arms of fleshlike weed, wavering, flowering in this brief spring. It was the color of rubber and ash, this jungle, from the many years without sun. It was the color of stones and white cheeses and ink, and it was the color of the moon.

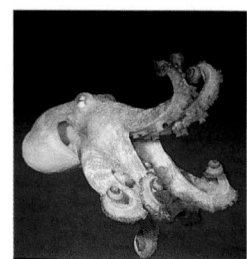

Did You Know?
Octopi (ok' tə pī) is the plural of *octopus.* An octopus is a sea creature that has, as the prefix *octo-* indicates, eight arms.

The children lay out, laughing, on the jungle mattress, and heard it sigh and squeak under them, resilient and alive. They ran among the trees, they slipped and fell, they pushed each other, they played hide-and-seek and tag, but most of all they squinted at the sun until tears ran down their faces, they put their hands up to that yellowness and that amazing blueness and breathed of the fresh, fresh air

Vocabulary
apparatus (ap' ə rat' əs) *n.* something created or invented for a particular purpose
tumultuously (too mul' chōō əs lē) *adv.* in a wildly excited, confused, or disturbed way
resilient (ri zil' yənt) *adj.* capable of springing back into shape or position after being bent, stretched, or compressed

AT THE CROSSROADS 465

M Active Reading

QUESTION Encourage students to discuss why the children put their hands to their ears before they step outdoors. *(They aren't used to the silence, and they feel their ears to see if something is wrong with their hearing.)*

N Literary Elements

SCIENCE FICTION: *Description* Have students discuss what clues indicate that this passage is a work of science fiction. *(One clue is that the children only have two hours of sun before the storms return.)*

O Literary Elements

SCIENCE FICTION: *Setting* Have your students describe the outdoor world on Venus when the sun shines. *(The jungle mattress grows and squeaks under the children when they lie down on it. There are trees, yellowness, blue skies, fresh air, and silence.)*

REAL-WORLD CONNECTION

Possible Jobs on Venus Ask students what skills astronauts will need to have in order to maintain and create a livable environment in future space stations.

Activity Encourage students to use information from the story and to find any more information they need through the Internet or the school library to create a chart of jobs for astronauts: meteorologists, aerospace engineers, mathematicians, physicists, electronics engineers, technicians, and so on. Have them explain why each profession is important to survival. **L2**

Critical Thinking

DRAWING CONCLUSIONS Have students explain why one of the girls wails and begins to cry. *(She feels a raindrop, which means the storms are returning and the sun will be gone. It makes her unhappy.)*

Literary Elements

SCIENCE FICTION: Setting Invite students to describe elements of this world that indicate it is a science fiction world. *(The children live in an underground house; the sky is dark as midnight most of the time; and rain falls in avalanches.)*

Critical Thinking

MAKING CRITICAL JUDGMENTS How do students think the children feel about what they did to Margot? What gestures indicate how the children feel? *(They are ashamed. They now know Margot was right about the sun and feel bad that they made her miss it. They look at their hands and feet; they won't look one another in the eyes; and their faces are solemn.)*

Thematic Focus

At the Crossroads Have students discuss how this story relates to the theme "At the Crossroads." What crossroads have Margot and her classmates reached?

✔ ASSESSMENT OPTIONS

📁 **Quick Checks,** p. 42

---

and listened and listened to the silence which suspended them in a blessed sea of no sound and no motion. They looked at everything and savored everything. Then, wildly, like animals escaped from their caves, they ran and ran in shouting circles. They ran for an hour and did not stop running.

And then—

In the midst of their running one of the girls wailed.

Everyone stopped.

The girl, standing in the open, held out her hand.

"Oh, look, look," she said, trembling.

They came slowly to look at her opened palm.

In the center of it, cupped and huge, was a single raindrop.

She began to cry, looking at it.

They glanced quietly at the sky.

"Oh. Oh."

A few cold drops fell on their noses and their cheeks and their mouths. The sun faded behind a stir of mist. A wind blew cool around them. They turned and started to walk back toward the underground house, their hands at their sides, their smiles vanishing away.

A boom of thunder startled them and like leaves before a new hurricane, they tumbled upon each other and ran. Lightning struck ten miles away, five miles away, a mile, a half mile. The sky darkened into midnight in a flash.

They stood in the doorway of the underground for a moment until it was raining hard. Then they closed the door and heard the gigantic sound of the rain falling in tons and avalanches, everywhere and forever.

Behind the closet door was only silence.

"Will it be seven more years?"

"Yes. Seven."

Then one of them gave a little cry.

"Margot!"

"What?"

"She's still in the closet where we locked her."

"Margot."

They stood as if someone had driven them, like so many stakes, into the floor. They looked at each other and then looked away. They glanced out at the world that was raining now and raining and raining steadily. They could not meet each other's glances. Their faces were solemn and pale. They looked at their hands and feet, their faces down.

"Margot."

One of the girls said, "Well . . . ?"

No one moved.

"Go on," whispered the girl.

They walked slowly down the hall in the sound of cold rain. They turned through the doorway to the room in the sound of the storm and thunder, lightning on their faces, blue and terrible. They walked over to the closet door slowly and stood by it.

Behind the closet door was only silence.

They unlocked the door, even more slowly, and let Margot out.

❖

Teaching Options

Grammar and Language *Minilesson*

Commas to Set Off Interrupters Write the following on the board:

The girl held out her hand.

Invite students to suggest ways one could add the phrase *standing in the open* to this sentence. One solution is to write *The girl, standing in the open, held out her hand.* Since *standing in the open* interrupts the flow of the sentence, it is set off by commas.

Activity Have students work in pairs to find five other examples of interrupters set off by commas on this page. Have students rewrite each of these sentences without the interrupters to prove that the sentences can indeed stand alone without the interrupters. Finally, have students write five sentences of their own that use interrupters set off by commas.

L2 **COLLAB. LEARN.**

Additional Resources

🖨 *Grammar and Language Transparency 40*

📓 *Grammar and Language Workbook,* pp. 255–256

📓 *Grammar and Composition Handbook,* Lesson 13.2

📓 *Writer's Choice,* Lesson 20.2

Responding to Literature

PERSONAL RESPONSE

◆ If you were Margot, how would you feel about missing the sun? What would you say to those who put you in the closet?
◆ What should be done to the students who locked Margot in the closet?

Analyzing Literature

RECALL

1. As the story begins, where are the children and what are they doing?
2. Why is the day a special one? How long has it rained?
3. Who is Margot, and why do the other children dislike her?
4. What do the children do when the rain stops? Why doesn't Margot go with them?

INTERPRET

5. How do you think the children felt as the special time approached? Support your opinion with details from the story.
6. What effect has the rain had on the planet?
7. Why is Margot different from the other children? Do you think her parents will take her back to Earth? Why or why not?
8. According to the author, when the children are playing outside, they act "like animals escaped from their caves." Why?

EVALUATE AND CONNECT

9. What do you think the title of the story means?
10. **Theme Connection** Do you know of situations in which children acted as cruelly as Margot's classmates do? How *should* young people behave with someone who is new to their school or neighborhood or who is in some way different from them?

LITERARY ELEMENTS

Science Fiction

Science fiction is a form of literature that explores imaginary worlds of the past, the present, and the future. Science fiction often has characters living in the future or shows people using technology that is not available today. Nevertheless, these characters deal with modern issues and problems, such as prejudice, fear, and isolation.

1. What is the modern problem faced by the main character in "All Summer in a Day"?
2. Describe a setting for a science-fiction story you might write someday.

● See **Literary Terms Handbook,** p. R9.

LITERARY ELEMENTS

1. The modern problem is Margot's not being liked by her peers because she is different from them.
2. Answers should describe a world that is different in some ways from our contemporary world.

Additional Resources

Literary Elements Transparency 42

Personal Response

Students should describe their reactions, positive or negative, their feelings about how Margot was treated, and what should be done about it.

Analyzing Literature

1. The children on the planet Venus are crowded at a window waiting for the sun.
2. It has rained for seven years. The day is special because the sun is supposed to appear.
3. Margot is a girl who misses the sun. The other children dislike her because she won't play games with them or participate in any other activities except singing songs about the sun.
4. The children go outside to play in the sun. Margot doesn't go because the children have locked her in a closet.
5. The children are excited, which is demonstrated by the way they crowd at the window waiting for the sun.
6. The rain has crushed thousands of forests. The landscape is gray, black, and white because the clouds block the sun.
7. Margot is different because she is the only child who remembers what the sun is like and she constantly longs for it. Her parents will probably take her back to Earth because she is miserable on Venus.
8. They have escaped from a world of underground tunnels and homes to play outdoors, which is rare. Usually they are cooped up indoors because of the rain.
9. It means that the sun (and summer) only last one day on Venus. It also means that things we associate with the sun—light, warmth, happiness—only last one day there.
10. Answers should include logical reasons to support ideas.

Literature and Writing

Writing About Literature

Students' paragraphs should

- explain how the setting of the story affects characters' actions and story events.
- contain examples from the story to support their ideas.
- have a clear topic sentence and conclusion.

Creative Writing

Students' sequels should

- use "All Summer in a Day" as a model for writing their science-fiction sequels.
- describe where Margot is, how she feels, and how others feel about her.
- use writing processes, such as prewriting, drafting, revising, editing, and proofreading to create the stories.

Extending Your Response

Literature Groups Before students meet as groups, encourage them to answer each of these questions themselves. Then in groups, have students share their ideas. The groups can then discuss and further explore each question. **COLLAB. LEARN.**

Learning for Life Before they start, encourage students to jot down ideas, sketch, doodle, and write snippets of snappy prose that could appear in the brochures.

Art Activity Have students plan the important features they want to include (terrain, roads and paths, buildings, plants and trees, rivers, and so on). Also, have them include a legend and a scale.

Literature and Writing

Writing About Literature

Setting How does the setting of "All Summer in a Day" play an important part in the story? Review your notes from the **Focus Activity** on page 460 and think about the effect such a setting would have on your own actions and moods. Then consider what effect the setting has on the story's events and on the actions of the characters. Write a paragraph explaining why the setting of "All Summer in a Day" is so important to the story.

Until very recently, this is all people could see of cloud-covered Venus. New radar imaging has allowed us to see through this cloud cover.

Creative Writing

A Sequel What will the children say to Margot after they let her out? What will happen to Margot in the days, months, or years ahead? Write a sequel to the story, starting with the unlocking of the door. Set the scene carefully. Be sure to describe the characters' facial expressions and gestures to help your readers understand what they are feeling.

Extending Your Response

Literature Groups

A Question of Innocence In small groups, discuss how Bradbury uses vivid details and memorable characterizations to build suspense in this story and to deal with the question of the children's innocence. As readers, when do you know that something will happen to Margot? Are you surprised by the children's cruelty? Why do the children treat Margot as an outsider? What do you think Bradbury is saying about children?

Learning for Life

A Brochure Imagine that you work for a travel agency that plans trips to Venus. Create a brochure describing the trip and what life is like on Venus. Use details from the story as a starting point, but make up any added details you need.

Art Activity

Make a Map Think about the setting of "All Summer in a Day." What do you think the school looks like? As the children look through the classroom window, what do they see? Draw a map of the schoolyard setting of this story. Use the story details and descriptions to help you, but feel free to use your imagination to add new details.

Reading Further

If you would like to read more by Ray Bradbury, try these books:
The Martian Chronicles
Twice Twenty-Two

📖 **Save your work for your portfolio.**

Skill Minilessons

GRAMMAR AND LANGUAGE • AVOIDING DOUBLE NEGATIVES

Negative words express the idea of "no." *Not* is a negative word. *Not* often appears in a shortened form as part of a contraction, such as *isn't* ("is not"). Other words—for example, *never, none, nobody, nowhere,* and *nothing*—may be used to express the negative. Two negatives used together in the same sentence create a **double negative**. Avoid using double negatives in your writing.

Nonstandard: You **shouldn't never** swim alone.

You can correct a sentence with a double negative in two ways:

1. Remove one of the negative words:
   Improved: You shouldn't swim alone.

2. Replace one of the negative words with a positive word:
   Improved: You shouldn't ever swim alone.

PRACTICE Revise the following paragraph by correcting each double negative you find.

The rain didn't never stop. It rained and rained until nobody could not remember the color of the sky. Plants couldn't never grow because they didn't never receive the warmth of the sun. Neither humans nor animals nor plants could never thrive in this rain-swept place.

● For more about negative adverbs, see **Language Handbook,** p. R27.

READING AND THINKING • INFERENCE FROM SETTING

You can use what you know about the setting to help you infer other details about life for the characters in this story. For example, since you know from the setting that it rains all the time, you can infer that most aspects of life take place indoors.

PRACTICE Reread "All Summer in a Day" and think about what you can infer about the kinds of activities and games the children in this story enjoy. Write a paragraph explaining your conclusions and how you arrived at them.

● For more about making inferences, see **Reading Handbook,** p. R89.

VOCABULARY • THE LATIN ROOTS *vit* AND *viv*

The root of *vital* is *vit,* which comes from a Latin word meaning "life." People must meet their *vital* needs, such as their needs for air, food, and water. *Vitamins* have that name because they are necessary for life. Over time, *vit* has come to have the somewhat broader meaning of "extremely important; absolutely necessary." Something of *vital* concern should receive immediate attention. The root *viv* is similar to *vit;* it means "live."

PRACTICE Use what you know about the roots *vit* and *viv* to answer each question.

1. Would someone show *vivacity* by leaping, coughing, or stumbling?
2. Does a *vivid* description of something make it seem frightening, boring, or real?
3. If there is a *revival* of an old-fashioned style, does it die out or become popular again?
4. What is the best synonym for *vitality—energy, hunger,* or *luck?*
5. Do people tend to feel *revitalized* after doing hard work, hearing a lullaby, or getting a good night's sleep?

Skill Minilessons

GRAMMAR AND LANGUAGE
AVOIDING DOUBLE NEGATIVES

Sample corrected paragraph:
The rain didn't stop. It rained and rained until nobody could remember the color of the sky. Plants couldn't grow because they didn't receive the warmth of the sun. No humans or animals or plants could thrive in this rain-swept place.

READING AND THINKING
INFERENCE FROM SETTING

Students' paragraphs should
- make logical inferences based on information in the story.
- use details from the story to support their inferences.
- contain a clear topic sentence and conclusion.

VOCABULARY
LATIN ROOTS: *vit* AND *viv*

1. leaping
2. real
3. become popular again
4. energy
5. getting a good night's sleep

Additional Resources

📖 *Grammar and Language Workbook,* pp. 135–136

📖 *Grammar and Composition Handbook,* Lesson 6.5

📖 *Writer's Choice,* Lesson 12.10

📁 *Reading Workbook,* pp. 73–74

📁 *Vocabulary Practice,* p. 28

✔️ ASSESSMENT OPTIONS

📁 *Quick Checks,* p. 42

📁 *Selection and Theme Assessment,* pp. 73–74

📁 *Performance Assessment,* p. 39

💾 *Testmaker*

Objective

- To recognize and use strategies for drawing conclusions

Teaching Strategies

After students read and discuss the passage in their books from "The Scholarship Jacket," ask them to think about Margot, the character who was locked in a closet by her classmates in "All Summer in a Day." The story ends without giving us a chance to hear how Margot felt or what her classmates said to her. Have students suggest a final paragraph to the story based on their own conclusions.

Exercise

1. Clues might include the fact that the boys worked out every chance they got and went running every morning.
2. Students might mention experiences in which a strict regimen, commitment to training, or daily discipline helped them achieve a dream.

Additional Resources

📁 *Reading Workbook*

Teaching Options

Drawing Conclusions

As a skillful reader, you are always **drawing conclusions**, or figuring out much more than an author states directly. To do this, you often must combine clues about characters and events in the text with your own knowledge and experience. For example, read the following passage from "The Scholarship Jacket."

> The next day when the principal called me into his office, I knew what it would be about. He looked uncomfortable and unhappy. I decided I wasn't going to make it any easier for him so I looked him straight in the eye. He looked away and fidgeted with the papers on his desk.

Details in this passage help you draw some conclusions about the feelings of the principal and the narrator. From the description of the principal looking "uncomfortable and unhappy" and fidgeting with his papers, you can draw the conclusion that he is nervous. From the description of the narrator, who "looked him straight in the eye," you can draw the conclusion that she is unwilling to be treated unfairly.

● For more about drawing conclusions, see **Reading Handbook,** p. R89.

EXERCISE

Read the following passage from "Amigo Brothers." Then answer the questions.

> Every chance they had, the boys worked out, sometimes at the Boys Club on 10th Street and Avenue A and sometimes at the pro's gym on 14th Street. Early morning sunrises would find them running along the East River Drive, wrapped in sweat shirts, short towels around their necks, and handkerchiefs Apache style around their foreheads.

1. What clues help you draw conclusions about how seriously the boys take their dreams?
2. How does your own experience, as well as the details in the passage, help you draw that conclusion?

MEETING INDIVIDUAL NEEDS

INCLUSION STRATEGIES

Less-Proficient Readers Have students dictate the last paragraph on page 465 as you write it on the board.

Activity Begin by erasing one or two key words from the first sentence. (You may wish to indicate missing words by drawing dots or dashes where words belong.) Then, ask a volunteer to read a sentence and fill in the missing words orally. Continue the process, with the remaining sentences, erasing words and asking students to read aloud. Make the complete paragraph reappear by having students write the words back in the blanks. **L1**

Additional Resources

📁 *Inclusion Strategies*

Before You Read
Primer Lesson and *The Bird Like No Other*

MEET CARL SANDBURG

Carl Sandburg first saw Chicago when he was eighteen. Those images of city life would later appear in his *Chicago Poems*. Most of his poems echo the poet's Midwestern values.

Carl Sandburg was born in 1878 in Galesburg, Illinois. He died in 1967.

MEET DOROTHY WEST

Just nineteen years old when she arrived in New York City, Dorothy West was known as "the Kid" by the other Harlem Renaissance writers. Her writing career has spanned eight decades. Her second novel, *The Wedding*, was published in 1995, when she was eighty-seven years old.

Dorothy West was born in 1907 in Boston, Massachusetts. She died in 1998.

FOCUS ACTIVITY

Have you ever said something in anger or frustration that you later regretted? What advice might you give to someone who is feeling angry or frustrated?

Journal
Take a moment to write your responses to these questions in your journal.

Setting a Purpose
Read these selections to discover what the writers have to say about the power of words.

BACKGROUND

Did You Know? A great surge of artistic activity took place in Harlem during the 1920s. This area in New York City became a magnet, attracting African American writers, artists, actors, musicians, and dancers. This artistic movement became known as the Harlem Renaissance.

VOCABULARY PREVIEW

obligation (ob′ lə gā′ shən) *n.* a sense of duty; a responsibility; p. 474

uncommitted (un′ kə mit′ id) *adj.* not having or showing a particular opinion, view, or course of action; p. 474

woe (wō) *n.* great sadness or suffering; great trouble or misfortune; p. 474

initiative (i nish′ ə tiv) *n.* the action of taking the first step; p. 476

soberly (sō′ bər lē) *adv.* very seriously; p. 476

Objectives
- To read and analyze a poem and a short story
- To identify details that authors use to create memorable portraits
- To write an evaluation

Skills
Reading/Thinking: Inferring; Synthesizing; Sequencing; Drawing Conclusions
Writing: Letter
Vocabulary: Word Mapping; Multiple Suffixes; Analogies
Grammar/Language: Troublesome Words: *Its* and *It's*
Listening/Speaking: Discussion
Collaboration: Literature Groups

Motivating
→ OPTIONS

Selection Focus Transparency 43: Have students read and discuss the quote by Thomas Jefferson.

Focus Activity: As an extension of the Focus Activity, have students write song lyrics about the power of words and the need to use caution when speaking.

RESOURCE MANAGER

Lesson Planning Resource
The **Theme Five Planning Guide** (pp. 35–40) provides additional lesson notes and reduced versions of all print resources.

📁 **Other Print Resources**
- Active Reading Guide, p. 43
- Vocabulary Practice, p. 29
- Reading Workbook, p. 75–76
- Grammar and Language Workbook, pp. 223–224

- Quick Checks, p. 43
- Selection and Theme Assessment, pp. 75–76
- Performance Assessment, p. 40
- Spanish Summaries, p.43
- Spanish Translations
- Inclusion Strategies
- English Language Learners Sourcebook

🖨 **Transparencies**
- Selection Focus 43
- Literary Elements 43
- Grammar and Language 41

Technology
🎧 Audio Library
🎧 Spanish Audio Library
💻 Glencoe Literature Web Site
💾 Testmaker

Reading the Selection

A Active Reading

PREDICT Ask students to think of words that are similar to *primer* to predict what the title of the poem might mean. *(The words prime and primary are similar, so a primer lesson might be a lesson upon which other lessons are based.)*

B Literary Elements

PERSONIFICATION Have students look at the details in lines 4–6. What traits does Sandburg give to proud words? *(He gives them human traits.)*

C Literary Elements

REPETITION Ask students to discuss why they think Sandburg repeats the first line at the end of the poem. *(This is the central message of the poem—to be careful about what you say because words are very powerful.)*

Vo•cab•u•lar•y Skills

Word Mappings Have students map the word *proud* as it is used in this poem. *(The word map should contain words that show scorn, disdain, and contempt.)*

Additional Resources

📁 *Active Reading Guide,* p. 43

🎧 *Audio Library*

🎧 *Spanish Audio Library*

🎧 *Spanish Summaries,* p. 43

Teaching Options

CONNECTING TO OTHER SELECTIONS
For a teaching strategy that connects "Primer Lesson" to "After Twenty Years," turn to page 23 in the *Theme Six Planning Guide.*

PRIMER LESSON

Carl Sandburg ∾

Look out how you use proud words.
When you let proud words go, it is
   not easy to call them back.
They wear long boots, hard boots; they
   walk off proud; they can't hear you
   calling—
Look out how you use proud words.

pretentious

selfish

foolish

vain

impolite

egotisti[c]

phoney

shallow

arrogan[t]

rude

lazy

thoughtless

inconsiderate

472 🐛 THEME 5

 ENGLISH LANGUAGE LEARNERS

MEETING INDIVIDUAL NEEDS

Forms of Address In "The Bird Like No Other," Aunt Emily is not actually Colby's aunt. Explain to English language learners that the words *aunt* and *uncle* are sometimes used as terms of endearment for close friends of a family.

Activity Invite students to talk about how they address family members and family friends in their own cultures.

Encourage them to compare them with those that are common in the United States. You might also point out that different regions and cultural groups in the United States also have different practices.

Additional Resources
📁 *English Language Learners Sourcebook*

472 🐛 THEME 5

The Bird Like No Other

Dorothy West ◦∿

Colby ran through the woods. He ran hard, as if he were putting his house and family behind him forever. The woods were not a dark forest of towering trees. They were just scrub oak and stunted pine with plenty of room for the sun to dapple[1] the road. The road, really a footpath worn by time, was so much a part of Colby's summers that at any point he knew how many trees to count before he reached the one with the hollow that caught the rain and gave the birds a drinking cup.

As the clearing came in sight with its cluster of cottages, Colby began to call Aunt Emily, the stridency[2] in his voice commanding her to shut out the sweeter sounds of summer.

Whatever Aunt Emily was doing, Colby knew, she would stop what she was

Haunted House, Aspen, 1996 (detail). Debby West. Acrylic on canvas, 24 x 18 in. Gallery Contemporanea, Jacksonville, FL.

doing. Wherever she was, she would start for the porch, so that by the time Colby pounded up the stairs, she would be sitting on her old porch glider, waiting for him to fling himself down beside her and cool his hot anger in her calm.

Aunt Emily was a courtesy aunt, a family friend of many years. When Colby's mother was a little girl, she played with Aunt Emily's little boy when they came on holiday from their separate cities. Then Aunt Emily lost her little boy in a winter accident on an icy street. When vacation time came again, it took all her courage to reopen her cottage. But she knew she must do it this saddest summer of all if she was ever to learn to live in a world that could not bend its tempo to the slow cadence[3] of grief.

---

1. The sun would *dapple* the road by casting spots of light into the shadows.
2. *Stridency* is a quality of being loud and harsh.

3. *Tempo* means "pace" or "speed," and *cadence* means "rhythm" or "beat."

D Critical Thinking

INFERRING Have students explain what feelings or emotions Colby seems to have in this scene. *(He is upset about something to do with his family.)*

E Literary Elements

DETAILS Have students revisit the details of this scene to describe the atmosphere of the woods. *(It is familiar and reassuring. Details include not a dark forest, sun to dapple, so much a part of Colby's summers, and gave the birds a drinking cup.)*

F Literary Elements

CHARACTER Ask students what they learn about Aunt Emily through these details. *(Aunt Emily is in tune with Colby's moods and feelings. He can depend on her ability to calm him down.)*

G Critical Thinking

SYNTHESIZING Have students think about the information West provides in this last paragraph. Ask them to synthesize the details. *(Aunt Emily is an old and trusted family friend whose young son died in an accident. She knows that life goes on despite grief, and she forces herself to open up her summer cottage.)*

Reading *Minilesson*

Sequencing Explain to students that an author often begins a story with action taking place in the present, then interrupts the story to give readers important background information.

Activity Suggest that groups each complete a chart to help distinguish background information from present action.

L2 **COLLAB. LEARN.**

Present Action	Background
Colby runs through the woods and calls for Aunt Emily as he approaches.	Aunt Emily's son and Colby's mother played together as children.

Additional Resources

📁 *Reading Workbook,* pp. 75–76

CONNECTING TO OTHER SELECTIONS

For a teaching strategy that connects "A Bird Like No Other" to "Strawberries," turn to page 38 in the *Theme Seven Planning Guide.*

Teaching Options

Active Reading

QUESTION Ask students why they think Aunt Emily feels that a little girl is no substitute for a little boy. *(She misses her son deeply; girls play differently.)*

Literary Elements

LITERARY LANGUAGE Ask students to picture being "at the bottom of a heap of scrapping sisters." Ask students to describe Colby's feelings in more matter-of-fact terms. *(Look for descriptions to convey a sense of being ignored or trapped.)*

Active Reading

VISUALIZE Ask students to picture this scene. Ask them to describe it in their own words or sketch it.

Vo•cab•u•lar•y Skills

Multiple Suffixes Review the concept that the suffix *-less* added to a noun signals "without." So *sound + less* means "without sound." Have students supply other examples of nouns that take *-less* *(care, window, noise, effort)*. Remind students that the suffix *-ly* forms a word that answers the question *How? Soundlessly* means "silently, without a sound."

Colby's sister made frequent visits with her dolls. She brought the dolls that didn't cry or didn't wet because they were always rewarded with a tea party for their good behavior. She eased the summer's sorrow for Aunt Emily, who felt an obligation to show this trusting child a cheerful face and to take an interest in her eager talk.

All the same, though Aunt Emily felt a bit ungrateful thinking it, a little girl dressing her dolls for a tea party is no substitute for a little boy playing cowboys and Indians at the top of his lungs.

Colby's family would have agreed with her. His mother adored him because he was her long-awaited son, five years younger than the youngest of his three sisters. His father was pleased and proud to have another male aboard.

But Colby couldn't see where he came first with anybody. As far as he was concerned he was always at the bottom of a heap of scrapping sisters. No matter how good he tried to be, his day most generally depended on how good his sisters decided to be. His rights were never mightier than their wrongs.

Aunt Emily had been Colby's sounding board[4] ever since the summer he was four. One day that summer, his mother postponed a promised boat ride because his sisters had fought with each other all morning over whose turn it was to use the paint box that somebody had given them together. When they began to make each other cry,

they were sent upstairs as punishment, and the outing was postponed.

Colby felt he was being punished for blows he hadn't struck and tears he hadn't caused. He had to tell somebody before he burst. Since he knew the way to Aunt Emily's, he went to tell her.

She took a look at his clouded-over face, plumped him down on her old porch glider, then went inside to telephone his mother that Colby wasn't lost, just decamped. His mother told her what had happened, and Aunt Emily listened with uncommitted little clucks. She wasn't any Solomon[5] to decide if it was more important to punish the bad than to keep a promise to the good.

She could hear him banging back and forth on the glider, waiting in hot impatience to tell his tale of woe. The old glider screeched and groaned at his assault on its unoiled joints.

Standing inside her screen door, wincing in sympathy, Aunt Emily knew that neither she nor any nearby neighbor could take that tortured sound much longer. She tried to think of something to distract Colby's mind until he calmed down. A blue jay flew across her line of vision, a bird familiar to the landscape, but the unexciting sight bloomed into an idea.

Shutting the screen door soundlessly, approaching Colby on whispering feet, she put her finger to her lips and sat down beside him.

---

4. A *sounding board* can be a person to whom one expresses opinions or ideas as a way of testing, or sounding them out.

5. Here, *decamped* refers to having run away, quickly and secretly. Famous for his great wisdom, *Solomon* was a king of Israel in the tenth century B.C.

Vocabulary
obligation (ob′ lə gā′ shən) *n.* a sense of duty; a responsibility
uncommitted (un′ kə mit′ id) *adj.* not having or showing a particular opinion, view, or course of action
woe (wō) *n.* great sadness or suffering; great trouble or misfortune

---

MEETING INDIVIDUAL NEEDS — INCLUSION STRATEGIES

Less-Proficient Readers Students who are having difficulties reading the selection may benefit from hearing you read passages aloud, then reading them aloud with you.

Activity Ask students to work in pairs to practice reading the first two paragraphs on this page aloud. Encourage them to make their reading sound as

natural as possible, using appropriate tone, pronunciation, and pauses. Students can select parts of the story and provide a dramatic reading for the class. **L1**

Additional Resources
📁 *Inclusion Strategies*

Full Moon Gossip, 1997. Gustavo Novoa. Acrylic on canvas, 36 x 36 in. Wally Findlay Galleries, New York.

Viewing the painting: Which aspects of this painting are realistic? Which are imaginative? Could any of these birds be "the bird like no other"? Explain your answer.

VIEWING THE PAINTING

Gustavo Novoa studied art in both France and his native country, Chile. Influenced by impressionism, surrealism, and ecology, Novoa's paintings bring together wild creatures from a variety of habitats, who often appear in unlikely urban settings. Another of his paintings can be seen on page 768.

Viewing Response *Given their vivid colors and unusual shapes, many of these birds could appear to be "the bird like no other" in most areas of the United States.*

On The Lighter Side

Do birds gossip? Some birds have a great capacity for learning language—particularly parrots. Some species of these brightly colored birds can learn from ten to sixty words, including family member's names and common household objects.

AT THE CROSSROADS 🦜 475

MULTIPLE LEARNING STYLES

MEETING INDIVIDUAL NEEDS

Spatial Students who have strong visual or spatial abilities may enjoy creating a bird mural. In creating the mural, students will better understand how Colby and Aunt Emily might have imagined "The Bird Like No Other."

Activity Using encyclopedias, Internet sites, or field guides, have students find out how different types of birds look.

Ask them to choose one image and sketch it in pencil. Point out that they should not be concerned with depicting the bird with great accuracy. Invite them, rather, to give the impressions of the bird's shape, colors, and movement. Finally, have students color or paint their birds on the mural, creating a fantasy landscape in which a "bird like no other" might appear. **L2**

K Active Reading

QUESTION Ask students why they think Aunt Emily claims that she has seen this unique bird. You may wish to model the thinking process involved in questioning.

Model: I know Aunt Emily just spoke with Colby's mother, so she knows he is upset. She is trying to think of something to distract Colby's attention until he calms down. I think this is why she tells him to look for the bird like no other.

L Literary Elements

DETAILS Have students identify the details that show that Colby is very upset and angry. *(He flings himself up the stairs and flings himself down on the poor old glider.)*

M Critical Thinking

DRAWING CONCLUSIONS Discuss with students why they think Aunt Emily has finally told Colby the truth about the bird. *(Some students might say that since Colby is eight, Aunt Emily thinks he is old enough to deal effectively with his angry feelings.)*

As he stared at her round-eyed, his swinging suspended, she said softly, "Colby, before you came the most beautiful bird I ever saw was sitting on my hydrangea bush. He almost took my breath. I never saw a bird of so many colors. When you came running, he flew away. But if we don't talk or make any noise, he may come back."

After a moment of reflection,[6] Colby's curiosity pulled out the plug in his sea of troubles, and he settled back.

That was the way this gentle fiction began. When Aunt Emily decided that the beautiful bird was gone for the day, Colby was wearing an agreeable face of a normal color. Taking the initiative, a shameless triumph over a small boy, Aunt Emily plunged into a story before Colby could get his mouth open to begin his own.

For the rest of that summer, and in the summers that followed, when Colby came glad or when Colby came only a little bit mad, the right to speak first was his automatically. But when Colby came breathing fire, by uncanny coincidence,[7] the bird like no other had just left the yard.

It was soon routine for Colby to seal his lips and settle down to wait.

Now he was eight, and on this angry morning when he flung himself up Aunt Emily's stairs, and flung himself down beside her on the poor old glider that responded as expected to a sudden shock, it was plainly a morning to search the sky for the bird like no other.

Before Aunt Emily could comb a fresh story out of her memory, Colby got a speech in ahead of her. He said in an excited whisper, "I see it, I see it. I see the bird you said was so beautiful. I guess he's every color in the world."

Jerking upright in stunned surprise, making the glider wearily protest, Aunt Emily asked in a shaken voice, "Where?"

"On that tree over there, see, over there."

By a confluence[8] of golden sunlight and blue sky and green leaves and shimmering summer air, a bird on a swinging bough took on an astonishing beauty.

For a moment Aunt Emily couldn't believe her eyes. But in another moment her eyes stopped playing tricks. And suddenly she wanted to stop playing tricks, too.

"Colby, look again. That's a jay. There never was a bird like the one I told you about. I made him up."

As if to give credence[9] to her confession, the bird on the bough released itself from its brief enchantment and flew away in the dress of a blue jay.

Colby spoke slowly. "Why did you make up a bird to tell me about?"

Aunt Emily started to answer, but asked instead, "Don't you know why, Colby?"

"I think so," he said soberly.

"Will you tell me?"

---

6. *Reflection* is serious and careful thinking.
7. An *uncanny coincidence* is a really strange occurrence of two things happening at the same time.
8. A *confluence* is a flowing together, or meeting, of two or more things.
9. Although *credence* (krēd′ əns) usually means "belief," here, the author is using the very old meaning of "believability" or "deserving trust."

Vocabulary
initiative (i nish′ ə tiv) *n.* the action of taking the first step
soberly (sō′ bər lē) *adv.* very seriously

476 🐦 THEME 5

Teaching Options

Grammar and Language *Minilesson*

Using Troublesome Words: Its and It's
Review the concept that one form indicates possession; the other is a shortened form of *it is*. Ask a volunteer to identify the word that is short for *it is*. Have a student explain what a contraction is. *(It is a word made by replacing some letters with an apostrophe to combine two words into one.)* Invite volunteers to indicate which form of the word completes each sentence below.

The dog wagged _____ tail as I approached. _____ time for my favorite show.

Activity Have students write one or two paragraphs about Colby and his Aunt Emily. Students should use at least three examples of *its* and three examples of *it's* in their writing. **L2**

Additional Resources

Grammar and Language Transparency 41

Grammar and Language Workbook, pp. 223–224

Writer's Choice, Lesson 17.2

When I Was a Child, 1996. Dr. Samella Lewis. Oil on canvas, 39¾ x 30 in. Stella Jones Gallery, New Orleans, LA.

Viewing the painting: How is the boy in the painting like or unlike Colby?

"To make me sit still so I wouldn't say bad things about my family when I was mad. But you didn't want to make me sit still like a punishment. So you made me sit still like we were waiting to see something wonderful."

"I see the wonderful thing I've been waiting for. I see a little boy who's learned about family loyalty. It's as beautiful to look at as that bird."

Colby got up. He scuffed his sneakers. "Well, I guess I'll go home now. See you, Aunt Emily."

He bounded down the stairs and began to run home, running faster and faster. Aunt Emily's eyes filled with sentimental tears. He was trying to catch up with the kind of man he was going to be. He was rushing toward understanding.

VIEWING THE PAINTING

Painter, graphic artist, sculptor, art historian, and educator Samella Lewis was born in New Orleans in 1924. She earned a Ph.D. in fine arts and art history from Ohio State University, and is regarded as the foremost authority on twentieth century African American art and artists.

Viewing Response *The boy in the painting looks solitary and lonely, as if he could use a friend like Aunt Emily.*

N Literary Elements

DETAILS Ask students to discuss the details on this page that describe how Colby has grown emotionally. *(Details include Colby's description of why Aunt Emily made up the bird, Aunt Emily's description of Colby, and the last two sentences of the story.)*

Thematic Focus

At the Crossroads Ask students to discuss times when they have had to go through difficult transitions or changes, or have had to make important decisions in their lives. Encourage them to think of older people who might have helped them during these times.

✔ ASSESSMENT OPTIONS

📁 *Quick Checks,* p. 43

REAL-WORLD CONNECTION

Extraordinary People Students might enjoy learning about real-life people who have inspired and affected others.

Activity Invite students to use the Internet or the school library to research a person who has made a strong impression on them, such as a poet, a writer, or a political leader. Some possible examples are Martin Luther King, Jr., Robert Frost, Maya Angelou, Nelson Mandela, and John F. Kennedy. Ask students to describe the character traits they most admire in the person they choose. Suggest they find one inspiring quotation from that person to share with the class. **L2**

Responding to the Selection

Personal Response

Some students might agree that it is best to avoid saying things in anger or out of pride. Others might suggest practical ways to calm down when angry.

Analyzing Literature

1. The speaker warns the reader of proud words.
2. He comes there to talk to her, often when he is angry or upset.
3. Aunt Emily tells Colby to sit quietly and look for a very beautiful and unusual bird.
4. The speaker might use "proud words" to describe words spoken in anger or arrogance.
5. Once proud words are spoken, they come to life. The person who spoke them no longer has control over them.
6. The central image is one of uncontrolled anger or arrogant words stomping away to do damage.
7. Aunt Emily is a mentor and a kind of substitute mother for Colby when he is feeling upset. She has lost her son, and Colby is searching for an understanding adult.
8. She thinks he is old enough to understand why she told the lie. She also feels that he has learned how to deal with his anger effectively.
9. Most students will agree that once words are spoken, other people remember them. Words are very powerful.
10. Colby learns the value of using positive rather than negative teaching and the importance of family loyalty. This helps him become a thoughtful, understanding, and caring person.

Responding to Literature

PERSONAL RESPONSE

Think back to the **Focus Activity** on page 471. How does your advice compare or contrast with the advice suggested in "Primer Lesson" or "The Bird Like No Other"? Add your latest thoughts to your journal.

Bird in Flight–Bird Series II, 1981. Freshman Brown. Prisma colors on bfk rives. Private collection.

Analyzing Literature

RECALL

1. About what kind of words does the speaker of "Primer Lesson" warn the reader?
2. What usually causes Colby to run to Aunt Emily's cottage?
3. What does Aunt Emily tell Colby whenever he arrives angry?

INTERPRET

4. What does the speaker in "Primer Lesson" mean by "proud words"?
5. According to "Primer Lesson," why is it not easy to call back proud words?
6. What is the central image of "Primer Lesson"? What does this image suggest?
7. How would you describe the relationship between Aunt Emily and Colby? Why do they share this relationship?
8. Why does Aunt Emily admit to Colby that she made up the story about the bird?

EVALUATE AND CONNECT

9. Do you agree that it isn't easy to call back proud words? Why or why not?
10. Theme Connection   In your opinion, what valuable lessons does Colby learn from Aunt Emily? Explain why those lessons are important.

LITERARY ELEMENTS

Descriptive Details

Writers use **descriptive details** to create memorable portraits of characters, places, objects, and events. Good writers help readers imagine what they describe by choosing details carefully and expressing them in vivid language. Dorothy West, for example, tells us that Colby "pounded up the stairs," and that Aunt Emily waited "for him to fling himself down beside her and cool his hot anger in her calm."

1. Describe two details in "The Bird Like No Other" that create a picture of the road leading to Aunt Emily's cottage.

2. Pick out a detail describing Colby that helps you imagine him more clearly.

● See **Literary Terms Handbook**, p. R3.

LITERARY ELEMENTS

1. The woods were not a dark forest, just scrub oak and stunted pine. Also, the road was just a footpath worn by time.
2. One possible response: "After a moment of reflection, Colby's curiosity pulled out the plug in his sea of troubles, and he settled back."

Additional Resources

Literary Elements Transparency 43

Extending Your Response

Writing About Literature

The Poet's Theme   Do you think that Sandburg was effective in getting across his **theme,** or central idea, in "Primer Lesson"? Write a paragraph or two explaining your opinion. Use details from the poem to support your assessment.

Literature Groups

Proud Words   Discuss with your group what Sandburg means by "proud words." What kind of person might use proud words? What kind of situation might cause someone to use them? Is the use of proud words ever warranted or justified? Share your group's thoughts with the rest of the class.

Art Activity

The Bird Like No Other   How do you see Aunt Emily's fictional bird? Create your own drawing or painting of the bird.

Creative Writing

Letter to Aunt Emily   Imagine that you are Colby as a teenager. Write a letter to Aunt Emily from Colby's point of view, describing some of the problems you now face. Express to Aunt Emily what her relationship has come to mean to you over the years and what advice you wish she could offer you now. Then trade letters with a partner. Next, imagine yourself as Aunt Emily, and answer your partner's letter.

Reading Further

Here are some other works by Carl Sandburg and Dorothy West you might enjoy:
The Complete Poems of Carl Sandburg
The Richer, the Poorer by Dorothy West

Save your work for your portfolio.

Skill Minilesson

VOCABULARY • ANALOGIES: DEFINING CHARACTERISTICS

One kind of **analogy** deals with "defining characteristics," that is, characteristics that are a necessary part of what makes the person or thing what it is.

fur : rabbit :: wool : sheep

Fur is a characteristic of a *rabbit* just as *wool* is a characteristic of a *sheep*. Every analogy contains two pairs of words. Decide what the relationship is between the first pair of words. Then find the word that will complete the second pair and show the same relationship.

PRACTICE   Choose the word that best completes each analogy.
1. wings : fly :: feet :
   a. legs   b. walk   c. person
2. dishonesty : thief :: initiative :
   a. leader   b. judge   c. coward
3. wall : house :: page :
   a. turn   b. book   c. read
4. displeasure : fury :: gloominess :
   a. delight   b. anger   c. woe
5. gift : present :: obligation :
   a. duty   b. decision   c. fault

Extending Your Response

Writing About Literature

Students' paragraphs should
• explain whether they think Sandburg was effective in communicating his message.
• include details from the poem to support their opinions.

Creative Writing

Students' reviews should
• describe some of the problems that Colby faces as a teenager.
• express to Aunt Emily what her relationship has come to mean and ask her for advice.
• respond to Colby's letter from Aunt Emily's point of view.

Literature Groups   Be sure that students explore the several definitions of the word *proud*. Help them distinguish between the kind of pride that is negative and that which is a positive and essential component of living. **COLLAB. LEARN.**

Art Activity   Provide students with bright colors for their drawings or paintings of the bird.

Skill Minilesson

VOCABULARY • ANALOGIES

1. b   3. b   5. a
2. a   4. c

Additional Resources
📁 *Vocabulary Practice,* p. 29

✓ ASSESSMENT OPTIONS

📁 *Quick Checks,* p. 43
📁 *Selection and Theme Assessment,* pp. 75–76
📁 *Performance Assessment,* p. 40
📁 *Testmaker*

Objectives

- To use and understand active viewing techniques
- To use the Internet to find screen-writing tips
- To rewrite a scene as a screenplay

Teaching Strategies

Use a video students might enjoy to model active viewing techniques. Help students observe the kinds of things that active viewers notice. For example, "They've just started playing scary music. I think that means something suspenseful is going to happen." Draw students' attention to various aspects of filmmaking:

- camera movements and angles
- how music affects a viewer's emotions
- transitions that move viewers from one setting to another, such as fades, dissolves, or cuts

Adapting to Available Technology

Encourage students to view particular scenes more closely by using features available on VCRs: freeze frame, advancing in slow motion, and advancing frame by frame. If your school's VCR has none of these features, have students use the rewind function and the counter to view a particular scene over and over again so that they can analyze it.

Teaching Options

Technology Skills

Becoming an Active Viewer

Did you know that directors of movies and television shows use many of the same story-telling elements that writers of novels and short stories do? Movies and television dramas are set in a particular time and place, or **setting**. They generally have a story line, or **plot**, that probably includes a **conflict** that leads to a **climax**. The actors help give the **characters** they play certain traits, which become part of their **characterization**. Camera work and lighting help establish the **mood** of the story, which may also include **suspense**. Even such literary elements as **symbolism, theme,** and **imagery** may be part of a movie or teleplay. (If any of the bold-faced terms above puzzle you, look for them in your Literary Terms Handbook on pages R1–R11.)

Practice Active Viewing Strategies

As you begin to recognize the techniques filmmakers use, you will need to practice active viewing strategies. For example, look at this still photo of a shot from the classic film *Citizen Kane.* In this shot, young Charles Foster Kane (the boy) is being introduced to the man who is about to become his guardian. Study the scene to answer the following questions.

Connect

- What emotion is the boy expressing? How can you tell? Have you ever felt this way?

Question

- Why is the guardian positioned between the boy and his father?
- Why do you think the boy is being sent away? What do you see in the scene that might suggest a reason?

> ### TECHNOLOGY TIP
> To discuss film, you need to know some of the vocabulary of filmmaking. A movie is made up of many—probably hundreds of—shots. A **shot** is a single sequence in which the camera films without interruption. The switch from one shot to another is called a **cut**. Cutting is the responsibility of the film editor. A **scene** in a movie is all the consecutive shots in a single setting. Movie cameras can **pan** (swing from one side to another), **zoom** (use a special lens to move toward or away from a subject), or move in a number of other ways, either carried by hand or on various mechanisms. As you learn more about filmmaking, your appreciation of the art will grow.

MEETING INDIVIDUAL NEEDS — MULTIPLE LEARNING STYLES

Musical Students with strong musical abilities may respond to movies more readily through sound than through visuals or words. These students can use active listening techniques to help them understand movie and television dramas.

Activity As students watch a movie, suggest they focus on the background music and sounds as well as on the images and dialogue. Have them create a two-column chart, noting each sound element in the left column and each emotion, mood, or idea created by that element in the right column. After their viewing is over, invite students to discuss how sound effects and music affect the viewing of a film. **L2**
COLLAB. LEARN.

Predict

* How might this scene relate to what will happen later in the movie?

Evaluate

* Why is this scene set outdoors on a cold winter day? Is there some connection between the setting and the action?
* What is your impression of the guardian? What gives you that impression?
* What do you think of the mother? Why?

Respond

* Can you identify with any of these characters? Why or why not?

The Art of Film

When you view a movie or TV drama, you should be aware of the filmmaker's art. Notice how a scene is framed, and how the actors are arranged. Looking at a single picture from a movie can start you thinking, but you need to remember that movies are *motion* pictures. How actors move may tell you something about their character. How they move in relation to one another can reveal relationships.

The camera can also move. It may pan from one character to another or from one place to another. It can follow a character as he or she moves. It can zoom in on something, drawing your attention to it, or zoom out to show you where something is taking place.

Look at camera angles. The camera can make a character seem smaller or weaker by looking down. Looking upward, it can make a person seem stronger or domineering. Tilted at an angle, it gives the viewer a sense of unease.

Watch for how a scene is edited. For example, cutting quickly from shot to shot can create excitement. A long scene with few or no cuts can create a sense of calm.

Listen to the background music. Does it add to or detract from the mood of what you're seeing? How?

All this doesn't mean that you need to strain to find meaning in everything you see. Viewing a situation comedy on TV doesn't require much care. But when you view a serious movie made by a good filmmaker, you'll find it a much richer experience if you view actively.

ACTIVITIES

1. Practice active viewing strategies when you watch television or a movie. What methods do directors and actors use to get their messages across? Write your conclusions in your journal.

2. Do an Internet search to find tips on screenwriting.

3. Rewrite a scene from one of the stories in this book as a screenplay. Describe how the scene should look, where actors should be, how they will move, and what sound effects or music should accompany the scene.

TECHNOLOGY TIP

When you see a movie on a television screen, you may not be seeing the movie as it was meant it to be seen. Most movies today are made in a wide-screen format. To fit the shape of a TV screen, the sides of the movie are cut off. Sometimes the movie may cut or pan back and forth between two characters who were originally shown on opposite sides of the wide screen. This adds cuts or pans that were not intended by the director, the film editor, or the director of photography. Until wide-screen digital TV becomes widely available, or unless you watch a wide-screen VHS or DVD version, keep in mind that you're not seeing exactly what the filmmakers intended.

Activities

You may wish to have the class generate a list on the board that students can copy into their notebooks for easy reference. Suggest that students pause in their viewing every fifteen or twenty minutes to think about the following:

* How does the filmmaker want me to feel?
* What is the camera doing?
* How does the filmmaker feel about the characters on screen right now? How can I tell?
* What kind of sounds and music am I hearing? How is that affecting me?

Students' rewritten scenes should

* describe what the scene looks like, where the actors are, and how they move.
* include sound effects or music to enhance the scene.
* describe unusual camera angles or camera movements.

TechnoTalk

Filmmaking Jargon Like any other profession, filmmaking has its own special vocabulary:

LS (long shot), in which the camera shows the entire setting, or shows the full figure of a person

MS (medium shot), in which one or more people are shown from the waist up

CU (closeup), in which only one person's face is shown, or in which a single body part or object is shown at close range

VO (voice-over), in which the audience hears the narrator but does not see the person speaking.

INTERDISCIPLINARY CONNECTION

Art Invite students interested in filmmaking to make a short film or video—a narrative, a music video, or a short documentary.

Activity Help students work in small groups to begin by planning their films. They may want to make a series of sketches (called a *storyboard*) that show what to shoot, where the actors will stand, how the shot will be framed, and how the camera will move. If your filmmakers are planning to use dialogue, they should also prepare a shooting script, which tells what each character says and does. Have students share their creations with the whole class. **L3** **COLLAB. LEARN.**

Objectives

- To read and analyze two short stories about facing challenges
- To uncover the implied themes
- To write a paragraph expressing an opinion on descriptive writing

Skills

Reading/Thinking: Drawing Conclusions; Inferring; Logical Reasoning; Synthesizing; Evaluating; Cause and Effect; Summarizing; Identifying Main Idea and Supporting Detail

Writing: Narrating Action

Vocabulary: Etymology; Suffixes; Prefixes: *mal-*

Grammar/Language: Verbs in the Past Tense; Participles and Participial Phrases

Listening/Speaking: Enacting a Dialogue; Oral Storytelling; Debate

Life Skills: Decision Making

Collaboration: Literature Groups

Motivating →OPTIONS

Literature Launchers: "Pearl Buck and Her World"

Videodisc Side B, Segment 15

Also available in VHS.

Selection Focus Transparency 44: Use the quotation to generate a discussion on old age.

Focus Activity: Have pairs of students tell how they would react in the face of danger.

Before You Read
The Old Demon *and* The Boy and His Grandfather

MEET PEARL S. BUCK

Pearl S. Buck was the first American woman to win the Nobel Prize for Literature. Many of her novels, stories, plays, and essays reflect her experience of growing up, living, and working in China for nearly forty years.

Pearl S. Buck was born in 1892 and died in 1973.

MEET RUDOLFO A. ANAYA

One of the founding fathers of modern Hispanic American literature, Rudolfo Anaya (rōō dôl′ fō ä nä′ yä) has written fiction, plays, and essays, mostly set in his native New Mexico. Anaya often weaves Hispanic legends and folktales into his work.

Rudolfo A. Anaya was born in 1937.

FOCUS ACTIVITY

Do you ever wonder how you would react in a time of danger or need? Could you be as courageous as you had to be?

Discuss

With a small group, discuss how you and people you know might respond to the needs of the sick or neglected.

Setting a Purpose

Read these stories to discover how others respond to danger or the needs of others.

BACKGROUND

The Time and Place "The Old Demon" takes place in China in the late 1930s, after Japan invaded China.

Did You Know? The Yellow River (Huang Ho in Chinese) got its name from the yellow silt that is carried with the current and gives the river a yellowish color. Once every twenty-five years or so, the river overflows its banks, and a massive flood destroys villages, livestock, and people. For this reason, the Yellow River is often referred to as "China's Sorrow."

VOCABULARY PREVIEW

malicious (mə lish′ əs) *adj.* having or showing a desire to harm another; p. 484

quavering (kwā′ vər ing) *adj.* trembling or shaking; p. 484

somberly (som′ bər lē) *adv.* in a gloomy manner; p. 490

tentatively (ten′ tə tiv lē) *adv.* hesitantly; uncertainly; p. 492

discern (di surn′) *v.* to detect or recognize; p. 492

acutely (ə kūt′ lē) *adv.* sharply and with intensity; p. 493

impetuous (im pech′ ōō əs) *adj.* marked by force or violent action; p. 494

RESOURCE MANAGER

Lesson Planning Resource
The *Theme Five Planning Guide* (pp. 41–46) provides additional lesson notes and reduced versions of all print resources.

📁 **Other Print Resources**
- Active Reading Guide, p. 44
- Vocabulary Practice, p. 30
- Reading Workbook, pp. 77–78
- Grammar and Language Workbook, pp. 83–86, 167–170

- Grammar and Composition Handbook, Lesson 3.5, 9.1
- Quick Checks, p. 44
- Selection and Theme Assessment, pp. 77–78
- Performance Assessment, pp. 41
- Spanish Summaries, p. 44
- Spanish Translations
- Inclusion Strategies
- English Language Learners Sourcebook

🖍 **Transparencies**
- Selection Focus 44
- Fine Art 44
- Literary Elements 42
- Grammar and Language 42

Technology

   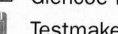

- Literature Launchers
- Audio Library
- Spanish Audio Library
- Glencoe Literature Web Site
- Testmaker

The Old Demon

Pearl S. Buck ~

Emperor Kuang Wu, of the Western Han Dynasty, Fording a River. Ch'iu Ying (active 1510–1551). Hanging scroll, ink and color on silk, height: 67¼ in. National Gallery of Canada, Ottawa.

A

Old Mrs. Wang knew, of course, that there was a war. Everybody had known for a long time that there was war going on and that Japanese were killing Chinese. But still it was not real and no more than hearsay since none of the Wangs had been killed. The Village of Three Mile Wangs on the flat banks of the Yellow River, which was old Mrs. Wang's clan village, had never seen a Japanese. This was how they came to be talking about Japanese at all.

AT THE CROSSROADS 🐚 483

SUMMARY

The Old Demon Mrs. Wang is the elderly leader of her village on the Yellow River during China's war with Japan. When Mrs. Wang sees the Japanese army coming across the plain, she opens the floodgates of the river, engulfing the Japanese army and saving the villagers.
The Boy and His Grandfather An old man is neglected by his son. The old man's grandson, through an act of kindness, reminds his father to treat the old man with care and dignity.

📁 *Spanish Summaries,* p. 44

A **Active Reading**

PREDICT Ask students to predict what "The Old Demon" might be.

Additional Resources

📁 *Active Reading Guide,* p. 44
🎧 *Audio Library*
🎧 *Spanish Audio Library*

CONNECTING TO OTHER SELECTIONS
For a teaching strategy that connects "The Old Demon" to "Rip Van Winkle," turn to page 49 in the *Theme Two Planning Guide.*

Teaching Options

MEETING INDIVIDUAL NEEDS — ENGLISH LANGUAGE LEARNERS

Describing a Setting Explain that the setting of a story often helps create an atmosphere or mood.

Activity Have students work in small groups. Ask them to read the first paragraph carefully and write down the details that describe the setting. Then suggest that they rewrite the paragraph in their own words. (*Old Mrs. Wang lives in the village of Three Mile Wangs along the banks of the Yellow River. Even though there is a war going on between China and Japan, the villagers have not yet experienced it.*)

Additional Resources

✏️ *Literary Elements Transparency 44*
📁 *English Language Learners Sourcebook*

FYI

The Yellow River Over many centuries the Yellow River has washed down soil, creating a large plain that is easily flooded when the river rises. The people have built dikes to hold back the water. The dikes have been made higher and higher, so that the river is now higher than the surrounding plains.

B Literary Elements

FIGURES OF SPEECH: *Simile* Ask students how water could be "curling along like a lot of snakes." *(This simile compares water to snakes, meaning that, instead of the water flowing in one direction, it breaks up, swirling this way and that, like a snake.)*

C Literary Elements

IMPLIED THEME Ask students what the apparent change of attitude toward things she has not seen reveals about Mrs. Wang. *(She is less reluctant to believe things just because she has not witnessed them.)*

D Critical Thinking

DRAWING CONCLUSIONS Though Little Pig probably knows about the reality of airplanes, he does not pursue the issue with Mrs. Wang. What does his going on to another song suggest about his attitude toward her? *(He respects her too much to persist in objecting.)*

The Old Demon

It was evening and early summer, and after her supper Mrs. Wang had climbed the dike steps, as she did every day, to see how high the river had risen. She was much more afraid of the river than of the Japanese. She knew what the river would do. And one by one the villagers had followed her up the dike, and now they stood staring down at the malicious yellow water, curling along like a lot of snakes, and biting at the high dike banks.

"I never saw it as high as this so early," Mrs. Wang said. She sat down on a bamboo stool that her grandson, Little Pig, had brought for her, and spat into the water.

"It's worse than the Japanese, this old devil of a river," Little Pig said recklessly.

"Fool!" Mrs. Wang said quickly. "The river god will hear you. Talk about something else."

So they had gone on talking about the Japanese. . . . How, for instance, asked Wang, the baker, who was old Mrs. Wang's nephew twice removed, would they know the Japanese when they saw them?

Mrs. Wang at this point said positively, "You'll know them. I once saw a foreigner. He was taller than the eaves of my house and he had mud-colored hair and eyes the color of a fish's eyes. Anyone who does not look like us—that is a Japanese."

Then Little Pig spoke up in his disconcerting[1] way. "You can't see them, Grandmother. They hide up in the sky in airplanes."

---

1. Little Pig's *disconcerting* way of speaking causes embarrassment, confusion, or frustration.

Mrs. Wang did not answer immediately. Once she would have said positively, "I shall not believe in an airplane until I see it." But so many things had been true which she had not believed—the Empress, for instance, whom she had not believed dead, was dead. The Republic, again, she had not believed in because she did not know what it was. She still did not know, but they had said for a long time there had been one. So now she merely stared quietly about the dike where they all sat around her. It was very pleasant and cool, and she felt nothing mattered if the river did not rise to flood.

"I don't believe in the Japanese," she said flatly.

They laughed at her a little, but no one spoke. Someone lit her pipe—it was Little Pig's wife, who was her favorite, and she smoked it.

"Sing, Little Pig!" someone called.

So Little Pig began to sing an old song in a high quavering voice, and old Mrs. Wang listened and forgot the Japanese. The evening was beautiful, the sky so clear and still that the willows overhanging the dike were reflected even in the muddy water. Everything was at peace. The thirty-odd houses which made up the village straggled along beneath them. Nothing could break this peace. After all, the Japanese were only human beings.

"I doubt those airplanes," she said mildly to Little Pig when he stopped singing.

But without answering her, he went on to another song.

Vocabulary

malicious (mə lish′ əs) *adj.* having or showing a desire to harm another
quavering (kwā′ vər ing) *adj.* trembling or shaking

Teaching Options

Reading *Minilesson*

Cause and Effect Cause is an action or event that directly results in or enables another action or event. Effect is the direct or logical outcome of an event or action. In this story, two threats to the village lead Mrs. Wang to make a very unusual decision.

Activity Start a cause-and-effect chart by having the class identify the two

threats. Ask them to work in small groups to develop the double chain of causes and effects that lead to Mrs. Wang's unusual decision. **L2 COLLAB. LEARN.**

Additional Resources

Reading Workbook, pp. 77–78

CAUSE 1		CAUSE 2
Threat of river floods		*Threat of the Japanese*

EFFECT		EFFECT
Mrs. Wang checks the dike every day.		*Mrs. Wang denies the threat.*

MRS. WANG'S DECISION

Year in and year out she had spent the summer evenings like this on the dike. The first time she was seventeen and a bride, and her husband had shouted to her to come out of the house and up the dike, and she had come, blushing and twisting her hands together, to hide among the women while the men roared at her and made jokes about her. All the same, they had liked her. "A pretty piece of meat in your bowl," they had said to her husband. "Feet a trifle big," he had answered deprecatingly.[2] But she could see he was pleased, and so gradually her shyness went away.

He, poor man, had been drowned in a flood when he was still young. And it had taken her years to get him prayed out of Buddhist purgatory.[3] Finally she had grown tired of it, what with the child and the land all on her back, and so when the priest said coaxingly, "Another ten pieces of silver and he'll be out entirely," she asked, "What's he got in there yet?"

"Only his right hand," the priest said, encouraging her.

Well, then, her patience broke. Ten dollars! It would feed them for the winter. Besides, she had had to hire labor for her share of repairing the dike, too, so there would be no more floods.

"If it's only one hand, he can pull himself out," she said firmly.

She often wondered if he had, poor silly fellow. As like as not, she had often thought gloomily in the night, he was still lying there, waiting for her to do

something about it. That was the sort of man he was. Well, some day, perhaps, when Little Pig's wife had had the first baby safely and she had a little extra, she might go back to finish him out of purgatory. There was no real hurry, though. . . .

"Grandmother, you must go in," Little Pig's wife's soft voice said. "There is a mist rising from the river now that the sun is gone."

"Yes, I suppose I must," old Mrs. Wang agreed. She gazed at the river a moment. The river—it was full of good and evil together. It would water the fields when it was curbed and checked, but then if an inch were allowed it, it crashed through like a soaring dragon. That was how her husband had been swept away—careless, he was, about his bit of the dike. He was always going to mend it, always going to pile more earth on top of it, and then in a night the river rose and broke through. He had run out of the house, and she had climbed on the roof with the child and had saved herself and it while he was drowned. Well, they had pushed the river back again behind its dikes, and it had stayed there this time. Every day she herself walked up and down the length of the dike for which the village was responsible and examined it. The men laughed and said, "If anything is wrong with the dikes, Granny will tell us."

It had never occurred to any of them to move the village away from the river. The Wangs had lived there for generations, and some had always escaped the floods and had fought the river more fiercely than ever afterward.

Little Pig suddenly stopped singing.

[2.] To speak *deprecatingly* is to express mild disapproval.
[3.] *Buddhism* is one of the major religions of the world. It grew out of the teachings of Gautama, called the Buddha. *Purgatory*, according to Roman Catholic doctrine, is a place where the souls of dead sinners are kept until they have been purged of sin and can enter heaven.

AT THE CROSSROADS 485

E Literary Elements
NARRATOR Ask students to identify who is telling the story. Explain that in this story the narrator reveals the thoughts of only one character, Mrs. Wang. *(The story is told from a third-person point of view.)*

On The Lighter Side
Help students see the humor in Mrs. Wang's response: "If it's only one hand, he can pull himself out." *(She is concerned about her deceased husband's resting in peace, but she thinks she should use the money on the living. He can pull himself out of purgatory.)*

F Literary Elements
IMPLIED THEME Ask students which quality of the river, good or evil, they expect to see demonstrated in the story and how this setting is important to the theme. *(The river is a critical element to the theme and the plot. It points to the potential for good and evil in all things.)*

G Literary Elements
IMPLIED THEME Ask students what personality trait Mrs. Wang best illustrates. What does she represent to village life? *(Even if the men laugh, they still depend on her sense of responsibility to protect them; she is seen as the guardian of the village.)*

INTERDISCIPLINARY CONNECTION

Social Studies Floods have always been a problem for some areas of the world, where they cause soil erosion, destroy property, and endanger lives. Though people have continually tried to control floods with new methods, they must often rely on those that are age-old.

Activity Have students research methods of flood control, perhaps in their area, if they live in a locality that floods from time to time. Have them find out what is being done to control floods on a permanent basis and what provisions are available during an emergency.

INFERRING Ask students what is revealed about how the other villagers feel toward Mrs. Wang. *(They seem to have the utmost respect for her.)*

Vo•cab•u•lar•y Skills

Etymology The word *wheedle* means "to persuade by flattery or smooth words; to coax." The word comes from an Old English word meaning "to beg."

I **Active Reading**

REVIEW Ask students to put in their own words what Mrs. Wang is thinking. *(At first, she says only coarse people want to fight and assumes the Japanese are not that way. Then she plans to be kind to them, thereby changing their minds about fighting. At the end, however, she is puzzled by their motives.)*

VIEWING THE PAINTING

Viewing Response *The painting shows a group of people who look stressed and exhausted. They appear to have left their homes on short notice because they are carrying very little. Perhaps they have been displaced by disaster, such as a war or a flood like the one in the story.*

Teaching Options

The Old Demon

"The moon is coming up!" he cried. "That's not good. Airplanes come out on moonlight nights."

"Where do you learn all this about airplanes?" old Mrs. Wang exclaimed. "It is tiresome to me," she said, so severely that no one spoke. In this silence, leaning upon the arm of Little Pig's wife she descended slowly the earthen steps which led down into the village, using her long pipe in the other hand as a walking stick. Behind her the villagers came down, one by one, to

bed. No one moved before she did, but none stayed long after her.

And in her own bed at last, behind the blue cotton mosquito curtains which Little Pig's wife fastened securely, she fell peacefully asleep. She had lain awake a little while thinking about the Japanese and H wondering why they wanted to fight. Only very coarse persons wanted wars. In her mind she saw large coarse persons. If they came one must wheedle them, she thought, invite them to drink tea, and explain to

Exiles, 1939. Chen Baoyi. Oil. Courtesy Dr. Michael Sullivan, St. Catherine's College, Oxford, England.
Viewing the painting: What story does the painting tell? What connection could you make between the painting and "The Old Demon"?

486 🦌 THEME 5

Listening and Speaking *Minilesson*

Enacting a Dialogue Remind students that in the culture of the story, elders allowed little dissent. In our culture, while respect for authority is still called for, disagreements are often permitted if they are raised in a respectful manner.

Activity Have students work in pairs to create a dialogue between Mrs. Wang and

Little Pig that is set in our culture today. Have Little Pig be more persistent in explaining the airplanes, while showing no disrespect. Have Mrs. Wang be as closed-minded as in the story. Have one student "play" Mrs. Wang and the other, Little Pig; then have them reverse the roles.
L2 COLLAB. LEARN.

them, reasonably—only why should they come to a peaceful farming village . . . ?

So she was not in the least prepared for Little Pig's wife screaming at her that the Japanese had come. She sat up in bed muttering, "The tea bowls—the tea—"

"Grandmother, there's no time!" Little Pig's wife screamed. "They're here—they're here!"

"Where?" old Mrs. Wang cried, now awake.

"In the sky!" Little Pig's wife wailed.

They had all run out at that, into the clear early dawn, and gazed up. There, like wild geese flying in autumn, were great bird-like shapes.

"But what are they?" old Mrs. Wang cried.

And then, like a silver egg dropping, something drifted straight down and fell at the far end of the village in a field. A fountain of earth flew up, and they all ran to see it. There was a hole thirty feet across, as big as a pond. They were so astonished they could not speak, and then, before anyone could say anything, another and another egg began to fall and everybody was running, running . . .

Everybody, that is, but Mrs. Wang. When Little Pig's wife seized her hand to drag her along, old Mrs. Wang pulled away and sat down against the bank of the dike.

"I can't run," she remarked. "I haven't run in seventy years, since before my feet were bound.[4] You go on. Where's Little Pig?" She looked around. Little Pig was

---

4. *[feet were bound]* The Chinese once believed that tiny feet added to a woman's beauty, so the feet of many Chinese girls were tightly wrapped to limit their growth. This painful process resulted in small but badly deformed feet. The practice was ended in the early 1900s.

already gone. "Like his grandfather," she remarked, "always the first to run."

But Little Pig's wife would not leave her, not, that is, until old Mrs. Wang reminded her that it was her duty.

"If Little Pig is dead," she said, "then it is necessary that his son be born alive." And when the girl still hesitated, she struck at her gently with her pipe. "Go on—go on," she exclaimed.

So unwillingly, because now they could scarcely hear each other speak for the roar of the dipping planes, Little Pig's wife went on with the others.

By now, although only a few minutes had passed, the village was in ruins and the straw roofs and wooden beams were blazing. Everybody was gone. As they passed they had shrieked at old Mrs. Wang to come on, and she had called back pleasantly:

"I'm coming—I'm coming!"

But she did not go. She sat quite alone watching now what was an extraordinary spectacle. For soon other planes came, from where she did not know, but they attacked the first ones. The sun came up over the fields of ripening wheat, and in the clear summery air the planes wheeled and darted and spat at each other. When this was over, she thought, she would go back into the village and see if anything was left. Here and there a wall stood, supporting a roof. She could not see her own house from here. But she was not unused to war. Once bandits had looted their village, and houses had been burned then, too. Well, now it had happened again. Burning houses one could see often, but not this darting silvery shining battle in the air. She understood none of it—not what those things were, nor how they

---

Critical Thinking

DRAWING CONCLUSIONS Ask students why Mrs. Wang says she can't run. *(Her feet were small and deformed as a result of being bound when she was a young girl. Running on them was not possible.)*

Critical Thinking

EVALUATING Ask students this question: Is Mrs. Wang's sending Little Pig's wife away consistent with what we know of Mrs. Wang? *(Yes. Here Mrs. Wang shows her leadership ability, as she has before. She concerns herself with the safety of others, as she did daily by checking the dikes.)*

Literary Elements

PERSONIFICATION Point out to that the description of the planes spitting on each other is an example of personification: objects (the planes) are given human characteristics.

Active Reading

RESPOND Ask students to imagine how Mrs. Wang perceives the burning of the village by bandits and its bombing by Japanese airplanes. *(She can probably understand the bandits better because they come as men, visible. The Japanese are represented by airplanes, which she has never seen before and does not understand.)*

Writing Minilesson

Narrating Action The bombing of the village creates chaos. To convey that chaos, the author crowds many different actions into a short space, as in the paragraph in column 1 beginning, "And then." Note that the sentences contain a number of events described rapidly without much detail.

Activity Write a paragraph narrating an action scene, such as the end-of-the-day dismissal from school, a storm, or a celebration after a championship game. Focus on the action, inserting many different actions in the paragraph to give the sense of uncontrolled activity. **L2 COLLAB. LEARN.**

Additional Resources

📕 *Writer's Choice*, Lesson 4.3

Viewing Response *The details in the painting look rather wild and ferocious, but the result of their stormy behavior, the rain, will be beneficial. The river in the story is beneficent when it stays within its banks and evil when it breaks through to cause disastrous floods.*

N Literary Elements

IMPLIED THEME: *Plot* Ask students what they think the complication to the story will be with the crash of a Japanese plane in Mrs. Wang's field. *(It raises the action to a new level and adds to the conflict.)*

V•o•cab•u•lar•y Skills

Suffixes The meaning of the word *doubtless* is "without doubt." Adding the suffix *-less* reverses the meaning of many words: *clueless, fearless.* Sometimes the spelling of the root word changes when the suffix is added: *mercy (merciless).*

O Active Reading

PREDICT Ask students who they think the pilot of the plane is. *(More than likely it is a Japanese pilot.)*

Beneficent Rain DETAIL #5 and #6. Chang Yu-ts'ai (1295–1316). Handscroll. Ink on silk. 10⅝ x 106¾ in. The Metropolitan Museum of Art, New York.

Viewing the painting: *Beneficent* means "doing or resulting in good." Do you find the details in the painting beneficent? Is the river in the story beneficent? Why or why not?

stayed up in the sky. She simply sat, growing hungry, and watching.

"I'd like to see one close," she said aloud. And at that moment, as though in answer, one of them pointed suddenly downward, and, wheeling and twisting as though it were wounded, it fell head down in a field which Little Pig had ploughed only yesterday for soybeans. And in an instant the sky was empty again, and there was only this wounded thing on the ground and herself.

She hoisted herself carefully from the earth. At her age she need be afraid of nothing. She could, she decided, go and see what it was. So, leaning on her bamboo pipe, she made her way slowly across the fields. Behind her in the sudden stillness two or three village dogs appeared and followed, creeping close to her in their terror. When they drew near to the fallen plane, they barked furiously. Then she hit them with her pipe.

488 🐌 THEME 5

"Be quiet," she scolded, "there's already been noise enough to split my ears!"

She tapped the airplane.

"Metal," she told the dogs. "Silver, doubtless," she added. Melted up, it would make them all rich.

She walked around it, examining it closely. What made it fly? It seemed dead. Nothing moved or made a sound within it. Then, coming to the side to which it tipped, she saw a young man in it, slumped into a heap in a little seat. The dogs growled, but she struck at them again and they fell back.

"Are you dead?" she inquired politely.

The young man moved a little at her voice, but did not speak. She drew nearer and peered into the hole in which he sat. His side was bleeding.

"Wounded!" she exclaimed. She took his wrist. It was warm, but inert, and when she let it go, it dropped against the side of the hole. She stared at him. He had black hair and a dark skin like a Chinese and still he did not look like a Chinese.

Teaching Options

Grammar and Language *Minilesson*

Verbs in the Past Tense The past tense of a verb names an action that has already happened. The past tense of most verbs is formed by adding *-ed* to the base form of the verb: *talk, talk-ed.* Irregular verbs, however, do not form their past tenses by adding *-ed.* These verbs change internally: *drink, drank; seek, sought.* A few verbs, such as *cut,* keep the same form for present and past: I *cut* the paper now; I *cut* the paper yesterday.

Activity Have students complete the table below, filling in the present or past tense verbs. **L2**

Present	Past
roar	roared
see	saw
know	knew
fight	fought
wrench	wrenched

Additional Resources

Grammar and Language Transparency 42

Grammar and Language Workbook, pp. 83–86

Grammar and Composition Handbook, Lesson 3.5

Writer's Choice, Lesson 10.5

P **Critical Thinking**

SYNTHESIZING Ask students why, based on what they learned of Mrs. Wang earlier, she does not think the pilot is Japanese. *(She had thought earlier of the Japanese as being big and coarse. Apparently this pilot is not. And he looks somewhat Chinese, she says.)*

Q **Critical Thinking**

DRAWING CONCLUSIONS Ask students why the dogs are so intent on growling at and even attacking the pilot. *(Perhaps they are hostile because he is a stranger; or perhaps the bombing has terrified them.)*

R **Literary Elements**

IMPLIED THEME Ask students what this description of Mrs. Wang's heaving the pilot "somehow on her back" tells them about her personality. *(The description tells us that Mrs. Wang is a determined, caring, and principled woman.)*

"He must be a Southerner," she thought. Well, the chief thing was, he was alive.

"You had better come out," she remarked. "I'll put some herb plaster on your side."

The young man muttered something dully.

"What did you say?" she asked. But he did not say it again.

"I am still quite strong," she decided after a moment. So she reached in and seized him about the waist and pulled him out slowly, panting a good deal. Fortunately he was rather a little fellow and very light. When she had him on the ground, he seemed to find his feet; and he stood shakily and clung to her, and she held him up.

"Now if you can walk to my house," she said, "I'll see if it is there."

Then he said something, quite clearly. She listened and could not understand a word of it. She pulled away from him and stared.

"What's that?" she asked.

He pointed at the dogs. They were standing growling, their ruffs up. Then he spoke again, and as he spoke he crumpled to the ground. The dogs fell on him, so that she had to beat them off with her hands.

"Get away!" she shouted. "Who told *you* to kill him?"

And then, when they had slunk back, she heaved him somehow onto her back; and, trembling, half carrying, half pulling him, she dragged him to the ruined village and laid him in the street while she went to find her house, taking the dogs with her.

Her house was quite gone. She found the place easily enough. This was where it should be, opposite the water gate into the dike. She had always watched that gate herself. Miraculously it was not injured now, nor was the dike broken. It would be easy enough to rebuild the house. Only, for the present, it was gone.

So she went back to the young man. He was lying as she had left him, propped

AT THE CROSSROADS 🐾 489

Active Reading

CONNECT Ask students what they think the pilot is trying to say to Mrs. Wang. *(He might be trying to explain where he is hurt, thanking her for helping him, or warning her about another attack.)*

Active Reading

VISUALIZE Ask students to visualize the destroyed bakery. Suggest that they recall some of the details without looking at the text.

Critical Thinking

EVALUATING Ask students to identify an admirable trait of Mrs. Wang's character. You may use the following model to illustrate the thinking process in evaluating character.

Model: Mrs. Wang's village has been bombed, her home destroyed, and her family sent running. For food, she has to fumble through a bombed-out bakery. She has lost just about everything, yet I see her resiliency, her ability to shrug off the devastation and joke about herself, "It's hard to kill an old thing like me." I think this is a strong person.

---

against the dike, panting and very pale. He had opened his coat and he had a little bag from which he was taking out strips of cloth and a bottle of something. And again he spoke, and again she understood nothing. Then he made signs and she saw it was water he wanted, so she took up a broken pot from one of many blown about the street, and, going up the dike, she filled it with river water and brought it down again and washed his wound, and she tore off the strips he made from the rolls of bandaging. He knew how to put the cloth over the gaping wound and he made signs to her, and she followed these signs. All the time he was trying to tell her something, but she could understand nothing.

"You must be from the South, sir," she said. It was easy to see that he had education. He looked very clever. "I have heard your language is different from ours." She laughed a little to put him at his ease, but he only stared at her somberly with dull eyes. So she said brightly, "Now if I could find something for us to eat, it would be nice."

He did not answer. Indeed he lay back, panting still more heavily, and stared into space as though she had not spoken.

"You would be better with food," she went on. "And so would I," she added. She was beginning to feel unbearably hungry.

> "It's hard to kill an old thing like me," she remarked cheerfully.

It occurred to her that in the baker's shop there might be some bread. Even if it were dusty with fallen mortar, it would still be bread. She would go and see. But before she went she moved the soldier a little so that he lay in the edge of shadow cast by a willow tree that grew in the bank of the dike. Then she went to the baker's shop. The dogs were gone.

The baker's shop was, like everything else, in ruins. No one was there. At first she saw nothing but the mass of crumpled earthen walls. But then she remembered that the oven was just inside the door, and the door frame still stood erect, supporting one end of the roof. She stood in this frame, and, running her hand in underneath the fallen roof inside, she felt the wooden cover of the iron caldron.[5] Under this there might be steamed bread. She worked her arm delicately and carefully in. It took quite a long time, but, even so, clouds of lime and dust almost choked her. Nevertheless she was right. She squeezed her hand under the cover and felt the firm smooth skin of the big steamed bread rolls, and one by one she drew out four.

"It's hard to kill an old thing like me," she remarked cheerfully to no one, and she began to eat one of the rolls as she walked

---

5. A *caldron* is a large kettle.

Vocabulary
somberly (som′ bər lē) *adv.* in a gloomy manner

Teaching Options

Less-Proficient Readers Suggest that students make use of callouts to help them grasp key ideas in a story or article before they actually read the text.

Activity Using the quote in the callout, have students explain what they expect to happen in the story. Does it foreshadow more difficulties for Mrs. Wang, or does it predict a happy ending? **L1**

Additional Resources
📁 *Inclusion Strategies*

back. If she had a bit of garlic and a bowl of tea—but one couldn't have everything in these times.

It was at this moment that she heard voices. When she came in sight of the soldier, she saw surrounding him a crowd of other soldiers, who had apparently come from nowhere. They were staring down at the wounded soldier, whose eyes were now closed.

"Where did you get this Japanese, Old Mother?" they shouted at her.

"What Japanese?" she asked, coming to them.

"This one!" they shouted.

"Is he a Japanese?" she cried in the greatest astonishment. "But he looks like us—his eyes are black, his skin—"

"Japanese!" one of them shouted at her.

"Well," she said quietly, "he dropped out of the sky."

"Give me that bread!" another shouted.

"Take it," she said, "all except this one for him."

"A Japanese monkey eat good bread?" the soldier shouted.

"I suppose he is hungry also," old Mrs. Wang replied. She began to dislike these men. But then, she had always disliked soldiers.

"I wish you would go away," she said. "What are you doing here? Our village has always been peaceful."

"It certainly looks very peaceful now," one of the men said, grinning, "as peaceful as a grave. Do you know who did that, Old Mother? The Japanese!"

"I suppose so," she agreed. Then she asked, "Why? That's what I don't understand."

"Why? Because they want our land, that's why!"

"Our land!" she repeated. "Why, they can't have our land!"

"Never!" they shouted.

But all this time while they were talking and chewing the bread they had divided among themselves, they were watching the eastern horizon.

"Why do you keep looking east?" old Mrs. Wang now asked.

"The Japanese are coming from there," the man replied who had taken the bread.

"Are you running away from them?" she asked, surprised.

"There are only a handful of us," he said apologetically. "We were left to guard a village—Pao An, in the county of—"

"I know that village," old Mrs. Wang interrupted. "You needn't tell me. I was a girl there. How is the old Pao who keeps the tea shop in the main street? He's my brother."

"Everybody is dead there," the man replied. "The Japanese have taken it—a great army of men came with their foreign guns and tanks, so what could we do?"

"Of course, only run," she agreed. Nevertheless she felt dazed and sick. So he was dead, that one brother she had left! She was now the last of her father's family.

But the soldiers were straggling away again leaving her alone.

"They'll be coming, those little black dwarfs," they were saying. "We'd best go on."

Nevertheless, one lingered a moment, the one who had taken the bread, to stare down at the young wounded man, who lay with his eyes shut, not having moved at all.

"Is he dead?" he inquired. Then, before Mrs. Wang could answer, he pulled a short knife out of his belt. "Dead or not, I'll give him a punch or two with this—"

INTERDISCIPLINARY CONNECTION

Social Studies Mention that many conflicts between nations have been caused by the desire for land. People, of course, need land to live on and grow food on, so land is vital to survival.

Activity Have students research conflicts between sets of states or nations and determine whether land was a major cause of the conflict. If so, have them identify the specific issues involved. Conflicts that students might look into are ones between mainland China and Taiwan or China and Tibet. Have students report on their findings orally or in a written paper. **L2**

With the founding of the People's Republic of China in 1949, much of the country's art was infused with political content. In recent years, however, Chinese art has been less political.

Viewing Response *Carte blanche means "the freedom to use one's own judgment," and the painting shows freedom in nature.*

The Noble Eightfold Path is a dominant theme in Buddhism. Following this path consists of: right views, right intentions, right speech, right action, right livelihood, right effort, right-mindedness, and right contemplation.

Y Author's Craft

CHARACTERIZATION Ask students for a word that identifies Mrs. Wang's thoughts on and actions toward this Japanese pilot. *(Motherly, caring, and kind describe Mrs. Wang's actions and her desire to make him better.)*

Teaching Options

LITERATURE & HUMANITIES

To help focus students' thinking on the themes and conflicts in this story, have them examine the painting *Both Members of This Club* on page 433 of *American Art History and Culture* and discuss its placement in an illustrated version of this story.

Carte Blanche, 1990. Bonnie Kwan Huo. Watercolor, 23.5 x 36.5 cm. Private collection.

Viewing the painting: Look up the meaning of this painting's title and discuss whether you think it is appropriate. How does this landscape differ from the one in the story?

But old Mrs. Wang pushed his arm away. "No, you won't," she said with authority. "If he is dead, then there is no use in sending him into purgatory all in pieces. I am a good Buddhist myself."

The man laughed. "Oh well, he is dead," he answered; and then, seeing his comrades already at a distance, he ran after them.

A Japanese, was he? Old Mrs. Wang, left alone with this inert figure, looked at him <u>tentatively</u>. He was very young, she could see, now that his eyes were closed. His hand, limp in unconsciousness, looked like a boy's hand, unformed and still growing. She felt his wrist but could <u>discern</u> no pulse. She leaned over him and held to his lips the half of her roll which she had not eaten.

"Eat," she said very loudly and distinctly. "Bread!"

Vocabulary
tentatively (ten′ tə tiv lē) *adv.* hesitantly; uncertainly
discern (di surn′) *v.* to detect or recognize

LIFE SKILLS CONNECTION

Decision Making Mrs. Wang is strong and consistent in protecting the young pilot. She never wavers in her decision.

Activity Have students work in groups to discuss how people make decisions when under pressure. Suggest that students consider ideas on the topic that they have heard and read about as well as those from their own experiences.

Encourage each group to make a list of character traits that may be helpful in difficult situations and a list of those that may be detrimental in the same situation. Let groups share their examples with the class as a whole. **L2 COLLAB. LEARN.**

But there was no answer. Evidently he was dead. He must have died while she was getting the bread out of the oven.

There was nothing to do then but to finish the bread herself. And when that was done, she wondered if she ought not to follow after Little Pig and his wife and all the villagers. The sun was mounting and it was growing hot. If she were going, she had better go. But first she would climb the dike and see what the direction was. They had gone straight west, and as far as the eye could look westward was a great plain. She might even see a good-sized crowd miles away. Anyway, she could see the next village, and they might all be there.

So she climbed the dike slowly, getting very hot. There was a slight breeze on top of the dike and it felt good. She was shocked to see the river very near the top of the dike. Why, it had risen in the last hour!

Z "You old demon!" she said severely. Let the river god hear it if he liked. He was evil, that he was—to threaten flood when there had been all this other trouble.

She stooped and bathed her cheeks and her wrists. The water was quite cold, as though with fresh rains somewhere. Then she stood up and gazed around her. To the west there was nothing except in the far distance the soldiers still half-running, and beyond them the blur of the next village, which stood on a long rise of ground. She had better set out for that village. Doubtless Little Pig and his wife were there waiting for her.

Just as she was about to climb down and start out, she saw something on the eastern horizon. It was at first only an immense cloud of dust. But, as she stared at it, very quickly it became a lot of black dots and shining spots. Then she saw what it was. It was a lot of men—an army. Instantly she knew what army.

"That's the Japanese," she thought. Yes, above them were the buzzing silver planes. They circled about, seeming to search for someone.

"I don't know who you're looking for," she muttered, "unless it's me and Little Pig and his wife. We're the only ones left. You've already killed my brother Pao."

She had almost forgotten that Pao was dead. Now she remembered it <u>acutely</u>. He had such a nice shop—always clean, and the tea good and the best meat dumplings to be had and the price always the same. Pao was a good man. Besides, what about his wife and his seven children? Doubtless they were all killed, too. Now these Japanese were looking for her. It occurred to her that on the dike she could easily be seen. So she clambered hastily down. **AA**

It was when she was about halfway down that she thought of the water gate. This old river—it had been a curse to them since time began. Why should it not make up a little now for all the wickedness it had done? It was plotting wickedness again, trying to steal over its banks. Well, why not? She wavered a moment. It was a pity, of course, that the young dead Japanese would be swept into the flood. He was a nice-looking boy, and she had saved him from being stabbed. It was not quite the same as saving his life, of course, but still it was a little the same. If he had been **BB**

Vocabulary

acutely (ə kūt′ lē) *adv.* sharply and with intensity

RESOLUTION Ask students how they feel about the falling action and what it suggests about the possible outcome of the story. *(Mrs. Wang's bravery and kindness to the very end will probably make them admire her character.)*

DD **Active Reading**

RESPOND Ask students how they feel about the story's ending. *(Some may feel sad and disappointed that Mrs. Wang dies. Others may feel she dies a hero's death; because her attitude was good, they do not feel bad.)*

At the MOVIES

The following video will tell students more about the author of this story. Be sure to preview the video for appropriateness for your class.

• *Pearl Buck: The Woman, the World, and Two Good Earths**

**Also available in the Glencoe Literature *Video Library*.

Teaching Options

Did You Know?
A *sluice* is a gate or valve used to control the flow of water through an artificial channel, which is also called a sluice.

CC

alive, he would have been saved. She went over to him and tugged at him until he lay well under the top of the bank. Then she went down again.

She knew perfectly how to open the water gate. Any child knew how to open the sluice for crops. But she knew also how to swing open the whole gate. The question was, could she open it quickly enough to get out of the way?

"I'm only one old woman," she muttered. She hesitated a second more. Well, it would be a pity not to see what sort of a baby Little Pig's wife would have, but one could not see everything. She had seen a great deal in this life. There was an end to what one could see, anyway.

She glanced again to the east. There were the Japanese coming across the plain. They were a long clear line of black, dotted with thousands of glittering points. If she opened this gate, the impetuous water would roar toward them, rushing into the plains, rolling into a wide lake, drowning them, maybe. Certainly they could not

keep on marching nearer and nearer to her, and to Little Pig and his wife who were waiting for her. Well, Little Pig and his wife—they would wonder about her—but they would never dream of this. It would make a good story—she would have enjoyed telling it.

She turned resolutely to the gate. Well, some people fought with airplanes and some with guns, but you could fight with a river, too, if it were a wicked one like this one. She wrenched out a huge wooden pin. It was slippery with silvery green moss. The rill[6] of water burst into a strong jet. When she wrenched one more pin, the rest would give way themselves. She began pulling at it, and felt it slip a little from its hole.

"I might be able to get myself out of purgatory with this," she thought, "and maybe they'll let me have that old man of mine, too. What's a hand of his to all this? Then we'll—"

The pin slipped away suddenly, and the gate burst flat against her and knocked her breath away. She had only time to gasp, to the river:

"Come on, you old demon!"

Then she felt it seize her and lift her up to the sky. It was beneath her and around her. It rolled her joyfully hither and thither, and then, holding her close and enfolded, it went rushing against the enemy. DD

---

6. A *rill* is a small stream.

Vocabulary
impetuous (im pech′ oo əs) *adj.* marked by force or violent action

---

MEETING INDIVIDUAL NEEDS **GIFTED AND TALENTED ACTIVITY**

Handscroll Painting Students might be interested in learning more about Chinese and Japanese cultures. Have students research handscroll painting in Chinese and Japanese art. Possible sources of information include encyclopedias, art histories, and Internet Web sites.

Activity Have students work in teams or individually, either to prepare a presentation on handscroll art, providing samples of this form, or to create their own handscroll painting or drawing. Students can share their information or artwork with the class. **L2** **COLLAB. LEARN.**

The Boy and His Grandfather

Rudolfo A. Anaya

In the old days it was not unusual to find several generations living together in one home. Usually, everyone lived in peace and harmony, but this situation caused problems for one man whose household included, besides his wife and small son, his elderly father.

It so happened that the daughter-in-law took a dislike to the old man. He was always in the way, she said, and she insisted he be removed to a small room apart from the house.

Because the old man was out of sight, he was often neglected. Sometimes he even went hungry. They took poor care of him, and in winter the old man often suffered from the cold. One day the little grandson visited his grandfather.

"My little one," the grandfather said, "go and find a blanket and cover me. It is cold and I am freezing."

The small boy ran to the barn to look for a blanket, and there he found a rug.

"Father, please cut this rug in half," he asked his father.

"Why? What are you going to do with it?"

"I'm going to take it to my grandfather because he is cold."

"Well, take the entire rug," replied his father.

"No," his son answered, "I cannot take it all. I want you to cut it in half so I can save the other half for you when you are as old as my grandfather. Then I will have it for you so you will not be cold."

His son's response was enough to make the man realize how poorly he had treated his own father. The man then brought his father back into his home and ordered that a warm room be prepared. From that time on he took care of his father's needs and visited him frequently every day.

❖

Active Reading

PREDICT In many stories a young person learns something from an older person. After reading the title, have students predict what this story is about.

FYI

The Aging of America
In 1996, 69 million Americans were under 18 years of age while almost 34 million were 65 or older. Over the next 50 years, those groups will become about equal in number: 95 million will be 18 and under; 96 million will be 65 and over.

Literary Elements

ALLEGORY This story is an allegory, a narrative in which characters and events stand for abstract ideas or forces, so that the literal sense has a parallel symbolic sense. Ask students who the grandfather and the father might represent. *(The grandfather might represent all old people; the father, the next generation.)*

Thematic Focus

At the Crossroads Have students discuss what type of crossroads face Mrs. Wang in "The Old Demon" and the father in "The Boy and His Grandfather"?

ASSESSMENT OPTIONS
📁 *Quick Checks,* p. 44

Reading Minilesson

Identifying Main Idea and Supporting Details A change of attitude is a significant human accomplishment and a common occurrence in fiction. Suggest that events leading to a major change in a character often point to the main idea.

Activity Have students use the questions below to identify the details that lead to the main idea of the story. **L2**

- Which character changes? *(The boy's father.)*
- In what way does the character change? *(He treats his own father with dignity.)*
- What is the story's main idea? *(Be kind to your elders.)*

Additional Resources
📁 *Reading Workbook,* pp. 77–78

CONNECTING TO OTHER SELECTIONS
For a teaching strategy that connects "The Boy and His Grandfather" to "A Crush," turn to page 27 in the *Theme Two Planning Guide.*

Personal Response

Some students may feel Mrs. Wang should have tried to save herself. Others may feel she was right to make sacrifices to save others. It would be hard to say the boy did not do the right thing. He was trying to be kind to his grandfather and to prepare to be kind years later to his father.

Analyzing Literature

1. The two forces endangering the village are the river and the Japanese army.
2. All the villagers except Mrs. Wang run.
3. Mrs. Wang's final action is to open the floodgates to keep the Japanese army from catching her family.
4. When the boy says he will keep half the rug for when his father becomes old, the father realizes how unkind he has been to his own father.
5. She fears the river more because she has seen its evil powers. She has never seen the Japanese army do anything.
6. Perhaps, as the leader of the village, she feels the need to patrol the area and see if anyone else remains. Perhaps she just doesn't want to run from her home.
7. She makes the decision because it is the only way she can preserve the next generation.
8. Be kind to old people because some day you will be old and will look for kindness.
9. The title reflects the story in that the demon, which had caused so much havoc for the villagers, now becomes their ally.
10. Remind students that the enemy need not be as threatening as a raging river or a hostile army.

Responding to Literature

PERSONAL RESPONSE

- ◆ Do you think Mrs. Wang took the correct action at the end of the story? Why or why not?
- ◆ Do you think the grandson in "The Boy and His Grandfather" did the right thing? Why or why not?

Analyzing Literature

RECALL

1. What two forces endanger the village in "The Old Demon"?
2. What do all the villagers do when the bombs begin to fall?
3. What is Mrs. Wang's final action?
4. What makes the father in "The Boy and His Grandfather" change his attitude about the grandfather?

INTERPRET

5. What does Mrs. Wang fear more—the river or the Japanese? Explain your answer.
6. In your opinion, why does Mrs. Wang choose to stay after the village is bombed?
7. In your opinion, why does Mrs. Wang make the decision she makes at the end of the story?
8. "The Boy and His Grandfather" is a story that teaches a lesson. Write that lesson in one sentence.

EVALUATE AND CONNECT

9. Why is the title "The Old Demon" appropriate for the story?
10. **Theme Connection** Do you think that decisions you have had to make in your life have prepared you to face an enemy with courage, as Mrs. Wang does in "The Old Demon"? Explain.

LITERARY ELEMENTS

Theme

Some stories, poems, or novels have a stated **theme** in which the main idea is expressed as a general statement. More frequently, however, literary works have an **implied theme,** which is revealed through plot, character, setting, or point of view. In "The Old Demon," the implied theme is revealed through the character of Mrs. Wang.

1. How do Mrs. Wang's actions throughout the story show that she feels it is her duty to protect her family and village?
2. What do you think is the implied theme of "The Old Demon"? What is the implied theme of "The Boy and His Grandfather"?

● See **Literary Terms Handbook,** p. R11.

LITERARY ELEMENTS

1. She looks after the dike and sends Little Pig's wife away to protect her.
2. The theme of "The Old Demon" is that some people live by their principles, regardless of the consequences. The theme of "The Boy and His Grandfather" is that we should care for the elderly because we too will be old some day.

Additional Resources

📖 *Literary Elements Transparency 44*

Literature and Writing

Writing About Literature
Analyzing Descriptions Pearl S. Buck knew the force of the Yellow River. She wanted to portray its power in her story. Write a paragraph that expresses your opinion about the effectiveness of her descriptions. Use examples from the story.

Personal Writing
Reflection on Personal Courage Recall the discussion you had in the **Focus Activity** on page 482. Then write a brief essay reflecting upon how you imagine you would respond to a needy person.

Chinese cities as well as the countryside were affected by this flood in the 1930s.

Extending Your Response

Literature Groups
Debating a Plan of Action Did Mrs. Wang make the right decision? Work with your group to decide whether you are for or against her action. Find another group that has chosen the opposite stand and hold a debate.

Interdisciplinary Activity
Social Studies Find out all you can about China's major rivers—their names, locations, tributaries (smaller rivers that flow into them), and how they are used by the Chinese. Then draw a map of the river systems for the class. Include the names of the rivers and any major cities along them.

Listening and Speaking
The Art of Storytelling "The Boy and His Grandfather" is the kind of story that one generation passes on to the next orally. Prepare your own telling of the story. Practice telling it until you no longer need notes. Then invite family, friends, or young children to hear your version.

Reading Further
To read more about China, try these books:

Homesick: My Own Story by Jean Fritz

The Remarkable Journey of Prince Jen by Lloyd Alexander

📖 **Save your work for your portfolio.**

Literature and Writing

Writing About Literature
Students' paragraphs should
- state their opinions of the effectiveness of the description.
- quote passages and tell why each is effective or not.

Personal Writing
Students' essays should
- be clear in telling how they would respond.
- illustrate with specific situations or circumstances.

Extending Your Response

Literature Groups Students might focus on Mrs. Wang's independence in making the decision alone and on her history of caring for others. **COLLAB. LEARN.**

Interdisciplinary Activity
Encyclopedias, the Internet, and atlases are some of the sources to which students can go for information. Treatments of China's agriculture and industry should cover the country's use of the rivers.

Listening and Speaking
Suggest that students may modify and modernize the story to suit their own situations.

AT THE CROSSROADS 🦋 497

Skill Minilessons

Skill Minilessons

GRAMMAR AND LANGUAGE
PARTICIPLES AND PARTICIPIAL PHRASES

Some possibilities

p. 484: "The evening was beautiful, the sky was so clear and still that the willows <u>overhanging the dike</u> were reflected even in the muddy water." Modifies *willows*.

p. 484: "and she had come, <u>blushing and twisting her hands together,</u> to hide among the women." Modifies *she*.

READING AND THINKING
SUMMARIZING

Key events: daughter-in-law dislikes old man; he is made to live apart from others; old man's request for a blanket; the boy's request of his father; the father's reaction.

VOCABULARY
THE PREFIX *-mal*

1. b   4. e
2. a   5. d
3. c

Additional Resources

Grammar and Language Workbook, pp. 167–170

Grammar and Composition Handbook, Lesson 9.1

Writer's Choice, Lesson 15.1

Reading Workbook, pp. 77–78

Vocabulary Practice, p. 30

GRAMMAR AND LANGUAGE • PARTICIPLES AND PARTICIPIAL PHRASES

A **present participle** is formed by adding *-ing* to a verb. A **past participle** is formed by adding *-ed* to a verb.

A participle often functions as an adjective to modify nouns or pronouns.

> *the ruined village*
> *burning houses*

A **participial phrase** is a group of words that includes a participle and other words that complete its meaning. For example:

So, *leaning on her bamboo pipe,* she made her way slowly across the fields.

The participial phrase *leaning on her bamboo pipe* modifies the pronoun *she.*

PRACTICE Review "The Old Demon" to find two sentences having participial phrases. Copy each sentence, underline the participial phrase, and tell what word or words it modifies.

● For more about participles, see **Language Handbook,** pp. R29–R30.

READING AND THINKING • SUMMARIZING

When you summarize a piece of writing, you state the main ideas of the selection in your own words. You omit unimportant details so that the summary is much briefer than the original piece. For example, in a summary of "The Old Demon," you would be sure to include that the pilot was a wounded Japanese soldier. You would not need to mention that he pointed to the dogs before he fell on the ground.

PRACTICE Write a summary of "The Boy and His Grandfather." Be sure to include all the key events in chronological order. When you edit your writing, check that you have written everything in your own words and that you have deleted any unimportant details.

● For more about summarizing, see **Reading Handbook,** p. R88.

VOCABULARY • THE PREFIX *mal-*

Something that is *malicious* always involves an effort to cause harm in a bad or evil way. The prefix *mal-,* which means "evil" or "bad," gives this word its meaning.

PRACTICE Use what you know about the prefix *mal-* and familiar base words to match each word on the left with its meaning.

1. malnutrition   a. dissatisfied
2. malcontent   b. poor nourishment
3. maltreatment   c. abuse; injury
4. malodorous   d. broken; not working
5. malfunctioning   e. bad-smelling

✔ ASSESSMENT OPTIONS

Quick Checks, p. 44

Selection and Theme Assessment, pp. 77–78

Performance Assessment, p. 41

Testmaker

Using Pronouns

Every pronoun gets its meaning from a noun, or another pronoun, called its antecedent. It must be clear exactly *which* antecedent a pronoun refers to. In addition, personal pronouns have different forms depending on whether they are used in a sentence as its subject or as the object of a verb or a preposition.

Subjective form:	I	he	she	we	they
Objective form:	me	him	her	us	them

Problem 1   A pronoun that can refer to more than one antecedent

Before Felix's fight with Antonio, he goes to stay with his aunt.

[Who goes to stay with Aunt Lucy? *He* could refer to *Felix* or *Antonio*.]

     Solution A   Use a noun in place of the pronoun.

Before his fight with Antonio, Felix goes to stay with his aunt.

     Solution B   Rewrite the sentence so that any pronoun reference is clear.

Felix goes to stay with his aunt before his fight with Antonio.

Problem 2   Confusion between subject pronouns and object pronouns

Him and Antonio know they must forget their friendship during the fight. After the bell, the trainers must pull Antonio and he apart.

     Solution   In the first sentence, use the subject pronoun *he* in the subject of the sentence. In the second sentence, "Antonio and he" is the object of the verb *pull.* Use the object pronoun *him.*

He and Antonio know they must forget their friendship during the fight. After the bell, the trainers must pull Antonio and him apart.

● For more about pronouns, see **Language Handbook,** p. R17.

EXERCISE

Rewrite each sentence as needed. If a sentence has no pronoun problems, write *C.*

1. The children saw raindrops as they fell from the sky.
2. The teacher assumed that Margot and them had gone outside.
3. As the children lay down on the jungle plants, they sighed and squeaked.
4. "All Summer in a Day" caused a disagreement between my friend Lucy and I.

Objective

• To recognize and use subjective and objective pronouns correctly

Teaching Strategies

After students read the problems and solutions, point out that another way to determine correct pronoun usage is to isolate the pronouns. For example: *She and I both love that song.* *(She loves that song; I love that song.)* They called him and me into the office. *(They called him into the office; They called me into the office.)*

Exercise

1. The children saw raindrops falling from the sky.
2. The teacher assumed that Margot and they had gone outside.
3. The children sighed and squeaked as they lay down on the jungle plants.
4. "All Summer in a Day" caused a disagreement between my friend Lucy and me.

Additional Resources

📖 *Grammar and Language Workbook,* pp. 107–108

📖 *Grammar and Composition Handbook,* Lesson 4.2

📖 *Writer's Choice,* Lesson 11.3

Teaching Options

Writing *Minilesson*

Plot Treatment Explain to students that a plot treatment is a short summary or outline of the main events in a story, a film, or a play.

Activity Ask students to imagine they are screenwriters and have them write brief plot treatments for the selections they have liked best so far in Theme Five. Have them work in pairs to discuss the plot of the selection they have chosen and to write a summary of its main events in ten complete sentences. To extend the activity, ask the partners to write a brief character description for each character in the story they choose. **L2**

Additional Resources

📖 *Writer's Choice,* Lesson 4.1

Objective

• To understand the elements of drama

Teaching Strategies

Help students make a list of all the places in their communities where drama can be seen. Have them use available resources to create a class phone book of all the theaters, play-houses, and dramatic arts organizations that operate locally. Encourage students to take advantage of performances that might be free to the public or to students.

Dialogue Deliver the following line of dialogue: "Nice shot, kid. That was one in a million!" Ask students if they can name the film in which the line was said. *(Star Wars)* Explain that bits of dialogue from plays and films often enter popular culture and become part of the way we speak. Play a game in which one student says a line of dialogue he or she likes and classmates guess which popular film, TV program, or play it comes from.

DRAMA

I f you've ever seen a live **drama,** you know that it can "grab" you. Drama, whether a stage play, a movie, or a TV show, brings literature to life.

These strangely shaped pillars are masses of gas and dust so enormous that any one of them would dwarf our sun with all of its planets. Scientists believe that new stars are born in such masses of interstellar matter.

FEATURES OF DRAMA

On the printed page, drama looks different from other literature. A drama appears as a **script**—a set of words and instructions to be used by actors. Longer scripts are divided into sections called **acts,** and each act may be divided into smaller sections called **scenes.** Each act or scene usually includes the following features:

MODEL: "The Monsters Are Due on Maple Street"

DIALOGUE—lines spoken by characters

STEVE. What do you mean? What are you talking about?

TOMMY. They don't want us to leave. That's why they shut everything off.

MEETING INDIVIDUAL NEEDS ENGLISH LANGUAGE LEARNERS

Understanding Drama The elements and features of drama can be culture-bound and therefore difficult for English language learners to grasp.

Activity You may wish to conduct an International Drama Festival in your class and have students work in groups to report on traditional theater from around the world. Examples might include shadow puppets in Indonesia,

Bunraku and Kabuki theater in Japan, Chinese opera, Cambodian ballet, and folkloric dancing in Mexico. Encourage students to create the elements of this theater in a live production of their own. **COLLAB. LEARN.**

Additional Resources
📁 *English Language Learners Sourcebook*

ELEMENTS OF DRAMA

Dramatic Conflicts in *Star Wars*		
Internal		
Luke Skywalker's obligation to stay home and help his uncle	vs.	his need to "try his wings"
Luke's desire to master the Force	vs.	his inexperience and lack of confidence
External		
Rebel Alliance	vs.	the Galactic Empire
Obi Wan Kenobe	vs.	Darth Vader
Han Solo's Millennium Falcon	vs.	the Storm Troopers' tie-fighters

The elements of drama, like the elements of fiction, include character, setting, theme, and plot. (For more about these elements, see **Literary Handbook,** pages R1–R11.) In a dramatic plot, look especially for **conflicts,** or problems that characters must deal with. Some conflicts are **external**—clashes between two characters, or between a character and an outside force. Other conflicts are **internal**—clashes between opposing feelings within a character. The chart shows some external and internal conflicts from a movie that you probably know.

STAGE DIRECTIONS—brief phrases, often in italics, telling actors how to move or speak; notes concerning sets, props, sound effects, lighting; and, for films and teleplays, camera instructions

> **STEVE.** [*Raising his voice and looking toward porch.*] Guess it was a meteor, honey. Came awful close, didn't it?
>
> **MRS. BRAND.** Too close for my money! Much too close.
>
> [*The camera pans across the various porches to people who stand there watching and talking in low tones.*]

CAST OF CHARACTERS—a list at the beginning of a play naming, and sometimes giving brief descriptions of, the characters

> **CHARACTERS**
> **NARRATOR**
> **STEVE BRAND**
> **MRS. BRAND**
> **DON MARTIN**
> **TOMMY**

AT THE CROSSROADS 🐾 501

Elements of Drama You may wish to prepare English language learners for the table on page 501 of their books by showing all or part of *Star Wars.* Write the names of the main characters on the board and familiarize students with the basic story line before they view the movie.

Stage Directions Enact a short scene and ask students to write what happened, using stage directions like the ones in their books. For example, you could enter the classroom, look at the class, exclaim that you are in the wrong room, and run out. Students might write: Teacher: [looking at the students with a shocked expression] "I'm in the wrong room!"

Cast of Characters Have students draw up a cast of characters for one of the selections they have read in Theme Five. Explain that this would be necessary if they were to rewrite the selection as a play, teleplay, or film script.

Technology Option

Drama Table

Students can use word processing software to create a table of the three main features of drama. Have each student open a new document and insert a four-column table with the following headings: *Title, Dialogue, Stage Directions,* and *Cast of Characters.*

For each new piece of drama students read, have them add a new row and complete the chart with their analysis of the three main features of drama. Students can use their tables to review the dramas they read or to help them compare and contrast various texts. **L2**

Title	Dialogue	Stage Directions	Cast of Characters

Active Reading Strategies

Objective

- To understand and apply strategies for reading drama

Teach the Strategies

Ask students to list the plays they have seen. Find out if they have ever read a play. Discuss the difference between watching and reading a play.

Predict

Have students watch the first half of a sitcom. Ask them to predict the outcome and write down the clues they used to predict what would happen. Then have them watch the second half of the sitcom. Discuss the accuracy of their predictions.

Visualize

Suggest that students imagine they are camera operators shooting the play. As they read, their imaginations "pan" the scene, action, and characters of the drama.

Question

Have students jot down questions that occur to them as they read.

Respond

Discuss how people respond to what they see, hear, and feel when they are watching a drama. Remind them that these same responses are felt when reading a drama.

ACTIVE READING MODEL

Active Reading Strategies

Tips for Reading a Drama

When reading a drama, skillful readers use strategies that help them follow the action of the play. These strategies also help readers by prompting them to question and evaluate what they read.

- For more about these and other reading strategies, see **Reading Handbook,** pp. R82–R96.

PREDICT

Combine clues in the play with what you already know to make educated guesses about what will happen next.

Ask Yourself . . .

- What action will this character take?
- What will happen next?

VISUALIZE

Reading the stage directions carefully will help you visualize the action of the play.

Ask Yourself . . .

- How does this scene look?

QUESTION

Keep asking yourself questions to help you clarify what is happening. Ask questions about the motivations of the characters.

Ask Yourself . . .

- What is really happening in this scene?
- What causes that character to act this way?

RESPOND

Don't wait until the play is over to respond to it. Think about what the play means to you while you are still reading it.

Say to Yourself . . .

- If I were this character, I would _____ .
- I'd like to ask the playwright why _____ .

Reading Journal

Who Are the Monsters?

Rod Serling's teleplay "The Monsters Are Due on Maple Street" provides readers with a glimpse of a small community unraveled by fears and prejudices. Invite students to discuss whether people should be more frightened by aliens and the world outside our universe or by the human race.

Activity As they read "The Monsters Are Due on Maple Street," invite students to create a chart in their reading journals that lists their predictions. After each prediction, have students jot down how each event actually turned out. After reading, invite students to tell what they think the major characters should have done.

REVIEW

Pause every page or two to think about what you have read. Summarize what is happening so you are sure you understand what has happened so far in the drama.

Ask Yourself . . .

- What happened in this scene?

- Do I understand what the playwright has written here?

EVALUATE

To evaluate means to make judgments. You can evaluate what the playwright has done during your reading as well as after you have finished the play.

Ask Yourself . . .

- Are these characters believable?

- Why did the playwright decide to have the plot take this turn?

- Would I enjoy seeing this play?

APPLYING THE STRATEGIES

Read the following teleplay, "The Monsters Are Due on Maple Street." Use the **Active Reading Model** notes in the margins as you read. Write your responses on a separate piece of paper or use stick-on notes.

AT THE CROSSROADS 503

Review

One way to help students review the drama "The Monsters Are Due on Maple Street" is to have them identify the scenes within each act. They can use stick-on notes to indicate where a new scene begins. Have them ask themselves the review questions in their books and other questions they come up with at the end of each scene. Encourage students to practice their review skills by reading a scene and summarizing it for a classmate who hasn't read the scene yet.

Evaluate

One way to help students evaluate the drama is to have them think about what they've learned about the characters' personality traits; what the sequence of events was before the plot took a certain turn; and whether the plot had a narrative hook to catch their attention.

Before Reading

Objectives

- To read and enjoy a television play
- To identify and understand the elements of a teleplay
- To write about conflict in the play

Skills

Reading/Thinking: Drawing Conclusions; Inferring; Making Critical Judgments; Classifying; Comparing and Contrasting; Visualizing; Evaluating; Judging the Credibility of a Source; Setting a Purpose for Reading; Synthesizing; Generalizing

Writing: Narrating; Different Point of View; Narrative; Analytical Writing

Vocabulary: Root Meanings; Synonyms; Idioms; Base Words

Grammar/Language: Using End Marks; Apostrophes; Complete Sentences

Listening/Speaking: Oral Reading; News Broadcast

Life Skills: Understanding Crowd Behavior

Collaboration: Literature Groups

Motivating
→OPTIONS

Selection Focus Transparency 45: Have students think about and discuss the concept of "monsters."

Focus Activity: Have students describe the personalities, hobbies, and oddities of people living in their neighborhoods.

ACTIVE READING MODEL

Before You Read
The Monsters Are Due on Maple Street

MEET ROD SERLING

Although Rod Serling became best known as the creator and host of *The Twilight Zone*, a popular fantasy and science-fiction television series, he was first and foremost a writer. Between 1951 and 1955, he wrote more than seventy TV dramas. Three of Serling's six Emmy Awards were for pre-*Twilight Zone* plays. In the five seasons *The Twilight Zone* was on the air from 1959 to 1964, Serling wrote nearly two out of every three of the show's 156 plays. The following selection was one of those plays.

Rod Serling was born in New York in 1924 and died in 1975.

FOCUS ACTIVITY

Lights flicker on and off. Cars start and stop. Telephones ring and go dead. Imagine these things happening in your town.

Journal
Describe how you think your neighbors would react to a series of strange occurrences on your street.

Setting a Purpose
Read to find out what happens on Maple Street.

BACKGROUND

Did You Know? "The Monsters Are Due on Maple Street" is a play written especially for television. The stage notes, written specifically for the television camera, include

- *pan* to turn the camera to follow a moving person or object
- *cut* to switch from one scene to another
- *close-up* to move the camera close to the subject, such as a person's face
- *long shot* to film a subject from a long distance away

VOCABULARY PREVIEW

reflective (ri flek′ tiv) *adj.* showing serious and careful thinking; thoughtful; p. 507

intimidated (in tim′ ə dāt′ əd) *adj.* made timid or fearful; bullied; p. 510

instill (in stil′) *v.* to put in gradually, little by little; p. 510

validity (və lid′ ə tē) *n.* state of being supported by facts; truth; p. 511

defiant (di fī′ ənt) *adj.* showing bold resistance to authority or an opponent; p. 511

antagonism (an tag′ ə niz′ əm) *n.* hostility; p. 511

incriminate (in krim′ ə nāt′) *v.* to show the guilt of; p. 515

legitimate (li jit′ ə mit) *adj.* that which follows the rules; lawful; p. 517

explicit (eks plis′ it) *adj.* clearly expressed; p. 524

prejudice (prej′ ə dis) *n.* an unfavorable opinion or judgment formed unfairly; p. 524

RESOURCE MANAGER

Lesson Planning Resource
The *Theme Five Planning Guide* (pp. 47–54) provides additional lesson notes and reduced versions of all print resources.

📁 **Other Print Resources**
- Active Reading Guide, p. 45
- Vocabulary Practice, p. 31
- Reading Workbook, p. 79–80
- Grammar and Language Workbook, pp. 55–56, 253–254, 273–274

- Grammar and Composition Handbook, Lessons 1.2, 13.1, 13.7
- Quick Checks, p. 45
- Selection and Theme Assessment, pp. 79–80
- Performance Assessment, p. 42
- Spanish Summaries, p. 45
- Spanish Translations
- Inclusion Strategies
- English Language Learners Sourcebook

🎮 **Transparencies**
- Selection Focus 45
- Literary Elements 45
- Grammar and Language 43–44

Technology
- 🎧 Audio Library
- 🎧 Spanish Audio Library
- 💻 Glencoe Literature Web Site
- 💾 Testmaker

THE MONSTERS ARE DUE ON MAPLE STREET

Rod Serling ∻

CHARACTERS

NARRATOR	FIGURE ONE	FIGURE TWO
STEVE BRAND	CHARLIE'S WIFE	MRS. GOODMAN
MRS. BRAND	TOMMY	WOMAN
DON MARTIN	SALLY, TOMMY'S MOTHER	MAN ONE
PETE VAN HORN	LES GOODMAN	MAN TWO
CHARLIE		

ACT I

[*Fade in on a shot of the night sky. The various nebulae[1] and planet bodies stand out in sharp, sparkling relief, and the camera begins a slow pan across the Heavens.*]

NARRATOR'S VOICE. There is a fifth dimension beyond that which is known to man. It is a dimension as vast as space, and as timeless as infinity. It is the middle ground between light and shadow—between science and superstition. And it lies between the pit of man's fears and the summit of his knowledge. This is the dimension of imagination. It is an area which we call The Twilight Zone.

---

1. The word *nebulae* (neb′ yə lē′) refers to bright, cloudlike masses of dust and gases that are visible in the night sky.

QUESTION

Why does the play begin with a shot of the night sky? What do the narrator's words tell you about the play that is about to begin?

A

A Active Reading

QUESTION (*The shot of the night sky indicates that the play is about outer space or the unknown. The narrator's words suggest it will be spooky.*)

Additional Resources

📁 *Active Reading Guide,* p. 45

🎧 *Audio Library*

🎧 *Spanish Audio Library*

SUMMARY

After a mysterious roar and a flash of light, all the homes on a suburban street lose power. What's more, the batteries in cars and radios go dead. People come into the street and discuss the situation. A boy says that in a similar situation he read about, monsters from outer space were responsible. When one neighbor's car starts, people accuse him of being responsible for the blackout or in league with those who are. They begin pointing the finger of blame at one another, and the accusations lead to physical violence. Figures observing the scene from far above explain that the best way to destroy a group of people is to plant a seed of dissension among them.

📁 *Spanish Summaries,* p. 45

Teaching Options

CONNECTING TO OTHER SELECTIONS

The chart at the right shows three ways to connect "The Monsters Are Due on Maple Street" to other selections in this book.

For specific teaching strategies, see the *Theme Five Planning Guide,* pages 50–51.

Connection	Title
Life Skills: Problem Solving	→ "Racing the Great Bear," p. 268
Thematic: A Delicate Balance	→ "We Are All One," p. 773
Literary: Dialogue	→ "Oh Broom, Get to Work," p. 383

B Active Reading

VISUALIZE (Ask students to visualize the street and then fill in the people: the man polishing his car; the neighbor watching; the Good Humor man.)

C Literary Elements

MOOD Ask students to describe the mood created by the narrator's exposition of the details in this setting. (It creates the calm, pleasant mood of a friendly neighborhood in a small town.)

D Literary Elements

NARRATOR Ask students what they think about the narrator's use of the future tense. (The narrator, unlike other characters, knows the future.)

E Literary Elements

TELEPLAY: *Stage Directions* Point out to students the detailed stage directions. Ask students what the purpose of these directions might be. (These directions indicate how characters move and act, and what sights and sounds are included in the scene.)

F Active Reading

PREDICT (It could have been a meteor, a large unidentified object, or a missile.)

At the MOVIES

"The Monsters Are Due on Maple Street" and another episode written by Rod Serling are available on the following video. Be sure to preview it for appropriateness for your class.

- *Twilight Zone: Volume 2*

Teaching Options

The Monsters Are Due On Maple Street

ACTIVE READING MODEL

▶ VISUALIZE

B Try to visualize the setting the playwright is describing. Can you see it?

[*The camera has begun to pan down until it passes the horizon and is on a sign which reads "Maple Street." Pan down until we are shooting down at an angle toward the street below. It's a tree-lined, quiet residential American street, very typical of the small town. The houses have front porches on which people sit and swing on gliders, conversing across from house to house.* STEVE BRAND *polishes his car parked in front of his house. His neighbor,* DON MARTIN, *leans against the fender watching him. A Good Humor man rides a bicycle and is just in the process of stopping to sell some ice cream to a couple of kids. Two women gossip on the front lawn. Another man waters his lawn.*]

C NARRATOR'S VOICE. Maple Street, U.S.A., late summer. A tree-lined little world of front porch gliders, hop scotch, the laughter of children, and the bell of an ice cream vendor.

[*There is a pause and the camera moves over to a shot of the Good Humor man and two small boys who are standing alongside, just buying ice cream.*]

D NARRATOR'S VOICE. At the sound of the roar and the flash of light it will be precisely 6:43 P.M. on Maple Street.

E [*At this moment one of the little boys,* TOMMY, *looks up to listen to a sound of a tremendous screeching roar from overhead. A flash of light plays on both their faces and then it moves down the street past lawns and porches and rooftops and then disappears. Various people leave their porches and stop what they're doing to stare up at the sky.* STEVE BRAND, *the man who's been polishing his car, now stands there transfixed,[2] staring upwards. He looks at* DON MARTIN, *his neighbor from across the street.*]

▶ PREDICT

F What do you think that flash of light was?

STEVE. What was that? A meteor?

DON. [*Nods.*] That's what it looked like. I didn't hear any crash though, did you?

STEVE. [*Shakes his head.*] Nope. I didn't hear anything except a roar.

MRS. BRAND. [*From her porch.*] Steve? What was that?

STEVE. [*Raising his voice and looking toward porch.*] Guess it was a meteor, honey. Came awful close, didn't it?

MRS. BRAND. Too close for my money! Much too close.

[*The camera pans across the various porches to people who stand there watching and talking in low tones.*]

---

2. To be *transfixed* is to be made motionless, as from wonder or fear.

MEETING INDIVIDUAL NEEDS — ENGLISH LANGUAGE LEARNERS

Idioms Explain to English language learners that idioms are expressions that should not be taken literally. For example "too close for my money" does not actually involve any money. It is an idiom, a way of saying "in my opinion."

Activity As students read the selection, have them look for additional examples of idioms. Other examples in the selection include *run a check on* (p. 512); *for laughs* (p. 516); *set a foot on* and *keep an eye on* (both on p. 517). Then have students work in small groups to compare the idioms they found and discuss what they mean. **COLLAB. LEARN.**

Additional Resources

📁 *English Language Learners Sourcebook*

Portrait of Orleans, 1950. Edward Hopper. Oil on canvas, 26 x 40 in. Fine Arts Museum of San Francisco.
Viewing the painting: In what ways is this street like the street in the teleplay?

G **NARRATOR'S VOICE.** Maple Street. Six-forty-four P.M. on a late September evening. [*A pause.*] Maple Street in the last calm and reflective moment . . . before the monsters came!

[*The camera slowly pans across the porches again. We see a man screwing a light bulb on a front porch, then getting down off the stool to flick the switch and finding that nothing happens.*
Another man is working on an electric power mower. He plugs in the plug, flicks on the switch of the power mower, off and on, with nothing happening.
Through the window of a front porch, we see a woman pushing her finger back and forth on the dial hook. Her voice is indistinct and distant, but intelligible and repetitive.]

WOMAN. Operator, operator, something's wrong on the phone, operator!

[*MRS. BRAND comes out on the porch and calls to STEVE.*]

MRS. BRAND. [*Calling.*] Steve, the power's off. I had the soup on the stove and the stove just stopped working.

WOMAN. Same thing over here. I can't get anybody on the phone either. The phone seems to be dead.

Vocabulary
reflective (ri flek′ tiv) *adj.* showing serious and careful thinking; thoughtful

QUESTION

What do these word-less actions suggest to you? What do you think is happening on Maple Street?

H

G **Critical Thinking**

MAKING CRITICAL JUDGMENTS Ask students why they think the author, through the narrator, tells us that the monsters came, eliminating any uncertainty and suspense about their coming. You may wish to share the following model to illustrate the thinking process in making critical judgments.

Model: The author tells us right away that the monsters came. So I have to conclude that the fact that they came was not the most important thing. Who they were, what they did, and why they came may be more important.

H **Active Reading**

QUESTION (*It seems that something has gone wrong in the neighborhood. Students may suggest that the monsters are planning to attack the people on Maple Street.*)

VIEWING THE PAINTING

Edward Hopper (1882–1967) worked for a time as a commercial illustrator, but he later gained fame as a central figure in the American Scene movement, expressing the emptiness and loneliness of town life.
Viewing Response *Like the street in the teleplay, Hopper's street looks normal and conventional on the surface.*

Reading *Minilesson*

Classifying Viewers of a teleplay often have to classify events based only on what they see. To help students do this, draw the diagram at the right on the board.

Happening at 1st House	Happening at 2nd House	Happening at 3rd House

Activity Ask students to identify the actions that take place at each house. Then have them tell what all these happenings have in common. **L2**

Additional Resources
📁 *Reading Workbook,* pp. 79–80

Literary Elements

I **Literary Elements**

TELEPLAY: *Stage Directions* Call attention to the word *VOICES*. Ask students what this word refers to. *(Various people on the street utter the short statements that follow. Because we do not see the people clearly, no names are associated with any of the utterances.)*

J **Active Reading**

PREDICT *(It couldn't be a power failure if the transistor radio is not working. Maybe more strange things will happen.)*

K **Literary Elements**

CHARACTERIZATION Ask students to give their impressions of the four characters, based on these comments. *(Steve seems inquisitive and thoughtful, trying to analyze the problem. Don seems more apt to come to a quick, simple conclusion. Charlie seems analytical, yet at the same time sounds a bit argumentative. The woman seems a bit of an alarmist—she is just restating the problem as everyone already knows it.)*

ACTIVE READING MODEL

PREDICT

Do you think it's just a power failure? What will happen next?

[*We look down on the street as we hear the voices creep up from below, small, mildly disturbed voices highlighting these kinds of phrases:*]

VOICES.
Electricity's off.
Phone won't work.
Can't get a thing on the radio.
My power mower won't move, won't work at all.
Radio's gone dead!

[*PETE VAN HORN, a tall, thin man, is seen standing in front of his house.*]

VAN HORN. I'll cut through the back yard . . . See if the power's still on on Floral Street. I'll be right back!

[*He walks past the side of his house and disappears into the back yard. The camera pans down slowly until we're looking at ten or eleven people standing around the street and overflowing to the curb and sidewalk. In the background is STEVE BRAND's car.*]

STEVE. Doesn't make sense. Why should the power go off all of a sudden, and the phone line?

DON. Maybe some sort of an electrical storm or something.

CHARLIE. That don't seem likely. Sky's just as blue as anything. Not a cloud. No lightning. No thunder. No nothing. How could it be a storm?

WOMAN. I can't get a thing on the radio. Not even the portable.

[*The people again murmur softly in wonderment and question.*]

CHARLIE. Well, why don't you go downtown and check with the police, though they'll probably think we're crazy or something. A little power failure and right away we get all flustered[3] and everything.

---

3. To be *flustered* is to be embarrassed, nervous, or confused.

Teaching Options

MEETING INDIVIDUAL NEEDS

MULTIPLE LEARNING STYLES

Spatial Mention that elements of setting and costumes can indicate the time of a story. Students can recognize television shows that were produced a number of years ago by the clothes people are wearing, hairstyles, furniture, cars, and so on.

Activity Draw a car that might replace the one on the page if the play were being staged today, or draw a costume that would indicate the present time or a much earlier time. **L2**

STEVE. It isn't just the power failure, Charlie. If it was, we'd still be able to get a broadcast on the portable.

[*There's a murmur of reaction to this. STEVE looks from face to face and then over to his car.*]

STEVE. I'll run downtown. We'll get this all straightened out.

[*He walks over to the car, gets in it, turns the key. Looking through the open car door, we see the crowd watching him from the other side. STEVE starts the engine. It turns over sluggishly and then just stops dead. He tries it again and this time he can't get it to turn over. Then, very slowly and reflectively, he turns the key back to "off" and slowly gets out of the car. The people stare at STEVE. He stands for a moment by the car, then walks toward the group.*]

STEVE. I don't understand it. It was working fine before . . .

DON. Out of gas?

STEVE. [*Shakes his head.*] I just had it filled up.

WOMAN. What's it mean?

CHARLIE. It's just as if . . . as if everything had stopped. [*Then he turns toward STEVE.*] We'd better walk downtown. [*Another murmur of assent[4] at this.*]

STEVE. The two of us can go, Charlie. [*He turns to look back at the car.*] It couldn't be the meteor. A meteor couldn't do this.

[*He and CHARLIE exchange a look, then they start to walk away from the group.*
We see TOMMY, a serious-faced fourteen-year-old in spectacles who stands a few feet away from the group. He is halfway between them and the two men, who start to walk down the sidewalk.]

TOMMY. Mr. Brand . . . you better not!

STEVE. Why not?

TOMMY. They don't want you to.

[*STEVE and CHARLIE exchange a grin, and STEVE looks back toward the boy.*]

STEVE. Who doesn't want us to?

TOMMY. [*Jerks his head in the general direction of the distant horizon.*] Them!

STEVE. Them?

CHARLIE. Who are them?

---

4. An expression of agreement is *assent.*

RESPOND

Would you walk downtown if you were Steve or Charlie?

QUESTION

Who is the "them" Tommy refers to? What makes you think so?

ACTIVE READING MODEL

L **Critical Thinking**

INFERRING Ask students why they think the reactions of the crowd are twice noted in the stage direction. *(Their faces show their concern or their dependence on Steve. Perhaps the author wants the audience to see the crowd as it grows.)*

M **Literary Elements**

DIALOGUE The playwright has limited space. Characters must say what has to be said to move the plot and reveal their personalities.

N **Active Reading**

RESPOND *(Students may say they would if they wanted to find answers. A person frozen by fear of the unknown would be unable to go anywhere.)*

O **Literary Elements**

CHARACTERIZATION What do the details of Tommy's appearance suggest about him? *(His serious face might suggest he is not a practical joker. Perhaps the author is implying he knows what he is talking about.)*

P **Active Reading**

QUESTION *("Them" might be referring to the monsters because Tommy looks off to the horizon.)*

Grammar and Language *Minilesson*

Using End Marks Explain to students that the period, the question mark, and the exclamation point all signal the end of a sentence. The end punctuation also helps readers identify the type of sentence being read. A period indicates a statement; a question mark indicates an interrogative sentence; and an exclamation point indicates a command or a sentence that expresses strong emotion.

Activity Write the following sentences on the board. Have students identify what type of sentence each is, based on the end punctuation.
1. Mr. Brand... you better not! *(strong emotion)*
2. Why not? *(interrogative)*
3. They don't want you to. *(statement)*
4. Who doesn't want us to? *(interrogative)*
5. Them! *(strong emotion)* **L2**

Additional Resources

🖊 ***Grammar and Language Transparency 43***

📖 ***Grammar and Language Workbook,*** pp. 253–254

📖 ***Grammar and Composition Handbook,*** Lesson 13.1

📕 ***Writer's Choice,*** Lesson 20.1

Literary Elements

Q

TELEPLAY: *Stage Directions* Call attention to the directions indicating the way Steve talks to the boy. Ask students why these directions are important. In what other way might the very same words be said? *(The directions are important because they ensure that Steve speaks to Tommy gently. The same words could be barked out, creating a totally different tone and relationship with the boy.)*

Active Reading

R

QUESTION *(Maybe Tommy, frightened by his reading, believes it to be true and not just science fiction.)*

Literary Elements

S

CHARACTERIZATION Ask students what they think of Sally, based on this one line. *(She is being protective of her son.)*

Critical Thinking

T

EVALUATING Ask students to identify the roles played by Steve, the Woman, and Tommy. *(Steve may be the hero; the Woman may be the antagonist, troublemaker, or "voice of the people"; and Tommy may be an instrument of either wisdom or fear.)*

Teaching Options

ACTIVE READING MODEL

TOMMY. [*Very intently.*] Whoever was in that thing that came by overhead.

[*STEVE knits his brows for a moment, cocking his head questioningly. His voice is intense.*]

STEVE. What?

TOMMY. Whoever was in that thing that came over. I don't think they want us to leave here.

[*STEVE leaves CHARLIE and walks over to the boy. He kneels down in front of him. He forces his voice to remain gentle. He reaches out and holds the boy.*]

STEVE. What do you mean? What are you talking about?

TOMMY. They don't want us to leave. That's why they shut everything off.

STEVE. What makes you say that? Whatever gave you that idea?

WOMAN. [*From the crowd.*] Now isn't that the craziest thing you ever heard?

QUESTION

R Why do you think Tommy is being so persistent?

TOMMY. [*Persistently but a little intimidated by the crowd.*] It's always that way, in every story I ever read about a ship landing from outer space.

WOMAN. [*To the boy's mother, SALLY, who stands on the fringe of the crowd.*] From outer space, yet! Sally, you better get that boy of yours up to bed. He's been reading too many comic books or seeing too many movies or something.

S **SALLY.** Tommy, come over here and stop that kind of talk.

STEVE. Go ahead, Tommy. We'll be right back. And you'll see. That wasn't any ship or anything like it. That was just a . . . a meteor or something. Likely as not— [*He turns to the group, now trying to weight his words with an optimism[5] he obviously doesn't feel but is desperately trying to instill in himself as well as the others.*] No doubt it did have something to do with all this power failure and the rest of it. Meteors can do some crazy things. Like sunspots.

T

DON. [*Picking up the cue.*] Sure. That's the kind of thing—like sunspots. They raise Cain[6] with radio reception all over the world. And this thing being so close—why, there's no telling the sort of stuff

---

5. *Optimism* means "a hopeful or cheerful view of things."
6. *[raise Cain]* This expression means "cause trouble."

Vocabulary
intimidated (in tim′ ə dāt′ əd) *adj.* made timid or fearful; bullied
instill (in stil′) *v.* to put in gradually, little by little

MEETING INDIVIDUAL NEEDS

INCLUSION STRATEGIES

Less-Proficient Readers Remind students that in the 1950s, people knew less about space and science than we do today. Anyone who sounded knowledgeable might be believed.

Activity Divide students into small groups containing both less-proficient readers and better readers. Ask each group to determine its area of exper-

tise, such as sports, TV shows, music, computer games. Have each group prepare a presentation for the rest of the class to convince them of their expertise. **L1**

Additional Resources
📁 *Inclusion Strategies*

it can do. [*He wets his lips, smiles nervously.*] Go ahead, Charlie. You and Steve go into town and see if that isn't what's causing it all.

ACTIVE READING MODEL

> [*STEVE and CHARLIE again walk away from the group down the sidewalk. The people watch silently.*
> *TOMMY stares at them, biting his lips, and finally calling out again.*]

U

TOMMY. Mr. Brand!

> [*The two men stop again. TOMMY takes a step toward them.*]

TOMMY. Mr. Brand . . . please don't leave here.

> [*STEVE and CHARLIE stop once again and turn toward the boy. There's a murmur in the crowd, a murmur of irritation and concern as if the boy were bringing up fears that shouldn't be brought up; words which carried with them a strange kind of <u>validity</u> that came without logic but nonetheless registered and had meaning and effect. Again we hear a murmur of reaction from the crowd.*
> *TOMMY is partly frightened and partly <u>defiant</u> as well.*]

TOMMY. You might not even be able to get to town. It was that way in the story. Nobody could leave. Nobody except—

STEVE. Except who?

TOMMY. Except the people they'd sent down ahead of them. They looked just like humans. And it wasn't until the ship landed that—

> [*The boy suddenly stops again, conscious of the parents staring at them and of the sudden hush of the crowd.*]

W

SALLY. [*In a whisper, sensing the <u>antagonism</u> of the crowd.*] Tommy, please son . . . honey, don't talk that way—

MAN ONE. That kid shouldn't talk that way . . . and we shouldn't stand here listening to him. Why this is the craziest thing I ever heard of. The kid tells us a comic book plot and here we stand listening—

> [*STEVE walks toward the camera, stops by the boy.*]

STEVE. Go ahead, Tommy. What kind of story was this? What about the people that they sent out ahead?

TOMMY. That was the way they prepared things for the landing. They sent four people. A mother and a father and two kids who looked just like humans . . . but they weren't.

Vocabulary
validity (və lid′ ə tē) *n.* state of being supported by facts; truth
defiant (di fī′ ənt) *adj.* showing bold resistance to authority or an opponent
antagonism (an tag′ ə niz′ əm) *n.* unfriendliness; hostility

U **Literary Elements**

FORESHADOWING Stories and plays often heighten suspense by foreshadowing, or conveying, a mood of impending doom. Could Tommy's statement be seen as a foreshadowing clue? *(Yes, Tommy's hesitancy and his use of the word "please" convey a fear of what can happen.)*

V **Active Reading**

EVALUATE

Does this make sense to you?

EVALUATE *(It makes sense because the crowd is influenced by the strange events. Maybe the two adults should not have been swayed by the fears of a young boy and should have gone for help anyway.)*

W **Critical Thinking**

JUDGING THE CREDIBILITY OF A SOURCE Ask students if they notice how Tommy is presenting the scenario in bits and pieces, giving more detail as he speaks. Ask students what kind of information makes a source credible. *(Someone is credible who gives detail, follows a logical pattern, and presents facts or solid sources for the information.)*

PREDICT

Will the person called "Man One" be an important character in the play? On what do you base your opinion?

X **Active Reading**

PREDICT *(The man will probably not be an important character in the play. He would probably have a name if he were.)*

Reading *Minilesson*

Setting a Purpose for Reading Explain that readers should begin to study the characters and weigh their impact.

Activity You may wish to have each student develop a table like the one at the right to take notes throughout the reading of the teleplay. **L2**

Additional Resources
📁 *Reading Workbook,* pp. 79–80

Character	What Character Thinks, Says, Does	What the Character Is Like
Tommy	*Concerned about his neighbors' safety; tells about sci-fi story*	*Serious, bookish, persistent in the face of opposition*
Steve	*Allows Tommy to talk.*	*Strong; a leader, takes charge*

Literary Elements

Y

TELEPLAY: Stage Directions Ask students why Steve is looking at the crowd. Why is the crowd repeatedly caught on camera? *(Steve wants to see the crowd's reaction to Tommy's comments. He's concerned about their behavior; conveying that concern to the audience may be why the director keeps putting the crowd on camera.)*

Critical Thinking

Z

EVALUATING Note that there is no answer to Charlie's question about Pete's getting back. Ask students why the author has a character raise the question but then interrupts with something else before there is an answer. *(Perhaps the author merely wants to remind the audience that Pete left and has not yet returned. Pete will more than likely play a critical role later in the play.)*

Vo•cab•u•lar•y Skills

Idioms Because a play's dialogue is written to sound much like ordinary speech, idioms will appear frequently. Recall that an idiom is an expression that means something other than its literal meaning. Here *no dice* is an idiom meaning "no" or "it didn't work."

Active Reading

PREDICT *(Because of the tension, the group might react with fear to the car's starting by itself.)*

**Teaching
Options**

**ACTIVE
READING
MODEL**

Y

[*There's another silence as* STEVE *looks toward the crowd and then toward* TOMMY. *He wears a tight grin.*]

STEVE. Well, I guess what we'd better do then is to run a check on the neighborhood and see which ones of us are really human.

[*There's laughter at this, but it's a laughter that comes from a desperate attempt to lighten the atmosphere. It's a release kind of laugh. The people look at one another in the middle of their laughter.*]

Z

CHARLIE. There must be somethin' better to do than stand around makin' bum jokes about it. [*Rubs his jaw nervously.*] I wonder if Floral Street's got the same deal we got. [*He looks past the houses.*] Where is Pete Van Horn anyway? Didn't he get back yet?

[*Suddenly there's the sound of a car's engine starting to turn over. We look across the street toward the driveway of* LES GOODMAN's *house. He's at the wheel trying to start the car.*]

SALLY. Can you get it started, Les?

[*He gets out of the car, shaking his head.*]

GOODMAN. No dice.

[*He walks toward the group. He stops suddenly as behind him, inexplicably[7] and with a noise that inserts itself into the silence, the car engine starts up all by itself.* GOODMAN *whirls around to stare toward it. The car idles roughly, smoke coming from the exhaust, the frame shaking gently.* GOODMAN's *eyes go wide, and he runs over to his car. The people stare toward the car.*]

MAN ONE. He got the car started somehow. He got his car started!

[*The camera pans along the faces of the people as they stare, somehow caught up by this revelation and somehow, illogically, wildly, frightened.*]

WOMAN. How come his car just up and started like that?

SALLY. All by itself. He wasn't anywheres near it. It started all by itself.

[DON *approaches the group, stops a few feet away to look toward* GOODMAN's *car and then back toward the group.*]

DON. And he never did come out to look at that thing that flew overhead. He wasn't even interested. [*He turns to the faces in the group, his face taut and serious.*] Why? Why didn't he come out with the rest of us to look?

---

7. Something that happens *inexplicably* (in′ iks plik′ ə blē) is impossible to understand or explain.

PREDICT

How will the group react to the car's starting by itself?

AA

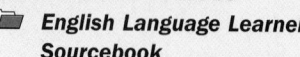

MEETING INDIVIDUAL NEEDS

ENGLISH LANGUAGE LEARNERS

Symbolism in Names Mention that the names of characters often suggest the types of people or roles they are to play.

Activity Divide the class into small groups that contain both English language learners and English-proficient students. Have them work together to create new, more descriptive names for characters in the teleplay. For example, Pete Van Horn could be renamed Pete Messenger, as he is to return with news for the neighbors. Have groups share their new names with each other.

COLLAB. LEARN.

Additional Resources

📁 *English Language Learners Sourcebook*

Rod Serling ∽

Did You Know?
A *metamorphosis* is a complete change, as when a caterpillar becomes a butterfly.

CHARLIE. He always was an oddball. Him and his whole family. Real oddball.

DON. What do you say we ask him?

[*The group suddenly starts toward the house. In this brief fraction of a moment they take the first step toward performing a metamorphosis that changes people from a group into a mob. They begin to head purposefully across the street toward the house at the end.* STEVE *stands in front of them. For a moment their fear almost turns their walk into a wild stampede, but* STEVE'*s voice, loud, incisive,*[8] *and commanding, makes them stop.*]

STEVE. Wait a minute . . . wait a minute! Let's not be a mob!

[*The people stop as a group, seem to pause for a moment, and then much more quietly and slowly start to walk across the street.* GOODMAN *stands alone facing the people.*]

GOODMAN. I just don't understand it. I tried to start it and it wouldn't start. You saw me. All of you saw me.

[*And now, just as suddenly as the engine started, it stops and there's a long silence that is gradually intruded upon by the frightened murmuring of the people.*]

GOODMAN. I don't understand. I swear . . . I don't understand. What's happening?

DON. Maybe you better tell us. Nothing's working on this street. Nothing. No lights, no power, no radio. [*And then meaningfully*] Nothing except one car—yours!

[*The people pick this up and now their murmuring becomes a loud chant filling the air with accusations and demands for action. Two of the men pass* DON *and head toward* GOODMAN, *who backs away, backing into his car and now at bay.*][9]

GOODMAN. Wait a minute now. You keep your distance—all of you. So I've got a car that starts by itself—well, that's a freak thing, I admit it. But does that make me some kind of a criminal or something? I don't know why the car works—it just does!

---

8. Steve's *incisive* voice is sharp and forceful.
9. *[at bay]* This describes the position of a cornered animal that is forced to turn and face its pursuers.

ACTIVE READING MODEL

VISUALIZE
Take a minute to picture this scene as if you were on the street but apart from the group.

REVIEW
What has happened up to this point? How have the characters reacted to these events? Can you tell yet who the main characters are?

BB **Active Reading**

TELEPLAY: *Stage Directions* Ask students how they would act if they were actors in this crowd. What kind of body language would they use to convey that, unbeknown to themselves, they were turning from a crowd into a mob. *(They would perhaps raise their arms, make angry faces, shout, surge forward, or shake their fists.)*

CC **Active Reading**

VISUALIZE *(Visualize the group, and then identify the different characters, such as Steve, commanding them to stop.)*

DD **Literary Elements**

CHARACTERIZATION In this one line Steve demonstrates his leadership qualities. Ask students what in particular shows his leadership. *(He's not afraid to oppose the group. A leader is a good communicator, and he uses the right word, mob, that his neighbors should react to.)*

EE **Active Reading**

REVIEW *(There was a loud noise in this peaceful neighborhood. Since then, the phone lines, electricity, and machines won't work. The characters are uneasy because of a science fiction story a young boy told, and they begin to suspect each other of wrongdoing. The main characters so far are Steve, Don, Charlie, Les, Tommy, Sally, and the Woman.)*

LIFE SKILLS CONNECTION

Lifelong Learning One of the most difficult things to do is to stand firm in one's beliefs when everyone else is thinking and acting in another way. Resisting the temptation to run with the herd is a major challenge. For example:
- Staying at home to study or baby-sit when everyone else is going to a concert.
- Not allowing someone to be bullied.

Activity Have small groups of students discuss incidents they know about in which an individual (perhaps themselves) had to fight the impulse to follow the crowd and do something opposed to their beliefs, principles, or wishes. Encourage each group to share their experiences with the class. **L2**

Hopper often used light to isolate people or objects, lending his paintings a feeling of loneliness.

Viewing Response *The artist combines light (the well-lit house front and lighted windows) with darkness (the shadowy background and dark awnings and bushes) to create a mysterious mood. A playwright might create a similar effect by combining "normal" settings and characters with hints of the strange and supernatural.*

FF Active Reading

QUESTION *(A "monster kick" means that the group is focused on the idea that monsters are responsible for these problems. Steve is trying to explain to Les why the group is behaving this way and might say "monster kick" to lighten the situation.)*

GG Active Reading

REVIEW Here Steve says "the general impression holds...." Ask what Steve's reaction to the notion of an alien family on the street had been before. *(Previously Steve didn't even acknowledge that as an option.)*

Teaching Options

Room for Tourists, 1945. Edward Hopper. Oil on canvas, 30¼ x 42⅛ in. Yale University Art Gallery, New Haven, CT.

Viewing the painting: What mood does the artist create in this painting? How might a playwright create a similar mood?

[*This stops the crowd momentarily and now* GOODMAN, *still backing away, goes toward his front porch. He goes up the steps and then stops to stand facing the mob.*
We see a long shot of STEVE *as he comes through the crowd.*]

FF **QUESTION**

What's a "monster kick"? Why does Steve say that?

514 🐾 THEME 5

STEVE. [*Quietly.*] We're all on a monster kick, Les. Seems that the general impression holds that maybe one family isn't what we think they **GG**

Writing *Minilesson*

Narrative A narrative is a story that usually answers the question "what happened." In a teleplay, the writer narrates in the present tense, using stage directions to tell what actors are doing and what is happening.

Activity Write the following short set of directions and ask students to add to them: *The door opens. The teacher comes in. Students rush to their desks.* Explain that the scene takes place in a classroom. Suggest that students describe what certain actors are doing and what sounds can be heard. Have them use verbs in the present tense in writing the directions. **L2**

Additional Resources

📙 *Writer's Choice,* Lessons 4.1–4.7

are. Monsters from outer space or something. Different than us. Fifth columnists[10] from the vast beyond. [*He chuckles.*] You know anybody that might fit that description around here on Maple Street?

GOODMAN. What is this, a gag or something? This a practical joke or something?

[*We see a close-up of the porch light as it suddenly goes out. There's a murmur from the group.*]

GOODMAN. Now I suppose that's supposed to incriminate me! The light goes on and off. That really does it, doesn't it?

[*He looks around the faces of the people.*] I just don't understand this— [*He wets his lips, looking from face to face.*] Look, you all know me. We've lived here five years. Right in this house. We're no different from any of the rest of you! We're no different at all. Really . . . this whole thing is just . . . just weird—

WOMAN. Well, if that's the case, Les Goodman, explain why— [*She stops suddenly, clamping her mouth shut.*]

GOODMAN. [*Softly.*] Explain what?

STEVE. [*Interjecting.*] Look, let's forget this—

CHARLIE. [*Overlapping him.*] Go ahead, let her talk. What about it? Explain what?

WOMAN. [*A little reluctantly.*] Well . . . sometimes I go to bed late at night. A couple of times . . . a couple of times I'd come out on the porch and I'd see Mr. Goodman here in the wee hours of the morning standing out in front of his house . . . looking up at the sky. [*She looks around the circle of*

10. *Fifth columnists* are traitors.

Vocabulary
incriminate (in krim′ ə nāt′) *v.* to show the guilt of

HH Active Reading

RESPOND *(Goodman probably feels betrayed and frightened because all the people he's known as neighbors for five years are lining up against him.)*

II Critical Thinking

EVALUATING Ask students to compare Steve's comment here with what he says at the top of the page. How has he changed? *(At the top of the page Steve was raising the issue most people were thinking, and he seemed to believe in it somewhat. Here, however, he seems to be rejecting it as a possibility.)*

RESPOND

How would you feel at this point if you were Goodman?

Vo•cab•u•lar•y Skills

Roots The stage directions have Steve "interjecting" a comment. *Interject* literally means "to throw" (*ject*) "between" (*inter*). Other words are built on the same roots: *eject* (throw out from within), *reject* (throw away as useless, or refuse to take), and *object* (to give a reason to oppose).

INTERDISCIPLINARY CONNECTION

Music Music can be a critical supporting force in a television play or series. It is another way of communicating. Music can create suspense or a sense of foreboding or indicate what will be happening next. Music used in a television series can also become a familiar part of our everyday lives.

Activity Ask students how many of them know the musical theme from *The Twilight Zone*. If possible, play a tape of the theme music for the class. Ask students to suggest other TV series whose theme music has become part of American culture. **L2**

Active Reading

EVALUATE *(Sometimes fear makes people want to blame someone for things that go wrong, even if that someone is a neighbor.)*

Active Reading

REVIEW *(So far, the lights have gone out, cars do not start, and there are no radio transmissions. A young boy has made them believe that they are the victims of aliens. The neighbors begin to suspect each other—especially Les.)*

Active Reading

QUESTION *(A few hours have passed since act 1. In act 1 we learned that it was 6:43 p.m. in late summer. In line 1 of act 2, it says that it is night and that Mrs. Goodman lights a candle, indicating that it is dark.)*

Teaching Options

ACTIVE READING MODEL

EVALUATE

JJ Would a person really say something like this about a neighbor?

REVIEW

KK So far, what has actually happened?

QUESTION

LL How much time has passed since the end of act 1? How can you tell?

The Monsters Are Due On Maple Street

faces.] That's right, looking up at the sky as if . . . as if he were waiting for something. [*A pause.*] As if he were looking for something.

[*There's a murmur of reaction from the crowd again. We cut suddenly to a group shot. As* GOODMAN *starts toward them, they back away frightened.*]

GOODMAN. You know really . . . this is for laughs. You know what I'm guilty of? [*He laughs.*] I'm guilty of insomnia.[11] Now what's the penalty for insomnia? [*At this point the laugh, the humor, leaves his voice.*] Did you hear what I said? I said it was insomnia. [*A pause as he looks around, then shouts.*] I said it was insomnia! You fools. You scared, frightened rabbits, you. You're sick people, do you know that? You're sick people—all of you! And you don't even know what you're starting because let me tell you . . . let me tell you—this thing you're starting—that should frighten you. As God is my witness . . . you're letting something begin here that's a nightmare!

ACT II

[*We see a medium shot of the Goodman entry hall at night. On the side table rests an unlit candle.* MRS. GOODMAN *walks into the scene, a glass of milk in hand. She sets the milk down on the table, lights the candle with a match from a box on the table, picks up the glass of milk, and starts out of scene.*

MRS. GOODMAN *comes through her porch door, glass of milk in hand. The entry hall, with table and lit candle, can be seen behind her.*

Outside, the camera slowly pans down the sidewalk, taking in little knots of people who stand around talking in low voices. At the end of each conversation they look toward LES GOODMAN's *house. From the various houses we can see candlelight but no electricity, and there's an all-pervading quiet that blankets the whole area, disturbed only by the almost whispered voices of the people as they stand around. The camera pans over to one group where* CHARLIE *stands. He stares across at* GOODMAN's *house.*

We see a long shot of the house. Two men stand across the street in almost sentry-like poses. Then we see a medium shot of a group of people.]

SALLY. [*A little timorously.*][12] It just doesn't seem right, though, keeping watch on them. Why . . . he was right when he said he was one of our neighbors. Why, I've known Ethel Goodman ever since they moved in. We've been good friends—

---

11. *Insomnia* is restless sleep or the inability to fall asleep.
12. *Timorously* (tim′ ər əs lē) means "lacking courage or self-confidence; timidly."

516 THEME 5

Reading Minilesson

Comparing and Contrasting The close of act 1 and the beginning of act 2 are very different, creating totally different moods. The mood at the close of act 1 is tense and charged with anger, as Goodman rants wildly at his neighbors in fearful defiance.

Activity Have students read the details from the opening of act 2 and describe

the mood those details create. *(Act 2 opens in a more subdued manner. Mrs. Goodman is carrying a glass of milk and a candle. People are standing and talking in quiet voices. The tension is still there, but the open hostility and anger have, for the moment, diminished.)* **L2**

Additional Resources
📁 *Reading Workbook*, pp. 79–80

CHARLIE. That don't prove a thing. Any guy who'd spend his time lookin' up at the sky early in the morning—well, there's something wrong with that kind of person. There's something that ain't legitimate. Maybe under normal circumstances we could let it go by, but these aren't normal circumstances. Why, look at this street! Nothin' but candles. Why, it's like goin' back into the dark ages or somethin'!

[STEVE *walks down the steps of his porch, walks down the street over to* LES GOODMAN's *house, and then stops at the foot of the steps.* GOODMAN *stands there, his wife behind him, very frightened.*]

GOODMAN. Just stay right where you are, Steve. We don't want any trouble, but this time if anybody sets foot on my porch, that's what they're going to get—trouble!

STEVE. Look, Les—

GOODMAN. I've already explained to you people. I don't sleep very well at night sometimes. I get up and I take a walk and I look up at the sky. I look at the stars!

MRS. GOODMAN. That's exactly what he does. Why this whole thing, it's . . . it's some kind of madness or something.

STEVE. [*Nods grimly.*] That's exactly what it is—some kind of madness.

CHARLIE'S VOICE. [*Shrill, from across the street.*] You best watch who you're seen with, Steve! Until we get this all straightened out, you ain't exactly above suspicion yourself.

STEVE. [*Whirling around toward him.*] Or you, Charlie. Or any of us, it seems. From age eight on up.

WOMAN. What I'd like to know is—what are we gonna do? Just stand around here all night?

CHARLIE. There's nothin' else we can do! [*He turns back looking toward* STEVE *and* GOODMAN *again.*] One of 'em'll tip their hand. They got to.

STEVE. [*Raising his voice.*] There's something you can do, Charlie. You could go home and keep your mouth shut. You could quit strutting around like a self-appointed hanging judge and just climb into bed and forget it.

CHARLIE. You sound real anxious to have that happen, Steve. I think we better keep our eye on you too!

ACTIVE READING MODEL

PREDICT

Toward what do events appear to be moving? What is going to happen next?

RESPOND

If you were Steve, how would you be feeling now?

Vocabulary
legitimate (li jit′ ə mit) *adj.* that which follows the rules; lawful

---

MM Literary Elements

IRONY Mention that a useful element in writing is *irony,* defined as a method of expression in which the conveyed meaning of the words is the opposite of what is in the speaker's mind. Ask students if they see anything ironic in Charlie's last sentence here. *(Students may see that, while Charlie is referring to the darkness as the absence of light, readers may see a different meaning in "dark ages," a meaning suggesting that these people may be behaving like primitives.)*

NN Critical Thinking

EVALUATING Ask students what is happening to these people. *(Students may see that, in their fear, the neighbors distrust one another: no one is above suspicion.)*

OO Active Reading

PREDICT *(It seems that the characters are so agitated that they might begin to act on their fear and distrust of one another. Something unfortunate will probably happen.)*

PP Active Reading

RESPOND *(Students would probably be feeling surprised that their longtime neighbor and friend would turn on them.)*

LIFE SKILLS CONNECTION

Understanding Crowd Behavior
Explain to students that "crowd control" has always been an issue around the world. Some organizations, such as the police, actually take classes in this skill.

Activity Ask students for their comments on crowd behavior and crowd control. Have them discuss incidents in which they feared or actually saw a crowd get-

ting out of control; for example, during a fire drill in school or a game in a large stadium. Have them explain what measures can be taken to protect oneself in such situations. **L2**

Literary Elements

PLOT Ask students why the author introduces new elements at different points in the play. *(The new elements add new twists and keep the audience attentive, trying to figure out where they will lead.)*

Active Reading

RESPOND *(Students may say they would feel angry and defiant.)*

Critical Thinking

EVALUATING Steve verbalizes the fear of monsters that many of his neighbors have been harboring. Is this statement going to help him or hurt him? You may wish to share the following model to illustrate the thinking process in evaluating.

Model: Steve is trying to help by bringing everyone's fears out into the open. He is trying to make people realize how silly the idea sounds. However, he could be hurting himself, as people may not see the sarcasm in his speech and take his words literally.

Vo•cab•u•lar•y Skills

Synonyms The use of the verb *whirls* in the stage direction is much more specific than the similar action verb *turns*. All good writers try to use the most specific verb to identify an action. Have students check a thesaurus for alternates for *look, walk,* and *speak.*

Teaching Options

The Monsters Are Due On Maple Street

ACTIVE READING MODEL

DON. [*As if he were taking the bit in his teeth, takes a hesitant step to the front.*] I think everything might as well come out now. [*He turns toward* STEVE.] Your wife's done plenty of talking, Steve, about how odd you are!

CHARLIE. [*Picking this up, his eyes widening.*] Go ahead, tell us what she's said.

[*We see a long shot of* STEVE *as he walks toward them from across the street.*]

STEVE. Go ahead, what's my wife said? Let's get it all out. Let's pick out every idiosyncrasy of every single man, woman, and child on the street. And then we might as well set up some kind of kangaroo court.[13] How about a firing squad at dawn, Charlie, so we can get rid of all the suspects? Narrow them down. Make it easier for you.

DON. There's no need gettin' so upset, Steve. It's just that . . . well . . . Myra's talked about how there's been plenty of nights you spent hours down in your basement workin' on some kind of radio or something. Well, none of us have ever seen that radio—

[*By this time* STEVE *has reached the group. He stands there defiantly close to them.*]

RESPOND

How would you react at this point if you were Steve?

CHARLIE. Go ahead, Steve. What kind of "radio set" you workin' on? I never seen it. Neither has anyone else. Who you talk to on that radio set? And who talks to you?

STEVE. I'm surprised at you, Charlie. How come you're so dense all of a sudden? [*A pause.*] Who do I talk to? I talk to monsters from outer space. I talk to three-headed green men who fly over here in what look like meteors.

[STEVE's *wife steps down from the porch, bites her lip, calls out.*]

MRS. BRAND. Steve! Steve, please. [*Then looking around, frightened, she walks toward the group.*] It's just a ham radio[14] set, that's all. I bought him a book on it myself. It's just a ham radio set. A lot of people have them. I can show it to you. It's right down in the basement.

STEVE. [*Whirls around toward her.*] Show them nothing! If they want to look inside our house—let them get a search warrant.

CHARLIE. Look, buddy, you can't afford to—

---

13. An *idiosyncrasy* (id' ē ə sing' krə sē) is a personal way of acting; an odd mannerism. A *kangaroo court* is an unofficial, irregular trial in which the verdict is often decided beforehand and fair legal procedures are ignored.
14. *Ham radio* is a hobby in which a person operates his or her own radio station, sending messages by voice or Morse code.

Listening and Speaking *Minilesson*

Oral Reading The author writes the dialogue, and the actors, with the help of the director, determine how to deliver the lines depending on the mood and action of the passage.

Activity Have students work with one or two classmates to rehearse and recite some of the dialogue on this page. Suggest that they try different ways of speaking, such as quickly, slowly, sharply, angrily, or calmly. Have each pair or team decide which is the best delivery to convey the meaning of each line. Have them keep in mind the character's personality as described by the author. After doing the recitation once, have them rotate the parts and do it again. **L2 COLLAB. LEARN.**

STEVE. [*Interrupting.*] Charlie, don't tell me what I can afford! And stop telling me who's dangerous and who isn't and who's safe and who's a menace. [*He turns to the group and shouts.*] And you're with him, too—all of you! You're standing here all set to crucify—all set to find a scapegoat[15]—all desperate to point some kind of a finger at a neighbor! Well now look, friends, the only thing that's gonna happen is that we'll eat each other up alive—

[*He stops abruptly as CHARLIE suddenly grabs his arm.*]

CHARLIE. [*In a hushed voice.*] That's not the only thing that can happen to us.

[*Cut to a long shot looking down the street. A figure has suddenly materialized in the gloom and in the silence we can hear the clickety-clack of slow, measured footsteps on concrete as the figure walks slowly toward them. One of the women lets out a stifled cry. The young mother grabs her boy as do a couple of others.*]

TOMMY. [*Shouting, frightened.*] It's the monster! It's the monster!

[*Another woman lets out a wail and the people fall back in a group, staring toward the darkness and the approaching figure.*
We see a medium group shot of the people as they stand in the shadows watching. DON MARTIN joins them, carrying a shotgun. He holds it up.]

DON. We may need this.

STEVE. A shotgun? [*He pulls it out of DON's hand.*] Good Lord—will anybody think a thought around here? Will you people wise up? What good would a shotgun do against—

[*Now CHARLIE pulls the gun from STEVE's hand.*]

CHARLIE. No more talk, Steve. You're going to talk us into a grave! You'd let whatever's out there walk right over us, wouldn't yuh? Well, some of us won't!

[*He swings the gun around to point it toward the sidewalk.*
The dark figure continues to walk toward them.
The group stands there, fearful, apprehensive, mothers clutching children, men standing in front of wives. CHARLIE slowly raises the gun. As the figure gets closer and closer he suddenly pulls the trigger. The sound of it explodes in the stillness. There is a long angle shot looking down at the figure, who suddenly lets out a small cry, stumbles forward onto his knees and then falls forward on his face. DON, CHARLIE, and STEVE race

---

15. A *scapegoat* is someone who is made to take the blame and suffer for the mistakes or misfortunes of another person or a group.

ACTIVE READING MODEL

 PREDICT

Who do you think the dark figure down the street is?

 UU

 EVALUATE

Take a minute to ask yourself if you think Charlie would really do this.

TT Active Reading

PREDICT *(The figure could be the monster or anyone from the neighborhood. Because of the darkness and the tenseness of the situation, anyone could look threatening.)*

UU Literary Elements

SYMBOL Until now, Steve has been the leader by virtue of his ability to control the group with his words. But when the gun appears, he seems to have lost that power to Charlie. Ask students what the gun might symbolize. *(The gun might symbolize a shift from a group governed by thought and discussion [Steve] to one governed by force [Charlie and the gun].)*

VV Active Reading

EVALUATE *(Students might say that this action is in character for Charlie because he's been consistently temperamental and quick to judge.)*

MEETING INDIVIDUAL NEEDS · INCLUSION STRATEGIES

Less-Proficient Readers To help students better understand the story, point out that no one in the group calls out, "Who's there?"

Activity Have students work in small groups to discuss why no one calls out to the figure. Ask the groups to share their observations. These may include

• People are too frightened to speak.
• If the figure hasn't seen them, a call might give away their position.
• In fiction, things are often allowed to happen for the sake of the story.
• In real life, people sometimes behave in explicable ways.

L2 COLLAB. LEARN.

Additional Resources
📁 *Inclusion Strategies*

FYI

War of the Worlds In 1938, Orson Welles created a panic with a radio adaptation of H. G. Wells's "War of the Worlds." The radio transmission, closely imitating the broadcasts of that time, described the invasion of New Jersey by Martian aliens so realistically that it caused thousands of people to leave their homes and try to escape.

Pop Culture

Rod Serling, the host of *The Twilight Zone,* was cocreator of another weekly series named *Night Gallery.* Its setting was a museum where Rod Serling would introduce tales of fantasy, horror, and science fiction.

Stormy Midnight, 1995. Jane Wilson. Oil on linen, 18 x 18 in. Courtesy Fischbach Gallery, New York.

Viewing the painting: If you were to add people to this scene, what would they be doing? Why? How does the mood of the painting compare with the mood of the play?

520 ❧ THEME 5

Teaching Options

Grammar and Language *Minilesson*

Complete Sentences Write the following sentence fragment on the board: *With few variations.* Note that in dialogue, characters often speak in sentence fragments. That is, the group of words may look like a sentence, but it lacks a subject or predicate to make it stand as an independent, complete thought. Written as a complete sentence, the fragment above could be

The pattern is always the same, with few variations.

Activity Have students find other sentence fragments in the text and write them as complete sentences (For example, Figure One's exchange: *"By no means."* should be, *"This place is by no means unique."*) **L2**

Additional Resources

Grammar and Language Transparency 44

Grammar and Language Workbook, pp. 55–56

Grammar and Composition Handbook, Lesson 1.2

Writer's Choice, Lesson 8.2

520

forward over to him. STEVE is there first and turns the man over. Now the crowd gathers around them.]

STEVE. [*Slowly looks up.*] It's Pete Van Horn.

DON. [*In a hushed voice.*] Pete Van Horn! He was just gonna go over to the next block to see if the power was on—

WOMAN. You killed him, Charlie. You shot him dead!

CHARLIE. [*Looks around at the circle of faces, his eyes frightened, his face contorted.*] But . . . but I didn't know who he was. I certainly didn't know who he was. He comes walkin' out of the darkness—how am I supposed to know who he was? [*He grabs STEVE.*] Steve—you know why I shot! How was I supposed to know he wasn't a monster or something? [*He grabs DON now.*] We're all scared of the same thing, I was just tryin' to . . . tryin' to protect my home, that's all! Look, all of you, that's all I was tryin' to do. [*He looks down wildly at the body.*] I didn't know it was somebody we knew! I didn't know—

[*There's a sudden hush and then an intake of breath. We see a medium shot of the living room window of CHARLIE's house. The window is not lit, but suddenly the house lights come on behind it.*]

WOMAN. [*In a very hushed voice.*] Charlie . . . Charlie . . . the lights just went on in your house. Why did the lights just go on?

DON. What about it, Charlie? How come you're the only one with lights now?

GOODMAN. That's what I'd like to know.

[*A pause as they all stare toward CHARLIE.*]

GOODMAN. You were so quick to kill, Charlie and you were so quick to tell us who we had to be careful of. Well, maybe you had to kill. Maybe Peter there was trying to tell us something. Maybe he'd found out something and came back to tell us who there was amongst us we should watch out for—

[*CHARLIE backs away from the group, his eyes wide with fright.*]

CHARLIE. No . . . no . . . it's nothing of the sort! I don't know why the lights are on, I swear I don't. Somebody's pulling a gag or something.

[*He bumps against STEVE, who grabs him and whirls him around.*]

STEVE. A gag? A gag? Charlie, there's a dead man on the sidewalk and you killed him. Does this thing look like a gag to you?

[*CHARLIE breaks away and screams as he runs toward his house.*]

CHARLIE. No! No! Please!

ACTIVE READING MODEL

VISUALIZE

Can you picture this scene?

REVIEW

How would you summarize what has happened so far?

WW Critical Thinking

SYNTHESIZING Ask students to synthesize the role of The Woman by adding what she says here to what she has said earlier. *(The Woman seems to be an instigator who sees the worst in every situation and highlights it, as she does here. She doesn't take sides but just stirs up trouble.)*

XX Active Reading

VISUALIZE *(Students can visualize the body of Pete Van Horn on the ground with all the neighbors around him. Then they can see the frightened face of Charlie when he realizes what he has done.)*

YY Critical Thinking

DRAWING CONCLUSIONS Ask students why Les Goodman feels no compassion for Charlie now that the crowd has turned against him. *(Probably because Charlie was encouraging the crowd to suspect Les of being a monster and did not support his own best friend, Steve.)*

ZZ Active Reading

REVIEW *(The crowd is still looking for the monster among them. Charlie in his wild fear takes a gun and shoots Pete Van Horn, a neighbor, and then the crowd turns on him.)*

MEETING INDIVIDUAL NEEDS

ENGLISH LANGUAGE LEARNERS

Nonverbal Language Facial expressions, body movements, and sounds are all part of nonverbal language that crosses language barriers. Remind English language learners that they are already "reading" nonverbal language, whether or not they are aware of it.

Activity Divide the class into small groups that include both English language learners and English-proficient students. Ask them to identify some nonverbal language and to put it into words. Then have students demonstrate their examples. Later, discuss any cultural differences that students have noted. **COLLAB. LEARN.**

Additional Resources
📁 *English Language Learners Sourcebook*

Critical Thinking

GENERALIZING Until now, except for Charlie's shooting the unidentified figure, all the aggression has been nonphysical. Now it is becoming physical and ugly. Ask students what is happening to these people. *(The people are so wrapped up in their fear they are not thinking clearly or thinking at all. They are acting like people from the "dark ages," when brute force determined every outcome.)*

Active Reading

VISUALIZE *(Students might want to shoot this scene from Charlie's house or from above to show the crowd scene and Charlie and his wife.)*

Active Reading

QUESTION *(No, Charlie doesn't really believe it. In his fear he is grasping at straws to save himself. He stammers and his speech is halting as he searches desperately for an answer that will shift the crowd's attention from him.)*

Teaching Options

The Monsters Are Due On Maple Street

ACTIVE READING MODEL

VISUALIZE

If you were the director, how would you have the camera operator shoot this scene?

[*A man breaks away from the crowd to chase* CHARLIE. *We see a long angle shot looking down as the man tackles* CHARLIE *and lands on top of him. The other people start to run toward them.* CHARLIE *is up on his feet, breaks away from the other man's grasp, lands a couple of desperate punches that push the man aside. Then he forces his way, fighting, through the crowd to once again break free, jumps up on his front porch. A rock thrown from the group smashes a window alongside of him, the broken glass flying past him. A couple of pieces cut him. He stands there perspiring, rumpled, blood running down from a cut on the cheek. His wife breaks away from the group to throw herself into his arms. He buries his face against her. We can see the crowd converging on the porch now.*]

VOICES.
It must have been him.
He's the one.
We got to get Charlie.

[*Another rock lands on the porch. Now* CHARLIE *pushes his wife behind him, facing the group.*]

CHARLIE. Look, look I swear to you . . . it isn't me . . . but I do know who it is . . . I swear to you, I do know who it is. I know who the monster is here. I know who it is that doesn't belong. I swear to you I know.

GOODMAN. [*Shouting.*] What are you waiting for?

WOMAN. [*Shouting.*] Come on, Charlie, come on.

MAN ONE. [*Shouting.*] Who is it, Charlie, tell us!

DON. [*Pushing his way to the front of the crowd*] All right, Charlie, let's hear it!

[CHARLIE's *eyes dart around wildly.*]

CHARLIE. It's . . . it's . . .

MAN TWO. [*Screaming.*] Go ahead, Charlie, tell us.

CHARLIE. It's . . . it's the kid. It's Tommy. He's the one.

[*There's a gasp from the crowd as we cut to a shot of* SALLY *holding her son* TOMMY. *The boy at first doesn't understand and then, realizing the eyes are all on him, buries his face against his mother.*]

SALLY. [*Backs away.*] That's crazy! That's crazy! He's a little boy.

WOMAN. But he knew! He was the only one who knew! He told us all about it. Well, how did he know? How *could* he have known?

[*The various people take this up and repeat the question aloud.*]

VOICES.
How could he know?

QUESTION

Does Charlie really believe what he is saying? What makes you think so?

Writing *Minilesson*

Narrating Action with Verbs In the stage directions at the top of the page, the sentences are relatively short and without much descriptive detail. But there are many action verbs: *tackles, breaks away, lands,* and *forces.*

Activity Narrate a scene with many people in it, such as in a cafeteria, at a game, or at a mall. Write short sentences that narrate the action through the use of strong, specific action verbs. Keep descriptive details to a minimum. **L2**

Additional Resources

Writer's Choice, Lesson 4.5

Who told him?
Make the kid answer.

DON. It was Charlie who killed old man Van Horn.

WOMAN. But it was the kid here who knew what was going to happen all the time. He was the one who knew!

[*We see a close-up of* STEVE.]

STEVE. Are you all gone crazy? [*Pause as he looks about.*] Stop.

[*A fist crashes at* STEVE's *face, staggering him back out of the frame of the picture.*
There are several close camera shots suggesting the coming of violence. A hand fires a rifle. A fist clenches. A hand grabs the hammer from VAN HORN's *body, etc. Meanwhile, we hear the following lines.*]

DON. Charlie has to be the one—Where's my rifle—

WOMAN. Les Goodman's the one. His car started! Let's wreck it.

MRS. GOODMAN. What about Steve's radio—He's the one that called them—

MR. GOODMAN. Smash the radio. Get me a hammer. Get me something.

STEVE. Stop—Stop—

CHARLIE. Where's that kid—Let's get him.

MAN ONE. Get Steve—Get Charlie—They're working together.

[*The crowd starts to converge around the mother, who grabs the child and starts to run with him. The crowd starts to follow, at first walking fast, and then running after him.*
We see a full shot of the street as suddenly CHARLIE's *lights go off and the lights in another house go on. They stay on for a moment, then from across the street other lights go on and then off again.*]

MAN ONE. [*Shouting.*] It isn't the kid . . . it's Bob Weaver's house.

WOMAN. It isn't Bob Weaver's house, it's Don Martin's place.

CHARLIE. I tell you it's the kid.

DON. It's Charlie. He's the one.

[*We move into a series of close-ups of various people as they shout, accuse, scream, interspersing these shots with shots of houses as the lights go on and off, and then slowly in the middle of this nightmarish morass[16] of sight and sound the camera starts to pull away, until once again we've*

---

16. *Interspersing* means "scattering or mixing in over brief periods." A *morass* (mə ras′) is any difficult, confused, or entangling condition or situation.

ACTIVE
READING
MODEL

EVALUATE

Has the playwright kept the character of Steve consistent throughout the story? How would you describe Steve?

EVALUATE

What mood does the playwright create with this scene? How does he create that mood?

DDD Literary Elements

TELEPLAY: *Stage Directions* Ask students what these close shots add to the story and the emotion. (*These close shots show individuals ready for physical violence, and they raise the tension level for the audience.*)

Active Reading

EVALUATE (*The playwright has always kept the character of Steve as the voice of reason throughout the story. Steve is presented as brave, reasonable, compassionate, and not easily swayed by the crowd or by fear.*)

Active Reading

EVALUATE (*The playwright creates an unsettling mood through chaos and confusion, with each character shouting and accusing and the lights going on and off.*)

LITERATURE &
HUMANITIES

Have students examine the painting *Catastrophe No. 2* in *Art Talk*, page 94. Ask them what will probably happen to the people and their houses. How does their reaction compare to the reactions of the characters in Serling's play?

REAL-WORLD CONNECTION

Riots Students may better understand the story by studying the dynamics of riots.

Activity Have students research *riots* in newspapers, in magazines, or on the Internet. Students may work in small groups to discuss their findings. Ask them to categorize the types of incidents that sparked the riots, and have them compare their findings. **L2**

*inter*NET
CONNECTION

Screenwriters Students can use a search engine to find out more about screenwriters. In addition to the word *screenwriting*, they might use such keywords as *play, film, TV, colleges,* or *guild.*

Active Reading

QUESTION *(It seems that the figures are creatures from outer space. They are trying to destroy humans by tricking them into destroying each other.)*

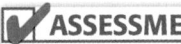 **Active Reading**

RESPOND *(Students might recognize that the play is trying to get a message across—that humans are too quick to judge and suspect each other of wrongdoing. Students might feel uncomfortable about the Narrator's observations.)*

Thematic Focus

At the Crossroads Ask students what they they think about the irrationality of the mob and how it relates to the theme. *(There are many opportunities for the characters in the story to make the right decision, control their fears, and work together for a solution to their dilemma. Instead, they allow themselves to become a mob and resort to violence.)*

✔ ASSESSMENT OPTIONS

📁 **Quick Checks,** p. 45

Teaching Options

The Monsters Are Due On Maple Street

ACTIVE READING MODEL

reached the opening shot looking at the Maple Street sign from high above. The camera continues to move away until we dissolve to a shot looking toward the metal side of a space craft, which sits shrouded in darkness. An open door throws out a beam of light from the illuminated interior. Two figures silhouetted against the bright lights appear. We get only a vague feeling of form, but nothing more <u>explicit</u> than that.]

QUESTION

Who are these figures? Where are they from? What are they doing?

FIGURE ONE. Understand the procedure now? Just stop a few of their machines and radios and telephones and lawn mowers . . . Throw them into darkness for a few hours, and then you just sit back and watch the pattern.

FIGURE TWO. And this pattern is always the same?

FIGURE ONE. With few variations. They pick the most dangerous enemy they can find . . . and it's themselves. And all we need do is sit back . . . and watch.

FIGURE TWO. Then I take it this place . . . this Maple Street . . . is not unique.

FIGURE ONE. *[Shaking his head.]* By no means. Their world is full of Maple Streets. And we'll go from one to the other and let them destroy themselves. One to the other . . . one to the other . . . one to the other—

[Now the camera pans up for a shot of the starry sky and over this we hear the NARRATOR'S VOICE.]

NARRATOR'S VOICE. The tools of conquest do not necessarily come with bombs and explosions and fallout.[17] There are weapons that are simply thoughts, attitudes, <u>prejudices</u>—to be found only in the minds of men. For the record, prejudices can kill and suspicion can destroy and a thoughtless frightened search for a scapegoat has a fallout all its own for the children . . . and the children yet unborn. *[A pause.]* And the pity of it is . . . that these things cannot be confined to . . . The Twilight Zone!

RESPOND

What is your reaction to the ending of this play?

---

17. *Fallout* is the radioactive dust particles that result from a nuclear explosion and fall to earth from the atmosphere.

Vocabulary
explicit (eks plis′ it) *adj.* clearly expressed
prejudice (prej′ ə dis) *n.* an unfavorable opinion or judgment formed unfairly

---

Writing *Minilesson*

Analytical Writing Many mysteries and horror stories take place at night. Is the nighttime more suited for such stories than daytime?

Activity Write a paragraph answering this question, giving reasons and examples to support your position. Complete the diagram to prepare for writing. **L2**

Your position on the subject: _____
Reason/Example: _____
Reason/Example: _____
Conclusion: _____

Additional Resources

🔖 *Writer's Choice,* Lesson 6.1–6.5

Responding to Literature

PERSONAL RESPONSE

What is your reaction to this play? Recall the **Focus Activity** on page 504. How do the reactions of the neighbors in the teleplay compare or contrast with how you imagined your own neighbors reacting to strange occurrences?

Active Reading Response

Review the strategies described in the **Active Reading Model** on pages 502–503. Choose one of the strategies and find three additional places in the teleplay where you could apply it.

Analyzing Literature

RECALL

1. What is the first sign of trouble on Maple Street?
2. Who is Tommy? Describe him and explain what he tells Steve.
3. Who is the first person the neighbors begin to suspect?
4. What events lead to the shooting?

INTERPRET

5. At the beginning of the play, what is the **mood** on Maple Street? What causes the mood to change?
6. What role do you think Tommy plays in this drama?
7. Why do the people on Maple Street begin to turn on each other?
8. At what point do the neighbors become a "mob"? Why does this happen? Use quotations from the play to support your ideas.

EVALUATE AND CONNECT

9. How do the aliens use their understanding of human nature to accomplish their goal? Explain.
10. The narrator says, "The tools of conquest do not necessarily come with bombs." How does the play portray that idea?

LITERARY ELEMENTS

Teleplay

"The Monsters Are Due on Maple Street" is a **teleplay**, or a play written especially for television. Its format is similar to that of a stage play. Like a play, the teleplay is divided into **scenes** and **acts**. Stage directions, meant for the actors and the studio crew, are in italic type and are enclosed in brackets. The main difference between the format of a play and a teleplay is the addition of camera directions.

1. Identify a stage direction that describes the setting of the teleplay.
2. Find where Act II begins. Tell why you think Serling divided the play at that particular point.

● See **Literary Terms Handbook**, p. R11.

Responding to the Selection

Personal Response

Some students may say that maybe their neighbors will react as the people in the play do. Others may feel that their neighbors would be more unified and rational.

Analyzing Literature

1. The first sign of trouble is the apparent power failure.
2. Tommy is a fourteen-year-old boy who reads a lot. He tells Steve he read a story in which the power failure was caused by aliens from space.
3. The neighbors first suspect Les Goodman.
4. Don Martin joins the group in the street, carrying a shotgun. When a figure comes walking toward them from the end of the street, the crowd cannot make out who it is in the dark. Charlie takes the gun and shoots the figure.
5. The mood is pleasant and calm. The mysterious power outage causes the mood to change.
6. Tommy triggers a line of thinking that eventually undoes the whole group. His mention of aliens gradually becomes a real possibility for some people, and then they act on it.
7. In their fear, they cannot accept the fact that they don't know the cause of this outage. They turn on each other because they want to find a culprit.
8. They become a mob when they accuse Les Goodman and follow him to his house. *"Now I suppose that's supposed to incriminate me! The light goes on and off."* There is no logical reason for accusing him, but they do.
9. The aliens know that the best way to destroy a human community is to set it against itself. The aliens plant the seed for disagreement, and people's fears grow into hostility toward one another.

LITERARY ELEMENTS

1. One example is page 505, act I.
2. Act I ends just as the crowd has decided Goodman is the villain. He says they are "sick" and letting a "nightmare" begin. Ending act I here enables the audience to reflect on what is happening. The audience can contemplate what Goodman means by this "nightmare."

Additional Resources

📖 *Literary Elements Transparency 45*

10. By exciting hostility among people, the aliens split the community, making it ripe for conquest without bombs or any other type of weapon.

Literature and Writing

Writing About Literature

Students' explanations should

- identify the two forces in the main conflict.
- identify other conflicts in the play.
- support their ideas with specific references and tell why these forces are in conflict.

Creative Writing

Students' messages should

- state what the aliens are trying to accomplish.
- explain their strategy for accomplishing it.
- summarize the effects of their strategy.

Extending Your Response

Learning for Life Students might gather information on the story by answering the *Where, When, Who, Why,* and *How* questions of good reporting. Also, encourage students to use quotes from those involved to help re-create the event.

Literature Groups Students might focus on the "evidence" people used to accuse one another and on the issue of what constitutes being a "monster." **COLLAB. LEARN.**

Literature and Writing

Writing About Literature

Thinking About Conflict **Conflict** is the struggle between two opposing forces at the center of a plot in a story or drama. What do you think is the main conflict in this teleplay? What other conflicts are portrayed? Write one or two paragraphs describing your ideas. Support your ideas with examples from the teleplay.

Creative Writing

From an Alien's Point of View Imagine that you are one of the aliens on the spacecraft. You are sending home a message about the events on Maple Street. Describe what you and your fellow aliens did and what happened as a result. Explain how you were able to get the "Earthlings" to accomplish your goals.

Extending Your Response

Learning for Life

News Broadcast Imagine that you are a television reporter who has arrived on Maple Street to interview as many people as possible and find out what happened there. Write a news story about this frightening event. Create diagrams, maps, or pictures to accompany your story. Present your story to your classmates as a TV news broadcast.

interNET CONNECTION

You can find out more about "The Twilight Zone," Rod Serling, and science fiction in general at many sites on the World Wide Web. Just type "twilight zone," "rod serling," or "science fiction" in the subject window of your search engine.

Literature Groups

Who Are the *Real* Monsters? "The Monsters Are Due on Maple Street" describes a neighborhood changed by fear. Do you agree with the author that human beings can be turned into "monsters"? Talk about the central question raised in this play: Who are the real monsters on Maple Street? How does fear change people? Support your ideas with examples from the play.

Reading Further

If you would like to read more by Rod Serling, try this book:
Stories from The Twilight Zone

Save your work for your portfolio.

Skill Minilessons

GRAMMAR AND LANGUAGE • APOSTROPHES

Do you know the difference between *its* and *it's?* The pronoun *its* shows possession. The word *it's* is a contraction of *it is.* The apostrophe (') in *it's* is used to indicate where the letter *i* has been left out.

Its setting is a typical American town. [possessive pronoun]

It's a drama about how fear destroys people's lives. [contraction of *it is*]

PRACTICE Write a paragraph describing "The Monsters Are Due on Maple Street" for someone who hasn't read it. Use the possessive pronoun *its* as well as the contraction *it's* in your paragraph.

● For more about using apostrophes, see **Language Handbook,** p. R19.

READING AND THINKING • VISUALIZING

A teleplay is meant to be seen on a screen. Therefore, when you read a teleplay, imagine that you are seeing the drama in your mind. Use the details to help you picture the different scenes as you read. Keep asking yourself:

How does this scene look? What is going on here? What is each character doing?

PRACTICE Work with a partner. Pick out one scene to read to your partner. As you read, your partner should draw a sketch showing what is going on in the scene. Then trade roles and draw a sketch as you listen to your partner read a different scene.

● For more about visualizing, see **Reading Handbook,** p. R84.

VOCABULARY • BASE WORDS

Base words are whole words that form the "base" of new words when prefixes or suffixes (or both) are attached to them. Familiar base words can help you unlock the meanings of unfamiliar words. For example, *timid* in *intimidated* is a very good clue to the meaning of *intimidated*.

   Spelling tip: A final *e* in a base word sometimes changes to another vowel when a suffix is added. For example: value → valuable.

PRACTICE Use what you know about base words and familiar prefixes and suffixes to match each word on the left to its meaning.

1. undesirable   a. cannot be avoided
2. inescapable   b. not wanted
3. nonexistent   c. determining worth again
4. revaluation   d. that which surrounds
5. encirclement   e. found nowhere

Skill Minilessons

GRAMMAR AND LANGUAGE
MECHANICS: APOSTROPHES

Students' paragraphs should contain the use of *its* and *it's*.

READING AND THINKING
VISUALIZING

The quality of the sketches is less critical than the details they captured.

VOCABULARY
BASE WORDS

1. b   3. e   5. d
2. a   4. c

Additional Resources

📕 *Grammar and Language Workbook,* pp. 273–274

📕 *Grammar and Composition Handbook,* Lesson 13.7

📕 *Writer's Choice,* Lesson 20.7

📕 *Reading Workbook,* pp. 79–80

📁 *Vocabulary Practice,* p. 21

✔ ASSESSMENT OPTIONS

📁 *Quick Checks,* p. 45

📁 *Selection and Theme Assessment,* pp. 79–80

📁 *Performance Assessment,* p. 42

💾 *Testmaker*

AT THE CROSSROADS 🐛 **527**

Objective

- To read and understand a Web site

Literature LINK

The Monsters Are Due on Maple Street This Web site connects to "The Monsters Are Due on Maple Street" (pp. 505–524). Explain to students that the Web site is a summary of Episode 42 of the television series *The Twilight Zone*, while the selection they have just read is a teleplay of an episode from the same series. In both episodes, characters' actions are dictated by a fear of the unusual and the unknown.

Respond

1. Students may say that keeping the characters' faces hidden allows viewers to assume Janet Tyler is the disfigured one.
2. The title is the second half of the expression "Beauty is in the eye of the beholder." The surprise is that a beautiful woman is considered ugly because she looks different from others.

Additional Resources

📁 *Media Connections*, p. 10

MEDIA
Connection

WEB SITE

"The Monsters Are Due on Maple Street" was written for the TV series *The Twilight Zone*. On some Web sites devoted to the series, you can find plot summaries of all the episodes. Here's an example.

The Eye of the Beholder

Address: ▼ http://www.the5thdimension.com/shows/

TWILIGHT ZONE

Episode 42 •
November 11, 1960

Janet Tyler is having her eleventh state-sponsored operation, the maximum allowed. The surgery is necessary because she is an outcast with a hideous face. The nurses commiserate with her, and her doctor is quite sympathetic. Janet believes the situation is hopeless and takes comfort in the bandages covering her face.

While talking with her doctor, Janet breaks down and starts crying because she just wants to look like everybody else and therefore enjoy the same privileges. However, if the surgery fails she will be forced to live in a village with other "freaks" away from normal society, which doesn't sit well with Janet, who calls it a "ghetto." She starts crying out against the state and pleads for her doctor to take off the bandages to see if the last experiment worked. He agrees to do so.

Slowly, the doctor starts to take off the bandages, layer by layer. The last layer is removed, the nurses cover their faces in horror, and the doctor drops his scissors: there has been no change. Janet Tyler raises her head, and appears to us to be quite beautiful. She tries to run and is

pinned against the wall by her doctor and nurse, who turns on the light. The faces of the others are revealed: pig-like nose, protruding lips, bone outlines, they are the ones that are "normal." Janet escapes their grasps and runs down many hall-ways, eventually stopping in front of Walter Smith, a similar outcast who has come to take her to the village. He tries to remind her to always remember that beauty is in the eye of the beholder.

Respond

1. In your opinion, why did the scriptwriter keep all the characters' faces hidden from viewers until the end of the teleplay?

2. What does the teleplay's title mean? Explain it in your own words.

Teaching Options

interNET CONNECTION

The Twilight Zone Have students enter this title in the search engines to locate other Web sites devoted to this series.

Writing Minilesson

Setting a Purpose for Reading Have students discuss the difference between reading the teleplay "The Monsters Are Due on Maple Street" and reading Episode 42 of *The Twilight Zone*.

Activity Divide students into small groups. Have each group take one paragraph of Episode 42, "The Eye of the Beholder." Suggest that students read the paragraph carefully, mining it for details. Then ask them to list the details in a chart under *Dialogue*, *Cast of Characters*, and *Stage Directions*. **L2 COLLAB. LEARN.**

Additional Resources

📁 *Reading Workbook*

Vo·cab·u·lar·y Skills

Idioms

When you step off a ladder, you put your foot down. When you firmly refuse to allow something, you put your foot down. In the first sentence, the words *put your foot down* have their ordinary, literal meaning. In the second, they do not. To "put one's foot down" is often used as an **idiom**—a word or phrase that has a special meaning different from the ordinary meaning of the word or words.

The English language contains many idioms. "He's on the ball." "She's really steamed." "They jumped the gun." "I'm all tied up." Many of them are so familiar they cause no problems. Unfamiliar idioms, however, can cause confusion.

There are two useful ways to figure out the meaning of an unfamiliar idiom. One is to think about what the ordinary meanings of the words suggest.

- If the father in "The Boy and His Grandfather" tried to defend his bad treatment of his own father, he wouldn't have a leg to stand on.

Even if you had never seen the underlined idiom, you could understand that it means not having any support. The father would have no basis for such a defense. A second way to approach idioms is to use context clues.

- Mrs. Wang had never worked out a plan for using the river's power against the enemy; her action resulted from a spur of the moment decision.

Context clues in the sentence suggest that "spur of the moment" means the opposite of "planned in advance."

EXERCISE

Write a short definition of each underlined idiom.

1. The villagers know that their only hope for survival is to flee, so they get out while the getting is good.
2. It is useless to argue with the hard-nosed Mrs. Wang.
3. Once Mrs. Wang has decided to open the sluice, she lets no grass grow under her feet.
4. It isn't easy for Mrs. Wang to rescue the injured pilot, but she sees it through.
5. Who would expect a sudden flood across dry land? When the enemy soldiers see the mighty river boiling toward them, the sight will throw them for a loop.

Vo·cab·u·lar·y Skills

Objective
- To recognize and use idiomatic expressions correctly

Teaching Strategies
Have students list some of the idiomatic expressions they use or hear everyday. Encourage them to spend a day listening for the expressions they, their classmates, their teachers, and their family members use. Ask students to keep a few notecards and jot down the expressions as they hear them. Create a class dictionary of all the idiomatic expressions heard in one day.

Exercise
1. They get out while they can.
2. Mrs. Wang is stubborn.
3. She moves quickly.
4. She finishes the task.
5. The sight will shock them.

Additional Resources
📁 *Vocabulary Power: Weekly Lessons and Activities*

Teaching Options

MEETING INDIVIDUAL NEEDS — ENGLISH LANGUAGE LEARNERS

Idioms Students who are not yet proficient in English may find idioms particularly challenging.

Activity Have students work in mixed groups. Ask them to create flip books for the idioms by folding a piece of paper in half lengthwise and making three cuts in one half. Students should select four idioms from any selection and write them, and their own definitions, one on each of the four flaps. Encourage students to add humorous illustrations as well. Beneath each flap, students can copy the sentence from the selection in which the idiom appears, or write a new sentence using the idiom. **COLLAB. LEARN.**

Additional Resources
📁 *English Language Learners Sourcebook*

Writing WORKSHOP

Objectives

- To create a personal response to literature
- To plan, draft, revise, edit, and present a definition essay
- To reflect on and assess the essay

Teaching Strategies

PREWRITING

Choose a Character and a Quality
Have students team up with partners to discuss the character traits and qualities that interest them most. Encourage them to talk to their partners about people from their own lives who possess these qualities. Suggest that they draw comparisons between a person they know and a character from one of the selections. Ask them to tell their partners something this person did or said that reveals an interesting personal quality.

Teaching Options

Writing WORKSHOP

Expository Writing: Definition Essay

What does loyalty mean to you? How would you define courage or cowardice, cruelty or compassion? Many of the characters in this book's selections demonstrate all these qualities, although the authors seldom define the qualities directly. To define a concept, you explain what it is and why it's important. You use examples to show your audience exactly what you mean.

Assignment: Follow the process explained in these pages to write an essay in which you define a personal quality. Use one or more characters from selections you've read in this book as examples to support your definition.

● As you write your expository essay, refer to **Writing Handbook,** pp. R48–R59.

The Writing Process

PREWRITING

PREWRITING TIP
To narrow down your selection of a character to write about, look at the titles of the selections in the table of contents. As you glance at each title, try to recall the character or characters involved in the selection. Which ones can you imagine most vividly? Which stand out as having a character trait you find appealing or especially interesting?

● **Choose a Character and a Quality**
To find a topic for your essay of definition, you can look through your journal or brainstorm with classmates. You can also ask yourself questions such as the following:

Rosa Parks

- What quality means the most to me in a friend? Which character shows that quality most or least?

- Which character do I remember best?

- Why has he or she stayed in my mind?

- What are his or her main qualities?

Choose one of the character's qualities that you understand, admire, or consider important.

530 ❧ THEME 5

ENGLISH LANGUAGE LEARNERS

(MEETING INDIVIDUAL NEEDS)

Preparing for Definition Essays
Help English language learners choose characters for their definition essays by creating a matching game.

Activity Have students work in small groups that include students at various levels of English proficiency. Ask each group to come up with a list of ten characters from the selections in this theme and write their names in a column numbered 1 to 10. Ask students to write one personal quality of each character in a second column, arranged A to J. Have students exchange papers and match each character with the appropriate trait. **COLLAB. LEARN.**

Additional Resources
📁 *English Language Learners Sourcebook*

Writing **WORKSHOP**

● Explore Your Ideas

You might start with a dictionary. Look up the quality you have chosen, and copy the dictionary definition into your journal. Then, in a focused freewriting, move beyond that definition, using your own words. Explore what the quality means to you and how you've seen it demonstrated. Write about people or characters who show that quality.

● Think About Audience and Purpose

Your teacher and classmates will read your essay, and you might aim at a wider audience as well. Your essay might interest a newspaper or magazine columnist exploring teens' viewpoints. It might inspire members of a special-interest group, or it might help a younger person learn about behavior choices. Target your chosen readers with writing that will appeal to them.

● Plan Your Approach

Look over your prewriting notes, and then create a sentence or two summing up your definition. This **thesis statement** will guide you as you plan and draft. Rough out main points explaining your thesis. You might discuss what the quality is and isn't, how it affects people's lives, and what it means to you. To illustrate each point, write notes on examples of actions by a character in this theme and by people in real life.

Stacy Allison

Lou Gehrig

Stacy Allison—Courageously climbed to top of Mount Everest on second attempt in spite of disappointing defeat on first try.

Lou Gehrig—Showed courage in facing a life-threatening disease. Gave "lucky man" speech in Yankee Stadium when forced to quit baseball while still a young man.

Rosa Parks—African American woman who showed courage in fighting against segregation in the early days of the Civil Rights movement.

Explore Your Ideas In addition to the focused free-writing suggested on this page, students may wish to build on their ideas by creating an acrostic, using the quality they have chosen to explore. Suggest that they write the word (*honesty,* for example) vertically and use each letter as part of a new word, phrase, or character name they wish to include in their essays.

Think About Audience and Purpose Remind students that if they are interested in publishing their essays in a newspaper or magazine, they may want to consider using well-known figures from public life as examples of their qualities. They will need to provide background information if they draw entirely from reading selections, since many readers will be unfamiliar with the characters.

Plan Your Approach If students are having difficulty planning their essays, suggest that they make a list of questions to answer when they write. For example:

- What quality will I define?
- Why have I chosen this quality?
- What does the quality mean to me?
- How does it affect my life?
- Have I ever met or read about a person who possesses this quality?

Additional Resources

📁 ***Writing and Proofreading Practice,*** pp. 1–7, 35–42

🖋 ***Writing and Proofreading Transparencies 1–6, 17–18, 33–34***

📘 ***Writer's Choice,*** Lesson 5.4

MEETING INDIVIDUAL NEEDS — MULTIPLE LEARNING STYLES

Logical/Mathematical Students who enjoy applying logical structure to their work may wish to plan and organize their definition essays on a three-pronged pitchfork graphic.

Activity Draw a three-pronged horizontal pitchfork on the board to model the use of this graphic. On the handle of the pitchfork, write the name of a personal quality, such as *loyalty.* On each of the three prongs, write a word or phrase about the topic, such as *Something I Admire; Mrs. Wang; Actions That Show Loyalty.* These serve as themes for students to develop in the main paragraphs of their essays. Encourage students to continue creating prongs until they have included all the information they plan to cover in their definition essays. **L2**

DRAFTING

Start with Flair Make a few books of famous quotations and/or traditional proverbs available to students. Encourage each to look up the personal quality he or she is writing about and find out what other people have said about it. Suggest that students look up related words as well. Remind students that if they decide to use quotations in their essays, they need to cite the authors of the quotes.

Follow Through Encourage students to use the graphics, word clusters, rough sketches, details, quotations, and notes they have created during the prewriting process as inspiration for their writing. While students shouldn't shy away from a new idea just because it isn't part of a plan, they should use the material they created during the prewriting phase as the basis for their essays.

REVISING

Plan Changes Have students read their essays aloud to themselves or to partners. In addition to the Questions for Revising that they find in their books, students should ask themselves how *they* feel about their own work: Does it express their ideas? Can they hear their own voice in the words they have written?

Teaching Options

Writing **WORKSHOP**

DRAFTING

DRAFTING TIP
If you get a new idea for your definition while drafting, try it out. You can always go back to your original prewriting plan if the new idea doesn't work out.

● Start with Flair

Capture your readers' interest with an intriguing statement, a meaningful quotation from a character, or an anecdote illustrating the quality you will define. To let your readers know what to expect from your essay, include a reworded version of your thesis statement in your first paragraph.

> **MODEL · DRAFTING**
>
> It doesn't require a white horse and a suit of armor. It doesn't usually bring fame or fortune. True heroism shows up in small things, but it has big effects.

● Follow Through

Each of your main points might be the topic sentence for a paragraph. The examples you have chosen can provide some of the supporting details. Link your sentences and paragraphs with appropriate transitions, such as *for example, for instance, in this way,* and so on. Wrap up your essay by restating your thesis in different words.

REVISING

REVISING TIP
As you revise, picture your readers. Choose words and images that you can imagine them responding to.

● Plan Changes

After a break, come back to your draft, perhaps with a partner. Use the **Questions for Revising** to plan improvements. You might write your planned changes in the margins of your first draft. Or you might set your first draft aside and write a fresh second draft, incorporating your ideas for improvement.

> **QUESTIONS FOR REVISING**
> ☑ How might I change my introduction to better catch my readers' interest?
> ☑ What transitions might I add to show my readers the connections between ideas?
> ☑ Where might I add examples to show my readers exactly what I mean?
> ☑ Which parts might I rearrange to make my ideas clearer?
> ☑ How might I change my conclusion to give my readers a sense of completion?

Writing *Minilesson*

Paragraph Development As students revise their work, remind them that each paragraph should contain a topic sentence and several supporting sentences.

Activity Have students read the first drafts of their essays and write the topic sentence of each paragraph on a separate sheet of paper. Beneath this, the students can list in bullet form at least three supporting ideas drawn from the paragraph. If there are not at least three supporting ideas, the students should consider further development of their paragraphs. Encourage students to include facts, personal opinions, anecdotes, and sensory details to develop and expand their ideas. **L2**

Additional Resources

📗 *Writer's Choice,* Lesson 2.7

Writing WORKSHOP

EDITING/PROOFREADING

Before writing your final draft, go over your essay once more to fix errors in grammar, usage, and mechanics. Pay special attention to your use of pronouns, as shown in the **Grammar Link** on page 499.

Grammar Hint

Use the comparative form of a modifier when comparing only two things. Use the superlative when comparing more than two things.

Which of the two forces is stronger?
Which of the four boys is strongest?

PROOFREADING CHECKLIST

☑ Modifiers are correctly used. (Double-check comparative forms.)

☑ Sentences are complete. There are no fragments or run-ons.

☑ Verbs agree with their subjects.

☑ Pronouns are in the correct form and agree with their antecedents.

☑ Spelling, capitalization, and punctuation are correct.

MODEL · EDITING/PROOFREADING

Martha and her history teacher are both brave‸
er
but I think Martha is brav‸est.

PUBLISHING/PRESENTING

In a small group, read your essay aloud, and listen to other group members' essays. Then discuss your definitions. Use the group discussion guidelines in the **Communications Skills Handbook,** page R69, to explore areas of agreement and disagreement with one another's views.

PRESENTING TIP
When reading aloud, pause at the ends of sentences and paragraphs to make eye contact with your listeners.

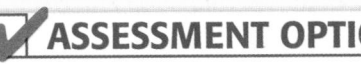

Reflecting

Take a few minutes to think about the questions below. Write your responses in your journal.

• How is your definition like and unlike the dictionary definition?

• Which part(s) of your essay do you consider especially effective? Why?

 Save your work for your portfolio.

AT THE CROSSROADS 🦢 533

EDITING/PROOFREADING

You may wish to assign a different color pencil to each item on the Proofreading Checklist. Have students exchange papers and mark corrections by underlining or circling words with the appropriate pencil. Papers can then be returned and the actual corrections made by the writers. Encourage collaboration through this part of the process and suggest that students ask their "editors" for clarification when necessary.

PUBLISHING/PRESENTING

Students may also be invited to read one another's essays aloud. One essay can be read in its entirety by a classmate, or the essay can be read by several students, each reading one paragraph. Have students talk about the experience of hearing their work read by others.

Reflecting

Portfolio Have students ask themselves these questions as they review their writing. Does my definition essay

• clearly state and define a personal quality?

• explain to my audience why this quality is important?

• use a character from literature as an example of the quality?

✔ ASSESSMENT OPTIONS

📁 ***Writing Assessment and Portfolio Management***
• Writing Assessment, pp. 1–16, 32–34
• Portfolio Management, pp. 17–19

Theme Wrap-Up

Objectives

- To offer a personal response to the selections, discussions, and activities in this theme
- To write a comparison of two characters
- To complete a self-evaluation, set a goal, and devise a plan for achieving the goal

Responding to the Theme

1. Students should be able to support their choices.
2. Accept all reasonable answers.
3. Allow time for students to share their interviews, presentations, and flow charts with the class.

Analyzing Literature

Students' writing should include

- an introductory paragraph that identifies the two characters and the selections(s) the characters come from.
- a comparison of the characters' problems and their ways of responding to them.
- examples and quotations from the text.

Evaluate and Set Goals

Evaluate

Have each student compile a list of activities completed for each task. Suggest that they add other tasks as well, such as accessing a Web site.

Set Goals

Have each student create a web to record their goals and the steps for achieving them. Discuss students' goals and plans in individual conferences.

AT THE CROSSROADS

Theme Wrap-Up

Responding to the Theme

1. Which story, poem, or play in this theme most helped you think about the kinds of crossroads people face at certain times in their lives? Explain your answer.

2. What new ideas do you have about the following as a result of reading the literature in this theme?
   - the points in people's lives when they must make difficult choices
   - how people go about making decisions when faced with a problem

3. Present your theme project to the class.

Analyzing Literature

COMPARE CHARACTERS

Compare two characters from this theme. You may compare the problems they encounter and how they respond to those problems. Remember to support your opinions with examples and quotations from the selections.

Evaluate and Set Goals

1. Which of the following tasks was most rewarding to you? Which was most difficult?
   - reading and thinking about selections
   - doing independent writing
   - analyzing the stories, poems, and teleplay in discussions
   - performing dramatizations
   - making presentations
   - doing research

2. Using the following scale, how would you assess your work in this unit? Give at least two reasons for your assessment.
   - 4 = outstanding   2 = fair
   - 3 = good   1 = weak

3. Based on what you found difficult in this theme, choose a goal to work toward in the next theme.
   - Write down your goal and three steps you will take to help you reach it.
   - Meet with your teacher to review your goal and your plan for achieving it.

Build Your Portfolio

SELECT

Select two pieces of work you did during this theme to include in your portfolio. Use the following questions to help you decide.

- ✦ Which work do you consider your best?
- ✦ From which work did you learn the most?
- ✦ Which work did you enjoy the most?

REFLECT

Write some notes to accompany the work you selected. Use these questions as guides.

- ✦ What do you like best about the piece?
- ✦ What did you learn from creating it?
- ✦ What might you do differently if you were beginning this piece again?

ASSESSMENT OPTIONS

📁 ***Writing Assessment and Portfolio Management***
- Writing Assessment, pp. 1–16
- Portfolio Management, pp. 17–19

GLENCOE

TECHNOLOGY

MINDJOGGER VIDEOQUIZZES
VIDEODISC

Use *MindJogger* to review the Theme 5 content.

Theme 5
Side A

 Also available in VHS.

Reading on Your Own

Have you enjoyed reading the literature in this theme?
If so, here are some other books you might like.

The Slave Dancer
by Paula Fox Jesse is kidnapped and forced to serve on a slave ship. He witnesses the horrors of slavery while providing music as the slaves are forced to exercise to keep themselves strong so they will remain "profitable investments."

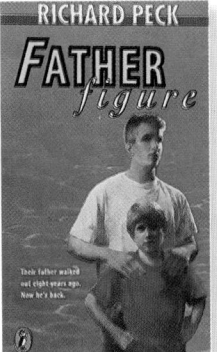

Father Figure
by Richard Peck Jim's role as a substitute father for his younger brother is threatened when, after their mother's death, the boys are sent to spend the summer with their long-absent father.

Sounder
by William Armstrong This award-winning novel deals with the hard lives of African American sharecroppers in the rural South a century ago and with a young boy's growth in understanding with the help of the family's devoted dog.

Running Out of Time
by Margaret Peterson Haddix This exciting thriller tells the story of a thirteen-year-old girl who makes a decision to escape from her community in order to save her family and friends.

Reading on Your Own

Glencoe Literature Library

The Slave Dancer by Paula Fox is one of the titles available in the *Glencoe Literature Library*. For a complete listing, see pp. 46–47 in this book.

The Glencoe Literature Library Study Guide: provides instructional support and student activities for works in the *Glencoe Literature Library*.

At the MOVIES

Be sure to preview the following video for appropriateness for your class.

• *Sounder* (1972, 105 minutes, G)

MEETING INDIVIDUAL NEEDS — INCLUSION STRATEGIES

You may wish to recommend *Sounder* by William Armstrong to students who are less-proficient readers. The simple, eloquent writing style makes this book appropriate for these students. **L1**

The following books are rated for average readers (**L2**) or for students who need more challenging reading material (**L3**):

• *The Slave Dancer* by Paula Fox **L2**
• *Father Figure* by Richard Peck **L2**
• *Running Out of Time* by Margaret Peterson Haddix **L3**

Additional Resources
📁 *Inclusion Strategies*

Answers and Analyses

1. **B** Since the first sentence begins in the present tense with the verb is, the second sentence should also be in the present tense and use visits.

2. **F** Since the sentence begins with the past tense reference *Last Tuesday* and the preceding verb is *rained,* the missing verb must also be in the past tense. H and J therefore can be eliminated. Further, soccer practice is not canceling something else but, instead, soccer practice is what is being cancelled, so the verb must be past tense and passive. The answer is F.

3. **D** The immediately preceding sentence is in the past tense, so the missing verb should also be in the past tense. Therefore students can eliminate choice A and B. And since the narrator is the person with the chance to attend the storyteller's meeting, the verb should be active. Choice D is the only remaining possibility.

4. **F** As with question 3, the immediately preceding sentence is in the past tense, so students should recognize that a past tense verb is required. The past tense of the verb, *craft,* choice F must be correct.

5. **B** Students should recognize that the blank is the subject of the second clause, since it describes who *will be known as the best in the country.* Therefore the pronouns must be the subject pronouns, she and I.

6. **J** Since this sentence asserts that the author will be better than everyone else in the country, the superlative form *best* is needed.

 TEST-TAKING TIP

Remind students that the verb tenses that they can establish the tense of a given verb by looking at the other verbs around it.

 THE PRINCETON REVIEW

Standardized Test Practice

Read the passage and choose the word or group of words that belongs in each space. Mark the letter for your answer on your paper.

My mother is the head storyteller in the town Tall Tale Club. She __(1)__ other clubs and libraries to tell stories. Last Tuesday it rained, and my soccer practice __(2)__. I finally __(3)__ a chance to go with Mom to her weekly meeting. After hearing my mother's stories for years at home, I was able to watch, listen, and learn how a tale was __(4)__.

I was thrilled by my afternoon with the storytellers. I enjoyed myself so much that I plan to ask Mom to teach me how to be a storyteller. Some day I will be a storyteller and __(5)__ will be known as the __(6)__ in the county!

1 **A** visited
   B visits
   C have been visiting
   D was visited

2 **F** was cancelled
   G cancelled
   H will be cancelled
   J could be cancelled

3 **A** have
   B has
   C was having
   D had

4 **F** crafted
   G crafting
   H crafty
   J craftily

5 **A** she and he
   B she and I
   C her and I
   D my mom and me

6 **F** better
   G most best
   H goodest
   J best

Read the passage and decide which type of error, if any, appears in each underlined section. Mark the letter for your answer on your paper.

    Bonsai, now a popular hobby that most people associate with Japan was
<u>(1)</u>
<u>created</u> in China many hundreds of years <u>ago to amuse emporers</u>. People <u>around</u>
    (2)   (3)
<u>the World spend hours</u> clipping branches and nipping leaves to ensure that their

trees stay small. Although the art of bonsai might seem <u>cruel to the trees it is</u>
                                                         (4)
<u>not</u>. By keeping them <u>trimmed, you ensure the trees health</u> and development.
                          (5)
The most important skill to master is watering the trees. Although watering

sounds simple, the tree will drown if it gets too much water, and it will dry out if

it gets too little water. <u>If you water your Tree</u> regularly, it will be on the path to a
                          (6)
long life.

---

1 A Spelling error
   B Capitalization error
   C Punctuation error
   D No error

2 F Spelling error
   G Capitalization error
   H Punctuation error
   J No error

3 A Spelling error
   B Capitalization error
   C Punctuation error
   D No error

4 F Spelling error
   G Capitalization error
   H Punctuation error
   J No error

5 A Spelling error
   B Capitalization error
   C Punctuation error
   D No error

6 F Spelling error
   G Capitalization error
   H Punctuation error
   J No error

Answers and Analyses

1. **C** The appositive *now a popular hobby that most people associate with Japan* should be set off with commas on both sides.
2. **F** The word *emperors* is misspelled.
3. **B** Since the word *world* is not a proper noun, it should not be capitalized.
4. **H** A comma should be placed after prepositional phrases such as *Although the art of bonsai might seem cruel to the trees.*
5. **C** Students should recognize that of the word *trees* is possessive, and needs an apostrophe.
6. **G** Since the word *tree* is not a proper noun, it should not be capitalized.

TEST-TAKING TIP

There are only three kinds of errors tested in this exercise: spelling, capitalization, and punctuation. Students should check carefully for these three errors; if none of the words is misspelled, no capitalization is erroneous or missing, and there are no punctuation errors, then they should pick No Error.

Theme 6 — At a Glance
Twists and Turns

THEME OPENING → Theme 6:
TWISTS AND TURNS

- **Introducing the Theme** (p. 539)
- **Exploring the Theme** (p. 540)
- **Theme Projects** (p. 541)

SELECTIONS

Media Connection: Calvin and Hobbes (p. 542)

Charles (p. 543)

No News (p. 543)

Who's On First (p. 554)

After Twenty Years (p. 564)

The Million-Pound Bank Note (p. 572)

The Force of Luck (p. 590)

Beware of the Dog (p. 602)

Active Reading Model: The Highwayman (p. 620)

Annabel Lee (p. 628)

Media Connection: *from* My Ninety Years (p. 634)

The Cremation of Sam McGee (p. 635)

SKILL FEATURES

Grammar Link (p. 553)

Technology Skills (pp. 562–563)

Listening, Speaking, and Viewing (p. 571)

Interdisciplinary Connection (p. 601)

Genre Focus: Poetry (pp. 616–617)

Active Reading Strategies (pp. 618–619)

Vocabulary Skills (p. 633)

Reading and Thinking Skills (p. 643)

WRITING WORKSHOP

Narrative Writing: Short Story (pp. 644–647)

THEME WRAP-UP

- **Responding to the Theme, Analyzing Literature, Evaluate and Set Goals** (p. 648)

- **Build Your Portfolio** (p. 648)

- **Reading on Your Own** (p. 649)

  The Adventures of Tom Sawyer by Mark Twain

  The Oxford Book of Story Poems edited by Michael Harrison and Christopher Stuart-Clark

  The One Who Came Back by Joan Mazzio

  Talking to the Sun selected by Kenneth Koch and Kate Farrell

- **Standardized Test Practice** (pp. 650–651)

KEYS TO LITERARY CONNECTIONS

 Comparing Selections

The **Comparing Selections** feature in this theme provides opportunities for addressing diverse aspects of the reading and literature curriculum.

For example, in Comparing Selections on page 600, students take a closer look at the characters and plots of "The Million-Pound Bank Note" by Mark Twain and "The Force of Luck" by Rudolfo A. Anaya. Through this comparison, students can gain insight into human instinct and motivation.

KEYS TO TEACHING OPTIONS

 Block Scheduling

Activities that are particularly suited to use within a block scheduling framework are identified throughout this theme by the following designation: For detailed suggestions on block scheduling, see the **Block Scheduling Guide** for this grade level.

Key to Ability Levels

The **Teaching Options** throughout this theme have been coded for students of various abilities.

L1 BASIC activities for all students

L2 AVERAGE activities for average to above-average students

L3 CHALLENGING activities for above-average students

Reading Skills in this theme

Variety of Texts

In addition to poetry, this theme includes the following text types:

- short story
- folktale
- comedy script
- drama
- cartoon strip
- oral history

Comprehension Skills

The following instructional support for comprehension skills appears in this theme of the Student Edition:

- **Reading and Thinking Minilessons** (pp. 552, 615, 642)
- **Active Reading Strategies and Model** (pp. 618–627)
- **Identifying Cause-and-Effect Relationships** (p. 643)

See also the **Reading Minilessons** throughout the theme in this Teacher's Wraparound Edition.

Reading Resources

Comprehension Skills Resources

Active Reading Guides

The **Active Reading Guide** provides graphic organizers and study guide questions to support students' reading of each selection (**Active Reading Guide**, pp. 46–54).

Reading Workbook

The **Reading Workbook** (pp. 81–96) includes additional instruction and reinforcement of reading strategies and skills.

Audio Library

Available both on tape and on CD, the **Audio Library** provides valuable comprehension support.

Resources for Reading Widely

Glencoe Literature Library

Each title in the *Glencoe Literature Library* includes a full-length novel or play plus related readings. A separate Study Guide is available for each title.

Literature Classics CD-ROM

The selections on this CD-ROM can be searched by author, theme, or genre.

A coproduction of Glencoe and Time, Inc., the *inTime* magazine includes a wealth of high interest nonfiction related to the selections in Theme Six.

✔ Assessment in this theme

Assessment Options in the Student Edition

Glencoe Literature offers a number of diverse ways to evaluate student understanding and skill proficiency. In the Student Edition, use the following:

- **Responding to Literature**
  Following each selection, students are asked to recall facts, interpret ideas, and evaluate concepts as they answer a variety of questions and complete activities to extend their understanding.
- **Theme Wrap-Up (pp. 648–649)**
  Here students respond to the selections on personal and analytical levels. They also assume ownership of their learning by setting and evaluating goals and by selecting work for their portfolios.

See also the many **Assessment Resources** listed on the facing page.

THE PRINCETON REVIEW

Standardized Test Practice

The Princeton Review has developed the Standardized Test Practice pages found at the end of this theme (pp. 650–651). These pages contain practice test questions that help students remain familiar with standardized test formats and content.

- ITBS Preparation and Practice
- SAT-9 Preparation and Practice
- TerraNova Preparation and Practice

Writing Skills in this theme

Writing Skills

The Student Edition of Theme Six offers strong instructional support for writing skills:

In **Extending Your Response**, which follows each selection:
- **Writing About Literature**
- **Personal/Creative Writing**

See also the **Writing Minilessons** throughout the theme in this Teacher's Wraparound Edition.

Writing Workshops

Theme Six concludes with a **Writing Workshop** that guides students through the process of writing a short story (pp. 644–647).

Writing Resources

Writer's Assistant CD-ROM
Each Writing Workshop is supplemented by an interactive writing guide on the Writer's Assistant CD-ROM. This easy-to-use writing guide provides prompts, templates, and other tools that lead students through the writing process.

Writing and Proofreading Practice
Blackline masters present in-depth instruction and practice on a specific step in the writing process and proofreading (pp. 1–7, 43–49).

Writing and Proofreading Transparencies
Transparencies provide graphic organizers and proofreading exercises for whole-class instruction (pp. 1–6, 21–22, 35–36).

Research and Report Writing Guide
This resource provides extensive tips and activities to guide students in their writing projects in the literature classroom as well as in classes across the curriculum.

Style and Documentation Sourcebook for Writers
This sourcebook is a combination reference and workbook, giving students the most up-to-date information and guidance regarding traditional as well as technological research strategies and documentation.

Grammar and Composition Handbook
The Grammar and Composition Handbook provides instruction that supplements activities in the student textbook.

Assessment Resources

Selection Quick Checks
For each selection, a Quick Check of three to five short-answer questions measures students' literal comprehension.

Selection and Theme Assessment
The Selection and Theme Assessment instrument tests students' abilities to recall, interpret, and evaluate what they've read. The tests consist of multiple-choice, short answer, and essay questions.

Performance Assessment
Alternative assessment instruments and rubrics for Theme Six are found in the Performance Assessment ancillary.

Writing Assessment and Portfolio Management
These notes and strategies, student models, and assessment tools assist with the task of measuring students' progress as writers and as monitors of their own writing.

Testmaker
Teachers can customize selection and Theme Six tests by accessing the Testmaker database.

Mindjogger Videoquizzes
Using a popular game show format, Mindjogger Videoquizzes enable teachers to evaluate student understanding of Theme Six in a quick and fun manner.

SELECTIONS	Literary Elements	Reading and Thinking	Writing	Vocabulary and Spelling	
Charles SHIRLEY JACKSON **No News** CONNIE REGAN-BLAKE AND BARBARA FREEMAN	Plot Twist, SE p. 550 *Plot, TWE pp. 545–549* *Character, TWE p. 545* *Point of View, TWE p. 548* *Irony, TWE p. 549*	Drawing Conclusions, SE p. 552 **COLLAB. LEARN.** *Comparing/ Contrasting, TWE p. 546* *Inferring, TWE p. 547*	Paragraph (Foreshadowing), SE p. 551 Personal Narrative, SE p. 551	The Prefix *re-*, SE p. 552	
Who's on First? BUD ABBOTT AND LOU COSTELLO	Dialogue, SE p. 560; *TWE pp. 556, 557, 559* *Conflict, TWE pp. 556, 558* *Comedy TWE p. 557* *Indirect Char., TWE p. 558*	**COLLAB. LEARN.** *Monitoring Comprehension, TWE p. 557* *Drawing Conclusions, TWE p. 558*	Paragraph (Puns and Humor), SE p. 561 Comedy Routine, SE p. 561	Homonyms, SE p. 561 *Dialect, TWE p. 557*	
After Twenty Years O. HENRY	Short Story, SE p. 569 *Characterization, TWE p. 566* *Plot, TWE pp. 566, 567, 568* *Dialogue, TWE p. 567* *Setting, TWE p. 567*	*Drawing Conclusions, TWE p. 567* *Comparing/Contrasting, TWE p. 567*	Paragraph (Analyzing Loyalty), SE p. 570 Paragraph (Irony), SE p. 570	The Suffix *-ity*, SE p. 570	
The Million-Pound Bank Note MARK TWAIN	Stage Directions, SE p. 588; *TWE pp. 578, 581, 582* *Narrator, TWE pp. 577, 579, 582, 585* *Irony, TWE p. 577*	*Synthesizing, TWE p. 575* *Drawing Conclusions, TWE pp. 576, 578, 579, 583* *Critical Judgments, TWE p. 580*	Dialogue and Monologue, SE p. 589 Newpaper Articles, SE p. 589 *Play as Story, TWE p. 579*	Etymology, SE p. 589 *Etymology, TWE p. 584*	
The Force of Luck RUDOLFO A. ANAYA	Folktales, SE p. 599 *Character, TWE p. 593* *Foreshadowing, TWE pp. 593, 595* *Folktales, TWE pp. 594, 596, 598*	*Using Text Struct., TWE p. 593* *Logical Reasoning, TWE p. 595* *Draw. Conc., TWE pp. 596, 597* *Sythesizing, TWE p. 597* *Analyze Argmnts., TWE p. 598*	Monologues, SE p. 599 *Different Ending to Story, TWE p. 596*	*Etymology, TWE pp. 596, 597*	
BEWARE OF THE DOG ROALD DAHL	Flashback, SE p. 613; *TWE pp. 605, 608, 612* *Setting, TWE p. 605* *Suspense, TWE pp. 606–608*	*Synthesizing, TWE p. 605* *Logical Reasoning, TWE pp. 609, 610*	Analysis, SE p. 614 Epilogue, SE p. 614 *Descriptive Scene, TWE p. 608*	Using Context Clues for Multiple-Meaning Words, SE p. 615	
The Highwayman ALFRED NOYES	Onomotopoeia, SE p. 626 *Onomotopoeia, TWE pp. 622* *Plot, TWE pp. 622, 624*	*Evaluating, TWE p. 623* **COLLAB. LEARN.** *Monitoring Comprehension, TWE p. 623*	Description (Narrative Elements), SE p. 627 Character Interview, SE p. 627		
ANNABEL LEE EDGAR ALLAN POE	Rhythm and Meter, SE p. 631: *TWE p. 630* *Stanza Types: Sestet, TWE p. 629*	*Critical Judgments, TWE p. 629* *Elaborating, TWE p. 630* *Paraphrasing, TWE p. 630*	Paragraph (Imagery), SE p. 632 Journal Entry, SE p. 632		
THE CREMATION OF SAM MCGEE ROBERT W. SERVICE	Rhyme, SE p. 641; *TWE pp. 637, 638;* *Foreshadow, TWE p. 637;* *Simile, TWE p. 637;* *Alliteration, TWE p. 638;* *Climax, TWE p. 639; Imagery,* *TWE p. 640; Point of View,* *TWE p. 640; Mood, TWE p. 640*	Sequence of Events, SE p. 642 *Main Ideas/Details, TWE p. 638* *Evaluating, TWE p. 639* *Drawing Conclusions, TWE p. 639*	Paragraph: Setting, SE p. 642 Television News Report, SE p. 642	*Slang, TWE p. 638*	

Key: Student material is in roman. Teacher material is in italic. Technology **COLLAB. LEARN.** Collaboration

Grammar and Language	Listening, Speaking, and Viewing	Life Skills	Study, Research, and Technology
Correct Pronoun Use, SE p. 552 *Apostrophes, TWE p. 548*	**COLLAB. LEARN.** Literature Groups, SE p. 551 **COLLAB. LEARN.** Performing (Dramatize a Scene), SE p. 551 Interviewing, SE p. 551	*Interpersonal (Chart New Experiences), TWE p. 545*	
Using Troublesome Words: Homophones, TWE p. 558	**COLLAB. LEARN.** Lit. Grps., SE p. 561 **COLLAB. LEARN.** Performing (Vaudeville Skit), SE p. 561 *Film, TWE p. 557* *Video, TWE p. 560*		
Adjective Clauses, TWE p. 568	**COLLAB. LEARN.** Literature Groups, SE p. 570	Newspaper Column, SE p. 570	
Using Commas to Join Main Clauses, TWE p. 586	**COLLAB. LEARN.** Literature Groups, SE p. 589 *Reading a Scene Aloud, TWE p. 578* *Video, TWE p. 587*	*Creating and Producing a Radio Play, TWE p. 583*	🖳 Internet Connection, SE p. 589 **COLLAB. LEARN.** *Research and Compare Exchange Rates, TWE p. 580*
Identifying the Subject of a Sentence, TWE p. 598	**COLLAB. LEARN.** Literature Groups, SE p. 599 *Storytelling, TWE p. 595*		🖳 *Folktales, TWE p. 597*
Complex Sentences, SE p. 615 *Troublesome Words: Lie, TWE p. 612*	**COLLAB. LEARN.** Literature Groups, SE p. 614 *Reading Scenes Aloud, TWE p. 611*	Learning for Life: Interviewing, SE p. 614	Research and Create a Map, SE p. 614
Colorful Adjectives, SE p. 627 *Compound Sentences, TWE p. 624*	**COLLAB. LEARN.** Lit. Grps., SE p. 627 **COLLAB. LEARN.** Choral Reading, SE p. 627		
Punctuating Poetry, SE p. 632	**COLLAB. LEARN.** Literature Groups, SE p. 632 Storytelling Festival, SE p. 632 *Video, TWE p. 631*		
Semicolons, TWE p. 640	**COLLAB. LEARN.** Literature Groups, SE p. 642 **COLLAB. LEARN.** Radio Performance of Poem, SE p. 642 *Poetry Reading, TWE p. 639*		

SELECTIONS	📂 Print Resources		
Charles SHIRLEY JACKSON **No News** CONNIE REGAN-BLAKE AND BARBARA FREEMAN	Theme Six Planning Guide, pp. 6–11 * Active Reading Guide, p. 46 Vocabulary Practice, p. 32	Grammar & Comp. Handbook, Lessons 4.2, 13.7 Grammar & Language Workbook, pp. 107–108, 273–274 Reading Workbook, pp. 81–82	* Quick Checks, p. 46 Sel. and Theme Assess., pp. 81–82 Performance Assessment, p. 43 Spanish Summaries, p. 46
Who's on First? BUD ABBOTT AND LOU COSTELLO	Theme Six Planning Guide, pp. 12–19 * Active Reading Guide, p. 47	Grammar & Comp. Handbook, Lesson 15.1 Grammar & Language Workbook, pp. 227–228, 295–296 Reading Workbook, pp. 83–84	* Quick Checks, p. 47 Sel. and Theme Assess., p. 83 Performance Assessment, p. 44 Spanish Summaries, p. 47
After Twenty Years O. HENRY	Theme Six Planning Guide, pp. 20–27 * Active Reading Guide, p. 48 Vocabulary Practice, p. 33	Grammar & Comp. Handbook, Lesson 8.3 Grammar & Language Workbook, pp. 157–158 Reading Workbook, pp. 85–86	* Quick Checks, p. 48 Sel. and Theme Assess., p. 84 Performance Assessment, p. 45 Spanish Summaries, p. 48 Spanish Translations
The Million-Pound Bank Note MARK TWAIN	Theme Six Planning Guide, pp. 28–35 * Active Reading Guide, p. 49 Vocabulary Practice, p. 34	Grammar & Comp. Handbook, Lesson 13.3 Grammar & Language Workbook, pp. 257–258 Reading Workbook, pp. 87–88	* Quick Checks, p. 49 Sel. and Theme Assess., pp. 85–86 Performance Assessment, p. 46 Spanish Summaries, p. 49 Spanish Translations
The Force of Luck RUDOLFO A. ANAYA	Theme Six Planning Guide, pp. 36–43 * Active Reading Guide, p. 50 Vocabulary Practice, p. 35	Grammar & Comp. Handbook, Lesson 1.3 Grammar & Language Workbook, pp. 51–52 Reading Workbook, pp. 89–90	* Quick Checks, p. 50 Sel. and Theme Assess., pp. 87–88 Performance Assessment, p. 47 Spanish Summaries, p. 50
BEWARE OF THE DOG ROALD DAHL	Theme Six Planning Guide, pp. 44–51 * Active Reading Guide, p. 51 Vocabulary Practice, p. 36	Grammar & Comp. Handbook, Lessons 8.2, 3.11, 3.12 Grammar & Language Workbook, pp. 155–156, 223–224 Reading Workbook, pp. 91–92	* Quick Checks, p. 51 Sel. and Theme Assess., pp. 89–90 Performance Assessment, p. 48 Spanish Summaries, p. 51 Spanish Translations
The Highwayman ALFRED NOYES	Theme Six Planning Guide, pp. 52–59 * Active Reading Guide, p. 52	Grammar & Comp. Handbook, Lessons 5.1, 14.1 Grammar & Language Workbook, pp. 117–118, 153–154 Reading Workbook, pp. 93–94	* Quick Checks, p. 52 Sel. and Theme Assess., pp. 91–92 Performance Assessment, p. 49 Spanish Summaries, p. 52
ANNABEL LEE EDGAR ALLAN POE	Theme Six Planning Guide, pp. 60–64 * Active Reading Guide, p. 53	Grammar & Comp. Handbook, Lesson 13.1 Grammar & Language Workbook, pp. 253–254	* Quick Checks, p. 53 Sel. and Theme Assess., p. 93 Performance Assessment, p. 50 Spanish Summaries, p. 53
THE CREMATION OF SAM McGEE ROBERT W. SERVICE	Theme Six Planning Guide, pp. 65–72 * Active Reading Guide, p. 54	Grammar & Comp. Handbook, Lesson 13.5 Grammar & Language Workbook, pp. 265–266 Reading Workbook, pp. 95–96	* Quick Checks, p. 54 Sel. and Theme Assess., p. 94 Performance Assessment, p. 51 Spanish Summaries, p. 54 Spanish Translations

*Also available in Spanish

Transparencies	Technology Resources
Selection Focus Transparency 46 Grammar and Language Transparency 45 Literary Elements Transparency 46 Fine Art Transparency 23	Audio Library Spanish Audio Library Vocabulary Puzzlemaker Web Site: lit.glencoe.com
Selection Focus Transparency 47 Grammar and Language Transparency 46 Literary Elements Transparency 47	Literature Launchers Audio Library Spanish Audio Library Vocabulary Puzzlemaker Web Site: lit.glencoe.com
Selection Focus Transparency 48 Grammar and Language Transparency 47 Literary Elements Transparency 48 Fine Art Transparency 11	Audio Library Spanish Audio Library Vocabulary Puzzlemaker Web Site: lit.glencoe.com
Selection Focus Transparency 49 Grammar and Language Transparency 48 Literary Elements Transparency 49	Literature Launchers Audio Library Spanish Audio Library Vocabulary Puzzlemaker Web Site: lit.glencoe.com
Selection Focus Transparency 50 Grammar and Language Transparency 49 Literary Elements Transparency 50 Fine Art Transparency 26	Audio Library Spanish Audio Library Vocabulary Puzzlemaker Web Site: lit.glencoe.com
Selection Focus Transparency 51 Grammar and Language Transparency 50 Literary Elements Transparency 51 Fine Art Transparency 13	Literature Launchers Audio Library Spanish Audio Library Vocabulary Puzzlemaker Web Site: lit.glencoe.com
Selection Focus Transparency 52 Grammar and Language Transparency 51 Literary Elements Transparency 52	Audio Library Spanish Audio Library Vocabulary Puzzlemaker Web Site: lit.glencoe.com
Selection Focus Transparency 53 Literary Elements Transparency 53	Audio Library Spanish Audio Library Vocabulary Puzzlemaker Web Site: lit.glencoe.com
Selection Focus Transparency 54 Grammar and Language Transparency 52 Literary Elements Transparency 54	Audio Library Spanish Audio Library Vocabulary Puzzlemaker Web Site: lit.glencoe.com

📁 Theme RESOURCES

- Listening and Speaking Activities (pp. 16–18)
- Viewing and Representing Activities (pp. 1–6, 22–24)
- Critical Thinking Skills (pp. 15–17)
- Media Connection Activities (pp. 11–12)
- Interdisciplinary Activities (pp. 22–25)
- Family and Community Activities (p. 16)
- Selection and Theme Assessment (pp. 135–136)

See also these additional planning resources:
- English Language Learners Sourcebook
- Inclusion Strategies Sourcebook
- Literature Groups Sourcebook

PRESENTATION Plus!

Use Glencoe's *Presentation Plus!* This multimedia teaching tool lets you present dynamic lessons that will engage your students. Using Microsoft PowerPoint®, you can customize the presentation to create your own personalized lessons.

Twists and Turns

Theme Objectives

- To enjoy reading about the tricks of fate that influence people's lives
- To analyze the literary elements in poetry, folktale, short story, and comedy selections
- To apply strategies for reading poetry

Teaching Strategies

Have students read the quote from "Nobody Knows My Name" by James Baldwin in preparation for the discussion questions on page 539.

VIEWING THE ART

Responding to the Art After discussing the Baldwin quotation, direct students to the photo of the maze. Ask:

- Have you ever seen or been in a maze like this one?
- James Baldwin says that life is like a waterwheel. In what way can life also be like a maze? (*Life is full of twists and turns. As in a maze, you must make choices, and you never know what might be around the next curve.*)

Twists and Turns

> ❝ . . . life is a water wheel. It turns. The trick is to hold your nose when you're under and not get dizzy when you're up. ❞
>
> —James Baldwin, *Nobody Knows My Name*

538

TEACHER to TEACHER

J.P. ELDER MIDDLE SCHOOL • FORTH WORTH, TEXAS

My students can be very one-sided in their observations. So, when introducing the theme "Twists and Turns," I have all the students stand on their chairs, and I ask, "How does the room look to you?" Next, I'll have a few students sit on the floor in a corner and ask, "How does the room look to you now?" We discuss how the classroom—a place where they sit every day and largely take for granted—can offer a different perspective. To reinforce the idea, I read the children's picture book *True Story of the Three Little Pigs,* which is told from the point of view of the Big Bad Wolf. We discuss how the book illustrates the fact that, when we change our perspective, the story changes. Then I talk about the twists and turns of life that they'll see if they keep their eyes open.

LEE A. FELTS

THEME
6

THEME CONTENTS

Charles • short story by Shirley Jackson 544

No News • folktale retold by
Connie Regan-Blake and Barbara Freeman 549

Who's on First? • comedy script
by Bud Abbott and Lou Costello 555

After Twenty Years • short story by O. Henry 565

The Million-Pound Bank Note •
drama based on a short story by Mark Twain 573

The Force of Luck •
folktale by Rudolfo A. Anaya 591

Beware of the Dog • short story by Roald Dahl 603

GENRE FOCUS *POETRY*

The Highwayman • poem by Alfred Noyes 621

Annabel Lee • poem by Edgar Allan Poe 629

The Cremation of Sam McGee •
poem by Robert Service 636

RESOURCE MANAGER

See the **Theme Six Planning Guide** (pp. 1–5) for additional teaching notes, strategies, and resources for introducing the theme "Twists and Turns."

GLENCOE
T E C H N O L O G Y

LITERATURE CLASSICS CD-ROM
Search for other selections related to the theme "Twists and Turns."

Introducing the Theme

Direct your students' attention to the **Theme Contents.** Ask them to read through the list of selections. Present these questions for discussion:

- Do any of the short story titles seem to suggest that the story might have a surprise ending? *(Students may mention that the stories by O. Henry, Mark Twain, and Rudolfo A. Anaya have mysterious titles and therefore could result in a surprise ending.)*
- Look at the list of authors in Theme 6. Have you read anything by these writers before? What kind of writing do you expect from Mark Twain? Edgar Allen Poe? Roald Dahl? *(Students might expect Mark Twain's writing to be comical, Edgar Allen Poe's writing to be dark and serious, and Roald Dahl's writing to be directed at children.)*
- As you read the titles, which selection interests you most? Why?

Additional Resources

- 📁 *Interdisciplinary Activities,* pp. 22–25
- 📁 *Viewing and Representing Activities,* pp. 22–24
- 📁 *Listening and Speaking Activities,* pp. 16–18
- 📁 *Critical Thinking Skills,* pp. 15–17
- 📁 *Selection and Theme Assessment,* pp. 135–136
- 📁 *Performance Assessment,* p. 74
- 📁 *Fine Art Transparency 12*

LITERATURE & HUMANITIES

💿 Have students examine *The Jungle* from the CD *National Museum of Women in the Arts,* and discuss why the artist might have chosen to show most of the figure but kept the face hidden. Is this twist meant to evoke curiosity or self-reflection?

Exploring the Theme

Twists and Turns

Introduce the phrase *sleight-of-hand* to students and discuss its meaning. *(Sleight-of-hand is a skill in using the hands to confuse, deceive, or perform tricks. It is also known as* legerdemain, *from the Old French for "light of hand.")* Ask students to work in groups or pairs to prepare card or "magic" tricks that employ sleight-of-hand to show the class.

Starting Points

A View with a Twist
Students may think the character in *Modern Times* appears to be taking it calmly. Students might respond that they would feel shocked, afraid, and angry.

Appreciating Life's Bumps
In some cultures, the saying *"May all your dreams come true"* is a blessing. In other cultures, it's a curse. Ask each student to choose a personal dream and ask what would happen if it unexpectedly came true.

Point out that a single event can impact the various people involved in it very differently. Ask students who know a "blessing in disguise" story to tell it from two viewpoints: their own and another person's.

After students draw their pictures, allow time for them to share their experiences in small groups.

FINE ART
TRANSPARENCY 12

You may wish to use *Fine Art Transparency 12* to enrich thinking.

Exploring the Theme

Twists and Turns

What makes literature interesting? The same twists and turns that make life interesting. In this theme, you will discover the surprising actions that characters take in order to deal with life's unexpected events. To begin your own thinking about the theme, choose one of the options below.

Starting Points

A VIEW WITH A TWIST
How often do you try looking at, reading, or thinking about something from a different point of view? Sometimes, by simply trying another viewpoint, your impression of reality can change dramatically.

- In Charlie Chaplin's classic comedy film *Modern Times,* his character gets pulled into the gears of a huge machine. How do you think he felt about this plot twist? How would you feel?

APPRECIATING LIFE'S BUMPS
Life doesn't always go smoothly. Sometimes, however, difficulties turn out to be surprise blessings. At other times, events you look forward to can turn out to be disasters. These all become the life experiences that make good stories.

- Think about an entertaining or dramatic event in your life that you have described more than once to

your family and friends. Draw a picture of this moment when, out of the blue, life surprised you in a positive or negative way.

Charlie Chaplin in the movie *Modern Times.*

Family and Community Activity

Have students create situations through which they can observe what happens when positive, unexpected events occur in people's lives. Ask each student to secretly choose a person for whom he or she would like to do something kind. Have students list ten things to do for this person and compile a schedule for when to do them. As they read the selections in

Theme 6, students should do their secret acts of kindness, and each should keep a short journal of the experience. Journal entries could include what the act was, when and how it was done, what the person's reaction was, and how long it was possible to remain anonymous.

Additional Resources
📁 *Family and Community Activities,* p. 16

Theme Projects

As you read the selections in this theme, complete one of the projects below. Work on your own, with a partner, or with a group.

LEARNING FOR LIFE
Writing an Incident Report
Events in real life are often the inspiration for events in fiction. Take notes about an actual news event that you have read or heard about.

1. Write a report as if you were an official investigating the incident. Describe the people involved, the series of events that led to the incident, the incident itself, and the outcome.
2. Share your report with the class. Ask classmates to help you check for any missing information.

PERFORMING
Storytelling
1. Choose a story with an unusual twist in the plot.
2. To learn the story, read it more than once. Then make an outline using your own words.
3. Practice telling the story in front of a mirror. Remember that facial expressions and gestures are important parts of the storyteller's art.
4. Perform your story in front of an audience. Make sure to use your voice to emphasize any surprises in the plot.

CRITICAL READING
Discovering the Unexpected
1. Review the plots of the stories and poems you have read recently.
2. Choose a plot with a turn of events that surprised you.
3. Rewrite the climax of the plot so that the outcome changes. Share your new story with your classmates.

interNET CONNECTION

You'll find more project ideas on the Web. You can also check out the Glencoe Web site to find out more about the literature selections in this theme. Here's the address: lit.glencoe.com

MULTIMEDIA PROJECT
Dramatizing
1. Working with a large group or the whole class, choose a story with a plot twist. It can be a story from this theme, from another theme, or from a source other than your literature book.
2. Discuss the story. Then work together to turn it into a script for a radio or television play.
3. Assign tasks to group members. You will need actors, a director, people to provide sound effects (for a radio play), scenery and perhaps costumes (for television), and background music. If you want to present your dramatization on audiotape or videotape, you will also need a technical crew to run the equipment.
4. Rehearse your script carefully. Then perform your story in front of an audience, or record it for presentation on audiotape or videotape.

TWISTS AND TURNS 541

Theme Projects

Teaching Strategies
The following suggestions may help your students plan and carry out their theme projects.

Learning for Life
- Bring in newspapers and magazines for students to look through to find events that interest them. Suggest that they use the Internet and other library resources to gather as much information as they can about the stories.
- Encourage students to report on historical events if current events do not interest them.
- Invite each student to write a rough draft of a fictionalized story based on the selected real-life incident. The draft could include who the main characters are, where the story takes place, what the main event is, and how the story ends.

Multimedia Project
- If students have difficulty thinking of a story with an unusual plot twist, recommend other stories written by this theme's authors, such as O. Henry, Edgar Allen Poe, and Shirley Jackson.
- Students may wish to videotape their storytelling performances individually or in a group and show them to the class.

Critical Reading
- Allow time for students to review the stories and poems in Themes 1–5.
- Students' papers should include the climax of the story as it appears in the book, with the new version beneath it.
- When students share their new stories with the class, have each one give a short synopsis of the original story to refresh classmates' memories.

Twists and Turns Students can use a search engine to find out more about unexpected turns of events. They might use such keywords as *exploration, invention, history, updated fairy tales,* or any other point of interest.

MEDIA
Connection

Objective

- To read and understand a comic strip

Literature — LINK

Charles This comic strip connects to the short story "Charles" by Shirley Jackson (pp. 544–548). In the comic strip, Calvin has created a portrait of himself that communicates to his parents something about how he's feeling in school. Laurie, the kindergartner in "Charles," is equally amusing when he creates an entire persona for himself as a way of letting his parents know what is happening at school.

Respond
Answers

1. Some students may think Calvin's mother expected to get a positive report from Calvin's teacher. Others may think she expected to hear that Calvin was having trouble in school.
2. Possible answers include that Calvin is a creative child, that his behavior is a bit wild, or that he sees himself as different from the other students.

Additional Resources
📁 *Media Connections*, p. 11

Teaching Options

interNET CONNECTION

Self-portraits Have students use a search engine to look for self-portraits by artists of their choice. Suggest that they try entering the name of the artist, such as: *Van Gogh, Monet, Warhol, Chagall;* or keywords such as *impressionism, painters, self-portraits.*

MEDIA
Connection

from Calvin and Hobbes
by Bill Watterson

Respond

1. What do you think Calvin's mother expected to happen at the meeting?
2. What does Calvin's self-portrait suggest about his behavior at school?

Reading *Minilesson*

Identifying Author's Purpose The twists and turns of everyday life are the raw material from which comic strip writers get their ideas.

Activity Ask students to do a comic strip treasure hunt over the next few days. Have students write a description of each comic strip they see, where they see it, and who the writer is. After students have collected a few days' worth of comic strips, ask them to share their findings with the class. Encourage them to try to identify the writer's purpose in writing the comic strip. **L2**

Additional Resources
📁 *Reading Workbook*

Before You Read
Charles and No News

MEET SHIRLEY JACKSON

Shirley Jackson's fiction is filled with strange twists and turns. In most of her novels and short stories, she explores the darker side of human life. However, Jackson also wrote humorously about family life, as she does in "Charles."

Shirley Jackson was born in 1919 and died in 1965.

MEET CONNIE REGAN-BLAKE AND BARBARA FREEMAN

Regan-Blake and Freeman are cousins who started telling stories as children. They have traveled around the country collecting and telling stories for more than twenty years. Many of their stories, like "No News," are set in the rural South.

Connie Regan-Blake was born in 1947; Barbara Freeman was born in 1944.

FOCUS ACTIVITY

Have you ever heard the expression *read between the lines?*

Sharing Ideas
In a small group, talk about the meaning of the expression and give examples of moments when the expression might be used in conversation.

Setting a Purpose
Try to read between the lines to discover the twists and turns in these two selections.

BACKGROUND

Did You Know? Children entering school must learn to get along with each other, follow directions, and help with classroom routines. In kindergarten, children become accustomed to a school setting and learn to play together.

VOCABULARY PREVIEW

raucous (rô′ kəs) *adj.* loud and rough-sounding; p. 544
insolently (in′ sə lənt lē) *adv.* in a boldly rude manner; p. 544
simultaneously (sī′ məl tā′ nē əs lē) *adv.* at the same time; p. 546
solemnly (sol′ əm lē) *adv.* seriously; p. 546
reformation (ref′ ər mā′ shən) *n.* a change for the better; improvement; p. 547
cynically (sin′ ə kəl lē) *adv.* in a way that shows doubt or disbelief; doubtfully; p. 547
primly (prim′ lē) *adv.* in a stiffly formal manner; p. 548
lapse (laps) *n.* a slipping or falling away; p. 548

Before Reading

Objectives

- To read and analyze two stories about dealing with bad news
- To identify plot elements in two stories
- To write a paragraph describing foreshadowing

Skills

Reading/Thinking: Comparing and Contrasting; Inferring; Drawing Conclusions
Writing: Narrative
Vocabulary: The Prefix *re-*
Grammar/Language: Apostrophes; Correct Pronoun Use
Listening/Speaking: Dramatization; Interview
Collaboration: Performance; Literature Groups

Motivating
→OPTIONS

Selection Focus Transparency 46: Have students read and discuss the quotation from William Shakespeare's *Antony and Cleopatra.*

Focus Activity: As an extension of the Focus Activity, have students work in small groups to create one or more cartoons that express the idea of reading between the lines.

RESOURCE MANAGER

Lesson Planning Resource
The *Theme Six Planning Guide* (pp. 6–11) provides additional lesson notes and reduced versions of all print resources.

📁 Other Print Resources
- Active Reading Guide, p. 46
- Vocabulary Practice, p. 32
- Reading Workbook, pp. 81–82
- Grammar and Language Workbook, pp. 107–108, 273–274

- Grammar and Composition Handbook, Lessons 4.2, 13.7
- Quick Checks, p. 46
- Selection and Theme Assessment, pp. 81–82
- Performance Assessment, p. 43
- Spanish Summaries, p. 46
- Inclusion Strategies
- English Language Learners Sourcebook

🔖 Transparencies
- Selection Focus 46
- Fine Art 23
- Literary Elements 46
- Grammar and Language 45

Technology
- 🎧 Audio Library
- 🎧 Spanish Audio Library
- 💻 Glencoe Literature Web Site
- 💾 Testmaker

Reading the Selection

SUMMARY

In these two humorous stories, the main characters must face new and unexpected situations. Laurie can only describe his difficult kindergarten experiences by attributing them to the fictional bad boy, "Charles." In "No News," Georgeanne explains to her friend in a very convoluted manner the many tragedies that have taken place in her absence.

📁 **Spanish Summaries,** p. 46

A **Active Reading**

PREDICT Ask students to use the title of the selection and details from the first paragraph to predict what they think the story is about. *(The crayons around the title "Charles" might help students predict that the story is about a young child.)*

Additional Resources

📂 *Active Reading Guide,* p. 46

🎧 *Audio Library*

🎧 *Spanish Audio Library*

Charles

Shirley Jackson

The day my son Laurie started kindergarten he renounced corduroy overalls with bibs and began wearing blue jeans with a belt; I watched him go off the first morning with the older girl next door, seeing clearly that an era of my life was ended, my sweet-voiced nursery-school tot replaced by a long-trousered, swaggering character who forgot to stop at the corner and wave good-bye to me.

He came home the same way, the front door slamming open, his cap on the floor, and the voice suddenly become <u>raucous</u> shouting, "Isn't anybody *here?*"

At lunch he spoke <u>insolently</u> to his father, spilled his baby sister's milk, and remarked that his teacher said we were not to take the name of the Lord in vain.

"How *was* school today?" I asked, elaborately casual.

"All right," he said.

"Did you learn anything?" his father asked.

Laurie regarded his father coldly. "I didn't learn nothing," he said.

"Anything," I said. "Didn't learn anything."

"The teacher spanked a boy, though," Laurie said, addressing his bread and butter. "For being fresh," he added, with his mouth full.

Vocabulary
raucous (rô′ kəs) *adj.* loud and rough-sounding
insolently (in′ sə lənt lē) *adv.* in a boldly rude manner

544 🌸 THEME 6

Teaching Options

CONNECTING TO OTHER SELECTIONS
For a teaching strategy that connects "Charles" to "A Crush," turn to page 28 in the *Theme Two Planning Guide.*

ENGLISH LANGUAGE LEARNERS

MEETING INDIVIDUAL NEEDS

Cultural Differences Some English language learners may be surprised by the way Laurie and Charles speak and act toward adults. You may wish to use the exchanges on these pages to discuss how adults and young children in various cultures relate to each other.

Activity Have students in small groups discuss what might have happened in their own cultures if they had behaved the way Laurie or Charles do in the story. Point out that there are many different standards of behavior, and that they can depend greatly upon individual cultural and family backgrounds.

COLLAB. LEARN.

Additional Resources
📂 *English Language Learners Sourcebook*

Viewing the photograph: What words would you use to describe this boy's personality? Would you use similar words to describe anyone in the story?

B
"What did he do?" I asked. "Who was it?"

Laurie thought. "It was Charles," he said. "He was fresh. The teacher spanked him and made him stand in a corner. He was awfully fresh."

"What did he do?" I asked again, but Laurie slid off his chair, took a cookie, and left, while his father was still saying, "See here, young man."

The next day Laurie remarked at lunch, as soon as he sat down, "Well, Charles was bad again today." He grinned enormously and said, "Today Charles hit the teacher."

"Good heavens," I said, mindful of the Lord's name, "I suppose he got spanked again?"

"He sure did," Laurie said. "Look up," he said to his father.

"What?" his father said, looking up.

"Look down," Laurie said. "Look at my thumb. Gee, you're dumb." He began to laugh insanely.

"Why did Charles hit the teacher?" I asked quickly.

"Because she tried to make him color with red crayons," Laurie said. "Charles wanted to

---

B **Literary Elements**

PLOT: *Exposition* Ask a volunteer to summarize the story's action thus far. *(Laurie has begun kindergarten and has immediately changed from a sweet boy into a rude child.)*

C **Active Reading**

QUESTION Ask students why they think Laurie "grins enormously" when he describes what Charles has done. *(Most students will think that Laurie is fascinated by the misbehaving Charles and seems to be entertained by the trouble he causes.)*

D **Literary Elements**

CHARACTER Discuss with students their reaction to Laurie's accounts of Charles's hitting the teacher. What do they think is driving him to enjoy this kind of unruly behavior? *(Laurie seems to be acting out some of Charles's unruliness and venting his own frustration about the new rules in school.)*

VIEWING THE PHOTOGRAPH

Viewing Response *Some possible descriptions are mischievous, naughty, sly, confident, and bold—words that might describe Charles.*

LIFE SKILLS CONNECTION

Interpersonal Skills Ask students how they feel when they are introduced to a new group of people for the first time.

Activity Ask students to work in pairs or small groups to discuss the best experiences and the worst experiences they have had when meeting new people, such as in a new school, a sports team, a club, or a family gathering. Were they angry,

uncomfortable, hopeful? Have them list their reactions on a *Good Feelings/Bad Feelings* chart. You may wish to have groups share their finds with one another.

E **Literary Elements**

PLOT: *Conflict* Ask students to discuss the central conflict that is described in this paragraph. *(Charles is having a difficult time adjusting to school; he doesn't get along with his teacher or the other students.)*

F **Active Reading**

RESPOND Ask students if they agree with Laurie's father that Laurie may as well meet people like Charles now as later. *(Some students may agree. Others will say that Charles may be a very bad role model for Laurie, who is still very young.)*

G **Active Reading**

CONNECT Ask students if they would be allowed to speak to their parents or guardians as Laurie speaks to his.

color with green crayons so he hit the teacher and she spanked him and said nobody play with Charles but everybody did."

The third day—it was Wednesday of the first week—Charles bounced a see-saw on to the head of a little girl and made her bleed, and the teacher made him stay inside all during recess. Thursday Charles had to stand in a corner during story-time because he kept pounding his feet on the floor. Friday Charles was deprived of blackboard privileges because he threw chalk.

On Saturday I remarked to my husband, "Do you think kindergarten is too unsettling for Laurie? All this toughness, and bad grammar, and this Charles boy sounds like such a bad influence."

"It'll be all right," my husband said reassuringly. "Bound to be people like Charles in the world. Might as well meet them now as later."

On Monday Laurie came home late, full of news. "Charles," he shouted as he came up the hill; I was waiting anxiously on the front steps. "Charles," Laurie yelled all the way up the hill, "Charles was bad again."

"Come right in," I said, as soon as he came close enough. "Lunch is waiting."

"You know what Charles did?" he demanded, following me through the door. "Charles yelled so in school they sent a boy in from first grade to tell the teacher she had to make Charles keep quiet, and so Charles had to stay after school. And so all the children stayed to watch him."

"What did he do?" I asked.

"He just sat there," Laurie said, climbing into his chair at the table. "Hi, Pop, y'old dust mop."

"Charles had to stay after school today," I told my husband. "Everyone stayed with him."

"What does this Charles look like?" my husband asked Laurie. "What's his other name?"

"He's bigger than me," Laurie said. "And he doesn't have any galoshes and he doesn't ever wear a jacket."

Monday night was the first Parent-Teachers meeting, and only the fact that the baby had a cold kept me from going; I wanted passionately to meet Charles's mother. On Tuesday Laurie remarked suddenly, "Our teacher had a friend come to see her in school today."

"Charles's mother?" my husband and I asked simultaneously.

"Naaah," Laurie said scornfully. "It was a man who came and made us do exercises, we had to touch our toes. Look." He climbed down from his chair and squatted down and touched his toes. "Like this," he said. He got solemnly back into his chair and said, picking up his fork, "Charles didn't even *do* exercises."

"That's fine," I said heartily. "Didn't Charles want to do exercises?"

"Naaah," Laurie said. "Charles was so fresh to the teacher's friend he wasn't *let* do exercises."

"Fresh again?" I said.

"He kicked the teacher's friend," Laurie said. "The teacher's friend told Charles to

Vocabulary
simultaneously (sī′ məl tā′ nē əs lē) *adv.* at the same time
solemnly (sol′ əm lē) *adv.* seriously

Teaching Options

Reading *Minilesson*

Comparing and Contrasting Review the processes of comparing and contrasting that help us analyze how things, ideas, facts, persons, or events are alike and how they are different. Students might benefit from comparing and contrasting Laurie and Charles.

Activity Have students work in small groups and revisit the story to look for details describing each boy's behavior. Ask them to create a Venn diagram to compare the boys. Then lead the class in a discussion about the similarities and differences between Laurie and Charles. **L2**
COLLAB. LEARN.

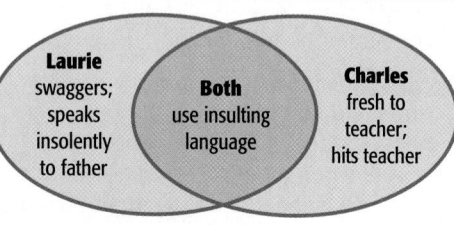

Laurie
swaggers; speaks insolently to father

Both
use insulting language

Charles
fresh to teacher; hits teacher

Additional Resources
📁 *Reading Workbook,* pp. 81–82

touch his toes like I just did and Charles kicked him."

"What are they going to do about Charles, do you suppose?" Laurie's father asked him.

Laurie shrugged elaborately. "Throw him out of school, I guess," he said.

Wednesday and Thursday were routine; Charles yelled during story hour and hit a boy in the stomach and made him cry. On Friday Charles stayed after school again and so did all the other children.

With the third week of kindergarten Charles was an institution[1] in our family; the baby was being a Charles when she cried all afternoon; Laurie did a Charles when he filled his wagon full of mud and pulled it through the kitchen; even my husband, when he caught his elbow in the telephone cord and pulled telephone, ash-tray, and a bowl of flowers off the table, said, after the first minute, "Looks like Charles."

During the third and fourth weeks it looked like a reformation in Charles; Laurie reported grimly at lunch on Thursday of the third week, "Charles was so good today the teacher gave him an apple."

"What?" I said, and my husband added warily, "You mean Charles?"

"Charles," Laurie said. "He gave the crayons around and he picked up the books afterward and the teacher said he was her helper."

"What happened?" I asked incredulously.

_____
1. Here, *institution* means "a regular feature or tradition."

"He was her helper, that's all," Laurie said, and shrugged.

"Can this be true, about Charles?" I asked my husband that night. "Can something like this happen?"

"Wait and see," my husband said cynically. "When you've got a Charles to deal with, this may mean he's only plotting."

He seemed to be wrong. For over a week Charles was the teacher's helper; each day he handed things out and he picked things up; no one had to stay after school.

"The P.T.A. meeting's next week again," I told my husband one evening. "I'm going to find Charles's mother there."

"Ask her what happened to Charles," my husband said. "I'd like to know."

"I'd like to know myself," I said.

On Friday of that week things were back to normal. "You know what Charles did today?" Laurie demanded at the lunch table, in a voice slightly awed. "He told a little girl to say a word and she said it and the teacher washed her mouth out with soap and Charles laughed."

"What word?" his father asked unwisely, and Laurie said, "I'll have to whisper it to you, it's so bad." He got down off his chair and went around to his father. His father bent his head down and Laurie whispered joyfully. His father's eyes widened.

"Did Charles tell the little girl to say *that?*" he asked respectfully.

"She said it *twice,*" Laurie said. "Charles told her to say it *twice.*"

Vocabulary
reformation (ref′ ər mā′ shən) *n.* a change for the better; improvement
cynically (sin′ ə kəl lē) *adv.* in a way that shows doubt or disbelief; doubtfully

---

H **Literary Elements**

PLOT: *Foreshadowing* Laurie reports Charles's good behavior "grimly." Ask students how this contrasts with the way he reports Charles's bad behavior. *(Laurie reported Charles's bad behavior with an enormous grin.)*

I **Active Reading**

QUESTION Ask students what Laurie's father means by the word *plotting.* *(Charles may be pretending to cooperate in order to lull the teacher into a false sense of security while he plans his next move.)*

J **Active Reading**

EVALUATE Ask students to describe how Charles's behavior has changed. *(Charles begins to behave himself and is very helpful in class.)*

K **Critical Thinking**

INFERRING Ask students to infer why Laurie takes so much joy in whispering the "bad word" to his father. *(Perhaps Laurie finds the opportunity exciting because it allows him to do something that is forbidden.)*

MEETING INDIVIDUAL NEEDS MULTIPLE LEARNING STYLES

Musical Students with strong musical abilities may better understand Charles by writing a song about him. All students may find that the song-writing activity gives them a deeper insight into Charles's character.

Activity Have students work in small groups to create a song about Charles. Have them discuss his character, and then have them write lyrics. Ask them to describe what he has done, what has happened to him, how it has affected the class, and how the teacher might feel about him. Some students may want to use a melody from a song they already know well. When students have finished their songs, ask volunteers to perform them for the class. **L2**

Literary Elements

L

PLOT: Climax Ask students how they think the P.T.A. meeting fits into the sequence of events. Could this be the turning point of the story? *(It could be the story's climax, since Laurie's mother will probably meet Charles's mother.)*

Author's Craft

M

POINT OF VIEW Ask students to discuss why the author might have written the story from the mother's point of view. *(Telling the story from the mother's point of view keeps the mystery of the story going.)*

Literary Elements

N

PLOT: Resolution Ask students to explain in their own words how the mystery of Charles is finally resolved. *(Guide students in understanding that all of Laurie's stories about Charles's bad behavior were really about Laurie's behavior. The mother that Laurie's mother is so anxious to meet is herself.)*

Charles

"What happened to Charles?" my husband asked.

"Nothing," Laurie said. "He was passing out the crayons."

Monday morning Charles abandoned the little girl and said the evil word himself three or four times, getting his mouth washed out with soap each time. He also threw chalk.

L My husband came to the door with me that evening as I set out for the P.T.A. meeting. "Invite her over for a cup of tea after the meeting," he said. "I want to get a look at her."

"If only she's there," I said prayerfully.

"She'll be there," my husband said. "I don't see how they could hold a P.T.A. meeting without Charles's mother."

M At the meeting I sat restlessly, scanning each comfortable matronly[2] face, trying to determine which one hid the secret of Charles. None of them looked to me haggard[3] enough. No one stood up in the meeting and apologized for the way her son had been acting. No one mentioned Charles.

---

2. Another word for *matronly* would be "motherly." It refers to a mature woman, especially one who is married and has children.
3. A *haggard* person looks worn out as a result of grief, worry, illness—or dealing with a Charles.

After the meeting I identified and sought out Laurie's kindergarten teacher. She had a plate with a cup of tea and a piece of chocolate cake; I had a plate with a cup of tea and a piece of marshmallow cake. We maneuvered up to one another cautiously, and smiled.

"I've been so anxious to meet you," I said. "I'm Laurie's mother."

"We're all so interested in Laurie," she said.

"Well, he certainly likes kindergarten," I said. "He talks about it all the time."

"We had a little trouble adjusting, the first week or so," she said <u>primly</u>, "but now he's a fine little helper. With occasional <u>lapses</u>, of course."

"Laurie usually adjusts very quickly," **N** I said. "I suppose this time it's Charles's influence."

"Charles?"

"Yes," I said, laughing, "you must have your hands full in that kindergarten, with Charles."

"Charles?" she said. "We don't have any Charles in the kindergarten."

Vocabulary
primly (prim′ lē) *adv.* in a stiffly formal manner
lapse (laps) *n.* a slipping or falling away

Teaching Options

Grammar and Language *Minilesson*

Apostrophes Write the following sentences from the story on the board:

> If only <u>she's</u> there. <u>She'll</u> be there. I <u>don't</u> see how they could hold a P.T.A. meeting without <u>Charles's</u> mother.

Review the use of an apostrophe to show possession and to substitute for a missing letter in a contraction.

Activity Have students make a list of words that use apostrophes in contractions and to show possession. Then tell them to write paragraphs that describe Laurie's mother telling his father about the P.T.A. meeting. Direct them to include in the paragraphs examples of apostrophes used in contractions and to show possession. **L2**

Additional Resources

📖 *Grammar and Language Transparency 45*

📓 *Grammar and Language Workbook,* pp. 273–274

📓 *Grammar and Composition Handbook,* Lesson 13.7

📓 *Writer's Choice,* Lesson 20.7

No News

Retold by Connie Regan-Blake and Barbara Freeman

A certain Southern lady was returning home after recuperating[1] in the mountains for three months. Her friend Georgeanne met her at the railway station.

"Georgeanne, has there been any news while I've been away?"

"Oh, no, there's no news."

"No news? Surely something has occurred in my absence. Why, I've been gone for nearly three months, and I'm anxious for any little bit of news you may have."

"Oh, now, since you mentioned it— 'course it don't amount to much—but since you've been away, your dog died."

"My dog died? How did my dog die?"

"He ate some of the burnt horseflesh, and that's what killed the dog."

"Burnt horseflesh?"

"Well, after the fire cooled off, the dog ate some of the burnt horseflesh, and that's what killed the dog."

"Fire cooled off?"

"Well, the barn burned down, burned up all of the cows and horses, and when the fire cooled down, the dog ate some of the burnt horseflesh, and that's what killed the dog."

"My barn burned down? How did my barn burn down?"

"Oh, it was a spark from the house. Blew over, lit the roof of the barn, burned down the barn, burned up all the cows and horses, and when the fire cooled off, the dog ate some of the burnt horseflesh, and that's what killed the dog."

"A spark from the house?"

"Oh, yes, now that's completely burned down."

"But how did my house burn down?"

"It was the candle flame that lit the curtains, shot up the side of the wall, and burned down the house; a spark flew over on the roof of the barn, burned down the barn, burned up all of the cows and horses, and when the fire cooled off, the dog ate some of the burnt horseflesh, and that's what killed the dog."

"Candles? I don't even allow candles in my house. How did the candles get into my house?"

"Oh, they were around the coffin."

"Coffin? Who died?"

"Oh, now you needn't worry about that. Since you've been away, your mother-in-law died."

"Oh, my mother-in-law. What a pity. How did she die?"

"Well, some folks say that it was the shock of hearing that your husband had run away with the choir leader. But other than that, there ain't been no news."

---

1. To *recuperate* (ri kōō′ pə rāt′) is to regain health or strength.

❖

O Literary Elements

PLOT: *Rising Action* Explain to students that this tale has an unusual plot structure. The events are exposed in reverse order—each effect in a chain of events is revealed before the cause.

P Active Reading

QUESTION Ask students to think about why Georgeanne is telling her friend the news in this way. *(Students may suggest that she does not want to tell all the terrible news at once.)*

Q Author's Craft

IRONY Have students discuss why Georgeanne's statement at the end of the story is ironic. *(She says that other than that, there's no news, but "that" turns out to be a series of terrible tragedies.)*

Thematic Focus

Twists and Turns Have students discuss how both of these selections illustrate the comic presentation of serious issues—a child's misbehaving in school and a woman's devastating loss. Invite students to share their responses to twists and turns of the plots.

FINE ART
TRANSPARENCY 23

You may wish to use *Fine Art Transparency 23* to extend the discussion.

REAL-WORLD CONNECTION

Humor Students might enjoy adding humor to a story about a real person who must accept unpleasant news. They can choose a news article or a story of someone they know.

Activity Ask students to create a cartoon that illustrates what happened in the article and how the person coped with what took place. Encourage students to create humorous, eye-catching titles for their cartoons. Then work with the class to create a "funny page" by pasting each cartoon on posterboard or butcher paper. **L2**

☑ **ASSESSMENT OPTIONS**

📁 *Quick Checks,* p. 46

Responding to the Selection

Personal Response

Encourage students to explain what first made them think that something unusual might be happening in these stories.

Analyzing Literature

1. He becomes raucous and insolent.
2. Laurie acts out at home to some extent, mostly with rude language, but is basically obedient. Charles is out of control, using rude language, hitting the teacher, and teasing other children.
3. They stay after school with Charles to watch him.
4. At first she wants to see what the mother of such a "bad" child could be like. Then she wants to know what made Charles change his ways.
5. Laurie probably feels that in order to defend himself against an unknown situation, he has to act bigger and stronger than he actually is.
6. Most likely Laurie wants to tell his parents what has been taking place at school but is afraid to admit that he is misbehaving.
7. At first because Laurie talks about him constantly. Later, Charles becomes a symbol for anything that goes wrong.
8. Georgeanne casually relates the tragedies of her friend's life in a series of drawn-out cause-and-effect relationships.
9. Both plots contain characters who are faced with new situations or unexpected events and end with a surprise twist.
10. Be sure that students support their opinions with concrete examples from the selections.

Responding to Literature

PERSONAL RESPONSE

Recall the **Focus Activity** on page 543. In each story, when did you first decide that you needed to read between the lines?

Analyzing Literature

RECALL

1. How does Laurie change when he starts kindergarten?
2. Compare Laurie's behavior at home with Charles's actions at school. How are their behaviors similar? How are they different?
3. According to Laurie, why do he and all the other children stay after school with Charles?
4. Why is Laurie's mother interested in meeting Charles's mother?

INTERPRET

5. Why do you think Laurie turns into a "swaggering character" when he begins kindergarten? Explain.
6. In your opinion, why does Laurie tell stories about Charles at home?
7. Why is Charles such a fascination in Laurie's household?
8. An *understatement* is a statement that plays down the importance of something. How does "No News" illustrate the word *understatement*?

EVALUATE AND CONNECT

9. Theme Connection   How do the **plots** of both selections reflect the theme of this unit? (For more about plot, see page R8.)
10. Which story do you prefer? Why?

LITERARY ELEMENTS

Plot Twist

The sequence of events in a story is called the **plot**. Usually the plot is built around a central **conflict** in which opposing sides are involved in a struggle or a problem that must be resolved. The turning point of the plot is called the **climax,** the point of highest interest. This is the point where the outcome of the conflict is determined. In some plots, the climax includes an unexpected turn of events, called a **plot twist.** "Charles" is an example of a story with a plot twist.

1. What is the plot twist in "Charles"?
2. In one or two sentences, describe the plot twist in "No News."
3. What does the plot twist at the end add to the story "No News"?

● See **Literary Terms Handbook,** p. R8.

LITERARY ELEMENTS

1. Laurie's mother learns that the mischievous Charles is really Laurie.
2. Georgeanne says that nothing has happened while her friend has been away, but then relates a chain of tragedies in her friend's life.
3. The last line adds a humorous touch to the end of the story.

Additional Resources

Literary Elements Transparency 46

Literature and Writing

Writing About Literature

Foreshadowing   When writers give clues or hints about something that will occur later, they are **foreshadowing** the later event or development. Reread "Charles" carefully. Identify the details that foreshadow the plot twist at the end. Write a paragraph describing how Jackson foreshadows the ending of her story.

Personal Writing

Time Travel   Think about yourself in your kindergarten or preschool days. Did you ever tell an exaggerated story—to your parents, your friends, or a teacher? Did you ever have a problem in school? How was it resolved? Write a narrative describing an early school experience.

Extending Your Response

Performing

Dramatization   With a partner or in a small group, choose either story to dramatize. If you choose "Charles," pick out one or two scenes to perform. Think about what Laurie says and does as well as how his body looks and moves.

Listening and Speaking

Interview   Interview a kindergarten student, a teacher, or someone else who works with young children. Find out what kindergarteners are like. Before the interview, make a list of questions that will help you find out about the thoughts, interests, and daily activities of a five- or six-year-old child.

Literature Groups

Turning Real Life into Fiction   How do you think authors turn real life into stories? In small groups, make a list of real-life events at your school. Work together to turn one or more of these events into a work of fiction. Share your story with your classmates.

 Save your work for your portfolio.

Literature and Writing

Writing About Literature

Students' paragraphs should
- describe how Jackson foreshadows the ending of her story.
- identify the details that foreshadow the plot twist at the end.

Personal Writing

Students' narratives should
- describe a problem or other early school experience.
- explain whether the problem was resolved and how.

Extending Your Response

Performing Encourage students to spend time preparing their dramatization by writing a script and rehearsing their parts.

Listening and Speaking As students prepare to conduct their interviews, encourage them to think of questions that will inspire another person to talk about his or her experience.

Literature Groups Encourage each group of students to work cooperatively in creating its own story, one that reflects the experiences of one or more members of the group. **COLLAB. LEARN.**

Skill Minilessons

GRAMMAR AND LANGUAGE
CORRECT PRONOUN USE

Practice

1. I	3. I	5. me
2. me	4. her	

READING AND THINKING
DRAWING CONCLUSIONS

Example: Laurie was unable to cope with the new school situation and was equally unable to ask his parents directly for help. Making up Charles was one way for Laurie to let his parents know that things were not entirely smooth at school. It was almost as if Laurie had two sides, one "good" and one "bad."

VOCABULARY
THE PREFIX *re-*

1. d	3. a	5. c
2. e	4. b	

Additional Resources

- *Grammar and Language Workbook,* pp. 107–108
- *Grammar and Composition Handbook,* Lesson 4.2
- *Writer's Choice,* Lesson 11.3
- *Reading Workbook,* p. 81–82
- *Vocabulary Practice,* p. 32

Skill Minilessons

GRAMMAR AND LANGUAGE • CORRECT PRONOUN USE

A **subject pronoun** is used as the subject of a sentence. An **object pronoun** is used as the object of a verb or a preposition. If you are unsure of which form of the pronoun to use, say the sentence aloud with only the pronoun as the subject or the object. Your ear should tell you which form is right.

He and his mother walked home. *(subject)*
Tell Laurie and **me** about school. *(object of verb)*
Mother read a story to **him**. *(object of preposition)*

Be especially careful when a sentence has two subjects or two objects.

Laurie and **I** played together. *(subject)*
Those games were fun for Laurie and **me**. *(object of preposition)*

PRACTICE Choose the correct form of the pronoun.
1. Laurie and (I, me) were in the same class.
2. Laurie told my husband and (I, me) story after story about Charles.
3. She and (I, me) were amazed at Charles's behavior.
4. The teacher asked for the crayon, but Charles refused to give it to (she, her).
5. Just between you and (I, me), I don't think Charles really existed.

● For more about pronouns, see **Language Handbook,** p. R17.

READING AND THINKING • DRAWING CONCLUSIONS

Stories include details about characters and events. By combining these details with your own knowledge and experience, you can draw conclusions that will help you understand a story.

● For more on drawing conclusions, see **Reading Handbook,** pp. R100–R101.

PRACTICE The author doesn't reveal why Laurie told stories about a boy that didn't exist. You have to draw conclusions to figure it out for yourself. Write a paragraph giving your conclusions about Laurie's tales about Charles.

VOCABULARY • THE PREFIX *re-*

Some prefixes have more than one meaning. The prefix *re-* can mean either "again" or "back."

When Charles's behavior improved, it looked like a *reformation.* It seemed that Charles had been "formed again." However, if you *recall* something, you don't call it again, you call it back. A ball that *rebounds* bounces back. When *re-* is attached to a word, think about the meaning of the word without the prefix and then add either "again" or "back."

PRACTICE Use what you know about the prefix *re-* to match each word to its definition.

1. repress	a. to say again
2. recoil	b. to copy or make again
3. restate	c. a coming back inside
4. reproduce	d. to push or hold back
5. reentry	e. to spring back when let go

✔ ASSESSMENT OPTIONS

- 📁 *Quick Checks,* p. 46
- 📁 *Selection and Theme Assessment,* pp. 81–82
- 📁 *Performance Assessment,* p. 43
- 💾 *Testmaker*

GRAMMAR LINK

Using Commas Correctly

Speakers use their voices to make their meanings clear. In writing, commas separate words or parts of sentences to make the meaning clear.

Problem 1 Missing commas in a series

Georgeanne met her friend answered questions and provided news.

 Solution Use commas to separate three or more items in a series.

Georgeanne met her friend, answered questions, and provided news.

Problem 2 Missing commas with direct quotations

"If the story weren't so funny" I said "it would be sad."

 Solution Use commas before and after words that interrupt a quotation.

"If the story weren't so funny," I said, "it would be sad."

Problem 3 Missing commas with nonessential appositives

The barn a wooden structure burned down.

 Solution Use commas to set off the nonessential appositive.

The barn, a wooden structure, burned down.

The **appositive,** *a wooden structure,* gives more information about the noun *barn.* Since it doesn't change the meaning of the sentence, it is a **nonessential appositive** and should be set off by commas.

● For more about commas, see **Language Handbook,** p. R19.

EXERCISE

Rewrite the sentences, adding commas wherever they are needed.

1. Laurie a kindergarten student told stories about Charles.
2. Charles sassed the teacher yelled pounded his feet and threw chalk.
3. "Charles" said Laurie "didn't do exercises hit a child and had to stay after school."
4. The narrator of the story Laurie's mother was eager to meet Charles's mother.
5. "When I got a chance to speak with his teacher" Laurie's mother said to her husband "I asked her about Charles."

TWISTS AND TURNS   553

GRAMMAR LINK

Objective

- To recognize and use commas correctly

Teaching Strategies

After reviewing the three rules of comma usage on page 553, you may wish to read aloud a few sentences from "Charles" and ask students to supply commas where they would be appropriate.

Exercise

1. Laurie, a kindergarten student, told stories about Charles.
2. Charles sassed the teacher, yelled, pounded his feet, and threw chalk.
3. "Charles," said Laurie, "didn't do exercises, hit a child, and had to stay after school."
4. The narrator of the story, Laurie's mother, was eager to meet Charles's mother.
5. "When I got a chance to speak with his teacher," Laurie's mother said to her husband, "I asked her about Charles."

Additional Resources

  Grammar and Language Workbook, pp. 255–256, 259–260

  Grammar and Composition Handbook, Lessons 13.2–13.4

  Writer's Choice, Lessons 20.2–20.4

Teaching Options

Writing *Minilesson*

Punctuating Quotations Choose three sentences of dialogue from "Charles" to read aloud. Have the class write the sentences in their notebooks exactly as they hear them, placing the proper punctuation.

Activity Ask students to write three quotations they like on index cards. Quotes can come from a famous person, a book of quotations, friends, or family members.

Have students write their quotations without punctuation and exchange cards with a partner. Partners can rewrite the quotes on the other side of the index card with the correct punctuation. Encourage pairs to check each other's work. **L2**

Additional Resources

  Writer's Choice, Lesson 20.6

TWISTS AND TURNS   553

Objectives

- To read and analyze a comedy sketch
- To explain how dialogue reveals characters' personalities
- To write a paragraph that explains how puns create humor

Skills

Reading/Thinking: Drawing Conclusions; Monitoring Comprehension
Writing: Comedy Routine
Vocabulary: Homonyms; Dialect
Grammar/Language: Using *Who's* and *Whose*
Listening/Speaking: Comedy Routine
Collaboration: Literature Groups; Performing

→ OPTIONS

Literature Launchers: "Abbot and Costello: Echoes of Laughter"

Videodisc Side B, Segment 16

Also available in VHS.

Selection Focus Transparency 47: Have students read the cartoon and respond to the questions. Help them connect the image with their own experience.

Focus Activity: As an extension of the Focus Activity, invite students to give examples of their favorite kinds of humor.

Before You Read
Who's on First?

MEET ABBOTT AND COSTELLO

Bud Abbott and Lou Costello were a slapstick comedy team who became two of the most popular film and television entertainers of the 1940s and 1950s. Their comedy routines featured Abbott as the witty straight man and Costello as the bumbling innocent. Their comedy skits were based on old vaudeville routines, but the comics freshened the material by ad-libbing, making up lines on the spot. Some say that they never performed a scene the same way twice.

Bud Abbott was born in 1895 and died in 1974. Lou Costello was born in 1906 and died in 1959.

FOCUS ACTIVITY

What makes you laugh? Do you like jokes, slapstick, plays on words?

Ask It!
Create a questionnaire about humor. Ask questions such as
- What different kinds of humor can you name?
- Which type of humor do you prefer? Why?
- What good examples of humor have you read or seen recently?
- Why is humor important to humans?

Make copies of your questionnaire, and have friends and family members fill it out. Compile your results, and share the information with others in your class.

Setting a Purpose
Read this comedy sketch for enjoyment. Then read it again to discover why it's funny.

BACKGROUND

Did You Know? "Who's on First?" is a comedy sketch created, performed, and made famous by the comedy team of Abbott and Costello. The team first performed this hilarious baseball skit on the Kate Smith Show, a radio program of the early 1940s. They performed it many, many times after that, including in a movie and on their television series *The Abbott and Costello Show.* The routine is memorialized on a plaque in the Baseball Hall of Fame in Cooperstown, New York.

Abbott and Costello with the Andrews Sisters, a popular singing trio, in the 1941 film *Buck Privates.*

RESOURCE MANAGER

Lesson Planning Resource
The *Theme Six Planning Guide* (pp. 12–19) provides additional lesson notes and reduced versions of all print resources.

📁 **Other Print Resources**
- Active Reading Guide, p. 47
- Reading Workbook, pp. 83–84
- Grammar and Language Workbook, pp. 227–228, 295–296
- Grammar and Composition

Handbook, Lesson 15.1
- Quick Checks, p. 47
- Selection and Theme Assessment, p. 83
- Performance Assessment, p. 44
- Spanish Summaries, p. 47
- Spanish Translations
- Inclusion Strategies
- English Language Learners Sourcebook

 Transparencies
- Selection Focus 47
- Literary Elements 47
- Grammar and Language 46

Technology
 Literature Launchers
 Audio Library
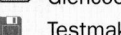 Spanish Audio Library
Glencoe Literature Web Site
Testmaker

SUMMARY

Sebastian asks Dexter to tell him the names of the baseball players on the St. Louis team. Dexter tells him that the first, second, and third basemen are named *Who, What,* and *I Don't Know.* Sebastian doesn't understand that these are actually the players' names, and a confused and hilarious dialogue begins when he innocently asks, "Who's playin' first?"

📁 *Spanish Summaries,* p. 47

Who's on First?

Bud Abbott and Lou Costello

A Active Reading

PREDICT Have students use the title, author credit, and photograph to predict what the story will be about. Suggest that they revisit their predictions at the end of the sketch.

Additional Resources
📁 *Active Reading Guide,* p. 47
🎧 *Audio Library*
🎧 *Spanish Audio Library*

SEBASTIAN. Peanuts!

DEXTER. Peanuts!

SEBASTIAN. Popcorn!

DEXTER. Popcorn!

SEBASTIAN. Crackerjack!

DEXTER. Crackerjack!

SEBASTIAN. Get your packages of Crackerjack here!

DEXTER. —Crackerjack—will you keep quiet? Sebastian! Sebastian, please! Don't interrupt my act!

SEBASTIAN. Ladies and gentlemen and also the children—will you excuse me for a minute, please? Thank you.

DEXTER. What do you want to do?

SEBASTIAN. Look, Mr. Broadhurst—

DEXTER. What are you doing?

TWISTS AND TURNS 🦅 555

Teaching Options

CONNECTING TO OTHER SELECTIONS

The chart at the right shows three ways to connect "Who's on First" to other selections in this book.

For specific teaching strategies, see the *Theme Six Planning Guide,* pages 15–16.

Connection	Title
Life Skills: Interpersonal	→ "How I Learned English," p. 377
Thematic: For Laughs	→ "The Night the Bed Fell," p. 399
Literary: Drama	→ "The Monsters Are Due on Maple Street," p. 505

DIALOGUE "Who's on First?" consists
entirely of dialogue. Engage students
in a discussion about the differences
between writing dialogue only and
writing a piece that consists of narrative and dialogue. *(Guide students in
understanding that when a piece consists of only dialogue, all details and
other information must be revealed
through the characters' words.
Narratives can provide details and
insights apart from what the characters say.)*

C Active Reading

QUESTION Ask students what
Sebastian thinks Dexter is telling
him when he uses the words *Who,
What,* and *I Don't Know.* What is
Dexter actually saying? *(Sebastian
thinks that Dexter doesn't know the
players' names. Dexter is saying the
real names of the players.)*

D Literary Elements

CONFLICT Have students explain the
conflict that is developing. What is
the conflict and why is it happening?
*(Sebastian and Dexter cannot under-
stand each other because they are
having a basic misunderstanding
about the word who's, a misunderstanding that neither of them can
clear up.)*

Teaching Options

Who's on First?

SEBASTIAN. I love baseball!

DEXTER. Well, we all love baseball.

SEBASTIAN. When we get to St. Louis,
will you tell me the guys' names on the
team so when I go to see them in that
St. Louis ballpark I'll be able to know
those fellows?

DEXTER. Then you'll go and peddle
your popcorn and won't interrupt the
act anymore?

SEBASTIAN. Yes, sir.

DEXTER. All right. But you know,
strange as it may seem, they give
ballplayers nowadays very peculiar
names.

SEBASTIAN. Funny names?

DEXTER. Nicknames. Nicknames.

SEBASTIAN. Not—not as funny as my
name—Sebastian Dinwiddie.

DEXTER. Oh, yes, yes, yes!

SEBASTIAN. Funnier than that?

DEXTER. Oh, absolutely. Yes. Now on
the St. Louis team we have Who's on
first, What's on second, I Don't Know is
on third—

SEBASTIAN. That's what I want to find
out. I want you to tell me the names of
the fellows on the St. Louis team.

DEXTER. I'm telling you. Who's on first,
What's on second, I Don't Know is on
third—

SEBASTIAN. You know the fellows'
names?

DEXTER. Yes.

SEBASTIAN. Well, then, who's playin'
first?

DEXTER. Yes!

SEBASTIAN. I mean the fellow's name
on first base.

DEXTER. Who.

SEBASTIAN. The fellow playin' first base
for St. Louis.

DEXTER. Who.

SEBASTIAN. The guy on first base.

DEXTER. Who is on first.

SEBASTIAN. Well, what are you askin'
me for?

DEXTER. I'm not asking you—I'm
telling you. *Who is on first.*

SEBASTIAN. I'm asking you—who's on
first?

DEXTER. That's the man's name!

SEBASTIAN. That's whose name?

DEXTER. Yes.

SEBASTIAN. Well, go ahead and tell me!

DEXTER. Who.

SEBASTIAN. The guy on first.

DEXTER. Who.

SEBASTIAN. The first baseman.

DEXTER. Who is on first.

SEBASTIAN. Have you got a first baseman on first?

DEXTER. Certainly.

SEBASTIAN. Then who's playing first?

DEXTER. Absolutely.

SEBASTIAN. When you pay off the first
baseman every month, who gets the
money?

DEXTER. Every dollar of it. And why
not, the man's entitled to it.

Understanding Humor To help
English language learners better understand "Who's on First?" you may wish
to show the layout of a baseball field.
Label the bases and the infield and outfield positions.

Activity Discuss the positions and
other baseball terms that may be confusing, such as *shortstop, pitcher,
catcher,* and *triple play.* If you have

students who know the game well, you
might wish to have them take turns
explaining the game and key terms to
their classmates. Encourage students
to listen to the audiotape as many
times as they wish.

Additional Resources

📁 *English Language Learners
Sourcebook*

SEBASTIAN. Who is?

DEXTER. Yes.

SEBASTIAN. So who gets it?

DEXTER. Why shouldn't he? Sometimes his wife comes down and collects it.

SEBASTIAN. Whose wife?

DEXTER. Yes. After all, the man earns it.

SEBASTIAN. Who does?

DEXTER. Absolutely.

SEBASTIAN. Well, all I'm trying to find out is what's the guy's name on first base.

DEXTER. Oh, no, no. What is on second base.

SEBASTIAN. I'm not asking you who's on second.

DEXTER. Who's on first.

SEBASTIAN. That's what I'm trying to find out.

DEXTER. Well, don't change the players around.

SEBASTIAN. I'm not changing nobody.

DEXTER. Now, take it easy.

SEBASTIAN. What's the guy's name on first base?

DEXTER. What's the guy's name on second base.

SEBASTIAN. I'm not askin' ya who is on second.

DEXTER. Who's on first.

SEBASTIAN. I don't know.

DEXTER. He's on third. We're not talking about him.

SEBASTIAN. How could I get on third base?

DEXTER. You mentioned his name.

SEBASTIAN. If I mentioned the third baseman's name, who did I say is playing third?

DEXTER. No, Who's playing first.

SEBASTIAN. Stay offa first, will ya?

DEXTER. Well, what do you want me to do?

SEBASTIAN. Now what's the guy's name on first base?

DEXTER. What's on second.

SEBASTIAN. I'm not asking ya who's on second.

DEXTER. Who's on first.

SEBASTIAN. I don't know.

DEXTER. He's on third.

SEBASTIAN. There I go back on third again.

DEXTER. Well, I can't change their names.

SEBASTIAN. Say, will you please stay on third base, Mr. Broadhurst.

DEXTER. Please. Now, what is it you want to know?

SEBASTIAN. What is the fellow's name on third base?

DEXTER. What is the fellow's name on second base.

SEBASTIAN. I'm not askin' ya who's on second.

DEXTER. Who's on first.

SEBASTIAN. I don't know.

DEXTER AND SEBASTIAN. *Third base!*

SEBASTIAN. You got a pitcher on the team?

557

Reading *Minilesson*

INDIRECT CHARACTERIZATION Ask
students what they learn about the
characters from the dialogue. *(Most
students will say that Sebastian is
very literal-minded and not too smart,
while Dexter is not very helpful and
may be having fun at Sebastian's
expense.)*

I **Literary Elements**

PLOT: *Rising Action* Remind students
that the rising action in a plot adds
to the conflict or problems in a story.
Point out that Sebastian says "Third
base" with Dexter. How does this
action build excitement? *(This builds
excitement because the audience
thinks Sebastian might be catching
on.)*

J **Critical Thinking**

DRAWING CONCLUSIONS Have students draw conclusions about what
Sebastian can understand and how
he has responded to Dexter. The following model illustrates the thinking
process involved in drawing conclusions.

Model: Sebastian does not seem to
be very smart. He's confused and
doesn't understand that *Who* and
What are names. However, when he
and Dexter both say "Third base,"
he seems to understand something. But then he says, "I don't
even know what I'm talking about."
I'd say he still doesn't understand.

Who's on First?

DEXTER. Wouldn't this be a fine team
without a pitcher?

SEBASTIAN. I don't know. Tell me the
pitcher's name.

DEXTER. Tomorrow.

SEBASTIAN. You don't want to tell me
today?

DEXTER. I'm telling you, man.

SEBASTIAN. Then go ahead.

DEXTER. Tomorrow.

SEBASTIAN. What time?

DEXTER. What time what?

SEBASTIAN. What time tomorrow are
you gonna tell me who's pitching?

DEXTER. Now listen, Who is not pitching. Who is on—

SEBASTIAN. I'll break your arm if you
say who's on first.

DEXTER. Then why come up here
and ask?

SEBASTIAN. I want to know what's the
pitcher's name.

DEXTER. What's on second.

SEBASTIAN. I don't know.

SEBASTIAN AND DEXTER. *Third base!*

SEBASTIAN. Gotta catcher?

DEXTER. Yes.

SEBASTIAN. I'm a good catcher, too, you
know.

DEXTER. I know that.

SEBASTIAN. I would like to play for the
St. Louis team.

DEXTER. Well, I might arrange that.

SEBASTIAN. I would like to catch.

Now, I'm being a good catcher,
Tomorrow's pitching on the team, and
I'm catching.

DEXTER. Yes.

SEBASTIAN. Tomorrow throws the ball
and the guy up bunts the ball.

DEXTER. Yes.

SEBASTIAN. Now, when he bunts the
ball—me being a good catcher—I want
to throw the guy out at first base, so I
pick up the ball and throw it to who?

DEXTER. Now that's the first thing
you've said right.

SEBASTIAN. I DON'T EVEN KNOW WHAT
I'M TALKING ABOUT.

DEXTER. Well, that's all you have to do.

SEBASTIAN. Is to throw it to first base.

DEXTER. Yes.

SEBASTIAN. Now who's got it?

DEXTER. Naturally.

SEBASTIAN. Who has it?

DEXTER. Naturally.

SEBASTIAN. Naturally.

DEXTER. Naturally.

SEBASTIAN. O.K.

DEXTER. Now you've got it.

SEBASTIAN. I pick up the ball and I
throw it to Naturally.

DEXTER. No you don't, you throw the
ball to first base.

SEBASTIAN. Then who gets it?

DEXTER. Naturally.

SEBASTIAN. O.K.

DEXTER. All right.

Teaching Options

Grammar and Language *Minilesson*

**Using Troublesome Words:
Homophones** Write the words *who's* and
whose on the board. Remind students that
homophones are words that sound the
same but are spelled differently. They are
entirely different words with different
meanings. *Who's* is a contraction of the
words *who is*. *Whose* is the possessive
form of *who*.

Activity Read the following sentences
aloud and ask students to write them
down, using the correct form of the homophones. Remind students to consider how
the word is used in the sentence to determine its spelling. **L2**

• *Who's* going to the game today?
• *Whose* ticket is this?
• *Who's* the first baseman for the team?
• *Whose* baseball glove is this?

Additional Resources

📖 *Grammar and Language Transparency 46*

📗 *Grammar and Language Workbook,*
pp. 227–228, 295–296

📗 *Grammar and Composition Handbook,*
Lesson 15.1

📘 *Writer's Choice,* Lessons 17.2, 23.5

Bud Abbott and Lou Costello

SEBASTIAN. I throw the ball to Naturally.

DEXTER. You don't. You throw it to Who.

SEBASTIAN. Naturally.

DEXTER. Well, naturally. Say it that way.

SEBASTIAN. That's what I said.

DEXTER. You did not.

SEBASTIAN. I said I'd throw the ball to Naturally.

DEXTER. You don't. You throw it to Who.

SEBASTIAN. Naturally.

DEXTER. Yes.

SEBASTIAN. So I throw the ball to first base and Naturally gets it.

DEXTER. No. You throw the ball to first base—

SEBASTIAN. Then who gets it?

DEXTER. Naturally.

SEBASTIAN. That's what I'm saying.

DEXTER. You're not saying that.

SEBASTIAN. Excuse me, folks.

DEXTER. Now, don't get excited. Now, don't get excited.

SEBASTIAN. I throw the ball to first base.

DEXTER. Then Who gets it.

SEBASTIAN. He better get it.

DEXTER. That's it. All right now, don't get excited. Take it easy.

SEBASTIAN. Now I throw the ball to first base, whoever it is grabs the ball, so the guy runs to second.

DEXTER. Uh-huh.

SEBASTIAN. Who picks up the ball and throws it to What. What throws it to I Don't Know. I Don't Know throws it back to Tomorrow—a triple play.

DEXTER. Yeah. It could be.

SEBASTIAN. And I don't care.

DEXTER. What was that?

SEBASTIAN. I said, *I don't care*.

DEXTER. Oh, that's our shortstop!

❖

K **Literary Elements**

DIALOGUE: *Comedy* Ask a pair of volunteers to read this fast-paced dialogue to get the flavor of a comedy skit that has its roots in vaudeville. Encourage students to reread aloud all or part of the skit, concentrating on their timing.

.... **FYI**

Triple Play A triple play takes place when the team in the field gets three men out in one play. Though this is always possible, it is a rare event in baseball.

....

L **Literary Elements**

DIALOGUE: *Comedy* Ask students if they were surprised by the "punch line" delivered at the end by Sebastian. *(The line, "I don't care," adds a new name to the confusion. It keeps the skit funny to the end.)*

Thematic Focus

Twists and Turns Simple twists and turns in communication between people are quite common. Have students describe a funny experience that was brought about by misunderstanding someone's directions or statements.

☑ **ASSESSMENT OPTIONS**

📁 ***Quick Checks,*** p. 47

REAL-WORLD CONNECTION

Mixed-up communication is a common cause of laughter. Have students use comic strips to discuss some other elements of humor in communication.

Activity Have students find a comic strip, such as *Calvin and Hobbes* or *Garfield,* about confused communication. When they have found examples, have students share their comic strips with the class and discuss what makes them funny. As an extension, students might enjoy creating their own comic strips or stories about mixed-up communication. **L2**

Responding to the Selection

Personal Response

- Students' responses should exhibit their own tastes and those of the people they have interviewed.
- Have students compare and contrast their favorite kind of humor with that of Abbott and Costello.

Analyzing Literature

1. Dexter is playing to the audience and already presenting himself as being in control of Sebastian's role.
2. He wants to be able to identify the players when he goes to the game.
3. He is confused, frustrated, and angry. By the end he says he doesn't care.
4. Sebastian associates "I don't know" with "Third base," but not as a name.
5. Sebastian seems to defer to Dexter. Dexter is calm and in control. Sebastian is easily excited.
6. They should understand the positions and simple terms of baseball.
7. The humor depends on a play on words. For example, *who* and *what* are used as pronouns and as people's names.
8. Most students will answer positively, since the play on words is still valid.
9. Most students will answer positively, because the play on words is well written and baseball is one of America's favorite sports.
10. Most students should be able to remember a situation in which communication was very difficult.

Responding to Literature

PERSONAL RESPONSE

- ◆ Take a look at your questionnaire results from the **Focus Activity** on page 554. Does "Who's on First?" fit into any of the categories you listed? Which ones?
- ◆ Who's your favorite comic or comedy team? How do Abbott and Costello compare with your favorite?

Analyzing Literature

RECALL

1. To what is Dexter referring when he says, "Don't interrupt my act"?
2. Why does Sebastian want to know the names of the players on the St. Louis team?
3. What is Sebastian's reaction to Dexter's information about the players? Does his reaction change by the end of the skit?
4. Does Sebastian ever understand any of the player's names? Give an example.

INTERPRET

5. What do you learn about Sebastian's personality from the opening of the skit? What do you learn about Dexter's personality?
6. What knowledge about baseball does the audience need in order to fully appreciate the skit?
7. On what does the humor of "Who's on First?" depend? Explain.

EVALUATE AND CONNECT

8. Do you think the skit is as funny today as it was in the 1940s? Why or why not?
9. "Who's on First?" has been included in a number of anthologies of great American humor. If you were an editor of such a book, would you include it? Why or why not?
10. Have you ever tried to explain something but had no luck in communicating your information? Describe the situation.

LITERARY ELEMENTS

Dialogue

In a play, the plot and the characters' personalities are revealed through the conversations between characters. These conversations are called **dialogue**. In the written form of a play, the dialogue appears following the characters' names. Quotation marks are not used around the characters' words.

Dialogue is not limited to drama. In fiction, writers move a plot along through the characters' own words and interactions. Dialogue also gives readers a break from writing in which a narrator tells everything.

1. What can you tell about Sebastian and Dexter from the dialogue?
2. Would "Who's on First?" be as funny if it were written as a story without dialogue? Why or why not?

● See **Literary Terms Handbook**, p. R3.

LITERARY ELEMENTS

1. Dexter is in control; Sebastian is innocent, literal, and slow to catch on. Dexter doesn't try to clear up the confusion; he may be making fun of Sebastian.
2. No. Though it is possible to describe what takes place, the humor lies in the way the two characters speak quickly back and forth.

Additional Resources

📖 *Literary Elements Transparency 47*

Extending Your Response

Writing About Literature

Puns   Most of the humor in "Who's on First?" is based on puns. A **pun** is a play on words based on two different meanings of the same word or two different words with the same pronunciation. For example, *who* is used both as a pronoun that asks a question and as a player's name. Choose one section of the routine and write a paragraph explaining how the puns create humor.

Literature Groups

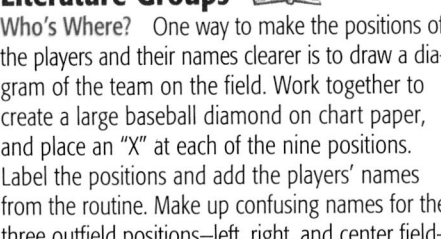

Who's Where?   One way to make the positions of the players and their names clearer is to draw a diagram of the team on the field. Work together to create a large baseball diamond on chart paper, and place an "X" at each of the nine positions. Label the positions and add the players' names from the routine. Make up confusing names for the three outfield positions—left, right, and center field—not mentioned in the script. Share your chart with the class.

Creative Writing

Further Confusion   Choose a team sport other than baseball. Write a comedy routine using the same names as "Who's on First?" but with positions and action to match the new sport.

Performing

Vaudeville Timing   Read "Who's on First?" with a partner, each of you taking one of the parts. You will soon find out that to make the skit truly funny, the dialogue must be spoken with split-second timing. Practice with the script until you feel you can make people laugh at every funny line. Then perform your routine for your classmates or another class.

Reading Further

Check out these other books full of puns:

The Laugh Book compiled by Joanna Cole and Stephanie Calmenson

Incognito Mosquito by E. A. Hass

📖 Save your work for your portfolio.

Skill Minilesson

VOCABULARY • HOMONYMS

The puns in "Who's on First?" are **homonyms**, words that sound or look alike. Here's another pun.

How do you get down off an elephant?
You don't. You get down off a duck.

To appreciate the pun, you must recognize that *down* can mean "from a higher to a lower place" or "the soft feathers of a duck." Puns have been used in literature dating back at least as far as biblical times. Some of the greatest writers have used them.

Puns are also used in jokes, everyday conversation, newspaper headlines, and advertising.

PRACTICE   Work alone or with a partner to practice punning.

1. Make a list of at least five pairs of homonyms. (Remember, many homonyms are spelled differently—for example *peace* and *piece*.)
2. Choose at least one pair of homonyms on your list to make a humorous pun. Share your pun with the class.

Writing About Literature

Students' paragraphs should
- focus on one section of the routine.
- explain how Abbott and Costello use puns to create the humor.

Creative Writing

Students' routines should
- use the same names as "Who's on First?" but apply them to positions in a different sport.
- match the action to the new sport.

Literature Groups   Have students who fully understand baseball help explain the positions to those who do not. Encourage groups to work together, sharing equally the tasks of setting up the paper, making up names, and creating the drawing. **COLLAB. LEARN.**

Performing   Have students spend an adequate amount of time rehearsing the piece. Encourage students to memorize part or all of the piece. 🎴

Skill Minilesson

VOCABULARY • HOMONYMS

1. *Examples:* ball/ball; tear/tear; pair/pear; meet/meat; deer/dear
2. *Example answer:* Where do golfers go to dance? To the golf ball.

✔️ ASSESSMENT OPTIONS

- 📁 *Quick Checks,* p. 47
- 📁 *Selection and Theme Assessment,* p. 83
- 📁 *Performance Assessment,* p. 44
- 💾 *Testmaker*

Technology Skills

Objectives

- To understand and use hypertext software
- To use hypertext software to complete a writing assignment
- To post a hypertext stack to a school Web site or Intranet site

Teaching Strategies

Help students see how hypertext can help readers follow a train of thought by demonstrating with a site on the Web that includes hypertext and clicking from link to link. You may want to include some or all of the following tasks in your demonstration of hypertext software:

- creating a new hypertext card
- linking cards to create a stack
- adding hyperlinks to graphics, sounds, and animation
- saving and printing a hypertext stack

Adapting to Available Technology

Hypertext software is available for both PCs and Macs. If your school computers do not have large amounts of memory, you may want to suggest that students create hypertext links only to additional text (rather than to videos, animation, or complicated graphics, which use large amounts of memory).

Teaching Options

Multimedia: Using Hypertext

When you learned to read, you trained your eyes to focus on letters that form words and words that form sentences. As you read, your eyes move from left to right and top to bottom on a page. But your mind may not always want to go along with your eyes. That's because the mind is capable of processing a lot of information at once. Suppose you're reading an article about cats. You may run across the line, "Cats, considered sacred by the ancient Egyptians, were often featured in Egyptian art." Before reading the next sentence, you may wonder briefly what such art looked like. But if the article doesn't have pictures, you have to put the thought out of your mind and continue reading.

Hypertext is a computer feature that allows you to follow such trains of thought by linking keywords with related data. You can click on words or phrases that will take you to more information. These clickable words are known as **hyperlinks,** or hotlinks, and they are usually differentiated from regular text through color, bold type, or underlining. If the story about cats were written on a computer in hypertext, it might look something like this:

Hyperlink to information on Egyptian art, with photo of an example

Hyperlink to a definition of *sacred*

Hyperlink to a photo of Bastet

Hyperlink to previous card

Hyperlink to next card

Hypertext Software

HyperStudio, Hypercard, and other hypertext software programs allow *you* to write stories, reports, or essays that contain many pages of linked text, graphics, sounds, and even animation! Each page is known as a card, and a group of cards is known as a stack.

MULTIPLE LEARNING STYLES

Customized Learning Methods
Hypertext software can allow students with different learning styles to make use of their particular approach.

Activity Invite students to create a hypertext stack in a format that suits their individual learning styles. For example, a logical/mathematical learner might create a timeline or flow chart with links that expand on key dates or important concepts. A spatial learner might create a map, with each site name linked to additional information about that site. A musical learner could create a report on music with links to songs or types of music. Linguistic learners could create stories or essays with links to important concepts. **L2**

To familiarize yourself with your hypertext software, open the program and click on its tutorial. The computer will lead you through the steps of creating a simple stack. (If your software lacks a tutorial, its manufacturer may offer one at its Web site on the Net. Otherwise, find the program's manual, ask your teacher or lab instructor for help, or use the topics in the Help index to learn how to use the program.)

Practice

Hypertext programs are fairly "intuitive." That means that you can figure out the items on their menus and toolbars from their names or by trying them out yourself. Many items and procedures are similar to those you will be familiar with from other software you use—word processing programs, for example.

The following chart may be useful. It tells you how to do some basic operations. The steps are separated by slash marks. For example, *File/New* means pull down the File menu and select New from the options on the menu.

To change a font size or style	Options/Text Style
To include a button that moves the reader to another card	Objects/Add a Button/Actions/Places to Go
To add graphics	File/Add Clip Art [or Photo, Movie]
To add sounds	Objects/Add a Button/Actions/Things to Do/ Play a Sound

1. To create your own hypertext stack, click on **File/New** and follow the prompts.

2. Explore the program by creating a stack that contains at least four linked cards. The stack can be about whatever you like: a short story, an autobiographical sketch, a review, essay, or article about literature, music, television, movies, or any other topic you wish.

3. If you have access to files of clip art, photos, or sounds (including music), add hyperlinks to appropriate graphics or sounds to your stack.

4. Save the stack when you have finished. (Your teacher or lab instructor will tell you where to save it.). Also, print out a copy to put in your portfolio.

ACTIVITIES

1. Complete one of the writing assignments from this unit using hypertext software. Present your work to your classmates.

2. Post your stack to your school's Web site or Intranet.

3. Volunteer to create stacks that describe your school's extracurricular activities. These stacks can be kept in the library and accessed by students who want to learn more about clubs and sports.

Activities

Before beginning, encourage students to suggest organizational strategies for different types of writing using hypertext. For example, some students might suggest creating a new card for each new concept. Others may suggest creating links for important vocabulary words or tangential information. And some may suggest links for visuals, sounds, or photos that augment or help explain the text.

Students' writing assignments should

• demonstrate an ability to use hypertext software to link several cards on one topic.

• include links to clip art, photographs, or sounds if these are available.

• be correctly posted to the school's Web site or Intranet site.

TechnoTalk

New Terms The word *hypertext* was first coined in 1965. It refers to text that is not linear and that contains links to additional text. The links are usually presented in a color and are sometimes underlined or in a different font. When a user double clicks on a link, they move to a new page or card. *Hypermedia* originally meant hypertext that included links to music, videos, animation, or other media in addition to text links. However, over time, the term *hypertext* has come to be virtually interchangeable with *hypermedia*.

INTERDISCIPLINARY CONNECTION

Science/Social Studies Invite small groups of students to create a hypertext dictionary of important concepts they are learning in science class or a hypertext map to explore a key idea in history or geography.

Activity Have students work in small groups to gather words or concepts to be defined in their dictionary, or to draw a map showing an important historical or geographical concept. Have students divide up the task of creating definitions or explaining places on the map. Finally, have each group create links to the information that group members have compiled. **L2** **COLLAB. LEARN.**

Objectives

- To read and analyze a short story about two friends who meet after twenty years
- To recognize how the elements of a short story create its overall impact
- To identify two examples of irony and explain what is ironic about each

Skills

Reading/Thinking: Drawing Conclusions; Comparing and Contrasting
Writing: Paragraph Analyzing Loyalty
Vocabulary: The Suffix -ity
Grammar/Language: Adjective Clauses
Life Skills: Newspaper Crime Report
Collaboration: Literature Groups

Motivating
→ OPTIONS

Selection Focus Transparency 48: Have students read the quote from O. Henry. Encourage them to think of times when a story has altered their views about a person, a place, or an event.

Focus Activity: As an extension of the Focus Activity, encourage students to work in small groups to debate the issue of loyalty and friendship.

Before You Read
After Twenty Years

MEET O. HENRY

William Sydney Porter, who used the pen name O. Henry, led a varied but difficult life. Many of his life experiences became material for his stories. He first worked in his uncle's drugstore in North Carolina, then as a sheepherder on a ranch in Texas. He was also a bank teller, a fugitive in Honduras, a prisoner, a magazine editor, and a newspaper writer before he began writing the stories that made him famous. Many of his stories contain a surprise ending or an ironic twist.

William Sydney Porter was born in 1862 and died in 1910.

FOCUS ACTIVITY

How do you feel about loyalty between friends?

QuickWrite
Write about whether you think a person should always expect loyalty from a friend, no matter what the situation.

Setting a Purpose
Read this story to find out what tests the loyalty of two old friends.

BACKGROUND

The Time and Place This story takes place in New York City in the late 1800s.

Did You Know? William Sydney Porter, writing under the name O. Henry, became one of America's most loved writers. Porter's first published stories were written in prison. He spent three years in prison for stealing money from the bank where he worked. He claimed he was innocent, but by using a pseudonym, he made sure his readers would not know about his past.

VOCABULARY PREVIEW

habitual (hə bich′ oo̅ əl) *adj.* done by habit; p. 565
intricate (in′ tri kit) *adj.* full of complicated detail; p. 565
artful (ärt′ fəl) *adj.* done with skill or cleverness; p. 565
correspond (kôr ə spond′) *v.* to communicate by exchanging letters; p. 567
dismally (diz′ məl lē) *adv.* in a gloomy, cheerless way; p. 567
absurdity (ab sur′ də tē) *n.* the state of being ridiculous, senseless, or irrational; p. 567
moderately (mod′ ər it lē) *adv.* neither too great nor too small; within limits; p. 568

RESOURCE MANAGER

Lesson Planning Resource
The *Theme Six Planning Guide* (pp. 20–27) provides additional lesson notes and reduced versions of all print resources.

📁 **Other Print Resources**
- Active Reading Guide, p. 48
- Vocabulary Practice, p. 33
- Reading Workbook, pp. 85–86
- Grammar and Language Workbook, pp. 157–158

- Grammar and Composition Handbook, Lesson 8.3
- Quick Checks, p. 48
- Selection and Theme Assessment, p. 84
- Performance Assessment, p. 45
- Spanish Summaries, p. 48
- Spanish Translations
- Inclusion Strategies
- English Language Learners Sourcebook

🏆 **Transparencies**
- Selection Focus 48
- Fine Art 11
- Literary Elements 48
- Grammar and Language 47

Technology
 🎧 Audio Library
 🎧 Spanish Audio Library
 💻 Glencoe Literature Web Site
💾 Testmaker

After Twenty Years

O. Henry

The policeman on the beat moved up the avenue impressively. The impressiveness was <u>habitual</u> and not for show, for spectators were few. The time was barely 10 o'clock at night, but chilly gusts of wind with a taste of rain in them had well nigh depeopled the streets.

A Trying doors as he went, twirling his club with many <u>intricate</u> and <u>artful</u> movements, turning now and then to cast his watchful eye adown the pacific thoroughfare, the officer, with his stalwart[1] form and slight swagger, made a fine picture of a guardian of the peace. The vicinity was one that kept early hours. Now and then you might see the lights of a cigar store or of an all-night lunch counter; but the majority of the doors belonged to business places that had long since been closed.

When about midway of a certain block the policeman suddenly slowed his walk. In the doorway of a darkened hardware store a man leaned, with an unlighted cigar in his mouth. As the policeman walked up to him the man spoke up quickly.

"It's all right, officer," he said, reassuringly. "I'm just waiting for a friend. It's an appointment made twenty years ago. Sounds a little funny to you, doesn't it? Well, I'll explain if you'd like to make certain it's all straight. About that long ago there used to be a restaurant where this store stands—'Big Joe' Brady's restaurant."

"Until five years ago," said the policeman. "It was torn down then."

---

1. *Pacific* means "calm; peaceful," and *stalwart* means "physically strong."

Vocabulary
habitual (hə bich' o͞o əl) *adj.* done by habit
intricate (in' tri kit) *adj.* full of complicated detail
artful (ärt' fəl) *adj.* done with skill or cleverness

A **Active Reading**

PREDICT Give students time to read the title and the first four paragraphs of the story. Encourage them to consider the setting and mood, then use what they know to predict whether the meeting will be a happy one.

Additional Resources
📁 *Active Reading Guide,* p. 48
🎧 *Audio Library*
🎧 *Spanish Audio Library*

Teaching Options

CONNECTING TO OTHER SELECTIONS

The chart at the right shows three ways to connect "After Twenty Years" to other selections in this book.

For specific teaching strategies, see the *Theme Six Planning Guide,* pages 23–24.

Connection	Title
Life Skills: Lifelong Learning	→ "To James," p. 253
Thematic: Humility	→ "Primer Lesson," p. 472
Literary: Character	→ "The Bird Like No Other," p. 473

VIEWING THE PAINTING

Charles Burchfield (1893–1967) was an artist who focused on urban scenes, such as docks, bridges, and industrial areas, in the poorer parts of small cities.

Viewing Response *The wet, empty night streets create a dark and foreboding mood. O. Henry also describes a bleak and lonely setting.*

Rainy Night, 1939. Charles Burchfield. Watercolor over pencil, 30 x 42 in. San Diego Museum of Art.
Viewing the painting: What mood does the painting create? What details help create that mood? What details does O. Henry use to create a mood in the story?

FYI

O. Henry named his 1906 book of stories about New York City *The Four Million.* A society leader said that there were only 400 people worth knowing in New York—the wealthiest citizens. O. Henry's title declared that all four million New Yorkers had stories worth telling.

B **Author's Craft**

CHARACTERIZATION Ask students to explain how O. Henry describes this man. *(He portrays the character as well-off in a showy way, but somehow shady because of the scar near his right eyebrow.)*

C **Literary Elements**

SHORT STORY: *Plot* Have students discuss why the man's explanation is important to the story. *(It introduces the story's characters, setting, and situation.)*

Teaching Options

B The man in the doorway struck a match and lit his cigar. The light showed a pale, square-jawed face with keen eyes, and a little white scar near his right eyebrow. His scarfpin was a large diamond, oddly set.

"Twenty years ago tonight," said the man, "I dined here at 'Big Joe' Brady's with Jimmy Wells, my best chum, and the finest chap in the world. He and I were raised here in New York, just like two brothers, together. I was eighteen and Jimmy was twenty. The next morning I was to start for the West to make my fortune. You couldn't have dragged Jimmy out of New York; he thought it was the only place on earth. Well, we agreed that night that we would **C**

566 ❧ THEME 6

---

meet here again exactly twenty years from that date and time, no matter what our conditions might be or from what distance we might have to come. We figured that in twenty years each of us ought to have our destiny worked out and our fortunes made, whatever they were going to be."

"It sounds pretty interesting," said the policeman. "Rather a long time between meets, though, it seems to me. Haven't you heard from your friend since you left?"

"Well, yes, for a time we corresponded," said the other. "But after a year or two we lost track of each other. You see, the West is a pretty big proposition, and I kept hustling around over it pretty lively. But I know Jimmy will meet me here if he's alive, for he always was the truest, staunchest[2] old chap in the world. He'll never forget. I came a thousand miles to stand in this door tonight, and it's worth it if my old partner turns up."

The waiting man pulled out a handsome watch, the lids of it set with small diamonds.

"Three minutes to ten," he announced. "It was exactly ten o'clock when we parted here at the restaurant door."

"Did pretty well out West, didn't you?" asked the policeman.

"You bet! I hope Jimmy has done half as well. He was a kind of plodder,[3] though, good fellow as he was. I've had to compete with some of the sharpest wits going to get my pile. A man gets in a groove in New York. It takes the West to put a razor-edge on him."

The policeman twirled his club and took a step or two.

"I'll be on my way. Hope your friend comes around all right. Going to call time on him sharp?"

"I should say not!" said the other. "I'll give him half an hour at least. If Jimmy is alive on earth he'll be here by that time. So long, officer."

"Good-night, sir," said the policeman, passing on along his beat, trying doors as he went.

There was now a fine, cold drizzle falling, and the wind had risen from its uncertain puffs into a steady blow. The few foot passengers astir in that quarter hurried dismally and silently along with coat collars turned high and pocketed hands. And in the door of the hardware store the man who had come a thousand miles to fill an appointment, uncertain almost to absurdity, with the friend of his youth, smoked his cigar and waited.

---

2. Here, *proposition* means "a challenging opportunity" and *staunchest* means "most loyal and dependable."

3. A *plodder* is someone who moves slowly, but the man means that Jimmy was not a quick thinker.

Vocabulary
correspond (kôr′ ə spond′) *v.* to communicate by exchanging letters
dismally (diz′ məl lē) *adv.* in a gloomy, cheerless way
absurdity (ab sur′ də tē) *n.* the state of being ridiculous, senseless, or irrational

---

D Literary Elements

DIALOGUE: *Short Story* Ask students what the dialogue reveals about the man in the doorway. *(The man feels that Jimmy Wells is still his best friend. He values loyalty and he trusts his friend.)*

E Literary Elements

FORESHADOWING Ask students what they think O. Henry is preparing readers to expect. *(He lets the reader know that the man in the doorway has become rich ("to get my pile"), and is sure his friend probably has not, foreshadowing a conflict.)*

F Critical Thinking

DRAWING CONCLUSIONS Encourage students to think about the policeman's question. Do they find it strange? *(Even though it sounds like a friendly chat, the policeman seems to have something in mind.)*

G Literary Elements

SHORT STORY: *Setting* Invite students to explain how they think this description affects the mood of the story. *(Details seem to build up tension in the story: the storm has increased in intensity; there are only a few people outdoors, and they are described as hurrying "dismally.")*

FINE ART
TRANSPARENCY 11

You may wish to use *Fine Art Transparency 11* to extend theme-related concepts.

Reading *Minilesson*

Comparing and Contrasting "After Twenty Years" focuses on two very different characters. Though they are old friends, their personalities are almost opposite, and their lives have gone in very different directions.

Activity Have students create a Venn diagram showing how Bob and Jimmy are different and similar. **L2**

Bob
quick;
ambitious;
dishonest

Both
grew up
together;
loyal

Jimmy
plodding;
honest

Additional Resources
📁 *Reading Workbook*, pp. 85–86

568

H Literary Elements

SHORT STORY: *Rising Action* Ask students to describe the rising action and its purpose in this story. *(After the long wait and all the discussion, Jimmy has finally arrived. The tension increases and readers will at last learn what is really happening.)*

I Literary Elements

FORESHADOWING It would be strange for Bob not to remember that his friend is so tall. Have students explain what O. Henry might be hinting. *(When the man thinks twice about this man being Jimmy, so should the reader.)*

J Literary Elements

SHORT STORY: *Climax* The climax of a story is the point of greatest emotional intensity or suspense. Have students explain where they think the climax of this story is. *(The climax occurs when Bob realizes the man is not Jimmy.)*

Thematic Focus

Twists and Turns Have students discuss the unexpected events that take place in this story and how they relate to the theme.

☑ ASSESSMENT OPTIONS

📁 *Quick Checks,* p. 48

Teaching Options

After Twenty Years

[H] About twenty minutes he waited, and then a tall man in a long overcoat, with collar turned up to his ears, hurried across from the opposite side of the street. He went directly to the waiting man.

"Is that you, Bob?" he asked, doubtfully.

"Is that you, Jimmy Wells?" cried the man in the door.

"Bless my heart!" exclaimed the new arrival, grasping both the other's hands with his own. "It's Bob, sure as fate. I was certain I'd find you here if you were still in existence. Well, well, well!—twenty years is a long time. The old restaurant's gone, Bob; I wish it had lasted, so we could have had another dinner there. How has the West treated you, old man?"

[I] "Bully;[4] it has given me everything I asked it for. You've changed lots, Jimmy. I never thought you were so tall by two or three inches."

"Oh, I grew a bit after I was twenty."

"Doing well in New York, Jimmy?"

"Moderately. I have a position in one of the city departments. Come on, Bob; we'll go around to a place I know of, and have a good long talk about old times."

The two men started up the street, arm in arm. The man from the West, his egotism[5] enlarged by success, was beginning to outline the history of his career. The other, submerged in his overcoat, listened with interest.

At the corner stood a drug store, brilliant with electric lights. When they came into this glare each of them turned simultaneously to gaze upon the other's face.

The man from the West stopped suddenly and released his arm.

"You're not Jimmy Wells," he snapped. "Twenty years is a long time, but not long enough to change a man's nose from a Roman to a pug."[6] [J]

"It sometimes changes a good man into a bad one," said the tall man. "You've been under arrest for ten minutes, 'Silky' Bob. Chicago thinks you may have dropped over our way and wires us she wants to have a chat with you. Going quietly, are you? That's sensible. Now, before we go on to the station here's a note I was asked to hand you. You may read it here at the window. It's from Patrolman Wells."

The man from the West unfolded the little piece of paper handed him. His hand was steady when he began to read, but it trembled a little by the time he had finished. The note was rather short.

> BOB: I was at the appointed place on time. When you struck the match to light your cigar I saw it was the face of the man wanted in Chicago. Somehow I couldn't do it myself, so I went around and got a plain clothes[7] man to do the job.
>
> JIMMY.

---

4. *Bully* is slang for "excellent; first-rate."
5. Here, *egotism* refers to an exaggerated sense of self-importance.

6. A *Roman nose* is long and bold, while a *pug* is short, thick, and turned-up.
7. *Plain clothes* refers to a police officer who does not wear a uniform while on duty.

Vocabulary
moderately (mod′ ər it lē) *adv.* neither too great nor too small; within limits

---

Grammar and Language *Minilesson*

Adjective Clauses Write the following example on the board:
• *Then a man who wore a long overcoat hurried across the street.*
Point out that *"who wore a long overcoat"* tells something about the noun *man.* An adjective clause adds information about a noun or a pronoun in the main clause and is usually introduced by a relative pronoun *(that, which, who, what,* etc.).

Activity Have students identify and underline the adjective clauses in these sentences, and double underline the nouns they describe. **L2**

1. The cabin that sits on the hill is our favorite vacation spot.
2. Susan is a person who excels at many different sports.
3. The chess game, which was very

challenging, lasted seven hours.

Additional Resources

📖 *Grammar and Language Transparency 47*

📕 *Grammar and Language Workbook,* pp. 157–158

📕 *Grammar and Composition Handbook,* Lesson 8.3

📕 *Writer's Choice,* Lesson 14.3

Responding to Literature

PERSONAL RESPONSE

- ◆ What surprised you most about the ending of the story?
- ◆ Can you think of an alternative ending for the story?

Analyzing Literature

RECALL

1. For whom is the man from the West waiting? What promise did he make twenty years ago?
2. What does the Westerner tell the police officer about Jimmy's character?
3. After the police officer leaves, who approaches the Westerner?
4. What does Jimmy reveal in his note?

INTERPRET

5. Why does the man from the West try so hard to reassure the police officer?
6. What is Jimmy Wells's internal conflict in the story?
7. What does the Westerner's physical reaction to the note tell you about his emotional state?
8. What do you think motivated Jimmy to do what he did to his old friend at the end?

EVALUATE AND CONNECT

9. In your opinion, what is the author saying about measuring success in a person's life? How has Jimmy been both more successful and less successful than Bob?
10. Theme Connection Did O. Henry surprise you? Why or why not?

Night Shadows. Edward Hopper (1882–1967). Etching, sheet: 12³⁄₁₆ x 15¹⁵⁄₁₆ in., plate: 7 x 8¼ in. Whitney Museum of American Art, New York. Josephine N. Hopper bequest.

LITERARY ELEMENTS

Short Story

A **short story** is a brief work of fiction that usually can be read in one sitting. Short stories have the usual elements of fiction—plot, character, setting, and theme. These are the events, people, places, and ideas that make a short story complete. The combination of these elements determines the story's overall impact on the reader.

1. What surprising facts do you learn about each character at the end of O. Henry's story?
2. What theme does the story communicate about the twists and turns of life and the way people can change?

● See **Literary Terms Handbook**, p. R10.

  569

Responding to the Selection

Personal Response

- Students will probably say that the policeman was Jimmy Wells or that Bob was a wanted man.
- Students may say that Bob could have recognized Jimmy and escaped.

Analyzing Literature

1. The man is waiting for his old friend. He promised twenty years ago to meet him at this spot.
2. He tells the policeman that Jimmy is a good fellow but a bit plodding.
3. Another man, who says he is Jimmy, approaches the Westerner.
4. Jimmy reveals that he had to do his duty as a policeman, but that he could not personally arrest his old friend.
5. He does not want the policeman to question him.
6. Jimmy Wells cannot bring himself to arrest his old friend even though he recognizes him as a wanted criminal.
7. The Westerner's hands begin to tremble when he realizes that his friend has turned him in. It tells that he is extremely shaken by the revelation.
8. Jimmy is motivated by his sense of duty as a policeman.
9. The author is saying that success can't be measured by wealth alone, since Bob, with all his money, has had to live in hiding. Most students will probably say that Jimmy has been more successful in leading an honest life, even though he has been less successful at making money.

LITERARY ELEMENTS

1. The man claiming to be Jimmy is not. The policeman is Bob's old friend who recognizes him as a wanted criminal.
2. Even people who begin their lives the same way can become very different, based on their personalities and the circumstances of their lives.

Additional Resources

📖 *Literary Elements Transparency 48*

10. Most students will say they were surprised by some aspect of the story. Encourage them to explain their answers with details from the story.

Extending Your Response

Personal Writing

Students' responses should
- describe how they feel about Jimmy's choice to do his duty and turn in a friend.
- draw examples from the story and from their own experience.

Literature Groups Before students complete the chart, have them discuss how they think each character might change in the future due to his life circumstances. **COLLAB. LEARN.**

Learning for Life To give students a sense of newspaper reporting style, show them examples of crime reports. Have them read their own reports aloud in small groups.

Writing About Literature

Students' paragraphs should
- identify two specific examples of irony in the story.
- explain what is ironic about each example.

Extending Your Response

Personal Writing

Judging Loyalty Look back at what you wrote about loyalty in the **Focus Activity** on page 564. Then write a response to Jimmy's choice in choosing between personal loyalty to a friend and loyalty to his duty as a police officer.

Literature Groups

Friend or Foe? Use examples from the story to create a chart that compares and contrasts Jimmy and Bob. Consider their physical and emotional characteristics and their past and future lives.

Characteristics	Jimmy	Bob
Physical		
Emotional		
Career		

Learning for Life

Crime Column Write a report for the crime section of the newspaper to inform the public of the arrest of "Silky" Bob. Include a description of the suspect and a tribute to the quick thinking of Officer Jimmy Wells.

Writing About Literature

Irony **Irony** is a difference between appearance and reality. A story is ironic when it focuses on the differences between the way things seem to be and the way they actually are. In a paragraph, identify two specific examples of irony in "After Twenty Years" and explain what is ironic about each.

Reading Further

If you would like to read other stories by O. Henry, try these books:
The Best Short Stories of O. Henry
The Gift of the Magi and Other Stories

Save your work for your portfolio.

Skill Minilesson

VOCABULARY • THE SUFFIX *-ity*

1. c   3. e   5. d
2. a   4. b

Additional Resources
Vocabulary Practice, p. 33

Skill Minilesson

VOCABULARY • THE SUFFIX *-ity*

When *-ity* is added to the end of a word, it adds the meaning "state or condition." *Absurd* means "ridiculous," and *absurdity* means "the state of being ridiculous." Adding the suffix *-ity* usually changes the way the base word sounds. For example, the first syllable is stressed in *rapid,* but the second syllable is stressed in *rapidity.*

PRACTICE Use what you know about familiar words and the suffix *-ity* to match each word with a word that has a similar meaning.
1. solidity   a. lawlessness
2. illegality   b. oldness
3. abnormality   c. hardness
4. antiquity   d. roundness
5. circularity   e. oddness

✔ ASSESSMENT OPTIONS

- *Quick Checks,* p. 48
- *Selection and Theme Assessment,* p. 84
- *Performance Assessment,* p. 45
- *Testmaker*

LISTENING, SPEAKING, and VIEWING

Storytelling

Is there a trick to telling a story aloud to an audience? Not really. All you have to do is practice. Learn your story well enough so that, even if you use notes, you don't have to read them word-for-word. Above all, practice. Practice in front of a mirror to be comfortable with yourself. Practice in front of a friend, and ask for feedback. Practice with a tape recorder or video camera to experiment with your voice and body language.

Whether you're spinning a tale you know by heart or telling a story you've written yourself, the following guidelines can help.

Storytelling Guidelines

- Stand or sit with good posture; it helps your voice to carry.
- Look at your listeners. When they return your gaze, you have their attention. Maintain eye contact as you speak.
- Change positions from time to time so that you don't tense up.

- Vary your volume and pacing to fit the story.
- Keep checking your listeners' responses. If they fidget, ask yourself why.
- Feel free to "talk with your hands." If you wish, take on characters' roles by changing your posture, gestures, and tone of voice.

ACTIVITIES

1. With a classmate, practice and take turns telling a story you both know well. Follow the above guidelines.

2. Tell classmates a story you have written. Score yourself afterward on how well you followed the **Storytelling Guidelines.**

Objective

- To recognize and apply strategies for storytelling

Teaching Strategies

After reading the storytelling guidelines on page 571, you may ask students to demonstrate the techniques with partners. They can use a typical opening line, such as, *Once upon a time, there lived a lonely prince...* over and over as they demonstrate standing and sitting with good/bad posture, looking/not looking at listeners, varying volume/speaking in a monotone. Encourage students to exaggerate the techniques as a way of becoming comfortable and having fun with the guidelines.

Activities

1. Students may decide to tell the same story or choose different stories both are familiar with.

2. Some students may wish to make a written checklist of the guidelines in order to score themselves in each category. Others may prefer to score themselves with an overall rating.

Teaching Options

MEETING INDIVIDUAL NEEDS — ENGLISH LANGUAGE LEARNERS

Group Storytelling Encourage English language learners to share a group story with the class, either orally or in written form.

Activity To encourage collaboration, have students form a circle, and explain that everyone will contribute one sentence to a class story. Begin with a simple story opener, such as, *Once, there was a girl who lived on a mountain.* Ask the next student to add a line. The story is always repeated from the beginning as it builds, giving English language learners plenty of opportunity to listen, understand, and contribute to creating the group story. **COLLAB. LEARN.**

Additional Resources
📁 *English Language Learners Sourcebook*

Objectives

- To read and analyze a radio drama
- To explain the effects of various kinds of stage directions
- To compare and contrast the functions of dialogues and monologues in a radio drama

Skills

Reading/Thinking: Inferring; Synthesizing; Drawing Conclusions; Making Critical Judgments; Verifying Predictions; Cause and Effect; Comparing and Contrasting

Writing: Rewriting a Play as a Short Story; Writing Newspaper Article

Vocabulary: Etymology

Grammar/Language: Using Commas to Join Main Clauses

Listening/Speaking: Reading a Scene Aloud

Life Skills: Creating and Producing

Collaboration: Creating a Radio Play; Literature Groups

Motivating

→OPTIONS

Literature Launchers: "An American Icon: Mark Twain"

Videodisc Side B, Segment 17

Also available in VHS.

Selection Focus Transparency 49: Have students view the transparency and discuss the questions.

Focus Activity: As an extension of the Focus Activity, have students discuss the needs and desires that many people have in common.

Before You Read

The Million-Pound Bank Note

MEET MARK TWAIN

Mark Twain found inspiration for his writing in childhood experiences along the Mississippi River, as well as from being a riverboat pilot, a gold panner, and a journalist. Generations of readers worldwide have enjoyed his work as a novelist, short-story writer, essayist, humorist, journalist, and literary critic. He is one of the great figures of American literature.

Samuel Langhorne Clemens, better known as Mark Twain, was born in 1835 and died in 1910.

FOCUS ACTIVITY

What would you do with a million dollars?

Graph It!
Gather suggestions from your classmates and work together to graph the class's responses.

Setting a Purpose
Read this play to find out how one man is affected by having a banknote worth a million British pounds.

BACKGROUND

The Time and Place The story takes place in the late 1800s.

This scene is from the 1954 film version of Twain's story, titled *Man with a Million.*

VOCABULARY PREVIEW

proposition (prop′ ə zish′ ən) *n.* something offered for consideration; proposal; p. 573

conceive (kən sēv′) *v.* to form an image or idea of; p. 577

competent (kom′ pət ənt) *adj.* having enough ability for the purpose; capable; p. 577

rebuke (ri būk′) *n.* an expression of sharp criticism or disapproval; p. 578

eccentric (ik sen′ trik) *adj.* not usual or normal in behavior; peculiar; p. 578

benefactor (ben′ ə fak′ tər) *n.* one who gives financial assistance; p. 584

shrewd (shrood) *adj.* sharp, clever, and practical; p. 584

RESOURCE MANAGER

Lesson Planning Resource
The ***Theme Six Planning Guide*** (pp. 28–35) provides additional lesson notes and reduced versions of all print resources.

📂 **Other Print Resources**
- Active Reading Guide, p. 49
- Vocabulary Practice, p. 34
- Reading Workbook, pp. 87–88
- Grammar and Language Workbook, pp. 257–258

- Grammar and Composition Handbook, Lesson 13.3
- Quick Checks, p. 49
- Selection and Theme Assessment, pp. 85–86
- Performance Assessment, p. 46
- Spanish Summaries, p. 49
- Spanish Translations
- Inclusion Strategies
- English Language Learners Sourcebook

 Transparencies
- Selection Focus 49
- Literary Elements 49
- Grammar and Language 48

Technology
  Literature Launchers
 Audio Library
 Spanish Audio Library
 Glencoe Literature Web Site
 Testmaker

The Million-Pound Bank Note

Mark Twain
Dramatized for radio by Walter Hackett

CAST OF CHARACTERS

HENRY ADAMS	SERVANT	SECOND MAN
LLOYD HASTINGS	TOD	WOMAN
FIRST COCKNEY	MR. SMEDLEY	THIRD MAN
GORDON FEATHERSTONE	HOTEL MANAGER	BUTLER
ABEL FEATHERSTONE	SECOND COCKNEY	PORTIA LANGHAM
ALBERT HAWKINS	FIRST MAN	SIR ALFRED

HENRY. When I was twenty-seven years old, I was a mining broker's clerk in San Francisco. I was alone in the world, and had nothing to depend upon but my wits and a clean reputation. These were setting my feet in the road to eventual fortune, and I was content with the prospect.[1] During my spare time, I did outside work. One of my part-time employers was Lloyd Hastings, a mining broker. During this period I was helping Hastings to verify[1] the Gould and Curry Extension papers, covering what seemed to be a highly valuable gold mine. One morning at two, after six hard hours of work on these papers, Lloyd Hastings and I went to the What Cheer restaurant in Frisco. As we lingered over our coffee, he offered me a proposition.

HASTINGS. Henry, how would you like to go to London?

HENRY. Thank you, no.

HASTINGS. Listen to me. I'm thinking of taking a month's option[2] on the Gould and Curry Extension for the locators.

HENRY. And—?

HASTINGS. They want one million dollars for it.

HENRY. Not too much—if the claim works out the way it appears it may.

HASTINGS. I'm going to try to sell it to London interests, which means a trip there, and I want you to go with me, because you know more about these papers than I.

---

1. Here, *prospect* means "possibility of future success." To *verify* the papers is to check the accuracy of their information.

2. In financial terms, an *option* is a right to buy or sell something for a certain price and within a certain time.

Vocabulary
proposition (prop′ ə zish′ ən) *n.* something offered for consideration; proposal

---

CONNECTING TO OTHER SELECTIONS

COMPARING selections

This selection is compared with "Force of Luck" on pages 591–598. A lesson for teaching a comparison of the two selections appears on page 600.

The chart at the right shows three other ways to connect "The Million-Pound Bank Note" to selections in this book.

For specific teaching strategies, see the *Theme Six Planning Guide,* pages 31–32.

Connection	Title
Life Skills: Interpersonal Skills	→ "The Teacher Who Changed My Life," p. 368
Thematic: Decisions	→ "Amigo Brothers," p. 433
Literary: Dialogue	→ "All Summer in a Day," p. 461

B Author's Craft

FORESHADOWING Ask students if they agree with Henry when he says, "I think you're doomed to failure." *(Many will think Henry will be right because he seems levelheaded, and Hastings seems to be a risk taker.)*

C Active Reading

PREDICT Encourage students to predict what may happen to Henry in London. You may wish to share the following model to illustrate the thinking process involved in predicting.

Model: I know Hastings went to London to try to sell the option. I also know Hastings had wanted Henry to explain the gold mine papers to potential buyers. I think that Henry and Hastings will reconnect in London, and Henry will help Hastings sell the gold mine option.

D Active Reading

EVALUATE Have students explain why Henry doesn't eat the pear. *(Henry doesn't want anyone to see him take the pear from the gutter; he is too proud to act desperate.)*

Teaching Options

The Million-Pound Bank Note

HENRY. No, thanks.

HASTINGS. I'll make it well worth your while. I'll pay all your expenses, and give you something over if I make the sale.

HENRY. I have a job.

HASTINGS. I'll arrange for you to get a leave of absence. What do you say?

HENRY. No.

HASTINGS. Why?

HENRY. If I go to London, I'll get out of touch with my work and with mining conditions here, and that means months getting the hang of things again.

HASTINGS. That's a pretty slim excuse, Henry.

HENRY. More important, perhaps, I think you're doomed to failure.

HASTINGS. But you just said the claim is valuable.

HENRY. It may well turn out that way, but right now its real value can't be proved. And even so, a month's option may leave you too little time to sell it; unless you sell it within the option time, you'll go stone broke.

HASTINGS. I'm willing to gamble.

HENRY. Well, I'm not.

HASTINGS. Think—a free trip to London.

HENRY. I've no desire to go to London. I'll remain right here in Frisco.

HASTINGS. [*Fading.*][3] Very well, but I know you're making a mistake, Henry.

HENRY. One of my few diversions[4] was sailing in the bay. One day I ventured too far, and was carried out to sea. Late that night, I was picked up by a freighter which was bound for London. It was a long voyage, and the captain made me work my passage without pay, as a common sailor. When I stepped ashore at London my clothes were ragged and shabby, and I had only a dollar in my pocket. This money fed and sheltered me for twenty-four hours. During the next twenty-four I went without food and shelter. I tried to get a job, doing manual labor. But the reply was always the same.

COCKNEY.[5] I'm not sure you'd do. You ain't the sort. [*Suspiciously.*] Look, 'ere, you're a Yank, ain't you?

HENRY. The next morning, seedy and hungry, I was dragging myself along Portland Place, when my desiring eye fell on a tempting treasure lying in the gutter. It was a luscious big pear—minus one bite. My mouth watered for it. But every time I made a move to get it, some passing eye detected my purpose. I was just getting desperate enough to brave all the shame, when a window behind me was raised.

GORDON. [*Away.*] I say, you there, will you step in here, please?

HENRY. It was a very sumptuous[6] house and an equally sumptuous room into which I was ushered by a servant. A couple of elderly gentlemen were sitting by the window. At that moment if I had known what they had in mind, undoubtedly I would have bolted for the door. They looked me over very thoroughly.

---

3. The *fading* of Hastings's voice indicates the end of the scene.
4. *Diversions* are activities that amuse and take one's mind away from work or worries.

5. A *cockney* is a person who speaks with an accent found only in a certain district of London.
6. Things that are *sumptuous* (sump′ chōō əs) are expensive, showy, and magnificent.

MEETING INDIVIDUAL NEEDS — ENGLISH LANGUAGE LEARNERS

Using a Flowchart Explain to students that Hastings has an *option*, or an opportunity, for one month to raise the money to buy the mine for one million dollars. Use the flowchart to help students understand the concept.

Activity Have students read the flowchart and explain in their own words what will happen if Hastings sells the mine or if he doesn't sell it on time. **L2**

Additional Resources

📁 *English Language Learners Sourcebook*

Bank of England
Promise to pay the Bearer on Demand the Sum of **One Million Pounds**
1890, May 27 London 27 May 1890

One Million

LONDON
For the Gov. and Company of the
BANK OF ENGLAND
Chief Cashier

E

GORDON. He looks poor enough, don't you think, brother?

ABEL. Very. Er, young man, you are poor?

HENRY. Extremely!

ABEL. Good! And honest, too?

HENRY. Honesty is about all I have left; that, and character.

ABEL. Splendid!

GORDON. If my brother and I are judges of people, we'd say you are just the man for whom we have been searching. By the way, you are also intelligent, I would say.

HENRY. Yes, sir, I am. But what do you mean by saying that I appear to be just the man for whom you have been searching?

GORDON. And we don't know you. You're a perfect stranger. And better still, an American.

HENRY. It's very kind of you gentlemen to call me into your home, but I'm a bit puzzled. Could you tell me what you have in mind?

ABEL. Might we inquire into your background?

HENRY. Pretty soon they had my full story. Their questions were complete and searching, and I gave them straightforward answers. Finally one said:

GORDON. Oh, yes, we're certain you will do, eh, brother?

ABEL. Definitely! He is elected.

HENRY. To what am I elected, please?

GORDON. This envelope will explain everything. Here, take it. [*Hastily.*] No, don't open it now. Take it to your lodgings and look it over carefully.

ABEL. Being sure not to be rash[7] or hasty.

HENRY. I'd like to discuss the matter.

GORDON. There is nothing to discuss at the moment.

HENRY. Is this a joke?

ABEL. Not at all. And now good day.

GORDON. And good luck.

ABEL. Cheerio!

HENRY. As soon as I was out of sight of the house I opened my envelope and saw it contained money. I lost not a moment, but shoved note and money into my pocket, and broke for the nearest cheap eating house. How I did eat! Finished, I took out my money and unfolded it. I took one glimpse and nearly fainted. It was a single million-pound bank note. Five millions of dollars! It made my head swim. The next

F

G

---

7. To be *rash* is to act without thought or preparation.

FYI

Bank Notes and Federal Reserve Notes Some nations have a central bank that issues paper money, called bank notes. The United States does not have a central bank; it has the Federal Reserve Bank, so U.S. bills are called Federal Reserve notes. If students look at a U.S. dollar, they will see the words *Federal Reserve Note* on the face of the bill.

E Literary Elements

DIALOGUE Have students explain what makes this dialogue engaging. *(It is funny, and it makes you wonder what is going to happen next.)*

F Critical Thinking

INFERRING Have students explain why the brothers don't want Henry to open the envelope until he gets back to his lodgings. *(Perhaps they are afraid Henry won't take the envelope if he opens it in the brothers' home.)*

G Active Reading

PREDICT Have students predict what Henry will do with all this money. *(Students might predict that Henry is honest and will give the money back, or that he is poor and desperate, and will use it for food and lodging, or to go back to San Francisco.)*

Reading *Minilesson*

Synthesizing Synthesizing is the ability to understand how ideas and information relate to other ideas and information. It involves collecting, connecting, and combining important details into something that makes sense.

Activity This play has a story (about Henry and the Featherstones) within a story (about Henry and Hastings). Have students create a two-column chart. One column should read *Henry and Hastings*; while the other reads *Henry and the Featherstones*. Have them work in small groups to select the most important details to create a synthesis of the plots.

L2 **COLLAB. LEARN.**

Additional Resources
📁 *Reading Workbook,* pp. 87–88

H Active Reading

QUESTION At the time of this story, twenty shillings equaled one English pound. Ask students to figure out how much change Henry would be owed if he paid for his meal with the million-pound bank note. *(Henry would be owed 999,999 pounds and 18 shillings.)*

Cultural Note

In the 1800s, twelve bronze pennies (or *pence* in British English) equaled one shilling. Stamped onto each penny were grooves shaped like a plus sign. The coins could be broken along the grooves into halves or fourths. One-quarter of this coin was a farthing. One-half of the coin was a half-pence.

I Critical Thinking

DRAWING CONCLUSIONS Have students explain why Hawkins treats Henry differently after he sees the bank note. *(Hawkins thinks Henry is rich and that he can certainly afford to pay for his meal, so Hawkins is willing to let Henry pay later.)*

J Literary Elements

CONFLICT Have students describe the conflict Henry faces. *(He thinks the brothers have accidentally given him too much money. He wants to return it, but the brothers are gone.)*

Teaching Options

thing I noticed was the owner of the eating house. His eyes were on the note, and he was petrified.[8] He couldn't stir hand or foot. I tossed the note toward him in careless fashion.

HAWKINS. I-is it real, sir! A million-pound note?

HENRY. [*Casually.*] Certainly. Let me have my change, please.

HAWKINS. Oh, I'm very sorry, sir, but I can't break the bill.

HENRY. Look here—

HAWKINS. Hawkins is the name, Albert Hawkins, proprietor.[9] It's only a matter of two shillings you owe, a trifling sum. Please owe it to me.

HENRY. I may not be in this neighborhood again for a good time.

HAWKINS. It's of no consequence, sir. And you can have anything you want, any time you choose, and let the account run as long as you please. I'm not afraid to trust as rich a gentleman as you, just because you choose to play larks[10] by dressing as a tramp.

HENRY. Well, thank you. I shall take advantage of your kindness.

HAWKINS. Not at all, sir, [*Fading.*] and please, sir, enter my humble restaurant place any time you wish. I shall be honored to receive you.

HENRY. I was frightened, afraid that the police might pick me up. I was afraid of the two brothers' reaction when they

discovered they had given me a million-pound note instead of what they must have intended giving—a one-pound note. I hurried to their house and rang the bell. The same servant appeared. I asked for the brothers.

SERVANT. They are gone.

HENRY. Gone! Where?

SERVANT. On a journey.

HENRY. But whereabouts?

SERVANT. To the Continent,[11] I think.

HENRY. The Continent?

SERVANT. Yes, sir.

HENRY. Which way—by what route?

SERVANT. I can't say, sir.

HENRY. When will they be back?

SERVANT. In a month, they said.

HENRY. A month! This is awful! Tell me how to get word to them. It's of great importance.

SERVANT. I can't, indeed. I've no idea where they've gone, sir.

HENRY. Then I must see some member of the family.

SERVANT. Family's been away too; been abroad months—in Egypt and India, I think.

HENRY. There's been an immense mistake made. They'll be back before night. Tell them I've been here, and that I'll keep coming till it's all made right, and they needn't worry.

SERVANT. I'll tell them, if they come back, but I'm not expecting them. They said you'd be here in an hour to make inquiries,

---

8. *Petrified* means "turned to stone." The man is struck rigid with astonishment.
9. As a *proprietor* (prə pri′ ə tər), Hawkins is the owner and operator of a small business.
10. The British expression *play larks* means "joke around."

11. *The Continent* is how the British often refer to mainland Europe.

MEETING INDIVIDUAL NEEDS — INCLUSION STRATEGIES

Less-Proficient Readers Students not used to reading plays may need some additional help.

Activity Have students label sheets of paper with the names of important characters they have encountered so far. *(Henry Adams, Lloyd Hastings)* Beneath each name, have students list the character's problem. *(Hastings*

needs to sell the option; Henry thinks he has been given a million-pound bank note by mistake.) As they encounter important new characters, have them create additional lists for the new characters. **L1**

Additional Resources
Inclusion Strategies

but I must tell you it's all right, they'll be here on time to meet you. [*Fading.*] And that's all they said.

HENRY. [*Slowly.*] I had to give it up and go away. What a riddle it all was! They would be here "on time." What could that mean? Then I thought of the letter. I got it out and read it. It said: "You are an intelligent and honest man, as one can see by your face. We <u>conceive</u> you to be poor and a stranger. Enclosed you will find a sum of money. It is lent to you for thirty days, without interest. Report to this house at the end of that time. I have a bet on you. If I win it you shall have any situation[12] that is in my gift, any, that is, that you shall be able to prove yourself familiar with and <u>competent</u> to fill." That was all. No signature, no address, no date. I hadn't the least idea what the game was, nor whether harm was meant me or kindness. The letter said there was a bet on me. What kind of a bet? Was the bet that I would abscond[13] with the million-pound bank note? Which brother was betting on my honesty? I reasoned this way: if I ask the Bank of England to deposit it to the credit of the man it belongs to, they'll ask me how I came by it, and if I tell the truth, they'll put me in the asylum; on the other hand, if I lie, they'll put me in jail. The same result would follow if I try to bank it anywhere or borrow money on it. Therefore, I have to carry this burden around until those men come back. A month's suffering without wages or profit—

unless I help win that bet, whatever it may be. If I do, I will get the situation I am promised. My hopes began to rise high. Then I looked at my rags. Could I afford a new suit? No, for I had nothing in the world but a million pounds. Finally I gave in and entered a fashionable tailor shop. The clerk looked at me very arrogantly.[14]

TOD. [*Icily.*] No chores to be done here. Get out!

HENRY. Perhaps you have a misfit suit.

TOD. We don't give away suits, even misfits.

HENRY. I can pay for it.

TOD. Follow me.

HENRY. He took me into a back room, and overhauled a pile of rejected suits. He tossed the rattiest looking one at me. I put it on. It didn't fit. It wasn't in any way attractive.

TOD. You may have that for four pounds, cash.

HENRY. It would be an accommodation to me if you could wait some days for the money. I haven't any small change about me.

TOD. [*Sarcastically.*][15] Oh, you haven't? Well, of course, I didn't expect it. I'd only expect gentlemen like you to carry large change.

HENRY. My friend, you shouldn't judge a stranger always by the clothes he wears. I am quite able to pay for this suit.

---

12. Here, *situation* means "a job or position of employment."
13. If Henry were to *abscond,* he would flee secretly and hide.

14. *Arrogantly* means "in a self-important way; proudly."
15. Tod speaks in a sharp, mocking way (*sarcastically*).

Vocabulary
conceive (kən sēv´) *v.* to form an image or idea of
competent (kom´ pət ənt) *adj.* having enough ability for the purpose; capable

---

Joseph Pennell was an American artist born in 1857. Like Henry in this drama, Pennell moved to London. Pennell created more than 1,500 works showing buildings and landscapes. His subjects ranged from English factories to Greek temples.

Viewing Response *Some students might choose to go on a shopping spree in the local shops. Others might opt for a meal at the best restaurant in London, a suite at a luxury hotel, a sightseeing tour, or any combination of these and other options.*

N **Critical Thinking**

DRAWING CONCLUSIONS Invite students to explain what Henry has learned from his experience in the restaurant that he may be remembering here. *(Henry has learned that stores cannot make change for his bank note and may, therefore, give him the goods he wants on credit.)*

O **Literary Elements**

STAGE DIRECTIONS Invite students to explain how these stage directions help the actors say their lines. *(Explanations like "he stutters and fumbles" and "raising voice" indicate that Tod should sound flustered and nervous. Until now he has seemed self-assured and condescending toward Henry.)*

Teaching Options

West Front of St. Paul's from Ludgate Hill. Joseph Pennell (1857–1926). Gouache en grisaille on paper laid down on board, 20 x 13¾ in. Private collection.

Viewing the painting: What would you want to see or do if you were in this scene with a million-pound bank note?

TOD. Hah!

N **HENRY.** I simply don't wish to put you to the trouble of changing a large note.

TOD. As long as <u>rebukes</u> are going around, I might say that it wasn't quite your affair to infer[16] that we couldn't change any note that you might happen to be carrying around. On the contrary, we *can.*

HENRY. Oh, very well. I apologize. Here you are.

TOD. Thank you. [*A complete change. He stutters and fumbles.*] Ah—it's—ah—that is—we—ah—you see—It's— [*Quickly.*] take it back, please. [*Raising voice.*] Mr. Smedley! Mr. Smedley! Help! Oh, Mr. Smedley. **O**

SMEDLEY. [*Coming in. A fussy man.*] What is it, Tod, what is it? Stop shouting!

TOD. Oh, but Mr. Smedley, I can't control myself.

SMEDLEY. What's up? What's the trouble? What's wanting? Who's this?

HENRY. I am a customer and I am waiting for my change.

SMEDLEY. Change, change! Tod, give him his change. Get it for him.

TOD. Get him his change! It's easy for you to say that, Mr. Smedley, but look at the bill yourself.

SMEDLEY. Bill, bill! Let me see it! [*Pause.*] Tod, you ass, selling an <u>eccentric</u> millionaire

16. Here, *infer* means "to come to a conclusion based on something assumed."

Vocabulary
rebuke (ri būk´) *n.* an expression of sharp criticism or disapproval
eccentric (ik sen´ trik) *adj.* not usual or normal in behavior; peculiar

Listening and Speaking *Minilesson*

Reading a Scene Aloud Work with students to list some guidelines on the board to help students read aloud a scene, such as the one between Tod and Henry. *(Practice. Read some parts slower or faster, louder or softer. Make eye contact. Don't rush. Read with feeling.)*

Activity Encourage pairs of students to examine the stage directions in the scene for ideas about how to say the lines. Then have pairs practice reading aloud the scene beginning with "No chores to be done here..." and ending with "Oh, Mr. Smedley." When pairs are ready, invite them to present their scenes to the class. Encourage audience members to listen attentively to help the performers feel confident. **L2** **COLLAB. LEARN.**

such an unspeakable suit as that. Tod, you're a fool—a born fool! Drives every millionaire away from this place, because he can't tell a millionaire from a tramp. Here, sir, are some suits more in keeping with your position.

HENRY. Thank you, but this one will do.

SMEDLEY. Of course it won't do! I shall burn it. Tod, burn this suit at once.

TOD. Yes, Mr. Smedley.

SMEDLEY. We shall be honored to outfit you completely, sir . . . morning clothes, evening dress, sack suits, tweeds, shetlands—everything you need. Come, Tod, book and pen. Now—length of leg, 32 inches; sleeve—

HENRY. But look here, I can't give you an order for suits, unless you can wait indefinitely,[17] or change this bill.

SMEDLEY. Indefinitely, sir. It's a weak word, a weak word. *Eternally, that's the* word, sir. Tod, rush these things through. Let the minor customers wait. Set down the gentleman's address and—

HENRY. I'm changing my quarters. I'll drop in and leave the new address.

SMEDLEY. Quite right, sir, quite right. One moment—allow me to show you out, sir. And don't worry about paying us. [*Fading.*] Your credit is the highest. Good day, sir, good day. You honor us greatly, sir.

HENRY. [*As though sighing.*] Well, don't you see what was bound to happen? I drifted naturally into whatever I wanted. Take my hotel, for example. I merely showed the resident manager my million-pound note, and he said:

MANAGER. We are honored to have you as a guest, sir. Now, I have just the suite for you. It consists of a bedroom, sitting room, a dressing room, a dining room, two baths and—

HENRY. I'll pay you a month in advance with this.

MANAGER. [*Laughing.*] You honor our simple hotel, sir. Pray, don't worry about the bill.

HENRY. But it may be several months before I can pay you.

MANAGER. We're not worried, Mr.—er—

HENRY. Henry Adams.

MANAGER. Mr. Adams, you are a most distinguished guest. [*Fading.*] Anything you desire, please name it and we shall procure it for you immediately. Thank you, sir.

HENRY. And there I was, sumptuously housed in an expensive hotel in Hanover Square. I took my dinners there, but for breakfast I stuck by Hawkins' humble feeding-house, where I had got my first meal on my million-pound bank note. I was the making of Hawkins.

[*SOUND. Rattle of dishes and silver, customers' voices ad-libbing[18] in background.*]

HAWKINS. Business is brisk, sir, very brisk, indeed, and has been ever since you and your million-pound bank note became patrons of my humble establishment. I've had to hire extra help, put in additional tables. Look for yourself, sir. There's a long line waiting to get in. Why, I'm famous and fair on my way to becoming wealthy.

17. To wait *indefinitely* would be for an unlimited length of time.

18. *Ad libbing* is saying things that are not written in a script.

TWISTS AND TURNS 579

P Active Reading
EVALUATE Encourage students to explain why shop owners treat Henry so differently once they see the bank note. (*They think Henry is rich and powerful, even though he dresses like a beggar.*)

Q Active Reading
QUESTION Have students explain why Henry says he is changing his quarters. (*Henry doesn't yet have a place to live, so he can't give an address.*)

R Literary Elements
NARRATOR Encourage students to offer an explanation of this monologue's purpose. Why does Henry speak directly to the radio audience? (*To help listeners realize that the action is moving from the tailor shop to a hotel.*)

S Critical Thinking
DRAWING CONCLUSIONS Have students explain how Henry is the "making of Hawkins." (*As word spreads that Henry, who people think is a millionaire, eats at Hawkins' eating-house, it becomes very popular.*)

Writing Minilesson

Rewriting a Play as a Short Story
Mark Twain's original version, written as a short story, described important elements through narration. This radio drama, on the other hand, has to depend exclusively on what the characters say.

Activity Invite students to rewrite one of the play's scenes as it might appear in a short story. Have them include a description of the setting to help readers understand or picture the scene. Students should also consider adding descriptions of each character's behavior, thoughts, and mannerisms. **L2**

Additional Resources
Writer's Choice, Lessons 4.1–4.4

COCKNEY 2. Pardon me, Guv'ner,[19] but aren't you the gentleman what owns the million-pound bank note?

HAWKINS. Look here, you, go away and stop bothering Mr.— Mr.—

HENRY. Adams.

HAWKINS. Mr. Adams.

COCKNEY 2. I was just anxious to get a look at him.

HAWKINS. Who? Mr. Adams?

COCKNEY 2. No. The bank note.

HENRY. Glad to oblige. There you are.

COCKNEY 2. By George, it *is* real. [*Fading.*] Now I can go home and tell me old lady I've seen it with me own eyes. I hopes she believes me, but she won't.

HAWKINS. Mr. Adams, I wonder if I couldn't force upon you a small loan— even a large one.

HENRY. Oh, no.

HAWKINS. Please allow me, sir.

HENRY. [*Relenting.*][20] Well, as a matter of fact, I haven't gotten around to changing this note.

HAWKINS. Fifty pounds might help tide you over. You know, a little spending money?

HENRY. It would help, a bit.

HAWKINS. I consider it a great honor. [*Fading.*] Indeed, a very great honor. Here you are, Mr. Adams, fifty pounds it is. [*Fading.*] And don't worry about repaying me.

HENRY. I was in, now, and must sink or swim. I walked on air. And it was natural,

for I had become one of the notorieties[21] of London. It turned my head, not just a little, but a great deal. The newspapers referred to me as the "Vest-Pocket Millionaire." Then came the climaxing stroke: "Punch" caricatured[22] me! Wherever I went, people cried:

MAN 1. There he goes!

MAN 2. That's him!

WOMAN 1. Morning, Guv'ner.

MAN 3. He's a bit of all right, he is.

HENRY. Why, I just swam in glory all day long. About the tenth day of my fame I fulfilled my duty to my country by calling upon the American Ambassador. He received me with enthusiasm, and insisted that I attend a dinner party he was giving the following night. Two important things happened at that dinner. I met two people who were to play important roles in the little drama I was living. Among the guests was a lovely English girl, named Portia Langham, whom I fell in love with in two minutes, and she with me; I could see it without glasses. And just before dinner, the butler announced:

[*BIZ. Guests ad-libbing in background, very politely.*]

BUTLER. [*Calling out.*] Mr. Lloyd Hastings.

HENRY. I stared at Hastings and he at me, his mouth open in surprise.

HASTINGS. I, er—pardon me, but are you? No, of course you can't be.

HENRY. [*Chuckling.*] But I am, Lloyd.

HASTINGS. Henry, I'm speechless. [*Suddenly.*] Don't tell me that you're also the Vest-Pocket Millionaire?

---

19. *Guv'ner* ("Governor") is Cockney dialect for addressing a man in authority or of a higher social class.
20. Here, *relenting* means "giving in."

21. A *notoriety* is someone who has become a celebrity.
22. *Punch* is a British humor magazine. It *caricatured* Henry in a cartoon that ridiculously exaggerated his features.

INTERDISCIPLINARY CONNECTION

Social Studies/Economics When this drama was written, one British pound equaled approximately five U.S. dollars.

Activity Students may work in pairs or small groups to examine exchange rates around the world today. Exchange rates are listed in many newspapers. They can also be found on the Internet. Have students first research how much one British pound is worth in U.S. dollars today. Then have students determine what unit of currency is used in Canada, Mexico, or any other country that interests them. Students can then find the worth of one unit of that currency in U.S. dollars. Encourage students to create a chart with their findings and share them with the rest of the class. **L2**

HENRY. Correct!

HASTINGS. I've seen your own name coupled with the nickname, but it never occurred to me you were *the* Henry Adams. Why, it isn't six months since you were clerking in Frisco, and sitting up nights helping me verify the Gould and Curry Extension papers. The idea of your being in London, and a vast millionaire, and a colossal celebrity! It's out of the Arabian Nights!

HENRY. I can't realize it myself.

HASTINGS. It was just three months ago that we were eating together, and I tried to persuade you to come to London with me. You turned me down and now here you are. How did you happen to come, and what gave you this incredible start?

HENRY. I'll tell you all about it, but not now.

HASTINGS. When?

HENRY. The end of this month.

HASTINGS. Make it a week.

HENRY. I can't. How's your business venture coming along?

HASTINGS. [*Sighing.*] You were a true prophet, Henry. I wish I hadn't come.

HENRY. Stop with me, when we leave here, and tell me all about it. I want to hear the whole story.

HASTINGS. You'll hear it, every last dismal word. [*Fading a bit.*] I'm so grateful to find a willing and sympathetic ear.[23]

[BIZ. *Background ad-libbing out. A pause, then:*]

---

23. One who listens in a caring way is said to have a *sympathetic ear.*

[PIANO. *Playing semi-classical tune in background.*]

HENRY. After dinner there was coffee and an informal piano recital and dear Miss Langham—lovely Portia Langham, the English girl. I eased her away from the music and the guests, to the library, where we talked.

[PIANO. *Out.*]

PORTIA. I'm really quite excited, Mr. Adams, meeting you like this. A millionaire!

HENRY. But I'm not one.

PORTIA. B-but of course you are.

HENRY. You're wrong.

PORTIA. I don't understand.

HENRY. You will! You will, that is, if you allow me to see you tomorrow.

PORTIA. [*As though smiling.*] Well, Mr. Adams—

HENRY. Henry.

PORTIA. Henry, then. I will give the invitation serious thought.

HENRY. Tomorrow is going to be a sunny day, just right for a picnic in the country. Yes?

PORTIA. Yes.

HENRY. I'll tell you the whole story then.

PORTIA. Do you think you should?

HENRY. Certainly! After all, we're going to be married.

PORTIA. [*Amazed.*] We—we're—going to—marry!

HENRY. Absolutely! I'll call for you at noon. Where?

PORTIA. Meet me here.

HENRY. You're a guest here?

Cultural Note

The Arabian Nights, or the *Thousand and One Nights*, is a series of ancient stories thought to be from Persia. Some of the most famous tales involve Aladdin and Ali Baba, who become wealthy with the help of a magic lamp, a magic ring, or the magic words *Open Sesame.*

W Active Reading

QUESTION Since Hastings and Henry last saw each other, three months earlier, have students figure out how long Henry must have spent on the ship coming to London. *(Since Henry has been in London for only eleven days, he must have been on the ship for more than two months.)* Using a wall map of the world, demonstrate—or have a student volunteer do so—the sea route from San Francisco to London before the Panama Canal existed.

X Literary Elements

STAGE DIRECTIONS Have students explain what the sounds of conversation, a pause, and then piano playing indicate to the radio audience. *(Dinner is over, and an after-dinner piano recital has begun.)*

Y Active Reading

EVALUATE Ask students if they think Henry is serious about marrying Portia. *(Students might note that Henry is in love with Portia and is boldly expressing his wishes.)*

Reading *Minilesson*

Cause and Effect Many events in this story cause other events to happen. For example, by not eating the pear, Henry causes two rich brothers to think he is a good candidate for their bet.

Activity Have students number a sheet of paper from 1 to 5. Beside each number have them list one cause from the story and its effect or effects. If students have trouble separating causes from effects, have them use this sentence to help: "Because of [something], [something else] happens." Encourage students to add to their lists as they read the rest of this play. **L2**

Additional Resources
📁 *Reading Workbook,* pp. 87–88

Literary Elements

STAGE DIRECTIONS Have students think about how Portia's speech probably sounds after the stage directions say "fading." *(Her voice gets quieter and quieter as she is leaving the scene.)*

Literary Elements

NARRATOR Ask students to discuss the purpose of this monologue. *(It lets listeners know that the setting has changed, and that Henry is now home. Also, it lets readers know Henry's state of mind: he is deep in thought, infatuated with Portia.)*

Literary Elements

CONFLICT Have students identify the conflict Hastings faces. *(The option on the mine expires at the end of the month, which is fast approaching, and the buyers have backed away from the deal.)*

Active Reading

QUESTION Have students explain why Henry doesn't take Hastings up on the deal. *(The money does not belong to him, so Henry does not want to take the risk of loosing it.)*

Teaching Options

PORTIA. N—no, but it will be more convenient.

HENRY. Do you like me?

PORTIA. Yes, Henry. [*Fading.*] You're a very unusual young man, even if you are a millionaire, and even if you claim you aren't.

HENRY. All the way home I was in the clouds, Hastings talking, and I not hearing a word. When we reached my suite, he said to me:

HASTINGS. This luxury makes me realize how poor, how defeated I am. Even the drippings of your daily income would seem like a tremendous fortune to me.

HENRY. Unreel your story, Lloyd.

HASTINGS. I told you the whole story on the way over here.

HENRY. You did?

HASTINGS. Yes.

HENRY. I'll be hanged if I heard a word of it.

HASTINGS. Are you well?

HENRY. Yes. I'm in love.

HASTINGS. That English girl you were speaking to?

HENRY. Yes. I'm going to marry her.

HASTINGS. Small wonder you didn't hear a word I said.

HENRY. Now I'm all attention.

HASTINGS. I came here with what I thought was a grand opportunity. I have an option to sell the Gould and Curry Mine and keep all I can get over a million dollars.

HENRY. Sounds like a good proposition.

HASTINGS. Yes, it's a fine claim.

HENRY. Well?

582 THEME 6

HASTINGS. The parties here whom I tried to interest have backed down. And so here I am trying to peddle a gold mine, but with nary a buyer in sight. In addition, I am almost penniless.

HENRY. Surely you'll find a buyer.

HASTINGS. My option on the mine expires in a matter of days; in fact, at the end of this month.

HENRY. You *are* in a fix.

HASTINGS. Henry, you can save me. Will you do it?

HENRY. I? How?

HASTINGS. Give me a million dollars and my passage home for my option.

HENRY. I can't.

HASTINGS. But you're wealthy.

HENRY. I—I—not really.

HASTINGS. You have a million pounds—five millions of dollars. Buy the mine and you'll double, maybe triple your investment.

HENRY. I'd like to help, but I can't.

HASTINGS. You know the value of this mine, as well as I do.

HENRY. [*Tired.*] Oh, Lloyd, I wish I could explain, but I can't. What you ask is impossible.

HASTINGS. That's quite all right. I'm sorry to have bothered you, Henry. [*Fading.*] You must have a good reason in turning me down, I'm sure.

HENRY. It hurt me to have to refuse Lloyd, but it made me comprehend my delicate and precarious[24] position. Here I was, deep in debt, not a cent in the world, in love

---

24. *Precarious* means "exposed to risk or danger."

---

with a lovely girl, and nothing in front of me but a promise of a position, if, *if* I won the bet for the nameless brother. Nothing could save me. The next day, Portia and I went on our picnic in the country. I told her the whole story, down to the last detail. Her reaction wasn't exactly what I thought it would be.

[SOUND. *Bird singing in background. Weave in and out of this scene.*]

PORTIA. [*Laughs.*] Oh, Henry, that's priceless.

HENRY. [*A bit stiffly.*] I fail to see the humor.

PORTIA. But I do, more than you can imagine.

HENRY. Here I am mixed up in a bet between two eccentric old men, and for all they care I might well be in jail.

PORTIA. [*Still laughing.*] Wonderful, the funniest thing I've ever heard.

HENRY. Pardon me if I don't laugh.

PORTIA. [*Stops laughing.*] Sorry, but it is both funny and pathetic.[25] But you say that one of the men is going to offer you a position?

HENRY. If I win the bet.

PORTIA. Which one is he?

HENRY. I don't know. But I have one solution. If I win, I get the position. Now, I've kept a very careful track of every cent I either owe or have borrowed, and I'm going to pay it back from my salary. If the position pays me six hundred pounds a year, I'll—I'll—

PORTIA. You'll what?

---

25. Something that's *pathetic* inspires pity or sadness.

HENRY. I'll— [*He whistles.*] To date I owe exactly six hundred pounds, my whole year's salary.

PORTIA. And the month isn't ended.

HENRY. If I'm careful, my second year's salary may carry me through. Oh, dear, that *is* going to make it difficult for us to get married immediately, isn't it?

PORTIA. [*Dreamily.*] Yes, it is. [*Suddenly.*] Henry, what are you talking about? Marriage! You don't know me.

HENRY. I know your name, your nationality, your age, and, most important, I know that I love you. I also know that you love me.

PORTIA. Please be sensible.

HENRY. I can't. I'm in love.

PORTIA. All this sounds like a play.

HENRY. It is—a wonderful one. I'll admit my owing my first two years' pay is going to pose a problem insofar as our getting married is concerned. [*Suddenly.*] I have it! The day I confront those two old gentlemen, I'll take you with me.

PORTIA. Oh, no. It wouldn't be proper.

HENRY. But so much depends upon that meeting. With you there, I can get the old boys to raise my salary—say, to a thousand pounds a year. Perhaps fifteen hundred. Say you'll go with me.

PORTIA. I'll go.

HENRY. In that case, I'll demand two thousand a year, so we can get married immediately.

PORTIA. Henry.

HENRY. Yes?

PORTIA. Keep your expenses down for the balance of the month. Don't dip into your third year's salary.

DD Critical Thinking

DRAWING CONCLUSIONS Portia thinks Henry's story is funny, but Twain doesn't have her explain why. Have students explain what this may indicate about Portia. *(Portia seems to know more than she is letting on. Perhaps she thinks the situation is funny because she knows something that Henry doesn't.)*

EE Active Reading

PREDICT Ask students whether they think Henry and Portia will get married. *(Portia doesn't care that Henry is not a millionaire, so perhaps they really will get married. Or, Portia knows something she isn't telling; whatever it is might interfere with their marriage plans.)*

FF Literary Elements

CHARACTER Have students explain how Portia feels. *(Portia is happy that Henry wants to marry her. She is amused by his financial situation but not alarmed, even though Henry is in debt.)*

LIFE SKILLS CONNECTION

Creating and Producing Invite students to use this play as a model to create their own brief scene for a radio play. Students can create a scene in which Henry shows the bank note to a local merchant to obtain something he needs, such as a haircut, shoes, or a taxi ride.

Activity Have small groups of students work together to think of a situation involving Henry Adams and a merchant.

Then have the group write dialogue and stage directions appropriate for a radio play. Next, have students think about sound effects or music and gather any props needed to make the sounds. Encourage students to practice their scenes and then to tape-record them. Have them play their audiotapes for the class. **L2 COLLAB. LEARN.**

Literary Elements

CONFLICT Have students explain in their own words Henry's problems now. *(Henry is heavily in debt. He doesn't know whether he will win the bet and be able to pay off his debts.)*

Active Reading

PREDICT Henry allows Hastings to use his name freely. Do students think this will help Hastings sell his option? You may wish to use the following model to illustrate the thinking process involved in predicting.

Model: Since Henry is now famous and people think he is rich, I think the use of Henry's name will help Hastings sell the mine. Most people will believe Henry's financial advice because they think he must be financially savvy to have become so rich.

Vo•cab•u•lar•y Skills

Etymology *Fortnight* comes from the Middle English word *fourtenight,* which meant "fourteen nights." Today a fortnight still means fourteen days and nights, or two weeks.

The Million-Pound Bank Note

HENRY. And that is how matters stood at that point. Thoughts raced through my mind. What if I lost the bet for my nameless benefactor? What if he failed to give me a position? Then the answer came to me, like a flash of lightning. I roused Lloyd Hastings from bed. He was a bit bewildered.

HASTINGS. I don't understand you. What are you getting at?

HENRY. Lloyd, I'm going to save you. Save you—understand!

HASTINGS. No.

HENRY. I'll save you, but not in the way you ask, for that wouldn't be fair, after your hard work and the risks you've run. Now, I don't need to buy a mine. I can keep my capital moving without that; it's what I'm doing all the time. I know all about your mine; I know its immense value and can swear to it if anybody wishes it. You shall sell it inside of the fortnight[26] for three million cash.

HASTINGS. Three million!

HENRY. Right!

HASTINGS. But how?

HENRY. By using my name freely—and right now my name is on the tip of everybody's tongue. We'll divide the profits, share and share alike.

HASTINGS. [*Overjoyed.*] I may use your name! Your name—think of it! Man, they'll flock in droves, these rich English. They'll fight for that stock. I'm a made

man,[27] a made man forever. [*Fading.*] I'll never forget you as long as I live . . . never, never . . .

HENRY. In less than twenty-four hours London was abuzz! I hadn't anything to do, day after day, but sit home, and wait for calls.

SIR ALFRED. Then I may assume, Mr. Adams, that you consider this mining property a sound investment?

HENRY. A very sound investment, Sir Alfred.

SIR ALFRED. And what of this American chap, Hastings?

HENRY. I know him very well, and he is as sound as the mine.

SIR ALFRED. Then I think I shall invest in this property. Your recommendation does it.

[*SOUND. Telephone bell.*]

HENRY. Excuse me, Sir Alfred.

[*SOUND. Receiver lifted from hook.*]

HENRY. [*Into phone.*] Yes, this is Henry Adams. Who? Sir John Hardcastle. Yes, Sir John. The Gould and Curry Extension? Yes, I know a great deal about it. I certainly would recommend it as a shrewd investment. The mine is worth far more than the asking price. Yes, Mr. Hastings is very well known in the States. Honest as the day is long, as they say. Yes, I suggest you contact Mr. Hastings. Thank you. Not at all. Good day, Sir John.

---

26. In financial terms, *capital* is wealth that is used to produce more wealth. A *fortnight* is two weeks.

27. *A made man* is one who is assured of success.

Vocabulary
benefactor (ben′ ə fak′ tər) *n.* one who gives financial assistance
shrewd (shrood) *adj.* sharp, clever, and practical

Teaching Options

Reading *Minilesson*

Comparing and Contrasting The interaction between Henry and Hastings on this page shows the ways in which the two men are alike and different. Draw a Venn diagram, like the one at the right, on the board. Label the left circle *HENRY* and the right circle *HASTINGS*.

Activity Have students complete the diagram and add their own ideas to it. Encourage students to think creatively as they compare the two men. Invite volunteers to share their best ideas with the rest of the class. **L2**

Additional Resources
📁 *Reading Workbook,* pp. 87–88

Indeed! Edward C. Clifford (1858–1910). Christopher Wood Gallery, London.

Viewing the painting: Compare this picture with the scene from the movie on page 572. Which do you think is truer to the story? Why?

[SOUND. *Receiver replaced onto hook.*]

SIR ALFRED. That clinches it. If Sir John is in, so am I. Do you suppose that your Mr. Hastings would mind if I brought in a few discreet friends on this venture?

HENRY. Er, no, in fact I'm sure he wouldn't. Mr. Hastings is a very democratic chap.

SIR ALFRED. Directly I shall go and call upon Mr. Hastings. By the way, exactly where is this mine?

HENRY. California.

SIR ALFRED. Is that near Washington, D.C.?

HENRY. Not exactly.

SIR ALFRED. A pity, for I had thought of asking the British Ambassador to look at

it. [*Fading.*] Well, I'm off. Thank you for your advice. Good day, Mr. Adams.

HENRY. And that's the way it went—a steady stream of wealthy Londoners asking my advice, which, of course, I gave freely. Meanwhile I said not a word to Portia about the possible sale of the mine. I wanted to save it as a surprise; and then there always was the possibility the sale might fall through. The day the month was up, she and I, dressed in our best, went to the house on Portland Place. As we waited for the two old gentlemen to enter, we talked excitedly.

PORTIA. You're certain you have the bank note with you?

VIEWING THE PAINTING

Viewing Response *Some students might say that the movie is truer because it was based on the story. Others might say that the painting is truer to the story because it was probably painted closer to the time of the story, and the clothing, hairstyles, and behavior of the couple would be more accurate.*

Active Reading

EVALUATE Have students explain what makes this scene funny. *(Sir Alfred is going to invest in the mine; in fact, he is even going to recommend the deal to friends. Yet, he doesn't know where the mine is. He wonders if the mine in California is near Washington, D.C.)*

Literary Elements

NARRATOR Have students explain the purpose of this monologue. *(It is to let listeners know that Henry hasn't told Portia about the deal, that time has passed and the month is up, and that Henry and Portia are on their way to see the two wealthy brothers.)*

MEETING INDIVIDUAL NEEDS — GIFTED AND TALENTED ACTIVITY

Mark Twain Students who are interested in Mark Twain might enjoy conducting research to learn more about him. The are many Twain resources available, including biographical information; *The New York Times* articles from the 1800s by and about Twain; the complete text of many short stories and books; information about Twain's influence on popular culture today; as well as photos, cartoons, and illustrations of Twain.

Activity Encourage students to use the school library, the public library, or the Internet to find more information on Twain. If students use the Internet, encourage them to use a variety of keywords, such as *Samuel Clemens, Huckleberry Finn,* and *The New York Times,* in addition to Twain's name. **L3**

Literary Elements

CHARACTER Encourage students to suggest words or phrases that describe what Gordon and Abel are like. *(The brothers are wealthy and competitive, but Abel is also a good loser.)*

Active Reading

QUESTION Have students explain why the brothers would not have given Henry the money if he had boldly eaten the pear. *(The brothers wanted someone with a sense of pride. If Henry had picked up the pear without hesitation, the brothers would have thought Henry reacted without thinking of the consequences.)*

Active Reading

REVIEW Tell students that 200,000 pounds equaled about one million U.S. dollars at the time. Based on this information, encourage students to figure out how much the mine sold for. *(Since Henry and Hastings split any money left over after the $1 million, the mine must have sold for $3 million.)*

HENRY. Right here. Portia, dearest, the way you look it's a crime to ask for a salary a single penny under three thousand a year.

PORTIA. You'll ruin us.

HENRY. Just trust in me. It'll come out all right.

PORTIA. [*Worried.*] Please remember if we ask for too much we may get no salary at all; and then what will become of us, with no way in the world to earn our living? [*Fading.*] Please handle this delicately, Henry.

HENRY. When the two old gentlemen entered, of course they were surprised to see Portia with me. I asked them to introduce themselves, which they did.

GORDON. I am Gordon Featherstone.

ABEL. And I am Abel Featherstone.

HENRY. Gentlemen, I am ready to report, but first may I ask which of you bet on me?

GORDON. It was I. Have you the million-pound note?

HENRY. Here it is, sir.

GORDON. Ah! I've won. *Now* what do you say, Abel?

ABEL. I say he did survive, and I've lost twenty thousand pounds. I never would have believed it.

HENRY. Perhaps you might enlighten[28] me as to the terms of the bet.

GORDON. Gladly! The Bank of England once issued two notes of a million pounds each. Only one of these had been used and cancelled; the other lay in the vaults. Well, Abel and I got to wondering what would happen to a perfectly honest and intelligent stranger turned adrift in London without a

friend and with no money in the world but the million-pound bank note. Abel said he would starve to death, and I claimed he wouldn't. My brother said he would be arrested if he offered the note at a bank. Well, we went on arguing until I bet him twenty thousand pounds that the man would live thirty days, *anyway*, on that million, and keep out of jail, too.

ABEL. And I took him up.

HENRY. How did you know I was the right choice?

ABEL. After talking with you, we decided you had all the qualifications.

GORDON. And that pear incident, if you had picked it up very boldly, it would have proved to us you were nothing but a tramp.

HENRY. You don't know how tempted I was to do just that.

GORDON. And so you shall receive your reward—a choice of any position you can fill.

HENRY. First I ask that you look at this scrap of paper, all of you. You, too, Portia.

GORDON. A certificate of deposit in the London and County Bank—

ABEL. In the sum of—

GORDON. Two hundred thousand pounds.

PORTIA. Henry, is it yours?

HENRY. It is. It represents my share of the sale of a mining property in California, sold by my friend Lloyd Hastings; a sort of commission, as it were. It all came about by thirty days' judicious[29] use of that little loan you gentlemen let me have. And the only use I made of it was to buy trifles and offer the bill in change.

---

28. To *enlighten* is to give or reveal knowledge or wisdom.

29. *Judicious* means "showing good judgment."

Teaching Options

Grammar and Language *Minilesson*

Using Commas to Join Main Clauses
Write the following complete sentence on the board: *Abel said he would starve to death, and I claimed he wouldn't.* Explain that there is a comma before *and* in the sentence because it separates main clauses. *(Abel said he would starve to death. I claimed he wouldn't.)* Commas are used to separate main clauses connected by *and, but,* or *or.*

Activity Have students, individually or in pairs, skim pages 574, 575, and 582 for other examples that use commas before *and, but,* or *or.* Ask them to rewrite each of these sentences as two separate sentences. Finally, have students write five sentences of their own that use commas to join two main clauses. **L2**

Additional Resources

- *Grammar and Language Transparency 48*
- *Grammar and Language Workbook,* pp. 257–258
- *Grammar and Composition Handbook,* Lesson 13.3
- *Writer's Choice,* Lesson 20.3

ABEL. Come, this is astonishing.

GORDON. It's incredible.

HENRY. [*Laughing.*] I can prove it.

PORTIA. Henry, is that really your money? Have you been fibbing to me?

HENRY. I have, indeed. But you'll forgive me, I know.

PORTIA. [*Half-smiling.*] Don't you be so sure.

HENRY. Oh, you'll get over it. Come, let's be going.

GORDON. Wait! I promised to give you a situation, you know.

HENRY. Thank you, but I really don't want one.

PORTIA. Henry, I'm ashamed of you. You don't even thank the good gentleman. May I do it for you?

HENRY. If you can improve upon it.

PORTIA. I shall. Uncle Abel, first, thank you for making this possible. And, dear Father—

HENRY. Hold on. You're her uncle?

ABEL. I am.

HENRY. And you—

GORDON. Yes, I'm her step-father.

PORTIA. And the dearest one that ever was. You understand now, don't you, Henry, why I was able to laugh when you told me the story of the bet with the two nameless gentlemen. Of course I couldn't miss knowing that it was this house and that the two men were Father and Uncle Abel.

HENRY. Sir, you *have* got a situation open that I want.

GORDON. Name it.

HENRY. Son-in-law.

GORDON. Well, well, well! But if you haven't ever served in that capacity, you of course can't furnish satisfactory recommendations to satisfy the conditions of the contract.

HENRY. Only just try me for thirty or forty years.

GORDON. What do you think, Abel?

ABEL. Well, he does look to be a satisfactory sort.

GORDON. And you, Portia?

PORTIA. I agree—heartily.

GORDON. Very well. Take her along. If you hurry, you can reach the license bureau before it closes. [*Fading.*] Hop to it now.

HENRY. Happy, we two? Indeed, yes! And when London got the whole history of my adventure for a month, how it did talk. My Portia's father took the million-pound bank note to the Bank of England, cashed it, had it cancelled, and he gave it to us at our wedding. Framed, it now hangs in our home. It gave me my Portia, but for it I could not have remained in London, would not have appeared at the American Ambassador's, never should have met her. And so I always say: Yes, it's a million-pounder; but it made but one purchase in its life, and then got the article for only about a tenth part of its value.

THE END

❖

TWISTS AND TURNS ❧ 587

NN **Author's Craft**

CHARACTERS Have students consider why Twain portrayed Gordon Featherstone as Portia's stepfather rather than her father. (*If Gordon were Portia's father, he would have the same last name as Portia. Readers might suspect that Portia and Gordon are related, which would spoil the surprise at the end.*)

00 **Active Reading**

REVIEW Encourage students to explain what they think the last sentence of this drama means. (*The only item the bank note ever bought Henry was Portia, and Portia is worth much more to Henry than the bank note was worth.*)

Thematic Focus

Twists and Turns Ask students how they feel about the twists and turns that occur in this drama. How do students think the moral of this play relates to those of the other stories in this theme?

✔ **ASSESSMENT OPTIONS**

📁 *Quick Checks,* p. 49

A&E HOME VIDEO ® The following videotape program is available from Glencoe. Be sure to preview it for appropriateness for your class.

• *Mark Twain: His Amazing Adventure**

Also available in the Glencoe Literature Video Library.

REAL-WORLD CONNECTION

Romance Throughout history, romance has been an engaging topic for artists to explore, for falling in love is an experience shared by many people throughout the world.

Activity Have students analyze a humorous treatment of a romance in a modern comic strip, a short story, or a movie or TV comedy. Encourage students to compare any humorous incidents they find with the humorous incidents in "The Million-Pound Bank Note." In what ways are Henry and Portia portrayed like the other characters students find? In what ways are the characters different? Ask students to discuss what characteristics of romance seem universal, and have them share their ideas with the class. **L2**

Personal Response

Students might find that their ideas are similar to Henry's since people the world over share the same basic wants and needs.

Analyzing Literature

1. Hastings wants Henry to go to London to help sell the mine claim because Henry knows the mine papers better than Hastings does.
2. The two wealthy men offer Henry money and bet on what he will do with it. Henry thinks they have made a mistake when he sees the note's value.
3. The shop people give Henry goods on credit when they see the note's value. The shop owners spread the word that Henry is a millionaire, and Henry becomes the talk of the town.
4. Henry lets Hastings use his name to sell the mine. Henry and Hastings divide the profits from the mine sale.
5. It is ironic because Henry has refused Hastings's expense-paid trip to London.
6. Gordon and Abel are trying to test both honesty and intelligence.
7. Henry doesn't look or act like a millionaire, but he has a million pounds in his vest pocket.
8. Henry's success shows that he is a creative problem solver and an astute businessman.
9. The ending is surprising, but Twain has given clues about the outcome. Twain portrays the brothers as good judges of character, and therefore believable when they bet on Henry's honesty. Portia's connection to the two gentlemen is made believable by her introduction to and relationship with Henry.

Responding to Literature

PERSONAL RESPONSE

Take a look at the graph you created in the **Focus Activity** on page 572. How do your ideas of what to do with a million dollars compare with how Henry uses the million-pound note?

Analyzing Literature

RECALL

1. Why did Hastings want Henry to travel to London, England?
2. What do the two wealthy gentlemen offer Henry? What is his response when he realizes the value of the bill?
3. How do the shop people respond to the million-pound note? How do they contribute to Henry's fame?
4. How does Henry manage to earn his own fortune?

INTERPRET

5. Why is it ironic that Henry finds himself on a freighter bound for London?
6. What do you think Gordon and Abel are trying to test?
7. Why does Henry achieve fame as the "Vest-Pocket Millionaire"?
8. What does Henry's success with the uncashed million-pound note tell you about his personality and business skills?

EVALUATE AND CONNECT

9. Were you surprised by the climax of the story? Do you think Twain gave enough clues to make the gentlemen's bet and Portia's connection to the two men believable? Explain.
10. **Theme Connection** How does having a million-pound bank note affect Henry? How would it affect you?

10. Having a million pounds doesn't affect Henry's integrity, but it does give him the confidence to achieve his goals. Students might say that it would enable them to afford many material things or allow them to achieve their own personal goals.

LITERARY ELEMENTS

Stage Directions

Mark Twain originally wrote "The Million-Pound Bank Note" as a short story. Many years later, Walter Hackett adapted the story as a radio play. Like a traditional play, a radio play includes **stage directions** written in italic type and set in brackets. However, directions about scenery, movement, lighting, or props are unnecessary. In a radio play, the audience must use its imagination to visualize the characters and the setting. The only stage directions deal with sound effects and how the actors should say their lines.

1. Compare Henry's first meal at Hawkins's restaurant on pages 575–576 with the stage directions on page 579 when he returns there. What difference would the addition of sound effects make to the listener?
2. A number of times in the play the word *fading* appears within a character's speech. What effect do you think the dramatist is trying to achieve in these places? What would the speech sound like?

● See **Literary Terms Handbook**, p. R10.

LITERARY ELEMENTS

1. The addition of sound effects makes listeners realize that the eating house is now packed with customers.
2. The word *fading* lets listeners know that the scene is ending and a new scene will soon begin. The speech would gradually become softer.

Additional Resources

Literary Elements Transparency 49

Extending Your Response

Writing About Literature

Dialogue and Monologue This dramatization contains **dialogue**—conversations between characters—and **monologues**—speeches Henry directs to the audience. From which of these do you learn more about Henry? From which do you learn more about the action in the play? Support your ideas with quotations from the play.

Creative Writing

Henry's Headlines Write a series of brief newspaper articles from the point of view of a London journalist hot on the trail to describe Henry's wealth, adventures, and romance.

Literature Groups

Making Judgments Discuss the assumptions people make about Henry when they see his shabby clothes and how those assumptions change when they see his million-pound note. What conclusions can be drawn about how the appearance of wealth affects our judgment of people?

interNET CONNECTION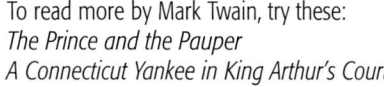

You can find out more about Mark Twain and his writings on the Internet. Just type *Mark Twain* or *Samuel Clemens* in the subject window of a search engine. You can even find the entire text of some of his novels and short stories if you'd like to read them.

Reading Further

To read more by Mark Twain, try these:
The Prince and the Pauper
A Connecticut Yankee in King Arthur's Court

💾 **Save your work for your portfolio.**

Skill Minilesson

VOCABULARY • ETYMOLOGY

Words have histories. Knowing where a word comes from can help you understand what it means now and why it means that. For example, *eccentric* comes from the Greek words *ek,* meaning "out of" and *kentron,* meaning "center." So an *eccentric* millionaire is one who is sort of "off center," or odd.

The history of a word is called its **etymology.** Here are the etymologies of some other words from "The Million-Pound Bank Note."

proposition: from the Latin *pro-* ("forward") and *positio* ("to place")
benefactor: from the Latin *bene-* ("well") and *facere* ("to do").
rebuke: from the Latin *re-* ("back") and the Old French *buchier* ("to beat")

PRACTICE Choose one of the words from the above list and briefly explain how the etymology of that word is connected to its present-day meaning.

Extending Your Response

Writing About Literature

Students' analyses should
- indicate that monologues tell most about Henry; dialogues tell most about the action.
- use quotations from the story.
- indicate that monologues also help listeners make the transition from one setting to another.

Creative Writing

Students' newspaper articles should
- describe Henry's adventures in London.
- contain opening paragraphs that stir interest in the story.
- be written from the point of view of a newspaper reporter in the mid-1800s.

Literature Groups Before students meet, encourage them to review the story to see what assumptions people make about Henry in his shabby clothes and how those assumptions change.
COLLAB. LEARN.

Skill Minilesson

VOCABULARY • ETYMOLOGY

Students should clearly explain how the meanings of the words in the etymologies provided relate to the words' modern definitions.

Additional Resources
📁 *Vocabulary Practice,* p. 34

✔ ASSESSMENT OPTIONS

📁 *Quick Checks,* p. 49
📁 *Selection and Theme Assessment,* pp. 85–86
📁 *Performance Assessment,* p. 46
💾 *Testmaker*

Objectives

- To read and analyze a folktale about a miller's changing fortune
- To recognize and discuss elements common to folktales
- To write two monologues comparing stages in a person's life

Skills

Reading/Thinking: Using Text Structures; Logical Reasoning; Drawing Conclusions; Synthesizing; Analyzing Arguments
Writing: Write a Different Ending
Vocabulary: Etymology
Grammar/Language: Identifying the Subject of a Sentence
Listening/Speaking: Storytelling
Collaboration: Literature Groups

Motivating
→OPTIONS

Selection Focus Transparency 50: Have students think about and discuss whether they have any control over their luck.

Focus Activity: As an extension of the Focus Activity, have students in small groups compare their ideas about good fortune, hard work, and honesty.

Before You Read
The Force of Luck

MEET RUDOLFO A. ANAYA

The land and culture of his native New Mexico has inspired Rudolfo A. Anaya (rōō dôl′ fō ä nä′yä) since he was a child. Anaya was born in Pastura, a village on a vast plain covered with small farming communities. He has written that "the most important elements of my childhood are the people of those villages and the wide open plains." In his short stories, novels, and plays, Anaya draws upon Mexican legends, myths, and symbolism to create an insight into the Mexican American community.

Rudolfo A. Anaya was born in 1937. This story is part of a collection called Cuentos: Tales from the Hispanic Southwest.

FOCUS ACTIVITY

Do you believe good fortune comes to those who are hard-working and honest or to those who are simply lucky?

Journal
In your journal, write your own ideas about good fortune.

Setting a Purpose
Read this story to find out what roles hard work and luck play in the life of one character.

BACKGROUND

Time and Place This story, like many folktales, takes place in a small village sometime in the past.

Did You Know? "The Force of Luck" is part of the oral tradition of the Hispanic people who lived in the American Southwest. The *cuentistas,* or oral storytellers, played an important role in the life of writer Rudolfo A. Anaya. Anaya comments, "[Storytelling] is a tradition one often loses when one moves into print, but its elements are strong and as valuable today as they have been historically."

VOCABULARY PREVIEW

prosperous (pros′ pər əs) *adj.* having wealth or good fortune; successful; p. 592
squander (skwon′ dər) *v.* to spend or use in a reckless or wasteful manner; p. 593
spendthrift (spend′ thrift′) *n.* one who spends money generously or wastefully; p. 594
novelty (nov′ əl tē) *n.* anything new and unusual; p. 595
jest (jest) *v.* to speak or act in a playful manner; joke; p. 596
intact (in takt′) *adj.* undamaged and whole; p. 598

RESOURCE MANAGER

Lesson Planning Resource
The *Theme Six Planning Guide* (pp. 36–43) provides additional lesson notes and reduced versions of all print resources.

📁 **Other Print Resources**
- Active Reading Guide, p. 50
- Vocabulary Practice, p. 35
- Reading Workbook, pp. 89–90
- Grammar and Language Workbook, pp. 51–52

- Grammar and Composition Handbook, Lesson 1.3
- Quick Checks, p. 50
- Selection and Theme Assessment, pp. 87–88
- Performance Assessment, p. 47
- Spanish Summaries, p. 50
- Inclusion Strategies
- English Language Learners Sourcebook

 Transparencies
- Selection Focus 50
- Fine Art 26
- Literary Elements 50
- Grammar and Language 49

Technology
🎧 Audio Library
🎧 Spanish Audio Library
💻 Glencoe Literature Web Site
💾 Testmaker

The Force of Luck

Retold by Rudolfo A. Anaya

Farmers (Agricultores), 1935. Antonio Gattorno. Gouache and ink on paper laid down on board, 17½ x 19½ in. Private collection.

SUMMARY

Two wealthy men give an honest but poor miller $200 to see whether it is luck or money that makes a man prosper. The miller loses the money. The men give him another $200. The miller again loses the money. The men then give the miller a worthless piece of lead, which leads the miller to a valuable diamond. This allows the miller to start his own business and become wealthy. Was it luck or money that made the miller prosper?

📁 *Spanish Summaries,* p. 50

A **Active Reading**

PREDICT Have students use the title of the story, what they know about folktales, and clues from the art to predict what they think the problem in the story may be. Suggest that students periodically revisit their predictions as they read to verify or revise them.

Additional Resources

📁 *Active Reading Guide,* p. 50

🎧 *Audio Library*

🎧 *Spanish Audio Library*

Teaching Options

CONNECTING TO OTHER SELECTIONS

COMPARING selections

This selection is compared with "The Million-Pound Bank Note" on page 573. A lesson for teaching a comparison of the two selections appears on page 600.

The chart at the right shows three other ways to connect "The Force of Luck" to selections in this book. For specific teaching strategies, see the *Theme Six Planning Guide,* pages 39–40.

Connection	Title
Life Skills: Supporting and Contributing →	"The Scholarship Jacket," p. 451
Thematic: Changes →	"Rip Van Winkle," p. 185
Literary: Folktale →	"Anansi and His Visitor, Turtle," p. 388

FYI

A *bit* is an amount equal to 1/8 of a dollar (or 12 1/2 cents). Since the United States does not have 1/2 cent coins, *bit* is almost always used in plural form: 2 bits (or 25 cents), 4 bits (or 50 cents), 6 bits (or 75 cents).

C **Active Reading**

PREDICT Have students predict whether the money will change the miller's life.

D **Active Reading**

REVIEW Ask students to name the developments up to this point in the story. *(We have been introduced to the characters, the setting, and the conflict.)*

Teaching Options

The Force of Luck

B
Once two wealthy friends got into a heated argument. One said that it was money which made a man prosperous, and the other maintained that it wasn't money, but luck, which made the man. They argued for some time and finally decided that if only they could find an honorable man then perhaps they could prove their respective points of view.[1]

One day while they were passing through a small village they came upon a miller who was grinding corn and wheat. They paused to ask the man how he ran his business. The miller replied that he worked for a master and that he earned only four bits a day, and with that he had to support a family of five.

The friends were surprised. "Do you mean to tell us you can maintain a family of five on only fifteen dollars a month?" one asked.

"I live modestly to make ends meet," the humble miller replied.

The two friends privately agreed that if they put this man to a test perhaps they could resolve their argument.

"I am going to make you an offer," one of them said to the miller. "I will give you two hundred dollars and you may do whatever you want with the money."

"But why would you give me this money when you've just met me?" the miller asked.

"Well, my good man, my friend and I have a long standing argument. He contends that it is luck which elevates a man

_____

1. *Prove their respective points of view* means that each man was interested in proving his opinion the correct one.

to high position, and I say it is money. By giving you this money perhaps we can settle our argument. Here, take it, and do with it what you want!"
C

So the poor miller took the money and spent the rest of the day thinking about the strange meeting which had presented him with more money than he had ever seen. What could he possibly do with all this money? Be that as it may, he had the money in his pocket and he could do with it whatever he wanted.

When the day's work was done, the miller decided the first thing he would do would be to buy food for his family. He took out ten dollars and wrapped the rest of the money in a cloth and put the bundle in his bag. Then he went to the market and bought supplies and a good piece of meat to take home.

On the way home he was attacked by a hawk that had smelled the meat which the miller carried. The miller fought off the bird but in the struggle he lost the bundle of money. Before the miller knew what was happening the hawk grabbed the bag and flew away with it. When he realized what had happened he fell into deep thought.
D

"Ah," he moaned, "wouldn't it have been better to let that hungry bird have the meat! I could have bought a lot more meat with the money he took. Alas, now I'm in the same poverty as before! And worse, because now those two men will say I am a thief! I should have thought carefully and bought nothing. Yes, I should have gone straight home and this wouldn't have happened!"

Vocabulary
prosperous (pros′ pər əs) *adj.* having wealth or good fortune; successful

MEETING INDIVIDUAL NEEDS ENGLISH LANGUAGE LEARNERS

Folktales Explain to English language learners that folktales are handed down from generation to generation and that they exist in almost every culture.

Activity Have students work in mixed groups to share stories about hard work, honesty, or luck leading to good fortune. Ask each group to select one story. Invite groups to present their tales orally to the class. Have students explain the characters in the story and what happens to them. Encourage the class to look for common features, themes, or values in these stories. **COLLAB. LEARN.**

Additional Resources
📁 *English Language Learners Sourcebook*

So he gathered what was left of his provisions[2] and continued home, and when he arrived he told his family the entire story.

When he was finished telling his story his wife said, "It has been our lot[3] to be poor, but have faith in God and maybe someday our luck will change."

The next day the miller got up and went to work as usual. He wondered what the two men would say about his story. But since he had never been a man of money he soon forgot the entire matter.

Three months after he had lost the money to the hawk, it happened that the two wealthy men returned to the village. As soon as they saw the miller they approached him to ask if his luck had changed. When the miller saw them he felt ashamed and afraid that they would think that he had squandered the money on worthless things. But he decided to tell them the truth and as soon as they had greeted each other he told his story. The men believed him. In fact, the one who insisted that it was money and not luck which made a man prosper took out another two hundred dollars and gave it to the miller.

"Let's try again," he said, "and let's see what happens this time."

The miller didn't know what to think. "Kind sir, maybe it would be better if you put this money in the hands of another man," he said.

"No," the man insisted, "I want to give it to you because you are an honest man,

and if we are going to settle our argument you have to take the money!"

The miller thanked them and promised to do his best. Then as soon as the two men left he began to think what to do with the money so that it wouldn't disappear as it had the first time. The thing to do was to take the money straight home. He took out ten dollars, wrapped the rest in a cloth, and headed home.

When he arrived his wife wasn't at home. At first he didn't know what to do with the money. He went to the pantry where he had stored a large earthenware jar filled with bran. That was as safe a place as any to hide the money, he thought, so he emptied out the grain and put the bundle of money at the bottom of the jar, then covered it up with the grain. Satisfied that the money was safe he returned to work.

That afternoon when he arrived home from work he was greeted by his wife.

"Look, my husband, today I bought some good clay with which to whitewash the entire house."

"And how did you buy the clay if we don't have any money?" he asked.

"Well, the man who was selling the clay was willing to trade for jewelry, money, or anything of value," she said. "The only thing we had of value was the jar full of bran, so I traded it for the clay. Isn't it wonderful, I think we have enough clay to whitewash these two rooms!"

The man groaned and pulled his hair.

"Oh, you crazy woman! What have you done? We're ruined again!"

---

2. The miller's *provisions* are his food supplies.
3. Here, *lot* means "fate; final outcome."

Vocabulary
squander (skwon′ dər) *v.* to spend or use in a reckless or wasteful manner

---

VIEWING THE PAINTING

Diego Rivera is one of Mexico's most famous artists. His subject matter often deals with life in Mexico, Mexican history, or social problems. Because Rivera believed that art should not be hidden away, he often painted large murals on the walls of public buildings.

Viewing Response *Most students will think the woman is similar to the miller's wife.*

H   Active Reading

QUESTION Have students recall what happened the first time the miller told the two men he lost the money. Do students think the two men will believe him again? *(The men believe him the first time because he seems honest. They will probably believe he had bad luck again.)*

I   Literary Elements

FOLKTALE Have students explain how the repetition in this story could help an oral storyteller tell this tale. *(It is easier to remember the events of a story if they happen in a predictable manner. The pattern allows the storyteller to stretch the story and keep his listeners interested.)*

Teaching Options

La Molendera I, 1924. Diego Rivera. *Encaustica sobre tela,* 90 x 117 cm. Museo de Arte Moderno, Bosque de Chapultepec, Mexico.

Viewing the painting: Which character in the story does this woman come closest to illustrating?

"But why?" she asked, unable to understand his anguish.

"Today I met the same two friends who gave me the two hundred dollars three months ago," he explained. "And after I told them how I lost the money they gave me another two hundred. And I, to make sure the money was safe, came home and hid it inside the jar of bran—the same jar you have traded for dirt! Now we're as poor as we were before! And what am I going to tell the two men? They'll think I'm a liar and a thief for sure!"

"Let them think what they want," his wife said calmly. "We will only have in our lives what the good Lord wants us to have. It is our lot to be poor until God wills it otherwise."

So the miller was consoled and the next day he went to work as usual. Time came and went, and one day the two wealthy friends returned to ask the miller how he had done with the second two hundred dollars. When the poor miller saw them he was afraid they would accuse him of being a liar and a spendthrift. But he

Vocabulary
spendthrift (spend′ thrift′) *n.* one who spends money generously or wastefully

MEETING INDIVIDUAL NEEDS   INCLUSION STRATEGIES

Less-Proficient Readers Some students may not understand what type of work the miller does. Explain that a miller grinds (or mills) grain into flour. A place where this is done is called a mill.

Activity Have students work in small groups to list what they think a miller's job entails. You may want to prompt them with questions like these:

- What does a miller have to do?
- What does the miller do with the ground grain?
- Why is ground grain important to people? **L1** **COLLAB. LEARN.**

Additional Resources
📁 *Inclusion Strategies*

decided to be truthful and as soon as they had greeted each other he told them what had happened to the money.

"That is why poor men remain honest," the man who had given him the money said. "Because they don't have money they can't get into trouble. But I find your stories hard to believe. I think you gambled and lost the money. That's why you're telling us these wild stories."

"Either way," he continued, "I still believe that it is money and not luck which makes a man prosper."

"Well, you certainly didn't prove your point by giving the money to this poor miller," his friend reminded him. "Good evening, you luckless man," he said to the miller.

"Thank you, friends," the miller said.

"Oh, by the way, here is a worthless piece of lead I've been carrying around. Maybe you can use it for something," said the man who believed in luck. Then the two men left, still debating their points of view on life.

Since the lead was practically worthless, the miller thought nothing of it and put it in his jacket pocket. He forgot all about it until he arrived home. When he threw his jacket on a chair he heard a thump and he remembered the piece of lead. He took it out of the pocket and threw it under the table. Later that night after the family had eaten and gone to bed, they heard a knock at the door.

"Who is it? What do you want?" the miller asked.

"It's me, your neighbor," a voice answered. The miller recognized the fisherman's wife. "My husband sent me to ask you if you have any lead you can spare. He is going fishing tomorrow and he needs the lead to weight down the nets."

The miller remembered the lead he had thrown under the table. He got up, found it, and gave it to the woman.

"Thank you very much, neighbor," the woman said. "I promise you the first fish my husband catches will be yours."

"Think nothing of it," the miller said and returned to bed. The next day he got up and went to work without thinking any more of the incident. But in the afternoon when he returned home he found his wife cooking a big fish for dinner.

"Since when are we so well off we can afford fish for supper?" he asked his wife.

"Don't you remember that our neighbor promised us the first fish her husband caught?" his wife reminded him. "Well this was the fish he caught the first time he threw his net. So it's ours, and it's a beauty. But you should have been here when I gutted him! I found a large piece of glass in his stomach!"

"And what did you do with it?"

"Oh, I gave it to the children to play with," she shrugged.

When the miller saw the piece of glass he noticed it shone so brightly it appeared to illuminate the room, but because he knew nothing about jewels he didn't realize its value and left it to the children. But the bright glass was such a novelty that the children were soon fighting over it and raising a terrible fuss.

Now it so happened that the miller and his wife had other neighbors who were

---

Vocabulary
novelty (nov′ əl tē) *n.* anything new and unusual

J Active Reading

RESPOND Ask students whether they agree with the man who says that people without money cannot get into trouble. *(Most students will think the statement is not true because people without money do get into trouble.)*

K Critical Thinking

LOGICAL REASONING Ask students to bring to mind what they know about folktales and apply it to the characters and events in this story. How do students think the story might develop after the miller meets the two men for the third time? *(The man who believes in luck gives the miller a piece of lead instead of $200. Perhaps luck will play a role this time.)*

L Active Reading

QUESTION Have students explain what usually happens to people who help others in stories. Do students think the miller will be rewarded for helping his neighbor? *(In folktales people are rewarded for helping others. Because this is a traditional tale, the miller will probably be rewarded.)*

M Literary Elements

FORESHADOWING Have students explain how this paragraph suggests that the piece of glass may be valuable. *(The glass shines so brilliantly it lights up the room, which indicates that it is special. The paragraph also says the miller knows nothing about jewels, which hints that the glass might be a jewel.)*

Listening and Speaking *Minilesson*

Storytelling Write on the board these guidelines for selecting a story to tell orally:

1. The story should have a good opening.
2. It shouldn't be very complicated.
3. It should be relatively short.
4. It should be interesting to listen to (i.e., funny, scary, suspenseful).

Activity Encourage each student to select a tale from this book or another source to tell out loud to a small group. Students should practice telling their stories several times. They may want to experiment with speaking loud, soft, fast, slow, high, or low to indicate the different characters they are portraying. Encourage listeners to listen carefully and try to visualize story events as they hear them. **L2**

Critical Thinking

DRAWING CONCLUSIONS Ask students why the jeweler and his wife think the miller will accept $50.00 for a piece of glass. *(They think that since the miller and his wife do not know the value of the "glass" they will accept anything.)*

Literary Elements

FOLKTALE Have students explain how this exchange is different from what might happen in contemporary realistic fiction. *(In realistic fiction, the jeweler's wife would not jump from offering $50 to offering $50,000. She would bargain her way up incrementally.)*

Vo•cab•u•lar•y Skills

Etymology The Greek and Latin word for the hardest imaginable substance was *adamas*. In later Latin, *diamas* was used to distinguish diamond, the hardest known substance in nature, from other meanings of *adamas*. These terms found their way into English. Today we use the noun *diamond* to mean the hard gem and the adjective *adamant* to mean something hard, inflexible, or immovable.

---

jewelers. The following morning when the miller had gone to work the jeweler's wife visited the miller's wife to complain about all the noise her children had made.

"We couldn't get any sleep last night," she moaned.

"I know, and I'm sorry, but you know how it is with a large family," the miller's wife explained. "Yesterday we found a beautiful piece of glass and I gave it to my youngest one to play with and when the others tried to take it from him he raised a storm."

The jeweler's wife took interest. "Won't you show me that piece of glass?" she asked.

"But of course. Here it is."

"Ah, yes, it's a pretty piece of glass. Where did you find it?"

"Our neighbor gave us a fish yesterday and when I was cleaning it I found the glass in its stomach."

"Why don't you let me take it home for just a moment. You see, I have one just like it and I want to compare them."

"Yes, why not? Take it," answered the miller's wife.

So the jeweler's wife ran off with the glass to show it to her husband. When the jeweler saw the glass he instantly knew it was one of the finest diamonds he had ever seen.

"It's a diamond!" he exclaimed.

"I thought so," his wife nodded eagerly. "What shall we do?"

"Go tell the neighbor we'll give her fifty dollars for it, but don't tell her it's a diamond!"

"No, no," his wife chuckled, "of course not." She ran to her neighbor's house. "Ah yes, we have one exactly like this," she

told the miller's wife. "My husband is willing to buy it for fifty dollars—only so we can have a pair, you understand."

"I can't sell it," the miller's wife answered. "You will have to wait until my husband returns from work."

That evening when the miller came home from work his wife told him about the offer the jeweler had made for the piece of glass.

"But why would they offer fifty dollars for a worthless piece of glass?" the miller wondered aloud. Before his wife could answer they were interrupted by the jeweler's wife.

"What do you say, neighbor, will you take fifty dollars for the glass?" she asked.

"No, that's not enough," the miller said cautiously. "Offer more."

"I'll give you fifty thousand!" the jeweler's wife blurted out.

"A little bit more," the miller replied.

"Impossible!" the jeweler's wife cried, "I can't offer any more without consulting my husband." She ran off to tell her husband how the bartering[4] was going, and he told her he was prepared to pay a hundred thousand dollars to acquire the diamond.

He handed her seventy-five thousand dollars and said, "Take this and tell him that tomorrow, as soon as I open my shop, he'll have the rest."

When the miller heard the offer and saw the money he couldn't believe his eyes. He imagined the jeweler's wife was jesting with him, but it was a true offer and

---

4. *Bartering* is trading goods for other goods without using money.

Vocabulary
jest (jest) *v.* to speak or act in a playful manner; joke

LITERATURE & HUMANITIES

To help students visualize a rural Central American village, show them the painting *San Antonio de Oriente* in the book *Introducing Art*, page 106. Ask students on which page the painting might serve as an illustration for this story.

Writing *Minilesson*

Writing a Different Ending Encourage students to imagine how this story might be different if, instead of giving the miller a piece of lead, the man gave the miller another object.

Activity Have students write a new ending to this story. Ask them to begin at the point where one of the wealthy men gives the miller an object and continue with how

that object changes the miller's life for better or for worse. Before starting to write, students should think about what they want their stories to teach about honesty and hard work. **L2**

Additional Resources

Writer's Choice, Lesson 1.1

Rudolfo A. Anaya ⁓

he received the hundred thousand dollars for the diamond. The miller had never seen so much money, but he still didn't quite trust the jeweler.

"I don't know about this money," he confided to his wife. "Maybe the jeweler plans to accuse us of robbing him and thus get it back."

"Oh no," his wife assured him, "the money is ours. We sold the diamond fair and square—we didn't rob anyone."

"I think I'll still go to work tomorrow," the miller said. "Who knows, something might happen and the money will disappear, then we would be without money and work. Then how would we live?"

So he went to work the next day, and all day he thought about how he could use the money. When he returned home that afternoon his wife asked him what he had decided to do with their new fortune.

"I think I will start my own mill," he answered, "like the one I operate for my master. Once I set up my business we'll see how our luck changes."

The next day he set about buying everything he needed to establish his mill and to build a new home. Soon he had everything going.

P Six months had passed, more or less, since he had seen the two men who had given him the four hundred dollars and the piece of lead. He was eager to see them again and to tell them how the piece of lead had changed his luck and made him wealthy.

Time passed and the miller prospered. His business grew and he even built a summer cottage where he could take his family on vacation. He had many employees who worked for him. One day while he was at his store he saw his two benefactors riding

by. He rushed out into the street to greet them and ask them to come in. He was overjoyed to see them, and he was happy to see that they admired his store.

"Tell us the truth," the man who had given him the four hundred dollars said. "You used that money to set up this business."

The miller swore he hadn't, and he told them how he had given the piece of lead to his neighbor and how the fisherman had in return given him a fish with a very large diamond in its stomach. And he told them **Q** how he had sold the diamond.

"And that's how I acquired this business and many other things I want to show you," he said. "But it's time to eat. Let's eat first then I'll show you everything I have now."

The men agreed, but one of them still doubted the miller's story. So they ate and then the miller had three horses saddled and they rode out to see his summer home. The cabin was on the other side of the river where the mountains were cool and beautiful. When they arrived the men admired the place very much. It was such a peaceful place that they rode all afternoon through the forest. During their ride they came upon a tall pine tree.

"What is that on top of the tree?" one of them asked.

"That's the nest of a hawk," the miller replied.

"I have never seen one; I would like to take a closer look at it!"

"Of course," the miller said, and he ordered a servant to climb the tree and bring down the nest so his friend could see how it was built. When the hawk's nest was on the ground they examined it carefully.

TWISTS AND TURNS 🦋 597

Vocabulary Skills

Etymology *Wif* is the oldest English word for "woman." In time it came to mean only a married woman, and *wifman* came to mean any woman, married or not. Over time the *f* in *wifman* blended into the word to become *wimman,* which in some dialects became *wummon.* Today both of these pronunciations still exist: in the singular word *woman* and the plural word *women.*

P **Critical Thinking**

SYNTHESIZING Have students express their ideas about what this story seems to be saying about the force of luck. The following model illustrates the process of synthesizing ideas.

Model: When the miller is given money, bad luck makes him lose it. When the miller is given a worthless piece of lead, good luck makes him rich. The story seems to be saying that luck is more important than money.

Q **Critical Thinking**

DRAWING CONCLUSIONS Ask students to identify which man doesn't believe the miller. Why doesn't he believe him? *(The man who believes in money doubts the miller's story because he will lose his bet if the story is true.)*

Folktales Students can use a search engine to find out more about folktales. They might use such keywords as *oral tradition, folklore,* and *legends.*

REAL-WORLD CONNECTION

The Force of Luck Although this story comes from an old storytelling tradition, luck is still a popular subject in many forms of media today.

Activity Invite students to find a modern comic strip, song, or TV show about luck. Ask students to compare the views of luck in their choice with those in this story. Have students discuss the similarities and differences between the two. **L2**

TWISTS AND TURNS 🦋 597

EVALUATE Why is the man who gave the miller the money not satisfied? *(He wants to believe that money, not luck, made the miller wealthy.)*

S **Literary Elements**

FOLKTALE What is the servant like and how is he typical of a character in a folktale? *(He is honest and loyal to his employer. Many folktale characters fit this description.)*

T **Critical Thinking**

ANALYZING ARGUMENTS Ask students whether they believe luck or money makes the miller rich. *(Bad luck makes him lose $200 twice, but good luck turns up the valuable diamond. However, the money he receives from the diamond is what actually makes him wealthy.)*

Thematic Focus

Twists and Turns Have students list some twists and turns that occur in this tale. Then encourage them to share any similar experiences they have heard about.

FINE ART
TRANSPARENCY 26

You may wish to use **Fine Art Transparency 26** to extend the discussion.

☑ **ASSESSMENT OPTIONS**

📁 **Quick Checks,** p. 50

Teaching Options

The Force of Luck

They noticed that there was a cloth bag at the bottom of the nest. When the miller saw the bag he immediately knew that it was the very same bag he had lost to the hawk which fought him for the piece of meat years ago.

"You won't believe me, friends, but this is the very same bag in which I put the first two hundred dollars you gave me," he told them.

"If it's the same bag," the man who had doubted him said, "then the money you said the hawk took should be there."

"No doubt about that," the miller said. "Let's see what we find."

The three of them examined the old, weatherbeaten bag. Although it was full of holes and crumbling, when they tore it apart they found the money <u>intact</u>. The two men remembered what the miller had told them and they agreed he was an honest and honorable man. Still, the man who had given him the money wasn't satisfied. He wondered what had really happened to the second two hundred he had given the miller.

They spent the rest of the day riding in the mountains and returned very late to the house.

As he unsaddled their horses, the servant in charge of grooming and feeding the horses suddenly realized that he had no grain for them. He ran to the barn and checked, but there was no grain for the hungry horses. So he ran to the neighbor's granary and there he was able to buy a large clay jar of bran. He carried the jar home and emptied the bran into a bucket to wet it before he fed it to the horses. When he got to the bottom of the jar he noticed a large lump which turned out to be a rag covered package. He examined it and felt something inside. He immediately went to give it to his master who had been eating dinner.

"Master," he said, "look at this package which I found in an earthenware jar of grain which I just bought from our neighbor!"

The three men carefully unraveled the cloth and found the other one hundred and ninety dollars which the miller had told them he had lost. That is how the miller proved to his friends that he was truly an honest man.

And they had to decide for themselves whether it had been luck or money which had made the miller a wealthy man!

❖

Eagle (Aquila), (detail). Diego Rivera (1886–1957). Overdoor mural, fresco. Secretaria de Education Publica, Mexico City.

Vocabulary
intact (in takt′) *adj.* undamaged and whole

Grammar and Language *Minilesson*

Identifying the Subject of a Sentence
Remind students that most statements begin with the subject.

- *The <u>dog</u> jumped into the lake.*

When a sentence begins with *Here is, Here are, There is,* or *There are,* the subject comes after the verb.

- *There was a <u>duck</u> in the lake.*

Questions begin with part of the predicate.

The subject is next, followed by the rest of the predicate.

- *Did the <u>duck</u> escape?*

Activity Ask students to refer to the models on the board and write five sentences in which the verb appears before the subject. Encourage students to write their sentences about "The Force of Luck."
L2

Additional Resources

🖥 *Grammar and Language Transparency 49*

📕 *Grammar and Language Workbook,* pp. 51–52

📕 *Grammar and Composition Handbook,* Lesson 1.4

📕 *Writer's Choice,* Lesson 8.4

Responding to Literature

PERSONAL RESPONSE

Look back at the **Focus Activity** on page 590. Did your ideas about hard work and luck change as you read the story? How?

Analyzing Literature

RECALL AND INTERPRET

1. What are the two wealthy men trying to prove? Is the miller a good test case for the men's theories? Explain your answers.
2. How does the miller lose his first and second gifts of two hundred dollars? Is his response to these events believable?
3. How does the miller's luck change? Why do the two benefactors assume he used their money to start his business?

EVALUATE AND CONNECT

4. Compare the responses of the miller and his wife to losing the first amount of money. Why does the storyteller include both responses?
5. What do you think you would do if you suddenly had an extra two hundred dollars to spend?
6. **Theme Connection** Reread the last line of the story. What is your opinion about the source of the twists and turns in the miller's fortunes?

LITERARY ELEMENTS

Folktales

Folktales, the world's most popular stories, have no known original authors. These stories have been passed down from person to person, generation to generation by word of mouth. Often folktales are told to reinforce the traditions and values of the culture that preserves them. The characters in folktales can be animals, people who have extraordinary powers, or ordinary people who have unusual or seemingly impossible experiences.

1. What values do you think the miller's story reinforces?
2. List two things that happen to the miller that would not occur in a more realistic story.

● See **Literary Terms Handbook,** p. R4.

Extending Your Response

Literature Groups
Plot With a group, create a chart that shows each twist and turn of the plot. Then color code each event according to whether you think it was caused by good luck, bad luck, plenty of money, or not enough money. Present your chart to the other groups.

Writing About Literature
Monologues Write two monologues for the miller. First, create a speech in which he describes his life at the beginning of the story. Then write a speech in which he explains how his life has changed since he opened his own mill.

TWISTS AND TURNS 🐌 599

LITERARY ELEMENTS

1. The miller's story reinforces the values of hard work, honesty, and helping your neighbor.
2. In a more realistic story, the miller would not be robbed by a hawk. He also would not find a diamond in the belly of a fish.

Additional Resources

Literary Elements Transparency 50

✓ ASSESSMENT OPTIONS

📁 *Quick Checks,* p. 50
📁 *Selection and Theme Assessment,* pp. 87–88
📁 *Performance Assessment,* p. 47
💾 *Testmaker*

Responding to the Selection

Personal Response

Answers should explain whether the students' ideas about the relationship between hard work and luck changed as they read.

Extending Your Response

1. They want to prove whether it is luck or money that makes a man prosper. The miller is a good test case because he is poor but also honest.
2. A hawk grabs the miller's first $200. His wife accidentally trades away the second. The miller doesn't get as upset as a real person might.
3. The miller's luck changes when he finds a diamond in a fish. The two men assume the miller used their money to start his business because he was too poor to have done so otherwise.
4. The miller is upset, but the wife believes they weren't meant to have money. This shows different attitudes toward bad fortune.
5. Students' answers may suggest conflicting values worth exploring further in a class discussion.
6. Students should support their opinions with examples from the story.

Extending Your Response

Literature Groups Before students meet, encourage them to review the story and list the main plot twists. Have the group discuss each twist further and come to an agreement on its cause. **COLLAB. LEARN.**

Writing About Literature

Students' monologues should
• be written from the miller's point of view, using facts from the story.
• show the differences in the miller's lifestyle at the beginning and end.

COMPARING selections

Objective
- To compare a radio drama and a folktale

COMPARE **GENRES**
Students' work should
- adapt the dialogue from "The Force of Luck" into a radio play.
- shorten "The Million-Pound Bank Note" for an oral storyteller.

COMPARE **CHARACTERS AND PLOTS**
1. Both plots are about wealthy men who settle a disagreement by giving money to a stranger. The men believe in Henry completely, whereas the miller's honesty is questioned.
2. Henry and the miller first buy food. This illustrates that both are very poor because food is a basic need.
3. Answers should take into account how each character has reacted to past events.

Additional Resources
📁 *Literature Groups Sourcebook*

COMPARE **IDEAS**
Students' plans should
- take into account the time and place in which each man lives.
- present causes that reflect each man's interests, lifestyle, and concerns.

Teaching Options

The Million-Pound Bank Note **and** The Force of Luck

COMPARE **GENRES**

"The Million-Pound Bank Note" is a dramatization of Twain's original story in the form of a radio play. "The Force of Luck" is a folktale. Both genres can be appreciated by either listening to the words or speaking them aloud. Working with a group, rewrite "The Force of Luck" as a radio play and shorten "The Million-Pound Bank Note" so that it can be told by a storyteller using just a few notes. Then present each new version to the class.

COMPARE **CHARACTERS AND PLOTS**

The plots of "The Million-Pound Bank Note" and "The Force of Luck" are similar in a number of ways. Both stories are about two men who decide to test a third person by giving him money.

1. What do the two men in "The Million-Pound Bank Note" and the two men in "The Force of Luck" have in common? How do the pairs differ?
2. What is the first thing Henry and the miller do with their gifts of money? What do their actions tell you about the state of their lives at the time?
3. What do you think would have happened to the miller if he had a million-pound bank note to cash? What do you think would have happened to Henry Adams if he had lost his bank note?

Indeed! (detail).

COMPARE **IDEAS**

Henry Adams and the miller both prove to be good, honest persons. Imagine that Henry and the miller became very rich. How do you think each might choose to give back to his community? What causes might they support? For each man, write a plan outlining his charity donations. Have each man's plan reflect the setting of the story as well as his previous experience.

 PORTFOLIO OPTIONS _____

Select and Reflect Have students reflect on the plans they wrote for the Compare Ideas activity by asking themselves these questions:
- Does my plan take into account each character's personality?
- Do I use events from the story to help me predict what the character might do with a large sum of money?

Students should clip their reflections to their plans and place them in their portfolios to revise and showcase at a later date. **L2**

Additional Resources
📁 *Writing Assessment and Portfolio Management,* pp. 17–19

Money Matters

Historically, paper money is a fairly recent development. At first, people traded or bartered for the things they wanted. Eventually, people needed a neutral item to trade, something they could use to buy anything, at any time. Shells were one of the early forms of money. They were used by both ancient Chinese people and Native Americans. In ancient Mexico, cacao beans served as money. In some parts of Africa, people exchanged salt. In the Caroline Islands of the western Pacific, people once traded giant stone rings.

Most of these early kinds of money wore out quickly or were awkward to carry. In what is now known as Turkey, people made the first coins. The idea spread to other places, and coins of gold or silver remained the most widely accepted form of money for centuries.

Eventually banks and governments issued "notes" and paper money. Paper money had the advantage of being easy to carry from place to place. However, whether money takes the form of shells, paper, or feathers, it all stands for the same thing—a symbol of value that you're willing to exchange for something else of value.

ACTIVITY

When Mark Twain's "The Million-Pound Bank Note" was published in 1893, a million British pounds was worth about $4,850,000 in U.S. currency.

1. Use a local bank, the travel section of a major newspaper, or the Internet to find out how much a million British pounds is worth in U.S. dollars today.

2. Using one of the same sources, find the exchange rate for at least two other countries listed at the right.

The United States, Canada, Australia, New Zealand, Zimbabwe, and more than a dozen other countries each have their own kind of dollar as a unit of exchange. Here are the units of exchange used by some other countries.

Brazil	cruzeiro
China	yuan
France	franc
Germany	mark
Great Britain	pound
Greece	drachma
Japan	yen
Mexico	peso
Russia	ruble
South Africa	rand

Objectives

- To read and analyze a story about an injured fighter pilot
- To recognize and understand the purpose of flashbacks
- To examine the way a writer creates suspense in a story

Skills

Reading/Thinking: Inferring; Synthesizing; Logical Reasoning; Identifying Author's Purpose
Writing: Descriptive Scene; Epilogue
Vocabulary: Using Context Clues for Multiple-Meaning Words
Grammar/Language: Troublesome Words: *Lie;* Complex Sentences
Listening/Speaking: Reading Aloud; Interviewing
Life Skills: Interviewing
Collaboration: Creating a Code; Creating a Map; Literature Groups

Motivating
→OPTIONS

Literature Launchers:
"The Life and Times of Roald Dahl"

Videodisc
Side B, Segment 18

Also available in VHS.

Selection Focus Transparency 51: Have students view the transparency and then discuss the questions provided.

Focus Activity: As an extension of the Focus Activity, have students tell how they feel when they are disoriented or uncertain about the time or day—for example, when they wake up after falling asleep at an unusual time.

Before You Read
Beware of the Dog

MEET ROALD DAHL

British author Roald Dahl (rōō äl′ dol′) is best known for his children's fiction. Dahl's stories and books—such as *James and the Giant Peach* and *Matilda*—are modern classics, loved by children throughout the world. About writing for children, Dahl said, "Children are a great discipline because they are highly critical. And they lose interest so quickly. You have to keep things ticking along. And if you think a child is getting bored, you must think up something that jolts it back. Something that tickles. You have to know what children like."

Roald Dahl was born in South Wales in 1916 and died in 1990.

FOCUS ACTIVITY

How would you feel if you woke up in an unfamiliar place?

Think/Pair/Share
Take a moment to jot down your thoughts and feelings about the question. Then share your ideas with a partner.

Setting a Purpose
The title of this story refers to something the main character discovers. Read the story to find out what it means.

BACKGROUND

The Time and Place   The story takes place in Europe during World War II, in the early 1940s. The British were at war with Germany, and German troops occupied France.

Did You Know?   The following story is fiction, but Roald Dahl's wartime experiences gave him plenty of background information for his story's plot. In 1939, at the beginning of World War II, Dahl joined the British Royal Air Force and was trained as a fighter pilot. His plane was brought down by enemy fire over Egypt, and Dahl crawled from the wreckage as the plane exploded. It took him six months to recuperate from his injuries.

A British fighter pilot of the early 1940s.

VOCABULARY PREVIEW

undulating (un′ jə lāt′ ing) *adj.* moving in waves; rippling; p. 603
giddy (gid′ dē) *adj.* dizzy or lightheaded; p. 604
precise (pri sīs′) *adj.* strictly accurate or clearly defined; exact; p. 604
intellectual (int′ əl ek′ chōō əl) *adj.* appealing to or involving mental ability; p. 608
intense (in tens′) *adj.* of a very high degree; very strong; p. 610

RESOURCE MANAGER

Lesson Planning Resource
The *Theme Six Planning Guide* (pp. 44–51) provides additional lesson notes and reduced versions of all print resources.

 Other Print Resources
- Active Reading Guide, p. 51
- Vocabulary Practice, p. 36
- Reading Workbook, pp. 91–92
- Grammar and Language Workbook, pp. 155–156, 223–224

- Grammar and Composition Handbook, Lessons 8.2, 3.11, 3.12
- Quick Checks, p. 51
- Selection and Theme Assessment, pp. 89–90
- Performance Assessment, p. 48
- Spanish Summaries, p. 51
- Spanish Translations
- Inclusion Strategies
- English Language Learners Sourcebook

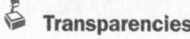 **Transparencies**
- Selection Focus 51
- Fine Art 13
- Literary Elements 51
- Grammar and Language 50

Technology
 Literature Launchers
 Audio Library
 Spanish Audio Library
 Glencoe Literature Web Site
 Testmaker

BEWARE OF THE DOG

Roald Dahl ~

Down below there was only a vast white undulating sea of cloud. Above there was the sun, and the sun was white like the clouds, because it is never yellow when one looks at it from high in the air.

He was still flying the Spitfire. His right hand was on the stick and he was working the rudder-bar[1] with his left leg alone. It was quite easy. The machine was flying well. He knew what he was doing.

Everything is fine, he thought. I'm doing all right. I'm doing nicely. I know my way home. I'll be there in half an hour. When I land I shall taxi in and switch off my engine and I shall say, help me to get out, will you. I shall make my voice sound ordinary and natural and none of them will take any notice. Then I shall say, someone help me to get out. I can't do it alone because I've lost one of my legs. They'll all laugh and think that I'm joking and I shall say, all right, come and have a look. Then Yorky will climb up onto the wing and look inside. He'll probably be sick because of all the blood and the mess. I shall laugh and say, for God's sake, help me get out.

---

1. The *Spitfire* was a British fighter plane used during World War II. Its *rudder-bar* controlled the movement of the tail rudder, which turned the plane left or right.

Vocabulary
undulating (un′ jə lāt′ ing) *adj.* moving in waves; rippling

SUMMARY

A British fighter pilot is shot down somewhere near the English Channel during World War II. He is severely injured, and as he regains consciousness he realizes he is in a hospital. The nurse tells him that he is in England. But is he? Through the window he sees a sign that reads, "Beware of the Dog" in French. He then realizes that he is a prisoner of war and his captors have been trying to get information from him by pretending to be British.

📁 *Spanish Summaries,* p. 51

A Active Reading

PREDICT Ask students to look at the title of this story and the image of the Spitfire plane. Then let volunteers read the text on this page aloud. Encourage students to describe the problem and predict whether events will unfold as the pilot imagines.

Additional Resources
📁 *Active Reading Guide,* p. 51
🎧 *Audio Library*
🎧 *Spanish Audio Library*

Teaching Options

CONNECTING TO OTHER SELECTIONS

The chart at the right shows three ways to connect "Beware of the Dog" to other selections in this book.

For specific teaching strategies, see the *Theme Six Planning Guide,* pages 47–48.

Connection	Title
Life Skills: Lifelong Learning	→ "Dreams," p. 261
Thematic: Courage	→ "I'll Walk the Tightrope," p. 231
Literary: Suspense	→ "Home," p. 361

Teaching Options

He glanced down again at his right leg. There was not much of it left. The cannon-shell had taken him on the thigh, just above the knee, and now there was nothing but a great mess and a lot of blood. But there was no pain.

He really felt fine, and because he still felt fine, he felt excited and unafraid.

Then he saw the sun shining on the engine cowling[2] of his machine. He saw the sun shining on the rivets in the metal, and he remembered the airplane and he remembered where he was. He realized that he was no longer feeling good; that he was sick and giddy. His head kept falling forward onto his chest because his neck seemed no longer to have any strength. But he knew that he was flying the Spitfire. He could feel the handle of the stick between the fingers of his right hand.

I'm going to pass out, he thought. Any moment now I'm going to pass out.

He looked at his altimeter. Twenty-one thousand. To test himself he tried to read the hundreds as well as the thousands. Twenty-one thousand and what? As he looked the dial became blurred and he could not even see the needle. He knew then that he must bail out; that there was not a second to lose, otherwise he would become unconscious. Quickly, frantically, he tried to slide back the hood with his left hand, but he had not the strength. For a second he took his right hand off the stick and with both hands he managed to push the hood back. The rush of cold air

on his face seemed to help. He had a moment of great clearness. His actions became orderly and precise. That is what happens with a good pilot. He took some quick deep breaths from his oxygen mask, and as he did so, he looked out over the side of the cockpit. Down below there was only a vast white sea of cloud and he realized that he did not know where he was.

It'll be the Channel, he thought. I'm sure to fall in the drink.[3]

He throttled back,[4] pulled off his helmet, undid his straps, and pushed the stick hard over to the left. The Spitfire dripped its port wing and turned smoothly over onto its back. The pilot fell out.

As he fell, he opened his eyes, because he knew that he must not pass out before he had pulled the cord. On one side he saw the sun; on the other he saw the whiteness of the clouds, and as he fell, as he somersaulted in the air, the white clouds chased the sun and the sun chased the clouds. They chased each other in a small circle; they ran faster and faster and there was the sun and the clouds and the clouds and the sun and the clouds came nearer until suddenly there was no longer any sun but only a great whiteness. The whole world was white and there was nothing in it. It was so white that sometimes it looked black, and after a time it was either white or black, but mostly it was white. He watched it as it turned from white

---

2. A *cowling* is a streamlined covering for the engine or another section of an airplane.

3. The *Channel* is the English Channel, a narrow part of the ocean, which separates the British Isles from France. To *fall in the drink* means to fall into the water.
4. When he *throttled back*, he "took his foot off the gas," so that the plane would slow down. The *throttle* is a valve that controls the supply of fuel to an engine.

Vocabulary
giddy (gid′ dē) *adj.* dizzy or lightheaded
precise (pri sīs′) *adj.* strictly accurate or clearly defined; exact

to black, then back to white again, and the white stayed for a long time, but the black lasted only for a few seconds. He got into the habit of going to sleep during the white periods, of waking up just in time to see the world when it was black. The black was very quick. Sometimes it was only a flash, a flash of black lightning. The white was slow and in the slowness if it, he always dozed off.

One day, when it was white, he put out a hand and he touched something. He took it between his fingers and crumpled it. For a time he lay there, idly letting the tips of his fingers play with the thing which they had touched. Then slowly he opened his eyes, looked down at his hand and saw that he was holding something which was white. It was the edge of a sheet. He knew it was a sheet because he could see the texture of the material and the stitchings on the hem. He screwed up his eyes and opened them again quickly.

This time he saw the room. He saw the bed in which he was lying, he saw the gray walls and the door and the green curtains over the window. There were some roses on the table by his bed.

Then he saw the basin on the table near the roses. It was a white enamel basin and beside it there was a small medicine glass.

This is a hospital, he thought. I am in a hospital. But he could remember nothing. He lay back on his pillow, looking at the ceiling and wondering what had happened. He was gazing at the smooth grayness of the ceiling which was so clean and gray, and then suddenly he saw a fly walking upon it. The sight of this fly, the suddenness of seeing this small black speck on a sea of gray, brushed the surface of his brain, and quickly, in that second, he remembered everything. He remembered the Spitfire,

and he remembered the altimeter showing twenty-one thousand feet. He remembered the pushing back of the hood with both hands and he remembered the bailing out. He remembered his leg.

It seemed all right now. He looked down at the end of the bed, but he could not tell. He put one hand underneath the bedclothes and felt for his knees. He found one of them, but when he felt for the other, his hand touched something which was soft and covered in bandages.

Just then the door opened and a nurse came in.

"Hello," she said. "So you've waked up at last."

She was not good-looking, but she was large and clean. She was between thirty and forty and she had fair hair. More than that he did not notice.

"Where am I?"

"You're a lucky fellow. You landed in a wood near the beach. You're in Brighton.[5] They brought you in two days ago, and now you're all fixed up. You look fine."

"I've lost a leg," he said.

"That's nothing. We'll get you another one. Now you must go to sleep. The doctor will be coming to see you in about an hour." She picked up the basin and the medicine glass and went out.

But he did not sleep. He wanted to keep his eyes open because he was frightened that if he shut them again everything would go away. He lay looking at the ceiling. The fly was still there. It was very energetic. It would run forward very fast for a few inches, then it would stop. Then it would run forward again, stop, run forward, stop, and every now and then it

---

5. *Brighton* is a seaside city in southeastern England.

F Critical Thinking

SYNTHESIZING Have students explain what seems to be going on here. *(The pilot is at first in a dream-like state; then slowly he awakens and realizes that he is holding onto a sheet.)*

G Literary Elements

SETTING Ask students to explain where the pilot is and describe the clues in the setting. *(The pilot is in a hospital somewhere. He's in a bed with a medicine glass nearby. He also has roses near his bedside.)*

H Literary Elements

FLASHBACK Have students describe the pilot's state of mind and how the flashback helps him remember what happened. *(The flashback helps the pilot remember bailing out of the plane and how he lost a leg. It helps to orient him.)*

I Literary Elements

CHARACTER Have students describe the nurse's character. *(The nurse seems cheerful and optimistic, but she doesn't give the pilot much information about his physical condition or how he got to the hospital.)*

Reading *Minilesson*

Identifying Author's Purpose Authors develop and organize story events to achieve a certain effect or to move the story forward in a particular direction.

Activity Have students create a chart. Ask them to list the unusual story events as they occur in the left column. The right column should have students' ideas about why the author included each event.

After students finish reading the entire story, have them revise their earlier responses. **L2**

Story Event	Author's Purpose
Pilot bails out on cloudy day.	Clouds prevent pilot and readers from telling where the pilot is.

Additional Resources
📁 *Reading Workbook,* pp. 91–92

J Active Reading

QUESTION Have students explain why the doctor tells the pilot that his buddies are not allowed to visit him. *(The doctor wants to provide a logical reason for the lack of visitors.)*

K Literary Elements

PLOT: *Rising Action* Ask students what the information about the Junkers 88 German bomber adds to the sequence of events. *(This description introduces a conflict and contributes to the rising action of the story.)*

L Active Reading

PREDICT What do your students think the answer is to the pilot's question: Why aren't there sirens and guns? *(Perhaps the pilot is still disoriented. Maybe Germany has captured Brighton.)*

Historical Note

The Junkers 88 (pronounced YOONG-kers 88) was a kind of bomber important to the German air force, or *Luftwaffe*, in World War II (1939–1945). Germany defeated France, Belgium, Holland, Norway, and Denmark, at least in part, because of its strong air support.

---

would take off and buzz around viciously in small circles. It always landed back in the same place on the ceiling and started running and stopping all over again. He watched it for so long that after a while it was no longer a fly, but only a black speck upon a sea of gray, and he was still watching it when the nurse opened the door, and stood aside while the doctor came in. He was an Army doctor, a major, and he had some last war ribbons on his chest. He was bald and small, but he had a cheerful face and kind eyes.

"Well, well," he said. "So you've decided to wake up at last. How are you feeling?"

"I feel all right."

"That's the stuff. You'll be up and about in no time."

The doctor took his wrist to feel his pulse.

"By the way," he said, "some of the lads from your squadron[6] were ringing up and asking about you. They wanted to come along and see you, but I said that they'd better wait a day or two. Told them you were all right and that they could come and see you a little later on. Just lie quiet and take it easy for a bit. Got something to read?" He glanced at the table with the roses. "No. Well, nurse will look after you. She'll get you anything you want." With that he waved his hand and went out, followed by the large clean nurse.

When they had gone, he lay back and looked at the ceiling again. The fly was still there and as he lay watching it, he heard the noise of an airplane in the distance. He lay listening to the sound of its engines. It was a long way away. I wonder what it is,

---

6. An air force *squadron* is a group of planes that fly into combat together.

---

he thought. Let me see if I can place it. Suddenly he jerked his head sharply to one side. Anyone who has been bombed can tell the noise of a Junkers 88. They can tell most other German bombers for that matter, but especially a Junkers 88. The engines seem to sing a duet. There is a deep vibrating bass voice and with it there is a high pitched tenor. It is the singing of the tenor which makes the sound of a JU-88 something which one cannot mistake.

He lay listening to the noise and he felt quite certain about what it was. But where were the sirens and where were the guns? That German pilot certainly had a nerve coming near Brighton alone in daylight.

The aircraft was always far away and soon the noise faded away into the distance. Later on there was another. This one, too, was far away, but there was the same deep undulating bass and the high singing tenor and there was no mistaking it. He had heard that noise every day during the Battle.[7]

He was puzzled. There was a bell on the table by the bed. He reached out his hand and rang it. He heard the noise of footsteps down the corridor. The nurse came in.

"Nurse, what were those airplanes?"

"I'm sure I don't know. I didn't hear them. Probably fighters or bombers. I expect they were returning from France. Why, what's the matter?"

"They were JU-88's. I'm sure they were JU-88's. I know the sound of the engines. There were two of them. What were they doing over here?"

The nurse came up to the side of his bed and began to straighten out the sheets and tuck them in under the mattress.

---

7. The *Battle* refers to the Battle of Britain, a series of air battles over Great Britain from June 1940 to April 1941.

Teaching Options

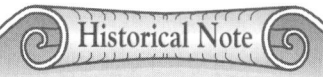

LITERATURE & HUMANITIES

To provide background about the music of the times, play *Boogie Woogie Bugle Boy* from *American Music: Cultural Traditions*, *Volume 2, Track 12*, which features some songs popular during World War II.

INCLUSION STRATEGIES

Less-Proficient Readers This story provides students with an opportunity to study words systematically across a content area.

Activity Have students work in pairs to sketch a Spitfire (using the image on the first page as a model). Then have them reread to find words with which to label their drawings. Finally, have them add any other labels for airplanes that they already know. **L1**

Additional Resources
  Inclusion Strategies

Bundles of Lictors Are Flying over England: Italian and German Bomber Wing in Operation, 1940. Hans Liska. Gouache. Berlin.

Viewing the painting: Imagine yourself as a pilot who had to fight against squadrons of enemy planes like these day after day. How would you feel?

Once toward evening he heard the noise of another aircraft. It was far away, but even so he knew that it was a single-engined machine. It was going fast; he could tell that. He could not place it. It wasn't a Spit, and it wasn't a Hurricane. It did not sound like an American engine either. They make more noise. He did not know what it was, and it worried him greatly. Perhaps I am very ill, he thought. Perhaps I am imagining things. Perhaps I am a little delirious.[9] I simply do not know what to think.

That evening the nurse came in with a basin of hot water and began to wash him.

"Well," she said, "I hope you don't still think that we're being bombed."

She had taken off his pajama top and was soaping his right arm with a flannel. He did not answer.

She rinsed the flannel in the water, rubbed more soap on it, and began to wash his chest.

"You're looking fine this evening," she said. "They operated on you as soon as you came in. They did a marvelous job. You'll be all right. I've got a brother in the R.A.F.,"[10] she added. "Flying bombers."

"Gracious me, what things you imagine. You mustn't worry about a thing like that. Would you like me to get you something to read?"

"No, thank you."

She patted his pillow and brushed back the hair from his forehead with her hand.

"They never come over in daylight any longer. You know that. They were probably Lancasters or Flying Fortresses."[8]

---

8. *Lancasters* were British bomber planes. American B-17 bombers were called *Flying Fortresses* because of their heavy armor and many guns.

9. The *Hurricane* was another type of British fighter plane. The pilot thinks he may be in a temporary state of confusion (*delirious*), which can result from a high fever.

10. *R.A.F.* stands for Royal Air Force.

Author's Craft

FLASHBACK Invite students to explain how the author uses this flashback to introduce more contradictions in the pilot's mind. *(The flashback allows the pilot to remember his childhood and to recall that the water in Brighton was extremely soft, not hard, as the nurse complains that this water is.)*

Critical Thinking

INFERRING What can readers begin to infer from some of the contradictions in the pilot's mind when he stops in mid-sentence here? *(Help students understand that things are not what they seem, and that the pilot is beginning to realize this.)*

Historical Note

To draw out British fighter planes, Germany first staged daylight raids against England. Later, after the Royal Air Force inflicted major losses, the Germans switched to nighttime raids.

Literary Elements

PLOT: Suspense Ask students what clues in this paragraph increase the level of suspense in the story. *(The clues about the Junkers 88s and the hard water contradict everything the pilot knows from personal experience.)*

He said, "I went to school in Brighton."

She looked up quickly. "Well, that's fine," she said. "I expect you'll know some people in the town."

"Yes," he said, "I know quite a few."

She had finished washing his chest and arms. Now she turned back the bedclothes so that his left leg was uncovered. She did it in such a way that his bandaged stump remained under the sheets. She began to wash his left leg and the rest of his body. This was the first time he had had a bed-bath and he was embarrassed. She laid a towel under his leg and began washing his foot with the flannel. She said, "This wretched soap won't lather at all. It's the water. It's as hard as nails."[11]

He said, "None of the soap is very good now and, of course, with hard water it's hopeless." As he said it he remembered something. He remembered the baths which he used to take at school in Brighton, in the long stone-floored bathroom which had four baths in a room. He remembered how the water was so soft that you had to take a shower afterwards to get all the soap off your body, and he remembered how the foam used to float on the surface of the water, so that you could not see your legs underneath. He remembered that sometimes they were given calcium tablets because the school doctor used to say that soft water was bad for the teeth.

"In Brighton," he said, "the water isn't . . ."

---

11. *Hard as nails* refers to hard water, which contains minerals that prevent soap from dissolving easily.

He did not finish the sentence. Something had occurred to him; something so fantastic and absurd that for a moment he felt like telling the nurse about it and having a good laugh.

She looked up. "The water isn't what?" she said.

"Nothing," he answered. "I was dreaming."

She rinsed the flannel in the basin, wiped the soap off his leg and dried him with a towel.

"It's nice to be washed," he said. "I feel better." He was feeling his face with his hand. "I need a shave."

"We'll do that tomorrow," she said. "Perhaps you can do it yourself then."

That night he could not sleep. He lay awake thinking of the Junkers 88's and of the hardness of the water. He could think of nothing else. They *were* JU-88's, he said to himself. I know they were. And yet it is not possible, because they would not be flying around so low over here in broad daylight. I know that it is true and yet I know that it is impossible. Perhaps I am ill. Perhaps I am behaving like a fool and do not know what I am doing or saying. Perhaps I am delirious. For a long time he lay awake thinking these things, and once he sat up in bed and said aloud, "I will prove that I am not crazy. I will make a little speech about something complicated and <u>intellectual</u>. I will talk about what to do with Germany after the war." But before he had time to begin, he was asleep.

He woke just as the first light of day was showing through the slit in the curtains over the window. The room was still

---

Vocabulary
intellectual (int′ əl ek′ chōō əl) *adj.* appealing to or involving mental ability

Teaching Options

Writing *Minilesson*

Writing a Descriptive Scene This story begins after the pilot has been wounded in battle. Encourage the class to discuss what might have happened to the pilot before the story begins. Let students use what they know about World War II, airplanes, and the story so far to present some possible scenarios.

Activity Have interested students create air battle scenes that describe what happened to the pilot before he got shot. Encourage students to use this story as a writing model for creating descriptive and realistic paragraphs. Have students write their scenes, as Dahl does, from the pilot's point of view. **L2**

Additional Resources

📘 *Writer's Choice,* Lesson 3.3

German Junker 88

dark, but he could tell that it was already beginning to get light outside. He lay looking at the gray light which was showing through the slit in the curtain and as he lay there he remembered the day before. He remembered the Junkers 88's and the hardness of the water; he remembered the large pleasant nurse and the kind doctor, and now a small grain of doubt took root in his mind and it began to grow.

He looked around the room. The nurse had taken the roses out the night before. There was nothing except the table. The room was bare. It was no longer warm or friendly. It was not even comfortable. It was cold and empty and very quiet.

Slowly the grain of doubt grew, and with it came fear, a light, dancing fear that warned but did not frighten; the kind of fear that one gets not because one is afraid, but because one feels that there is something wrong. Quickly the doubt and the fear grew so that he became restless and angry, and when he touched his forehead with his hand, he found that it was damp with sweat. He knew then that he must do something; that he must find some way of proving to himself that he was either right or wrong, and he looked up and saw again the window and the green curtains. From where he lay, that window was right in front of him, but it was fully ten yards away. Somehow he must reach it and look out. The idea became an obsession with him and soon he could think

of nothing except the window. But what about his leg? He put his hand underneath the bedclothes and felt the thick bandaged stump which was all that was left on the right hand side. It seemed all right. It didn't hurt. But it would not be easy.

He sat up. Then he pushed the bedclothes aside and put his left leg on the floor. Slowly, carefully, he swung his body over until he had both hands on the floor as well; then he was out of bed, kneeling on the carpet. He looked at the stump. It was very short and thick, covered with bandages. It was beginning to hurt and he could feel it throbbing. He wanted to collapse, lie down on the carpet and do nothing but he knew that he must go on.

With two arms and one leg, he crawled over toward the window. He would reach forward as far as he could with his arms, then he would give a little jump and slide his left leg along after them. Each time he did it, it jarred his wound so that he gave a soft grunt of pain, but he continued to crawl across the floor on two hands and one knee. When he got to the window he reached up, and one at a time he placed both hands on the sill. Slowly he raised himself up until he was standing on his left leg. Then quickly he pushed aside the curtains and looked out.

He saw a small house with a gray tiled roof standing alone beside a narrow lane, and immediately behind it there was a plowed field. In front of the house there was

R Critical Thinking

LOGICAL REASONING The hospital room has not changed much. Have students explain why the pilot is no longer at ease there. *(The pilot's attitude has changed. The room no longer feels warm and friendly to him because he is beginning to doubt the doctor and nurse.)*

S Active Reading

RESPOND Encourage students to discuss the pilot's view of his situation. *(He has become worried that something is wrong, but he doesn't know what it is.)* Have students explain what they would do if they were the pilot. *(Students may say that they would ask the doctor or nurse questions about Brighton that anyone living there would know, ask why there are no other patients in the hospital, insist on personally contacting family, and insist that buddies be allowed to visit.)*

T Active Reading

PREDICT Have students predict what the pilot will see when he looks out the window. *(The pilot may see that the town is occupied by German soldiers, that Brighton has been destroyed, or that he is not in Brighton.)*

MEETING INDIVIDUAL NEEDS

MULTIPLE LEARNING STYLES

Logical/Mathematical Students with strong logical/mathematical abilities may respond to this story in an analytical and conceptual way. They can use coded messages to help them understand the frustration and danger inherent in the pilot's situation.

Activity Encourage students to work in small groups to analyze how the pilot might get a coded message to people in the outside world. Students can create codes or ciphers and exchange coded messages with partners. Students can explain to the class how they coded their messages and the problems they encountered in the process. **L2 COLLAB. LEARN.**

TWISTS AND TURNS ❧ 609

Critical Thinking

LOGICAL REASONING Encourage students to explain the importance of the *garde au chien* sign. *(The sign helps the pilot resolve his confusion: He is in France; that's why the water is hard and he hears Junkers 88s.)*

Historical Note

When this story takes place, Germany controlled France and the Atlantic Coast. If the pilot is in France, he is in territory controlled by England's enemy, Germany.

Active Reading

QUESTION Discuss with students why the nurse tells the pilot he was in Brighton when he is in France. *(The nurse wants him to feel at home and let his guard down.)*

Active Reading

CONNECT Have students describe situations in which they get nervous. Then have them explain why the nurse might be nervous. *(The nurse may be nervous because she is hiding something from the pilot.)*

Teaching Options

---

an untidy garden, and there was a green hedge separating the garden from the lane. He was looking at the hedge when he saw the sign. It was just a piece of board nailed to the top of a short pole, and because the hedge had not been trimmed for a long time, the branches had grown out around the sign so that it seemed almost as though it had been placed in the middle of the hedge. There was something written on the board with white paint. He pressed his head against the glass of the window, trying to read what it said. The first letter was a G, he could see that. The second was an A, and the third was an R. One after another he managed to see what the letters were. There were three words, and slowly he spelled the letters out aloud to himself as he managed to read them. G–A–R–D–E A–U C–H–I–E–N. *Garde au chien.* That is what it said.

Did You Know?
Along a hedge near a house in France, the words *garde au chien* (gard ō shyen) would warn visitors to "beware of the dog."

He stood there balancing on one leg and holding tightly to the edges of the window sill with his hands, staring at the sign and at the white-washed lettering of the words. For a moment he could think of nothing at all. He stood there looking at the sign, repeating the words over and over to himself. Slowly he began to realize the full meaning of the thing. He looked up at the cottage and at the plowed field. He looked at the small orchard on the left of the cottage and he looked at the green countryside beyond. "So this is France," he said. "I am in France."

Now the throbbing in his right thigh was very great. It felt as though someone was pounding the end of his stump with a hammer and suddenly the pain became so intense that it affected his head. For a moment he thought he was going to fall. Quickly he knelt down again, crawled back to the bed and hoisted himself in. He pulled the bedclothes over himself and lay back on the pillow, exhausted. He could still think of nothing at all except the small sign by the hedge and the plowed field and the orchard. It was the words on the sign that he could not forget.

It was some time before the nurse came in. She came carrying a basin of hot water and she said, "Good morning, how are you today?"

He said, "Good morning, nurse."

The pain was still great under the bandages, but he did not wish to tell this woman anything. He looked at her as she busied herself with getting the washing things ready. He looked at her more carefully now. Her hair was very fair. She was tall and big-boned and her face seemed pleasant. But there was something a little uneasy about her eyes. They were never still. They never looked at anything for more than a moment and they moved too quickly from one place to another in the room. There was something about her movements also. They were too sharp and nervous to go well with the casual manner in which she spoke.

Vocabulary
intense (in tens´) *adj.* of a very high degree; very strong

INCLUSION STRATEGIES
MEETING INDIVIDUAL NEEDS

Learning Disabled Some students may not fully comprehend why being in France is dangerous for this pilot. They may better understand this concept by looking at a map of Europe.

Activity On the map, point out Brighton, England, France, and Germany. Explain that in World War II, England and France both fought against Germany. Then Germany overran France and took control of it. Ask students to discuss why it is dangerous for the pilot to be in France. *(If the pilot is in France, he is in the hands of the enemy.)* **L2**

Additional Resources
📁 *Inclusion Strategies*

Roald Dahl ﹌

She set down the basin, took off his pajama top and began to wash him.

"Did you sleep well?"

"Yes."

"Good," she said. She was washing his arms and his chest.

"I believe there's someone coming down to see you from the Air Ministry after breakfast," she went on. "They want a report or something. I expect you know all about it. How you got shot down and all that. I won't let him stay long, so don't worry."

He did not answer. She finished washing him and gave him a toothbrush and some toothpowder. He brushed his teeth, rinsed his mouth and spat the water out into the basin.

Later she brought him his breakfast on a tray, but he did not want to eat. He was still feeling weak and sick and he wished only to lie still and think about what had happened. And there was a sentence running through his head. It was a sentence which Johnny, the Intelligence Officer of his squadron, always repeated to the pilots every day before they went out. He could see Johnny now, leaning against the wall of the dispersal hut[12] with his pipe in his hand, saying,

---

12. An *Intelligence Officer* gathers and studies information about the enemy. He informs the R.A.F. pilots of enemy activities that would affect their missions and trains them to safeguard information from the enemy. The pilots get their flight instructions in the *dispersal hut.*

Trees Near Douarnenez. Jules Eugene Pages (1867–1946). Oil on canvas, 21¼ x 25¾ in. Private collection.

Viewing the painting: This could be the scene the British pilot saw from his window. Why do you suppose he was sent to a place like this?

X **Active Reading**

QUESTION Have students recall whether the pilot has really slept well that night. Ask students why the pilot might lie to the nurse about how he slept. *(The pilot has not slept well and does not share the information with the nurse because he no longer trusts her.)*

Y **Active Reading**

EVALUATE Have students explain why someone from the British Air Ministry would want to talk to the pilot about getting shot down. Have students explain whether this information would also be valuable to the enemy. *(All pilots are debriefed after a mission. The intelligence is also very important to the enemy because it would provide information about the other side's strength, tactics, and methods of operation.)*

VIEWING THE PAINTING

Douamenez, the town this scene is near, is along the Atlantic coast in Brittany, at the far western part of France.

Viewing Response *Students might suggest that the location is quiet, not heavily populated, and presumably away from any military action that might arouse suspicion in the British airman.*

Listening and Speaking *Minilesson*

Reading Aloud Have students develop some guidelines for reading a scene aloud. Record them on the board. *(Read some parts slower or faster, louder or softer. Don't rush. Read with feeling.)*

Activity Assign pairs of students one of the scenes to read aloud to the rest of the class. Have students think about how the pilot would feel in each situation and then read aloud to show those emotions. The class should listen for the way the pilot's emotions and attitudes change as the scenes progress. **L2** **COLLAB. LEARN.**

Belgian painter René Magritte (1898–1967) was a well-known Surrealist who delighted in symbols and illogical images. *La Grande Famille* includes three of his favorite motifs: sky, clouds, and sea.

Viewing Response *Students may say the dove is a symbol of peace and might suggest that its flight could symbolize the British airman's desire for freedom.*

Literary Elements

FLASHBACK Encourage your students to explain how remembering the Intelligence Officer prepares the pilot for the resolution of the story. *(The pilot realizes he has been captured by the enemy; the flashback reminds him to give only his name, rank, and number.)*

Thematic Focus

Twists and Turns Review with students the different twists and turns this story takes and how it relates to the theme.

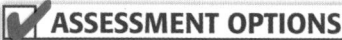

FINE ART
TRANSPARENCY 13

You may wish to use *Fine Art Transparency 13* to enrich the discussion.

✓ ASSESSMENT OPTIONS

📁 **Quick Checks**, p. 51

Teaching Options

La Grande Famille, 1947. René Magritte. Oil on canvas, 100 x 81 cm. Copyright ARS, New York. Private collection.

Viewing the painting: What does this painting say to you? How would you connect it with the story?

Z "And if they get you, don't forget, just your name, rank, and number. Nothing else. For God's sake, say nothing else."

"There you are," she said as she put the tray on his lap. "I've got you an egg. Can you manage all right?"

"Yes."

She stood beside the bed. "Are you feeling all right?"

"Yes."

"Good. If you want another egg I might be able to get you one."

"This is all right."

"Well, just ring the bell if you want any more." And she went out.

He had just finished eating, when the nurse came in again.

She said, "Wing Commander Roberts is here. I've told him that he can only stay for a few minutes."

She beckoned with her hand and the Wing Commander came in.

"Sorry to bother you like this," he said.

He was an ordinary R.A.F. officer, dressed in a uniform which was a little shabby. He wore wings and a D.F.C.[13] He was fairly tall and thin with plenty of black hair. His teeth, which were irregular and widely spaced, stuck out a little even when he closed his mouth. As he spoke he took a printed form and pencil from his pocket and he pulled up a chair and sat down.

"How are you feeling?"

There was no answer.

"Tough luck about your leg. I know how you feel. I hear you put up a fine show before they got you."

The man in the bed was lying quite still, watching the man in the chair.

The man in the chair said, "Well, let's get this stuff over. I'm afraid you'll have to answer a few questions so that I can fill in this combat report. Let me see now, first of all, what was your squadron?"

The man in the bed did not move. He looked straight at the Wing Commander and he said, "My name is Peter Williamson. My rank is Squadron Leader, and my number is nine seven two four five seven."

---

13. An R.A.F. pilot would wear a small badge shaped like flying wings. The *D.F.C.*, or *Distinguished Flying Cross*, was a medal awarded for heroism.

Grammar and Language *Minilesson*

Troublesome Words: Lie Write these sentences on the board to illustrate how to use *lie* in the past, present, and future tenses:
1. Yesterday the pilot lay listening to the Junkers 88s.
2. Today he lies in bed.
3. Tomorrow he will still lie in bed.

Have volunteers explain why Dahl sometimes used *lie* and other times *lay* to mean "reclining" in bed. (*Lay is the past tense. Lie is the present tense.*)

Activity Have students write five sentences using lie in the present, past and future tenses. Have them include the words *yesterday, today,* or *tomorrow* in each sentence to show that they understand when the action occurs. **L2**

Additional Resources

📠 *Grammar and Language Transparency 50*

📕 *Grammar and Language Workbook,* pp. 223–224

📕 *Grammar and Composition Handbook,* Lessons 3.11, 3.12

📕 *Writer's Choice,* Lesson 17.2

Responding to Literature

PERSONAL RESPONSE

What was your reaction to this story? Did you find this story suspenseful, mysterious, both? How does the story relate to your response to the **Focus Activity** on page 602? Describe your impressions in your journal.

Analyzing Literature

RECALL

1. Briefly describe the main character in the story. Who is he and what is he doing as the story opens?
2. Where does the pilot end up? What are his injuries?
3. Describe the things that make the pilot become suspicious about his location. What does he decide to do to test his suspicions?

INTERPRET

4. What is the importance of the French phrase *garde au chien?*
5. What sort of person is the pilot? How does he come to realize what has happened to him? Support your ideas with examples from the story.
6. How does the author inform you about the pilot's misfortune?
7. In describing the **setting** of the story, Dahl uses details that intensify the mood of suspense. Pick out details that help create this mood. (See **Literary Terms Handbook,** page R10.)
8. Why do you think Dahl named the story "Beware of the Dog"?

EVALUATE AND CONNECT

9. In the last paragraph of the story, why does the pilot respond the way he does to the wing commander? If you were the pilot, what would you have done?
10. At what point in the story did you begin to suspect that the pilot was not where the nurse said he was? How does Dahl build toward that suspicion?

LITERARY ELEMENTS

Flashback

A **flashback** is an interruption in the sequence of a piece of writing to describe a scene that happened at an earlier time. Skillful writers sometimes use flashbacks to give background information to readers so they can better understand what is happening at the present time.

For example, a character in a story may meet someone he or she knew years earlier. A flashback to that earlier time could tell the reader about the relationship between the two characters.

1. How is a flashback used in "Beware of the Dog"? Describe the scene that is presented in the flashback.

2. Sometimes a flashback can appear in the form of a dream. Why do you think Roald Dahl chose to begin the story the way he did?

● See **Literary Terms Handbook,** p. R4.

Personal Response

Students should describe their reactions to the story as well as how the story relates to their ideas about waking up in an unfamiliar place.

Analyzing Literature

1. The main character is a Spitfire pilot for the Royal Air Force. He is piloting his plane back to England after having been wounded in battle.
2. The pilot has been shot in a leg, which has been amputated. At first he thinks he is in a hospital in Brighton, England.
3. He hears Junkers 88s flying overhead and he remembers Brighton had soft water. He decides he must look out the window to see where he is.
4. The fact that this "Beware of the Dog" sign is in French makes the pilot realize that he is in France.
5. The pilot is perceptive and wary. He hears the Junkers 88 and remembers that Brighton has soft water. He looks out the window and realizes that he is in enemy territory in France.
6. The pilot daydreams and imagines landing, injured, in England and surprising his buddies.
7. After the pilot's doubts begin to grow, Dahl describes his room as "cold and empty and very quiet." It is no longer warm and friendly.
8. The French sign helps the pilot figure out where he is. The sign might also mean "Beware of the Enemy."

LITERARY ELEMENTS

1. Flashback is used to describe how the pilot is forced to bail out and to hook readers' interest.
2. It creates interest and intrigue. It also tells the reader how the main character got into this situation.

Additional Resources

Literary Elements Transparency 51

9. He realizes that the enemy has captured him, and he doesn't want to give them any information.
10. Suspicion might begin when the pilot discovers that the water is hard. Dahl adds to the suspicion by having Junkers 88s fly overhead in daylight.

Literature and Writing

Writing About Literature

Students' analyses should

- describe specific techniques Dahl uses to build suspense in this story.
- use examples from the story to support ideas.
- describe general techniques Dahl uses that students could incorporate into their own writing.

Personal Writing

Students' epilogues should

- describe what happens to the pilot after this story ends.
- use what they already know about the pilot to accurately describe his responses.
- incorporate descriptions of the setting and the war into a plausible scenario.

Extending Your Response

Interdisciplinary Activity

Encourage students to color-code their map so it is easy for others to understand. In addition, have them include a legend and a compass rose. **COLLAB. LEARN.**

Learning for Life

Remind students to develop questions that require more than a yes-or-no answer. When they answer questions, encourage them to base their answers on what they know about World War II and the pilot in this story.

Literature Groups

Before students meet, encourage them to jot down some initial impressions about the options available to the pilot. **COLLAB. LEARN.**

Literature and Writing

Writing About Literature

Suspense   Suspense, a state of uncertainty or fear about how something will turn out, is an essential element of this story. How does the writer build suspense? How does he raise questions in your mind about what will happen next? Write a brief analysis of how suspense is created in this story. Use examples from the story.

Personal Writing

An Epilogue   An **epilogue** is a passage added to the end of a written work. What do you think will happen to the pilot after the end of this story? Write a brief epilogue describing what happens to the pilot and why.

Extending Your Response

Interdisciplinary Activity

Social Studies: Map It!   With a partner or in a small group, research the role of British fighter pilots in World War II. Using your research and the information in the story, create a map that shows the possible route of the ill-fated flight, a possible point of origin, and where the pilot might have ended up in France.

Learning for Life

Interview a Vet   Imagine you are a journalist sent to interview the pilot after the end of the war. Write a list of the questions you would ask the pilot. Then work with a partner, taking turns as pilot and interviewer as you answer each other's questions.

Literature Groups

A Difficult Decision   The main character in this story faces a difficult decision. Once he realizes that he is in enemy hands, what should he do? What are his options? In small groups, discuss the pilot's situation, his options, and his decision. Support your ideas with examples and quotations from the story.

Reading Further

If you would like to read more Roald Dahl stories like this one, try:
Over to You: Ten Stories of Flyers and Flying

📖 **Save your work for your portfolio.**

✔ ASSESSMENT OPTIONS

- 📁 *Quick Checks,* p. 51
- 📁 *Selection and Theme Assessment,* pp. 89–90
- 📁 *Performance Assessment,* p. 48
- 💾 *Testmaker*

Skill Minilessons

GRAMMAR AND LANGUAGE • COMPLEX SENTENCES

A **complex sentence** is a sentence with one main clause and one or more subordinate clauses. In the following examples, the main clauses are in regular type, and the subordinate clauses are in *italic* type.

When he woke up, the pilot looked around.
The room had one light, *which was very dim.*
The pilot knew *that his options were limited.*

PRACTICE Write a paragraph describing the main character in "Beware of the Dog." Use at least three complex sentences in your description. Then trade paragraphs with a partner and read his or her paragraph. As you read, find the complex sentences and underline each main clause once and each subordinate clause twice.

● For more about complex sentences, see **Language Handbook,** p. R32.

READING AND THINKING • MONITORING COMPREHENSION

As a skillful reader, you should always ask questions about what you read and also evaluate the characters, actions, and events to make sure you understand what is happening. Remember to question and evaluate while you are reading—not just after you have finished. As you read, ask yourself questions such as these:

• Does this event make sense?
• What's really going on here?
• Would this character really say or do this?
• What is the writer describing? Why?

PRACTICE Review "Beware of the Dog." Write at least five questions about the characters, events, and setting of the story. Make them questions that require more than a simple yes or no for answers. Next, trade your questions with a partner. Answer each other's questions and then discuss your answers.

● For more about monitoring comprehension, see **Reading Handbook,** pp. R82–R93.

VOCABULARY • USING CONTEXT CLUES FOR MULTIPLE-MEANING WORDS

Some words have multiple meanings that are similar. In "Beware of the Dog," *giddy* means "dizzy or lightheaded." It describes the kind of whirling feeling a person gets after spinning around or from being very sick. *Giddy* can also mean "causing dizziness." It can also mean "not serious or steady; silly."

To know which definition of a multiple-meaning word is correct, look for context clues in the sentence or paragraph the word is in.

PRACTICE Use context clues to decide which meaning of *giddy* is the right one in each sentence.

a. dizzy or lightheaded   c. not serious, silly
b. causing dizziness

1. Lisa looked down from her *giddy* perch near the top of the tree.
2. I must have sounded foolish, giggling in such a *giddy* way.
3. Harry complained of feeling *giddy,* and then he fell backwards in a faint.
4. How can figure skaters spin as they do without becoming *giddy*?
5. The children could not calm down and listen; they were too *giddy* with excitement.

Skill Minilessons

GRAMMAR AND LANGUAGE
COMPLEX SENTENCES

If students have difficulty distinguishing main from subordinate clauses in their partner's paragraphs, have them read the clauses out loud to hear which can stand alone as sentences. These are main clauses.

READING AND THINKING
MONITORING COMPREHENSION

Students questions should

• help clarify the significance of story events.
• require the one who responds to form opinions or make judgments.
• provide insight into the author's purpose or the pilot's motivation.

VOCABULARY
USING CONTEXT CLUES FOR MULTIPLE-MEANING WORDS

1. b   **3.** a   **5.** c
2. c   **4.** a

Additional Resources

▮ *Grammar and Language Workbook,* pp. 155–156

▮ *Grammar and Composition Handbook,* Lesson 8.2

▮ *Writer's Choice,* Lesson 14.2

▮ *Reading Workbook,* pp. 91–92

🗀 *Vocabulary Practice,* p. 36

Objective

- To understand the elements of poetry

Teaching Strategies

Ask students if they can remember any poetry from their childhood, such as nursery rhymes, prayers, jump rope chants, or clapping games. Ask students if any of these elements helped them remember those poems and chants even after many years: rhythm, rhyme, images, colorful language, the sound of the words.

Form Explain that the form of a poem can make the poem visually interesting on the page. Students may wish to experiment with form by writing a poem that has an unusual shape.

Imagery An image in poetry can be thought of as a picture painted with words. Ask students to describe the image that comes to mind when they read the stanza of "The Highwayman" on the bottom of the page. Which senses does this stanza appeal to? Ask them to do quick sketches of the picture brought to mind by the words.

Teaching Options

POETRY

Poetry is a form of writing that uses not only words, but also form, patterns of sound, imagery, and figurative language to convey its message. Any poem will include some or all of the elements described on these two pages.

● For more about the various elements of poetry, see **Literary Terms Handbook**, p. R8.

The Arch of Nero, 1846. Thomas Cole. Oil on canvas, 60 x 48 in. The Newark Museum, Newark, NJ.

ELEMENTS OF POETRY	MODEL
FORM A poem's form is its appearance. Poems are divided into lines. Many poems, especially longer ones, may also be divided into groups of lines called **stanzas**. Stanzas function like paragraphs in a story. Each one contains a single idea or takes the idea one step further. The opening stanza of "The Highwayman," for example, sets the scene for the narrative poem.	The wind was a torrent of darkness among the gusty trees. The moon was a ghostly galleon tossed upon cloudy seas. The road was a ribbon of moonlight over the purple moor, And the highwayman came riding— Riding—riding— The highwayman came riding, up to the old inn door.
IMAGERY Poets use words and phrases that appeal to the reader's senses of sight, sound, touch, taste, and smell. Notice in the model from "The Highwayman" how the poet uses words to help you "see" an angry man on horseback.	Back, he spurred like a madman, shouting curses to the sky, With the white road smoking behind him and his rapier brandished high.

MEETING INDIVIDUAL NEEDS — ENGLISH LANGUAGE LEARNERS

World Poetry Some English language learners will find it challenging to understand the elements of poetry and identify them in English-language poems. Images, metaphors, and similes often require advanced-level vocabulary skills. The spirit of poetry, however, is something that is universal.

Activity Ask each student to bring in a favorite poem that is written either in English or in their native language. Have the students work in groups. Ask them to read each poem aloud, translating if necessary. Have each student choose one image from the poem and draw a picture that represents the image.

Additional Resources

📁 *English Language Learners Sourcebook*

SOUND Some poems use techniques of sound such as the following.

- **Rhythm** is the pattern of beats or stresses in a poem. Poets use patterns of stressed and unstressed syllables to create a regular rhythm. In the model, the stressed syllables are printed in **bold** type. Try beating out the rhythm with a finger as you read these lines.

- **Rhyme** is the repetition of the same or similar sounds, usually in stressed syllables at the ends of lines, but sometimes within a line as well, as in this model.

- **Alliteration** is the repetition of consonant sounds at the beginnings of words. Read aloud the model example to hear its alliteration.

> - **She** was a **child** and **I** was a **child**,
>   In this **king**dom **by** the **sea**:
>   But we **loved** with a **love** that was
>   **more** than **love**—
>   **I** and my **Ann**abel **Lee**;
>
> - There are strange things **done** in the midnight **sun**
>   By the men who moil for gold;
>
> - Over the **c**obbles he **c**lattered and **c**lashed . . .

FIGURES OF SPEECH Figures of speech are a special kind of imagery. They create pictures by making comparisons.

- A **simile** is a comparison using *like* or *as*.

- A **metaphor** describes one thing as if it *were* another.

- **Personification** gives human characteristics to something nonhuman.

> - Talk of your cold! through the parka's fold it stabbed like a driven nail.
> - The moon was a ghostly galleon tossed upon cloudy seas.
> - 	. . . and the stars o'erhead were dancing heel and toe . . .

In "The Highwayman," images create a picture of Tim. Which figures are used to describe his eyes and his hair?

His eyes were hollows of madness, his hair like
*   mouldy hay,*

THEME The **theme** of a poem is its central or main idea. To identify a poem's theme, ask yourself what ideas or insights about life or human nature you have found in the poem.

Sound If students have difficulty discerning the difference between stressed and unstressed syllables, have them clap out the stressed syllables in their full names, or in short couplets they write that include their names, such as, *My name's Pat/ Where's my cat?* After they clap out the words, ask them to write what they have said, underlining the stressed syllables.

Figures of Speech Write the following sentences on the board:
- My love is like a rose.
- Our love bloomed in the garden.
- The rose tipped its head as we passed by.

After students have read about figures of speech on page 617, ask them to identify which of the above is an example of a simile, metaphor, and personification. Encourage students to write their own examples of each.

Theme Explain that the theme of a poem is often hard to find on first reading. The reader may have a general sense of what the poem is about, but additional readings of the poem often help clarify thoughts and feelings about it.

Technology Option

Poetry Table

Students can use a word processing program to create a table of poetry elements as they read the poems in this unit.

Activity Ask each student to open a new document and insert a six-column table as shown. For each poem, a new row can be added to the table and information can be keyed in about each of the five elements of that poem. Encourage the use of quotation marks when including direct examples of imagery and figures of speech from the poems. **L2**

Title	Form	Sound	Imagery	Figures of Speech	Theme

Active Reading Strategies

Objective
- To understand and apply strategies for reading and comprehending poetry

Teach the Strategies
Remind students that poetry is all around them, not only in a literature class, but also in song lyrics, raps, jazz chants, and childhood rhymes. Poems come in all lengths, forms, and levels of language.

Preview
Tell students that previewing will make a poem seem familiar to them before they actually read it.

Listen
Suggest that students take turns reading the poems to each other. Listeners should just listen rather than read along.

Visualize
Suggest that students make a habit of visualizing favorite images as they read through a poem. Visualizing will help them remember the image.

Question
Point out to students that they may have many questions when they first read a poem since the language and images are often more compressed and intense in poetry than in prose.

Teaching Options

Active Reading Strategies

Tips for Reading Poetry

Poetry is a kind of imaginative writing in which thoughts and feelings are expressed in rhythmic, compressed language. Skillful readers use strategies that help them understand the meaning of a poem.

- For more about reading strategies, see **Reading Handbook,** pp. R70–R101.

PREVIEW

Before reading the poem, just stop to look at it. Think about its form.

Ask Yourself . . .
- How long is the poem? Is it broken into stanzas?
- Are the individual lines short or long?
- How does the poet use punctuation?

LISTEN

Read the poem aloud. Listen for patterns of rhythm and rhyme.

Ask Yourself . . .
- Does the poet use rhyme? What rhythm and rhyming patterns can I discover?

VISUALIZE

Look for the poet's use of imagery and figures of speech.

Ask Yourself . . .
- What images does the poem contain? Can I imagine what the poet describes?

QUESTION

Since poetry is such a compact form of literature, poets think very carefully about each word they use. As a skillful reader, you, too, should think about each word.

Ask Yourself . . .
- Why did the poet choose this particular word or phrase?
- Why does the poet use this image or comparison?

618 THEME 6

Reading Journal

Does Love Conquer All?
The poet Alfred Noyes presents in "The Highwayman" a tale about a robber and the woman he loves. Invite students to discuss whether people have any control over whom they fall in love with.

Activity As they read "The Highwayman," invite students to copy into their reading journals the rhymes and images they especially like. After reading, have students give their opinions of the choices made by Bess and the highwayman.

CONNECT

As you read, think about the theme of the poem. Discuss the poem with your class-mates. There is no "right answer" when you read a poem.

Ask Yourself . . .

- How do the events and images in the poem connect to my own experience?
- What message is the poet trying to get across?

RESPOND

Think about whether feelings, events, or images from the poem remind you of something in your own life. Think about what the poem means to you.

Ask Yourself . . .

- Do I like the sound of the rhyme pattern?
- Is the poet's imagery appropriate for the poem's theme?

EVALUATE

Read the poem several times. As you read, think about your reactions to the poem. Evaluate what the poem has to say.

Ask Yourself . . .

- Who is the speaker? What does the speaker feel or think?
- Do I agree with the message of the poem?

APPLYING THE STRATEGIES

Read the following poem, "The Highway-man." Use the **Active Reading** notes in the margins as you read. Write your responses on a separate piece of paper or use stick-on notes.

TWISTS AND TURNS 🐾 619

Connect

Encourage students to share their impressions of the poem with each other. Ask them to focus on images, scenes, and characters in the poem with which they feel a connection, and to explain why.

Respond

Have students imagine that the poet has sent the poem to each of them in the mail. As they read the poem, they may wonder what the events and images have to do with them and their lives. If they read the poem as if it has been written specifically for them, their experience as readers may be sharpened.

Evaluate

Some students may need to read the poem several times before they can evaluate its meaning. Suggest that they jot down impressions as they read to help their comprehension.

Before Reading

Objectives

- To read and appreciate the twists and turns in a narrative poem
- To recognize and understand the purpose of onomatopoeia
- To write about narrative elements in a poem

Skills

Reading/Thinking: Evaluating; Monitoring Comprehension; Drawing Conclusions
Writing: Interview Questions
Vocabulary: Multiple-Meaning Words
Grammar/Language: Compound Sentences; Colorful Adjectives
Listening/Speaking: Choral Reading
Collaboration: Literature Groups

Motivating OPTIONS

Selection Focus Transparency 52: Have students view the quote and discuss its figurative meaning.

Focus Activity: As an extension of the Focus Activity, have students in small groups discuss what made their favorite adventure books or movies exciting.

Before You Read
The Highwayman

MEET ALFRED NOYES

Alfred Noyes was one of the most popular British poets of the early twentieth century. Because he became a successful poet while still in his twenties, Noyes was able to continue a career as a full-time poet. While many other British poets writing at that time were thoroughly modern in their writing styles, Noyes chose to write traditional poetry in the manner of the great nineteenth-century Romantic poets.

Alfred Noyes was born in England in 1880 and died in 1958.

FOCUS ACTIVITY

Do you enjoy dramatic adventure stories?

Sharing Ideas
Think about adventure stories you have enjoyed reading or seeing as movies. Jot down the titles of a few favorites to share with your classmates.

Setting a Purpose
Read this poem to enjoy its story.

BACKGROUND

By the eighteenth century, horse-drawn coaches traveled regularly on English roads. They were preyed upon by armed thieves on horseback called highwaymen, who would stop coaches at gunpoint and demand that the passengers surrender their money and other valuables. A few highwaymen, such as Dick Turpin, became legends in their time, inspiring songs, poems, and stories in the popular newspapers of the time—at least until they were caught and hanged for their crimes.

RESOURCE MANAGER

Lesson Planning Resource
The *Theme Six Planning Guide* (pp. 52–59) provides additional lesson notes and reduced versions of all print resources.

Other Print Resources
- Active Reading Guide, p. 52
- Reading Workbook, pp. 93–94
- Grammar and Language Workbook, pp. 117–118, 153–154

- Grammar and Composition Handbook, Lessons 5.1, 14.1
- Quick Checks, p. 52
- Selection and Theme Assessment, pp. 91–92
- Performance Assessment, p. 49
- Spanish Summaries, p. 52
- Spanish Translations
- Inclusion Strategies
- English Language Learners Sourcebook

 Transparencies
- Selection Focus 52
- Literary Elements 52
- Grammar and Language 51

Technology
- Audio Library
- Spanish Audio Library
- Glencoe Literature Web Site
- Testmaker

The Highwayman

Alfred Noyes

ACTIVE READING MODEL

SUMMARY

The highwayman is a thief in eighteenth-century England. He promises to return to his love, Bess, by moonlight. King George's redcoats learn of his planned return. They capture Bess and lie in wait for the highwayman. When Bess hears the highwayman returning, she shoots herself to warn the highwayman away. The highwayman retreats, but soon finds out Bess is dead. Enraged, he rides back to avenge her death and is killed himself.

📁 *Spanish Summaries,* p. 52

PART 1

The wind was a torrent of darkness among the gusty trees.
The moon was a ghostly galleon° tossed upon cloudy seas.
The road was a ribbon of moonlight over the purple moor,°
And the highwayman came riding—
5   Riding—riding—
The highwayman came riding, up to the old inn door.

He'd a French cocked hat on his forehead, a bunch of lace at his chin,
A coat of the claret velvet, and breeches of brown doeskin.
They fitted with never a wrinkle. His boots were up to the thigh.
10 And he rode with a jewelled twinkle,
         His pistol butts a-twinkle,
His rapier° hilt° a-twinkle, under the jewelled sky.

---

2 A *galleon* (gal′ yən) is a large sailing ship of the 1400s–1600s.
3 A *moor* is an area of open, rolling, wild land, usually a grassy wetland.
12 A *rapier* is a long, lightweight sword, and the *hilt* is its handle.

PREVIEW

Take a minute to think about the shape of this poem. How are the lines of the poem grouped? How many parts does it have?

VISUALIZE

How does this description help you "see" the highwayman?

A Active Reading

PREVIEW *(The lines are grouped in paragraphs called stanzas. Each stanza has six lines. The poem has two parts.)*

B Active Reading

VISUALIZE *(The details give a clear image of the highwayman. Details include his hat, his suede boots, his pistol, and his sword.)*

Additional Resources

📁 *Active Reading Guide,* pp. 52

🎧 *Audio Library*

🎧 *Spanish Audio Library*

Teaching Options

CONNECTING TO OTHER SELECTIONS

The chart at the right shows three ways to connect "The Highwayman" to other selections in this book.

For specific teaching strategies, see the *Theme Six Planning Guide,* pages 55–56.

Connection	Title
Life Skills: Making Decisions →	"The Wreck of the Hesperus," p. 227
Thematic: Outcasts →	"Antaeus," p. 347
Literary: Repetition →	"Growing Pains," p. 133

The Highwayman

Teaching Options

C Literary Elements

ONOMATOPOEIA Have students list examples of onomatopoeia in this stanza, and explain what effect these words have on the poem. *(The words* clattered, clashed, *and* tapped *help the reader "hear" the action of the poem.)*

D Active Reading

QUESTION *(The images describe a lovelorn, pale, and jealous man. They set a mood of dread.)*

E Author's Craft

FORESHADOWING Ask students why they think the poet describes Tim by saying that "His eyes were hollows of madness." *(Tim loves Bess and is crazed because she loves the high-wayman. The poet is foreshadowing something dark.)*

F Literary Elements

PLOT: *Rising Action* Have students read lines 25–30 and discuss how these lines add to the tension in the poem. *(The reader knows Tim is lis-tening as the highwayman explains his plans to steal gold and return before morning.)*

G Active Reading

QUESTION *(These lines illustrate the love the highwayman and Bess feel for each other.)*

ACTIVE READING MODEL

QUESTION

D What do these images tell us about Tim?

QUESTION

G What is happening here?

Over the cobbles he clattered and clashed in the dark inn yard.
He tapped with his whip on the shutters, but all was locked and
  barred.
15 He whistled a tune to the window, and who should be waiting
  there
But the landlord's black-eyed daughter,
      Bess, the landlord's daughter,
Plaiting° a dark red love-knot into her long black hair.

And dark in the dark old inn yard a stable wicket° creaked
20 Where Tim the ostler° listened. His face was white and peaked.°
His eyes were hollows of madness, his hair like mouldy hay,
But he loved the landlord's daughter,
      The landlord's red-lipped daughter.
Dumb as a dog he listened, and he heard the robber say—

25 "One kiss, my bonny° sweetheart, I'm after a prize tonight,
But I shall be back with the yellow gold before the morning
  light;
Yet, if they press me sharply, and harry° me through the day,
Then look for me by moonlight,
      Watch for me by moonlight,
30 I'll come to thee by moonlight, though hell should bar the way."

He rose upright in the stirrups. He scarce could reach her hand,
But she loosened her hair in the casement.° His face burnt like a
  brand°
As the black cascade of perfume came tumbling over his breast;
And he kissed its waves in the moonlight,
35   (O, sweet black waves in the moonlight!)
Then he tugged at his rein in the moonlight, and galloped away
  to the west.

---

18 Bess is braiding *(plaiting)* a red ribbon into her hair.
19 A *wicket* is a small door or gate; this one leads into the stable.
20 As the *ostler* (a shorter form of *hostler*), it's Tim's job to take care of the horses at the inn. A *peaked* face looks pale and sickly.
25 *Bonny* (a Scottish word) means "good-looking, fine, or admirable."
27 To *harry* is to trouble, bother, or worry.
32 The *casement* is the window frame, and the *brand* is a burning torch.

MEETING INDIVIDUAL NEEDS — ENGLISH LANGUAGE LEARNERS

Picture the Highwayman English lan-guage learners might find it easier to understand this poem if they can visual-ize the highwayman. Begin by having students look up the word *highwayman* in the dictionary.

Activity Have students work in small groups to create illustrations of the highwayman. Ask each group to look up unfamiliar words or phrases in the poem that describe the highwayman's appearance and include these details in their drawings. Encourage them to label the drawings and display them so oth-ers can refer to them as they read the poem. **L2** **COLLAB. LEARN.**

Additional Resources
📁 *English Language Learners Sourcebook*

Moon Landing, 1977. Jamie Wyeth. Oil on canvas, 29 x 43 in. Private collection.
Viewing the painting: What lines of the poem might this painting illustrate?

PART 2

He did not come in the dawning. He did not come at noon;
And out of the tawny° sunset, before the rise of the moon,
When the road was a gypsy's ribbon, looping the purple moor,
40 A red coat troop° came marching—
        Marching—marching—
King George's men came marching, up to the old inn door.

They said no word to the landlord. They drank his ale instead,
But they gagged his daughter, and bound her, to the foot of her
    narrow bed.
45 Two of them knelt at her casement, with muskets at their side!
There was death at every window;
        And hell at one dark window;
For Bess could see, through her casement, the road that *he*
    would ride.

QUESTION

Why have the red-
coats appeared?

H

LISTEN

Why does the poet
repeat the word
marching? Where
else does he use
repetition?

I

J

---

38 *Tawny* is a brownish-gold color.
40 The *red coat troop* is a group of soldiers wearing bright red coats.

Reading *Minilesson*

Monitoring Comprehension To help students comprehend the poem, you may wish to have them work with the following questions while reading the selection: What is the conflict?; What is happening?; and What can I predict?

<u>Activity</u> Have students use a three-column chart to write their responses to the questions as they read the poem. They can use their charts to answer the questions that follow the selection.
L2 COLLAB. LEARN.

What is the conflict?	What is happening?	What can I predict?

Additional Resources

 Reading Workbook pp. 93–94

Teaching Options (left column)

K Literary Elements

CHARACTER Have students describe the character of the redcoats. *(They are bullies. They tie Bess up and laugh disrespectfully at her. They put a gun under her rib cage when she cannot defend herself.)*

L Author's Craft

FORESHADOWING Have students explain what this line may indicate: "She heard the doomed man say...." *(Bess believes the highwayman is doomed—foreshadowing that something bad will happen to him.)*

M Active Reading

VISUALIZE *(The poet uses vivid verbs and exclamation marks to help the reader see Bess's struggle to free herself and warn the highwayman.)*

N Active Reading

LISTEN *(The poet uses "Tlot-tlot; tlot-tlot!" repeatedly to create the sound of the horse galloping toward the inn.)*

The Highwayman

ACTIVE READING MODEL

50   They had tied her up to attention, with many a sniggering jest.°
    They had bound a musket beside her, with the muzzle beneath her breast!
    "Now, keep good watch!" and they kissed her. She heard the doomed man say—
    Look for me by moonlight;
            Watch for me by moonlight;
    I'll come to thee by moonlight, though hell should bar the way!

55   She twisted her hands behind her; but all the knots held good!
    She writhed° her hands till her fingers were wet with sweat or blood!
    They stretched and strained in the darkness, and the hours crawled by like years,
    Till, now, on the stroke of midnight,
            Cold, on the stroke of midnight,
60   The tip of one finger touched it! The trigger at last was hers!

    The tip of one finger touched it. She strove no more for the rest.
    Up, she stood up to attention, with the muzzle beneath her breast.
    She would not risk their hearing; she would not strive again;
    For the road lay bare in the moonlight;
65   Blank and bare in the moonlight;
    And the blood of her veins, in the moonlight, throbbed to her love's refrain.°

    Tlot-tlot; tlot-tlot! Had they heard it: The horsehoofs ringing clear;
    Tlot-tlot, tlot-tlot, in the distance? Were they deaf that they did not hear?
    Down the ribbon of moonlight, over the brow of the hill,
70   The highwayman came riding—
            Riding—riding—
    The red-coats looked to their priming!° She stood up, straight and still!

VISUALIZE (M) How does the poet help you visualize this scene?

LISTEN (N) How does the poet create the sound of the highwayman on horseback?

---

49 Bess is tied to a pole, arms at her sides in what a soldier would call "at attention," while the soldiers laugh disrespectfully *(many a sniggering jest)*.
56 To *writhe* is to twist and turn.
66 In a song or poem, the *refrain* is a phrase or verse that is repeated regularly.
72 The soldiers are *priming* their weapons, or loading their muskets with ammunition.

Grammar and Language *Minilesson*

Compound Sentences Write the following sentence on the board:

- *He tapped with his whip on the shutters, but all was locked and bare.*

Remind students to note that compound sentences joined by a conjunction require a comma before the conjunction.

Activity Have students rewrite these compound sentences as pairs of complete sentences:

- *He whistled a tune to the window, and who should be waiting there.*
- *They stretched and strained in the darkness, and the hours crawled like years.*

To extend the activity, have students create five compound sentences of their own.

L2 **COLLAB. LEARN.**

Additional Resources

📖 **Grammar and Language Transparency 151**

📕 **Grammar and Language Workbook,** pp. 153–154

📕 **Grammar and Composition Handbook,** Lesson 14.1

📕 **Writer's Choice,** Lesson 20.3

Alfred Noyes ～

Tlot-tlot, in the frosty silence! *Tlot-tlot*, in the echoing night!
Nearer he came and nearer. Her face was like a light.
75   Her eyes grew wide for a moment; she drew one last deep breath,
      Then her finger moved in the moonlight,
            Her musket shattered the moonlight,
      Shattered her breast in the moonlight and warned him—with
         her death.

      He turned. He spurred to the westward; he did not know who
         stood
80   Bowed, with her head o'er the musket, drenched with her own
         red blood!
      Not till the dawn he heard it, and his face grew grey to hear
      How Bess, the landlord's daughter,
            The landlord's black-eyed daughter,
      Had watched for her love in the moonlight, and died in the
         darkness there.

85   Back, he spurred like a madman, shrieking a curse to the sky,
      With the white road smoking behind him and his rapier
         brandished° high.
      Blood-red were his spurs in the golden noon, wine-red was his
         velvet coat;
      When they shot him down on the highway,
            Down like a dog on the highway,
90   And he lay in his blood on the highway, with a bunch of lace at
         his throat.

And still of a winter's night, they say, when the wind is in the trees,
When the moon is a ghostly galleon tossed upon cloudy seas,
When the road is a ribbon of moonlight over the purple moor,
A highwayman comes riding—
95   *Riding—riding—*
A highwayman comes riding, up to the old inn door.

Over the cobbles he clatters and clangs in the dark inn yard.
He taps with his whip on the shutters, but all is locked and barred.
He whistles a tune to the window, and who should be waiting there
100 *But the landlord's black-eyed daughter,*
            Bess, the landlord's daughter,
Plaiting a dark red love-knot into her long black hair.

---

86 The highwayman waved his sword threateningly *(brandished)*.

ACTIVE READING MODEL

RESPOND

What mood does the poet create in this stanza?

O

QUESTION

What do you learn about the highwayman's character in this stanza?

P

RESPOND

What do these final stanzas mean to you?

Q

O Active Reading

RESPOND *(The poet creates a mood of despair, loss, and loyalty.)* Have students explain what Bess's actions show about her feelings toward the highwayman.

P Active Reading

QUESTION *(The highwayman is brave and would risk his own safety to avenge Bess's death. He feels he has nothing to live for now that Bess is dead.)*

Q Active Reading

RESPOND *(Some students may think that the highwayman and Bess meet again at the inn as ghosts on moonlit winter nights.)*

Thematic Focus

Twists and Turns Have students discuss some of the twists and turns that occur in this poem.

☑ ASSESSMENT OPTIONS

📁 *Quick Checks,* p. 52

REAL-WORLD CONNECTION

Music Folksinger Phil Ochs set "The Highwayman" to music. Other musicians have recorded the poem as a song, too. You may want to play such a recording for your class.

Activity Locate or ask students to locate the sheet music for a performance of "The Highwayman." Ask a music student to volunteer to play the song for the class.

Responding to the Selection

Personal Response

Student responses should explain whether "The Highwayman" could be made into a good action movie.

Active Reading Response

Students should list three places in the poem where they could apply one active reading strategy.

Analyzing Literature

1. The setting of this poem is an eighteenth-century inn in England. The main characters are the highwayman and Bess.

2. The highwayman loves Bess and vows to return after a night of robbery. The redcoats learn of this vow and try to ambush him. Bess kills herself to save the highwayman, and the highwayman is killed trying to avenge her death.

3. In the beginning and end, the poet uses such eerie words as *darkness, gusty trees, ghostly galleon,* and *ribbon of moonlight.*

4. Central conflict: Tim loves Bess, but she loves the highwayman. When Tim hears the highwayman will be back at the inn, he brings in the redcoats to capture him.

5. Bess shoots herself to warn the highwayman. Students might think Bess's act is heroic because she makes the ultimate sacrifice. Others might think it is unacceptable to end one's own life.

6. The highwayman is enraged and wants to avenge her death. This shows the highwayman cares deeply about Bess.

7. Tim tells the redcoats when the highwayman will return. Tim was hiding in the barn when he heard the highwayman tell Bess he would return.

8. It would be less eerie because readers would not know of the rumor that the highwayman continues to roam the area on certain nights.

9. Examples of metaphors include "the moon was a ghostly galleon" and "the road was a ribbon of moonlight." Some similes are "his hair like mouldy hay" and "his face burnt like a brand."

10. The repetition of words helps give the poem its form, emphasizes the rhythm as well as the words, and stresses certain actions or ideas. In some lines, it is used for onomatopoetic effect.

Responding to Literature

PERSONAL RESPONSE

Take a look at your list from the **Focus Activity** on page 620. How does "The Highwayman" compare with your favorite adventure stories? Could it be made into a good action movie? Explain why or why not.

Active Reading Response

Review the strategies described in the **Active Reading Model** notes on pages 618–619. Choose one strategy and find three places in the poem where you could apply it.

Analyzing Literature

RECALL

1. What is the setting of this poem? Who are the main characters?

2. Summarize what happens in "The Highwayman."

INTERPRET

3. How does the poet create a mysterious mood in the opening stanza? How do the closing stanzas echo that same mood?

4. What is the central conflict in the plot of this poem? Use words and images from the poem to support your ideas.

EVALUATE AND CONNECT

5. What sacrifice does Bess make? Do you think her act is foolish or heroic? Why?

6. Why do you think the highwayman reacts as he does when he finds out what has happened to Bess? What does his action reveal about him?

7. How did the redcoats know that the highwayman would return to the inn? On what do you base your opinion?

8. How would the poem be different if it ended just before the final two stanzas?

9. Identify two examples of simile or metaphor the poet uses.

10. What effect does the poet's repetition of words create?

LITERARY ELEMENTS

Onomatopoeia

Onomatopoeia (on′ ə mat′ ə pē′ ə) is the use of words or phrases whose sounds suggest their meanings. The sound of the word *boom,* for example, suggests an explosion. The use of onomatopoeia begins as early as infancy. Often, some of the first words children learn are words such as *woof* or *meow.*

Onomatopoeia plays an important role in the sounds of poetry. In "The Highwayman," for example, *tlot-tlot* represents the sound of a horse's hooves.

1. What other examples of onomatopoeia can you find in "The Highwayman"?

2. Reread another poem from this book and pick out an example of onomatopoeia. Explain what you think the word or phrase adds to the meaning of the poem.

● See **Literary Terms Handbook,** p. R7.

LITERARY ELEMENTS

1. Other examples of onomatopoeia include *clattered, clashed, creaked, gagged, sniggering, throbbed, shattered,* and *whistles.*

2. Examples from other poems should include an explanation about what each adds to the meaning of the poem.

Additional Resources

 Literary Elements Transparency 52

Extending Your Response

Writing About Literature

Narrative Poetry A **narrative poem** tells a story. In "The Highwayman," the poet creates a vivid story with a mysterious setting, strong characters, and a plot with twists and turns. Write a paragraph describing one of the narrative elements used in this poem—setting, character, or plot—as you picture the place, the person, or the series of actions.

Creative Writing

Character Interview Imagine that you are to interview one of the characters in this poem. Write a series of questions to ask that character. With a partner, dramatize the interview for your classmates.

Literature Groups

Prose or Poetry? The plot of this poem could have been written in **prose,** the language of ordinary writing and speech. Which version would you prefer? Why? Discuss what the poem's story would lose or gain if it were written in prose.

Performing

Choral Reading With a small group, plan a choral reading of "The Highwayman." Group members can take turns reading parts of the poem. They can read other parts together as a chorus. Begin by planning how you will divide the parts. Then practice reading the poem a few times before presenting it to the class.

Reading Further

If you would like to read more narrative poems, here are a few suggestions. You can find these and other poems in poetry books or on the Internet.

"The Walrus and the Carpenter" by Lewis Carroll

"The Shooting of Dan McGrew" by Robert W. Service

"The Charge of the Light Brigade" by Alfred, Lord Tennyson

"Casey at the Bat" by Ernest Lawrence Thayer

 Save your work for your portfolio.

Skill Minilesson

GRAMMAR AND LANGUAGE • COLORFUL ADJECTIVES

"The Highwayman" is filled with adjectives that help readers visualize the nouns described. For example, think about the opening lines:

The wind was a torrent of darkness among the gusty trees.
The moon was a ghostly galleon tossed upon cloudy seas.
The road was a ribbon of moonlight over the purple moor,

You can "see" the wind-blown trees, the fierce sea, and the dimly lit road winding through the dark moor because the poet has chosen adjectives to create vivid images.

PRACTICE Reread the poem. As you do, list the adjectives that help you to visualize the images in the poem. In your journal, keep an ongoing list of colorful adjectives you find in your reading.

● For more about adjectives, see **Language Handbook,** p. R27.

Writing About Literature

Students' paragraphs should
- clearly describe one narrative element in this poem.
- use vivid examples from the poem to support the description.
- explain how students can incorporate this element into their own writing.

Creative Writing

Students' questions should
- require in-depth rather than yes-or-no responses.
- explore a character's motivations, feelings, and actions.

Literature Groups Before students meet, encourage them to jot down some initial impressions about how this poem would be different if it were written in prose.
COLLAB. LEARN.

Performing Encourage students to use stress to emphasize the rhythm of the poem. In addition, have them practice reading loudly or softly and using low voices for serious or scary parts.

Skill Minilesson

GRAMMAR AND LANGUAGE
• COLORFUL ADJECTIVES
Invite students to list their favorite adjectives on the board and to read them aloud with feeling.

Additional Resources
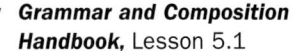 *Grammar and Language Workbook,* pp. 117–118
Grammar and Composition Handbook, Lesson 5.1
Writer's Choice, Lessons 3.2–3.3

✓ ASSESSMENT OPTIONS

📂 *Quick Checks,* p. 52

📂 *Selection and Theme Assessment,* pp. 91–92

📂 *Performance Assessment,* p. 49

💾 *Testmaker*

Objectives

- To read and analyze a poem about a loving relationship
- To recognize rhythm and meter
- To write a paragraph on the poet's use of imagery

Skills

Reading/Thinking: Making Critical Judgments; Elaborating; Paraphrasing
Writing: Paragraph About Imagery; Journal Entry
Vocabulary: Word Roots
Grammar/Language: Punctuating Poetry
Listening/Speaking: Reading Poetry and Short Stories Aloud
Collaboration: Literature Groups

Motivating
→ OPTIONS

Selection Focus Transparency 53: Discuss how the watercolor *A Rocky Coast* might reflect the mood of this selection.

Focus Activity: As an extension of the Focus Activity, have pairs of students share their thoughts on how they would react in the face of a difficult experience.

Before You Read
Annabel Lee

MEET EDGAR ALLAN POE

Death played a large part in Edgar Allan Poe's life, his fiction, and his poetry. Poe is best known for his detective stories (a form of fiction he helped invent) and tales of horror and madness. He wished, however, to be remembered for his poetry. "Annabel Lee," one of the poet's best-loved poems, was published two days after his early death.

Edgar Allan Poe was born in 1809 and died in 1849.

FOCUS ACTIVITY

Do you think that writing about a difficult experience can help you better deal with the experience?

Journal
Jot down your thoughts about whether writing can help you deal with difficult experiences.

Setting a Purpose
Read this poem to find out how the speaker responds to an unexpected experience.

BACKGROUND

Did You Know? Edgar Allan Poe lived a life as tragic as those he described in some of his famous horror tales. The one bright shining light in his life was his love for his young wife Virginia. It is believed that Poe wrote "Annabel Lee" after his beloved wife died tragically of tuberculosis, the same illness that had robbed him of his natural mother when he was only two years old. Later, his foster mother died of the same disease.

Virginia Poe

RESOURCE MANAGER

Lesson Planning Resource
The **Theme Six Planning Guide** (pp. 60–64) provides additional lesson notes and reduced versions of all print resources.

📁 **Other Print Resources**
- Active Reading Guide, p. 53
- Reading Workbook
- Grammar and Language Workbook, pp. 253–254

- Grammar and Composition Handbook, Lesson 13.1
- Quick Checks, p. 53
- Selection and Theme Assessment, p. 93
- Performance Assessment, p. 50
- Spanish Summaries, p. 53
- Inclusion Strategies
- English Language Learners Sourcebook

 Transparencies
- Selection Focus 53
- Literary Elements 53

Technology
 🎧 Audio Library
 🎧 Spanish Audio Library
🖥 Glencoe Literature Web Site
 💾 Testmaker

ANNABEL LEE

Edgar Allan Poe

A Rocky Coast, 1877. William Trost Richards. Watercolor and gouache on gray oatmeal wove paper, 22³⁄₁₆ x 36 in. Metropolitan Museum of Art, New York.

It was many and many a year ago,
    In a kingdom by the sea,
That a maiden there lived whom you may know
    By the name of Annabel Lee;—
5 And this maiden she lived with no other thought
    Than to love and be loved by me.

She was a child and *I* was a child,
    In this kingdom by the sea,
But we loved with a love that was more than love—
10   I and my Annabel Lee—
With a love that the wingéd seraphs° of Heaven
    Coveted° her and me.

11–12 *Seraphs,* the highest-ranking angels, are said to burn with love for God. Even these angels were jealous of *(coveted)* a love as strong as that between the speaker and Annabel Lee.

And this was the reason that, long ago,
   In this kingdom by the sea,
15 A wind blew out of a cloud by night
   Chilling my Annabel Lee;
So that her high-born kinsmen came
   And bore her away from me,
To shut her up in a sepulcher°
20   In this kingdom by the sea.

The angels, not half so happy in Heaven,
   Went envying her and me;
Yes! that was the reason (as all men know,
   In this kingdom by the sea)
25 That the wind came out of the cloud, chilling
   And killing my Annabel Lee.

But our love it was stronger by far than the love
   Of those who were older than we—
   Of many far wiser than we—
30 And neither the angels in Heaven above
   Nor the demons down under the sea
Can ever dissever° my soul from the soul
   Of the beautiful Annabel Lee:—

For the moon never beams without bringing me dreams
35   Of the beautiful Annabel Lee;
And the stars never rise but I see the bright eyes
   Of the beautiful Annabel Lee;
And so, all the night-tide, I lie down by the side
Of my darling, my darling, my life and my bride
40   In her sepulcher there by the sea—
   In her tomb by the side of the sea.

19 A *sepulcher* (sep′ əl kər) is a tomb or burial place.
32 To *dissever* is to separate or split apart.

Responding to Literature

PERSONAL RESPONSE

What are your thoughts about the relationship between the speaker and Annabel Lee?

Analyzing Literature

RECALL

1. What is the relationship between the poem's speaker and Annabel Lee?
2. Where is the speaker at the end of the poem?

INTERPRET

3. To be *idealized* means "to be made a model of perfection." Do you think the speaker of the poem has idealized Annabel Lee? Why or why not?
4. From whose point of view is this poem told? How does this point of view affect what the poem tells?
5. What are the basic themes of this poem?

Storm Light, 1995. Jane Wilson. Oil on linen, 80 x 74 in. Courtesy Fischbach Gallery, New York.

EVALUATE AND CONNECT

6. How does Poe use rhyme and repetition in the poem, and to what effect?
7. Give an example of **alliteration** in "Annabel Lee" and tell why you think Poe uses it in this poem. (See **Literary Terms Handbook,** page R1.)
8. Does this poem seem true to life? Why or why not?
9. Theme Connection   What unexpected event do the lovers in the poem face? How does the poem's speaker deal with it?
10. Think of a time when you lost something or someone you felt very strongly about. How did the experience affect you?

LITERARY ELEMENTS

Rhythm and Meter

Like a song, a poem has rhythm. In poetry, **rhythm** is the pattern of beats made by stressed and unstressed syllables. Some poems have a predictable rhythm, called **meter.** To find the meter of a poem, try scanning, or reading the poem to find the pattern of stressed (ˊ) and unstressed (˘) syllables. For example:

It wăs mány ănd mány ă
    yéar ăgó,
In ă kíngdŏm bý thĕ séa,

When you read a poem, pay attention to the rhythm, but don't stress the beats so much that the poem sounds sing-song.

1. With a partner, practice reading aloud a stanza of "Annabel Lee." Then work together to copy the stanza and mark its pattern of stressed and unstressed syllables.

2. Choose another poem from this book and mark the rhythm pattern of a stanza or several lines.

● See **Literary Terms Handbook,** pp. R9 and R6.

LITERARY ELEMENTS

1. Suggest that students exaggerate the stressed syllables to determine the meter, and then reduce the stress, reading the lines with natural emphasis.
2. Suggest that students choose a poem with a different rhythm and meter from "Annabel Lee."

Additional Resources

 Literary Elements Transparency 53

Personal Response

Some students may be moved by such a close, loving relationship. Others may think the speaker idealizes the relationship.

Analyzing Literature
---

1. The two were married and loved each other.
2. The speaker says he is lying in the tomb with her.
3. Some may say he has not idealized her because he truly loves her. Others may say he does idealize her, as being so perfect that the angels took her life out of jealousy.
4. The poem is told from the point of view of Annabel's lover. He has been so emotionally shaken by her death that he cannot be objective.
5. One theme is that even death cannot separate the spirits of two lovers.
6. Poe rhymes the last words of every other line of each stanza, but varies the pattern for emphasis. He uses internal rhyme in some lines, such as line 32 (*ever dissever*), line 34 (*beams* and *dreams*), and line 36 (*rise* and *eyes*). He repeats "Annabel Lee" and "the kingdom by the sea," which give a musical quality to the poem.
7. An example is "kinsmen came" (line 17). The *k* sound has a harshness that reinforces the harshness of the action being described.
8. Some may say it is because Poe accurately expresses the pain of loss. Others may say it isn't, because the poet's idealization of the woman and their love is excessive.
9. The unexpected event is Annabel Lee's death. The speaker blames the angels and sleeps in her tomb at night.
10. Answers will depend on the experiences of the student.

Extending Your Response

Writing About Literature

Students' explanations should

- refer to the imagery of the wind and the clouds and their impact on Annabel.
- quote passages and explain how each affects the theme.
- not overlook images of touch, such as the word *chilling*.

Literature Groups

Students may have different opinions on the validity of the idea. As for the speaker, more than likely he would agree with it. **COLLAB. LEARN.**

Personal Writing

Suggest that students include the details of the event as well as their handling of it.

Listening and Speaking

Students might add to the festivities with costumes and props of one kind or another.

Skill Minilesson

GRAMMAR AND LANGUAGE

- **PUNCTUATING POETRY**

Suggest that students focus on the poet's use of punctuation as a means of telling readers when to pause or stop. This kind of direction can help readers understand poetry more readily.

Additional Resources

- *Grammar and Language Workbook,* pp. 253–254
- *Grammar and Composition Handbook,* Lesson 13.1
- *Writer's Choice,* Lesson 20.1

Extending Your Response

Writing About Literature

Imagery Imagery is the use of words that appeal to the senses. What kinds of images does the poet use in "Annabel Lee"? How do these images support the themes of the poem? Write a paragraph exploring these questions.

Literature Groups

Poet's Corner Have you ever heard the expression, "It is better to have loved and lost than never to have loved at all"? What does it mean? Do you agree or disagree? How do you think the speaker in "Annabel Lee" would feel about the expression? In a small group, discuss the expression and how it relates to the poem.

Personal Writing

Facing the Unexpected Review your notes from the **Focus Activity** on page 628. Then write a journal entry about a time when something difficult or unexpected happened to you or someone you know. Describe how you dealt with the situation.

Listening and Speaking

A Poe Festival Find copies of other poems by Poe, such as "The Raven," as well as some of his famous horror stories, such as "The Tell-Tale Heart." Bring in appropriate background music to play as you take turns reading stories and poems aloud to one another.

Edgar Allan Poe, 1915. Charles Claude Buck. Pen and ink, ink wash, and charcoal on paper, 25.2 x 17.8 cm. National Museum of American Art, Smithsonian Institution, Washington, DC. Gift of Mrs. Claude Buck.

Reading Further

If you would like to read more by Edgar Allan Poe, try these books:
Great Tales and Poems of Edgar Allan Poe
Six Tales of Mystery and Imagination

Save your work for your portfolio.

Skill Minilesson

GRAMMAR AND LANGUAGE • PUNCTUATING POETRY

In some poems, each line ends with some kind of punctuation; other poems use no punctuation at all, not even a final period. In writing, most punctuation takes the place of pauses in speech. A poet's punctuation will help you read and understand the poem. When a poet does not use punctuation, you need to think more carefully about the meanings of the words and about the ideas the words express.

PRACTICE Choose two or three poems from this book or elsewhere. Examine the kinds of punctuation used by the poets. Quote examples of the different kinds of punctuation you found and explain how effective each one is in communicating the poet's ideas.

● For more about punctuation, see **Language Handbook,** pp. R36–R43.

✔ ASSESSMENT OPTIONS

- *Quick Checks,* p. 53
- *Selection and Theme Assessment,* p. 93
- *Performance Assessment,* p. 50
- *Testmaker*

Vo·cab·u·lar·y Skills

Multiple-Meaning Words

Most words have more than one meaning. The meanings may be different only in terms of what parts of speech they are. "I saw a *beam* of light" (noun) and "The moon never *beams* without bringing me dreams" (verb) both use meanings of *beam* that have to do with rays of light. The meanings also may be quite different. "I hit my head on a *beam*" uses a meaning that has nothing to do with light.

Sometimes one meaning of a word is familiar and another is not. A reader who assumes that the familiar meaning is the right one may misunderstand what he or she is reading. In "The Highwayman," Tim the ostler is described as "*dumb* as a dog." This doesn't mean that Tim (or a dog) is stupid. It means that Tim is silent. He says nothing, and his silence allows him to eavesdrop. The context of a sentence reveals what part of speech a word is and may also give clues to the meaning of the word.

EXERCISE

Look at the definition for each word. Then choose the sentence that uses a *different* meaning for the word.

1. catch: *to seize and hold; capture*

   a. I hope I catch my train.

   b. I hope the police catch the criminal.

2. safe: *free from harm.*

   a. She felt safe once she had locked the door behind her.

   b. She opened the safe and removed her diamond bracelet.

3. graze: *to feed on grass*

   a. The horse grazed all afternoon in the pasture.

   b. The horse just grazed me as he galloped past.

4. return: *a profit from an investment*

   a. I look forward to your return from school.

   b. I invested my savings and made a good return.

5. medium: *something in the middle*

   a. I need this sweater in a medium, not a large.

   b. Copper is a good medium for conducting electricity.

Vo·cab·u·lar·y Skills

Objective

- To recognize multiple-meaning words and use them correctly

Teaching Strategies

Have students list as many multiple-meaning words, or homographs, as they can. Point out that multiple-meaning words are different from homophones, since homophones may sound the same but can be spelled differently, such as *seize* and *seas*. Multiple-meaning words, homographs, are spelled alike.

Have students work in pairs to come up with riddles describing multiple-meaning words. For example: *I can draw a pig and keep it from running away. (I am the word* pen.) Encourage them to pose their riddles to the class or to other pairs of students.

Exercise

1. a
2. b
3. b
4. a
5. b

Additional Resources

📁 *Vocabulary Power: Weekly Lessons and Activities*

Teaching Options

MEETING INDIVIDUAL NEEDS — ENGLISH LANGUAGE LEARNERS

Multiple-Meaning Words English language learners may need extra practice to understand multiple-meaning words.

Activity Have English language learners and English-proficient students work in small groups to write sentences with alternate meanings of each of the words defined on this page: *catch, safe, graze, return,* and *medium.* Students may also wish to create charts listing other words with multiple meanings. Make dictionaries available to aid students.

Additional Resources

📁 *English Language Learners Sourcebook*

Objective

- To read and understand an oral history

Respond

1. Some students may mention the snow that begins to melt in the spring and causes flooding, avalanches, and landslides.
2. Students who would like to live in the Yukon might appreciate the natural beauty of the region, the wildlife, the northern lights, and the fact that it is an unusual place—not too developed or populated. Students who would not like to live there would probably find the Yukon too cold, isolated, and barren.

Additional Resources

Media Connections, p. 12

Teaching Options

interNET CONNECTION

The Yukon Have students use a search engine to find information about traveling in the Yukon. Suggest that they try entering keywords such as *Yukon* and *Yukon Territory.*

MEDIA
Connection

ORAL HISTORY

Oral history is based on the spoken words of people who lived through an event or an era. This account relates an experience in the Yukon in the 1890s.

from My Ninety Years

by Martha Louise Black (as told to Elizabeth Bailey Price)

I was still on the lookout for my first bear and was thinking what glory would be mine if I should kill one while alone in camp. Absorbed in these thoughts, still conscious of the rustling, grinding noises, I had not looked toward the hill. When I did, to my horror I saw the whole hillside slowly moving toward the cabin, and gaining momentum. A landslide! The quick thaw had loosened the upper stratum of earth and made it into a river of mud that was carrying everything before it.

I dashed into the cabin again. I seized the baby, wrapped him in a shawl, put on my own coat, and paralyzed with fright, stood at the corner of the cabin, wondering desperately what move to make, if any. I knew I was in terrible danger. . . .

The onrushing avalanche was halted by a clump of trees seventy feet above the cabin. The mud, rocks, snow, and small trees piled up

against them. Deeply rooted, they held firmly. In a moment the roaring river of mud started to move again, but the trees had split the avalanche. The heavier right half cleared our cabin, uprooted a tree, and swept with it two cabins below, depositing its debris on the bosom of the Yukon. The left passed more closely, carried with it our outhouses, and finally lost itself in the more securely frozen ground below us.

Realizing our narrow escape from a horrible death, and trembling from head to foot, I tottered into the cabin. . . . Looking out, I knew that it was not a bad dream, for the hillside was cleared of its surface, and gleamed like the earth of a new-cut furrow.

Hearing the terrific barking of dogs, I went to the door. I gazed upon a scene of magnificent beauty—enormous iceblocks coursing down the river, swirling in swift-frothing eddies. And, sitting on a huge ice-cake, hurtling by in mid-stream, was a bobcat, with a frantic pack of huskies in hot pursuit along the river bank.

Respond

1. Why might early spring be an especially dangerous time in the Yukon?
2. Martha Louise Black not only survived, but she thrived in the Yukon Territory. Would you like to live in the Yukon? Why or why not?

Reading Minilesson

Sequencing This selection describes a situation in which a dangerous sequence of events leads Martha to fear for her life and the life of her infant son.

Activity Have students work in groups to create a pictorial sequence of events for the story. Suggest that they use their own illustrations or pictures cut out of magazines to create storyboards that detail the sequence of events described in *My Ninety Years*. The events should be numbered in sequence, and a brief description of each event should be included with the illustration or magazine photo. **L2 COLLAB. LEARN.**

Additional Resources

Reading Workbook

Before You Read
The Cremation of Sam McGee

MEET ROBERT W. SERVICE

While writing poems about the rugged Yukon Territory and the wild, colorful characters found there, Robert Service was working in the unromantic job of bank teller. His life, however, was certainly not dull. At one time or another, he tried working in professional sports, the theater, construction, journalism, and several other jobs. As a writer, he produced poetry, novels, and autobiography. He is best remembered today as the author of "The Cremation of Sam McGee" and a few other poems set in the Yukon Territory.

Robert W. Service was born in England in 1874 and died in France in 1958.

FOCUS ACTIVITY

Have you ever been *really* cold—so cold that you thought you would never get warm again?

Chart It!

Think about your experiences in bitter cold weather, or close your eyes and imagine how it feels. Chart the sensory details that describe the cold you remember or imagine.

Sight	Sound	Touch	Smell	Taste

Setting a Purpose

Read the following narrative poem to find out what happens to Sam McGee.

BACKGROUND

Did You Know? The Yukon Territory of Canada, named for the Yukon River, is north of British Columbia and east of Alaska. Winters there are long and hard, with average temperatures between 0 and −20 degrees Fahrenheit. As in Alaska, the far northern part of the territory is often called "the land of the midnight sun" because in summer the sun never sets. Mining has been the leading economic activity in the territory since a gold strike in 1896 brought more than thirty thousand adventurers to the region.

Before Reading

Objectives

- To read a poem for entertainment
- To read and understand the use of end and internal rhyme
- To write about the use of vivid adjectives and figurative language

Skills

Reading/Thinking: Evaluating; Drawing Conclusions; Identifying Main Idea and Supporting Details; Sequence of Events
Writing: Television News Report
Vocabulary: Slang
Grammar/Language: Semicolons
Listening/Speaking: Radio Show; Reading Aloud
Collaboration: Radio Show; Literature Groups

Motivating
→OPTIONS

Selection Focus Transparency 54: Use the transparency to have students think about what it is to feel bitterly cold.

Focus Activity: As an extension of the Focus Activity, have pairs of students share their experiences with cold as well as the sensory details they have charted.

RESOURCE MANAGER

Lesson Planning Resource
The *Theme Six Planning Guide* (pp. 65–72) provides additional lesson notes and reduced versions of all print resources.

📁 **Other Print Resources**
- Active Reading Guide, p. 54
- Reading Workbook, pp. 95–96
- Grammar and Language Workbook, pp. 265–266
- Grammar and Composition

Handbook, Lesson 13.5
- Quick Checks, p. 54
- Selection and Theme Assessment, p. 94
- Performance Assessment, p. 51
- Spanish Summaries, p. 54
- Spanish Translations
- Inclusion Strategies
- English Language Learners Sourcebook

🖨 **Transparencies**
- Selection Focus 54
- Literary Elements 54
- Grammar and Language 52

Technology
🎧 Audio Library
🎧 Spanish Audio Library
💻 Glencoe Literature Web Site
💾 Testmaker

Reading the Selection

A Active Reading

VISUALIZE Ask students to read the first stanza and visualize the setting of the poem. Have them use text clues such as the *midnight sun, men prospecting for gold,* and *northern lights* to help them visualize the scene.

Additional Resources

📁 *Active Reading Guide,* p. 54

🎧 *Audio Library*

🎧 *Spanish Audio Library*

Teaching Options

North (Greenland). (detail). Rockwell Kent (1882–1971). 33¹⁵⁄₁₆ x 44¹⁄₁₆ in. Peter Brady Collection, Rockwell Kent Legacies, Au Sable, NY. Service's poem begins: "There are strange things done in the midnight sun." Does this painting give you any ideas about why people might do strange things in the far north? How would you feel if you lived in a place where it was always cold and the sun never set in summer and never rose in winter?

CONNECTING TO OTHER SELECTIONS

The chart at the right shows three ways to connect "The Cremation of Sam McGee" to other selections in this book.

For specific teaching strategies, see the **Theme Six Planning Guide,** pages 68–69.

Connection	Title
Life Skills: Problem Solving	→ "After Twenty Years," p. 565
Thematic: Death	→ "Annabel Lee," p. 629
Literary: Narrative Poem	→ "The Wreck of the Hesperus," p. 227

THE CREMATION OF SAM MCGEE

Robert Service ❧

There are strange things done in the midnight sun
   By the men who moil° for gold;
The Arctic trails have their secret tales
   That would make your blood run cold;
5 The Northern Lights have seen queer sights,
   But the queerest they ever did see
Was that night on the marge,° of Lake Lebarge
   I cremated Sam McGee.

Now Sam McGee was from Tennessee,
   where the cotton blooms and blows.
10 Why he left his home in the South to roam 'round the Pole,
   God only knows.
He was always cold, but the land of gold seemed to hold him
   like a spell;
Though he'd often say in his homely° way that
   "he'd sooner live in hell."

On a Christmas Day we were mushing° our way
   over the Dawson° trail.
Talk of your cold! through the parka's fold it stabbed
   like a driven nail.

---

2 To *moil* is to work hard.
7 *Marge* is an old word for *margin,* or edge.
12 Here, *homely* means "simple; ordinary."
13 Driving a dogsled is *mushing* because the driver says "Mush!" to order the dogs to begin pulling or to move faster. Early French fur traders in Canada used the command *Marchons!* (meaning "March! Go!"), but English and American dogsledders mispronounced it, saying "Mush on!" *Dawson* is a city in the old gold-mining region of Canada's Yukon Territory.

B Literary Elements

FORESHADOW Ask students how the first two lines of the poem foreshadow a strange event in the narrative. *(They warn that "strange things" happen in the midnight sun.)*

VIEWING THE PAINTING

Rockwell Kent (1882–1971), artist, author, and political activist, was born in Tarrytown, New York. His work, which was a reflection of his life in the harsh climates of Maine, Alaska, Greenland, and the Adirondacks, often portrayed the bleak and rugged aspects of nature.

Viewing Response *Anyone who lives in the isolation imposed by a bitterly cold, harsh climate in a bleak landscape of such monumental proportions might be driven to do strange things.*

C Literary Elements

RHYME: *Internal* Ask students to find examples of internal rhyme in the poem. *(Some examples of internal rhyme include done/sun, trails/tales, lights/sights, marge/Lebarge, McGee/Tennessee, home/roam, cold/gold/hold.)*

D Literary Elements

FIGURES OF SPEECH: *Simile* Ask students what two things are being compared in line 14. Ask how the two, which are not similar in nature, are alike. *(The cold and a driven nail are compared. The cold pierces the body so sharply that it feels like a nail being driven into the skin.)*

ENGLISH LANGUAGE LEARNERS

Ancient Burial Rites English language learners may not appreciate the poem unless they fully understand the meaning of the word *cremation.* Explain that, after people die, their corpses are burned instead of buried. It is a practice that dates back thousands of years and is still practiced by some groups and individuals.

Activity Have students discuss in small groups their knowledge of cremation. Have each student research his or her family's or religion's view of cremation and report back to the group. **L2**
COLLAB. LEARN.

Additional Resources
📁 *English Language Learners Sourcebook*

E Literary Elements

RHYME: *Internal* Point out to students that each line of the poem actually takes up two lines on the page. To help them understand this, ask them to count the lines between the line numbers 20 and 25. Explain that line 21 begins with the word *Well* and ends with *moan.* Challenge them to identify the internal rhyme in line 21. *(The internal rhyme is low/no.)*

Vo•cab•u•lar•y Skills

Slang The phrase *cash in* (line 19) is a slang expression that means *"die." Cash in* comes from gambling and refers to gamblers turning in their chips for cash when they are finished gambling.

F Literary Elements

SOUND DEVICES: *Alliteration* Point out that much of the entertainment value of the poem comes from its use of sound devices, such as alliteration. Alliteration is the repetition of a sound, most often a consonant sound, at the beginning of words. Ask students to identify alliterative words in this stanza. *(Alliterative words are hurried/horror and half/hid.)*

15 If our eyes we'd close, then the lashes froze till
      sometimes we couldn't see;
    It wasn't much fun, but the only one to whimper
      was Sam McGee.

    And that very night, as we lay packed tight
      in our robes beneath the snow,
    And the dogs were fed, and the stars o'erhead
      were dancing heel and toe,
    He turned to me, and "Cap," says he,
      "I'll cash in this trip, I guess;
20 And if I do, I'm asking that you won't refuse
      my last request."

    Well, he seemed so low that I couldn't say no;
      then he says with a sort of moan:
    "It's the cursèd cold, and it's got right hold till
      I'm chilled clean through to the bone.
    Yet 'tain't being dead—it's my awful dread of the
      icy grave that pains;
    So I want you to swear that, foul or fair, you'll
      cremate° my last remains."

25 A pal's last need is a thing to heed,° so I swore
      I would not fail;
    And we started on at the streak of dawn; but God!
      he looked ghastly pale.
    He crouched on the sleigh, and he raved all day
      of his home in Tennessee;
    And before nightfall a corpse was all that was left
      of Sam McGee.

    There wasn't a breath in that land of death,
      and I hurried, horror driven,
30 With a corpse half hid that I couldn't get rid,
      because of a promise given;

---

24 To *cremate* a body is to burn it rather than bury it.
25 To *heed* is to give careful attention.

638

Teaching Options

Reading *Minilesson*

Identifying Main Idea and Supporting Details Remind students that in a poem, every detail serves to help convey the main idea or some aspect supporting the main idea, such as an image or a mood. Explain that readers must keep track of these details as they read to fully appreciate the poem.

Activity Have students use a chart to jot down details from the poem that convey how cold it is and Sam's condition. Then have students gather in small groups to discuss how the author's use of details made the narrative more believable. **L2** COLLAB. LEARN.

How Cold	Sam's Condition
line 14, (cold) stabbed like a driven nail	line 15, lashes frozen
line 17, robes beneath the snow	line 22, chilled to the bone; dreads an icy grave

Additional Resources

Reading Workbook, pp. 95–96

638

It was lashed to the sleigh, and it seemed to say:
  "You may tax° your brawn° and brains,
But you promised true, and it's up to you
  to cremate those last remains."

Now a promise made is a debt unpaid,
  and the trail has its own stern code.
In the days to come, though my lips were dumb,
  in my heart how I cursed that load.
35 In the long, long night, by the lone firelight,
  while the huskies, round in a ring,
Howled out their woes to the homeless snows—O God!
  how I loathed° the thing.

And every day that quiet clay° seemed to
  heavy and heavier grow;
And on I went, though the dogs were spent
  and the grub was getting low;
The trail was bad, and I felt half mad,
  but I swore I would not give in;
40 And I'd often sing to the hateful thing, and
  it hearkened with a grin.

Till I came to the marge of Lake Lebarge,
  and a derelict° there lay;
It was jammed in the ice, but I saw in a trice°
  it was called the "Alice May."
And I looked at it, and I thought a bit, and
  I looked at my frozen chum;
Then "Here," said I, with a sudden cry,
  "is my cre-ma-tor-eum."

45 Some planks I tore from the cabin floor,
  and I lit the boiler fire;
Some coal I found that was lying around,
  and I heaped the fuel higher;

---

31 Here, *tax* means "place a heavy burden on," and *brawn* means "muscle; strength."
36 To *loathe* is to feel great hatred.
37 The *quiet clay* is Sam's body.
41 A *derelict* is an abandoned ship.
42 Here, *trice* means "a very short time; a moment."

639

G Critical Thinking

EVALUATING Ask students what is implied by the speaker's use of the word *it* here. *(Sam is dead now—a corpse—not a living person.)*

H Critical Thinking

DRAWING CONCLUSIONS Ask students what conclusions they can draw about the speaker's feelings toward Sam. *(The speaker hates carrying Sam's body around, and the promise weighs heavily on his conscience.)*

I Active Reading

RESPOND Ask students what the speaker refers to when he swears "I would not give in." *(The speaker is exhausted physically. It would be easier for him to leave the corpse to lighten his load, but he plans to honor his promise to Sam.)*

J Literary Elements

PLOT: *Climax* Ask students if they think that finding the "cre-ma-tor-eum" can be considered the climax in this narrative poem. *(Students will probably agree, since it provides a solution to the speaker's problem of how to fulfill the promise he made to Sam.)*

Listening and Speaking *Minilesson*

Reading Aloud Explain to students that the content and the musical quality of the poem render it a perfect poem for reading aloud. It is a perfect poem for sharing around a campfire at night with a group of friends.

Activity Individually or in small groups, have students practice giving a dramatic reading of the poem. Encourage them to practice emphasizing the most interesting rhymes and the lines they want their friends to enjoy most. Then have individuals or groups perform their readings for the class. **L2** **COLLAB. LEARN.**

Literary Elements

K **IMAGERY** Ask students how the imagery in this stanza reflects the internal struggle of the speaker. *(The speaker's distaste for the cremation is reflected in the images of the fire, the wind blowing, and the black smoke streaking the sky.)*

Author's Craft

L **POINT OF VIEW** Ask students if the poet's use of the first-person point of view makes this story more exciting to the reader. *(Some students will say it does, because they feel the speaker's struggle and discomfort with the promise he made to a dying man.)*

Literary Elements

M **MOOD** Ask students how the mood in the tale has changed from one of anguish to one of joy. *(The speaker describes Sam McGee as looking "cool and calm" instead of raving and ghostly, creating an uplifting mood.)*

Thematic Focus

Twists and Turns Have students discuss other strange twists and turns they have experienced or heard about, whether in real life or in stories.

✔ ASSESSMENT OPTIONS

📁 **Quick Checks**, p. 54

The flames just soared, and the furnace roared—
    such a blaze you seldom see;
And I burrowed a hole in the glowing coal,
    and I stuffed in Sam McGee.

Then I made a hike, for I didn't like
    to hear him sizzle so;
50 And the heavens scowled, and the huskies howled,
    and the wind began to blow.
It was icy cold, but the hot sweat rolled down my cheeks,
    and I don't know why;
And the greasy smoke in an inky cloak
    went streaking down the sky.

I do not know how long in the snow
    I wrestled with grisly fear;
But the stars came out and they danced about
    ere° again I ventured near;
55 I was sick with dread, but I bravely said:
    "I'll just take a peep inside.
I guess he's cooked, and it's time I looked,"
    . . . then the door I opened wide.

And there sat Sam, looking cool and calm,
    in the heart of the furnace roar;
And he wore a smile you could see a mile, and he said:
    "Please close that door.
It's fine in here, but I greatly fear
    you'll let in the cold and storm—
60 Since I left Plumtree, down in Tennessee,
    it's the first time I've been warm."

There are strange things done in the midnight sun
    By the men who moil for gold;
The Arctic trails have their secret tales
    That would make your blood run cold;
65 *The Northern Lights have seen queer sights,*
    But the queerest they ever did see
Was that night on the marge of Lake Lebarge
    I cremated Sam McGee.

---

54 *Ere* (âr) is an old word for *before.*

640

Teaching Options

Grammar and Language *Minilesson*

Semicolons Point out the author's frequent use of the semicolon. The semicolon is generally used to join parts of a compound sentence or two independent clauses closely related in thought. Explain the thought relationship of the clauses joined by the semicolon in lines 51–52. *(These lines describe the cold and smoke— images of the setting.)*

Activity Have students work with partners to determine the thought relationships in the following lines:
1. lines 15–16 *(describe responses to the bitter cold)*
2. lines 19–20 *(Sam knows he is about to die and asks the narrator to honor his last request.)*
3. lines 45–46 *(describe how the narrator builds a fire)* **L2** **COLLAB. LEARN.**

Additional Resources

🖌 *Grammar and Language Transparency 52*

📕 *Grammar and Language Workbook,* pp. 265–266

📕 *Grammar and Composition Handbook,* Lesson 13.5

📕 *Writer's Choice,* Lesson 20.5

Responding to Literature

PERSONAL RESPONSE

: Were you surprised by the ending of the poem? Why or
: why not?

Analyzing Literature

RECALL

1. Where did Sam McGee come from?
2. Why did Sam request that he be cremated?
3. Describe the twist at the end of the poem.

INTERPRET

4. What phrases in the opening stanza (lines 1–8) of "The Cremation of Sam McGee" **foreshadow** the strange plot twist in the poem? (See **Literary Terms Handbook,** page R4.)
5. How does Service use **humor** in the narration of this strange tale? Give examples to support your opinion.
6. What is the central conflict in the plot of the poem? How is the conflict resolved?

EVALUATE AND CONNECT

7. Describe the relationship between the speaker and Sam McGee. What attitude toward friendship is expressed in the poem?
8. Imagery plays an important part in this poem. Pick out your favorite image from the poem and explain why you like it.
9. Personal Connection   Does reading this poem make you want to visit the Yukon? Why or why not?
10. Theme Connection   How does the speaker of the poem deal with the unexpected event that occurs during the trip?

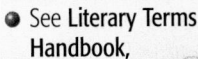

LITERARY ELEMENTS

Rhyme

The most common type of rhyme in poetry is **end rhyme**, rhyme that occurs at the ends of lines. An example is the words *gold* and *cold* at the ends of lines 2 and 4. **Internal rhyme,** on the other hand, occurs within a single line of poetry—for example, the words *done* and *sun* in line 1.

1. Find and quote at least two other examples of internal and end rhymes in the poem.
2. Write a short poem about cold (or hot) weather. Then mark the rhyme pattern of your poem.

● See **Literary Terms Handbook,** p. R9.

Personal Response

If they were surprised, encourage students to discuss how they thought the poem might end.

Analyzing Literature

1. Sam came from Tennessee.
2. Sam wanted to be cremated because he hated the cold and dreaded the thought of being buried in an icy grave.
3. At the end of the poem, after building a fire and throwing Sam's body into it, the speaker returns to find Sam sitting up and talking.
4. The strange plot twist at the end may be foreshadowed by phrases such as: "strange things done," "queer sights," and "queerest."
5. Part of Service's humor comes from the situation and the speaker's manner of telling about it. For example: in lines 42–44, he rhymes "frozen chum" with "cre-ma-tor-eum."
6. The central conflict is in the speaker's distaste for the act of cremating his friend and his obligation to do it.
7. The men do not seem to be close, and the speaker even seems annoyed by Sam's "whimpering," but there is a bond and a loyalty formed by their being together for so long in a challenging environment.
8. Favorite imagery may include: lines 13–14, the cold "stabbed like a driven nail"; line 15, "lashes froze"; lines 36–37, huskies "howled"; lines 49–50, "to hear him sizzle" and "the heavens howled."

9. Some may want to visit the Yukon because they are attracted by nature; others may not fancy the idea of experiencing such cold temperatures.
10. The speaker agonizes over his promise, but he fulfills it.

LITERARY ELEMENTS

1. *End rhyme* includes: "blows/knows"; "spell/hell"; and "trail/nail." *Internal rhyme* includes: "fed/o'erhead"; "me/he"; and "dead/dread."
2. Suggest that students try to use both end and internal rhyme.

Additional Resources

Literary Elements Transparency 54

Extending Your Response

Literature Groups

Students might have different opinions about the poem's being a tall tale. Have students use specifics in making a case for or against the poem's being a tall tale. **COLLAB. LEARN.**

Performing

Some students may do the reading and others the sound effects, then reverse roles.

Writing About Literature

Students' paragraphs should
- begin with a topic sentence expressing the writer's attitude in general terms.
- refer to the imagery of the wind and cold, including images of sound and touch as well as sight.
- explain how each image affects them.

Creative Writing

Students' paragraphs should
- include quotations from eyewitnesses.
- give background information about the members of the Yukon dogsled teams.
- provide background information about the towns or territory.

Skill Minilesson

READING AND THINKING
• SEQUENCE OF EVENTS

Suggest that students focus on the major elements of each event, not on the minor details.

Additional Resources
📁 *Reading Workbook,* pp. 95–96

Extending Your Response

Literature Groups

Tall Tales   A **tall tale** is a kind of folktale in which the characters, their physical traits, and their deeds are often greatly exaggerated in a humorous fashion. Paul Bunyan and John Henry are examples of tall tale heroes. In small groups, talk about whether or not "The Cremation of Sam McGee" is a tall tale. Use examples from the poem to support your opinion.

His Hammer in His Hand. Palmer C. Hayden (1870–1973). From the John Henry Series, Museum of African American Art, Los Angeles. Palmer C. Hayden Collection. Gift of Miriam A. Hayden. Photo by Armando Solis.

Performing

Audio Only   As a class activity, divide the poem into sections and work in small groups to prepare the different sections for a performance of the poem for radio. On radio, you can't depend on an actor's gestures—everything must be done with the voice. However, you can add sound effects, such as blowing wind or the sound of a dogsled. To give the illusion of a radio show, have each group present its segment *behind* the rest of the class.

Writing About Literature

Setting   Pick out examples of vivid adjectives or figurative language that describe either the bitter cold setting or the Yukon landscape. Then review your notes from the **Focus Activity** on page 635. In a short paragraph, explain how the writer's vivid language helps you to "feel" the icy temperatures of the setting as if you were there.

Creative Writing

Wilderness Report   Turn the plot of "The Cremation of Sam McGee" into a television news report. Add any details you need to create the report, including eyewitness interviews with members of other Yukon dogsled trips as well as local weather reports.

Reading Further

If you would like to read more by Robert Service, try *The Best of Robert Service*

📖 **Save your work for your portfolio.**

Skill Minilesson

READING AND THINKING   • SEQUENCE OF EVENTS

The events in a story should take place in a logical order. That is, the reader should be able to see how each event leads to the next one. Most stories follow chronological order, the time order in which the events naturally happen.

PRACTICE   Reread the poem. As you do, make a list of the events in the poem in the order in which they occur.

● For more on sequence, see **Reading Handbook,** p. R87.

642   🐾   THEME 6

✓ ASSESSMENT OPTIONS

📁 *Quick Checks,* p. 54

📁 *Selection and Theme Assessment,* p. 94

📁 *Performance Assessment,* p. 51

💾 *Testmaker*

Reading and Thinking Skills

Identifying Cause-and-Effect Relationships

In a **cause-and-effect relationship,** one event or action causes other things to happen. For example, a character does something wrong (cause) and then feels guilty about what he or she did (effect). The character may then try to correct the wrong that was done (a new effect caused by the character's feelings of guilt).

For example, consider this passage from "After Twenty Years."

> The policeman on the beat moved up the avenue impressively. . . . The time was barely 10 o'clock at night, but chilly gusts of wind with a taste of rain in them had well-nigh depeopled the streets.

This passage contains a cause and its effect. The effect, or result, is the almost empty streets. The cause, or reason, is that chilly winds and the possibility of rain have kept people indoors.

As you try to identify cause-and-effect relationships in the literature you read, always look for clue words like *because, since, as a result,* and *so.* However, the causes of narrative events are not always stated directly. When the cause is not obvious to you, look back over the selection to identify it.

● For more on cause and effect, see **Reading Handbook,** p. R85.

ACTIVITY

Read the following passage from "The Force of Luck." Then answer the questions.

> On the way home he [the miller] was attacked by a hawk that had smelled the meat which the miller carried. The miller fought off the bird but in the struggle he lost the bundle of money. Before the miller knew what was happening the hawk grabbed the bag and flew away with it.

1. What caused the hawk to attack the miller?
2. What effect did the hawk's actions have on the miller?

Reading and Thinking Skills

Objective

• To recognize and use strategies for identifying cause-and-effect relationships

Teaching Strategies

Ask students to identify one cause-and-effect relationship for each of the selections in this theme. For example:

Charles
Cause: Laurie's behavior at school
Effect: Laurie invented Charles

No News
Cause: The candle flame lit the curtains
Effect: The house burned down

Who's on First
Cause: A baseball player named "Who"
Effect: Confusion about players' names

The Million-Pound Bank Note
Cause: A bet between two brothers
Effect: A man becomes rich

Activity

1. The hawk smelled the meat that the miller was carrying.
2. The miller fought off the bird, but in the struggle he lost the money he had been given.

Additional Resources
📂 *Reading Workbook,* pp. 95–96

Teaching Options

MEETING INDIVIDUAL NEEDS INCLUSION STRATEGIES

Less-proficient readers may find it challenging to identify cause-and-effect relationships in what they read, especially in long selections.

Activity Have students complete the diagram as shown. Then have them work in groups to complete diagrams for a different story. **L1** **COLLAB. LEARN.**

Cause	Effect
The hawk smelled the meat.	The hawk attacked the miller.

Additional Resources
 Inclusion Strategies

Writing WORKSHOP

Objectives

- To create a personal response to literature
- To plan, draft, revise, edit, and present a short story
- To reflect on and assess one's short story

GLENCOE
TECHNOLOGY

WRITER'S ASSISTANT CD-ROM
Students can use Glencoe's templates and guidelines software for narrative writing to aid them in working through the steps in the writing process in the lesson.

Teaching Strategies

PREWRITING

Search for story ideas In addition to answering the questions in their books, students should consider the mysterious elements contained in each poem. Exploring a mysterious character or situation can be an intriguing task for a short story writer.

Writing WORKSHOP

Narrative Writing: Short Story

As you've learned from the narrative poems in this theme, a poem can tell a story—and it can hint at stories left untold. When you explore these untold stories, you gain deeper insight into the poem and into your imagination. Take a few moments to review the three narrative poems in this theme. Whose stories do they tell? What stories do they leave untold?

Assignment: Follow the process explained in this Workshop to write a short story based on a poem.

● As you write your short story, refer to the **Writing Handbook,** pp. R48–R53.

The Writing Process

PREWRITING

PREWRITING TIP
Imagine a meeting between characters from two poems. What if the speaker in "Annabel Lee" met Bess, of "The Highwayman"? What story might unfold then?

TECHNOLOGY TIP
Use your computer to create separate files for several story ideas. If one doesn't work out, you can switch to another.

● Search for Story Ideas

Look again at "The Highwayman," "Annabel Lee," and "The Cremation of Sam McGee." Notice that each poem tells the stories of at least two characters, including the speakers. Use questions like the following to find story ideas to explore:

- With which character do I most identify?
- Which character do I find most interesting?
- What might have happened before the events in the poems?
- What might happen after the events in the poems?
- What new endings might I give the poems?
- What might a character from one poem do in the setting of another poem?

MEETING INDIVIDUAL NEEDS
ENGLISH LANGUAGE LEARNERS

Elements of Poems Expand the prewriting activity on page 644 to help English language learners recall aspects of the poems they have read.

Activity Have students work in small groups to complete information sheets on each of the three poems in Theme Six. Write the following questions on the board:
1. What is the title of the poem and who is the poet?
2. Who are the main characters?
3. What words does the poet use to describe the setting?
4. What happens in the poem?
COLLAB. LEARN.

Additional Resources
📁 *English Language Learners Sourcebook*

Writing WORKSHOP

● Make a Plan

Choose a story idea that intrigues you. Then explore it by filling in a story map like the following one. You can borrow details of setting, characters, point of view, and plot from the poem(s) in this theme, or you might create your own variations.

Characters:	The highwayman, Bess, Tim (the ostler), captain, soldiers
Setting:	an old inn in the late 1700s
Point of view:	third person; Tim's
Plot:	Tim, jealous of the highwayman, informs the captain of the thief's pledge to return to Bess, but his plot results in Bess's death.

● Choose Your Audience and Purpose

Will your story entertain, amuse, or perhaps provide some chills? Will it be a children's story, a tale for your classmates to enjoy, or a story for a mixed audience, such as the readers of a popular magazine? These decisions help you plan your writing. Children may need vivid action and simple language. A mixed audience might not understand the same literary terms or references that your classmates would.

● Put Events in Order

The events in a story may or may not be given in chronological order. Filling in a sequence chart like the one below can help you organize the events.

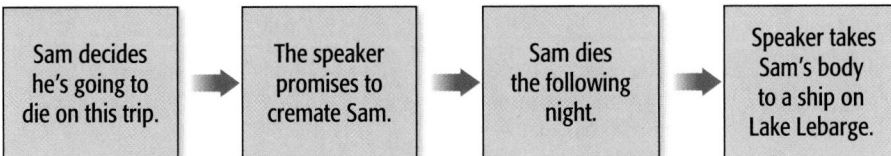

Sam decides he's going to die on this trip. → The speaker promises to cremate Sam. → Sam dies the following night. → Speaker takes Sam's body to a ship on Lake Lebarge.

Make a plan Suggest that students work in pairs to bounce their story ideas around. Point out that the planning phase of the writing process is the one that many writers love most—the possibilities are endless. A story starts with an idea but has a way of taking on a life of its own once the writer begins writing. A good plan helps the writer stay focused on the story yet remain open to colorful details and plot twists as they arise.

Choose your audience and purpose Remind students to consider their audience as they write their stories. The poems in Theme Six have elements in them that might frighten children, but these same elements could provide chilling excitement for older readers.

Put events in order Encourage students to fill in sequence charts like the one in their book. They may wish to expand the charts to include supporting details for each event.

Additional Resources

📁 ***Writing and Proofreading Practice,*** pp. 1–7, 43–49

🖋 ***Writing and Proofreading Transparencies 1–6, 21–22, 35–36***

📘 ***Writer's Choice,*** Lesson 4.3

MEETING INDIVIDUAL NEEDS — MULTIPLE LEARNING STYLES

Intrapersonal While certain steps in the writing process can be enhanced by group or pair activities, the act of writing itself is often a quiet, personal pursuit. Students who display strong intrapersonal learning capabilities may find it necessary to create a nonclassroom environment conducive to creative writing.

Activity Give students time to list places they like to go when they are alone. Have each student imagine or draw the ideal writing place: a place to be alone with one's thoughts. Help students explore the options available at school, such as the library, an office, or an outdoor space. Encourage each of them to find or make a special place in which to write a story. **L2**

Create an opening Write a few opening lines from stories you like on the board and tell students why you like them. You may wish to have an anthology of short stories in the classroom for students to look through to see how other writers started their stories.

Draft your story Suggest that students write the first drafts of their stories without being too critical of their writing. If they have followed the prewriting steps in the Writing Workshop, they have already done a lot of preparation for the assignment. As they sit down with pen and paper, they should think of themselves as writers—not editors.

Map out changes During the revision process, students should work with partners to discuss the changes they want to make in their stories. Since this may be the first time the class has written stories with plots, partners can help each other find "holes" in the plots—where an event seems out of sequence or is missing altogether. You may wish to have students read their stories aloud and invite partners to tell the stories back to the writers.

Teaching Options

Writing WORKSHOP

DRAFTING

DRAFTING TIP
Don't try to explain too much about your characters. Instead, reveal details about them through their actions, thoughts, and words.

● Create an Opening

You can pull readers into your story with any of several types of openers:

- an intriguing line of dialogue
- an image of a character in action (even a small action, such as a sigh)
- a mysterious comment about the story to come

Then move right into your chain of events.

● Draft Your Story

Be sure to include transitions, such as *next, soon, before that, afterwards, later,* or *meanwhile* to keep the order of events clear for your readers.

MODEL · DRAFTING

Meanwhile, Tim had devised a plan to capture the highwayman. First, Bess must be prevented from signaling the scoundrel.

"Only later will she appreciate my heroic deed," thought Tim.

REVISING

REVISING TIP
One way to give your story a "finished" feel is to refer again to something from the opening, perhaps showing it in a new light.

● Map Out Changes

Plan a short break before you revise. Then take a new look at your story. Is it on its way toward creating the effects you had hoped for? Using the **Questions for Revising,** map out improvements. A peer reader can offer useful feedback and ideas.

QUESTIONS FOR REVISING
☑ Which other part of my story might create a more interesting opening?
☑ Which parts move too slowly?
☑ Where might I add details to make my characters or setting easier to visualize?
☑ What transitions might I add to make the order of events clearer?
☑ How do I create a sense of completion at the end of my story?

Writing *Minilesson*

Character Development Introduce techniques that writers use to develop their characters by asking students to list ways in which they get to know people. An opinion of someone, for example, may be based on what the person says, how old the person is, what the person looks like, where the person is from. Explain that a good way to develop a character in fiction is to let the character speak.

Activity Ask students to read aloud the dialogue they have written in their short stories. If their stories do not contain dialogue, encourage students to experiment with putting a few lines of dialogue in. Have students work in pairs to read the dialogue to a partner. Encourage the partner to give his or her impression of the character. Suggest that the writer evaluate this impression and check whether it

matches the way he or she meant the character to be. If not, they should revise their dialogue accordingly. **L2** **COLLAB. LEARN.**

Additional Resources

📖 ***Writer's Choice,*** Lesson 4.4

Writing WORKSHOP

EDITING/PROOFREADING

Use the **Proofreading Checklist** to help you spot and correct errors in grammar, usage, and mechanics. Pay special attention to comma usage, as shown in the **Grammar Link** on page 553.

Grammar Hint

The words *someone, anyone,* and *everyone* are singular. With these words, use singular possessive pronouns such as *his* or *her* instead of the plural pronoun *their.*

In the Yukon, everyone chased his or her dreams of gold.

PROOFREADING CHECKLIST

☑ All pronouns agree with their antecedents. (Double-check agreement with the word *everyone.*)

☑ There are no sentence fragments or run-ons.

☑ All verbs agree with their subjects.

☑ Punctuation is correct.

☑ Spelling and capitalization are correct.

MODEL · EDITING/PROOFREADING

Noyes, Poe, and Robert Service, the three poets in this theme, all wrote narrative poetry, but their poetry is very different.

PUBLISHING/PRESENTING

Read your story aloud to your class, using the guidelines on pages 644–645. If you wrote for children, you might also offer to read your story to an elementary school class. If you wrote for magazine readers, consider submitting your story for publication.

Reflecting

Take time to think over the following questions before writing your responses.

- What was the trickiest part of writing your story? How might you do it differently next time?

- Do you prefer writing fictional stories, like this one, or nonfiction narratives? Explain your preference.

Save your work for your portfolio.

Explain to students that it is often difficult for writers to proofread and edit their own work. Writers often ask a friend to read their writing and circle spelling, grammar, or usage errors. Suggest that students work in pairs or small groups to help one another proofread their stories.

Additional Resources
📁 *Grammar and Composition Handbook,* Lesson 16.4

PUBLISHING/PRESENTING

Students may wish to do readings of their work, the way many writers conduct readings in bookstores, schools, and libraries. You may wish to set up a literary night, when students simulate the experience of "giving a reading." Short stories could also be compiled into a class literary anthology.

Reflecting

Portfolio Have students ask themselves these questions as they review their writing:

- Is my story based on one of the poems we have read in class?
- Does it have a clear sequence of events?
- Does my story include setting, characters, and plot?

✔ ASSESSMENT OPTIONS

📁 *Writing Assessment and Portfolio Management*
- Writing Assessment, pp. 1–16, 35–37
- Portfolio Management, pp. 17–19

Theme Wrap-Up

Objectives

- To offer a personal response to the writers' craft in this theme
- To write a comparison of two narrative poems
- To complete a self-evaluation, set a goal, and devise a plan for achieving the goal

---

Responding to the Theme

1. Students should be able to support their choices with specific examples.
2. Accept all thoughtful answers and observations.
3. Allow time for students to share their incident reports, storytelling performances, and rewritten stories with classmates.

Analyzing Literature

Students' writing should include

- an introductory paragraph that identifies the two poems and the elements they plan to compare.
- examples and details from the poems to support their conclusions.

Evaluate and Set Goals

Evaluate

Have students list the activities they have completed for each task on this page. Suggest that they add other tasks as well, such as interviewing people.

Set Goals

Have each student create a chart on which to record their goals and the steps for achieving them. Discuss students' goals and plans in individual conferences.

Theme Wrap-Up

Responding to the Theme

1. Which selection helped you notice how writers add a spark of the unexpected to their work? Explain your answer.

2. What new ideas do you have about the following as a result of reading the literature in this theme?
   - the role of luck in people's lives
   - how life's ups and downs are part of the normal course of human events

3. Present your theme project to the class.

Analyzing Literature

COMPARE NARRATIVE POEMS

Compare two of the narrative poems from this theme. You may compare the speakers, setting, plot, other characters, or the unexpected turn of events in the plot. Include quotations from the selections in your comparisons.

Evaluate and Set Goals

1. Which of the following tasks was most rewarding to you? Which was most difficult?
   - reading and thinking about the stories, poems, and plays
   - doing independent writing
   - analyzing the selections in discussions
   - performing dramatizations

2. Using the following scale, how would you assess your work in this theme? Give at least two reasons for your assessment.
   4 = outstanding   2 = fair
   3 = good   1 = weak

3. Based on what you found difficult in this theme, choose a goal to work toward in the next theme.
   - Write down your goal and three steps you will take to reach it.
   - Meet with your teacher to review your goal and your plan for achieving it.

Build Your Portfolio

SELECT

Select two pieces of work you did during this theme to include in your portfolio. Use the following questions to help you decide.

- ✦ Which do you consider your best work?
- ✦ From which did you learn the most?
- ✦ Which work challenged you the most?
- ✦ Which work did you enjoy the most?

REFLECT

Write some notes to accompany the work you selected. Use the following questions to guide you.

- ✦ What do you like best about the piece?
- ✦ What did you learn from creating it?
- ✦ What might you do differently if you were beginning this piece again?

 ASSESSMENT OPTIONS

 Writing Assessment and Portfolio Management
- Writing Assessment, pp. 1–16
- Portfolio Management, pp. 17–19

 GLENCOE
TECHNOLOGY

 MINDJOGGER VIDEOQUIZZES
VIDEODISC

Use *MindJogger* to review the Theme 6 content.

Theme 6
Side B

Also available in VHS.

Reading on Your Own

Have you enjoyed reading the literature in this theme? If so, you might be interested in reading the following books.

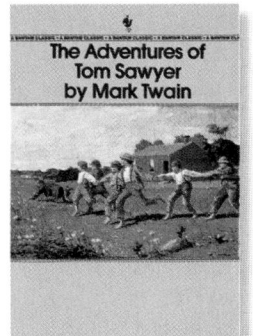

The Adventures of Tom Sawyer

by Mark Twain Twain's classic story has plenty of comic trickery, twists, and turns, including Tom's attending his own funeral.

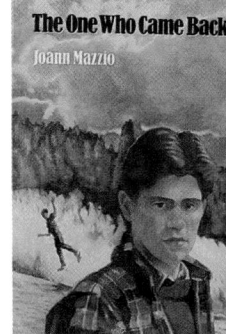

The One Who Came Back

by Joann Mazzio This novel is an adventure story of a friendship between two boys in the mountains of New Mexico. When one of the boys disappears, no one believes the other boy's version of what happened.

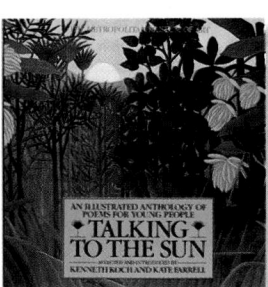

Talking to the Sun

selected by Kenneth Koch and Kate Farrell This anthology of poetry from ancient times to the present is illustrated with reproductions of art works from the Metropolitan Museum of Art in New York.

The Oxford Book of Story Poems

edited by Michael Harrison and Christopher Stuart-Clark This collection of narrative poetry includes classic and modern poems that will make you laugh, poems that will amaze you, and poems that will thrill and chill you.

Reading on Your Own

Glencoe Literature Library

The Adventures of Tom Sawyer by Mark Twain is one of the titles available in the *Glencoe Literature Library*. For a complete listing, see pages T46–T47 in this book.

The *Glencoe Literature Library: Study Guide* provides instructional support and student activities for works in the *Glencoe Library*.

MEETING INDIVIDUAL NEEDS — INCLUSION STRATEGIES

You may wish to recommend to your less-proficient readers *The Oxford Book of Story Poems* edited by Michael Harrison and Christopher Stuart-Clark.

The following books are rated for average readers (**L2**) or for students who need more challenging reading (**L3**):

- *The Adventures of Tom Sawyer* by Mark Twain **L2**
- *The One Who Came Back* by Joann Mazzio **L2**
- *Talking to the Sun* selected by Kenneth Koch and Kate Farrell **L3**

Additional Resources
📁 *Inclusion Strategies*

Standardized Test Practice

Read the following passage. Then read each question on page 651. Decide which is the best answer to each question. Mark the letter for that answer on your paper.

Captain Thomas's Last Flight?

When the first explosion hit the hull of his starship, Captain Hunter Thomas grabbed for the shipwide microphone and began yelling. "Damage report! Blakely! What's happening?"

There was a moment of static on the line before Blakely's voice crackled into Thomas's cabin. "You'd better get to the bridge, Captain. We've got company."

Thomas was already off his bunk, jamming his feet into his flight boots and groping for his tunic. His hands found the belt with his phaser holstered on it, and he slipped it around his waist. He was halfway out the door when Blakely's voice crackled over the intercom again.

"Pirates, Captain. It looks like the Derellians."

Thomas's voice came out in a growl. "How many?"

Another static-filled pause, until Thomas heard, "Five."

Then the ship rocked horribly to starboard, another explosion tearing like a claw into the vital flight and life support mechanisms. With another few blasts like that one, the hull might crack like an eggshell.

Thomas tucked his head and sprinted for the bridge. He arrived to find Blakely whirling about, <u>careening</u> from one control panel to the next, trying to keep the ship's many automated systems running. The look on the first mate's face told Thomas all he needed to know. They were in trouble—very deep trouble.

"What does the damage look like, Blakely?"

Blakely didn't look up. His eyes were glued to a computer screen. His fingers punched furiously at buttons and switches. "Third engine gone. Navigation computer damaged. Pulsar guns disabled."

"Life support status?"

Blakely sighed. "Holding."

Blakely punched the emergency distress signal on the communications console. A red light began to flash, signifying that an all-purpose emergency broadcast was being sent out to any ships in the vicinity. Blakely didn't have much hope that anyone would come, though. Few ships could tangle with a fleet of Derellian pirates.

Thomas gripped the steering controls and aimed straight for the first of the five ships he saw screeching through the deep space outside the glass portal, hoping to avoid its firing range. "Signal all hands to abandon ship, Blakely. Get the crew to safety. See to it personally. I'm going to hold out as long as I can."

Blakely looked at his captain and friend, but said nothing. Thomas was already veering through the inky space between two more ships, dodging their fire. The two men had flown together for two years. Now, seated in the big chair with the top of his head barely visible from behind, Captain Hunter Thomas appeared impossibly small and alone in the sudden gloom that had befallen the bridge.

"Move it, Blakely! Now!"

When Blakely spoke, his voice was little more than a whisper. "Yes, Captain Thomas." He forced his legs to carry him toward the gangway to the escape pods.

The ship rocked once again under the weight of a crushing explosion. Warning lights began to flash, sirens screamed, smoke hissed from the computer consoles of the bridge like steam escaping a cooking pot. Blakely stood straight to salute his good friend Captain Thomas once more before he turned and ran down the gangway, screaming for his crew to board the escape pods and fly away to safety.

A few minutes later, from several miles distance, Blakely stared through the portal of his escape pod and watched distant explosions flower in the infinite night of space. *Goodbye, Captain*, he thought.

Then the loudspeaker squawked and a familiar voice echoed through the cabin of the pod. "Don't give up on me now, Blake. They've given up! We're free and clear!"

The Captain!

"Hang tight, Blakely. I'll be back on my next pass to pick you all up!"

Blakely cheered triumphantly and ran to tell the crew.

---

1   How did Blakely feel at the end of the story?

   A   Elated

   B   Amused

   C   Embarrassed

   D   Confused

2   In this story, the word <u>careening</u> means —

   F   walking slowly

   G   wandering

   H   lurching

   J   fainting

3   What will probably happen next?

   A   Blakely will help Captain Thomas fight off the Derellians.

   B   Captain Thomas will go down with his ship.

   C   Captain Thomas will fly to where the crew's pods are.

   D   The crew members will rebel against Captain Thomas for making them leave the ship.

4   Which of these is the best summary of the story?

   F   A starship captain saves his ship and his crew from destruction at the hands of pirates.

   G   A first mate saves the crew members of his ship by getting them to the escape pods.

   H   A captain steers his ship and crew safely out of the way of an asteroid.

   J   The pulsar guns of a ship are not working.

5   The author would probably describe Captain Thomas as —

   A   bossy and arrogant

   B   nervous and inhibited

   C   happy and charming

   D   brave and selfless

Answers and Analyses

1. **A** Students should look back to the end of the story to find evidence to support their choice. In the last sentence of the story Blakely *cheered triumphantly and ran to tell the crew*. The best inference is that he was *happy* or *elated*. If students do not know the word *elated*, they should still be able to eliminate choices B, C, and D, and to arrive at the correct answer by process of elimination.

2. **H** This is another good example to teach process of elimination. Students should look for clues in the immediate vicinity of the word *careening*. Blakely is described as *whirling about, careening from one control panel to the next.* Therefore the word *careening* must have something to do with a great deal of motion. This should allow students to eliminate choices F, G, and J. Even if they do not know the word *lurching*, it is the only remaining possibility, and the best choice.

3. **C** Clues to what will happen next can be found at the end of the story. Captain Thomas survives and says *I'll be back on my next pass to pick you all up*. Therefore, the most reasonable inference is that Captain Thomas will come and pick up the crew.

4. **F** The title should give students a good clue that the story is about Captain Thomas. Therefore we can eliminate choices G and J. Since the story describes a battle against space pirates, and never mentions an asteroid, the most reasonable summary is F.

5. **D** In the middle of the story, Captain Thomas says *Get the crew to safety... I'm going to hold out as long as I can.* He is prepared to sacrifice his life to save the crew, so the best choice is D.

Theme 7 At a Glance
A Different Dimension

THEME OPENING ➡️ **Theme 7: A DIFFERENT DIMENSION** ➡️

- Introducing the Theme (p. 653)
- Exploring the Theme (p. 654)
- Theme Projects (p. 655)

SELECTIONS

Media Connection: Seizure-Alert: Dog Is Girl's Lifeline (pp. 656–657)

Lob's Girl (p. 658) 🔘🔘

Key Item (p. 674)

The Smallest Dragonboy (p. 682)

Active Reading Model: Aunty Misery (p. 700) 🔘🔘

Strawberries (p. 706)

Atalanta's Race (p. 713) 🔘🔘

Atalanta (p. 713)

Cat and Rat: The Legend of the Chinese Zodiac (p. 725) 🔘🔘

Icarus and Daedalus (p. 736) 🔘🔘

Prometheus (p. 742) 🔘🔘

Media Connection: First Ballad Interlude from Benjamin Britten's *Paul Bunyan* (p. 748)

The Bunyans (p. 749)

Brer Rabbit and Brer Lion (p. 749)

SKILL FEATURES

Reading and Thinking Skills (p. 672)

Writing Skills (p. 673)

Interdisciplinary Connection (p. 681)

Genre Focus: Legends, Myths, and Folklore (p. 698)

Active Reading Strategies (p. 699)

Grammar Link (p. 712)

Vocabulary Skills (p. 735)

WRITING WORKSHOP

Expository Writing: Book Review (pp. 760–763)

THEME WRAP-UP

- **Responding to the Theme, Analyzing Literature, Evaluate and Set Goals** (p. 764)
- **Build Your Portfolio** (p. 764)
- **Reading on Your Own** (p. 765)

  A Wrinkle in Time by Madeleine L'Engle

  Maniac Magee by Jerry Spinelli

  Big Men, Big Country: A Collection of American Tall Tales by Paul Robert Walker

  Cut from the Same Cloth: American Women of Myth, Legend, and Tall Tale by Robert D. San Souci

- **Standardized Test Practice** (pp. 766–767)

KEYS TO LITERARY CONNECTIONS

Comparing Selections

The **Comparing Selections** feature in this theme provides opportunities for addressing diverse aspects of the reading and literature curriculum.

For example, in Comparing Selections on page 747, students take a closer look at the ideas in "Icarus and Daedalus" by Josephine Preston Peabody and "Prometheus" by Bernard Evslin. Through this comparison students can develop insights about the importance of myths in certain cultures.

KEYS TO TEACHING OPTIONS

Block Scheduling

Activities that are particularly suited to use within a block scheduling framework are identified throughout this theme by the following designation: For detailed suggestions on block scheduling, see the **Block Scheduling Guide** for this grade level.

Key to Ability Levels

The Teaching Options throughout this theme have been coded for students of various abilities.

L1 BASIC activities for all students

L2 AVERAGE activities for average to above-average students

L3 CHALLENGING activities for above-average students

Theme 7   At a Glance

A Different Dimension

Reading Skills in this theme

Variety of Texts

In addition to legend, myth, and folklore, this theme includes the following text types:

- short story
- cartoon
- magazine article
- opera libretto

Comprehension Skills

The following instructional support for comprehension skills appears in this theme of the Student Edition:

- **Reading and Thinking Minilessons** (pp. 671, 697, 705, 724, 734, 759)
- **Monitoring Comprehension** (p. 672)
- **Active Reading Strategies and Model** (pp. 699–705)

See also the **Reading Minilessons** throughout the theme in this Teacher's Wraparound Edition.

Reading Resources

Comprehension Skills Resources

📂 **Active Reading Guides**

The **Active Reading Guide** provides graphic organizers and study guide questions to support students' reading of each selection (**Active Reading Guide**, pp. 55–64).

📂 **Reading Workbook**

The Reading Workbook (pp. 97–116) includes additional instruction and reinforcement of reading strategies and skills.

🎧 **Audio Library**

Available both on tape and on CD, the Audio Library provides valuable comprehension support.

Resources for Reading Widely

Glencoe Literature Library

Each title in the *Glencoe Literature Library* includes a full-length novel or play plus related readings. A separate Study Guide is available for each title.

💿 **Literature Classics CD-ROM**

The selections on this CD-ROM can be searched by author, theme, or genre.

 *in*TIME

A coproduction of Glencoe and Time, Inc., the *inTime* magazine includes a wealth of high interest nonfiction related to the selections in Theme Seven.

✓ Assessment in this theme

Assessment Options in the Student Edition

Glencoe Literature offers a number of diverse ways to evaluate student understanding and skill proficiency. In the Student Edition, use the following:

- **Responding to Literature**
  Following each selection, students are asked to recall facts, interpret ideas, and evaluate concepts as they answer a variety of questions and complete activities to extend their understanding.
- **Theme Wrap-Up (pp. 764–765)**
  Here students respond to the selections on personal and analytical levels. They also assume ownership of their learning by setting and evaluating goals and by selecting work for their portfolios.

See also the many **Assessment Resources** listed on the facing page.

THE PRINCETON REVIEW

Standardized Test Practice

The Princeton Review has developed the Standardized Test Practice pages found at the end of this theme (pp. 766–767). These pages contain practice test questions that help students remain familiar with standardized test formats and content.

- ITBS Preparation and Practice
- SAT-9 Preparation and Practice
- TerraNova Preparation and Practice

Writing Skills in this theme

Writing Skills

The Student Edition of Theme Seven offers strong instructional support for writing skills:

In **Extending Your Response**, which follows each selection:
- **Writing About Literature**
- **Personal/Creative Writing**

See also the **Writing Minilessons** throughout the theme in this Teacher's Wraparound Edition.

Writing Workshops

Theme Seven concludes with a **Writing Workshop** that guides students through the process of writing a book review (pp. 760–763).

Writing Resources

Writer's Assistant CD-ROM
Each Writing Workshop is supplemented by an interactive writing guide on the Writer's Assistant CD-ROM. This easy-to-use writing guide provides prompts, templates, and other tools that lead students through the writing process.

Writing and Proofreading Practice
Blackline masters present in-depth instruction and practice on a specific step in the writing process and proofreading. (pp. 1–7, 50–56).

Writing and Proofreading Transparencies
Transparencies provide graphic organizers and proofreading exercises for whole-class instruction (pp. 1–6, 37–38).

Research and Report Writing Guide
This resource provides extensive tips and activities to guide students in their writing projects in the literature classroom as well as in classes across the curriculum.

Style and Documentation Sourcebook for Writers
This sourcebook is a combination reference and workbook, giving students the most up-to-date information and guidance regarding traditional as well as technological research strategies and documentation.

Grammar and Composition Handbook
The Grammar and Composition Handbook provides instruction that supplements activities in the student textbook.

Assessment Resources

Selection Quick Checks
For each selection, a Quick Check of three to five short-answer questions measures students' literal comprehension.

Selection and Theme Assessment
The Selection and Theme Assessment instrument tests students' abilities to recall, interpret, and evaluate what they've read. The tests consist of multiple-choice, short answer, and essay questions.

Performance Assessment
Alternative assessment instruments and rubrics for Theme Seven are found in the Performance Assessment ancillary.

Writing Assessment and Portfolio Management
These notes and strategies, student models, and assessment tools assist with the task of measuring students' progress as writers and as monitors of their own writing.

Testmaker
Teachers can customize selection and Theme Seven tests by accessing the Testmaker database.

Mindjogger Videoquizzes
Using a popular game show format, Mindjogger Videoquizzes enable teachers to evaluate student understanding of Theme Seven in a quick and fun manner.

Theme 7 SKILLS SCOPE AND SEQUENCE

SELECTIONS	Literary Elements	Reading and Thinking	Writing	Vocabulary and Spelling
Lob's Girl JOAN AIKEN	Suspense, SE pp. 669; *TWE pp. 664, 666, 667* *Foreshadowing, TWE p. 660* *Hyperbole, TWE p. 662* *Characterization, TWE p. 662* *Mood, TWE p. 663*	Scanning, SE p. 671 *Logical Reasoning, TWE pp. 661, 663* *Graphic Aids, TWE p. 661* *Inferring, TWE p. 666* *Evaluating, TWE p. 668*	Resolution, SE p. 670 Journal Entry, SE p. 670 *Creating Suspense, TWE p. 664*	Unlocking Meaning, SE p. 671 *Multiple-Meaning Words, TWE pp. 661, 662*
KEY ITEM ISAAC ASIMOV	Irony, SE p. 679 *Irony, TWE p. 677*	*Inferring, TWE p. 676* Compare and Contrast, *TWE p. 677* *Synthesizing, TWE p. 678*	Paragraph (Characters), SE p. 680 Description: Personal View of the Future, SE p. 680	Etymology, SE p. 680
The Smallest Dragonboy ANNE McCAFFREY	Fantasy, SE p. 695; *TWE pp. 684, 687, 694* *Character, TWE p. 685* *Fantasy, TWE p. 692*	*Graphic Aids, TWE p. 685* *Draw. Conclu., TWE pp. 686, 689, 690, 691, 694* *Analyze Arguments, TWE p. 688*	Setting, SE p. 696 Sequel, SE p. 696 *Another Point of View, TWE p. 689*	Synonyms: Shades of Meaning, SE p. 697
Aunty Misery JUDITH ORTIZ COFER	Fable, SE p. 703	Generalizing, SE p. 705 *Comparing and Contrasting, TWE p. 702*	Identify Short Story Elements, SE p. 704 Write a Fable, SE p. 704	Analogies, SE p. 705
Strawberries GAYLE ROSS	Tone, SE p. 710 *Tone, TWE pp. 708, 709*	*Cause and Effect, TWE p. 709*	Conflict, SE p. 711 Write a Myth, SE p. 711	Synonyms: Thesaurus, SE p. 711
Atalanta's Race REX WARNER **Atalanta** BETTY MILES	Description, SE p. 722; *TWE pp. 715, 716, 717, 719, 721* *Characterization, TWE pp. 717, 718, 719* *Foreshadowing, TWE p. 717* *Simile, TWE p. 720*	Chronological Order, SE p. 724 *Draw. Conclu., TWE p. 715* *Inferring, TWE pp. 716, 717* *Sequencing, TWE p. 716* *Synthesizing, TWE p. 719* *Verifying Predict., TWE p. 721*	Characterization, SE p. 723 Journal Entry, SE p. 723 **COLLAB. LEARN.** *Description of the Setting, TWE p. 715*	Analogies, SE p. 724 *Prefix -twi, TWE p. 720*
Cat and Rat ED YOUNG	Legend, SE p. 732 *Imagery, TWE p. 728* *Legend, TWE p. 729*	Using Graphic Aids, SE p. 734 *Analyze Argumts., TWE p. 727* *Purpose for Rdg., TWE p. 727* *Critical Judgments, TWE p. 730* *Elaborating, TWE p. 731*	Diagram Plot, SE p. 733 Write and Illustrate Legend, SE p. 733	The Suffix -ful, SE p. 734
Icarus and Daedalus JOSEPHINE PRESTON PEABODY	Myth, SE p. 740 *Myth, TWE pp. 738, 739*	*Identifying Spatial Relationships, TWE p. 738*	Description (Character), SE p. 741 News Report, SE p. 741	Dictionary Skills: Definitions, SE p. 741
PROMETHEUS BERNARD EVSLIN	Theme, SE p. 746 *Theme, TWE pp. 744, 745* *Personification, TWE p. 745*		Explanation (Myth), SE p. 746	
The Bunyans AUDREY WOOD **Brer Rabbit and Brer Lion** JULIUS LESTER	Folktales and Tall Tales, SE pp. 757; *TWE pp. 751–754* *Mood, TWE p. 751* *Trickster Tale, TWE p. 755*	Paraphrasing, SE p. 759 *Problem and Solution, TWE p. 750* *Drawing Conclusions, TWE p. 753* *Synthesizing, TWE p. 756*	Paragraph (Dialogue), SE p. 758 Sequel, SE p. 758 *Tall Tale, TWE p. 751*	Etymology, SE p. 759

Key: Student material is in roman. Teacher material is in italic.   Technology   **COLLAB. LEARN.** Collaboration

Grammar and Language	Listening, Speaking, and Viewing	Life Skills	Study, Research, and Technology
Apostrophes in Possessives, SE p. 671 *Using Troublesome Words, TWE p. 668*	**COLLAB. LEARN.** Literature Groups, SE p. 670 **COLLAB. LEARN.** *Creating a Radio Drama, TWE p. 663* *Film, TWE p. 667*	Learning for Life: Community Service Plan, SE p. 670 *Leading and Organizing, TWE p. 665*	Interdisciplinary Activity: Research Dogs, SE p. 670
Compound Predicates, TWE p. 678	**COLLAB. LEARN.** Literature Groups, SE p. 680	Learning for Life: User's Manual, SE p. 680	
Writing Numbers, SE p. 697 **COLLAB. LEARN.** *Infinitives, TWE p. 694*	**COLLAB. LEARN.** Literature Groups, SE p. 696 **COLLAB. LEARN.** News Story, SE p. 696 **COLLAB. LEARN.** *Debate, TWE p. 688*	*Creating and Producing, TWE p. 690*	*Interdisciplinary Connection: Research Planets, TWE p. 691*
Frequently Misspelled Words, SE p. 705	**COLLAB. LEARN.** Literature Groups, SE p. 704		Interdisciplinary Activity: Research Puerto Rico, SE p. 704
	COLLAB. LEARN. Literature Groups, SE p. 711 **COLLAB. LEARN.** Role-Play, SE p. 711		
Spelling Compound Words, SE p. 724 **COLLAB. LEARN.** *Irregular Verbs, TWE p. 720*	**COLLAB. LEARN.** Lit. Grp., SE p. 723 **COLLAB. LEARN.** Role-Play, SE p. 723 **COLLAB. LEARN.** *Narration, TWE p. 717* *Video, TWE, p. 719* **COLLAB. LEARN.** *Survey, TWE p. 721*		Interdisciplinary Activity: Research Fitness, SE p. 723
Apostrophes in Contractions, SE p. 734 *Commas in a Series, TWE p. 730*	**COLLAB. LEARN.** Literature Groups, SE p. 733 **COLLAB. LEARN.** Story Dramatization, SE p. 733	**COLLAB. LEARN.** *Decision Making, TWE p. 729*	Interdisciplinary Activity: Research Calendars, SE p. 733 *Real-World Connection: Research Legends, TWE p. 731*
	COLLAB. LEARN. Literature Groups, SE p. 741		
Dashes, TWE p. 744	**COLLAB. LEARN.** Literature Groups, SE p. 746		
Quotation Marks, SE p. 759 *Apostrophes, TWE p. 756*	**COLLAB. LEARN.** Literature Groups, SE p. 758 **COLLAB. LEARN.** Dramatization, SE p. 758		Research Natural Wonders, SE p. 758 **COLLAB. LEARN.** *Real-World Connection: Research Fairy Tales, TWE p. 754*

Theme 7 RESOURCE MANAGER

SELECTIONS	Print Resources		
Lob's Girl JOAN AIKEN	Theme 7 Plan. Guide, pp. 6–13 * Active Reading Guide, p. 55 Vocabulary Practice, p. 37	Gr. & Comp. Hdbk., Lessons 4.4, 13.7 Gr. & Lang. Wkbk., pp. 223–224, 227–228, 273–274 Reading Workbook, pp. 97–98	* Quick Checks, p. 55 Sel. and Th. Assess., pp. 95–96 Performance Assessment, p. 52 Spanish Summaries, p. 55
KEY ITEM ISAAC ASIMOV	Theme 7 Plan. Guide, pp. 14–21 * Active Reading Guide, p. 56 Vocabulary Practice, p. 38	Gr. & Comp. Hdbk., Lesson 1.5 Gr. & Lang. Wkbk., pp. 53–54 Reading Workbook, pp. 99–100	* Quick Checks, p. 56 Sel. and Th. Assess. pp. 97–98 Performance Assessment, p. 53 Spanish Summaries, p. 56 Spanish Translations
The Smallest Dragonboy ANNE McCAFFREY	Theme 7 Plan. Guide, pp. 22–29 * Active Reading Guide, p. 57 Vocabulary Practice, p. 39	Gr. & Comp. Hdbk., Lessons 9.3, 13.10 Gr. & Lang. Wkbk., pp. 175–178, 279–280 Reading Workbook, pp. 101–102	* Quick Checks, p. 57 Sel. and Th. Assess., pp. 99–100 Performance Assessment, p. 54 Spanish Summaries, p. 57 Spanish Translations
Aunty Misery JUDITH ORTIZ COFER	Theme 7 Plan. Guide, pp. 30–34 * Active Reading Guide, p. 58 Vocabulary Practice, p. 40	Gr. & Comp. Hdbk., Lessons 15.1–15.2 Gr. & Lang. Wkbk., pp. 297–300 Reading Workbook, pp. 103–104	* Quick Checks, p. 58 Sel. and Th. Assess., p. 101 Performance Assessment, p. 55 Spanish Summaries, p. 58 Spanish Translations
Strawberries GAYLE ROSS	Theme 7 Plan. Guide, pp. 35–42 * Active Reading Guide, p. 59 Vocabulary Practice, p. 41	Reading Workbook, pp. 105–106	* Quick Checks, p. 59 Sel. and Th. Assess., p. 102 Performance Assessment, p. 56 Spanish Summaries, p. 59 Spanish Translations
Atalanta's Race REX WARNER **Atalanta** BETTY MILES	Theme 7 Plan.Guide, pp. 43–48 * Active Reading Guide, p. 60 Vocabulary Practice, p. 42	Gr. & Comp. Hdbk.k, Lessons 3.11, 3.12, 15.1 Gr. & Lang. Wkbk., pp. 95–100, 297–300 Reading Workbook, pp. 107–108	* Quick Checks, p. 60 Sel. and Th. Assess., pp. 103–104 Performance Assessment, p. 57 Spanish Summaries, p. 60
Cat and Rat ED YOUNG	Theme 7 Plan. Guide, pp. 49–56 * Active Reading Guide, p. 61 Vocabulary Practice, p. 43	Gr. & Comp. Hdbk., Lsns. 13.2, 13.7 Gr. & Lang. Wkbk., p. 255–256, 273–274; Rdg. Wkbk., pp. 109–110	* Quick Checks, p. 61; Sel. and Th. Assess., pp. 105–106; Perf. Assess., p. 58; Sp. Sum., p. 61; Sp. Trans.
Icarus and Daedalus JOSEPHINE PRESTON PEABODY	Theme 7 Plan. Guide, pp. 57–64 * Active Reading Guide, p. 62 Vocabulary Practice, p. 44	Reading Workbook, pp. 111–112	* Quick Checks, p. 62; Sel. and Th. Assess., pp. 107–108; Perf. Assess., p. 59; Sp. Sum., p. 62; Sp. Trans.
PROMETHEUS BERNARD EVSLIN	Theme 7 Plan. Guide, pp. 65–72 * Active Reading Guide, p. 63 Vocabulary Practice, p. 45	Gr. & Comp. Hdbk., Lesson 13.8 Gr. & Lang. Wkbk., pp. 275–276 Reading Workbook, pp. 113–114	* Quick Checks, p. 63 Sel. and Th. Assess., pp. 107–108 Performance Assessment, p. 59 Sp. Sum., p. 63; Sp. Trans.
The Bunyans AUDREY WOOD **Brer Rabbit and Brer Lion** JULIUS LESTER	Theme 7 Plan. Guide, pp. 73–78 * Active Reading Guide, p. 64 Vocabulary Practice, p. 46	Gr. & Comp. Hdbk., Lsns. 13.6, 13.7 Gr. & Lang. Wkbk., pp. 267–270, 273–274; Rdg. Wkbk., pp. 115–116	* Quick Checks, p. 64 Sel. and Th. Assess., pp. 109–110 Perf. Assess., p. 60; Sp. Sum., p. 64

*Also available in Spanish

Transparencies	Technology Resources
Selection Focus Transparency 55 Grammar and Language Transparency 53 Literary Elements Transparency 55	Literature Launchers Spanish/Audio Library Vocabulary Puzzlemaker Web Site: lit.glencoe.com
Selection Focus Transparency 56 Grammar and Language Transparency 55 Literary Elements Transparency 56	Literature Launchers Spanish/Audio Library Vocabulary Puzzlemaker Web Site: lit.glencoe.com
Selection Focus Transparency 57 Grammar and Language Transparency 56 Literary Elements Transparency 57	Spanish/Audio Library Vocabulary Puzzlemaker Web Site: lit.glencoe.com
Selection Focus Transparency 58 Literary Elements Transparency 58	Spanish/Audio Library Vocabulary Puzzlemaker Web Site: lit.glencoe.com
Selection Focus Transparency 59 Literary Elements Transparency 59 Fine Art Transparency 28	Literature Launchers Spanish/Audio Library Vocabulary Puzzlemaker Web Site: lit.glencoe.com
Selection Focus Transparency 60 Grammar and Language Transparency 57 Literary Elements Transparency 60	Spanish/Audio Library Vocabulary Puzzlemaker Web Site: lit.glencoe.com
Selection Focus Transparency 61 Grammar and Language Transparency 58 Literary Elements Transparency 61	Spanish/Audio Library Vocabulary Puzzlemaker Web Site: lit.glencoe.com
Selection Focus Transparency 62 Literary Elements Transparency 62 Fine Art Transparency 25	Spanish/Audio Library Vocabulary Puzzlemaker Web Site: lit.glencoe.com
Selection Focus Transparency 63 Grammar and Language Transparency 59 Literary Elements Transparency 63	Spanish/Audio Library Vocabulary Puzzlemaker Web Site: lit.glencoe.com
Selection Focus Transparency 64 Grammar and Language Transparency 60 Literary Elements Transparency 64	Spanish/Audio Library Vocabulary Puzzlemaker Web Site: lit.glencoe.com

Theme RESOURCES

- Listening and Speaking Activities (pp. 19–21)
- Viewing and Representing Activities (pp. 1–6, 25–27)
- Critical Thinking Skills (pp. 18–19)
- Media Connection Activities (pp. 13–14)
- Interdisciplinary Activities (pp. 26–29)
- Family and Community Activities (p. 17)
- Selection and Theme Assessment (pp. 137–138)

See also these additional planning resources:
- English Language Learners Sourcebook
- Inclusion Strategies Sourcebook
- Literature Groups Sourcebook

Use Glencoe's *Presentation Plus!* This multi-media teaching tool lets you present dynamic lessons that will engage your students. Using Microsoft PowerPoint®, you can customize the presentation to create your own personalized lessons.

THEME 7

A Different Dimension

Theme Objectives

- To enjoy reading about magical and mythical events
- To analyze the literary elements in folktale, myth, legend, and short story selections
- To apply strategies for reading legends, myths, and folklore

Teaching Strategies

Have students read the quotation from *"Magic Words"* in preparation for the questions below.

VIEWING THE PAINTING

The title of the painting by Maria Angelica Ruiz-Tagle means "Yesterday, I had a dream."

Responding to the Painting
Discussion Questions:

- Why would this painting be chosen to represent the theme? What mythical horses do you know of? *(Students may mention Pegasus, the winged horse in Greek mythology.)*
- How might the images in the painting relate to the quote "That was the time when ... the human mind had mysterious powers"?

A Different Dimension

Ayer Tuve un Sueño, 1990. Maria Angelica Ruiz-Tagle. Oil on canvas, 100 x 120 cm. Kactus Foto, Santiago, Chile.

652

TEACHER to TEACHER

NAUTILUS MIDDLE SCHOOL • MIAMI, FLORIDA

I introduce the theme "A Different Dimension" with a short lesson on Greek mythology that focuses on the different qualities possessed by the Greek pantheon of deities. In Greek mythology, gods and goddesses had certain characteristics that defined them. For example, Athena, the goddess of wisdom, was represented by an owl, the symbol for wisdom. Following class discussion, students choose various teachers and staff people to be "school gods and goddesses" by designating a special quality to each along with a representative symbol. For example, a student may designate a teacher the "god of detention" with a watch and chain as his symbol. Each student then draws a picture of the chosen god or goddess and his or her symbol and writes an essay that supports the illustration.

CYNTHIA CASTILLO

THEME 7

> *That was the time when words were like magic. The human mind had mysterious powers. A word spoken by chance might have strange consequences.*
>
> —"Magic Words," Songs and Stories of the Netsilik Eskimos

THEME CONTENTS

Lob's Girl • short story by Joan Aiken 659

Key Item • short story by Isaac Asimov 675

The Smallest Dragonboy •
short story by Anne McCaffrey 683

 GENRE FOCUS *LEGENDS, MYTHS, AND FOLKLORE*

Aunty Misery • folktale by Judith Ortiz Cofer 701

Strawberries • myth retold by Gayle Ross 707

Atalanta's Race • myth retold by Rex Warner 714

Atalanta • myth retold by Betty Miles 718

Cat and Rat: The Legend of the Chinese Zodiac •
legend retold by Ed Young 726

Icarus and Daedalus •
myth retold by Josephine Preston Peabody 737

Prometheus • myth retold by Bernard Evslin 743

The Bunyans • folktale by Audrey Wood 750

Brer Rabbit and Brer Lion •
folktale retold by Julius Lester 755

A DIFFERENT DIMENSION 653

RESOURCE MANAGER

See the ***Theme Seven Planning Guide*** (pp. 1–5) for additional teaching notes, strategies, and resources for introducing the theme "A Different Dimension."

Introducing the Theme

Direct your students' attention to the **Theme Contents.** Ask them to read through the list of selections. Present these questions for discussion:

- What do several of the selections have in common? *(Students may say that many are familiar myths and legends passed down through storytelling.)*
- As you read the table of contents, can you tell where some of the stories in this theme originated? *(Students may mention Greece, China, and the United States.)*
- Do you know what special powers or attributes any of these mythical figures possess? *(Students may know of Paul Bunyan and his extraordinary size or of Prometheus stealing fire from the gods.)*

 LITERATURE & HUMANITIES

Have students examine the painting *Plate 69...* on the CD *National Museum of Women in the Arts* and create their own myths using these two characters.

GLENCOE TECHNOLOGY

 LITERATURE CLASSICS CD-ROM
Search for other selections related to the theme "A Different Dimension."

Exploring the Theme

A Different Dimension

In addition to the power of words to transport and transform us, children in many parts of the world use "magic words" that are supposed to make wonderful or startling things happen. *Abracadabra* is a magic word common in the United States.

Starting Points

When the Moon Is Full

After students describe what is happening in the cartoon, ask them what they think Maynard's wife usually means when she asks him to come out and look at the moon.

- Prompt a discussion about the romantic relationship people have with the moon. Find out whether students think the moon is romantic, and why.
- Have students talk about things that are known or believed to happen at the time of the full moon. *(Students may say that animals howl, people act strangely, tides are affected, and creatures like werewolves and vampires come out.)*
- You may wish to post students' cartoons around the classroom and refer to the various fates of Maynard and his wife as students read the selections in this theme.

Traveling to Another Dimension

Suggest that students turn to their dreams for ideas about magical places. They may want to talk to partners about dreams they have had that took place in strange or wonderful realms and regions.

- Invite students to draw or paint pictures of the settings for their fantasies.
- Remind students that many parts of our earthly landscape have taken on mythical characteristics in poems and stories through the years. You may wish to use Fine Art Transparency 22 to enrich students' thinking about the theme.

Exploring the Theme

A Different Dimension

The magical power of words has always been able to transport listeners and readers to other worlds. In this theme, you will discover how the magic of words can carry you to places such as ancient Greece and China, the imaginary planet of Pern, and the legendary American frontier. Begin thinking about the theme by selecting one of the activities below.

Starting Points

WHEN THE MOON IS FULL

Writers and artists like to imagine life in different dimensions. The couple in this cartoon are certainly about to enter a new dimension!

- What do you think is happening? Draw a cartoon strip with two or three more panels showing what might happen next to Maynard and his wife.

TRAVELING TO ANOTHER DIMENSION

Have you ever used your imagination to travel to another dimension?

- Describe a setting for a fantasy you might write. It can take place in the past, in the future, on another planet, or even on an Earth that never really existed. The place can be as strange or as magical as you can imagine.

"Maynard, I do think that just this once you should come out and see the moon!"

Drawing by Chas. Addams; ©1983. The New Yorker Magazine, Inc.

Family and Community Activity

Mapping the Stars Ask students to make star maps at least three times a week throughout the course of Theme 7. They will need construction paper, colored pencils, markers or small stick-on stars, and a flashlight. Students should select a patch of sky that is visible from home and stand in exactly the same place each time they observe and record the stars. Have them mark the positions of the brightest stars on a sheet of construction paper and write the date and time of each observation. Observing at the same time each night is the best way to detect how the star map changes. Encourage students to compare maps and compile booklets of their own star maps at the end of the theme.

Additional Resources
📁 *Family and Community Activities,* p. 17

Theme Projects

As you read the selections in this theme, complete one of the projects below. Work on your own, with a partner, or with a group.

CRITICAL READING
Different Dimensions in Literature

1. Alone or with a partner, brainstorm a list of fantasy or science-fiction novels, short stories, TV episodes, or movies you have read or seen. Then choose at least four of them that you think are especially good.
2. Plan a chart to prepare a detailed comparison of your choices. Use headings such as Title, Author(s), Setting (time and place), Plot Summary, Characters, Theme(s), and Evaluation.
3. Use your completed chart to write an essay telling what elements good science-fiction or fantasy stories have in common. Use examples from the stories to back up your opinions.
4. Decorate your chart with drawings or pictures clipped from old magazines or downloaded from the Internet and display it for the class along with your essay.

For more project ideas, check out some fantasy, science-fiction, myth, legend, or folklore sites on the Web. You can begin with the Glencoe Literature site at lit.glencoe.com

LEARNING FOR LIFE
Travel Itinerary

1. Plan an itinerary, or traveler's guide, for a trip to a different dimension.
2. Decide how you will travel: in a time machine, a spacecraft, or even on the back of a dragon. Decide what sights you will see and what people or creatures you will meet there.
3. Make a map of your journey. Use it for a presentation in which you describe your visit.

MULTIMEDIA PROJECT
Creating an Imaginary World

1. Working in a small group, collect pictures of places that would make good settings for a story set in a different dimension.
2. Create a diorama using or adapting the scenery you found. Use modeling clay or cutouts to add to your display the kinds of people or creatures who might live in your "different dimension."
3. Share your world with your classmates. If you wish, use the scene you have created as an inspiration for writing or dramatizing a story.

A DIFFERENT DIMENSION 655

Greek Mythology Students may wish to use a search engine to find more information about Ancient Greece. They may use keywords such as *Greek Gods*, *Mount Olympus*, or *Troy*.

Theme Projects

Teaching Strategies
The following suggestions may help students with their theme projects.

Critical Reading
- Students may wish to compare and contrast print and film versions of the same story.
- In step 2, have students add a heading for notes on the stories' social implications.
- Suggest that students create book and movie lists based on the selections they have chosen.

Learning for Life
- Have students create names for the dimension, the creatures that inhabit it, and the language they speak.
- Ask students to translate a few "useful phrases" for travelers who visit this dimension.
- Invite students to make travel posters advertising future trips to this dimension.

Multimedia Project
Help students develop a list of worlds they would like to create, such as a recycled world, or a world where everything is reversed.
- Ask groups to write brief histories of the worlds they create.
- Have students read or perform their stories.

Additional Resources
- *Interdisciplinary Activities,* pp. 26–29
- *Viewing and Representing Activities,* pp. 25–27
- *Listening and Speaking Activities,* pp. 19–21
- *Critical Thinking Skills,* pp. 18–19
- *Selection and Theme Assessment,* pp. 137–138
- *Performance Assessment,* p. 75

Objective

- To understand and apply strategies for reading a magazine article

Literature —— LINK

Lob's Girl "Seizure-Alert Dog Is Girl's Lifeline" connects to the literature selection "Lob's Girl" (pp. 658–668). In each story, a young girl inspires love, devotion, and lifelong companionship in her dog.

Service-Dog Training Have students use a search engine to find out how dogs are trained to help humans. Suggest that students enter key words such as *seeing-eye dogs, dog training, guide dogs,* and *Canine Partners for Life.*

Teaching Options

MEDIA Connection

MAGAZINE ARTICLE

This article comes from a magazine for dog lovers. Why do you think it appeared in a section called "Dogs That Make a Difference"?

Seizure-Alert Dog Is Girl's Lifeline

by Sarah Christie—Dog Fancy, June 1997

Emily Ramsey's world just grew a little bigger. For the first time in her life, the 13-year-old middle school student from Racine, Wis., is now able to cruise the mall, ride the school bus, and participate in after-school sports without constant supervision. That's standard operating procedure for most teenagers, but for one with epilepsy, the world is a perilous place.

Seizures strike without warning, making simple acts such as walking down stairs, crossing the street, or going for a swim potentially life-threatening. These days Emily can do all that and more, thanks to her constant companion, Watson.

Watson is a seizure-alert dog, able to warn his owner of epileptic attacks before they strike.

The skill goes beyond regular service-dog training. It can't be taught or bred for. Nobody knows how Watson is able to predict these spells—one theory is that dogs sense

chemical changes preceding the attacks—but the details don't matter to Emily. She knows only that her dog's intuition is a lifeline she almost didn't dare hope for.

Watson was an improbable candidate for service dog school. He had been left at a veterinarian's office to be put to sleep for a broken foot at 6 months of age. A clinic employee saved him. The sympathetic veterinary technician, who also

worked as a volunteer at CPL [Canine Partners for Life], saw promise in the lame pup.

Thus began the education of Watson. During his year at CPL, he mastered the arts of pushing wheelchairs, opening refrigerator and sliding glass doors, paying cashiers, and retrieving coins off cement floors. But the only way to know if Watson could predict Emily's seizures was to pair the two and wait and see.

656 ❧ THEME 7

Reading *Minilesson*

Problem and Solution Many of the problems Emily used to face can now be solved, thanks to Watson.

Activity Draw the following chart on the board and ask students to help complete the steps from problem to solution. Ask students to identify a problem and outline the steps they could take to solve the problem, with or without the help of another. **L2**

Problem: Emily couldn't go to the mall because of her seizures.
Step 1
Step 2
Step 3
Solution:

Additional Resources
📂 *Reading Workbook*

When dog met girl, there was no turning back. "It was love at first sight for both of them," [Emily's mother, Mary] Ramsey said. "He knew this was his person. They bonded very strongly, very quickly."

A month later, Emily returned to the CPL kennel for three weeks' training. Watson was put to the test right away.

"It was the middle of the night in the motel when Emily started seizuring," Ramsey said. "And Watson woke me up barking. I turned on the light and he was straddling her on the bed, looking straight down at her."

Eventually Watson learned that Emily's spells, frightening as they are, were only temporary. His concern turned to vigilance as he realized the importance of remaining with her at all times. After only three or four episodes, he began signaling coming attacks by whining and licking Emily's face. This has been refined into a deep, throaty whine, alerting Emily that she has about 45 minutes to prepare herself for a seizure.

But Watson's protectiveness goes beyond his special early-warning system. If Emily has had a particularly bad night, Watson won't allow her to exert herself the next day. He will forgo his morning walk and refuse to let her off the property. Nor will he allow her to go into the pool for a swim. "The uncanny thing is, he makes these decisions all by himself," Ramsey said. "He's decided that he knows what's best for Emily, and nobody would think about questioning his judgment."

Emily's mother credits Watson for improving her daughter's quality of life in ways nothing else has. Emily has her own reasons for loving Watson. "He's always there for me," she said without hesitation. "He's my best friend."

Respond

1. Describe the difference Watson makes in Emily's life.

2. How did this article affect your understanding of the relationship between dogs and humans?

FYI

The German shepherd, the Labrador retriever, the St. Bernard, and the Siberian husky are a few examples of dog breeds most often used as police dogs, seeing-eye dogs, and rescue dogs. These dogs are valued for their intelligence, obedience, and loyalty.

Respond

1. Possible answers: Emily can ride the school bus, go to the mall, participate in sports, and do things on her own.

2. Students may mention the "non-verbal" relationship that is evident between Watson and Emily, the strong connection dogs form with their owners, or the way dogs are willing to use their instincts to help humans.

Additional Resources
📁 *Media Connections,* p. 13

MEETING INDIVIDUAL NEEDS

INCLUSION STRATEGIES

Special Needs These students may benefit from working with other students to discuss the physical and mental challenges they face in the classroom.

Activity Have special needs students and their classmates work together in groups. Ask each group to discuss the challenges special needs students face and to create a list of suggestions about how to resolve them. Then, have students write a magazine article explaining the issues and possible solutions.

Additional Resources
📁 *Inclusion Strategies*

Objectives

- To read and analyze a short story
- To recognize and understand the purpose of suspense in a story
- To analyze a story's resolution

Skills

Reading/Thinking: Graphic Aids; Reasoning; Inferring; Drawing Conclusions; Evaluating; Scanning
Writing: Suspense; Journal Entry
Vocabulary: Multiple-Meaning Words; Unlocking Meaning
Grammar/Language: Troublesome Words; Apostrophes
Listening/Speaking: Radio Drama
Life Skills: Leading and Organizing; Community Service Plan
Collaboration: Literature Groups

Motivating OPTIONS

Literature Launchers: "Getting to Know Joan Aiken"

Videodisc Side B, Segment 21

Also available in VHS.

Selection Focus Transparency 55: Have students view the transparency and then discuss the questions provided.

Focus Activity: Have groups share stories about devoted animals.

Before You Read

Lob's Girl

MEET JOAN AIKEN

British author Joan Aiken says that she writes "the sort of thing I should have liked to read myself." She began creating poems and stories when she was five years old. Aiken's first work was published when she was seventeen, and she has since written more than eighty books and short-story collections. She is best known for historic fiction with mysterious or enchanted characters and settings.

Joan Aiken was born in 1924. This story was published in 1982.

FOCUS ACTIVITY

Do you think the bond between an animal and a human can be as strong as the bond between two humans?

QuickWrite

Write about what it is like, or would be like, to have an animal as a devoted friend.

Setting a Purpose

Read this story to find out about the powerful bond between a young girl and her dog.

BACKGROUND

The Time and Place   The story takes place over the course of nine years in a fishing village in southwestern England.

Did You Know?   Dogs have been known to travel great distances to find their owners or to return to their original homes. Scientists are unsure of how dogs manage to find their way, but they know that a dog's sense of smell is a powerful tool. Their scent memory is probably stronger than their sight memory. For example, dogs remember the arrangement of objects in a room by their different scents rather than by how they look.

VOCABULARY PREVIEW

secretive (sē′ kri tiv) *adj.* keeping one's thoughts and feelings to oneself; p. 663
hurtle (hurt′ əl) *v.* to move rapidly, especially with much force; p. 664
aggrieved (ə grēvd′) *adj.* feeling wronged, as by an insult or unfair treatment; p. 666
succeed (sək sēd′) *v.* to come or happen after in time, place, or order; p. 666
haggard (hag′ ərd) *adj.* looking worn as a result of grief, worry, or illness; p. 666
agitated (aj′ ə tāt′ əd) *adj.* excited, nervous, or disturbed; stirred up; p. 667

RESOURCE MANAGER

Lesson Planning Resource
The *Theme Seven Planning Guide* (pp. 6–13) provides additional lesson notes and reduced versions of all print resources.

📁 Other Print Resources

- Active Reading Guide, p. 55
- Vocabulary Practice, p. 37
- Reading Workbook, pp. 97–98
- Grammar and Language Workbook, pp. 223–224, 227–228, 273–274

- Grammar and Composition Handbook, Lessons 13.7, 4.4
- Quick Checks, p. 55
- Selection and Theme Assessment, pp. 95–96
- Performance Assessment, p. 52
- Spanish Summaries, p. 55
- Inclusion Strategies
- English Language Learners Sourcebook

 Transparencies

- Selection Focus 55
- Literary Elements 55
- Grammar and Language 53

Technology

 Literature Launchers
 Audio Library
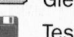 Spanish Audio Library
Glencoe Literature Web Site
Testmaker

Lob's Girl

Joan Aiken

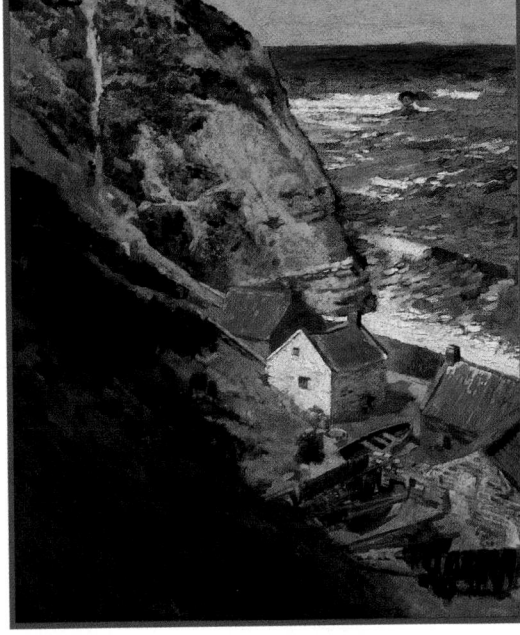

Straithes, Yorkshire. Dame Laura Knight, 1877–1970. Oil on canvas, 29½ x 24½ in. Private collection. How does the artist show the isolation of this home and yard?

Some people choose their dogs, and some dogs choose their people. The Pengelly family had no say in the choosing of Lob; he came to them in the second way, and very decisively.

It began on the beach, the summer when Sandy was five, Don, her older brother, twelve, and the twins were three. Sandy was really Alexandra, because her grandmother had a beautiful picture of a queen in a diamond tiara[1] and high collar of pearls. It hung by Granny Pearce's kitchen sink and was as familiar as the doormat. When Sandy was born everyone agreed that she was the living spit[2] of the picture, and so she was called Alexandra and Sandy for short.

On this summer day she was lying peacefully reading a comic and not keeping an eye on the twins, who didn't need it because they were occupied in seeing which of them could wrap the most seaweed around the other one's legs. Father—Bert Pengelly—and Don were up on the

---

1. A *tiara* (tē ar′ ə) is a woman's crownlike headdress, often made with jewels and precious metals.

2. *Living spit* is British slang for "exact likeness," which Americans would call "spitting image."

B Active Reading

CONNECT Have students describe how this family is like and different from the family or families they know. (*Sandy is like many other big sisters who are supposed to keep an eye on younger siblings but don't watch too closely. The father works as a fisherman. The mother is a home-maker.*)

FYI

German Shepherds
The word *shepherd* comes from the words *sheep* and *herder*. Originally German shepherds were used to herd and protect flocks of sheep. German shepherds are intelligent, loyal, and courageous. For these reasons, they are often used as seeing-eye dogs.

C Literary Elements

FORESHADOWING Ask students what they think the author means when she says that Lob gave himself, as well as the stick, to Sandy. (*Lob is somehow going to become Sandy's dog.*)

D Active Reading

VISUALIZE Have students visualize the setting and explain how the narrow, steep, twisting road contrasts with the fishing village. (*The village seems peaceful and safe, but the access road is treacherous.*)

Teaching Options

Lob's Girl

[B] Hard[3] painting the bottom boards of the boat in which Father went fishing for pilchards. And Mother—Jean Pengelly—was getting ahead with making the Christmas puddings[4] because she never felt easy in her mind if they weren't made and safely put away by the end of August. As usual, each member of the family was happily getting on with his or her own affairs. Little did they guess how soon this state of things would be changed by the large new member who was going to erupt into their midst.

Sandy rolled onto her back to make sure that the twins were not climbing on slippery rocks or getting cut off by the tide. At the same moment a large body struck her forcibly in the midriff and she was covered by flying sand. Instinctively she shut her eyes and felt the sand being wiped off her face by something that seemed like a warm, rough, damp flannel. She opened her eyes and looked. It was a tongue. Its owner was a large and bouncy young Alsatian, or German shepherd, with topaz[5] eyes, black-tipped prick ears, a thick, soft coat, and a bushy black-tipped tail.

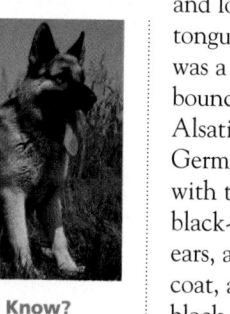

Did You Know?
Alsatians, also called German shepherds, were originally bred in Germany. They are noted for their intelligence and loyalty.

"*Lob!*" shouted a man farther up the beach. "Lob, come here!"

3. The *Hard* is a place for landing and launching boats. *Pilchards* are small herring-like fish.
4. *Christmas puddings* are a traditional British dessert similar to a fruitcake.
5. *Topaz* eyes are a bright, clear yellow-gold.

660 🐾 THEME 7

But Lob, as if trying to atone for the surprise he had given her, went on licking the sand off Sandy's face, wagging his tail so hard while he kept on knocking up more clouds of sand. His owner, a gray-haired man with a limp, walked over as quickly as he could and seized him by the collar.

"I hope he didn't give you a fright?" the man said to Sandy. "He meant it in play—he's only young."

"Oh, no, I think he's *beautiful*," said Sandy truly. She picked up a bit of driftwood and threw it. Lob, whisking easily out of his master's grip, was after it like a sand-colored bullet. He came back with the stick, beaming, and gave it to Sandy. At the same time he gave himself, though no one else was aware of this at the time. But with Sandy, too, it was love at first sight, and when, after a lot more stick-throwing, she and the twins joined Father and Don to go home for tea, they cast many a backward glance at Lob being led firmly away by his master.

"I wish we could play with him every day," Tess sighed.

"Why can't we?" said Tim.

Sandy explained, "Because Mr. Dodsworth, who owns him, is from Liverpool, and he is only staying at the Fisherman's Arms till Saturday."

"Is Liverpool a long way off?"

"Right at the other end of England from Cornwall, I'm afraid."

[D] It was a Cornish fishing village where the Pengelly family lived, with rocks and cliffs and a strip of beach and a little round harbor, and palm trees growing in the gardens of the little whitewashed stone houses. The village was approached by a narrow, steep, twisting hill-road, and

---

ENGLISH LANGUAGE LEARNERS

Life in a Fishing Village For some English language learners from other parts of the world, or for their families, fishing may have been, or may still be, an important part of life.

Activity Have small groups of students work together to share stories about fishing in other parts of the world and locally: where people fish, what they fish for, when they fish, what tools they use (nets, boats, line, bait), and how they prepare the fish once they catch them. Some students may want to make illustrations of certain fish or how they are caught. Invite groups to share their findings. **COLLAB. LEARN.**

Additional Resources
📁 *English Language Learners Sourcebook*

guarded by a notice that said LOW GEAR FOR 1 1/2 MILES, DANGEROUS TO CYCLISTS.

The Pengelly children went home to scones[6] with Cornish cream and jam, thinking they had seen the last of Lob. But they were much mistaken. The whole family was playing cards by the fire in the front room after supper when there was a loud thump and a crash of china in the kitchen.

"My Christmas puddings!" exclaimed Jean, and ran out.

"Did you put TNT in them, then?" her husband said.

But it was Lob, who, finding the front door shut, had gone around to the back and bounced in through the open kitchen window, where the puddings were cooling on the sill. Luckily only the smallest was knocked down and broken.

Lob stood on his hind legs and plastered Sandy's face with licks. Then he did the same for the twins, who shrieked with joy.

"Where does this friend of yours come from?" inquired Mr. Pengelly.

"He's staying at the Fisherman's Arms—I mean his owner is."

"Then he must go back there. Find a bit of string, Sandy, to tie to his collar."

"I wonder how he found his way here," Mrs. Pengelly said when the reluctant Lob had been led whining away and Sandy had explained about their afternoon's game on the beach. "Fisherman's Arms is right round the other side of the harbor."

Lob's owner scolded him and thanked Mr. Pengelly for bringing him back. Jean Pengelly warned the children that they had better not encourage Lob any more if they met him on the beach, or it would only lead to more trouble. So they dutifully

took no notice of him the next day until he spoiled their good resolutions by dashing up to them with joyful barks, wagging his tail so hard that he winded Tess and knocked Tim's legs from under him.

They had a happy day, playing on the sand.

The next day was Saturday. Sandy had found out that Mr. Dodsworth was to catch the half-past-nine train. She went out secretly, down to the station, nodded to Mr. Hoskins, the stationmaster, who wouldn't dream of charging any local for a platform ticket, and climbed up on the footbridge that led over the tracks. She didn't want to be seen, but she did want to see. She saw Mr. Dodsworth get on the train, accompanied by an unhappy-looking Lob with drooping ears and tail. Then she saw the train slide away out of sight around the next headland, with a melancholy wail that sounded like Lob's last good-bye.

Sandy wished she hadn't had the idea of coming to the station. She walked home miserably, with her shoulders hunched and her hands in her pockets. For the rest of the day she was so cross and unlike herself that Tess and Tim were quite surprised, and her mother gave her a dose of senna.[7]

A week passed. Then, one evening, Mrs. Pengelly and the younger children were in the front room playing snakes and ladders. Mr. Pengelly and Don had gone fishing on the evening tide. If your father is a fisherman, he will never be home at the same time from one week to the next.

Suddenly, history repeating itself, there was a crash from the kitchen. Jean Pengelly leaped up, crying, "My blackberry jelly!"

6. *Scones* are sweet biscuits.

7. *Senna* is a medicine made from senna plants and used as a laxative.

H Literary Elements

FIGURES OF SPEECH: *Hyperbole*
Explain to students that hyperbole is a figure of speech that uses exaggeration to express strong emotion, make a point, or evoke humor. What effect is exaggeration supposed to have here? *(Lob's tongue cannot be a yard long. It adds humor and emphasizes how happy Lob is.)*

I Author's Craft

CHARACTERIZATION Have students describe Lob's personality. *(Lob is determined and persistent; he loves Sandy and will not be separated from her.)*

Vo•cab•u•lar•y Skills

Multiple-Meaning Words *Draft* has at least fourteen different meanings. Have students volunteer definitions, then select the one that fits here. *("Planning, doing a rough sketch of a written piece" fits here.)*

J Active Reading

CONNECT Have students explain how they would feel if they had to say goodbye forever to someone they loved. How do the children show their feelings? *(Don, an adolescent, walks out of the house. The young twins cry. Sandy feels bruised.)*

Teaching Options

Lob's Girl

She and the children had spent the morning picking and the afternoon boiling fruit.

But Sandy was ahead of her mother. With flushed cheeks and eyes like stars she had darted into the kitchen, where she and Lob were hugging one another in a frenzy of joy. About a yard of his tongue was out, and he was licking every part of her that he could reach.

"Good heavens!" exclaimed Jean. "How in the world did *he* get here?"

"He must have walked," said Sandy. "Look at his feet."

They were worn, dusty, and tarry. One had a cut on the pad.

"They ought to be bathed," said Jean Pengelly. "Sandy, run a bowl of warm water while I get the disinfectant."

"What'll we do about him, Mother?" said Sandy anxiously.

Mrs. Pengelly looked at her daughter's pleading eyes and sighed.

"He must go back to his owner, of course," she said, making her voice firm. "Your dad can get the address from the Fisherman's tomorrow, and phone him or send a telegram. In the meantime he'd better have a long drink and a good meal."

Lob was very grateful for the drink and the meal, and made no objection to having his feet washed. Then he flopped down on the hearthrug and slept in front of the fire they had lit because it was a cold, wet evening, with his head on Sandy's feet. He was a very tired dog. He had walked all the way from Liverpool to Cornwall, which is more than four hundred miles.

The next day Mr. Pengelly phoned Lob's owner, and the following morning Mr. Dodsworth arrived off the night train, decidedly put out, to take his pet home. That parting was worse than the first. Lob

whined, Don walked out of the house, the twins burst out crying, and Sandy crept up to her bedroom afterward and lay with her face pressed into the quilt, feeling as if she were bruised all over.

Jean Pengelly took them all into Plymouth to see the circus on the next day and the twins cheered up a little, but even the hour's ride in the train each way and the Liberty horses and performing seals could not cure Sandy's sore heart.

She need not have bothered, though. In ten days' time Lob was back—limping this time, with a torn ear and a patch missing out of his furry coat, as if he had met and tangled with an enemy or two in the course of his four-hundred-mile walk.

Bert Pengelly rang up Liverpool again. Mr. Dodsworth, when he answered, sounded weary. He said, "That dog has already cost me two days that I can't spare away from my work—plus endless time in police stations and drafting newspaper advertisements. I'm too old for these ups and downs. I think we'd better face the fact, Mr. Pengelly, that it's your family he wants to stay with—that is, if you want to have him."

Bert Pengelly gulped. He was not a rich man; and Lob was a pedigreed[8] dog. He said cautiously, "How much would you be asking for him?"

"Good heavens, man, I'm not suggesting I'd sell him to you. You must have him as a gift. Think of the train fares I'll be saving. You'll be doing me a good turn."

"Is he a big eater?" Bert asked doubtfully.

By this time the children, breathless in the background listening to one side of this conversation, had realized what was in

---

8. A *pedigreed* dog has papers showing that its ancestors were the same breed.

Less-Proficient Readers Less-proficient readers might need help interpreting some of the British expressions in the story. Write these sentences on the board:

- *For the rest of the day she was so cross and unlike herself...*
- *Bert Pengelly rang up Liverpool again.*
- *You'll be doing me a good turn.*

Activity Encourage pairs of students to use context clues to write brief definitions for the underlined phrases. **L1**

Additional Resources
📁 *Inclusion Strategies*

Joan Aiken

the wind and were dancing up and down with their hands clasped beseechingly.[9]

"Oh, not for his size," Lob's owner assured Bert. "Two or three pounds of meat a day and some vegetables and gravy and biscuits—he does very well on that."

Alexandra's father looked over the telephone at his daughter's swimming eyes and trembling lips. He reached a decision. "Well, then, Mr. Dodsworth," he said briskly, "we'll accept your offer and thank you very much. The children will be overjoyed and you can be sure Lob has come to a good home. They'll look after him and see he gets enough exercise. But I can tell you," he ended firmly, "if he wants to settle in with us he'll have to learn to eat a lot of fish."

So that was how Lob came to live with the Pengelly family. Everybody loved him and he loved them all. But there was never any question who came first with him. He was Sandy's dog. He slept by her bed and followed her everywhere he was allowed.

K Nine years went by, and each summer Mr. Dodsworth came back to stay at the Fisherman's Arms and call on his erstwhile dog. Lob always met him with recognition and dignified pleasure, accompanied him for a walk or two—but showed no signs of wishing to return to Liverpool. His place, he intimated,[10] was definitely with the Pengellys.

In the course of nine years Lob changed less than Sandy. As she went into her teens he became a little slower, a little stiffer, there was a touch of gray on his nose, but

he was still a handsome dog. He and Sandy still loved one another devotedly.

One evening in October all the summer visitors had left, and the little fishing town looked empty and secretive. It was a wet, windy dusk. When the children came home from school—even the twins were at high school[11] now, and Don was a full-fledged fisherman—Jean Pengelly said, "Sandy, your Aunt Rebecca says she's lonesome because Uncle Will Hoskins has gone out trawling,[12] and she wants one of you to go and spend the evening with her. You go, dear; you can take your homework with you."

Sandy looked far from enthusiastic.

"Can I take Lob with me?"

"You know Aunt Becky doesn't really like dogs— Oh, very well." Mrs. Pengelly sighed. "I suppose she'll have to put up with him as well as you."

Reluctantly Sandy tidied herself, took her schoolbag, put on the damp raincoat she had just taken off, fastened Lob's lead to his collar, and set off to walk through the dusk to Aunt Becky's cottage, which was five minutes' climb up the steep hill.

M The wind was howling through the shrouds of boats drawn up on the Hard.

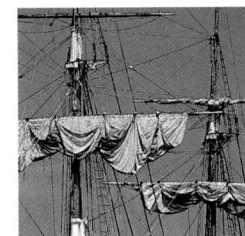

Did You Know?
A boat's *shrouds* are ropes that help support the masts.

L

---

9. *Beseechingly* means "in a begging or pleading manner."
10. Lob belonged to Mr. Dodsworth in earlier times *(erstwhile)*. To *intimate* is to hint at something without stating it directly.

11. An English *high school* starts with what would be the sixth or seventh grade in the United States.
12. *Trawling* is fishing with large nets that are dragged across the water's bottom.

Vocabulary
secretive (sē′ kri tiv) *adj.* keeping one's thoughts and feelings to oneself

---

K **Active Reading**

PREDICT Invite students to predict what may be about to happen. *(Since nine years is a long time for a dog, students may predict that the aging Lob will die soon. Others may predict that something will happen on the steep hill.)*

L **Critical Thinking**

LOGICAL REASONING Have students explain why the story now focuses on one day in October nine years after Lob comes to live with the Pengellys. *(Something important is going to happen.)*

M **Literary Elements**

MOOD Invite your students to describe the story's mood at this point. *(It is dark; the wind howls; the mood is ominous.)*

Listening and Speaking *Minilesson*

Creating a Radio Drama As you name a sound, have students suggest feelings that it can evoke in listeners. For example, if you say *laughter*, students might say *happiness*. If you say *howling wind*, students might say *fear* or *suspense*.

Activity Have small groups of students select one scene from the story to read as a radio drama. Encourage them to cre-

ate sound effects to accompany their drama. The sound effects should capture the mood or atmosphere of the passage. Encourage groups to practice their dramas and then perform them for the class. Have class members close their eyes as they listen. After each performance, have listeners describe the feelings and images each scene created in their minds. **L2** **COLLAB. LEARN.**

Literary Elements

[N] Literary Elements

SUSPENSE Invite students to explain how suspense builds in this paragraph. *(On a dark and rainy night, a truck has just hurtled down the hill Sandy and Lob climbed; but they aren't mentioned.)*

[O] Literary Elements

REPETITION Have students explain why they think the author again mentions the steep hill. *(Perhaps it is to remind readers how dangerous it is or to build suspense over Sandy and Lob.)*

[P] Literary Elements

SUSPENSE Encourage students to explain why the author describes the object by the wall as a pile of clothes or maybe the body of a child. *(The author doesn't spell out what has happened and builds suspense by withholding details.)*

[Q] Active Reading

PREDICT Invite students to predict what has happened to Lob. *(Perhaps Lob was killed by the truck; perhaps he ran away to get help; or maybe he is injured.)*

Teaching Options

Lob's Girl

"Put some cheerful music on, do," said Jean Pengelly to the nearest twin. "Anything to drown that wretched sound while I make your dad's supper." So Don, who had just come in, put on some rock music, loud. Which was why the Pengellys did not hear the truck <u>hurtle</u> down the hill and crash against the post office wall a few minutes later.

Dr. Travers was driving through Cornwall with his wife, taking a late holiday before patients began coming down with winter colds and flu. He saw the sign that said STEEP HILL. LOW GEAR FOR 1 1/2 MILES. Dutifully he changed into second gear.

"We must be nearly there," said his wife, looking out her window. "I noticed a sign on the coast road that said the Fisherman's Arms was two miles. What a narrow, dangerous hill! But the cottages are very pretty— Oh, Frank, stop, *stop!* There's a child, I'm sure it's a child—by the wall over there!"

Dr. Travers jammed on his brakes and brought the car to a stop. A little stream ran down by the road in a shallow stone culvert,[13] and half in the water lay something that looked, in the dusk, like a pile of clothes—or was it the body of a child? Mrs. Travers was out of the car in a flash, but her husband was quicker.

"Don't touch her, Emily!" he said sharply. "She's been hit. Can't be more than a few minutes. Remember that truck that overtook us half a mile back, speeding like the devil? Here, quick, go into that cottage and phone for an ambulance. The girl's in a bad way. I'll stay here and do what I can to stop the bleeding. Don't waste a minute."

Doctors are expert at stopping dangerous bleeding, for they know the right places to press. This Dr. Travers was able to do, but he didn't dare do more; the girl was lying in a queerly crumpled heap, and he guessed she had a number of bones broken and that it would be highly dangerous to move her. He watched her with great concentration, wondering where the truck had got to and what other damage it had done.

Mrs. Travers was very quick. She had seen plenty of accident cases and knew the importance of speed. The first cottage she tried had a phone; in four minutes she was back, and in six an ambulance was wailing down the hill.

Its attendants lifted the child onto a stretcher as carefully as if she were made of fine thistledown. The ambulance sped off to Plymouth—for the local cottage hospital[14] did not take serious accident cases—and Dr. Travers went down to the police station to report what he had done.

He found that the police already knew about the speeding truck—which had suffered from loss of brakes and ended up with its radiator halfway through the post office wall. The driver was concussed and shocked, but the police thought he was the only person injured— until Dr. Travers told his tale.

---

13. A *culvert* is a drainage ditch.

14. *Cottage hospital* is a British term for a small hospital with a staff of local doctors.

Vocabulary
hurtle (hurt′ əl) *v.* to move rapidly, especially with much force

---

Writing Minilesson

Creating Suspense Encourage students to help you list ways the author creates suspense in this story:
- by not telling readers what is happening and making them guess
- by creating a setting that seems spooky and dangerous
- by having characters perform an action that seems dangerous

Activity Have students write suspenseful stories. They may want to plan their tales by thinking about an event involving a dog or other pet, a scary event, or a setting that creates a mood of fear or worry.

Encourage students to use "Lob's Girl" as a writing model for creating suspense and mood. **L2**

Additional Resources

▌ *Writer's Choice,* Lesson 3.3

Viewing the photograph: Compare the home shown here with the painting *Straithes, Yorkshire,* on page 659. Which of the two pictures is closer to your image of the story's setting? Why?

FYI

Accident "Culprits"

What really caused this truck accident? The answer is momentum, gravity, and lack of friction. The moving truck had *momentum*—the tendency to maintain its speed and overcome resistance. On the steep hill, the truck's speed was increased by *gravity*—the natural force that causes objects to have weight and move toward the center of the earth. The heavier an object is and the faster it moves, the harder it is to stop. Failed brakes left the truck without a source of *friction*—resistance to motion of things that touch. So the truck gathered momentum and kept going until the post office wall—a stronger opposing force—stopped it.

LIFE SKILLS CONNECTION

Leading and Organizing Invite a group of students to think about a dangerous place in their community, such as an intersection in need of a stop sign, a residential street that drivers speed through, a place that needs a streetlight, or a bridge with a missing railing.

Activity Have students analyze the problem and decide what they think

should be done about it (such as installing speed bumps or lights). Then have students attend a neighborhood association meeting or set up an appointment with the mayor to discuss the problem and its solution. The mayor or association members may have ideas about the next step students can take to help solve the problem. **L2**

Critical Thinking

R

INFERRING Have students explain why Aunt Rebecca's attitude changes. *(Aunt Rebecca learns that Sandy has been hit by a truck and may die.)*

Literary Elements

S

SUSPENSE Have students explain why the author has not mentioned Lob until now. *(She builds suspense by not revealing where Lob is.)*

Critical Thinking

T

DRAWING CONCLUSIONS Ask students to explain why it is bad that Sandy has shown no signs of regaining consciousness. *(The doctor told Bert and Jean that Sandy had a chance if she showed signs of coming out of the coma.)*

R

At half-past nine that night Aunt Rebecca Hoskins was sitting by her fire thinking <u>aggrieved</u> thoughts about the inconsiderateness of nieces who were asked to supper and never turned up when she was startled by a neighbor, who burst in exclaiming, "Have you heard about Sandy Pengelly, then, Mrs. Hoskins? Terrible thing, poor little soul, and they don't know if she's likely to live. Police have got the truck driver that hit her—ah, it didn't ought to be allowed, speeding through the place like that at umpty miles an hour, they ought to jail him for life— not that that'd be any comfort to poor Bert and Jean."

Horrified, Aunt Rebecca put on a coat and went down to her brother's house. She found the family with white shocked faces; Bert and Jean were about to drive off to the hospital where Sandy had been taken, and the twins were crying bitterly. Lob was nowhere to be seen. But Aunt Rebecca was not interested in dogs; she did not inquire about him.

S

"Thank the lord you've come, Beck," said her brother. "Will you stay the night with Don and the twins? Don's out looking for Lob and heaven knows when we'll be back; we may get a bed with Jean's mother in Plymouth."

"Oh, if only I'd never invited the poor child," wailed Mrs. Hoskins. But Bert and Jean hardly heard her.

That night seemed to last forever. The twins cried themselves to sleep. Don came home very late and grim-faced. Bert and Jean sat in a waiting room of the Western Counties Hospital, but Sandy was unconscious, they were told, and she remained so. All that could be done for her was done. She was given transfusions to replace all the blood she had lost. The broken bones were set and put in slings and cradles.[15]

"Is she a healthy girl? Has she a good constitution?"[16] the emergency doctor asked.

"Aye, doctor, she is that," Bert said hoarsely. The lump in Jean's throat prevented her from answering: she merely nodded.

"Then she ought to have a chance. But I won't conceal from you that her condition is very serious, unless she shows signs of coming out from this coma."

T

But as hour <u>succeeded</u> hour, Sandy showed no signs of recovering consciousness. Her parents sat in the waiting room with <u>haggard</u> faces; sometimes one of them would go to telephone the family at home, or try to get a little sleep at the home of Granny Pearce, not far away.

At noon next day Dr. and Mrs. Travers went to the Pengelly cottage to inquire how Sandy was doing, but the report was gloomy: "Still in a very serious condition." The twins were miserably unhappy. They forgot that they had sometimes called their elder sister bossy and only remembered how often she had shared her pocket money with them, how she read to them and took them for picnics and helped with their homework.

---

15. Here, the *cradles* are frames that keep Sandy's bedclothes from touching her injuries.
16. Here, *constitution* refers to a person's physical condition.

Vocabulary

aggrieved (ə grēvd´) *adj.* feeling wronged, as by an insult or unfair treatment
succeed (sək sēd´) *v.* to come or happen after in time, place, or order
haggard (hag´ ərd) *adj.* looking worn as a result of grief, worry, or illness

Teaching Options

MEETING INDIVIDUAL NEEDS — MULTIPLE LEARNING STYLES

Linguistic Students with linguistic skills may enjoy interviewing in order to learn more about careers in which people care for dogs, such as dog training or dog grooming.

Activity Have students work in pairs or small groups to set up an interview with a veterinarian, a dog trainer, or a dog groomer. Have the class help the interviewer brainstorm a list of questions for the interview. Encourage students to ask their interviewee questions such as how to examine a dog's teeth, how to teach a dog one command (such as *heel*), or how to groom a dog. Then have students prepare a demonstration to illustrate what they've learned to the class. **L2** **COLLAB. LEARN.**

Joan Aiken ~

Now there was no Sandy, no Mother and Dad, Don went around with a gray, shuttered face, and worse still, there was no Lob.

The Western Counties Hospital is a large one, with dozens of different departments and five or six connected buildings, each with three or four entrances. By that afternoon it became noticeable that a dog seemed to have taken up position outside the hospital, with the fixed intention of getting in. Patiently he would try first one entrance and then another, all the way around, and then begin again. Sometimes he would get a little way inside, following a visitor, but animals were, of course, forbidden, and he was always kindly but firmly turned out again. Sometimes the guard at the main entrance gave him a pat or offered him a bit of sandwich—he looked so wet and beseeching and desperate. But he never ate the sandwich. No one seemed to own him or to know where he came from: Plymouth is a large city and he might have belonged to anybody.

At tea time Granny Pearce came through the pouring rain to bring a flask of hot tea with brandy in it to her daughter and son-in-law. Just as she reached the main entrance the guard was gently but forcibly shoving out a large, <u>agitated</u>, soaking-wet Alsatian dog.

"No, old fellow, you can *not* come in. Hospitals are for people, not for dogs."

"Why, bless me," exclaimed old Mrs. Pearce. "That's Lob! Here, Lob. Lobby boy!"

Lob ran to her, whining. Mrs. Pearce walked up to the desk.

"I'm sorry, madam, you can't bring that dog in here," the guard said.

Mrs. Pearce was a very determined old lady. She looked the porter in the eye.

"Now, see here, young man. That dog has walked twenty miles from St. Killan to get to my granddaughter. Heaven knows how he knew she was here, but it's plain he knows. And he ought to have his rights! He ought to get to see her! Do you know," she went on, bristling, "that dog has walked the length of England—*twice*—to be with that girl? And you think you can keep him out with your fiddling rules and regulations?"

"I'll have to ask the medical officer," the guard said weakly.

"You do that, young man." Granny Pearce sat down in a determined manner, shutting her umbrella, and Lob sat patiently dripping at her feet. Every now and then he shook his head, as if to dislodge something heavy that was tied around his neck.

Presently a tired, thin, intelligent-looking man in a white coat came downstairs, with an impressive, silver-haired man in a dark suit, and there was a low-voiced discussion. Granny Pearce eyed them, biding her time.

"Frankly . . . not much to lose," said the older man. The man in the white coat approached Granny Pearce.

"It's strictly against every rule, but as it's such a serious case we are making an exception," he said to her quietly. "But only *outside* her bedroom door—and only for a moment or two."

Without a word, Granny Pearce rose and stumped upstairs. Lob followed close to her skirts, as if he knew his hope lay with her.

Vocabulary
agitated (aj′ ə tāt′ əd) *adj.* excited, nervous, or disturbed; stirred up

Active Reading

EVALUATE Ask students to explain why Bert and Jean are "white-faced and shocked" when they see Lob.
(The hospital is far from their home; they thought Lob was lost; or they thought Lob was killed.)

Critical Thinking

EVALUATING Have students explain whether or not they think the dog in the hospital was Lob. You may wish to share the following model.

Model: Now I know Lob was killed, but Lob has a history of overcoming obstacles to be with Sandy. The dog in the hospital shook his head as if to dislodge something heavy around his neck. I now know that Don tied concrete to Lob's collar and buried him at sea. Perhaps Lob has made his most difficult journey of all.

Thematic Focus

A Different Dimension Have students explain how this story relates to the theme. *(Lob seems to have returned from a different dimension to help Sandy.)*

✔ ASSESSMENT OPTIONS

📁 *Quick Checks,* p. 55

Lob's Girl

They waited in the green-floored corridor outside Sandy's room. The door was half shut. Bert and Jean were inside. Everything was terribly quiet. A nurse came out. The white-coated man asked her something and she shook her head. She had left the door ajar, and through it could now be seen a high, narrow bed with a lot of gadgets around it. Sandy lay there, very flat under the covers, very still. Her head was turned away. All Lob's attention was riveted on the bed. He strained toward it, but Granny Pearce clasped his collar firmly.

"I've done a lot for you, my boy, now you behave yourself," she whispered grimly. Lob let out a faint whine, anxious and pleading.

At the sound of that whine Sandy stirred just a little. She sighed and moved her head the least fraction. Lob whined again. And then Sandy turned her head right over. Her eyes opened, looking at the door.

"Lob?" she murmured—no more than a breath of sound. "Lobby, boy?"

The doctor by Granny Pearce drew a quick, sharp breath. Sandy moved her left arm—the one that was not broken—from below the covers and let her hand dangle down, feeling, as she always did in the mornings, for Lob's furry head. The doctor nodded slowly.

"All right," he whispered. "Let him go to the bedside. But keep ahold of him."

Granny Pearce and Lob moved to the bedside. Now she could see Bert and Jean, white-faced and shocked, on the far side of the bed. But she didn't look at them. She looked at the smile on her granddaughter's face as the groping fingers found Lob's wet

ears and gently pulled them. "Good boy," whispered Sandy, and fell asleep again.

Granny Pearce led Lob out into the passage again. There she let go of him and he ran off swiftly down the stairs. She would have followed him, but Bert and Jean had come out into the passage, and she spoke to Bert fiercely.

"I don't know why you were so foolish as not to bring the dog before! Leaving him to find the way here himself—"

"But, Mother!" said Jean Pengelly. "That can't have been Lob. What a chance to take! Suppose Sandy hadn't—" She stopped, with her handkerchief pressed to her mouth.

"Not Lob? I've known that dog nine years! I suppose I ought to know my own granddaughter's dog?"

"Listen, Mother," said Bert. "Lob was killed by the same truck that hit Sandy. Don found him—when he went to look for Sandy's schoolbag. He was—he was dead. Ribs all smashed. No question of that. Don told me on the phone—he and Will Hoskins rowed a half mile out to sea and sank the dog with a lump of concrete tied to his collar. Poor old boy. Still—he was getting on. Couldn't have lasted forever."

"*Sank him at sea? Then what—?*"

Slowly old Mrs. Pearce, and then the other two, turned to look at the trail of dripping-wet footprints that led down the hospital stairs.

In the Pengellys' garden they have a stone, under the palm tree. It says: "Lob. Sandy's dog. Buried at sea."

❖

Teaching Options

Grammar and Language *Minilesson*

Using Troublesome Words Put the following chart on the board and discuss each word's meaning:

Word	Meaning	Example
its	the possessive form of it	The dog wags its tail.
it's	the contraction of it is	It's raining cats and dogs.
their	the possessive form of they	Their raincoats are completely soaked.
they're	the contraction of they are	See if they're dry yet.

Activity Have students choose the correct form to complete each of the following sentences.
- Some people choose *(they're, their)* dogs.
- *(It's, Its)* tongue was a yard long.
- Sandy helped them with *(they're, their)* homework.
- *(It's, Its)* against the rules. **L2**

Additional Resources

🖊 *Grammar and Language Transparency 53*

📕 *Grammar and Language Workbook,* pp. 223–224, 227–228

📕 *Grammar and Composition Handbook,* Lesson 4.4

📕 *Writer's Choice,* Lesson 17.2

Responding to Literature

PERSONAL RESPONSE

What do you think really happened in the hospital room?

Analyzing Literature

RECALL

1. How far does Lob travel to reach the Pengelly family after his owner returns to Liverpool?
2. Why does Lob's owner give the dog away?
3. What happens to Sandy nine years after she meets Lob?
4. What visitor does Granny Pearce see outside the hospital? How does Sandy respond to the visitor?

INTERPRET

5. What do you think would motivate a dog like Lob to travel great distances to return to a place he had once visited?
6. Describe the difference between the former owner's and Sandy's attachment to Lob.
7. The author includes a detailed description of the accident scene. In your opinion, why doesn't the author reveal at that point that the victim is Sandy?
8. Why are Sandy's parents especially shocked at Sandy's response to the dog?

EVALUATE AND CONNECT

9. Do you believe a pet could actually cause a medical change in a patient? Explain.
10. Theme Connection What does the story's ending suggest about the power of Sandy's and Lob's feelings for each other?

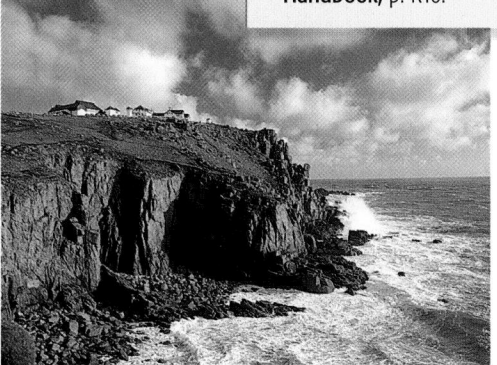

LITERARY ELEMENTS

Suspense

Have you ever been so anxious while reading a story that you've held your breath or bitten your nails? That feeling of uncertainty about what will happen next in a story is caused by the **suspense** a writer creates. Writers can build suspense by raising questions in a reader's mind about characters and their motivations, by describing a mood that is threatening or mysterious, or by including hints about possible developments.

1. How does the author build suspense about whether Lob will get to Sandy's hospital room?

2. Describe briefly how suspense was created in another story you have read.

● See **Literary Terms Handbook**, p. R10.

Responding to the Selection

Personal Response

Students' ideas about what happened in the hospital room should be supported by evidence from the story.

Analyzing Literature

1. Lob travels four hundred miles.
2. Lob's owner gives the dog to the Pengellys because Lob keeps returning to them.
3. Sandy is hit by a truck nine years after she meets Lob.
4. Granny Pearce sees Lob outside the hospital. Sandy responds to Lob in the hospital by recovering from her coma.
5. Lob is motivated by a strong bond with Sandy.
6. The former owner was nice to Lob, but Sandy deeply loves Lob.
7. The author doesn't reveal that the accident victim is Sandy because she wants to build suspense.
8. Sandy's parents are shocked because they know that Lob was killed by the truck.
9. Sample: A pet could cause a medical change in a patient if the patient loves the animal.
10. The ending suggests that Sandy's and Lob's love was so strong that Lob returned from a different dimension to help Sandy.

LITERARY ELEMENTS

1. The author describes Lob's persistent but unsuccessful attempts to get into the hospital.
2. Students should use examples from the selected stories to support their ideas about how the authors create suspense.

Additional Resources

Literary Elements Transparency 55

Literature and Writing

Writing About Literature

Students' paragraphs should
- explain what occurs during the story's resolution.
- analyze the effectiveness of the resolution.
- describe the effect other methods of resolving the story would have on readers.

Personal Writing

Students' journal entries should
- describe their reactions to Lob.
- use examples from the story to explain whether Lob was believable.
- explain whether they could be as close to an animal as Sandy was to Lob.

Extending Your Response

Literature Groups Before students meet, encourage them to think about what may happen next in the story. Have them each create a brief illustration showing one idea to share with the group. **COLLAB. LEARN.**

Learning for Life Encourage students to develop plans that could really be put into action. When they are finished, encourage pairs to work together with the animals to implement their plans.

Interdisciplinary Activity

Students will find many sites on the Internet devoted to specific dog breeds and their special talents. Students may want to define their search terms with breed names, such as *Labrador Retriever, Beagle,* or *Golden Retriever.*

Literature and Writing

Writing About Literature

Resolution Do you think Joan Aiken wrote a satisfying conclusion to the story? Write a paragraph that analyzes the effectiveness of the story's **resolution.**

Personal Writing

Special Connections Look back at what you wrote about animals and people in the **Focus Activity** on page 658. Then write about your reaction to the character of Lob in a journal entry. Do you think he was believable? Can you imagine being as close to an animal as Sandy was to Lob?

Extending Your Response

Literature Groups

The Next Chapter By the end of the story, Sandy's fate is still unclear. With a group, brainstorm ideas for an added chapter for the story. Build on what you already know about the characters and setting. Draw pictures to illustrate your concept. Choose the one that best illustrates your group's ideas, and share it with the class.

Learning for Life

Community Service Plan Visits from animals can have a beneficial effect on the sick and elderly. Work with a partner to write a plan for your own community that involves students, their pets, and people who could be cheered by visits.

Interdisciplinary Activity

Science Alsatians are used frequently as guide dogs for the sight-impaired. Research ways in which another dog breed has been used to help humans. Consider such skills as hunting, herding, rescuing, guarding, and assisting the disabled. Present your findings as a television reporter.

Reading Further

If you would like to read other mysterious stories by Joan Aiken, try these:
The Wolves of Willoughby Chase
Night Fall

📖 **Save your work for your portfolio.**

Skill Minilessons

GRAMMAR AND LANGUAGE • APOSTROPHES IN POSSESSIVES

An **apostrophe** can be used to show possession. Follow these rules for forming possessives:

- Use an apostrophe and an *s* to form the possessive of a singular noun.
  Lob + 's = Lob's
- Use an apostrophe and an *s* to form the possessive of a plural noun that does not end in *s*.
  children + 's = children's
- Use an apostrophe alone to form the possessive of a plural noun that ends in *s*.
  dogs + ' = dogs'

PRACTICE Write the possessive form of each word below.

1. Sandy	5. houses
2. ambulances	6. train
3. ears	7. women
4. people	8. telegram

- For more about apostrophes, see **Language Handbook,** p. R40.

READING AND THINKING • SCANNING

Scanning is a method of rapid reading in which you search quickly through a piece of writing for a particular piece of information. You can scan to look for the answer to a specific question. When scanning, run your eyes across each page of the story until they fall on the word or words you need.

- For more about scanning and related reading strategies, see **Reading Handbook,** pp. R82–R83.

PRACTICE Scan "Lob's Girl" to find the following information:

1. whose picture hangs by Granny Pearce's kitchen sink
2. a physical description of Lob
3. the names of two people who stayed at the Fisherman's Arms
4. the number of years Lob is a member of the family

VOCABULARY • UNLOCKING MEANING

Within *secretive,* you can see the word *secret.* These two words are related words. Using what you know about one can help you understand the other. Use what you know about each italicized word to complete each statement correctly.

PRACTICE Use what you know about each italic word to complete the item.

1. *agitated* If an <u>agitator</u> spoke to a crowd of people, he or she would
   a. stir them up
   b. make them laugh
   c. calm them down
2. *succeed* The <u>successor</u> to the president of the United States is the
   a. Congress
   b. Supreme Court
   c. next president
3. *resolution* A <u>resolute</u> person could be described as
   a. worried
   b. determined
   c. confused
4. *aggrieved* If you write down your <u>grievances</u>, you make a list of
   a. possessions
   b. complaints
   c. assignments

Skill Minilessons

GRAMMAR AND LANGUAGE
APOSTROPHES IN POSSESSIVES

1. Sandy's
2. ambulances'
3. ears'
4. people's
5. houses'
6. train's
7. women's
8. telegram's

READING AND THINKING
SCANNING

1. a queen in a diamond tiara and pearls
2. topaz eyes; black-tipped ears; a thick, soft coat; bushy black-tipped tail
3. Mr. Dodsworth; Dr. Travers and his wife
4. nine years

VOCABULARY
UNLOCKING MEANING

1. a   2. c   3. b   4. b

Additional Resources

- *Grammar and Language Workbook,* pp. 273–274
- *Grammar and Composition Handbook,* Lesson 13.7
- *Writer's Choice,* Lesson 20.7
- *Reading Workbook,* pp. 97–98
- *Vocabulary Practice,* p. 37

✔ ASSESSMENT OPTIONS

- *Quick Checks,* p. 55
- *Selection and Theme Assessment,* pp. 95–96
- *Performance Assessment,* p. 52
- *Testmaker*

Objective

• To recognize and use strategies for monitoring comprehension

Teaching Strategies

Dramatize the question-asking strategies suggested on page 672 by having students practice asking their questions aloud. Use the sample paragraph, or any paragraph from the previous story. Have students read silently, but ask the questions they have out loud, as if they were speaking directly to the writer. Questions don't have to be formed completely. For example, if students practice using the sample paragraph they may ask: *How do they know that? Why didn't he do more?*

Exercise

1. Answers may include: I wonder what the hospital looks like? Who is the dog? What happened to the dog after the accident? Why is the dog hanging around the hospital?
2. Students may say that the dog doesn't give up easily. He is determined to get into the hospital even if he has to wait patiently or try unsuccessfully many times.

Additional Resources
📁 *Reading Workbook*

Teaching Options

Reading and Thinking Skills

Monitoring Comprehension

To get the most out of their reading, active readers ask questions as they read. By asking questions, they monitor their comprehension of a piece of writing. Ask yourself questions as you read the following passage from "Lob's Girl."

> Doctors are experts at stopping dangerous bleeding, for they know the right places to press. This Dr. Travers was able to do, but he didn't dare do more; the girl was lying in a queerly crumpled heap, and he guessed she had a number of bones broken and that it would be highly dangerous to move her. He watched her with great concentration, wondering where the truck had got to and what other damage it had done.

What does the doctor do for the injured girl? What does the writer mean by a "crumpled heap"? Why does the doctor wonder about the truck? If you can answer these kinds of questions about the scene, then you understand exactly what is happening. If not, stop and reread the passage until you can figure out what is going on.

● For more about monitoring comprehension, see **Reading Handbook**, pp. R82–R83.

EXERCISE

Read the following excerpt from "Lob's Girl." Then answer the questions.

> By that afternoon it became noticeable that a dog seemed to have taken up position outside the hospital, with the fixed intention of getting in. Patiently he would try first one entrance and then another, all the way around, and then begin again. Sometimes he would get a little way inside, following a visitor, but animals were, of course, forbidden, and he was always kindly but firmly turned out again.

1. Write at least two questions you might ask yourself as you monitor your comprehension of the passage.

2. From reading this description, what do you learn about the determination of the dog?

MEETING INDIVIDUAL NEEDS — INCLUSION STRATEGIES

Less-Proficient Readers Write this sentence from "Lob's Girl" on the board: *Some people choose their dogs, and some dogs choose their people.*

Activity Ask each student to choose an opening sentence from a paragraph in "Lob's Girl" and write it on an index card, along with as many questions that relate to it as possible. Have students exchange cards and hunt for the answers to one another's questions in the story. **L1**

Additional Resources
📁 *Inclusion Strategies*

Writing Skills

Using Sentence Variety

What do these sentences from "Lob's Girl" have in common?

He must have walked.

He was a very tired dog.

Bert Pengelly rang up Liverpool again.

If you guessed that they are all fairly short sentences, you're right. There's nothing wrong with short sentences, but good writers like to vary their sentence patterns to avoid monotony. Notice the varied lengths in the following sentences from "Lob's Girl." You can add variety to your sentences by using techniques like these.

Alternate shorter sentences and longer sentences:

She opened her eyes and looked. It was a tongue. Its owner was a large and bouncy young Alsatian, or German shepherd, with topaz eyes, black-tipped prick ears, a thick, soft coat, and a bushy black-tipped tail.

Combine short sentences into long ones:

Lob's owner scolded him. He thanked Mrs. Pengelly for bringing him back.

Lob's owner scolded him and thanked Mrs. Pengelly for bringing him back.

Start with an adjective or adverb:

Horrified, Aunt Rebecca put on a coat and went down to her brother's house.

Start with an adverb phrase:

Without a word, Granny Pearce rose and stumped upstairs.

Start with a subordinate clause:

Just as she reached the main entrance, the guard was gently but forcibly shoving out a large, agitated, soaking-wet Alsatian dog.

EXERCISES

1. Look over something you have written. Revise it to increase the variety of your sentence patterns. Use the techniques shown above.

2. Write a paragraph describing a scene from your favorite animal story, television show, or movie. Vary your sentence patterns, using the techniques shown above.

Objective

- To recognize and use sentence variety in writing

Teaching Strategies

Remind students that it is acceptable to use short sentences, but that it is important not to use *only* short sentences. You may wish to have students practice their sentence-combining skills with the following sentences: *The man was tired. The man swung hard. The man swung fast. The man had a rope. The man reached the summit.*

Exercises

1. Students should be able to identify which of the techniques they used to vary sentence patterns.
2. Some students may be able to write paragraphs with varied sentence patterns in a first draft. Others may wish to rewrite their paragraphs focusing specifically on this task after a first draft has been written.

Additional Resources

📕 *Writer's Choice,* Lesson 2.8

Teaching Options

Grammar and Language *Minilesson*

Identifying Lively Sentence Patterns
Writers use a mix of simple, compound, and complex sentences when they write, just as we do when we speak.

Activity Have students work in small groups. Ask each group to find and read aloud a paragraph or poem that demonstrates lively sentence patterning, tell why they chose it, and explain how sentence variety affects its impact. **L2** **COLLAB. LEARN.**

Additional Resources

🖇 *Grammar and Language Transparency 54*

📕 *Grammar and Language Workbook,* pp. 323–324

📕 *Grammar and Composition Handbook,* Lesson 1.6

📕 *Writer's Choice,* Lesson 2.8

Objectives

- To read and analyze a short story about a computer
- To recognize and understand the purpose of irony
- To write a paragraph about a computer as a main character

Skills

Reading/Thinking: Inferring; Drawing Conclusions; Synthesizing; Comparing and Contrasting
Writing: Vision of the Future
Vocabulary: Etymology
Grammar/Language: Compound Predicates
Life Skills: User's Manual
Collaboration: Literature Groups

Motivating
→OPTIONS

Literature Launchers:
"The Many Worlds of Isaac Asimov"

Videodisc Side B, Segment 19

Also available in VHS.

Selection Focus Transparency 56: Have students discuss whether scientists of the future will be able to alter people's personalities.

Focus Activity: As an extension of the Focus Activity, have students work in small groups to discuss whether computers could become as smart as people one day.

Before You Read
Key Item

MEET ISAAC ASIMOV

Isaac Asimov (ī′ zək a′ zi môf) described his talent for explaining scientific principles as the ability to "read a dozen dull books and make one interesting book out of them." Asimov wrote or edited more than 500 books in his lifetime—far more than millions of Americans will read in a lifetime. Born in Russia, Asimov was raised in Brooklyn, New York. In addition to writing, he worked as a biochemist and taught biochemistry at Boston University.

Isaac Asimov was born in 1920 and died in 1992. "Key Item" was first published in 1968.

FOCUS ACTIVITY

Are computers becoming more and more human-like?

Graph It!
Ask ten people whether computers will ever be as smart as humans, and if so, how soon. Compile your results in a graph and share it with the class.

Setting a Purpose
Read this story to find out what the "key item" is.

BACKGROUND

The modern digital computer was first imagined by British mathematician Alan Turing in 1936. It looked like an automatic typewriter with math symbols instead of letters. Today, computers can turn appliances on and off, direct satellites, and create three-dimensional models of machines that do not exist. Chess-playing supercomputers can compute more than 100 million chess positions per second and have won games against world chess champions.

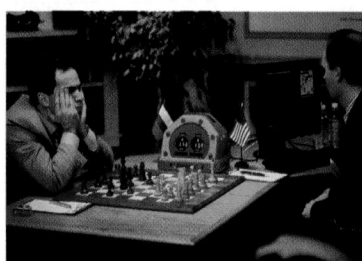

VOCABULARY PREVIEW

therapy (ther′ ə pē) *n.* treatment of an injury, disease, or mental disorder; p. 676
efficient (i fish′ ənt) *adj.* producing a desired effect with a minimum of effort or waste; p. 677
sufficient (sə fish′ ənt) *adj.* adequate; enough; p. 677
accede (ak sēd′) *v.* to give in; go along with; p. 677
collective (kə lek′ tiv) *adj.* having to do with a group of persons or things; common; shared; p. 677

RESOURCE MANAGER

Lesson Planning Resource
The ***Theme Seven Planning Guide*** (pp. 14–21) provides additional lesson notes and reduced versions of all print resources.

📁 **Other Print Resources**
- Active Reading Guide, p. 56
- Vocabulary Practice, p. 38
- Reading Workbook, pp. 99–100
- Grammar and Language Workbook, pp. 53–54

- Grammar and Composition Handbook, Lesson 1.5
- Quick Checks, p. 56
- Selection and Theme Assessment, pp. 97–98
- Performance Assessment, p. 53
- Spanish Summaries, p. 56
- Spanish Translations
- Inclusion Strategies
- English Language Learners Sourcebook

 Transparencies
- Selection Focus 56
- Literary Elements 56
- Grammar and Language 55

Technology
 Literature Launchers
 Audio Library
 Spanish Audio Library
 Glencoe Literature Web Site
 Testmaker

KEY ITEM

Isaac Asimov

Jack Weaver came out of the vitals[1] of Multivac looking utterly worn and disgusted.

From the stool, where the other maintained his own stolid[2] watch, Todd Nemerson said, "Nothing?"

"Nothing," said Weaver. "Nothing, nothing, nothing. No one can find anything wrong with it."

"Except that it won't work, you mean."

"You're no help sitting there!"

"I'm thinking."

"Thinking!" Weaver showed a canine[3] at one side of his mouth.

Nemerson stirred impatiently on his stool. "Why not? There are six teams of computer technologists roaming around in the corridors of Multivac. They haven't come up with anything in three days. Can't you spare one person to think?"

"It's not a matter of thinking. We've got to look. Somewhere a relay is stuck."

"It's not that simple, Jack!"

"Who says it's simple. You know how many million relays we have there?"

---

1. *Vitals* are parts that are necessary to keep a body alive or a machine operating. Here, the word refers to small chambers containing such parts inside Multivac.
2. A *stolid* (stol′ id) person is behaving unemotionally, without excitement.
3. Weaver shows his disgust by curling his upper lip, revealing a tooth. The two pointed teeth on each side of the top front teeth are called *canine* (kā′ nīn) teeth.

A DIFFERENT DIMENSION ✿ 675

SUMMARY

The world's economy depends on Multivac, a huge computer. One day, Multivac refuses to answer a question. Six teams of computer scientists wander inside the computer for three days looking for the problem. They can't find anything wrong. Todd Nemerson thinks the computer has become too human-like. He thinks the key to solving the problem is to figure out why a human, in Multivac's position, would not answer.

📁 *Spanish Summaries,* p. 56

A **Active Reading**

PREDICT Invite students to look at the title of this story. Then let volunteers read the first page of text aloud. Ask students to describe the problem. Then, using the title of the story and what they already know about computers as a clues, have students predict how this problem may be solved. Suggest that students periodically revisit their predictions as they read to verify or revise them.

Additional Resources
📁 *Active Reading Guide,* p. 56
🎧 *Audio Library*
🎧 *Spanish Audio Library*

Teaching Options

CONNECTING TO OTHER SELECTIONS

The chart at the right shows three ways to connect "Key Item" to other selections in this book.

For specific teaching strategies, see the *Theme Seven Planning Guide,* pages 17–18.

Connection	Title
Life Skills: Problem Solving	→ "The Million-Pound Bank Note," p. 573
Thematic: Surprises	→ "Beware of the Dog," p. 603
Literary: Science Fiction	→ "All Summer in a Day," p. 461

B Active Reading

EVALUATE If Nemerson had finished this sentence, he might have said "...*Multivac becomes human?*" You may wish to use the following model.

Model: I know Multivac is just a machine. It doesn't have nerves and other biological features that contribute to human emotions. On the other hand, Multivac has become as complex as a human brain, so perhaps it can have some complex human feelings, too.

C Critical Thinking

INFERRING Have students explain why the world's economy depends on knowing the price of wheat next summer. *(Nations can plan better. For example, if the price will be high, governments that need wheat can raise the cash needed. If the price will be low, governments can spend their money on other things.)*

D Active Reading

EVALUATE Encourage students to explain what the key item is. *(The key item is whatever is causing the computer to fail—whatever is preventing it from functioning the way people want it to.)*

Teaching Options

"That doesn't matter. If it were just a relay, Multivac would have alternate circuits, devices for locating the flaw, and facilities to repair or replace the ailing part. The trouble is, Multivac won't only not answer the original question, it won't tell us what's wrong with it. —And meanwhile, there'll be panic in every city if we don't do something. The world's economy depends on Multivac, and everyone knows that."

"I know it, too. But what's there to do?"

"I told you, *think*. There must be something we're missing completely. Look, Jack, there isn't a computer bigwig in a hundred years who hasn't devoted himself to making Multivac more complicated. It can do so much now—hell, it can even talk and listen. It's practically as complex as the human brain. We can't understand the human brain, so why should we understand Multivac?"

"Aw, come on. Next you'll be saying Multivac is human."

"Why not?" Nemerson grew absorbed and seemed to sink into himself. "Now that you mention it, why not? Could we tell if Multivac passed the thin dividing line where it stopped being a machine and started being human? *Is there a dividing line, for that matter? If the brain is just more complex than Multivac, and we keep making Multivac more complex, isn't there a point where . . .*" He mumbled down into silence.

Weaver said impatiently, "What are you driving at? Suppose Multivac were human. How would that help us find out why it isn't working?"

"For a human reason, maybe. Suppose *you* were asked the most probable price of

wheat next summer and didn't answer. Why wouldn't you answer?"

"Because I wouldn't know. But Multivac would know! We've given it all the factors. It can analyze futures in weather, politics, and economics. We know it can. It's done it before."

"All right. Suppose I asked the question and you knew the answer but didn't tell me. Why not?"

Weaver snarled, "Because I had a brain tumor. Because I had been knocked out. Doggone it, because my machinery was out of order. That's just what we're trying to find out about Multivac. We're looking for the place where its machinery is out of order, for the key item."

"Only you haven't found it." Nemerson got off his stool. "Listen, ask me the question Multivac stalled on."

"How? Shall I run the tape through you?"

"Come on, Jack. Give me the talk that goes along with it. You do talk to Multivac, don't you?"

"I've got to. Therapy."

Nemerson nodded. "Yes, that's the story. Therapy. That's the official story. We talk to it in order to pretend it's a human being so that we don't get neurotic[4] over having a machine know so much more than we do. We turn a frightening metal monster into a protective father image."

"If you want to put it that way."

"Well, it's wrong and you know it. A computer as complex as Multivac *must* talk

---

4. *Neurotic* (noo rot′ ik) having symptoms of an emotional disorder.

Vocabulary
therapy (ther′ ə pē) *n.* treatment of an injury, disease, or mental disorder

---

ENGLISH LANGUAGE LEARNERS

MEETING INDIVIDUAL NEEDS

Computer Terminology This story provides an opportunity for English language learners to become familiar with words related to computers.

Activity Encourage small groups of students to complete sketches of the inside of the Multivac computer and the control wall with its dials and lights. Then have students reread the selection to find words with which to label

their drawings. *(relay, program, tape with coded dots, control wall, dials, lights, valves)* Encourage students to add computer terms they already know. They can refer to their drawings as they complete the Responding to Literature pages.
COLLAB. LEARN.

Additional Resources
📁 *English Language Learners Sourcebook*

and listen to be efficient. Just putting in and taking out coded dots isn't sufficient. At a certain level of complexity, Multivac must be made to seem human because, by God, it *is* human. Come on, Jack, ask me the question. I want to see my reaction to it."

Jack Weaver flushed. "This is silly."

"Come on, will you?"

It was a measure of Weaver's depression and desperation that he acceded. Half sullenly, he pretended to be feeding the program into Multivac, speaking as he did so in his usual manner. He commented on the latest information concerning farm unrest, talked about the new equations describing jet-stream contortions, lectured on the solar constant.

He began stiffly enough, but warmed to this task out of long habit, and when the last of the program was slammed home, he almost closed contact with a physical snap at Todd Nemerson's waist.

He ended briskly, "All right, now. Work that out and give us the answer pronto."

For a moment, having done, Jack Weaver stood there, nostrils flaring, as though he was feeling once more the excitement of throwing into action the most gigantic and glorious machine ever put together by the mind and hands of humans.

Then he remembered and muttered, "All right. That's it."

E Nemerson said, "At least I know now why *I* wouldn't answer, so let's try that on Multivac. Look, clear Multivac; make sure the investigators have their paws off it. Then run the program into it and let me do the talking. Just once."

Weaver shrugged and turned to Multivac's control wall, filled with its somber, unwinking dials and lights. Slowly he cleared it. One by one he ordered the teams away.

Then, with a deep breath, he began once more feeding the program into Multivac. It was the twelfth time all told, the dozenth time. Somewhere a distant news commentator would spread the word that they were trying again. All over the world a Multivac-dependent people would be holding its collective breath.

Nemerson talked as Weaver fed the data silently. He talked diffidently,[5] trying to remember what it was that Weaver had said, but waiting for the moment when the key item might be added.

Weaver was done and now a note of tension was in Nemerson's voice. He said, "All right, now, Multivac. Work that out and give us the answer." He paused and added the key item. He said, *"Please!"*

And all over Multivac, the valves and relays went joyously to work. After all, a machine has feelings—when it isn't a machine anymore.

_____

5. *Diffidently* means "in a way that shows a lack of confidence; shyly."

Vocabulary
efficient (i fish′ ənt) *adj.* producing a desired effect with a minimum of effort or waste
sufficient (sə fish′ ənt) *adj.* adequate; enough
accede (ak sēd′) *v.* to give in; go along with
collective (kə lek′ tiv) *adj.* having to do with a group of persons or things; common; shared

FYI

Jet stream is a high-speed air current, usually found between seven and nine miles above the earth's surface, that moves generally west to east at speeds reaching over 200 miles per hour. **Solar constant** is the amount of radiation coming from the sun, measured at the outside of the atmosphere.

E **Active Reading**

PREDICT Encourage students to explain why they think Nemerson would not answer the question if he were asked to do so. *(He thinks Weaver is not asking politely.)*

F **Critical Thinking**

DRAWING CONCLUSIONS Have students explain what the key item is. *(The word* please *is the key item.)* Why do students think it is needed now and never before? *(The computer thinks more like a human and expects common courtesy.)*

G **Literary Elements**

IRONY Have students explain why the ending to this story is ironic. *(Six teams of computer technologists spent three days looking for a way to fix the computer, when all that was needed was one little word: please.)*

Reading *Minilesson*

Comparing and Contrasting Explain that the name Multivac suggests that the computer, like other early computers, uses vacuum tubes instead of chips. So many vacuum tubes were needed in early computers that they filled entire rooms.

Activity Have students work in small groups to list other ways Multivac is similar to and different from computers today.

Then have them create a Venn diagram that compares Multivac to a modern computer. **L2**

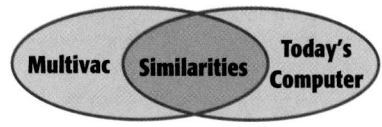

Multivac | Similarities | Today's Computer

Additional Resources
📁 *Reading Workbook,* pp. 99–100

Dan Piraro, born in Oklahoma and raised in Texas, is a nationally syndicated cartoonist whose work appears in newspapers and in several books of cartoons. His humor is based on improbable combinations of the real and the unreal.

Viewing Response *Similar: The computer has humanlike feelings. It talks. Different: The computer is small. It doesn't have a control wall or dials.*

Ⓗ Active Reading

RESPOND Have students discuss whether they think computers will ever have human emotions.

Ⓘ Critical Thinking

SYNTHESIZING Have students explain the humor in this cartoon. *(The cartoon uses a play on words. "The computer is down" usually means that the computer is broken. But* down *also means "sad.")*

Thematic Focus

A Different Dimension Have students explain how this story relates to the theme. *(The story is about a computer that crosses the line dividing computers and humans.)*

✔ ASSESSMENT OPTIONS

🗀 *Quick Checks,* p. 56

Teaching Options

Bizzaro

I don't feel very good about myself right now. I don't know what it is, I just feel sort of..... oh, I don't know. Could I just be alone for a little while?

THE COMPUTER IS DOWN AGAIN.

Dan Piraro/Universal Press Syndicate.

Viewing the cartoon: In what ways is the theme of this cartoon similar to and different from Asimov's story?

678 ❧ THEME 7

Grammar and Language *Minilesson*

Compound Predicates A compound predicate has two or more simple predicates, or verbs, that have the same subject. Write this sentence on the board and ask a volunteer to identify the compound predicate: *Weaver shrugged and turned to Multivac's control wall.*

Activity Have students work independently to write five sentences with compound predicates about this story. **L2**

Additional Resources

📠 *Grammar and Language Transparency 55*

📙 *Grammar and Language Workbook,* pp. 53–54

📗 *Grammar and Composition Handbook,* Lesson 1.5

📘 *Writer's Choice,* Lesson 8.5

Responding to Literature

PERSONAL RESPONSE

Did the story end the way you expected it would? Why or why not?

Analyzing Literature

RECALL

1. What is Multivac and what does it do?
2. Why is the breakdown causing panic in every city?
3. What does Nemerson ask Weaver to do to help solve the problem of finding the key item?
4. What does the key item turn out to be?

INTERPRET

5. Why does Nemerson think Multivac could be human?
6. How is the future world of this story different from our world?
7. How does Weaver's attitude toward Multivac differ from Nemerson's?
8. In your opinion, how did Nemerson figure out what the key item was?

EVALUATE AND CONNECT

9. Theme Connection   Some of the technologies in Asimov's stories have been invented or were discovered years after he wrote about them. In your opinion, could the events in "Key Item" ever really happen? Explain why or why not.
10. How would your life be affected if you lived in a world where computers were nearly human?

LITERARY ELEMENTS

Irony

Irony is the difference between the way things seem to be and the way they actually are. Irony can also contrast what is expected with what actually happens. Authors use irony to create humor or strong emotion. Surprise endings often involve irony. In "Key Item," for example, the answer to why the computer isn't responding is ironic.

1. Why is the title of this story an example of irony? Explain fully.
2. Think about some of the other selections you have read in this book. Explain how irony is used in one of them.

● See **Literary Terms Handbook**, p. R5.

A DIFFERENT DIMENSION ✂ 679

Personal Response

Students should use examples from the story to fully explain their ideas.

Analyzing Literature

1. Multivac is a huge computer that the world depends on for important information.
2. Every city in the world depends on Multivac's calculations.
3. Nemerson wants Weaver to ask him the question that Multivac stalled on.
4. The key item turns out to be the word *please*.
5. Nemerson thinks Multivac could be human because scientists have been making it more and more complex, just like a human brain.
6. The world in the story is different because our entire world does not rely on one huge computer.
7. Weaver thinks of Multivac as an inanimate tool. Nemerson thinks Multivac may have human emotions.
8. Nemerson realizes that he doesn't like the way Weaver talked to him.
9. Sample: The events in "Key Item" could not happen because humans are smarter than computers. Or: The events could happen. It is only a matter of time before scientists build computers that have humanlike emotions.
10. Computers would be doing more complex tasks in every area of human endeavor.

LITERARY ELEMENTS

1. The "key item" seems to be some complicated technical fix. Instead, it's the word *please*.
2. Examples should show a difference between the way things seem to be and the way they actually are.

Additional Resources

✎ *Literary Elements Transparency 56*

Extending Your Response

Writing About Literature

Students' paragraphs should
- describe important qualities of main characters.
- explain why Multivac has the qualities of a main character.
- include examples from the story to show Multivac's qualities.

Personal Writing

Students' visions should
- incorporate results they graphed based on the question in the Focus Activity.
- describe a world of the future.
- show the future world as exciting, frightening, or something else.

Learning for Life
Encourage students to organize their manuals like real computer manuals. Have them write their instructions step by step. Explain that the user manuals cannot be too simple.

Literature Groups
Students might extend this activity by using the dictionary to find definitions for the terms. **COLLAB. LEARN.**

Skill Minilesson

VOCABULARY • ETYMOLOGY

1. umbrella   2. give up land
3. one that is operated by a group

Additional Resources
Vocabulary Practice, p. 38

Extending Your Response

Writing About Literature

Main Characters   Although Jack Weaver and Todd Nemerson are the first two characters readers meet in "Key Item," there is also a third character in the story. Write a paragraph explaining why Multivac should be viewed as an important character.

Learning for Life

User's Manual   Computers usually come with a user's manual to help people operate them. Find an example of a computer user's manual. Use it as a model to write part of the instructions for a Multivac User's Manual. Using what you have learned from the story, tell how to operate Multivac smoothly.

Literature Groups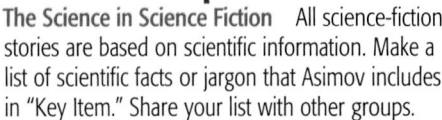

The Science in Science Fiction   All science-fiction stories are based on scientific information. Make a list of scientific facts or jargon that Asimov includes in "Key Item." Share your list with other groups.

Personal Writing

Life in a Technological Future   Some people are excited to imagine a life in which humans depend on smarter and smarter machines. Others are fearful about what a super-technological world might be like. Drawing upon the results of your questionnaire in the **Focus Activity** on page 674, create a vision of how you believe people may use computers many years from now. Write a description of your vision.

Reading Further

Try these other robot stories by Isaac Asimov:
I, Robot
Robot Dreams

■ **Save your work for your portfolio.**

Skill Minilesson

VOCABULARY • ETYMOLOGY

The etymology, or history, of the word *collective* shows that it comes from the Latin *com,* meaning "together," and *legere,* "to gather." To gather things together is to *collect* them.

When Weaver *acceded* to Nemerson, he gave in. *Accede* comes from the Latin *ad,* meaning "to," and *cedere,* "to yield," which combine to mean "to yield to."

The dials and lights of the unworking Multivac are described as *somber,* which comes from the Latin *sub,* meaning "under," and *umbra,* "shade."

PRACTICE   Use the information about etymologies to answer the questions.

1. What word comes from the Latin *umbra* and names something that can block the sun or the rain?
2. When a nation *cedes* land, does that nation buy land, give up land, or use land wisely?
3. Is a *collective* farm one that is successful, one that is operated by a group, or one that specializes in multiple crops?

✔ ASSESSMENT OPTIONS

- 📁 *Quick Checks,* p. 56
- 📁 *Selection and Theme Assessment,* pp. 97–98
- 📁 *Performance Assessment,* p. 53
- 💾 *Testmaker*

Interdisciplinary Connection

Communicating on the Net

Netiquette

"Netiquette" is a set of rules for behavior on the Internet. Many of these rules are not much different from the rules of etiquette for any other behavior. Put simply, you should behave toward others on the Net as you'd like them to behave toward you.

Other rules are unique to the Net. For example, DON'T SHOUT! Using all capital letters is considered shouting. It's also considered impolite and the sign of a "newbie," or newcomer. To emphasize a word or phrase, put *asterisks* before and after it.

Speaking of newbies, if you visit a new newsgroup or chat room, don't start out by asking too many questions. First read the FAQs (pronounced "faks"). FAQs stands for Frequently Asked Questions, and you'll nearly always find a set of them (with answers) at a newsgroup or chat site.

Smileys and Emoticons

In face-to-face communication, you can read people's expressions or body language to tell if they are happy, sad, or joking. But how do you know whether people are joking or serious on-line? Two popular tools that help relay such information on the computer screen are *smileys* and *emoticons*.

Smileys are images made with the characters found on a keyboard. Viewed sideways, they make pictures. Examples: a happy face :) a happy face with a nose :-)

Emoticons (a word made by putting together *emotion* and *icons*) tell your on-line penpal how you feel. For instance, instead of writing *I'm sad that I have to miss art class on Thursday,* you could write: *I have to miss art class on Thursday <sad>.* You create emoticons by putting < > symbols around a word that tells a reader what you're doing or feeling. Here are a few more examples:

<blush>   <angry>   <giggle>   <wink>   <silly grin>

Acronyms

FAQ is an **acronym**. An acronym uses initials to stand for a phrase. Here are some examples often used on the Net.

ASAP	as soon as possible
B4N	[good]bye for now
BRB	be right back
BTW	by the way
CUL	see you later
F2F	face to face
IMHO	in my humble opinion
KWIM	know what I mean?
TIA	thanks in advance

Smileys

:-)	= happy
:-(	= sad
:'-(	= crying
'-)	= a wink
:-x	= my lips are sealed

ACTIVITIES

1. Make up at least two emoticons and two acronyms that could be added to those on this page.

2. Compose an E-mail to a real or an imaginary friend. Use your made-up emoticons and acronyms in your message. If you wish, use additional ones from the lists.

Interdisciplinary Connection

Objective

• To understand and apply strategies for communicating on the Net

Teaching Strategies

Work with students to list some differences between Netiquette and face-to-face (F2F) etiquette. Discuss the advantages and disadvantages of communicating with a friend using E-mail. In addition to the activities on the student page, ask students to create a "smiley" or facial expression using keyboard icons and punctuation marks. You may wish to draw the icons on the board if students do not have access to computers in the classroom.

Activities

1. Students might create emotions such as <shrug> or <confused>. They may also use words that are familiar to peers, such as popular Spanish words or lingo. Sample acronyms could include TMA (twist my arm) or WMB (write me back).

2. E-mail message based on activity 1 might read *Anna: I'm not sure I want to go to the party. <confused> Let me know who else is going. WMB, okay?*

Teaching Options

MEETING INDIVIDUAL NEEDS — MULTIPLE LEARNING STYLES

Linguistic Students who think linguistically will find that the focus on words, wordplay, and creative use of language in computer communication offers them new opportunities for self-expression.

Activity Have students work in pairs to describe memorable experiences they have had. Encourage students to to prepare E-mails about their experiences.

Their E-mails should include as many emotions, invented words, acronyms, and expressions as possible. Have students exchange E-mails or send them to their partners. **L2 COLLAB. LEARN.**

Objectives

- To read and analyze a fantasy
- To identify elements that are common to fantasy stories
- To explain how the setting of a story influences its plot

Skills

Reading/Thinking: Judging the Credibility of a Source; Using Graphic Aids; Drawing Conclusions; Analyzing Arguments; Inferring; Classifying
Writing: Another Point of View; Summarizing a Sequel; TV News Story
Vocabulary: Synonyms
Grammar/Language: Infinitives; Writing Numbers
Listening/Speaking: Debating; Performing a News Story
Life Skills: Creating and Producing; Magazine Article
Collaboration: Literature Groups

Motivating
→OPTIONS

Selection Focus Transparency 57: Have students discuss other types of stories that "speak the language of the night." (*Science fiction, horror stories, mysteries*)

Focus Activity: As an extension of the Focus Activity, list on the board suggestions from volunteers about situations in which peer pressure occurs.

Before You Read
The Smallest Dragonboy

MEET ANNE McCAFFREY

Sometimes called science fiction's "Dragon Lady," Anne McCaffrey lives in Ireland, in a home called Dragonhold. It is there that she weaves her rich tales. In order to create the world of Pern, McCaffrey returned to graduate school to study physics. Although dragons are more common in fantasy stories, McCaffrey's dragon stories have become popular with readers of science fiction. "If you write a good story," she says, "anybody will read it."

Anne McCaffrey was born in Massachusetts in 1926.

FOCUS ACTIVITY

What kinds of pressures can peers place on one another?

Think/Pair/Share
Take a moment to jot down notes about your own peer-pressure experiences and what you have learned from them. Then share your thoughts with a partner.

Setting a Purpose
Read to find out how the smallest dragonboy deals with peer pressure.

BACKGROUND

The Time and Place The setting is the imaginary planet Pern, sometime in the future.

Did You Know? This fantasy story takes place in a world created by the imagination of the writer Anne McCaffrey. Pern is the setting of many of McCaffrey's stories. A former colony of Earth, Pern is protected from deadly spores, referred to as "Thread," by fire-breathing dragons and human dragonriders, who live together in communities called Weyrs.

Carved dragon-head post from the ship burial at Oseberg, c. 850. Viking Ship Museum, Bygdoy, Norway.

VOCABULARY PREVIEW

enticing (en tīs′ ing) *adj.* offering pleasure or reward; p. 684
jeer (jēr) *v.* to make fun of (someone or something) rudely and openly; p. 684
enviable (en′ vē ə bəl) *adj.* good enough to be highly desired; p. 685
replenish (ri plen′ ish) *v.* to provide a new supply; p. 687
exasperation (ig zas′ pə rā′ shən) *n.* anger or great irritation; p. 689
desolation (des′ ə lā′ shən) *n.* sadness; loneliness; p. 689

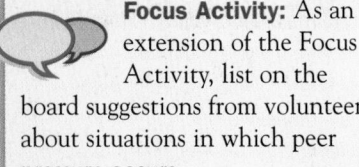

RESOURCE MANAGER

Lesson Planning Resource
The *Theme Seven Planning Guide* (pp. 22–29) provides additional lesson notes and reduced versions of all print resources.

📁 **Other Print Resources**
- Active Reading Guide, p. 57
- Vocabulary Practice, p. 39
- Reading Workbook, pp. 101–102
- Grammar and Language Workbook, pp. 175–178, 279–280

- Grammar and Composition Handbook, Lessons 9.3, 13.10
- Quick Checks, p. 57
- Selection and Theme Assessment, pp. 99–100
- Performance Assessment, p. 54
- Spanish Summaries, p. 57
- Spanish Translations
- Inclusion Strategies
- English Language Learners Sourcebook

🖥 **Transparencies**
- Selection Focus 57
- Literary Elements 57
- Grammar and Language 56

Technology
🎧 Audio Library
🎧 Spanish Audio Library
💻 Glencoe Literature Web Site
💾 Testmaker

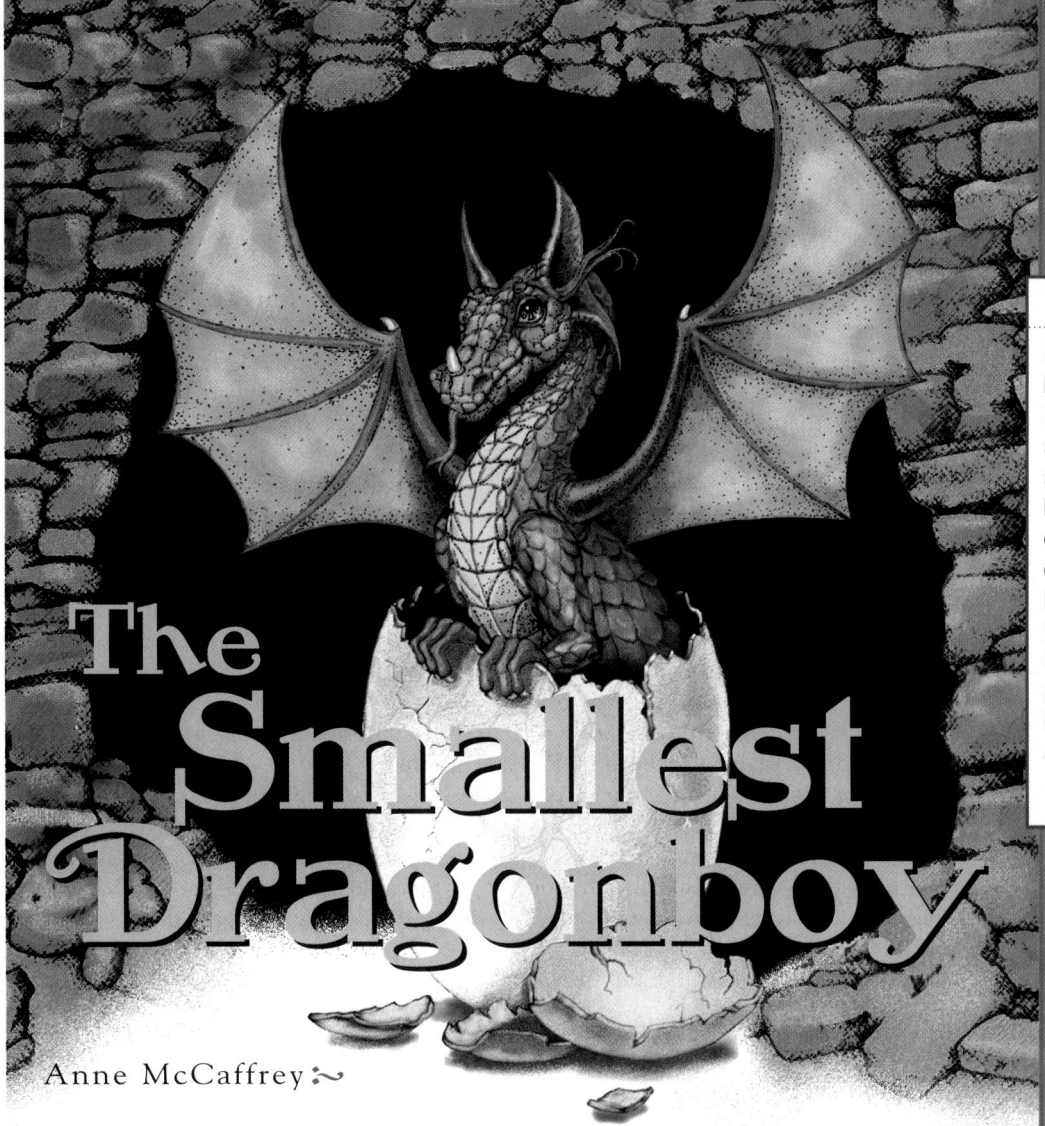

The Smallest Dragonboy

Anne McCaffrey

Although Keevan lengthened his walking stride as far as his legs would stretch, he couldn't quite keep up with the other candidates. He knew he would be teased again.

Just as he knew many other things that his foster mother told him he ought not to know, Keevan knew that Beterli, the most senior of the boys, set that spanking pace just to embarrass him, the smallest dragonboy. Keevan would arrive, tail fork-end of the group, breathless, chest heaving, and maybe get a stern look from the instructing wingsecond.

683

SUMMARY

Keevan is one of seventy-two boys eligible to become a dragonrider. But Keevan is the smallest and youngest of all the candidates. Forty dragons are about to hatch. Each will choose one boy. Keevan desperately wants to be chosen, because the other boys, especially Beterli, tease and bully him about his small size and unworthiness. Beterli injures Keevan, who is hospitalized when the hatching begins. In great pain, Keevan drags himself to the hatching. The highest-ranking dragon of all chooses Keevan.

📁 *Spanish Summaries,* p. 57

A Active Reading

PREDICT Invite students to look at the title of this story and the illustration. Then have volunteers read the first two paragraphs aloud. Encourage students to predict who Keevan is and what the conflict in the story will be. Suggest that students periodically revisit their predictions as they read to verify or revise them.

Additional Resources
📁 *Active Reading Guide,* p. 57
🎧 *Audio Library*
🎧 *Spanish Audio Library*

Teaching Options

CONNECTING TO OTHER SELECTIONS

The chart at the right shows three ways to connect "The Smallest Dragonboy" to other selections in this book.

For specific teaching strategies, see the *Theme Seven Planning Guide,* pages 25–26.

Connection	Title
Life Skills: Lifelong Learning	→ "Hollywood and the Pits," p. 117
Thematic: Growing Up	→ "Fish Cheeks," p. 77
Literary: Fantasy	→ "Rikki-tikki-tavi," p. 789

LITERATURE & HUMANITIES

To help students better understand the importance of ritual in some cultures, have them view the images on the *Coming of Age Hat,* page 252 of *Introducing Art.* Ask students what role such ornate ritual clothing plays in preserving a culture.

B Active Reading

EVALUATE Have students explain what Keevan's goal is and how that goal is achieved. (*Keevan wants to become a dragonrider. When the dragons hatch, each chooses a boy to be its lifetime companion, or dragonrider.*)

C Literary Elements

FANTASY Have students explain what elements of this story indicate that it is a fantasy. Encourage students to explain what in the story could exist in real life. (*In real life dragons, dragon eggs, and dragonriders falling from the skies do not exist, but conflict between a small boy and larger boys who tease him could happen.*)

D Active Reading

RESPOND Have students explain Keevan's disadvantages and advantages in being chosen as a dragonrider. (*Keevan is smaller, younger, and weaker than the other candidates. But Keevan works twice as hard as they do and can run faster, too.*)

E Active Reading

QUESTION Invite students to think about what qualities might be important to a dragon. (*Some qualities include: loyalty, courage, intelligence, and patience.*)

The Smallest Dragonboy

Dragonriders, even if they were still only hopeful candidates for the glowing eggs which were hardening on the hot sands of the Hatching Ground cavern, were expected to be punctual and prepared. Sloth was not tolerated by the weyrleader of Benden Weyr. A good record was especially important now. It was very near hatching time, when the baby dragons would crack their mottled shells and stagger forth to choose their lifetime companions. The very thought of that glorious moment made Keevan's breath catch in his throat. To be chosen—to be a dragonrider! To sit astride the neck of the winged beast with the jeweled eyes: to be his friend in telepathic communion[1] with him for life; to be his companion in good times and fighting extremes; to fly effortlessly over the lands of Pern! Or, thrillingly, *between* to any point anywhere on the world! Flying *between* was done on dragonback or not at all, and it was dangerous.

Keevan glanced upward, past the black mouths of the weyr caves in which grown dragons and their chosen riders lived, toward the Star Stones that crowned the ridge of the old volcano that was Benden Weyr. On the height, the blue watch dragon, his rider mounted on his neck, stretched the great transparent pinions[2] that carried him on the winds of Pern to fight the evil Thread that fell at certain times from the sky. The many-faceted rainbow jewels of his eyes glistened momentarily in the greeny sun. He folded his great wings to his back, and the watchpair resumed their statuesque pose of alertness.

Then the <u>enticing</u> view was obscured as Keevan passed into the Hatching Ground cavern. The sands underfoot were hot, even through heavy wher-hide boots. How the bootmaker had protested having to sew so small! Keevan was forced to wonder again why being small was reprehensible.[3] People were always calling him "babe" and shooing him away as being "too small" or "too young" for this or that. Keevan was constantly working, twice as hard as any other boy his age, to prove himself capable. What if his muscles weren't as big as Beterli's? They were just as hard. And if he couldn't overpower anyone in a wrestling match, he could outdistance everyone in a footrace.

"Maybe if you run fast enough," Beterli had <u>jeered</u> on the occasion when Keevan had been goaded[4] to boast of his swiftness, "you could catch a dragon. That's the only way you'll make a dragonrider!"

"You just wait and see, Beterli, you just wait," Keevan had replied. He would have liked to wipe the contemptuous[5] smile from Beterli's face, but the guy didn't fight fair even when the wingsecond was watching. "No one knows what Impresses a dragon!"

"They've got to be able to *find* you first, babe!"

---

1. In *telepathic communion,* thoughts are shared directly between two minds.
2. A bird's *pinions* are its wings or wing feathers.

3. Something that's *reprehensible* is deserving of sharp criticism.
4. To *goad* means "to pressure someone to do something; urge on."
5. *Contemptuous* means "proud and scornful."

Vocabulary
enticing (en tīs′ ing) *adj.* offering pleasure or reward
jeer (jēr) *v.* to make fun of (someone or something) rudely and openly

---

Dragon Stories Dragons are found in stories from many cultures around the world. In some stories, dragons breathe fire and are evil. In others, dragons are friendly and good. Invite English language learners to think of stories they know from their cultures about dragons or other fantastic creatures.

Activity Ask small groups of students to work together to share and discuss dragon stories. Have each group work together to create a comic strip that tells a story about one dragon. Have students display their dragon comics for the rest of the class to read. **COLLAB. LEARN.**

Additional Resources
📁 *English Language Learners Sourcebook*

Anne McCaffrey

Yes, being the smallest candidate was not an enviable position. It was therefore imperative[6] that Keevan Impress a dragon in his first hatching. That would wipe the smile off every face in the cavern, and accord him the respect due any dragon-rider, even the smallest one.

Besides, no one knew exactly what Impressed the baby dragons as they struggled from their shells in search of their life-time partners.

"I like to believe that dragons see into a man's heart," Keevan's foster mother, Mende, told him. "If they find goodness, honesty, a flexible mind, patience, courage—and you've that in quantity, dear Keevan—that's what dragons look for. I've seen many a well-grown lad left standing on the sands, Hatching Day, in favor of someone not so strong or tall or handsome. And if my memory serves me" (which it usually did—Mende knew every word of every Harper's tale worth telling, although Keevan did not interrupt her to say so), "I don't believe that F'lar, our weyrleader, was all that tall when bronze Mnementh chose him. And Mnementh was the only bronze dragon of that hatching."

Dreams of Impressing a bronze were beyond Keevan's boldest reflections, although that goal dominated[7] the thoughts of every other hopeful candidate. Green dragons were small and fast and more numerous. There was more prestige[8] in Impressing a blue or a brown than a green. Being practical, Keevan seldom

dreamed as high as a big fighting brown, like Canth, F'nor's fine fellow, the biggest brown on all Pern. But to fly a bronze? Bronzes were almost as big as the queen, and only they took the air when a queen flew at mating time. A bronze rider could aspire to become weyrleader! Well, Keevan would console himself, brown riders could aspire to become wingseconds, and that wasn't bad. He'd even settle for a green dragon: they were small, but so was he. No matter! He simply had to Impress a dragon his first time in the Hatching Ground. Then no one in the weyr would taunt[9] him anymore for being so small.

"Shells," thought Keevan now, "but the sands are hot!"

"Impression time is imminent, candidates," the wingsecond was saying as everyone crowded respectfully close to him. "See the extent of the striations[10] on this promising egg." The stretch marks *were* larger than yesterday.

Everyone leaned forward and nodded thoughtfully. That particular egg was the one Beterli had marked as his own, and no other candidate dared, on pain of being beaten by Beterli on the first opportunity, to approach it. The egg was marked by a large yellowish splotch in the shape of a dragon backwinging to land, talons outstretched to grasp rock. Everyone knew that bronze eggs bore distinctive markings. And naturally, Beterli, who'd been presented at eight Impressions already and

---

6. If something is *imperative*, it is absolutely necessary.
7. To *dominate* is to control.
8. Someone with *prestige* is admired and respected by others.

9. To *taunt* is to make fun of in a scornful, insulting way.
10. Something *imminent* is likely to happen soon. The *striations* are grooves or marks—as used here, they are probably cracks that appear as the eggs begin to hatch.

Vocabulary
enviable (en′ vē ə bəl) *adj.* good enough to be highly desired

---

F Active Reading
CONNECT Have students think about how they feel when others tease or belittle them. Then have students explain how Keevan probably feels and why being a dragonrider is important to him. *(Keevan probably feels unhappy and frustrated. He wants to be chosen a dragonrider so the other boys will treat him with respect.)*

G Critical Thinking
JUDGING THE CREDIBILITY OF A SOURCE Have students explain why Mende's ideas about what dragons look for may be more credible than the other boys' ideas. *(Mende has seen many hatchings and knows from experience that the strongest boys are not always picked. She knows dragons look for courage, goodness, honesty, and patience.)*

H Literary Elements
CHARACTER Using what they know about Keevan so far, invite students to describe his character. *(Keevan tries hard. According to Mende, he is courageous; he is humble and practical; and he wants the other boys to respect him.)*

I Active Reading
EVALUATE Have students explain whether Beterli's efforts to keep the other boys away from "his" egg will have an effect on who the hatchling chooses. *(If the hatchling doesn't like Beterli, it will not choose him even if he guards the egg.)*

Reading Minilesson

Using Graphic Aids Students might better understand the relationship between Keevan and Beterli if they create a chart to summarize and keep track of encounters between them.

Activity Have students answer these questions to help them begin the chart.
• Why does Beterli walk fast?
• What does Beterli say to Keevan about his swiftness?
• What does Beterli do in the Hatching Ground? **L2**

Keevan and Beterli's Relationship	
1. Why does Beterli walk fast?	Beterli walks fast so Keevan will have trouble keeping up.

Additional Resources
📁 *Reading Workbook,* pp. 101–102

J Critical Thinking

DRAWING CONCLUSIONS Have students explain why Beterli treats Keevan poorly. *(Beterli is probably ashamed that he has been passed over eight times. It makes him feel tough to tease Keevan.)*

K Active Reading

PREDICT Have students predict whether they think Keevan and Beterli will be chosen by a dragon and why. *(Students may say that Keevan seems to have all of the qualities that a dragon looks for in a companion. Also, Beterli has been passed over before.)*

VIEWING THE PAINTING

Viewing Response *Yes, these dragons are intentionally frightening. They look mean and ready to fight. They are not like the dragons in the story, who are friendly to humans and presumably to each other.*

L Active Reading

RESPOND Ask students if they think Keevan's stroking of Beterli's egg will have an effect on the dragon inside. *(Some may think the dragon will establish a bond with Keevan and choose him.)*

Teaching Options

---

was the biggest of the candidates, had chosen it.

"I'd say that the great opening day is almost upon us," the wingsecond went on, and then his face assumed a grave expression. "As we well know, there are only forty eggs and seventy-two candidates. Some of you may be disappointed on the great day. That doesn't necessarily mean you aren't dragonrider material, just that *the* dragon for you hasn't been shelled. You'll have other hatchings, and it's no disgrace to be left behind an Impression or two. Or more."

Keevan was positive that the wingsecond's eyes rested on Beterli, who'd been stood off at so many Impressions already. Keevan tried to squinch down so the wingsecond wouldn't notice him. Keevan had been reminded too often that he was eligible to be a candidate by one day only. He, of all the hopefuls, was most likely to

The Two Mythical Dragons. Sir Roy Calne, F. R. S. Private collection.
Viewing the painting: Are these mythical dragons intended to be frightening? Do they fit with your image of dragons in the story? Give reasons for your answer.

686 THEME 7

be left standing on the great day. One more reason why he simply had to Impress at his first hatching.

"Now move about among the eggs," the wingsecond said. "Touch them. We don't know that it does any good, but it certainly doesn't do any harm."

Some of the boys laughed nervously, but everyone immediately began to circulate among the eggs. Beterli stepped up officiously to "his" egg, daring anyone to come near it. Keevan smiled, because he had already touched it . . . every inspection day . . . as the others were leaving the Hatching Ground, when no one could see him crouch and stroke it.

Keevan had an egg he concentrated on, too, one drawn slightly to the far side of the others. The shell bore a soft greenish blue tinge with a faint creamy swirl design. The consensus[11] was that this egg contained a mere green, so Keevan was rarely bothered by rivals. He was somewhat perturbed then to see Beterli wandering over to him.

"I don't know why you're allowed in this Impression, Keevan. There are enough of us without a babe," Beterli said, shaking his head.

"I'm of age." Keevan kept his voice level, telling himself not to be bothered by mere words.

"Yah!" Beterli made a show of standing on his

---

11. A *consensus* is an opinion shared by most members of a group.

MEETING INDIVIDUAL NEEDS — INCLUSION STRATEGIES

Less-Proficient Readers Some students may find the language that the inhabitants of Pern speak confusing. They may need practice using context clues to understand words. Write the following sentences from the story on the board: *Any boy who is over twelve turns has the right to stand in the Hatching Ground.* (years)

Activity Have students use context clues to write a brief definition for each of these words: *wher, shelled, tuff,* and *babes.* **L2**

Additional Resources
📁 *Inclusion Strategies*

toe tips. "You can't even see over an egg; Hatching Day, you better get in front or the dragons won't see you at all. 'Course, you could get run down that way in the mad scramble. Oh, I forget, you can run fast, can't you?"

"You'd better make sure a dragon sees *you*, this time, Beterli," Keevan replied. "You're almost overage, aren't you?"

Beterli flushed and took a step forward, hand half-raised. Keevan stood his ground, but if Beterli advanced one more step, he would call the wingsecond. No one fought on the Hatching Ground. Surely Beterli knew that much.

Fortunately, at that moment the wingsecond called the boys together and led them from the Hatching Ground to start on evening chores.

There were "glows" to be <u>replenished</u> in the main kitchen caverns and sleeping cubicles, the major hallways, and the queen's apartment. Firestone sacks had to be filled against Thread attack, and black rock brought to the kitchen hearths. The boys fell to their chores, tantalized[12] by the odors of roasting meat. The population of the weyr began to assemble for the evening meal, and the dragonriders came in from the Feeding Ground or their sweep checks.

It was the time of day Keevan like best: once the chores were done, before dinner was served, a fellow could often get close to the dragonriders and listen to their talk. Tonight Keevan's father, K'last, was at the main dragonrider table. It puzzled Keevan how his father, a brown rider and a tall man, could *be* his father—because he, Keevan, was so small. It obviously never puzzled K'last when he deigned to notice his small son: "In a few more turns, you'll be as tall as I am—or taller!"

K'last was pouring Benden drink all around the table. The dragonriders were relaxing. There'd be no Thread attack for three more days, and they'd be in the mood to tell tall tales, better than Harper yarns, about impossible maneuvers they'd done a-dragonback. When Thread attack was closer, their talk would change to a discussion of tactics of evasion, of going *between*, how long to suspend there until the burning but fragile Thread would freeze and crack and fall harmlessly off dragon and man. They would dispute the exact moment to feed firestone to the dragon so he'd have the best flame ready to sear Thread midair and render[13] it harmless to ground—and man—below. There was such a lot to know and understand about being a dragonrider that sometimes Keevan was overwhelmed. How would he ever be able to remember everything he ought to know at the right moment? He couldn't dare ask such a question; this would only have given additional weight to the notion that he was too young yet to be a dragonrider.

"Having older candidates makes good sense," L'vel was saying, as Keevan settled down near the table. "Why waste four to five years of a dragon's fighting prime until his rider grows up enough to stand the rigors?" L'vel had Impressed a blue of Ramoth's

---

12. To *tantalize* is to tempt or tease someone with something that person cannot have.

13. *Sear* means "scorch or burn," and *render,* as used here, means "make."

Vocabulary
replenish (ri plen' ish) *v.* to provide a new supply

Teaching Options

first clutch. Most of the candidates thought L'vel was marvelous because he spoke up in front of the older riders, who awed them. "That was well enough in the Interval when you didn't need to mount the full weyr complement to fight Thread. But not now. Not with more eligible candidates than ever. Let the babes wait."

"Any boy who is over twelve turns has the right to stand in the Hatching Ground," K'last replied, a slight smile on his face. He never argued or got angry. Keevan wished he were more like his father. And oh, how he wished he were a brown rider! "Only a dragon . . . each particular dragon . . . knows what he wants in a rider. We certainly can't tell. Time and again the theorists," and K'last's smile deepened as his eyes swept those at the table, "are surprised by dragon choice. *They* never seem to make mistakes, however."

"Now, K'last, just look at the roster this Impression. Seventy-two boys and only forty eggs. Drop off the twelve youngest, and there's still a good field for the hatchlings to choose from. Shells! There are a couple of weyrlings unable to see over a wher egg much less a dragon! And years before they can ride Thread."

"True enough, but the weyr is scarcely under fighting strength, and if the youngest Impress, they'll be old enough to fight when the oldest of our current dragons go *between* from senility."[14]

"Half the weyrbred lads have already been through several Impressions," one of the bronze riders said then. "I'd say drop some of *them* off this time. Give the untried a chance."

"There's nothing wrong in presenting a clutch with as wide a choice as possible," said the weyrleader, who had joined the table with Lessa, the weyrwoman.

"Has there ever been a case," she said, smiling in her odd way at the riders, "where a hatchling didn't choose?"

Her suggestion was almost heretical[15] and drew astonished gasps from everyone, including the boys.

F'lar laughed. "You say the most outrageous things, Lessa."

"Well, *has* there ever been a case where a dragon didn't choose?"

"Can't say as I recall one," K'last replied.

"Then we continue in this tradition," Lessa said firmly, as if that ended the matter.

But it didn't. The argument ranged from one table to the other all through dinner, with some favoring a weeding out of the candidates to the most likely, lopping off those who were very young or who had had multiple opportunities to Impress. All the candidates were in a swivet,[16] though such a departure from tradition would be to the advantage of many. As the evening progressed, more riders were favoring eliminating the youngest and those who'd passed four or more Impressions unchosen. Keevan felt he could bear such a dictum if only Beterli was also eliminated. But this seemed less likely than that Keevan would be tuffed out, since the weyr's need was for fighting dragons and riders.

By the time the evening meal was over, no decision had been reached, although the weyrleader had promised to give the matter due consideration.

---

14. *Senility* refers to a loss of mental abilities that sometimes comes with old age.

15. Something that is *heretical* goes against what most people consider to be right, true, or proper.

16. A *swivet* (swiv′ ət) or (swiv′ it) is a condition of strain and confusion.

Listening and Speaking *Minilesson*

Debating Have students help you list on the board some of the reasons for and against allowing all seventy-two boys to stand before the dragons.

Activity Create two teams. Encourage each team to prepare to debate one side of this issue: *The age for dragonrider candidates should be raised to thirteen turns.* Have each team prepare arguments for its stance on the issue. Team members should also discuss the arguments the other team is likely to use and prepare counterarguments. Each side should elect a captain to present its best ideas. After captains present the cases, the teams should huddle to consider how to counter the other team's arguments. Finally, judges can decide which team has won the debate. **L2 COLLAB. LEARN.**

Anne McCaffrey

He might have slept on the problem, but few of the candidates did. Tempers were uncertain in the sleeping caverns next morning as the boys were routed out of their beds to carry water and black rock and cover the "glows." Mende had to call Keevan to order twice for clumsiness.

"Whatever is the matter with you, boy?" she demanded in exasperation when he tipped black rock short of the bin and sooted up the hearth.

"They're going to keep me from this Impression."

"What?" Mende stared at him. "Who?"

"You heard them talking at dinner last night. They're going to tuff the babes from the hatching."

Mende regarded him a moment longer before touching his arm gently. "There's lots of talk around a supper table, Keevan. And it cools as soon as the supper. I've heard the same nonsense before every hatching, but nothing is ever changed."

"There's always a first time," Keevan answered, copying one of her own phrases.

"That'll be enough of that, Keevan. Finish your job. If the clutch does hatch today, we'll need full rock bins for the feast, and you won't be around to do the filling. All my fosterlings make dragonriders."

"The first time?" Keevan was bold enough to ask as he scooted off with the rockbarrow.

Perhaps, Keevan thought later, if he hadn't been on that chore just when Beterli was also fetching black rock, things might have turned out differently. But he had dutifully trundled the barrow to the

outdoor bunker for another load just as Beterli arrived on a similar errand.

"Heard the news, babe?" asked Beterli. He was grinning from ear to ear, and he put an unnecessary emphasis on the final insulting word.

"The eggs are cracking?" Keevan all but dropped the loaded shovel. Several anxieties flicked through his mind then; he was black with rock dust—would he have time to wash before donning the white tunic[17] of candidacy? And if the eggs were hatching, why hadn't the candidates been recalled by the wingsecond?

"Naw! Guess again!" Beterli was much too pleased with himself.

With a sinking heart Keevan knew what the news must be, and he could only stare with intense desolation at the older boy.

"C'mon! Guess, babe!"

"I've no time for guessing games," Keevan managed to say with indifference. He began to shovel black rock into his barrow as fast as he could.

"I said, 'guess'." Beterli grabbed the shovel.

"And I said I'd no time for guessing games."

Beterli wrenched the shovel from Keevan's hands. "Guess!"

"I'll have the shovel back, Beterli." Keevan straightened up, but he didn't come up to Beterli's bulky shoulder. From somewhere, other boys appeared, some with barrows, some mysteriously alerted to

---

17. A *tunic* is a garment resembling a long shirt.

Vocabulary
exasperation (ig zas′ pə rā′ shən) *n.* anger or great irritation
desolation (des′ ə lā′ shən) *n.* sadness; loneliness

A DIFFERENT DIMENSION 🦂 689

Writing *Minilesson*

Another Point of View Readers learn how Keevan, the other candidates, and the dragonriders feel about many issues.

Activity Invite students to write about the hatching from a dragon's point of view. Have students explain what the hatchlings see, feel, and think as they choose dragonriders to be their lifelong companions. Students may want to consider this ques-

tion before they write: How do the dragons feel about their role in Pern society and about their future as Thread fighters? When writers finish their scenes, invite them to share them with the class. **L2**

Additional Resources

📖 *Writer's Choice,* Lesson 4.5

Critical Thinking

X **DRAWING CONCLUSIONS** Have students explain why Keevan should or should not believe Beterli. *(Keevan should not believe Beterli because Beterli would say anything to bother and upset Keevan.)*

Active Reading

Y **QUESTION** Encourage students to explain who Mende is talking about when she says, "...some won't be at any hatching again." *(She's probably talking about Beterli. Perhaps injuring Keevan has made Pern's leaders decide Beterli cannot be a dragonrider candidate anymore.)*

Critical Thinking

Z **INFERRING** Have students explain whether they think Keevan will be eliminated this year because of his broken skull and leg.

Model: I think these injuries would keep many other candidates from attending the Impression, but Keevan is exceptionally determined. I think Keevan will do everything in his power to attend the Impression.

Active Reading

AA **QUESTION** Have students explain whether Keevan has been officially eliminated from being a candidate. *(Keevan is not officially eliminated, but his injuries seem serious enough to stop him from attending the Impression.)*

Teaching Options

---

the prospect of a confrontation among their numbers.

X "Babes don't give orders to candidates around here, babe!"

Someone sniggered and Keevan knew, incredibly, that he must've been dropped from the candidacy.

He yanked the shovel from Beterli's loosened grasp. Snarling, the older boy tried to regain possession, but Keevan clung with all his strength to the handle, dragged back and forth as the stronger boy jerked the shovel about.

With a sudden, unexpected movement, Beterli rammed the handle into Keevan's chest, knocking him over the barrow handles. Keevan felt a sharp, painful jab behind his left ear, an unbearable pain in his right shin, and then a painless nothingness.

Mende's angry voice roused him, and startled, he tried to throw back the covers, thinking he'd overslept. But he couldn't move, so firmly was he tucked into his bed. And then the constriction of a bandage on his head and the dull sickishness in his leg brought back recent occurrences.

"Hatching?" he cried.

Y "No, lovey," said Mende, and her voice was suddenly very kind, her hand cool and gentle on his forehead. "Though there's some as won't be at any hatching again." Her voice took on a stern edge.

Keevan looked beyond her to see the weyrwoman, who was frowning with irritation.

"Keevan, will you tell me what occurred at the black-rock bunker?" Lessa asked, but her voice wasn't angry.

He remembered Beterli now and the quarrel over the shovel and . . . what had

690 🦎 THEME 7

Mende said about some not being at any hatching? Much as he hated Beterli, he couldn't bring himself to tattle on Beterli and force him out of candidacy.

"Come, lad," and a note of impatience crept into the weyrwoman's voice. "I merely want to know what happened from you, too. Mende said she sent you for black rock. Beterli—and every weyrling in the cavern—seems to have been on the same errand. What happened?"

"Beterli took the shovel. I hadn't finished with it."

"There's more than one shovel. What did he *say* to you?"

"He'd heard the news."

"What news?" The weyrwoman was suddenly amused.

"That . . . that . . . there'd been changes."

"Is that what he said?"

"Not exactly."

"What did he say? C'mon, lad. I've heard from everyone else, you know."

"He said for me to guess the news."

"And you fell for that old gag?" The weyrwoman's irritation returned.

"Consider all the talk last night at supper, Lessa," said Mende. "Of course the boy would think he'd been eliminated."

Z "In effect, he is, with a broken skull and leg." She touched his arm, a rare gesture of sympathy in her. "Be that as it may, Keevan, you'll have other Impressions. Beterli will not. There are certain rules that must be observed by all candidates, and his conduct proves him unacceptable to the weyr."

She smiled at Mende and then left.

"I'm still a candidate?" Keevan asked urgently.

AA "Well, you are and you aren't, lovey," his foster mother said. "Is the numb weed

---

LIFE SKILLS CONNECTION

Creating and Producing Students might be interested in trying to bring this fantasy story to life. Invite students to think about how this story could be made into a movie.

Activity Have small groups of students work together to rewrite some part of this story as a screenplay. Have each group decide what kind of movie it wants to create: a cartoon, a Claymation feature, a full-length feature film, and so on. Then have each group describe the setting and stage directions that are appropriate for its movie script. Encourage students to think of as many details as possible, even describing specific actors and materials they'd use for production. **L2**

working?" she asked, and when he nodded, she said, "You just rest. I'll bring you some nice broth."

Dragonmen don't cry! Dragonmen learn to live with pain. . . .

At any other time in his life, Keevan would have relished such cosseting,[18] but he lay there worrying. Beterli had been dismissed. Would the others think it was his fault? But everyone was there! Beterli provoked the fight. His worry increased, because although he heard excited comings and goings in the passageway, no one tweaked back the curtain across the sleeping alcove[19] he shared with five other boys. Surely one of them would have to come in sometime. No, they were all avoiding him. And something else was wrong. Only he didn't know what.

Mende returned with broth and beach-berry bread.

"Why doesn't anyone come see me, Mende? I haven't done anything wrong, have I? I didn't ask to have Beterli tuffed out."

Mende soothed him, saying everyone was busy with noontime chores and no one was mad at him. They were giving him a chance to rest in quiet. The numb weed made him drowsy, and her words were fair enough. He permitted his fears to dissipate.[20] Until he heard the humming. It started low, too low to be heard. Rather he felt it in the broken shin bone and his sore head. And thought, at first, it was an effect of the numb weed. Then the hum grew, augmented by additional sources. Two things registered suddenly in Keevan's groggy mind: The only

white candidate's robe still on the pegs in the chamber was his; and dragons hummed when a clutch was being laid or being hatched. Impression! And he was flat abed.

Bitter, bitter disappointment turned the warm broth sour in his belly. Even the small voice telling him that he'd have other opportunities failed to alleviate[21] his crushing depression. *This* was the Impression that mattered! This was his chance to show *everyone* from Mende to K'last to L'vel and even the weyrleaders that he, Keevan, was worthy of being a dragonrider.

He twisted in bed, fighting against the tears that threatened to choke him. Dragonmen don't cry! Dragonmen learn to live with pain. . . .

Pain? The leg didn't actually pain him as he rolled about on his bedding. His head felt sort of stiff from the tightness of the bandage. He sat up, an effort in itself since the numb weed made exertion difficult. He touched the splinted leg, but the knee was unhampered. He had no feeling in his bone, really. He swung himself carefully to the side of his bed and slowly stood. The room wanted to swim about him. He closed his eyes, which made the dizziness worse, and he had to clutch the bedpost.

Gingerly he took a step. The broken leg dragged. It hurt in spite of the numb weed, but what was pain to a dragonman?

No one had said he couldn't go to the Impression. "You are and you aren't," were Mende's exact words.

Clinging to the bedpost, he jerked off his bedshirt. Stretching his arm to the

---

18. *Cosseting* means "pampering."
19. An *alcove* (al′ kōv) is a small room or shallow opening off a larger room.
20. Keevan's fears gradually disappear (*dissipate*).

21. To *alleviate* is to lessen, relieve, or make easier to bear.

INTERDISCIPLINARY CONNECTION

Biology Students might be interested in finding out which planets could support human life.

Activity Have students work in small groups to research the different planets and the different types of atmospheres they have. Have students describe specific environmental factors and how humans could manage to live there. Ask them to describe the climate, what type of shelter would have to be built, and where humans would find nourishment. Students may also explore whether the length of the days are similar to the length of days on Earth. **L2**

Cultural Note

Unusual Eggs Just over a hundred years ago, some Germans used elaborately decorated eggs as birth certificates. The baby's name and birth date were etched on the egg. Astonishingly, courts of law honored these unusual documents.

FF Literary Elements

FANTASY: *Figurative Language* Have students explain what the phrase "the room wanted to tip over his ears" means. Ask students why they think the author uses these words to describe the situation. *(It's an unusual description, so readers are more likely to notice it and think about it than if the author said "the room was spinning.")*

GG Critical Thinking

INFERRING Have students explain why the humming may have stopped. *(The eggs are ready to hatch, or they have already started to hatch.)*

HH Active Reading

EVALUATE Have students explain what qualities Keevan shows by attempting to overcome his pain and get to the hatching ground before it is too late. *(He shows great courage, perseverance, and determination. He is fit to be a dragonrider.)*

Teaching Options

The Smallest Dragonboy

utmost, he jerked his white candidate's tunic from the peg. Jamming first one arm and then the other into the holes, he pulled it over his head. Too bad about the belt. He couldn't wait. He hobbled to the door, hung on to the curtain to steady himself. The weight on his leg was unwieldy.[22] He'd not get very far without something to lean on. Down by the bathing pool was one of the long crook-necked poles used to retrieve clothes from the hot washing troughs. But it was down there, and he was on the level above. And there was no one nearby to come to his aid: everyone would be in the Hatching Ground right now, eagerly waiting for the first egg to crack.

The humming increased in volume and tempo, an urgency to which Keevan responded, knowing that his time was all too limited if he was to join the ranks of the hopeful boys standing about the cracking eggs. But if he hurried down the ramp, he'd fall flat on his face.

He could, of course, go flat on his rear end, the way crawling children did. He sat down, the jar sending a stab of pain through his leg and up to the wound on the back of his head. Gritting his teeth and blinking away the tears, Keevan scrabbled down the ramp. He had to wait a moment at the bottom to catch his breath. He got to one knee, the injured leg straight out in front of him. Somehow, he managed to push himself erect, though the room wanted to tip over his ears. It wasn't far to the crooked stick, but it seemed an age before he had it in his hand.

Then the humming stopped!

Keevan cried out and began to hobble frantically across the cavern, out to the bowl of the weyr. Never had the distance between the living caverns and the Hatching Ground seemed so great. Never had the weyr been so silent, breathless. As if the multitude of people and dragons watching the hatching held every breath in suspense. Not even the wind muttered down the steep sides of the bowl. The only sounds to break the stillness were Keevan's ragged breathing and the thump-thud of his stick on the hard-packed ground. Sometimes he had to hop twice on his good leg to maintain his balance. Twice he fell into the sand and had to pull himself up on the stick, his white tunic no longer spotless. Once he jarred himself so badly he couldn't get up immediately.

Then he heard the first exhalation of the crowd, the ooohs, the muted cheer, the susurrus[23] of excited whispers. An egg had cracked, and the dragon had chosen his rider. Desperation increased Keevan's hobble. Would he never reach the arching mouth of the Hatching Ground?

Another cheer and an excited spate of applause spurred Keevan to greater effort. If he didn't get there in moments, there'd be no unpaired hatchling left. Then he was actually staggering into the Hatching Ground, the sands hot on his bare feet.

No one noticed his entrance or his halting progress. And Keevan could see nothing but the backs of the white-robed candidates, seventy of them ringing the area around the eggs. Then one side would surge forward or back and there'd be a cheer. Another dragon had been Impressed. Suddenly a large gap appeared in the white human wall, and Keevan had his first sight of the eggs. There didn't seem to be *any* left uncracked, and he

---

22. *Unwieldy* means "clumsy and difficult to control."

23. A *susurrus* (sōō sur' əs) is a hum or whisper.

(MEETING INDIVIDUAL NEEDS) **GIFTED AND TALENTED ACTIVITY**

Dragon Lore Dragons are found in stories from many parts of the world. In the Middle Ages, sailors were afraid to sail into unknown seas because of dragons and other creatures who were thought to live there.

Activity Invite students interested in dragons or mythology to research several dragon stories from various cultures. Encourage students to prepare a chart or poster illustrating the different characteristics of the dragons in each society. **L3**

Rainbow Bridge by Moonlight. William Robinson Leigh (1866–1955). Oil on canvas, 35¾ x 47¾ in. Private collection.
Viewing the painting: What life would you expect to find in a setting like this? How might that life be connected to storybook dragons?

could see the lucky boys standing beside wobble-legged dragons. He could hear the unmistakable plaintive crooning of hatchlings and their squawks of protest as they'd fall awkwardly in the sand.

Suddenly he wished that he hadn't left his bed, that he'd stayed away from the Hatching Ground. Now everyone would see his ignominious[24] failure. He scrambled now as desperately to reach the shadowy walls of the Hatching Ground as he had struggled to cross the bowl. He mustn't be seen.

He didn't notice, therefore, that the shifting group of boys remaining had begun to drift in his direction. The hard pace he had set himself and his cruel disappointment took their double toll of Keevan. He tripped and collapsed sobbing to the warm sands. He didn't see the consternation[25]

in the watching weyrfolk above the Hatching Ground, nor did he hear the excited whispers of speculation. He didn't know that the weyrleader and weyrwoman had dropped to the arena and were making their way toward the knot of boys slowly moving in the direction of the archway.

"Never seen anything like it," the weyrleader was saying. "Only thirty-nine riders chosen. And the bronze trying to leave the Hatching Ground without making Impression!"

"A case in point of what I said last night," the weyrwoman replied, "where a hatchling makes no choice because the right boy isn't there."

"There's only Beterli and K'last's young one missing. And there's a full wing of likely boys to choose from. . . ."

"None acceptable, apparently. Where is the creature going? He's not heading for

---

24. *Ignominious* (ig′ nə min′ ē əs) means "shameful; disgraceful."
25. *Consternation* is amazement or confusion.

Critical Thinking

DRAWING CONCLUSIONS Have students explain where the words in italic type are coming from and why. *(They are coming from the dragon. Early in the story, the author mentioned that dragons can communicate telepathically with their riders.)*

Active Reading

RESPOND Invite students to explain how Impressing a bronze dragon may change Keevan's life. *(Bronze dragons are the highest-ranking dragons. To ride a bronze dragon means that Keevan will be respected and admired by others. In addition, it means Keevan may one day become a leader of Pern.)*

Literary Elements

FANTASY Have students explain what makes this paragraph a fantasy. *(Not only is the paragraph about a dragon, it is about a dragon that communicates telepathically with people.)*

Thematic Focus

A Different Dimension Have students explain how this story relates to the theme. *(Dragons, dragonriders, and the other fantasy elements of this story are from another dimension.)*

ASSESSMENT OPTIONS

📁 *Quick Checks,* p. 57

The Smallest Dragonboy

the entrance after all. Oh, what have we there, in the shadows?"

Keevan heard with dismay the sound of voices nearing him. He tried to burrow into the sand. The mere thought of how he would be teased and taunted now was unbearable.

Don't worry! Please don't worry! The thought was urgent, but not his own.

Someone kicked sand over Keevan and butted roughly against him.

"Go away. Leave me alone!" he cried.

Why? was the injured-sounding question inserted into his mind. There was no voice, no tone, but the question was there, perfectly clear, in his head.

Incredulous, Keevan lifted his head and stared into the glowing jeweled eyes of a small bronze dragon. His wings were wet; the tips hung drooping to the sand. And he sagged in the middle on his unsteady legs, although he was making a great effort to keep erect.

Keevan dragged himself to his knees, oblivious to the pain of his leg. He wasn't even aware that he was ringed by the boys passed over, while thirty-one pairs of resentful eyes watched him Impress the dragon. The weyrleaders looked on, amused and surprised at the draconic[26] choice, which could not be forced. Could not be questioned. Could not be changed.

Why? asked the dragon again. *Don't you like me?* His eyes whirled with anxiety, and his tone was so piteous that

---

26. Keevan either doesn't notice or doesn't pay attention to (is *oblivious* to) the pain. *Draconic* means "having to do with a dragon."

Keevan staggered forward and threw his arms around the dragon's neck, stroking his eye ridges, patting the damp, soft hide, opening the fragile-looking wings to dry them, and assuring the hatchling wordlessly over and over again that he was the most perfect, most beautiful, most beloved dragon in the entire weyr, in all the weyrs of Pern.

"What's his name, K'van?" asked Lessa, smiling warmly at the new dragonrider. K'van stared up at her for a long moment. Lessa would know as soon as he did. Lessa was the only person who could "receive" from all dragons, not only her own Ramoth. Then he gave her a radiant smile, recognizing the traditional shortening of his name that raised him forever to the rank of dragonrider.

My name is Heath, thought the dragon mildly and hiccuped in sudden urgency: *I'm hungry.*

"Dragons are born hungry," said Lessa, laughing. "F'lar, give the boy a hand. He can barely manage his own legs, much less a dragon's."

K'van remembered his stick and drew himself up. "We'll be just fine, thank you."

"You may be the smallest dragonrider ever, young K'van, but you're the bravest," said F'lar.

And Heath agreed! Pride and joy so leaped in both chests that K'van wondered if his heart would burst right out of his body. He looped an arm around Heath's neck and the pair—the smallest dragonboy, and the hatchling who wouldn't choose anybody else—walked out of the Hatching Ground together forever.

Teaching Options

Grammar and Language *Minilesson*

Infinitives An infinitive is a verb form (verbal) most commonly used as a noun in a sentence, but it is also used as an adjective or an adverb. Knowing how to use infinitives gives writers tools to vary their sentences and keep their readers interested.

Activity Have students work in pairs to identify the infinitive in each sentence

below and tell how it is used.

1. Keevan didn't have the strength to fight Beterli. *(adjective)*
2. Keevan bent to hear the hatching sounds better. *(adverb)*
3. Heath was born hungry and wanted to eat. *(noun)*

Ask each student to write three story-related sentences using infinitives. **L3**
COLLAB. LEARN.

Additional Resources

📖 *Grammar and Language Transparency 56*

📕 *Grammar and Language Workbook,* pp. 175–178

📕 *Grammar and Composition Handbook,* Lesson 9.3

📕 *Writer's Choice,* Lesson 15.3

Responding to Literature

PERSONAL RESPONSE

What was your reaction to this story? Record your responses in your journal. Describe your thoughts and feelings as you followed Keevan through his experience.

Analyzing Literature

RECALL

1. What is a dragonrider, and how does someone become one?
2. Why is Keevan teased by the other dragonboys?
3. What are the different colors of dragons? Which ones were the most desirable?
4. According to Keevan's foster mother, what do dragons look for in their lifetime partners?

INTERPRET

5. Why are the dragons and their riders so important to the people of Pern?
6. Why does Keevan's "breath catch in his throat" at the thought of the moment of hatching time? Explain.
7. Why does Keevan hope to ride a brown dragon?
8. In your opinion, why does Heath choose Keevan? Explain.

EVALUATE AND CONNECT

9. How would most people cope with the cruel teasing Keevan faced daily? How would you?
10. Theme Connection
    Would you like to live on Pern? Why or why not?

Paisaje con Volcano en Primer Plano. Dr. Atl (aka Gerard Murillo) (1875–1964). Atl colors on Masonite, 15¾ x 15¾ in. Galeria de Arte Misrachi, Mexico City.

LITERARY ELEMENTS

Fantasy

Anne McCaffrey's Pern stories combine science fiction (the setting on another planet in the future) with fantasy (fire-breathing dragons). Much like science fiction, **fantasy** explores unreal worlds or the real world with unreal elements, like dragons, ghosts, magic, or characters with superhuman qualities. The emotions and conflicts of characters in a fantasy, however, are often those of ordinary people. Readers can recognize themselves in the personal struggles and adventures of the characters.

1. Which elements in "The Smallest Dragonboy" are fantastic rather than realistic?

2. What is the realistic problem faced by Keevan?

● See **Literary Terms Handbook**, p. R4.

A DIFFERENT DIMENSION 🐚 695

Personal Response

Students should describe the thoughts and feelings they had as they read about Keevan's experiences.

Analyzing Literature

1. A dragonrider is a person who rides a flying dragon to protect the people of Pern from dangerous Thread. A rider is chosen by a dragon when it hatches.
2. Keevan is teased because he is smaller than the other boys.
3. Dragons can be green, blue, brown, or bronze. It is good to Impress a blue or brown dragon, but bronze dragons are the most desirable.
4. Dragons look for boys who are good, honest, patient, courageous, and have flexible minds.
5. Dragons and their riders fly above Pern to destroy deadly Thread before it falls on the people of Pern.
6. Keevan very much wants to be chosen by a dragon. The thought of being picked is very emotional for him.
7. Brown dragons are respected, high-ranking dragons—not the highest, though. Riders of brown dragons could become wingseconds, which was respectable.
8. Heath chooses Keevan because he is brave, determined, and caring. Bravery and determination would be important in the dangerous job of fighting Thread.
9. Students may say that they'd ignore the teaser, try to avoid him, or do something nice for him in the hope that he would stop teasing.

LITERARY ELEMENTS

1. *Fantastic elements:* flying, fire-breathing dragons, dragonriders, and telepathic communication.
2. *Realistic problem:* Keevan is teased because he is smaller than the other boys.

Additional Resources

📖 *Literary Elements Transparency 57*

10. Samples: Yes, because it seems an exciting life. No, because it seems like a primitive world without modern conveniences or equal rights for males and females.

Literature and Writing

Writing About Literature

Students' paragraphs should
- describe the setting of the story.
- explain how the setting affects the story's events.
- analyze why the setting is so important to the story.

Creative Writing

Students' sequels should
- use what they already know about Pern, Keevan, and Heath.
- have a beginning, a middle, and an end.
- contain elements of fantasy.

Extending Your Response

Literature Groups Before students meet, encourage them to review their notes about peer-pressure experiences. Have each group member describe one peer-pressure experience Keevan had and compare it to an experience a person in real life might have.
COLLAB. LEARN.

Performing Have each student prepare a script that describes what occurs. Students may want to interview Keevan or another eyewitness for their stories.

Interdisciplinary Activity Invite students to try methods of drawing or mapping that they have never tried before, such as using chalk or creating a geologic map.

Literature and Writing

Writing About Literature

Setting What is the setting of "The Smallest Dragonboy"? Think about how the setting affects events in the plot. Then write a paragraph explaining why setting is so important to the story.

Creative Writing

A Sequel What might happen to Keevan and his dragon sometime in the future? Will they be called upon to defend Pern against the evil Thread? Write a summary of a sequel telling of a later adventure.

Extending Your Response

Literature Groups

Hopes and Dreams Think about Keevan's hopes and dreams. Think about his relationship with his family and his interactions with the other dragonboys. Review your notes from the **Focus Activity** on page 682. Then work together to create a chart comparing and contrasting Keevan's experiences with his peers with the experiences you and your classmates discussed.

Performing

Eyewitness News: Hatching Day! Imagine that you are a TV news reporter sent to cover this year's Hatching Day. What do you see? Whom do you interview? Write a TV news story based on the events in "The Smallest Dragonboy." Feel free to make up any details you wish. Perform your news story for your classmates in an oral presentation.

Interdisciplinary Activity

Art Imagine what the setting of "The Smallest Dragonboy" looks like. Make a list of the places mentioned in the story, and then draw a picture or map of the setting. Use the story details and descriptions to help you, but feel free to use your imagination to add new details.

Reading Further

If you would like to read more by Anne McCaffrey, try these:
The Dolphins of Pern
Dragonseye

Save your work for your portfolio.

Dragon's Handiwork. Gregory Blake Larson (b. 1961). Pencil and watercolor, 16 x 13 in. Private collection.

Skill Minilessons

GRAMMAR AND LANGUAGE • WRITING: NUMBERS

In writing, you either spell out numbers, or you write them as numerals. Follow these rules.

- Spell out numbers you can write in one or two words.

  The city is **twenty-five** miles from here.
- Spell out any number that begins a sentence.

  One hundred and thirty-four children came to school in spite of the snowstorm.
- Use numerals for numbers of more than two words not at the beginning of a sentence.

  The city is **465** miles away.

- Write a very large number as a numeral followed by the word *million* or *billion.*

  The planet is **3 billion** miles away.
- If related numbers appear in the same sentence and one of them should be written as numerals, use all numerals.

  She wrote **10** novels and more than **150** short stories.

PRACTICE Write a sentence of your own to demonstrate each one of the previous rules.

● For more about similar usage problems, see **Language Handbook,** p. R43.

READING AND THINKING • CLASSIFYING

Skillful readers organize information by classifying things into categories. When you **classify,** you think about how things are alike and then put similar things into groups. In "The Smallest Dragonboy," for example, Keevan and the other boys could be classified as dragonboys.

PRACTICE Skim "The Smallest Dragonboy" and find two other groups of things that can be put into categories.

● For more about organizing information, see **Reading Handbook,** pp. R84–R85.

VOCABULARY • SYNONYMS: SHADES OF MEANING

Synonyms differ in their meanings—sometimes in important ways. For example, you could be pleasant and gentle while you *urge* someone to do something, but not while you *goad* someone. A *goaded* person feels forced or driven to do something he or she most likely doesn't want to do.

PRACTICE Think about what the underlined word means in each sentence. Then choose the better synonym for that word *that makes sense in the sentence.*

1. The neighborhood bully <u>ridiculed</u> Billy when he came outside holding his sister's hand.
   a. teased   b. mocked
2. The <u>enticing</u> sign said "Everything half price."
   a. inviting   b. charming
3. As the phone interrupted her for the fifth time, Mrs. Frye groaned in <u>exasperation.</u>
   a. annoyance   b. rage
4. After the tornado, their <u>desolated</u> town needed to be almost totally rebuilt.
   a. ruined   b. gloomy

Skill Minilessons

GRAMMAR AND LANGUAGE
WRITING: NUMBERS

Samples:
1. I live ten minutes from school.
2. Eight hundred and fifty-three students go to my school.
3. We drove 1132 miles on our vacation.
4. Approximately 7 million people live in New York City.
5. I have 6 quarters and 133 pennies.

READING AND THINKING
CLASSIFYING

Sample categories:
- Dragons: green, blue, brown, and bronze
- Dragonriders: green riders, blue riders, brown riders, and bronze riders

VOCABULARY
SYNONYMS: SHADES OF MEANING

1. b
2. a
3. a
4. a

Additional Resources

📙 *Grammar and Language Workbook,* pp. 279–280

📙 *Grammar and Composition Handbook,* Lesson 13.10

📙 *Writer's Choice,* Lesson 20.10

📙 *Reading Workbook,* pp. 101–102

📁 *Vocabulary Practice,* p. 39

ASSESSMENT OPTIONS

📁 *Quick Checks,* p. 57

📁 *Selection and Theme Assessment,* pp. 99–100

📁 *Performance Assessment,* p. 54

💾 *Testmaker*

Objective

• To understand the elements of legends, myths, and folklore

Teaching Strategies

Ask students to share stories they have heard that fit the descriptions in their books. Have them list legendary figures or mythical heroes they have heard about. Encourage students to explore their own cultural heritage for folkloric tales they could bring in and share with classmates.

Legends Have students talk about modern-day legends and describe what they consider "legendary behavior" to be. Encourage them to find pictures in magazines of people they think of as the living legends of their generation.

Myths Point out to students that the word *myth* has come to mean something that isn't true. People might say, "That's just a myth," meaning "That's just a falsehood."

Folklore Point out to students that *folklore* can be thought of as the collection of stories, songs, tales, and jokes that helps members of a culture stay connected to one another. Folkloric expression is a way of preserving the shared past of a people or nation.

LEGENDS, MYTHS, AND FOLKLORE

Long before there was written language, there was folklore. One storyteller calls myths, legends, and folk stories "stories that aren't true on the outside, but are true on the inside." Some of these stories are humorous; some are serious, even tragic, and filled with the power of ancient cultures and the spoken word.

Most of these stories were passed down orally from one teller to the next over hundreds of years. They are still evolving today. They may change a little each time the speaker or writer adds his or her own touches. In this way, the oldest stories in the world stay new.

LEGENDS, which relate amazing events or accomplishments, are stories known throughout a cultural group. Their heroes may be humans, animals, or even plants, enchanted objects, or forces of nature. Some legendary human heroes actually lived, but over the years their reputations grew larger than life. In this theme, you'll read the Chinese legend "Cat and Rat" and learn about the Chinese calendar.

MYTHS are traditional stories about gods and goddesses or how things came to be. These stories usually reflect a culture's religious or other deeply held beliefs. In the myth "Icarus and Daedalus," two mortals try to fly like the god Apollo. They learn that, unlike their gods, humans have limits.

FOLKLORE is a general term covering folktales, proverbs, ritual speeches, folk songs, fables, and many other forms of literature handed down by word of mouth. "The Bunyans," a story about Paul Bunyan and his family, is an example of a type of folktale called the tall tale. Some scholars classify legends and myths as forms of folklore.

The Two Mythical Dragons (detail).

Some Common Types of Folklore	
jokes	fables
riddles	fairy tales
proverbs	folktales
anecdotes	legends
animal tales	myths

Technology Option

Folklore Table

Students can use word processing software to create tables of folkloric elements as they read the stories in this unit. Have each student create a table like the one below.

Title	Type of Story	Cultural Origin	Hero(es)	Fantastic Elements	Main Event	Outcome

Activity For each myth, legend, or folktale, students can add a new row to the table and type in information about each of the six elements of that story. Students can use their completed tables as tools for study and review. **L2**

Active Reading Strategies

Legends, myths, and folklore are part of the earliest and longest-lasting literature—the ancient stories that tell about the beliefs, histories, joys, and sorrows of people from every corner of the world. When reading legends, myths, and folktales, skillful readers use strategies that help them understand how the characters—human and imaginary—respond to their settings and situations.

● For more about reading strategies and reading across cultures, see **Reading Handbook,** pp. R70–R77.

PREVIEW

Before reading a legend, myth, or folktale, look at the title and the illustrations. Previewing helps you get an overall look at, or sense of, the text before you begin reading it.

VISUALIZE

As you read, use the author's descriptions to try to imagine the setting and characters.

CONNECT

Even a legend, myth, or folktale from another place or time can have great meaning to a modern reader. Connect the story to experiences in your own life.

QUESTION

As you read the story, ask yourself questions about the characters, the events, and the ideas.

PREDICT

Even while reading a story with magical events, you should try to predict what might happen next or how the tale might end.

APPLYING THE STRATEGIES

Read the following folktale, "Aunty Misery." Use the Active Reading Model notes in the margins as you read. Write your responses on a separate piece of paper or use stick-on notes.

699

Objective

• To understand and apply strategies for reading and comprehending myths, legends, and folklore

Teach the Strategies

Remind students that most myths, legends, and folktales come to us through the oral tradition. Readers, like listeners, remain actively engaged in these stories by practicing the following techniques.

Preview Ask students to look at the story as they would look at a story-teller. What do they think the title means? Can they tell where the story comes from?

Visualize The supernatural world is often a natural part of myths, legends, and folk stories. Students may wish to visualize and draw pictures of the spirits they read about.

Connect Although the external settings and circumstances of many myths and legends may be unfamiliar to students, the internal truths they reveal are often universal. Encourage students to relate these truths to beliefs they have formed.

Question Point out to students that they may wish to practice questioning the capabilities of the characters within the "fantastic" context of the story rather than questioning the possibility of their existence.

Teaching Options

Reading Journal

Universal Notions

The author Judith Ortiz Cofer presents in "Aunty Misery" a Puerto Rican folktale about misery and death. Invite students to discuss how death is portrayed in this country. (Frequently as the grim reaper, a person dressed in black with a scythe.) Invite students to share any sayings they know about death. (*Sample: two things are certain in life: death and taxes.*)

Activity As they read, ask students to draw a flow chart in which they show the order of the story events. After reading, have students list the pros and cons of Aunty Misery's decision to keep Death stuck in the pear tree.

Objectives

- To read a fable about two things in life that everyone experiences
- To recognize the characteristics of a fable
- To write about the story elements found in a fable

Skills

Reading/Thinking: Comparing and Contrasting; Generalizing
Writing: Fable
Vocabulary: Analogies
Grammar/Language: Frequently Misspelled Words
Listening/Speaking: Group Presentation
Collaboration: Literature Groups

Motivating

→OPTIONS

Selection Focus Transparency 58: Have students discuss the quotation and list things in life that happen to everyone whether they are prepared or not (*such as birth, death, fortune, misfortune*).

Focus Activity: As an extension of the Focus Activity, have students in small groups list two good things that happen in everyone's life.

ACTIVE READING MODEL

Before You Read
Aunty Misery

MEET JUDITH ORTIZ COFER

English was not Judith Ortiz Cofer's first language. Born in Puerto Rico, she learned English only after her family moved to the United States. "It was a challenge," she said, "not only to learn English, but to master it enough to teach it and—the ultimate goal—to write poetry in it." Cofer's writing reflects the split between her two childhood homes: the island of Puerto Rico and the United States. She has written, "My family is one of the main topics of my poetry. In tracing their lives, I discover more about mine."

Judith Ortiz Cofer was born in Puerto Rico in 1952.

FOCUS ACTIVITY

What do you imagine would happen if human beings could live forever?

Sharing Ideas

In a small group, talk about how the world would change if people lived forever. Discuss the positive and negative results of such a change in the human life cycle.

Setting a Purpose

Read to enjoy this Puerto Rican tale.

BACKGROUND

The Time and Place "Aunty Misery" is set in a Spanish-speaking country sometime in the distant past.

Did You Know? The Commonwealth of Puerto Rico is made up of one large and several smaller islands located about 1,000 miles southeast of Florida. It has been a part of the United States since 1898. The island's culture is a blend of the people who have lived there—the Native Americans, the Spanish who conquered the island in 1509, and the Africans who were first brought there as slaves to work on the sugar plantations. The majority of today's Puerto Rican population is of Hispanic background.

VOCABULARY PREVIEW

sorcerer (sor′ sər ər) *n.* a person who practices magic with the aid of evil spirits; p. 701
taunt (tônt) *v.* to make fun of in a scornful, insulting way; p. 701
gnarled (närld) *adj.* rough, twisted, and knotty, as a tree trunk or branches; p. 702
potion (pō′ shən) *n.* a drink, especially of a liquid that is supposed to have magical powers; p. 702

RESOURCE MANAGER

Lesson Planning Resource
The ***Theme Seven Planning Guide*** (pp. 30–34) provides additional lesson notes and reduced versions of all print resources.

📂 **Other Print Resources**
- Active Reading Guide, p. 58
- Vocabulary Practice, p. 40
- Reading Workbook, pp. 103–104

- Grammar and Language Workbook, pp. 297–300
- Grammar and Composition Handbook, Lessons 15.1–15.2
- Quick Checks, p. 58
- Selection and Theme Assessment, p. 101
- Performance Assessment, p. 55
- Spanish Summaries, p. 58
- Spanish Translations
- Inclusion Strategies

- English Language Learners Sourcebook

🔖 **Transparencies**
- Selection Focus 58
- Literary Elements 58

Technology
🎧 Audio Library
🎧 Spanish Audio Library
💻 Glencoe Literature Web Site
💾 Testmaker

Aunty Misery
A Folktale from Puerto Rico

Judith Ortiz Cofer ✎

This is a story about an old, a very old woman who lived alone in her little hut with no other company than a beautiful pear tree that grew at her door. She spent all her time taking care of this tree. The neighborhood children drove the old woman crazy by stealing her fruit. They would climb her tree, shake its delicate limbs, and run away with armloads of golden pears, yelling insults at *la Tia Miseria*,[1] Aunty Misery, as they called her.

One day, a traveler stopped at the old woman's hut and asked her for permission to spend the night under her roof. Aunty Misery saw that he had an honest face and bid the pilgrim come in. She fed him and made a bed for him in front of her hearth. In the morning the stranger told her that he would show his gratitude for her hospitality by granting her one wish.

"There is only one thing that I desire," said Aunty Misery.

"Ask, and it shall be yours," replied the stranger, who was a <u>sorcerer</u> in disguise.

"I wish that anyone who climbs up my pear tree should not be able to come back down until I permit it."

"Your wish is granted," said the stranger, touching the pear tree as he left Aunty Misery's house.

And so it happened that when the children came back to <u>taunt</u> the old woman and to steal her fruit, she stood at her window watching them. Several of them shimmied[2] up the trunk of the pear tree and

---

1. *La Tia Miseria* (lä tē′ ə mē′ ze rē′ ə)
2. *Shimmied* means "shook or vibrated," which is what the tree might have done as the children shinnied up it. To *shinny* is to climb by using the hands, arms, feet, and legs to pull and push oneself up.

Vocabulary
sorcerer (sôr′ sər ər) *n.* a person who practices magic with the aid of evil spirits
taunt (tônt) *v.* to make fun of in a scornful, insulting way

ACTIVE READING MODEL

PREVIEW

What is the origin of this folktale? — A

VISUALIZE

Can you picture Aunty Misery? What words does the author use to help you see the character? — B

QUESTION

What does the fact that the traveler can grant wishes tell you about the tale? — C

CONNECT

Have you ever known someone like Aunty Misery? — D

Reading the Selection

SUMMARY

Aunty Misery cares only for her beautiful pear tree; however, the neighborhood children keep stealing its fruit. A sorcerer grants Aunty Misery's wish that tree climbers can come down only with her permission. The wish works well when Death gets stuck in the tree. He can come down only when he promises never to come for her again. This is why there is always misery and death in the world.

📁 *Spanish Summaries,* p. 58

A **Active Reading**
PREVIEW *(It is from Puerto Rico.)*

B **Active Reading**
VISUALIZE Have students draw Aunty Misery and her house.

C **Active Reading**
QUESTION *(It will probably be about extraordinary events.)*

D **Active Reading**
CONNECT *(Students should compare Aunty Misery with someone they know.)*

Additional Resources
📁 *Active Reading Guide,* p. 58
🎧 *Audio Library*
🎧 *Spanish Audio Library*

Teaching Options

CONNECTING TO OTHER SELECTIONS
For a teaching strategy that connects "Aunty Misery" to "Lob's Girl," turn to page 10 in the *Theme Seven Planning Guide.*

LITERATURE & HUMANITIES

To introduce students to another woman who personifies a painful human emotion, play the song "La Llorona" (track 26) from the second CD of *The World of Music.* This song is about the Latino myth of a woman who represents grief.

Aunty Misery

Active Reading sidebar (left column)

E **Active Reading**

CONNECT *(Students can share their experiences with the class.)*

F **Active Reading**

PREDICT *(Aunty Misery will probably trick Death into getting stuck in the tree. Aunty Misery is old, but she might live as long as death is stuck in the tree.)*

G **Active Reading**

QUESTION *(No one dies in the world because Death is stuck in the pear tree. People whose livelihood is connected in some way to death are out of work.)*

H **Active Reading**

EVALUATE *(It explains why misery and death are always in the world. They may or may not retell this story to a friend depending on how they feel about the topic.)*

Thematic Focus

A Different Dimension Have students explain how this story relates to the theme.

☑ **ASSESSMENT OPTIONS**

📁 *Quick Checks,* p. 58

Teaching Options

Sidebar prompts (center)

CONNECT

E — Have you ever had to think quickly to get out of a sticky situation?

PREDICT

F — What do you think Aunty Misery has in mind for Death? What will happen to Aunty Misery?

QUESTION

G — What cause-and-effect situation is the author describing here?

EVALUATE

H — What lesson about misery and death does this tale explain? Would you retell this tale to a friend? Why or why not?

---

immediately got stuck to it as if with glue. She let them cry and beg her for a long time before she gave the tree permission to let them go on the condition that they never again steal her fruit, or bother her.

Time passed and both Aunty Misery and her tree grew bent and <u>gnarled</u> with age. One day another traveler stopped at her door. This one looked untrustworthy to her, so before letting him into her home the old woman asked him what he was doing in her village. He answered her in a voice that was dry and hoarse, as if he had swallowed a desert: "I am Death, and I have come to take you with me."

Thinking fast Aunty Misery said, "All right, but before I go I would like to pluck some pears from my beloved tree to remember how much pleasure it brought me in this life. But I am a very old woman and cannot climb to the tallest branches where the best fruit is. Will you be so kind as to do it for me?"

With a heavy sigh like wind through a tomb, Señor[3] Death climbed the pear tree. Immediately he became stuck to it as if with glue. And no matter how much he cursed and threatened, Aunty Misery would not allow the tree to release Death.

Many years passed and there were no deaths in the world. The people who make their living from death began to protest loudly. The doctors claimed no one bothered to come in for examinations or treatments anymore, because they did not fear dying; the pharmacists' business suffered too because medicines are, like magic <u>potions</u>, bought to prevent or postpone the inevitable; priests and undertakers were unhappy with the situation also, for obvious reasons. There were also many old folks tired of life who wanted to pass on to the next world to rest from miseries of this one.

La Tia Miseria was blamed by these people for their troubles, of course. Not wishing to be unfair, the old woman made a deal with her prisoner, Death: if he promised not ever to come for her again, she would give him his freedom. He agreed. And that is why there are two things you can always count on running into in this world: Misery and Death: *La miseria y la muerte.*[4]

---

3. *Señor* (sen yôr´) is the Spanish equivalent of "Mister."
4. *Y la muerte* (ē   lä   mwer´ tä)

Vocabulary

gnarled (närld) *adj.* rough, twisted, and knotty, as a tree trunk or branches

potion (pō´ shən) *n.* a drink, especially of a liquid that is supposed to have magical powers

---

Reading *Minilesson*

Comparing and Contrasting Have students discuss how Señor Death and Aunty Misery are alike and different.

Activity Encourage students to use Venn diagrams to compare and contrast Aunty Misery and Señor Death. When students have completed the comparison, have them put an asterisk in front of those characteristics that are often found in folktales. **L2**

Aunty Misery
owns a beautiful pear tree
*sorcerer grants her a wish

*live forever
*have special powers

Señor Death
untrustworthy
*is stuck in tree for years

Additional Resources

📁 *Reading Workbook,* pp. 103–104

Responding to Literature

Responding to the Selection

PERSONAL RESPONSE

How does this story add to your thoughts about life and death?

Active Reading Response
Review the strategies described in the **Active Reading Model** notes on page 699. Choose one of the strategies, and find two places in the story where you could apply it.

Analyzing Literature

RECALL
1. How does Aunty Misery punish the neighborhood children who steal her pears?
2. How did Aunty Misery treat the first stranger?
3. Who is the second stranger who visits Aunty Misery?
4. How does Aunty Misery manage to trick Death?

INTERPRET
5. Why do you think the neighborhood children call the old woman "Aunty Misery"?
6. In your opinion, why does the first stranger grant Aunty Misery's wish?
7. Explain how Aunty Misery's wisdom about the second stranger saves her life.
8. What causes Aunty Misery finally to make a deal with Death?

EVALUATE AND CONNECT
9. **Theme Connection** How does this story fit the theme of "a different dimension"?
10. Recall your discussion in the **Focus Activity** on page 700. How did reading "Aunty Misery" influence your ideas about a world without death?

LITERARY ELEMENTS

Fable

A **fable** is a kind of folklore in which a brief story is used to teach a lesson about human nature. Some of the most famous fables were written by Aesop, who is thought to have been a slave in ancient Greece. The characters in fables are often animals who speak and act like people. Usually a fable—"Aunty Misery," for example—concludes with a clearly stated moral, or lesson.

1. Two strangers visit Aunty Misery. Describe how she wisely treats them differently. What are the results of her actions?

2. What is the moral, or stated lesson, of "Aunty Misery"?

● See **Literary Terms Handbook**, p. R4.

A DIFFERENT DIMENSION 🐾 703

Personal Response

Students may realize that life and death are closely related or that death is important for life.

Active Reading Response
Students should explain how to apply the strategy in two different places.

Analyzing Literature

1. She causes them to stick to the tree as if with glue.
2. Aunty Misery treated the first stranger with kindness and hospitality.
3. The second stranger is Death.
4. Aunty Misery convinces Death to climb the tree and pick some pears for her before she dies.
5. They call her Aunty Misery because she is old and alone and seems miserable to them.
6. The first stranger grants Aunty Misery's wish because Aunty Misery was very kind to him.
7. Because she doesn't trust him, she maneuvers him into a position where he can't harm her.
8. Aunty Misery makes a deal with Death because she realizes the world cannot function properly without death.
9. The story fits the theme because it contains people with special powers, such as the ability to grant wishes or to live forever.
10. Answers may indicate that students hadn't considered the negative aspects of a world without death.

LITERARY ELEMENTS

1. After being treated kindly, the first stranger grants Aunty Misery one wish. By tricking the second stranger, Aunty Misery is spared from Death.
2. The moral of "Aunty Misery" is that people can always count on death and misery in the world.

Additional Resources
 Literary Elements Transparency 58

Literature and Writing

Writing About Literature

Students' writing should

- accurately identify the characters, plot, setting, and lesson of "Aunty Misery."
- explain how these elements work together in a fable.
- explain how a fable is different from other kinds of stories.

Creative Writing

Students' fables should

- contain elements of a short story: characters, plot, and setting.
- contain elements of a fable, such as a moral.
- use this fable as a writing model to create characters, such as Death and Misery, who represent aspects of the human experience.

Extending Your Response

Literature Groups Before students meet, encourage them to jot down a few ideas or to review the Venn diagrams they created for the Reading Minilesson on page 702. Then, in groups, have each member briefly contribute and summarize a comparison or a contrasting idea. **COLLAB. LEARN.**

Art Activity Encourage students to try drawing tools they haven't used before, such as charcoal or pastels. Then have them focus on the feeling their scenes create in their minds.

Interdisciplinary Activity Encourage students to share what they already know about Puerto Rico. Remind students that an interview with someone who is part of the Puerto Rican culture is valuable research. **COLLAB. LEARN.**

Literature and Writing

Writing About Literature

Story Elements Although fables are brief, they usually contain all the elements of a short story. Briefly identify the characters, plot, setting, and theme (or lesson) of "Aunty Misery."

Creative Writing

Folktale Write your own fable about two things "you can always count on running into in this world." Choose two things other than misery and death that you believe are always part of the human experience.

Extending Your Response

Literature Groups

Spiritual Effects Aunty Misery isn't the only human character in the story whose life is changed by supernatural characters. Using examples from the text, compare and contrast the roles of the two supernatural characters. How do these spiritual strangers affect the lives of the human characters?

Art Activity

Scene Illustration Create an illustration of a descriptive scene from the story. Choose a scene that is especially vivid—such as the children stuck in the pear tree or Aunty Misery, as bent and gnarled as her pear tree.

Interdisciplinary Activity

Social Studies Working with a small group, study the culture of Puerto Rico. Have each group member research one of the following: the history of the people, the geography of their homeland, their religious beliefs, art and music, their relationship to the government of the United States. To combine what you have learned, plan a group presentation that includes pictures, maps, and music.

Reading Further

If you would like to read more folktales, try these:

Perez and Martina: A Puerto Rican Folktale by Pura Belpré

The Terrible EEK: A Japanese Tale retold by Patricia A. Compton

📖 **Save your work for your portfolio.**

Dona Rosita Morillo, 1944. Frida Kahlo. Oil on canvas mounted on Masonite, 30½ x 28½ in. Fundacion Dolores Olmedo, Mexico City, D.F., Mexico.

Skill Minilessons

GRAMMAR AND LANGUAGE • FREQUENTLY MISSPELLED WORDS

Simple words may be misspelled because a word is mistaken for a similar one–for example, confusing *they're* (a contraction for *they are*) for *their* or *there*. Some other often-confused words are *whose* and *who's; its* and *it's;* and *your* and *you're*. If you are confused about which to use, use a dictionary for help.

PRACTICE Write the word that should be used in each sentence.
1. There once was a woman (whose, who's) pear tree attracted all the children in the neighborhood.
2. "Those children over (their, there, they're) are stealing my pears," she complained.
3. "(Your, You're) pears will remain untouched," the stranger promised.
4. "(Its, It's) branches will remain unbroken," he added.
5. "(Your, You're) very kind," Aunty Misery replied.

● For more about frequently misspelled words, see **Language Handbook,** p. R44.

READING AND THINKING • GENERALIZING

Generalizing is forming a general rule or conclusion based on particular facts or examples. For example, based on "Aunty Misery" and similar stories, you might generalize that many folktales try to explain why some condition exists in the real world.

● For more about generalizing, see **Reading Handbook,** p. R88.

PRACTICE Based on your own experience and reading, make a generalization about each of the following.
1. why people enjoy fantasy or science fiction
2. the main difference between folklore and modern fiction

VOCABULARY • ANALOGIES

An **analogy** is a comparison based on the relationships between things or ideas. Each of the two pairs of words in an analogy illustrates the same relationship.

eyes : vision :: ears : hearing

The relationship between the words can be expressed in a sentence. "*Eyes* are used for *vision* as *ears* are used for *hearing*." The phrase "are used for" describes the relationship, which is the same in each half, or word pair, of the analogy.

PRACTICE Choose the word that best completes each analogy.
1. puppy : dog :: child :
   a. baby   b. adult   c. person
2. taunt : scorn :: praise :
   a. approval   b. complaint   c. gratitude
3. man : woman :: rooster :
   a. egg   b. crow   c. hen
4. potion : drink :: song :
   a. notes   b. music   c. sing

● For more about analogies, see **Communications Skills Handbook,** p. R65.

Skill Minilessons

GRAMMAR AND LANGUAGE
FREQUENTLY MISSPELLED WORDS
1. whose
2. there
3. Your
4. Its
5. You're

READING AND THINKING
GENERALIZING
1. Students should make generalizations based on their own experiences.
2. Students should cite examples from folklore and modern fiction to support their ideas.

VOCABULARY
ANALOGIES
1. b
2. a
3. c
4. b

Additional Resources
Grammar and Language Workbook, pp. 297–300
Grammar and Composition Handbook, Lessons 15.1, 15.2
Writer's Choice, Lesson 23.8
Reading Workbook, pp. 103–104
Vocabulary Practice, p. 40

ASSESSMENT OPTIONS
Quick Checks, p. 58
Selection and Theme Assessment, pp. 101
Performance Assessment, p. 55
Testmaker

Before Reading

Objectives

- To read and analyze a folktale
- To recognize transitions that indicate chronological order
- To write about the cause and resolution of a conflict in a story

Skills

Reading/Thinking: Cause and Effect
Writing: Myth
Vocabulary: Synonyms
Listening/Speaking: Role-Playing
Collaboration: Literature Groups

Motivating →OPTIONS

Literature Launchers: "A Few Minutes with Gayle Ross"

Videodisc Side B, Segment 20

Also available in VHS.

Selection Focus Transparency 59: Have students think about and discuss the quotation by Marc Chagall. Encourage them to think about what color love is to them.

Focus Activity: As an extension of the Focus Activity, have pairs of students list favorite features of the plants they drew and why those features express love to them.

Before You Read
Strawberries

MEET GAYLE ROSS

The role of storyteller is not limited to people who lived in earlier societies that lacked writing. Many people today carry on the oral story-telling tradition. Gayle Ross is one of them. A descendent of John Ross, a famous chief of the Cherokee nation, Gayle Ross first heard tales of her heritage from her grand-mother. Ross has worked in radio and television and has performed as a storyteller all over the United States. Her audiences have included the president and vice president of the United States and other world leaders. She is the author of five books.

Gayle Ross was born in 1951.

706 🐿 THEME 7

FOCUS ACTIVITY

If you could create a flower, fruit, or plant that expressed your idea of love, what would it be?

Think/Pair/Share
Think about what you would create, then draw a picture of it. Share your creation with a partner.

Setting a Purpose
Read to find out how strawberries came to be, according to this Cherokee myth.

BACKGROUND

Did You Know? The Cherokee language was one of the first Native American languages to have a system of writing. A Cherokee named Sequoyah invented an alphabet in 1821. Remarkably, Sequoyah himself was unable to read in any language when he began. To create letters for the sounds of Cherokee, Sequoyah borrowed from the Roman alphabet (the alphabet used for English), modified other Roman letters, and made up some additional symbols. Before long, the Cherokee had books and a news-paper in their own language.

VOCABULARY PREVIEW

despair (di spār′) *n.* complete loss of hope; desperation; p. 708
overtake (ō′ vər tāk′) *v.* to catch up with or to reach and then pass; p. 708
fixed (fikst) *adj.* steadily directed and unchanging; p. 708
aroma (ə rō′ mə) *n.* a pleasant smell; odor; p. 708

RESOURCE MANAGER

Lesson Planning Resource
The ***Theme Seven Planning Guide*** (pp. 35–42) provides additional lesson notes and reduced versions of all print resources.

📁 **Other Print Resources**
- Active Reading Guide, p. 59
- Vocabulary Practice, p. 41
- Reading Workbook, pp. 105–106
- Quick Checks, p. 59

- Selection and Theme Assessment, p. 102
- Performance Assessment, p. 56
- Spanish Summaries, p. 59
- Spanish Translations
- Inclusion Strategies
- English Language Learners Sourcebook

👆 **Transparencies**
- Selection Focus 59
- Fine Art 28

- Literary Elements 59

Technology
 Literature Launchers
 Audio Library
 Spanish Audio Library
 Glencoe Literature Web Site
 Testmaker

706 🐿 THEME 7

Strawberries

Retold by Gayle Ross

Long ago, in the very first days of the world, there lived the first man and the first woman. They lived together as husband and wife, and they loved one another dearly. But one day, they quarreled. Although neither later could remember what the quarrel was about, the pain grew stronger with every word that was spoken, until finally, in anger and in grief, the woman left their home and began walking away—to the east, toward the rising sun.

A

SUMMARY

A man and his wife quarrel. In anger and grief, the woman walks away from their home. The man regrets the quarrel and tries to catch his wife, but she walks too fast. A spirit makes huckleberries bloom in the woman's path, but she doesn't slow down for them. The spirit makes all the trees bloom, but the woman still does not slow down. Finally, the spirit creates a new plant—strawberries. The woman stops to pick the berries. Anger leaves her heart, and love returns. The husband catches up to his wife. After the two pick and eat the berries, they return home to live in happiness and love.

📁 *Spanish Summaries,* p. 59

A Active Reading

PREDICT Have a volunteer read the first paragraph of this story aloud. Then ask students to describe the conflict and predict how the title "Strawberries" may play a role in its resolution. Suggest that students periodically revisit their predictions as they read to verify or revise them.

Additional Resources
📁 *Active Reading Guide,* p. 59
🎧 *Audio Library*
🎧 *Spanish Audio Library*

Teaching Options

CONNECTING TO OTHER SELECTIONS

The chart at the right shows three ways to connect "Strawberries" to other selections in this book.

For specific teaching strategies, see the *Theme Seven Planning Guide,* pages 38–39.

Connection	Title
Life Skills: Lifelong Learning	→ "Bird Like No Other," p. 473
Thematic: Where the Heart Is	→ "Oh, Broom Get to Work," p. 383
Literary: Folktale	→ "The Force of Luck," p. 591

B Literary Elements

TONE Ask students to think about what the lean detail and absence of any emotional words other than *pity* might imply about the author's attitude toward the characters and events. *(She's serious and generally matter-of-fact, impartial.)*

C Active Reading

VISUALIZE Ask students to describe how the couple looks. *(She walks angrily, gazing straight ahead. The man may look sad as he follows her, his shoulders drooping.)*

D Active Reading

PREDICT Ask students to predict what the woman will do when she sees the new fruit. The following model illustrates the thinking process involved in predicting.

Model: I think the spirit will be successful this time; the woman will be curious about this new fruit. When she stops to look, her husband may catch up to her.

FYI

Strong emotions, such as anger, cause the brain to secrete adrenaline, a strong hormone that stimulates the body to produce extra glucose quickly. This natural sugar helps supply additional energy to respond to stress, allowing a person to walk for a long time.

Teaching Options

Strawberries

The man sat alone in his house. But as time went by, he grew lonelier and lonelier. The anger left him, and all that remained was a terrible grief and <u>despair</u>, and he began to cry.

B

A spirit heard the man crying and took pity on him. The spirit said, "Man, why do you cry?"

The man said, "My wife has left me."

The spirit said, "Why did your woman leave?"

The man just hung his head and said nothing.

The spirit asked, "You quarreled with her?"

And the man nodded.

"Would you quarrel with her again?" asked the spirit.

The man said, "No." He wanted only to live with his wife as they had lived before—in peace, in happiness, and in love.

"I have seen your woman," the spirit said. "She is walking to the east toward the rising sun."

The man followed his wife, but he could not <u>overtake</u> her. Everyone knows an angry woman walks fast.

Finally, the spirit said, "I'll go ahead and see if I can make her slow her steps." So the spirit found the woman walking, her footsteps fast and angry and her gaze <u>fixed</u> straight ahead. There was pain in her heart.

C

The spirit saw some huckleberry bushes growing along the trail, so with a wave of

his hand, he made the bushes burst into bloom and ripen into fruit. But the woman's gaze remained fixed. She looked neither to the right nor to the left, and she didn't see the berries. Her footsteps didn't slow.

Again, the spirit waved his hand, and one by one, all of the berries growing along the trail burst into bloom and ripened into fruit. But still, the woman's gaze remained fixed. She saw nothing but her anger and pain, and her footsteps didn't slow.

And again, the spirit waved his hand, and, one by one, the trees of the forest—the peach, the pear, the apple, the wild cherry—burst into bloom and ripened into fruit. But still, the woman's eyes remained fixed, and even still, she saw nothing but her anger and pain. And her footsteps didn't slow.

Then finally, the spirit thought, "I will create an entirely new fruit—one that grows very, very close to the ground so the woman must forget her anger and bend her head for a moment." So the spirit waved his hand, and a thick green carpet began to grow along the trail. Then the carpet became starred with tiny white flowers, and each flower gradually ripened into a berry that was the color and shape of the human heart.

D

As the woman walked, she crushed the tiny berries, and the delicious <u>aroma</u> came up through her nose. She stopped and

---

Vocabulary
despair (di spār′) *n.* complete loss of hope; desperation
overtake (ō′ vər tāk′) *v.* to catch up with or to reach and then pass
fixed (fikst) *adj.* steadily directed and unchanging
aroma (ə rō′ mə) *n.* a pleasant smell; odor

ENGLISH LANGUAGE LEARNERS

Folktales Almost every culture has stories that have been passed down orally from generation to generation. Some of these stories are about love or about how things first came to be.

Activity Have students break into small groups to share stories from their cultures about love or about how something came to be. Then have each group select one story and act it out for the

rest of the class. Allow students ample time to practice. Students may want to make some visuals to enhance the stories. Encourage the class to notice which values are important in each story.
COLLAB. LEARN.

Additional Resources
📁 *English Language Learners Sourcebook*

Strawberry Dance, 1983. G. Peter Jemison. Mixed media on handmade paper, 22 x 30 in. Private collection, by permission of the artist.

Viewing the painting: How does the mood of this artwork reflect the mood of the story's ending?

E looked down, and she saw the berries. She picked one and ate it, and she discovered its taste was as sweet as love itself. So she began walking slowly, picking berries as she went, and as she leaned down to pick a berry, she saw her husband coming behind her.

F The anger had gone from her heart, and all that remained was the love she had always known. So she stopped for him, and together, they picked and ate the berries. Finally, they returned to their home, where they lived out their days in peace, happiness, and love.

And that's how the world's very first strawberries brought peace between men and women in the world and why to this day they are called the berries of love.

A DIFFERENT DIMENSION 🐿 709

VIEWING THE PAINTING

Viewing Response *The colors and style of the art, with the subjects nesting and "dancing" among the strawberries, convey the same bright, peaceful mood found at the end of the story.*

E Literary Elements

TONE Have a volunteer read this passage aloud as a newswriter might deliver it. Ask students to discuss what would make this passage be even more matter-of-fact. *(Take out the comparison and just say that the strawberry tasted sweet.)*

F Active Reading

RESPOND Ask students which human values are portrayed in this story. *(This story portrays forgiveness, love, the letting go of anger, and the wisdom to appreciate the importance of another person.)*

Thematic Focus

A Different Dimension Have students explain what this story has to do with the theme. *(A spirit from a different dimension helps resolve the story's conflict.)*

FINE ART
TRANSPARENCY 28

You may wish to use *Fine Art Transparency 28* to help students think about the theme.

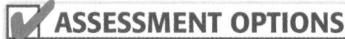

☑ ASSESSMENT OPTIONS

📁 *Quick Checks,* p. 59

Reading *Minilesson*

Cause and Effect Draw the following chart on the board and invite students to help fill in the first causes and effects from the story.

Activity Have students reread the story to identify and to list cause and effect transitions on the chart. Have the class discuss any disagreements and reach a consensus on the major causes and effects in this story. **L2**

Cause	Effect
1. *A man and wife fight.*	*The woman leaves in anger.*
2. *The man misses his wife.*	*He hurries after her.*

Additional Resources
📁 *Reading Workbook,* pp. 105–106

Responding to the Selection

Personal Response

Students should explain how their thoughts have changed or expanded.

Analyzing Literature

1. The woman leaves her husband because a quarrel makes her angry.
2. A spirit tries to slow the woman down so her husband can catch up to her.
3. The berries and trees in bloom have no effect on the woman.
4. Strawberries finally slow her down.
5. The man cannot overtake his wife because her anger causes her to walk very fast.
6. The woman cannot see the blossoming bushes and trees because her gaze is fixed straight ahead.
7. The spirit decides to create a new fruit that grows close to the ground so the woman will bend her head for a moment and forget her anger.
8. The woman crushes the strawberries under her feet as she walks, releasing a pleasant scent. She stops to look at the berries she has never seen before.
9. "Strawberries" teaches the reader that by holding onto anger you prevent yourself from seeing the beautiful things in life. In this story, the woman missed the beautiful huckleberries and fruit trees.
10. "Strawberries" indicates that the Cherokee may have believed that without love, life is lonely and unhappy. It also indicates that letting go of anger helps you enjoy life, and that the ability to forget quarrels is an important human value.

Responding to Literature

PERSONAL RESPONSE

How did this tale change or add to your thoughts about love?

Analyzing Literature

RECALL

1. What causes the woman to leave her husband?
2. Why does the spirit want to slow the angry woman's steps?
3. What effect do the blooming huckleberries and trees of the forest have upon the woman?
4. What finally slows the woman down?

INTERPRET

5. Why is the man unable to overtake his wife?
6. Why isn't the woman able to see the blossoming bushes and trees?
7. Why does the spirit decide to create a new fruit?
8. Why do the strawberries make the woman slow down?

EVALUATE AND CONNECT

9. What does "Strawberries" teach the reader about letting go of anger?
10. Theme Connection "Strawberries" is a Cherokee myth. What does it tell you about what the Cherokee people believe about love?

710 THEME 7

LITERARY ELEMENTS

Tone

The **tone** of a piece of writing expresses to readers the author's feelings and attitude toward his or her subject, ideas, theme, or characters. A written piece may express seriousness, humor, nostalgia, or any number of other feelings. Formal writing, for example, usually creates a serious tone; colloquial writing can create a light, humorous tone. Factors that contribute to tone are the writer's sentence construction and choice of words, the kinds of details used, and the images created. In poetry, the rhythm may help to create a tone. A rhythm can encourage readers to skip lightly along the poet's words or mournfully drag them out.

1. Reread the first paragraphs of "Auntie Misery" and "Strawberries." What tone does each author create? How?

2. Choose a poem you read earlier in this book. How does the poet create its tone?

● See **Literary Terms Handbook,** p. R11.

LITERARY ELEMENTS

1. The authors create a serious tone by presenting a problem that needs to be solved.
2. Students should be able to support their answers with examples.

Additional Resources

 Literary Elements Transparency 59

Literature and Writing

Writing About Literature

Conflict **Conflict** refers to the struggle between two opposing forces. Write briefly about the conflict that is central to "Strawberries." Explain what caused the conflict and how it was resolved.

Creative Writing

The First . . . "Strawberries" is a Cherokee myth about how strawberries came to be. Write a myth to explain the origin of the fruit, flower, or plant you illustrated for the **Focus Activity** on page 706.

Extending Your Response

Literature Groups
Anger Management In addition to telling about the origin of strawberries, the myth also presents the idea that anger can ruin love. Do you agree? How could the man and woman in the myth have prevented their quarrel or dealt with their anger? Share your group's opinions with the class.

Performing
Role-Playing What do the husband and wife in "Strawberries" argue about? What do they say to each other as they walk back home? With a partner,

consider these questions. Then role-play one of these two dialogues from the story.

Reading Further

If you would like to read more Native American tales, try these:

How Rabbit Tricked Otter and Other Cherokee Trickster Stories, told by Gayle Ross

Mai'ii and Cousin Horned Toad: A Traditional Navajo Story by Shonto Begay

 Save your work for your portfolio.

Skill Minilesson

VOCABULARY • SYNONYMS: THESAURUS

The angry woman in "Strawberries" would not have tasted berries that had a *stink.* What made her stop was the berries' *aroma. Smell, stink, aroma,* and *scent* are synonyms, but each word has its own distinctive meaning. A **thesaurus** is a dictionary of synonyms. It can help you find differences among synonyms so that you can use the one best suited to your purpose.

PRACTICE For each sentence, decide whether *smell, scent, stink,* or *aroma* is the best choice.
1. The kitchen filled with the ___ of apple pie.
2. Even blindfolded, I would know I was in the barn by the familiar ___ .
3. The ___ in my room was a mixture of wet dog and dirty socks.
4. The ___ of her favorite perfume told me that my mother had been in my room.

A DIFFERENT DIMENSION 711

Literature and Writing

Writing About Literature
Students' writing should
- explain that the conflict is about a husband trying to reconcile with his wife after a fight.
- indicate that a quarrel causes the conflict and that help from a spirit resolves it.
- use examples from the story to support their ideas.

Creative Writing
Students' myths should
- indicate how a fruit, a flower, or a plant came to be.
- show an important human value, such as forgiveness or love.
- teach a lesson about human behavior.

Extending Your Response

Literature Groups Have each group create a chart showing the most effective ways to deal with anger. Have groups share their charts and explain their ideas.
COLLAB. LEARN.

Performing Partners may want to improvise the scene a few times to figure out what the characters are likely to say. Then they can memorize and rehearse their lines.

Skill Minilesson

VOCABULARY
• SYNONYMS: THESAURUS
1. aroma   3. stink
2. smell   4. scent

Additional Resources
📁 *Vocabulary Practice,* p. 41

✔ ASSESSMENT OPTIONS

📁 *Quick Checks,* p. 59
📁 *Selection and Theme Assessment,* p. 102
📁 *Performance Assessment,* p. 56
💾 *Testmaker*

Objective

• To recognize and apply strategies for using capitalization correctly

Teaching Strategies

Point out to students that sometimes people mistakenly capitalize words in order to emphasize their importance. Remind students that there are other ways to emphasize importance, such as underlining the word, and that capitalization should not be used in this case.

Exercise

1. correct
2. call Aunt Millie
3. speak Spanish
4. the Empire State Building
5. tell Mom and Dad
6. a German composer
7. correct
8. correct
9. the Puerto Rican flag
10. correct

Additional Resources

📖 **Grammar and Language Workbook,** pp. 235–246

📖 **Grammar and Composition Handbook,** Lessons 12.1–2.4

📖 **Writer's Choice,** Lessons 19.1–19.4

Teaching Options

Capitalization

A proper noun names a particular person, place, or thing. A proper adjective is formed from a proper noun. Proper nouns and proper adjectives are capitalized.

Problem 1 Words referring to ethnic groups, nationalities, and languages
Some french folk songs are sung in english in the United States.

Solution Capitalize names of ethnic groups, nationalities, and languages and the adjectives formed from them.
Some French folk songs are sung in English in the United States.

Problem 2 Words that name family relationships
I told mom, aunt Martha, and my grandfather about "Aunty Misery."

Solution Capitalize the word that names a family relationship only if it is part of the person's name or used in place of the person's name.
I told Mom, Aunt Martha, and my grandfather about "Aunty Misery."

Problem 3 Names of organizations and structures
The American folklore society seeks to study and preserve folklore.
There are songs about the Brooklyn bridge but not the sears tower.

Solution Capitalize the names of organizations and structures.
The American Folklore Society seeks to study and preserve folklore.
There are songs about the Brooklyn Bridge but not the Sears Tower.

● For more about capitalization, see **Language Handbook,** p. R20.

EXERCISE

Write *Correct* if the phrase is capitalized correctly. If it is capitalized incorrectly, rewrite the phrase to correct it.

1. my sister, Sue
2. call aunt Millie
3. speak spanish
4. the empire state building
5. tell mom and dad
6. a german composer
7. my favorite uncle
8. the U.S. Congress
9. the puerto rican flag
10. a mother's worries

Writing Minilesson

Writing an Exercise Work with students to create a list of word categories that are routinely capitalized in English. Some categories are days of the week, months of the year, planets, countries, languages, and song titles.

Activity Have students work in groups of three to five "teachers." Explain that each group will prepare a short capitalization lesson and writing exercise for students in another group. Exercises can include sentences, stories, poems, "test questions," or any other writing activities students feel will help their peers learn and practice capitalization. **L2**
COLLAB. LEARN.

Additional Resources

📖 **Writer's Choice,** Lessons 19.1–19.4

Before You Read
Atalanta's Race and *Atalanta*

MEET REX WARNER

A novelist, Greek scholar, poet, translator, and critic, Rex Warner spent the early days of his career as a schoolteacher in England and Egypt. He later served as director of the British Institute in Athens, Greece. In 1961 Warner moved to the United States. His novels, often written as allegories, focus on the power of government.

Rex Warner was born in England in 1905 and died in 1986.

MEET BETTY MILES

Betty Miles's first full-time job, as an assistant kindergarten teacher, inspired her to write children's books. When asked about her writing, Miles replied, "I put my own feelings into my characters, and say things through them that I might be too shy to say in person. . . . For me, the greatest reward of writing is being told that 'you know just how I feel.'"

Betty Miles was born in Chicago in 1928.

FOCUS ACTIVITY

The ancient Greeks believed that fate was an all-powerful force in everyday life. More people today believe that their fate depends on their own actions and decisions. How do you feel about what influences people's futures?

Think/Pair/Share
Take a moment to jot down your thoughts and feelings about the question. Then share your ideas with a partner, and discuss how we can influence our future lives.

Setting a Purpose
Read two versions of the same myth to see how they differ.

BACKGROUND

Did You Know? Greek myths have had a long-lasting influence on literature, including classic Greek and Roman dramas based on these myths. The borrowing of these themes continues today, not only in drama, poetry, and fiction but in motion pictures and television features. Even many of the comic book or TV superheroes can be traced back to such ancient Greek models as Hercules and Achilles.

VOCABULARY PREVIEW

condemn (kən dem′) *v.* to criticize sharply; p. 715
envious (en′ vē əs) *adj.* having resentment over, and a wish to possess for oneself, something possessed by another; p. 715
parched (pärcht) *adj.* severely in need of moisture; p. 717
hallowed (hal′ ōd) *adj.* regarded as sacred or holy; p. 717
fleetest (flēt′ əst) *adj.* swiftest; fastest; p. 719
jubilant (joō′ bə lənt) *adj.* filled with great joy; p. 721
claim (klām) *v.* to ask for or demand possession of one's right to something; p. 721

A DIFFERENT DIMENSION 713

Objectives

- To read and understand two versions of a myth
- To see how details are used to describe people, places, things, and events
- To write a paragraph describing a character

Skills

Reading/Thinking: Sequencing; Drawing Conclusions; Inferring; Synthesizing; Verifying Predictions
Writing: Description of the Setting; Journal Entry
Vocabulary: The Prefix *twi-*; Analogies
Grammar/Language: Irregular Verbs; Spelling Compound Words
Listening/Speaking: Radio Narration
Collaboration: Literature Groups

Motivating
→OPTIONS

Selection Focus Transparency 60: Have students interpret and discuss the cartoon in the Selection Focus Transparency.

 Focus Activity: As an extension of the Focus Activity, have pairs of students share their thoughts on the forces that shape their lives and on what part the roles of free will and self-determination play in them.

RESOURCE MANAGER

Lesson Planning Resource
The ***Theme Seven Planning Guide*** (pp. 43–48) provides additional lesson notes and reduced versions of all print resources.

📁 **Other Print Resources**
- Active Reading Guide, p. 60
- Vocabulary Practice, p. 42
- Reading Workbook, pp. 107–108
- Grammar and Language Workbook, pp. 95–100, 297–300

- Grammar and Composition Handbook, Lessons 3.11, 3.12, 15.1
- Quick Checks, p. 60
- Selection and Theme Assessment, pp. 103–104
- Performance Assessment, p. 57
- Spanish Summaries, p. 60
- Inclusion Strategies
- English Language Learners Sourcebook

🖐 **Transparencies**
- Selection Focus 60
- Literary Elements 60
- Grammar and Language 57

Technology
- 🎧 Audio Library
- 🎧 Spanish Audio Library
- 💻 Glencoe Literature Web Site
- 💾 Testmaker

SUMMARY

In "Atalanta's Race," the oracle warns Atalanta that marrying will bring her disaster. Terrified, she says that she will marry the man who beats her in a foot race, but all the losers must die. Venus helps Hippomenes win, but he forgets to thank her. Venus punishes him and Atalanta by luring them into spending the night at the forbidden temple of Cybele. Angry, Cybele transforms them into lions.

"Atalanta" is a modern spin on the same myth. The race between Atalanta and a young admirer named John is a tie. The king offers her in marriage to John, who leaves the decision to Atalanta. In the end, they become friends.

📁 *Spanish Summaries,* p. 60

Active Reading

PREDICT Ask students to use the title and the first two paragraphs to predict whom and what they think the "race" will involve.

Additional Resources
📁 *Active Reading Guide,* p. 60
🎧 *Audio Library*
🎧 *Spanish Audio Library*

Teaching Options

CONNECTING TO OTHER SELECTIONS
For a teaching strategy that connects "Atalanta's Race" to "Rosa Parks: My Story," turn to page 72 in the *Theme One Planning Guide.*

Atalanta's Race

Rex Warner ◡

The huntress Atalanta,[1] whom Meleager,[2] before he died, had loved, could run faster even than the fastest runners among men. Nor was her beauty inferior to her swiftness of foot; both were beyond praise.

When Atalanta asked the oracle[3] about whom she ought to marry, the god replied: "Do not take a husband, Atalanta. If you do, it will bring disaster on you. Yet you will not escape, and though you will continue to live, you will not be yourself."

---

1. According to Greek myths, the Greek heroine *Atalanta* was abandoned at birth and rescued by a bear. Later found by hunters who raised her, Atalanta grew into a daring child who excelled at all physical activities.
2. In Greek mythology, *Meleager* (mel´ ē ā´ gər) was the son of a king whose country was ravaged by a wild boar. Meleager put together a band of heroes to drive the boar away, and he himself killed it.
3. In ancient Greece, an *oracle* was a priest through whom the gods sometimes answered the questions of worshipers.

714 🐾 THEME 7

ENGLISH LANGUAGE LEARNERS

MEETING INDIVIDUAL NEEDS

Women in Society The story raises many cultural issues. Depending on their backgrounds, English language learners may find issues that are either familiar or puzzling to them.

Activity Separate the class into small groups. Have students think about and discuss male attitudes toward females who are able to run faster than men.

Encourage students to share their experiences in and knowledge of different cultures. Discussions can be expanded to include other competitive situations, such as earning better grades and making larger salaries. **COLLAB. LEARN.**

Additional Resources
📁 *English Language Learners Sourcebook*

Terrified by these words, Atalanta lived in the dark woods unmarried. There were many men who wished to marry her, but to them, in their eagerness, she said: "No one can have me for his wife unless first he beats me in a race. If you will, you may run with me. If any of you wins, he shall have me as a prize. But those who are defeated will have death for their reward. These are the conditions for the race."

Cruel indeed she was, but her beauty had such power that numbers of young men were impatient to race with her on these terms.

There was a young man called Hippomenes,[4] who had come to watch the contest. At first he had said to himself: "What man in his senses would run such a risk to get a wife?" and he had condemned the young men for being too madly in love. But when he saw her face and her body all stripped for the race—a face and a body like Venus's[5] own—he was lost in astonishment and, stretching out his hands, he said: "I had no right to blame the young men. I did not know what the prize was for which they were running."

As he spoke his own heart caught on fire with love for her and, in jealous fear, he hoped that none of the young men would be able to beat her in the race. Then he said to himself: "But why should not I try my fortune? When one takes a risk, the gods help one."

By now the race had started, and the girl sped past him on feet that seemed to have wings. Though she went fast as an arrow, he admired her beauty still more. Indeed she looked particularly beautiful when running. In the breeze her hair streamed back over her ivory shoulders; the ribbons with their bright borders fluttered at her knees; the white of her young body flushed rose-red, as when a purple awning is drawn over white marble and makes the stone glow with its own color. While Hippomenes fixed his eyes on her, she reached the winning post and was crowned with the victor's garland. The young men, with groans, suffered the penalty of death according to the agreement which they had made.

Did You Know?
The victor's *garland* was a small wreath of flowers, leaves, or vines worn about the head as a symbol of honor.

Their fate, however, had no effect on Hippomenes. He came forward and, fixing his eyes on Atalanta, said: "Why do you win an easy glory by conquering these slow movers? Now run with me. If I win, it will be no disgrace to you. I am a king's son and Neptune[6] is my great-grandfather. And, if you defeat me, it will be an honor to be able to say that you defeated Hippomenes."

As he spoke, Atalanta looked at him with a softer expression in her eyes. She wondered whether she really wanted to conquer or to be conquered. She thought to herself: "What god, envious of beautiful

---

4. *Hippomenes* (hi pom′ ə nēz′)
5. *Venus* was the goddess of beauty and love.

6. *Neptune* was the god of the sea.

Vocabulary
condemn (kən dem′) *v.* to criticize sharply
envious (en′ vē əs) *adj.* having resentment over, and a wish to possess for oneself, something possessed by another

A DIFFERENT DIMENSION 715

B Critical Thinking

DRAWING CONCLUSIONS Ask students why Atalanta sets such drastic conditions for the runners. The following model illustrates the thinking process involved in drawing conclusions.

> **Model:** Atalanta is terrified by the oracle's warning, so she tries to avoid marriage. She probably thinks that by threatening the losers with death, they won't want to race her.

C Active Reading

EVALUATE Invite students to share their opinions on the wisdom of risking one's life to acquire something based exclusively on its outward appearance. *(Some students may think it is all right to take such a risk, but others may point to examples in history where such a risk proved fatal.)*

D Author's Craft

DESCRIPTION The author chooses specific details to convey personalities and atmosphere in this story. How is Atalanta "beautiful while running"? *(Atalanta's hair "streamed back over her ivory shoulders," bright ribbons "fluttered at her knees," and her body glowed.)*

Writing Minilesson

Description of the Setting Writers usually include details about the settings of their stories. Have students skim page 715 (col. 2) to the very top of page 717 and note details of the setting. *(The race course is sandy and the people shout.)*

Activity Have students work in small groups. Encourage them to visualize the setting of the race and brainstorm to fill in the details. Ask each group to work together to write a brief description of the setting of the race. Encourage them to use their imaginations to create vivid details. **L2** **COLLAB. LEARN.**

Additional Resources

📓 ***Writer's Choice,*** Lesson 3.2

A DIFFERENT DIMENSION 715

VIEWING THE PHOTOGRAPH

Viewing Response *The photo collage suggests various stages of a race and gives an impression of movement that a single shot of a runner could not convey. Like Atalanta, this present-day runner is probably the goal-oriented product of self-discipline and intense training.*

E **Critical Thinking**

INFERRING Atalanta does not show the same compassion for the other men who race her as she does for Hippomenes. Ask students what that might imply. *(It implies that she feels something special for this young man.)*

Cultural Note

Love Goddess Venus (called Aphrodite by the Greeks) was worshipped in ancient Greece and Rome as the goddess of love.

F **Literary Elements**

DESCRIPTION Ask students how this long description of the golden apple tree might increase a reader's interest in the story. *(Students may say that readers will be curious to see what role it plays in the story.)*

Viewing the photograph: What does this photo-collage suggest that could not be shown with a single photograph? What might this present-day runner have in common with Atalanta?

young men, wants to destroy this one and makes him seek marriage with me at the risk of his dear life? In my opinion, I am not worth it. It is not his beauty that touches me (though I might easily be touched by that); it is because he is still only a boy. And then there is his courage, and the fact that he is willing to risk so much for me. Why should he die, simply because he wants to live with me? I wish he would go, while he still may, and realize that it is fatal to want to marry me. Indeed he deserves to live. If only I were happier, if only the fates[7] had not forbidden me to marry, he would be the man that I would choose."

Meanwhile Atalanta's father and the whole people demanded that the race should take place. Hippomenes prayed to Venus and said: "O goddess, you put this love into my heart. Now be near me in my trial and aid me!"

A gentle breeze carried his prayer to the goddess and she was moved by it. Little time, however, remained in which she could help him. But it happened that she had just returned from her sacred island of Cyprus,[8] where in one of her temple gardens grows a golden apple tree. The leaves are gold; the branches and the fruit rattle with metal as the wind stirs them. Venus had in her hand three golden apples which she had just picked from this tree. Now she came down to earth, making herself visible only to Hippomenes, and showed him how to use the apples.

Then the trumpets sounded and the two runners darted forward from the starting post, skimming over the sandy course with feet so light that it would seem they might have run over the sea or over the waving heads of standing corn. The crowd shouted their applause.[9] "Now, Hippomenes," they

7. The *fates* were three goddesses who controlled human lives and fortunes.

8. *Cyprus* is an island in the Mediterranean Sea, south of Turkey.
9. Here, *applause* means simply "praise."

716 ❦ THEME 7

Teaching Options

Reading *Minilesson*

Sequencing Explain that a myth, like other traditional stories, has a plot. Readers can better understand the plot of a story by analyzing the story's sequence of events.

Activity Have each student develop a graphic organizer to keep track of the sequence of events in the story. When the graphic organizers are complete, ask stu-

dents whether there are events or details that confuse them. Have them discuss whether they think the sequence of events led to a logical conclusion. Students can use their charts to answer the questions that follow the selection. **L2** **COLLAB. LEARN.**

Additional Resources

📁 *Reading Workbook,* pp. 107–108

Atalanta's Race

1. Oracle warns Atalanta. → 2. Men woo her. → 3. She invents the rules of a race.

cried, "run as you have never run before! You are winning." It would be difficult to say whether Hippomenes or Atalanta herself was most pleased with this encouragement. For some time Atalanta, though she might have passed the young man, did not do so. She ran by his side, looking into his face. Then, half unwillingly, she left him behind. He, with <u>parched</u> throat and straining lungs, followed after; still the winning post was far in the distance; and now he took one of the golden apples which Venus had given him and threw it in her way. The girl looked with wonder at the shining fruit and, longing to have it, stopped running so that she could pick it up. Hippomenes passed her and again the spectators shouted out their applause. Soon, however, Atalanta made up the ground that she had lost and again left Hippomenes behind. He threw the second apple, once more took the lead and once more was overtaken. Now they were in sight of the winning post, and Hippomenes, with a prayer to Venus, threw the last apple rather sideways, so that it went some distance from the course. Atalanta seemed to hesitate whether she should go after it or not, but Venus made her go, and, when she had picked up the apple, she made it heavier, handicapping the girl not only by the time she had lost but by the weight of what she was carrying. This time she could not catch up Hippomenes. He passed the winning post first and claimed her as his bride.

Then, indeed, Hippomenes should have offered thanks to Venus, but he forgot entirely the goddess who had helped him, neither giving thanks nor making sacrifice.

Venus was angry and determined to make an example of them both. On their way to the home of Hippomenes they came to a holy temple, sacred to the mother of the gods, great Cybele. No mortal[10] was allowed to pass the night in this temple, so <u>hallowed</u> was the spot; but Venus put it into the hearts of Hippomenes and Atalanta, who were tired from their journey, to rest there all night and treat the temple of the goddess as though it were a common inn. So in the most holy of the temple's shrines, where wooden images of the ancient gods turned away their eyes in horror at the profanation,[11] they rested together. But the terrible goddess, her head crowned with a crown of towers, appeared to them. She covered their necks, which had been so smooth, with tawny manes of hair; their fingers became sharp claws, and their arms turned to legs. Most of their weight went to their chests, and behind them they swept the sandy ground with long tails. Instead of the palace they had hoped for, they lived in the savage woods, a lion and a lioness, terrible to others but, when Cybele needed them, tame enough to draw her chariot, champing the iron bits between their gnashing jaws.

---

10. *Cybele* (sib' ə lē) and the other gods were *immortals*—beings who would never die. A *mortal* is a human being.
11. *Profanation* is an act of disrespect or scorn for sacred beings or objects, such as this holy shrine.

Vocabulary
parched (pärcht) *adj.* severely in need of moisture
hallowed (hal' ōd) *adj.* regarded as sacred or holy

G **Literary Elements**

CHARACTERIZATION Ask students what Atalanta's actions here reveal about her. *(She seems to have good intentions, but is torn by her love for Hippomenes and fear of the oracle's warning.)*

Cultural Note

Cybele is the Phrygian name for the mother of the gods. (Phrygia was across the Aegean Sea from Greece, in Asia Minor.) The Greeks also called her Rhea, and to the Romans, she was Magna Mater ("Great Mother").

H **Critical Thinking**

INFERRING Ask students to what degree Venus is involved in the outcome of the race. *(Venus tells Hippomenes where and when to throw the apples and makes Atalanta pick them up. She even makes the third apple heavier.)*

I **Author's Craft**

FORESHADOWING What development could this negative description of Hippomenes' action possibly foreshadow? *(It foreshadows doom for Hippomenes for being ungrateful to Venus.)*

J **Literary Elements**

DESCRIPTION: *Plot Resolution* Ask what the description of Venus's anger and her choice of punishment reveals. *(The harshness of the punishment conveys the importance of gratitude, respect, and obedience to rules.)*

Listening and Speaking *Minilesson*

Radio Narration of the Race This race, with its exciting action, competitive spirit, and cheering crowd, is very similar to the athletic events witnessed today. In fact, the scene of the race lends itself nicely to oral narration.

Activity Have students work in pairs or small groups to prepare radio scripts of the race between Atalanta and Hippomenes. Encourage students to use descriptions that make listeners "see" the action in their minds. Then they may tape their scripts, reading aloud the text in the voice of a radio announcer or a pair of announcers. **L2** **COLLAB. LEARN.**

Atalanta

Betty Miles ～

K Once upon a time, not long ago, there lived a princess named Atalanta, who could run as fast as the wind.

She was so bright, and so clever, and could build things and fix things so wonderfully, that many young men wished to marry her.

L "What shall I do?" said Atalanta's father, who was a powerful king. "So many young men want to marry you, and I don't know how to choose."

"You don't have to choose, Father," Atalanta said. "I will choose. And I'm not sure that I will choose to marry anyone at all."

"Of course you will," said the king. "Everybody gets married. It is what people do."

"But," Atalanta told him, with a toss of her head, "I intend to go out and see the world. When I come home, perhaps I will marry and perhaps I will not."

The king did not like this at all. He was a very ordinary king; that is, he was powerful and used to having his own way. So he did not answer Atalanta, but simply told her, "I have decided how to choose the young man you will marry. I will hold a great race, and the winner—the swiftest, fleetest young man of all—will win the right to marry you."

Now Atalanta was a clever girl as well as a swift runner. She saw that she might win both the argument and the race—provided that she herself could run in the race, too. "Very well," she said. "But you must let me race along with the others. If I am not the winner, I will accept the wishes of the young man who is."

The king agreed to this. He was pleased; he would have his way, marry off his daughter, and enjoy a fine day of racing as well. So he directed his messengers to travel throughout the kingdom announcing the race with its wonderful prize: the chance to marry the bright Atalanta.

As the day of the race drew near, flags were raised in the streets of the town, and banners were hung near the grassy field where the race would be run. Baskets of ripe plums and peaches, wheels of cheese, ropes of sausages and onions, and loaves of crusty bread were gathered for the crowds.

Meanwhile, Atalanta herself was preparing for the race. Each day at dawn, dressed in soft green trousers and a shirt of yellow silk, she went to the field in secret and ran across it—slowly at first, then fast and faster, until she could run the course more quickly than anyone had ever run it before.

As the day of the race grew nearer, young men began to crowd into the town. Each was sure he could win the prize, except for one; that was Young John, who lived in the town. He saw Atalanta day by day as she bought nails and wood to make a pigeon house, or chose parts for her telescope, or laughed with her friends. Young John saw the princess only from a distance, but near enough to know how bright and clever she was. He wished very much to race with her, to win, and to earn the right to talk with her and become her friend.

"For surely," he said to himself, "it is not right for Atalanta's father to give her away to the winner of the race. Atalanta herself must choose the person she wants to marry, or whether she wishes to marry at all. Still, if I could only win the race, I would be free to speak to her, and to ask for her friendship."

Each evening, after his studies of the stars and the seas, Young John went to the field in secret and practiced running across

---

Vocabulary

fleetest (flēt′ əst) *adj.* swiftest; fastest

Vo·cab·u·lar·y Skills

Prefix twi- The prefix *twi-*, means two, as in *twice* and *twin*. The word *twilight* is built on the word light coupled with *twi*. *Twilight* is formed by the light of day and nightfall. The word *twilight* as used here means "the soft, diffused light from the sky when the sun is below the horizon, either from daybreak to sunrise, or, more commonly, from sunset to nightfall."

P Active Reading

VISUALIZE Ask students to visualize the starting line of the race with all the young men and Atalanta, dressed in red pants and a blue shirt, looking them over with disdain.

Q Literary Elements

FIGURES OF SPEECH: *Simile* Point out the author's use of a simile to describe the color of Atalanta's shirt. Ask students to find another simile in this passage. (*"I will run as fast as the wind."*)

VIEWING THE PAINTING

In the opening ceremonies of the Olympic Games, participating athletes bear the Olympic flag into the stadium, where it flies while the games go on.

Viewing Response *Given what we know about her ability, Atalanta would probably win medals in one or more of the running events.*

it. Night after night, he ran fast as the wind across the twilight field, until he could cross it more quickly than anyone had ever crossed it before.

At last, the day of the race arrived.

Trumpets sounded in the early morning, and the young men gathered at the edge of the field, along with Atalanta herself, the prize they sought. The king and his friends sat in soft chairs, and the townspeople stood along the course.

The king rose to address them all. "Good day," he said to the crowds. "Good luck," he said to the young men. To Atalanta he said, "Good-bye. I must tell you farewell, for tomorrow you will be married."

"I am not so sure of that, Father," Atalanta answered. She was dressed for the race in trousers of crimson and a shirt of silk as blue as the sky, and she laughed as she looked up and down the line of young men.

"Not one of them," she said to herself, "can win the race, for I will run fast as the wind and leave them all behind."

And now a bugle sounded, a flag was dropped, and the runners were off!

The crowds cheered as the young men and Atalanta began to race across the field. At first they ran as a group, but Atalanta soon pulled ahead, with three of the young men close after her. As they neared the halfway point, one young man put on a great burst of speed and seemed to pull ahead for an instant, but then he gasped and fell back. Atalanta shot on.

Soon another young man, tense with the effort, drew near to Atalanta. He

Viewing the photograph: Today, a runner as fast as Atalanta would probably run in the Olympic Games. How do you think she would do against today's competitors?

Teaching Options

Grammar and Language *Minilesson*

Irregular Verbs Explain to students that many verbs form their past tense by adding *-ed* to the present form of the verb, but some do not. The past tense of irregular verbs is formed by changing the spelling of the word itself.

Activity Ask students to reread this page and list examples of irregular verbs in the past tense and then write the pre-

sent tense of those verbs. Students may use a dictionary to find each verb's present tense. **L2** COLLAB. LEARN.

Past	Present
ran	run
sat	sit
stood	stand
rose	rise
said	say
began	begin
shot	shoot
fell	fall

Additional Resources

- *Grammar and Language Transparency 56*

- *Grammar and Language Workbook,* pp. 95–100

- *Grammar and Composition Handbook,* Lessons 3.11, 3.12

- *Writer's Choice,* Lesson 10.9

reached out as though to touch her sleeve, stumbled for an instant, and lost speed. Atalanta smiled as she ran on. I have almost won, she thought.

But then another young man came near. This was Young John, running like the wind, as steadily and as swiftly as Atalanta herself. Atalanta felt his closeness, and in a sudden burst she dashed ahead.

Young John might have given up at this, but he never stopped running. Nothing at all, thought he, will keep me from winning the chance to speak with Atalanta. And on he ran, swift as the wind, until he ran as her equal, side by side with her, toward the golden ribbon that marked the race's end. Atalanta raced even faster to pull ahead, but Young John was a strong match for her. Smiling with the pleasure of the race, Atalanta and Young John reached the finish line together, and together they broke through the golden ribbon.

Trumpets blew. The crowd shouted and leaped about. The king rose. "Who is that young man?" he asked.

"It is Young John from the town," the people told him.

"Very well. Young John," said the king, as John and Atalanta stood before him, exhausted and jubilant from their efforts. "You have not won the race, but you have come closer to winning than

any man here. And so I give you the prize that was promised—the right to marry my daughter."

Young John smiled at Atalanta, and she smiled back. "Thank you, sir," said John to the king, "but I could not possibly marry your daughter unless she wished to marry me. I have run this race for the chance to talk with Atalanta, and, if she is willing, I am ready to claim my prize."

Atalanta laughed with pleasure. "And I," she said to John, "could not possibly marry before I have seen the world. But I would like nothing better than to spend the afternoon with you."

Then the two of them sat and talked on the grassy field, as the crowds went away. They ate bread and cheese and purple plums. Atalanta told John about her telescopes and her pigeons, and John told Atalanta about his globes and his studies of geography. At the end of the day, they were friends.

On the next day, John sailed off to discover new lands. And Atalanta set off to visit the great cities.

By this time, each of them has had wonderful adventures, and seen marvelous sights. Perhaps some day they will be married, and perhaps they will not. In any case, they are friends. And it is certain that they are both living happily ever after.

❖

Vocabulary
jubilant (jōō′ bə lənt) *adj.* filled with great joy
claim (klām) *v.* to ask for or demand possession of one's right to something

---

R Literary Elements

DESCRIPTION: Symbolism Ask students what the fact that Atalanta and John are running side by side "as equals" symbolizes. *(The fact that Atalanta and John run side by side symbolizes that they view each other as equals in all things.)*

S Critical Thinking

VERIFYING PREDICTIONS Ask students whether the ending of the story matches their predictions. How does the story's closing line coincide with what its opening lines foreshadowed? *(Some students will say that their predictions were correct, but that it is not the happy ending they imagined.)*

Thematic Focus

A Different Dimension Discuss with students how these two versions of this myth illustrate the theme of this section. *("Atalanta's Race" includes the involvement of the gods and similar mythological occurrences that are quite "magical" and removed from modern life. "Atalanta" offers a different dimension by putting a modern twist on the myth.)*

✔ ASSESSMENT OPTIONS

📁 *Quick Checks*, p. 60

REAL-WORLD CONNECTION

Attitudes Have students discuss which attitudes toward women exhibited in these selections still relate to attitudes toward women in the world today.

Activity Have students work in small groups to create short questionnaires that can be used to survey the opinions of their classmates on the attitudes discussed. Students may wish to pool their efforts and produce only two different questionnaires. Then half the class can answer one and the other half can answer the other. It would be interesting to compare the results of the two. **L2**
COLLAB. LEARN.

Responding to the Selection

Personal Response

Encourage students to discuss human dependence or independence, particularly in relation to authority figures.

Analyzing Literature

1. The warning was that she would bring disaster on herself if she married.
2. Her strategy was to race her suitors and win. Whoever lost the race died. They took that risk because of her great beauty.
3. In the first version, she is less assertive and self-sufficient than in the second.
4. Betty Miles' version leaves out the oracle's warning, Venus's assistance to Hippomenes, and the disastrous ending.
5. Her attempt to avoid marriage simply because of the oracle's warning shows her respect for the power of the gods.
6. It meant that she would continue to live, but in a different form.
7. In both, she showed her determination and courage by working hard to avoid something she did not want. In the first version, Atalanta used her running ability to "escape" marriage. In the second, she relied more on her intelligence and her assertiveness.
8. Perhaps because Miles is writing for a modern audience, she wants to convey a message about the equality of women. Her message would not be as effective if the gods have the power to override a person's will no matter what that person does.
9. Some readers may prefer the first for its magical quality and suspense. Others may like the second version for its modern messages.

Responding to Literature

PERSONAL RESPONSE

What was your reaction to these stories? How do these tales relate to your response for the **Focus Activity** on page 713? Describe your impressions in your journal.

Analyzing Literature

RECALL

1. In "Atalanta's Race," what warning did the oracle give Atalanta?
2. In "Atalanta's Race," what strategy did Atalanta use to avoid marriage? Why were young men willing to risk their lives for her?
3. How does the character of Atalanta differ in the two versions of the myth?
4. What parts of the myth included in Rex Warner's version are left out of Betty Miles's version?

INTERPRET

5. How did Atalanta's actions in "Atalanta's Race" show her respect for the oracle and the decrees of fate? Explain.
6. Explain what the oracle's warning that "though you will continue to live, you will not be yourself" meant.
7. In either version, what does the reader discover about Atalanta's sense of determination and courage in dealing with her life? Identify details to support your ideas.
8. Why, do you think, did Betty Miles leave out parts of the Atalanta myth that are included in Rex Warner's version?

EVALUATE AND CONNECT

9. Which version of the myth did you enjoy more? Why?
10. Think of someone who would enjoy reading these myths. What about these stories would appeal to that person?

LITERARY ELEMENTS

Description

A **description** is a carefully detailed portrayal of a person, place, thing, or event. Strong description is an important element in both fiction and nonfiction writing. Skillful writers select details carefully so that their readers can see, hear, smell, taste, and feel what is being described. Both of these myths come alive through the vivid descriptions of the main characters and their worlds.

1. Skim the myths and pick out a description that helps you imagine a particular character or scene. Explain which details help you imagine the character or scene clearly.

2. Choose your favorite description in either myth and explain why it appeals to you.

● See **Literary Terms Handbook**, p. R3.

10. This person would probably also enjoy learning about other cultures, especially ancient Greece and the power of the gods.

LITERARY ELEMENTS

1. On page 715, Warner describes Atalanta's hair in the breeze, touching her shoulders while she runs.
2. Students should use specific examples from the text to support their choices.

Additional Resources

 Literary Elements Transparency 60

Literature and Writing

Writing About Literature

Characterization In both myths, the two main characters are revealed through their actions as well as their words. Write a paragraph describing either Atalanta or Hippomenes/John as you picture that person.

Creative Writing

Journal Entry Imagine you are either Atalanta or Hippomenes/John right before the race. What are you thinking and feeling? Write a journal entry describing your thoughts and feelings. Use the myth as a jumping-off point, but feel free to make up details of your own.

Extending Your Response

Literature Groups

Discussing Conflict You know that conflict, the struggle between two or more forces, makes stories interesting. There are four common types of conflict in literature: with nature; with fate; with other people or society; and with oneself. Working in small groups, discuss the kinds of conflicts present in both versions of the Atalanta myth, and talk about which conflict is the most difficult. Support your thoughts and ideas with examples from the myths.

Interdisciplinary Activity

Health Physical fitness is good for anyone, not just professional athletes or competitive runners like Atalanta. What are some ways in which people your age can keep fit? Work with a small group to plan a fitness program for average teenagers who don't wish to be competitive athletes. Present your plan to the class.

Performing

Live from Ancient Greece! Imagine you are a reporter sent to cover the race by the Hellenic News Network. Interview either Atalanta or Hippomenes before or after the race. With a partner, develop a script. Then share your interview with your classmates by presenting it as a "live" news report.

Reading Further

If you would like to read other myths or folktales, try these books:

Island of the Mighty: Stories of Old Britain by Haydn Middleton

A Treasury of Stories from Around the World chosen by Linda Jennings

 Save your work for your portfolio.

Writing About Literature
Students' paragraphs should
- use their own words in giving their impressions of the characters.
- not be limited to physical features but should also include character traits.

Creative Writing
Students' journal entries should
- explain the student's thoughts and feelings clearly, not the character's.
- be personal and imaginative in handling this topic.

Extending Your Response

Literature Groups Students may focus on Atalanta's conflict with the gods, on her competition with the men pursuing her, on her difference of opinion with her father, or on her contradictory inner feelings about Hippomenes/John. **COLLAB. LEARN.**

Interdisciplinary Activity Internet sources, health magazines, and physical education instructors are some sources of information. In presenting a fitness plan to the class, perhaps one student can demonstrate an exercise while another explains it.

Performing Suggest that students may modify the story to suit their own situations. Remind them that a script is important, even if the interview is supposed to look spontaneous.

GRAMMAR AND LANGUAGE
SPELLING COMPOUND WORDS

Students may use additional words such as:

god + mother = godmother
hind + sight = hindsight
hitch + hike = hitchhike

READING AND THINKING
CHRONOLOGICAL ORDER

"Atalanta's Race "

1. Atalanta receives a warning from the oracle.
2. To discourage her suitors, she sets up the conditions of the race.
3. Hippomenes wins with the help of Venus.
4. Venus punishes the couple.

VOCABULARY
ANALOGIES

1. a   3. a   5. b
2. c   4. b

Additional Resources

📕 *Grammar and Language Workbook,* pp. 297–300

📕 *Grammar and Composition Handbook,* Lesson 15.1

📕 *Writer's Choice,* Lesson 23.7

📕 *Reading Workbook,* pp. 107–108

📁 *Vocabulary Practice,* p. 42

GRAMMAR AND LANGUAGE • SPELLING COMPOUND WORDS

The word *grandfather* is a compound word made up of the words *grand* and *father.* The rule for spelling compound words is simple. Keep the original spelling of both words, no matter how the words begin or end.

> night + time = nighttime
> easy + going = easygoing

PRACTICE Write a paragraph describing the race held to find a worthy husband for Atalanta. Make up any details you wish to describe the race. Use at least three compound words in your description. Then trade paragraphs with a partner and read each other's paragraphs. As you read, underline each compound word you find, and check that it is spelled correctly.

● For more about compound words, see **Language Handbook,** Spelling, p. R44.

READING AND THINKING • CHRONOLOGICAL ORDER

The events in both myths are told in chronological order, or the order in which they occur. As a skillful reader, you should always ask questions so you are sure you understand what is going on. As you read, ask yourself questions such as the following.
• What happened first?
• What happened next?
• Do the steps, or the events, occur in an order that makes sense?

PRACTICE Review either myth. Outline the steps taken to find a suitable mate for Atalanta. Write the steps in the order in which they happened in the myth.

● For more about sequencing and chronological order, see **Reading Handbook,** p. R87.

VOCABULARY • ANALOGIES

An analogy is a type of comparison that is based on the relationships between things or ideas. To complete analogies, you must figure out what relationships exist between words. For example, choose an answer for this incomplete analogy:

> toe : foot :: finger : ?

Is the answer *nail, thumb,* or *hand?* All three of these words "go with" *finger,* but only one is related in the same way that *foot* goes with *toe.* A *finger* is part of a *hand,* just as a *toe* is part of a *foot.*

● For more about analogies, see **Communications Skills Handbook,** p. R65.

PRACTICE Choose the word that best completes each analogy.
1. lift : drop :: condemn :
   a. praise   b. scold   c. ban
2. starving : hunger :: parched :
   a. throat   b. rain   c. thirst
3. cheetah : fleetest :: giraffe :
   a. tallest   b. biggest   c. rarest
4. terrified : fearful :: jubilant :
   a. relieved   b. joyful   c. sorry
5. irritable : grouchy :: envious :
   a. sad   b. jealous   c. suspicious

✔ ASSESSMENT OPTIONS

📁 *Quick Checks,* p. 60

📁 *Selection and Theme Assessment,* pp. 103–104

📁 *Performance Assessment,* p. 57

💾 *Testmaker*

Before You Read
Cat and Rat: The Legend of the Chinese Zodiac

MEET ED YOUNG

Ed Young, who provides both the words and the pictures for "Cat and Rat," says, "There are things that words do that pictures never can, and likewise, there are images that words can never describe." Young was born in China and lived there until he attended college in the United States. He often uses the traditional Chinese technique of brushing ink on rice paper for his artwork. Young was encouraged to become a children's book illustrator after years of sketching animals at New York City's Central Park Zoo.

Ed Young was born in 1931 in Tientsin, China. This story was published in 1995.

FOCUS ACTIVITY

Why do you think cats are so good at catching rats?

Think/Pair/Share

Think about a quick explanation for a cat's talents. Share your ideas with a partner.

Setting a Purpose

Read this story to find out about the legendary origins of the relationship between cats and rats.

BACKGROUND

The Time and Place This legend is set in China more than 5,000 years ago.

Did You Know? The traditional Chinese calendar is arranged in twelve-year cycles. Each year in the zodiac (the twelve constellations seen in the sky around the earth's orbit) is named after an animal. The zodiac was first introduced to the Chinese people nearly 5,000 years ago by the Emperor Huang Di. According to Chinese astrology, people's personalities share characteristics with the animal that rules their birth year.

VOCABULARY PREVIEW

resourceful (ri sôrs′ fəl) *adj.* capable or skillful in dealing with new or difficult situations; p. 727
podium (pō′ dē əm) *n.* a small, raised platform or stand with a slanted shelf for holding a speaker's papers; p. 728
pounce (pouns) *v.* to swoop down, spring, or leap suddenly in attack; p. 729

A DIFFERENT DIMENSION 725

Objectives

- To read and understand a legend about another place and time
- To read and identify elements of the legend
- To write an animal tale

Skills

Reading/Thinking: Analyzing Arguments; Drawing Conclusions; Inferring; Making Critical Judgments; Elaborating; Using Graphic Aids; Setting a Purpose for Reading
Writing: Legend
Vocabulary: Using Graphic Aids
Grammar/Language: Commas in a Series; Apostrophes
Listening/Speaking: Dramatization
Life Skills: Decision-Making
Collaboration: Literature Groups

Motivating
→OPTIONS

Selection Focus Transparency 61: Show students the transparency of the Aztec calendar stone. Discuss the skill and perseverance, as well as the knowledge, that were needed to create such an instrument in 400 B.C.

Focus Activity: As an extension of the Focus Activity, have pairs of students share their thoughts on the personalities and traits of cats.

RESOURCE MANAGER

Lesson Planning Resource
The **Theme Seven Planning Guide** (pp. 49–56) provides additional lesson notes and reduced versions of all print resources.

📁 **Other Print Resources**
- Active Reading Guide, p. 61
- Vocabulary Practice, p. 43
- Reading Workbook, pp. 109–110
- Grammar and Language Workbook, pp. 255–256, 273–274

- Grammar and Composition Handbook, Lessons 13.2, 13.7
- Quick Checks, p. 61
- Selection and Theme Assessment, pp. 105–106
- Performance Assessment, p. 58
- Spanish Summaries, p. 61
- Spanish Translations
- Inclusion Strategies
- English Language Learners Sourcebook

🖋 **Transparencies**
- Selection Focus 61
- Literary Elements 61
- Grammar and Language 58

Technology
- 🎧 Audio Library
- 🎧 Spanish Audio Library
- 💻 Glencoe Literature Web Site
- 💾 Testmaker

Reading the Selection

SUMMARY

In China, many years ago, Cat and Rat were good friends. Then the Emperor announced a race in which the first twelve animals to cross the finish line would be honored by having a year of the calendar named after them. Cat and Rat entered the race, and decided to ride across the river on the back of Buffalo. Rat lured Cat into the water and tricked Buffalo out of the lead. Other animals came in one at a time, but Cat arrived too late to be included in the list of the first twelve animals. This is why, to this day, Cat and Rat are enemies.

📁 **Spanish Summaries,** p. 61

A **Active Reading**

PREDICT Ask students what they know about the zodiac and in what way they think a story about a cat and a rat might be linked to the Chinese calendar. *(Students may know that the names of animals are an element in the Chinese zodiac and may predict that the story tells how that came about.)*

Additional Resources

📁 *Active Reading Guide,* p. 61

🎧 *Audio Library*

🎧 *Spanish Audio Library*

Teaching Options

A

From: CAT AND RAT: THE LEGEND OF THE CHINESE ZODIAC by Ed Young, © 1995 by Ed Young. Reprinted by permission of Henry Holt and Company, Inc.

CONNECTING TO OTHER SELECTIONS

The chart at the right shows three ways to connect "Cat and Rat: The Legend of the Chinese Zodiac" to other selections in this book.

For specific teaching strategies, see the *Theme Seven Planning Guide,* pages 52–53.

Connection		Title
Life Skills: Supporting and Contributing	→	"Beyond the Limits," p. 281
Thematic: Twists and Turns	→	"The Cremation of Sam McGee," p. 636
Literary: Legend	→	"Rip Van Winkle," p. 185

Cat and Rat:
The Legend of the Chinese Zodiac

Ed Young ∿

In China, a long, long time ago, there lived a cat and a rat. They were best friends. They ate together. They played together. They slept together.

One day, the Emperor decided to hold a race among all the animals in the land. The first twelve animals to cross the finish line would have a year in the Chinese calendar named after them. This would be quite an honor.

"But winning the race will not be easy," warned the Emperor. "You must run through the thickest part of the forest and then swim across the river at its widest point."

Cat and Rat each wanted to be the first to cross the finish line. But they knew that they would be two of the smallest animals in the race.

"We will never make it," Rat complained to Cat.

"Oh, I think we will," replied the resourceful cat.

"We'll ask the water buffalo to help us," said the cat. "He could give us a head start. He always wakes

---

Vocabulary
resourceful (ri sôrs′ fəl) *adj.* capable or skillful in dealing with new or difficult situations

---

Historical Note

Astrology, developed as early as 3000 B.C., is the study of how events on earth correspond to the movements of astronomical objects. Astrologers map the positions of these objects on charts called horoscopes. A circle represents the plane on which the earth orbits the sun. The circle is divided into twelve sections—the signs of the Zodiac.

FYI

Calendars Not all calendars are the same. New Year's Day, for example, is celebrated January 1 in the Gregorian calendar, which was introduced in 1582. Prior to that, most European countries observed New Year's Day on March 25. The Jewish New Year is celebrated between mid-September and early October. The Chinese New Year is celebrated between January 10 and February 19.

B Critical Thinking

ANALYZING ARGUMENTS Ask students why Rat and Cat, being the smallest animals in the race, are at a disadvantage. *(Their short legs put them at a disadvantage because the race involves crossing a forest and a river.)*

Reading *Minilesson*

Setting a Purpose for Reading The initial purpose for reading may change depending on what new questions arise. Explain to students that some good questions to ask when they begin reading are *Who are the characters? Where does the story take place? What is the situation?*

Activity Invite volunteers to model processes for setting and revising purposes for reading fiction. The process should include these steps: 1. Identify the material as fiction or nonfiction. 2. When setting a purpose, skim the illustrations and the first page or two to find out what the selection is about. 3. Decide what information is important to find out. **L2**

Additional Resources
📁 *Reading Workbook,* pp. 109–110

C Critical Thinking

DRAWING CONCLUSIONS Ask students to describe Buffalo's personality and use story details to support their conclusions. *(Buffalo seems to have an easy-going, generous personality. Even though they are in a competition, Buffalo is willing to help his friends.)*

D Active Reading

QUESTION Encourage students to raise questions about Rat's treatment of his friend Cat. *(It is unrealistic to suggest that a friend would do such a thing, although that sometimes happens to friends when a prize is involved.)*

E Literary Elements

IMAGERY Through a careful choice of verbs, the author gives a clear picture of each animal at the finish line. Each picture is accurate for that animal, and each is different from the others. For example, "Tiger came roaring." Ask students to identify verbs describing other animals' crossing of the line. *(Rabbit darted, snake slithered, and horse thundered. All of these verbs indicate the way these animals actually move.)*

---

up before sunrise. Maybe we could even ride on his back."

So Cat and Rat convinced Buffalo to wake them up early on the day of the race. The next morning, Buffalo was up long before dawn. "Wake up, lazybones," he said to the sleeping cat and rat. "We had better get started."

Cat and Rat climbed on the buffalo's back. But they were so sleepy that by the time they had fully awakened, they were half way across the river.

Rat woke up first. He saw the Emperor standing at the finish line far, far away. Why should I share the glory of first place with Cat and Buffalo? thought the rat selfishly.

"Wake up, my friend," he cried to Cat. "Look at all the tasty fish swimming in the water."

Cat licked her lips. She leaned over for a closer look, and Rat gave her a little push. SPLASH! She tumbled into the water.

Buffalo turned his head to see what had made the splash. He didn't see the cat, though. What he saw instead were the other animals in the race—and they were close behind him. Without giving Cat or Rat another thought, he sped toward the Emperor.

Just as Buffalo neared the riverbank, the clever rat leaped from behind his ear and crossed the finish line in first place.

"How did such a small animal win the race?" asked the Emperor in surprise.

"I may be small but I am also smart," replied the rat. He scampered up onto the winner's <u>podium</u>. Buffalo knew he had

been tricked into second place, but he could only grunt in dismay.

Back in the river, Cat tried to swim along with the other animals. She hated water. But if she had to swim in it to win the race, she would do so.

Far ahead of her, Tiger came roaring across the finish line. "Am I first?" he growled.

"No," said the rat smugly. "You'd have to be awfully clever to beat me."

"And you'd have to get up extra early to beat me," added the buffalo.

Cat scrambled onto a log. She paused to shake herself off and to catch her breath.

By then the sky was dark and a great storm was blowing. A dragon appeared in the clouds above. He was much, much too big to run through woods or swim across a river, so the Emperor had told him he could race through the sky, braving the rains and the wind.

But no sooner had he begun his descent to the earth, than the rabbit darted across the finish line in front of him, taking fourth place. The dragon had to be content with fifth.

In the river, the cat heaved a great sigh, then plunged into the water again. "I can still make it," she told herself. But Snake slithered across the finish line next and hissed a silvery greeting to the five animals who had arrived before him. Snake was number six.

Cat swam as fast as she could. A few moments later, she heard the sound of galloping hooves in the distance. Horse thundered across the finish line in seventh place.

Vocabulary

podium (pōʹ dē əm) *n.* a small, raised platform or stand with a slanted shelf for holding a speaker's papers

---

MEETING INDIVIDUAL NEEDS — ENGLISH LANGUAGE LEARNERS

Beastly English Explain to English language learners that the English language is full of words and phrases inspired by animal behavior and characteristics. In fact, certain animal words are used to describe human behavior or character traits that resemble the animal's characteristics.

Activity Have a mixed group of students find out what human behavior or

traits each of the following animal words describes: *ape, badger, bug, chicken, duck, parrot, rat,* and *worm.* Students can then use three or four of these terms in sentences. **L2**
COLLAB. LEARN.

Additional Resources

📁 *English Language Learners Sourcebook*

Teaching Options

Goat and Monkey weren't far behind. They jumped onto the log on which Cat had rested and paddled across the finish line almost at the same time. But Goat beat Monkey by a hair.

While the nine winners waited patiently with the Emperor, Cat watched Rooster struggle toward the finish line. Dog could easily have swum ahead of Rooster, but she couldn't resist playing in the water for just a few minutes longer.

"Number ten!" called the Emperor as Rooster staggered in. "Number eleven!" he cried when Dog arrived.

"Who will be number twelve?" asked the Emperor. "I need just one more animal."

"Me! I will!" called Cat, and she swam even faster.

Unfortunately for Cat, Pig rushed across the finish line in front of her.

"Number twelve!" cried the Emperor, but Cat was still too far away.

"Congratulations to all the winners!" said the Emperor. "One of the twelve years will be named after each of you."

Suddenly, up rushed Cat. She was tired and wet and more than a little unhappy

From CAT AND RAT: THE LEGEND OF THE CHINESE ZODIAC by Ed Young, ©1995 by Ed Young. Reprinted by permission of Henry Holt and Company, Inc.

Viewing the painting: What event in the legend does this painting show? Does the mood of the painting match the mood of the story? Explain.

about swimming across the river on her own. "How did I do?" she asked anxiously. "Am I one of the winners?"

"Sorry, dear Cat," replied the Emperor. "All twelve places have been filled."

Upon hearing this news, Cat let out a yowl and tried to <u>pounce</u> on Rat. Her claws scratched the tip of his tail, but Rat squeezed under the Emperor's chair just in time.

And that is why, to this very day, Cat and Rat are enemies.

Vocabulary
pounce (pouns) *v.* to swoop down, spring, or leap suddenly in attack

LIFE SKILLS CONNECTION

Decision Making Mention that Rat's selfish action destroys a friendship which is never restored. He won glory, but lost a friend.

Activity Have students in small groups identify situations in which people have to choose between things and friends. Have them write decision-making guidelines that lie somewhere between these two extremes. **L2** **COLLAB. LEARN.**

Extreme	Middle	Extreme
Never do anything to upset a friend	Talk to friend about conflicting interests and decide together	Do what ever feels good at the time

Critical Thinking

MAKING CRITICAL JUDGMENTS Have students read the description of the Buffalo (Ox) in the graphic and explain how the description does or does not match Buffalo's personality in the story. *(In the story, Buffalo is patient and dependable, waking the Cat and Rat and carrying them across the river. Buffalo shows perseverance in completing the race.)*

Active Reading

CONNECT Have students read the personality descriptions in the graphics and then have each create a composite of an ideal friend, choosing the most appealing characteristics of each animal.

Cat and Rat

R a t

*1996, 1984, 1972, 1960,
1948, 1936, 1924, 1912, 1900*

Rats are innovative and know how to use opportunities to their advantage. They love to collect and organize and tend to be most active while others are at rest. Rats need to be careful not to lose their tempers or to become greedy. Rats get along best with Dragons and Monkeys and least with Horses.

R a b b i t

*1999, 1987, 1975, 1963,
1951, 1939, 1927, 1915, 1903*

This is the luckiest sign of all. Rabbits are gentle, talented, gracious, and friendly. Because of these qualities, they are popular wherever they go as mediators of conflicts. Sometimes Rabbits are overly shy and sentimental, but they almost always succeed at what they do. Their best friends are Goats or Pigs. Roosters may be enemies.

O x (B u f f a l o)

*1997, 1985, 1973, 1961,
1949, 1937, 1925, 1913, 1901*

Ox are honest, conservative, and patient by nature. They are happy when alone. Since friends and family find them dependable, they will make good mothers or fathers. Ox can be stubborn when pushed. They may be slow in starting things, but always complete what they begin. Ox are better friends with Snakes and Roosters and can get into trouble with Goats.

D r a g o n

*2000, 1988, 1976, 1964,
1952, 1940, 1928, 1916, 1904*

Dragons have a superimagination and are unique, energetic, and dramatic. Dragons are also moody and can be too perfectionistic. They make good friends with Monkeys and Rats but should beware of Dogs.

T i g e r

*1998, 1986, 1974, 1962,
1950, 1938, 1926, 1914, 1902*

Tigers are powerful, courageous, and like to take chances—qualities that make them natural leaders. Because of this, they must weigh matters before taking action on them. Tigers need to be careful not to let their brashness offend others. Dogs and Horses are friends with Tigers, but Monkeys are not.

S n a k e

*2001, 1989, 1977, 1965,
1953, 1941, 1929, 1917, 1905*

Snakes are talented and graceful, intuitive and wise. They are subtle in their ways and care about their looks. Snakes can be stingy at times, but if they use their good qualities to help others, many people will benefit. Snakes' best friends are Roosters and Ox, while their enemies are Pigs.

Teaching Options

Grammar and Language *Minilesson*

Commas in a Series Remind students to use commas to separate three or more items in a series. Write these sentences on the board:

1. An ox is honest conservative and patient by nature.
2. Their energy high spirits and optimism make horses popular among friends.
3. Snakes are talented graceful and wise.

Ask for volunteers to come up to the board to insert commas where they belong.

Activity Then, have students select five animals from the story and write a descriptive sentence about each. Every sentence must include at least three items in a series, *i.e.*, three adjectives, three verbs, or three nouns. **L2**

Additional Resources

- *Grammar and Language Transparency 58*
- *Grammar and Language Workbook,* pp. 255–256
- *Grammar and Composition Handbook,* Lesson 13.2
- *Writer's Choice,* Lesson 20.2

Ed Young ～

Horse

2002, 1990, 1978, 1966,
1954, 1942, 1930, 1918, 1906

Horses' energy, high spirits, and optimism make them popular among friends. They have a very independent streak and like to travel alone. Horses must learn patience and learn to finish what they start. They should marry Tigers or Dogs but not Rats.

Rooster

2005, 1993, 1981, 1969,
1957, 1945, 1933, 1921, 1909

Roosters are punctual, reliable, independent, and enjoy being on center stage. They are careful and unique but sometimes conceited. Snakes and Ox are friends but Rabbits are trouble.

Goat

2003, 1991, 1979, 1967,
1955, 1943, 1931, 1919, 1907

Although Goats are sometimes shy, they are always loving, gentle, elegant, and creative. They must learn to be direct and to venture out of comfortable situations. Goats get along well with Pigs and Rabbits but are not as friendly with Ox.

Dog

2006, 1994, 1982, 1970,
1958, 1946, 1934, 1922, 1910

Dogs are gregarious, loyal, honest, fun-loving team players. They are also helpful and optimistic but may spend too much time worrying about things. For friendship, Dogs should look to Horses or Tigers. Watch out for Dragons.

Monkey

2004, 1992, 1980, 1968,
1956, 1944, 1932, 1920, 1908

People pay attention to Monkeys because they are very smart. They are confident, energetic, happy, and curious. However, Monkeys can become overly confident, getting ahead of themselves and becoming confused. Monkeys should stay away from Tigers and look for Dragons or Rats as friends.

Pig

2007, 1995, 1983, 1971,
1959, 1947, 1935, 1923, 1911

Pigs are noble and physically strong and will sacrifice anything for the welfare of their family. Their friendships are long-lasting, even though they may not always be easy. Pigs can sometimes be reckless. They should stay away from other Pigs and make friends with Rabbits or Goats.

From CAT AND RAT: THE LEGEND OF THE CHINESE ZODIAC by Ed Young. ©1995 by Ed Young. Reprinted by permission of Henry Holt and Company, Inc.

A DIFFERENT DIMENSION ❧ 731

ELABORATING Have students explain why they think "Roosters may be enemies" of Rabbits, and "Snakes and Ox are friends" of Roosters. *(Perhaps because rabbits are shy, whereas roosters enjoy being the center of the stage. Roosters are reliable and snakes can be helpful to others. The Ox is also dependable.)*

Thematic Focus

A Different Dimension Ask students how this selection relates to the theme. *(It provides a different dimension of understanding of the Chinese zodiac.)*

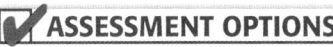

☑ ASSESSMENT OPTIONS

📁 *Quick Checks,* p. 61

REAL-WORLD CONNECTION

Legends Students may learn about legends by listening to people tell them, by researching them on the Internet, or by reading about them in history books or other reliably documented resources. Legends serve to teach and to instill in people the important values of their culture.

Activity Have students research legends, such as George Washington and the cherry tree, Abraham Lincoln reading by firelight, or Paul Revere and his midnight ride. Have each group report to the class on the legend, telling what it is about and what cultural or national values the legend fosters among people. **L2**

A DIFFERENT DIMENSION ❧ 731

Responding to the Selection

Personal Response

Some students may have expected a more realistic explanation of the relationship between the cat and rat.

Analyzing Literature

1. The Emperor will name a year of the calendar after each of the first twelve animals that finish the race.
2. Cat's plan is for Rat and Cat to ride on the back of Buffalo.
3. Rat tricks Cat into looking at the fish and then pushes her into the water. When Buffalo brings Rat close to shore, Rat jumps off his back and scampers ahead of him to finish first.
4. Twelve animals finish before Cat. She lets out a yowl and chases Rat.
5. We learn that Rat says, "We will never make it," showing his pessimism. Cat is more positive and resourceful, thinking up a plan.
6. The legend teaches us that rats are selfish, sneaky creatures.
7. Cats and rats are enemies because Rat tricked Cat out of a great honor.
8. Rat in the story is innovative, opportunistic, and active while others rest. Rat shows a tendency toward greediness.
9. Some students may feel this kind of story may help children remember at least some of the animals because the story puts the abstract concept into concrete form.
10. Students will probably say that their choices are based on more than the generalizations given in the zodiac.

Responding to Literature

PERSONAL RESPONSE

How does the ancient Chinese explanation about cats and rats compare with the ideas you shared in the **Focus Activity** on page 725?

Analyzing Literature

RECALL

1. How does the emperor plan to use the results of the race?
2. What is Cat's plan for succeeding in the race?
3. How does Rat manage to finish the race?
4. How many animals cross the finish line before Cat? How does she react to the results of the race?

INTERPRET

5. What do you learn about the personalities of Cat and Rat when they first hear about the race?
6. What does the legend teach about rats in general?
7. According to this tale, why are cats and rats enemies?

EVALUATE AND CONNECT

8. Read the description of people born under the sign of the Rat in the zodiac chart. Which characteristics does Rat in the story share with this description?
9. In your opinion, would this kind of imaginative explanation for the Chinese calendar help children remember the animals associated with each year? Why or why not?
10. **Personal Connection** Would you use the Chinese Zodiac or something similar to it as a guide for choosing your friends? Why or why not?

LITERARY ELEMENTS

Legend

Legends, folktales, and myths are part of folk literature—the collected beliefs and traditions of a people. A **legend** is a story, handed down from generation to generation, about a specific person or thing. Legends usually deal with or explain something that exists or existed historically. For example, the twelve-month zodiac in "Cat and Rat" has been the center of Chinese astrology for thousands of years.

1. How does the "Cat and Rat" legend explain why cats are great rat catchers?
2. Do you think the twelve zodiac animals were really chosen as a result of a race? Why or why not?

● See **Literary Terms Handbook,** p. R6.

LITERARY ELEMENTS

1. Rat tricked Cat out of having a year in the Chinese calendar named after her. Ever since, Cat has sought revenge.
2. The legend of the race was probably written to promote knowledge of the already-existing calendar.

Additional Resources

 Literary Elements Transparency 61

Literature and Writing

Writing About Literature

Plot   The plot of "Cat and Rat" begins with Cat and Rat as friends and ends when they become ene- mies. Using the diagram on pages 144–145 as a model, draw and label a diagram identifying the five stages of the legend's plot.

Creative Writing

Why Do . . . ?   Think of your favorite animal. Then choose one of the animal's more interesting traits or physical characteristics to explain in a legend. Illustrate your tale with pictures that call attention to the characteristic you explained.

Extending Your Response

Literature Groups

Reality and Fantasy   Myths, legends, and folktales combine reality and fantasy. For example, an emperor inventing a new calendar could be a realis- tic event. However, a cat and a rat having a conver- sation is fantasy. List other examples of reality and fantasy in "Cat and Rat." Compare your findings with those of the rest of the class.

Performing

Dramatize   Form an acting troupe to perform "Cat and Rat." Adapt the story so that it takes place in a present-day setting. Write a script, and then choose students to take the parts of the emperor, the vari- ous animals, and a narrator. You may want to design and build simple scenery and make costumes that suggest the various characters as well. Perform the legend for another class.

Interdisciplinary Activity

Social Studies   Our Western calendar is not the only one used by large numbers of people. Use library resources to find out about other calendars (for example, Hindu, Jewish, and Muslim calendars). Choose one to investigate further. Find out how and when it developed and how it differs from your calendar.

Reading Further

If you would like to read other Chinese legends, try these:
How the Ox Star Fell from Heaven by Lily Toy Hong
Min-Yo and the Moon Dragon by Elizabeth Hillman

📖 **Save your work for your portfolio.**

Writing About Literature

Students' diagrams should
- identify and label the five stages of the legend's plot.
- identify the events at each stage.

Creative Writing

Students' tales should
- portray the animals' general characteristics as accurately as possible.
- use illustrations that convey an idea without being attempts at great artistic creation.

Literature Groups Students may view the animosity between the cat and the rat as realism, but their competing in a race as fantasy.
COLLAB. LEARN.

Performing Suggest that students use their imaginations in adapting the story. For example, because it is not possible to use a river in their performance, students may create another type of obstacle the "animals" must overcome.

Interdisciplinary Activity
Internet sources and encyclopedias can provide the information needed. Suggest that in starting their research students prepare lists of questions that they can use but not be limited to as they work.

Skill Minilessons

GRAMMAR AND LANGUAGE
APOSTROPHES IN CONTRACTIONS

1. They'd
2. We'll
3. We'd
4. They'd
5. I'm

READING AND THINKING
USING GRAPHIC AIDS

Students may find some points of agreement and disagreement when matching their personalities to the one described in the graphic. They can include both in their paragraphs. Encourage them to give explanations or examples of how their personalities do or do not match the zodiac profile.

VOCABULARY
THE SUFFIX -ful

1. having much skill
2. brilliant, well-worked
3. policy that leads to waste
4. response accompanied by tears
5. number of coins that would fit in one hand

Additional Resources

📕 *Grammar and Language Workbook,* pp. 273–274

📕 *Grammar and Composition Handbook,* Lesson 13.7

📕 *Writer's Choice,* Lesson 20.7

📕 *Reading Workbook,* p. 109–110

📕 *Vocabulary Practice,* p. 43

Skill Minilessons

GRAMMAR AND LANGUAGE • APOSTROPHES IN CONTRACTIONS

A **contraction** is a word made by putting two words together and replacing one or more letters with an apostrophe.

it + is = it's   we + are = we're
I + will = I'll   she + would = she'd

PRACTICE Copy each sentence from the story. Then find and underline two words that could be combined into a contraction. Write the contraction above the words.

1. They would be two of the smallest.
2. We will never make it.
3. We had better get started.
4. They had fully awakened.
5. But I am also smart.

● For more about apostrophe usage, see **Language Handbook,** p. R19.

READING AND THINKING • USING GRAPHIC AIDS

Stories and novels are most often illustrated by drawings or paintings, but sometimes a story includes a graphic aid. A **graphic aid** is a chart, graph, map, or other illustration that organizes information for the reader. The graphic aid in "Cat and Rat" is the chart of the zodiac. Without this chart, the purpose of the legend would be difficult to understand. The zodiac chart shows the order of the twelve year names, the Chinese symbol for each year, the birth years for anyone born between 1900 and 2007, as well as the personality traits for people born in each of the twelve years.

PRACTICE In what year were you born? Look up your birth year on the zodiac chart on pages 730–731. Then write a paragraph explaining how your personality does or does not match the one described in the graphic. Find out the birth years of members of your family, and compare their personality traits with those described under the matching animals.

● For more about interpreting graphic aids, see **Reading Handbook,** p. R97.

VOCABULARY • THE SUFFIX -FUL

A *hopeful* person is full of hope; a *cheerful* one is full of cheer; a *fearful* one is full of fear. In each of these cases, you could define the word by simply adding "full of" to the base word. However, you can't always define a word this way. For example, a *dreadful* sight is not a sight that is full of dread; it's a sight that fills the viewer with dread. An area with many natural resources, such as oil, is "rich in resources" or "resource rich," but not *resourceful.*

PRACTICE Briefly explain what each underlined word means.

1. a skillful athlete
2. a masterful plan
3. a wasteful policy
4. a tearful response
5. a handful of coins

● For more about adding suffixes, see **Language Handbook,** Spelling, pp. R44–R45.

✔ ASSESSMENT OPTIONS

📂 *Quick Checks,* p. 61

📂 *Selection and Theme Assessment,* pp. 105–106

📂 *Performance Assessment,* p. 58

💾 *Testmaker*

Vo·cab·u·lar·y Skills

Analyzing Word Parts

The best source of information for the meaning of an unfamiliar word is a dictionary, but a dictionary is not always handy. Context clues are often useful, but in many cases, there are not enough context clues to provide adequate help. Many words themselves contain clues to their meanings. Familiar base words, roots, or other word parts can provide information about the meaning of the word.

"The Smallest Dragonboy" says, "Being the youngest candidate was not an enviable position." The sentence provides little help for the meaning of *enviable*. It could mean "lucky" or "common" or many other things. However, the word itself is helpful because it is made up of the base word *envy* and the suffix *-able*. Putting these clues together provides an idea very close to the actual meaning of "able to be envied."

A word may have a familiar root. For example, look at *spectacle* in this sentence:

"The Bunyan family must have been quite a spectacle."

If you remember having seen *spec* in *spectator* or *inspect,* you should know that a *spectacle* is something that is seen.

Analyzing words is not a substitute for looking them up in a good dictionary. A word part may look like a familiar root, but it might not be one. Also, the meaning of the word may have changed over time. Still, analyzing words can sometimes provide real help when you need to guess at a meaning.

EXERCISE

Analyze the underlined words, using whatever clues they contain to help you. Then match each word to its meaning on the right.

1. a new modification
2. to dislocate a knee
3. a migratory way of life
4. to be a noncombatant
5. to identify a precondition
6. behave like an ingrate
7. an injurious act
8. to use some leverage
9. to maltreat someone
10. a snippet of information

a. to abuse
b. harmful or damaging
c. one who is not thankful
d. a slight change in form
e. characterized by moving from place to place
f. a small piece or fragment
g. to put out of the proper position
h. increased means of accomplishing a purpose
i. one whose duties do not include actual fighting
j. something required before something else can occur

Vo·cab·u·lar·y Skills

Objective

- To recognize and use strategies for analyzing words

Teaching Strategies

Ask students to conduct a vocabulary hunt through the stories in this theme to find a word they don't know the meaning of. Have them write the word down and try to figure out its meaning by analyzing the base, root, prefix and/or suffix of the word. Encourage students to use one another as resources in analyzing their words.

Exercise

1. d
2. g
3. e
4. i
5. j
6. c
7. b
8. h
9. a
10. f

Additional Resources
📁 *Vocabulary Power: Weekly Lessons and Activities*

Teaching Options

MEETING INDIVIDUAL NEEDS — ENGLISH LANGUAGE LEARNERS

Word Families Exposure to word families can help English language learners analyze new words and expand their vocabularies. Write these roots and their meanings on the board: *geo* (earth), *luna* (moon), *therme* (heat), and *bios* (life).

Activity Have students work in mixed groups. Ask them to choose one of the root words listed on the board and write six words that contain that root, one per card, on index cards and to illustrate the words on the other sides of the cards. **COLLAB. LEARN.**

Additional Resources
📁 *English Language Learners Sourcebook*

Objectives

- To read and analyze a myth about a boy who ignores his father's advice
- To learn and identify the important elements of myths
- To describe one of the characters as pictured in the author's characterization

Skills

Reading/Thinking: Identifying Spatial Relationships
Writing: News Report
Vocabulary: Dictionary Skills: Definitions
Collaboration: Literature Groups

Motivating
→OPTIONS

Selection Focus Transparency 62: Have students view the transparency and discuss the questions provided.

Focus Activity: As an extension of the Focus Activity, have small groups discuss how they distinguish good advice from poor advice and identify which factors influence their decisions.

Before You Read
Icarus and Daedalus

MEET JOSEPHINE PRESTON PEABODY

Josephine Preston Peabody's parents introduced her to literature and the theater at a young age. As a result, Peabody grew up reading and writing constantly. She published her first poem when she was fourteen years old. Six years later, the publication of her poems in magazines helped her to attend Radcliffe College. One of her verse dramas, "The Piper," was based on the Pied Piper legend and was produced at theaters in New York City and London.

Josephine Preston Peabody was born in Brooklyn, New York, in 1874 and died in Cambridge, Massachusetts, in 1922.

FOCUS ACTIVITY

Have you ever known someone who ignored caution and did something dangerous?

Journal
Write your thoughts and feelings about failing to heed good advice. Then share your ideas in a small-group discussion.

Setting a Purpose
Read this story to find out what happens to Icarus and Daedalus.

BACKGROUND

The Time and Place This story takes place on the Greek island of Crete in the legendary time when both mortals and gods inhabited ancient Greece.

Did You Know? The word *myth* comes from *mythos,* a Greek word meaning "story." A myth is a special kind of story, usually involving gods and goddesses. The origins of the Greek myths are unknown, but they likely developed over many hundreds of years of oral retellings before the Greeks developed writing. They were already very old by around 850 B.C., when the Greek writer Homer referred to them in his poems. The Greek myths tell the stories of the gods and goddesses, their lives on Mount Olympus, and their interactions with the mortals on earth.

VOCABULARY PREVIEW

veer (vēr) *v.* to shift or change direction; p. 737
waver (wā′ vər) *v.* to become unsteady; p. 738
rash (rash) *adj.* done without thought or preparation; reckless; p. 738
reel (rēl) *v.* to turn or seem to turn round and round; whirl; p. 739
quench (kwench) *v.* to satisfy or put an end to a need or desire; p. 739
vainly (vān′ lē) *adv.* without success; uselessly; p. 739

RESOURCE MANAGER

Lesson Planning Resource
The *Theme Seven Planning Guide* (pp. 57–64) provides additional lesson notes and reduced versions of all print resources.

📁 **Other Print Resources**
- Active Reading Guide, p. 62
- Vocabulary Practice, p. 44
- Reading Workbook, pp. 111–112

- Quick Checks, p. 62
- Selection and Theme Assessment, pp. 107–108
- Performance Assessment, p. 59
- Spanish Summaries, p. 62
- Spanish Translations
- Inclusion Strategies
- English Language Learners Sourcebook

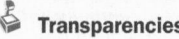 **Transparencies**
- Selection Focus 62
- Fine Art 25
- Literary Elements 62

Technology
🎧 Audio Library
🎧 Spanish Audio Library
💻 Glencoe Literature Web Site
💾 Testmaker

Icarus and Daedalus

Josephine Preston Peabody

Among all those mortals who grew so wise that they learned the secrets of the gods, none was more cunning than Daedalus.[1]

He once built, for King Minos of Crete, a wonderful Labyrinth of winding ways so cunningly tangled up and twisted around that, once inside, you could never find your way out again without a magic clue. But the king's favor veered with the wind, and one day he had his master architect imprisoned in a tower. Daedalus managed to escape from his cell; but it seemed impossible to leave the island, since every ship that came or went was well guarded by order of the king.

At length, watching the sea gulls in the air—the only creatures that were sure of liberty—he thought of a plan for himself and his young son Icarus,[2] who was captive with him.

_____

1. *Daedalus* (ded' əl əs)
2. *Icarus* (ik' ər əs)

Vocabulary
veer (vēr) *v.* to shift or change direction

A DIFFERENT DIMENSION 737

Did You Know?
The *Labyrinth* (lab' ə rinth') was a huge maze in which a complicated, twisted path enclosed by high walls made it impossible for people to find the way out once they had entered it.

SUMMARY

King Minos has imprisoned the master architect, Daedalus, and his son, Icarus. Trapped on the island of Crete, Daedalus builds wings to help them escape by flying away. He warns Icarus not to fly too high or low, but once in the air, Icarus ignores the warning. Flying too close to the sun, his wings melt and he falls to his death in the ocean. Daedalus is filled with grief for his son. He travels to Sicily where he hangs his wings at the temple of Apollo and never again tries to fly.

📁 *Spanish Summaries,* p. 62

A **Active Reading**
PREDICT Have students read this page and then use the title and text clues to predict what they think will happen to Daedalus and his son Icarus. *(Students will probably use the title, the setting in a prison tower, and the context clues, which inform them that Daedalus was an ingenious inventor, to predict that they will escape somehow.)*

Additional Resources
📁 *Active Reading Guide,* p. 62
🎧 *Audio Library*
🎧 *Spanish Audio Library*

Teaching Options

CONNECTING TO OTHER SELECTIONS

COMPARING *selections*

This selection is compared with "Prometheus" on page 742. A lesson for teaching a comparison of the two selections appears on page 747.

The chart at the right shows three ways to connect "Icarus and Daedalus" to other selections in this book.

For specific teaching strategies, see the *Theme Seven Planning Guide,* pages 60–61.

Connection	Title
Life Skills: Teaching and Mentoring	→ "Racing the Great Bear," p. 268
Thematic: Facing Challenge	→ "Dreams," p. 261
Literary: Narrator	→ "The Wreck of Hesperus," p. 227

B Literary Elements

MYTH: *Character* Ask students what this passage reveals about Daedalus' relationship with his son. *(He is a careful and caring father.)*

C Literary Elements

MYTH: *Point of View* Ask students who is telling the story and what he reveals about the characters. *(There is a nameless narrator who lets readers in on the characters' thoughts and conversations.)*

LITERATURE & HUMANITIES

Have students examine the portrayal of Icarus in *Introducing Art*, page 76. Discuss why Matisse might have chosen to portray Icarus in this way and how the artist creates a sense of movement.

Icarus, 1947. Henri Matisse. From the *Jazz* series. Gouache on paper, 42 x 32.5 cm. COPYRIGHT ARS, New York, Ecole des Beaux Arts, Paris.

Viewing the painting: How is the flight of Icarus, as described in the myth, like the Icarus painted by Matisse? What important differences do you see?

Little by little, he gathered a store of feathers great and small. He fastened these together with thread, molded them in with wax, and so fashioned two great wings like those of a bird. When they were done, Daedalus fitted them to his own shoulders, and after one or two efforts, he found that by waving his arms he could winnow the air and cleave[3] it, as a swimmer does the sea. He held himself aloft, wavered this way and that with the wind, and at last, like a great fledgling,[4] he learned to fly.

Without delay, he fell to work on a pair of wings for the boy Icarus, and taught him carefully how to use them, bidding him beware of rash adventures among the stars. "Remember," said the father, "never to fly very low or very high, for the fogs about the earth

B

C

---

3. Here, *winnow* and *cleave* both mean "to separate or divide."
4. A *fledgling* is a young bird that hasn't yet grown the feathers it needs to fly.

Vocabulary
waver (wā′ vər) *v.* to become unsteady
rash (rash) *adj.* done without thought or preparation; reckless

738 ❧ THEME 7

Teaching Options

Reading *Minilesson*

Identifying Spatial Relationships
Words that refer to location or distance help readers visualize the setting, plot events, and characters' actions in a story. Some words that are clues to location or distance include *between, below, about, left, alongside, here, outside, around, close to, far, right, over, near, in, into, beside, middle, next to, beyond, north, east, on, opposite, there, inside, in front of, under, out,* behind, across, above, toward, by,* and *away from.* These words help answer the question, "Where?"

Activity Have students work in small groups and have each group choose a scene from the story. Ask each group to develop stage directions and write details for scenery and the location of characters for a play based on the scene they choose from the story. When they have completed their work, engage them in a discussion about how understanding spatial relationships in a selection can help readers understand that selection better.
L3 COLLAB. LEARN.

Additional Resources

Reading Workbook, pp. 111–112

would weigh you down, but the blaze of the sun will surely melt your feathers apart if you go too near."

For Icarus, these cautions went in at one ear and out by the other. Who could remember to be careful when he was to fly for the first time? Are birds careful? Not they! And not an idea remained in the boy's head but the one joy of escape.

The day came, and the fair wind that was to set them free. The father bird put on his wings, and, while the light urged them to be gone, he waited to see that all was well with Icarus, for the two could not fly hand in hand. Up they rose, the boy after his father. The hateful ground of Crete sank beneath them; and the country folk, who caught a glimpse of them when they were high above the treetops, took it for a vision of the gods—Apollo, perhaps, with Cupid[5] after him.

At first there was a terror in the joy. The wide vacancy of the air dazed them—a glance downward made their brains reel. But when a great wind filled their wings, and Icarus felt himself sustained, like a halcyon-bird[6] in the hollow of a wave, like a

child uplifted by his mother, he forgot everything in the world but joy. He forgot Crete and the other islands that he had passed over: he saw but vaguely that winged thing in the distance before him that was his father Daedalus. He longed for one draft[7] of flight to quench the thirst of his captivity: he stretched out his arms to the sky and made toward the highest heavens.

Alas for him! Warmer and warmer grew the air. Those arms, that had seemed to uphold him, relaxed. His wings wavered, drooped. He fluttered his young hands vainly—he was falling—and in that terror he remembered. The heat of the sun had melted the wax from his wings; the feathers were falling, one by one, like snowflakes; and there was none to help.

He fell like a leaf tossed down the wind, down, down, with one cry that overtook Daedalus far away. When he returned, and sought high and low for the poor boy, he saw nothing but the bird-like feathers afloat on the water, and he knew that Icarus was drowned.

The nearest island he named Icaria, in memory of the child; but he, in heavy grief, went to the temple of Apollo in Sicily, and there hung up his wings as an offering. Never again did he attempt to fly.

---

5. In mythology, *Apollo* is the god of the sun, and *Cupid* is the god of love.
6. Here, *sustained* means to be kept from sinking or falling. The *halcyon-bird* (hal′ sē ən), or kingfisher, glides slowly and smoothly near the water's surface as it hunts for fish.

7. Here, *draft* means "taste."

Vocabulary
reel (rēl) *v.* to turn or seem to turn round and round; whirl
quench (kwench) *v.* to satisfy or put an end to a need or desire
vainly (vān′ lē) *adv.* without success; uselessly

A DIFFERENT DIMENSION 🐿 739

Responding to the Selection

Personal Response

Students might explain that Icarus was young and did not know how to listen; he also became overwhelmed with joy when he began to fly.

Analyzing Literature

1. King Minos locks them in a tower on the island and guards all the ships.
2. Daedalus loves his son Icarus.
3. Icarus flies too close to the sun, melting his wings. He drowns in the sea.
4. Daedalus goes to the temple of Apollo in Sicily, hangs up his wings, and never flies again.
5. Since Crete is an island, there are only two ways for Daedalus and his son to escape: by sea or by air. King Minos guards all the ships, so the only way left for them to escape is to fly.
6. Yes. Daedalus makes wings for Icarus and warns him about the dangers he is to avoid. He is heartbroken when he loses his son and never flies again.
7. Because Icarus gets carried away with his sense of freedom, he forgets his father's words of warning.
8. Some students may think that Daedalus feels responsible. Perhaps he should not have flown so far ahead of his son.
9. Students will probably say yes, they would listen to the father's advice. He is known to be a genius and he would not warn about the risk of flying if it were not a real danger.
10. Students will probably feel sad about the tragic ending of this story. It is a tragedy that Daedalus escapes imprison-ment but loses his son.

Responding to Literature

PERSONAL RESPONSE

Why didn't Icarus listen to his father's words of wisdom? Describe your impressions in your journal.

Analyzing Literature

RECALL

1. What does King Minos do to keep Daedalus and Icarus from escaping Crete?
2. Describe the relationship between Daedalus and Icarus.
3. What happens to Icarus?
4. What does Daedalus do once he reaches safety?

INTERPRET

5. How does the setting of the story influence the plot? Support your ideas with details from the story.
6. Do you think that Daedalus is a concerned father? Why or why not? Support your opinion with examples.
7. Why does Icarus disobey his father's words of caution?
8. Do you think Daedalus feels responsible for what happens to his son? Why or why not?

EVALUATE AND CONNECT

9. Imagine that you are Icarus. Would you listen to your father's advice? Why or why not?
10. How do you feel about what happens to the main characters in this myth? Explain.

LITERARY ELEMENTS

Myth

People in every culture through-out the world have created myths. A **myth** is an ancient story of unknown origins, often involving gods and heroes. Myths originally helped people try to explain how natural events and human actions happened. There are myths about every facet of human life, from the creation of the world to an understanding of why things grow. In fact, collections of myths, called mythologies, generally account for everything in the experience of a particular culture.

1. What elements in "Icarus and Daedalus" fit the definition of a myth?
2. What can you learn about ancient Greek culture from reading this myth?

● See **Literary Terms Handbook**, p. R6.

LITERARY ELEMENTS

1. The story refers to the Greek gods and describes how humans can fly with bird feathers.
2. In ancient Greece they believed in the gods Apollo and Cupid; King Minos ruled the island of Crete; and Daedalus built the famous Labyrinth.

Additional Resources

 Literary Elements Transparency 62

Literature and Writing

Writing About Literature

Characterization Characterization refers to the ways in which an author informs readers about the characters in a story. You learn about characters through their thoughts, words, actions, and interactions with other characters, and from what other characters say about them. Describe one of the characters as you picture him from the author's characterization.

Creative Writing

The Greek Gazette Imagine that you have been assigned to write a news story about Daedalus and his flight to freedom. Interview Daedalus just as he and Icarus are preparing for their journey. Then write a news report based on the interview and the results of the flight. Share your news story with your classmates in an oral presentation.

Extending Your Response

Literature Groups

Thinking About Theme Discuss the theme of "Icarus and Daedalus." Focus on the questions: What did Daedalus fear would happen to his son? Why did Icarus choose to ignore his father's words of caution? Review your notes from the **Focus Activity** on page 736, and talk about the meaning of this myth as it relates to life today.

Art Activity

Modeling Create a model or draw a diagram of Daedalus's flying machine as you picture it.

📕 **Save your work for your portfolio.**

Skill Minilesson

VOCABULARY • DICTIONARY SKILLS: DEFINITIONS

vain (vān) *adj.* **1.** too interested in, or proud of, one's own abilities, appearance, or accomplishments: *a vain man.* **2.** not successful or effective: *a vain attempt.* **3.** of no real value or meaning; empty: *a vain promise. adv.* vainly

PRACTICE Study the dictionary definitions above. Decide which meaning of *vain* (or *vainly*) is used in each sentence and write the number of that meaning.

1. One might expect *vain* satisfaction in a man who had accomplished what no other had ever done.
2. After all, Daedalus triumphed over King Minos's *vain* efforts to confine him.
3. Instead of *vainly* showing off his ability, however, Daedalus never flew again.
4. Liberty itself seemed *vain* to him when achieved at the cost of his son.
5. Could he have known how *vain* his warnings would be?

Literature and Writing

Writing About Literature

Students' descriptions should
- tell how they picture one of the characters.
- use the author's characterization as a basis for the description.

Creative Writing

Students' news reports should
- include an interview with Daedalus as he and Icarus are preparing for their escape.
- describe what took place during and after the flight.

Extending Your Response

Literature Groups As students discuss the myth, be sure they see its universal aspect: everyone has opportunities to heed or ignore the advice of others. Have students share examples from their own experience. **COLLAB. LEARN.**

Art Activity Provide students with time and materials to complete their models or diagrams. When they have finished, have them share their work with the class. 🗄

Skill Minilesson

VOCABULARY • DICTIONARY SKILLS: DEFINITIONS

1. 1	**3.** 1	**5.** 2
2. 2	**4.** 3	

Additional Resources

📁 *Vocabulary Practice*, p. 44

📁 *Quick Checks*, p. 62
📁 *Selection and Theme Assessment,* pp. 107–108
📁 *Performance Assessment*, p. 59
💾 *Testmaker*

Objectives

- To read and analyze a Greek myth about how fire was given to humans
- To identify the theme of a Greek myth
- To explain how "Prometheus" might have been an ancient Greek explanation for the origins of civilization

Skills

Reading/Thinking: Drawing Conclusions
Writing: Journal Writing
Grammar/Language: Dashes
Collaboration: Literature Groups

Motivating
→OPTIONS

Selection Focus Transparency 63: Have students read and discuss the quote by Joseph Campbell. Invite them to think of examples of both heroes and celebrities.

Focus Activity: As an extension of the Focus Activity, invite students to create a poster with the caption "Knowledge is power." After students have discussed the expression, encourage them to develop images that fit their ideas.

Before You Read
Prometheus

MEET BERNARD EVSLIN

Having written plays for the stage and screen and published a novel for adults, Bernard Evslin (əv′ slin) decided on a career shift. In the mid-1960s, he began retelling myths and other ancient stories for an audience of young readers. His gift was his ability to retell ancient tales, whether from Greek mythology or the Bible, with such colorful details and contemporary language that some of the oldest stories in the world captured the interests of young readers.

Bernard Evslin was born in Pennsylvania in 1916 and died in Hawaii in 1993. This story was published in 1966.

FOCUS ACTIVITY

Think about the expression "Knowledge is power." What does it mean? Do you agree or disagree with it? Why?

Sharing Ideas
Jot down your ideas about the meaning of the expression, and then share them in a small-group discussion.

Setting a Purpose
Read this myth to find out what a giant thinks about knowledge.

BACKGROUND

The Time and Place This story takes place in Greece in the days when the gods and goddesses of Greek mythology were thought to rule the lives of mortals.

Did You Know? In Greek art, Prometheus is often pictured chained to a rock, his body attacked by vultures.

Coppa laconica con punizione di Atlante e Prometeo, 630–100 B.C. Pottery. Museo Gregoriano Etrusco, Vaticano.

VOCABULARY PREVIEW

decree (di krē′) *n.* an official rule, order, or decision; p. 743
aptitude (ap′ tə tōōd′) *n.* a natural ability; talent; p. 743
humility (hū mil′ ə tē) *n.* the quality of being humble or modest; p. 744
spite (spīt) *n.* a desire to hurt or annoy another person; p. 744
agony (ag′ ə nē) *n.* great pain and suffering of the mind or body; p. 745
hover (huv′ ər) *v.* to remain as if suspended in the air over a particular spot; p. 745

OVERSET—CHANNEL

 Glencoe Literature Web Site
Testmaker

RESOURCE MANAGER

Lesson Planning Resource
The *Theme Seven Planning Guide* (pp. 65–72) provides additional lesson notes and reduced versions of all print resources.

📁 **Other Print Resources**
- Active Reading Guide, p. 63
- Vocabulary Practice, p. 45
- Reading Workbook, pp. 113–114
- Grammar and Language

Workbook, pp. 275–276
- Grammar and Composition Handbook, Lesson 13.8
- Quick Checks, p. 63
- Selection and Theme Assessment, pp. 107–108
- Performance Assessment, p. 59
- Spanish Summaries, p. 63
- Spanish Translations
- Inclusion Strategies

- English Language Learners Sourcebook

 Transparencies
- Selection Focus 63
- Literary Elements 63
- Grammar and Language 59

Technology
🎧 Audio Library
🎧 Spanish Audio Library

PROMETHEUS

Retold by Bernard Evslin ～

Prometheus was a young Titan, no great admirer of Zeus.[1] Although he knew the great lord of the sky hated explicit questions, he did not hesitate to beard[2] him when there was something he wanted to know.

One morning he came to Zeus and said, "O Thunderer, I do not understand your design. You have caused the race of man to appear on earth, but you keep him in ignorance and darkness."

"Perhaps you had better leave the race of man to me," said Zeus. "What you call ignorance is innocence. What you call darkness is the shadow of my decree. Man is happy now. And he is so framed that he will remain happy unless someone persuades him that he is unhappy. Let us not speak of this again."

But Prometheus said, "Look at him. Look below. He crouches in caves. He is at the mercy of beast and weather. He eats his meat raw. If you mean something by this, enlighten me with your wisdom. Tell me why you refuse to give man the gift of fire."

Zeus answered, "Do you not know, Prometheus, that every gift brings a penalty? This is the way the Fates weave destiny—by which gods also must abide.[3] Man does not have fire, true, nor the crafts which fire teaches. On the other hand, he does not know disease, warfare, old age, or that inward pest called worry. He is happy, I say, happy without fire. And so he shall remain."

"Happy as beasts are happy," said Prometheus. "Of what use to make a separate race called man and endow[4] him with little fur, some wit, and a curious charm of unpredictability? If he must live like this, why separate him from the beasts at all?"

"He has another quality," said Zeus, "the capacity for worship. An aptitude for admiring our power, being puzzled by our riddles and amazed by our caprice.[5] That is why he was made."

"Would not fire, and the graces he can put on with fire, make him more interesting?"

"More interesting, perhaps, but infinitely more dangerous. For there is this in man

---

1. According to Greek myths, *Prometheus* (prə mē′ thē əs) and the other *Titans* (tīt′ ənz) belonged to a race of giants who once ruled the world. They were overthrown by *Zeus* (zōōs) and other gods.
2. To *beard* Zeus was to meet him boldly, face-to-face.
3. The ancient Greeks believed that three goddesses, sisters called the *Fates,* controlled human lives and fortunes. Even the gods had to go along with, or *abide,* the sisters' decisions.
4. To *endow* is to give a quality, ability, or talent to someone.
5. The gods' *caprice* was their tendency to change their minds suddenly and for little or no reason.

Vocabulary
decree (di krē′) *n.* an official rule, order, or decision
aptitude (ap′ tə tōōd′) *n.* a natural ability; talent

A DIFFERENT DIMENSION ❧ 743

Prometheus Giving Fire to Man. 1st century A.D. Mosaic tile. Museo delle Terme, Rome.

Viewing the mosaic: The ancient Greeks considered the gift of fire an important event. They celebrated the Prometheus myth in their literature and their art. Can you think of any modern "gift" that has had such an influence?

too: a vaunting pride that needs little sustenance to make it swell to giant size. Improve his lot,[6] and he will forget that which makes him pleasing—his sense of worship, his humility. He will grow big and poisoned with pride and fancy himself a god, and before we know it, we shall see him storming Olympus. Enough, Prometheus! I have been patient with you, but do not try me too far. Go now and trouble me no more with your speculations."

Prometheus was not satisfied. All that night he lay awake making plans. Then he left his couch at dawn and, standing tiptoe on Olympus, stretched his arm to the eastern horizon where the first faint flames of the sun were flickering. In his hand he held a reed filled with a dry fiber; he thrust it into the sunrise until a spark smoldered. Then he put the reed in his tunic and came down from the mountain.

At first men were frightened by the gift. It was so hot, so quick; it bit sharply when you touched it and for pure spite made the shadows dance. They thanked Prometheus and asked him to take it away. But he took the haunch of a newly killed deer and held it over the fire. And when the meat began to sear and sputter, filling the cave with its rich smells, the people felt themselves

---

6. *Vaunting* pride is boastful. *Sustenance* means "support or assistance." Here, *lot* refers to humans' situations in life or the conditions in which they live.

Vocabulary
humility (hū mil′ ə tē) *n.* the quality of being humble or modest
spite (spīt) *n.* a desire to hurt or annoy another person

744   THEME 7

Teaching Options

Grammar and Language *Minilesson*

Dashes Write these sentences on the board:
- *Then you must stop, or it will eat everything in sight—and you too.*
- *Prometheus was a Titan—a brash youth—who suffered a terrible fate.*

Explain that the dash shows a sudden break or change in thought or speech. If the sentence continues, a second dash marks the end of the interruption.

Activity Write these sentences—without the dashes—on the board. Have students add dashes where needed.
1. This is the way the Fates weave destiny—the gods' destinies, too.
2. Zeus refused Prometheus's request—a thoughtful one.
3. Men suspected—no, they knew—a terrible thing happened on the mountain.
L2

Additional Resources

 Grammar and Language Transparency 59

Grammar and Language Workbook, pp. 275–276

Grammar and Composition Handbook, Lesson 13.8

Writer's Choice, Lesson 20.8

Retold by Bernard Evslin ~

melting with hunger and flung themselves on the meat and devoured it greedily, burning their tongues.

D "This that I have brought you is called 'fire,'" Prometheus said. "It is an ill-natured spirit, a little brother of the sun, but if you handle it carefully, it can change your whole life. It is very greedy; you must feed it twigs, but only until it becomes a proper size. Then you must stop, or it will eat everything in sight—and you too. If it escapes, use this magic: water. It fears the water spirit, and if you touch it with water, it will fly away until you need it again."

He left the fire burning in the first cave, with children staring at it wide-eyed, and then went to every cave in the land.

Then one day Zeus looked down from the mountain and was amazed. Everything had changed. Man had come out of his cave. Zeus saw woodmen's huts, farmhouses, villages, walled towns, even a castle or two. He saw men cooking their food, carrying torches to light their way at night. He saw forges blazing, men beating out ploughs, keels,[7] swords, spears. They were making ships and raising white wings of sails and daring to use the fury of the winds for their journeys. They were wearing helmets, riding out in chariots to do battle, like the gods themselves.

Zeus was full of rage. He seized his largest thunderbolt. "So they want fire," he said to himself. "I'll give them fire—more than they can use. I'll turn their miserable little ball of earth into a cinder." But then another thought came to him, and he lowered his arm. "No," he said to himself, "I shall have vengeance—and entertainment too. Let them destroy themselves with their new skills. This will make a long, twisted game, interesting to watch. I'll attend to them later. My first business is with Prometheus."

He called his giant guards and had them seize Prometheus, drag him off to the Caucasus, and there bind him to a mountain peak with great chains specially forged by Hephaestus[8]—chains which even a Titan in agony could not break. And when the friend of man was bound to the mountain, Zeus sent two vultures to hover about him forever, tearing at his belly and eating his liver.

Men knew a terrible thing was happening on the mountain, but they did not know what. But the wind shrieked like a giant in torment and sometimes like fierce birds.

Many centuries he lay there—until another hero was born brave enough to defy the gods. He climbed to the peak in the Caucasus and struck the shackles from Prometheus and killed the vultures. His name was Heracles.[9]

E

---

7. A blacksmith uses a *forge* to heat and soften metal so that it can be hammered into desired shapes. A shipbuilder makes a *keel,* the main timber that runs the length of a boat's bottom.

8. The *Caucasus* Mountains, in southeastern Russia between the Black and Caspian Seas, separate Europe and Asia. *Hephaestus* (hi fes' tas) was the god of fire and metalworking.

9. *Heracles* (her' ə klēz') is the Greek name for Hercules, who was the son of Zeus and a human woman.

Vocabulary

agony (ag' ə nē) *n.* great pain and suffering of the mind or body
hover (huv' ər) *v.* to remain as if suspended in the air over a particular spot

---

Responding to the Selection

Personal Response

Students will probably mention man's first encounter with fire or Prometheus and the vultures.

Analyzing Literature

1. Prometheus requests fire. He feels sorry for humans.
2. Zeus's refusal is not justified. Fire's benefits would outweigh its disadvantages.
3. Prometheus asks Zeus to give fire to humans; Zeus refuses, but Prometheus gives it to them; humans change a great deal; Zeus chains Prometheus to a mountain where vultures attack him. The fire symbolizes knowledge which can also be dangerous if misused.
4. Fire enables people to stay warm, make tools, cook food, and frighten away animals.
5. He was a hero. He helped humans even though he was afraid.

Extending Your Response

Literature Groups

Have students state whether they agree with Prometheus and then relate to the expression theme.
COLLAB. LEARN.

Writing About Literature

Students' paragraphs should
- describe how the myth was an ancient explanation for the origins of the civilized world.
- include things students think are essential to civilization.

Responding to Literature

PERSONAL RESPONSE

What images from the myth linger in your mind? Record them in your journal.

Analyzing Literature

RECALL AND INTERPRET

1. What gift for human beings does Prometheus request from Zeus? Why do you think he makes such a request?
2. What is Zeus's response to the request? Do you think this response was justified? Explain your answer.
3. What series of events make up the plot of this myth? Why do you think this myth was created?

EVALUATE AND CONNECT

4. Why was fire so important to the development of human civilization?
5. Do you think Prometheus was a hero or a fool? Use examples to support your opinion.

LITERARY ELEMENTS

Theme

A **theme** is the message, or general truth about life, expressed in a work of literature. A piece of writing may have a **stated theme**, which is expressed directly, or an **implied theme**, which is revealed gradually through the thoughts and actions of the characters. There may be one theme or several in a single piece of writing.

1. What is the theme of "Prometheus"? Support your ideas with examples and quotations from the myth.
2. In a paragraph, discuss the theme of another selection you have read.

● See **Literary Terms Handbook**, p. R11.

Extending Your Response

Literature Groups

Is Knowledge Power?   In this myth, Prometheus argues that human beings need the gift of fire to bring them out of ignorance and darkness. Do you agree with him? Review your notes from the **Focus Activity** on page 742. Then discuss how the expression "Knowledge is power" relates to the theme of this myth.

Writing About Literature

Myth   Brainstorm a list of things you think are essential to civilization. Then write one or two paragraphs describing how this myth might have been the ancient Greeks' explanation for the origins of the civilized world.

✓ ASSESSMENT OPTIONS

📁 *Quick Checks,* p. 63

📁 *Selection and Theme Assessment* pp. 107–108

📁 *Performance Assessment,* p. 59

💾 *Testmaker*

LITERARY ELEMENTS

1. Knowledge can be both a useful and a dangerous tool. The givers of knowledge must take responsibility for their actions.
2. Answers will depend upon student's choice of selection.

Additional Resources

📠 *Literary Elements Transparency 63*

COMPARING SELECTIONS

Icarus and Daedalus and PROMETHEUS

COMPARE **MYTHS**

"Icarus and Daedalus" and "Prometheus" are Greek myths that portray characters attempting to use intelligence to outwit their fates. The themes of knowledge and freedom play an important role in both these myths.

1. How does Daedalus use his intelligence? Does he succeed in reaching his goal? Why or why not?
2. How does Prometheus use his intelligence? Does he succeed in reaching his goal? Why or why not?
3. How are these myths alike? How are they different?
4. Which myth do you prefer? Why?

Icarus, 1947 (detail).

COMPARE **IDEAS**

What is the meaning of the word *hero?* Are any of the characters in these two myths heroes?

- In small groups, talk about the kinds of personal characteristics, qualities, and actions that define a hero. Make a list of the characteristics of a hero. List some fictional as well as real-life examples.
- Look at each of the main characters in the two myths, and talk about whether or not each character's actions and personal qualities were heroic.
- Share your ideas and definitions in a discussion with your classmates.

COMPARE **ENDINGS**

Compare the endings of these myths. How are they alike? How are they different? How else might each of these selections have ended?

- What else might have happened to Icarus and Daedalus? Perhaps they stayed on the island of Crete or they escaped by boat. What about Prometheus? What else might have happened to him?
- Use your imagination to write an alternate ending to either myth. Feel free to use Zeus or any other Greek god or goddess in your ending, and make up any new details you wish.

A DIFFERENT DIMENSION 747

COMPARING *selections*

Objective

- To compare myths that deal with how knowledge and power can be both beneficial and dangerous

COMPARE **MYTHS**

1. He makes wings with which he can fly. He escapes from the island with Icarus, but in the end he loses his son.
2. He steals fire and gives it to human beings. He reaches his goal but is punished terribly.
3. Because ignorant Icarus and defiant Prometheus ignore advice, they suffer terrible consequences.
4. Students should support their opinions with examples.

COMPARE **IDEAS**

Students' definitions should

- include characteristics, qualities, and actions that define a hero.
- state whether the main characters in the two myths were heroes.
- support ideas with examples from each myth.

Additional Resources
📁 *Literature Groups Sourcebook*

COMPARE **ENDINGS**

Students' alternate endings should

- be based on the plot and characters in one of these myths.
- be consistent with what they know about gods and goddesses.

Teaching Options

 PORTFOLIO OPTIONS _____

Select and Reflect Have students reflect on the endings they wrote for the activity above by answering these questions:

- Is my ending based on the characters and plot of the myth?
- Have I included new elements that create a logical and very different conclusion to the story?

Students should place their alternate endings in their portfolios along with their reflections. You may wish at a later time to have them revise their work and present the endings as portfolio showcase pieces. **L2**

Additional Resources
📁 *Writing Assessment and Portfolio Management,* pp. 17–19

MEDIA Connection

Objective
- To read and understand an opera libretto

Literature LINK

The Bunyans This libretto connects to "The Bunyans," pages 750–756. While the opera text describes the magical beginning of Paul Bunyan's life and his legendary size, "The Bunyans" recounts, in tall-tale fashion, the fantastic feats of the whole Bunyan family. Explain that the text of an opera is contained in the libretto.

Respond
Possible answers include:
1. Paul Bunyan grew six inches every day, gained 346 pounds a week, was as tall as the Empire State Building, had a 3.7-mile stride, and scratched his shin with a pine tree.
2. Some students may say that since *Paul Bunyan* is a folk story, a folk singer is an appropriate choice. Others may say the composer wanted to make the song sound informal and down-to-earth, so he chose a folk singer.

Additional Resources
Media Connections, p. 14

Teaching Options

interNET CONNECTION

Opera Have students use a search engine to find out more about Benjamin Britten's opera *Paul Bunyan*. Suggest they try entering keywords like *Britten, Bunyan, opera,* and *American opera.*

MEDIA Connection

OPERA LIBRETTO
The poet W. H. Auden wrote the libretto, or text, for Benjamin Britten's opera about the American folk hero Paul Bunyan. This ballad is sung by a folk singer in the opera.

First Ballad Interlude from Benjamin Britten's *Paul Bunyan*
by W. H. Auden

The cold wind blew through the crooked thorn,
Up in the North a boy was born.

His hair was black, and his eyes were blue,
His mouth turned up at the corners too.

A fairy stood beside his bed;
"You shall never, never grow old," she said,

"Paul Bunyan is to be your name";
Then she departed whence she came.

You must believe me when I say,
He grew six inches every day.

You must believe me when I speak,
He gained 346 pounds every week.

He grew so fast, by the time he was eight,
He was as tall as the Empire State.

The length of his stride's a historical fact;
3.7 miles to be exact.

When he ordered a jacket, the New England mills
For months had no more unemployment ills.

When he wanted a snapshot to send to his friends,
They found they had to use a telephoto lens.

But let me tell you in advance,
His dreams were of greater significance.

His favorite dream was of felling trees,
A fancy which grew by swift degrees.

One night he dreamt he was to be
The greatest logger in history.

He woke to feel something stroking his brow,
And found it was the tongue of an enormous cow.

From horn to horn or from lug to lug,
Was forty-seven axe-heads and a baccy plug.

But what would have most bewildered you
Was the color of her hide, which was bright bright blue.

But Bunyan wasn't surprised at all;
Said, "I'll call you Babe, you call me Paul."

He pointed to a meadow, said, "Take a bite:
For you're leaving with me for the South tonight."

Over the mountains, across the streams
They went to find Paul Bunyan's dreams.

The bear and the beaver waved a paw,
The magpie chattered, the squirrel swore.

The trappers ran out from their lonely huts
Scratching their heads with their rifle-butts.

For a year and a day they traveled fast.
"This is the place," Paul said at last.

The forest stretched for miles around,
The sound of their breathing was the only sound.

Paul picked a pine-tree and scratched his shins,
Said, "This is the place where our work begins."

Respond
1. Paul Bunyan is a tall-tale hero, and tall tales exaggerate, or go beyond the truth. What details in the ballad are clearly exaggerations?
2. In the opera, the ballad is performed by a folk singer rather than an opera singer. Why do you think the composer might prefer that kind of voice?

Reading Minilesson

Cause and Effect Much of the humor in the Paul Bunyan stories is drawn from silly cause-and-effect relationships, as shown in the chart to the right.

Activity Have students work in small groups to create cause-and-effect "towers" for the fabled causes of Mammoth Cave, Big Sur, Bryce Canyon, the Great Sand Dunes of Colorado, the Rocky Mountains, and Old Faithful. **L2**

Cause	Teeny spills a silo of syrup in her hair.
Effect	Bears burrow into her sticky, hair.
Cause	The Bunyans cannot get the bears out of Teeny's curls.
Effect	Paul creates Niagara Falls to wash them out.

Additional Resources
Reading Workbook

Before You Read

The Bunyans and Brer Rabbit and Brer Lion

MEET AUDREY WOOD

An artist and a children's book writer, Audrey Wood created this new Paul Bunyan story to add to the wonderful tradition of the American tall tale. Wood has written and illustrated many other books in collaboration with her husband, Don Wood.

Audrey Wood lives in Santa Barbara, California.

MEET JULIUS LESTER

Julius Lester's fiction and nonfiction focuses on preserving the history and heritage of African Americans. Lester has been a professional musician and singer, a host of radio and television programs, a university professor, and a writer of both adult and children's books.

Julius Lester was born in 1939. He lives in Amherst, Massachusetts.

FOCUS ACTIVITY

Think about your favorite fictional characters. Are they realistic characters, or are they fantasy creatures or clever animals that inhabit the world of folktales and myths?

Think/Pair/Share

List some of your favorite fictional characters, and explain why you like them. Then share your ideas with a partner.

Setting a Purpose

Read to enjoy these two folktales.

BACKGROUND

Did You Know? Stories about the legendary giant Paul Bunyan were first published in Minnesota in 1910, but they were told years earlier in lumber camps around the country. As the stories were passed on, Paul's deeds grew more and more incredible until the stories developed into the type of folklore called tall tales.

The character of the trickster has appeared in the folktales of many cultures throughout the world. In Theme 4 you read a story about Anansi, a trickster in African folktales. Brer Rabbit is a version of Anansi that developed in America. (*Brer,* also spelled *br'er,* is a shortened form of *brother.*) The Brer Rabbit stories were passed on orally by African Americans for generations before anyone put them into writing.

VOCABULARY PREVIEW

cordially (kôr′ jəl lē) *adv.* in a genuinely warm and friendly way; p. 752

barren (bar′ ən) *adj.* having little or no plant life; bare; empty; p. 753

fanciful (fan′ si fəl) *adj.* showing imagination in design or construction; imaginative; p. 753

sensation (sen sā′ shən) *n.* a cause of excitement or great interest; a wonder; p. 754

colossal (kə los′ əl) *adj.* extraordinarily or awesomely large; p. 754

A DIFFERENT DIMENSION 749

Objectives

- To read and analyze a tall tale and a folktale
- To identify important elements in tall tales and folktales
- To explain what is revealed through dialogue about a story's main characters

Skills

Reading/Thinking: Problem and Solution; Drawing Conclusions; Synthesizing; Paraphrasing
Writing: Tall Tale; Sequel
Vocabulary: Etymology
Grammar/Language: Apostrophes; Quotation Marks
Listening/Speaking: Trickster Tale Dramatization
Collaboration: Literature Groups

Motivating
→OPTIONS

 Selection Focus Transparency 64: Have students view the transparency and then discuss the questions provided.

 Focus Activity: As an extension of the Focus Activity, have students write new stories that combine two or more of their favorite characters from different sources.

RESOURCE MANAGER

Lesson Planning Resource
The **Theme Seven Planning Guide** (pp. 73–78) provides additional lesson notes and reduced versions of all print resources.

📁 Other Print Resources
- Active Reading Guide, p. 64
- Vocabulary Practice, p. 46
- Reading Workbook, pp. 115–116
- Grammar and Language Workbook, pp. 267–270,

273–274
- Grammar and Composition Handbook, Lesson 13.6, 13.7
- Quick Checks, p. 64
- Selection and Theme Assessment, pp. 109–110
- Performance Assessment, p. 60
- Spanish Summaries, p. 64
- Spanish Translations
- Inclusion Strategies
- English Language Learners

Sourcebook

🖨 Transparencies
- Selection Focus 64
- Literary Elements 64
- Grammar and Language 60

Technology
- 🎧 Audio Library
- 🎧 Spanish Audio Library
- 💻 Glencoe Literature Web Site
- 💾 Testmaker

Reading the Selection

SUMMARY

"The Bunyans" is a modern retelling of the tall tale about how the famous giant woodsman, Paul Bunyan, and his family create some of the natural wonders of North America.

"Brer Rabbit and Brer Lion" is a folktale about how the cunning Rabbit outwits Lion by convincing him that a hurricane is coming. Lion lets Rabbit tie him to a tree for safety only to discover that Rabbit will not untie him. The other animals are very impressed by Rabbit's feat.

📁 *Spanish Summaries,* p. 64

A Active Reading

CONNECT Have students tell what they already know about some of the deeds that have been attributed to Paul Bunyan. Then explain that the story they will read is a modern version that adds new elements to the traditional tale.

Additional Resources

📁 *Active Reading Guide,* p. 64

🎧 *Audio Library*

🎧 *Spanish Audio Library*

Teaching Options

[A] The Bunyans

Audrey Wood

The Bunyans. Illustration by David Shannon from THE BUNYANS by Audrey Wood. Published by the BLUE SKY PRESS. Illustrations © 1996 by David Shannon. Reprinted by permission of Scholastic Inc. The BLUE SKY PRESS is a registered trademark of Scholastic Inc.

750 🐾 THEME 7

Reading *Minilesson*

Problem and Solution "The Bunyans" is a tall tale that focuses on how a family of giants solves a series of challenging problems. The result of some of their actions is the creation of some very famous American landmarks. Draw the following chart on the board.

Activity As students read the story, have them fill in the chart with the four different "problems" encountered by the Bunyans, the solutions found by the Bunyans, and the end results of their actions. **L2**

Additional Resources

📁 *Reading Workbook,* pp. 115–116

Problem	Solution	Result
Carrie loses her lucky wishbone.	She digs in the ground to find it.	Mammoth Cave is created.

Storyteller's Note

Now I suppose that you have heard about the mighty logger Paul Bunyan and his great blue ox named Babe. In the early days of our country, Paul and Babe cleared the land for the settlers, so farms and cities could spring up. And you probably know that Paul was taller than a redwood tree, stronger than fifty grizzly bears, and smarter than a library full of books. But you may not know that Paul was married and had two fine children.

A DIFFERENT DIMENSION 🦫 751

VISUALIZE Have students look carefully at the illustrations of Paul Bunyan and Babe. Encourage students to visualize how Paul and Babe would fit in a hallway of their school. Would Paul's boots fit in the average school locker?

C **Author's Craft**

MOOD Ask students who is speaking and to whom they are speaking. What atmosphere is created in the story? *(The storyteller is addressing the reader directly. The atmosphere is informal and relaxed, which helps to draw the reader in.)*

D **Literary Elements**

TALL TALE: *Character* As students read this page, ask them to identify details of a tall tale. *(Paul was taller than a redwood tree, stronger than fifty grizzly bears, and smarter than a library full of books.)*

Writing *Minilesson*

Tall Tale Explain to students that a tall tale needs to have a beginning, a middle, and an end peppered with humor and exaggeration. Readers have to be able to visualize the setting, the character(s), and the plot.

Activity Have each student write an episode in which one or more of the Bunyans produce another natural wonder, preferably a North American natural wonder that they have seen or know something about. Encourage them to make the new adventures consistent with what they know about the character traits of the Bunyan family. **L2**

Additional Resources

📕 *Writer's Choice,* Lesson 4.5

E Literary Elements

AUTHOR'S PURPOSE Have students discuss what the author's purpose is in rewriting an old American tall tale. *(Students might say that the author's primary purpose is to humorously relate the Bunyan's deeds to familiar landmarks, entertaining today's readers.)*

FYI

Mammoth Cave, located in Kentucky, is one of the largest caves in the world. It contains more than 191 miles of passageways on five levels and is thought to be over 300 million years old. The limestone from which it is formed was once the bottom of a sea.

F Active Reading

VISUALIZE Have students take a moment to visualize the humorous scene of Teeny wrestling with a big purple puma and accidentally pouring a silo of syrup on her head.

G Literary Elements

TALL TALE Ask students to list the exaggerated details in the story up to this point. *(They include Paul digging up an acre of cane; Carrie digging the cavern; the wedding invitations; Teeny wrestling a puma; the silo of syrup; bears burrowing in Teeny's curls; and Paul digging a hole in the riverbed to create Niagara Falls.)*

Teaching Options

E One day when Paul Bunyan was out clearing a road through the forests of Kentucky, a great pounding began to shake the earth. Looking around, Paul discovered an enormous hole in the side of a hill. The lumberjack pulled up an acre of dry cane and fashioned a torch to light his way.

Paul climbed inside the hole and followed the sound underground for miles, until he came to a large cavern glistening with crystals. By the flickering light of his torch, he saw a gigantic woman banging a behemoth[1] pickax against a wall.

It was love at first sight.

"I'm Carrie McIntie," the gigantic woman said. "I was sitting on the hill when my lucky wishbone fell down a crack into the earth. I've been digging all day trying to find it."

With a grin on his face as wide as the Missouri River, Paul reached into his shirt pocket. "I've got one too," he said, pulling out *his* lucky wishbone. "Marry me, Carrie, and we'll share mine."

Carrie agreed, and their wedding invitations were mailed out right away.

The invitations were so large, only one needed to be sent to each state. Everyone could read them for miles!

The invitations said: *You are cordially invited to the mammoth wedding of Paul Bunyan and Carrie McIntie.* The couple were married in the enormous crystal chamber that Carrie had carved, and after the ceremony, folks began to call it "Mammoth Cave." The giantess had dug more than two hundred miles, making it

the longest cave in the world, so the name fit perfectly.

Paul and Carrie settled down on a farm in Maine, and soon there were two new Bunyans. While Pa Bunyan traveled with his logging crew, Ma Bunyan worked the farm and cared for their jumbo boy, named Little Jean, and their gigantic girl, named Teeny.

One morning when Pa Bunyan was home between jobs, Ma Bunyan cooked up a hearty breakfast of pancakes and syrup. Teeny was wrestling with her big purple puma[2] named Slink and accidentally dumped a silo of syrup on her head. Teeny's hair was so sweet, bears crawled into it and burrowed deep in her curls. Try as they might, Pa and Ma Bunyan couldn't wash them out. **F**

"We'll need a forceful shower of water to get rid of those varmints!"[3] Ma Bunyan declared.

Pa Bunyan had an idea. He placed his daughter on Babe, and he led them to the Niagara River in Canada. The gargantuan[4] father scooped out a huge hole in the middle of the riverbed. As the great river roared down into the deep hole, Teeny cried out in delight, "Niagara falls!" Teeny showered in the waterfall, and the pesky bears were washed downstream. **G**

When Little Jean was five, he wanted to work too, so he followed his pa out to his logging camp in Montana. Thinking his son was too young to do much of

---

1. A *behemoth* (bi hē´ məth) object is monstrously large.

2. The *puma* (pū´ mə) is a mountain lion.
3. Here, *varmint* means "a pesky animal."
4. From the name of a fictional giant, *gargantuan* means "enormous; huge."

Vocabulary
cordially (kôr´ jəl lē) *adv.* in a genuinely warm and friendly way

---

INCLUSION STRATEGIES
MEETING INDIVIDUAL NEEDS

Less-Proficient Readers To help students monitor their comprehension while reading the story, you may wish to provide them with some clues to connect the play on words with actual landmarks in the United States.

Activity As students read this story, have them fill in a chart with the other stories of landmark creations.

Additional Resources
📁 *Inclusion Strategies*

Bunyan Action	Landmark Connection
Carrie McIntie was looking for her wishbone and dug an enormous crystal chamber in the side of a hill.	Mammoth Cave

anything, Paul set Little Jean down in a barren canyon in Utah to play for the day. When the lumberjack went to fetch him, he couldn't believe his eyes. Little Jean had carved the canyon into a wonderland of fanciful shapes.

Pa Bunyan got tongue-tied and said, "That's a mighty *brice* nanyon, coy, I mean, a mighty nice canyon, boy!" Somehow part of the mix-up stuck.

To this day the canyon is known as Bryce Canyon.

After all that sculpting, Little Jean's shoes were full of sand. Pa knew Ma Bunyan wouldn't want her clean floors dirtied up, so he told Little Jean to sit down and empty out his shoes.

The Bunyans. Illustration by David Shannon from THE BUNYANS by Audrey Wood. Published by the BLUE SKY PRESS. Illustrations ©1996 by David Shannon. Reprinted by permission of Scholastic, Inc. The BLUE SKY PRESS is a registered trademark of Scholastic, Inc.

Viewing the painting: This illustration was created for Audrey Wood's story. How does it add to the reader's appreciation of the tale?

H The sand from Little Jean's shoes blew away on the eastern wind and settled down a state away. It covered a valley ten miles long, making sand dunes eight hundred feet high. Everyone knows that's how the Great Sand Dunes of Colorado came to be.

I One summer, Little Jean and Teeny wanted to go to the beach. Ma Bunyan told them to follow a river to the ocean. But all the rivers flowed west back then, so they missed the Atlantic Ocean and ended up on the other side of the country instead.

Ma Bunyan tracked them out to the Pacific Ocean, where she found Teeny riding on the backs of two blue whales and Little Jean carving out fifty zigzag miles of the California coast.

When Ma Bunyan saw what her son had done, she exclaimed, "What's the big **J**

Vocabulary
barren (bar′ ən) *adj.* having little or no plant life; bare; empty
fanciful (fan′ si fəl) *adj.* showing imagination in design or construction; imaginative

A DIFFERENT DIMENSION 🐾 753

H Literary Elements

HYPERBOLE Have students identify a hyperbole in the events that take place in Utah. *(Little Jean creates sand dunes 800 feet high by dumping out his shoes.)*

V IEWING THE PAINTING

In 1998, writer and illustrator David Shannon won the prestigious Caldecott Medal for *No, David*, a book based on one he wrote and illustrated when he was only five years old.

Viewing Response *The illustration helps readers appreciate Ma Bunyan's energy and her size in relation to the trees and mountains around her.*

I Literary Elements

TALL TALE: Setting Encourage students to identify story elements that make this tall tale American. *(The story takes place entirely in the United States and describes the formation of a few famous American natural landmarks.)*

J Critical Thinking

DRAWING CONCLUSIONS Ask students to discuss how tall the Bunyans might be. *(Students might guess that the Bunyans are hundreds of feet tall based on their adventures and accomplishments.)*

MEETING INDIVIDUAL NEEDS GIFTED AND TALENTED ACTIVITY

Telling Tales "The Bunyans" is a wildly imaginative story about the fantastic adventures of the Bunyan family. This American tall tale has been passed down orally, each generation adding a little more to it, as happens in this selection.

Activity Have students work alone or in pairs to create oral presentations of

tall tales. They can be about any subject or personality they choose, but the narrators must speak directly to the listeners. Encourage students to have the characters use authentic dialect or idioms to make the presentations more interesting. When their creations are ready, the students may present them orally to the whole class. **L3**

Old Faithful's Schedule
Scientists can predict the length of time between Old Faithful's eruptions. If the geyser erupts for about two minutes, the next eruption will come between 45 and 55 minutes later. If the eruption lasts between three to five minutes, the next spouting takes longer to occur, about 70 to 80 minutes.

Historical Note

The first world's fair in London took place in 1851. It was held in an enormous structure called the Crystal Palace where an estimated six million people visited the exposition. There were about eight miles of displays. The United States sent more than 500 products, including the McCormick reaper and Goodyear rubber products.

 Author's Craft

TALL TALE Have students explain how the author modernizes this American frontier tall tale. *(The author has Little Jean Bunyan go into outer space where he seems to have left a colossal carving of his face on Mars.)*

Teaching Options

idea, sir!?" From that time on, the scenic area was known as Big Sur.

Ma Bunyan knew she had to put up a barrier to remind her children not to wander off too far. So, on the way home, everyone pitched in and built the Rocky Mountains. Teeny gathered up and sorted out all the rivers, letting some flow east and others west. After that, the children had no trouble following the eastern rivers down to the Atlantic Ocean. And when they wanted to go out exploring, Ma Bunyan would call out, "Now don't cross the Continental Divide, children!"

The best thing about camping is sleeping outdoors, and the worst thing is not having enough hot water. That's why the Bunyans always camped in Wyoming. By the time their camping years were over, Ma Bunyan had poked more than three hundred holes in the ground with her pickax and released tons of hot water from geysers. But Ma got tired of poking so many holes, so she made a geyser that blew every hour on the hour. After that, there was a steady supply of hot water to keep the giants' clothes and dishes sparkling clean.

Teeny named the geyser Old Faithful, and to this day, Old Faithful still blows its top every hour in Yellowstone National Park.

As our great country grew up, so did the Bunyan children. When the kids left home, Ma and Pa Bunyan retired to a wilderness area, where they still live happily.

Teeny hitched a ride on a whale over to England and became a famous fashion designer. Her colorful skirts made from air balloons and her breezy blouses cut from ship sails were a sensation at the first World's Fair in London.

Little Jean traveled to Venice, Italy, where he studied astronomy and art. Every day, the gondoliers would take their passengers down the Grand Canal[5] to watch the giant artist chiseling his marble sculptures.

After graduation, Little Jean decided to explore new lands, as his parents had done. So he took two great jumps and one flying leap and bounded up into outer space.

In 1976, the year of our country's bicentennial,[6] a spacecraft sent by the National Aeronautics and Space Administration was on a mission to study Mars. The spacecraft was named *Viking I,* and it took many photographs of the surface of the planet. One mysterious photo looked like a face carved out of colossal rock.

Some say the photograph is not a face, but an illusion caused by light and shadows on the rock. Others think the famous "Martian face" is just the spitting image of Little Jean Bunyan. If that's so, who knows what he's up to on the other planets.

Only time will tell!

K

---

5. *Venice* (ven' is) is a city that has canals for streets, and the *Grand Canal* is its Main Street. A *gondolier* (gon' də lēr') operates a gondola—a long, narrow, flat-bottomed boat with high peaks at the ends.
6. A *bicentennial* is a two hundredth anniversary.

Vocabulary
sensation (sen sā' shən) *n.* a cause of excitement or great interest; a wonder
colossal (kə los' əl) *adj.* extraordinarily or awesomely large

REAL-WORLD CONNECTION

Opera Libretto There are many examples of fairy tales or children's stories that have been adapted to write an opera libretto or to compose a symphonic work.

Activity Students should work in pairs to research, either in the school library or on the Internet, the different categories in which fairy tales, legends, or children's stories have been adapted for the stage.

One celebrated example is the children's fairy tale "Hansel and Gretel" that has been adapted as an opera and is performed all over the world. Students may then present their lists to the class and post them on the class bulletin board.
L2 COLLAB. LEARN.

Brer Rabbit and Brer Lion

Retold by Julius Lester ⤷

Brer Rabbit was in the woods one afternoon when a great wind came up. It blew on the ground and it blew in the tops of the trees. It blew so hard that Brer Rabbit was afraid a tree might fall on him, and he started running.

L Literary Elements

FOLKTALES: *Trickster Tale* Point out that "Brer Rabbit and Brer Lion" is one of many trickster tales that have been passed down for generations by African Americans. Tricksters are found in cultures throughout the world and they teach lessons about living.

Cultural Note

African American oral folktales were first recorded by Joel Chandler Harris in the late 1800s. In his book, a slave character named Uncle Remus told the stories. As a literary device, Harris used an exaggerated phonetic dialect. The fractured English was difficult to read. Harris's version inaccurately recorded the language and the tales themselves.

M Active Reading

PREDICT Have students use text clues and what they know about folktales to predict what might happen in this story.

Model: I know that folktales usually have a lesson to teach readers. Perhaps the rabbit will be threatened by the great winds and have to be clever to save himself. Or perhaps he will find a greater danger as he tries to take cover in the woods.

MEETING INDIVIDUAL NEEDS — ENGLISH LANGUAGE LEARNERS

Dialect "Brer Rabbit and Brer Lion" contains examples of unusual grammar, words, and spellings that may be unfamiliar to English language learners. Because this story has been told aloud for years, some parts are written in dialect.

Activity Have mixed groups work together to find other examples of words or sentences they find confusing.

Have students use a two-column chart to list the words or phrases and their meanings. **COLLAB. LEARN.**

Word or Phrase	Meaning
Ain't none here now.	There aren't any here now.

Additional Resources
📁 ***English Language Learners Sourcebook***

A DIFFERENT DIMENSION 🐾 755

SYNTHESIZING Have students discuss what they think the message of this story is. *(The message is that if you are clever enough, you can outsmart others who are more powerful.)*

VIEWING THE PAINTING

Christian Pierre, now working in Jacksonville, Florida, has had her work reproduced as book covers, on brochures, and as editorial illustrations. Another of her paintings can be seen on page 223.

Viewing Response *Lions are thought of as strong and fierce. In the tale, the unhappy Brer Lion is fearful and bumbling. The lion in the painting looks pleasant and friendly.*

Thematic Focus

A Different Dimension Have students review both stories and identify elements that take the reader into another dimension. Then invite them to discuss how the characters and events in "Brer Rabbit and Brer Lion" relate to aspects of modern life.

☑ASSESSMENT OPTIONS

📁 **Quick Checks,** p. 64

Brer Rabbit and Brer Lion

He was trucking through the woods when he ran smack into Brer Lion. Now, don't come telling me ain't no lions in the United States. Ain't none here now. But back in yonder times, all the animals lived everywhere. The lions and tigers and elephants and foxes and what 'nall run around with each other like they was family. So that's how come wasn't unusual for Brer Rabbit to run up on Brer Lion like he done that day.

"What's your hurry, Brer Rabbit?"

"Run, Brer Lion! There's a hurricane coming."

Brer Lion got scared. "I'm too heavy to run, Brer Rabbit. What am I going to do?"

"Lay down, Brer Lion. Lay down! Get close to the ground!"

Brer Lion shook his head. "The wind might pick me up and blow me away."

"Hug a tree, Brer Lion! Hug a tree!"

"But what if the wind blows all day and into the night?"

"Let me tie you to the tree, Brer Lion. Let me tie you to the tree."

Brer Lion liked that idea. Brer Rabbit tied him to the tree and sat down next to it. After a while, Brer Lion got tired of hugging the tree.

"Brer Rabbit? I don't hear no hurricane."

Brer Rabbit listened. "Neither do I."

"Brer Rabbit? I don't hear no wind."

Brer Rabbit listened. "Neither do I."

"Brer Rabbit? Ain't a leaf moving in the trees."

Brer Rabbit looked up. "Sho' ain't."

"So untie me."

"I'm afraid to, Brer Lion."

Brer Lion began to roar. He roared so loud and so long, the foundations of the Earth started shaking. Least that's what it seemed like, and the other animals came from all over to see what was going on.

When they got close, Brer Rabbit jumped up and began strutting around the tied-up Brer Lion. When the animals saw what Brer Rabbit had done to Brer Lion, you'd better believe it was the forty-eleventh of Octorerarry before they messed with him again.

Emma's Lion, 1994. Christian Pierre. Acrylic on Masonite, 16 x 20 in. Private collection.
Viewing the painting: What qualities do you usually attribute to lions? Which of these qualities does the lion in the folktale show? Which qualities do you see in the painting?

Teaching Options

Grammar and Language *Minilesson*

Apostrophes Point out Julius's frequent use of contractions in this story. Write these examples on the board:
Now, don't come telling me ain't no lions in the United States. Sho' ain't.
Discuss each contraction with students, pointing out that *ain't* is a common word in several American dialects, though it is not accepted as correct in formal English. Explain that *sho'* is short for "sure."

Activity Have students form a contraction for each word in parentheses. **L2**
1. "(I am) too heavy to run, Brer Rabbit." *(I'm)*
2. "I (do not) hear no hurricane." *(don't)*
3. "Marry me, Carrie, and (we will) share mine." *(we'll)*
4. "(What is) the big idea, sir!?" *(What's)*
L2

Additional Resources

🖥 *Grammar and Language Transparency 60*

📗 *Grammar and Language Workbook,* pp. 273–274

📗 *Grammar and Composition Handbook,* Lesson 13.7

📗 *Writer's Choice,* Lesson 20.7

Responding to Literature

PERSONAL RESPONSE

What was your reaction to these tales? Record your responses in your journal.

Analyzing Literature

RECALL

1. Describe the Bunyan family.
2. What are some of the natural features of North America that the Bunyans built?
3. What lesson does Brer Lion learn?

INTERPRET

4. Compare and contrast the ordinary actions of the Bunyans and the extraordinary results of their actions.
5. What personality traits does Brer Rabbit have that help him get the better of a much larger animal?
6. What does the final sentence in "Brer Rabbit and Brer Lion" mean? When exactly is the "forty-eleventh of Octorerarry"? Explain.
7. How do you think Brer Rabbit feels at the end of this tale? Compare his feelings with those of Brer Lion.
8. If you could add a moral, or lesson, to the end of "Brer Rabbit and Brer Lion," what would it be?

EVALUATE AND CONNECT

9. What role does humor play in these tales? Explain.
10. Which tale did you prefer? Why?

LITERARY ELEMENTS

Folktales and Tall Tales

Folktales are stories that have been passed down from generation to generation. In many folktales, the characters are animals or ordinary people who have unusual experiences. **Tall tales** are a specific kind of American folktale that often describes one aspect of frontier life, such as logging (Paul Bunyan) or cattle ranching (Pecos Bill). In tall tales, the characters, their physical attributes, and their deeds are greatly exaggerated for humorous effect.

1. Give at least two reasons why "The Bunyans" would be considered a tall tale.
2. What message about life is illustrated in "Brer Rabbit and Brer Lion"?

● See **Literary Terms Handbook,** pp. R4 and R11.

Personal Response

Students may find these tales entertaining and see that they also offer insights into how people think and live.

Analyzing Literature

1. Paul and Carrie are two giants who have two giant children, Teeny and Little Jean.
2. They are Mammoth Cave, Niagara Falls, Bryce Canyon, The Great Sand Dunes of Colorado, Big Sur, the Rocky Mountains, and Old Faithful.
3. He learns not to believe everything he hears, especially from Brer Rabbit.
4. Carrie digs in the ground and creates a huge cavern; Paul washes Teeny's hair and makes Niagara falls; Little Jean empties sand out of his shoes and makes 800-foot-high dunes.
5. He is innocent-looking but clever.
6. It means that the other animals will never bother Brer Rabbit. The date is one that doesn't exist.
7. He is very proud and full of himself, whereas Brer Lion is humiliated and angry.
8. Most students will say something like "Be very careful what you believe."
9. "The Bunyans" is funny because everything is so exaggerated, which is entertaining. The humor in Brer Rabbit helps the reader enjoy the story and get its message.

LITERARY ELEMENTS

1. The main characters are enormous giants, and they created many huge natural features.
2. Cunning can win out over brute strength.

Additional Resources

 Literary Elements Transparency 64

10. Students should explain their choices with examples from one or both of the stories.

Literature and Writing

Writing About Literature

Students' paragraphs should

- explain what they learned from dialogue about the main characters in one of the tales.
- use examples from the tale to illustrate their ideas.

Creative Writing

Students' sequels should

- describe events that may have happened after the end of one of the stories.
- include new details that are consistent with the characters of the story as it is.

Extending Your Response

Literature Groups Before students compare characters, have them list important traits for each of the main characters in "The Bunyans" and "Brer Rabbit and Brer Lion."

COLLAB. LEARN.

Performing Allow students plenty of time to research and prepare their dramatizations. You might want to have students create masks for the main characters in the story.

Interdisciplinary Activity Help students locate sources of information on wind and water erosion, rivers, geothermal activity, the formation of mountain ranges, and relevant natural forces.

◆ RESPONDING TO LITERATURE

Literature and Writing

Writing About Literature

Dialogue   Readers learn a great deal through the dialogue in a story. Write a paragraph explaining what you learned about the main characters from the dialogue in one of these folktales.

Creative Writing

Writing a Sequel   Choose one of the stories and write a sequel, or continuation, of that tale. What else might happen to the Bunyans or Brer Rabbit? Feel free to make up any details you wish.

Extending Your Response

Literature Groups

Lovable Literary Characters   Look back at your notes from the **Focus Activity** on page 749. Then discuss some of your favorite fictional characters and why you like them. Make a list of all-time favorite characters. Then compare and contrast the characters in these two tales with the characters on the list. How are they alike? How are they different?

Performing

Trickster Tale Dramatization   The trickster is a familiar figure in folktales of many cultures. The sly coyote is as well-known a trickster in Native American folklore as Brer Rabbit is in African American folktales. Working in small groups, find a trickster tale, and dramatize the tale for another class.

Interdisciplinary Activity

Science   Trace a map of the United States, and highlight the locations of the natural wonders "created" by the Bunyans. In an oral presentation, using your map as a guide, describe a tour that stops at each site. When appropriate, include information about what caused each natural wonder.

Reading Further

To read more stories by Audrey Wood or Julius Lester, try these books:
The Napping House by Audrey Wood
More Tales of Uncle Remus by Julius Lester

📖 **Save your work for your portfolio.**

Skill Minilessons

GRAMMAR AND LANGUAGE • QUOTATION MARKS

Remember these rules when using quotation marks in your writing.

- Use quotation marks before and after the exact words in a direct quotation.

  "I'm Carrie McIntie," the gigantic woman said.

- Use quotation marks with both parts of a divided quotation.

  "Brer Rabbit," said Brer Lion, "I don't hear no hurricane."

- Use commas to separate phrases such as *he said* from the quotation (as in the example above).

- Always place commas and periods inside closing quotation marks (as in the examples). Place a question mark or an exclamation point inside the quotation marks only if it is part of the quotation.

  "Hug a tree!!" Brer Rabbit exclaimed. Why do you think he told Brer Lion to "Hug a tree"?

PRACTICE In pairs, create a dialogue between two characters from either selection. Once you have written your dialogue, proofread it to check for correct punctuation. Dramatize it for the class.

- For more about the use of quotation marks, see **Language Handbook,** p. R39.

READING AND THINKING • PARAPHRASING

When you paraphrase, you use your own words to briefly restate the content of a piece of writing. Paraphrasing a written work, or a portion of it, can help you understand the writer's meaning.

PRACTICE Reread "Brer Rabbit and Brer Lion" or "The Bunyans." Then write a paragraph paraphrasing what happens in the story.

- For more about paraphrasing, see **Reading Handbook,** p. R88.

VOCABULARY • ETYMOLOGY

The word *fanciful* is related to *fancy* and *fantasy,* all of which come from the Latin word *phantasia. Phantasia,* in turn, came from the Greek word *phantasie,* which means something like "a making visible." The Greeks used the word to describe the mind's ability to "picture" something that is just an idea or isn't really there.

PRACTICE Use the etymology given above to answer the questions.

1. Which would a *fanciful* person be able to do—see long distances, see through a phony smile, or see animals in the shapes made by clouds?
2. What do you need in order to *fantasize*—a pencil, an imagination, or a camera?
3. Which word do you think comes from the same root as *fanciful*—*phantom* or *fan?*
4. Which word does not come from the same root as *fanciful*—*fantastic* or *fanatic?*

Skill Minilessons

GRAMMAR AND LANGUAGE
QUOTATION MARKS

Possible answer: "Dad, could you make a lake for me tomorrow?" asked Teeny. "I could, but I think you could do it yourself," replied Paul. "You're right," said Teeny, "but it would take me all day."

READING AND THINKING
PARAPHRASING

Brer Rabbit runs from high winds straight into Brer Lion. To save himself, he convinces Brer Lion that a hurricane is coming and that the only way to save himself is to let Rabbit tie him to a tree. After Lion is tied up, he notices that there is no storm. He asks Brer Rabbit to untie him, and when Brer Rabbit refuses, he roars with anger. This attracts all the animals, who arrive and think that Brer Rabbit is someone to be reckoned with since he has overpowered Brer Lion.

VOCABULARY
ETYMOLOGY

1. see animals in the shapes made by clouds
2. an imagination
3. phantom
4. fanatic

Additional Resources

- *Grammar and Language Workbook,* pp. 267–270
- *Grammar and Composition Handbook,* Lesson 13.6
- *Writer's Choice,* Lesson 20.6
- *Reading Workbook,* pp. 115–116
- *Vocabulary Practice,* p. 46

✔ ASSESSMENT OPTIONS

- *Quick Checks,* p. 64
- *Selection and Theme Assessment,* pp. 109–110
- *Performance Assessment,* p. 60
- *Testmaker*

Writing WORKSHOP

Objectives

- To create a personal response to literature
- To plan, draft, revise, edit, and present a book review
- To reflect on and assess one's book review

Teaching Strategies

PREWRITING

Pick a Book Point out to students that if they choose a book they feel strongly about, it will make the reviewing process easier and more interesting. A review is based in large part on the opinion of the reviewer. Therefore, the more passionately a reviewer feels about a book, the more dynamic his or her review might be.

Teaching Options

Writing WORKSHOP

Expository Writing: Book Review

Almost any book can take you to a different dimension. Yet some books grab you from the beginning, while others leave you cold. What makes the difference? After reading a book, you probably express your own thumbs-up or thumbs-down opinion. In a book review, you need to back up your opinion and help your audience decide whether to read the book.

Assignment: Follow the process explained in these pages to develop your own book review.

- As you write your book review, refer to **Writing Handbook,** pp. R48–R59.

The Writing Process

PREWRITING

PREWRITING TIP
Choose a book that you respond to strongly, either positively or negatively. Such feelings will help give your review a strong focus.

Pick a Book

To choose a book to review, try searching the library catalog for books by authors in this theme. The books listed under Reading Further will give you a good start. As an alternative, brainstorm for books that you've already read. List them under categories such as Funniest, Most Confusing, Most Predictable, Most Thought Provoking, Most True to Life, or even Most Disappointing. Then look over your list to choose a book you feel strongly about. Your teacher or a librarian may be able to help you.

Look at the Elements

After you have read or reread the book, sum up your opinion of it. To support your opinion, examine the book's literary elements. Consider its theme or themes—the insights or lessons about life that the book provides. The chart on the next page shows other elements that you might evaluate.

MEETING INDIVIDUAL NEEDS — ENGLISH LANGUAGE LEARNERS

Creating Book Jackets Depending on his or her level of proficiency, an English language learner can follow the steps in the writing process to create a book jacket for one of the selections in the theme, rather than write a book review.

Activity Review the selections students have read in this theme. Have each English language learner choose one story and create a book jacket that includes the title, the author, an illustration, a short synopsis, and the opinion of at least one reader. Students can follow the same steps as their English-proficient peers as they proceed through the Writing Workshop.

Additional Resources
📁 *English Language Learners Sourcebook*

Writing WORKSHOP

Evaluating Literary Elements

For Fiction	For Nonfiction	For Poetry
• Plot and Conflict: fast moving? suspenseful? complex?	• Point of View: biased? consistent? understandable?	• Language: sensory? emotional? creative?
• Characters: lifelike? believable? exaggerated?	• Style: formal? personal? humorous?	• Form: narrative or lyric? short? long? unusual?
• Setting: realistic? imaginative?	• Content: clear? detailed?	• Sound: rhyme? meter?

● Know Your Purpose and Audience

If you review a young-adult book, your audience will probably be your classmates. For other books, your audience may be younger children, older people, or a mixed group. Since your purpose is to persuade your audience, you'll need to supply basic information about the book. Include examples or quotations to back up each point you make. Choose examples with your readers in mind. Consider their interests, their age, and their concerns.

● Organize

Get ready to draft by filling in a form like the one below.

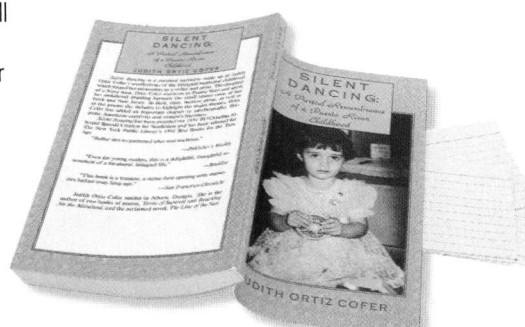

About the Book

Title: *So Far from the Bamboo Grove*

Author: *Yoko Kawashima Watkins*

Summary: *A Japanese family escapes from communist North Korea after World War II.*

My Opinion: *I like this book. It was exciting, and the people seemed real.*

Elements and Evaluation

Point of View: *Watkins wrote from the point of view of the eleven-year-old Yoko.*

Style: *Personal and realistic.*

Content: *The novel, based on the author's real-life experiences, gives a picture of a family going through difficult times.*

Look at the Elements Suggest that students make notes for their reviews as they read or reread the book. The chart on page 761 can serve as a guide for elements to keep in mind as they prepare to write. Students may also wish to create logs of quotes, images, or supporting details with page numbers for easy reference.

Know Your Purpose and Audience Point out that most people who read book reviews are readers who might be persuaded either to read or <u>avoid</u> reading the book that has been reviewed. They will be interested in the opinion of the reviewer as well as in a concise summary of the book.

Organize Have students use the form to keep track of all the information they want to include in their reviews. Point out that many book reviews present a balanced view of the book first and the opinion of the reviewer last. Others start off with the reviewer's opinion and remarks. Either way, organizing information in an efficient manner beforehand can help the reviewer write with confidence and conviction.

Additional Resources

📁 ***Writing and Proofreading Practice,*** pp. 1–7, 50–56

📋 ***Writing and Proofreading Transparencies 1–6, 37–38***

📓 ***Writer's Choice,*** Lesson 5.9

MULTIPLE LEARNING STYLES
MEETING INDIVIDUAL NEEDS

Interpersonal Students who learn best in cooperative groups may wish to work together during the organizational phase of the writing process. Establishing a book club will offer students a chance to socialize, give advice, and state opinions.

Activity Have students form small groups and pass their books around for other book club members to see and discuss. Book club members may wish to decide how to organize their reviews orally, bouncing ideas off each other. Students can take notes, create graphic organizers, or listen and organize their ideas mentally before writing. After the reviews have been written, students may wish to discuss what they learned by writing them. **L2** **COLLAB. LEARN.**

DRAFTING

Start with the Book Point out to students that a book reviewer can use wordplay in a review by create a pun out of the title of the book, such as "Readers will want to join *The Joy Luck Club* (by Amy Tan)." This is a way of mentioning the book in the beginning of the review while also hinting at the reviewer's opinion.

Support Your Opinion Remind students that it is important for a reviewer to balance information about the book with their opinions regarding it. Readers will feel frustrated if a reviewer focuses too sharply on one area and neglects another. A good reviewer is able to state his or her opinion clearly and then support it with examples from the book.

REVISING

Take a Second Look Students may wish to use stick-on notes during the revision process. This can be particularly helpful if they want to insert quotes from the books or opinions they have forgotten. Students who benefit from reading their work aloud might read to partners and ask their partners' opinions, using the "Questions for Revising" guidelines. They should also ask their partners if the reviews make them think favorably about the books or not.

Teaching Options

Writing WORKSHOP

DRAFTING

DRAFTING TIP
Include your personal responses. Writing whether you laughed out loud, yawned, were angered by the author's opinions, or couldn't put the book down will help persuade your audience.

● Start with the Book

Catch your readers' attention with a surprising quotation from the book, or with an intriguing statement about it. Then provide the basic information: the book's title and author and your summary. You can also state your opinion directly at this point—or you can save it for the end.

● Support Your Opinion

Evaluate each of the elements in your prewriting plan. Comment on strong points as well as weak points, choosing words that make your opinions clear. Back up your statements with examples or quotations. Close with a recommendation to readers.

> **MODEL · DRAFTING**
>
> Judith Ortiz Cofer's sense of humor is like a spotlight. It shows how parts of her childhood just didn't make sense. If you like to laugh, and at the same time learn about life between two cultures, read Silent Dancing.

REVISING

REVISING TIP
Keep your evaluation fair. If your opinion seems unreasonably positive or negative, you may lose your readers' trust.

TECHNOLOGY TIP
If you're revising on a computer, keep in mind that your word processor's spell-check can't distinguish between correctly spelled homonyms. If you mean *their* but type *there,* the spell-check will not detect the error.

● Take a Second Look

Take a break. Then return to your draft, looking for parts that need improvement. Use the **Questions for Revising** as guidelines. On your own or with a partner, experiment with changes until your draft satisfies you.

QUESTIONS FOR REVISING
- ☑ In my first paragraph, what other information about the book might my readers need?
- ☑ In the body of my review, which literary elements might I evaluate in more detail?
- ☑ Where might I add examples to illustrate my points?
- ☑ Which parts might be more effective if I moved them?
- ☑ Which wording could I change to reveal my opinions more clearly?

MEETING INDIVIDUAL NEEDS — INCLUSION STRATEGIES

Special Needs Any student who is visually impaired or who has a learning disability that prevents full participation in the Writing Workshop may wish to complete an adapted version of the book review assignment.

Activity Encourage the student to listen to an audiotaped version of a book of interest. Then have him or her prepare an oral book review. The final version of the book review can be taped on a cassette and "aired" for the class during the Publishing/Presenting phase of the workshop. **L1**

Additional Resources
📁 *Inclusion Strategies*

EDITING/PROOFREADING

Use the **Proofreading Checklist** to go over your revision once more, correcting errors in grammar and mechanics. Pay special attention to capitalization, as shown in the **Grammar Link** on page 712.

Grammar Hint

As you know, verbs must agree with subjects. Don't be tricked by phrases that come between subject and verb:

One of the authors <u>was</u> a famous scientist.

PROOFREADING CHECKLIST

☑ Subjects and verbs agree (double-check when a phrase comes between subject and verb).

☑ Sentences are complete; there are no fragments or run-ons.

☑ Pronouns agree with their antecedents.

☑ Modifiers are used correctly.

☑ Spelling, punctuation, and capitalization are correct.

MODEL · EDITING/PROOFREADING

Not one of those other books ~~were~~ *was* as memorable as this one.

PUBLISHING/PRESENTING

You and your classmates might compile your book reviews into a literary supplement for your school newspaper. Give your supplement a name, display the name in an eye-catching way on the first page, and lay out your reviews in columns. Invite readers' comments.

PRESENTING TIP
A literary supplement for your school newspaper might become an ongoing class project.

Reflecting

Think about the following questions, and then write responses.

- Which part of your review do you consider most persuasive? Why?

- How has writing your review changed your understanding of the book you chose? Explain.

 Save your work for your portfolio.

EDITING/PROOFREADING

Point out that many writers give their work to friends for editing and proofreading. It is sometimes difficult to see one's own errors. The "Proofreading Checklist" on the student page can help students edit their own work and can serve as a guide when they proofread their peers' reviews.

PUBLISHING/PRESENTING

Encourage students to present their book reviews to the class. Classmates can create a personal reading list based on books that were reviewed. Encourage students who created audio book reviews to play them for classmates at this time.

Reflecting

Portfolio Suggest that students ask themselves the following questions as they review their writing:

Does my book review

- provide a clear, concise summary of the book?
- present my opinion in an interesting, well-supported manner?
- persuade readers to read the book?

OR

- discourage readers from reading the book?

✔ ASSESSMENT OPTIONS

📁 ***Writing Assessment and Portfolio Management***
- Writing Assessment, pp. 1–16, 38–40
- Portfolio Management, pp. 17–19

Theme Wrap-Up

Objectives

- To offer a personal response to the stories, myths, and folklore in this theme
- To write a comparison of two stories
- To complete a self-evaluation, set a goal, and devise a plan for achieving the goal

Responding to the Theme

1. Students should provide insight into the reasons for their choices.
2. Accept all thoughtful answers and observations.
3. Allow time for students to share their charts, travel itineraries, and dioramas with classmates.

Analyzing Literature

Students' writing should include

- an introductory paragraph identifying the characters and stories to be compared.
- an analysis of the characters' differences and similarities.
- examples and details from the stories.

Evaluate

Have students list activities they have completed for each task on this page. Suggest that they add other tasks as well, such as creating a graphic.

Have students use the class rubric they developed in the first theme's evaluation to assess their work.

Set Goals

Have students record their goals and plot steps for achieving them on a timeline. Discuss students' goals and plans in individual conferences.

 A DIFFERENT DIMENSION

Theme Wrap-Up

Responding to the Theme

1. Which myth, legend, folktale, or story in this theme did you most enjoy reading? What was it about the story that you particularly liked?

2. What new ideas do you have about the following as a result of reading the literature in this theme?
   - the use of supernatural characters to further the plot of a story
   - the way imaginative settings or situations add interest to a story

3. Present your theme project to the class.

Analyzing Literature

COMPARE TALES

Compare the characters from any two stories in this theme. How are they alike? How do they differ? How do they cope with any problems or difficulties they encounter? Support your analysis with quotations from the selections.

Evaluate and Set Goals

1. Which of the following tasks did you find most rewarding? Which was most difficult?
   - reading and thinking about the stories
   - doing independent writing
   - analyzing the stories in discussions
   - performing dramatizations
   - doing research

2. Using the following scale, how would you assess your work in this theme? Give at least two reasons for your assessment.

   4 = outstanding   2 = fair
   3 = good   1 = weak

3. Based on what you found difficult in this theme, choose a goal to work toward in the next theme.
   - Write your goal and three steps you will take to help you reach it.
   - Meet with your teacher to review your goal and your plan for achieving it.

 Build Your Portfolio

SELECT	REFLECT
Select two pieces of work you did during this theme to include in your portfolio. Use the following questions to help you decide.	Write some notes to accompany the work you selected. Use the following questions to guide you.

SELECT
- Which work do you consider your best work?
- From which work did you learn the most?
- Which work "stretched" you the most?
- Which work did you enjoy the most?

REFLECT
- What do you like best about the piece?
- What did you learn from creating it?
- What might you do differently if you were beginning this piece again?

764   THEME 7

 ASSESSMENT OPTIONS

📁 ***Writing Assessment and Portfolio Management***
- Writing Assessment, pp. 1–16, 38–40
- Portfolio Management, pp. 17–19

GLENCOE
TECHNOLOGY

 MINDJOGGER VIDEOQUIZZES
VIDEODISC

Use *MindJogger* to review the Theme 7 content.

Theme 7
Side B

 Also available in VHS.

Reading on Your Own

Have you enjoyed reading the literature in this theme? If so, you might be interested in the following books.

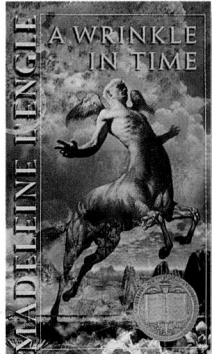

A Wrinkle in Time
by Madeleine L'Engle In this award-winning novel, Meg and Charles, along with their friend Calvin, search through time and space for their missing father.

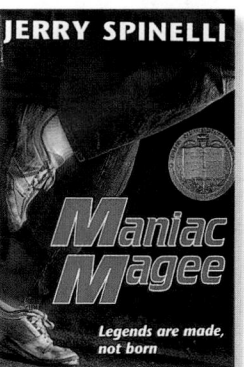

Maniac Magee
by Jerry Spinelli A modern-day folktale about a twelve-year-old boy who appears in a town, amazes everyone with his deeds, and becomes a legend.

Big Men, Big Country: A Collection of American Tall Tales
by Paul Robert Walker Stories portray nine American tall-tale heroes, including Paul Bunyan, Pecos Bill, Sluefoot Sue, and Davy Crockett.

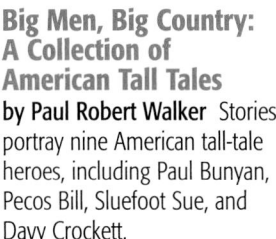

Cut from the Same Cloth: American Women of Myth, Legend, and Tall Tale
by Robert D. San Souci The author retells stories about legendary, larger-than-life women from various American cultures.

Reading on Your Own

Glencoe Literature Library

Wrinkle in Time by Madeline L'Engle is one of Literature titles available in the *Glencoe Library*. For a complete listing, see pages 46–47 in this book.

The *Glencoe Literature Library: Study Guide* provides instructional support and student activities for works in the *Glencoe Literature Library*.

At the MOVIES

Be sure to preview the following video for appropriateness for your class.

• *The Day the Earth Stood Still* (1951, 88 minutes, G) concentrates more on characters and its message then on special effects. Many regard it as a science fiction classic.

MEETING INDIVIDUAL NEEDS — INCLUSION STRATEGIES

You may wish to recommend Madeleine L'Engle's *A Wrinkle in Time* to your less-proficient readers. The storyline is easy to follow, and the narrative writing and dialogue are quite manageable. **L1**

Activity The following books are rated for average readers (L2) or for students who need more challenging material (L3).

• *Big Men, Big Country: A Collection of American Tall Tales* by Paul Robert Walker **L2**
• *Cut from the Same Cloth: American Women of Myth, Legend, and Tall Tale* by Robert D. San Souci **L2**
• *Maniac Magee* by Jerry Spinelli **L3**

Additional Resources
📁 *Inclusion Strategies*

Standardized Test Practice

Answers and Analyses

1. **D** Choices A and C contain sentence fragments and can be eliminated. As written, choice B is a run-on sentence. Independent clauses should be separated by a conjunction and a comma. Therefore the best choice is D.

2. **J** Choices F and H are awkward constructions. There is no reason to join the clauses with the word, *and,* or to add the word, *or.* Choice G contains sentence fragments and can be eliminated.

 TEST-TAKING TIP

Each new question on a test should be done as if on a clean slate. Once students have read a question, considered the choices and picked an answer, they should put that question behind. Students can always go back for a second look, but they should not let troublesome questions distract them while they're working on other questions.

 TEST-TAKING TIP

Part of training for any verbal or reading test should include as much reading as possible. Students should challenge themselves with books or newspapers that will require them to use a dictionary. The New York Times is a good example of one such source.

Standardized Test Practice

Read the passage. Some sections are underlined. The underlined sections may be one of the following:

- Incomplete sentences
- Run-on sentences
- Correctly written sentences that should be combined
- Correctly written sentences that do not need to be rewritten

Choose the best way to write each underlined section. Mark the letter for your answer on your paper. If the underlined section needs no change, mark the choice "Correct as is."

> According to new research, the number of North American adults using the
> (1)
> Internet has surged to 79 million, an increase of 21 million, or 36 percent, since
>
> this time last year. Web-savvy kids are teaching their parents about cyberspace.
>
> Only 18 million adults were using the Internet when the research was first
> (2)
> conducted in 1995.

1 A According to new research, the number of North American adults using the Internet has surged to 79 million. An increase from 21 million, or 36 percent, since this time last year.

B According to new research, the number of North American adults using the Internet has surged to 79 million and this is an increase of 21 million, or 36 percent, since this time last year.

C According to new research, the number of North American adults using the Internet has surged to 79 million. Increased 21 million, or 36 percent, since this time last year.

D Correct as is

2 F Only 18 million adults were using the Internet and the research was first conducted in 1995.

G Only 18 million adults were using the Internet. The research first conducted in 1995.

H Only 18 million adults were using the Internet and only the research was first conducted in 1995.

J Correct as is.

Read the passage and decide which type of error, if any, appears in each underlined section. Mark the letter for your answer on your paper.

Dear Sven,

<u>Its been a long time</u> since we last spoke. <u>I hope you are doing well</u> in Norway.
(1)   (2)
I enjoyed <u>visitting you and your</u> family last month. Please thank your parents for
(3)
letting us stay with you <u>and for cooking that great european food!</u> We had a
(4)
wonderful time. My sister was especially impressed with the tall mountains going

straight down into the sea.

I have been telling <u>my friends here in Provo Utah about you.</u> They all want
(5)
to go to Norway now! Maybe next year you and your family can come to my

house and see where we live. Thanks again for the fun trip.

<u>your friend,</u>
(6)
Carnelo

---

1 **A** Spelling error

   B Capitalization error

   C Punctuation error

   D No error

2 **F** Spelling error

   G Capitalization error

   H Punctuation error

   J No error

3 **A** Spelling error

   B Capitalization error

   C Punctuation error

   D No error

4 **F** Spelling error

   G Capitalization error

   H Punctuation error

   J No error

5 **A** Spelling error

   B Capitalization error

   C Punctuation error

   D No error

6 **F** Spelling error

   G Capitalization error

   H Punctuation error

   J No error

STOP

Answers and Analyses

1. **C** Since this occurrence of the word *its* is intended as a contraction of *it has,* an apostrophe is required.
2. **J** There is no error in this sentence.
3. **A** The word *visiting* is misspelled.
4. **G** The word European, like any adjective denoting a nationality, should be capitalized.
5. **C** Students should recognize that a comma is needed before and after the name of a state when it is used with a city.
6. **G** The opening and closing formalities in a letter, such as *Yours Truly* and *Your Friend,* should be capitalized.

THE PRINCETON REVIEW **TEST-TAKING TIP**

Students do not have to answer the questions in the order they are presented. They should answer the questions in the order that they feel most comfortable with. If a student is having trouble with the first question, he or she should skip it and come back to it later. Often a difficult question will be easy to answer after a student has completed the easier questions.

Theme 8 At a Glance
A Delicate Balance

THEME OPENING ➜ **Theme 8: A DELICATE BALANCE**

- Introducing the Theme (p. 769)
- Exploring the Theme (p. 770)
- Theme Projects (p. 771)

SELECTIONS

We Are All One (p. 772)

Media Connection: *from* "See Bobby Run" (p. 780)

Birdfoot's Grampa (p. 782)

Miracles (p. 782)

Media Connection: The Jungle Book (p. 787)

Rikki-tikki-tavi (p. 788)

Uncle Tony's Goat (p. 806)

 Loo-Wit (p. 818)

The Flower-Fed Buffaloes (p. 822)

Turkeys (p. 826)

The Pasture (p. 834)

Short Poems (p. 840)

SKILL FEATURES

Vocabulary Skills (p. 781)

Interdisciplinary Connection (p. 805)

Grammar Link (p. 816)

Listening, Speaking, and Viewing (p. 817)

Making Inferences (p. 833)

Genre Focus: Short Forms of Poetry (pp. 838–839)

WRITING WORKSHOP

Expository Writing: Cause-and-Effect Essay (pp. 846–849)

THEME WRAP-UP

- **Responding to the Theme, Analyzing Literature, Evaluate and Set Goals** (p. 850)
- **Build Your Portfolio** (p. 850)
- **Reading on Your Own** (p. 851)

  The Call of the Wild by Jack London

  Cricket Never Does: A Collection of Haiku and Tanka by Myra Cohn Livingston

  Hatchet by Gary Paulsen

  My Life with the Chimpanzees by Jane Goodall

- **Standardized Test Practice** (pp. 852–853)

KEYS TO LITERARY CONNECTIONS

 Comparing Selections

The **Comparing Selections** feature in this theme provides opportunities for addressing diverse aspects of the reading and literature curriculum.

For example, in Comparing Selections on page 825, students compare the themes and poetic language of "Loo-Wit" and "The Flower-Fed Buffaloes." Students are asked to consider the relationship human beings have with nature.

KEYS TO TEACHING OPTIONS

 Block Scheduling

Activities that are particularly suited to use within a block scheduling framework are identified throughout this theme by the following designation: For detailed suggestions on block scheduling, see the **Block Scheduling Guide** for this grade level.

Key to Ability Levels

The Teaching Options throughout this theme have been coded for students of various abilities.

L1 BASIC activities for all students

L2 AVERAGE activities for average to above-average students

L3 CHALLENGING activities for above-average students

Theme 8 At a Glance
A Delicate Balance

Reading Skills in this theme

Variety of Texts
In addition to short forms of poetry, this theme includes the following text types:
- folktale
- short story
- humorous essay
- cartoon
- journal entry
- movie review

Comprehension Skills
The following instructional support for comprehension skills appears in this theme of the Student Edition:
- **Reading and Thinking Minilessons** (pp. 804, 815, 821, 832, 845)
- **Making Inferences** (p. 833)

See also the **Reading Minilessons** throughout the theme in this Teacher's Wraparound Edition.

Reading Resources

Comprehension Skills Resources

📂 **Active Reading Guides**
The **Active Reading Guide** provides graphic organizers and study guide questions to support students' reading of each selection (**Active Reading Guide**, pp. 65–73).

📂 **Reading Workbook**
The **Reading Workbook** (pp. 117–124) includes additional instruction and reinforcement of reading strategies and skills.

🎧 **Audio Library**
Available both on tape and on CD, the **Audio Library** provides valuable comprehension support.

Resources for Reading Widely

Glencoe Literature Library
Each title in the *Glencoe Literature Library* includes a full-length novel or play plus related readings. A separate Study Guide is available for each title.

💿 **Literature Classics CD-ROM**
The selections on this CD-ROM can be searched by author, theme, or genre.

 *in*TIME
A coproduction of Glencoe and Time, Inc., the *inTime* magazine includes a wealth of high interest nonfiction related to the selections in Theme Eight.

✔ Assessment in this theme

Assessment Options in the Student Edition
Glencoe Literature offers a number of diverse ways to evaluate student understanding and skill proficiency. In the Student Edition, use the following:
- **Responding to Literature**
  Following each selection, students are asked to recall facts, interpret ideas, and evaluate concepts as they answer a variety of questions and complete activities to extend their understanding.
- **Theme Wrap-Up (pp. 850–851)**
  Here students respond to the selections on personal and analytical levels. They also assume ownership of their learning by setting and evaluating goals and by selecting work for their portfolios.

See also the many **Assessment Resources** listed on the facing page.

 THE PRINCETON REVIEW

Standardized Test Practice
The Princeton Review has developed the Standardized Test Practice pages found at the end of this theme (pp. 852–853). These pages contain practice test questions that help students remain familiar with standardized test formats and content.
- **ITBS Preparation and Practice**
- **SAT-9 Preparation and Practice**
- **TerraNova Preparation and Practice**

Writing Skills in this theme

Writing Skills

The Student Edition of Theme Eight offers strong instructional support for writing skills:

In **Extending Your Response**, which follows each selection:
• **Writing About Literature**
• **Personal/Creative Writing**

See also the **Writing Minilessons** throughout the theme in this Teacher's Wraparound Edition.

Writing Workshops

Theme Eight concludes with a **Writing Workshop** that guides students through the process of writing a cause-and-effect essay (pp. 846–849).

Writing Resources

⊙ Writer's Assistant CD-ROM

Each Writing Workshop is supplemented by an interactive writing guide on the Writer's Assistant CD-ROM. This easy-to-use writing guide provides prompts, templates, and other tools that lead students through the writing process.

📁 Writing and Proofreading Practice

Blackline masters present in-depth instruction and practice on a specific step in the writing process and proofreading (pp. 1–7, 57–63).

Writing and Proofreading Transparencies

Transparencies provide graphic organizers and proofreading exercises for whole-class instruction (pp. 1–6, 23–24, 39–40).

📕 Research and Report Writing Guide

This resource provides extensive tips and activities to guide students in their writing projects in the literature classroom as well as in classes across the curriculum.

📕 Style and Documentation Sourcebook for Writers

This sourcebook is a combination reference and workbook, giving students the most up-to-date information and guidance regarding traditional as well as technological research strategies and documentation.

📕 Grammar and Composition Handbook

The Grammar and Composition Handbook provides instruction that supplements activities in the student textbook.

Assessment Resources

📁 Selection Quick Checks

For each selection, a Quick Check of three to five short-answer questions measures students' literal comprehension.

📁 Selection and Theme Assessment

The Selection and Theme Assessment instrument tests students' abilities to recall, interpret, and evaluate what they've read. The tests consist of multiple-choice, short answer, and essay questions.

📁 Performance Assessment

Alternative assessment instruments and rubrics for Theme Eight are found in the Performance Assessment ancillary.

📁 Writing Assessment and Portfolio Management

These notes and strategies, student models, and assessment tools assist with the task of measuring students' progress as writers and as monitors of their own writing.

💾 Testmaker

Teachers can customize selection and Theme Eight tests by accessing the Testmaker database.

📼 Mindjogger Videoquizzes

Using a popular game show format, Mindjogger Videoquizzes enable teachers to evaluate student understanding of Theme Eight in a quick and fun manner.

SELECTIONS	Literary Elements	Reading and Thinking	Writing	Vocabulary and Spelling	

We Are All One
 	
LAURENCE YEP
	Plot, SE p. 778
	Character, TWE p. 774
	Plot: Sequence of Events,
	  TWE pp. 774, 775
	Repetition, TWE p. 775
	Theme, TWE p. 777
	Folktale, TWE p. 777
		Drawing Conclusions,
		  TWE p. 774
		Inferring, TWE p. 775
		Monitoring Comprehension,
		  TWE p. 775
			Paragraph (Imagery),
			  SE p. 779
			Journal Entry, SE p. 779
				Synonyms, SE p. 779
				Etymology, TWE p. 776	

Birdfoot's Grampa JOSEPH BRUCHAC Miracles WALT WHITMAN	Theme, SE p. 785 *Characterization, TWE p. 783*	*Using Graphic Aids, TWE p. 784*	Describing a Character, SE p. 786 Short Poem, SE p. 786		

Rikki-tikki-tavi
 	
RUDYARD KIPLING
	Anthropomorphism, SE p. 802;
	  TWE pp. 790, 791, 796,
	  797, 798, 799, 801
	Narrator, TWE p. 790
	Characteriztion, TWE p. 793
	Humor, TWE p. 796
	Mood, TWE p. 797
	Onomatopoeia, TWE p. 799
		Evaluating, SE p. 804
		Inferring, TWE pp. 791, 794
		Using Graphic Aids,
		  TWE p. 791
		Drawing Conclusions,
		  TWE p. 792
		Identifying Bias, TWE p. 795
		Evaluating, TWE p. 798
			Explanation (Setting),
			  SE p. 803
			News Article, SE p. 803
			Writing from Another Point of
			  View, TWE p. 797
				Dictionary Skills: Definitions,
				  SE p. 804
				Word Origins, TWE p. 792
				Etymology, TWE p. 795	

Uncle Tony's Goat
 	
LESLIE MARMON SILKO
	Narrator, SE p. 813;
	  TWE p. 808, 811
	Foreshadowing, TWE p. 809
		Problem/Solution, SE p. 815
		Logical Reasoning, TWE p. 808
		Graphic Aids, TWE p. 809
		Drawing Conclusions,
		  TWE pp. 811, 812
			Paragraph (Setting), SE p. 814
			Rewrite Story, SE p. 814
				Unlocking Meaning,
				  SE p. 815	

Loo-Wit
 	
WENDY ROSE
	Extended Metaphor,
	  SE p. 820
	Extended Metaphor,
	  TWE p. 819
		Elaborating, SE p. 821	Describing a Poem's Impact,
			  SE p. 821
			Metaphor, SE p. 821		

The Flower-Fed Buffaloes VACHEL LINDSAY	Alliteration, SE p. 824 *Alliteration, TWE p. 823*	*Identifying Assumptions,* *TWE p. 823*			

TURKEYS
 	
BAILEY WHITE
	Author's Purpose, SE p. 830
	Author's Purpose,
	  TWE pp. 828, 829
		Cause and Effect, SE p. 832
		Evaluating, TWE p. 829
		Problem and Solution,
		  TWE p. 829
			Another Point of View,
			  SE p. 831
			Journal Entry, SE p. 831
				The Prefix *de–*, SE p. 832	

The **Pasture**
 	
ROBERT FROST
	Rhythm: End-Stopped Lines,
	  SE p. 836; TWE p. 835
	End-Stopped Lines,
	  TWE p. 835
	Assonance, TWE p. 835
			Paragraph (Mood), SE p. 837
			Poem, SE p. 837
				Mechanics: Semicolon, Colon,
				  SE p. 837	

Short Poems
 	
MATSUO BASHŌ   MYRA COHN LIVINGSTON
RAYMOND R. PATTERSON   ANNE ATWOOD
	Personification, SE p. 843;
	  TWE pp. 841, 842
	Symbol, TWE p. 841
	Haiku, TWE p. 841
		Spatial Rel./Order, SE p. 845
		Comparing and Contrasting,
		  TWE p. 842
			Imagery/Mood, SE p. 844
			Cinquain or Limerick,
			  SE p. 844
				Compound Words, SE p. 845	

Key: Student material is in roman. Teacher material is in italic.   💻 Technology   **COLLAB. LEARN.** Collaboration

Grammar and Language	Listening, Speaking, and Viewing	Life Skills	Study, Research, and Technology
Past Perfect Tense, TWE p. 776	**COLLAB. LEARN.** Literature Groups, SE p. 779 **COLLAB. LEARN.** Storytelling, SE p. 779		Interdisciplinary Activity: Research Buddhism, SE p. 779 *Nature,* TWE p. 777
Sensory Language, SE p. 786	**COLLAB. LEARN.** Literature Groups, SE p. 786 Appreciating Poetry, SE p. 786		
Personal Pronouns, SE p. 804 *Using Semicolons,* TWE p. 800	**COLLAB. LEARN.** Literature Groups, SE p. 803 Performing: Readers Theater, SE p. 803 **COLLAB. LEARN.** *Analyzing a Video,* TWE p. 796 *Interviewing,* TWE p. 799	*Interviewing,* TWE p. 799	Interdisciplinary Activity: Research Snakes, SE p. 803 *Research Animals,* TWE p. 795
Consistent Verb Tenses, SE p. 815 *Apostrophes in Contractions,* TWE p. 812	**COLLAB. LEARN.** Literature Groups, SE p. 814	Learning for Life: Police Report, SE p. 814	🖥 Internet Connection, SE p. 814
	COLLAB. LEARN. Literature Groups, SE p. 821 Role-Play, SE p. 821		
Using Hyphens, TWE p. 823	**COLLAB. LEARN.** Literature Groups, SE p. 824 Poetry Reading, SE p. 824		
Run-On Sentences, SE p. 832	**COLLAB. LEARN.** Literature Groups, SE p. 831		Interdisciplinary Activity: Research Birds, SE p. 831 🖥 Internet Connection, SE p. 831
COLLAB. LEARN. Literature Groups, SE p. 837 Read Poems Aloud, SE p. 837 **COLLAB. LEARN.** *Choral Speaking,* TWE p. 835			
Prepositional Phrases, SE p. 845	**COLLAB. LEARN.** Lit. Grp., SE p. 844 **COLLAB. LEARN.** Readers' Theater, SE p. 844 **COLLAB. LEARN.** Literature Groups, SE p. 844		

SELECTIONS	📁 Print Resources		
We Are All One LAURENCE YEP	Theme Eight Planning Guide, pp. 6–13 * Active Reading Guide, p. 65 Vocabulary Practice, p. 47	Grammar & Comp. Handbook, Lesson 3.8 Grammar & Language Workbook, pp. 93–94 Reading Workbook, pp. 117–118	* Quick Checks, p. 65 Sel. and Th. Assess., pp. 111–112 Performance Assessment, p. 61 Spanish Summaries, p. 65 Spanish Translations
Birdfoot's Grampa JOSEPH BRUCHAC **Miracles** WALT WHITMAN	Theme Eight Planning Guide, pp. 14–18 * Active Reading Guide, p. 66	Grammar & Comp. Handbook, Lesson 5.1 Grammar & Language Workbook, pp. 117–118	* Quick Checks, p. 66 Sel. and Th. Assess., pp. 113–114 Performance Assessment, p. 62 Spanish Summaries, p. 66
Rikki-tikki-tavi RUDYARD KIPLING	Theme Eight Planning Guide, pp. 19–26 * Active Reading Guide, p. 67 Vocabulary Practice, p. 48	Grammar & Comp. Handbook, Lessons 4.1, 13.5 Grammar & Language Workbook, pp. 103–104, 265–266 Reading Workbook, pp. 119–120	* Quick Checks, p. 67 Sel. and Th. Assess., pp. 115–116 Performance Assessment, p. 63 Spanish Summaries, p. 67 Spanish Translations
Uncle Tony's Goat LESLIE MARMON SILKO	Theme Eight Planning Guide, pp. 27–34 * Active Reading Guide, p. 68 Vocabulary Practice, p. 49	Grammar & Comp. Handbook, Lessons 3.5, 13.7 Grammar & Language Workbook, pp. 83–84, 273–274 Reading Workbook, pp. 121–122	* Quick Checks, p. 68 Sel. and Th. Assess., pp. 117–118 Performance Assessment, p. 64 Spanish Summaries, p. 68
Loo-Wit WENDY ROSE	Theme Eight Planning Guide, pp. 35–39 * Active Reading Guide, p. 69		* Quick Checks, p. 69 Sel. and Th. Assess., pp. 119–120 Performance Assessment, p. 65 Spanish Summaries, p. 69
The Flower-Fed Buffaloes VACHEL LINDSAY	Theme Eight Planning Guide, pp. 40–44 * Active Reading Guide, p. 70	Grammar and Comp. Handbook, Lesson 13.8 Grammar and Language Workbook, pp. 275–276	* Quick Checks, p. 70 Sel. and Th. Assess., pp. 119–120 Performance Assessment, p. 65 Spanish Summaries, p. 70 Spanish Translations
TURKEYS BAILEY WHITE	Theme Eight Planning Guide, pp. 45–51 * Active Reading Guide, p. 71 Vocabulary Practice, p. 50	Grammar & Comp. Handbook, Lesson 1.6 Grammar & Language Workbook, pp. 26–27, 57–58 Reading Workbook, pp. 123–124	* Quick Checks, p. 71 Sel. and Th. Assess., pp. 121–122 Performance Assessment, p. 66 Spanish Summaries, p. 71 Spanish Translations
The Pasture ROBERT FROST	Theme Eight Planning Guide, pp. 52–56 * Active Reading Guide, p. 72	Grammar & Comp. Handbook, Lesson 13.5 Grammar & Language Workbook, pp. 265–266	* Quick Checks, p. 72 Sel. and Th. Assess., p. 123 Performance Assessment, p. 67 Spanish Summaries, p. 72 Spanish Translations
Short Poems MATSUO BASHŌ MYRA COHN LIVINGSTON RAYMOND R. PATTERSON ANNE ATWOOD	Theme Eight Planning Guide, pp. 57–61 * Active Reading Guide, p. 73	Grammar & Comp. Handbook, Lesson 7.1 Grammar & Language Workbook, pp. 141–142	* Quick Checks, p. 73 Sel. and Th. Assess., p. 124 Performance Assessment, p. 68 Spanish Summaries, p. 73 Spanish Translations

*Also available in Spanish

Transparencies	Technology Resources
Selection Focus Transparency 65 Grammar and Language Transparency 61 Literary Elements Transparency 65	Audio Library Spanish Audio Library Vocabulary Puzzlemaker Web Site: lit.glencoe.com
Selection Focus Transparency 66 Literary Elements Transparency 66 Fine Art Transparency 19	Literature Launchers Audio Library Spanish Audio Library Vocabulary Puzzlemaker Web Site: lit.glencoe.com
Selection Focus Transparency 67 Grammar and Language Transparency 62 Literary Elements Transparency 67	Literature Launchers Audio Library Spanish Audio Library Vocabulary Puzzlemaker Web Site: lit.glencoe.com
Selection Focus Transparency 68 Grammar and Language Transparency 63 Literary Elements Transparency 68	Literature Launchers Audio Library Spanish Audio Library Vocabulary Puzzlemaker Web Site: lit.glencoe.com
Selection Focus Transparency 69 Literary Elements Transparency 69	Audio Library Spanish Audio Library Vocabulary Puzzlemaker Web Site: lit.glencoe.com
Selection Focus Transparency 70 Literary Elements Transparency 70	Audio Library Spanish Audio Library Vocabulary Puzzlemaker Web Site: lit.glencoe.com
Selection Focus Transparency 71 Literary Elements Transparency 71	Audio Library Spanish Audio Library Vocabulary Puzzlemaker Web Site: lit.glencoe.com
Selection Focus Transparency 72 Literary Elements Transparency 72	Audio Library Spanish Audio Library Vocabulary Puzzlemaker Web Site: lit.glencoe.com
Selection Focus Transparency 73 Literary Elements Transparency 73 Fine Art Transparency 6	Audio Library Spanish Audio Library Vocabulary Puzzlemaker Web Site: lit.glencoe.com

Theme RESOURCES

- Listening and Speaking Activities (pp. 22–24)
- Viewing and Representing Activities (pp. 1–6, 28–30)
- Critical Thinking Skills (pp. 20–22)
- Media Connection Activities (pp. 15–16)
- Interdisciplinary Activities (pp. 30–33)
- Family and Community Activities (pp.18–19)
- Selection and Theme Assessment (pp. 139–140)

See also these additional planning resources:
- English Language Learners Sourcebook
- Inclusion Strategies Sourcebook
- Literature Groups Sourcebook

Use Glencoe's *Presentation Plus!* This multi-media teaching tool lets you present dynamic lessons that will engage your students. Using Microsoft PowerPoint®, you can customize the presentation to create your own personalized lessons.

A Delicate Balance

Theme Objectives

- To enjoy reading about the natural world and people's place within it
- To analyze the literary elements in nonfiction, poetry, folktale, and short story selections
- To apply strategies for reading short forms of poetry

Teaching Strategies

Have students read the quotation from Woody Guthrie's song in preparation for the questions below.

VIEWING THE PAINTING

In Chilean-born Gustavo Novao's dreamlike paintings, predators and their prey coexist peacefully in the wild, and even in modern urban settings.

Responding to the Art Discussion Questions:
- What animals do you see in this paining? *(lion, ostrich, zebras)*
- Where are they? *(in Central Park)*
- How would you relate the painting to the theme? *(Wild animals appear to be at home in a city park—in balance with each other and with an urban setting.)*

A Delicate Balance

Central Park. Gustavo Novoa (b. 1941). 24 x 18 in. Wally Findlay Galleries, New York.

768

TEACHER to TEACHER

To impress upon students the importance of balance, I have them all stand with their left foot and left shoulder touching a wall. On command they are to lift their right foot off the floor. In this off-balanced position, anyone managing to lift his/her foot would fall, but most students don't even try because the brain realizes the body is unbalanced and automatically communicates that to the foot. Then, we brainstorm all the activities and catch phrases in which balance plays a part and discuss how prevalent the idea of balance is in our lives. I use the idea of the scales of justice as a jumping off point for another class discussion. I ask them about their thoughts and ideas concerning balance as it relates to the scales of justice.

KAREN D. THOMPSON

THEME 8

THEME CONTENTS

We Are All One • folktale by Laurence Yep 773

Birdfoot's Grampa • poem by Joseph Bruchac 783

Miracles • poem by Walt Whitman 784

Rikki-tikki-tavi • short story by Rudyard Kipling 789

Uncle Tony's Goat •
    short story by Leslie Marmon Silko 807

Loo-Wit • poem by Wendy Rose 819

The Flower-Fed Buffaloes •
    poem by Vachel Lindsay 823

Turkeys • humorous essay by Bailey White 827

The Pasture • poem by Robert Frost 835

GENRE FOCUS *SHORT FORMS OF POETRY*

Glory, Glory;
Birds Circling at Dusk; and
Bamboo Grove •
    haiku by Raymond R. Patterson, Anne Atwood,
    and Matsuo Bashō 841
T-Shirt and
There Was a Young Fellow of Ealing •
    cinquain by Myra Cohn Livingston and
    anonymous limerick 842

A DELICATE BALANCE 769

> ❝ *This land is your land, this land is my land . . . This land was made for you and me.* ❞
>
> —Woody Guthrie

Introducing the Theme

Direct your students' attention to the **Theme Contents.** Ask them to read through the list of selections. Present these questions for discussion:

- Does the tone of the theme seem friendly or unfriendly toward the natural world? Explain your response. *(Students may say that titles such as "We Are All One," "Miracles," "Turkeys," "The Pasture," and "Flower-Fed Buffaloes" seem to be friendly toward nature.)*
- Are there any words in these titles that sound nonsensical to you? *(possibly "Rikki-tikki-tavi" and "Loo-Wit")* What might they mean?
- Do you recognize the name of the man who wrote "Birdfoot's Grandpa"? Where have you read the words of Joseph Bruchac before? *(Students may recall discussing Joseph Bruchac's words from* Flying with the Eagle, Racing the Great Bear *in Theme 3, page 216: "Sooner or later, each of us must… challenge our own monsters, with our survival in the balance.")*

FINE ART
TRANSPARENCY 16

You may wish to use **Fine Arts Transparency 16** to explore what *delicate balance* connotes.

LITERATURE & HUMANITIES

Have students examine the painting *Summer and Winter* from the CD *National Museum of Women in the Arts* and use these two mythical characters as a starting point for writing a short myth of their own.

RESOURCE MANAGER

See the *Theme Eight Planning Guide* (pp. 1–5) for additional teaching notes, strategies, and resources for introducing the theme "A Delicate Balance."

GLENCOE
TECHNOLOGY

LITERATURE CLASSICS
CD-ROM
Search for other selections related to the theme "A Delicate Balance."

Exploring the Theme

A Delicate Balance

- Some students may think that we interact responsibly and compassionately with the natural world, while others may disagree, citing a history of environmentally dangerous practices.
- Students may say that the world as seen through the eyes of other creatures would differ from the way it looks to us. Animals who are hunted or killed for food and skins are probably afraid of humans and find the world a treacherous place; our pets, on the other hand, probably see the world as a safe and comfortable environment.

Starting Points

Escape to Nature
Some students may say that animals are happy to be free, while others may worry that the animals will not know how to fend for themselves in their natural habitats. They have been given their freedom because the pet shop is going out of business.

- Allow time for students to share their captions with each other and their ideas about people's relationships with animals.

Through the Lens
Talk with students about anthropomorphism—the attribution of human form or characteristics to animals or objects. Prepare them to see role reversal when, in "The Dog Diaries," a human takes on the behavior and characteristics of an animal. Have students be aware of anthropomorphism when they write about their experiences from an animal's perspective.

Exploring the Theme

We share the planet Earth with a great number and variety of other creatures. How do we interact with the natural world? How might the world look through the eyes of the other creatures who share this planet with us? In the stories, poems, and essays in this theme, you will find a variety of possible responses to these questions. Try one of the options below to start your own thinking about the theme.

Starting Points

ESCAPE TO NATURE
Human beings today often feel removed from the natural world. We spend many more hours indoors than outside. In this cartoon, assorted animals who have also been separated from nature are released into a new life outdoors.

- What might happen to the creatures in this picture? Why have they been given their freedom? Write a caption for the cartoon that expresses some of your ideas about people's relationships with animals.

THROUGH THE LENS OF EXPERIENCE
Think about an experience you've had with an animal—a pet, a farm animal, an animal in a zoo, or one in the wild. If you haven't had an interesting animal experience, use your imagination to make one up.

- Put yourself in the animal's place and write a few notes about how the experience may have seemed from the animal's point of view. (For an example of writing from an animal's point of view, you might want to reread "The Dog Diaries," pages 411–416.)

---

interNET CONNECTION

Students can use a search engine to find out more about endangered species and their habitats. Suggest that they use such keywords as *rain forest, endangered species,* and *conservation.*

Theme Projects

As you read the selections in this theme, try your hand at one of the projects below. Work on your own, with a partner, or with a group.

LEARNING FOR LIFE
Policy Statement

1. Develop a policy for the ethical treatment of animals as pets or in zoos. Start by listing your own ideas.
2. Gather input from teachers, other students, pet owners, zookeepers, the local humane society, or books and magazines. Draft your policy statement. Share it with the class.

CRITICAL VIEWING
Animals in Nature

1. Collect ten or more photos and other illustrations of animals in their natural habitats. Look through magazines, catalogs, and old calendars for a variety of animals and environments.
2. Study the images. What kind of connection do you make between each animal and its habitat? Write an introduction to your collection that describes the connection between animals and their environments.

interNET CONNECTION

Check out the Web for more project ideas. On the Web you can also find out about the selections in this theme. Look for Glencoe Literature at this Web site: lit.glencoe.com

MULTIMEDIA PROJECT
Author Presentation

1. Gather data about an author from this theme. Use HyperStudio or similar software to create a multimedia presentation about the author you choose.
2. Present interesting facts about the author's life using a visual format such as a time line. If possible, include a picture of the author.
3. Organize and present your work to the class.

A DELICATE BALANCE 771

Theme Projects

Teaching Strategies

The following suggestions may help your students plan and carry out their theme projects.

Learning for Life

- Begin by having students discuss the advantages and disadvantages of zoos. Ask them each to draw up two lists: one of reasons why we should continue to keep animals in zoos and another of reasons why we should end the practice.
- Help students identify some of the issues involved in the ethical treatment of animals. You may wish to create a web on the board with topics such as leash laws, neutering, or pet shops vs. shelters.
- Encourage students to gather policy statements from local organizations that deal with animals.

Critical Viewing

- Students may wish to do this project in pairs or small groups.
- Students can alter the activity by choosing a habitat, such as a jungle, plain, desert, or forest, and finding pictures of ten animals that share the habitat.
- Suggest that students include insects, amphibians, fish, and birds in their studies.

Multimedia Project

As students gather material, suggest that they read other works by the author and try to get a sense of what his or her major themes are.

Additional Resources

📁 *Interdisciplinary Activities,* pp. 30–33
📁 *Viewing and Representing Activities,* pp. 1–6, 28–30
📁 *Listening and Speaking Activities,* pp. 22–24
📁 *Critical Thinking Skills,* pp. 20–22
📁 *Selection and Theme Assessment,* pp. 139–140
📁 *Performance Assessment,* p. 76

Family and Community Activity

Volunteer Work Ask students to spend two hours volunteering at the local chapter of the Humane Society, an animal shelter, a veterinary clinic, a sanctuary, a zoo, or an organization that deals with the care of animals. Have students prepare posters based on their experiences. Each poster should include a picture of the student in a volunteer capacity, pictures or descriptions of the animals the student worked with, and a brief summary of what the student did as a volunteer. A list of tasks volunteers could do at this organization and the name of a volunteering coordinator would also be of interest.

Additional Resources
📁 *Family and Community Activities,* pp. 18–19

Before Reading

Objectives

- To read and appreciate a folktale about a man who respects the delicate balance of nature
- To list events that make up the plot of a short story
- To write about how the story's imagery reflects the storyteller's point of view

Skills

Reading/Thinking: Drawing Conclusions; Inferring; Monitoring Comprehension
Writing: Journal Writing
Grammar/Language: Past Perfect Tense
Vocabulary: Synonyms; Word Origins
Listening/Speaking: Storyteller's Circle; Oral Report
Collaboration: Literature Groups

Motivating
→ OPTIONS

Selection Focus Transparency 65: Have students view the quote by Jacob Bronowski and discuss how humans and animals are interconnected.

Focus Activity: As an extension of the Focus Activity, have students in small groups discuss whether they believe plant life is as important as human life and the reasons for their beliefs.

---

772 ❧ THEME 8

Before You Read
We Are All One

MEET LAURENCE YEP

Identity is an important issue in many of Laurence Yep's award-winning novels. He has explained, "In a sense I have no one culture to call my own since I exist . . . in several. However, in my writing I can create my own." Yep grew up as a Chinese American in an African American neighborhood in San Francisco. He attended school first in Chinatown, then in a white neighborhood. Those early experiences contributed to his sense that he is "always pursuing the theme of being an outsider."

Laurence Yep was born in 1948. This story was first published in 1973.

FOCUS ACTIVITY

Do you believe animal life is as important as human life? If given the opportunity, would you provide food, shelter, or protection for an animal? for an insect? Why or why not?

Think/Pair/Share
Jot down your responses to these questions. Then share your thoughts and feelings with a partner.

Setting a Purpose
Read this folktale to find out how a person's good deeds toward the natural world are rewarded.

BACKGROUND

The Time and Place   The tale takes place in some legendary time in China.

Did You Know?   During the Great Depression of the 1930s, the U.S. government created work projects to help the unemployed. Jon Lee was given the job of gathering and translating into English traditional stories from Chinese immigrants living in Chinatown in Oakland, California. Yep's "We Are All One" is a retelling of one of those stories.

VOCABULARY PREVIEW

scurry (skur′ ē) *v.* to run or move briskly or in an agitated way; p. 774
regretfully (ri gret′ fəl lē) *adv.* in a way that shows sorrow, distress, or disappointment; p. 774
omen (ō′ mən) *n.* a sign or event thought to foretell good or bad fortune; p. 774
frustration (frus trā′ shən) *n.* disappointment or irritation at being kept from doing or achieving something; p. 777

RESOURCE MANAGER

Lesson Planning Resource
The **Theme Eight Planning Guide** (pp. 6–13) provides additional lesson notes and reduced versions of all print resources.

📁 **Other Print Resources**
- Active Reading Guide, p. 65
- Vocabulary Practice, p. 47
- Reading Workbook, pp. 117–118
- Grammar and Language Workbook, pp. 93–94
- Grammar and Composition

Handbook, Lesson 3.8
- Quick Checks, p. 65
- Selection and Theme Assessment, pp. 111–112
- Performance Assessment, p. 61
- Spanish Summaries, p. 65
- Spanish Translations
- Inclusion Strategies
- English Language Learners Sourcebook

 Transparencies
- Selection Focus 65
- Literary Elements 65
- Grammar and Language 61

Technology
🎧 Audio Library
🎧 Spanish Audio Library
💻 Glencoe Literature Web Site
💾 Testmaker

We Are All One

Laurence Yep

Long ago there was a rich man with a disease in his eyes. For many years, the pain was so great that he could not sleep at night. He saw every doctor he could, but none of them could help him.

"What good is all my money?" he groaned. Finally, he became so desperate that he sent **A** criers[1] through the city offering a reward to anyone who could cure him.

Now in that city lived an old candy peddler. He would walk around with his baskets of candy, but he was so kind-hearted that he gave away as much as he sold, so he was always poor.

---

1. Since few people could read in ancient times, the rich man had to employ *criers,* people who shouted out announcements or news, to make his offer known.

SUMMARY

A kind candy peddler knows of a magic herb that can cure the eye disease of a rich man. He interrupts his search in the forest to divert a small stream of water away from an ants' nest. Later he protects a centipede from being eaten by a bird. The peddler cannot find the herb; but the centipede tells him where to find a magical bead to cure the rich man. Since the bead is covered in pine needles, he calls on the ants to join the search. They find the bead, which cures the rich man, and the peddler is rewarded.

📁 *Spanish Summaries,* p. 65

A **Active Reading**

PREDICT Invite students to look at the title of this story and the illustration. Then ask a volunteer to read the first three paragraphs aloud. Encourage students to predict what the kindhearted peddler will do and what will happen to the rich man. Suggest that students periodically verify or revise their predictions.

Additional Resources
📁 *Active Reading Guide,* p. 65
🎧 *Audio Library*
🎧 *Spanish Audio Library*

Teaching Options

CONNECTING TO OTHER SELECTIONS

The chart at the right shows three ways to connect "We Are All One" to other selections in this book.

For specific teaching strategies, see the ***Theme Eight Planning Guide,*** pages 9–10.

Connection	Title
Life Skills: Supporting and Contributing	→ "A Boy and His Dog," p. 243
Thematic: Journeys	→ "Too Soon a Woman," p. 235
Literary: Folktale	→ "Strawberries," p. 707

B Author's Craft

CHARACTER Ask students how the author presents the peddler's character and possible future actions in this passage. *(The author shows him to be a kind person who cares about what is happening around him, even to the ants he encounters along the way in his quest for the magical herb.)*

C Literary Elements

PLOT: Sequence of Events Have students summarize the most important events of the story so far. *(A peddler hears of a rich man's eye disease. He goes into the forest to find a magic herb to cure the man. He interrupts his search to help some ants in trouble.)*

D Critical Thinking

DRAWING CONCLUSIONS Have volunteers explain who the queen and soldiers are in the peddler's dream. *(They represent the ant queen and the soldier ants.)*

When the old peddler heard the announcement, he remembered something his mother had said. She had once told him about a magical herb that was good for the eyes. So he packed up his baskets and went back to the single tiny room in which his family lived.

When he told his plan to his wife, she scolded him, "If you go off on this crazy hunt, how are we supposed to eat?"

Usually the peddler gave in to his wife, but this time he was stubborn. "There are two baskets of candy," he said. "I'll be back before they're gone."

The next morning, as soon as the soldiers opened the gates, he was the first one to leave the city. He did not stop until he was deep inside the woods. As a boy, he had often wandered there. He had liked to pretend that the shadowy forest was a green sea and he was a fish slipping through the cool waters.

As he examined the ground, he noticed ants scurrying about. On their backs were larvae[2] like white grains of rice. A rock had fallen into a stream, so the water now spilled into the ant's nest.

"We're all one," the kind-hearted peddler said. So he waded into the shallow stream and put the rock on the bank. Then with a sharp stick, he dug a shallow ditch that sent the rest of the water back into the stream.

Without another thought about his good deed, he began to search through the forest.

He looked everywhere; but as the day went on, he grew sleepy. "Ho-hum. I got up too early. I'll take just a short nap," he decided, and lay down in the shade of an old tree, where he fell right asleep.

In his dreams, the old peddler found himself standing in the middle of a great city. Tall buildings rose high overhead. He couldn't see the sky even when he tilted back his head. An escort of soldiers marched up to him with a loud clatter of their black lacquer armor. "Our queen wishes to see you," the captain said.

The frightened peddler could only obey and let the fierce soldiers lead him into a shining palace. There, a woman with a high crown sat upon a tall throne. Trembling, the old peddler fell to his knees and touched his forehead against the floor.

But the queen ordered him to stand. "Like the great Emperor Yü of long ago, you tamed the great flood. We are all one now. You have only to ask, and I or any of my people will come to your aid."

The old peddler cleared his throat. "I am looking for a certain herb. It will cure any disease of the eyes."

The queen shook her head regretfully. "I have never heard of that herb. But you will surely find it if you keep looking for it."

And then the old peddler woke. Sitting up, he saw that in his wanderings he had come back to the ants' nest. It was there he had taken his nap. His dream city had been the ants' nest itself.

"This is a good omen," he said to himself, and he began searching even harder. He was so determined to find the herb that

---

2. *Larvae* (lär′ vē) is the plural of *larva*, which is the early, worm-like form of an insect; a caterpillar is the larva of a butterfly or moth.

Vocabulary
scurry (skur′ ē) *v.* to run or move briskly or in an agitated way
regretfully (ri gret′ fəl lē) *adj.* in a way that shows sorrow, distress, or disappointment
omen (ō′ mən) *n.* a sign or event thought to foretell good or bad fortune

---

Teaching Options

LITERATURE & HUMANITIES

Have students examine *The Peaceable Kingdom*, in the book *Introducing Art*, page 140, portraying different kinds of people and animals living in harmony. Ask students what similarities exist between the messages of the story and the painting.

MEETING INDIVIDUAL NEEDS — ENGLISH LANGUAGE LEARNERS

Folktales Every culture has stories that have been passed down from generation to generation. Some of these stories tell about respecting nature or being kind to people and animals.

Activity Ask small groups of students to share stories from their cultures about kindness to people or animals or about respecting nature. Then have each group select one story and draw a comic strip showing major story events. Invite groups to display their comic strips for the rest of the class and explain who the people in the story are and what happens to them.

Additional Resources
📁 *English Language Learners Sourcebook*

he did not notice how time had passed. He was surprised when he saw how the light was fading. He looked all around then. There was no sight of his city—only strange hills. He realized then that he had searched so far he had gotten lost.

Night was coming fast and with it the cold. He rubbed his arms and hunted for shelter. In the twilight, he thought he could see the green tiles of a roof.

He stumbled through the growing darkness until he reached a ruined temple. Weeds grew through cracks in the stones and most of the roof itself had fallen in. Still, the ruins would provide some protection.

As he started inside, he saw a centipede with bright orange skin and red tufts of fur along its back. Yellow dots covered its sides like a dozen tiny eyes. It was also rushing into the temple as fast as it could, but there was a bird swooping down toward it.

The old peddler waved his arms and shouted, scaring the bird away. Then he put down his palm in front of the insect. "We are all one, you and I." The many feet tickled his skin as the centipede climbed onto his hand.

Inside the temple, he gathered dried leaves and found old sticks of wood and soon he had a fire going. The peddler even picked some fresh leaves for the centipede from a bush near the temple doorway.

Did You Know?
A *centipede* is a long, flat insect with many pairs of legs. The prefix *centi-* means either "hundred" or "hundredth part of," and *pede* comes from the Latin word for "foot."

"I may have to go hungry, but you don't have to, friend."

Stretching out beside the fire, the old peddler pillowed his head on his arms. He was so tired that he soon fell asleep, but even in his sleep he dreamed he was still searching in the woods. Suddenly he thought he heard footsteps near his head. He woke instantly and looked about, but he only saw the brightly colored centipede.

"Was it you, friend?" The old peddler chuckled and, lying down, he closed his eyes again. "I must be getting nervous."

"We are one, you and I," a voice said faintly—as if from a long distance. "If you go south, you will find a pine tree with two trunks. By its roots, you will find a magic bead. A cousin of mine spat on it years ago. Dissolve that bead in wine and tell the rich man to drink it if he wants to heal his eyes."

The old peddler trembled when he heard the voice, because he realized that the centipede was magical. He wanted to run from the temple, but he couldn't even get up. It was as if he were glued to the floor.

But then the old peddler reasoned with himself: If the centipede had wanted to hurt me, it could have long ago. Instead, it seems to want to help me.

So the old peddler stayed where he was, but he did not dare open his eyes. When the first sunlight fell through the roof, he raised one eyelid cautiously. There was no sign of the centipede. He sat up and looked around, but the magical centipede was gone.

He followed the centipede's instructions when he left the temple. Traveling south, he kept a sharp eye out for the pine tree with two trunks. He walked until late in the afternoon, but all he saw were normal pine trees.

E Literary Elements

PLOT: *Sequence of Events* Have students describe what important event occurs after the peddler finds the ruined temple. *(The peddler saves a centipede and feeds it, even though he has no food himself.)*

F Author's Craft

REPETITION Have students think about how the author uses repetition to develop the story. *(He presents a pattern of behavior for the peddler that gives the reader insight into what might happen in the story.)*

G Critical Thinking

INFERRING Have students explain whether they think the peddler will find the pine tree with two trunks. You may wish to share the following model to illustrate the process of making inferences.

Model: I think the peddler will find the pine tree eventually because good people in folktales are usually rewarded. But the peddler still has not been helped by the ants. I think the ants will have to help him before the story can be resolved. Perhaps the ants will help the peddler find the pine tree with two trunks.

Reading Minilesson

Monitoring Comprehension Review with students the process of detecting when something doesn't make sense and then the steps that can be taken to remedy the situation. Jot important points on the board: *Identify the problem or question; Adjust reading rate; Reread; Self-question; Paraphrase; Visualize.*

Activity Have students work in small groups. They can use "We Are All One" as the basis to develop think-aloud models explaining how to detect and remedy comprehension breakdowns. Each group should model the process for the class. **L2** **COLLAB. LEARN.**

Additional Resources
Reading Workbook, pp. 117–118

Vo•cab•u•lar•y Skills

Etymology The Middle English word *bede* comes from the Old English word *gebed*, which meant "a prayer." To keep track of prayers, people used a string of small round balls (today called a rosary). Since each round ball stood for one *bede* (or prayer), the word eventually came to mean the round balls themselves. Today *bead* means a small object that can be threaded on a string.

River Scene. 18th century, China. Free Library, Philadelphia, PA.

Viewing the painting: What does this painting add to your understanding of the setting of "We Are All One"?

776 🐿 THEME 8

Grammar and Language *Minilesson*

Past Perfect Tense Write this sentence from the story on the board to illustrate the concept of past perfect tense: *He remembered something his mother had said.* The past perfect tense of a verb names an action that happened before another action or event in the past. What the peddler's mother said happened before the peddler remembered. Invite students to identify what happened before the weeds

grew through the cracks in this example: *Weeds grew through the cracks and most of the roof had fallen in.* (The roof fell in.)

Activity Have students look for other examples of the past perfect tense in this story. (There are many examples on pages 774 and 775.) Then have students list which event happened first and which event happened second. **L2**

Additional Resources

📖 *Grammar and Language Transparency 61*

📕 *Grammar and Language Workbook,* pp. 93–94

📗 *Grammar and Composition Handbook,* Lesson 3.8

📙 *Writer's Choice,* Lesson 10.8

776

Laurence Yep

Wearily he sat down and sighed. Even if he found the pine tree, he couldn't be sure that he would find the bead. Someone else might even have discovered it a long time ago.

But something made him look a little longer. Just when he was thinking about turning back, he saw the odd tree. Somehow his tired legs managed to carry him over to the tree, and he got down on his knees. But the ground was covered with pine needles and his old eyes were too weak. The old peddler could have wept with frustration, and then he remembered the ants.

H He began to call, "Ants, ants, we are all one."

Almost immediately, thousands of ants came boiling out of nowhere. Delighted, the old man held up his fingers. "I'm looking for a bead. It might be very tiny."

Then, careful not to crush any of his little helpers, the old man sat down to wait. In no time, the ants reappeared with a tiny bead. With trembling fingers, the **I** old man took the bead from them and examined it. It was colored orange and looked as if it had yellow eyes on the sides.

There was nothing very special about the bead, but the old peddler treated it like a fine jewel. Putting the bead into his

pouch, the old peddler bowed his head. "I thank you and I thank your queen," the old man said. After the ants disappeared among the pine needles, he made his way out of the woods.

The next day, he reached the house of the rich man. However, he was so poor and ragged that the gatekeeper only laughed at him. "How could an old beggar like you help my master?"

The old peddler tried to argue. "Beggar or rich man, we are all one."

But it so happened that the rich man was passing by the gates. He went over to the old peddler. "I said anyone could see me. But it'll mean a stick across your back if you're wasting my time."

The old peddler took out the pouch. "Dissolve this bead in some wine and drink it down." Then, turning the pouch upside down, he shook the tiny bead onto his palm and handed it to the rich man.

The rich man immediately called for a cup of wine. Dropping the bead into the wine, he waited a moment and then drank it down. Instantly the pain vanished. Shortly after that, his eyes healed.

The rich man was so happy and grateful that he doubled the reward. And the **J** kindly old peddler and his family lived comfortably for the rest of their lives.

❖

Vocabulary
frustration (frus trā′ shən) *n.* disappointment or irritation at being kept from doing or achieving something

A DELICATE BALANCE 777

Sidebar

H **Literary Elements**
THEME Have students explain what they think the theme of this story is. *(The theme is the story's title—we are all one. Humans and animals are all a vital part of the world, and we should all help each other whenever we get a chance.)*

I **Active Reading**
VISUALIZE Have students describe what the colors of the bead remind them of. *(The bead is orange with yellow spots, the same colors and pattern as on the centipede.)*

J **Author's Craft**
FOLKTALE Based on other folktales students have read, have them explain how the ending the author uses is typical. *(Goodness and kindness are rewarded. The rich man rewards the peddler with a comfortable lifestyle. The peddler and his family live happily ever after.)*

Thematic Focus

A Delicate Balance Have students explain how this selection relates to the theme "A Delicate Balance." *(The delicate balance of nature includes life and death. In this story, the peddler interferes with death by helping the ants keep water out of their nest and preventing a bird from eating the centipede.)*

☑ ASSESSMENT OPTIONS
📁 *Quick Checks,* p. 65

REAL-WORLD CONNECTION

Journals Journals can tell a story, record personal change, or simply keep track of observations from day to day.

Activity Encourage students to look closely at the natural world around them. They do not need to go into a forest to see the natural world. They can find insects in a schoolyard, birds in a parking lot, or people in a mall. Invite students to choose one spot to observe nature (human or animal). Have students take notes in a journal. Encourage students to visit the same spot several times and to record how nature changes at different times of day or different days of the week. Finally, have students draw some conclusions about what they see and share their observations with the rest of the class. **L2**

Responding to the Selection

Personal Response

Some students may have enjoyed the magical aspects of this story; others may have felt that the magic made the story too farfetched.

Analyzing Literature

1. The peddler thinks he can cure the rich man because he remembers something his mother told him. His wife does not believe he will find the herb. She calls the hunt "crazy."
2. The peddler first saves an ants' nest.
3. The centipede tells the peddler where to find a magic bead.
4. The peddler says, "We are all one."
5. The peddler is kindhearted; he gives away as much candy as he sells, so he is always poor. The peddler wants to win the reward because the money will help his family.
6. The dream had a queen and soldiers, who are the ants. The queen tells the peddler that because he saved them from a flood, he only has to ask and the queen or her helpers will come to his aid.
7. The ants help the peddler find the bead. This was foreshadowed by the peddler's dream.
8. Sample: No, wealth will not change the peddler. He is so kindhearted he will probably use his money to help those less fortunate than he is.
9. Sample: This story's moral, we are all one, can help people recognize that although there are differences, whether someone is rich or poor, Chinese-speaking or English-speaking, we all deserve respect.
10. Sample: Wars would end. Different opinions would be tolerated. Wealthier people would share with poorer people.

Responding to Literature

PERSONAL RESPONSE

What were your thoughts about the magical aspects of this folktale?

Analyzing Literature

RECALL

1. Why does the peddler believe he can win the reward? Does his wife believe in his idea?
2. What is the peddler's first gesture of kindness toward another creature?
3. What is the centipede's advice to the peddler?
4. How does the peddler sum up his belief about the difference between the rich and the poor?

INTERPRET

5. What details does the author reveal to explain why the peddler wanted to win the reward?
6. How was the peddler's dream connected to his rescuing the ant's nest?
7. Who helped the peddler follow the centipede's advice? How was this event **foreshadowed** earlier in the tale?
8. By the end of the tale, the peddler has plenty of money. Do you believe his behavior will change now that he is rich? Explain how the author's description of the character led you to your opinion.

EVALUATE AND CONNECT

9. In your opinion, why did Chinese immigrants continue to tell this ancient tale after they arrived in America? How might the folktale have been a "strategy" for living among strangers in a different country?
10. Theme Connection   The title of the tale summarizes the philosophy of the peddler. How do you imagine the world would change if most people shared this belief?

Landscape, early 18th century. Yao Song. Private collection.

Plot

A **plot** is the series of events in a story that shows the characters in action, trying to resolve one or more conflicts or problems. One way to determine a story's plot is first to identify the problems. In "We Are All One," for example, the rich man's problem with his eyes sets the story's events in motion. Next, ask yourself: What characters are involved? What will happen next? What is the solution to the problem?

1. Why does the peddler become involved in the rich man's problem? What other problems does the peddler face?

2. Briefly list the series of events that make up the plot of "We Are All One."

● See **Literary Terms Handbook,** p. R8.

LITERARY ELEMENTS

1. The peddler gets involved to help the rich man. The peddler is poor and ragged.
2. While hunting for a magic healing herb, a peddler saves an ant colony and a centipede. They help him find a magic bead that cures a rich man, who rewards the peddler by making him well-off for life.

Additional Resources

 Literary Elements Transparency 65

Extending Your Response

Writing About Literature

Imagery One of the points of the story is that all of nature is interconnected. Scan the story, looking for images of the landscape and the animals. Write a paragraph using the imagery you found to show the storyteller's love and respect for the natural world.

Personal Writing

Life's Connections How does the candy peddler's treatment of all living things compare with your own response in the **Focus Activity** on page 772? Did the story make you look at this issue in a different way? Answer these questions in a journal entry.

Performing

Storyteller's Circle "We Are All One" began as an oral tale. Working in a small group, divide the story into sections, one section for each group member. Perform the story for another class.

Literature Groups

Literary Quests The **quest,** a search or pursuit to find some object or achieve some goal, is a theme found in literature and popular media ranging from the Greek myths to *The Lord of the Rings* and the *Star Wars* movies. What is the quest in "We Are All One"? With your group, share ideas about stories you know that are based on a quest. What do these stories have in common?

Interdisciplinary Activity

Social Studies The belief that animal life is as sacred as human life is important in many religions, including Buddhism. Research Buddhism. Discover how it is practiced in China and in America. Then present your findings in an oral report.

Reading Further

If you would like to read other books by Laurence Yep, try *Tongues of Jade* and *Child of the Owl*

 Save your work for your portfolio.

Skill Minilesson

VOCABULARY • SYNONYMS

Just because two words are synonyms does not mean that one can be substituted for the other in every situation. Thinking carefully about words will help you use them accurately.

PRACTICE In each question, the italicized words are synonyms. For each, choose the more accurate word.

1. Does a rocket *scurry* or *zoom* into the sky?
2. If you can't go to a party you want to go to, do you stay home *regretfully* or *apologetically?*
3. If a friend told you you would be lucky today and you believed it, would you regard your friend's comment as an *omen* or a *fore-warning?*
4. If you receive a radio as a gift instead of the camera you had hoped for, do you feel *frustration* or *disappointment?*

Extending Your Response

Writing About Literature
Students' paragraphs should
- describe how imagery shows the author's love and respect for the natural world.
- contain a clear topic sentence and concise closing.

Personal Writing
Students' journal entries should
- compare the peddler's treatment of living things with their ideas.
- explain how this story alters their ideas about the treatment of living things.
- contain their thoughts about the interconnectedness of all living things.

Performing Before students perform, have them experiment with varying the volume, rate, pitch, and rhythm of their voices for dramatic effect.

Literature Groups
Encourage students to recall other quest stories. Then, in groups, have each member briefly describe one quest story. **COLLAB. LEARN.**

Interdisciplinary Activity
Encourage students to visit a library and use a card or computer catalog to find books on Buddhism.

Skill Minilesson
VOCABULARY • SYNONYMS
1. zoom   3. omen
2. regretfully   4. disappointment
Additional Resources
Vocabulary Practice, p. 47

✔ ASSESSMENT OPTIONS
- *Quick Checks,* p. 65
- *Selection and Theme Assessment,* pp. 111–112
- *Performance Assessment,* p. 61
- *Testmaker*

MEDIA Connection

Objective
- To read and understand journal excerpts

Respond
Possible answers include being better than others, doing something to the best of one's ability, gaining material rewards, and feeling good about an achievement.

Additional Resources
📁 **Media Connections,** p. 15

interNET CONNECTION

Down's Syndrome Have students use a search engine to find out more about Down's syndrome. They might use such keywords as *Down's syndrome, adapted sports for kids,* or *children with disabilities.*

Teaching Options

MEDIA Connection

from "See Robby Run"
by Edie Scher—*Runner's World,* March 1998

May 30: Heading toward my driveway at the end of a run, I hear the rhythm of sneakered foot-falls behind me and turn to see a father and his young son engaged in a coaching session.
"Come on, Robby, that's good. Keep up those arms!" Words of encouragement for a beginning runner, I figure. . . .
"Great morning for a run!" I say.
The boy stops in his tracks and grins. His father smiles at me and gently places a hand on his son's shoulder. "C'mon Robby. Let's keep going." Robby waves happily, and they continue down the block, a tall, handsome father and his 10-year-old Down's syndrome son, whose spanking-clean running shoes and freshly ironed T-shirt announce his newness to the sport.

June 28: Robby has a different partner this morning. His mother does not jog, but instead walks purposefully beside him. When Robby sees me and becomes distracted, she

encourages him as her husband would. "His father's on a business trip, and I don't want to stop the momentum," she tells me.

July 5: Robby's father is back, and it looks as if Mom will continue to join them. She walks a few steps behind while her husband talks Robby through his workout. In the middle of the block, Robby stops and turns to ask his mother to run, too. His father cheerfully urges him to continue.

August 11: I look forward to my daily encounter with Robby and his parents. His athletic improvement, while minimal, inspires me by the lesson it teaches. We each run our race and push forward for our own reasons; winning means something different for each runner.

August 22: Robby's two sisters have returned from summer camp and now join his team. Robby's running style has not changed much, but his stride seems to have more bounce. He points to his sisters with

obvious pride, stopping to tell me their names. . . . Robby's feet will never leave the pavement with the grace and speed of theirs, but he is not aware of that; his spirit is not competitive, only joyful, as he pushes himself to catch up with them.

September 10: School has resumed, and Robby's sisters and mother no longer run with him. I look at Robby carefully today. He seems a little taller, a little slimmer. Is it my imagination that his stride is a little smoother?
I wait to wave to them before I head up my driveway. They both wave back, but this time Robby does not stop running, and his father lovingly cheers him on for this new personal best.

Respond
The writer says, "We each run our race and push forward for our own reasons; winning means something different for each runner." What does winning mean to you?

Reading Minilesson

Setting a Purpose for Reading
Readers who enjoy reading journals and diaries are often interested in the viewpoint of the writer as well as in the writer's experience.

Activity Suggest that students go to the library and find a book or magazine article written in journal/diary form. Have students read several entries and write a

journal entry of their own in which they describe what they have read. Encourage them to make candid observations about the writer's perspective as well as the topic. **L2**

Additional Resources
📁 **Reading Workbook**

Vo·cab·u·lar·y Skills

Dictionary Skills: Pronunciation

One of the most important kinds of information you can find in a dictionary is how to pronounce words.

Any vowel letter can be pronounced in different ways. In a dictionary pronunciation, a vowel without any symbol has its normal "short" sound, like the vowels in *pat, pet, pit, hot,* and *hut.* Other vowel sounds are shown by symbols, such as a straight line above the vowel to show that it is "long." (Long vowels "say their own name.")

Following are some additional pronunciation symbols:

ä	an **ah** sound, as in **father**
ô	an **aw** sound, as in **coffee** and **law**
oo	the vowel sound in **wood**
o͞o	the vowel sound in **fool**
oi	the vowel sound in **toy**
ou	an **ow** sound, as in **cow** and **out**
ə	the unaccented vowel sound at the end of **pencil, lemon, taken**
th	**th** as in **thin**
th	**th** as in **this**
zh	the sound in the middle of **treasure** or the end of **garage**

An accent mark (′) follows the syllable you should stress. Emphasizing the correct syllable is important in pronunciation.

EXERCISES

1. Use the pronunciation given for each word to answer the question.
   a. Does *brood* (bro͞od) rhyme with *rude, road,* or *rod?*
   b. Does the first syllable of *scuttle* (skut′ əl) rhyme with *cute* or *cut?*
   c. Does *cower* (kou′ ər) rhyme with *lower* or *power?*
   d. Does the *g* in *lunge* (lunj) sound like the *g* in *rage* or in *rag?*
   e. Does the first syllable of *valiant* (val′ yənt) rhyme with *sale, pal,* or *call?*
2. Decide which word is represented by each dictionary pronunciation.
   a. lo͞os   Is this word *lose* or *loose?*
   b. i rās′   Is this word *erase* or *earache?*
   c. kwī′ it   Is this word *quite, quiet,* or *quit?*
   d. hal′ lōd   Is this word *hollowed, halo,* or *hallowed?*
   e. kon′ stənt   Is this word *consonant, constant,* or *consent?*

Objective

• To recognize and use strategies for pronouncing words correctly

Teaching Strategies

Have students locate a pronunciation key at the beginning of their dictionaries. Then, ask them to locate the International Phonetic Alphabet (IPA), which often appears alongside the pronunciation key.

Have students familiarize themselves with the IPA and write their names in phonetic transcription. Point out that anyone who can read and use the IPA could pronounce these student names correctly. Knowledge of pronunciation symbols and phonetic transcription can help, not only in English pronunciation, but also in learning how to pronounce words in other languages.

Exercises

1. a. rude
   b. cut
   c. power
   d. rage
   e. pal

2. a. loose
   b. erase
   c. quiet
   d. hallowed
   e. constant

Additional Resources

📁 *Vocabulary Power: Weekly Lessons and Activities*

Teaching Options

MEETING INDIVIDUAL NEEDS
ENGLISH LANGUAGE LEARNERS

Sound/Symbol Correlation

Pronunciation keys and phonetic symbols can be especially difficult for English language learners. Students whose first language is not based on a Roman alphabet face even more difficulty.

Activity Have mixed groups of students open their dictionaries to any page, close their eyes, and point to a word. Ask them to copy the pronunciation for the word selected on the front of an index card and the word itself on the back of the card. Have students exchange cards and use the Pronunciation Key in the dictionary to figure out how the word should be pronounced.

Additional Resources

📁 *English Language Learners Sourcebook*

Before Reading

Objectives

- To read and enjoy two poems about the natural world
- To state the theme of two poems
- To write a description of a character

Skills

Reading/Thinking: Using Graphic Aids
Writing: Writing a Poem
Grammar/Language: Sensory Language
Listening/Speaking: Oral Reading
Collaboration: Literature Groups

Motivating
→OPTIONS

Literature Launchers: *Native American Storytelling*

Videodisc Side B, Segment 24

Also available in VHS.

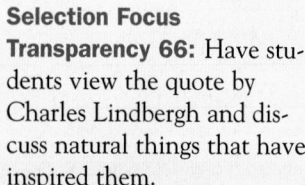

Selection Focus Transparency 66: Have students view the quote by Charles Lindbergh and discuss natural things that have inspired them.

Focus Activity: As an extension of the Focus Activity, have students in small groups examine whether their lists contain more natural objects or human-made objects.

Before You Read
Birdfoot's Grampa and *Miracles*

MEET JOSEPH BRUCHAC

Joseph Bruchac (brōō′ shak) did not learn of his Native American ancestry until he was an adult. His grandfather, who raised him, kept it a secret. Now Bruchac proudly bears his Abenaki name, *Gahnegohheyoh*, which means "the good mind."

Joseph Bruchac was born in 1942. This poem was first published in 1978.

MEET WALT WHITMAN

Walt Whitman worked at everything from carpentry to teaching. He loved variety, not only in jobs, but also in the people and places of America. *Leaves of Grass*, his famous collection of poetry, celebrates the variety and vastness of this country.

Walt Whitman was born in New York in 1819 and died in 1892.

FOCUS ACTIVITY

Do you ever stop to think about the beauty and the wonder in everyday life?

QuickWrite
Make a quick list of things in everyday life that you think are extraordinary or beautiful.

Setting a Purpose
Read these poems to find out how two poets express their reverence for life.

BACKGROUND

Joseph Bruchac writes out of a long Native American tradition of viewing one's relationship to Earth in terms of family. Here are his words about that tradition.

"The Okanagan people of the Pacific Northwest speak of the Earth as Mother; the Sun as Father, and the animals as our brothers and sisters. This view of the world was held by the Navajo and the Abenaki, the Sioux and the Anishinabe, and most of the aboriginal people of this continent. They saw their role on this earth, not as rulers of Creation, but as beings entrusted with a special mission—to maintain the natural balance, to take care of our Mother, to be Keepers of the Earth."

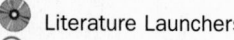

RESOURCE MANAGER

Lesson Planning Resource
The *Theme Eight Planning Guide* (pp. 14–18) provides additional lesson notes and reduced versions of all print resources.

📁 **Other Print Resources**
- Active Reading Guide, p. 66
- Grammar and Language Workbook, pp. 117–118
- Grammar and Composition Handbook, Lesson 5.1
- Quick Checks, p. 66

- Selection and Theme Assessment, pp. 113–114
- Performance Assessment, p. 62
- Spanish Summaries, p. 66
- Inclusion Strategies
- English Language Learners Sourcebook

 Transparencies
- Selection Focus 66
- Fine Art 19
- Literary Elements 66

Technology
 Literature Launchers
🎧 Audio Library
🎧 Spanish Audio Library
💻 Glencoe Literature Web Site
💾 Testmaker

Birdfoot's Grampa

Joseph Bruchac ~

The old man
must have stopped our car
two dozen times to climb out
and gather into his hands
5 the small toads blinded
by our lights and leaping,
live drops of rain.

The rain was falling,
a mist about his white hair
10 and I kept saying
you can't save them all,
accept it, get back in
we've got places to go.

But, leathery hands full
15 of wet brown life,
knee deep in the summer
roadside grass,
he just smiled and said
they have places to go to
20 *too.*

D Active Reading

VISUALIZE Invite students to close their eyes while a volunteer reads aloud the poem's first fifteen lines. Encourage students to visualize each image. Discuss which images are most striking.

E Active Reading

REVIEW Have students explain what Whitman thinks is a miracle. *(He thinks everything in life is a miracle.)*

F Active Reading

EVALUATE Invite students to explain what the miracles in the final stanza have in common. *(All are related to the sea.)*

Thematic Focus

A Delicate Balance Invite students to explain how these two poems relate to the theme "A Delicate Balance." *(Both poems are about the delicate balance of nature.)*

FINE ART
TRANSPARENCY 19

You may wish to use *Fine Arts Transparency 19* to enrich the development of theme concepts.

☑ **ASSESSMENT OPTIONS**

📁 *Quick Checks,* p. 66

Miracles

Walt Whitman ∾

Why, who makes much of a miracle?
As to me I know of nothing else but miracles,
Whether I walk the streets of Manhattan,
Or dart my sight over the roofs of houses toward the sky,
5 Or wade with naked feet along the beach just in the edge of the water,
Or stand under trees in the woods,
Or talk by day with any one I love . . .
Or sit at table at dinner with the rest,
Or look at strangers opposite me riding in the car.
10 Or watch honey-bees busy around the hive of a summer forenoon,
Or animals feeding in the fields,
Or birds, or the wonderfulness of the sundown, or of stars shining so quiet and
    bright,
Or the exquisite° delicate thin curve of the new moon in spring;
These with the rest, one and all, are to me miracles,
15 The whole referring, yet each distinct and in its place.°

To me every hour of the light and dark is a miracle,
Every cubic inch of space is a miracle,
Every square yard of the surface of the earth is spread with the same,
Every foot of the interior swarms with the same.

20 To me the sea is a continual miracle,
The fishes that swim—the rocks—the motion of the waves—the ships with men
    in them,
What stranger miracles are there?

---

13 Something that is *exquisite* has a rare beauty, charm, or perfection.
15 This line suggests that all of these small, separate miracles are involved in, or refer to, some greater miracle.

784

Teaching Options

Reading *Minilesson*

Using Graphic Aids Some students may understand this poem better if they can visualize the images Whitman describes.

Activity Place a large sheet of butcher paper or mural paper on a bulletin board, table, or floor. Label it *Miracles*. Ask each student to draw one image from this poem on the paper. Encourage students to try to show the emotion and sense of awe Whitman feels about each of these images. When students have finished adding to the mural, read the poem aloud while listeners locate each image. **L2**

Additional Resources
📁 *Reading Workbook*

Responding to Literature

PERSONAL RESPONSE

Reread your QuickWrite from the **Focus Activity** on page 782. How did these two poems reinforce, or change, your own thoughts and feelings about the extraordinary nature of daily life?

Analyzing Literature

RECALL

1. In "Birdfoot's Grampa," why does the old man stop the car "two dozen times"?
2. List four events in "Miracles" that the speaker identifies as miracles relating to human beings and four relating to nature.
3. Give an example of imagery from each poem.

INTERPRET

4. What conflict takes place in "Birdfoot's Grampa"? How does it affect your feelings about the speaker or the old man?
5. How many of the five senses does Whitman include in his list of miracles? Give an example of each.

EVALUATE AND CONNECT

6. In "Birdfoot's Grampa," do you identify more with the speaker or the old man? Why?
7. What other miracles might be included in Whitman's list? Give at least three possibilities.
8. What are your favorite images from each of these poems? Explain why you like them.
9. Theme Connection   What attitude toward life and nature do these poems convey?
10. Think of someone you know who would enjoy reading these poems. Why would the poems appeal to that person?

Responding to the Selection

Personal Response

Some students may say that Whitman expands on their ideas about beauty. Others may say that Bruchac forces them to look at nature in a new way.

Analyzing Literature

1. The old man stops the car to pick up toads in the road and carry them to the tall grass beside the road.
2. Human miracles include the streets of Manhattan, roofs of houses, talking with loved ones, and eating dinner with friends. Nature's miracles include beaches, trees, honeybees, animals feeding, birds, sundown, stars, new moons, fish, rocks, and waves.
3. Examples of imagery include Grampa, the rain creating a "mist about his white hair," and the "delicate thin curve of the new moon in spring."
4. In "Birdfoot's Grampa" the old man wants to move toads from the road to safety. The young man doesn't want to waste time saving toads. This conflict may make students appreciate the way the old man takes time to think about other beings in nature.
5. Whitman includes sight: *sundown*; hearing: *stars shining so quiet*; touch: *wade with naked feet*; smell: *trees in the woods*; and taste: *sit at table at dinner*.
6. Students may identify with either character, depending on their personal beliefs.

LITERARY ELEMENTS

1. The theme is that everything in nature has a purpose. The theme is implied. Grampa replies, "They have places to go to too."
2. The theme of "Miracles" is that everything in life is awe-inspiring. The concept is stated in the title.

Additional Resources

  Literary Elements Transparency 66

7. Other possible miracles include laughter, flowers, and icicles.
8. Encourage students to explain why they like their chosen image.
9. The poems convey an attitude of appreciation of life and nature.
10. Students should explain why these poems would appeal to the person they choose.

Extending Your Response

Writing About Literature

Students' paragraphs should
- contain a topic sentence.
- describe what the old man is like.
- contain a sentence that succinctly wraps up the paragraph.

Creative Writing

Poems or paragraphs should
- focus on one incident involving another person.
- reveal a person's character by describing his or her actions.
- contain sensory imagery.

Literature Groups
Before students meet, encourage them to jot down observations on how the two poems are alike and different. Then, in groups, have each member briefly describe one observation.
COLLAB. LEARN.

Listening and Speaking
Encourage students to experiment with their voices to create varying effects. Encourage them to experiment with pauses.

Skill Minilesson

GRAMMAR AND LANGUAGE
- SENSORY LANGUAGE

Each sentence should appeal to at least two senses.

Additional Resources

Grammar and Language Workbook, p. 117

Grammar and Composition Handbook, Lesson 6.4

Writer's Choice, Lesson 3.2

Extending Your Response

Writing About Literature
Characterization In "Birdfoot's Grampa," the poet packs a lot of information about the old man into very few words. Write a paragraph describing the old man as you picture him.

Creative Writing
Poem Write your own short poem or prose paragraph telling about a person. Focus on one incident that shows this person's character, as Joseph Bruchac does in "Birdfoot's Grampa."

Literature Groups
Poet's Choice Although both of these poems deal with the beauty and wonder in life, the two poems are very different. Compare and contrast the two poems. Pick out examples from the poems that show how the poems are alike and how they are different.

Listening and Speaking
Appreciating Poetry Take turns reading these poems aloud to one another. Pay attention to how different readings affect your experience of each poem.

Reading Further
If you would like to read more by these poets, try these books:
The Girl Who Married the Moon, by Joseph Bruchac
Walt Whitman: Poetry for Young People

📖 **Save your work for your portfolio.**

Skill Minilesson

GRAMMAR AND LANGUAGE • SENSORY LANGUAGE

Joseph Bruchac's description of the old man's "leathery hands full of wet brown life" is a fine example of **sensory language**–language that appeals to the senses. Sensory language describes how something looks, sounds, feels, smells, or tastes.

PRACTICE Write a sentence about each of the following items. Try to use sensory language that appeals to at least two senses in each sentence.
1. a car   4. a banana
2. a dog   5. a beach
3. a tree

● For more about sensory language and imagery, see **Literary Terms Handbook,** p. R9.

✔ ASSESSMENT OPTIONS

📁 *Quick Checks,* p. 66

📁 *Selection and Theme Assessment,* pp. 113–114

📁 *Performance Assessment,* p. 62

💾 *Testmaker*

MOVIE REVIEW

David Ansen reviews a film adaptation of Rudyard Kipling's *The Jungle Book*. One of the stories included in Kipling's book is "Rikki-tikki-tavi."

The Jungle Book

by David Ansen—*Newsweek*, January 16, 1995

Kipling purists may not cotton to Disney's new live-action version of *The Jungle Book*, but it's hard to think of anyone else who won't be enchanted. Jason Scott Lee's Mowgli, raised in the jungle by wild animals, uncontaminated by civilization, is no longer the boy Kipling imagined. He's sprouted into a buff young man whose best friends happen to be bears and wolves, but he's not unappreciative of the beauty of the English girl Kitty (Lena Headey), engaged to the dastardly Captain Boone (Cary Elwes). Director Stephen Sommers and his co-writers, Ronald Yanover and Mark D. Geldman, have imposed a taut, cliffhanging story structure upon Kipling's episodic stories, turning *The Jungle Book* into an action-packed

love story with something for everyone: hidden treasures, death by quicksand, a Spielbergian lost temple, ecological mysticism, swinish colonialist villains, an irresistible supporting cast of cackling monkeys, a treacherous tiger, a loyal bear, and one very deadly serpent.

It's Lee's ingratiating innocence that holds it all together. He's a figure of the purest fantasy, and he plays Mowgli with a wide-eyed, silent-movie exuberance so disarming it compels belief (even as you wonder where in the overgrown jungle he gets his wardrobe).

Respond

1. Do you think you would like to see this movie? Why or why not?

2. What is your opinion of the kind of "action-packed love story" the reviewer describes? Use examples of movies you know in your answer.

Reading *Minilesson*

Identifying Author's Purpose Words and phrases from movie reviews are often used to advertise the movie and entice moviegoers.

Activity Have students work in groups to locate and read a review of a G- or PG-rated movie. Ask students to discuss the review and decide whether the reviewer's purpose was: 1) to present a balanced

view of the film, 2) to encourage people to see the film, or 3) to discourage people from seeing the film. **L2 COLLAB. LEARN.**

Additional Resources
📁 *Reading Workbook*

Objective

• To read and understand a movie review

Literature ▸ LINK

Rikki-tikki-tavi This review of *The Jungle Book* connects to the story "Rikki-tikki-tavi," pages 789–801.

Respond
Answers

1. Students who enjoy action, romance, and exotic locations might say they would like to see the movie. Other students may prefer more realistic movies.

2. Movies might include *Titanic, Star Wars, Indiana Jones.*

Additional Resources
📁 *Media Connections,* p. 16

At the

The movie mentioned in the review (*The Jungle Book*, 1994, 50 minutes, NR) is available for rental. The 1942 version (*Jungle Book*, 109 minutes, NR) is even better, and probably less violent. Be sure to preview any movies beforehand to determine if they are suitable for your class.

Teaching Options

*inter*NET CONNECTION

Movie Reviews Have students use a search engine to find reviews of movies they have seen. They might use the name of the movie and then add the word *review*.

Objectives

- To read and analyze a short story about the delicate balance between two types of predators
- To recognize anthropomorphism
- To write about how setting contributes to a story's effect

Skills

Reading/Thinking: Inferring; Using Graphic Aids; Drawing Conclusions; Identifying Bias; Evaluating

Writing: Writing from Another Point of View; Writing a News Article

Vocabulary: Definitions; Word Origins

Grammar/Language: Using Semicolons; Personal Pronouns

Listening/Speaking: Analyzing a Video; Readers Theater

Life Skills: Interviewing

Collaboration: Literature Groups

Motivating
OPTIONS

Literature Launchers: The Mongoose: A Snake's Deadly Enemy

Videodisc Side B, Segment 22

Also available in VHS.

Selection Focus Transparency 67: Have students help create two lists on the board: animals that are often portrayed in stories as evil and animals that are often portrayed as good.

Focus Activity: As an extension of the Focus Activity, have students in small groups share facts about snakes found locally and around the world.

Before You Read
Rikki-tikki-tavi

MEET RUDYARD KIPLING

Shortly after writing "Rikki-tikki-tavi," Rudyard Kipling became involved in a family feud. After an argument with his brother-in-law that stopped just short of a fistfight, Kipling and his American wife left Vermont for England. Kipling lived the rest of his life in England and India. As a boy, and again as a young adult, he lived in India with his parents in bungalows like the one described in this story. In 1907 Kipling became the first British writer to win the Nobel Prize for Literature.

Rudyard Kipling was born in Bombay, India, in 1865 and died in England in 1936. This story was published in 1894.

FOCUS ACTIVITY

What feelings do you have when you think about snakes?

Think/Pair/Share
Take a moment to jot down your response to this question. Then share your ideas with a partner.

Setting a Purpose
Read this story to find out what happens when a mongoose meets a snake.

BACKGROUND

The Time and Place   The story takes place in India during the late 1800s, a time when the country was ruled by the British. It was not unusual for snakes and other animals to find their way inside people's houses.

Did You Know?   A mongoose is a small mammal of India and Africa, famous for its ability to kill snakes. Mongooses grow to an average length of only about sixteen inches, but their lightning speed makes them fearsome enemies of snakes.

VOCABULARY PREVIEW

scuttle (skut′ əl) *v.* to move with short, rapid steps; p. 789
cower (kou′ ər) *v.* to crouch down, as in fear or shame; p. 792
flinch (flinch) *v.* to draw back, as from something painful, dangerous, or unpleasant; p. 793
gait (gāt) *n.* a particular manner of moving on foot; p. 793
lunge (lunj) *v.* to make a sudden forward movement; charge; p. 794
fancy (fan′ sē) *v.* to picture mentally; imagine; p. 796
valiant (val′ yənt) *adj.* brave; courageous; p. 797
brood (brōōd) *n.* all of the young of an animal that are born or cared for at the same time; p. 799

RESOURCE MANAGER

Lesson Planning Resource
The *Theme Eight Planning Guide* (pp. 19–26) provides additional lesson notes and reduced versions of all print resources.

 Other Print Resources
- Active Reading Guide, p. 67
- Vocabulary Practice, p. 48
- Reading Workbook, pp. 119–120
- Grammar and Language Workbook, pp. 103–104, 265–266

- Grammar and Composition Handbook, Lessons 4.1, 13.5
- Quick Checks, p. 67
- Selection and Theme Assessment, pp. 115–116
- Performance Assessment, p. 63
- Spanish Summaries, p. 67
- Spanish Translations
- Inclusion Strategies
- English Language Learners Sourcebook

 Transparencies
- Selection Focus 67
- Literary Elements 67
- Grammar and Language 62

Technology
 Literature Launchers
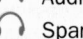 Audio Library
 Spanish Audio Library
 Glencoe Literature Web Site
 Testmaker

Rikki-tikki-tavi

Rudyard Kipling

T his is the story of the great war that Rikki-tikki-tavi fought
single-handed, through the bathrooms of the big bungalow
in Segowlee cantonment.[1] Darzee, the tailorbird, helped him,
and Chuchundra, the muskrat, who never comes out into the middle
of the floor, but always creeps round by the wall, gave him advice;
but Rikki-tikki did the real fighting.

He was a mongoose, rather like a little cat in his fur and his tail,
but quite like a weasel in his head and his habits. His eyes and the end
of his restless nose were pink; he could scratch himself anywhere he
pleased, with any leg, front or back, that he chose to use; he could
fluff up his tail till it looked like a bottle brush, and his war cry, as he
scuttled through the long grass, was *"Rikk-tikk-tikki-tikki-tchk!"*

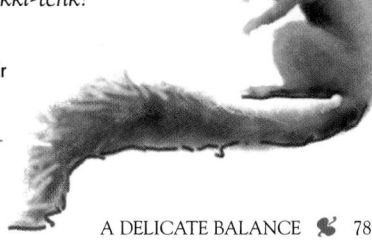

1. In India, a *cantonment* was a British military "town" where servicemen and their
families lived in separate *bungalows,* or cottages.

Vocabulary
scuttle (skut′ əl) *v.* to move with short, rapid steps

SUMMARY

Rikki-tikki-tavi is a young mongoose. He moves into a new territory where a pair of deadly cobras live. Rikki-tikki manages to surprise and kill Nag, the male cobra. Nagaina, the female cobra, blames the humans that Rikki-tikki befriends for Nag's death; she corners the humans on their veranda. When Rikki-tikki battles Nagaina, he is dragged down a rat hole and presumed dead. But surprisingly, Rikki-tikki emerges victorious. From that day forward, no cobras dare enter the garden that Rikki-tikki-tavi guards.

📁 *Spanish Summaries,* p. 67

A Active Reading

QUESTION Invite students to look at the title of this story and identify the animals in the illustrations. After volunteers read the first two paragraphs aloud, ask them to predict whom Rikki-tikki-tavi fights in the great war. Suggest that students periodically revisit their predictions to verify or revise them.

Additional Resources
📁 *Active Reading Guide,* p. 67
🎧 *Audio Library*
🎧 *Spanish Audio Library*

Teaching Options

CONNECTING TO OTHER SELECTIONS

The chart at the right shows three ways to connect "Rikki-tikki-tavi" to other selections in this book.

For specific teaching strategies, see the *Theme Eight Planning Guide,* pages 22–23.

Connection	Title
Life Skills: Problem Solving	→ "Beware of the Dog," p. 603
Thematic: Parents and Children	→ "Mother to Son," p. 342
Literary: Setting	→ "The Smallest Dragonboy," p. 683

B **Literary Elements**

POINT OF VIEW: *Narrator* Have students notice that the narrator reveals the thoughts of several of the characters.

C **Active Reading**

QUESTION Ask students to think what it might mean that Rikki-tikki likes the raw meat "immensely." *(It is a clue that mongooses are carnivores.)*

D **Author's Craft**

ANTHROPOMORPHISM Have students describe how Kipling makes Rikki-tikki-tavi seem like a person. *(The paragraph contains Rikki-tikki's thoughts, which seem like something a person might think. Rikki-tikki thinks about his family and why he wants to stay in the house.)*

E **Active Reading**

VISUALIZE Invite students to visualize this paragraph as you or a volunteer read it aloud. Encourage students to form mental images of Rikki-tikki-tavi nearly drowning in the bathtub, putting his nose in the ink, or burning his nose on a cigar.

Teaching Options

Rikki-tikki-tavi

One day, a high summer flood washed him out of the burrow where he lived with his father and mother, and carried him, kicking and clucking, down a roadside ditch. He found a little wisp of grass floating there, and clung to it till he lost his senses. When he revived, he was lying in the hot sun on the middle of a garden path, very draggled[2] indeed, and a small boy was saying: "Here's a dead mongoose. Let's have a funeral."

"No," said his mother: "let's take him in and dry him. Perhaps he isn't really dead."

They took him into the house, and a big man picked him up between his finger and thumb and said he was not dead but half choked; so they wrapped him in cotton wool and warmed him, and he opened his eyes and sneezed.

"Now," said the big man (he was an Englishman who had just moved into the bungalow), "don't frighten him, and we'll see what he'll do."

It is the hardest thing in the world to frighten a mongoose, because he is eaten up from nose to tail with curiosity. The motto of all the mongoose family is "Run and find out"; and Rikki-tikki was a true mongoose. He looked at the cotton wool, decided that it was not good to eat, ran all round the table, sat up and put his fur in order, scratched himself, and jumped on the small boy's shoulder.

"Don't be frightened, Teddy," said his father. "That's his way of making friends."

"Ouch! He's tickling under my chin," said Teddy.

Rikki-tikki looked down between the boy's collar and neck, snuffed at his ear,

and climbed down to the floor, where he sat rubbing his nose.

"Good gracious," said Teddy's mother, "and that's a wild creature! I suppose he's so tame because we've been kind to him."

"All mongooses are like that," said her husband. "If Teddy doesn't pick him up by the tail, or try to put him in a cage, he'll run in and out of the house all day long. Let's give him something to eat."

They gave him a little piece of raw meat. Rikki-tikki liked it immensely, and when it was finished he went out into the veranda and sat in the sunshine and fluffed up his fur to make it dry to the roots. Then he felt better.

Did You Know?
A *veranda* is a long porch, usually with a roof, along one or more sides of a house.

"There are more things to find out about in this house," he said to himself, "than all my family could find out in all their lives. I shall certainly stay and find out."

He spent all that day roaming over the house. He nearly drowned himself in the bathtubs, put his nose into the ink on a writing table, and burned it on the end of the big man's cigar, for he climbed up in the big man's lap to see how writing was done. At nightfall he ran into Teddy's nursery to watch how kerosene lamps[3] were lighted, and when Teddy went to bed Rikki-tikki climbed up too; but he was a restless companion, because he had to get up and attend to every noise all through the night and find out what made it.

---

2. *Draggled* means "wet and dirty."

---

3. A *kerosene lamp* burns a liquid fuel made from petroleum.

Understanding Long Sentences For some English language learners, the length of the sentences in this story may make comprehension difficult. By breaking the sentences into smaller, more manageable units, students may find the story easier to understand.

Activity Have groups of students read this story together. Encourage students to stop whenever they see a comma or

semicolon and summarize the action that has occurred until that point. By discussing the action with other group members, students can discover whether their ideas about the events are accurate. **COLLAB. LEARN.**

Additional Resources
📁 *English Language Learners Sourcebook*

Teddy's mother and father came in, the last thing, to look at their boy, and Rikki-tikki was awake on the pillow. "I don't like that," said Teddy's mother; "he may bite the child."

"He'll do no such thing," said the father. "Teddy's safer with that little beast than if he had a bloodhound to watch him. If a snake came into the nursery now—"

But Teddy's mother wouldn't think of anything so awful.

Early in the morning Rikki-tikki came to early breakfast in the veranda, riding on Teddy's shoulder, and they gave him banana and some boiled egg; and he sat on all their laps one after the other, because every well-brought-up mongoose always hopes to be a house mongoose someday and have rooms to run about in, and Rikki-tikki's mother (she used to live in the general's house at Segowlee) had carefully told Rikki what to do if ever he came across Englishmen.

Then Rikki-tikki went out into the garden to see what was to be seen. It was a large garden, only half cultivated, with bushes as big as summer houses of roses, lime and orange trees, clumps of bamboos, and thickets of high grass. Rikki-tikki licked his lips. "This is a splendid hunting

Tent Hanging. Early 18th century, Mughal (Jaipur?). Cotton quilt embroidered in silk. Victoria and Albert Museum, London.

Viewing the artifact: How might the characters in Rikki-tikki-tavi have used a tent hanging? What do you think would have been its original use?

ground," he said, and his tail grew bottle-brushy at the thought of it, and he scuttled up and down the garden, snuffling here and there till he heard very sorrowful voices in a thornbush.

It was Darzee, the tailorbird, and his wife. They had made a beautiful nest by pulling two big leaves together and stitching them up the edges with fibers, and had

---

F Critical Thinking

INFERRING Have students finish the father's sentence for him. *(...the snake would kill Teddy.)* What might happen if a snake came into the nursery when Rikki-tikki-tavi was on the pillow? *(Rikki-tikki-tavi might attack and kill the snake.)*

G Literary Elements

ANTHROPOMORPHISM Ask students to describe the humanlike behaviors and thoughts of Rikki-tikki-tavi in this paragraph. *(Rikki-tikki is well-brought-up and has hopes for a better life. His mother has told him how to behave if he ever runs across English people.)*

VIEWING THE ARTIFACT

The Mughals invaded India in the sixteenth century, bringing the influence of Islamic art with them. Because Islam discourages the portrayal of human figures in art, their rugs and hangings made use of animals, geometrical figures, or floral motifs, usually repeated in a continuous pattern.

Viewing Response *The tent hanging might have been used for decoration. Originally, it might have been used as a partition or hung on the tent wall for decoration.*

Reading Minilesson

Using Graphic Aids Kipling gives the animals in this story human emotions and characteristics. On the board, begin a web for Rikki-tikki. Have students list human characteristics that they have noticed so far in Rikki-tikki. Add these ideas to the web on the board.

Rikki-tikki-tavi: *curious; restless; hopes to be a proper house mongoose; well-brought-up, knows etiquette*

Activity Have students create their own webs: one for Rikki-tikki-tavi and, later, one for Nag and Nagaina. On the web, ask students to keep track of the human emotions, characteristics, and thoughts that these animals display. **L2**

Additional Resources
📁 *Reading Workbook,* pp. 119–120

Author's Craft

DESCRIPTION Encourage students to identify phrases Kipling uses to make Nag seem evil. *(Phrases include "horrid cold sound," and "wicked snake's eyes.")*

Vo•cab•u•lar•y Skills

Word Origins The Portuguese navigator Vasco da Gama landed in India in 1498. There the Portuguese first saw a poisonous hooded snake, which Indians called *nag*. The Portuguese, however, called the snake *cobra de capello*, or "snake with the small cape, or hood." The English borrowed *cobra de capello* in the 1600s. By the 1800s, they had shortened the name to *cobra*.

Literary Elements

FORESHADOWING Ask students what clues in this paragraph make them think that there will be conflict between Nag and Rikki-tikki. *(Rikki-tikki and Nag will probably have a fight. The paragraph says that a mongoose's business in life is to fight and eat snakes.)*

Critical Thinking

DRAWING CONCLUSIONS Ask students whether a snake that eats birds is really more evil than a mongoose that eats snakes. *(Students may say that neither is more evil than the other. They are both using their instincts to survive.)*

Teaching Options

Rikki-tikki-tavi

filled the hollow with cotton and downy fluff. The nest swayed to and fro, as they sat on the brim and cried.

"What is the matter?" asked Rikki-tikki.

"We are very miserable," said Darzee. "One of our babies fell out of the nest yesterday, and Nag ate him."

"H'm!" said Rikki-tikki; "that is very sad—but I am a stranger here. Who is Nag?"

Darzee and his wife only <u>cowered</u> down in the nest without answering, for from the thick grass at the foot of the bush came a low hiss—a horrid cold sound that made Rikki-tikki jump back two clear feet. Then inch by inch out of the grass rose up the head and spread hood of Nag, the big black cobra, and he was five feet long from tongue to tail. When he had lifted one third of himself clear of the ground, he stayed balancing to and fro exactly as a dandelion tuft balances in the wind, and he looked at Rikki-tikki with the wicked snake's eyes that never change their expression, whatever the snake may be thinking of.

"Who is Nag?" he said. "*I* am Nag. The great god Brahm put his mark upon all our people when the first cobra spread his hood to keep the sun off Brahm as he slept. Look, and be afraid!"

He spread out his hood more than ever, and Rikki-tikki saw the spectacle mark on the back of it that looks exactly like the eye part of a hook-and-eye fastening. He was afraid for the minute; but it is impossible for a mongoose to stay frightened for any length of time, and though Rikki-tikki had never met

a live cobra before, his mother had fed him on dead ones, and he knew that all a grown mongoose's business in life was to fight and eat snakes. Nag knew that too, and at the bottom of his cold heart he was afraid.

"Well," said Rikki-tikki, and his tail began to fluff up again, "marks or no marks, do you think it is right for you to eat fledglings[4] out of a nest?"

Nag was thinking to himself, and watching the least little movement in the grass behind Rikki-tikki. He knew that mongooses in the garden meant death sooner or later for him and his family, but he wanted to get Rikki-tikki off his guard. So he dropped his head a little and put it on one side.

"Let us talk," he said. "You eat eggs. Why should not I eat birds?"

"Behind you! Look behind you!" sang Darzee.

Rikki-tikki knew better than to waste time in staring. He jumped up in the air as high as he could go, and just under him whizzed by the head of Nagaina, Nag's wicked wife. She had crept up behind him as he was

---

4. Young birds that haven't yet grown the feathers needed to fly are called *fledglings*.

Vocabulary
cower (kou′ ər) *v.* to crouch down, as in fear or shame

792 ❧ THEME 8

Cobra

Special Needs Visually-impaired students may have difficulty keeping track of the new vocabulary words introduced in the story.

Activity Have a proficient reader work with a visually impaired student. Ask the proficient reader to read the story, pausing when he or she reads a word they do not understand. Together they can find the definitions and tape-record each of the vocabulary words along with its definition. The special-needs student can use the audiotape for future reference in the classroom or at home.

L2 COLLAB. LEARN.

Additional Resources
📁 *Inclusion Strategies*

Author's Craft

CHARACTERIZATION Ask students how the author describes Nagaina and why. *(She is Nag's wicked wife, with a "savage hiss." Kipling does not seem to want the reader to have any sympathy for her.)*

talking, to make an end of him; and he heard her savage hiss as the stroke missed. He came down almost across her back, and if he had been an old mongoose, he would have known that then was the time to break her back with one bite; but he was afraid of the terrible lashing return stroke of the cobra. He bit, indeed, but did not bite long enough, and he jumped clear of the whisking tail, leaving Nagaina torn and angry.

"Wicked, wicked Darzee!" said Nag, lashing up as high as he could reach toward the nest in the thornbush; but Darzee had built it out of the reach of snakes, and it only swayed to and fro.

Rikki-tikki felt his eyes growing red and hot (when a mongoose's eyes grow red, he is angry), and he sat back on his tail and hind legs like a little kangaroo, and looked all around him, and chattered with rage. But Nag and Nagaina had disappeared into the grass. When a snake misses its stroke, it never says anything or gives any sign of what it means to do next. Rikki-tikki did not care to follow them, for he did not feel sure that he could manage two snakes at once. So he trotted off to the gravel path near the house, and sat down to think. It was a serious matter for him.

If you read the old books of natural history, you will find they say that when the mongoose fights the snake and happens to get bitten, he runs off and eats some herb that cures him. That is not true. The victory is only a matter of quickness of eye and quickness of foot—snake's blow against mongoose's jump—and as no eye can follow the motion of a snake's head when it strikes, that makes things much more wonderful than any magic herb. Rikki-tikki knew he was a young mongoose, and it made him all the more pleased to think that he had managed to escape a blow from behind. It gave him confidence in himself, and when Teddy came running down the path, Rikki-tikki was ready to be petted.

But just as Teddy was stooping, something flinched a little in the dust, and a tiny voice said: "Be careful. I am death!" It was Karait, the dusty brown snakeling that lies for choice on the dusty earth; and his bite is as dangerous as the cobra's. But he is so small that nobody thinks of him, and so he does the more harm to people.

Rikki-tikki's eyes grew red again, and he danced up to Karait with the peculiar rocking, swaying motion that he had inherited from his family. It looks very funny, but it is so perfectly balanced a gait that you can fly off from it at any angle you please; and in dealing with snakes this is an advantage. If Rikki-tikki had only known, he was doing a much more dangerous thing than fighting Nag, for Karait is so small, and can turn so quickly, that unless Rikki bit him close to the back of the head, he would get the return stroke in his eye or lip. But Rikki did not know: his eyes were all red, and he rocked back and forth, looking for a good place to hold. Karait struck out. Rikki jumped sideways and tried to run in, but the wicked little dusty gray head lashed within a fraction of his shoulder, and he had to jump over the body, and the head followed his heels close.

Active Reading

PREDICT Invite students to predict whether Karait will bite Teddy or Rikki-tikki. *(Students may think that since Karait is more dangerous than a cobra, Rikki-tikki may be harmed. Others may think that if Rikki-tikki can defeat Karait, he can defeat Nag and Nagaina.)*

FYI

Cobras and Kraits The *king cobra* of southern Asia is the largest poisonous snake in the world. It can reach sixteen feet in length, but its bite is not usually fatal. The *krait* (pronounced *krite*) is a small snake in Southeast Asia. Fifty percent of the people it bites die, even if antivenom is given.

Vocabulary

flinch (flinch) *v.* to draw back, as from something painful, dangerous, or unpleasant

gait (gāt) *n.* a particular manner of moving on foot

A DELICATE BALANCE 793

Teddy shouted to the house: "Oh, look here! Our mongoose is killing a snake"; and Rikki-tikki heard a scream from Teddy's mother. His father ran out with a stick, but by the time he came up, Karait had lunged out once too far, and Rikki-tikki had sprung, jumped on the snake's back, dropped his head far between his forelegs, bitten as high up the back as he could get hold, and rolled away. That bite paralyzed Karait, and Rikki-tikki was just going to eat him up from the tail, after the custom of his family at dinner, when he remembered that a full meal makes a slow mongoose, and if he wanted all his strength and quickness ready, he must keep himself thin.

He went away for a dust bath under the castor-oil bushes, while Teddy's father beat the dead Karait. "What is the use of that?" thought Rikki-tikki. "I have settled it all"; and then Teddy's mother picked him up from the dust and hugged him, crying that he had saved Teddy from death, and Teddy's father said that he was a providence,[5] and Teddy looked on with big scared eyes. Rikki-tikki was rather amused at all the fuss, which, of course, he did not understand. Teddy's mother might just as well have petted Teddy for playing in the dust. Rikki was thoroughly enjoying himself.

That night, at dinner, walking to and fro among the wineglasses on the table, he could have stuffed himself three times over with nice things; but he remembered Nag and Nagaina, and though it was very pleasant to be patted and petted by Teddy's

mother, and to sit on Teddy's shoulder, his eyes would get red from time to time, and he would go off into his long war cry of *"Rikk-tikk-tikki-tikki-tchk!"*

Teddy carried him off to bed and insisted on Rikki-tikki sleeping under his chin. Rikki-tikki was too well bred to bite or scratch, but as soon as Teddy was asleep he went off for his nightly walk round the house, and in the dark he ran up against Chuchundra, the muskrat, creeping round by the wall. Chuchundra is a broken-hearted little beast. He whimpers and cheeps all the night, trying to make up his mind to run into the middle of the room, but he never gets there.

"Don't kill me," said Chuchundra, almost weeping. "Rikki-tikki, don't kill me."

"Do you think a snake-killer kills muskrats?" said Rikki-tikki scornfully.

"Those who kill snakes get killed by snakes," said Chuchundra, more sorrowfully than ever. "And how am I to be sure that Nag won't mistake me for you some dark night?"

"There's not the least danger," said Rikki-tikki; "but Nag is in the garden, and I know you don't go there."

"My cousin Chua, the rat, told me—" said Chuchundra, and then he stopped.

"Told you what?"

"H'sh! Nag is everywhere, Rikki-tikki. You should have talked to Chua in the garden."

"I didn't—so you must tell me. Quick, Chuchundra, or I'll bite you!"

Chuchundra sat down and cried till the tears rolled off his whiskers. "I am a very

---

5. A *providence* (prov′ ə dəns) is a blessing from God or nature.

Vocabulary
lunge (lunj) *v.* to make a sudden forward movement; charge

GIFTED AND TALENTED ACTIVITY
MEETING INDIVIDUAL NEEDS

Cobras and the Mongoose Have interested students read reference materials to find out more about cobras and the mongoose.

Activity Invite students to work in pairs and search a library database or the Internet to find information on the habits and habitats of these creatures. Suggest students take notes in order to present an oral report that highlights their most interesting findings. Encourage students to include visuals when they present their findings to the rest of the class. **L3** **COLLAB. LEARN.**

poor man," he sobbed. "I never had spirit enough to run out into the middle of the room. H'sh! I mustn't tell you anything. Can't you *hear*, Rikki-tikki?"

Rikki-tikki listened. The house was as still as still, but he thought he could just catch the faintest *scratch-scratch* in the world—a noise as faint as that of a wasp walking on a window-pane—the dry scratch of a snake's scales on brickwork.

"That's Nag or Nagaina," he said to himself; "and he is crawling into the bathroom sluice.[6] You're right, Chuchundra; I should have talked to Chua."

He stole off to Teddy's bathroom, but there was nothing there, and then to Teddy's mother's bathroom. At the bottom of the smooth plaster wall there was a brick pulled out to make a sluice for the bath water, and as Rikki-tikki stole in by the masonry curb where the bath is put, he heard Nag and Nagaina whispering together outside in the moonlight.

Q "When the house is emptied of people," said Nagaina to her husband, "*he* will have to go away, and then the garden will be our own again. Go in quietly, and remember that the big man who killed Karait is the first one to bite. Then come out and tell me, and we will hunt for Rikki-tikki together."

"But are you sure there is anything to be gained by killing the people?" said Nag.

The house was as still as still, but he thought he could just catch the faintest scratch-scratch in the world—a noise as faint as that of a wasp walking on a windowpane—

"Everything. When there were no people in the bungalow, did we have any mongoose in the garden? So long as the bungalow is empty, we are king and queen of the garden; and remember that as soon as our eggs in the melon bed hatch (as they may tomorrow), our children will need room and quiet."

R "I had not thought of that," said Nag. "I will go, but there is no need that we should hunt for Rikki-tikki afterward. I will kill the big man and his wife, and the child if I can, and come away quietly. Then the bungalow will be empty, and Rikki-tikki will go."

Rikki-tikki tingled all over with rage and hatred at this, and then Nag's head came through the sluice, and his five feet of cold body followed it. Angry as he was, Rikki-tikki was very frightened as he saw the size of the big cobra. Nag coiled himself up, raised his head, and looked into the bathroom in the dark, and Rikki could see his eyes glitter.

"Now, if I kill him there, Nagaina will know; and if I fight him on the open floor, the odds are in his favor. What am I to do?" said Rikki-tikki-tavi.

Nag waved to and fro, and then Rikki-tikki heard him drinking from the biggest water jar that was used to fill the bath. "That is good," said the snake. "Now, when Karait was killed, the big man had a stick. He may have that stick still, but when he comes in to bathe in the morning he will

6. Here, the *sluice* is a drainpipe.

INTERDISCIPLINARY CONNECTION

Science How did Rikki-tikki-tavi know who his mother was? Konrad Lorenz (1893–1989) studied animal behavior, particularly how animal instinct and learned behavior worked together. He pioneered studies on how a young animal instinctively becomes attached to a parent.

Activity Interested students may wish to look into imprinting in more detail.

Although Lorenz did his experiments with goslings and ducklings, studies were replicated using mammals. Students could prepare a report, complete with visuals including diagrams, graphs, and photographs downloaded from a reliable Web site. **L3**

Literary Elements

ANTHROPOMORPHISM Ask students to describe Rikki-tikki-tavi's human-like thoughts in this paragraph. *(He analyzes the situation much as a person would; he thinks about his strategy and where the best place to get a good hold is. He recognizes the consequences if he doesn't get a good hold in the proper place.)*

Active Reading

QUESTION Ask students to discuss what has just happened here. What is the thunderclap and the red fire? *(The fight must have been noisy enough to wake up the Englishman, who shoots at the cobra. The thunderclap is the booming of the gun. The red fire is the bullet whizzing close to Rikki-tikki-tavi's fur.)*

Literary Elements

HUMOR Have students explain what is funny or amusing about this situation. *(Rikki-tikki-tavi is probably badly bruised after the fight, but he clearly is not broken into forty pieces. His exaggerated evaluation creates humor.)*

Teaching Options

not have a stick. I shall wait here till he comes. Nagaina—do you hear me? I shall wait here in the cool till daytime."

There was no answer from outside, so Rikki-tikki knew Nagaina had gone away. Nag coiled himself down, coil by coil, round the bulge at the bottom of the water jar, and Rikki-tikki stayed still as death. After an hour he began to move, muscle by muscle, toward the jar. Nag was asleep, and Rikki-tikki looked at his big back, wondering which would be the best place for a good hold. "If I don't break his back at the first jump," said Rikki, "he can still fight; and if he fights—O Rikki!" He looked at the thickness of the neck below the hood, but that was too much for him; and a bite near the tail would only make Nag savage.

"It must be the head," he said at last; "the head above the hood; and when I am once there, I must not let go."

Then he jumped. The head was lying a little clear of the water jar, under the curve of it; and, as his teeth met, Rikki braced his back against the bulge of the red earthenware to hold down the head. This gave him just one second's purchase,[7] and he made the most of it. Then he was battered to and fro as a rat is shaken by a dog—to and fro on the floor, up and down, and round in great circles; but his eyes were red, and he held on as the body cartwhipped[8] over the floor, upsetting the tin dipper and the soap dish and the

---

7. In this context, the *purchase* is an advantageous position for applying force.
8. Rikki's body is being thrown about like a whip (*cartwhipped*) as the cobra lashes.

fleshbrush, and banged against the tin side of the bath. As he held, he closed his jaws tighter and tighter, for he made sure he would be banged to death, and, for the honor of his family, he preferred to be found with his teeth locked. He was dizzy, aching, and felt shaken to pieces when something went off like a thunderclap just behind him; a hot wind knocked him senseless, and red fire singed his fur. The big man had been wakened by the noise, and had fired both barrels of a shotgun into Nag just behind the hood.

Rikki-tikki held on with his eyes shut, for now he was quite sure he was dead; but the head did not move, and the big man picked him up and said: "It's the mongoose again, Alice; the little chap has saved *our* lives now." Then Teddy's mother came in with a very white face, and saw what was left of Nag, and Rikki-tikki dragged himself to Teddy's bedroom and spent half the rest of the night shaking himself tenderly to find out whether he really was broken into forty pieces, as he fancied.

When morning came he was very stiff, but well pleased with his doings. "Now I have Nagaina to settle with, and she will be worse than five Nags, and there's no knowing when the eggs she spoke of will hatch. Goodness! I must go and see Darzee," he said.

Without waiting for breakfast, Rikki-tikki ran to the thornbush where Darzee was singing a song of triumph at the top of his voice. The news of Nag's death was all over the garden, for the sweeper had thrown the body on the rubbish heap.

Vocabulary
fancy (fan′ sē) *v.* to picture mentally; imagine

Listening and Speaking *Minilesson*

Analyzing a Video The story of Rikki-tikki-tavi has been recreated on film. Students may enjoy comparing a video version of this story with the print version.

Activity You may want to show the class the thirty-minute cartoon *Rikki-tikki-tavi,* created by renowned cartoonist Chuck Jones. As students view the video, have them take notes on how the two

stories are similar and how they are different. After the viewing, divide the class into small groups. Have each group list similarities and differences between the two versions of the story. Finally, have each group decide which version they liked better and explain why.
L2 **COLLAB. LEARN.**

"Oh, you stupid tuft of feathers!" said Rikki-tikki angrily. "Is this the time to sing?"

"Nag is dead—is dead—is dead!" sang Darzee. "The valiant Rikki-tikki caught him by the head and held fast. The big man brought the bang-stick, and Nag fell in two pieces! He will never eat my babies again."

"All that's true enough; but where's Nagaina?" said Rikki-tikki, looking carefully round him.

"Nagaina came to the bathroom sluice and called for Nag," Darzee went on; "and Nag came out on the end of a stick—the sweeper picked him up on the end of a stick and threw him upon the rubbish heap. Let us sing about the great, the red-eyed Rikki-tikki!" And Darzee filled his throat and sang.

"If I could get up to your nest, I'd roll all your babies out!" said Rikki-tikki. "You don't know when to do the right thing at the right time. You're safe enough in your nest there, but it's war for me down here. Stop singing a minute, Darzee."

"For the great, the beautiful Rikki-tikki's sake I will stop," said Darzee. "What is it, O Killer of the terrible Nag?"

"Where is Nagaina, for the third time?"

"On the rubbish heap by the stables, mourning for Nag. Great is Rikki-tikki with the white teeth."

"Bother my white teeth![9] Have you ever heard where she keeps her eggs?"

---

9. *Bother my white teeth* is a British way of saying, "Don't concern yourself with my teeth."

Vocabulary
valiant (val′ yənt) *adj.* brave; courageous

V Literary Elements

ANTHROPOMORPHISM Have students describe how this paragraph makes Rikki-tikki-tavi and Darzee seem like people. *(Rikki-tikki knows the fight is not over yet, so he is angry with Darzee for being so happy. Darzee is empty-headed and has no common sense. Rikki-tikki is more practical and needs to get answers from Darzee, who is too busy celebrating to answer his questions.)*

W Literary Elements

MOOD Ask students to discuss what they think the mood of this scene is. Do some find it comical? frantic? chaotic? Pairs of students might be interested in dramatizing this scene for the class.

X Active Reading

PREDICT Have students predict what Rikki-tikki will do if he finds out where Nagaina keeps her eggs. *(Rikki-tikki will destroy the eggs, so the garden will not be overrun by cobras.)*

Writing *Minilesson*

Writing from Another Point of View
Invite students to try their hand at giving voice to one of the cobras' thoughts and concerns.

Activity Have students choose one dramatic scene involving Rikki-tikki-tavi and Nag or Nagaina. Invite students to work in pairs to rewrite this scene from the point of view of Nag or Nagaina. When students have finished, ask them to share their scenes with the rest of the class. Students can discuss whether this new perspective changes their ideas about the story. **L2 COLLAB. LEARN.**

Additional Resources

📖 *Writer's Choice*, Lesson 4.5

EVALUATING Ask students to contrast Darzee and his wife. *(Darzee is foolish, unfocused, and opposed to destroying the eggs. His wife is sensible and sees the big picture: baby cobras mean danger to her young.)*

Z Literary Elements

ANTHROPOMORPHISM Have students describe the human qualities that Nagaina and Darzee's wife display here. *(Darzee's wife pretends; Nagaina blames, holds a grudge, and wants revenge.)*

FYI

Snake Facts Most reptiles abandon their eggs, which do not have to be kept warm all the time. Baby reptiles have an "egg tooth" which they use to break through the egg. The tooth falls off shortly after hatching. Snakes have no eyelids. Their eyes are protected by a permanent see-through covering. Snakes have internal ears.

Teaching Options

Rikki-tikki-tavi

"In the melon bed, on the end nearest the wall, where the sun strikes nearly all day. She hid them there weeks ago."

"And you never thought it worthwhile to tell me? The end nearest the wall, you said?"

"Rikki-tikki, you are not going to eat her eggs?"

"Not eat exactly; no. Darzee, if you have a grain of sense you will fly off to the stables and pretend that your wing is broken, and let Nagaina chase you away to this bush! I must get to the melon bed, and if I went there now she'd see me."

Darzee was a featherbrained little fellow who could never hold more than one idea at a time in his head; and just because he knew that Nagaina's children were born in eggs like his own, he didn't think at first that it was fair to kill them. But his wife was a sensible bird, and she knew that cobras' eggs meant young cobras later on; so she flew off from the nest, and left Darzee to keep the babies warm, and continue his song about the death of Nag. Darzee was very like a man in some ways.

She fluttered in front of Nagaina by the rubbish heap and cried out, "Oh, my wing is broken! The boy in the house threw a stone at me and broke it." Then she fluttered more desperately than ever.

Nagaina lifted up her head and hissed, "You warned Rikki-tikki when I would have killed him. Indeed and truly, you've chosen a bad place to be lame in." And she moved toward Darzee's wife, slipping along over the dust.

"The boy broke it with a stone!" shrieked Darzee's wife.

"Well! It may be some consolation to you when you're dead to know that I shall settle accounts with the boy. My husband lies on the rubbish heap this morning, but

before night the boy in the house will lie very still. What is the use of running away? I am sure to catch you. Little fool, look at me!"

Darzee's wife knew better than to do *that*, for a bird who looks at a snake's eyes gets so frightened that she cannot move. Darzee's wife fluttered on, piping sorrowfully, and never leaving the ground, and Nagaina quickened her pace.

Rikki-tikki heard them going up the path from the stables, and he raced for the end of the melon patch near the wall. There, in the warm litter about the melons, very cunningly hidden, he found twenty-five eggs, about the size of a bantam's eggs, but with whitish skin instead of shell.

Did You Know?
A *bantam* is a small breed of chicken.

"I was not a day too soon," he said; for he could see the baby cobras curled up inside the skin, and he knew that the minute they were hatched they could each kill a man or a mongoose. He bit off the tops of the eggs as fast as he could, taking care to crush the young cobras, and turned over the litter from time to time to see whether he had missed any. At last there were only three eggs left, and Rikki-tikki began to chuckle to himself, when he heard Darzee's wife screaming:

"Rikki-tikki, I led Nagaina toward the house, and she has gone into the veranda, and—oh, come quickly—she means killing!"

Rikki-tikki smashed two eggs, and tumbled backward down the melon bed

---

MEETING INDIVIDUAL NEEDS — ENGLISH LANGUAGE LEARNERS

Predators All over the world, some predators are seen as helpful to humans while others are seen as pests or enemies. Write the words *predator* and *prey* on the board. Have volunteers define each word.

Activity In mixed groups, have students list animals that are helpful to humans and animals that are seen as pests or dangerous enemies. Have

students explain why those animals are enemies of humans. Finally, have each group draw a picture of one predator that is considered especially dangerous to people. Encourage groups to display their drawings for the rest of the class.

Additional Resources
📁 *English Language Learners Sourcebook*

Rudyard Kipling

with the third egg in his mouth, and scuttled to the veranda as hard as he could put foot to the ground. Teddy and his mother and father were there at early breakfast; but Rikki-tikki saw that they were not eating anything. They sat stone-still, and their faces were white. Nagaina was coiled up on the matting by Teddy's chair, within easy striking distance of Teddy's bare leg, and she was swaying to and fro singing a song of triumph.

"Look at your friends, Rikki-tikki. They are still and white; they are afraid. They dare not move, and if you come a step nearer I strike."

AA "Son of the big man that killed Nag," she hissed, "stay still. I am not ready yet. Wait a little. Keep very still, all you three. If you move I strike, and if you do not move I strike. Oh, foolish people, who killed my Nag!"

Teddy's eyes were fixed on his father, and all his father could do was to whisper, "Sit still, Teddy. You mustn't move. Teddy, keep still."

Then Rikki-tikki came up and cried: "Turn round, Nagaina; turn and fight!"

"All in good time," said she, without moving her eyes. "I will settle my account with *you* presently. Look at your friends, Rikki-tikki. They are still and white; they are afraid. They dare not move, and if you come a step nearer I strike."

"Look at your eggs," said Rikki-tikki, "in the melon bed near the wall. Go and look, Nagaina."

The big snake turned half round and saw the egg on the veranda. "Ah-h! Give it to me," she said.

Rikki-tikki put his paws one on each side of the egg, and his eyes were blood-red. "What price for a snake's egg? For a young cobra? For a young king cobra? For the last—the very last of the <u>brood</u>? The ants are eating all the others down by the melon bed." **BB**

Nagaina spun clear round, forgetting everything for the sake of the one egg; and Rikki-tikki saw Teddy's father shoot out a big hand, catch Teddy by the shoulder, and drag him across the little table with the teacups, safe and out of reach of Nagaina.

"Tricked! Tricked! Tricked! *Rikk-tck-tck!*" chuckled Rikki-tikki. "The boy is safe, and it was I—I—I that caught Nag by the hood last night in the bathroom." Then he began to jump up and down, all four feet together, his head close to the floor. "He threw me to and fro, but he could not shake me off. He was dead before the big man blew him in two. I did it. *Rikki-tikki-tck-tck!* Come then, Nagaina. Come and fight with me. You shall not be a widow long."

Nagaina saw that she had lost her chance of killing Teddy, and the egg lay between Rikki-tikki's paws. "Give me the egg, Rikki-tikki. Give me the last of my eggs, and I will go away and never come **CC**

Vocabulary
brood (brood) *n.* all of the young of an animal that are born or cared for at the same time

---

Literary Elements

SIMILE Ask students to discuss the similes in these paragraphs. What do the two unlike things have in common? *(Examples include eyes/hot coals: red and glowing; tail rustle/dry leaves: sound.)*

EE **Active Reading**

QUESTION Invite students to explain what will happen if Rikki-tikki-tavi does not catch Nagaina. *(She and her baby will pose a constant danger.)*

FF **Active Reading**

RESPOND Encourage students to discuss why Kipling never explains what happens underground. *(He wants it to remain mysterious.)* Invite students to describe what they think happened underground. *(Rikki-tikki-tavi must somehow have bitten her and held on until she was dead.)*

FYI

The Mongoose Since mongooses are such fierce and destructive hunters, it is illegal to import them into this country. It is feared they will do great damage if they ever get loose. Even U.S. zoos are not allowed to import mongooses.

Rikki-tikki-tavi

back," she said, lowering her hood.

"Yes, you will go away, and you will never come back; for you will go to the rubbish heap with Nag. Fight, widow! The big man has gone for his gun! Fight!"

Rikki-tikki was bounding all round Nagaina, keeping just out of reach of her stroke, his little eyes like hot coals. Nagaina gathered herself together and flung out at him. Rikki-tikki jumped up and backward. Again and again and again she struck, and each time her head came with a whack on the matting of the veranda, and she gathered herself together like a watchspring. Then Rikki-tikki danced in a circle to get behind her, and Nagaina spun round to keep her head to his head, so that the rustle of her tail on the matting sounded like dry leaves blown along by the wind.

He had forgotten the egg. It still lay on the veranda, and Nagaina came nearer and nearer to it, till at last, while Rikki-tikki was drawing breath, she caught it in her mouth, turned to the veranda steps, and flew like an arrow down the path, with Rikki-tikki behind her. When the cobra runs for her life, she goes like a whiplash flicked across a horse's neck.

Rikki-tikki knew that he must catch her, or all the trouble would begin again. She headed straight for the long grass by the thornbush, and as he was running Rikki-tikki heard Darzee singing his foolish little song of triumph. But Darzee's wife was wiser. She flew off her nest as Nagaina came along,

. . . very few mongooses, however wise and old they may be, care to follow a cobra into its hole.

and flapped her wings about Nagaina's head. If Darzee had helped they might have turned her; but Nagaina only lowered her hood and went on. Still, the instant's delay brought Rikki-tikki up to her, and as she plunged into the rathole where she and Nag used to live, his little white teeth were clenched on her tail, and he went down with her—and very few mongooses, however wise and old they may be, care to follow a cobra into its hole. It was dark in the hole; and Rikki-tikki never knew when it might open out and give Nagaina room to turn and strike at him. He held on savagely and struck out his feet to act as brakes on the dark slope of the hot, moist earth.

Then the grass by the mouth of the hole stopped waving, and Darzee said: "It is all over with Rikki-tikki! We must sing his death song. Valiant Rikki-tikki is dead. For Nagaina will surely kill him underground."

So he sang a very mournful song that he made up all on the spur of the minute, and just as he got to the most touching part the grass quivered again, and Rikki-tikki, covered with dirt, dragged himself out of the hole leg by leg, licking his whiskers. Darzee stopped with a little shout. Rikki-tikki shook some of the dust out of his fur and sneezed. "It is all over," he said. "The widow will never come out again." And the red ants that live between the grass stems heard him, and began to troop down one after another to see if he had spoken the truth.

Teaching Options

Grammar and Language *Minilesson*

Using Semicolons If two main clauses are connected by *and, but,* or *or,* a comma precedes the conjunction: *All of the eggs were exposed, and only one survived.* However, if two main clauses do not each have an end mark and are not joined by a conjunction, a semicolon can be used as the connector: *All of the eggs were exposed; only one survived.*

Activity Write the following sentences on the board without semicolons. Ask students to punctuate them.
1. They are still and white; they are afraid.
2. His eyes at the end of his restless nose were pink; he could scratch himself anywhere he pleased; he could fluff up his tail till it looked like a bottlebrush.
3. You will go away, and you will never come back; you will go to the rubbish

heap with Nag. **L2**

Additional Resources

 Grammar and Language Transparency 62

📙 ***Grammar and Language Workbook,*** pp. 265–266

📙 ***Grammar and Composition Handbook,*** Lesson 13.5

📙 ***Writer's Choice,*** Lesson 20.5

Rikki-tikki curled himself up in the grass and slept where he was—slept and slept till it was late in the afternoon, for he had done a hard day's work.

"Now," he said, when he awoke, "I will go back to the house. Tell the coppersmith, Darzee, and he will tell the garden that Nagaina is dead."

The coppersmith is a bird who makes a noise exactly like the beating of a little hammer on a copper pot; and the reason he is always making it is because he is the town crier to every Indian garden, and tells all the news to everybody who cares to listen. As Rikki-tikki went up the path, he heard his "attention" notes like a tiny dinner gong; and then the steady "*Ding-dong-tock!* Nag is dead—*dong!* Nagaina is dead! *Ding-dong-tock!*" That set all the birds in the garden singing, and the frogs croaking, for Nag and Nagaina used to eat frogs as well as little birds.

When Rikki got to the house, Teddy and Teddy's mother (she still looked very white, for she had been fainting) and Teddy's father came out and almost cried over him; and that night he ate all that was given him till he could eat no more, and went to bed on Teddy's shoulder, where Teddy's mother saw him when she came to look late at night.

"He saved our lives and Teddy's life," she said to her husband. "Just think, he saved all our lives!"

Viewing the photograph: Did you imagine Darzee, the tailorbird, looking anything like this tailorbird? Why or why not?

Rikki-tikki woke up with a jump, for all mongooses are light sleepers.

"Oh, it's you," said he. "What are you bothering for? All the cobras are dead; and if they weren't, I'm here."

Rikki-tikki had a right to be proud of himself; but he did not grow too proud, and he kept that garden as a mongoose should keep it, with tooth and jump and spring and bite, till never a cobra dared show its head inside the walls.

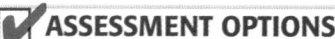

GG Literary Elements

ANTHROPOMORPHISM Ask students for examples of human characteristics Kipling is using to portray Rikki-tikki. *(He is tired after the fight and needs to sleep to recover his energy; he is a little smug at having beaten a strong competitor; he now thinks he can take care of any cobras that might threaten the garden or the family.)*

VIEWING THE PHOTOGRAPH

The *tailorbird* is a warbler, a family of birds famous for its song. More than 100 species of warblers exist in Europe, Asia, Africa, and the Americas.

Viewing Response *Some students may have imagined Darzee as larger, or perhaps more comic in appearance.*

Thematic Focus

A Delicate Balance Have students explain how this story fits the theme "A Delicate Balance." *(The story is about the delicate balance in the natural world between animals that prey on one another, and other animals that help one another.)*

✔ ASSESSMENT OPTIONS

📁 *Quick Checks,* p. 67

REAL-WORLD CONNECTION

Review A review quickly highlights the main idea of a book, story, movie, or play. Reviews help people decide whether they want to read a book, see a movie, or go to a play. Explain to students that when they tell a friend about something they've seen or read, they are essentially providing a review.

Activity Invite students to work in pairs or groups to write a review of "Rikki-tikki-tavi." They might provide the review to groups that have not read the story, or send it to a friend or relative in a letter. **L2 COLLAB. LEARN.**

Responding to the Selection

Personal Response

Some students may find the fight between Nagaina and Rikki-tikki-tavi the most exciting moment. Some may feel that the English family shares their attitude about snakes.

Analyzing Literature

1. Rikki-tikki-tavi lives in the house of a family from England.
2. Darzee, a tailorbird, relays important information to Rikki-tikki-tavi about when Nagaina is about to attack him and where she hides her eggs. Chuchundra, a muskrat, tells Rikki to listen to Nag crawling through the house. This information helps Rikki in his great war against the cobras.
3. The cobras think that if the people leave the house, Rikki-tikki-tavi will, too.
4. Rikki-tikki-tavi kills both Nag and Nagaina.
5. It provides the reader with a description of Rikki and his characteristics. Also, since the English family saved Rikki's life, it is only fitting that Rikki return the favor.
6. Darzee and Chuchundra are both cowardly. Rikki-tikki-tavi contrasts sharply with them.
7. Kipling presents Nagaina as being a protective mother. She gives up on killing Teddy to get her last egg back.
8. Even though Rikki is a young, inexperienced mongoose, he figures out how to kill Nag in the bathroom and Nagaina in the rat hole.
9. If Rikki had been killed, then evil would have triumphed, and the ending of the story would not have been satisfactory.
10. Students may say they like stories of good versus evil because they know exactly whom to root for.

Responding to Literature

PERSONAL RESPONSE

- ◆ What moment in the story did you find the most exciting? Why?
- ◆ Look back at the notes you made in the Focus Activity on page 788. Do any of the characters in the story share your thoughts and feelings about snakes?

Analyzing Literature

RECALL

1. In whose house does Rikki live?
2. Who are Darzee and Chuchundra? How do they help Rikki in his "great war"?
3. Why do the cobras decide they have to kill the people in the house?
4. What finally happens to Nag and Nagaina?

INTERPRET

5. Why do you think Kipling starts the story with an account of the rescue of Rikki?
6. How does the author use Darzee and Chuchundra to call attention to Rikki's bravery?
7. Does Kipling present one of the cobras more sympathetically than the other? Use examples to support your answer.
8. How does Rikki's cleverness help protect the family?

EVALUATE AND CONNECT

9. For the **climax** of the story, Kipling could have chosen to have Rikki killed in Nagaina's hole. How would that change affect your response to the story?
10. "Rikki-tikki-tavi" is a story of "good versus evil." Do you like that kind of story, or do you prefer stories in which the characters are not so easy to classify? Why?

LITERARY ELEMENTS

Anthropomorphism

Kipling gives the animal characters in "Rikki-tikki-tavi" human emotions, characteristics, and intelligence. Authors use this technique, called **anthropomorphism,** to help readers feel a connection to characters who are not human. The conflict between Rikki-tikki-tavi and Nag is told through their actions, their words, and their thoughts.

1. How does the use of anthropomorphism contribute to the level of interest and suspense in the story?
2. How would your reaction to "Rikki-tikki-tavi" be changed if it were written as a newspaper story about a real fight between a snake and a mongoose?

● See **Literary Terms Handbook,** p. R1.

LITERARY ELEMENTS

1. It helps the readers know exactly what Rikki-tikki-tavi is thinking and planning. It makes the reader an active participant in the story.
2. If "Rikki-tikki-tavi" were written like a newspaper article about a fight, reactions might not be as sharp. Reporters would present the story from both sides.

Additional Resources

📖 *Literary Elements Transparency 67*

Writing About Literature

Setting   The **setting** is the time and place in which a story takes place. Explain how the descriptions of the setting contribute to the story. What details help you to visualize the house, the garden, and the action between characters?

Creative Writing

News Article   Imagine you have been assigned to write a news article about Rikki's heroics. Choose one character to interview. Then write a short article using quotations from your imaginary interview.

Extending Your Response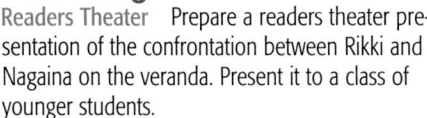

Literature Groups

A Fan of Snakes   Robert Bakker wrote in *The Dinosaur Heresies,* "Whenever I read Kipling's 'Rikki-tikki-tavi,' I root for the snake. . . ." An authority on reptiles, Bakker thinks that Kipling is biased against snakes. Do you agree? Share your group's opinions with the class.

Performing

Readers Theater   Prepare a readers theater presentation of the confrontation between Rikki and Nagaina on the veranda. Present it to a class of younger students.

Interdisciplinary Activity

Science   Not every snake is life-threatening to humans. Do some research on harmful and harmless snakes in your area. Make a two-column chart that identifies and illustrates the two categories of snakes you have researched.

Reading Further

If you would like to read other books by Rudyard Kipling, try these:
Kim
The Jungle Book

 Save your work for your portfolio.

Writing About Literature

Students' paragraphs should
- list specific descriptive details.
- explain how the description affects their understanding of the story.
- contain a clear topic sentence and conclusion.

Creative Writing

Students' news articles should
- list *who, what, where, when,* and *why.*
- contain quotations from one of the characters in the story.
- contain an engaging hook, an intriguing title, and an appropriate conclusion.

Literature Groups Encourage students to jot down story details that show a bias for or against snakes. Then, have each group come to a consensus about Kipling's attitude toward snakes. **COLLAB. LEARN.**

Performing Ask students to experiment with dramatic pauses, yells, whispers, rapid speech, slow speech, rhythm, and evil, calm, and hysterical voices before they perform.

Interdisciplinary Activity Encourage students to consult a library computer catalog or an Internet search engine to find material on snakes.

A DELICATE BALANCE   803

 ASSESSMENT OPTIONS

📁 *Quick Checks,* p. 67
📁 *Selection and Theme Assessment,* pp. 115–116
📁 *Performance Assessment,* p. 63
💾 *Testmaker*

GRAMMAR AND LANGUAGE
PERSONAL PRONOUNS

1. He lived in a burrow with his father and mother.
2. After the flood, Rikki never saw them again.
3. They wanted everyone to fear them.
4. "When they are gone," Nagaina said to Nag, "the garden will belong to us."

READING AND THINKING
EVALUATING

Students' paragraphs should take a clear stand on Kipling's purpose for writing "Rikki-tikki-tavi." Then they should decide whether he has achieved his purpose. Students should use details from the story to support their ideas.

VOCABULARY
DEFINITIONS

1. noun, 4   3. verb, 1   5. verb, 2
2. noun, 3   4. adjective, 1

Additional Resources

- *Grammar and Language Workbook,* pp. 103–104
- *Grammar and Composition Handbook,* Lesson 4.1
- *Writer's Choice,* Lesson 11.1
- *Reading Workbook,* pp. 119–120
- *Vocabulary Practice,* p. 48

GRAMMAR AND LANGUAGE • PERSONAL PRONOUNS

Personal pronouns refer to people or things. These pronouns have different forms depending on whether they are used in a sentence as subjects or as the objects of verbs or prepositions.

Singular subject pronouns: I, you, he, she, it

Plural subject pronouns: we, you, they

Singular object pronouns: me, you, him, her, it

Plural object pronouns: us, you, them

● For more about pronouns, see **Language Handbook,** p. R31.

PRACTICE Write each sentence, replacing each underlined word or phrase with a personal pronoun.

1. <u>Rikki-tikki-tavi</u> lived in a burrow with his father and mother.
2. After the flood, Rikki never saw <u>his father and mother</u> again.
3. <u>Nag and Nagaina</u> wanted everyone to fear <u>Nag and Nagaina.</u>
4. "When <u>the people</u> are gone," Nagaina said to Nag, "the garden will belong to <u>Nag and Nagaina.</u>"

READING AND THINKING • EVALUATING

When you evaluate a piece of writing, one of the things you determine is whether or not the author has achieved his or her purpose.

● For more about evaluating what you read, see **Reading Handbook,** pp. R82–R96.

PRACTICE Was Kipling trying to entertain, to inform, or to persuade his audience with "Rikki-tikki-tavi"? Write a short paragraph stating the author's purpose and evaluating how well he achieved it. Use specific examples from the story to support your opinion.

VOCABULARY • DICTIONARY SKILLS: DEFINITIONS

When you see an unfamiliar word in your reading, the first thing you must do is decide how the word is being used. Is it a noun? a verb? an adjective or adverb? Then look at the **dictionary entry** to find the meanings that are given for the word as that part of speech. Use **context clues** to decide which meaning is the appropriate one.

fancy *n.* **1.** imagination, especially a playful imagination. **2.** something imagined; a mental image. **3.** a sudden wish or notion. **4.** a liking or fondness. —*adj.* **1.** decorated; not plain. **2.** showing expert skill: *fancy dancing.* **3.** of high quality and, therefore, more expensive: *a fancy brand of soup.* —*v.* **1.** to picture mentally; imagine. **2.** to have a liking for. **3.** to suppose; think without being sure: *I fancied she was about twelve.*

PRACTICE Review the dictionary definitions for the word *fancy.* Then decide which meaning of *fancy* is used in each sentence below. Write the part of speech (noun, adjective, or verb) and then the number of the appropriate definition.

1. I've always had a *fancy* for cats and dogs.
2. After reading "Rikki-tikki-tavi," I had a *fancy* to own a mongoose.
3. I could *fancy* myself feeding it and brushing its furry coat.
4. It wouldn't need a *fancy* collar and leash; plain ones would do.
5. My parents, however, didn't *fancy* the idea of another pet, especially a mongoose.

SCIENCE

Endangered Species

You've probably heard the slogan "Save the whales!" or read it on a bumper sticker. Do you know why this slogan began? It started as a protest from people who wanted to ban whale-hunting. Some types of whales are among the hundreds of endangered species. A species of animal or plant at risk of becoming extinct is called *endangered.*

Many people, such as naturalists who study the environment, believe it is important to save endangered species to maintain the balance of nature. Already, the passenger pigeon, dodo bird, and Labrador duck are extinct. Of course, dinosaurs are extinct too. However, dinosaurs did not disappear because of humans. Today, as the human population increases all over the planet, less space remains for other species to live in their natural habitats.

Species become endangered for many reasons. For example, the cutting down of forests destroys the natural habitats of forest animals. Some animals have been hunted to extinction or near extinction. Overfishing has endangered many fish species. Pesticides kill insects regarded by humans as pests, but they also endanger birds that depend on those insects for food. Pesticide-sprayed insects may also harm birds that feed on them.

Since the 1800s, people have been trying to protect wildlife with special programs. In 1973 the United States passed the Endangered Species Act. An important part of this law made it illegal for people in the United States to buy animals (or animal parts, such as furs) endangered anywhere in the world.

As of June 30, 1998, 350 animal species in the U.S. and another 521 elsewhere in the world were listed as endangered. A few are shown above.

ACTIVITY

Pick an endangered animal to "adopt." Learn everything you can about this animal. Then share with classmates a picture of your adopted animal and your ideas about why and how it should be protected.

Objective

• To understand basic conditions that affect endangered animal species

Teaching Strategies

You may wish to illustrate one of the points made in the text by connecting the situation of endangered species to consumer decisions. For example, bring in a piece of fruit bought at a grocery store. Explain that fruit growers often use pesticides to kill insects that eat the fruit. Birds eat the dead insects and are poisoned. Eventually, these birds could lose great numbers of their population, putting them at risk.

Ask students to come up with ways in which they can help break the cycle. One possibility is looking for fruits and vegetables grown organically. Another is to create and support sanctuaries where birds and other animals can thrive without threat of being poisoned.

Activity

Some students may choose animals that can be protected locally; others may share information on animals found in other parts of the world.

Teaching Options

MEETING INDIVIDUAL NEEDS

MULTIPLE LEARNING STYLES

Bodily/Kinesthetic Bodily/kinesthetic learners will appreciate the chance to act out the drama of animals who experience loss of habitat.

Activity Designate each of the four corners of the classroom as a habitat: *jungle, forest, desert,* and *river.* Ask students to choose an animal indigenous to one of the habitats and go to that habitat. Label a series of index cards *Natural Disaster, Development, Pollution,* and *Poaching.* Hand the cards to different students and have them decide whether their animal can survive the threat or must flee to a different available habitat. Students can flee and go from habitat to habitat. When this is no longer possible, they must decide what to do to survive. **L2**

Objectives

- To read and analyze a short story about the balance between human and animal needs on a farm
- To recognize point of view in a first-person narrative
- To write about how the setting brings a story to life

Skills

Reading/Thinking: Using Graphic Aids; Logical Reasoning; Drawing Conclusions; Problem and Solution
Writing: Telling a Story from Another Point of View
Vocabulary: Unlocking Meaning
Grammar/Language: Apostrophes in Contractions; Consistent Verb Tenses
Listening/Speaking: Literature Groups
Collaboration: Literature Groups

Motivating

→OPTIONS

Literature Launchers: *A Conversation with Leslie Marmon Silko*

Videodisc Side B, Segment 23

Also available in VHS.

Selection Focus Transparency 68: Have students discuss the temperaments and reputations of different animals.

Focus Activity: To extend the Focus Activity, have students brainstorm English expressions that involve animals, e.g., *ponytail; stubborn as a mule, wily as a coyote,* and *to pig out.*

Before You Read

Uncle Tony's Goat

MEET LESLIE MARMON SILKO

Leslie Marmon Silko, who describes herself as Laguna, Pueblo, Mexican, and white, grew up on the Laguna Pueblo Reservation in New Mexico, listening to tales told by her female relatives. These stories gave Silko a sense of identity and inspired her writing. Silko's own stories explore her Pueblo heritage and the conflicts between traditional and modern ways. Silko decided to write "Uncle Tony's Goat" after a phone conversation with a friend, the poet Simon J. Ortiz, who told her a story about goats.

Leslie Marmon Silko was born in 1948. This story was first published in 1981.

806 🐐 THEME 8

FOCUS ACTIVITY

Imagine meeting a large, unfamiliar animal. You feel the threat of its presence as it follows your movements with a watchful eye.

QuickWrite
How would such an experience make you feel? Jot down your response in a few sentences.

Setting a Purpose
Read this story to find out what one boy learns from his experience with a goat.

BACKGROUND

The Time and Place   The story is set on a small family farm in New Mexico.

Did You Know?   Some people think goats are "garbage disposals" that chew tin cans and other trash. Actually, goats spend their days leisurely munching grass and weeds. Hardy animals, goats can live on sparse vegetation and produce milk even under extreme climatic conditions. Some types of goats are also valued for their wool, hides, and meat. Male goats are often called billy goats. A female goat is called a nanny or doe. A young goat is a kid.

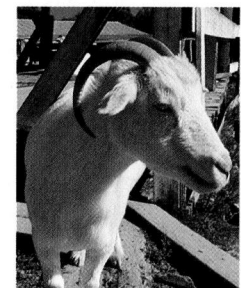

VOCABULARY PREVIEW

compensate (kom′ pən sāt′) *v.* to make up for; balance in force, weight, or effect; p. 808
hostile (host′ əl) *adj.* feeling or showing dislike; unfriendly; p. 808
conspicuously (kən spik′ ū əs lē) *adv.* in a way that draws attention or is easily seen; p. 809

RESOURCE MANAGER

Lesson Planning Resource
The ***Theme Eight Planning Guide*** (pp. 27–34) provides additional lesson notes and reduced versions of all print resources.

📂 **Other Print Resources**
- Active Reading Guide, p. 68
- Vocabulary Practice, p. 49
- Reading Workbook, pp. 121–122
- Grammar and Language Workbook, pp. 83–84, 273–274

- Grammar and Composition Handbook, Lessons 3.5, 13.7
- Quick Checks, p. 68
- Selection and Theme Assessment, pp. 117–118
- Performance Assessment, p. 64
- Spanish Summaries, p. 68
- Inclusion Strategies
- English Language Learners Sourcebook

 Transparencies
- Selection Focus 68
- Literary Elements 68
- Grammar and Language 63

Technology
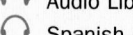 Literature Launchers
Audio Library
Spanish Audio Library
 Glencoe Literature Web Site
 Testmaker

Uncle Tony's Goat

Leslie Marmon Silko ∿

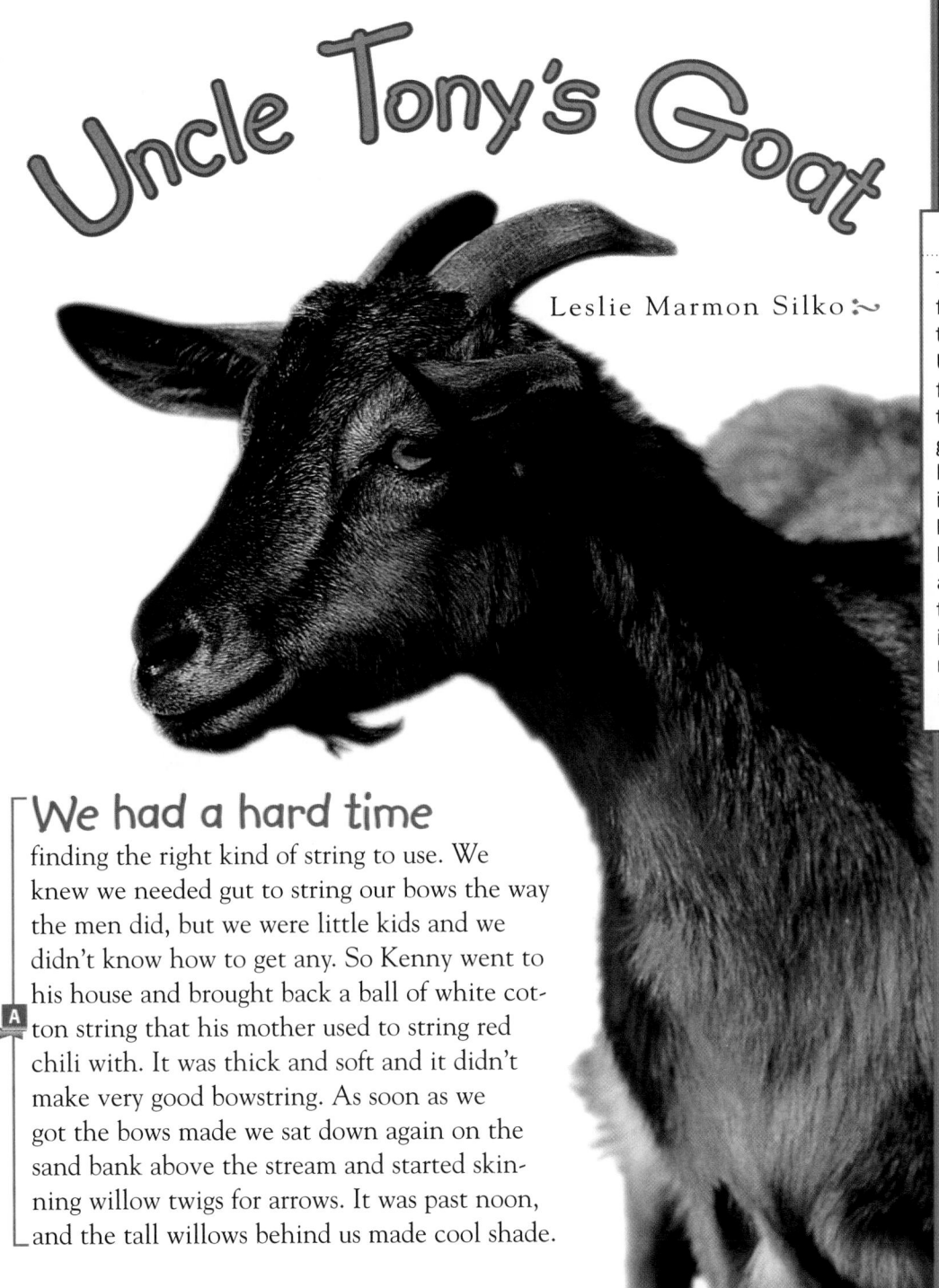

We had a hard time

finding the right kind of string to use. We knew we needed gut to string our bows the way the men did, but we were little kids and we didn't know how to get any. So Kenny went to his house and brought back a ball of white cotton string that his mother used to string red chili with. It was thick and soft and it didn't make very good bowstring. As soon as we got the bows made we sat down again on the sand bank above the stream and started skinning willow twigs for arrows. It was past noon, and the tall willows behind us made cool shade.

SUMMARY

The narrator and his friends make flimsy bows and arrows and shoot them harmlessly at Uncle Tony's goats. Uncle Tony's big, black billy goat never forgets the incident. Much later, when the narrator is asked to chase the billy goat out of his pen, the goat refuses to leave and charges the narrator, knocking him down and opening a cut above his eye. Uncle Tony, as much as he loves the goat, knows he can't have an animal that harms humans. He decides to kill the goat. The goat, sensing what is coming, jumps out of his pen and runs far away.

📁 *Spanish Summaries,* p. 68

A Active Reading

PREDICT Ask a volunteer to read the title and the first paragraph aloud. Encourage students to predict how Uncle Tony's goat will interact with the narrator. Suggest that students periodically verify or revise their predictions.

Additional Resources
📁 *Active Reading Guide,* p. 68
🎧 *Audio Library*
🎧 *Spanish Audio Library*

Teaching Options

CONNECTING TO OTHER SELECTIONS

The chart at the right shows three ways to connect "Uncle Tony's Goat" to other selections in this book.

For specific teaching strategies, see the *Theme Eight Planning Guide,* pages 30–31.

Connection		Title
Life Skills: Lifelong Learning	→	"Lob's Girl," p. 659
Thematic: Remembering	→	"Last Cover," p. 163
Literary: Narrative	→	"Atalanta," p. 718

B Literary Elements

NARRATOR: *First-Person Narrative*
Ask students who is narrating the story and how they know. *(An older boy or man is telling about an incident that happened when he was younger. The narrator uses the pronouns we, I, and my, which show that the story is a first-person narrative.)*

C Critical Thinking

LOGICAL REASONING Have students explain whether the children's arrows are a threat to the goats. *(Possibly yes. However, the goats don't even seem to notice; the arrows do not take a direct path.)*

D Active Reading

QUESTION Have students explain why the billy goat takes the narrator into his memory. *(He doesn't want to forget who participated in the arrow shooting.)* Do students think goats can remember for a long time, hold a grudge, or plot revenge? *(Some may think goats can remember who has harmed them in the past.)*

Teaching Options

Uncle Tony's Goat

There were lots of little minnows that day, flashing in the shallow water, swimming back and forth wildly like they weren't sure if they really wanted to go up or down the stream; it was a day for minnows that we were always hoping for—we could have filled our rusty coffee cans and old pickle jars full. But this was the first time for making bows and arrows, and the minnows weren't much different from the sand or the rocks now. The secret is the arrows. The ones we made were crooked, and when we shot them they didn't go straight—they flew around in arcs and curves; so we crawled through the leaves and branches, deep into the willow groves, looking for the best, the straightest willow branches. But even after we skinned the sticky wet bark from them and whittled the knobs off, they still weren't straight. Finally we went ahead and made notches at the end of each arrow to hook in the bowstring, and we started practicing, thinking maybe we could learn to shoot the crooked arrows straight.

We left the river each of us with a handful of damp, yellow arrows and our fresh-skinned willow bows. We walked slowly and shot arrows at bushes, big rocks, and the juniper tree that grows by Pino's sheep pen. They were working better just like we had figured; they still didn't fly straight, but now we could compensate for that by the way we aimed them. We were going up to the church to shoot at the cats old Sister Julian kept outside the cloister.[1] We didn't want to hurt anything, just to have new kinds of things to shoot at.

But before we got to the church we went past the grassy hill where my uncle Tony's goats were grazing. A few of them were lying down chewing their cud[2] peacefully, and they didn't seem to notice us. The billy goat was lying down, but he was watching us closely like he already knew about little kids. His yellow goat eyes didn't blink, and he stared with a wide, hostile look. The grazing goats made good deer for our bows. We shot all our arrows at the nanny goats and their kids; they skipped away from the careening[3] arrows and never lost the rhythm of their greedy chewing as they continued to nibble the weeds and grass on the hillside. The billy goat was lying there watching us and taking us into his memory. As we ran down the road toward the church and Sister Julian's cats, I looked back, and my uncle Tony's billy goat was still watching me.

My uncle and my father were sitting on the bench outside the house when we walked by. It was September now, and the farming was almost over, except for bringing home the melons and a few pumpkins. They were mending ropes and bridles

Did You Know?
A *bridle* is the headgear for a horse. It includes the bit that fits in the horse's mouth and the reins the rider uses to guide the horse.

---

1. Here, the *cloister* is a convent, the building in which nuns live.

2. *Cud* is partially digested food brought back up from an animal's stomach for a second, more thorough, chewing.
3. *Careening* arrows would sway from side to side while moving, as if out of control.

Vocabulary
compensate (kom′ pən sāt′) *v.* to make up for; balance in force, weight, or effect
hostile (host′ əl) *adj.* feeling or showing dislike; unfriendly

---

MEETING INDIVIDUAL NEEDS — ENGLISH LANGUAGE LEARNERS

Possessives English language learners may confuse possessives with plurals. To illustrate how possessives are formed, write the chart at right on the board. Use the examples to demonstrate word order and possession.

Activity Have students work in small groups to find other examples of possessives in the story to add to the chart. Then have students write five

more possessives using the names of students in the group. **COLLAB. LEARN.**

What	Whose It Is	This Is _____.
goat	Uncle Tony	Uncle Tony's goat
neck	the goat	the goat's neck

Additional Resources
📁 *English Language Learners Sourcebook*

and feeling the afternoon sun. We held our bows and arrows out in front of us so they could see them. My father smiled and kept braiding the strips of leather in his hand, but my uncle Tony put down the bridle and pieces of scrap leather he was working on and looked at each of us kids slowly. He was old, getting some white hair—he was my mother's oldest brother, the one that scolded us when we told lies or broke things.

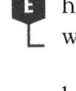

"You'd better not be shooting at things," he said, "only at rocks or trees. Something will get hurt. Maybe even one of you."

We all nodded in agreement and tried to hold the bows and arrows less <u>conspicuously</u> down at our sides; when he turned back to his work we hurried away before he took the bows away from us like he did the time we made the slingshot. He caught us shooting rocks at an old wrecked car; its windows were all busted out anyway, but he took the slingshot away. I always wondered what he did with it and with the knives we made ourselves out of tin cans. When I was much older I asked my mother, "What did he ever do with those knives and slingshots he took away from us?" She was kneading[4] bread on the kitchen table at the time and was probably busy thinking about the fire in the oven outside. "I don't know," she said; "you ought to ask him yourself." But I never did. I thought about it lots of times, but I never did. It would have been like getting caught all over again.

The goats were valuable. We got milk and meat from them. My uncle was careful to see that all the goats were treated properly; the worst scolding my older sister ever got was when my mother caught her and some of her friends chasing the newborn kids. My mother kept saying over and over again, "It's a good thing I saw you; what if your uncle had seen you?" and even though we kids were very young then, we understood very well what she meant.

The billy goat never forgot the bows and arrows, even after the bows had cracked and split and the crooked, whittled arrows were all lost. This goat was big and black and important to my uncle Tony because he'd paid a lot to get him and because he wasn't an ordinary goat. Uncle Tony had bought him from a white man, and then he'd hauled him in the back of the pickup all the way from Quemado.[5] And my uncle was the only person who could touch this goat. If a stranger or one of us kids got too near him, the mane on the billy goat's neck would stand on end and the goat would rear up on his hind legs and dance forward trying to reach the person with his long, spiral horns. This billy goat smelled bad, and none of us cared if we couldn't pet him. But my uncle took good care of this goat. The goat would let Uncle Tony brush him with the horse brush and scratch him around the base of his horns. Uncle Tony talked to the billy goat—in the morning when he unpenned the goats and in the evening when he gave them their hay and closed the gate for the night. I never paid too much attention to what he said to the billy goat; usually it was something like

---

4. The mother was pressing and squeezing, or *kneading*, bread dough.

5. *Quemado* (kā mä′ dō)

Vocabulary
conspicuously (kən spik′ ū əs lē) *adv.* in a way that draws attention or is easily seen

---

E **Author's Craft**

FORESHADOWING Ask students to note how the author is introducing the possibility of one of the children getting hurt if they shoot any arrows at the goats.

F **Active Reading**

EVALUATE Ask students to think about possible reasons the narrator would have for mentioning that the goat never forgot. You may wish to share the following model to illustrate the thinking process involved in evaluating.

Model: I know that the narrator is a character in the story. He is probably leading up to a dramatic scene with the goat later in the story. It will probably have to do with the incident of shooting arrows at the goats.

G **Active Reading**

RESPOND Invite students to describe Uncle Tony's feelings about the goat and how they differ from the narrator's attitude. *(Uncle Tony is grateful to the goat for what he provides and takes good care of him; the narrator treats the goat as a "thing" he can use to entertain himself, without a thought that the goat is a living creature.)*

Reading Minilesson

Using Graphic Aids As this story progresses, readers find out more and more about the narrator, Uncle Tony, and the billy goat.

Activity Invite students to begin a word web for each of these characters. At the end of the story, students can mark in color the character traits that they were most surprised to discover. **L2**

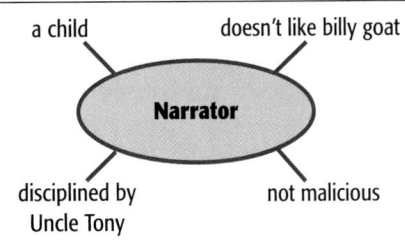

Additional Resources
📁 *Reading Workbook*, pp. 121–122

🅷 Active Reading

EVALUATE Uncle Tony never says how he feels about the billy goat. What do students think Tony's actions show about his feelings? *(Uncle Tony thinks of the goat as more than just livestock. Uncle Tony treats the goat much like a pet.)*

🅸 Active Reading

PREDICT Invite students to predict what may happen when the narrator tries to run the goats out of the pen. *(The females and young goats are docile and will do what the narrator wants, but the billy goat does not like the narrator. It may pose a problem, perhaps even hurt the narrator.)*

Crescent Moon Over the Southwest, 1990. Sherri Silverman. Pastel, 25¾ x 36 in. Private collection.
Viewing the painting: How is the scene in the painting similar to and different from the story's setting?

🅷 "Get up, big goat! You've slept long enough," or "Move over, big goat, and let the others have something to eat." I think Uncle Tony was proud of that billy goat.

We all had chores to do around home. My sister helped out around the house mostly, and I was supposed to carry water from the hydrant and bring in kindling. I helped my father look after the horses and pigs, and Uncle Tony milked the goats and fed them. One morning near the end of September I was out feeding the pigs their table scraps and pig mash;[6] I'd given the

pigs their food, and I was watching them squeal and snap at each other as they crowded into the feed trough. Behind me I could hear the milk squirting into the eight-pound lard pail that Uncle Tony used for milking.

When he finished milking he noticed me standing there; he motioned toward the goats still inside the pen. "Run the rest of them out," he said as he untied the two milk goats and carried the milk to the house.

I was seven years old, and I understood that everyone, including my uncle, expected me to handle more chores; so I hurried over to the goat pen and swung the tall wire gate open. The does and kids 🅸

---

6. *Mash* is animal feed that consists of a mixture of ground grains.

810 🐾 THEME 8

MEETING INDIVIDUAL NEEDS — MULTIPLE LEARNING STYLES

Musical Students with strong musical abilities can use music to help them appreciate the mood, tone, and feelings generated by the story.

Activity Invite musical learners to imagine they are turning this story into a movie. As they read, have them stop whenever the action suggests to them a background song, a type of music, or a

sound. Have them jot down a description of the music or sound, along with the emotions or mood it makes them feel. Students may find their notes useful when they complete the Responding to Literature activities on pages 813–815. Some students may want to tape-record music or sound effects to accompany a reading of an important scene from the story. **L2**

Leslie Marmon Silko

came prancing out. They trotted daintily past the pigpen and scattered out, intent on finding leaves and grass to eat. It wasn't until then I noticed that the billy goat hadn't come out of the little wooden shed inside the goat pen. I stood outside the pen and tried to look inside the wooden shelter, but it was still early and the morning sun left the inside of the shelter in deep shadow. I stood there for a while, hoping that he would come out by himself, but I realized that he'd recognized me and that he wouldn't come out. I understood right away what was happening and my fear of him was in my bowels and down my neck; I was shaking.

Finally my uncle came out of the house; it was time for breakfast. "What's wrong?" he called out from the door.

"The billy goat won't come out," I yelled back, hoping he would look disgusted and come do it himself.

"Get in there and get him out," he said as he went back into the house.

I looked around quickly for a stick or broom handle, or even a big rock, but I couldn't find anything. I walked into the pen slowly, concentrating on the darkness beyond the shed door; I circled to the back of the shed and kicked at the boards, hoping to make the billy goat run out. I put my eye up to a crack between the boards, and I could see he was standing up now and that his yellow eyes were on mine.

My mother was yelling at me to hurry up, and Uncle Tony was watching. I stepped around into the low doorway, and the goat charged toward me, feet first. I had dirt in my mouth and up my nose and there was blood running past my eye; my head ached. Uncle Tony carried me to the

house; his face was stiff with anger, and I remembered what he'd always told us about animals; they won't bother you unless you bother them first. I didn't start to cry until my mother hugged me close and wiped my face with a damp wash rag. It was only a little cut above my eyebrow, and she sent me to school anyway with a Band-Aid on my forehead.

Uncle Tony locked the billy goat in the pen. He didn't say what he was going to do with the goat, but when he left with my father to haul firewood, he made sure the gate to the pen was wired tightly shut. He looked at the goat quietly and with sadness; he said something to the goat, but the yellow eyes stared past him.

"What's he going to do with the goat?" I asked my mother before I went to catch the school bus.

"He ought to get rid of it," she said. "We can't have that goat knocking people down for no good reason."

I didn't feel good at school. The teacher sent me to the nurse's office and the nurse made me lie down. Whenever I closed my eyes I could see the goat and my uncle, and I felt a stiffness in my throat and chest. I got off the school bus slowly, so the other kids would go ahead without me. I walked slowly and wished I could be away from home for a while. I could go over to Grandma's house, but she would ask me if my mother knew where I was and I would have to say no, and she would make me go home first to ask. So I walked very slowly, because I didn't want to see the black goat's hide hanging over the corral fence.

When I got to the house I didn't see a goat hide or the goat, but Uncle Tony was on his horse and my mother was standing

A DELICATE BALANCE 811

J Literary Elements
NARRATOR: *Foreshadowing* Invite students to explain how the narrator is presenting clues to prepare for what may happen between the goat and the boy. *(The goat has recognized the narrator as the person involved in the arrow-shooting incident. The goat does not like him and will not do what the boy wants. This foreshadows an unpleasant incident.)*

K Critical Thinking
DRAWING CONCLUSIONS Have students explain why Uncle Tony watches the narrator as he tries to get the goat out of the pen. *(Uncle Tony wants to see how the boy and the goat get along. Uncle Tony knows the goat is mean and probably recalls the arrow-shooting incident.)*

L Critical Thinking
DRAWING CONCLUSIONS Remind students that the narrator doesn't like the goat. Why might he feel sick at the thought of the goat's being killed? *(The narrator feels guilty because he believes he is responsible for the goat's fate. If he hadn't shot arrows at the goat, which he knew he wasn't supposed to do, the goat might not have misbehaved.)*

GIFTED AND TALENTED ACTIVITY
MEETING INDIVIDUAL NEEDS

Interview People who live on farms have many things to care for. In this story, the boy, who is only seven, feeds the pigs and helps look after the horses. Uncle Tony milks and feeds the goats. Invite students to find out more about daily life on a farm.

Activity Have students work in pairs to read about farm life or interview someone their age who lives and works on a farm in the region. Encourage students to find out what chores and activities must be done each day, and how chores and activities change, season by season. **L3** COLLAB. LEARN.

A DELICATE BALANCE 811

M Critical Thinking

DRAWING CONCLUSIONS Have students draw on story details and their prior knowledge of animal behavior to explain why the goat runs away on this day. *(Students may say that animal instinct is at work, and the goat somehow senses danger or threat.)*

N Critical Thinking

DRAWING CONCLUSIONS Encourage students to explain why Uncle Tony's voice is strong and happy now that the goat is gone. *(He knows that the goat has escaped alive and he will not have to kill it. He also knows that the goat is gone for good, so it will not harm people.)*

Thematic Focus

A Delicate Balance Have students explain how this story fits the theme "A Delicate Balance." *(The story is about the balance between human needs and animal needs on a farm.)*

☑ **ASSESSMENT OPTIONS**

📁 *Quick Checks,* p. 68

---

beside the horse holding a canteen and a flour sack bundle tied with brown string. I was frightened at what this meant. My uncle looked down at me from the saddle.

"The goat ran away," he said. "Jumped out of the pen somehow. I saw him just as he went over the hill beyond the river. He stopped at the top of the hill and he looked back this way."

Uncle Tony nodded at my mother and me and then he left; we watched his old roan gelding[7] splash across the stream and labor up the steep path beyond the river. Then they were over the top of the hill and gone.

Uncle Tony was gone for three days. He came home early on the morning of the fourth day, before we had eaten breakfast or fed the animals. He was glad to be home, he said, because he was getting too old for such long rides. He called me over and looked closely at the cut above my eye. It had scabbed over good, and I wasn't wearing a Band-Aid any more; he examined it very carefully before he let me go. He stirred some sugar into his coffee.

"That miserable goat," he said. "I followed him for three days. He was headed south, going straight to Quemado. I never

could catch up to him." My uncle shook his head. "The first time I saw him he was already in the piñon forest, halfway into the mountains already. I could see him most of the time, off in the distance a mile or two. He would stop sometimes and look back." Uncle Tony paused and drank some more coffee. "I stopped at night. I had to. He stopped too, and in the morning we would start out again. The trail just gets higher and steeper. Yesterday morning there was frost on top of the blanket when I woke up and we were in the big pines and red oak leaves. I couldn't see him any more because the forest is too thick. So I turned around." Tony finished the cup of coffee. "He's probably in Quemado by now."

I looked at him again, standing there by the door, ready to go milk the nanny goats.

"There wasn't ever a goat like that one," he said, "but if that's the way he's going to act, O.K. then. That stubborn goat was just too mean anyway."

He smiled at me and his voice was strong and happy when he said this.

Did You Know?
Piñon (pin' yun), a Spanish word, refers to any of several small pine trees found in Mexico and the southwestern United States.

---

7. *Roan* describes the horse's color, a reddish-brown mixed with gray or white. A *gelding* is a male horse that's been surgically "fixed" so that it cannot breed.

Teaching Options

Grammar and Language *Minilesson*

Apostrophes in Contractions Write the following words on the board:
it is = it's   he would = he'd
The apostrophe has two primary uses: to signal a possession or to form a contraction. In a contraction, the apostrophe replaces one or more letters dropped when two words are combined into one.

Activity Have students add an apostrophe to each contraction they find, and identify the words that were combined.
1. Its a good thing I saw you. *(It's, it is)*
2. Its eyes were yellow. *(no contraction)*
3. He wasnt an ordinary goat. *(wasn't, was not)*
4. Whats wrong? *(What's, What is)*

Additional Resources

🔖 *Grammar and Language Transparency 63*

📘 *Grammar and Language Workbook,* pp. 273–274

📘 *Grammar and Composition Handbook,* Lesson 13.7

📘 *Writer's Choice,* Lesson 20.7

Responding to Literature

PERSONAL RESPONSE

Review your notes from the **Focus Activity** on page 806. How do your thoughts and feelings compare with those of the story's narrator?

Analyzing Literature

RECALL

1. What do Kenny and the narrator do when they encounter the goats on the hill? Why do you think they do that?
2. What is the billy goat's reaction to the boys' behavior?
3. What happens when the narrator attempts to run the goats from the pen?
4. What is the narrator afraid he will find when he returns from school? What happens instead?

INTERPRET

5. Why do you think the billy goat acts as he does when the narrator attempts to run the goats from the pen? Do you think Uncle Tony understands the goat's behavior? Why or why not?
6. Does the goat deserve to be killed as Uncle Tony seems to plan? Why or why not?
7. How does the narrator's attitude toward the goat change in the course of the story? Explain.
8. What do you think the narrator learned from his experience with Uncle Tony's goat?

EVALUATE AND CONNECT

9. Were you satisfied with the story's ending? Why or why not? Suggest two other possible endings for the story.
10. Theme Connection What does the story communicate to you about the relationship between humans and animals?

LITERARY ELEMENTS

Narrator

Narrative is a type of writing that tells a story. The person who tells the story is called the **narrator**. Because the narrator in "Uncle Tony's Goat" tells the events in his own words, using the pronoun *I,* this story is a **first-person narrative**. In a first-person narrative, all information about the story's characters and events comes from the narrator. A skillful reader must determine how the narrator's experience and opinions influence the telling of the story.

1. What affects the narrator's description of Uncle Tony?
2. If Uncle Tony were telling the story, how might he have described the goat?

● See **Literary Terms Handbook**, p. R7.

Responding to the Selection

Personal Response

Students should use examples from the story to compare their thoughts and feelings with those of the narrator.

Analyzing Literature

1. They shoot arrows at the goats because they want to try out their arrows on moving targets.
2. The billy goat doesn't do anything at the time, but he remembers the incident and the boys involved.
3. All the goats except the billy goat leave the pen.
4. The narrator is afraid the billy goat will have been killed. Instead, he finds out that the goat has run away.
5. The goat remembers the arrow-shooting incident. He does not like the narrator and will not do what the narrator wants him to do. It seems that Uncle Tony understands that the goat does not like the narrator, which is why he watches to see what will happen.
6. Some students may say the goat deserves to be killed because he is dangerous to humans. Others may say the goat does not deserve to be killed because the narrator had picked on the goat.
7. The narrator dislikes the goat and is afraid of him. But later, when he thinks the goat will be killed, he is very unhappy. He doesn't want the goat to be killed because he knows he has at least partially caused the goat's behavior.

LITERARY ELEMENTS

1. The narrator's description is affected by his respect for Uncle Tony and by Uncle Tony's respect for his farm animals.
2. *Example:* He is stubborn, smart, and takes care of other goats in the herd.

Additional Resources

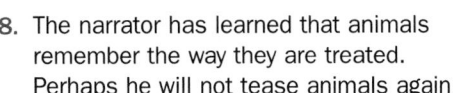
Literary Elements Transparency 68

8. The narrator has learned that animals remember the way they are treated. Perhaps he will not tease animals again.
9. Other possible endings include Tony's killing the goat or the narrator's working with the goat until the goat trusts him.
10. *Example:* Both human needs and animal needs are important, but on a farm, you must put the needs of humans first.

Literature and Writing

Writing About Literature

Students' paragraphs should
- list specific details of setting.
- describe techniques the author uses to bring the setting to life for readers.
- use examples from the story.

Creative Writing

Students' stories should
- be written from the goat's point of view.
- describe the goat's thoughts about the narrator and Uncle Tony.
- explain why the goat runs away.

Extending Your Response

Art Activity Have students work together to create a story map that includes foreshadowing and share it with the class. **COLLAB. LEARN.**

Literature Groups Have each member share one thought about how animals are portrayed in the two stories and discuss which method they prefer. **COLLAB. LEARN.**

Learning for Life Encourage students to review the story if they have difficulty remembering the sequence of events.

Literature and Writing

Writing About Literature

Setting What is the setting of the story? How does the author bring the setting to life for her readers? Write a paragraph about the story's setting. Use examples and quotations from the story.

Creative Writing

Retelling the Story Rewrite the story as if the goat were narrating it. Be sure to include the goat's thoughts and feelings toward Uncle Tony, as well as his response to the boys' activities.

Extending Your Response

Art Activity

Story Map Leslie Marmon Silko uses foreshadowing when she offers her readers clues about what will occur next in the story. If you recognize these clues, you can predict what will happen. Reexamine the story. As a group, use chart paper to create a large story map that illustrates and charts the evidence foreshadowing the goat's attack on the narrator. Present your story map to the class.

*inter*NET CONNECTION

Leslie Marmon Silko grew up on a pueblo in New Mexico. If you would like to learn more about the Pueblo people, type "Pueblo Indians" or "Anasazi" into a search engine to find some informative sites.

Literature Groups

Animal Portraits Compare the way animals are portrayed in "Rikki-tikki-tavi" and "Uncle Tony's Goat." Which animal portrait do you prefer? From which did you learn the most? Give reasons for your opinions.

Learning for Life

Incident Report Imagine you are Uncle Tony. Write a report for the police about your missing goat. Summarize the events that lead to the goat's escape. Also describe the goat and your nephew. Read your report to the class.

Reading Further

To learn more about the Pueblos and other Native Americans of the Southwest, try these books:

Mother Earth, Father Sky: Pueblo Indians of the American Southwest by David Lavender

Desert Dwellers: Native People of the American Southwest by Scott S. Warren

Save your work for your portfolio.

✔ ASSESSMENT OPTIONS

- *Quick Checks,* p. 68
- *Selection and Theme Assessment,* pp. 117–118
- *Performance Assessment,* p. 64
- *Testmaker*

Skill Minilessons

GRAMMAR AND LANGUAGE • CONSISTENT VERB TENSES

It is important to keep the verb tenses consistent in your writing. If you jump from one tense to another, readers will be confused about when events take place.

CONFUSING: Uncle Tony **works** hard on the farm. The narrator **worked** on the farm too.

BETTER: Uncle Tony **works** hard on the farm. The narrator **works** on the farm too.

PRACTICE Write a paragraph summarizing the events in "Uncle Tony's Goat." Keep your verbs in the same tense unless you have a strong reason to change them. Exchange paragraphs with a partner and check for consistent verb tenses.

● For more about verb tense, see **Language Handbook,** pp. R15–R16.

READING AND THINKING • PROBLEM/SOLUTION

Most plots in fiction focus on one or more problems that the characters try to solve. Often, readers learn about characters by the way in which they respond to problems in their lives. In "Uncle Tony's Goat," there are a number of related problems. How do the different characters respond to the problems? How do they try to solve the problems?

PRACTICE Reread "Uncle Tony's Goat." Write a paragraph describing how two of the characters in the story respond to problems in their lives and how they finally solve them.

● To learn more about the problem/solution organization of text, see **Reading Handbook,** pp. R85–R86.

VOCABULARY • UNLOCKING MEANING

You can often use what you know about one word to figure out what another related word means. The narrator of "Uncle Tony's Goat" has the chore of gathering *kindling*. You know that *kindling* is small sticks or other material used to start a fire. You could use that information to figure out that the expression "kindled my anger" means "made me start to get angry."

PRACTICE Use what you know about the words on the left and familiar prefixes and suffixes to answer the questions.

1. *hostile* Hostilities are sure to occur during _____ .
   a. wars   b. parties   c. contests
2. *conspicuous* You might try to be inconspicuous to avoid being _____ .
   a. noticed   b. alone   c. neglected
3. *compensate* If your brother lost your jacket, what might he do to recompense you?
   a. apologize b. laugh   c. buy you another

● For more about using word parts to unlock meaning, see **Reading Handbook,** pp. R72 and R79–R80.

Skill Minilessons

GRAMMAR AND LANGUAGE
CONSISTENT VERB TENSES

Students' paragraphs should
• accurately summarize the story.
• use consistent verb tenses throughout.
• switch verb tenses only for compelling reasons, such as to describe an incident that happened much earlier than the rest.

READING AND THINKING
PROBLEM/SOLUTION

Students' paragraphs should
• describe the problems of two characters in the story.
• explain how the two characters solve the problems.
• contain a clear topic sentence and effective conclusion.

VOCABULARY
UNLOCKING MEANING

1. a   **2.** a   **3.** c

Additional Resources

📘 *Grammar and Language Workbook,* pp. 83–84

📘 *Grammar and Composition Handbook,* Lesson 3.5

📘 *Writer's Choice,* Lesson 10.5
📁 *Reading Workbook,* pp. 121–122
📁 *Vocabulary Practice,* p. 49

A DELICATE BALANCE 815

Objective

• To recognize and apply strategies for forming possessive nouns and pronouns

Teaching Strategies

Before reading the problems and solutions on page 816, explain to students that they are in charge of proofreading signs that will be posted around town. Write the following texts on the board and ask students to make any necessary corrections: *Womens' Shoes* *(Women's)*; *Rays Tire Shop (Ray's)*; *Pet's Welcome (Pets)*; *Dollys' Snack Shop (Dolly's)*; *Eat at Joes' (Joe's)*; *Teacher's Parking Lot (Teachers')*.

Exercise

a. dresses'   e. horns'   h. ours
b. sheep's   f. story's   i. ladies'
c. men's   g. James's   j. family's
d. class's

Additional Resources

Teaching Options

Using Apostrophes to Show Possession

The **apostrophe** is used to show possession. Sometimes it is used alone, but it is usually combined with the letter *s*.

Problem 1   Singular, possessive nouns

Leslie Marmon Silkos story about the goat is humorous.

Solution   Use an apostrophe and an *-s* to make a singular noun possessive, even if the noun ends in *-s*.

Leslie Marmon Silko's story about the goat is humorous.

Problem 2   Plural nouns ending in *-s*

Are your classmates responses the same as yours?

Solution   If a plural noun ends in *-s,* make it possessive by adding only an apostrophe.

Are your classmates' responses the same as yours?

Problem 3   Plural nouns not ending in *-s*

Peoples ideas about goats have not changed much over time.

Solution   If a plural noun does not end in *-s,* add an apostrophe and an *-s.*

People's ideas about goats have not changed much over time.

Problem 4   Possessive personal pronouns

The boys don't realize that the problem with the goat is their's.

Solution   Apostrophes are not used in possessive pronouns, such as *yours* and *hers.*

The boys don't realize that the problem with the goat is theirs.

● For more about using apostrophes, see **Language Handbook,** p. R40.

EXERCISE

Write the possessive form of each word.
a. dresses   **c.** men   **e.** horns   **g.** James   **i.** ladies
b. sheep   **d.** class **f.** story   **h.** our   **j.** family

Writing *Minilesson*

Writing a Tercet Explain that a tercet is a group of three lines that form a group. For example:

I like frogs' eyes,
Twinkling like starry skies,
Big and shiny, bright and wise.

Write a few tercets as a class. Encourage students to experiment with different line lengths and rhyming words.

Activity Have students work individually to write a tercet about something in nature. Ask that the tercet include at least one possessive noun formed with an apostrophe. **L2**

Additional Resources

📕 ***Writer's Choice,*** Lesson 3.6

LISTENING, SPEAKING, and VIEWING

Critical Viewing

How can you judge the accuracy of things you view on television, on film, or on the Internet? The following tips can help.

Critical Viewing Guidelines

Ask Why
- When you view a presentation, ask yourself about its purpose. Is it designed to entertain, to inform, or to persuade? Material should be accurate, but material intended to persuade may be one-sided.

Digital composite by John Lund/Tony Stone Images.

Ask Who
- Who created the presentation? Is the creator an expert? Does he or she have a reputation for quality?

Ask When
- When was the presentation created? Older material may not be up-to-date. On the other hand, very new information may not yet have been reliably confirmed. Can you check key facts?

Ask How
- How is the material presented? Do you detect fuzzy thinking, sensationalism, one-sidedness, or other attempts to manipulate viewers?

ACTIVITIES

1. On your own or with a partner, view a television commercial and use the Critical Viewing Guidelines to evaluate it. Make notes of your evaluation, and share your results with classmates.

2. Use the Critical Viewing Guidelines to evaluate a television program or video designed to inform. Write a paragraph explaining your evaluation.

A DELICATE BALANCE 817

Objective
- To recognize and apply strategies for critical viewing

Teaching Strategies

Have students role-play two television spots: one a public service announcement urging viewers to take care of their bodies; the second an advertisement for a health club. Ask students to use their critical faculties and the guidelines on page 817 to discuss the differences between the two spots.

Activities

1. Some students may find that they already apply the critical viewing guidelines to their television watching, while others may be surprised by the results of their evaluation.
2. Students may wish to read their paragraphs aloud or share them in small groups.

Teaching Options

MEETING INDIVIDUAL NEEDS ENGLISH LANGUAGE LEARNERS

Focus Groups Diverse cultural perspectives can provide all students with valuable insights into how an American television program might be perceived outside America.

Activity Have small groups of students choose a popular television program to analyze. Ask the groups to imagine they are living in a country where the only information they have about American culture comes from that television program. Have students view the program critically and use it to make assumptions about American life: What do Americans look like? How do they act? What is their family life like?

Additional Resources
📁 *English Language Learners Sourcebook*

Objectives

- To read and enjoy a poem about the power of the natural world
- To understand and describe an extended metaphor
- To write about one's reaction to a poem

Skills

Reading/Thinking: Elaborating
Writing: Creating an Extended Metaphor
Listening/Speaking: Performing
Collaboration: Literature Groups

Motivating → OPTIONS

Selection Focus Transparency 69: Have students discuss a construction project that is occurring locally. Who benefits? Who is harmed?

Focus Activity: As an extension of the Focus Activity, have students in small groups list forces of nature that change the earth suddenly and forces of nature that change the earth steadily over thousands of years.

Before You Read
Loo-Wit

MEET WENDY ROSE

Wendy Rose's mother was of Miwok descent, and her father was a full-blood Hopi. Her poems often reflect her personal search for tribal and personal identity. About her need to write, Rose once said, "Writing is just something that always has been and just is. For everything in this universe there is a song to accompany its existence; writing is another way of singing these songs. . . . Some people have tried to say I sing my songs because I'm half-Hopi; that's not true . . . I sing them because I hear them."

Wendy Rose was born in California in 1948.

FOCUS ACTIVITY

Think about the extraordinary power of natural elements, such as a volcano, tornado, or the ocean tides. What words might describe that kind of power?

Sharing Ideas
Write down your ideas. Then share your thoughts in a small group discussion.

Setting a Purpose
Read this poem to discover how one poet describes a volcano.

BACKGROUND

Loo-Wit is the Cowlitz Indian name for Mount St. Helens, the volcano that erupted in Washington in 1980. A volcano is a vent in the Earth from which molten rock and gas sometimes erupt. The molten rock that erupts, called lava, forms a hill or mountain around the vent. The lava sometimes flows out as liquid, or it may explode as solid particles. The fierce eruption of Mount St. Helens was the most violent volcanic event within the continental United States in recorded history.

RESOURCE MANAGER

Lesson Planning Resource
The *Theme Eight Planning Guide* (pp. 35–39) provides additional lesson notes and reduced versions of all print resources.

📁 **Other Print Resources**
- Active Reading Guide, p. 69
- Quick Checks, p. 69
- Selection and Theme Assessment, pp. 119–120
- Performance Assessment, p. 65

- Spanish Summaries, p. 69
- Inclusion Strategies
- Block Scheduling Guide
- English Language Learners Sourcebook

 Transparencies
- Selection Focus 69
- Literary Elements 69

Technology
- 🎧 Audio Library
- 🎧 Spanish Audio Library
- 💻 Glencoe Literature Web Site
- 💾 Testmaker

Loo-Wit

Wendy Rose

The way they do
this old woman
no longer cares
what others think
5 but spits her black tobacco
any which way
stretching full length
from her bumpy bed.
Finally up
10 she sprinkles
ashes on the snow,
cold buttes°
promising nothing
but the walk
15 of winter.
Centuries of cedar
have bound her
to earth,
huckleberry ropes
20 lay prickly
on her neck.
Around her
machinery growls,
snarls and ploughs
25 great patches
of her skin.
She crouches
in the north,
her trembling
30 the source
of dawn.
Light appears
with the shudder
of her slopes,
35 the movement
of her arm.

Blackberries unravel,°
stones dislodge.°
It's not as if
40 they weren't warned.

She was sleeping
but she heard
the boot scrape,
the creaking floor,
45 felt the pull of the blanket
from her thin shoulder.
With one free hand
she finds her weapons
and raises them high;
50 clearing the twigs
from her throat
she sings, she sings,
shaking the sky
like a blanket about her
55 Loo-Wit sings and sings and sings!

---

37 Here, *unravel* means "untangle; separate; come apart."
38 To *dislodge* is to move out of position.

---

12 *Buttes* (būts) are steep, isolated, flat-topped hills.

COMPARING selections

This selection is compared with "The Flower-Fed Buffaloes" on page 823. A lesson for teaching a comparison of the two selections appears on page 825.

A Active Reading

PREDICT Ask a volunteer to read the first sentence aloud. Have students suggest what the black tobacco is and what event is taking place. *(The black tobacco is volcanic ash spewing from Mount St. Helens.)*

Additional Resources

📁 *Active Reading Guide,* p. 69

🎧 *Audio Library*

🎧 *Spanish Audio Library*

📁 *Spanish Summaries,* p. 69

B Literary Elements

EXTENDED METAPHOR Mount St. Helens, or Loo-Wit, is described as a woman throughout this poem. Have students describe why Loo-Wit sings in the last stanza. *(Loo-Wit is angry at the scraping boots on her skin, the tearing off of her blanket of trees. She expresses her anger with her singing—a volcanic eruption.)*

Thematic Focus

A Delicate Balance Invite students to explain the delicate balance in this poem. *(The balance is between people and nature. Nature is stronger.)*

Teaching Options

✔ ASSESSMENT OPTIONS

📁 *Quick Checks,* p. 69

Responding to the Selection

Personal Response

The poet demonstrates her connection by describing her understanding of Loo-Wit and treating her as a woman with emotions.

Analyzing Literature

1. The poet describes the volcano as an old woman who is upset at what is happening to her.
2. The metaphor helps readers understand that humans and nature are sometimes in conflict.
3. Loo-Wit is erupting. The author describes the volcanic eruption with words like "shaking the sky" and "singing."
4. The message is that humans are destructive and that nature fights back when things get bad.
5. Examples include "huckleberry ropes lay prickly on her neck"—huckleberries grow on the mountainsides; "the shudder of her slopes"—an earthquake that causes stones to dislodge; "the pull of the blanket from her thin shoulder"—removing trees or other vegetation blanketing the mountainside.
6. The poet uses the phrase *centuries of cedar* because it is less wordy and sounds melodious.
7. The poem relates to the theme because it shows what can happen when the balance of nature gets disturbed by humans. In this case, Loo-Wit fights back by creating a volcanic eruption.
8. Students should list elements of the poem that would appeal to the person they choose.

Responding to Literature

PERSONAL RESPONSE

Could you feel the poet's connection to the subject of this poem? How would you describe her connection?

Analyzing Literature

RECALL AND INTERPRET

1. What metaphor does the poet use to describe the volcano?
2. How does the metaphor help you to understand the **theme** of the poem?
3. What is really happening in lines 50–55 of the poem?
4. What message about nature does the poem express?

EVALUATE AND CONNECT

5. In lines 5–6, the poet uses an image of an old woman who "spits her black tobacco." The poet's words are figurative, or metaphoric. She is really describing a volcano throwing out black ashes. That is the literal, or nonfigurative, meaning of the lines. Give three more examples of the poet's use of figurative language, explaining what each one means literally.
6. Find an example of **alliteration** in "Loo-Wit." (See **Literary Terms Handbook,** page R1.) Why do you think the poet uses this poetic device?
7. Theme Connection   How is the poem related to the theme of "A Delicate Balance"? Explain.
8. Think of someone who would enjoy reading this poem. What about the poem would appeal to that person?

LITERARY ELEMENTS

Extended Metaphor

A **metaphor** is a comparison of two basically different things. Like similes, metaphors create unique, unexpected images that bring a poem to life. In a metaphor, however, the comparison is stated directly, and the words *as* or *like* are not used. In a metaphor, one thing is not *like* another thing; it *is* another thing. In an **extended metaphor,** the comparison is extended through a long passage. In a poem, it may be carried throughout the entire piece. The comparison between an old woman and a volcano in "Loo-Wit" is an extended metaphor.

1. Describe how the poet first introduces the extended metaphor in "Loo-Wit."

2. Explain how the actions of the old woman in the poem mirror the actions of a volcano.

● See **Literary Terms Handbook,** p. R4.

LITERARY ELEMENTS

1. In lines 2–4 of "Loo-Wit," the poet writes, "this old woman/no longer cares/what others think."
2. She spits black tobacco (volcanic ash); her slopes shudder and her arm moves (an earthquake); she sings (erupts).

Additional Resources

📖 *Literary Elements Transparency 69*

Extending Your Response

Writing About Literature

Analyzing Impressions   In a paragraph or two, write about your own reaction as you read "Loo-Wit." First describe the poem's overall impact. Were you confused? challenged? intrigued? excited? Then give examples of how the poet's use of language helped to create the effect the poem had on you.

Literature Groups

Poet's Corner   How does the poem's extended metaphor allow you to see a volcano in an entirely new way? In small groups, discuss the poem's unique comparison and how it offers readers an opportunity to think about nature in a different way. Then make a list of other natural elements that might become the subjects of poems. Brainstorm possible comparisons for each element on your list.

Personal Writing
Extended Metaphor   Using the notes you wrote for the **Focus Activity** on page 818, write your own extended metaphor. It can be a poem or a prose paragraph. Compare something in the natural world, such as a volcano or a hurricane, to something else, such as a train or an unruly student. Be creative in your comparison. Use sensory language and vivid imagery in your extended metaphor.

Performing

Role-Play   Work with a partner. While one of you reads the poem aloud, the other will role-play the actions of the old woman described in the poem. Use props such as a blanket, a boot, twigs, stones, or chairs pushed together to make a "bumpy bed." Practice until you feel comfortable sharing your dramatization with your classmates.

Reading Further
If you would like to read more poetry by Native Americans, try these books:

In the Trail of the Wind: American Indian Poems and Ritual Orations by John Bierhorst

Rising Voices: Writings of Young Native Americans ed. by Arlene B. Hirschfelder

 Save your work for your portfolio.

Skill Minilesson

READING AND THINKING • ELABORATING

What is the meaning of the poem "Loo-Wit"? You might respond in a simple sentence: *"Loo-Wit" is about the eruption of a volcano.* But a skillful thinker will consider a more elaborate response to the question. As you read, try to keep expanding, or elaborating your understanding of a poem by thinking about the different details and images that add rich texture to its meaning.

PRACTICE Reread "Loo-Wit." As you do, pay attention to the details that help you understand the rich texture of the meaning of the poem. In a short paragraph, elaborate on your understanding of the meaning of the poem.

● For more about main idea and details, see **Reading Handbook,** p. R87.

A DELICATE BALANCE 🐛 821

Extending Your Response

Writing About Literature
Students' paragraphs should
• contain a topic sentence that states how their feelings changed.
• use examples from the poem.
• contain a summarizing sentence.

Literature Groups
Have students list natural events, such as hurricanes. In groups, have them make a combined list. Finally, have them identify comparisons.
COLLAB. LEARN.

Personal Writing
Student poems or paragraphs should
• compare and contrast something in the natural world with something else.
• help others see the subject in a new way.

Performing Encourage students to experiment with their voices to create varying effects. Encourage them to experiment with movement as well.

Skill Minilesson

READING AND THINKING
• ELABORATING

Students' paragraphs should describe details that add additional layers of meaning and that deepen their understanding.

Additional Resources
📁 *Reading Workbook*

 ## ASSESSMENT OPTIONS

📁 *Quick Checks,* p. 69
📁 *Selection and Theme Assessment,* pp. 119–120
📁 *Performance Assessment,* p. 65
📁 *Testmaker*

Objectives

- To read and enjoy a poem about the delicate balance between machines and nature
- To recognize and appreciate alliteration

Skills

Reading/Thinking: Identifying Assumptions
Listening/Speaking: Performing
Collaboration: Literature Groups

Motivating
→OPTIONS

Selection Focus Transparency 70: Have students list ways in which trains helped and harmed the prairies and the West.

Focus Activity: As an extension of the Focus Activity, have students in small groups think about how the United States would be different if locomotives hadn't carried people westward in the 1800s.

Before You Read
The Flower-Fed Buffaloes

MEET VACHEL LINDSAY

Vachel Lindsay earned the nickname the Vagabond Poet because as a young man he walked from Illinois to Colorado and New Mexico. Along the way, he performed his poems in return for food and shelter. Lindsay's sense of pride in his country is evident in the patriotic images, strong rhythms, and whimsical folklore found in his poetry. Like Walt Whitman, another poet who traveled widely and wrote about the full panorama of American life, Lindsay felt that poetry should touch upon every kind of human experience.

Vachel Lindsay was born in Springfield, Illinois, in 1879 and died in 1931.

FOCUS ACTIVITY

Imagine the nineteenth-century landscape of the plains west of the Mississippi River. How do you think the locomotive changed that landscape?

Sharing Ideas
Jot down your ideas and then share them in a small-group discussion.

Setting a Purpose
Read this poem to find out how the speaker views the impact of the locomotive upon the natural environment.

BACKGROUND

Did You Know? The word *buffalo* is commonly used to refer to the North American bison, a species of wild cattle. These majestic animals may weigh more than two thousand pounds each and stand more than six feet high. Bison once roamed freely throughout much of North America. There were more than 30 million bison in the grasslands west of the Mississippi River when white settlers first arrived. By the end of the nineteenth century, the bison population had been reduced to about five hundred, and many people feared their extinction. Today, the animals are raised on ranches and protected on refuges, and the bison population is increasing.

RESOURCE MANAGER

Lesson Planning Resource
The *Theme Eight Planning Guide* (pp. 40–44) provides additional lesson notes and reduced versions of all print resources.

📁 **Other Print Resources**
- Active Reading Guide, p. 70
- Grammar and Language Workbook, pp. 275–276
- Grammar and Composition Handbook, Lesson 13.8
- Quick Checks, p. 70

- Selection and Theme Assessment, pp. 119–120
- Performance Assessment, p. 65
- Spanish Summaries, p. 70
- Spanish Translations
- Inclusion Strategies
- Block Scheduling Guide
- English Language Learners Sourcebook

 Transparencies
- Selection Focus 70
- Literary Elements 70

Technology
🎧 Audio Library
🎧 Spanish Audio Library
💻 Glencoe Literature Web Site
💾 Testmaker

The Flower-Fed Buffaloes

Vachel Lindsay

View in the 'Grand Detour', 1852. George Catlin. Oil on canvas, 11⅛ x 14¾ in. Thomas Gilcrease Institute of American History and Art, Tulsa, OK.

The flower-fed buffaloes of the spring
In the days of long ago,
Ranged where the locomotives sing
And the prairie flowers lie low:—
5 The tossing, blooming, perfumed grass
Is swept away by the wheat,
Wheels and wheels and wheels spin by
In the spring that still is sweet.
But the flower-fed buffaloes of the spring
10 Left us, long ago.
They gore° no more, they bellow no more,
They trundle° around the hills no more:—
With the Blackfeet,° lying low,
With the Pawnees,° lying low,
15 Lying low.

11 **gore:** to pierce with a horn, tusk, or sharp weapon.
12 **trundle:** to move or roll along on, or as if on, wheels.
13 The **Blackfeet** are Native Americans who lived east of the Rocky Mountains in what are now Montana and Saskatchewan, Canada. The homeland of the **Pawnees** was what is now west-central Nebraska.

Grammar and Language *Minilesson*

Using Hyphens Explain that hyphens are used in a compound adjective before a noun (as in "flower-fed buffaloes"), in some compound nouns ("father-in-law"), and in fractions ("two-thirds") and compound numbers ("forty-one").

Activity Ask students to supply hyphens where needed in the following.
1. great-grandmother
2. pitch-black night
3. junior high school
4. twenty-three
5. two-thirds **L2** **COLLAB. LEARN.**

Additional Resources

📙 *Grammar and Language Workbook,* p. 275–276

📙 *Grammar and Composition Handbook,* Lesson 13.8

📙 *Writer's Choice,* Lesson 20.8

Responding to the Selection

Personal Response

In their journals, students should describe the images, along with the feelings they evoke.

Analyzing Literature

1. The buffaloes ranged on the prairie. The wheat has swept away the prairie grass.
2. The wheels of trains spin by where the buffalo once roamed. The spring is still sweet.
3. The buffaloes left long ago. The Pawnee and the Blackfeet left with them.
4. The term *flower-fed* makes the buffalo seem peaceful and gentle. It maintains the harmonious and gentle mood of the poem.
5. Lindsay describes the buffalo as bellowing, trundling, goring, and feeding on flowers. The present has locomotives with "wheels and wheels and wheels" that spin by through massive wheat fields.
6. Lindsay uses *lying low* to mean that something is gone, suppressed, or near extinction.

Extending Your Response

Literature Groups Encourage group members to take turns, so that all the students have a chance to express their ideas. **COLLAB. LEARN.**

Performing Encourage students to use their voices to create varying effects. Students may want to speak softly, loudly, slowly, or quickly.

Responding to Literature

PERSONAL RESPONSE

What images from the poem linger in your mind? Record them in your journal.

Analyzing Literature

RECALL AND INTERPRET

1. Where did the buffaloes range in the "days of long ago"? What has the wheat swept away?
2. What spins by now where the buffalo once roamed? What is still sweet?
3. When did the buffaloes leave? Who left with them?

EVALUATE AND CONNECT

4. How does the phrase "flower-fed" affect your image of the buffaloes? What effect does it have on the overall **mood** of the poem?
5. What comparisons does Lindsay make between the past and the present?
6. What meanings do you think Lindsay intended for the phrase "lying low"?

Extending Your Response

Literature Groups

Theme Discussion Review your notes from the **Focus Activity** on page 822. Then, working in small groups, discuss the theme of "The Flower-Fed Buffaloes."

Performing

Poetry Reading Give your own reading of this poem. Listen to the sounds and rhythms of the poem as you practice reading aloud. When you are ready, read the poem aloud to the class.

📖 **Save your work for your portfolio.**

824 🦬 THEME 8

LITERARY ELEMENTS

Alliteration

Alliteration is the repetition of the same or very similar consonant sounds in words that are close together—most often, but not always, at the beginnings of words. In "The Flower-Fed Buffaloes," for example, the *f* sound is repeated in the words *flower* and *fed*. Poets use alliteration to emphasize particular words, to establish a mood, or to give their writing a musical tone.

1. Find and list three other examples of alliteration in "The Flower-Fed Buffaloes."
2. Find another poem that contains alliteration. Describe how alliteration affects the poem.

● See **Literary Terms Handbook,** p. R1.

LITERARY ELEMENTS

1. Examples of alliteration are: lie low; spring that still is sweet; wheels and wheels and wheels; left us, long ago
2. Paragraphs should use examples from the poem to support their ideas about alliteration.

Additional Resources

💾 *Literary Elements Transparency 70*

✓ ASSESSMENT OPTIONS

📁 *Quick Checks,* p. 70
📁 *Selection and Theme Assessment,* pp. 119–120
📁 *Performance Assessment,* p. 65
📁 *Testmaker*

COMPARING SELECTIONS

Loo-Wit and The Flower-Fed Buffaloes

COMPARE THEMES

"Loo-Wit" and "The Flower-Fed Buffaloes" are poems that portray the power and beauty of nature. The theme of nature and its relationship to human beings and civilization plays an important role in both poems.

- How does "Loo-Wit" portray the force of nature? What role do humans play in the poem?
- How does "The Flower-Fed Buffaloes" portray the power and beauty of nature? What role do humans play in this poem?
- Compare and contrast how the relationship between nature and human beings is portrayed in these poems.

View in the 'Grand Detour', 1852 (detail).

COMPARE POETIC LANGUAGE

Both poems are filled with sounds, imagery, and figurative language that help readers appreciate the total effect of the poem.

1. In small groups, talk about the total effect of each poem.
2. Pick out your favorite images, sounds, similes, or metaphors from each poem. Talk about each of your examples and why you chose them.
3. Share your thoughts and feelings with your classmates in a full-class forum.

COMPARE RESPONSES

Compare your overall feelings and attitudes about these poems. In one or two paragraphs, explain your thoughts and feelings as you answer the following questions:

- How are these poems alike? How are they different?
- Which poem do you prefer? Why?
- Which poem did you learn more from? What did you learn?

 A DELICATE BALANCE 825

Objective
- To compare two poems that deal with the theme of nature and its relationship to civilization

COMPARE THEMES
- "Loo-Wit" portrays nature as something that can strike back at humans if they take advantage of it. Humans are destructive.
- "The Flower-Fed Buffaloes" portrays nature as something that humans can destroy or change.
- In "Loo-Wit" nature can defend itself, but in "Buffaloes," nature is at the mercy of civilization. In both poems, humans alter nature.

COMPARE POETIC LANGUAGE
Student groups should
- allow each member to present reasons for liking a favorite image, sound, simile, or metaphor.
- present the group's ideas in a full-class forum.

COMPARE RESPONSES
Students' paragraphs should
- describe how the two poems are alike and different.
- explain which poem the student prefers and why.
- analyze which poem the student learned more from and describe what was learned.

Additional Resources
📁 *Literature Groups Sourcebook*

Teaching Options

PORTFOLIO OPTIONS

Select and Reflect Have students reflect on the paragraphs they wrote for the Compare Responses activity by asking themselves these questions:
- Do my paragraphs contain examples to show how the two poems are alike and different?
- Have I given careful thought to what I can learn from each poem?

Students should clip their reflections to their paragraphs and place them in their portfolios.

Additional Resources
📁 *Writing Assessment and Portfolio Management,* pp. 17–19

Objectives

- To read and analyze an essay
- To identify the author's purpose
- To rewrite the essay from a different point of view

Skills

Reading/Thinking: Evaluating; Problem and Solution; Cause and Effect
Writing: Journal Entry
Vocabulary: Prefix *de-*
Grammar/Language: Run-on Sentences
Listening/Speaking: Literature Groups; Oral Report
Collaboration: Literature Groups

Motivating
→OPTIONS

Selection Focus Transparency 71: Have students read and discuss the quote about the threat of extinction for some bird species.

Focus Activity: As an extension of the Focus Activity, invite students to work in small groups and create a dramatization of one of their humorous stories. Then have them perform it for the class.

Before You Read
Turkeys

MEET BAILEY WHITE

Not many first-grade teachers become famous radio celebrities or have books on the national bestseller list, but Bailey White is no ordinary first-grade teacher. She calls teaching first graders in her south Georgia town her "honorable job." After school she entertains listeners with her regular commentaries on National Public Radio's *All Things Considered*. White has written two collections of humorous autobiographical stories, *Mama Makes Up Her Mind* and *Sleeping at the Starlite Motel*.

Bailey White was born in 1948. This essay was published in 1993.

FOCUS ACTIVITY

What amusing events do you remember from when you were a very young child? Choose one amusing event from that time in your life.

QuickWrite
Make a list of at least three details that you recall about that past event.

Setting a Purpose
Read this humorous essay to find out about the author's childhood experience with turkeys and ornithologists.

BACKGROUND

The Time and Place   It is the 1950s in a small town in southern Georgia.

Did You Know?   An *ornithologist* is a scientist who studies birds. The ornithologists in this selection study birds native to the southeastern United States, including wild turkeys and several kinds of woodpeckers. The chuck-will's-widow, another bird mentioned in the essay, is shown here. These birds resemble whippoorwills but are somewhat larger.

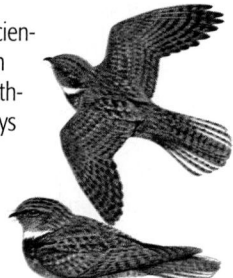

VOCABULARY PREVIEW

domestic (də mes′ tik) *adj.* describes animals living with or near human beings and cared for by them; p. 828
degrade (di grād′) *v.* to lower in character or quality; make less pure; p. 828
demise (di mīz′) *n.* death; end; p. 828
sluggish (slug′ ish) *adj.* lacking energy or alertness; p. 828
elaborate (i lab′ ər it) *adj.* worked out carefully and thoroughly; detailed; complicated; p. 829
undertake (un′ dər tāk′) *v.* to enter into (a task); attempt; p. 829

RESOURCE MANAGER

Lesson Planning Resource
The *Theme Eight Planning Guide* (pp. 45–51) provides additional lesson notes and reduced versions of all print resources.

📁 **Other Print Resources**
- Active Reading Guide, p. 71
- Vocabulary Practice, p. 50
- Reading Workbook, pp. 123–124
- Grammar and Language Workbook, pp. 26–27, 57–58
- Grammar and Composition

Handbook, Lesson 1.6
- Quick Checks, p. 71
- Selection and Theme Assessment, pp. 121–122
- Performance Assessment, p. 66
- Spanish Summaries, p. 71
- Spanish Translations
- Inclusion Strategies Sourcebook
- Block Scheduling Guide
- English Language Learners Sourcebook

 Transparencies
- Selection Focus 71
- Literary Elements 71

Technology
🎧 Audio Library
🎧 Spanish Audio Library
💻 Glencoe Literature Web Site
💾 Testmaker

TURKEYS

Bailey White

Something about my mother attracts ornithologists.[1]
It all started years ago when a couple of them discovered she had
a rare species of woodpecker coming to her bird feeder. They came
in the house and sat around the window, exclaiming and taking
pictures with big fancy cameras. But long after the red cockaded
woodpeckers had gone to roost in their sticky little holes in the
red hearts of our big old pine trees, and the chuck-will's-widows had
started to sing their night chorus, the ornithologists were still there.

---

1. *Ornithologists* (ôr′ nə thol′ ə jists) are people who study birds or are experts on
   birds.

SUMMARY

When Bailey White was growing up, there were often ornithologists in and around her house, looking for rare birds. They were especially concerned with keeping wild and domestic turkeys from mixing. Once, when Bailey was in bed with a high fever, the ornithologists rescued eggs from an abandoned turkey nest and to keep them warm put them in her bed. She awoke with six-teen wild turkey chicks snuggling against her. Years later, she is happy to report that the woods are full of pure wild turkeys.

📁 *Spanish Summaries,* p. 71

A Active Reading

CONNECT Ask students what they know about turkeys. Have a volun-teer read the first paragraph and dis-cuss what the class knows about the different types of birds men-tioned. Ask if any students have bird feeders, what kinds of birds come to them, and what they look like or what kinds of sound they make.

Additional Resources
📁 *Active Reading Guide,* p. 71

🎧 *Audio Library*

🎧 *Spanish Audio Library*

Teaching Options

CONNECTING TO OTHER SELECTIONS

The chart at the right shows three ways to connect "Turkeys" to other selections in this book.

For specific teaching strategies, see The *Theme Eight Planning Guide*, pages 48–49.

Connection	Title
Life Skills: Problem Solving	→ "Oh Broom, Get to Work," p. 383
Thematic: Challenges	→ "The Fish Crisis," p. 295
Literary: Humor	→ "Who's on First?" p. 555

B **Literary Elements**

AUTHOR'S PURPOSE: *Setting* Ask students to think about the time and place the events take place. *(The events probably take place in the Carolina region in the 1950s.)*

C **Literary Elements**

AUTHOR'S PURPOSE What is Bailey White trying to convey to the readers in this paragraph? *(Bailey describes the demise and degradation of the birds, which upsets her, and she wants to share this information.)*

D **Active Reading**

PREDICT What text clues can help students predict why the ornithologists are interested in the girl's health? *(The "102 fever" is a context clue that might help them predict what the ornithologists' purpose might be.)*

Teaching Options

TURKEYS

There always seemed to be three or four of them wandering around our place, discussing the body fat of hummingbirds, telling cruel jokes about people who couldn't tell a pileated woodpecker from an ivory bill,[2] and staying for supper.

B In those days, during the 1950s, the big concern of ornithologists in our area was the wild turkey. They were rare, and the pure-strain wild turkeys had begun to interbreed with farmers' domestic stock. The species was being degraded. It was extinction by dilution,[3] and to the ornithologists it was just as tragic as the more dramatic demise of the passenger pigeon or the Carolina parakeet.[4]

C One ornithologist had devised a formula to compute the ratio of domestic to pure-strain wild turkey in an individual bird by comparing the angle of flight at takeoff and the rate of acceleration. And in those sad days, the turkeys were flying low and slow.[5]

It was during that time, the spring when I was six years old, that I caught the measles. I had a high fever, and my mother was worried about me. She kept the house quiet and dark and crept around silently, trying different methods of cooling me down.

Even the ornithologists stayed away—but not out of fear of the measles or respect for a household with sickness. The fact was, they had discovered a wild turkey nest. According to the formula, the hen was pure-strain wild—not a taint of the sluggish domestic bird in her blood—and the ornithologists were camping in the woods, protecting her nest from predators and taking pictures.

One night our phone rang. It was one of the ornithologists. "Does your little girl still have measles?" he asked. **D**

"Yes," said my mother. "She's very sick. Her temperature is 102."

"I'll be right over," said the ornithologist.

In five minutes a whole carload of them arrived. They marched solemnly into the house, carrying a cardboard box. "A hundred two, did you say? Where is she?" they asked my mother.

They crept into my room and set the box down on the bed. I was barely conscious, and when I opened my eyes, their worried faces hovering over me seemed to float out of the darkness like giant, glowing eggs.

---

2. The *cockaded woodpeckers* have red crests. The *chuck-will's-widows* are night-flying birds. The *pileated woodpecker* has a bright red crest on the top of its head. Ornithologists use the adjective *pileated* to describe any bird with a bright red crest. *Cockaded* indicates a small tuft of feathers on the top of the head; *ivory bill* refers to an ivory-colored bill.
3. After generations of interbreeding, the wild turkeys became less wild, a weakening *(dilution)* that could lead to their gradual dying out *(extinction)*.
4. Once common in the eastern United States, the *passenger pigeon* and the *Carolina parakeet* are now extinct.
5. Wild turkeys can fly, but domestic turkeys cannot. Their *low and slow* flight indicates that the wild birds have lost much of their pure strain.

Vocabulary
domestic (də mes' tik) *adj.* describes animals living with or near human beings and cared for by them
degrade (di grād') *v.* to lower in character or quality; make less pure
demise (di mīz') *n.* death; end
sluggish (slug' ish) *adj.* lacking energy or alertness

Bailey White ~

They snatched the covers off me and felt me all over. They consulted in whispers.

"Feels just right, I'd say."

"A hundred two—can't miss if we tuck them up close and she lies still."

I closed my eyes then, and after a while the ornithologists drifted away, their pale faces bobbing up and down on the black wave of fever.

The next morning I was better. For the first time in days I could think. The memory of the ornithologists with their whispered voices and their bony, cool hands was like a dream from another life. But when I pulled down the covers, there staring up at me with googly eyes and wide mouths, were sixteen fuzzy baby turkeys and the cracked chips and caps of sixteen brown speckled eggs.

 I was a sensible child. I gently stretched myself out. The eggshells crackled, and the turkey babies fluttered and cheeped and snuggled against me. I laid my aching head back on the pillow and closed my eyes. "The ornithologists," I whispered. "The ornithologists have been here."

It seems the turkey hen had been so disturbed by the <u>elaborate</u> protective measures that had been <u>undertaken</u> in her behalf that she had abandoned her nest on the night the eggs were due to hatch. It was a cold night. The ornithologists, not having an incubator to hand, used their heads and came up with the next best thing.

The baby turkeys and I gained our strength together. When I was finally able to get out of bed and feebly creep around the house, the turkeys peeped and cheeped around my ankles, scrambling to keep up with me and tripping over their own big spraddle-toed[6] feet. When I went outside for the first time, the turkeys tumbled after me down the steps and scratched around in the yard while I sat in the sun.

Finally, in late summer, the day came when they were ready to fly for the first time as adult birds. The ornithologists gathered. I ran down the hill, and the turkeys ran too. Then, one by one, they took off. They flew high and fast. The ornithologists made V's with their thumbs and forefingers, measuring angles. They consulted their stopwatches and paced off distances. They scribbled in their tiny notebooks. Finally they looked at each other. They sighed. They smiled. They jumped up and down and hugged each other. "One hundred percent pure wild turkey!" they said.

Nearly forty years have passed since then. In many ways the world is a worse place now. But there's a vaccine for measles. And the woods where I live are full of pure wild turkeys. I like to think they are all descendants of those sixteen birds I saved from the vigilance of the ornithologists.

---

6. The toes of a *spraddle-toed* bird spread out in different directions.

❖

Vocabulary

elaborate (i lab′ ər it) *adj.* worked out carefully and thoroughly; detailed; complicated

undertake (un′ dər tāk′) *v.* to enter into (a task); attempt

A DELICATE BALANCE ❦ 829

E Active Reading

VISUALIZE Have students visualize the scene of a six-year-old in bed with sixteen fuzzy baby turkeys and cracked chips and caps of eggshells around her. What do they think of the scene? *(Most students will recognize that this is a very humorous scene.)*

F Critical Thinking

EVALUATING What serious miscalculation do the ornithologists make and how could it have affected the outcome? *(They think that protecting the turkey hen from strangers would save the eggs, not realizing they also were "strangers" to the hen—they are surprised when she abandons her nest. If they had not thought quickly to use Bailey as the "incubator," all their hopes of a pure breed would have been dashed.)*

G Literary Elements

AUTHOR'S PURPOSE: *Point* of *View*
Ask students to discuss Bailey's feelings for the ornithologists. Have them support their statements with examples from the essay. *(Bailey seems to have an admiration for the ornithologists even though she presents them with humor and shows how much they care about the birds, especially in saving the "One hundred percent pure wild turkey!")*

Thematic Focus

A Delicate Balance Ask students how this selection relates to the theme. *(The ornithologists are trying to restore the balance of nature.)*

✓ ASSESSMENT OPTIONS

📁 *Quick Checks,* p. 71

Reading *Minilesson*

Problem and Solution Even though "Turkeys" is presented in a humorous tone, the author's purpose is to bring attention to the serious issue of bird extinction. She presents the reader with some basic survival problems birds face and presents some funny solutions.

Activity Have students work in small groups to discuss the story's main prob-lems and how they were resolved. Suggest that students use a chart to keep track of the problems and their solutions. They can use the chart to help them answer the questions that follow the selection. **L2** **COLLAB. LEARN.**

Additional Resources

📁 *Reading Workbook,* pp. 123–124

A DELICATE BALANCE ❦ 829

Responding to the Selection

Personal Response

Some students may think that it would be fun to have ornithologists and baby turkeys in the house. Others might object to having to share their backyard with sixteen turkeys.

Analyzing Literature

1. They discovered a rare species of woodpecker there.
2. They were breeding with domestic turkeys and losing the ability to fly.
3. "She kept the house quiet and dark and crept around silently, trying different methods of cooling me down."
4. Bailey's high body temperature would keep them warm enough to survive.
5. Yes. She describes in a humorous way the results of the "elaborate protective measures" taken on behalf of the mother turkey.
6. They took time to protect the mother and rescue the eggs, putting them in Bailey's bed.
7. Yes. She lets the ornithologists stay around her house and use her sick daughter's bed to save the birds.
8. Vigilance refers to the way they watched the mother turkey and eventually scared her away. Bailey provided a way to save the birds once the mother was gone.
9. She creates a mystery and says something funny all at once, which gives the story a light-hearted and humorous feeling.
10. Students' answers should rely on humor to explain the reasons for their responses.

Responding to Literature

PERSONAL RESPONSE

Do you think you would have enjoyed living with Bailey White's family? Why or why not?

Analyzing Literature

RECALL

1. Why did the ornithologists first start coming to Bailey White's house?
2. Why were the scientists concerned about the wild turkeys?
3. Find and quote a passage that tells you something about Bailey White's mother.
4. Why did the ornithologists need Bailey to incubate the eggs?

INTERPRET

5. Do you think Bailey found the ornithologists amusing? Support your opinion.
6. In what ways does the author make clear the scientists' concern for wild turkeys?
7. Do you think Bailey's mother is a generous person? Why or why not?
8. The author says she saved the turkeys "from the vigilance of the ornithologists." What does she mean?

EVALUATE AND CONNECT

9. **Tone** is the attitude a writer expresses about his or her subject. How does White's first sentence help to set the tone of the story?
10. How would you react if a group of scientists barged into your bedroom when you were sick?

LITERARY ELEMENTS

Author's Purpose

The **author's purpose** is the writer's goal in writing a particular work. For example, the author of the humorous essay "Turkeys" probably wanted to **entertain** readers. An author's purpose in writing a newspaper editorial is probably to **persuade** readers of a viewpoint. The purpose of an encyclopedia article is usually to **inform**. Sometimes, especially in serious poetry, an author's purpose is to **express** an idea, a feeling, or a truth.

1. How well does Bailey White achieve her purpose of entertaining her readers? Support your opinion with examples from the selection.

2. What other purpose or purposes does White seem to have? How do you know?

● See **Literary Terms Handbook**, p. R1.

LITERARY ELEMENTS

1. She presents many funny scenes, such as putting the chicks into her bed, but she also makes clear how birds face extinction.
2. White's purpose is to educate people about endangered species. She cites and describes several examples.

Additional Resources

📖 *Literary Elements Transparency 71*

Extending Your Response

Personal Writing

Childhood Memories   Look back at your QuickWrite list from the **Focus Activity** on page 826. Use the details on the list to write a journal entry about that humorous event in your life. Be sure to explain why that event has stayed in your memory. You may share your entry with your friends or family if you wish.

Literature Groups

Picture This   Imagine that an article about young Bailey's adventures with the turkeys is going to appear in a wildlife magazine. Design a cover for the magazine that features a drawing and brief "teaser" to interest readers in the story. Post all the covers in the room. Discuss how they succeed at grabbing the attention of readers.

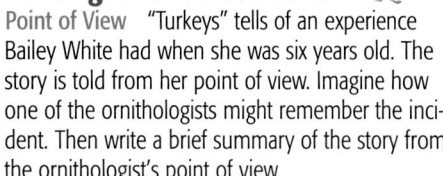
CONNECTION

Did you know that Benjamin Franklin wanted to make the turkey, rather than the bald eagle, our national bird? To learn more about turkeys or other birds, type "birds," or the name of a type of bird, into a search engine.

Writing About Literature

Point of View   "Turkeys" tells of an experience Bailey White had when she was six years old. The story is told from her point of view. Imagine how one of the ornithologists might remember the incident. Then write a brief summary of the story from the ornithologist's point of view.

Interdisciplinary Activity

Science   Sharpen your own ornithological skills. Do some research on birds, and prepare a brief oral report for your class on how to tell the difference between a pileated woodpecker and an ivory-billed woodpecker–or between any other pair of birds common in your area. If you can, illustrate your report with photos or drawings of the birds. If appropriate, and you're a good whistler, you might also demonstrate how their songs differ.

Reading Further

Here are some more humorous autobiographies you might want to read:
My Life and Hard Times by James Thurber
Growing Up by Russell Baker

 Save your work for your portfolio.

Extending Your Response

Personal Writing

Students' journal entries should
- describe a humorous event in their lives from when they were very young.
- explain why the event has stayed in their memories.

Writing About Literature

Students' summaries should
- describe the events of the story.
- be told from one of the ornithologists' point of view.

Literature Groups

Encourage students to make several sketches, trying to give a strong feeling about the characters and events in the story. Then have them create their cover and write the "teaser."
COLLAB. LEARN.

Interdisciplinary Activity

Help students locate information in library reference books or on the Internet. Before they begin, you might have them list birds that are found in your area and identify the times of year they can observe specific types.

✔ ASSESSMENT OPTIONS

📁 *Quick Checks,* p. 71
📁 *Selection and Theme Assessment,* pp. 121–122
📁 *Performance Assessment,* p. 66
📁 *Testmaker*

Skill Minilessons

GRAMMAR AND LANGUAGE
RUN-ON SENTENCES

1. At the age of six Bailey caught the measles. She went to bed with a high fever.
2. A mother hen had abandoned her eggs, and the ornithologists thought Bailey's high body temperature could hatch them.
3. She awoke in the morning to find sixteen baby turkeys in her bed; she gently stretched herself out.
4. The eggshells crackled, and the turkey babies fluttered and cheeped and snuggled against her.

READING AND THINKING
CAUSE AND EFFECT

Practice

1. The ornithologists were too close to the nest, and they scared her away.
2. They rescued the eggs and put them in Bailey's bed to keep them warm.
3. Bailey awoke to find sixteen turkey chicks in bed with her. They snuggled against her and later followed her around.

VOCABULARY
ANTONYMS THE PREFIX *de-*

1. b   3. a   5. c
2. e   4. d

Additional Resources

📘 ***Grammar and Language Workbook,*** pp. 26–27, 57–58

📘 ***Grammar and Composition Handbook,*** Lesson 1.6

📘 ***Writer's Choice,*** Lesson 7.2

📂 ***Reading Workbook,*** pp. 123–124

📂 ***Vocabulary Practice,*** p. 50

Skill Minilessons

GRAMMAR AND LANGUAGE • RUN-ON SENTENCES

A **run-on sentence** has two (or more) main clauses run together or separated by only a comma. Correct a run-on sentence in one of these ways:

1. Make two sentences out of it.
2. Turn the run-on sentence into a compound sentence by adding a comma followed by a conjunction (such as *and* or *but*).
3. Use a semicolon to separate the two main clauses.

● For more about run-on sentences, see **Language Handbook,** p. R13.

PRACTICE Use the most appropriate of the three methods to correct each of the following run-ons.

1. At the age of six Bailey caught the measles, she went to bed with a high fever.
2. A mother hen had abandoned her eggs the ornithologists thought Bailey's high body temperature could hatch them.
3. She awoke in the morning to find sixteen baby turkeys in her bed, she gently stretched herself out.
4. The eggshells crackled, the turkey babies fluttered and cheeped and snuggled against her.

READING AND THINKING • CAUSE AND EFFECT

Many events in stories that you read are connected by cause-and-effect relationships. Each event causes others to happen, as this example from "Turkeys" illustrates.

Cause	Effect
Rare woodpecker appears near Bailey's house.	Ornithologists go to Bailey's house and study birds.

PRACTICE Answer these questions about other causes and effects in "Turkeys."

1. What caused the mother turkey to abandon her nest?
2. What action did the ornithologists take because the nest was abandoned?
3. What effects did their action have on Bailey?

● For more about cause and effect, see **Reading Handbook,** p. R85.

VOCABULARY • THE PREFIX *de-*

The two most common meanings of the prefix *de-* are "down or away from" and "reverse or undo." In *degrade,* the prefix has the "down" meaning. When wild turkeys are *degraded,* their quality is lowered. In *decode,* the prefix has the "undo" meaning. If you *decode* a message, you undo the code it was written in.

● For more about prefixes, see **Reading Handbook,** pp. R79–R80.

PRACTICE Use the two common meanings of *de-* to match each word with its meaning.

1. depress   a. to bleach
2. devalue   b. to push down
3. decolorize   c. to remove a bad smell
4. deforest   d. to cut down all the trees
5. deodorize   e. to make (something) worth less

Making Inferences

Skillful writers provide many details about the characters, events, and action in a piece of writing. By reading carefully, however, you can figure out even more than you're directly told. Read and think about this passage from "Uncle Tony's Goat."

> I stepped around into the low doorway, and the goat charged toward me, feet first. I had dirt in my mouth and up my nose and there was blood running past my eye: my head ached.

From the details about the dirt and the blood, you can figure out that the goat knocked the narrator to the ground. When you use what you know to figure out what you think is happening in a story, you are inferring, or **making inferences**. An inference is a conclusion based on details that are known.

● For more about making inferences, see **Reading Handbook,** p. R89.

EXERCISE

Read the following excerpt from "Turkeys." Then answer the questions.

Something about my mother attracts ornithologists. It all started years ago when a couple of them discovered she had a rare species of woodpecker coming to her bird feeder. They came in the house and sat around the window, exclaiming and taking pictures with big fancy cameras. But long after the red cockaded woodpeckers had gone to roost in their sticky little holes in the red hearts of our big old pine trees, and the chuck-will's-widows had started to sing their night chorus, the ornithologists were still there.

1. What inferences can you make about the narrator's mother? What clues helped you make that inference?

2. What inferences can you make about the place where the narrator grew up?

3. What inferences can you make about how the narrator feels about the ornithologists? How do your experience and the details in the selection help you make this inference?

Objective

• To recognize and use strategies for making inferences

Teaching Strategies

Point out that students make inferences on a daily basis. Show a few photographs from the local newspaper and ask students what they might infer by looking at the photos. Make a game out of seeing how accurately students can guess what led up to the photo.

Exercise

1. Students might infer that she is a bird-lover, that she is open and hospitable, and that she likes company. Clues include that she has bird feeders and that she invited the ornithologists into her home.
2. Students could infer that the narrator grew up in a rural or wooded area.
3. Students may think that the narrator finds the ornithologists strange, based on their own experiences with unusual guests. Details that contribute to this inference include the big fancy cameras and the fact that the ornithologists linger even after the birds have gone home.

Additional Resources
📂 *Reading Workbook*

Teaching Options

 INCLUSION STRATEGIES

Less-Proficient Readers Hearing a selection read aloud before reading it silently may help less-proficient readers make stronger inferences.

Activity Read Robert Frost's poem "The Pasture" (p. 835) aloud. As students listen to the poem, ask them to visualize the setting and speaker. Have them draw or paint a picture based on the images they visualized. They have could illustrate the poem's setting, speaker, or even their interpretation of its mood. **L2**

Additional Resources
📂 *Inclusion Strategies*

Objectives

- To read and analyze a poem
- To identify the effect of end-stopped rhymes
- To describe the effect of repetition in a poem

Skills

Reading/Thinking: Inferring
Writing: Poem
Grammar/Language: Mechanics: Semicolon, Colon
Listening/Speaking: Oral Reading; Choral Speaking
Collaboration: Listening and Speaking; Literature Groups

Motivating
→OPTIONS

Selection Focus Transparency 72: Have students read and discuss the quote about how poems can have multiple meanings and evoke a range of feelings.

Focus Activity: As an extension of the Focus Activity, have students write a paragraph about what it means to be a part of a family or group and share responsibilities.

Before You Read
The Pasture

MEET ROBERT FROST

R obert Frost worked as a mill worker, a shoemaker, a schoolteacher, a newspaper editor, and a farmer before he finally became a published poet. He lived most of his adult life on farms in Vermont and New Hampshire. "Three things have followed me," he wrote, "writing, teaching, and a little farming." His poems, inspired by the rural life and scenery of New England, are known for their plain language and natural rhythms.

Robert Frost was born in 1874 and died in 1963.

FOCUS ACTIVITY

How do you feel about chores you're asked to do? Do you think it's possible to enjoy doing chores?

Sharing Ideas
Think about the questions above. Then share your thoughts in a small-group discussion. Does everyone feel the same way?

Setting a Purpose
Read this poem to discover how the speaker feels about his chores.

BACKGROUND

Robert Frost, one of the most honored poets in America, won the Pulitzer Prize for Poetry four times. In 1961, when John F. Kennedy was elected president of the United States, Frost made history. At age eighty-seven, he became the first poet to read a poem at a presidential inauguration. His poem, "The Gift Outright," was heard by millions of people.

RESOURCE MANAGER

Lesson Planning Resource
The *Theme Eight Planning Guide* (pp. 52–56) provides additional lesson notes and reduced versions of all print resources.

📁 **Other Print Resources**
- Active Reading Guide, p. 72
- Grammar and Language Workbook, pp. 265–266
- Grammar and Composition Handbook, Lesson 13.5
- Quick Checks, p. 72
- Selection and Theme

Assessment, p. 123
- Performance Assessment, p. 67
- Spanish Summaries, p. 72
- Spanish Translations
- Inclusion Strategies
- Block Scheduling Guide
- English Language Learners Sourcebook

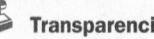 **Transparencies**
- Selection Focus 72
- Literary Elements 72

Technology
- 🎧 Audio Library
- 🎧 Spanish Audio Library
- 💻 Glencoe Literature Web Site
- 💾 Testmaker

The Pasture

Robert Frost

I'm going out to clean the pasture spring;
I'll only stop to rake the leaves away
(And wait to watch the water clear, I may):
I sha'n't be gone long.—You come too.

I'm going out to fetch the little calf
That's standing by the mother. It's so young,
It totters when she licks it with her tongue.
I sha'n't be gone long.—You come too.

Autumn, 1958. Eric Sloane. Oil on Masonite, 26¾ x 21¾ in. Private collection. Would the title "You Come Too" be appropriate for this painting? Why or why not?

A DELICATE BALANCE 🐏 835

Reading the Selection

A Active Reading

VISUALIZE Encourage students to read each stanza carefully to picture as many details as possible.

Additional Resources

📁 *Active Reading Guide,* p. 72

🎧 *Audio Library*

🎧 *Spanish Audio Library*

📁 *Spanish Summaries,* p. 72

B Literary Elements

RHYTHM: *End-Stopped Lines* Help students see how Frost creates a natural pause at the end of each line. *(He also repeats the rhyme scheme in the second and third lines of each stanza: abbc/deec.)*

C Author's Craft

ASSONANCE Frost uses this technique by repeating the words *you* and *too* in the last line of each stanza.

Thematic Focus

A Delicate Balance Ask students how this poem relates to the theme "A Delicate Balance."

✓ ASSESSMENT OPTIONS

📁 *Quick Checks,* p. 72

Teaching Options

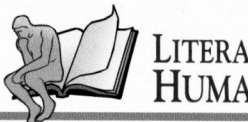

LITERATURE & HUMANITIES

📖 Have students compare the poem with the painting *Crossing the Pasture,* in *Introducing Art,* page 68. Ask students which elements of the pasture each work might be celebrating.

Listening and Speaking *Minilesson*

Choral Speaking As performers, students must read critically, making a new language style and tone their own.

Activity Break the class into two groups for a choral reading of the poem. During rehearsal, encourage students to work on such vocal traits as musicality, dynamics, enunciation, and expressiveness to communicate meaning. Encourage them to use appropriate intonations (clued by punctuation) and reflect Frost's tone (clued by Frost's word choice and sentence construction). **COLLAB. LEARN.**

A DELICATE BALANCE 🐏 835

Personal Response

Frost describes these chores in an inviting way and names jobs that are important to do; many students may think they would enjoy doing them.

Analyzing Literature

1. The speaker is going to clean the pasture spring. He will watch the water clear.
2. He must also fetch the little calf.
3. Most students will say that the speaker is an adult man or woman who lives on a farm and loves the pasture.
4. The poem is an invitation; repeating the last line reinforces its intent.
5. The speaker might be inviting a younger person, perhaps the speaker's child, though it could also be the reader.
6. They signify a pause. Omitting the pause would lessen the emphasis on the words "You come too."
7. An example of alliteration is: "And wait to watch the water clear, I may." The alliterations make the sound of the poem flow easily.
8. He describes the chore in a very caring way; his descriptions evoke a reverence for life and the land: "and wait to watch the water clear, I may;" "It's so young,/It totters when she licks it with her tongue."
9. He cares about them a great deal.
10. Students should name examples and explain why the chores might make them feel happy and satisfied.

Responding to Literature

PERSONAL RESPONSE

Did the poem make you rethink the ideas that you shared in the **Focus Activity** on page 834? Explain.

Analyzing Literature

RECALL

1. What is the speaker going out to clean? What might he wait for?
2. What is the other chore the speaker is planning?

INTERPRET

3. Imagine and describe the speaker of "The Pasture."
4. Why do you think the poet ends both stanzas with the same line?

EVALUATE AND CONNECT

5. Whom do you think the speaker is inviting to "come too"?
6. What is the purpose of the dashes in lines 4 and 8? How would the poem sound different without the dashes?
7. Find an example of **alliteration** in the poem. (See **Literary Terms Handbook,** page R1.) How does this poetic device affect the way you read the poem aloud?
8. How does Frost make a common farm chore seem interesting? Use examples from the poem to explain your answer.
9. Theme Connection   What can you infer from the second stanza about the speaker's attitude toward his farm animals?
10. Personal Connection   What chores could you do that might make you feel happy and satisfied?

LITERARY ELEMENTS

Rhythm: End-Stopped Lines

When a pause occurs naturally at the end of a line of poetry, it is called an **end-stopped line.** The length of the stop, as you read or recite the poem, depends on the sense of the words and the kind of punctuation used. A period, question mark, exclamation point, colon, or semicolon generally call for a somewhat longer stop than a comma or dash. When a poet uses no punctuation at all, readers need to use the sense of the words to figure out whether lines are end-stopped. Because end-stops at every line can make a poem, especially a long one, seem monotonous, most poets generally avoid using them at every line.

1. Which lines in "The Pasture" are end-stopped? What punctuation marks does Frost use to indicate the pauses?

2. Read "The Pasture" out loud twice. First stop at the end of each line. Then pause only when the punctuation directs you to do so. Which reading makes the poem easier to understand?

● See **Literary Terms Handbook,** p. R9.

LITERARY ELEMENTS

1. Lines 1, 3, 4, 7, and 8 are end-stopped. Frost uses a semicolon, colon, and period to indicate the pauses.
2. The punctuation makes it easier to understand; stopping at the end of every line breaks up the connected thoughts.

Additional Resources

Literary Elements Transparency 72

Extending Your Response

Writing About Literature

Mood   The speaker in the poem seems to anticipate enjoying his chores. Write a paragraph describing the mood of the poem. How does the invitation at the end of each stanza contribute to the mood?

Listening and Speaking

A Frost Menagerie   Many of Robert Frost's poems mention animals. Collect a few of these poems and read them aloud with a partner.

Creative Writing

An Invitation   Try to think about your own chores in a more interesting way. Write a poem inviting someone to join you as you go about your work.

Literature Groups

Pastoral Images   The images in "The Pasture" are vivid and concrete. Draw a picture of the image created in one of the stanzas. Then compare your work with others and choose the drawing that best conveys the poet's vision of farm life.

Reading Further

Here are some other books by and about Robert Frost you might enjoy reading:
You Come, Too by Robert Frost
A Restless Spirit by Natalie S. Bober

 Save your work for your portfolio.

Skill Minilesson

GRAMMAR AND LANGUAGE • MECHANICS: SEMICOLON, COLON

The semicolon and colon separate parts of a sentence that might otherwise be confused.

Rule 1: Use a semicolon to join parts of a compound sentence when a conjunction, such as *and, but,* or *or* is not used.

> Frost wrote poetry; he also worked a farm.

Rule 2: Use a colon to introduce a list of items that end a sentence. Use words such as *these* or *the following* to signal that a list is coming.

> Try these books by Frost: *Birches; You Come, Too; Christmas Trees.*

PRACTICE   Practice the rules by adding a semicolon or colon to each sentence.
1. This bicycle comes in the following colors red, blue, silver, and black.
2. Soccer clubs are very popular these clubs often play clubs from other cities.
3. We bought a new computer I'm eager to try it.
4. When you pack for the camping trip take these items flashlight, sleeping bag, warm clothes.

● For more about semicolons and colons, see **Language Handbook,** p. R38.

✔ ASSESSMENT OPTIONS

📁 *Quick Checks,* p. 72
📁 *Selection and Theme Assessment,* p. 123
📁 *Performance Assessment,* p. 67
📁 *Testmaker*

Extending Your Response

Writing About Literature

Students' paragraphs should
• describe the mood of the poem.
• explain how the end of each stanza contributes to the mood.

Creative Writing

Students' poems should
• invite another person to join them as they work on a project or chore.
• describe the work in terms that would convince someone to join in.

Listening and Speaking   Help students find other Frost poems. Tell them to read each poem more than once to see how new details emerge with each reading.

Literature Groups   Have students take time to clearly visualize the scene before they begin drawing. When they compare images, discuss how the same words can evoke different impressions. **COLLAB. LEARN.**

Skill Minilesson

GRAMMAR AND LANGUAGE
• **MECHANICS:** SEMICOLON, COLON

1. This bicycle comes in the following colors: red, blue, silver, and black.
2. Soccer clubs are very popular; these clubs often play clubs from other cities.
3. We bought a new computer; I'm eager to try it.
4. When you pack for the camping trip take these items: flashlight, sleeping bag, warm clothes.

Additional Resources

📖 *Grammar and Language Workbook,* pp. 265–266

📖 *Grammar and Composition Handbook,* Lesson 13.5

📖 *Writers Choice,* Lesson 20.5

Objective

- To understand the elements of short forms of poetry

Teaching Strategies

Write the following lines on the board:

> Yesterday, I bought
> A cat at the pet shelter
> On Main Street downtown.

Ask students to discuss whether they think these lines qualify as poetry or not. Some students might find something poetic in the lines, but many won't. After students have read the haiku poem on page 838, point out that the "poem" on the board has three lines, the appropriate number of syllables in each line, and an image from nature. Does that make it a haiku? Why or why not? *(No, it is a sentence broken up into lines and syllables, lacking interesting language, emotion, and imagery. It has the form of haiku, but not the content.)*

Refer students to the elements that comprise the essence of haiku, described on pages 838–839: simplicity, depth, and a bond between human beings and the natural world.

Teaching Options

SHORT FORMS OF POETRY

Haiku, cinquains, and limericks are all short forms of poetry. Do you know this classic haiku?

> An old silent pond . . .
> A frog jumps into the pond,
> splash! Silence again.
>
> —*Matsuo Bashō*

Over three centuries old, this haiku was written in Japanese by Matsuo Bashō (mät sü′ ō̄ bä′ shō), the poet who perfected the haiku form.

HAIKU

Haiku originated in Japan. A traditional haiku has only three lines made up of five syllables, seven syllables, and five syllables. Within this compact form, poets present simple images, often linked by unstated connections. It's left up to readers to discover, or to imagine, what the connections might be. What connections can you discover in the following haiku by an American writer?

> A balmy spring wind
> Reminding me of something
> I cannot recall
>
> —*Richard Wright*

Haiku are as striking for what they don't include as for what they do. Traditional haiku have no rhyme and no figures of speech. They usually include at least one nature image and one, often subtle, reference to a specific season of the year. (In the haiku by Bashō, the frog suggests summer.)

Translators of haiku sometimes maintain the traditions and sometimes alter them. In English translation, some haiku have fewer or more than seventeen syllables, and some even include rhyme:

> A morning-glory vine
> all blossoming, has thatched
> this hut of mine.
>
> —*Kobayashi Issa,*
>   *translated by Harold G. Henderson*

MEETING INDIVIDUAL NEEDS — ENGLISH LANGUAGE LEARNERS

Translation A group translation project can give English language learners a chance to bring artistic works from their first language into class and practice explaining the words and images to others.

Activity Ask students to find a short poem written in their native language. Have students work in small groups to translate and illustrate these poems.

Make bilingual dictionaries available if possible. Each group can work on one or two poems, depending on how many non-English poems students have brought into class. **COLLAB. LEARN.**

Additional Resources
📂 *English Language Learners Sourcebook*

As poets of many eras and cultures work with haiku, they may change the form, adding new features, such as titles, or creating more modern images using figures of speech.

> **The New and the Old**
>
> Railroad tracks; a flight
> of wild geese close above them
> in the moonlit night.
>
> —*Shiki*

What remains unchanged, despite any gulf of time or culture, is the essence of haiku: simplicity, depth, and a bond between human beings and the natural world.

CINQUAINS

Over time, haiku has influenced many forms of poetry, including one form called the **cinquain.** Invented by Adelaide Crapsey, the cinquain consists of five lines made up of two, four, six, eight, and two syllables, respectively. What elements of haiku do you recognize in the following cinquain?

> **A Warning**
>
> Just now,
> Out of the strange
> Still dusk . . . as strange, as still . . .
> A white moth flew. Why am I grown
> So cold?
>
> —*Adelaide Crapsey*

Like haiku, the five-line, unrhymed cinquain uses imagery to suggest its real topic or theme and evoke emotion in the reader. In this case, the speaker suddenly, "just now,"

becomes aware of her own mortality. The theme of mortality is suggested by the time of day, dusk; by the short-lived white moth; and by the speaker's sensation of growing cold.

LIMERICKS

Another short poetic form is the **limerick.** While the haiku and cinquain usually suggest a more serious or delicate topic and tone, the limerick is *always* funny. Part of the fun of a limerick is its rhyme pattern.

> No matter how grouchy you're feeling,
> A smile is always quite healing;
>   It grows like a wreath
>   All around the front teeth,
> Thus preventing the face from
>   congealing.

The limerick consists of five lines rhyming *aabba.* (See *rhyme* in **Literary Terms Handbook,** page R9.) Many limericks begin with some variation of the opening lines "There was a young lady of. . . ." or "There was a young man from. . . ."

The limerick's origin is unknown, but it may have come from an eighteenth-century Irish song. In the early twentieth century, the limerick became quite popular. Followers of the form made the verse more complicated by creating tongue twisters. How quickly can you read aloud this anonymous limerick?

> A tutor who taught on the flute
> Tried to teach two tooters to toot.
>   Said the two to the tutor,
>   "Is it harder to toot, or
> To tutor two tooters to toot?"

Haiku Have students read the haiku by Matsuo Bashō on page 838 aloud. Before reading the description of haiku that follows the poem, ask if they can deduce the elements of the form based on the haiku they have just read. You may want to prompt with questions such as: How many lines are there? How many syllables are in each line? What are the two most visual images in the poem? *(Many haiku poets juxtapose two contrasting images to create emotion in their poetry, as Basho does in this haiku with the old silent pond and the lively frog.)*

Cinquain Point out to students the cyclical nature of the cinquain. Use "A Warning" as an example. The poem begins with two syllables, builds steadily in line length and dramatic tension, and then ends with two syllables. Students may find elements of haiku in the way Adelaide Crapsey contrasts the image of the "strange, still dusk" with the image of the white moth.

Limericks Have students practice writing quick limericks using their own names or regions. *(There once was a young girl named Anna...; An eager young student from Dallas...)* Encourage them to play with language and humor, but to keep the form and rhyme scheme of the limerick.

Technology Option

Poetry Table

Students can use a word processing program to create a six-column table of poetry elements as they read the poems in this unit. Ask students to insert the headings shown below. Students can use their tables as tools for study and review or as a valuable set of data for writing a comparison-and-contrast essay. **L2**

Title	Author	Type of Poem	Number of Lines/Syllables	Images	Emotion

Objectives

- To read and analyze five short poems
- To identify personification and explain how it contributes to a poem's power.
- To explain how a poem's imagery supports its mood

Skills

Reading/Thinking: Comparing and Contrasting; Spatial Relationships
Writing: Haiku; Cinquain or Limerick
Vocabulary: Compound Words
Grammar/Language: Prepositional Phrases
Listening/Speaking: Reciting Haiku; Readers Theater
Collaboration: Literature Groups

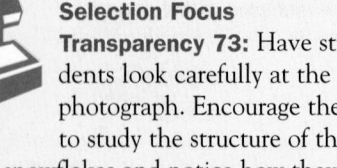

Motivating
→OPTIONS

Selection Focus Transparency 73: Have students look carefully at the photograph. Encourage them to study the structure of the snowflakes and notice how they are similar and different.

Focus Activity: As an extension of the Focus Activity, have students make a drawing of the object they described. Then have them write their description again and compare it with the first.

Before You Read
Short Poems

MEET THE POETS

Matsuo Bashō, who was born into the samurai, or warrior class, started writing poetry at the age of nine. Bashō taught poetry to many devoted students.

Bashō was probably born in 1644 and died in 1694.

Raymond R. Patterson was born in New York City. A former director of Black Poets Reading, Patterson also wrote a newspaper column on African American history.

Raymond R. Patterson was born in 1929.

Ann Atwood has been influenced by nature throughout her life. Many of her books and films fuse poetry with nature photography.

Ann Atwood was born in 1913.

Myra Cohn Livingston edited dozens of books of poetry for younger readers and taught the writing of poetry to both children and adults.

Myra Cohn Livingston was born in 1926 and died in 1996.

FOCUS ACTIVITY

Have you ever heard the expression "Less is more"? Using as few words as possible, how would you describe an ordinary object, such as your locker or a chair?

QuickWrite

Jot down a few words describing an object you can see right now.

Setting a Purpose

Read these short poems first for enjoyment and then to become familiar with their forms.

BACKGROUND

Did You Know? The seventeenth-century Japanese poet Matsuo Bashō is generally acknowledged as the innovator and master of the haiku form. One story about Bashō illustrates his approach to haiku. While walking one day, Bashō and a young student watched dragonflies darting through the fields. The student quickly made up a poem: "Red dragonflies! / Take off their wings, / and they are pepper pods!" Bashō responded, "No! That is not haiku. If you wish to make a haiku on the subject, you must say: "Red pepper pods! / Add wings to them, / and they are dragonflies!"

Matsuo Bashō

Raymond R. Patterson

Ann Atwood

Myra Cohn Livingston

RESOURCE MANAGER

Lesson Planning Resource
The *Theme Eight Planning Guide* (pp. 57–61) provides additional lesson notes and reduced versions of all print resources.

📁 **Other Print Resources**
- Active Reading Guide, p. 73
- Grammar and Language Workbook, pp. 141–142
- Grammar and Composition Handbook, Lesson 7.1
- Quick Checks, p. 73
- Selection and Theme

Assessment, p. 124
- Performance Assessment, p. 68
- Spanish Summaries, p. 73
- Spanish Translations
- Inclusion Strategies Sourcebook
- Block Scheduling Guide
- English Language Learners Sourcebook

 Transparencies
- Selection Focus 73
- Fine Art 6
- Literary Elements 73

Technology
🎧 Audio Library
🎧 Spanish Audio Library
💻 Glencoe Literature Web Site
💾 Testmaker

Glory, Glory...

Haiku by Raymond R. Patterson 〜

Across Grandmother's knees
A kindly sun
Laid a yellow quilt.

Birds Circling at Dusk

Haiku by Ann Atwood 〜

Birds circling at dusk.
The first night of my journey—
yet how far from home!

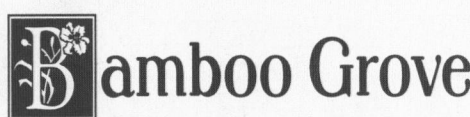

Bamboo Grove

Haiku by Matsuo Bashō 〜

Song of the cuckoo:
in the grove of great bamboos,
moonlight seeping through.

A DELICATE BALANCE 🦢 841

Reading the Selection

A **Literary Elements**

PERSONIFICATION Have students note how the sun is personified in "Glory, Glory." *(The sun places a yellow quilt across the grandmother's knee.)*

B **Literary Elements**

SYMBOL Ask students what the journey might symbolize in "Birds Circling at Dusk." *(The journey might be emotional—not just physical.)*

C **Literary Elements**

HAIKU This type of poetry has three lines and seventeen syllables. The first and third line have five syllables each; the middle line has seven syllables. Point out how the translator of Matsuo Bashō's haiku has maintained the count.

Additional Resources
📁 *Active Reading Guide,* p. 73
🎧 *Audio Library*
🎧 *Spanish Audio Library*
📁 *Spanish Summaries,* p. 73

Teaching Options

MEETING INDIVIDUAL NEEDS **GIFTED AND TALENTED ACTIVITY**

Haiku Haiku is a challenge to write since it restricts expression to three lines and seventeen syllables.

Activity Have students work in pairs to write a three-line Haiku. The first and third lines should have five syllables each and the middle line, seven syllables. Have students write each line separately and count the syllables. Students may then illustrate their haiku poem on the same page to reinforce the imagery of the poem they created.

L3 **COLLAB. LEARN.**

D Literary Elements

FIGURES OF SPEECH: *Personification*
Draw out the subtley of the T-shirt's personification. *(It "said something when it was new," probably with letters or symbols; "no one knows what you said..." implies that the shirt could speak.)*

E Literary Elements

RHYTHM AND RHYME Write the words *brighter* and *writer* on the board. Help students notice that these rhyming words end with an unstressed syllable. Explain that this is called a feminine rhyme. Rhyming on a stressed syllable is called a masculine rhyme. Feminine rhymes always consist of two or more syllables, while masculine rhymes consist of a single syllable. Have students find the masculine and feminine rhymes in the limerick. *(masculine: door, floor; feminine: Ealing, feeling, ceiling)*

Thematic Focus

A Delicate Balance Which of the poems most directly relate to the theme? *(The haiku, which contain images of nature—and often of nature in balance with itself and with the poet—most directly involve the theme.)* To enrich and extend the discussion, you might use *Fine Art Transparency 6.* Would a form other than poetry be as effective here?

✔ **ASSESSMENT OPTIONS**

📁 *Quick Checks,* p. 73

Teaching Options

T-Shirt

Cinquain by
Myra Cohn Livingston ∼

T-shirt,
you're my best thing
though you've faded so much
no one knows what you said when you
were new.

D

There Was a Young Fellow of Ealing

Anonymous Limerick ∼

There was a young fellow of Ealing,
Endowed with such delicate feeling,
    When he read, on the door,
    "Don't spit on the floor,"
He jumped up and spat on the ceiling.

E

842 THEME 8

Reading Minilesson

Comparing and Contrasting Haiku, cinquains, and limericks are distinct in many ways. The three haiku and the cinquain are fairly serious in tone, while the limerick is lighthearted and funny.

Activity After students have read the poems, have them work in small groups to fill in a chart comparing and contrasting

these poetic elements: rhyme scheme, tone, imagery, and mood. **L2** **COLLAB. LEARN.**

Additional Resources
📁 *Reading Workbook*

Characteristics	Haiku	Cinquain	Limerick
Rhyme scheme	none	none	a, a, b, b, a
Tone	serious	serious	funny
Imagery			
Mood			

842

Responding to Literature

PERSONAL RESPONSE

Which of the poems did you enjoy most? Explain why.

Analyzing Literature

RECALL

1. What are the **settings** of the three haiku?
2. In what condition is the T-shirt in the cinquain?
3. What funny event occurs in the limerick?

INTERPRET

4. In each haiku, what words or phrases provide clues to the time of day?
5. What might the T-shirt have said when it was new?
6. Why does the event make the limerick funny?

EVALUATE AND CONNECT

7. In your opinion, how does the Japanese poet Bashō feel about nature? Explain your answer.
8. In what ways are the three haiku similar and different?
9. Which poem do you think makes the most effective use of the least number of words? Why?
10. Which poem would you most like to share with another person? Explain why.

LITERARY ELEMENTS

Personification

Personification is a figure of speech in which an idea, object, or animal is given human form or human characteristics. The sentence *The impatient alarm clock shook me out of bed.* is an example of personification. An object, an alarm clock, is described as though it were an impatient parent trying to get a sleepy child out of bed. Authors use personification to make their writing more vivid and to describe things in a way that people can imagine and understand.

1. Identify how personification is used in one of the poems.

2. Paraphrase the poem in one sentence without using personification. Do you think your image is as powerful as the poem's? Why or why not?

3. Using the photo at the left, write a haiku of your own using personification.

● See **Literary Terms Handbook,** p. R7.

A DELICATE BALANCE 843

Personal Response

Encourage students to discuss imagery, form, content, and tone when they explain which poem they like best.

Analyzing Literature

1. The first setting is a relaxing sunny day. The next setting is dusk somewhere far from the speaker's home. The last is at night in a grove of bamboo trees.
2. The T-shirt is very faded.
3. The young fellow jumped up and spat on the ceiling.
4. *Kindly sun* implies daytime; *dusk* indicates evening; *moonlight seeping through* indicates nighttime.
5. Students will probably suggest currently popular slogans or styles.
6. Because spitting on the ceiling would be much more difficult than spitting on the floor.
7. Most students will recognize that Bashō has a strong and intimate connection with nature; the entire poem focuses on images of the natural world.
8. All the poems include images of nature; the first two include the interaction between nature (personification) and humans; the third does not.
9. Most students will probably choose one of the haiku. (The first has the least number of words.)
10. Students should explain their choice.

LITERARY ELEMENTS

1. In "Glory, Glory" the sun is shown placing a quilt on a woman's knees.
2. *Sunlight shone on Grandmother's knees.* The personification of the sun provides a more powerful description.
3. Students should use a figure of speech in which an animal, an object, or an idea is given human form or characteristics.

Additional Resources

 Literary Elements Transparency 73

✓ ASSESSMENT OPTIONS

📁 *Quick Checks,* p. 73

Extending Your Response

Writing About Literature

Students' paragraphs should
- describe the mood of the poem.
- explain how the imagery builds or supports the poem's mood.

Creative Writing

Students' poems should
- be short, possibly in the form of a cinquain or limerick.
- create an image of a particular moment in time.

Literature Groups As students discuss the poems, encourage them to list the details in each. Then have them make sketches and compare how each person's interpretation of a poem can be very different.
COLLAB. LEARN.

Listening and Speaking Before the students recite, have them read their poems two or three times.

Performing Have students read slowly and clearly, making sure that their audience can understand their words.

Writing About Literature

Imagery and Mood Choose one of the three haiku. Decide what mood the poem creates. Then think about the poem's imagery. Write a paragraph telling how the imagery builds or supports the poem's mood.

Listening and Speaking

Inspired by Nature Traditional haiku always contains an image from nature. With a partner, look around your classroom and out the window. Find a class pet or plant or a glimpse of the sky, a tree, an insect—any natural object or being—for inspiration. Collaborate with your partner to write a haiku about what you observe. Recite your haiku to the class.

Literature Groups

Snapshots If you think of a short poem as a snapshot of a moment, what would the snapshots look like from each of the five poems? Work with your group to discuss your ideas. Sketch them if you wish. Which snapshot contains the least detail and which contains the most? Compare your group's ideas with those of other groups.

Performing

Readers Theater Work with a small group to collect five or six short poems on a specific theme. Try to include a variety of short forms, such as haiku, cinquain, limerick, or any other short poem. Read your collection of poems aloud to the class. Have the class guess the theme of your collection and suggest a title for it.

Creative Writing

Short Poem Use one of the poems as a model for writing your own cinquain or limerick about the object you described in the **Focus Activity** on page 840.

Reading Further

If you wish to read more short poems, try these books:

O Sliver of Liver by Myra Cohn Livingston

Red Dragonfly on My Shoulder, translated by Sylvia Cassedy and Kunihiro Suetake

📖 **Save your work for your portfolio.**

✔ ASSESSMENT OPTIONS

- 📁 *Quick Checks,* p. 73
- 📁 *Selection and Theme Assessment,* p. 124
- 📁 *Performance Assessment,* p. 68
- 📁 *Testmaker*

Skill Minilessons

GRAMMAR AND LANGUAGE • PREPOSITIONAL PHRASES

A **preposition** is a word that relates a noun or a pronoun to some other word in the sentence. A **prepositional phrase** is a group of words that begins with a preposition and ends with a noun or pronoun, which is called the **object of the preposition.**

> He jumped up and spat on the ceiling.

In this sentence, *on* is a preposition, and *on the ceiling* is the prepositional phrase. The object of the preposition is *ceiling.*

Commonly Used Prepositions			
about	before	for	on
above	behind	from	out
across	below	in	since
against	between	like	through
at	during	near	with

PRACTICE Write the prepositional phrase from each of the following sentences. Underline the preposition.

1. Haiku and cinquain are two short forms of poetry.
2. Centuries have passed since Bashō wrote his poems.
3. Within every classic haiku, there is one powerful image.
4. I'm looking for a startling image.
5. Across Grandmother's knees / A kindly sun / Laid a yellow quilt.

● For more about prepositional phrases, see **Language Handbook,** p. R30.

READING AND THINKING • SPATIAL RELATIONSHIPS/SPATIAL ORDER

Spatial relationships describe how things relate to one another in physical space. Matsuo Bashō's description of the "moonlight seeping *through*" helps readers imagine the image of the moonlight in the bamboo grove. Writers use words like *through, across, above, below, under,* and *next to* help the reader understand the spatial order of the images in the poem and the relationship between the speaker and the things described.

PRACTICE Reread the three haiku and think about where the images the poets describe are in relationship to one another and to the speaker. Write a sentence or two about each poem using words that describe spatial relationships. Then underline those words.

● For more about spatial order, see **Reading Handbook,** p. R87.

VOCABULARY • COMPOUND WORDS

Moonlight is a common image in haiku. *Moonlight* is a **compound word,** a word made by joining two words to make a new word. Words that form compounds can be spelled closed *(birthday),* hyphenated *(worn-out),* or open *(high school).* When writing compound words, remember to keep the original spelling of both words.

PRACTICE Combine words from both columns to make five compound words.

1. grand   berry
2. row   board
3. touch   mother
4. blue   down
5. card   boat

Skill Minilessons

GRAMMAR AND LANGUAGE
PREPOSITIONAL PHRASES

1. <u>of</u> poetry
2. <u>since</u> Bashō wrote his poems
3. <u>Within</u> every classic haiku,
4. <u>for</u> a startling image
5. <u>Across</u> Grandmother's knees

READING AND THINKING
SPATIAL RELATIONSHIPS/SPATIAL ORDER

1. "Glory, Glory…" The sunlight is shining <u>across</u> the grandmother's knees.
2. "Birds Circling at Dusk" The birds are circling <u>in</u> the speaker's sight. The speaker is far <u>from</u> home.
3. "Bamboo Grove" The moonlight is seeping <u>through</u> a grove of trees; the cuckoo is <u>in</u> the grove.

VOCABULARY
COMPOUND WORDS

1. grandmother
2. rowboat
3. touchdown
4. blueberry
5. cardboard

Additional Resources

📖 ***Grammar and Language Workbook,*** pp. 141–142

📖 ***Grammar and Composition Handbook,*** Lesson 7.1

📖 ***Writer's Choice,*** Lesson 13.1

📁 ***Reading Workbook***

📁 ***Vocabulary Practice***

Writing WORKSHOP

Objectives
- To create a personal response to literature
- To plan, draft, revise, edit, and present a cause-and-effect essay
- To reflect on and assess the essay

Teaching Strategies

PREWRITING

Select an Issue Have students create a list of issues that arise from common conflicts between people and nature. They may identify issues such as vegetarianism, animal rights, or the environment. Have them research a topic until they find a focus.

Look at Causes and Effects Encourage students to contact organizations involved in the issue they have chosen. Special-interest groups and organizations often provide educational information free to the public.

Teaching Options

Writing WORKSHOP

Expository Writing: Cause-and-Effect Essay

In a national park, heavy smog damage causes officials to consider banning cars from the park. In a city, a decision about airport sites affects a rare animal's survival. Nature's way and people's way—how are they connected? Sometimes we don't find out until they clash. By investigating the causes and effects of a conflict, you can clarify your own position on the issue and maybe gain new insights as well.

Assignment: Follow the process explained in these pages to develop your own cause-and-effect essay about a conflict between people and nature.

● As you write your cause-and-effect essay, refer to **Writing Handbook,** pp. R48–R53.

The Writing Process

PREWRITING

PREWRITING TIP
Don't be fooled by coincidences. Remember that an event that came before another event hasn't necessarily caused it. Make sure a genuine cause-and-effect relationship exists.

● **Select an Issue**

You may find issues in selections from this theme. For other ideas, watch television news and scan newspapers and magazines for environmental issues. Talk with parents and friends about issues affecting your community. Choose an issue that you care about.

● **Look at Causes and Effects**

Identify some causes and effects surrounding your issue. Don't forget that many events have multiple causes and effects. If you need more details, you might view television nature programs, interview knowledgeable people, visit the library, or research your issue on the Internet. To evaluate information from television or the Internet, use the critical viewing guidelines from **Listening, Speaking, and Viewing** on page 817.

MEETING INDIVIDUAL NEEDS: ENGLISH LANGUAGE LEARNERS

Discussing the Issue After students have selected an issue for their cause-and-effect essay, have them form small discussion groups with other students who are writing about similar topics. Make sure the groups include English language learners as well as more-proficient speakers of English.

Activity Ask students to take turns talking about their topics and explaining the cause-and-effect relationships they plan to explore. Encourage them to share resources and information, to help each other create graphic organizers like the one shown on page 847, and to develop position statements.

Additional Resources
📁 *English Language Learners Sourcebook*

Writing WORKSHOP

Issue: Florida's manatees are endangered.

Causes	Effects
Manatees need warm, clean water.	Manatee habitats are declared off-limits to boaters.
Water skiers and jetskiers like warm, clean water.	Pollution controls are enacted for cities near manatee areas.
Manatees don't know propellers are dangerous.	
Manatees eat water plants.	
Pollution from cities kills water plants.	

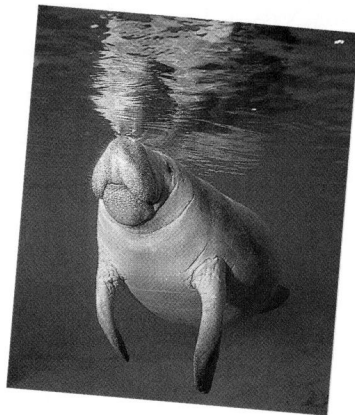

● Customize for Audience and Purpose

Will you write for people who might take action, such as government officials or supporters in the general public? Or will you write to increase awareness among students? Gear your writing to your audience. Decide which details will mean the most to your readers, and make those details stand out.

● Use Graphics

Causes and effects can form a chain: causes lead to effects, which in turn become new causes, leading to further effects. Create a graphic similar to the one at the bottom of this page to keep cause-and-effect relationships clear. Then write a position statement to set the direction of your draft.

Issue: Endangered Manatees

Causes
Manatees need Florida coast ecosystem.

Boat propellers kill manatees.

Pollution from coastal cities kills manatees.

Manatee population declines.	➡	Manatees declared endangered.	➡	Restrictions on coastal use protect manatees.	➡	Restrictions interfere with sports and city growth.	➡	Boaters and city dwellers oppose restrictions.
Effect/Cause		**Effect/Cause**		**Effect/Cause**		**Effect/Cause**		**Effect/Cause**

Position Statement: Manatees need some of the same kinds of things people need. If we make the coast safer for them, in the long run it will be safer for us too.

A DELICATE BALANCE 🐾 847

Customize for Audience and Purpose Point out to students that it is important to gather information from a wide variety of sources and to present it in a way that will engage their target audience. Readers will feel more receptive to a writer's point of view if it is balanced and draws on accurate, up-to-date information gathered from both sides of an issue.

Use Graphics Students may want to create their graphic organizers in pairs or groups. Encourage them to discuss whether the cause-and-effect chain makes sense. They should strive to make the links between the causes and their effects as strong and clear as they can. Write a few position statements on the board as models. For example:

- Without hunting, wild animals like deer and moose soon exhaust their food supplies.
- Hunting is an unnecessary sport that hurts and kills animals in their natural habitats.

Explain to students that they may decide not to use their position statement as the opening sentence in their essay, but they should write it out for themselves before drafting.

Additional Resources

📁 *Writing and Proofreading Practice,* pp. 1–7, 57–63

🖊 *Writing and Proofreading Transparencies 1–6, 23–24, 39–40*

📙 *Writer's Choice,* Lesson 5.3

MULTIPLE LEARNING STYLES

Spatial Students who have strong spatial abilities can express their ideas by using images and pictures. Write a few common slogans on the board and ask students to talk about the kind of image or picture they would create to accompany the slogan. Slogans might be something like: *The Earth Is Your Mother; Keep Wildlife Wild; Think Globally, Act Locally.*

Activity Have students work in small groups to design posters advocating their position on the issue they have chosen. Students can use paint, collage, photographs, recycled materials, or anything else they can think of to get their point across. Encourage students to create a slogan from their position statement and include it on the poster.

L2 COLLAB. LEARN.

A DELICATE BALANCE 🐾 847

DRAFTING

Start with an Anecdote Remind students that a story or anecdote that grabbed their attention will probably affect their readers the same way. A well-chosen story or anecdote can give the reader a glimpse into what possessed the writer to explore this particular topic to begin with.

Explain Connections Write this example on the board: *Run-off from cattle herds pollutes rivers and streams.* Ask students if they can answer the following questions after reading the statement: *What is run-off? Where does the run-off come from? What is the polluting substance?*

Writers should not assume that their readers know a lot about the subject matter. Connections need to be explained. A better example of explaining connections might be:

Herds of cattle are washed down daily with industrial hoses. Water runs off their bodies to the ground where it gathers dirt, feed, and manure. Some water soaks into the ground. The rest can find its way to nearby rivers or streams and cause pollution.

REVISING

Make Adjustments Suggest that students read their essays aloud to a partner and ask the partner to restate the cause-and-effect relationships described in the essay.

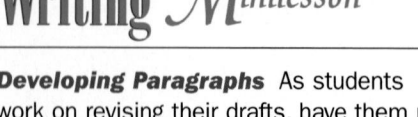

Teaching Options

Writing **WORKSHOP**

DRAFTING

DRAFTING TIP
To grab your readers' attention, choose an anecdote that touches some aspect of their lives.

● **Start with an Anecdote**

A brief, vivid story illustrating your issue can be a powerful opener. Put your position statement at the end of this introductory anecdote.

● **Explain Connections**

Go on to explain causes and effects, as you planned in your prewriting graphic. Discuss multiple causes, multiple effects, and cause-and-effect chains. Include details that will be memorable for your readers. You might conclude with a restatement of your position or with a prediction about the future.

MODEL · DRAFTING

Maybe we don't need manatees, but we need the kind of environment in which they can thrive. Their deaths are warnings. A world unsafe for manatees may soon become unsafe for humans too.

REVISING

REVISING TIP
Some transitional words or phrases you can use to show cause and effect include *as a result of, because, so, therefore, consequently, this is why, the result is,* and *for this reason.*

● **Make Adjustments**

This is the time to fine-tune. Look over your draft and consider possible improvements, using the **Questions for Revising** as a guide. Ask a classmate to read your draft and to give you feedback.

QUESTIONS FOR REVISING
☑ How can I make my introduction more directly related to my readers' lives?
☑ How might I make my position statement clearer to my readers?
☑ Where can I add details to help readers see causes and effects?
☑ Should I rearrange any sentences or paragraphs to make my draft easier to understand?
☑ What changes might make my conclusion more memorable?

Writing *Minilesson*

Developing Paragraphs As students work on revising their drafts, have them pay special attention to individual paragraphs within the essay. Remind them that their finished essay should reflect and support their position statement. Each paragraph contributes to this goal and should contain an identifiable topic sentence as well as supporting sentences.

Activity Ask students to work in pairs as they revise their drafts. Suggest that they exchange essays and read each other's work. Have them use note cards to identify and write down the topic sentence and supporting sentences in the paragraphs of their partner's essay. Afterward, encourage students to help each other add or delete information to improve their essays, paragraph by paragraph. Students can do this

activity with the entire draft or focus on paragraphs they are having trouble with. **L2**
COLLAB. LEARN.

Additional Resources

📕 *Writer's Choice,* Lesson 2.7

Writing **WORKSHOP**

EDITING/PROOFREADING

Find and correct errors in grammar and mechanics. The **Proofreading Checklist** can help. Watch especially for incorrect use of apostrophes, as shown in the **Grammar Link** on page 816.

Grammar Hint

When you use commas with a series of words or phrases, be sure to put in all the commas—not just the first one:

Rain forests exist in Africa, South America, North America, and Southeast Asia.

PROOFREADING CHECKLIST
- ☑ Commas are used correctly. (Double-check commas with words in a series.)
- ☑ Modifiers are used correctly.
- ☑ There are no fragments or run-ons.
- ☑ Verbs agree with subjects.
- ☑ Pronouns agree with antecedents.
- ☑ Spelling and capitalization are correct.

MODEL · EDITING/PROOFREADING

Manatees are gentle, playfulintelligent mammals.

TECHNOLOGY TIP
Some word processing programs let you design graphics and insert them into your essay.

PUBLISHING/PRESENTING

Try creating graphic visual aids, such as graphs or cause-and-effect diagrams, to illustrate your ideas. Then share your writing with classmates. You and others who explored related issues might present your papers in a panel discussion.

PRESENTING TIP
For a panel discussion, make your visual aids poster-sized.

Reflecting

After thinking about the following questions, write your responses.

- Does your writing focus more on causes or on effects? Why?

- For what other classes might you write papers exploring cause-and-effect connections? What topics might you examine?

 Save your work for your portfolio.

A DELICATE BALANCE 🦢 849

EDITING/PROOFREADING

Students may wish to edit and proof-read their essays in a group. Encourage them to ask peers for help with grammar and punctuation questions. Suggest that students read their essays aloud if a sentence or paragraph doesn't seem right to them and ask for feedback from the group.

PUBLISHING/PRESENTING

Encourage students who have chosen conflicting sides of the same issue to present their essays in a debate format. In addition to creating graphic visual aids, students might want to take or describe a photograph they would use if they were to publish their essay in a magazine.

Reflecting

 Portfolio Suggest that students ask themselves the following questions as they review their writing:

Does my cause-and-effect essay
- provide a clear position statement?
- present well-explained connections between cause and effect?
- engage the audience I targeted?

✅ ASSESSMENT OPTIONS

📁 **Writing Assessment and Portfolio Management**
- Writing Assessment, pp. 1–16, 41–43
- Portfolio Management, pp. 17–19

Theme Wrap-Up

Objectives

- To offer a personal response to the selections in this theme
- To write a comparison of two selections
- To complete a self-evaluation, set a goal, and devise a plan for achieving the goal

---

Responding to the Theme

1. Students should provide evidence from the selections to support their opinions.
2. Accept all thoughtful answers and observations.
3. Allow time for students to share their policy statements, wildlife series, and multimedia presentations with classmates.

Analyzing Literature

Students' writing should include

- an introductory paragraph identifying the selections and elements chosen for comparison.
- an analysis of how the selections illustrate the theme.
- examples and details from the stories.

Evaluate and Set Goals

Evaluate

Have students review their work and list activities they have completed for each task on this page. Suggest that they add other tasks as well, such as using desktop publishing software.

Have students use the rubric they developed in the first theme's evaluation to assess their work.

Set Goals

Have each student write the goal and the steps on a boxed equation graphic, using:
STEP 1 + STEP 2 + STEP 3 = GOAL

Discuss students' goals and plans in individual conferences.

Theme Wrap-Up

Responding to the Theme

1. Which story, poem, or narrative in this theme helped you to better understand the relationships between humans and nature? Explain your answer.

2. What new ideas do you have about the following as a result of reading the literature in this theme?
   - people's attitudes and actions toward animals and nature
   - the importance of the relationship between nature and human beings

3. Present your theme project to the class.

Analyzing Literature

COMPARE SELECTIONS

Choose pieces from this unit to compare. You may compare the characters, settings, descriptions, or themes. You may compare how two pieces in different forms—such as a poem and a short story—illustrate the theme "A Delicate Balance." Support your ideas with quotations from the selections.

Evaluate and Set Goals

1. Which of the following tasks was most rewarding to you? Which was most difficult?
   - reading and thinking about the selections
   - doing independent writing
   - analyzing the selections in discussions
   - making presentations
   - performing dramatizations

2. Using the following scale, how would you assess your work in this theme? Give at least two reasons for your assessment.
   4 = outstanding   2 = fair
   3 = good   1 = weak

3. Based on what you found difficult in this theme, choose a goal to work toward to increase your understanding of literature next year.
   - Write down your goal and three steps you will take to try to reach it.
   - Next fall, meet with your teacher to review your goal and your plan for achieving it.

Build Your Portfolio

SELECT

Select two pieces of work you did during this theme to include in your portfolio. Use the following questions to help you decide.

- ✦ Which do you consider your best work?
- ✦ Which work "stretched" you the most?
- ✦ Which work did you enjoy the most?

REFLECT

Write some notes to accompany the work you selected. Use these questions to guide you.

- ✦ What do you like best about the piece?
- ✦ What did you learn from creating it?
- ✦ What might you do differently if you were beginning this piece again?

ASSESSMENT OPTIONS

📁 ***Writing Assessment and Portfolio Management***
- Writing Assessment, pp. 1–16
- Portfolio Management, pp. 17–19

GLENCOE
TECHNOLOGY

MINDJOGGER VIDEOQUIZZES
VIDEODISC

Use *MindJogger* to review the Theme 8 content.

Theme 8
Side B

Also available in VHS.

Reading on Your Own

If you have enjoyed the literature in this theme, you might also be interested in the following books.

The Call of the Wild
By Jack London Buck, a domestic dog, is taken from his home to serve as a sled dog during the Klondike gold rush. Amidst the wolves of the Far North, he begins to hear "the call of the wild."

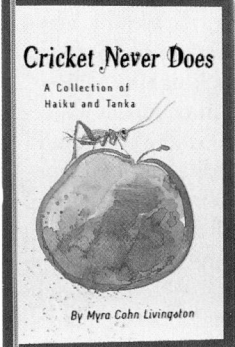

Cricket Never Does: A Collection of Haiku and Tanka
by Myra Cohn Livingston This collection of modern poems using the traditional Japanese forms of haiku and tanka presents poems for each of the seasons.

Hatchet
by Gary Paulsen Brian, the only survivor of a plane crash in the Canadian wilderness, must try to stay alive with nothing more than the clothes on his back and a hatchet.

My Life with the Chimpanzees
by Jane Goodall The world's leading authority on chimpanzees describes her thirty years of living with and studying the chimpanzees of Tanzania.

Glencoe Literature Library

The Call of the Wild by Jack London is one of the titles available in the *Glencoe Library*. For a complete listing, see pages 46–47 in this book.

The *Study Guides for Glencoe Literature* provide instructional support and student activities for works in the *Glencoe Library*.

At the MOVIES

• *Born Free* (1966, 95 minutes, PG) is based on the true story of a woman and her game-warden husband in Kenya who raise a lion cub and later must reeducate the grown animal to survive in the wild. Be sure to preview the movie to decide if it is suitable for your class.

MEETING INDIVIDUAL NEEDS INCLUSION STRATEGIES

You may wish to recommend *Cricket Never Does:* by Myra Cohn Livingston for less-proficient readers. The limited scope, concrete imagery, and vivid language of these short poems may inspire and build the confidence of students who find reading long selections difficult. **L1**

The following books are rated for average readers (**L2**) or for students who need more challenging reading (**L3**):
• *The Call of the Wild* by Jack London **L2**
• *Hatchet* by Gary Paulsen **L2**
• *My Life with the Chimpanzees* by Jane Goodall **L3**

Additional Resources
📁 *Inclusion Strategies*

Standardized Test Practice

Read the following passage. Then read each question on page 853. Decide which is the best answer to each question. Mark the letter for that answer on your paper.

Why Have Flatbreads Always Been So Popular?

In many parts of the world, bread is not baked in the loaves that we are most used to in the United States. Instead, it is baked in thin sheets. This type of bread is known as "flatbread." One of the most familiar types of flatbread is *pita*, which comes from the eastern Mediterranean. Pita bread is soft and is often used as a pocket of bread, into which meat or vegetables are placed to make a sandwich. Pita is gaining popularity and recognition as more people experiment with this new type of baked good. Many types of flatbread can be found in supermarkets and bakeries today. However, flatbreads are not new grain products.

The history of flatbread goes back more than six thousand years. It is one of the oldest known prepared foods. People have eaten flatbread wherever there was grain available because it is nourishing, it is easy to prepare, and it keeps well over time.

Flatbread Ingredients

Many types of grain are used in the creation of flatbread, including rye, oats, corn, wheat, rice, and buckwheat. Sometimes vegetables are used as well; potatoes, chickpeas, and lentils add flavor and texture to the bread. Flatbreads can have unusual and <u>distinctive</u> tastes depending on the ingredients used. For example, "Sweet Armenian" bread is flavored with *maleb,* a black cherry pit.

In Asia, a black onion seed, *nigella,* is added to the mixture. Ethiopians use *teff flour* for a unique molasses flavor. In addition to providing interesting flavor, the additional ingredients provide nutrients that grain cannot offer by itself.

Preparing Flatbread

The way in which a flatbread is baked varies from place to place. No matter how it is done, flatbread is considered one of the world's great fast foods because of its rapid cooking time. This is an important quality in countries where fuel is scarce and needs to be conserved. In Asia, flatbread is baked in a *tandoor.* This barrel-shaped oven has hot coals in its center. The bread is slapped to the sides of the oven, and heat transfers rapidly from the oven sides to the bread. On the other hand, *injeras* (an Ethiopian sourdough), *chapatis* (an Indian bread), and *tortillas* (a Latin American bread) are often baked in a large, hot skillet over an open fire or on the flat surface of a wood-burning stove. The skillet can be curved as we are accustomed to, or it can be arched the other way, creating a concave bump on which the bread is baked. Amazingly, Algerians and Tunisians can bake bread right on the fiery desert sand, and Malaysians throw the dough up in the air over and over again until it becomes paper thin. Then they twist it and cook it on a griddle.

The Hopi of North America made special *piki* stones that they used for baking flatbreads, a tradition that was passed down from generation to generation.

Flatbread's Longevity

Another important quality of flatbreads is that they are easy to store and preserve. In countries where the winters are long, people dry the bread after it is baked to help preserve a grain supply that needs to endure many cold months.

Flatbreads have varied ingredients and preparation techniques, and they can be used in many ways. Today we are rediscovering the nutritious, fast, and long-lasting flatbreads of many different cultures, enriching our own culinary offerings.

---

1 According to the passage, *maleb* and *nigella* can be used as ingredients in flatbreads to make them —

   A rise slowly

   B taste good

   C last longer

   D cook faster

2 Why did the author start the passage by mentioning pita bread?

   F To help readers recall what they already know about flatbreads

   G To show that pita bread is not as popular as other flatbreads

   H To persuade readers to eat pita bread

   J To describe how pita bread is used

3 Based on the information in the passage, you can predict that —

   A flatbreads will no longer be baked soon

   B new ways of cooking flatbreads will continue to be found

   C flatbreads will continue to be baked for a long time

   D all breads will now be flatbreads

4 The word <u>distinctive</u> in this passage means —

   F different

   G unpleasant

   H commonplace

   J delicious

5 Which is a FACT in the passage?

   A All flatbreads are crunchy and grainy.

   B Flatbreads are the perfect food.

   C Pita bread is a type of flatbread.

   D Flatbreads have been around for ten thousand years.

6 The author provides evidence to suggest that —

   F pita bread is the most popular flatbread in the world

   G flatbreads are more common in South America than in Central Asia

   H flatbreads need many flavorings to make them tasty

   J flatbreads have been popular for a long time throughout the world

 STOP

Answers and Analyses

1. **B** This is an excellent opportunity to point out how helpful the titles within the passage can be. The third paragraph says that one type of bread *is flavored with maleb, a black cherry pit. In Asia, a black onion seed, nigella, is added to the mixture.* It can be inferred that these ingredients are added for flavor, answer choice B.

2. **F** In the first paragraph the author states *One of the most familiar types of flatbread is pita.* The author therefore feels that pita is familiar. The best choice is F.

3. **C** The end of the story claims that we are rediscovering the nutritious, fast, and long-lasting flatbreads of many different cultures. This contradicts choice A, and choice D seems unreasonable and there is no evidence in the text to support such a claim. The most reasonable inference is that we will continue to eat them for many years to come.

4. **F** The third paragraph states *Flatbreads can have unusual and distinctive tastes depending on the ingredients used.* Therefore the word *distinctive* must be a word which accords with the word *unusual.* The closest choice is F.

5. **C** Only choice C is explicitly stated in the passage. According to the first paragraph *One of the most familiar types of flatbread is pita.*

6. **J** Students should be careful to make sure that the author provided evidence to support a claim. Choice J is a paraphrase of the information in the second paragraph.

Reference Section

● **Literary Terms Handbook** **R1**

● **Language Handbook** **R12**

    Troubleshooter R12
    Troublesome Words R22
    Grammar Glossary R27
    Mechanics R34
    Spelling R44

● **Writing Handbook** **R48**

    The Writing Process R48
    Writing Modes R52
    Research Paper Writing R54
    Business Writing R58

● **Communications Skills Handbook** **R60**

    Using Electronic Resources R60
    Study and Test-Taking Skills R62
    Listening, Speaking, and Viewing Skills R66

● **Reading Handbook** **R70**

    Vocabulary Development R77
    Comprehension R82
    Literary Response R93
    Inquiry and Research R96

Glossary R102

Spanish Glossary R111

Index of Skills R120

Index of Authors and Titles R129

Index of Art and Artists R132

Acknowledgments R134

Literary Terms Handbook

A

Act A major unit of a drama. A play may be subdivided into several acts. Many modern plays have two or three acts. A short play can be composed of one or more scenes but only one act—for example, Walter Hackett's adaptation of Mark Twain's *The Million-Pound Bank Note.*

> See page 500.
> See also SCENE.

Alliteration The repetition of consonant sounds at the beginnings of words. Alliteration gives emphasis to words. For example, the following line from "The Highwayman," by Alfred Noyes, contains an example of alliteration:

Over the cobbles he clattered and clashed in the dark innyard. . . .

> See page 824.

Allusion A reference in a work of literature to a well-known character, place, or situation from another work of literature, music, or art or from history. For example, there is an allusion to the biblical story of Noah's Ark in Ann Stanford's poem "The Flood":

Could we float on that Ark
Through the corn fields. . . .

> See page 357.

Antagonist A person or force that opposes the protagonist, or central character, in a story or drama. The reader is generally meant not to sympathize with the antagonist. For example, Margot's entire class is her antagonist in "All Summer in a Day" by Ray Bradbury.

> See also CONFLICT, PROTAGONIST.

Anthropomorphism Representing animals as if they had human emotions and intelligence. Fables and fairy tales often contain anthropomorphism. "Rikki-tikki-tavi," by Rudyard Kipling, is another example of this technique.

> See page 802.

Aside In a play, a comment made by a character who is heard by the audience but not by the other characters on stage. The speaker turns to one side, or "aside," away from the other characters on stage. Asides are common in older theatrical forms—you will find them throughout Shakespeare's plays—but are infrequent in modern drama.

Assonance The repetition of vowel sounds, especially in a line of poetry. For example, the following line from "The Women's 400 Meters," by Lillian Morrison, contains an example of assonance:

they flex knees, drum heels and/shiver at the starting line

> See also ALLITERATION, CONSONANCE, RHYME, SOUND DEVICES.

Author's purpose The intention of the writer. For example, the purpose of a story may be to entertain, to describe, to explain, to persuade, or a combination of these purposes. "A Crush," by Cynthia Rylant, both tells an entertaining story and describes.

> See page 830.

Autobiography The story of a person's life written by that person. *Rosa Parks: My Story,* by Rosa Parks with Jim Haskins, is an example of autobiography.

> See pages 62–63.
> See also BIOGRAPHY, MEMOIR.

B

Ballad A short, musical narrative song or poem. Folk ballads, which usually tell of an exciting or dramatic episode, were passed on by word of mouth for generations before being written down. Literary ballads are written in imitation of folk ballads. "Annabel Lee," by Edgar Allan Poe, is an example of a literary ballad.

> See also NARRATIVE POETRY.

Biography The account of a person's life written by someone other than the subject. Biographies can be short or book-length. In "New Directions," Maya Angelou writes a biographical sketch of her grandmother.

> See page 223.
> See also AUTOBIOGRAPHY, MEMOIR.

C

Character A person in a literary work. (If a character is an animal, it displays human traits.) Characters who show varied and sometimes contradictory traits, such as the alternately stern and compassionate Mary in Dorothy M. Johnson's "Too Soon a Woman," are called **round.** Characters who reveal only one personality trait, like the flinty father in the same story, are called **flat.** A **stereotype** is a flat character of a familiar and often-repeated type. A **dynamic** character changes during the story. A **static** character remains primarily the same throughout the story.

> See page 180.
> See also CHARACTERIZATION.

Characterization The methods a writer uses to develop the personality of the character. In **direct characterization** the writer makes direct statements about a character's personality. In **indirect characterization,** the writer reveals a character's

personality through the character's words and actions and through what other characters think and say about the character. These techniques are frequently blended together, as is the case with Margot in Ray Bradbury's "All Summer in a Day."

> See page 406.

Climax The point of greatest emotional intensity, interest, or suspense in a narrative. Usually the climax comes at the turning point in a story or drama, the point at which the resolution of the conflict becomes clear, as in O. Henry's "After Twenty Years," when Bob discovers that the man he thinks is Jimmy Wells is actually someone else.

> See page 550.
> See also FALLING ACTION, PLOT, RISING ACTION.

Comedy A type of drama that is humorous and has a happy ending. A heroic comedy focuses on the exploits of a larger-than-life hero. In American popular culture, comedy can take the form of scripted performances involving one or more performers—either as a skit that is part of a variety show, as in vaudeville, or as a stand-up monologue. "Who's on First," by Bud Abbott and Lou Costello, is an example of skit comedy with roots in vaudeville.

> See also HUMOR.

Conflict The struggle between two opposing forces that lies at the center of a plot in a story or drama. An **external conflict** exists when a character struggles against some outside force, such as another person, nature, society, or fate—for example, the struggle of the two scientists with the Multivac computer in Isaac Asimov's "Key Item." An **internal conflict** exists within the mind of a character who is torn between opposing feelings or goals—as Antonio and Felix grapple with their desire for the championship and their reluctance to fight each other in "The Amigo Brothers" by Piri Thomas.

> See page 53.
> See also ANTAGONIST, PLOT, PROTAGONIST.

Consonance A pleasing combination of sounds, especially in poetry. Consonance usually refers to the repetition of consonant sounds in stressed syllables. Notice, for example, the echoing *p* sounds in the following lines from "Slam, Dunk, & Hook" by Yusef Komunyakaa:

. . . Trouble / was there slapping a blackjack / Against an open palm. . . .

　　See also ALLITERATION, ASSONANCE, RHYME, SOUND DEVICES.

D

Description Writing that seeks to convey the feeling of any external experience: a setting, a person, an animal, and so on. Almost all writing, fiction and nonfiction, contains elements of description. The following example of descriptive writing comes from "Lob's Girl" by Joan Aiken:

Instinctively she shut her eyes and felt the sand being wiped off her face by something that seemed like a warm, rough, damp flannel. . . . It was a tongue. Its owner was a large and bouncy young Alsatian, or German shepherd, with topaz eyes, black-tipped pick ears, a thick, soft coat, and a bushy black-tipped tail

　　See page 73.

Details Particular features of things used to make descriptions more accurate and vivid. Authors use details to help readers imagine the characters, scenes, and actions they describe, as in this description of a boy in Borden Deal's "Antaeus."

He was a stocky, robust kid with a shock of white hair, nothing sissy about him except his voice; he talked in this slow, gentle voice like you never heard before.

Dialect A variation of language spoken by a particular group, often within a particular region. Dialects differ from standard language because they may contain different pronunciations, forms, and meanings. There is an example of

dialect in these lines from "Mother to Son" by Langston Hughes:

I'se been a-climbin' on,
And reachin' landin's,
And turnin' corners. . . .

　　See page 240.

Dialogue Conversation between characters in a literary work. The following lines from "Uncle Tony's Goat," by Leslie Marmon Silko, are an example of dialogue:

　　Finally my uncle came out of the house; it was time for breakfast. "What's wrong?" he called out from the door.
　　"The billy goat won't come out, " I yelled back. . . .
　　"Get in there and get him out," he said. . . .

　　See page 560.
　　See also MONOLOGUE.

Drama A story usually performed by actors on a stage or before movie or TV cameras. Most dramas before the modern period can be divided into two basic types: tragedy and comedy. The script of a drama includes dialogue—the words the actors speak—and stage directions—descriptions of the action and scenery. "The Monsters Are Due on Maple Street," by Rod Serling, is an example of a modern television drama.

　　See pages 500–501.
　　See also COMEDY, TRAGEDY.

E

Essay A short piece of nonfiction writing on a single topic. The purpose of the essay is to communicate an idea or opinion. The **formal essay** is serious and impersonal. The **informal essay** entertains while it informs, usually in a light, conversational style. "The Fish Crisis," by J. Madeleine Nash, is an example of a formal essay.

　　See page 396.

Extended metaphor An implied comparison that continues through an entire poem. "Loo-Wit," by Wendy Rose, contains an extended metaphor.

> See page 820.
> See also METAPHOR.

F

Fable A short, usually simple tale that teaches a moral and sometimes uses animal characters. Themes of fables are usually stated outright, as in "Anansi and His Visitor, Turtle," as retold by Edna Mason Kaula.

> See page 703.
> See also THEME.

Falling action In a play or story, the action that follows the climax.

> See also PLOT, RISING ACTION.

Fantasy A form of literature that explores unreal worlds of the past, the present, and the future. "The Smallest Dragonboy," by Anne McCaffrey, is fantasy.

> See page 695.

Fiction A prose narrative in which situations and characters are invented by the writer. Some aspects of a fictional work may be based on fact or experience. Fiction includes both short stories and novels.

> See also NOVEL, SHORT STORY.

Figurative language Language used for descriptive effect, often to imply ideas indirectly. Expressions of figurative language are not literally true but express some truth beyond the literal level. Although it appears in all kinds of writing, figurative language is especially prominent in poetry, for example, in "The Courage That My Mother Had" by Edna St. Vincent Millay.

> See page 343.
> See also FIGURE OF SPEECH, METAPHOR, PERSONIFICATION, SIMILE, SYMBOL.

Figure of speech A specific kind of figurative language such as **metaphor, personification, simile,** or **symbol.**

> See also FIGURATIVE LANGUAGE, METAPHOR, PERSONIFICATION, SIMILE, SYMBOL.

First-person narrative. See POINT OF VIEW.

Flashback An interruption in a chronological narrative that tells about something that happened before that point in the story or before the story began. A flashback gives readers information that might help explain the main events of the story, as when the author, Ray Bradbury, fills in details of Margot's life in "All Summer in a Day."

> See page 613.

Folklore The traditional beliefs, customs, stories, songs, and dances of a culture. Folklore is from the oral tradition and is based in the concerns of ordinary people.

> See also FOLKTALE, LEGEND, MYTH, ORAL TRADITION.

Folktale An anonymous, traditional story passed down orally long before being written down. The author of a folktale is generally anonymous. Folktales include animal stories, trickster stories, fairy tales, myths, legends, and tall tales. "Aunty Misery," by Judith Ortiz Cofer, is an example of a folktale retold by a modern author.

> See page 599.
> See also LEGEND, MYTH, ORAL TRADITION, TALL TALE.

Foreshadowing The use of clues by the author to prepare readers for events that will happen in a story. An example of foreshadowing is Daedalus's warning to Icarus about not flying too high in "Icarus and Daedalus" by Josephine Preston Peabody.

> See page 248.
> See also PLOT, RISING ACTION.

Free verse Poetry that has no fixed pattern of meter, rhyme, line length, or stanza arrangement. "Without Commercials," by Alice Walker, is an example of free verse.

See page 255.
See also RHYTHM.

G

Genre A division of literature. The main literary genres are prose, poetry, and fiction. Each of these is divided into smaller genres. For example: **Prose** includes fiction (such as novels, short stories, and folktales) and nonfiction (such as biography, autobiography, and essays). **Poetry** includes lyric poetry, dramatic poetry, narrative poetry, and so on. **Drama** includes tragedy, comedy, historical drama, melodrama, farce, and so on.

H

Haiku An originally Japanese form of poetry that has three lines and seventeen syllables. The first and third line have five syllables each; the middle line has seven syllables. "Birds Circling at Dusk," by Ann Atwood, is an example of a haiku.

See page 838.

Hero A literary work's main character, usually one with admirable qualities. Although the word hero is applied only to males in traditional usage—the female form is heroine—the term now applies to both sexes. Prometheus is the hero of the myth of the same name as retold by Bernard Evslin.

See also LEGEND, MYTH, PROTAGONIST, TALL TALE.

Historical fiction A novel, play, short story, or narrative poem that sets fictional characters against a historical backdrop and contains many details about the period in which it is set.

See also GENRE.

Humor The quality of a literary work that makes the characters and their situations seem funny, amusing, or ludicrous. Humorous writing can be as effective in nonfiction as in fiction, as shown in Merrill Markoe's "Dog Diaries."

See also COMEDY.

I

Imagery Language that emphasizes sensory impressions that help the reader of a literary work to see, hear, feel, smell, and taste the scenes described in the work.

See page 336.
See also FIGURATIVE LANGUAGE.

Informational text One kind of nonfiction. This kind of writing conveys facts and information without introducing personal opinion. "Hurricanes," by Patricia Lauber, is an example of informational text.

See page 312.

Irony A contrast between reality and what seems to be real. Situational irony exists when the actual outcome of a situation is the opposite of someone's expectations, as in the ending of O. Henry's "After Twenty Years." Verbal irony exists when a person says one thing and means another—for example, saying "Nice guy!" about someone you dislike.

See page 21.

L

Legend A traditional story handed down orally, based on history and an actual hero. A legend is usually exaggerated and gains elements of fantasy over the years. Stories about Daniel Boone and Davy Crockett are American legends.

> See page 732.
> See also FABLE, FOLKLORE, FOLKTALE, MYTH, ORAL TRADITION, TALL TALE.

Limerick A light, usually humorous poem with a regular metrical scheme and a rhyme scheme of *aabba*.

> See page 839.
> See also HUMOR, RHYME SCHEME.

Local color The fictional portrayal of a region's distinctive ways of talking and behaving, usually as a way of adding a realistic flavor to a story. "Rip Van Winkle," by Washington Irving, is notable for its touches of local color.

Lyric The words of a song, usually with a regular rhyme scheme.

> See also RHYME SCHEME.

Lyric poetry Poems, usually short, that express personal feelings about a subject or event. Emily Dickinson's "I'm Nobody" is a lyric poem.

M

Main idea The most important idea expressed in a paragraph or an essay. It may or may not be directly stated. In "The Teacher Who Changed My Life," by Nicholas Gage, the main idea is expressed in the title.

> See page 374.

Memoir A biographical or autobiographical narrative; an account of an event or period emphasizing the narrator's personal experience of it. "The Teacher Who Changed My Life," by Nicholas Gage, is an example of a memoir.

> See page 39.
> See also AUTOBIOGRAPHY, BIOGRAPHY.

Metaphor A figure of speech that compares or equates seemingly unlike things. In contrast to a simile, a metaphor implies the comparison instead of stating it directly; hence, there is no use of connectives such as *like* or *as*. The following line from "The Highwayman," by Alfred Noyes, contains an example of metaphor:

The moon was a ghostly galleon tossed upon cloudy seas. . . .

> See page 391.
> See also FIGURE OF SPEECH, IMAGERY, SIMILE.

Meter A regular pattern of stressed and unstressed syllables that gives a line of poetry a predictable rhythm. For example, the meter is marked in the following lines from "The Courage That My Mother Had" by Edna St. Vincent Millay:

The golden brooch my mother wore
She left behind for me to wear. . . .

> See page 631.
> See also RHYTHM

Monologue A long speech by a single character in a play or a solo performance.

Mood The emotional quality or atmosphere of a story.

> See page 134.
> See also SETTING.

Myth A traditional story of anonymous origin that deals with goddesses, gods, heroes, and supernatural events. For example, "Atalanta's Race," by Rex Warner, is a retelling of an ancient Greek myth.

> See page 740.
> See also FOLKLORE, FOLKTALE, HERO, LEGEND, ORAL TRADITION, TALL TALE.

N

Narration The kind of writing or speech that tells a story. Narration is used in novels, short stories, and narrative poetry. Narration can also be an important element in biographies, autobiographies, and essays.

> See also NARRATIVE POETRY.

Narrative poetry Verse that tells a story. "The Highwayman," by Alfred Noyes, is an example of a narrative poem.

> See page 232.
> See also NARRATION.

Narrator The person who tells a story. In some cases the narrator is a character in the story—for example, the narrator in "Uncle Tony's Goat" by Leslie Marmon Silko.

> See page 813.
> See also POINT OF VIEW.

Nonfiction Factual prose writing. Nonfiction deals with real people and experiences. Among the categories of nonfiction are biographies, autobiographies, and essays. Patricia Lauber's "Hurricanes: Big Winds and Big Damage" is an example of nonfiction.

> See pages 290–291.
> See also AUTOBIOGRAPHY, BIOGRAPHY, ESSAY, FICTION.

Novel A book-length fictional prose narrative. The novel has more scope than a short story in its presentation of plot, character, setting, and theme. Because novels are not subject to any limits in their presentation of these elements, they encompass a wide range of narratives.

> See also FICTION, SHORT STORY.

O

Onomatopoeia The use of a word or phrase that actually imitates or suggests the sound of what it describes. The following lines from "The Women's 400 Meters," by Lillian Morrison, contain an example of onomatopoeia:

Bang! they're off / careening down the lanes / each chased by her own bright tiger.

> See page 626.
> See also SOUND DEVICES.

Oral tradition Literature that passes by word of mouth from one generation to the next. "Racing the Great Bear," as retold by Joseph Bruchac, is an example of a story passed down through oral tradition among Native Americans.

> See page 276.
> See also FOLKLORE, FOLKTALE, LEGEND, MYTH.

P

Parallelism The use of a series of words, phrases, or sentences that have similar grammatical form. Parallelism emphasizes the items that are arranged in the similar structures. Gwendolyn Brooks uses parallelism in these lines from "Home."

They watched his progress. He passed the Kennedy's, he passed the vacant lot, he passed Mrs. Blakemore's

> See also REPETITION.

Personification A figure of speech in which an animal, object, or idea is given human form or characteristics. The following lines from "old age sticks," by E. E. Cummings, contain examples of personification:

old age sticks / up Keep / Off / signs&youth yanks them / down. . . .

> See page 843.
> See also FIGURATIVE LANGUAGE, FIGURE OF SPEECH, METAPHOR.

Plot The sequence of events in a story, novel, or play. The plot begins with **exposition,** which introduces the story's characters, setting, and situation. The plot catches the reader's attention with a **narrative hook.** The **rising action** adds complications to the story's conflicts, or problems, leading to the **climax,** or point of highest emotional pitch. The **falling action** is the logical result of the climax, and the **resolution** presents the final outcome.

> See page 171.
> See also CONFLICT, FALLING ACTION, RISING ACTION.

Plot twist An unexpected turn of events in a plot. Surprise endings in stories such as O. Henry's "After Twenty Years," are examples of plot twists.

> See page 550.

Poetry A form of literary expression that differs from prose in emphasizing the line as the unit of composition. Many other traditional characteristics of poetry apply to some poems but not others: emotional, imaginative language; use of metaphor and simile; division into stanzas; rhyme; regular pattern or meter; and so on.

> See pages 616–617.

Point of view The relationship of the narrator, or storyteller, to the story. In a story with **first-person point of view,** the story is told by one of the characters, referred to as "I," as in "Too Soon a Woman" by Dorothy M. Johnson. The reader generally sees everything through that character's eyes. In a story with a **limited third-person point of view,** the narrator reveals the thoughts of only one character, but refers to that character as "he" or "she," as in "Broken Chain" by Gary Soto. In a story with an **omniscient point of view,** like "Amigo Brothers" by Piri Thomas, the narrator reveals the thoughts of several characters.

> See page 61.

Props Theater slang (a shortened form of *properties*) for objects and elements of the scenery of a stage play or movie set.

Prose Writing that is similar to everyday speech and written language, as opposed to poetry or drama. Fiction and nonfiction are the major categories of prose.

> See also FICTION, NONFICTION.

Protagonist The central character in a story, drama, or dramatic poem. Usually the action revolves around the protagonist, who undergoes the main conflict. For example, Keevan is the protagonist of "The Smallest Dragonboy" by Anne McCaffrey.

> See page 144.
> See ANTAGONIST, CONFLICT.

Pun A humorous play on two or more meanings of the same word or on two different words with the same sound. Today puns often appear in advertising headlines and slogans—for example, "Our hotel rooms give you suite feelings."

> See page 561.
> See also HUMOR.

R

Refrain A line or lines repeated regularly, usually in a poem or song.

Repetition The recurrence of sounds, words, phrases, lines, or stanzas in a speech or piece of writing. Repetition increases the feeling of unity in a work. When a line or stanza is repeated in a poem, it is called a refrain. The following lines from "the 1st," by Lucille Clifton, make use of repetition:

nothing about the emptied rooms
nothing about the emptied family

> See also PARALLELISM, REFRAIN.

Resolution The part of a plot that concludes the falling action by revealing or suggesting the outcome of the conflict.

> See page 456.
> See also CONFLICT, PLOT.

Rhyme The repetition of sounds in words that appear close to each other in a poem. **End rhymes** occur at the ends of lines. **Internal rhyme** occurs within a single line. **Slant rhymes** occur when words include sounds that are similar but not identical. Slant rhyme usually involves some variation of **consonance** (the repetition of consonant sounds) or **assonance** (the repetition of vowel sounds). The following lines from "The Cremation of Sam McGee" have both internal and end rhymes.

On a Christmas Day we were mushing our way
     over the Dawson trail.
Talk of your cold! through the parka's fold it
     stabbed like a driven nail.

> See page 641.
> See also ASSONANCE, CONSONANCE, RHYME
>   SCHEME, SOUND DEVICES.

Rhyme scheme The pattern of rhymes formed by the end rhyme in a poem. The rhyme scheme is designated by the assignment of a different letter of the alphabet to each new rhyme. For example, the opening stanza of "Annabel Lee," by Edgar Allan Poe, has a rhyme scheme of *ababcb*.

> See page 262.
> See also RHYME.

Rhythm The pattern created by the arrangement of stressed and unstressed syllables, especially in poetry. Rhythm gives poetry a musical quality that helps convey its meaning. Rhythm

can be regular, with a predictable pattern or meter, or irregular.

> See page 631.
> See also METER.

Rising action The part of a plot that adds complications to the problems in the story and increases reader interest.

> See also FALLING ACTION, PLOT.

S

Scene A subdivision of an act in a play. Each scene usually takes place in a specific setting and time. A scene is either as long as or shorter than an act.

> See also ACT.

Science fiction Fiction dealing with the impact of real science or imaginary superscience on human or alien societies of the past, present, or future. Although science fiction is mainly a product of the twentieth century, nineteenth-century authors such as Mary Shelley, Jules Verne, and Robert Louis Stevenson were pioneers of the genre.

> See page 467.

Screenplay The script of a film, which, in addition to dialogue and stage directions, usually contains detailed instructions about camera shots and angles. A screenplay for an original television show is called a teleplay, of which Rod Serling's "The Monsters Are Due on Maple Street" is an example.

> See also DRAMA, STAGE DIRECTIONS.

Sensory imagery Language that appeals to a reader's five senses: hearing, sight, touch, taste, and smell. In the following lines from "Fish Cheeks," Amy Tan includes images that appeal to several senses:

The kitchen was littered with appalling mounds of raw food: A slimy rock cod with bulging fish eyes that pleaded not to be thrown into a pan of hot oil.

> See page 80.
> See also VISUAL IMAGERY.

Sequence of events The order in which the events in a story take place. In *Rosa Parks: My Story,* the sequence is established by including dates and times.

> See page 101.

Setting The time and place in which the events of a story, novel, or play occur. The setting often helps create an atmosphere or mood.

> See page 201.

Short story A brief fictional narrative in prose. Elements of the short story include plot, character, setting, point of view, theme, and sometimes symbol and irony. O. Henry wrote numerous short stories, including "After Twenty Years."

> See pages 144–145.

Simile A figure of speech using *like* or *as* to compare seemingly unlike things. The following lines from Henry Wadsworth Longfellow's "Wreck of the Hesperus" contain an example of a simile:

The snow fell hissing in the brine,
And the billows frothed like yeast.

> See page 617.
> See also FIGURATIVE LANGUAGE, FIGURE OF
> SPEECH, IMAGERY, METAPHOR.

Sound devices Techniques used to create a sense of rhythm or to emphasize particular sounds in writing. For example, sound can be controlled through the use of onomatopoeia, alliteration, consonance, assonance, and rhyme.

> See also RHYTHM.

Speaker The voice of a poem, sometimes that of the poet, sometimes that of a fictional person or even a thing. The speaker's words communicate a particular tone or attitude toward the subject of the poem. For example, in "To James," by Frank Horne, an adult male offers earnest advice about life to a young man, perhaps the speaker's son.

> See page 157.

Stage directions Instructions written by the dramatist to describe the appearance and actions of characters, as well as sets, costumes, and lighting. Examples of stage directions can be found in "The Monsters Are Due on Maple Street" by Rod Serling.

> See page 588.

Stanza A group of lines forming a unit in a poem. Stanzas are, in effect, the paragraphs of a poem.

> See page 616.

Stereotype A character who is not developed as an individual, but as a collection of traits and mannerisms supposedly shared by all members of a group.

Style The author's choice and arrangement of words and sentences in a literary work. Style can reveal an author's purpose in writing and attitude toward his or her subject and audience.

> See also GENRE.

Suspense A feeling of curiosity, uncertainty, or even dread about what is going to happen next. Writers increase the level of suspense in a story by giving readers clues to what might happen.

> See page 669.
> See also FORESHADOWING, RISING ACTION.

Symbol Any object, person, place, or experience that means more than what it is. **Symbolism** is the use of images to represent internal realities. For example, in "Prometheus," as retold by Bernard Evslin, Prometheus symbolizes the rebellious, defiant side of the human spirit.

> See page 446.

T

Tall tale A wildly imaginative story, usually passed down orally, about the fantastic adventures or amazing feats of folk heroes in realistic local settings. In "The Bunyans," Audrey Wood tells a story based on Paul Bunyan, a character from American folklore around whom many tall tales arose.

> See page 757.
> See also FOLKLORE, FOLKTALE, HERO, LEGEND, MYTH, ORAL TRADITION.

Teleplay A play written or adapted for television. "The Monsters Are Due on Maple Street," by Rod Serling, was written for television.

> See page 525.

Theme The main idea of a story, poem, novel, or play, usually expressed as a general statement. Some works have a stated theme, which is expressed directly. More frequently works have an implied theme, which is revealed gradually through other elements such as plot, character, setting, point of view, symbol, and irony.

> See page 785.

Third-person narrative. See POINT OF VIEW.

Title The name of a literary work.

Tone The elements of style that express to readers an author's feelings and attitude toward his or her subject, ideas, theme, or characters. A factual article would most likely have an objective tone, while an editorial on the same topic could be argumentative or satiric. Edgar Allan Poe's poem "Annabel Lee" could be described as having a tone of despair.

> See page 710.

Tragedy A play in which the main character suffers a downfall. That character often is a person of dignified or heroic stature. The downfall may result from outside forces or from a weakness within the character, which is known as a **tragic flaw.**

V

Visual imagery Details that appeal to the sense of sight. These lines from the poem "One," by James Berry, contain visual imagery:

And mirrors can show me multiplied
many times, say, dressed up in green
or dressed up in blue.

> See page 16.

Voice An author's distinctive style, or the particular speech patterns of a character in a story.

> See also STYLE, TONE.

Language Handbook

Troubleshooter

Use the Troubleshooter to recognize and correct common writing errors.

Sentence Fragment

A sentence fragment does not express a complete thought. It may lack a subject or verb or both.

Problem: Fragment that lacks a subject

The lion paced the floor of the cage. (Looked hungry.) *frag*

Solution: Add a subject to the fragment to make a complete sentence.

The lion paced the floor of the cage. He looked hungry.

Problem: Fragment that lacks a predicate

I'm painting my room. (The walls yellow.) *frag*

Solution: Add a predicate to make the sentence complete.

I'm painting my room. The walls are going to be yellow.

Problem: Fragment that lacks both a subject and a predicate

We walked around the reservoir. (Near the parkway.) *frag*

Solution: Combine the fragment with another sentence.

We walked around the reservoir near the parkway.

Rule of Thumb

You can use fragments when talking with friends or writing personal letters. Some writers use fragments to produce a special effect. Use complete sentences, however, for school or business writing.

Run-on Sentence

A run-on sentence is two or more sentences written incorrectly as one sentence.

Problem: Two main clauses separated only by a comma

Roller coasters make me dizzy, I don't enjoy them. *run-on*

Solution A: Replace the comma with a period or other end mark. Start the second sentence with a capital letter.

Roller coasters make me dizzy. I don't enjoy them.

Solution B: Replace the comma with a semicolon.

Roller coasters make me dizzy; I don't enjoy them.

Problem: Two main clauses with no punctuation between them

Acid rain is a worldwide problem there are no solutions in sight. *run-on*

Solution A: Separate the main clauses with a period or other end mark. Begin the second sentence with a capital letter.

Acid rain is a worldwide problem. There are no solutions in sight.

Solution B: Add a comma and a coordinating conjunction between the main clauses.

Acid rain is a worldwide problem, but there are no solutions in sight.

Problem: Two main clauses with no comma before the coordinating conjunction

Our chorus has been practicing all month but we still need another rehearsal. *run-on*

Solution: Add a comma before the coordinating conjunction.

Our chorus has been practicing all month, but we still need another rehearsal.

Lack of Subject-Verb Agreement

A singular subject calls for a singular form of the verb. A plural subject calls for a plural form of the verb.

Problem: A subject that is separated from the verb by an intervening prepositional phrase

The two policemen at the construction site (looks) bored. *agr*

The members of my baby-sitting club (is) saving money. *agr*

Solution: Make sure that the verb agrees with the subject of the sentence, not with the object of the preposition. The object of a preposition is never the subject.

The two policemen at the construction site look bored.

The members of my baby-sitting club are saving money.

Rule of Thumb

When subject and verb are separated by a prepositional phrase, check for agreement by reading the sentence without the prepositional phrase.

Problem: A sentence that begins with *here* or *there*

Here (come) the last bus to Pelham Heights. *agr*

There (is) my aunt and uncle. *agr*

Solution: In sentences that begin with *here* or *there,* look for the subject after the verb. Make sure that the verb agrees with the subject.

Here comes the last bus to Pelham Heights.

There are my aunt and uncle.

Problem: An indefinite pronoun as the subject

Each of the candidates (are) qualified. *agr*

All of the problems on the test (was) hard. *agr*

Solution: Some indefinite pronouns are singular; some are plural; and some can be either singular or plural, depending on the noun they refer to. Determine whether the indefinite pronoun is singular or plural, and make sure the verb agrees with it.

Each of the candidates is qualified.

All of the problems on the test were hard.

Problem: A compound subject that is joined by *and*

Fishing tackle and a life jacket (was) stowed in the boat. *agr*

Peanut butter and jelly (are) delicious. *agr*

Solution A: If the compound subjects refer to different people or things, use a plural verb.

Fishing tackle and a life jacket were stowed in the boat.

Solution B: If the parts of a compound subject name one unit or if they refer to the same person or thing, use a singular verb.

Peanut butter and jelly is delicious.

Problem: A compound subject that is joined by *or* or *nor*

Either my aunt or my parents (plans) to attend parents' night. *agr*

Neither onions nor pepper (improve) the taste of this meatloaf. *agr*

Solution: Make the verb agree with the subject that is closer to it.

Either my aunt or my parents plan to attend parents' night.

Neither onions nor pepper improves the taste of this meatloaf.

Incorrect Verb Tense or Form

Verbs have different tenses to show when the action takes place.

Problem: An incorrect or missing verb ending

The Parks Department (install) a new water fountain last week. *tense*

They have also (plant) flowers in all the flower beds. *tense*

Solution: To form the past tense and the part participle, add *-ed* to a regular verb.

The Parks Department installed a new water fountain last week.

They have also planted flowers in all the flower beds.

Problem: An improperly formed irregular verb

Wendell (has standed) in line for two hours. *tense*

I (catched) the fly ball and (throwed) it to first base. *tense*

Solution: Irregular verbs vary in their past and past participle forms. Look up the ones you are not sure of.

Wendell has stood in line for two hours.

I caught the fly ball and threw it to first base.

Problem: Confusion between the past form and the past participle

The cast for *The Music Man* (has began) rehearsals. *tense*

Solution: Use the past participle form of an irregular verb, not its past form, when you use the auxiliary verb *have*.

The cast for *The Music Man* has begun rehearsals.

Problem: Improper use of the past participle

Our seventh grade (drawn) a mural for the wall of the cafeteria. *tense*

Solution: Add the auxiliary verb *have* to the past participle of an irregular verb to form a complete verb.

Our seventh grade has drawn a mural for the wall of the cafeteria.

Rule of Thumb

Because irregular verbs vary, it is useful to memorize the verbs that you use most often.

Incorrect Use of Pronouns

The noun that a pronoun refers to is called its **antecedent**. A pronoun must refer to its antecedent clearly. Subject pronouns refer to subjects in a sentence. Object pronouns refer to objects in a sentence.

Problem: A pronoun that could refer to more than one antecedent

Gary and Mike are coming, but *he* doesn't know the other kids. *ant*

Solution: Substitute a noun for the pronoun to make your sentence clearer.

Gary and Mike are coming, but Gary doesn't know the other kids.

Problem: Personal pronouns as subjects

Him and John were freezing after skating for three hours. *pro*

Lori and *me* decided not to audition for the musical. *pro*

Solution: Use a subject pronoun as the subject part of a sentence.

He and John were freezing after skating for three hours.

Lori and I decided not to audition for the musical.

Problem: Personal pronouns as objects

Ms. Wang asked Reggie and *I* to enter the science fair. *pro*

Ms. Wang helped *he* and *I* with the project. *pro*

Solution: Use an object pronoun as the object of a verb or a preposition.

Ms. Wang asked Reggie and me to enter the science fair.

Ms. Wang helped him and me with the project.

Rule of Thumb

When a pronoun is part of a compound subject or object, it is sometimes hard to choose the correct pronoun. Try saying the sentence with only the pronoun as the subject or object. That often makes the correct choice clear. For example, change *Dad gave Ronny and I a new basketball* to *Dad gave I a new basketball.* The pronoun *I* sounds wrong and should be changed to *me.*

Incorrect Use of Adjectives

Some adjectives have irregular forms: comparative forms for comparing two things and superlative forms for comparing more than two things.

Problem: Incorrect use of *good, better, best*

Their team is (more good) at softball than ours. *adj*

They have (more better) equipment too. *adj*

Solution: The comparative and superlative forms of *good* are *better* and *best*. Do not use *more* or *most* before irregular forms of comparative and superlative adjectives.

Their team is better at softball than ours.

They have better equipment too.

Problem: Incorrect use of *bad, worse, worst*

The flooding on East Street was the (baddest) I've seen. *adj*

Mike's basement was in (badder) shape than his garage. *adj*

Solution: The comparative and superlative forms of *bad* are *worse* and *worst*. Do not use *more* or *most* or the endings *-er* or *-est* with *bad*.

The flooding on East Street was the worst I've seen.

Mike's basement was in worse shape than his garage.

Problem: Incorrect use of comparative and superlative adjectives

The Appalachian Mountains are (more older) than the Rockies. *adj*

Mount Washington is the (most highest) of the Appalachians. *adj*

Solution: Do not use both *-er* and *more* or *-est* and *most* at the same time.

The Appalachian Mountains are older than the Rockies.

Mount Washington is the highest of the Appalachians.

Incorrect Use of Commas

Commas signal a pause between parts of a sentence and help to clarify meaning.

Problem: Missing commas in a series of three or more items

Sergio put mustard₍catsup₎and bean sprouts on his hot dog. *s com*

Solution: If there are three or more items in a series, use a comma after each one, including the item preceding the conjunction.

Sergio put mustard, catsup, and bean sprouts on his hot dog.

Problem: Missing commas with direct quotations

"A little cold water₎" the swim coach said₎ "won't hurt you." *com*

Solution: The first part of an interrupted quotation ends with a comma followed by quotation marks. The interrupting words are also followed by a comma.

"A little cold water," the swim coach said, "won't hurt you."

Problem: Missing commas with nonessential appositives

My sneakers₎a new pair₎are covered with mud. *com*

Solution: Determine whether the appositive is important to the meaning of the sentence. If it is not essential, set off the appositive with commas.

My sneakers, a new pair, are covered with mud.

Incorrect Use of Apostrophes

An apostrophe shows possession. It can also indicate missing letters in a contraction.

Problem: Singular possessive nouns

A ⟨parrots⟩ toes are used for gripping. *poss*

The ⟨bus⟩ color was bright yellow. *poss*

Solution: Use an apostrophe and an -*s* to form the possessive of a singular noun, even one that ends in -*s*.

A parrot's toes are used for gripping.

The bus's color was bright yellow.

Problem: Plural possessive nouns ending in *-s*

The (visitors) center closes at five o'clock. *poss*

The guide put several (tourists) luggage in one compartment. *poss*

Solution: Use an apostrophe alone to form the possessive of a plural noun that ends in *-s.*

The visitors' center closes at five o'clock.

The guide put several tourists' luggage in one compartment.

Problem: Plural possessive nouns not ending in *-s*

The (peoples) applause gave courage to the young gymnast. *poss*

Solution: Use an apostrophe and an *-s* to form the possessive of a plural noun that does not end in *-s.*

The people's applause gave courage to the young gymnast.

Problem: Possessive personal pronouns

Jenny found the locker that was (her's;) she waited while her friends found (their's.) *poss*

Solution: Do not use apostrophes with possessive personal pronouns.

Jenny found the locker that was hers; she waited while her friends found theirs.

Incorrect Capitalization

Proper nouns, proper adjectives, and the first words of sentences always begin with a capital letter.

Problem: Words referring to ethnic groups, nationalities, and languages

Many (canadians) in the province of (quebec) speak (french.) *cap*

Solution: Capitalize proper nouns and adjectives that refer to ethnic groups, nationalities, and languages.

Many Canadians in the province of Quebec speak French.

Problem: Words that refer to a family member

Yesterday (aunt) Doreen asked me to baby-sit. *cap*

Don't forget to give (dad) a call. *cap*

Solution: Capitalize words that are used as part of or in place of a family member's name.

Yesterday Aunt Doreen asked me to baby-sit.

Don't forget to give Dad a call.

Rule of Thumb

Do not capitalize a word that identifies a family member when preceded by a possessive adjective: *My father bought a new car.*

Problem: The first word of a direct quotation

The judge declared, "(the) court is now in session." *cap*

Solution: Capitalize the first word in a direct quotation.

The judge declared, "The court is now in session."

Rule of Thumb

If you have difficulty with a rule of usage, try rewriting the rule in your own words. Check with your teacher to be sure you understand the rule.

Troublesome Words

This section will help you choose between words and expressions that are often confusing or misused.

---

accept, except

Accept means "to receive." *Except* means "other than."

Phillip walked proudly to the stage to **accept** the award.

Everything fits in my suitcase **except** my sleeping bag.

---

affect, effect

Affect is a verb meaning "to cause a change in" or "to influence." *Effect* as a verb means "to bring about or accomplish." As a noun, *effect* means "result."

Bad weather will **affect** our plans for the weekend.

The new medicine **effected** an improvement in the patient's condition.

The gloomy weather had a bad **effect** on my mood.

---

ain't

Ain't is never used in formal speaking or writing unless you are quoting the exact words of a character or a real person. Instead of using *ain't*, say or write *am not, is not, are not;* or use contractions such as *I'm not, she isn't.*

The pizza **is not** going to arrive for another half hour.

The pizza **isn't** going to arrive for another half hour.

---

a lot, alot

The expression *a lot* means "very much" and should always be written as two words. Some authorities discourage its use in formal writing.

A lot of my friends are learning Spanish.

Many of my friends are learning Spanish.

---

all ready, already

All ready, written as two words, is a phrase that means "completely ready." *Already,* written as one word, is an adverb that means "before" or "by this time."

By the time the fireworks display was **all ready**, we had **already** arrived.

---

all right, alright

The expression *all right* should be written as two words. Some dictionaries do list the single word *alright* but usually not as a preferred spelling.

Tom hurt his ankle, but he will be **all right.**

all together, altogether

All together means "in a group." *Altogether* means "completely."

The Minutemen gathered **all together** at the end of Lexington Green.

The rebel farmers were not **altogether** sure that they could fight the British soldiers.

among, between

Use *among* for three or more people, things, or groups. Use *between* for two people, things, or groups.

Mr. Kendall divided the jobs for the car wash **among** the team members.

Our soccer field lies **between** the gym and Main Street.

amount, number

Use *amount* with nouns that cannot be counted. Use *number* with nouns that can be counted.

This recipe calls for an unusual **amount** of pepper.

A record **number** of students attended last Saturday's book fair.

bad, badly

Bad is an adjective and modifies a noun. *Badly* is an adverb and modifies a verb, an adjective, or another adverb.

The **badly** burnt cookies left a **bad** smell in the kitchen.

Joseph **badly** wants to be on the track team.

beside, besides

Beside means "next to." *Besides* means "in addition to."

The zebra is grazing **beside** a wildebeest.

Besides the zoo, I like to visit the aquarium.

bring, take

Bring means "to carry from a distant place to a closer one." *Take* means "to carry from a nearby place to a more distant one."

Please **bring** a bag lunch and subway money to school tomorrow.

Don't forget to **take** your art projects home this afternoon.

can, may

Can implies the ability to do something. *May* implies permission to do something.

Rule of Thumb

Although *can* is sometimes used in place of *may* in informal speech, a distinction should be made when speaking and writing formally.

You **may** take a later bus home if you **can** remember which bus to get on.

choose, chose

Choose means "to select." *Chose,* the past tense of *choose,* means "selected."

Dad helped me **choose** a birthday card for my grandmother.

Dad **chose** a card with a funny joke inside.

doesn't, don't

The subject of the contraction **doesn't** *(does not)* is the third-person singular (*he* or *she*). The subject of the contraction **don't** *(do not)* is *I, you, we,* or *they.*

Tanya **doesn't** have any tickets for the concert.

We **don't** need tickets if we stand in the back row.

farther, further

Farther refers to physical distance. *Further* refers to time or degree.

Our new apartment is **farther** away from the school.

I will not continue this argument **further.**

fewer, less

Fewer is used to refer to things or qualities that can be counted. *Less* is used to refer to things or qualities that cannot be counted. In addition, *less* is used with figures that are regarded as single amounts.

Fewer people were waiting in line after lunch.

There is **less** fat in this kind of peanut butter.

Try to spend **less** than ten dollars on a present. [The money is treated as a single sum, not as individual dollars.]

good, well

Good is often used as an adjective meaning "pleasing" or "able." *Well* may be used as an adverb of manner telling how ably something is done or as an adjective meaning "in good health."

That is a **good** haircut.

Marco writes **well.**

Because Ms. Rodriguez had a headache, she was not **well** enough to correct our tests.

in, into

In means "inside." *Into* indicates a movement from outside toward the inside.

Refreshments will be sold **in** the lobby of the auditorium.

The doors opened, and the eager crowd rushed **into** the auditorium.

it's, its

Use an apostrophe to form the contraction of *it is.* The possessive of the personal pronoun *it* does not take an apostrophe.

It's hard to keep up with computer technology.

The computer industry seems to change **its** products daily.

lay, lie

Lay means "to place." *Lie* means "to recline."

I will **lay** my beach towel here on the warm sand.

Help! I don't want to **lie** next to a hill of red ants!

learn, teach

Learn means "to gain knowledge." *Teach* means "to give knowledge."

I don't **learn** very quickly.

My uncle is **teaching** me how to juggle.

leave, let

Leave means "to go away." *Let* means "to allow." With the word *alone* you may use either *let* or *leave.*

Huang has to **leave** at eight o'clock.

Mr. Davio **lets** the band practice in his basement.

Leave me alone. **Let** me alone.

like, as

Use *like,* a preposition, to introduce a prepositional phrase. Use *as,* a subordinating conjunction, to introduce a subordinate clause. Many authorities believe that *like* should not be used before a clause in formal English.

Andy sometimes acts **like** a clown.

The detective looked carefully at the empty suitcase **as** she examined the room.

Rule of Thumb

As can be a preposition in cases like the following: *Jack went to the costume party as a giant pumpkin.*

loose, lose

Loose means "not firmly attached." *Lose* means "to misplace" or "to fail to win."

If you keep wiggling that **loose** tooth, you might **lose** it.

raise, rise

Raise means to "cause to move up." *Rise* means "to move upward."

Farmers in this part of Florida **raise** sugarcane.

The hot air balloon began to **rise** slowly in the morning sky.

set, sit

Set means "to place" or "to put." *Sit* means "to place oneself in a seated position."

I **set** the tips of my running shoes against the starting line.

After running the fifty-yard dash, I had to **sit** down and catch my breath.

than, then

Than introduces the second part of a comparison. *Then* means "at that time" or "after that."

I'd rather go to Disney World in the winter **than** in the summer.

The park is too crowded and hot **then.**

their, they're

Their is the possessive form of *they*. *They're* is the contraction of *they are*.

They're visiting Plymouth Plantation during **their** vacation.

to, too , two

To means "in the direction of." *Too* means "also" or "to an excessive degree." *Two* is the number after one.

I bought **two** tickets **to** the concert.

The music was **too** loud.

It's my favorite group, **too.**

who, whom

Who is a subject pronoun. *Whom* is an object pronoun.

Who has finished the test already?

Mr. Russo is the man to **whom** we owe our thanks.

who's, whose

Who's is the contraction of *who is*. *Whose* is the possessive form of *who*.

Who's going to wake me up in the morning?

The policeman discovered **whose** car alarm was making so much noise.

Grammar Glossary

This glossary will help you quickly locate information on parts of speech and sentence structure.

A

Abstract noun. *See* Noun.

Action verb. *See* Verb.

Adjective A word that modifies a noun or a pronoun. An adjective may answer one of these questions: *What kind? Which one? How many? How much?* (My *playful* dog splashed *cold* water in my face.)

Many adjectives have different forms to indicate degree of **comparison.** *(bright, brighter, brightest)*

The **comparative degree** compares two persons, places, things, or ideas. *(worse, sadder)*

The **superlative degree** compares more than two persons, places, things, or ideas. *(worst, saddest)*

A **predicate adjective** always follows a linking verb. It modifies the subject of the sentence. (Marathon running is *difficult.*)

A **proper adjective** is formed from a proper noun. It always begins with a capital letter. Most proper adjectives are formed by using the following endings: *-an, -ian, -ese, -ish.* (Chin**ese**)

Sometimes **pronouns** are used as adjectives.
Possessive adjectives are possessive pronouns that answer the question *Which one? (my, your, her, his, its, our, their)*

Demonstrative adjectives are pronouns that answer the questions *Which one? How many?* and *How much?* (Jane read *that* book.)

Adverb A word that modifies a verb, an adjective, or another adverb. Adverbs answer the questions *How? When?* and *Where?* When modifying a verb, an adverb may appear in various positions in a sentence. (The van rocked *dangerously* on the bumpy road. *Gradually,* we slowed down.)

When modifying an adjective or another adverb, an adverb appears directly before the modified word. (The driver stopped *quite* suddenly.) The negatives *no* and *not* and *-n't,* the contraction for *not,* are adverbs. (I could *not* see through the fog.) Other negative words, such as *nowhere, hardly,* and *never* can function as adverbs of time, place, and degree. (She would *hardly* endorse such an idea.)

Some adverbs have different forms to indicate **degree of comparison.** *(loud, louder, loudest; sweetly, more sweetly, most sweetly)* Many adverbs are formed by adding *-ly* to adjectives. *(calmly)* However, not all words that end in *-ly* are adverbs. *(friendly)*

Antecedent. *See* Pronoun.

Appositive An **appositive** is a noun placed next to another noun to identify it or add information about it. (My basketball coach, *Ms. Lopes,* called for a time out.)

Appositive phrase. *See* Phrase.

Article The adjectives *a, an,* and *the.*

A and *an* are **indefinite** articles. They refer to any one item of a group. (She bought *a* ticket.)

The is a **definite** article. It indicates that the noun is a specific person, place or thing. (She liked *the* movie.)

B C

Base form. *See* Verb.

Clause A group of words that has a subject and a predicate and that is used as part of a sentence. Clauses fall into two categories: **main clauses,** which are also called **independent clauses,** and **subordinate clauses,** which are also called **dependent clauses.**

A **main clause** has a subject and a predicate and can stand alone as a sentence. There must be at least one main clause in every sentence. *(The water was cold.)*

A **subordinate clause** has a subject and a predicate, but it cannot stand alone as a sentence. A subordinate clause makes sense only when attached to a main clause. Many subordinate clauses begin with subordinating conjunctions or relative pronouns. (She returned the book *although she hadn't finished it.*) The best way to distinguish between a main clause and a subordinate clause is to see whether the clause can stand alone outside the sentence. Main clauses can stand alone; subordinate clauses cannot.

Collective noun. *See* Noun.

Common noun. *See* Noun.

Comparative degree. *See* Adjective; Adverb.

Complement A word or phrase that completes the meaning of a verb. Three kinds of complements are *direct objects, indirect objects,* and *subject complements.*

A **direct object** answers the question *What?* or *Whom?* after an action verb. (He ate *a hamburger.* She mailed *the letter.*)

An **indirect object** answers the question *To whom? For whom? To what?* or *For what?* after an action verb. (Marcia gave *the baby* a bath.)

A **subject complement** follows a subject and a linking verb. It identifies or describes a subject. The two kinds of subject complements are *predicate nouns* and *predicate adjectives.*

A **predicate noun** is a noun that follows a linking verb and gives more information about the subject. (The first prize is a medal.)

A **predicate adjective** is an adjective that follows a linking verb and gives more information about the subject. (The day is *cloudy.* It looks *cold.*)

Complete predicate. *See* Predicate.

Complete subject. *See* Subject.

Complex sentence. *See* Sentence.

Compound predicate. *See* Predicate.

Compound preposition. *See* Preposition.

Compound sentence. *See* Sentence.

Compound subject. *See* Subject.

Conjunction A word that joins single words or groups of words.

A **coordinating conjunction** *(and, but, or, nor, for, yet)* joins words or groups of words that are equal in grammatical importance. (Pizza *and* spaghetti are the choices for lunch today.)

Correlative conjunctions *(both . . . and, just as . . . so, not only . . . but also, either . . . or, neither . . . nor)* are pairs of words used to connect words or phrases in a sentence. (Anna is *either* brilliant *or* very studious.)

A **subordinating conjunction** *(after, although, because, before, if, in order that, since, than, though, until, when, while)* joins a subordinate idea or clause to a main clause. (I read a book *while* I was waiting for you.)

Coordinating conjunction. *See* Conjunction.

Correlative conjunction. *See* Conjunction.

Declarative sentence. *See* Sentence.

Definite article. *See* Article.

Demonstrative. *See* Adjective; Pronoun.

Direct object. *See* Complement.

Exclamatory sentence. *See* Sentence.

Future tense. *See* Verb.

Gerund A verb form that is used as a noun. A gerund always ends in *-ing.* A gerund may function as a subject, an object of a verb, or the object of a preposition. (*Walking* is good exercise. I prefer *walking* to *running.*) One identification test is to replace the gerund or gerund phrase with the singular pronoun *it.* When you replace a gerund with *it,* the sentence still makes sense. Participles fail this test.

Gerund phrase. *See* Phrase.

Helping verb. *See* Verb.

Imperative sentence. *See* Sentence.

Indefinite article. *See* Article.

Indefinite pronoun. *See* Pronoun.

Indirect object. *See* Complement.

Infinitive A verb that is usually preceded by the word *to.* An infinitive often functions as a noun in a sentence. The word *to* may also begin a prepositional phrase. However, when *to* precedes a verb, it is not a preposition but instead signals an infinitive. (*To achieve* a goal is very satisfying.)

Infinitive phrase. *See* Phrase.

Intensive pronoun. *See* Pronoun.

Interjection A word or phrase that expresses strong feeling. An interjection has no grammatical connection to other words in the sentence. Commas follow mild ones; exclamation points follow stronger ones. (*Darn!* I left my subway pass at home! *Well,* we should leave anyway.)

Interrogative pronoun. *See* Pronoun.

Interrogative sentence. *See* Sentence.

Intransitive verb. *See* Verb.

Inverted order In most sentences in English, the subject comes before the predicate. In a sentence written in **inverted order,** the predicate comes before the subject. Some sentences are written in inverted order for variety or special emphasis. (In the middle of the park *grew a large oak tree.*) The subject generally follows the predicate in a sentence that begins with *there* or *here.* (*There* is a new girl in the class. *Here* come the clowns.) Questions, or interrogative sentences, are generally written in inverted order. Questions that begin with *who* or *what* follow normal word order.

Irregular verb. *See* Verb.

Linking verb. *See* Verb.

Main clause. *See* Clause.

Noun A word that names a person, a place, a thing, or an idea. The chart on page R30 shows the main types of nouns.

Number A noun, pronoun, or verb is **singular** in number if it refers to one; **plural** if it refers to more than one.

Object. *See* Complement.

Object pronoun. *See* Pronoun.

Participle A verb form that can function as an adjective. Present participles always end in *-ing.* Although past participles often end in *-ed,* they can take other forms as well. (I loved the actor's *engrossing* performance. Lori stared down the road with a *worried* expression on her face.)

Past tense. *See* Verb.

Types of Nouns

Noun	Function	Examples
Abstract noun	Names an idea, a quality, or a characteristic	beauty, love
Collective noun	Names a group of people or things	audience, class
Common noun	Names a general, not a particular, name of a person, place, thing, or idea	writer, city, desk, fear
Compound noun	Is made up of two or more words	hairbrush
Concrete noun	Names a thing that you can see or touch	pheasant, water
Possessive noun	Shows possession, ownership, or the relationship between two nouns	*Chris's* paper
Predicate noun	Follows a linking verb and gives information about the subject	The movie is *a comedy.*
Proper noun	Names a particular person, place, thing, or idea	Marco Polo, Chicago, Eiffel Tower

Perfect tenses. *See* Verb.

Personal pronoun. *See* Pronoun.

Phrase A group of words that acts in a sentence as a single part of speech.

An **appositive phrase** includes an appositive and other words that describe the appositive. Many appositives are set off by commas. (My next fish, *a striped bass,* was the biggest catch of the day.)

A **gerund phrase** includes a gerund and any complements and modifiers needed to complete its meaning. (*Watching the clock* doesn't make time move faster.)

An **infinitive phrase** includes an infinitive and any complements and modifiers. (I prefer *to wake up slowly by listening to music.*)

A **participial phrase** contains a participle and any modifiers necessary to complete its meaning. (*Huddled together in the damp cave,* the hikers waited for the storm to end.)

A **prepositional phrase** begins with a preposition and ends with a noun or a pronoun called the **object of the preposition.** A prepositional phrase can function as an adjective, modifying a noun or a pronoun. (Bach was a great composer *of the eighteenth century.*) A prepositional phrase may also function as an adverb when it modifies a verb, an adverb, or an adjective. (*Throughout his life,* Bach wrote sacred music.)

A **verb phrase** consists of one or more helping verbs followed by a main verb. (I *have been studying* all night.)

A **verbal phrase** contains a verbal plus any complements and modifiers. The three kinds of verbals are participles, gerunds, and infinitives. *See* Gerund; Infinitive; Participle.

Plural. *See* Number.

Possessive noun. *See* Noun.

Possessive pronoun. *See* Pronoun.

Predicate The verb or verb phrase and any modifiers that express the essential thought about the subject of a sentence.

A **simple predicate** is a verb or verb phrase that tells something about the subject. (The carpenter *left.*)

A **complete predicate** includes the simple predicate and any words that modify or complete it. (The carpenter left very early. The carpenter built a beautiful cabinet.)

A **compound predicate** has two or more verbs or verb phrases that are joined by a conjunction and share the same subject. (The receiver *caught the pass and headed for the end zone.*)

Predicate adjective. *See* Adjective; Complement.

Predicate noun. *See* Complement; Noun.

Preposition A word that shows the relationship of a noun or pronoun to some other word in the sentence. Prepositions include *about, above, across, among, as, behind, below, beyond, but, by, down, during, except, for, from, into, like, near, of, on, outside, over, since, through, to, under, until, with.* (We skated *across* the ice.)

A **compound preposition** is made up of more than one word. Compound prepositions include *according to, across from, ahead of, as to, because of, by means of, in addition to, in spite of, on account of.* (*Because of* our

late start, we had to park at a distance from the rink.)

Prepositional phrase. *See* Phrase.

Present tense. *See* Verb.

Progressive form. *See* Verb.

Pronoun A word that takes the place of a noun, a group of words acting as a noun, or another pronoun. The word or group of words that a pronoun refers to is called its **antecedent.** (In the following sentence, *girls* is the antecedent of *they. When the girls camped on the mountain, they slept well.*)

A **demonstrative pronoun** points out specific persons, places, things, or ideas. *(this, that, these, those)*

An **indefinite pronoun** refers to persons, places, or things in a more general way than a noun does. *(all, another, any, both, each, either, enough, everything, few, many, most, much, neither, nobody, none, one, other, others, plenty, several, some)*

An **intensive pronoun** adds emphasis to another noun or

pronoun. If an intensive pronoun is omitted, the meaning of the sentence will be the same. (The mayor *himself* gave the diplomas to the graduates.)

An **interrogative pronoun** is used to form questions. *(Who? Whom? Whose? What? Which?)*

A **personal pronoun** refers to a specific person or thing. The form of the personal pronoun depends on its use in the sentence. The chart on this page shows the different forms of personal pronouns.

A **reflexive pronoun** reflects back to a noun or pronoun used earlier in the sentence, indicating that the same person or thing is involved. (We congratulated *ourselves* on winning the pennant.)

A **relative pronoun** is used to begin a subordinate clause. *(who, whose, whomever, that, what, whom, whoever, whomever, whichever, whatever)*

Proper adjective. *See* Adjective.

Proper noun. *See* Noun.

Personal Pronouns		
Singular Pronouns	**Plural Pronouns**	**Use in Sentence**
I, you, she, he, it	we, you, they	subject or predicate nominative
me, you, her, him, it	us, you, them	direct object, indirect object, or object of a preposition
my, your, her, his, its	our, your, their	possessive used before nouns (*our* car)
mine, yours, hers, his, its	ours, yours, theirs	possessive used alone (The car is *ours*.)

R

Reflexive pronoun. *See* Pronoun.

Regular verb. *See* Verb.

Relative pronoun. *See* Pronoun.

S

Sentence A group of words expressing a complete thought. Every sentence has a subject and a predicate. *See also* Clause; Predicate; Subject.

A **simple sentence** has only one main clause and no subordinate clauses. A simple sentence may contain a compound subject or a compound predicate or both. The subject and the predicate can be expanded with adjectives, adverbs, prepositional phrases, appositives, and verbal phrases. As long as the sentence has only one main clause, however, it remains a simple sentence. *(Doreen swam and snorkled. Doreen and David swam and snorkled. Students in grades seven and eight will plant a vegetable garden this spring and sell vegetables next fall.)*

A **compound sentence** has two or more main clauses. Each main clause of a compound sentence has its own subject and predicate, and these main clauses are usually joined by a comma and a coordinating conjunction. *(The spacecraft landed on Mars, and a special camera took pictures of rocks.)* A semicolon can also be used to join the main clauses in a compound sentence. *(The play ended late; we missed the last bus home.)*

A **complex sentence** has one main clause and one or more subordinate clauses. *(I'll be glad when this day is over.)*

The chart on this page shows the kinds of sentences by function.

Simple predicate. *See* Predicate; Sentence; Subject.

Subject The key noun or pronoun that tells what the sentence is about.

A **simple subject** is the main noun or pronoun. (*Leaves* covered the yard.)

A **complete subject** includes the simple subject and any words that modify it. (*Wet leaves from the old maple tree* covered the front yard.)

A **compound subject** has two or more simple subjects that are joined by a conjunction. The subjects share the same verb. (*Lee, Kim, and Andrew* won prizes in the spelling bee.)

Subordinate clause. *See* Clause.

Subordinating conjunction. *See* Conjunction.

Superlative degree. *See* Adjective; Adverb.

T

Tense. *See* Verb tense.

Transitive verb. *See* Verb.

Types of Sentences			
Sentence Type	**Function**	**Ends with . . .**	**Examples**
Declarative sentence	Makes a statement	A period	The red kangaroo lives in Australia.
Exclamatory sentence	Expresses strong emotion	An exclamation point	How loud that thunder is!
Imperative sentence	Gives a command or makes a request	A period or an exclamation point	Please leave a message.
Interrogative sentence	Asks a question	A question mark	When does the movie begin?

Verb A word that expresses action or a state of being and is necessary to make a statement. *(sing, is, had)*

An **action verb** names an action and tell what a subject does. Action verbs can express either physical or mental action. (He *plays* the piano. Linda *prefers* this movie.)

A **helping verb** helps the main verb tell about an action or make a statement. (Naomi *is* playing the lead in the spring musical.) The forms of *be* and *have* are the most common helping verbs. *(am, is, are, was, were, being, been; has, have, had, having)* Other helping verbs are *can, could; do, does, did, may, might; must; shall, should; will, would.* Helping verbs are also called auxiliary verbs.

An **intransitive verb** is an action verb that is *not* followed by a direct object. (The horse *ran* across the field.) A dictionary will indicate whether a verb is transitive or intransitive.

A **linking verb** links, or connects, the subject of a sentence with a noun or adjective that identifies or describes the subject. The predicate tells what the subject *is,* or *is like.* (The Lincoln Memorial *is* a national monument. The Lincoln Memorial *is* huge.) A linking verb does not show action. *To be* in all its forms is the most common linking verb. *(am, is, are, was, were, will be, been, being)* Other linking verbs are *appear, become, feel, grow, look, remain, seem, sound, smell, stay, taste.*

A **transitive verb** is an action verb that is followed by a direct object that answers the question *What?* or *Whom?* (The Pony Express rider *delivered* the mail.)

Verb phrase. *See* Phrase.

Verb tense The tense of a verb indicates when the action or state of being occurs. All the verb tenses are formed from the four principal parts of a verb: a base form *(freeze),* a present participle *(freezing),* a simple past form *(froze)* and a past participle *(frozen).*

A **regular verb** forms its simple past and past participle by adding -ed to the base form.

Verbs that form their past and past participle in some other way are called **irregular verbs.** *(begin, began, begun; am, is, are, was, were, been; win, won, won)*

In addition to present, past, and future tenses, there are three perfect tenses.

The **present perfect** tense expresses an action or condition that occurred at some indefinite time in the past. This tense also shows an action or condition that began in the past and continues into the present. (Naomi *has played* important roles in school plays every year.)

The **past perfect tense** indicates that one past action or condition began *and* ended before another past action started. (The guests *had called* us before they heard about the storm.)

The **future perfect tense** indicates that one future action or condition will begin *and* end before another future event starts. Use *will have* or *shall have* with the past participle of a verb. (By the time you are finally ready, the bus *will have left.*)

Each of the six tenses has a **progressive** form that expresses a continuing action. To make the progressive forms, use the appropriate tense of the verb *be* with the present participle of the main verb. (Maria *will be working.*)

Verbal A verb form that functions in a sentence as a noun, an adjective, or an adverb. The three kinds of verbals are participles, gerunds, and infinitives.

Mechanics

This section will help you use correct capitalization, punctuation, and abbreviations in your writing.

Capitalization

Capitalizing Sentences, Quotations, and Salutations	
Rule	**Example**
A capital letter appears at the beginning of a sentence.	**A**nother gust of wind shook the house.
A capital letter marks the beginning of a direct quotation that is a complete sentence.	Sabrina said, "**T**he lights might go out."
When a quoted sentence is interrupted by explanatory words, such as *she said,* do not begin the second part of the sentence with a capital letter.	"There's a rainbow," exclaimed Jeffrey, "**o**ver the whole beach."
When the second part of a quotation is a new sentence, put a period after the explanatory words; begin the new part with a capital letter.	"Please come inside," Justin said. "**W**ipe your feet."
Do not capitalize an indirect quotation.	Jo said that **t**he storm was getting worse.
Capitalize the first word in the salutation and closing of a letter. Capitalize the title and name of the person addressed.	**D**ear **D**r. **M**enino **D**ear **E**ditor **S**incerely

Capitalizing Names and Titles of People	
Rule	**Example**
Capitalize the names of people and the initials that stand for their names.	**M**alcolm **X** **J. F. K.** **R**obert **E**. Lee **Q**ueen **E**lizabeth I
Capitalize a title or an abbreviation of a title when it comes before a person's name or when it is used in direct address.	**D**r. **S**alinas "Your patient, **D**octor, is waiting."
Do not capitalize a title that follows or is a substitute for a person's name.	Marcia Salinas is a good **d**octor. He asked to speak to the **d**octor.

Rule	Example
Capitalize the names and abbreviations of academic degrees that follow a person's name. Capitalize *Jr.* and *Sr.*	Marcia Salinas, **M.D.** Raoul Tobias, **A**ttorney Donald Bruns **Sr.** Ann Lee, **Ph.D.**
Capitalize words that show family relationships when used as titles or as substitutes for a person's name.	We saw **U**ncle Carlos. She read a book about **M**other **T**eresa.
Do not capitalize words that show family relationships when they follow a possessive noun or pronoun.	Your **b**rother will give us a ride. I forgot my **m**other's phone number.
Always capitalize the pronoun *I*.	After **I** clean my room, **I**'m going swimming.

Capitalizing Names of Places

Rule	Example
Rule of Thumb Do not capitalize articles and prepositions in proper nouns: *the Rock of Gibraltar, the Statue of Liberty*	
Capitalize the names of cities, counties, states, countries, and continents.	**S**t. **L**ouis, **M**issouri **M**arin **C**ounty **A**ustralia **S**outh **A**merica
Capitalize the names of bodies of water and other geographical features.	the **G**reat **L**akes **C**ape **C**od the **D**ust **B**owl
Capitalize the names of sections of a country and regions of the world.	**E**ast **A**sia **N**ew **E**ngland the **P**acific **R**im the **M**idwest
Capitalize compass points when they refer to a specific section of a country.	the **N**orthwest the **S**outh
Do not capitalize compass points when they indicate direction.	Canada is **n**orth of the United States.
Do not capitalize adjectives indicating direction.	**w**estern Utah
Capitalize the names of streets and highways.	**D**orchester **A**venue **R**oute 22
Capitalize the names of buildings, bridges, monuments, and other structures.	**W**orld **T**rade **C**enter **C**hesapeake **B**ay **B**ridge

LANGUAGE HANDBOOK R35

Capitalizing Other Proper Nouns and Adjectives

Rule	Example
Capitalize the names of clubs, organizations, businesses, institutions, and political parties.	Houston Oilers the Food and Drug Administration Boys and Girls Club
Capitalize brand names but not the nouns following them.	Zippo brand energy bar
Capitalize the names of days of the week, months, and holidays.	Saturday June Thanksgiving Day
Do not capitalize the names of seasons.	winter, spring, summer, fall
Capitalize the first word, the last word, and all important words in the title of a book, play, short story, poem, essay, article, film, television series, song, magazine, newspaper, and chapter of a book.	*Not Without Laughter* *World Book Encyclopedia* "Jingle Bells" *Star Wars* Chapter 12
Capitalize the names of ethnic groups, nationalities, and languages.	Latino Japanese European Spanish
Capitalize proper adjectives that are formed from the names of ethnic groups and nationalities.	Shetland pony Jewish holiday

Punctuation

Using the Period and Other End Marks

Rule	Example
Use a period at the end of a declarative sentence.	My great-grandfather fought in the Mexican Revolution.
Use a period at the end of an imperative sentence that does not express strong feeling.	Please set the table.
Use a question mark at the end of an interrogative sentence.	How did your sneakers get so muddy?
Use an exclamation point at the end of an exclamatory sentence or a strong imperative.	How exciting the play was! Watch out!

Using Commas

Rule	Example
Use commas to separate three or more items in a series.	The canary eats bird seed, fruit, and suet.
Use commas to show a pause after an introductory word and to set off names used in direct address.	Yes, I offered to take care of her canary this weekend. Please, Stella, can I borrow your nail polish?
Use a comma after two or more introductory prepositional phrases or when the comma is needed to make the meaning clear. A comma is not needed after a single, short prepositional phrase, but it is acceptable to use one.	From the back of the balcony, we had a lousy view of the stage. After the movie we walked home. (no comma needed)
Use a comma after an introductory participle and an introductory participial phrase.	Whistling and moaning, the wind shook the little house.
Use commas to set off words that interrupt the flow of thought in a sentence.	Tomorrow, I think, our projects are due.
Use a comma after conjunctive adverbs such as *however, moreover, furthermore, nevertheless,* and *therefore.*	The skating rink is crowded on Saturday; however, it's the only time I can go.
Use commas to set off an appositive if it is not essential to the meaning of a sentence.	Ben Wagner, a resident of Pittsfield, won the first round in the golf tournament.
Use a comma before *and, or,* or *but* when it joins main clauses.	We can buy our tickets now, or we can take a chance on buying them just before the show.
Use a comma after an introductory adverb clause.	Because I stayed up so late, I'm sleepy this morning.
In most cases, do not use a comma with an adverb clause that comes at the end of a sentence.	The picnic will be canceled unless the weather clears.
Use a comma or a pair of commas to set off an adjective clause that is not essential to the meaning of a sentence.	Tracy, who just moved here from Florida, has never seen snow before.
Do not use a comma or pair of commas to set off an essential clause from the rest of the sentence.	Anyone who signs up this month will get a discount.

Rule	Example
Use commas before and after the year when it is used with both the month and the day. If only the month and the year are given, do not use a comma.	On January 2, 1985, my parents moved to Dallas, Texas. I was born in May 1985.
Use commas before and after the name of a state or a country when it is used with the name of a city. Do not use a comma after the state if it is used with a ZIP code.	The area code for Concord, New Hampshire, is 603. Please forward my mail to 6 Madison Lane, Topsham, ME 04086
Use commas or a pair of commas to set off an abbreviated title or degree following a person's name.	The infirmary was founded by Elizabeth Blackwell, M.D., the first woman in the United States to earn a medical degree.
Use a comma or commas to set off *too* when *too* means "also."	We bought groceries for this week and for next week, too.
Use a comma or commas to set off a direct quotation.	"My nose," exclaimed Pinocchio, "is growing longer!"
Use a comma after the salutation of a friendly letter and after the closing of both a friendly and a business letter.	Dear Gary, Sincerely, Best regards,
Use a comma when necessary to prevent mis-reading of a sentence.	In math, solutions always elude me.

Using Semicolons and Colons

Rule	Example
Use a semicolon to join the parts of a compound sentence when a coordinating conjunction, such as *and, or, nor,* or *but,* is not used.	Don't be late for the dress rehearsal; it begins at 7 o'clock sharp.
Use a semicolon to join parts of a compound sentence when the main clauses are long and are subdivided by commas. Use a semicolon even if these clauses are already joined by a coordinating conjunction.	In the gray light of early morning, on a remote airstrip in the desert, two pilots prepared to fly on a dangerous mission; but accompanying them were a television camera crew, three newspaper reporters, and a congressman from their home state of Nebraska.

Rule	Example
Use a semicolon to separate main clauses joined by a conjunctive adverb. Be sure to use a comma after the conjunctive adverb.	We've been climbing all morning; therefore, we need a rest.
Use a colon to introduce a list of items that ends a sentence. Use a phrase such as *these, the following,* or *as follows* to signal that a list is coming.	Remember to bring the following items: a backpack, a bag lunch, sunscreen, and insect repellent.
Do not use a colon to introduce a list preceded by a verb or preposition.	Remember to bring a backpack, a bag lunch, sunscreen, and insect repellent. (No colon is used after *bring*.)
Use a colon to separate the hour and the minutes when you write the time of day.	My Spanish class starts at 9:15.
Use a colon after the salutation of a business letter.	Dear Dr. Coulombe: To the Personnel Dept.:

Using Quotation Marks and Italics	
Rule	**Example**
Use quotation marks before and after a direct quotation.	"Curiouser and curiouser," said Alice.
Use quotation marks with both parts of a divided quotation.	"This gymnastics trick," explained Amanda, "took me three months to learn."
Use a comma or commas to separate a phrase such as *she said* from the quotation itself. Place the comma that precedes the phrase inside the closing quotation marks.	"I will be late for my appointment," said the cable technician.
Place a period that ends a quotation inside the closing quotation marks.	Scott said, "Thanks for letting me borrow your camping tent."
Place a question mark or an exclamation point inside the quotation marks when it is part of the quotation.	"Why is the door of your snake's cage open?" asked my mother.

Rule	Example
Place a question mark or an exclamation point outside the quotation marks when it is part of the entire sentence.	How I love "The Pit and the Pendulum"!
Use quotation marks for the title of a short story, essay, poem, song, magazine or newspaper article, or book chapter.	short story: "The Necklace" poem: "The Fish" article: "Fifty Things to Make from Bottlecaps"
Use italics or underlining for the title of a book, play, film, television series, magazine, newspaper, or work of art.	book: *To Kill a Mockingbird* magazine: *The New Republic* painting: *Sunflowers*
Use italics or underlining for the names of ships, trains, airplanes, and spacecraft.	ship: *Mayflower* airplane: *Air Force One*

Using Apostrophes

Rule	Example
Use an apostrophe and an -*s* ('*s*) to form the possessive of a singular noun.	my brother**'s** rock collection Chris**'s** hat
Use an apostrophe and an -*s* ('*s*) to form the possessive of a plural noun that does not end in -*s*.	the geese**'s** feathers the oxen**'s** domestication

Rule of Thumb

If a thing is jointly owned by two or more individuals, only the last name needs an apostrophe: *Mom and Dad's car.* If the ownership is not joint, each name needs an apostrophe: *Mom's and Dad's parents are coming for Thanksgiving.*

Rule	Example
Use an apostrophe alone to form the possessive of a plural noun that ends in -*s*.	the animal**s'** habitat the instrument**s'** sound
Use an apostrophe and an -*s* ('*s*) to form the possessive of an indefinite pronoun.	everyone**'s** homework someone**'s** homework
Do not use an apostrophe in a possessive pronoun.	The dog knocked over **its** dish. **Yours** is the best entry in the contest. One of these drawings must be **hers.**

Rule	Example
Use an apostrophe to replace letters that have been omitted in a contraction.	it + is = it**'s** can + not = can**'t** I + have = I**'ve**
Use an apostrophe to form the plural of letters, figures, and words when they are used as themselves.	Write three *7***'s.** The word is spelled with two *m***'s.** The sentence contains three *and***'s.**
Use an apostrophe to show missing numbers in a year.	the class of **'02**

Using Hyphens, Dashes, and Parentheses

Rule	Example
Use a hyphen to show the division of a word at the end of a line. Always divide the word between its syllables.	With the new recycling pro- gram, more residents are recycling their trash.

Rule of Thumb

One-letter divisions are not permissible. Proper nouns should not be divided.

Rule	Example
Use a hyphen in compound numbers.	He sold forty-six ice creams in one hour.
Use a hyphen in a fraction that is used as a modifier. Do not use a hyphen in a fraction used as a noun.	We won the vote by a two-thirds majority. Two thirds of the votes have been counted.
Use a hyphen or hyphens in certain compound nouns.	great-grandmother merry-go-round
Hyphenate a compound modifier only when it precedes the word it modifies.	A well-known musician visited our school. The story was well written.
Use a hyphen after the prefixes *all-, ex-,* and *self-* when they are joined to any noun or adjective.	all-star ex-president self-conscious
Use a hyphen to separate any prefix from a word that begins with a capital letter.	un-American mid-January

Rule	Example
Use a dash or dashes to show a sudden break or change in thought or speech.	Daniel—he's kind of a pest—is my youngest cousin.
Use parentheses to set off words that define or helpfully explain a word in the sentence.	The transverse flute (transverse means "sideways") is a wind instrument.

Abbreviations

Rule	Example
Abbreviate the titles *Mr., Mrs., Ms.,* and *Dr.* before a person's name. Also abbreviate any professional or academic degree that follows a name, along with the titles *Jr.* and *Sr.*	**Dr.** Stanley Livingston (doctor) Luisa Mendez, **M.A.** (Master of Arts)
Use capital letters and no periods with abbreviations that are pronounced letter by letter or as words. Exceptions are *U.S.* and *Washington, D.C.,* which do use periods.	**NAACP** National Association for the Advancement of Colored People **UFO** unidentified flying object **MADD** Mothers Against Driving Drunk
With exact times use *A.M.* (*ante meridiem,* "before noon") and *P.M.* (*post meridiem,* "after noon"). For years use *B.C.* (before Christ) and, sometimes, *A.D.* (*anno Domini,* "in the year of the lord," after Christ).	8:15 **A.M.** 6:55 **P.M.** 5000 **B.C.** **A.D.** 235
Abbreviate days and months only in charts and lists.	School will be closed on **Sept.** 3 **Nov.** 11 **Nov.** 27
In scientific writing abbreviate units of measure. Use periods with English units but not with metric units.	inch(es) **in.** yard(s) **yd.** meter(s) **m** milliliter(s) **ml**
On envelopes only, abbreviate street names and state names. In general text, spell out street names and state names.	Ms. Karen Holmes 347 Grandville **St.** Tilton, **NH** 03276 Karen lives on Grandville **Street** in Tilton, **New Hampshire.**

Writing Numbers

Rule	Example
In charts and tables, always write numbers as numerals. Other rules apply to numbers not in charts or tables.	Student Test Scores Student Test **1** Test **2** Test **3** Lai, W. **82** **89** **94** Ostos, A. **78** **90** **86**
Spell out numbers that you write in one or two words.	We carried enough supplies for **twenty-three** days.
Use numerals for numbers of more than two words.	The tallest mountain in Mexico rises **17,520** feet.
Spell out any number that begins a sentence, or reword the sentence so that it does not begin with a number.	**One hundred forty-three** days later the baby elephant was born. The baby elephant was born **143** days later.
Write very large numbers as a numeral followed by the word *million* or *billion*.	There are **15 million** people living in or near Mexico City.
If related numbers appear in the same sentence, use all numerals.	There are **365** days in the year, but only **52** weekends.
Spell out ordinal numbers (*first, second,* and so forth).	Welcome to our **fifteenth** annual convention.
Use words to express the time of day unless you are writing the exact time or using the abbreviation *A.M.* or *P.M.*	My guitar lesson is at **five o'clock**. It ends by 5:45 **P.M.**
Use numerals to express dates, house and street numbers, apartment and room numbers, telephone numbers, page numbers, amounts of money of more than two words, and percentages. Write out the word *percent*.	August **5, 1999** **9** Davio Dr. Apartment **9**F **24 percent**

Spelling

The following rules, examples, and exceptions can help you master the spelling of many words.

Spelling *ie* and *ei*

Put *i* before *e* except when both letters follow *c* or when both letters are pronounced together as an **a** sound.

believe	sieve	weight
receive	relieve	neighborhood

It is helpful to memorize exceptions to this rule. Exceptions include the following words: *species, science, weird, either, seize, leisure,* and *protein.*

Spelling unstressed vowels

Notice the vowel sound in the second syllable of the word *won-d_r-ful.* This is the unstressed vowel sound; dictionary respellings use the schwa symbol (ə) to indicate it. Because any of several vowels can be used to spell this sound, you might find yourself uncertain about which vowel to use. To spell words with unstressed vowels, try thinking of a related word in which the syllable containing the vowel sound is stressed.

Unknown Spelling	Related Word	Word Spelled Correctly
wond_rful	wonder	wonderful
fort_fications	fortify	fortifications
res_dent	reside	resident

Suffixes and the silent *e*

For most words with silent *e,* keep the *e* when adding a suffix. When you add the suffix *-ly* to a word that ends in *l* plus silent *e,* drop the *-le.* Also drop the silent *e* when you add a suffix beginning with a vowel or a *y.*

wise + ly = wisely	peaceful + ly = peacefully
skate + ing = skating	gentle + ly = gently

There are exceptions to the rule, including the following:

awe + ful = awful	judge + ment = judgment
true + ly = truly	noise + y = noisy
dye + ing = dyeing	mile + age = mileage

Suffixes and the final *y*

When you are adding a suffix to words ending with a vowel + *y*, keep the *y*. For words ending with a consonant + *y*, change the *y* to *i* unless the suffix begins with *i*. To avoid having two *i*'s together, keep the *y*.

enjoy + ment = enjoyment   merry + ment = merriment
display + ed = displayed   lazy + ness= laziness
play + ful = playful   worry + ing = worrying

Note: For some words, there are alternate spellings:

sly + er = slyer *or* slier
shy + est = shyest *or* shiest

Adding prefixes

When you add a prefix to a word, do not change the spelling of the word.

un + done = undone   re + schedule = reschedule
il + legible = illegible   semi + sweet = semisweet

Doubling the final consonant

Double the final consonant when a word ends with a single consonant following one vowel and the word is one syllable, or when the last syllable of the word is accented both before and after adding the suffix.

sit + ing = sitting   rub + ing = rubbing
commit + ed = committed   confer + ed = conferred

Do not double the final consonant if the suffix begins with a consonant, if the accent is not on the last syllable, or if the accent moves when the suffix is added.

cancel + ing = canceling   commit + ment = commitment
travel + ed = traveled   defer + ence = deference

Do not double the final consonant if the word ends in two consonants or if the suffix begins with a consonant.

climb + er = climber   nervous + ness = nervousness
import + ance = importance   star + dom = stardom

When adding -*ly* to a word that ends in *ll*, drop one *l*.

hill + ly = hilly   full + ly = fully

Forming Plurals

GENERAL RULES FOR PLURALS		
If the noun ends in	**Rule**	**Example**
s, ch, sh, x or z	add -es	loss, losses latch, latches box, boxes bush, bushes quiz, quizzes
a consonant + y	change y to i and add -es	ferry, ferries baby, babies worry, worries
a vowel + y	add -s	chimney, chimneys monkey, monkeys toy, toys
a vowel + o	add -s	cameo, cameos radio, radios rodeo, rodeos
a consonant + o	add -es but sometimes add -s	potato, potatoes echo, echoes photo, photos solo, solos
f or ff	add -s but sometimes change f to v and add -es	proof, proofs bluff, bluffs sheaf, sheaves thief, thieves hoof, hooves
lf	change f to v and add -es	calf, calves half, halves loaf, loaves
fe	change f to v and add -s	knife, knives life, lives

SPECIAL RULES FOR PLURALS

Rule	Example
To form the plural of most proper names and one-word compound nouns, follow the general rules for plurals.	Jones, Joneses Thomas, Thomases Hatch, Hatches
To form the plural of hyphenated compound nouns or compound nouns of more than one word, make the most important word plural.	credit card, credit cards mother-in-law, mothers-in-law district attorney, district attorneys
Some nouns have irregular plural forms and do not follow any rules.	man, men foot, feet tooth, teeth
Some nouns have the same singular and plural forms	deer, deer species, species sheep, sheep

Forming compound words

When forming compound words, keep the original spelling of both words.

home + work = homework
scare + crow = scarecrow
pea + nut = peanut

Writing Handbook

The Writing Process

The writing process consists of five stages: *prewriting, drafting, revising, editing/proofreading,* and *publishing/presenting.* By following the stages in order, you can turn your ideas into polished pieces of writing. Most writers take their writing through all five stages, and repeat stages when necessary.

The Writing Process

Prewriting

Prewriting is the process of gathering and organizing your ideas. It begins whenever you start to consider what you will write about or what will interest your readers. Try keeping a small notebook with you for several days and using it to jot down possible topics. Consult the chart below for tips on using the prewriting techniques, known as listing, questioning, and clustering.

Listing	Questioning	Clustering
List as many ideas as you can—whatever comes into your head on a particular subject. This is called brainstorming. Then go back over the list and circle the ideas you like best. Eventually you'll hit on an idea you can use.	If your audience is your classmates, ask yourself questions such as the following: *What do my friends like to learn about? What do my friends like to read about? What have I done that my friends might like to hear about?*	Write your topic in the middle of a piece of paper. Organize related ideas around the topic in a cluster of circles, with lines showing how the ideas are related. Clustering can help you decide which part of a topic to write about.

When you have selected your topic, organize your ideas around the topic. Identify your main ideas and supporting ideas. Each main idea needs examples or facts to support it. Then write a plan for what you want to say. The plan might be an organized list or outline. It does not have to use complete sentences.

Drafting

Drafting is the stage that turns your list into sentences and paragraphs. Use your prewriting notes to remember what you want to say. Begin by writing an introduction that gets the reader's attention. Move ahead through the topic, paragraph by paragraph. Let your words flow. This is the time to express yourself or try out a new idea. Don't worry about mistakes in spelling and grammar; you can correct them later. If you get stuck, try one of the tricks below.

Tips for drafting

- Work on the easiest part first. You don't have to begin at the beginning.
- Make a diagram, sketch, or drawing of the topic.
- Focus on just one sentence or paragraph at a time.
- Freewrite your thoughts and images. You can organize them later.
- Pretend that you are writing to a friend.
- Ask more questions about your topic.
- Speak your ideas into a tape recorder.
- Take a break. Take a walk or listen to music. Return to your writing later.

Revising

The goal of revising is to make your writing clearer and more interesting. When you revise, look at the whole piece of writing. Ask whether the parts go together smoothly and whether anything should be added or deleted. You may decide to organize the draft in a different way. Some writers make several revisions before they are satisfied.

☑ Did I stick to my topic?

☑ Did I accomplish my purpose?

☑ Did I keep my audience in mind?

☑ Does my main idea come across clearly?

☑ Do all the details support the main idea?

☑ Did I give enough information? too much?

☑ Did I use transition words such as *first, then* and *next* to make my sentences flow smoothly?

WRITING HANDBOOK R49

- Step back. If you have the time, set your draft aside for a while. When you look at it again, you may see it from a new point of view. You may notice that some information is missing or that part of the paper is disorganized.
- Read your paper aloud. Listen carefully as you read your paper aloud. How does it sound?
- Have a writing conference with a peer reviewer, one of your friends or classmates. A second opinion helps. Your reader can offer a fresh point of view.

Peer review

You can direct peer responses in one or more of the following ways.

- Ask readers to tell you what they have read in their own words. If you do not hear your ideas restated, revise your writing for clarity.
- Ask readers to tell you the part they liked best and why. You may want to expand those parts.
- Repeat what the readers have told you in your own words. Ask the readers if you have understood their suggestions.
- Discuss your writing with your readers. Listen to their suggestions carefully.

As you confer, make notes of your reviewers' comments. Then revise your draft, using your own judgment and including what is helpful from your reviewers' comments.

Editing/Proofreading

When you are satisfied with the changes you've made, edit your revised draft. Replace dull, vague words with lively verbs and precise adjectives. Vary the length of your sentences. Take time to correct errors in spelling, grammar, capitalization, and punctuation. Refer to the Proofreading Checklist on page R139 and on the inside back cover of this book.

Editing for style

Use the following checklist:

☑ Have I avoided clichés?
☑ Have I avoided wordiness?
☑ Is the tone of my writing appropriate to my purpose?
☑ Have I made clear connections between ideas?
☑ Do my sentences and paragraphs flow smoothly?

Publishing/Presenting

Now your writing is ready for an audience. Make a clean, neat copy, and add your name and date. Check that the paper has a title. If you wish, enclose the paper in a folder or binder to give it a professional look. Hand it in to your teacher, or share it in one of the ways described below. When the paper is returned, keep it in your writing portfolio.

Ideas for presenting

- **Illustrations** A photograph, diagram, or drawing can convey helpful information.
- **Oral presentation** Almost any writing can be shared aloud. Try including music, slides, or a group oral reading.
- **Class book** A collection of class writing is a nice contribution to the school library.
- **Newspaper** Some schools have a school newspaper. Local newspapers often publish student writing, especially if it is about local people and events.
- **Literary magazine** Magazines such as *Cricket* and *Stone Soup* publish student writing. Some schools have a literary magazine that publishes student writing once or twice a year.
- **Bulletin board** A rotating display of student writing is an effective way to see what your classmates have written. Illustrations and photographs add interest.

Some writing, such as journal writing, is private and not intended for an audience. However, even if you don't share your paper, don't throw it away. It might contain ideas that you can use later.

Writing Modes

There are four different types, or modes, of writing—expository, descriptive, narrative, and persuasive. Each mode has its own purpose and characteristics.

Expository Writing

Expository writing communicates knowledge. It provides and explains information; it may also give general directions or step-by-step instructions on any activity.

☑ Is the opening paragraph interesting?

☑ Are my explanations accurate and complete? Is information clear and easy to read?

☑ Is information presented in a logical order?

☑ Does each paragraph have a main idea? Does all the information in the paragraph support the main idea?

☑ Does my essay have an introduction, a body, and a conclusion?

☑ Have I defined any unfamiliar terms?

☑ Are my comparisons clear and logical?

Kinds of expository writing

Expository writing covers a wide range of styles. The chart below describes some of the possibilities.

Kinds of Expository Writing	Examples
Give general instructions on how to do something.	Explain how to train for a cross-country race, how to arrange a surprise party, or how to avoid cleaning up your room.
Compare and contrast two things in an essay.	Compare two athletes or two sports, two fictional characters, two books or movies, two places, or two kinds of vacations.
Give step-by-step directions.	Give directions for building a model plane, making lemon meringue pie, or drawing on a computer screen.
Inform and explain how something works; show cause and effect in a chain of events.	Explain what causes sunspots, how plants grow in the desert, or why camels have a hump.
Write a report or essay.	Write a book report, a report on the Buddhist religion, or a report on a new wildlife center.

Descriptive Writing

Descriptive writing can make a person, place, or thing come to life. The scene described may be as unfamiliar and far away as the bottom of the sea or as familiar and close as the gym locker room. By presenting details that awaken the reader's senses, descriptive writing can help your readers see the world more clearly.

☑ Does my introduction identify the person or place that will be described?

☑ Are my details vivid? Are nouns and adjectives precise?

☑ Do all the details contribute to the same impression?

☑ Is it clear why this place or person is special?

☑ Are transitions clear? Do the paragraphs follow a logical order?

☑ Does each paragraph contain a main idea?

☑ Have I communicated a definite impression or mood?

Narrative Writing

Narrative writing tells a story, either real or fictional. It answers the question *What happened?* A well-written narrative holds the reader's attention by presenting interesting characters in a carefully ordered series of events.

☑ Does my first sentence get the reader's attention?

☑ Are the characters and setting introduced with enough detail?

☑ Does the story have a satisfactory conclusion?

☑ Are the events narrated in an order clear enough for the reader to follow?

☑ Are there places where dialogue should be added?

☑ Is my ending satisfying to the reader?

Persuasive Writing

Persuasive writing presents an opinion. Its goal is to make readers feel or think a certain way about a situation or an idea. The writer includes facts and opinions often designed to urge readers to take action. Good persuasive writing can sometimes be hard to resist.

☑ Is my main idea expressed in a clear statement?

☑ Have I presented good reasons to support my point of view?

☑ Have I supported my reasons with facts and opinions?

☑ Have I taken account of the opposing points of view?

☑ Have I addressed the interests of my audience?

☑ Have I ended with a strong closing statement?

Research Report Writing

When you write a research report, you explore a topic by gathering factual information from several different resources. Through your research, you develop a point of view or draw a conclusion. This point of view or conclusion becomes the main idea, or thesis, of your report.

Select a Topic

Because a research report usually takes time to prepare and write, your choice of topic is especially important. Follow these guidelines.

- Brainstorm a list of questions about a subject you would like to explore. Choose one that is neither too narrow nor too broad for the length of paper you will write. Use that question as your topic.
- Select a topic that genuinely interests you.
- Be sure you can find information on your topic from several different sources.

Do Research

Start by looking up your topic in an encyclopedia to find general information. Then find specific information in books, magazines, and newspapers, on CD-ROMs and the Internet, and from personal interviews when this seems appropriate. Use the computerized or card catalog in the library to locate books on your topic. Then search for up-to-date information in periodicals (magazines) or newspapers and from electronic sources, such as CD-ROMs or the Internet. If you need help in finding or using any of these resources, ask the librarian.

As you gather information, make sure each source you use relates closely to your topic. Also be sure that your source is reliable. Be extra careful if you are using information from the Internet. If you are not sure about the reliability of a source, consult the librarian or your teacher.

Make Source Cards

In a research report, you must document the source of your information. To keep track of your sources, write the author, title, publication information, and location of each source on a separate index card. Give each source card a number and write it in the upper right-hand corner. These cards will be useful for preparing a bibliography.

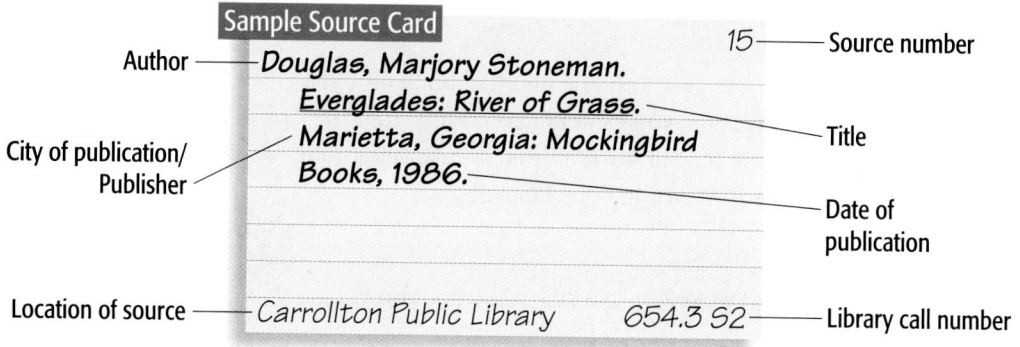

Sample Source Card

Author — **Douglas, Marjory Stoneman.**
Everglades: River of Grass.
Marietta, Georgia: Mockingbird
Books, 1986.

15 — Source number

Title

City of publication/Publisher

Date of publication

Location of source — *Carrollton Public Library* — 654.3 S2 — Library call number

Take Notes

As you read, you encounter many new facts and ideas. Taking notes will help you keep track of information and focus on the topic. Here are some helpful suggestions:

- Use a new card for each important piece of information. Separate cards will help you to organize your notes.
- At the top of each card, write a key word or phrase that tells you about the information. Also, write the number of the source you used.
- Write only details and ideas that relate to your topic.
- Summarize information in your own words.
- Write down a phrase or a quote only when the words are especially interesting or come from an important source. Enclose all quotes in quotation marks to make clear that the ideas belong to someone else.

This sample note card shows information to include.

Sample Note Card

Write a key word or phrase that tells you what the information is about. —

Functions of wetlands
Besides furnishing a home for a variety of wildlife, the wet, spongy soil of wetlands maintains the level of the water table. p. 79

15 — Write the source number from your source card.

Write the number of the page or pages on which you found the information.

Develop Your Thesis

As you begin researching and learning about your topic, think about the overall point you want to make. Write down a thesis statement, and keep it in mind as you continue your research. The thesis will help you determine what information is important. However, be prepared to change your thesis if the information you find does not support it.

WRITING HANDBOOK R55

WRITING HANDBOOK

R55

Write an Outline

When you finish taking notes, organize the information in an outline. Write down the main ideas that you want to cover. Write your thesis statement at the beginning of your outline. Then list the supporting details. Follow an outline form like the one below.

Sample Outline

Everglades National Park is a beautiful but endangered animal habitat.

  I. Special aspects of the Everglades

    A. Characteristics of wetlands

    B. Endangered birds and animals

 II. Pressures on the Everglades

    A. Florida agriculture

    B. Carelessness of visitors

III. How to protect the Everglades

    A. Change agricultural practices

    B. Educate visitors who come to the park

        1. Mandatory video on safety for individuals and environment

        2. Instructional reminders posted throughout the park

The thesis statement identifies your topic and the overall point you will make.

If you have subtopics under a main topic, there must be at least two. They must relate directly to your main topic.

If you wish to divide a subtopic, you must have at least two divisions. Each must relate to the subtopic above it.

Document Your Information

You must document, or show the source of, information you use in your paper. Only information that can be found in several widely available sources does not need to be documented. Place the source in parentheses immediately following its appearance in the text. If the author's name is given in the text, only the page number should be placed in parentheses. The chart that follows shows how to credit other sources. Additional information about the source should be placed in the list of sources at the end of the paper.

Types of Sources	How to Credit Source
Book with one author	(Knox 49)
Book with more than one author	(Chadwick and Sartore 18)
No author given	("Keystone Ride" 1)

Bibliography or Works Cited

At the end of your paper, list all the sources of information that you documented in your parenthetical notes. Arrange them alphabetically by the author's last name, as shown below. If no author is given, alphabetize according to the first word in the title. If your sources are all print media (books, magazines, newspapers), label your list *Bibliography.* If you used other media, such as on-line articles, videotapes, or interviews, label your list *Works Cited.*

Works Cited

Magazine article → Gore, Rick. "Neanderthals." National Geographic January 1996: 2–35.

Book with one author → Gould, Stephen J. The Panda's Thumb. New York: W. W. Norton & Co., 1982.

On-line article → "Governor Chiles Vetoes Anti-Everglades Bills–5/13/98." Friends of the Everglades. May 1998. 26 Aug 1998 <http://www.everglades.org/pressrel_may28.htm>.

Encyclopedia → "Neanderthal man." The Columbia Encyclopedia. 5th Edition. New York: Columbia University Press, 1993.

Interview → Pabst, Laura (Curator of Natural History Museum), Interview. March 11, 1998.

Indent all but the first line of each item.

Include page numbers for a magazine article but not for a book, unless the book is a collection of essays by different authors.

Include database (underlined), publication medium (on-line), computer service, and date of access.

Business Writing

Two standard formats for business letters are block style and modified block style. In block style all the parts of the letter begin at the left-hand margin.

The following business letter uses modified block style.

> 10 Pullman Lane
> Cromwell, CT 06416
> January 16, 1999
>
> Mr. Philip Fornaro
> Principal
> Cromwell School
> 179 West Maple St.
> Cromwell, CT 06416
>
> Dear Mr. Fornaro:
>
> My friends and I in the seventh grade at Brimmer Middle School feel that there is not enough to do in Cromwell during the winter vacation week. Some students can afford to go away for vacation. Many families, however, cannot afford to go away, or the parents have to work.
>
> I would like to suggest that you keep the Brimmer Middle School gym open during the vacation week. If the gym were open, the basketball teams could practice. The fencing club could meet. We could meet our friends there instead of going to the mall.
>
> Thanks for listening to my request. I hope you will think it over.
>
> Sincerely,
>
> *Kim Goodwin*
>
> Kim Goodwin

- In the heading, write your address and the date on separate lines.
- In the inside address, write the name and address of the person to whom you are sending the letter.
- Use a colon after the greeting.
- In Kim's introduction she lets Mr. Fornaro know who she is and why she is writing.
- In the body of her letter, Kim provides details concerning her request.
- Kim concludes by restating her purpose and thanking Mr. Fornaro.
- In the closing, use *Sincerely, Sincerely yours,* or *Yours truly* followed by a comma. Include both your signature and your printed or typed name.

General guidelines

Follow these guidelines when writing a business letter.

- Use correct business-letter form, as shown on page R58. Whether you write, type, or use a word processor, use 8½-by-11-inch white or off-white paper. Be sure your letter is neat and clean.
- Use Standard English. Check your spelling carefully.
- Be polite, even if you are making a complaint or expressing a negative opinion.
- Be brief and to the point. State your reason for writing within the first two or three sentences.
- Include all necessary information.
- If you are making a request, be specific. Make sure what you are asking is reasonable. Express your appreciation at the end of the letter.
- Be considerate. Request only information you cannot get another way.
- When expressing an opinion or a complaint, state your reasons clearly and logically. Avoid emotional language.
- When requesting an interview, make it easy for the interviewee to meet with you. Suggest a few dates.

Writing a Memo

A memo, or memorandum, is a brief, efficient way of communicating information to another person or group of people. It begins with a header that provides basic information. A memo does not have a formal closing.

TO: *Brimmer Banner* newspaper staff
FROM: Terry Glinski
SUBJECT: Winter issue
DATE: January 18, 1999

Articles for the winter issue of the *Brimmer Banner* are due by February 1. Please see Terry about your assignment as soon as possible! The following articles or features have not yet been assigned:

Cafeteria Mess: Who Is Responsible?
Teacher Profile: Mr. Jinks, Ms. Magee
Sports roundup

Communications Skills Handbook

Using a Computer for Writing

Using a computer to write offers advantages at every stage of the writing process.

Prewriting

A computer can help you gather and organize ideas and information.

Brainstorming

While brainstorming for topics or details, you can dim the computer screen and do "invisible writing." Some writers find that this technique allows their ideas to flow more freely.

Researching

CD-ROMs are disks that store large amounts of text, graphics, and sounds. If your computer has a CD-ROM player, you can use a CD-ROM encyclopedia to find not only text and pictures, but also sound, animated cartoons or graphics, and live-action video clips.

If you have a modem and are connected with an on-line service, you can access material from an on-line encyclopedia, magazine, or Web site.

Outlining

Some word-processing programs offer an outlining feature that automatically indents headings and uses different type styles for main headings and subheadings.

Drafting/Revising

Most word-processing programs make it easy to do the following.

- *insert* new text at any point in your document
- *delete* or *copy* text
- *move* text from one position to another
- *undo* a change you just made
- *save* each draft or revision of your document
- *print* copies of your work-in-progress for others to read

Editing/Proofreading

You can edit and proofread directly on the computer, or you can mark your changes on a printout, or hard copy, and then input the changes on screen. The following word-processing features are helpful.

- **Grammar checker** The computer finds possible errors in grammar and suggests revisions.
- **Spelling checker** The computer finds misspellings and suggests corrections.
- **Thesaurus** If you want to replace an inappropriate or overused word, you can highlight the word and the computer will suggest synonyms.
- **Search and replace** If you want to change or correct something that occurs several times in your document, the computer can quickly make the change throughout the document.

Rule of Thumb: The grammar checker, spelling checker, and thesaurus cannot replace your own careful reading and judgment. Because English grammar is so complex, the suggestions that the grammar checker makes may not be appropriate. Also, the spelling checker will not tell you that you have typed *brake* when you meant *break,* for example, because both are valid words. The thesaurus may offer you several synonyms for a word, but you need to consider the connotations of each before deciding which, if any, fits your context.

Presenting

The computer allows you to enhance the readability, attractiveness, and visual interest of your document in many ways.

Formatting your text

The computer gives you a variety of options for the layout and appearance of your text. You can easily add or change the following elements.

- margin width
- number of columns
- type size and style
- page numbering
- header or footer (information such as a title that appears at the top or bottom of every page)

Visual aids

Some word-processing programs have graphic functions that allow you to create graphs, charts, and diagrams. Collections of clip art, pictures you can copy and paste into your document, are also available.

COMMUNICATIONS SKILLS HANDBOOK R61

Study and Test-Taking Skills

Study Skills

Good study skills grow out of good habits. Try making the following suggestions part of your daily school routine. Write down each subject and each assignment daily in an assignment notebook. For each assignment, set a study goal. Decide how long it will take you to meet each goal. Divide long assignments into smaller tasks.

Tips for good study habits

- Keep an assignment notebook. Keep it up to date.
- Keep your notes for each course together in one place.
- Find a good place to study. Choose a place that has as few distractions as possible. Try to study in the same place each day.
- Try to study at the same time each day.
- Don't study one subject too long. If you haven't finished after thirty minutes, switch to another subject.
- Take notes on your reading. Keep your notes in one place.

Taking Tests

How well you perform on a test is not a matter of chance. Some specific strategies can help you answer test questions. This section of the handbook will show how to improve your test-taking skills.

Tips for preparing for tests

Here are some useful suggestions:

- Gather information about the test. When will it be given? How long will it take? Exactly what material will it cover?
- Review material from your textbook, class notes, homework, quizzes, and handouts. Review the study questions at the end of each section of a textbook. Try to define terms in boldface type.
- Make up some sample questions and answer them. As you skim selections, try to predict what may be asked.
- Draw charts and cluster or Venn diagrams to help you remember information and to picture how one piece of information relates to another.
- Give yourself plenty of time to study. Avoid cramming for a test. Several short review sessions are more effective than one long one.
- In addition to studying alone, study with a partner or small group. Quiz one another on topics you think the test will cover.

Tips for using test time

Try following these steps:

- Read all directions carefully. Understanding the directions can prevent mistakes.
- Ask for help if you have a question.
- Answer the easier items first. By skipping the hard items, you will have time to answer all the easy ones.
- In the time that is left, return to the items you skipped. Answer them as best you can. If you won't be penalized for doing so, guess at an answer.
- If possible, save some time at the end to check your answers.

Taking objective tests

An objective test is a test of factual information. The questions are usually either right or wrong; there is no difference of opinion. On an objective test, you are asked to recall information, not to present your ideas. Objective test questions include true-or-false items, multiple-choice items, fill-in-the-blanks statements, short-answer items, and matching items. At the beginning of an objective test, scan the number of items. Then budget your time.

Multiple-choice items Multiple-choice questions ask you to answer a question or complete a sentence. They are the kind of question you will encounter most often on objective tests. Read all the choices before answering. Pick the best response.

> What is a peninsula?
>   (a) a range of mountains
>   (b) a circle around the moon
>   (c) **a body of land surrounded by water on three sides**
>
> Correct answer: (c)

- Read the question carefully. Be sure that you understand it.
- Read all the answers before selecting one. Reading all of the responses is especially important when one of the choices is "all of the above" or "none of the above."
- Eliminate responses that are clearly incorrect. Focus on the responses that might be correct.
- Look for absolute words, such as *never, always, all, none.* Most generalizations have exceptions. Absolute statements are often incorrect. (Note: This tip applies to true/false items also.)

Answering essay questions

Essay questions ask you to think about what you have learned and to write about it in one or more paragraphs. Some tests present a choice of essay questions. If a test has both an objective part and an essay part, answer the objective questions first, but leave yourself enough time to work on the essay.

Read the essay question carefully. What does it ask you to do? Discuss? Explain? Define? Summarize? Compare and contrast? These key words tell what kind of information you must give in your answer.

Key Verbs in Essay Questions	
Argue	Give your opinion and supporting reasons.
Compare and contrast	Discuss likenesses and differences.
Define	Give details that show exactly what something is like.
Demonstrate	Give examples to support a point.
Describe	Present a picture with words.
Discuss	Show detailed information on a particular subject.
Explain	Give reasons.
Identify	Give specific characteristics.
List (also outline, trace)	Give details, give steps in order, give a time sequence.
Summarize	Give a short overview of the most important ideas or events.

Tips for answering essay questions

You might wish to consider the following suggestions:

- Read the question or questions carefully. Determine the kind of information required by the question.
- Plan your time. Do not spend too much time on one part of the essay.
- Make a list of what you want to cover.
- If you have time, make revisions and proofreading corrections.

Taking standardized tests

Standardized tests are taken by students all over the country. Your performance on the test is compared with the performance of other students at your grade level. There are many different kinds of standardized tests. Some measure your progress in such subjects as English, math, and science, while others measure how well you think. Standardized tests can show how you learn and what you do best.

Preparing for standardized tests

There is no way to know exactly what information will be on a standardized test, or even what topics will be covered. The best preparation is to do the best you can in your daily schoolwork. However, you can learn the *kinds* of questions that will appear on a standardized test. Some general tips will also help.

Tips for taking standardized tests

You might find the following suggestions helpful.

- Get enough sleep the night before the test. Eat a healthful breakfast.
- Arrive early for the test. Try to relax.
- Listen carefully to all test directions. Ask questions if you don't understand the directions.
- Complete easy questions first. Leave harder items for the end.
- Be sure your answers are in the right place on the answer sheet.
- If points are not subtracted for wrong answers, guess at questions that you aren't sure of.

Analogies Analogy items test your understanding of the relationships between things or ideas. On standardized tests, analogies are written in an abbreviated format, as shown below.

man : woman :: buck : doe

The symbol : means "is to"; the symbol :: means "as."

This chart shows some word relationships you might find in analogy tests.

Relationship	Definition	Example
Synonyms	Two words have a similar meaning.	huge : gigantic :: scared : afraid
Antonyms	Two words have opposite meanings.	bright : dull :: far : near
Use	Words name a user and something used.	farmer : tractor :: writer : computer
Cause-Effect	Words name a cause and its effect.	tickle : laugh :: polish : shine
Category	Words name a category and an item in it.	fish : tuna :: building : house
Description	Words name an item and a characteristic of it.	knife : sharp :: joke : funny

Listening, Speaking, and Viewing Skills

Listening Effectively

A large part of the school day is spent either listening or speaking to others. By becoming a better listener and speaker, you will know more about what is expected of you, and understand more about your audience.

Listening to instructions in class

Some of the most important listening in the school day involves listening to instructions. Use the following checklist to help you.

- First, make sure you understand what you are listening for. Are you receiving instructions for homework or for a test? What you listen for depends upon the type of instructions being given.
- Think about what you are hearing, and keep your eyes on the speaker. This will help you stay focused on the important points.
- Listen for key words, or word clues. Examples of word clues are phrases such as *above all, most important,* or *the three basic parts.* These clues help you identify important points that you should remember.
- Take notes on what you hear. Write down only the most important parts of the instructions.
- If you don't understand something, ask questions. Then, if you're still unsure about the instructions, repeat them aloud to your teacher to receive correction on any key points that you may have missed.

Interpreting nonverbal clues

Understanding nonverbal clues is part of effective listening. Nonverbal clues are everything you notice about a speaker *except* what the speaker says. As you listen, ask yourself these questions:

- Where and how is the speaker standing?
- Are some words spoken more loudly than others?
- Does the speaker make eye contact?
- Does he or she smile or look angry?
- What message is sent by the speaker's gestures and facial expression?

Speaking Effectively

- Speak slowly, clearly, and in a normal tone of voice. Raise your voice a bit, or use gestures to stress important points.
- Pause a few seconds after making an important point.
- Use words that help your audience picture what you're talking about. Visual aids such as pictures, graphs, charts, and maps can also help make your information clear.
- Stay in contact with your audience. Make sure your eyes move from person to person in the group you're addressing.

Speaking informally

Most oral communication is informal. When you speak casually with your friends, family, and neighbors, you use informal speech. Human relationships depend on this form of communication.

- Be courteous. Listen until the other person has finished speaking.
- Speak in a relaxed and spontaneous manner.
- Make eye contact with your listeners.
- Do not monopolize a conversation.
- When telling a story, show enthusiasm.
- When giving an announcement or directions, speak clearly and slowly. Check that your listeners understand the information.

Presenting an oral report

The steps in preparing an oral report are similar to the steps in the writing process. Complete each step carefully and you can be confident of presenting an effective oral report.

Steps in Preparing an Oral Report	
Prewriting	Determine your purpose and audience. Decide on a topic and narrow it.
Drafting	Make an outline. Fill in the supporting details. Write the report.
Revising and editing	Review your draft. Check the organization of ideas and details. Reword unclear statements.
Practicing	Practice the report aloud in front of a family member. Time the report. Ask for and accept advice.
Presenting	Relax in front of your audience. Make eye contact with your audience. Speak slowly and clearly.

COMMUNICATIONS SKILLS HANDBOOK R67

Viewing Effectively

Critical viewing means thinking about what you see while watching a TV program, newscast, film, or video. It requires paying attention to what you hear and see, and deciding whether information is true, false, or exaggerated. If the information *seems* to be true, try to determine whether it is based on a fact or an opinion.

Fact versus opinion

A fact is something that can be proved. An opinion is what someone *believes* is true. Opinions are based on feelings and experiences, but cannot be proved.

Television commercials, political speeches, and even the evening news contain both facts and opinions. They use emotional words and actions to persuade the viewer to agree with a particular point of view. They may also use faulty reasoning, such as linking the wrong cause and effect. Think through what is being said. The speaker may seem sincere, but do his or her reasons make sense? Are the reasons based on facts or on unfair generalizations?

Commercials contain both obvious and hidden messages. The obvious message is the spoken words of the commercial. The hidden message comes across in *how* the message is presented. Look carefully at commercials to see whether a product is really worth buying.

Working in Groups

Working in a group is an opportunity to learn from others. Whether you are planning a group project such as a class trip or solving a math problem, each person in a group brings specific strengths and interests to the task. When a task is large, such as planting a garden, a group provides the necessary energy and talent to get the job done.

Small groups vary in size according to the nature of the task. Three to five students is a good size for most small-group tasks. Your teacher might assign you to a group, or you might be asked to form your own group. Don't work with your best friend if you are likely to chat too much. Successful groups often have a mix of student abilities and interests.

Individual role assignments give everyone in a group something to do. One student, the group recorder, might take notes. Another might lead the discussion, and another report the results to the rest of the class.

Roles for a Small Group	
Reviewer	Reads or reviews the assignment and makes sure everyone understands it
Recorder 1 (of the process)	Takes notes on the discussion
Recorder 2 (of the results)	Takes notes on the final results
Reporter	Reports results to the rest of the class
Discussion leader	Asks questions to get the discussion going; keeps the group focused
Facilitator	Helps the group resolve disagreements and reach a compromise

For a small group of three or four students, some of these roles can be combined. Your teacher might assign a role to each student in your group. Or you might be asked to choose your own role.

Tips for working in groups

- Review the group assignment and goal. Be sure that everyone in the group understands the assignment.
- Review the amount of time allotted for the task. Decide how your group will organize its time.
- Check that all the group members understand their roles in the group.
- When a question arises, try to solve it as a group before asking a teacher for help.
- Listen to other points of view. Take turns during a discussion.
- When it is your turn to talk, address the subject, and help the project move forward.

Reading Handbook

The Reading Process

As reading materials get more difficult, you'll need to use a variety of active reading strategies to understand texts. This handbook is designed to help you find and use the tools you'll need before, during, and after reading.

Word Identification

Word identification skills are a necessary building block for understanding what you read. They prepare you to deal with unknown words you'll encounter as you read.

Look before, at, and after a new word. Use the other words and sentences around an unknown word to help you make an educated guess about what that word might be. Think about the following questions as you try to read new words.

- What other word would make sense in this sentence?
- Can I sound this new word out?
- Can I figure out this word from its place in the sentence?

Using letter-sound cues

One way to figure out a new word is to try to sound it out. Use the following tips when sounding out new words.

- Look at the beginning of the word. What letter or group of letters makes up the beginning sound or beginning syllable of the word?

  Example: In the word *coagulate, co-* looks like and rhymes with *so.*

- Look at the end of the word. What letter or group of letters makes up the ending sound or syllable? Knowing how a word begins and ends will help you take a better guess at the whole word.

  Example: In the word *coagulate, late* is a word you know.

- Look at the middle of the word. What are the sounds of the letters and groups of letters within the word? Is there a word you already know inside the new word? Is the middle of the word similar to other words you know? What vowel or vowel pattern is represented in each syllable?

Example: In the word *coagulate,* the syllable *ag* has the same vowel sound as *bag; u* is pronounced like the letter.

Now try pronouncing the whole word: *co ag u late.*

Using language structure cues

Word order, or **syntax,** helps you make sense of a sentence, so looking at the position of a new word in a sentence can help you identify a word. For instance, look at the following nonsense sentence.

The drazzy lurds miffled the bonkee blams.

Your experience with English sentence patterns and parts of speech tells you that the action word, or verb, in this sentence is *miffled.* Who did the *miffling?*–the *lurds.* What kind of *lurds* were they?–*drazzy.* Whom did they *miffle?*–the *blams.* What kind of blams were they?–*bonkee.* Even though you do not know word meanings in the nonsense sentence, you can make some sense of the entire sentence by using syntax.

Using context clues

When you read on your own, you can often figure out the meaning of a new word by looking at its **context,** the other words and sentences that surround it. For instance, look at the following example.

The area suffered an earthquake followed by a flood. After such *cataclysms,* it took some time to return to normal.

You can see from the first sentence that *cataclysms* refers to both an earthquake and a flood. It is a general word for violent change in the forces of nature. The context provides examples of the unknown word.

Tips for Using Context

- Look before, at, and after the unknown word for
  - a synonym or definition of the unknown word in a sentence.
    *To avoid a collision, the car **swerved,** or **turned aside.***
  - a clue to what the word is like or not like.
    ***Like a human top,** the little dancer **pirouetted** gracefully.*
  - a general topic associated with the word.
    *The **gardener** shoveled **mulch** onto all the flower beds.*
  - a description or action associated with the word.
    *The seamstress used **pinking shears** to **trim** the seams of the dress.*
- Connect what you know with what the author has written.
- Predict a possible meaning.
- Apply the meaning in the sentence.
- Try again if your guess does not make sense.

Using word parts to read new words

Noticing word parts can help you sound out unknown words. Look at some of the following word parts.

- **Roots** The base part of a word is called its root. If you know a root within a new word, start from there to sound out the rest of the word. *(speculate)*

- **Plurals** Many times nouns are changed from singular to plural by adding *-s, -es,* or *-ies.* Some nouns have irregular plurals *(ox, oxen).*

- **Comparative endings** The endings *-er* and *-est,* used for adjectives and adverbs, make comparisons *(abler, ablest).*

- **Inflectional endings** Other endings, such as *-ing* or *-ed,* can be important parts of both the meaning and pronunciation of a word *(strut, strutted, strutting).*

- **Prefixes** These syllables, added to the beginning of a word, change the meaning of the word. For example, *semi-* means "half," so *semicircle* means "half circle."

- **Suffixes** These syllables are added to the ends of words. For example, *-ful* means "full of," so *fearful* means "full of fear."

Using reference materials

When looking at or around an unknown word does not help you identify it, dictionaries, glossaries, and other reference sources can be useful tools.

A **dictionary** provides the pronunciation and literal meaning or meanings of a word. It may also give other forms of the word, its part of speech, alternate spellings, examples, synonyms, origins, and other useful information. Look at the dictionary entry below.

Pronunciation

Part of speech

Numbered definitions

Synonyms

Examples of use

Informal idiom

Origin

hap·pen (hap′ ən) *v.i.* **1.** to take place; occur: *The accident happened last week.* **2.** to be or occur by chance; take place without planning or apparent reason: *His birthday just happens to be the same day as mine.* **3.** to have the occasion or luck; chance: *I happened to be there at the right time.* **4.** to come or go by chance (with *along* or *by*). **5. to happen on** (or **upon**). to meet or find accidentally. **6. to happen to. a.** to be done to: befall: *Something terrible must have happened to the family.* **b.** to be the fate of; become of: *What ever happened to old-fashioned gallantry?* [Middle English *happenen* to befall, from *happen,* from *hap* chance. See HAP.]
Syn. 1. Happen, occur denote to take place. **Happen** is the more common word and means to come to pass with or without cause: *Those terrible traffic jams usually happen around Christmas.* **Occur** is slightly more formal and may be more specific in terms of place or event: *The accident occurred at the intersection.*

A **glossary** is a condensed dictionary within a specific text. It provides an alphabetical listing of words used within that text, together with their definitions and other information necessary to understand the word as it appears in the text. Look at the example below.

A

abolitionist a person who favors doing away with slavery (p. 416)

abstain to not take part in some activity, such as voting (p. 440)

abode a sun-dried mud brick used to build the homes of Native Americans (p. 31)

affirmative action an active effort to improve educational and employment opportunities for minority groups and women (p. 887)

affluence the state of having much wealth (p. 808)

airlift a system of transporting food and supplies by aircraft into an area otherwise impossible to reach (p. 777)

A **thesaurus** is a dictionary of synonyms and antonyms. It can be especially useful for choosing precise, descriptive language. Some thesauruses are available on CD-ROM and on the Internet.

Reading Fluency

Becoming an accomplished reader is like learning a sports skill or a musical instrument: the more you practice, the better you'll get. The more you read aloud, the less attention you will need to pay to sounding words out, and the more attention you can give to understanding the meaning in a selection.

Tips for Becoming a Fluent Reader

- Develop a good sight vocabulary.
- Practice reading aloud on independent level materials.
- Begin with a short, interesting passage.
- Reread the same passage aloud at least three times.
- As your reading sounds smoother, move on to a longer or slightly more difficult passage.

Reading in appropriate level materials

How do you decide if something is too easy, too hard, or just right for you to read? If you want to develop into a smooth, fluent reader, it is important to read regularly in materials that are easy for you. However, it is also important to grow as a strategic reader, and to do that, you will want to read materials that are challenging but manageable.

To decide what level of reading material is right for each reading task, look at the following chart:

Reading level	Definition/Criteria	When to use
Independent level	Fewer than 3 difficult words per 100 words read	On your own, anytime To practice smooth reading
Instructional level	Between 3 and 10 difficult words per 100 words read	With support from teacher, parent, or other more experienced reader To challenge yourself
Beyond instructional level	More than 10 difficult words per 100 words read	As material read to you by someone else To develop new vocabulary through listening

Adjusting reading rate—skimming, scanning, and careful reading

It is important to adjust your reading speed to suit your purposes and the task you face. When you read something for enjoyment you might read quickly. If you want to refresh your memory of a passage or get a quick impression of new material, skim the selection. **Skimming** is reading quickly over a piece of writing to find its main idea or to get a general overview of it. When you need to find a particular piece or type of information, scan the selection. In **scanning,** you run your eyes quickly over the material, looking only for key words or phrases that have to do with the information you seek.

When you read a chapter of a textbook filled with new concepts, when you follow complex written directions, or when you study for a test, read slowly, take notes, make a graphic organizer, and even reread passages in order to remember them later.

Look at the following models.

It was a perfect day at Bowen Lake. At noon the woods and the lake were warm in the sun. Seated on a rock at the top of a hill, the boy watched the scene below him. The lake was a mirror of glass, occasionally broken by a leaping fish or a swooping bird. Far across the lake, he could sometimes see a canoe gliding by. He felt at peace with himself and the world, absorbed in the magic of being alone with nature.

Osmosis is the tendency of a liquid, usually water, to flow through a semipermeable membrane that blocks the transport of salts or other solutes through it. Osmosis is a fundamental effect in all biological systems. When two volumes of liquid are separated by a semipermeable membrane, water will flow from the side of low solute concentration to the side of high solute concentration.

Which paragraph could you read more quickly? Why? What would you do to be sure you remembered the information in each paragraph?

Reading aloud

Reading out loud, alone or with others, can make a writer's work come to life and can be an enjoyable way of sharing a selection. Reading a complicated paragraph aloud can also be a powerful aid to understanding. Here are some suggestions for reading aloud:

- First, read the selection silently a number of times.
- Think about the best way to make the main ideas understandable to your listeners.
- Use pauses to separate complete thoughts, and be sure you observe all punctuation marks.
- Read carefully and clearly. Vary your speed and volume to reflect the important ideas in a passage.
- Use a lively voice. Emphasize important words and phrases to make the meaning clear.
- Practice difficult words and phrases until you've mastered them.
- Practice in front of another person if possible, or use a tape recorder to hear how you sound.

Reading silently

Be sure to avoid any distractions or interruptions when you read silently.

Tips for Sustained Silent Reading

- Be sure you're comfortable, but not too comfortable.
- Check your concentration regularly by asking yourself **questions** about the selection.
- **Summarize** what you've read from time to time.
- Use a **study guide** or **story map** while reading difficult passages.
- Make a **graphic organizer,** if necessary, to understand and remember important concepts or a sequence of events.
- Take regular breaks when you need them, and vary your reading rate with the demands of the text.

TRY THE STRATEGIES

With a partner, choose a selection from your text. Read the selection silently, adjusting your speed to the difficulty of the text. When both of you are finished, take turns asking questions to check your comprehension. Finally, choose a small section of the passage and take turns reading it aloud. Exchange suggestions about your oral reading.

Reading a Variety of Texts

Learn to read a wide range of materials for a variety of purposes. Throughout this textbook, you've read both classic and contemporary writing. From "Rip Van Winkle" to "The Scholarship Jacket," you have seen how a variety of selections broadens your knowledge and deepens your appreciation of people and cultures.

Reading varied sources

Strategic readers take advantage of a variety of sources for information and for entertainment. For instance, to create a detailed and interesting portrait of a famous person from your hometown or state, you might refer to sources like those listed below.

- **Textbooks** provide a basic foundation of information.
- **Letters, memos, speeches, newspapers,** and **magazines** add valuable information as well as personal perspectives.
- **Databases, library indexes,** and **Internet sites** often supply interesting information.
- **Novels, poems, plays,** and **anthologies,** or collections of literature, provide excellent opportunities to read for pleasure as well as to explore the ideas of a writer in a particular time.

Reading for various purposes

Active reading begins with thinking about a reason for reading. You may find that you have more than one purpose or that your purposes overlap. For instance, you might enjoy reading an intense and thrilling mystery and, at the same time, discover how police detectives work. The reading strategies you use to guide you through a text will depend on your purposes.

When your purpose for reading is

- **to be informed,** read slowly, take notes, construct a graphic organizer, reread, and review difficult sections.
- **to be entertained,** read at a faster rate.
- **to appreciate a writer's craft,** read simply to admire how well others write.
- **to discover models for your own writing,** look at other writers' works to help stimulate your own ideas.
- **to take action,** be sure you understand all facts and instructions.

TRY THE STRATEGIES

Choose a topic that interests you, and read about it in at least three different sources. Decide on some sort of action to take as a result of your reading. You may write a short report, give a speech, demonstrate how something works, or try to persuade your classmates to believe or do something. Make a short presentation to your class, explaining your purpose for reading and the value of each of your sources.

Vocabulary Development

Having a good vocabulary means more than just knowing the meanings of isolated words. It means knowing the larger concepts that surround those words. The very best way to build a good vocabulary is to read widely, listen carefully, and participate actively in discussions in which new words and concepts are used.

Listening

Books that may be just a little too hard for you to read on your own are often excellent choices as selections to be read aloud to you. They provide a good way to learn new vocabulary. "Read-alouds" also give you a model for your own future oral reading. As you hear new words, try to pay attention to their **context**—the words and ideas surrounding the unknown words. Try to guess at what meaning would make sense for new words. Many times you will guess accurately if you pay careful attention.

Using experience and prior knowledge

Because of your life experiences, you know certain things and understand the meanings of certain words and ideas. Those experiences, called **prior knowledge,** help you determine word meanings. For instance, if you have had experience using computers, you'll understand the following sentence.

> *She needed to clean her mouse in order to make her cursor move.*

Sometimes you'll need to look beyond the exact meaning of words in a selection and consider some of the following variations of language.

- **Idioms** An expression that has a meaning apart from the literal meaning of the words is called an idiom. If a comedian's jokes *bring down the house,* it means that he or she has made the audience applaud or laugh loudly. When someone is *stretching a point,* he or she is making an exception. In each case, combine the words with your own prior knowledge to interpret what the expression really means.
- **Multiple meanings** Words can have more than one meaning, so check the context to be sure the meaning you have chosen makes sense. Look at these examples:
  The **stops** on the organ were jammed, so the organist had to **stop** *playing.*
  Jay **spoke** *to his dad about the loose* **spoke** *on his bicycle wheel.*
- **Figurative language** Writers sometimes make comparisons by using figurative language, such as similes and metaphors. A **simile** uses *like* or *as* to compare two unlike things, while a **metaphor** compares two unlike things without using *like* or *as.*
  Simile: *Snow* **like** *small white feathers floated down from the sky.*
  Metaphor: *Her eyes were stars that sparkled at the good news.*
- **Analogies** A comparison based on the relationship between two things or ideas is called an analogy. Analogies sometimes are written like this: *carpenter : saw :: painter : brush.* To understand the analogy, try turning it into short identical sentences. For instance, *A carpenter uses a saw. A painter uses a brush.*

Clarifying meanings with reference aids

Sometimes meanings of words and phrases can remain unclear even after using context, drawing on your personal background, and listening carefully. In that case, look to other reference aids to help clarify the meanings and usage of difficult terms.

- **Thesauruses** and books of synonyms can clarify a word by listing other words that have similar meanings.
- **Dictionaries** will often be able to clear up word meanings because they provide a variety of definitions for a word and examples of

each definition in a sentence. You can often find the meaning of an idiom by looking in a dictionary under the main word in the phrase. Look at the idioms listed under the word *time*.

> **against time.** in an effort to finish within or before a certain time: *Police were working against time in their search for the hidden bomb.*
>
> **ahead of time.** before the time due or expected; early: *She arrived at the appointed place ahead of time.*
>
> **at the same time.** however; nevertheless.
>
> **at times.** sometimes; occasionally.
>
> **behind the times.** old-fashioned.
>
> **for the time being.** for the present; temporarily.
>
> **from time to time.** now and then; occasionally.
>
> **in good time. a.** at the proper time; within reasonable time. **b.** when or sooner than expected; quickly.
>
> **in no time.** almost instantly; very rapidly.
>
> **in time. a.** before it is too late. *Do you think we can get there in time for the first act?* **b.** in the course of time; eventually: *In time, all this will be forgotten.* **c.** in the correct or corresponding rhythm or tempo: *to clap in time to music.*
>
> **on time. a.** at the correct or appointed time; punctual or punctually. **b.** payable in installments over time.
>
> **time after time.** repeatedly. Also, **time and again.**
>
> **time out of mind.** longer than can be remembered.
>
> **to keep time.** to record time, as a clock.
>
> **to make time. a.** to move rapidly, as in attempting to recover lost time. **b.** *Slang.* to progress in gaining favor or acceptance, as in carrying on a flirtation.

- **Software** for a computer will often include reference materials that can clarify meanings and usage for difficult words.

Using word parts and origins to determine meaning

Another way to determine the meaning of a word is to take the word itself apart. If you understand the meaning of the **base,** or **root** part, of a word and also know the meanings of key syllables added either to the beginning or end of the base, you can usually figure out what a word means.

Word Part	Definition	Example
Root or base	the most basic part of a word means "lead together"	*ced* means "go"
Prefix	a syllable used before a root word to add to or change its meaning	*pre-* means "before" *precede* means "go before"
Suffix	a syllable used after a root word to add to or change its meaning	*ous* means "full of" *joyous* means "full of joy"

Word origins English contains many words based on roots from ancient languages like Greek and Latin. Having some knowledge of word derivations in either of these languages can help you determine meanings, pronunciations, and spellings in English. Look at the following examples.

Root	Meaning	Example
astro (Greek)	star	astronaut, astronomy, asterisk
ped (Latin)	foot	pedal, pedestrian
vid (Latin)	see	video, evidence
hydr (Greek)	water	hydrant, dehydrate

Affixes These syllables are added either to the beginning or end of a word. For example, the word *unusually* is made up of the root *usual* and the affixes *un-* and *-ly.* The prefix *un-* means "not." The suffix *-ly* means "in a particular manner." If you put them together, *unusually* means "not in the usual manner."

Using word meanings across subjects

Have you ever learned a new word and then noticed it in many different places and across many different subjects? The word may not mean exactly the same thing in each place, but you can often use what you know about a word meaning to help you interpret its meaning in a different context. Look at the following example from two different subjects:

Social studies: *Altitude is one of the **factors** affecting climate.*

Math: *The numbers 2 and 3 are **factors** of 6.*

A factor is something that contributes to something else, so in geography, altitude causes a climate to be warmer or cooler. In math, a factor is a number that can be multiplied by another number to produce a product.

When you learn vocabulary across subject areas, you may learn one of the following things.

- new meaning for a word you know
- new word for a concept or idea you know about
- new word for a completely new concept or idea

Listening to news stories and current events is a good way to increase your vocabulary. Actively discuss ideas as well as new vocabulary that you hear in news reports. Friends, teachers, and parents will have their own ideas about the subtle meanings of words, so careful listening will add to your vocabulary development. Look at the model below. Can you figure out the meaning of the italicized word in the first sentence of this news report?

> The President pledged to continue with his economic *agenda*, beginning with the reform of the Social Security Administration.

What strategies did you use to determine that *agenda* means "plan"? How could you use the word in another context?

TRY THE STRATEGIES

Find a science or social studies textbook that includes a list of key vocabulary at the beginning of a chapter. Use prior knowledge or word parts and origins to predict what the words might mean. Then read the passages where the words are located and use syntax or context to check or further refine the meanings you predicted.

Determining connotation and denotation

Determining special meanings of words is an important aid to understanding. Look at these two ways to distinguish between word meanings:

- Denotation A **denotation** expresses the literal, or dictionary, meaning of a word. A word may have more than one denotation, but all of its denotations will be listed in the dictionary.
- Connotation When a word has an implied meaning or association in addition to its dictionary meaning, it has a **connotation.** You may say that flowers have a *fragrance,* but that garbage has a *stench.* Both words have a denotation that means "smell," but *fragrance* has a pleasant connotation, while the word *stench* connotes something unpleasant.

Understanding historical influences of words

In addition to giving you word spellings, pronunciations, and meanings, a dictionary will give you the historical background of a word. Many English words have Greek, Latin, or Anglo-Saxon origins. The Earl of Sandwich devised a way of eating meat between two pieces of bread so he would not have to interrupt his card game for meals. Did you realize that the word *sandwich* originated from this historical fact? or that the *martial* in *martial arts* recalls the name of Mars, the Roman god of warfare?

Comprehension

The main job you have in reading is to understand what you have read. Using the best strategies at the right times will improve your understanding of what you are reading.

Previewing

Before you begin to read, it's helpful to **preview** a selection.

- **Look** at the title and the illustrations that are included.
- **Read** the headings, subheadings, and anything in bold letters.
- **Skim** the passage; that is, take a quick look at the whole thing.
- **Decide** what the author's purpose might be for writing.
- **Predict** what the selection will be about.
- **Set a purpose** for your own reading.

Using knowledge and experience to understand

Reading is an interactive process between you and a writer. Even the youngest child has a body of information and personal experiences that are important and uniquely his or her own. When you use your own knowledge and experience and combine it with the words on a page, you create meaning in a selection. Drawing on this personal background is called **activating prior knowledge.** As you read, ask yourself:

- What do I know about this **topic?**
- Have I been to places similar to the **setting** described by this writer?
- What **experiences** have I had that compare or contrast with what I am reading?
- What **characters** from life or literature remind me of the characters or narrator in the selection?

Establishing and adjusting purposes for reading

Think about these possible purposes that you might have for reading.

- to find out something
- to understand a process or an idea
- to interpret a writer's work and create meaning in a passage
- to enjoy a selection or be entertained by a story
- to solve problems or to perform a task

Each purpose allows for different active reading strategies. To find information for a report, you might skim an entire passage until you find the section you're looking for and then read more slowly. To understand new information, you might read slowly from beginning to end, or even reread passages that are unclear. To simply enjoy a piece of good writing, you may allow yourself to read quickly or slow yourself down to appreciate something beautifully written.

It's also important to be able to adjust your purposes as well as your strategies to get the most out of your reading.

Making and verifying predictions

As you read, take educated guesses about story events and outcomes. **Make predictions** before and during your reading. Using your prior knowledge and the information you have gathered in your preview, predict what you will learn or what might happen in a selection. Then, as you read, **adjust your prediction.** Finally, **verify your prediction.** Whether your original prediction is precisely accurate or not does not matter, but careful predictions and later verifications or adjustments, based on your reading, increase your understanding of a selection.

Monitoring and modifying reading strategies

No matter what your purposes for reading, your most important task is to understand what you have read. Ask yourself questions as you read. Monitor or check your understanding using the following strategies.

- **Summarize** what you read by answering *who, what, where, why,* and *when.*
- **Clarify** what you don't understand by careful rereading.
- **Question** important ideas and story elements.
- **Predict** what will happen next.
- **Evaluate** what you have read so far.

You might practice a strategy once or twice in an easy, entertaining selection, or after every paragraph in a nonfiction passage.

Tips for Monitoring Understanding

- **Reread.** If silently rereading a passage several times does not help, read it aloud. Observe punctuation marks, and slow your rate.
- **Map out the main thoughts or ideas.** A graphic organizer like a story map or Venn diagram can help get your thoughts on track.
- **Look for context clues.** Often a writer will include an example or a definition of a difficult word or idea somewhere in the surrounding sentences. Synonyms or antonyms also provide clues.
- **Ask questions.** Teachers, parents, and other classmates can shed light on difficult written passages.
- **Write comments** as well as questions on another piece of paper for later review or discussion.
- **Use reference aids.** Sometimes looking up one word is all it takes to clear up a difficult passage. Dictionaries, glossaries, thesauruses, and encyclopedias provide access to most information.

Visualizing

Creating pictures in your mind as you read is a powerful aid to understanding. According to your imagination and the text, what do characters look like? Can you picture the steps in a process when you read nonfiction? If you can visualize what you read, selections will be more vivid, and you'll recall them better later on. Be sure, though, that what you picture is accurately based on information from the text.

TRY THE STRATEGIES

During a time when your teacher is reading aloud to you, either from a piece of fiction or nonfiction, try sketching what you're hearing. If the selection is fiction, draw a character, setting, or action, based on text description. If the selection is nonfiction, see if you can draw the steps in a process or make a small diagram of the place or thing described. Compare your sketch with a partner and talk about similarities and differences. Go back to the text to adjust or verify your information.

Constructing graphic organizers

Graphic organizers help you draw a picture of what you're reading, so you can sort ideas out, clear up difficult passages, and remember important ideas in a selection. Look at the following examples of good graphic organizers and notice how they are used.

Web You can show a main idea and supporting details by using a web. Put the main idea in the middle circle and the supporting details in the surrounding circles. Notice how you might include other circles branching off from the detail circles. Use those for further information about your details.

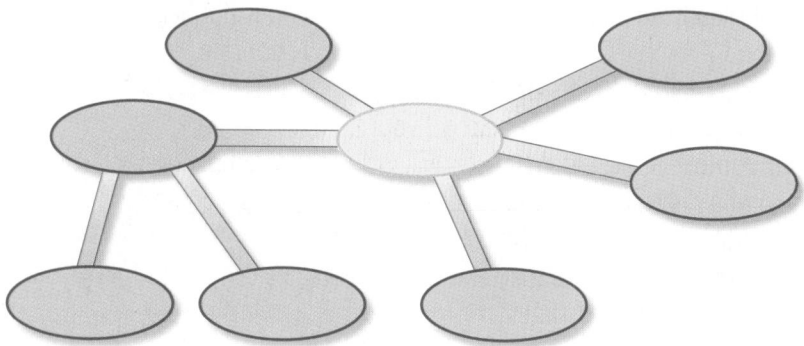

Flow chart When you want to keep track of events in a time order or show a cause-and-effect relationship between events, use a flow chart. Arrange your ideas or events in the boxes, putting them in their logical order. Then draw arrows between the boxes to show how one idea or event flows into another.

Venn diagram To look at the similarities and differences between two ideas, characters, or events, use a Venn diagram. The outer portions of each circle will show how two items contrast or are different. Use the overlapping portion of the circles to show how they are the same.

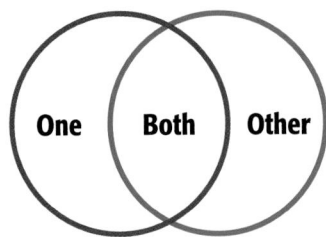

Using text structures

Writers organize their ideas in a variety of ways, depending on their topic and their purpose for writing. When you find that pattern of organization or **text structure** within a selection, it's easier to locate and recall a writer's ideas. Here are three ways that writers structure or organize text, together with word clues that characterize those text structures.

Kind of Organization	Purpose	Clues
Comparison and contrast	To determine similarities and differences	Words and phrases such as *similarly, on the other hand, in contrast to, but, however*
Cause and effect	To explore the reasons for something and to examine the results of events or actions	Words and phrases such as *so, because, as a result*
Chronological order	To present events in time order	Words and phrases such as *first, next, then, later, finally*
Problem/Solution	To examine how conflicts or obstacles are overcome	Words and phrases such as *need, attempt, help, obstruction*

Writers might use one text structure within another, but it is usually possible to figure out one main pattern of organization that will focus your attention on the important ideas in a selection. Look for **signal words,** the clues that lead you to the text structure. Read the two models below.

> Melissa carefully planned her experiment in baking. One Saturday morning, when everyone in the family had left for the day, she took out the recipe she had tucked away. First, she assembled the ingredients she would need for butterscotch cookies and carefully adjusted the oven to the required temperature. Next, she sprayed two baking sheets with nonstick vegetable oil. Then she prepared the batter and dropped it by teaspoonfuls onto the baking sheets. After setting the timer, she went into the living room to watch TV.

> For twelve hours, the snow fell steadily throughout the city. An army of snowplows and salt trucks were ready to roll, but because of the heavy snow, plowed streets were clogged an hour after they had been cleared. As soon as the snow stopped, subzero temperatures set in, causing the salting operation to have minimal results. Because of the difficulty in traveling, many plants and offices were closed. School was cancelled as well. The entire city was at a standstill.

What is the basic text structure of the first model? of the second? Explain how you determined your answers.

Determining main ideas and supporting details

The most important idea in a paragraph or passage is called the **main idea.** The examples or ideas that further explain the main idea are called **supporting details.** Some main ideas are clearly stated in sentences within a passage. Other times, without directly stating a main idea, an author will suggest it by providing a variety of clues.

Many times the main idea will be the first sentence of a paragraph, but not always. A main idea might be anywhere, even in the last sentence in a passage.

A selection can have a number of main ideas in it. Each paragraph might contain a main idea, as in most nonfiction, or entire passages can have a main idea, as in both fiction and nonfiction.

When you need to find the main idea, ask yourself these questions:

- What is each sentence about?
- Is there one sentence that tells about the whole passage or that is more important than the others?
- If the main idea is not directly stated, what main idea do the supporting details point out?

Finding the main ideas will help you understand a selection. Look at the following model.

Main idea —— **Hibernation is important for the survival of animals like the bear.** By going into hibernation—a dormant, sleep-like state—the bear can bypass winter. Bears would find it extremely difficult to find enough food when the temperatures grow cold. During hibernation Supporting details —— the bear cuddles up in a cave or in a hollowed-out tree, safe from the dangers of winter. In order to survive this long period of inactivity, the bear must build up its body weight by accumulating fat.

Sequencing

The order in which thoughts are arranged is called **sequence.** A good sequence is one that is logical, given the ideas in a selection. Here are three common forms of sequencing.

- **Chronological order**—time order
- **Spatial order**—the order in which things would be arranged within a certain space
- **Order of importance**—going from most important to least important or the other way around

Recognizing the sequence of something is very important when you have to follow **directions.** If you fail to follow steps in a certain order, you may not be able to accomplish your task.

READING HANDBOOK 🐾 R87

Paraphrasing

When you retell something using your own words you are **paraphrasing.** You might paraphrase just the main ideas of a selection or you might retell an entire story in your own words. Paraphrasing is a useful strategy for reviewing and for checking comprehension.

Original text: *The key to developing a healthy eating plan you can live with—one that you can easily incorporate into your daily life—is to discover your personal obstacles to healthy eating, and then to make one or two small changes at a time.*

Paraphrase: *To make healthy eating a regular part of your daily routine, change your unhealthy eating habits gradually.*

Summarizing

When you **summarize,** you relate the main ideas of a selection in a logical sequence and in your own words. To create a good summary, include all the main ideas and only essential supporting details.

A good summary can be easily understood by someone who has not read the whole selection. Look at the following model and summary.

The Dead Sea is not dead. It is not a sea, either. Even though the water of the Dead Sea is too salty for fish and other animals to live there, some microscopic organisms that use the sun to photosynthesize, and others from which petroleum can be made make the waters of the Dead Sea their home. This body of water is not a sea but is instead a salt lake. It has the lowest elevation of any place on earth. The water contains more salt and other minerals than any other body of water.

Summary: The Dead Sea, a salt lake, is the saltiest body of water in the world and the lowest place on earth. Even though fish and other animals cannot live there, microscopic plants call the Dead Sea home.

TRY THE STRATEGIES

Read "The Teacher Who Changed My Life" on page 368 of this book. On separate paper, list the main ideas in the selection. Under each main idea, list the supporting details that explain it. Use this information to write a one-paragraph summary of what you have read.

Drawing and supporting inferences

Writers don't always directly state what they want you to understand in a selection. By providing clues and interesting details, they suggest certain information. Whenever you combine those clues with your own background and knowledge, you are drawing an inference. An **inference** involves using your reason and experience to come up with an idea, based on what an author implies or suggests. The following active reading behaviors are examples of drawing an inference.

- Inferring You infer when you use context clues and your own knowledge to figure out what an author is suggesting.
- Predicting When you guess what a story will be about or what will happen next, you are drawing an inference.
- Drawing conclusions A conclusion is a general statement you can make and explain with reasoning or with supporting details from a selection.
- Generalizing When you draw an inference that can apply to more than one item or group, you are making a generalization.
- Classifying When you recognize something as fitting into a category, you classify it.

Finding similarities and differences across texts

As your reading takes you across a variety of sources, **compare and contrast** the things you've read. When you look for similarities and differences in your reading selections, you'll gain a better understanding of all the material you've read. Ask yourself in what ways sources might be alike or different. What is included in one selection that might be left out of another? Why might that be?

Here are some of the ways you can compare and contrast writers' works:

- Scope Take a broad look at each selection. How would you compare the time periods covered? How much information is given in each nonfiction selection? How many characters and settings are involved in fiction pieces? How extended is the entire selection?
- Treatment Look at how each writer presents important ideas. Who tells the story? Is the narrator's attitude serious or funny? How would you compare the writers' purposes? styles?
- Organization Compare selections in terms of how writers arrange their thoughts. Is a writer using **chronological order? comparing and contrasting? cause and effect? problem and solution?**

When you look for similarities and differences in what you've read, you'll learn to read more critically and get more out of each selection.

READING HANDBOOK R89

Distinguishing fact from opinion

When deciding whether to believe what a writer has written, you need to distinguish between fact and opinion. A **fact** is a statement that can be proved with supporting information. An **opinion,** on the other hand, is what a writer believes, based on his or her personal viewpoint. Writers can support their opinions with facts, but an opinion is something that cannot be proved. Look at the following examples of fact and opinion.

Fact: *New York State produces fruits and other agricultural products.*
Opinion: *New York is a wonderful place for a vacation.*

When interpreting anything you read, be sure that you distinguish between statements of fact and opinion.

Answering questions

Most of the time you'll need to answer questions about selections you've read. Look at the chart below to help you decide.

Type of question	What is it?	Example	How to find the answer
Literal	Has a definite answer	What color was Snow White's hair?	Look for direct statement in text.
Interpretive	Answer based on text and prior knowledge	Why was Snow White a threat to the queen?	Use text information and/or prior knowledge.
Open-ended	No right or wrong answer	Is Snow White a role model for girls today?	Use personal background and opinions.

You may find a different type of question on a test.

Tips for Answering Test Questions

- **True or false questions** If any part of a true or false question is false, the correct answer is "false."
- **Short answer** Use complete sentences so your responses will be clear. Try to put your thoughts in a logical sequence.
- **Multiple choice** First read all the responses. Eliminate the answers you know are incorrect. Choose the best remaining answer.

Representing text information

After you've read in various sources, you may need to reproduce what you have learned in a visual way, perhaps to present it to your class or to show the teacher that you have understood it.

- **Outlines** An **outline** is helpful if you are organizing information for a report. Roman numerals, together with upper- and lower-case letters show the basic structure of the report. Look at this sample model of a topic outline.

Each main topic is one of the big ideas of your subject. Suppose that your subject is surfing. The first main topic could be the history of surfing.

If you have subtopics under a main topic, there must be at least two. They must relate directly to the main topic.

I. Main topic

  A. First subtopic

    1. Division of a subtopic

    2. Division of a subtopic

  B. Second subtopic

If you wish to divide a subtopic, you must have at least two divisions. Each division must relate to the subtopic above it.

- **Time lines** A time line shows the chronological order of events over a period of time. Use a line to document the amount of time you want to cover. Add events above or below the line to show the order in which they occurred. Look at the example below.

The title shows the subject of the time line. It also may include the dates covered.

Space between events shows the amount of time that passed between them. Which two events came closest together?

Developments in Electronic Communication, 1844–1960

| 1850 | 1875 | 1900 | 1925 | 1950 |

1844 Telegraph — 1906 First voice message by radio — 1947 Transistor

1876 Telephone — 1877 Phonograph — 1895 Wireless telegraph (radio) — 1936 First TV broadcasts — 1960 First communications satellite

- **Graphic organizers** Word webs, flow charts, Venn diagrams, and other kinds of graphic organizers can help you present information in a visual way so that both you and your audience can easily see, understand, and remember what is presented.

Using study strategies

If you're preparing for a quiz or test or getting ready for a class presentation, you'll want to use a study strategy that helps you organize and remember the material you've read. Here are some useful strategies.

- Using story maps A **story map** can help you sort out important literary elements in works of fiction. Look at the model below to see how a story map works as a tool for review.

STORY MAP

Characters	Setting
Plot Conflict (problem)	**Plot** Resolution (solution)

- Using KWL **KWL** is a good way to keep track of what you are learning when you read informational text. Make three columns on a page. Label the first column *What I Know,* the second column *What I Want to Know,* and the third column *What I Learned.* Before reading, list the things you already know about a topic in the first column. List your questions in the second column. When you've finished reading, record what you've learned in the third column. You can add more columns to record places where you found information and places to look for more.

KWL

What I Know	What I Want to Know	What I Learned	Where I Got Information
			Where I Can Get More

- Using SQ3R A useful study strategy for studying subject areas like science or social studies is **SQ3R.** This stands for **s**urvey, **q**uestion, **r**ead, **r**ecord, and **r**eview. Here's how it works.
  1. **Survey** Take a quick look over the entire selection you need to study. Notice anything boldfaced. Look at any headings, subheadings, or pictures.
  2. **Question** Think of a number of questions you'll want to answer as you read.

3. **Read** Read the selection carefully. Vary your reading rate as you encounter easy or difficult passages.
4. **Record** Take notes about important ideas. Record your comments and any additional questions that come up as you read.
5. **Review** When you've finished reading, go back over the text once again to be sure you've understood important ideas. Add any other information you'll need to remember.

- Creating and using study guides Your teacher may provide you with a guide to focus your attention on important vocabulary and ideas, or you may create your own using end-of-chapter questions.

TRY THE STRATEGIES

Select a chapter from your social studies or science text. Use SQ3R as you read the material. Have a classmate quiz you by using end-of-chapter questions to see how well you remember what you studied.

Literary Response

Whenever you share your thoughts and feelings about something you've read, you are responding to text. You have your own learning style, so you will want to respond in ways that are comfortable for you. Some students learn best when speaking and writing, while others enjoy moving around or creating something artistic. Your responses can take a variety of forms. You can offer an observation, draw a connection to your life or to another work you've read, or question a character's actions or motives.

Tips for Responding to and Interpreting Literature

- **Discuss** what you have read, and share your views in active classroom discussions or at home.
- **Keep a journal** about what you read. Record your thoughts and feelings as well as what you've learned. Write down your impressions of a selection as well as questions you might have about it.
- **Take part in dramatizations, oral interpretations,** and **readers theater.** These activities can allow you to present characters through actions and dialogue and give you the opportunity to use your voice, facial expressions, and body language to convey meaning.
- **Tape record or videotape** your oral readings or dramatizations.

Supporting responses and interpretations

Whether you respond with your mind or with your emotions, you need to support your responses by going back to the text itself. Make sure you provide details from the author's work to back up your thoughts and feelings. It is not enough to say, "I really liked the main character." You must show what you liked about him or her. Look for specific descriptions and information. Ask yourself questions like these:

- What is interesting about this story's setting?
- What do I like or dislike about this character?
- How is the overall theme or idea expressed?
- What specific details account for my views about this selection?
- How have my own experiences and prior knowledge influenced my feelings in this selection?

Whenever you make a connection, or compare and contrast themes, ideas, and issues across texts, you need to support your thoughts with the writer's own words. If you can't provide adequate text proofs, you may need to rethink your response.

Identifying the purpose of a text

Authors have a variety of reasons for writing. They may simply want to **entertain** you. They may want to **inform** you about a topic. They may feel the need to **express** thoughts and emotions through a narrative or biographical essay. They also may want to **influence** your thinking so that you believe something or are motivated to act in a certain way. How can you tell what a writer's purpose is? To identify the purposes of different types of texts, use the following tips.

Tips for Identifying the Purpose of a Text

- **Look at word choices.** Authors select words according to their connotations, which carry emotional or implied meanings, as well as their denotations, or dictionary meanings. For example, a writer's opinion of a character called *bold* and *adventurous* is different from that of a character described as *weird* and *reckless*.
- **Consider the intended audience.** Most selections are written with an audience in mind. A speech at a pep rally might have a different purpose from one given before a committee of student council members.
- **Look at the structure of the text.** Writers use patterns of organization to clearly present their messages. By figuring out if a writer has used chronological order, comparison-and-contrast structure, or perhaps cause- and-effect structure, you can help determine his or her purpose.

Comparing elements across genres

Have you ever seen a movie or a television program that was based on a book you have read? How were they similar? How were they different? If you read the book *Sarah Plain and Tall* and then saw the made-for-TV movie, you might have noticed that some scenes were left out of the movie in order to make the story fit into a particular time frame. Some characters in movies are not represented precisely as they are described in books. As you look to see how the same story may vary across genres, look at similarities and differences in the following story elements:

- **Characters** Are all characters represented? Are some characters combined?
- **Settings** Is the setting presented similarly in each work? What differences affect the story as a whole?
- **Plot** How is the plot adjusted to fit the strengths and limitations of the genre?
- **Themes or ideas** Are important ideas well developed?
- **Author's point of view** Does the author's attitude affect how the story is told?
- **Author's purpose** Why is the author telling this story?
- **Author's style** What format and word choices are used?

Analyzing inductive and deductive reasoning

As you think about works you've read, ask yourself whether the reasoning behind an author's ideas are logical. Here are two kinds of logical reasoning writers use.

Inductive reasoning When you consider a certain number of examples a writer gives you, or if you can see a particular number of cases to illustrate a point or an idea, you may be able to arrive at a **generalization**— a conclusion or general statement—by using **inductive reasoning.** For instance, if the tulips your class planted on the shady side of your school building did not grow, there is never any grass on that side of the building, and a bush planted there last year still has no leaves, you can inductively reason that the shady side of your school building may not be the best place to plant things. This logic moves from the **specific** to the **general.**

Deductive reasoning When you take a general statement and apply it through reasoning to a number of specific situations, you are using **deductive reasoning**. For example, you know that plants do not grow well in shady places. Therefore, you can deductively reason that it might not be wise to plant tulips or expect grass to grow well on the shady side of a building. This logic moves from the **general** to the **specific**.

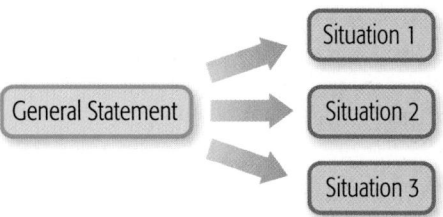

Inquiry and Research

Whenever you read to learn, you'll need to come up with interesting and useful questions. As you read in a variety of sources, you will think of new questions or revise the ones you started with to take into account new information. When you ask important questions and carefully research thorough answers, you will draw conclusions about your topic, and in the best situations, the process will lead you to other interesting questions and areas for further study.

Forming and revising questions

Finding an interesting and relevant question or topic is a very important first step in doing research and deserves your careful attention.

> **Tips for Asking Research Questions**
>
> - Think of a question or topic that interests you.
> - Choose a question that helps you focus on one main idea.
> - Be sure the question is not too broad or too narrow.
>   **Too broad:** *What can cause mummification?*
>   **Better:** *Why did the Egyptians mummify the remains of their Pharaohs?*

Using text organizers

Once you've found an interesting question to investigate, the next step is to locate and then organize information you find. Textbooks, references, magazines, and other sources use a variety of ways to help you find what you need quickly and efficiently.

- Tables of contents Look at a table of contents first to see whether a resource offers information you need.

- **Indexes** An index, found in the back of a book, is a more detailed, alphabetical listing of all people, places, events, and topics.
- **Headings and subheadings** The headings often identify the information that follows.
- **Graphic features** Photos, maps, graphs, and other graphic features can convey a large amount of information at a glance.

Using multiple sources for research

Any research you do will be more interesting and balanced when you include different types of sources. To find the most recent information, it may be necessary to use sources other than books. The following are some helpful resources for conducting research.

- **Print resources:** textbooks, magazines, reference books, and other specialized references
- **Nonprint information:** films, videos, and recorded interviews
- **Electronic texts:** CD-ROM encyclopedias and the Internet
- **Experts:** people who are specialists on the topic you have chosen

Interpreting graphic aids

When you're researching a topic, be sure to read and interpret the graphic aids included. **Graphic aids** let you see information at a glance.

Reading a map Maps are flat representations of land. A **compass rose** allows you to determine direction. A **legend** explains the map's symbols, and a **scale** shows you how the size of the map relates to the actual distances covered. Look at the map below.

Compass rose

The United States in 1824

Legend

Scale

Reading a graph Graphs show information pictorially. Graphs can use circles, dots, bars, or lines. It is very important to read and understand the labels. Look at the title and the labels on the bar graphs below. They compare types of crops produced in the South. Next, look at the labels along the bottom of the graphs. Each bar represents a different decade. The numbers along the side represent millions of pounds, bales, or bushels. Can you interpret the information?

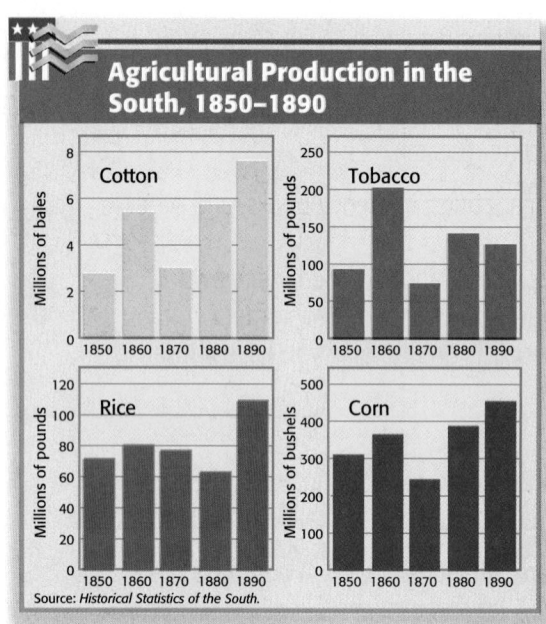

Agricultural Production in the South, 1850–1890

Source: *Historical Statistics of the South.*

Reading a table A table allows you to compare numbers or facts by putting them into categories. Look at the table below. Read the title first. You can read the table to find just one piece of information—for instance, how much per gallon gasoline cost in 1973—or you can compare the consumption of gasoline across the years. What other information can you gather from this table?

Gasoline Consumption and Prices

Year	Consumption (billions of gallons)	Cost per Gallon		
		Reg.	Prem.	No lead
1973	110.5	$.40	.45	NA
1974	106.3	.53	.57	.55
1975	109.0	.57	.61	.60
1976	115.7	.59	.64	.61
1977	119.6	.62	.67	.66
1978	125.1	.63	.69	.67
1979	122.1	.86	.92	.90
1980	115.0	1.19	1.28	1.25

Source: *Statistical Abstract of the United States.*

TRY THE STRATEGIES

Look in a current newspaper or newsmagazine to find an example of a chart, graph, or table. Explain the graphic aid briefly to the class, and analyze the information presented.

Organizing information

Now that you've read about your research topic in a variety of sources, how will you put it all together? Here are some suggestions.

- **Record** information on note cards. Use a new card for each main idea or important fact so you can organize and rearrange them.
- **Summarize** information before you write it on a card. That way you'll have the main ideas in your own words.
- **Outline ideas** by putting your note cards in order and creating a written outline so you can see how subtopics and supporting information will fit under the main ideas.
- **Make a table or graph** to compare items or categories of information.

Tips for Charting Information

- Decide what information you want your audience to see at a glance.
- Decide what kind of table or graph will best show the information you've chosen.
- Choose a title for your graphic aid, and label the categories horizontally and vertically.
- Check the accuracy of your information, and then plot it carefully.
- Use different colors, if possible, to distinguish between items.

Producing projects and reports

How should you present the information you've gathered? Before you decide, think about these questions.

- How can I briefly and clearly convey important information? What would best capture the attention of my audience?
- What graphic aids can I use to illustrate my main ideas?
- What pattern of organization would suit this information—chronological order? compare and contrast? cause-and-effect?
- Would an illustration or even a cartoon help to make a point?

When considering a format to use for your report, you might consider a **written** or an **oral report**, a **debate**, an **interview**, or a **dramatic** or **video presentation**. Ask yourself which format would most creatively and completely present your ideas.

Drawing conclusions and asking further questions

You will certainly form opinions about your topic after you've finished your research. A **conclusion** is a general statement that you'll make about what you have learned. Remember that you started your research with an important question, so your answer to that question may help to form your conclusion. In the best situations, a conclusion will lead you to other interesting questions and areas for further reading.

Explain your conclusions with good reasons and with supporting details from your sources. Read the following excerpts and the conclusion that follows. Then look at the question for further research.

> Ancient Egyptians are perhaps the best known mummy-makers—though initially, it was their climate, not their skill, that preserved the dead. Arid desert winds and blazing hot sand occasionally dried corpses out quickly enough to mummify them. In fact, the oldest-known Egyptian mummy, dated around 3500 B.C., is believed to have been created in this way.
>
> The first "artificial" Egyptian mummies were made around 3000 B.C. These early efforts at embalming were crude but reflected the culture's emerging beliefs about preserving the dead to achieve eternal life.

> He has delicate fingers and hugs his knees, one foot over the other, as if to keep warm. His hair is plaited in more than 200 braids, and miniature idols and keep-sakes accompany him in his frozen tomb. Dead for 500 years, this Inca sacrificial mummy found on Chile's El Plomo Peak has opened the door to further inquiry into the strange and mysterious ritual life of the Inca.

Conclusion: Ancient civilizations used various means of mummification, but mummification always seems to have been connected with ritual.

Question for further research: What can archaeologists learn about ancient civilizations from examining mummified remains?

Tips for Drawing Conclusions

- Don't try to twist the facts to support your ideas.
- Don't make statements that go beyond the facts you've gathered.
- Recognize that your conclusions might be different than you originally thought.
- Be sure to record accurately where you got your information.
- Never present ideas that aren't yours as your own.

Glossary

This glossary lists the vocabulary words found in the selections in this book. The definition given is for the word as it is used in the selection; you may wish to consult a dictionary for other meanings of these words. The key below is a guide to the pronunciation symbols used in each entry.

a	at	**ō**	hope	**ng**	sing
ā	ape	**ô**	fork, all	**th**	thin
ä	father	**oo**	wood, put	**th**	this
e	end	**ōo**	fool	**zh**	treasure
ē	me	**oi**	oil	**ə**	ago, taken, pencil,
i	it	**ou**	out		lemon, circus
ī	ice	**u**	up	**′**	indicates primary stress
o	hot	**ū**	use	**′**	indicates secondary stress

A

absurdity (ab sur′ də tē) *n.* the state of being ridiculous, senseless, or irrational; p. 567

accede (ək sēd′) *v.* to give in; go along with; p. 677

acutely (ə kūt′ lē) *adv.* sharply and with intensity; p. 493

aggrieved (ə grēvd′) *adj.* feeling wronged, as by an insult or unfair treatment; p. 666

agility (ə jil′ ə tē) *n.* quickness and ease in motion or thought; p. 282

agitated (aj′ ə tāt′ ed) *adj.* 1. upset; disturbed; p. 36. 2. excited, nervous, stirred up; p. 667

agony (ag′ ə nē) *n.* great pain and suffering of the mind or body; p. 745

amplify (am′ plə fī′) *v.* to increase; extend; p. 300

anguished (ang′ gwisht) *adj.* having or showing extreme mental or physical suffering; p. 286

antagonism (an tag′ ə niz′ əm) *n.* hostility; p. 511

anticipation (an tis′ ə pā′ shən) *n.* a feeling of excited expectation; p. 390

appalling (ə pô′ ling) *adj.* shocking; horrifying; p. 79

apparatus (ap′ ə rat′ əs) *n.* something created or invented for a particular purpose; p. 465

aptitude (ap′ tə tōod′) *n.* a natural ability; talent; p. 743

aroma (ə rō′ mə) *n.* a pleasant smell; odor; p. 708

artful (ärt′ fəl) *adj.* done with skill or cleverness; p. 565

ascertain (as′ ər tān′) *v.* to find out with certainty; determine; p. 413

assess (ə ses′) *v.* to determine the meaning or importance of; analyze; p. 222

authoritarian (ə thôr′ ə tār′ ē ən) *adj.* having or expecting complete obedience to authority; p. 369

avert (ə vurt′) *v.* to keep from happening; prevent; p. 401

avidly (av′ id lē) *adv.* eagerly; enthusiastically; p. 372

awe (ô) *n.* wonder combined with respect; p. 351

B

balmy (bä′ mē) *adj.* mild; soothing; p. 222

barrage (bə räzh′) *n.* a heavy concentration or great outpouring, as of words; p. 119

barren (bar′ ən) *adj.* having little or no plant life; bare; empty; p. 753

benefactor (ben′ ə fak′ tər) *n.* one who gives financial assistance; p. 584

bewildered (bi wil′ dərd) *adj.* very confused; p. 118

bleak (blēk) *adj.* cheerless; depressing; p. 164

boycott (boi′ kot) *n.* an organized protest in which the participants refuse to buy, sell, or use a product or service; p. 90

bravado (brə vä′ dō) *n.* a false show of bravery; p. 353

brink (bringk) *n.* the point at which something may begin; p. 282

brood (brōōd) *n.* all of the young of an animal that are born or cared for at the same time; p. 799

C

casually (kazh′ ōō əl lē) *adv.* in a relaxed, informal way; p. 362

chaotic (kā ot′ ik) *adj.* confused and disorganized; in great disorder; p. 8

charismatic (kar′ iz mat′ ik) *adj.* having personal qualities that enable one to inspire loyalty and devotion; p. 283

claim (klām) *v.* to ask for or demand possession of one's right to something; p. 721

clamor (klam′ ər) *n.* a loud, continuous noise; uproar; p. 79

clan (klan) *n.* a group of families descended from a common ancestor; p. 270

coincidence (kō in′ si dəns) *n.* an accidental occurrence of events, ideas, or circumstances at the same time, without one causing the other; p. 452

collaborator (kə lab′ ə rā′ tər) *n.* one who works or cooperates with another; p. 415

collective (kə lek′ tiv) *adj.* having to do with a group of persons or things; common; shared; p. 677

colossal (kə los′ əl) *adj.* extraordinarily or awesomely large; p. 754

commencement (kə mens′ mənt) *n.* a beginning; start; graduation ceremonies; p. 9

compact (kəm pakt′) *adj.* occupying a relatively small space or area; tightly packed; p. 306

compensate (kom′ pən sāt′) *v.* to make up for; balance in force, weight, or effect; p. 808

competent (kom′ pət ənt) *adj.* having enough ability for the purpose; capable; p. 577

comply (kəm plī′) *v.* to go along with a request; p. 86

comprehend (kom′ pri hend′) *v.* to grasp mentally; understand fully; p. 413

concede (kən sēd′) *v.* to admit to be true or proper; p. 221

conceive (kən sēv′) *v.* to form an image or idea of; p. 577

condemn (kən dem′) *v.* to express strong disapproval of; criticize sharply; p. 715

confront (kən frunt′) *v.* to come face to face with; stand facing; p. 416

consecutive (kən sek′ yə tiv) *adj.* following one after another in order without interruption; p. 27

consequence (kon′ sə kwens′) *n.* importance; significance; p. 464

consolation (kon′ sə lā shən) *n.* a comfort; p. 373

conspicuously (kən spik′ ū əs lē) *adv.* in a way that draws attention or is easily seen; p. 809

contemplate (kon′ təm plāt′) *v.* to give intense attention to; consider carefully; p. 296

converge (kən vurj′) *v.* to come together at a place; p. 299

cordially (kôr′ jəl lē) *adv.* in a genuinely warm and friendly way; p. 752

correspond (kôr ə spond′) *v.* to communicate by exchanging letters; p. 567

cower (kou′ ər) *v.* to crouch down, as in fear or shame; p. 792

culprit (kul′ prit) *n.* one guilty of some offense; p. 405

cunning (kun′ ing) *adj.* crafty; sly; p. 390

cynically (sin′ ə kəl lē) *adv.* in a way that shows doubt or disbelief; doubtfully; p. 547

D

deception (di sep′ shən) *n.* that which fools or misleads; p. 125

decree (di krē′) *n.* an official rule, order, or decision; p. 743

defiant (di fī′ ənt) *adj.* showing bold resistance to authority or an opponent; p. 511

degrade (di grād′) *v.* to lower in character or quality; make less pure; p. 828

delectable (di lek′ tə bəl) *adj.* highly pleasing or delightful, especially to the taste; delicious; p. 389

demise (di mīz′) *n.* death; end; p. 828

depleted (di plēt′ id) *adj.* greatly reduced in amount; p. 296

desolation (des′ ə lā′ shən) *n.* sadness; loneliness; p. 689

despair (di spār′) *n.* complete loss of hope; desperation; p. 708

desperation (des′ pə rā′ shən) *n.* distress caused by great need or loss of hope; p. 50

destine (des′ tin) *v.* to determine beforehand; p. 400

devastating (dev′ əs tāt ing) *adj.* causing great pain, damage, or destruction; overwhelming; p. 434

devise (di vīz′) *v.* to think out; invent; plan; p. 384

diligently (dil′ ə jənt lē) *adv.* in a way that shows great attention, care, and effort; p. 301

discern (di surn′) *v.* to detect or recognize; p. 492

discreetly (dis krēt′ lē) *adv.* in a manner showing good judgment; cautiously; p. 155

discrepancy (dis krep′ ən sē) *n.* a lack of agreement, as between facts; p. 28

dismally (diz′ məl lē) *adv.* in a gloomy, cheerless way; p. 567

dismay (dis mā′) *n.* a feeling of alarm or uneasiness; p. 453

dispense (dis pens′) *v.* to give out in portions; p. 385

distinct (dis tingkt′) *adj.* different in quality or kind; p. 285

divulge (di vulj′) *v.* to make known; give away; p. 38

domestic (də mes′ tik) *adj.* describes animals living with or near human beings and cared for by them; p. 828

E

eccentric (ik sen′ trik) *adj.* not usual or normal in behavior; peculiar; p. 578

ecology (ē kol′ ə jē) *n.* the relationship of living things to their environment and to each other; p. 309

ecstatic (ek stat′ ik) *adj.* overwhelmed with joy; p. 371

efficient (i fish′ ənt) *adj.* producing a desired effect with a minimum of effort or waste; p. 677

elaborate (i lab′ ər it) *adj.* worked out carefully and thoroughly; detailed; complicated; p. 829

elicit (i lis′ it) *v.* to draw forth or bring out; p. 29

eloquent (el′ ə kwənt) *adj.* expressive, effective, and stirring in speech or writing; p. 29

embrace (em brās′) *v.* to hug or hold in the arms, especially as a sign of love or affection; p. 275

emerge (i murj′) *v.* to come out; p. 52

emphatic (em fat′ ik) *adj.* strongly expressive; forceful; p. 361

endeavor (en dev′ ər) *n.* a serious attempt to accomplish something; undertaking; p. 404

endure (en door′) *v.* to put up with; undergo, as pain, stress, or other hardship; p. 238

enticing (en tīs′ ing) *adj.* offering pleasure or reward; p. 684

enviable (en′ vē ə bəl) *adj.* good enough to be highly desired; p. 685

envious (en′ vē əs) *adj.* having resentment over, and a wish to possess for oneself, something possessed by another; p. 716

esteem (es tēm′) *n.* favorable opinion; high regard; p. 29

etiquette (et′ i kit) *n.* the rules of good manners and polite behavior; p. 414

evacuate (i vak′ ū āt′) *v.* to leave or clear an area; p. 307

evading (i vād′ ing) *adj.* escaping or avoiding; p. 440

eventually (i ven′ choo ə lē) *adv.* in the end; finally; p. 153

exasperation (ig zas′ pə rā′ shən) *n.* anger or great irritation; p. 689

excavated (eks′ kə vāt′ əd) *adj.* uncovered or removed by digging; unearthed; p. 119

excess (ek′ ses) *adj.* more than usual or necessary; p. 149

exotic (ig zot′ ik) *adj.* strangely attractive; foreign; p. 8

explicit (eks plis′ it) *adj.* clearly expressed; p. 524

exploit (iks ploit′) *v.* to use or develop for profit, often in a selfish, unjust, or unfair way; p. 299

extricate (eks′ trə kāt′) *v.* to release from entanglement or difficulty; set free; p. 404

F

faltering (fôl′ tər ing) *adj.* shaky because of uncertainty; p. 199

fanciful (fan′ si fəl) *adj.* showing imagination in design or construction; imaginative; p. 753

fancy (fan′ sē) *v.* to picture mentally; imagine; p. 795

fixed (fikst) *adj.* steadily directed and unchanging; p. 708

flail (flāl) *v.* to wave or swing, especially swiftly or violently; p. 440

fleetest (flēt′ əst) *adj.* swiftest; fastest; p. 719

flinch (flinch) *v.* to draw back, as from something painful, dangerous, or unpleasant; p. 793

flourishing (flur′ ish ing) *adj.* growing or developing successfully; doing very well; p. 354

formidable (for′ mi də bəl) *adj.* causing fear or dread by reason of size, strength, or power; p. 69

fortitude (fôr tə tood′) *n.* firm courage or strength of mind in the face of pain or danger; p. 401

frail (frāl) *adj.* lacking in strength; weak; p. 463

frenzy (fren′ zē) *n.* a state of intense excitement or disturbance; p. 246

frustration (frus trā′ shən) *n.* disappointment or irritation at being kept from doing or achieving something; p. 777

G

gait (gāt) *n.* a particular manner of moving on foot; p. 793

gaunt (gônt) *adj.* looking like skin and bones; p. 237

giddy (gid′ dē) *adj.* dizzy or light-headed; p. 604

gnarled (närld) *adj.* rough, twisted, and knotty, as a tree trunk or branches; p. 702

grim (grim) *adj.* fierce; severe; stern; forbidding; p. 237

grimace (grim′ əs) *v.* to twist the face, as in pain or displeasure; p. 79

grudging (gruj′ ing) *adj.* given or allowed unwillingly or resentfully; p. 236

gruffly (gruf′ lē) *adv.* in a rough, stern manner; p. 239

H

habitual (hə bich′ oo əl) *adj.* done by habit; p. 565

haggard (hag′ ərd) *adj.* looking worn as a result of grief, worry, or illness; p. 666

hallowed (hal′ ōd) *adj.* regarded as sacred or holy; p. 717

hardy (här' dē) *adj.* able to endure hardship; strong and healthy; p. 155

hindrance (hin' drəns) *n.* something that holds back progress or movement; obstacle; p. 30

hostile (host' əl) *adj.* feeling or showing dislike; unfriendly; p. 808

hover (huv' ər) *v.* to remain as if suspended in the air over a particular spot; p. 745

humility (hū mil' ə tē) *n.* the quality of being humble or modest; p. 744

hurtle (hurt' əl) *v.* to move rapidly, especially with much force; p. 664

I

illuminated (i lōō' mə nāt id) *adj.* lit up; p. 152

immobilize (i mō' bə līz') *v.* to make unable to move; fix in place; p. 119

impetuous (im pech' ōō əs) *adj.* marked by force or violent action; p. 494

impose (im pōz') *v.* to apply legally; enforce; p. 100

impoverished (im pov' ər isht) *adj.* reduced to poverty; made very poor; p. 370

improbable (im prob' ə bəl) *adj.* not likely; p. 151

improvise (im' prə vīz') *v.* to invent, compose, or do without much preparation; p. 438

impulse (im' puls) *n.* an internal force that causes one to act without thinking; p. 50

impunity (im pū' nə tē) *n.* freedom from punishment, harm, or bad effects; p. 187

incessantly (in ses' ənt lē) *adv.* endlessly; constantly; p. 188

incomprehensible (in' kom prē hen' sə bəl) *adj.* not understandable; p. 191

inconvenience (in' kən vēn' yəns) *v.* to cause someone difficulty, bother, or hassle; p. 93

incredulous (in krej' ə ləs) *adj.* unwilling or unable to believe something; p. 170

incriminate (in krim' ə nāt') *v.* to show the guilt of; p. 515

indifferent (in dif' ər ənt) *adj.* having or showing a lack of feeling, concern, or care; p. 385

indignity (in dig' nə tē) *n.* an offense against one's pride or dignity; humiliation; p. 94

indiscriminately (in' dis krim' ə nit lē) *adv.* in a way that does not pay attention to differences; carelessly; p. 300

inert (i nurt') *adj.* without power to move or act; p. 352

inevitably (i nev' ə tə blē) *adv.* in a way that cannot be avoided or prevented; p. 7

infantile (in' fən tīl') *adj.* like an infant; childish; p. 413

infinite (in' fə nit) *adj.* boundless; limitless; extremely great; p. 177

initial (i nish' əl) *adj.* at the beginning; first; p. 7

initiative (i nish' ə tiv) *n.* the action of taking the first step; p. 476

insistent (in sis' tənt) *adj.* demanding attention or notice; p. 176

insolently (in' sə lənt lē) *adv.* in a boldly rude manner; p. 544

instill (in stil') *v.* to put in gradually, little by little; p. 510

instinct (in' stingkt) *n.* a way of knowing, behaving, or reacting that comes naturally rather than through learning; p. 167

intact (in takt') *adj.* undamaged and whole; p. 597

intellectual (int' əl ek' chōō əl) *adj.* appealing to or involving mental ability; p. 608

intense (in tens') *adj.* of a very high degree; very strong; p. 610

intently (in tent' lē) *adv.* in a firmly focused way; with concentration; p. 154

intimidated (in tim' ə dāt' əd) *adj.* made timid or fearful; bullied; p. 510

intricate (in' tri kit) *adj.* full of complicated detail; p. 565

intrusion (in trōō' zhən) *n.* a sudden interruption; p. 384

invalid (in' və lid) *n.* one who is disabled by disease or injury; p. 165

invariably (in vār' ē ə blē) *adv.* without exception; p. 194

ironically (ī ron' i kəl ē) *adv.* in a way that is different from what would be expected; p. 6

J

jeer (jēr) *v.* to make fun of (someone or something) rudely and openly; p. 684

jest (jest) *v.* to speak or act in a playful manner; joke; p. 596

jubilant (jōō′ bə lənt) *adj.* filled with great joy and excitement; high-spirited; p. 721

juncture (jungk′ chər) *n.* a critical point of time; p. 36

K

keen (kēn) *adj.* highly sensitive; sharp; p. 272

L

laden (lād′ ən) *adj.* loaded; weighed down; burdened; p. 386

lapse (laps) *n.* a slipping or falling away; p. 548

legitimate (li jit′ ə mit) *adj.* that which follows the rules; lawful; p. 517

lolling (lol′ ing) *adj.* hanging down loosely; drooping; p. 246

loom (lōōm) *v.* to appear to the mind as threatening; p. 222

lunge (lunj) *v.* to make a sudden forward movement; charge; p. 794

M

malicious (mə lish′ əs) *adj.* having or showing a desire to harm another; p. 484

maneuver (mə nōō′ vər) *v.* to move or handle skillfully, as into a position or toward a goal; p. 68

meek (mēk) *adj.* patient and mild in manner; gentle; p. 389

menace (men′ əs) *n.* a threat or danger; p. 68

merge (murj) *v.* to join together so as to become one; unite; p. 7

meticulously (mi tik′ yə ləs lē) *adv.* in a way that shows careful attention to details; p. 221

mobilize (mō′ bə līz′) *v.* to become prepared, as for war or an emergency; p. 91

moderately (mod′ ər it lē) *adv.* neither too great nor too small; within limits; p. 568

mortified (môr′ tə fīd′) *adj.* greatly embarrassed; p. 370

murky (mur′ kē) *adj.* dark; not clear; p. 414

muse (mūz) *v.* to think or reflect; p. 190

muster (mus′ tər) *v.* to find and gather together; collect; p. 453

N

naive (nä ēv′) *adj.* simple in nature; childlike; p. 37

narrative (nar′ ə tiv) *n.* story; storytelling; p. 37

negotiate (ni gō′ shē āt′) *v.* to discuss in order to bring about an agreement; p. 97

nimble (nim′ bəl) *adj.* light and quick in movement; p. 439

novelty (nov′ əl tē) *n.* anything new and unusual; p. 595

nurture (nur′ chər) *v.* to care for and help grow; p. 356

O

obligation (ob′ lə gā′ shən) *n.* a sense of duty; responsibility; p. 474

obligingly (ə blī′ jing lē) *adv.* helpfully; agreeably; p. 244

obnoxious (ob nok′ shəs) *adj.* annoying and disagreeable; p. 69

obscure (əb skyoor′) *adj.* difficult to understand; p. 350

obsessed (əb sesd′) *adj.* overly concentrated or focused on a single emotion or idea; p. 118

obsession (əb sesh′ ən) *n.* a single emotion or idea that occupies or troubles the mind; p. 414

obstinate (ob′ stə nit) *adj.* stubborn; difficult to overcome or control; p. 361

omen (ō′ mən) *n.* a sign or event thought to foretell good or bad fortune; p. 774

ominous (om′ ə nəs) *adj.* threatening harm or evil; p. 222

oppression (ə presh′ ən) *n.* the act of controlling or governing by the cruel and unjust use of force or authority; p. 95

overtake (ō′ vər tāk′) *v.* to catch up with or to reach and then pass; p. 708

P

painstaking (pānz′ tā′ king) *adj.* requiring close, careful labor or attention; p. 123

parched (pärcht) *adj.* severely in need of moisture; very dry; p. 717

passive (pas′ iv) *adj.* not participating or active; p. 166

perilous (per′ ə ləs) *adj.* dangerous; risky; p. 403

perpetual (pər pech′ o͞o əl) *adj.* constant; unceasing; p. 437

perplexity (pər plek′ sə tē) *n.* doubt or uncertainty; puzzlement; p. 194

perseverance (pur′ sə vēr′ əns) *n.* continuation despite difficulty; determination; p. 187

persistently (pər sis′ tənt lē) *adv.* repeatedly; p. 70

perspective (pər spek′ tiv) *n.* point of view; p. 370

pinnacle (pin′ ə kəl) *n.* a high point, or peak; p. 285

pious (pi′ əs) *adj.* having either genuine or pretended religious devotion; p. 385

plummet (plum′ it) *v.* to fall or drop straight downward; plunge; p. 296

podium (pō′ dē əm) *n.* a small, raised platform or stand with a slanted shelf for holding a speaker's papers; p. 728

pompous (pom′ pəs) *adj.* showing an exaggerated sense of self-importance; p. 385

portly (pôrt′ lē) *adj.* having a stout but dignified appearance; p. 369

possessively (pə zes′ iv lē) *adv.* in a way that shows ownership or control; p. 361

potion (pō′ shən) *n.* a drink, especially of a liquid that is supposed to have magical powers; p. 702

pounce (pouns) *v.* to swoop down, spring, or leap suddenly in attack; p. 729

precise (pri sīs′) *adj.* strictly accurate or clearly defined; exact; p. 605

predator (pred′ ə tər) *n.* an animal, such as a lion or hawk, that kills other animals for food; p. 125

prejudice (prej′ ə dis) *n.* an unfavorable opinion or judgment formed unfairly; p. 524

premonition (prē′ mə nish′ ən) *n.* a feeling that something is about to happen; warning or sign; p. 400

primly (prim′ lē) *adv.* in a formal and proper manner; p. 548

principle (prin′ sə pəl) *n.* a basic law, truth, or belief; rule of personal conduct; p. 354

proposition (prop′ ə zish′ ən) *n.* something offered for consideration; proposal; p. 573

prosperous (pros′ pər əs) *adj.* having wealth or good fortune; successful; p. 592

pursue (pər so͞o′) *v.* to chase; p. 273

Q

quavering (kwā′ vər ing) *adj.* trembling or shaking; p. 484

quench (kwench) *v.* to satisfy or put an end to a need or desire; p. 739

R

rash (rash) *adj.* done without thought or preparation; reckless; p. 738

raucous (rô′ kəs) *adj.* loud and rough-sounding; p. 544

ravenous (rav′ ə nəs) *adj.* extremely hungry; p. 390

rebuke (ri būk′) *n.* an expression of sharp criticism or disapproval; p. 578

reel (rēl) *v.* to turn or seem to turn round and round; whirl; p. 739

reflective (ri flek′ tiv) *adj.* showing serious and careful thinking; thoughtful; p. 507

reformation (ref′ ər mā′ shən) *n.* a change for the better; improvement; p. 547

regretfully (ri gret′ fəl lē) *adv.* in a way that shows sorrow, distress, or disappointment; p. 774

reluctantly (ri luk′ tənt lē) *adv.* unwillingly; p. 247

replenish (ri plen′ ish) *v.* to provide a new supply; p. 687

resigned (ri zīnd′) *adj.* giving in without resistance; p. 88

resilient (ri zil′ yənt) *adj.* capable of springing back into shape or position after being bent, stretched, or compressed; p. 465

resolute (rez′ ə lōōt′) *adj.* determined; stubborn; p. 348

resourceful (ri sôrs′ fəl) *adj.* capable or skillful in dealing with new or difficult situations; p. 727

retrieve (ri trēv′) *v.* to locate and bring back; recover; fetch; p. 50

ritual (rich′ ōō əl) *n.* an established form of doing something; ceremony; p. 37

robust (rō bust′) *adj.* strong and full of energy; p. 341

S

sanction (sangk′ shən) *v.* to give support or encouragement to; approve; p. 168

sanctuary (sangk′ chōō er′ ē) *n.* a place of safety or protection; p. 170

saunter (sôn′ tər) *v.* to walk in a relaxed way; p. 246

savor (sā′ vər) *v.* to take great delight in; p. 239

scavenger (skav′ in jər) *n.* an animal, such as a hyena or vulture, that feeds on dead, decaying animals; p. 125

scurry (skur′ ē) *v.* to run or move briskly or in an agitated way; p. 774

scuttle (skut′ əl) *v.* to move with short, rapid steps; p. 789

secretive (sē′ kri tiv) *adj.* keeping one's thoughts and feelings to oneself; p. 663

sedately (si dāt′ lē) *adv.* in a quiet, restrained style or manner; calmly; p. 239

sensation (sen sā′ shən) *n.* a cause of excitement or great interest; a wonder; p. 754

shrewd (shrōōd) *adj.* sharp, clever, and practical; p. 584

simultaneously (sī′ məl tā′ nē əs lē) *adv.* at the same time; p. 546

sinewy (sin′ ū ē) *adj.* physically tough, or powerful; p. 274

singularity (sing′ gyə lar′ ə tē) *n.* that which is remarkable or out of the ordinary; unusualness; p. 191

skimpy (skim′ pē) *adj.* lacking in quantity, fullness, or size; barely enough or not quite enough; p. 236

slither (sli<u>th</u>′ ər) *v.* to move along with a sliding or gliding motion, as a snake; p. 246

sluggish (slug′ ish) *adj.* lacking energy, liveliness, or alertness; p. 828

soberly (sō′ bər lē) *adv.* very seriously; p. 476

solemnly (sol′ əm lē) *adv.* seriously; p. 546

somberly (som′ bər lē) *adv.* in a gloomy manner; p. 490

sorcerer (sor′ sər ər) *n.* a person who practices magic with the aid of evil spirits; p. 701

spare (spār) *v.* to treat with mercy; hold back from harming or injuring; p. 274

spasm (spaz′ əm) *n.* a sudden uncontrollable tightening of a muscle; p. 243

specify (spes′ ə fī′) *v.* to state or describe in detail; p. 7

speculation (spek′ yə lā′ shən) *n.* the act of forming an opinion or conclusion based on guesswork; p. 150

spendthrift (spend′ thrift′) *n.* one who spends money generously or wastefully; p. 594

spite (spīt) *n.* a desire to hurt or annoy another person; p. 744

squander (skwon′ dər) *v.* to spend or use in a reckless or wasteful manner; p. 593

staccato (stə kä′ tō) *adj.* made of short, sharp sounds or movements; p. 362

staple (stā′ pəl) *adj.* important; main; p. 38

stark (stärk) *adv.* completely; harshly or grimly; p. 177

subsidize (sub′ sə dīz′) *v.* to aid or support with a contribution of money; p. 301

subtle (sut′ əl) *adj.* not open or direct; not obvious; p. 178

succeed (sək sēd′) *v.* to come or happen after in time, place, or order; p. 666

sufficient (sə fish′ ənt) *adj.* adequate; enough; p. 677

sullen (sul′ ən) *adj.* stubbornly withdrawn or gloomy; sulky; p. 45

surge (surj) *v.* to rise or increase suddenly; move with a violent swelling motion, as waves; p. 441

surly (sur′ le) *adj.* rude and bad tempered; gruff; p. 164

swagger (swag′ ər) *v.* to walk or behave in a bold, rude, or overly proud way; p. 45

T

tact (takt) *n.* the ability to handle people or situations without causing displeasure or resentment; p. 370

taunt (tônt) *v.* to make fun of in a scornful, insulting way; p. 701

taut (tôt) *adj.* stretched tight; p. 150

tentatively (ten′ tə tiv le) *adv.* hesitantly; uncertainly; p. 492

therapy (ther′ ə pē) *n.* treatment of an injury, disease, or mental disorder; p. 676

tumultuously (too mul′ choo əs le) *adv.* in a wildly excited, confused, or disturbed way; p. 465

U

ultimately (ul′ tə mit le) *adv.* in the end; finally; p. 369

uncanny (un kan′ e) *adj.* so strange as to cause fear or wonder; weird; p. 404

uncommitted (un′ kə mit′ id) *adj.* not having or showing a particular opinion, view, or course of action; p. 474

undermine (un′ dər mīn′) *v.* to weaken, wear away, or destroy slowly; p. 298

undertake (un′ dər tāk′) *v.* to enter into (a task); attempt; p. 829

undulating (un′ jə lāt′ ing) *adj.* moving in waves; rippling; p. 603

unique (ū nēk′) *adj.* highly uncommon; rare; one-of-a-kind; p. 309

unpalatable (un pal′ ə tə bəl) *adj.* not agreeable to the taste, mind, or feelings; unacceptable; p. 222

V

vaguely (vāg′ lē) *adv.* in a way that is not clear, exact, or definite; p. 7

vainly (vān′ lē) *adv.* without success; uselessly; p. 739

valiant (val′ yənt) *adj.* brave; courageous; p. 797

validity (və lid′ ə tē) *n.* state of being supported by facts; truth; p. 511

veer (vēr) *v.* to shift or change direction; p. 737

venture (ven′ chər) *v.* to do something in spite of possible risk or danger; p. 152

vigor (vig′ ər) *n.* strength and energy; p. 246

vile (vīl) *adj.* very bad; unpleasant; foul; p. 455

vital (vīt′ əl) *adj.* of primary importance; essential; p. 464

W

wary (wār′ ē) *adj.* cautious; on the alert; p. 437

waver (wā′ vər) *v.* to become unsteady; p. 738

wholeheartedly (hōl′ här′ tid lē) *adv.* completely; sincerely; enthusiastically; p. 68

wily (wī′ lē) *adj.* full of tricks; crafty; sly; p. 170

wince (wins) *v.* to draw back slightly, as in pain; p. 48

withdrawn (with drôn′) *adj.* shy, reserved, or unsociable; p. 454

woe (wō) *n.* great sadness or suffering; great trouble or misfortune; p. 474

Spanish Glossary

A

absurdity/absurdo s. cualidad de disparatado o ridículo; irracional; p. 567

accede/acceder v. aceptar; consentir; p. 677

acutely/agudamente adv. de modo punzante e intenso; p. 493

aggrieved/apesadumbrado adj. afligido o apenado, por ejemplo por un insulto o un trato injusto; p. 666

agility/agilidad s. rapidez y ligereza de movimiento o pensamiento; p. 282

agitated/agitado adj. 1. molesto; turbado; p. 36. 2. excitado; nervioso; trastornado; p. 667

agony/agonía s. gran dolor y sufrimiento mental o físico; p. 745

amplify/ampliar v. aumentar; extender; p. 300

anguished/angustiado adj. que siente o demuestra un gran sufrimiento mental o físico; p. 286

antagonism/antagonismo s. hostilidad; p. 511

anticipation/anticipación s. expectación; sensación de esperar algo con interés o ilusión; p. 390

appalling/pasmoso adj. impactante; horrorizante; p. 79

apparatus/aparato s. algo creado o inventado con un fin particular; p. 465

aptitude/aptitud s. habilidad natural; talento; p. 743

aroma/aroma s. olor agradable; fragancia; p. 708

artful/habilidoso adj. hecho con habilidad o ingenio; p. 565

ascertain/averiguar v. cerciorarse; comprobar; p. 413

assess/evaluar v. determinar el significado o la importancia de algo; analizar; p. 222

authoritarian/autoritario adj. que tiene o exige total obediencia a la autoridad; dominante; p. 369

avert/prevenir v. impedir que ocurra; evitar; p. 401

avidly/ávidamente adv. de modo intenso; ansiosamente; con mucho ánimo; p. 372

awe/veneración s. admiración combinada con respeto; p. 351

B

balmy/suave adj. balsámico; calmante; p. 222

barrage/descarga s. concentración o efusión grande, como de palabras; p. 119

barren/yermo adj. que tiene poca o ninguna vegetación; árido; vacío; p. 753

benefactor/benefactor s. quien brinda ayuda financiera; p. 584

bewildered/perplejo adj. muy confundido; p. 118

bleak/sombrío adj. triste; deprimente; p. 164

boycott/boicot s. protesta organizada en la que los participantes se niegan a comprar, vender o usar un producto o servicio; p. 90

bravado/bravuconería s. falsa demostración de valentía; p. 353

brink/margen s. borde; a punto de; p. 282

brood/camada s. crías de un animal que nacen a un mismo tiempo; p. 799

C

casually/casualmente adv. de modo informal o imprevisto; p. 362

chaotic/caótico adj. confuso y desorganizado; muy desarreglado; p. 8

charismatic/carismático adj. con cualidades personales que inspiran lealtad y admiración; p. 283

claim/reclamar v. solicitar o exigir la posesión o el derecho de algo; p. 721

clamor/algarabía *s.* ruido fuerte y continuo; griterío; p. 79

clan/clan *s.* grupo de familias descendientes de un antepasado común; p. 270

coincidence/coincidencia *s.* acontecimientos, circunstancias o ideas que ocurren al mismo tiempo por accidente; casualidad; p. 452

collaborator/colaborador *s.* alguien que trabaja o coopera con otro; p. 415

collective/colectivo *adj.* relativo a un grupo de personas o cosas; común; compartido; p. 677

colossal/colosal *adj.* extraordinaria o asombrosamente grande; p. 754

commencement/comienzo *s.* principio; ceremonia de graduación; p. 9

compact/compacto *adj.* que ocupa un espacio o área relativamente pequeño; macizo; p. 306

compensate/compensar *v.* dar algo a cambio; equilibrar en fuerza, peso o efecto; p. 808

competent/competente *adj.* que tiene suficiente habilidad para un fin concreto; capaz; p. 577

comply/acatar *v.* aceptar una solicitud; cumplir con algo; p. 86

comprehend/comprender *v.* captar mentalmente; entender por completo; p. 413

concede/conceder *v.* admitir que algo es cierto o apropiado; p. 221

conceive/concebir *v.* formarse una imagen o idea de algo; p. 577

condemn/condenar *v.* expresar total desacuerdo; criticar agudamente; p. 715

confront/confrontar *v.* encontrarse cara a cara; enfrentar; p. 416

consecutive/consecutivo *adj.* seguido uno de otro en orden y sin interrupción; p. 27

consequence/consecuencia *s.* importancia; significación; p. 464

consolation/consolación *s.* aliento; alivio; p. 373

conspicuously/conspicuamente *adv.* de modo que capta atención o notoriedad; p. 809

contemplate/contemplar *v.* prestar gran atención a algo; considerar cuidadosamente; p. 296

converge/converger *v.* reunirse en un lugar; p. 299

cordially/cordialmente *adv.* de modo cálido y amistoso; p. 752

correspond/cartearse *v.* comunicarse mediante cartas; p. 567

cower/encogerse *v.* agacharse, como cuando se siente miedo o vergüenza; p. 792

culprit/culpable *s.* el que ha cometido una ofensa; p. 405

cunning/astuto *adj.* vivo; engañoso; p. 390

cynically/cínicamente *adv.* de un modo que muestra duda o incertidumbre; dudosamente; p. 547

D

deception/engaño *s.* mentira o enredo; p. 125

decree/decreto *s.* regla, orden o decisión oficial; p. 743

defiant/desafiante *adj.* que se enfrenta atrevidamente a la autoridad o a un oponente; p. 511

degrade/degradar *v.* rebajar las características o la calidad; hacer menos puro; p. 828

delectable/deleitable *adj.* muy placentero o agradable, especialmente al gusto; delicioso; p. 389

demise/defunción *s.* muerte; fin; p. 828

depleted/disminuido *adj.* muy reducido en cantidad; p. 296

desolation/desolación *s.* tristeza; soledad; p. 689

despair/desesperanza *s.* pérdida total de la esperanza; desesperación; desconsuelo; p. 708

desperation/desesperación *s.* angustia causada por una gran necesidad o pérdida de la esperanza; p. 50

destine/destinar *v.* determinar con anticipación; asignar; p. 400

devastating/devastador *adj.* que causa gran dolor, daño o destrucción; abrumador; p. 434

devise/ingeniar *v.* pensar; inventar; planear; p. 384

diligently/diligentemente *adv.* de modo que muestra gran atención, cuidado y esfuerzo; p. 301

discern/discernir *v.* distinguir o reconocer; p. 492

discreetly/discretamente *adv.* de un modo sensato y cuidadoso; p. 155

discrepancy/discrepancia *s.* desacuerdo, como cuando dos hechos no concuerdan; p. 28

dismally/desconsoladamente *adv.* de un modo melancólico y triste; p. 567

dismay/consternación *s.* sentimiento de alarma o intranquilidad; p. 453

dispense/dispensar *v.* dar en porciones; distribuir; p. 385

distinct/distinto *adj.* diferente en calidad o tipo; p. 285

divulge/divulgar *v.* dar a conocer; emitir; p. 38

domestic/doméstico *adj.* relativo a los animales que conviven con los seres humanos; p. 828

E

eccentric/excéntrico *adj.* que no es común o normal en su comportamiento; peculiar; p. 578

ecology/ecología *s.* relación de los seres vivientes entre sí y con su medio ambiente; p. 309

ecstatic/extasiado *adj.* encantado; lleno de júbilo; p. 371

efficient/eficiente *adj.* que produce un efecto deseado con un mínimo de esfuerzo o gasto; p. 677

elaborate/elaborado *adj.* hecho con cuidado y esmero; detallado; complicado; p. 829

elicit/sacar *v.* revelar; p. 29

eloquent/elocuente *adj.* expresivo, efectivo y conmovedor, ya sea al hablar o escribir; p. 29

embrace/abrazar *v.* estrechar entre los brazos en demostración de amor o afecto; p. 275

emerge/emerger *v.* salir; surgir; brotar; p. 52

emphatic/enfático *adj.* que se expresa con intensidad o fuerza; p. 361

endeavor/empeño *s.* deseo intenso de hacer o lograr algo y tesón para alcanzarlo; p. 404

endure/soportar *v.* resistir o aguantar algo, como por ejemplo dolor, tensión u otra dificultad; p. 238

enticing/tentador *adj.* que ofrece placer o recompensa; p. 684

enviable/envidiable *adj.* suficientemente bueno como para que se desee mucho; ansiado; p. 685

envious/envidioso *adj.* que siente resentimiento por la suerte ajena o desearía algo que le pertenece a otra persona; p. 716

esteem/estima *s.* opinión favorable; aprecio; p. 29

etiquette/etiqueta *s.* normas de buenos modales y buena educación; p. 414

evacuate/evacuar *v.* despejar o limpiar un área; p. 307

evading/evasivo *adj.* que evita o escapa; p. 440

eventually/con el tiempo *adv.* al final; por último; p. 153

exasperation/exasperación *s.* rabia o gran irritación; p. 689

excavated/excavado *adj.* desenterrado o descubierto al cavar; p. 119

excess/exceso *adj.* más de lo usual o de lo necesario; p. 149

exotic/exótico *adj.* que tiene un atractivo extraño; foráneo; p. 8

explicit/explícito *adj.* expresado claramente; p. 524

exploit/explotar *v.* usar o aprovechar, a menudo de manera egoísta o injusta; p. 299

extricate/desembrollar *v.* sacar de un problema o dificultad; p. 404

F

faltering/titubeante *adj.* que muestra inseguridad, duda o vacilación; p. 199

fanciful/fantástico *adj.* con un diseño o construcción imaginativo y atrayente; p. 753

fancy/idear *v.* visualizar; imaginar; p. 795

fixed/fijo *adj.* asegurado; que no cambia; p. 708

flail/zarandear *v.* agitar o sacudir, especialmente de modo rápido o brusco; p. 440

fleetest/apresurado *adj.* el más rápido; el más veloz; p. 719

flinch/recular *v.* retroceder o echarse hacia atrás, ya sea por algo doloroso, peligroso o desagradable; p. 793

flourishing/floreciente *adj.* que crece o se desarrolla con éxito; que progresa; p. 354

formidable/formidable *adj.* que causa temor o asombro debido a su tamaño, fuerza o poder; p. 69

fortitude/fortaleza *s.* valor y tranquilidad ante el sufrimiento o el peligro; p. 401

frail/frágil *adj.* que carece de fuerza; débil; p. 463

frenzy/frenesí *s.* estado de intenso entusiasmo o enojo; p. 246

frustration/frustración *s.* desilusión o irritación por no poder hacer o alcanzar algo; p. 777

G

gait/andadura *s.* modo particular de caminar; p. 793

gaunt/esquelético *adj.* excesivamente flaco; p. 237

giddy/aturdido *adj.* mareado o atontado; p. 604

gnarled/retorcido *adj.* torcido y nudoso, como el tronco o las ramas de un árbol; p. 702

grim/severo *adj.* estricto; austero; inflexible; p. 237

grimace/hacer muecas *v.* hacer gestos con la cara, como cuando se siente dolor o desagrado; p. 79

grudging/de mala gana *adj.* que se da o permite sin querer o con resentimiento; p. 236

gruffly/rudamente *adv.* de modo severo o grosero; p. 239

H

habitual/habitual *adj.* que se hace por hábito o costumbre; p. 565

haggard/demacrado *adj.* de aspecto enfermizo o cansado debido a una pena, preocupación o enfermedad; p. 666

hallowed/sagrado *adj.* que se considera santificado o bendito; p. 717

hardy/resistente *adj.* capaz de soportar dificultades; fuerte y saludable; p. 155

hindrance/estorbo *s.* algo que impide el progreso o movimiento; obstáculo; p. 30

hostile/hostil *adj.* que siente o muestra antipatía o desagrado; p. 808

hover/revolotear *v.* permanecer en un sitio como si estuviera suspendido del aire; p. 745

humility/humildad *s.* cualidad de ser humilde o modesto; p. 744

hurtle/precipitarse *v.* moverse rápidamente, especialmente con fuerza o ansiedad; p. 664

I

illuminated/iluminado *adj.* encendido; p. 152

immobilize/inmovilizar *v.* impedir que se mueva; fijar en un sitio; p. 119

impetuous/impetuoso *adj.* que actúa con fuerza o violencia; p. 494

impose/imponer *v.* llevar a cabo legalmente; aplicar; p. 100

impoverished/empobrecido *adj.* reducido a la pobreza; arruinado; p. 370

improbable/improbable *adj.* que no es probable; incierto; p. 151

improvise/improvisar *v.* inventar, componer o hacer sin mucha preparación; p. 438

impulse/impulso *s.* fuerza interna que obliga a actuar sin pensar; p. 50

impunity/impunidad *s.* exención de castigo, perjuicio o consecuencias negativas; p. 187

incessantly/incesantemente *adv.* de modo constante; sin parar; p. 188

incomprehensible/incomprensible *adj.* que no se entiende; p. 191

inconvenience/estorbar *v.* causar molestias o dificultades a alguien; p. 93

incredulous/incrédulo *adj.* que no quiere o no puede creer en algo; p. 170

incriminate/incriminar *v.* demostrar culpabilidad; p. 515

indifferent/indiferente *adj.* que no demuestra interés, sentimiento o preocupación; p. 385

indignity/oprobio *s.* ofensa contra el orgullo o dignidad; humillación; p. 94

indiscriminately/indiscriminadamente *adv.* de un modo que no presta atención a las diferencias; sin hacer distinciones; p. 300

inert/inerte *adj.* incapaz de moverse o actuar; p. 352

inevitably/inevitablemente *adv.* de un modo que no se puede evitar o prevenir; p. 7

infantile/infantil *adj.* como lo haría un niño; pueril; p. 413

infinite/infinito *adj.* sin fronteras; ilimitado; inmenso; p. 177

initial/inicial *adj.* al comienzo; lo primero; p. 7

initiative/iniciativa *s.* acción de dar el primer paso o iniciar una acción; p. 476

insistent/insistente *adj.* que exige atención a toda costa; p. 176

insolently/insolentemente *adv.* de modo atrevido o rudo; p. 544

instill/instilar *v.* verter gradualmente o poco a poco; p. 510

instinct/instinto *s.* modo natural de saber, comportarse o reaccionar que no se ha aprendido; p. 167

intact/intacto *adj.* que no se ha dañado; que está completo; p. 597

intellectual/intelectual *adj.* relativo a la habilidad mental o a la inteligencia; p. 608

intense/intenso *adj.* acentuado o potente; muy fuerte; p. 610

intently/resueltamente *adv.* de un modo firme y decidido; con concentración; p. 154

intimidated/intimidado *adj.* atemorizado o asustado; p. 510

intricate/intrincado *adj.* con muchos detalles complicados; p. 565

intrusion/intrusión *s.* interrupción repentina; p. 384

invalid/inválido *s.* alguien que está incapacitado debido a una enfermedad o herida; p. 165

invariably/invariablemente *adv.* sin excepción; p. 194

ironically/irónicamente *adv.* de un modo diferente al que se espera; p. 6

J

jeer/mofarse *v.* burlarse de algo o alguien de manera brusca y abierta; p. 684

jest/chancear *v.* hablar o actuar de manera jocosa; bromear; p. 596

jubilant/jubiloso *adj.* que está muy contento o emocionado; p. 721

juncture/coyuntura *s.* momento o punto crítico; p. 36

K

keen/agudo *adj.* muy sensible; despierto; p. 272

L

laden/cargado *adj.* abrumado; agobiado; atiborrado; p. 386

lapse/traspié *s.* caída o resbalón; p. 548

legitimate/legítimo *adj.* que sigue las reglas; legal; p. 517

lolling/oscilante *adj.* que cuelga flojamente; colgante; p. 246

loom/vislumbrarse *v.* que surge en la mente como algo temible; p. 222

lunge/arremeter *v.* moverse repentinamente hacia adelante; atacar; p. 794

M

malicious/malicioso *adj.* que tiene o muestra el deseo de perjudicar a alguien; p. 484

maneuver/maniobrar *v.* desempeñarse con destreza, por ejemplo para obtener un cargo o alcanzar una meta; p. 68

meek/apacible *adj.* paciente y tranquilo; gentil; p. 389

menace/amenaza *s.* peligro o riesgo; p. 68

merge/fusionar *v.* unir; agrupar; p. 7

meticulously/meticulosamente *adv.* de un modo que muestra mucha atención a los detalles; p. 221

mobilize/movilizar *v.* prepararse, como para una guerra o emergencia; p. 91

moderately/moderadamente *adv.* ni mucho ni poco; dentro de los límites; p. 568

mortified/mortificado *adj.* muy avergonzado; p. 370

murky/lóbrego *adj.* obscuro o sombrío; p. 414

muse/meditar *v.* pensar o reflexionar; p. 190

muster/congregar *v.* buscar y reunir; agrupar; p. 453

N

naive/ingenuo *adj.* simple por naturaleza; infantil; p. 37

narrative/narración *s.* cuento; relato; p. 37

negotiate/negociar *v.* discutir con el fin de llegar a un acuerdo; p. 97

nimble/ágil *adj.* ligero y rápido de movimiento; p. 439

novelty/novedad *s.* algo nuevo e inusual; p. 595

nurture/criar *v.* cuidar y ayudar a crecer; p. 356

O

obligation/obligación *s.* sentido del deber; responsabilidad; p. 474

obligingly/servicialmente *adv.* que muestra el deseo de ser útil o servir; cortésmente; p. 244

obnoxious/odioso *adj.* molesto y desagradable; p. 69

obscure/confuso *adj.* difícil de entender; p. 350

obsessed/obsesionado *adj.* demasiado concentrado o dedicado a una sola emoción o idea; p. 118

obsession/obsesión *s.* emoción o idea fija que ocupa la mente; p. 414

obstinate/obstinado *adj.* terco; difícil de controlar o superar; p. 361

omen/presagio *s.* suceso visto como señal de buena o mala suerte; p. 774

ominous/ominoso *adj.* algo que anuncia temor o daño; p. 222

oppression/opresión *s.* acto de controlar o gobernar mediante el uso cruel e injusto de la fuerza o autoridad; p. 95

overtake/alcanzar *v.* dar alcance y rebasar; p. 708

P

painstaking/esmerado *adj.* que requiere de mucha atención o trabajo; p. 123

parched/reseco *adj.* que necesita humedad con urgencia; muy seco; p. 717

passive/pasivo *adj.* que no participa ni es activo; p. 166

perilous/peligroso *adj.* azaroso; arriesgado; p. 403

perpetual/perpetuo *adj.* constante; incesante; p. 437

perplexity/perplejidad *s.* duda o incertidumbre; aturdimiento; p. 194

perseverance/perseverancia *s.* voluntad para continuar haciendo algo aunque sea difícil; determinación; p. 187

persistently/persistentemente *adv.* repetidamente; una y otra vez; p. 70

perspective/perspectiva *s.* punto de vista; p. 370

pinnacle/pináculo *s.* cumbre o cima; punto más alto; p. 285

pious/piadoso *adj.* que tiene o finge devoción religiosa; p. 385

plummet/desplomarse *v.* caer verticalmente; derrumbarse; p. 296

podium/podio *s.* plataforma pequeña con una repisa para sostener los papeles de la persona que habla; p. 728

pompous/pomposo *adj.* que muestra exagerado orgullo o vanidad; p. 385

portly/corpulento *adj.* que tiene una figura robusta y respetable; p. 369

possessively/posesivamente *adv.* de un modo que muestra control o posesión sobre algo o alguien; p. 361

potion/poción *s.* bebida, especialmente referente a líquidos con poderes mágicos; p. 702

pounce/abalanzarse *v.* saltar o caer encima de repente con intención de atacar; embestir; p. 729

precise/preciso *adj.* muy claro o definido; exacto; p. 605

predator/depredador *s.* animal, tal como el león o el halcón, que mata a otros animales para alimentarse; p. 125

prejudice/prejuicio *s.* opinión o juicio desfavorable sin bases justas; p. 524

premonition/premonición *s.* sensación de que algo está por ocurrir; señal o advertencia; p. 400

primly/formalmente *adv.* de modo formal y apropiado; p. 548

principle/principio *s.* ley, verdad o creencia básica; norma de conducta personal; p. 354

proposition/proposición *s.* algo que se ofrece o propone; propuesta; oferta; p. 573

prosperous/próspero *adj.* que tiene riquezas o buena suerte; exitoso; acaudalado; p. 592

pursue/perseguir *v.* dar caza; p. 273

Q

quavering/trémulo *adj.* tembloroso; p. 484

quench/aplacar *v.* satisfacer o mitigar una necesidad o deseo; p. 739

R

rash/apresurado *adj.* hecho a la carrera sin pensarlo ni prepararlo; p. 738

raucous/estridente *adj.* sonido fuerte y áspero; p. 544

ravenous/hambriento *adj.* con mucha hambre; p. 390

rebuke/reproche *s.* expresión severa de crítica o desacuerdo; p. 578

reel/remolinar *v.* dar vueltas o parecer como si diera vueltas; girar; p. 739

reflective/reflexivo *adj.* que piensa seria y cuidadosamente; pensativo; p. 507

reformation/reforma *s.* cambio positivo; mejora; p. 547

regretfully/lamentablemente *adv.* de un modo que muestra pesar o desilusión; p. 774

reluctantly/a regañadientes *adv.* sin querer; de mala gana; p. 247

replenish/reabastecer *v.* dar nuevo suministro; volver a llenar; p. 687

resigned/resignado *adj.* que cede o acepta sin oponer resistencia; p. 88

resilient/flexible *adj.* capaz de volver a su forma o posición original después de que se dobla, estira o comprime; p. 465

resolute/resuelto *adj.* determinado; decidido; p. 348

resourceful/recursivo *adj.* hábil para enfrentarse a situaciones nuevas o difíciles; p. 727

retrieve/recobrar *v.* localizar y traer de nuevo; recuperar; p. 50

ritual/ritual *s.* forma establecida de hacer algo; ceremonia; p. 37

robust/robusto *adj.* fuerte y lleno de energía; p. 341

S

sanction/ratificar *v.* respaldar o aprobar algo; p. 168

sanctuary/santuario *s.* lugar de resguardo o protección; p. 170

saunter/deambular *v.* caminar tranquilamente; pasearse; p. 246

savor/saborear *v.* gozar de algo con gran placer; p. 239

scavenger/carroñero *s.* animal que se alimenta de cadáveres descompuestos de animales, como por ejemplo las hienas o los buitres; p. 125

scurry/escurrirse *v.* correr o moverse rápida o agitadamente; p. 774

scuttle/apresurarse *v.* caminar con pasos rápidos y cortos; p. 789

secretive/reservado *adj.* que no expresa sus pensamientos o emociones; p. 663

sedately/sosegadamente *adv.* de modo tranquilo y silencioso; calmadamente; p. 239

SPANISH GLOSSARY

sensation/sensación *s.* motivo de asombro o gran interés; maravilla; p. 754

shrewd/sagaz *adj.* astuto, listo y práctico; p. 584

simultaneously/simultáneamente *adv.* al mismo tiempo; p. 546

sinewy/vigoroso *adj.* físicamente fuerte o poderoso; p. 274

singularity/singularidad *s.* cualidad de notorio o fuera de lo ordinario; peculiaridad; p. 191

skimpy/escaso *adj.* de poca cantidad o tamaño; incompleto; insuficiente o que apenas alcanza; p. 236

slither/deslizarse *v.* avanzar resbalándose como una serpiente; p. 246

sluggish/flojo *adj.* sin energía, vitalidad o ánimo; p. 828

soberly/severamente *adv.* muy seriamente; p. 476

solemnly/solemnemente *adv.* seriamente; p. 546

somberly/lúgubremente *adv.* de modo sombrío o tétrico; p. 490

sorcerer/hechicero *s.* persona que practica la magia con la ayuda de espíritus malignos; p. 701

spare/perdonar *v.* tener misericordia de alguien; desistir de hacerle daño; p. 274

spasm/espasmo *s.* tirantez repentina e incontrolable de un músculo; p. 243

specify/especificar *v.* establecer o describir en detalle; p. 7

speculation/especulación *s.* acto de formarse una opinión o conclusión basándose en suposiciones; p. 150

spendthrift/derrochador *s.* aquél que gasta dinero de modo generoso o que lo desperdicia; p. 150

spite/rencor *s.* deseo de herir o molestar a otra persona; p. 744

squander/malgastar *v.* gastar o usar de forma imprudente o innecesaria; p. 593

staccato/entrecortado *adj.* hecho de ruidos o movimientos cortos y agudos; p. 362

staple/principal *adj.* importante; prominente; p. 38

stark/absolutamente *adv.* completamente; rígida o severamente; p. 177

subsidize/subsidiar *v.* ayudar o respaldar con dinero; p. 301

subtle/sutil *adj.* que no es abierto o directo; que no es obvio; p. 178

succeed/seguir *v.* ocurrir después, ya sea en tiempo, orden o lugar; p. 666

sufficient/suficiente *adj.* adecuado; bastante; p. 677

sullen/hosco *adj.* malhumorado, retraído o sombrío; resentido; p. 45

surge/surgir *v.* elevarse de repente; moverse con agitación violenta, como el oleaje; p. 441

surly/arisco *adj.* rudo y de malhumor; hosco; p. 164

swagger/contonearse *v.* caminar o comportarse de modo altanero, brusco o demasiado orgulloso; p. 45

T

tact/tacto *s.* habilidad para manejar situaciones o personas sin causar desagrado ni herir sentimientos; p. 370

taunt/mofarse *v.* burlarse de manera despreciativa e insultante; p. 701

taut/tirante *adj.* tenso; estirado; p. 150

tentatively/tentativamente *adv.* de modo dudoso; inciertamente; posiblemente; p. 492

therapy/terapia *s.* tratamiento de una herida, enfermedad o desorden mental; p. 676

tumultuously/tumultosamente *adv.* de un modo agitado o confuso; p. 465

U

ultimately/por último *adv.* al final; finalmente; p. 369

uncanny/extraño *adj.* que produce asombro; misterioso; p. 404

uncommitted/imparcial *adj.* que no demuestra una opinión o punto de vista particular o definido; p. 474

undermine/socavar *v.* debilitar, desgastar o destruir lentamente; p. 298

undertake/emprender *v.* iniciar una labor o proyecto; intentar; acometer; p. 829

undulating/ondulante *adj.* que se mueve como las olas; fluctuante; p. 603

unique/único *adj.* muy particular; raro; singular; p. 309

unpalatable/desagradable *adj.* que no es agradable al gusto, la mente o los sentidos; inaceptable; p. 222

V

vaguely/vagamente *adv.* de un modo que no es claro, exacto o definido; p. 7

vainly/vanamente *adv.* sin éxito; ineficaz; p. 739

valiant/valiente *adj.* intrépido; valeroso; p. 797

validity/validez *s.* condición de ser apoyado por los hechos; verdad; p. 511

veer/virar *v.* girar o cambiar de dirección; p. 737

venture/aventurarse *v.* hacer algo a pesar de los posibles riesgos o peligros; p. 152

vigor/vigor *s.* fortaleza y energía; p. 246

vile/vil *adj.* muy malo; perverso; desagradable; p. 455

vital/vital *adj.* de enorme importancia; esencial; p. 464

W

wary/cauteloso *adj.* cuidadoso; prudente; p. 437

waver/tambalear *v.* perder el equilibrio; p. 738

wholeheartedly/sinceramente *adv.* francamente; con gusto; p. 68

wily/taimado *adj.* hipócrita; engañoso; p. 170

wince/recular *v.* retroceder ligeramente, como cuando se siente dolor; p. 48

withdrawn/retraído *adj.* tímido, reservado o poco sociable; p. 454

woe/aflicción *s.* gran tristeza o sufrimiento; gran preocupación o desdicha; p. 474

Index of Skills

Boldface page references indicate an extensive treatment of the topic.

References beginning with R refer to handbook pages.

Literary Concepts

Act 500, R1
Alliteration 140, 446, 631, 824, R1
Allusion 357, R1
Anecdote 62, 104–107, 408
Antagonist R1
Anthropomorphism 802, R1
Aside R1
Assonance R1, R9
Author's purpose 32, 396, 830, R1
Autobiography 62–63, 104, 288, R1
Ballad R2
Bias 359
Biography 223, 288, R2
Cast of characters 501
Character 62, 63, 144, 180, 202, 359, R2
Characterization 172, 406, R2
  direct 406, R2
  indirect R2
Chronological order 62
Cinquain 839
Climax 145, 171, 407, 550, 802, R2
Comedy R2
Conflict 21, 53, 145, 171, 232, 442, 501, 526, 550, R2
  external 53, 442, 501, R2
  internal 53, 442, 501, R2
Consonance R3, R9
Description 10, 73, 80, 722, R3
Details 478, R3
Dialect 240, R3
Dialogue 23, 277, 500, 560, 589, R3
Diary entry 62
Direct characterization 406, R2

Drama 500–501, R3, R5
Dynamic character R2
End rhyme 262, R9
End-stopped line 836
Epilogue 358
Essay 302, 396, R3
  formal R3
  informal R3
  persuasive 32, 302
Exposition 144, 171, R8
Extended metaphor 820, R4
External conflict 53, 442, 501, R2
Eyewitness account 62
Fable 703, R4
Falling action 145, R4
Fantasy 695, R4
Fiction 144, R4
Figurative language (Figures of speech) 343, 391, R4
  imagery 291, 336, R5
  metaphor 232, 262, 343, 391, 446, 626, 820, R4
  personification R4
  simile 343, 391, 626, 820, R4, R10
  symbol/symbolism 127, R4, R10
  understatement 550
First-person narrative 330, R4
First-person point of view 62, 330, 813, R8
Flashback 62, 144, 613, R4
Flash-forward 62
Flat character R2
Folklore 698, R4
  folktale 599, 757, R4
  legend 698, 732, R6
  myth R6
  tall tale 757, R11
Foreshadowing 248, 551, R4
Free verse 255, R5
Genre R5
Haiku 838–839, R5
Hero/heroine R5
Historical fiction R5
Humor R5
Imagery 291, 336, R5

Indirect characterization R2
Informational text 312, R5
Internal conflict 53, 442, 501, R2
Internal rhyme R9
Irony 21, 570, 679, R5
  situational 21
  verbal 21
Legend 698, 732, R6
Limerick 839, R6
Limited third-person point of view R8
Local color R6
Lyric R6
Lyric poetry R6
Main character 62, 144, 180
Main idea 374, R6
Memoir 39, 62, 288, R6
Metaphor 232, 262, 343, 391, 446, 626, 820, R4, R6
  extended metaphor 820, R4
Meter 631, R6
Minor character 180
Monologue 589, R6
Mood 134, 201, R6
Myth 698, R6. *See also* Legend.
Narration R7
Narrative 374, 813
  first-person 330, R8
  third-person R11
Narrative hook R8
Narrative poetry 232, R7
Narrator 145, 813, R7
Nonfiction 32, 290–291, R7
  autobiography 62–63, 104, 288, R1
  biography 223, 288, R2
  essay 302, 396, R3
    formal R3
    informal R3
    persuasive 32, 302
  informative nonfiction 292, 312
  memoir 39, 62, 288, R6
Novel R7
Omniscient point of view R8
Onomatopoeia 626, R7

Oral tradition **276**, R7
Parallelism R7
Personification R4, R7–R8
Persuasive essay 32, 302
Plot **145, 171**, 550, **778,** R8
   climax 145, 171, 407, 550,
     R2, R8
   exposition 144, 171, R8
   falling action 145, R4, R8
   plot twist **550,** R8
   resolution 145, 171, **456,**
     R8, R9
   rising action 145, 171,
     R8, R9
Poetry **616–617,** R5, R9
   alliteration 140, 446,
     824, R1
   assonance R1, R9
   ballad R2
   cinquain **839**
   consonance R3, R9
   end-stopped line **836**
   free verse **255**
   haiku **836–837,** R5
   limerick **839,** R6
   lyric R6
   meter **631,** R6
   narrative **232,** R7
   onomatopoeia **626,** R7
   rhyme 262, **641,** R9
   rhyme scheme **262,** R9
   rhythm **631,** 836, R9
   short forms **838–839**
   speaker R10
   stanza R10
Point of view 62, 63, 73, 74,
   145, 417, R8
   first-person 62, 145, 330,
     417, 813, R8
   limited third-person R8
   third-person 145, **157**
   omniscient R8
Props R8
Prose 627, R5, R8
Protagonist 144, R8
Pun 561, R8
Quest 779
Refrain R8
Repetition 53, R8–R9
Resolution 145, 171, **456,** R9

Rhyme 262, **641,** R9
Rhyme scheme **262,** R9
Rhythm **631,** R9
Rising action 145, 171, R9
Round character R2
Scene **500,** R9
Science-fiction **467,** R9
Screenplay R9
Script 500
Sensory details 73, 395
Sensory imagery 11, **80,** 141,
   R9–R10
Sequence of events 101, R10
Setting **62,** 63, 144, **201,**
   379, 803, R10
Short story **144–145, 569,**
   R10
Simile 343, 391, 626, 820, R4,
   R10
Situational irony 21
Slant rhyme R9
Sound devices R10
   alliteration 140, 446, 631,
     824, R1
   assonance R1, R9
   consonance R3, R9
   onomatopoeia R7
   rhyme 262, **641,** R9
Speaker **61,** 134, R10
Stage directions **501, 588,**
   R10
Stanza R10
Static character R2
Stereotype 202, 359, R2, R10
Style **206, 396,** R10
Suspense 614, **669,** R10
Symbol/symbolism 127, **446,**
   R4, R10
Tall tale 642, **757,** R11
Teleplay **525,** R11
Theme 10, 17, 21, **63, 145,**
   171, 223, 330, 343, **364,**
   396, 746, 785, 820, R11
   implied 10, 63, 145, **496,**
     746, 785
   stated 10, 63, 145, 746, 785
Thesis 209, 396
Third-person narrative R11
Third-person point of view
   145, **157**

Title R11
Tone 101, **396,** 830
Tragedy R11
Tragic flaw R11
Transition 710
Travel journal 62
Understatement 550
Verbal irony 21
Visual imagery **16,** 61, R11
Voice R11

Reading and Thinking

Activating prior knowledge
   2, 4, 18, 34, 40, 61, 76, 116,
   132, 174, 184, 251, 280, 326,
   333, 398, 430, 432, 444, 450,
   471, 826, **R78,** R82
Active reading strategies
   64–65, 146–147, 292–293,
   397, 502–503, 618–619,
   699, R83
   connecting **147,** 152, 154,
     301, 401, 404, 619, 699,
     701, 702
   evaluating **147,** 151, 154,
     155, **293,** 299, 300, 301,
     397, 404, **503,** 511, 516,
     519, 523, 619, 702
   listening 618, 623, 624, **R77**
   predicting **64,** 67, 68, 70,
     146, 150, 153, 156, 295,
     296, 298, **397,** 400, 403,
     404, **502,** 506, 508, 511,
     512, 517, 519, 699, 702
   previewing **64, 292,** 295,
     618, 621, 699, 701. *See
     also* Scanning.
   questioning **64,** 72, 149,
     151, 153, 156, **292,** 296,
     299, 300, 301, **397,** 399,
     400, 404, **502,** 505, 507,
     509, 510, 514, 516, 522,
     524, 618, 622, 623, 625,
     699, 701, 702
   responding **65,** 68, 70, 71,
     72, 151, 155, 156, 300,
     403, 405, **502,** 509, 515,
     517, 518, 524, 619, 625

reviewing **146,** 152, 155, **293,** 299, 403, **503,** 513, 516, 521

visualizing **65,** 67, 71, **146,** 150, 152, 156, **397,** 403, 405, **502,** 506, 513, 521, 522, 618, 621, 624, 699, 701, R84

Analysis

anthropomorphism 802

bias 359

character 32, 54, 180, 219, 249, 359, 534, 569, 600

details 478

figurative language (figures of speech) 343, 446, 820, 843

humor 409, 417, 560, 843

imagery 336, 478, 785, 843, 845

irony 21

mood 201, 525, 824, 837

narrator's perspective 330, 813

plot 232, 456, 550, 600, 778

point of view 157, 330, 417

problem and solution **393**

punctuation 836

rhyme scheme 262

rhythm 255, 446, 836

setting 201, 232, 379, 469, 814, 843

spatial relationships 845

speaker 255, 336, 478, 836

stereotype **359**

text structure 364, 836

theme 206, 207, 223, 364, 447, 496, 569, 785, 820, 825

title 10, 140, 223, 240, 374, 496, 528, 785

tone 830

word choice 843, R79–R81

Assumption 263

Author's purpose 32, 80, **419,** 525, 830

Cause and effect (as a text structure) **129, 832**

Cause-effect relationships **103, 643,** 832, 846–847

Chronological order 83

Clarifying **458**

Classifying 697, 785

Comparing and contrasting **17, 40,** 54, 108, 206, **207,** 212, 219, 232, **249,** 289, 336, 343, **380,** 391, 409, **447,** 525, 534, 599, **600,** 648, **747,** 764, **825,** 840, 850

Comparison and contrast (as a text structure) 343, R85

Comprehension strategies **64–65, 146–147, 292–293, 397, 502–503, 672, R82**

Connecting 10, 16, 21, 32, 39, 53, 61, 73, 80, 101, 127, 134, 140, 157, 171, 180, 201, 206, 223, 232, 240, 248, 255, 262, 276, 288, 302, 312, 330, 336, 343, 357, 364, **366,** 374, 379, 391, 406, 417, 442, 446, 456, 467, 478, 496, 525, 550, 560, 569, 588, 599, 613, 626, 631, 641, 669, 679, 695, 703, 710, 722, 732, 740, 746, 757, 778, 785, 802, 813, 820, 824, 830, 836, 840

Connotation/denotation R74

Context R71

Cultures, 10, 61, 73, 80, 276, 330, 379, 380

Drawing conclusions 39, 61, 73, 134, 157, 248, 327, **337, 470, 552,** 778, R100

Elaborating 21, 39, 108, 140, 171, 201, 232, 302, 379, 446, 778, **821**

Evaluating 10, 16, 21, 32, 39, 53, 61, 73, 101, 127, 134, 140, 157, 171, 180, 201, **203,** 206, 223, 232, 240, 248, 255, 262, 276, 288, 302, 312, 330, 336, 343, 357, 364, 374, 379, 391, 406, 417, 424, 442, 446, 456, 467, 478, 496, 525, 550, 560, 569, 588, 599, 613, 626, 631, 641, 669, 679, 695, 703, 710, 722, 732, 740, 746, 757, 778, 785, 802, **804,** 813, 820, 824, 830, 836, 840, 850

Exaggeration 408

Fact and opinion 314, 338–339, R68

Generalizing 705

Graphic aids 734, 847

charts 18, 54, 83, 242, 376, 432, 561, 570, 599, 635, 696, R97–R99

diagram 233, 303, 407

graph 40, 572, 674

story map 105, 814

word map 2, R84

Identifying assumptions 263

Inferring 159, 180, 240, 391, 456, **469, 833,** 836

Interpreting 10, 16, 21, 32, 39, 53, 61, 73, 101, 127, 134, 140, 157, 171, 180, 201, 206, 223, 232, 240, 248, 255, 262, 276, 288, 302, 312, 330, 336, 343, 357, 364, 374, 379, 391, 406, 417, 442, 446, 456, 467, 478, 496, 525, 550, 560, 569, 588, 599, 613, 626, 631, 641, 669, 679, 695, 703, 710, 722, 732, 740, 746, 757, 778, 785, 802, 813, 820, 824, 830, 836, 840

Listening 22, 344, 407, 786, 824, R66, **R77**

Main idea and supporting details 39, **142,** 171, 201, 223, 224, 233, 302, 312, 320, 357, 364, 785, 802, 830

Monitoring comprehension 615, R82–R83

Paraphrasing 759, 843, **R88**

Personal background. *See* Activating prior knowledge.

Personal response 10, 16, 21, 32, 33, 39, 53, 61, 73, 101, 127, 134, 140, 157, 171, 180, 201, 223, 232, 240, 248, 255, 262, 276, 288,

302, 312, 330, 336, 343,
357, 364, 374, 379, 391,
406, 417, 424, 442, 446,
456, 467, 478, 496, 525,
550, 560, 569, 588, 599,
613, 626, 631, 641, 669,
679, 695, 703, 710, 722,
732, 740, 746, 757, 778,
785, 802, 813, 820, 824,
830, 836, 843

Predicting 173, R83

Problem and solution (as a
text structure) 364, **393,
815,** R85

Purpose for reading. *See*
Setting a purpose for
reading.

Questioning 64, 292, 397,
458, 502

Reading aloud 22, 135, 140,
141, 233, 255, 263, 333,
344, 407, 446, 527, 786,
824, 836, **R75**

Recalling 10, 16, 21, 32, 39,
53, 61, 73, 80, 101, 127,
134, 140, 157, 171, 180,
201, 206, 223, 232, 240,
248, 255, 262, 276, 288,
302, 312, 330, 336, 343,
357, 364, 374, 379, 391,
406, 417, 442, 446, 456,
467, 478, 496, 525, 550,
560, 569, 588, 599, 613,
626, 631, 641, 669, 679,
695, 703, 710, 722, 732,
740, 746, 757, 778, 785,
802, 813, 820, 824, 830,
836, 840

Research
locating information 3, 54,
115, 219, 779, **R72**
organizing information 3,
40, 54, 115, 219, 779
presenting 3, 40, 115, 212,
219, 320, 779

Responding 65, 68, 70, 71, 72,
151, 155, 156, 300, 403,
405, **502,** 509, 515, 517,
518, 524, 619, 625, **R93**

Reviewing 146, 293, 503

Scanning 208, 671, 779, R74

Self-assessment 108, 212, 320,
424, 534, 850

Sequence of events (as a text
structure) 63, **101, 135,** 778

Sequencing 83, 105, **R87**

Setting a purpose for reading
4, 13, 18, 25, 34, 43, 58, 66,
76, 84, 116, 132, 137, 148,
162, 174, 184, 204, 220,
226, 234, 242, 251, 258,
267, **278,** 280, 294, 305,
328, 333, 340, 346, 360,
367, 376, 382, 398, 410,
432, 444, 450, 460, 471,
482, 504, 543, 554, 564,
590, 602, 620, 628, 635,
658, 674, 682, 700, 706,
713, 725, 736, 742, 749,
772, 782, 788, 806, 818,
822, 826, 834, 840, **R82**

Skimming 391, R74

Spatial order 233, R71, R87

Spatial relationships 233, 845

Summarizing 21, 56, 81, 102,
140, 232, 302, 312, 364,
446, **498,** 814, **R88**

Visualizing 22, 250, 344, 527

Grammar
and Language

Abbreviations R42

Abstract nouns R30

Action verb R33

Adjectives 182, 458, 627,
R18, R27
comparative 182, R18, R27
demonstrative R27
possessive R27
predicate R27, R28
proper R27
superlative 182, R18, R27

Adverb clause 159

Adverbs 182, 203, 458, R27
comparative 182, R27
superlative 182

Antecedent 331, R27, R31

Apostrophes 527, 671, 734,
816, R40, R41

Appositives 553, R27

Article R27
definite R27
indefinite R27

**Capitalization 712, R20–R21,
R34–R36**

Clauses and sentence structure
R27–R28
adverb **159**
main R13, R28
subordinate R28

Collective nouns R30

Colons 837, R38–R39

Commas 173, 359, 553, R13,
R19–R20, R37–R38

Common nouns R30

Complements R28

Complex sentence 615, R32

Compound sentences 359, R32

Compound subject R15

Concrete nouns R30

Conjunctions R28
coordinating R13, R28
correlative R28
subordinating **159,** R28

Coordinating conjunctions
R13, R28

Correlative conjunctions R28

Dashes R41–R42

Declarative sentences R32

Demonstrative pronouns R27,
R31

Direct object R28

Double negative 469

Ellipsis 256

Exclamation marks R36

Exclamatory sentences R32

Fragments 12, R12

Future perfect tense R33

Gerunds R29

Helping verb R33

Hyphens R41–R42

Imperative sentences R32

Indefinite pronouns R14, R31

Indirect object R28

Infinitive phrases R30

Infinitives R29

Intensive pronouns R31

Interjections R29

Interrogative pronouns R31

Interrogative sentences R31
Intransitive verb R33
Inverted order R29
Irregular verb 381, R16, R33
Italics 129, R39–R40
Linking verbs R33
Nonessential appositive 553, R19
Nouns 103, 314, R20, R29–R30
Number R29
  plural R29
  singular R29
Numbers 697, R43
Object of the preposition 845, R30
Parentheses 408, R41–R42
Participial phrase 498, R30
Participles 498, R16, R29
Parts of speech
  adjectives 182, 458, 627, R18, R27
  adverbs 182, 203, 458, R27
  conjunctions 159, R13, R28
  interjections R29
  nouns 103, 314, R29, R30
  prepositions 845, R30
  pronouns 331, R31
    demonstrative R31
    indefinite R14, R31
    intensive R31
    interrogative R31
    personal 804, R20, R31
    reflexive R31
    relative R31
  verbs 12, 55, 315, R14, R33
    action R33
    helping R33
    intransitive R33
    irregular 381, R16, R33
    linking R33
    regular 381, R33
    transitive R33
Past perfect tense R33
Periods R36
Personal pronouns 804, R17, R20, R31
Phrases R30
  appositive phrase R27

infinitive phrase R30
  participial phrase 498, R30
  prepositional phrase 845, R30
  verb phrase R30
  verbal phrase R30
Plural nouns 314, R20, R30
Possessive apostrophe 816
Possessive pronoun 278, R20, R27
Predicates 12, R12, R30–R31
  complete R30–R31
  simple R30
Prepositional phrases 845, R30
Prepositions 845, R31
Present perfect tense R33
Pronoun use 278, 331, 499, 552, R17, R20, R27
Pronouns 331, R31
  demonstrative R27, R31
  indefinite R14, R31
  intensive R31
  interrogative R31
  personal 804, R17, R20, R31
  reflexive R31
  relative R31
Punctuation 632, R36–R43
  apostrophes 527, 671, 734, 816, R40–R41
  colons 837, R38–R39
  commas 359, 553, R13, R19–R20, R37–R38
  dashes R41–R42
  ellipsis 256
  exclamation marks R36
  hyphens R41–R42
  italics R39–R40
  parentheses 408, R41–R42
  periods R36
  question marks R36
  quotation marks 759, R19, R39–R40
  semicolons 837, R38–R39
Question marks R36
Quotation marks 759, R19, R39–R40
Reflexive pronouns R31
Regular verbs 381, R33
Relative pronouns R31
Run-on sentences 832, R13

Semicolons 837, R38–R39
Sensory language 786
Sentence R32
  complex 615, R32
  compound 359, R32
  declarative R32
  exclamatory R32
  fragment 12, R12
  imperative R32
  interrogative R32
  run-on 832, R13
  simple R32
Simple sentences R32
Spelling 314, 393, 705, 724, R44–R47
Subject complement R28
Subjects 12, 55, 315, R12, R14, R17, R32
  complete R32
  compound R32
  simple R32
Subject-verb agreement 55, 315, R14–R15
Subordinating conjunctions 159, R28
Transitive verb R33
Verb phrase R30
Verb tense 815, R15–R16, R33
Verbal phrase R30
Verbals R33
  gerunds R29
  infinitives R29
  participles R16
Verbs 12, 55, 141, 315, R14, R33
  action R33
  helping R33
  intransitive R33
  irregular 381, R16, R33
  linking R33
  regular 381, R33
  transitive R33

Vocabulary

Acquisition strategies 33, 103, 443, 671
Analogies 224, 359, 479, 705, 724

Antonyms 11, 203, **408**
Base words **75**, 289, **527**
Compound words **74, 845**
Context clues **143, 615**, 815
Dictionary skills
  definition 741, **804**
  pronunciation **781**
Etymology **589**, 680, 759
Homonyms **561**
Homophones **225**
Multiple meaning words **278**, 615, **633**
Prefixes **181**, 314, **419, 458, 498**, 552, 832
Pronunciation **781**
Related forms of words **129**
Roots **173, 394, 469**
Suffixes 75, 159, 289, **303**, 375, 570, **734**
Synonyms **55**, 203, **393, 697, 711, 779**
Usage **365**
Word parts (roots, prefixes, suffixes) **735**

Writing

Advice 158, 206, 344
Analysis 746
  assumption 263
  author's purpose 375, 419, 443, 804
  character 22, 615, 627, 680, 704
  characterization 172, 406, 723, 741, 786
  compare and contrast 17, 392
  conflict 442, 526, 711
  description 158, 497
  details 33, 54
  dialogue 277, 365, 589, 758
  drawing conclusions 159, 337, 552
  ending 241
  grammar 256
  humor 561
  imagery 233, 446, 632, 779, 884
  irony 570

monologue 589
mood 837, 844
plot 407, 670, 733
poetry 17, 627
point of view 81, 128
problem and solution 815
rhythm 135
sensory imagery 11, 141, 263
sequence of events 135
setting 181, 468, 469, 642, 696, 803, 814
sources 303
style 331
suspense 614
theme 17, 202, 256, 357, 446, 479, 704
Anecdote 408, 848
Arrest report 570
Audience and purpose 105, 209, 317, 421, 531, 847
Business letter **R58–R59**
Business writing **R58–R59**
Cartoon caption 770
Cause-and-effect essay **846–849**
Character
  interpretation of 22, 358
  sketch 337
Comic book 392
Compare-and-contrast essay **208–211**
Creative writing 141, 704, 733, 786
Critical review 33, 457, 817
Definitions 129, 529, **530–533**
Descriptive writing 22, **420–423**, 654, **R53**
Details 40, 104, 106, **395**, 422
Dialogue 2, **23**, 106, 380, 430
Diary entries 202
Drafting **106, 210, 318, 422, 532, 848, R49**, R60
Editing/proofreading **107, 211, 319, 423, 533, 849**, R50, R60
Editorial **316–319**
Ending of story 207
Epilogue 358, 614

Essay 655
  cause-and-effect **846–849**
  compare-and-contrast **208–211**
  expository **530–533**
  personal 375, 497
  persuasive 279
Expository writing **530–533, 760–763, 846–849, R52**
Finding/focusing topic 104, 316–317, 420, 530, 846, R54, R60
Haiku 843, 844
Humorous writing 408, 418, 561
Incident report 541, 814
Interview 219, 614, 627, 723
Introduction 241, 771
Journal entry 11, 53, 76, 101, 116, 127, 141, 171, 172, 173, 201, 218, 223, 224, 251, 256, 265, 277, 288, 289, 327, 330, 331, 339, 367, 444, 457, 471, 478, 504, 533, 590, 613, 628, 632, 670, 723, 736, 779, 824, 831
Letter 54, 74, 128, 158, 303, 379, 392, 447, 479
Memo 219, 365, R59
Monologue 599
Myth 711
Narrative writing 23, **104–107**, 551, **644–647, R53**
News story 128, 313, 526, 642, 741
Newspaper article 202, 233, 443, 589, 803
Peer review/editing 106, 210, 318, 422, 848
Personal essay 375, 497
Personal writing 11, 17, 33, 81, 128, 680, 821, 850
Persuasive essay 279, 303
Persuasive writing 219, **316–319, R53**
Picture storybook 102
Play 365
Plot 541

Poetry 22, 135, 140, 141, 207, 263, 337, 379, 446, 786, 821, 837, 844

Point of view 157, 172, 379, 407, 526, 770, 813, 831

Policy statement 327, 771

Position statement 847

Postcard 313

Prewriting 104–105, 208–209, 316–317, 420–421, 530–531, 644–645, 760–761, 846–847, R48–R49, R60

Proposal 115, 358

Publishing/presenting 107, 211, 319, 423, 533, 647, 763, 849, R51, R60

Quickwrite 13, 137, 174, 204, 305, 328, 382, 398, 564, 658, 782, 806, 826, 840

Radio play 600

Research report writing 241, R54–R57

Review 33, 458

Revising 12, 106, 210, 318, 422, 532, 848, R49–R50, R60

Script 418, 443, 733

Sentence variety 673

Sequel 392, 468, 758

Short story 181, 644–647

Speech 181, 457, 599

Summarizing 82, 102, 313, 317, 498, 815, 831

Technical writing 54

Thesis statement 531

Travel brochure 468

Writing about literature. See Analysis.

Writing modes R52–R53

Writing process 104–107, 208–211, 316–319, 420–423, 530–533, 644–647, 846–849, R48–R51

Writing skills
comparison and contrast 183
details 395
dialogue 23
sentence variety 673

Listening, Speaking, and Viewing

Advertising/persuasive speech 279

Choral reading 627

Critical viewing 327, 771, **817**

Debate 141, 202, 289, 358, 392, 497

Discourse (discussing literature)
assumptions 589
author's purpose (or attitude) 680, 803
character 135, 614
compare and contrast 344, 627, 704, 786, 814, 825
conflict 723
humor 249, 418
imagery 17, 837, 844
literary techniques 468
meaning 181, 263, 365
metaphors 821
narrator 331
persuasive effect **279**
philosophical thought 392
poetic devices 825
poetry 263
scene 102
speaker 337
stereotype 202
theme 741, 779, 824
tone 249
viewpoints 81

Dramatic presentations 758
dialogue 430
one-act play 365
play 541, 733
readers theater 11, 206
role-playing 114, 207, 218, 821
scene 54, 141, 172, 551
skit 102, 249, 561
tableau 337

Group discussions (sharing ideas, personal response) 4, 11, 22, 25, 34, 40, 66, 128, 132, 158, 184, 220, 226, 234, 248, 256, 258, 267, 280, 313, 333, 340, 346, 360, 407, 410, 443, **449**, 450, 457, 460, 482, 541, 543, 602, 620, 632, 700, 746, 772, 788, 805, 817, 818, 822, 831, 834, 849
brainstorm 224, 303, 326, 375, 655, 670, 821
cultural preservation 58, 380
imagery 17, 22
opinions 33, 43, 127, 141, 181, 241, 803
roles 162, 207

Interviewing 11, 57, 82, 128, 256, 614

Listening techniques R66

Newscast 696

Nonverbal clues R66

Oral reading
essay 407
poetry 22, 141, 233, 344, 786, 821, 824, 837, 844

Oral report 779, 831, R67

Paintings. See Viewing.

Performing
choral reading 627
dialogue 430
one-act play 365
play 541
poetry reading 22, 141, 233, 344, 786, 821, 824, 837, 844
readers theater 11, 206, 803, 844
scene 54, 141, 172, 551
sportscast 443
storytelling 277, 375, 497, 541, **571,** 779

Photographs. See Viewing.

Play 541

Poetry reading 22, 141, 233, 344, 786, 821, 824, 837, 844

Public speaking R67

Readers theater 11, 206, 803, 844

Role-playing 114, 207, 218, 821

Scene 54, 141, 172, 551

Sculpture. See Viewing.

Skit 102, 249, 561

Sportscast 443

Storytelling 277, 375, 497, 541, **571,** 779

Tableau 337
Television commercial 817
Television show 418, 541
Viewing
    painting 8, 78, 154, 165,
        178, 188, 193, 195, 196,
        229, 245, 341, 349, 352,
        389, 412, 435, 439, 454,
        462–463, 475, 477, 486,
        488–489, 492, 507,
        514–515, 520, 566–567,
        578, 585, 594, 607, 610,
        612, 623, 636, 659, 686,
        709, 729, 738, 753, 756,
        776, 810
    photograph 46, 69, 286,
        308, 371, 414, 545, 665,
        693, 716, 720, 801
    sculpture 100
    sketch 190, 770
    other media 28, 51, 678,
        744, 791, 817

Research and Study Skills

CD-ROM R54, R60
Crediting sources R56–R57
Drawing conclusions 241
Generating questions 248,
    344, 431, 551
Graphic organizers 102, 304,
    771, 803, R61
Internet 81, 115, 219, 241,
    266, 277, 327, 338–339, 418,
    771, R54
Library/reference resources 3,
    54, 241, 266, 277, 327, 431,
    771, R54
Locating information 130,
    158, 219, 327, 771
Note taking 65, 102, 147, 219,
    293, 397, 503, R55
Organizing information 3, 40,
    102, 104, 219, 771
Outlining 102, 171, 358, 541,
    600, R56, R60
Presenting information 3, 40,
    115, 212, 219, 320, 327, 431,
    771

Research reports 241, 327,
    831, R54–R57
Test-taking skills 214–215,
    322–323, 536–537,
    650–651, 766–767,
    852–853, R62–R65
Time line 102, 202, 771

Media and Technology

Advertising 40
Audiotapes 319, 541
Comic strip 409, 642
Critical viewing 115, 327, 771,
    817
E-mail 264–265
Internet 115, 128, 219,
    264–265, 266, 277, 327,
    338–339, 418, 431, 526,
    541, 589, 601, 655, 814,
    817, 831
Internet connection 3, 81,
    115, 128, 219, 241, 277,
    327, 418, 431, 526, 541,
    589, 655, 771, 814, 831
Interview 219, 256, 431
Journal 780
Magazine article 136, 656–657
Media connection
    comic strip 409, 542
    journal 780
    magazine article 136,
        656–657
    movie review 787
    newspaper column 24
    newspaper story 345
    oral history 634
    public opinion poll 304
    song 131, 748
    television script 41–42
    Web site 266, 458, 528
Movie review 787
Multimedia presentation 3,
    115, 219, 431, 541, 563, 655,
    771
Newspaper column 24
Radio news show 219
Song 131
Tape recording 135, 431

Technology skills
    active viewing strategies
        480–481
    E-mail 264–265
    hyperlinks 562
    hypertext 562
    internet 338–339
    multimedia 562–563
    spreadsheets 160–161
    word processing 56–57
Videotapes 219, 319, 431, 541
Web site 266, 458, 528

Life Skills

Brochure 17, 468
Career choices 3, 248
Collaborating (team member
    and partner) 3, 11, 17, 22,
    25, 40, 54, 56, 57, 58, 66,
    84, 102, 106, 107, 114, 127,
    128, 132, 135, 141, 158, 161,
    162, 172, 181, 202, 207, 210,
    211, 219, 220, 224, 233, 234,
    248, 249, 258, 263, 264, 265,
    267, 277, 279, 280, 294, 303,
    304, 313, 331, 337, 340, 344,
    358, 360, 365, 379, 380, 392,
    407, 410, 418, 430, 443, 446,
    457, 458, 460, 468, 479, 482,
    497, 526, 527, 533, 541, 543,
    551, 561, 570, 571, 572, 589,
    599, 614, 615, 771, 772, 779,
    788, 805, 817, 818, 821, 822,
    824, 831, 834, 837, 844, 849,
    R68–R69
Community resources 115,
    158, 313, 358, 670, 771,
    846
Chart 18, 54, 83, 161, 183,
    242, 248, 303, 395, 431, 448,
    561, 570, 599, 803
Creating and producing
    banner 17
    booklet 102, 680
    brochure 17, 468
    chart 18, 54, 83, 161, 183,
        242, 248, 303, 313, 431,
        448, 561, 570, 599, 803
    diagram 183, 327, 407

incident report 541, 814
letter 54, 74, 158, 303, 339, 379, 392, 447, 479, R58–R59
memo 219, 365, R59
news broadcast 128, 313
newspaper article 202
poster 102, 158, 303
proposal 115, 358
Decision making 431
Diagram 183, 303, 327, 407
Incident report 541, 814
Interview 11, 82, 256, 431, 551, 614
Leading and organizing 207, 541
Memo 219, 365
News article 202
News broadcast 128, 313
Planning and designing 115, 209, 313, 317, 358
Problem solving 431
Supporting and contributing 207, 313, 541
Responsibilities 771

Interdisciplinary Studies

Advertisement 40
Art 704
advertisement 40
cartoon 407
collage 115
comic book 392
comic strip 654
diorama 655
drawing, sketching 74, 224, 240, 241, 327, 418, 479, 540, 696, 741, 831, 837, 844
floor plan 331, 332
magazine cover 831
map 289, 468, 497, 614, 696
model 277, 327, 741
mural 313, 358
painting 479
picture book 102
story map 814
timeline 202
wrapping paper 181

Cartoon 407
Comic book 392
Comic strip 654
Communication 681
Drawing, sketching 74, 224, 240, 241, 289, 327, 418, 479, 540, 696, 831, 837, 844
Environmental science 805
Health **448,** 723
History 115
Magazine covers 831
Math **257,** 303
Multimedia 3, 115, 219, 771
Murals 313, 358
Music 3, 17, 263
Paintings 479
Picture book 102
Science and technology 54, **130,** 248, 303, 313, **332,** 358, 670, 758, 803, **805,** 831
Social studies **82,** 102, 158, 202, 289, 497, **601,** 614, 704, 733, 779
Sports 40, 141

Index of Authors and Titles

A

Abbott, Bud 555
Adoff, Arnold 20
After Twenty Years 565
Aiken, Joan 659
Alarcón, Francisco X. 334
All Summer in a Day 461
Allison, Stacy, with Carlin, Peter 281
Almost Ready 20
Alvarez, Julia 5
Americans Continue to Worry About the Decline of the Oceans 304
Amigo Brothers 433
Anansi and His Visitor, Turtle 388
Anaya, Rudolfo A. 495, 591
Angelou, Maya 221
Annabel Lee 629
Annixter, Paul 163
Ansen, David 787
Antaeus 347
Asimov, Isaac 675
Atalanta 718
Atalanta's Race 714
Atwood, Ann 841
Auden, W. H. 748
Aunty Misery 701

B

Bamboo Grove 841
Barrio Boy, from 67
Bashō, Matsuo 841
Berry, James 14
Beware of the Dog 603
Beyond the Limits, from 281
Bird Like No Other, The 473
Birdfoot's Grampa 783
Birds Circling at Dusk 841
Birthday Box 175
Black, Carol 41
Black, Martha Louise 634

Bloodworth, Raymond 131
Bombeck, Erma 24
Boy and His Dog, A 243
Boy and His Grandfather, The 495
Bradbury, Ray 461
Brer Rabbit and Brer Lion 755
Broken Chain 44
Brooks, Gwendolyn 361
Brooks, Martha 243
Bruchac, Joseph 268, 783
Buck, Pearl S. 483
Bums in the Attic 329
Bunyans, The 750

C

Cat and Rat: The Legend of the Chinese Zodiac 726
Charles 544
Christie, Sarah 656
Cisneros, Sandra 329
Clifton, Lucille 363
Cofer, Judith Ortiz 701
Cosgrove, Benedict 26
Costello, Lou 555
Courage That My Mother Had, The 341
Cremation of Sam McGee, The 636
Crush, A 149
Cummings, E. E. 205

D

Dahl, Roald 603
Danner, Margaret 231
Deal, Borden 347
Dickinson, Emily 15
Djanikian, Gregory 377
Dodds, Paisley 345
Dog Diaries, The 411
Dreams 261

E

En un Barrio de Los Angeles 334
Evslin, Bernard 743
Eye of the Beholder, The 528

F

Face It 19
Face of Venus, The 459
1st, the 363
First Ballad Interlude from Benjamin Britten's Paul Bunyan 748
Fish Cheeks 77
Fish Crisis, The 295
Flower-Fed Buffaloes, The 823
Force of Luck, The 591
Freeman, Barbara 549
Frost, Robert 835

G

Gage, Nicholas 368
Galarza, Ernesto 67
Giovanni, Nikki 259
Glory, Glory 841
Goodwin, Doris Kearns 35
Growing Pains 133

H

Henry, O. 565
Heroes 24
Highwayman, The 621
Hollywood and the Pits 117
Home 361
Horne, Frank 253
How I Learned English 377
Hughes, Langston 261, 342
Hurricanes 306

I

Icarus and Daedalus 737
I'll Walk the Tightrope 231
I'm Nobody! Who are you? 15
In a Neighborhood in Los Angeles 334
Irving, Washington 185

J

Jackson, Shirley 544
Johnson, Dorothy M. 235
Johnson, Georgia 445
Jungle Book, The 787

K

Kaula, Edna Mason 388
Key Item 675
Kids from Chicago's Cabrini Green Learn Urban Farming in Arkansas 345
Kipling, Rudyard 789
Komunyakaa, Yusef 138

L

Last Cover 163
Lauber, Patricia 306
Lee, Cherylene 117
Lester, Julius 755
Lindsay, Vachel 823
Little, Jean 133
Livingston, Myra Cohn 842
Lob's Girl 659
Longfellow, Henry Wadsworth 227
Loo-Wit 819

M

Markoe, Merrill 411
Marlens, Neal 41

McCaffrey, Anne 683
Meshel, Billy 131
Miles, Betty 718
Millay, Edna St. Vincent 341
Million-Pound Bank Note, The 573
Miracles 784
Monsters Are Due on Maple Street, The 505
Morrison, Lillian 252
Mother to Son 342
My Ninety Years, from 634

N

N.B.A.'s Sister Act, The, from 136
Names/Nombres 5
Nash, J. Madeleine 295
New Directions 221
Night the Bed Fell, The 399
No News 549
Noyes, Alfred 621

O

Oh Broom, Get to Work 383
old age sticks 205
Old Demon, The 483
One 14

P

Parks, Rosa, with Haskins, Jim 85
Pasture, The 835
Patterson, Raymond 841
Peabody, Josephine Preston 737
Poe, Edgar Allan 629
poem (for langston hughes), a 259

Primer Lesson 472
Prometheus 743

R

Racing the Great Bear 268
Regan-Blake, Connie 549
Rikki-tikki-tavi 789
Rip Van Winkle 185
Rosa Parks: My Story, from 85
Rose, Wendy 819
Ross, Gayle 707
Rylant, Cynthia 149

S

Salinas, Marta 451
Sandburg, Carl 472
Scher, Edie 780
Scholarship Jacket, The 451
Seaway Ocean Update 304
See Robby Run, from 780
Seizure-Alert Dog Is Girl's Lifeline 656
Serling, Rod 505
Service, Robert 636
Silko, Leslie Marmon 807
Slam, Dunk, and Hook 138
Smallest Dragonboy, The 683
Soto, Gary 44
Strawberries 707
Strong Men Weep 26

T

TallMountain, Mary 179
Tan, Amy 77
Teacher Who Changed My Life, The 368
There Is No Word for Goodbye 179
There Was a Young Fellow of Ealing 842
Thomas, Piri 433

Thurber, James 399
Time to Change 131
To James 253
Too Soon a Woman 235
T-Shirt 842
Turkeys 827
Twain, Mark 573

U

Uchida, Yoshiko 383
Uncle Tony's Goat 807

W

Wait Till Next Year, from 35
Walker, Alice 59
Warner, Rex 714
We Are All One 773
Welch, Chris 131
West, Dorothy 473
White, Bailey 827
Whitman, Walt 784
Who's on First? 555
Without Commercials 59
Women's 400 Meters, The 252

Wonder Years, The, from 41
Wong, Janet S. 19
Wood, Audrey 750
Wreck of the Hesperus, The 227
Wulf, Steve 136

Y

Yep, Lawrence 773
Yolen, Jane 175
Young, Ed 726
Your World 445

Index of Art and Artists

Angresano, Bill, *Vinny Pazienza* 435

Atl, Dr., *Paisaje con Volcano en Primer Plano* 695

Baeder, John, *Boulevard Diner—Worcester, MA* 154

Beasley, Phoebe, *Sibling Rivals* 51

Bellows, George, *My House, Woodstock* 421

Berni, Antonio, *New Chicago Athletic Club* 352

Birch, Thomas, *Shipwreck* 226

Blumenschein, Ernest L., *New Mexico Peon* 454

Boetticher, Otto, *Union Prisoners at Salisbury, N.C.* 376

Botero, Fernando, *The Musicians* 8

Botnyik, Sandor, *Bokszolok* 442

Brown, Freshman, *Bird in Flight—Bird Series II* 478

Bunker, John S., *Emerging Angel* 178

Burchfield, Charles, *Rainy Night* 566–567

Calne, Sir Roy, *The Two Mythical Dragons* 686, 698

Catlett, Elizabeth, *Survivor* 342

Catlin, George, *View in the 'Grand Detour'* 823, 825

Ch'iu Ying, *Emporor Kuang Wu, of the Western Han Dynasty, Fording a River* 483

Chang Yu-ts'ai, *Beneficent Rain DETAIL #5 and #6* 488–489

Charles, James, *Companions* 245

Chen Baoyi, *Exiles* 486

Clifford, Edward C., *Indeed!* 585, 600

Cole, Thomas, *The Arch of Nero* 616

Cominetti, G., *Boxing* 439

Cummings, E. E., *Self-portrait* 204

Freilicher, Jane, *Early New York Evening* 349

Gattorno, Antonio, *Farmers (Agricultores)* 591

Glass, Andrew, Illustrations from *Ananse's Feast* 388, 389

Griffiths, Diane, *Hawthorne Dusk* 112–113

Gwathmey, Robert, *Children Dancing* 360

Hassam, Childe, *A Back Road* 235

Hayden, Palmer C., *His Hammer in His Hand* 642

Hodges, Elizabeth Barakah, *Fatima* 231

Homer, Winslow, *Fox Hunt* 165

Hopper, Edward, *Night Shadows* 569

Hopper, Edward, *Portrait of Orleans* 507

Hopper, Edward, *Room for Tourists* 514–515

Huo, Bonnie Kwan, *Carte Blanche* 492

Jemison, G. Peter, *Strawberry Dance* 709

Johnson, William H., *Midnight Sun, Lofoten* 462–463

Jones, Loïs Mailou, *The Ascent of Ethiopia* 444

Kahlo, Frida, *Dona Rosita Morillo* 704

Kahlo, Frida, *Portrait of Virginia* 5

Kent, Rockwell, *North (Greenland)* 636–637

Kingman, Eduardo, *Lugar Natal* 324–325

Knight, Dame Laura, *Straithes, Yorkshire* 659

Kopilak, GG, *The Way It Is* 341

Larson, Gregory Blake, *Dragon's Handiwork* 696

Lawrence, Jacob, *The Apartment* 363

Leibovitz, Annie, *Soccer player* 216–217

Leigh, William Robinson, *Rainbow Bridge by Moonlight* 693

Lewis, Dr. Samella, *When I Was a Child* 477

Liska, Hans, *Bundles of Lictors Are Flying over England: Italian and German Bomber Wing in Operation* 607

Magritte, René, *La Grande Famille* 612

Matisse, Henri, *Icarus* 738, 747

Novoa, Gustavo, *Central Park* 768

Novoa, Gustavo, *Full Moon Gossip* 475

Ong, Diana, *Sun Shower* 14–15

Pages, Jules Eugene, *Trees Near Douarnenez* 611

Pennell, Joseph, *West Front of St. Paul's from Ludgate Hill* 578

Perry, Lilla Cabot, *Fuji from Lava Beach* 383

Pierre, Christian, *Dawn Raid* 755

Pierre, Christian, *Emma's Lion* 756

Pierre, Christian, *The Storyteller* 223

Porter, James A., *Woman Holding a Jug* 361

Qui Ti, *Portrait of Pang Tao* 78

Quidor, John, *The Return of Rip Van Winkle* 196

Reinagle, George Philip, *First Rate Man of War Foundering in a Gale* 232

Reiss, Winold, *Portrait of Langston Hughes, 1902–1967, Poet* 261

Richards, William Trost, *A Rocky Coast* 629

Ring, Lauritz Anderson, *Old Man Walking in a Rye Field* 205

Rivera, Diego, *Cabeza de Nino* 67

Rivera, Diego, *Eagle (Aquila)* 598

Rivera, Diego, *La Molendera I* 594

Rockwell, Norman, *Girl at Mirror* 1

Rodrigue, George, *My Favorite Part of Town* 412

Ruiz-Tagle, Maria Angelica, *Ayer Tuve un Sueño* 652

Rumbaugh, Marshall D., *Civil Rights Activist* 100

Rungius, Carl, *Grizzly Bear in a Mountainous Landscape* 268–269

Shannon, David, Illustrations from *The Bunyans* 750–751, 753

Silverman, Sherri, *Crescent Moon Over the Southwest* 810

Sloane, Eric, *Autumn* 835

Soyer, Raphael, *Girl with a Red Hat* 22

Unknown, Contemporary Zuni alabaster carving 275

Unknown, Early eighteenth-century Mughal tent hanging 791

Unknown, Haida carving of female figure 179

Unknown, Iroquois wampum belts 270, 271

Unknown, Native American bear claw necklace 274

Unknown, *Prometheus Giving Fire to Man*, first-century Roman mosaic tile 744

Unknown, River scene, eighteenth-century Chinese painting 776

West, Debby, *Haunted House, Aspen* 473

Wibberley, John D., *Spokes* 53

Wilson, Jane, *Storm Light* 631

Wilson, Jane, *Stormy Midnight* 520

Wyeth, Jamie, *Moon Landing* 623

Wyeth, N. C., *Dog with Broom Thrown at Him* 201

Wyeth, N. C., *Gnomes Bowling* 192–193

Wyeth, N. C., *Rip as Old Man* 202

Wyeth, N. C., *Rip Fishing* 203

Wyeth, N. C., *Rip Hunting* 207

Wyeth, N. C., *Rip Van Winkle Returns Home* 195

Wyeth, N. C., *Rip With Dog Under Tree* 190

Wyeth, N. C., *Termagant Wife* 188

Wyeth, N. C., Title page from *Rip Van Winkle* 185

Yao Song, *Landscape* 778

Young, Ed, Illustrations from *Cat and Rat: The Legend of the Chinese Zodiac* 726–727, 729, 731–732

Acknowledgments

(Continued from page iv)

Literature

Theme 1

"Names/Nombres" Copyright © 1985 by Julia Alvarez. First published in *Nuestro,* March 1985. Reprinted by permission of Susan Bergholz Literary Services, New York. All rights reserved.

"One" from *When I Dance,* copyright © 1991, 1988 by James Berry, reprinted by permission of Harcourt Brace & Company.
"One" from *When I Dance,* copyright © 1991, 1988 by James Berry. Reprinted by permission of The Peters Fraser Dunlop Group Limited on behalf of the author.

"I'm Nobody! Who are you?" reprinted by permission of the publishers and the Trustees of Amherst College from *The Poems of Emily Dickinson,* Thomas H. Johnson, ed., Cambridge, Mass.: The Belknap Press of Harvard University Press, Copyright © 1951, 1955, 1979, 1983 by the President and Fellows of Harvard College.

"Face It" reprinted with the permission of Margaret K. McElderry Books, an imprint of Simon & Schuster Children's Publishing Division from *A Suitcase of Seaweed and Other Poems* by Janet S. Wong. Copyright © 1996 Janet S. Wong.

"Almost Ready" from *Slow Dance Heart Break Blues* by Arnold Adoff. Copyright © 1995 by Arnold Adoff. Reprinted by permission of Lothrop, Lee & Shepard Books, a division of William Morrow & Company, Inc.

"Heroes" by Erma Bombeck, reprinted by permission of the Aaron Priest Literary Agency, Inc.

Foreword by Ron Rapaport from *Covering the Bases* by Benedict Cosgrove, © 1997, published by Chronicle Books, San Francisco.

"Strong Men Weep" by Shirley Povitch. Copyright © 1939 The Washington Post. Reprinted with permission.

Reprinted with the permission of Simon & Schuster from *Wait Till Next Year* by Doris Kearns Goodwin. Copyright © 1997 by Blithedale Productions.

"Broken Chain" from *Baseball in April and Other Stories,* copyright © 1990 by Gary Soto, reprinted by permission of Harcourt Brace & Company.

"Without Commercials" from *Horses Make a Landscape Look More Beautiful,* copyright © 1984 by Alice Walker, reprinted by permission of Harcourt Brace & Company.

From *Barrio Boy* by Ernesto Galarza. Copyright © 1971 by the University of Notre Dame Press: Notre Dame, Indiana. Reprinted by permission of the publisher.

"Fish Cheeks" Copyright © 1987 by Amy Tan. First appeared in *Seventeen* Magazine. Reprinted by permission of Amy Tan and the Sandra Dijkstra Literary Agency.

From *Rosa Parks: My Story* by Rosa Parks with Jim Haskins. Copyright © 1992 by Rosa Parks. Used by permission of Dial Books for Young Readers, a division of Penguin Books USA Inc.

Theme 2

"Hollywood and the Pits," copyright © 1992 by Cherylene Lee. Reprinted by permission of Bret Adams Ltd.

"Time to Change" by Raymond Bloodworth, Chris Welch and Billy Meshel. Copyright © 1971 by Famous Music Corporation. Reprinted by permission.

"Growing Pains" from *Hey World, Here I Am!* Copyright © 1986 by Jean Little. Used by permission of HarperCollins Publishers.
"Growing Pains" from *Hey World, Here I Am!* by Jean Little used by permission of Kids Can Press Ltd., Toronto. Copyright © 1986 by Jean Little. Available in the U.S. from HarperCollins.

"NBA's Sister Act" by Steve Wulf. Copyright © 1997 Time Inc. Reprinted by permission.

Yusef Komunyakaa, "Slam, Dunk and Hook" from *Magic City,* © 1992 by Yusef Komunyakaa, Wesleyan University Press by permission of the University Press of New England.

"A Crush" from *A Couple of Kooks and Other Stories About Love* by Cynthia Rylant. Copyright © 1990 by Cynthia Rylant. Reprinted by permission of Orchard Books, New York.

"Last Cover" from *The Best Nature Stories of Paul Annixter.* Copyright © 1974 by Jane and Paul Annixter. Reprinted by permission of Lawrence Hill Books, an imprint of Chicago Review Press, Inc.

"Birthday Box" by Jane Yolen. Copyright © 1995 by Jane Yolen. First appeared in *Birthday Surprises: Ten Great Stories to Unwrap,* published by Morrow Junior Books. Reprinted by permission of Curtis Brown, Ltd.

"There Is No Word for Goodbye" by Mary TallMountain. Copyright © 1994 TallMountain Estate, previously published in *Light on the Tent Wall,* LA:AISC, 1990. Reprinted by permission of the TallMountain Circle.

"old age sticks," copyright © 1958, 1986, 1991 by the Trustees for the E. E. Cummings Trust, from *Complete Poems: 1904–1962* by E. E. Cummings. Edited by George J. Firmage. Reprinted by permission of Liveright Publishing Corporation.

Theme 3

"New Directions" from *Wouldn't Take Nothing For My Journey Now* by Maya Angelou. Copyright © 1993 by Maya Angelou. Reprinted by permission of Random House, Inc.

"Too Soon a Woman" by Dorothy M. Johnson. Copyright © 1953 and renewed © 1981 by Dorothy M. Johnson. By permission of McIntosh and Otis, Inc.

"A Boy and His Dog" from *Paradise Café and Other Stories* by Martha Brooks. Copyright © 1988 by Martha Brooks. By permission of Little, Brown and Company.
"A Boy and His Dog" by Martha Brooks, from *Paradise Café and Other Stories* (Thistledown Press Ltd., 1988).

"The Women's 400 Meters" from *The Sidewalk Racer and Other Poems of Sports and Motion* by Lillian Morrison. Copyright © 1968, 1977 Lillian Morrison. Used by permission of Marian Reiner for the author.

"A Poem (for langston hughes)", copyright © 1995 by Nikki Giovanni, from *The Selected Poems of Nikki Giovanni*.

"Dreams" from *Collected Poems* by Langston Hughes. Copyright © 1994 by the Estate of Langston Hughes. Reprinted by permission of Alfred A. Knopf, Inc.

"Racing the Great Bear" from *Flying with the Eagle, Racing the Great Bear*. Copyright © 1993 by Joseph Bruchac. Reprinted by permission of Bridgewater Books, an imprint of Troll Communications, L.L.C.

"Blown Away" from *Beyond the Limits* by Stacy Allison. Copyright © 1993 by Stacy Allison and Peter Carlin. By permission of Little, Brown and Company.

"Fish Crisis" by J. Madeline Nash. Copyright © 1997 Time Inc. Reprinted by permission.

"Americans Continue to Worry About the Decline of the Oceans" a SeaWeb Ocean Update, February 1998. © 1998 SeaWeb.

"There aren't many of us left . . ." (cartoon). The *Washington Post* National Weekly Edition, December 8, 1997. Reprinted by permission of Scott Bateman.

"Big Winds and Big Damage" from *Hurricanes* by Patricia Lauber. Copyright © 1996 by Patricia Lauber. Reprinted by permission of Scholastic, Inc.

Theme 4

"Bums in the Attic" from *The House on Mango Street*. Copyright © 1984 by Sandra Cisneros. Published by Vintage Books, a division of Random House, Inc., and in hardcover by Alfred A. Knopf. Reprinted by permission of Susan Bergholz Literary Services, New York. All rights reserved.

"En un Barrio de Los Angeles/In a Neighborhood in Los Angeles" from *Body in Flames: Cuerpo en Llamas* by Francisco Alarcon, © 1990, published by Chronicle Books, San Francisco.

"The Courage That My Mother Had" by Edna St. Vincent Millay. From *Collected Poems*, HarperCollins. Copyright © 1954, 1982 by Norma Millay Ellis. All rights reserved. Used by permission of Elizabeth Barnett, literary executor.

"Mother to Son" from *Collected Poems* by Langston Hughes. Copyright © 1994 by the Estate of Langston Hughes. Reprinted by permission of Alfred A. Knopf, Inc.

"Kids from Chicago's Cabrini Green Learn Urban Farming in Arkansas" by Paisley Dodds. *Associated Press,* August 19, 1997. Reprinted by permission of Associated Press.

"Home" from the novel *Maud Martha* by Gwendolyn Brooks. Copyright © 1991 by Gwendolyn Brooks Blakely. Published by Third World Press, Chicago. Reprinted by permission of the author.

"the 1st" copyright © 1969 by Lucille Clifton. First appeared in *Good Times,* published by Random House. Reprinted by permission of Curtis Brown, Ltd.

"The Teacher Who Changed My Life" by Nicholas Gage. Reprinted with permission of the author and *Parade,* copyright © 1989.

"How I Learned English" by Gregory Djanikian, from *Falling Deeply into America,* Carnegie-Mellon University Press, 1989. Reprinted by permission of Gregory Djanikian.

"Oh Broom, Get to Work" reprinted with the permission of Simon & Schuster Books for Young Readers, an imprint of Simon & Schuster Children's Publishing Division from *The Invisible Thread* by Yoshiko Uchida. Copyright © 1991 by Yoshiko Uchida.

"The Night the Bed Fell," copyright © 1933 by James Thurber. Copyright © renewed 1961 by Hellen Thurber and Rosemary A. Thurber. Reprinted by arrangement with Rosemary A. Thurber and the Barbara Hogenson Agency.

"Dog Diaries" from *What the Dogs Have Taught Me* by Merrill Markoe. Copyright © 1992 by Merrill Markoe. Used by permission of Viking Penguin, a division of Penguin Books USA Inc.

Theme 5

"Amigo Brothers" from *Stories from the Barrio* by Piri Thomas. Copyright © 1978 by Piri Thomas. Reprinted by permission of the author.

"The Face of Venus" from *Views of the Solar System*. Copyright © Calvin J. Hamilton. Reprinted by permission.

"All Summer in a Day" by Ray Bradbury. Reprinted by permission of Don Congdon Associates, Inc. Copyright © 1954, renewed 1982 by Ray Bradbury.

"The Bird Like No Other" from *The Richer, The Poorer,* by Dorothy West. Copyright © 1995 by Dorothy West. Used by permission of Doubleday, a division of Bantam Doubleday Dell Publishing Group, Inc.

"The Old Demon" by Pearl S. Buck. Reprinted by permission of Harold Ober Associates Inc. Copyright © 1939 by Pearl S. Buck. Copyright renewed 1966 by Pearl S. Buck.

"The Boy and His Grandfather" by Rudolfo Anaya, from *Cuentos: Tales from the Hispanic Southwest.* Copyright © 1980 by the Museum of New Mexico Press.

"The Monsters Are Due On Maple Street" by Rod Serling. Reprinted by permission of The Rod Serling Trust. All rights reserved. © 1960 Rod Serling; © 1988 by Carolyn Serling, Jodi Serling and Anne Serling.

Theme 6

"Charles" from *The Lottery* by Shirley Jackson. Copyright © 1948, 1949 by Shirley Jackson, and copyright renewed © 1976 by Laurence Hyman, Barry Hyman, Mrs. Sarah Webster and Mrs. Joanne Schnurer. Reprinted by permission of Farrar, Straus & Giroux, Inc.

"No News" retold by Connie Regan-Blake and Barbara Freeman. Reprinted by permission of Connie Regan-Blake and Folktellers.

"Who's on First?" by Bud Abbott and Lou Costello reprinted by permission of TCA Television Corp., The Estate of Bud Abbott Jr. and Hi Neighbor.

"The Million-Pound Bank Note" reprinted by permission from *Radio Plays for Young People,* by Walter Hackett. Copyright © 1950 by Walter Hackett. Publishers: Plays, Inc., Boston, MA.

"The Force of Luck" by Rudolfo A. Anaya, from *Cuentos.* Copyright © 1980 by the Museum of New Mexico Press. Reprinted by permission.

"Beware of Dog" from *Over to You,* copyright © 1946 by Roald Dahl. Reprinted by permission of the Estate of Roald Dahl and the Watkins/Loomis Agency.

Excerpted from *Martha Black,* edited by Flo Whyard, Copyright © 1976, 1980, 1986 and 1988. Reprinted with permission of Alaska Northwest Books™.

Theme 7

Excerpt from "Seizure-Alert Dog Is Girl's Lifeline" by Sarah Christie, from *Dog Fancy,* June 1997. Reprinted by permission of the author.

"Lob's Girl" from *A Whisper in the Night* by Joan Aiken. Copyright © 1984 by Joan Aiken. Used by permission of Bantam Doubleday Dell Books for Young Readers.
"Lob's Girl," copyright © Joan Aiken Enterprises Ltd., 1984. Reprinted by permission of A. M. Heath.

"Key Item" from *Buy Jupiter and Other Stories* by Isaac Asimov. Copyright © 1975 by Isaac Asimov. Used by permission of Doubleday, a division of Bantam Doubleday Dell Publishing Group, Inc.

"The Smallest Dragonboy" by Anne McCaffrey. Reprinted by permission of Checkerboard Press.

"Aunty Misery: A Folktale from Puerto Rico" by Judith Ortiz Cofer. Reprinted by permission of the author.

"Strawberries," a traditional Cherokee story retold by Gayle Ross. Reprinted by permission of the author.

"Atalanta's Race" from *Men and Gods* by Rex Warner. Copyright © 1950 by MacGibbon & Kee. Reprinted by permission of Michigan State University Press.

"Atalanta" by Betty Miles. Copyright © 1973 Free To Be Foundation, Inc.

Cat and Rat: The Legend of the Chinese Zodiac by Ed Young. Copyright © 1995 by Ed Young. Reprinted by permission of Henry Holt and Company, Inc.

"Prometheus" from *Heroes, Gods and Monsters of Greek Myths* by Bernard Evslin. Copyright © 1966, 1977 by Scholastic, Inc. Reprinted by permission of Scholastic, Inc.

"First Battle Interlude from Paul Bunyan" from *The Complete Works of W. H. Auden: Libretti.* Reprinted by permission of Faber & Faber.

The Bunyans by Audrey Wood, illustrated by David Shannon. Text copyright © 1996 by Audrey Wood, illustrations copyright © 1996 by David Shannon. All rights reserved. Reprinted by permission of Scholastic, Inc. Published by The Blue Sky Press, an imprint of Scholastic, Inc.

"Brer Rabbit and Brer Lion" from *The Tales of Uncle Remus* by Julius Lester. Copyright © 1987 by Julius Lester. Used by permission of Dial Books for Young Readers, a division of Penguin Books USA Inc.

Theme 8

"We Are All One" from *The Rainbow People* by Laurence Yep. Copyright © 1989 by Laurence Yep. Used by permission of HarperCollins Publishers.

"See Robby Run" by Edie Scher. Reprinted by permission of Runner's World Magazine. Copyrighted 1998, Rodale Press, Inc., all rights reserved.

"Birdfoot's Grampa" from *Entering Onondaga,* copyright © 1975 by Joseph Bruchac. Reprinted by permission of Barbara S. Kouts.

"The Jungle Book" review by David Ansen, from *Newsweek,* January 16, 1995. Copyright © 1995 Newsweek, Inc. All rights reserved. Reprinted by permission.

"Uncle Tony's Goat" Copyright © 1981 by Leslie Marmon Silko. Reprinted from *Storyteller* by Leslie Marmon Silko, published by Seaver Books, New York, New York.

"Loo-Wit" copyright © 1985 by Wendy Rose. Reprinted by permission of West End Press.

"The Flower-Fed Buffaloes," from *Going to the Stars* by Vachel Lindsay. Copyright 1926 by D. Appleton & Co., renewed 1954 by Elizabeth C. Lindsay. A Hawthorn Book. Used by permission of Dutton's Children's Books, a division of Penguin Books USA Inc.

"Turkeys" from B. White, *Mama Makes Up Her Mind,* © 1993 by Bailey White. Reprinted by permission of Addison-Wesley Longman, Inc.

Reprinted with the permission of Atheneum Books for Young Readers, an imprint of Simon & Schuster Children's Publishing division from *Haiku-Vision* by Ann Atwood. Copyright © 1977 Ann Atwood.

"Bamboo Grove" from *An Introduction to Haiku* by Harold G. Henderson. Copyright © 1958 by Harold G. Henderson. Used by permission of Doubleday, a division of Bantam Doubleday Dell Publishing Group, Inc.

"Glory, Glory," from *26 Ways of Looking at a Black Man and Other Poems* by Raymond R. Patterson. Copyright © 1969 by Raymond R. Patterson. Reprinted by permission of the author.

"T-Shirt" from *O Sliver of Liver* by Myra Cohn Livingston. Copyright © 1979 by Myra Cohn Livingston. Used by permission of Marian Reiner.

"There was a young fellow of ealing . . ." from *Peter Pauper's Limerick Book.* Reprinted by permission of Peter Pauper Press, Inc.

Maps

Ortelius Design, Inc.

Photography

Abbreviation key: **AH**=Aaron Haupt Photography; **AR**=Art Resource, New York; **BAL**=Bridgeman Art Library, London/New York; **CB**=Corbis/Bettmann; **CI**=Christie's Images; **LPBC/AH**=book provided by Little Professor Book Company. Photo by AH; **LOC**=Library of Congress; **PR**=Photo Researchers; **SIS**=Stock Illustration Source; **SS**=SuperStock; **TSI**=Tony Stone Images; **TSM**=The Stock Market.

Cover (guitar)Doug Martin, (painting)*The Guitar Player,* 1897. Pierre Auguste Renoir. Oil on canvas. Musée des Beaux Arts, Lyon, France/SS; **vii** (t to b)Bob Fitch/Black Star, Millport Conservancy, SS, SS, Bill Angresano, Photofest, Scholastic, Inc., Jeff & Alexa Henry/Peter Arnold, Inc.; **viii** Printed by permission of the Norman Rockwell Family Trust ©1954 the Norman Rockwell Family; **ix** (l)Rich Brommer, (r)The Grand Design/SS; **x** (t)Amanita Pictures, (b)Stuart Kingston Gallery; **xi** Annie Leibovitz/Contact Press Images; **xii** Reproduced by permission of the IDB; **xiii** (t)Ken Chernus/FPG, (b)Glencoe photo; **xiv** Larry Hamill; **xv** Mark Burnett; **xvi** (t)Jason Hawkes/TSI, (b)Mark Burnett; **xvii** (l)Imperial War Museum, (r)Kactus Foto, Santiago, Chile/SS; **xviii** Dan Bosler/TSI; **xix** Wally Findlay Galleries, New York/SS; **xx** Jeff Lynch/Mendola Ltd./TSM; **xxi** (t)The Newark Museum/AR, (b)UPI/CB; **xxii** (l)Jade Albert/FPG, (r)Sid and Diana Avery Trust; **xxiii** John Lund/TSI; **1** Printed by permission of the Norman Rockwell Family Trust ©1954 the Norman Rockwell Family; **2** Drawing by Chas. Addams, ©1977 The New Yorker Magazine, Inc.; **3** (t)Lisa Quinones/

Black Star, (cl)Al Rendon/CB, (cr)Eric Lars/Black Star, (b)Fred Ward/ Black Star; **4** Theo Westernberger/Gamma Liaison; **5** Schalkwijk/AR; **6** Chuck Pefley/TSI; **7** Robert Van Der Hilst/TSI; **8** CI; **9, 10** Mark Burnett; **13** (tl)courtesy Harper Collins, (r)Trustees of Amherst College, (bl)CB; **14–15** Diana Ong/SS; **16** Joseph T. Collins/PR; **18** (t)courtesy Simon & Schuster, (b)Virginia Hamilton Adoff; **19** Mark Burnett; **20** SS; **22** AR; **24** AP/Wide World; **25** (l)courtesy Benedict Cosgrove, (r)courtesy *The Washington Post;* **26** UPI/CB; **27** FPG; **28** Photo File; **31** UPI/ CB; **32, 33** Mark Burnett; **34** (l)AP Photo/Steve Herbert, (r)FPG; **35** Mark Burnett; **36** CB; **37** UPI/CB; **38, 39** FPG; **40** CB; **41, 42** Photofest; **43** (l)courtesy Gary Soto, (r)Walter Bibikow/FPG; **44** Mark Gottlieb/FPG; **46** Richard Laird/FPG; **47** Alan & Sandy Carey/PR; **49** Mark Burnett; **51** Phoebe Beasley; **53** John D. Wibberley; **54** Mark Gottlieb/FPG; **58** (t)Adam Scull/Globe Photos, (b)Chris Brown/Stock Boston; **64** AH; **66** Courtesy Stanford University News Service; **67** CI; **68** FPG; **69** City of Sacramento Archives and Museum Collection Center; **70** Rich Brommer; **74** City of Sacramento Archives and Museum Collection Center; **76** (l)Andrea Renault/Globe Photos, (r)FoodPix; **77** Mark Burnett; **78** Courtesy Dr. Michael Sullivan, St. Catherine's College, Oxford, England; **80** Flip Nicklin/Minden Pictures; **82** (t)E.R. Degginger/PR, (cl)Geoff Butler, (cr)courtesy John Scott & Son Haggis, Fife, Scotland, (b)Kelvin Aitken/Peter Arnold, Inc.; **84** Bob Fitch/Black Star; **85** Brian Lanker; **86** The publisher wishes to thank The National Association for the Advancement of Colored People for authorizing the use of this photograph; **88** AP/Wide World Photos; **92, 95** Dan Weiner, courtesy Sandra Weiner; **98, 99** AP/Wide World Photos; **100** National Museum of American Art, Washington DC/AR; **101** AP/Wide World Photos; **102** CB; **105** Mark Burnett; **109** (br)Mark Burnett, (others)AH; **112–113** The Grand Design/SS; **115** (t)Ray Ellis/ PR, (b)Rafael Macia/PR; **116, 120** Courtesy Cherylene Lee; **117** Ken Biggs/TSI; **119** Tom McHugh/PR; **123** Greg Vaughn/Tom Stack & Associates; **124,126** Natural History Museum of Los Angeles County/ Tom McHugh/PR; **127, 130** Tom McHugh/PR; **128** Amanita Pictures; **131** Photofest; **132** (l)courtesy Penguin Books, Toronto, (r)Rick Rusing/ TSI; **135** Jeffrey Myers/FPG; **136** DUOMO/Darren Carroll; **137** (l)Tony Getsug, (r)David Madison/TSI; **139** Carl Schneider/Gamma Liaison; **140** Glencoe photo; **146–147** Mark Burnett; **148** (l)courtesy Blue Sky Press, (r)LPI/FPG; **149** Mark Burnett; **150** Hulton Getty/TSI; **152, 153** Mark Burnett; **154** O.K. Harris Works of Art, New York; **157** Derek Fell; **158** Amanita Pictures; **163** Gene Frazier; **165** Museum of American Art, Philadelphia; **168** John W. Warden/SS; **172** Alvin E. Staffan; **174** (t)Jason Stemple, (bl)University of Fairbanks AK, (br)Amanita Pictures; **175–176** Mark Steinmetz; **178** SS; **179** John Bigelow Taylor, New York/Thaw Collection, Fenimore House Museum, Cooperstown NY; **180** Geoff Butler; **184** FPG; **185** The Millport Conservancy; **186** Glencoe photo; **188** The Millport Conservancy; **190** Stuart Kingston Gallery; **193, 195** The Millport Conservancy; **196** National Gallery of Art, Washington DC; **201, 202, 203** Stuart Kingston Gallery; **204** CB; **205** SS; **207** Stuart Kingston Gallery; **213** AH; **216–217** Annie Leibovitz/Contact Press Images; **219** Ray Pfortner/Peter Arnold, Inc.; **220** Thomas Lau/Outline; **221** James Selkin/Gamma Liaison; **222** Mark Burnett; **223** Private collection/ Christian Pierre/SS; **226** (t)*Harper's Weekly*/CB, (c)CI, (b)courtesy Pinkie Gardner; **229** The Metropolitan Museum of Art, New York; **231** Elizabeth Barakah Hodges/SS; **232** Royal Albert Memorial Museum, Exeter, England/BAL/SS; **234** Mansfield Library Archives, University of MT, Missoula; **235** The Brooklyn Museum: Polhemus Fund; **236** Bob Daemmrich/The Image Works; **240** Ed Reschke/Peter Arnold, Inc.; **242** (l)courtesy Martha Brooks, (r)Kent Knudson/Stock Boston; **243** Glencoe photo; **245** Oldham Art Gallery, Manchester, England/BAL/SS; **249** (t)Ed Reschke/Peter Arnold, Inc., (b)Mark Burnett; **252–253** Spencer Rowell/FPG; **254** Blair Seitz/PR; **255** Jim Cummins/FPG; **256** Glencoe photo; **258** (t)Barron Claiborne/Outline, (bl)LOC/Corbis, (br)Sherry Suris/PR; **259** Glencoe photo; **261** National Portrait Gallery, Smithsonian Institution/AR; **262** William J. Weber; **263** Doug Martin; **266** (t)James Firmiss, *The Wonderful Skunk & Opossum Web Site v. 4,* (b)David M. Dennis; **267** (l)courtesy Joseph

Bruchac, (r)courtesy the British Museum; **268–269** CI; **270** Courtesy The NY State Museum, Albany; **271** Newberry Library, Chicago/SS; **272, 273, 274** CI; **275** Catherine Gehm; **276** Glencoe photo; **279** (tr)Larry Moore/SIS, (others)Glencoe photo; **280** Courtesy Stacy Allison; **281** Nova Online/Gamma Liaison; **282** Tom McHugh/PR; **284, 286** Nova Online/Gamma Liaison; **292–293** Jeff Greenberg/PR; **294** Time, Inc.; **295** Matt Johnson/Alaska Stock; **297** Vanessa Vick/PR; **298** ©1997 Time, Inc. Reprinted by permission; **301** Rondi/Tani Church/PR; **302** Glencoe photo; **303** Richard Ellis/PR; **304** Scott Bateman; **305** Courtesy Scholastic, Inc.; **307** Len Kaufman/Black Star; **308** Ben Van Hook/Black Star; **310** Larry Lipsky/Tom Stack & Associates; **311** Steven Jaffe/Reuters/CB; **312** Bill Hoyt/Panoramic Images; **321** (b)Mark Burnett; (others)AH; **324–325** Reproduced by permission of the IDB; **326** The Cartoon Bank; **328** (t)M. Toussaint/Gamma Liaison, (b)LPBC/AH; **329** Vic Huber/Corbis Los Angeles; **332** (tl br)SS, (tr)Hans Blohm/Masterfile, (bl)Chris Salvo/FPG, (inset)AH; **333** Annie Valva/Chronicle Books; **334–335** Comstock; **340** LOC/Corbis; **341** SS; **342** Armistad Research Center, Tulane University; **343** Bob Daemmrich/ TSI; **345** Danny Johnston/AP/Wide World Photos; **346** Babs H. Deal/ AP/Wide World Photos; **347** Glencoe photo; **348** SS; **348–356** (grass) Glencoe photo; **349** Jane Freilicher, courtesy Tibor de Nagy Gallery, New York; **352** Photograph ©1997 The Museum of Modern Art, New York. Inter-American Fund; **357** Alan & Linda Detrick/PR; **358** Renato Rotolo/Gamma Liaison; **360** (t)UPI/CB, (bl)Gerardo Somoza/Outline, (br)Butler Institute of American Art, Youngstown OH; **361** Fisk University Art Gallery; **363** Hunter Museum of American Art, Chattanooga TN; **367** Allen/Gamma Liaison; **368** Eddie Adams; **371, 372** Courtesy Nicholas Gage; **373** J. Noelker/The Image Works; **374** Courtesy Nicholas Gage; **376** (t)Tommy Leonardi, (b)Print Collection, Miriam and Ira D. Wallach Division of Arts, Prints and Photographs. The New York Public Library. Astor, Lennox and Tilden Foundation; **377** Glencoe photo; **378** Ken Chernus/FPG; **379** John Goodman/FPG; **380** (t)courtesy Nicholas Gage, (b)Glencoe photo; **382** (l)courtesy McMillan, (r)Mark Burnett; **383** Courtesy Mr. and Mrs. Jay Peter Moffat; **384** Glencoe photo; **386** Mark Burnett; **387** Tomomi Saito/Dunq/PR; **388, 389** From *Ananse's Feast: An Ashanti Tale* by Tolowa M. Mollel. Jacket illustration ©1997 by Andrew Glass. Reprinted by permission of Clarion Books/ Houghton Mifflin Company. All rights reserved; **390** Bonnie Sue/PR; **391** Mark Burnett; **398** (l)CB, (r)©1933 by James Thurber. ©Renewed 1960 by James Thurber. Reprinted by arrangement with Rosemary A. Thurber and the Barbara Hogenson Agency; **401, 402** ©1933 by James Thurber. ©Renewed 1960 by James Thurber. Reprinted by arrangement with Rosemary A. Thurber and the Barbara Hogenson Agency; **403** Carey/The Image Works; **405, 407** ©1933 by James Thurber. ©Renewed 1960 by James Thurber. Reprinted by arrange-ment with Rosemary A. Thurber and the Barbara Hogenson Agency; **410** Michael Ferguson/Globe Photos; **411** Mark Steinmetz; **412** Courtesy Rodrigue Studio; **414** Sandy Skoglund/SS; **416** Mark Steinmetz; **418** Stephanie Rausser/FPG; **421** Sid and Diana Avery Trust; **425** (br)Mark Burnett, (others)AH; **428–429** Larry Hamill; **431** Glencoe photo; **432** Courtesy Piri Thomas; **433** Spencer/ Jones/FPG; **435** Bill Angresano; **439** Fratelli Alinari/SS; **442** CI; **444** (l)Photographs and Prints Division, Schomburg Center for Research in Black Culture. The New York Public Library. Astor, Lenox and Tilden Foundations, (r)Milwaukee Art Museum; **445** M. Angelo/ Corbis Los Angeles; **447** Mark Burnett; **448** (t)Arthur Tilley/FPG, (b)Jade Albert/FPG; **449** (t)Larry Moore/SIS, (b)Rosanne Olson/ TSI; **450** Bob Daemmrich/The Image Works; **451** Mark Burnett; **453** Walter H. Hodge/Peter Arnold, Inc.; **454** Gerald Peters Gallery, Sante Fe NM; **456** Mark Burnett; **457** Bob Daemmrich/Stock Boston; **459** Jack Zehrt/FPG; **460** Satelight/Gamma Liaison; **461** Jeffrey Myers/FPG; **462–463** AR; **464** SS; **465** Glencoe photo; **466** Jeffrey Myers/FPG; **467** Freeman Patterson/Masterfile; **468** Glencoe photo; **471** (t)FPG, (b)Vincent Frye; **473, 475** SS; **477** Stella Jones Gallery, New Orleans LA; **478** Louise Freshman Brown/SS; **482** (t)Wide World Photo, (b)Miriam Berkley; **483** National Gallery of Canada; **486** Courtesy Dr. Michael Sullivan, St. Catherine's College, Oxford,

England; **488–489** The Metropolitan Museum of Art, New York. Photograph by Malcolm Varon; **492** Private collection/Bonnie Kwan Huo/SS; **494** Mark Burnett; **495** Bjorn Bolstad/Peter Arnold, Inc.; **496** Jim Cummins/FPG; **497** AP/Wide World Photos; **500** Masterfile; **502–503** Geoff Butler; **504** UPI/CB; **507** Fine Arts Museums of San Francisco; **508** FPG; **513** E.T. Archive, London/SS; **514–515** Yale University Art Gallery; **520** Peter Jacobs, New York; **525** Photofest; **526** FPG; **528** CBS Photo Archive; **530** Bob Fitch/Black Star; **531** (t)courtesy Stacy Allison, (b)CB; **535** (br)Lawrence Migdale, (others)AH; **538–539** Jason Hawkes/TSI; **540** Photofest; **543** (t)Lawrence J. Hyman, courtesy Bantam Books, (bl)courtesy Barbara Freeman, (br)Laura Dwight/Peter Arnold, Inc.; **544** Amanita Pictures; **545** Hulton Getty/TSI; **548–549** From the Permanent Collection of the Museum of American Folk Art; **551** Julianne Fringado, age 5; **554** (t)CB, (b)Culver Pictures; **555** CB; **557** Mark Burnett; **560** Photofest/Jagarts; **564** CB; **565** Doug Martin; **566–567** San Diego Museum of Art; **569** Whitney Museum of American Art, New York; **571** (t)Larry Moore/SIS, (b)Lawrence Migdale; **572** (l)AP/Wide World Photos, (r)Photofest; **578** CI; **585** Christopher Wood Gallery, London/BAL/SS; **588** Photofest/Jagarts; **590** (l)Miriam Berkley, (r)Kathy Plunkett Versluys/FPG; **591, 594** CI/SS; **598** Schalkwijk/AR; **601** G. Randall/FPG, (inset)Christian Michaels/FPG; **602** (l)Horst Tappe/Camera Press London, (r)Salamander Picture Library; **607** A.K.G. Berlin/SS; **609** Imperial War Museum; **610** Geoff Butler; **611** CI; **612** Charly Herscovici/AR; **614** Salamander Picture Library; **616** The Newark Museum/AR; **618–619** Lawrence Migdale; **620** (t)AP/Wide World Photos, (b)Farrell Grehan/FPG; **621** Hermann Eisenheiss/PR; **623** James Wyeth; **626** Richard Pasley/Viesti Associates; **628** (t)FPG, (b)CB; **629** The Metropolitan Museum of Art, New York. Photograph by Geoffrey Clements; **630** J.H. Robinson/PR; **631** Peter Jacobs, New York; **632** National Museum of American Art, Washington DC/AR; **634** Culver Pictures; **635** UPI/CB; **636–637** Courtesy Rockwell Kent Legacies; **638–640** NSPI/Mauritius/Nawrocki; **641** SS; **642** Collection of The Museum of African American Art, Los Angeles CA. Palmer C. Hayden Collection, Gift of Marian A. Hayden; **649** (br)Mark Burnett, (others)AH; **652–635** Kactus Foto, Santiago, Chile/SS; **654** The New Yorker Magazine, Inc.; **655** Icon Images; **656, 657** Mark Hertzberg/*Racine Journal Times;* **658** Rod Delroy; **659** CI; **660** Franz Gorski/Peter Arnold, Inc.; **663** Onne Van Der Wal/Stock Newport; **665** Peter Henschel/FPG; **669** John Chard/TSI; **670** Lawrence Migdale/PR; **674** (l)Peter C. Jones/Alex Gotfryd/CB, (r)Jonathan Elderfield/Gamma Liaison; **678** Dan Piraro/Universal Press Syndicate; **679** Paul Shambroom/PR; **680** Glencoe photo; **681** Alex Bartel/Science Photo Library/PR; **682** (l)Tara Heinemann/Camera Press London, (r)Werner Forman/AR; **686** Roy Calne/SS; **693, 695** CI; **696** Private collection/Greg Larson/SS; **698** Roy Calne/SS; **699** Mark Burnett; **700** Miriam Berkley; **701** Glencoe photo; **703** Charles Benes/FPG; **704** Schalkwijk/AR; **706** (l)courtesy Gayle Ross, (r)Newberry Library, SS; **707** (t)Michael P. Gadomski/PR,

(b)Miyoko Komine/Photonica; **709** (t)G. Peter Jemison, (b)Miyoko Komine/Photonica; **710** Larry Hamill; **713** Glencoe photo; **714** Melanie Carr/The Viesti Collection; **715** Gianni Dagli/CB; **716, 718–719** Dan Bosler/TSI; **720** T. Zimmerman/FPG; **722** Amanita Pictures; **723** Arthur Tilley/FPG; **725** (l)courtesy Henry Holt and Co., Inc., (r)Dennis Cox/FPG; **726 through 731** Reprinted by permission of Henry Holt and Co., Inc.; **733** Vanessa Vick/PR; **736** Courtesy Radcliffe College Archives; **737** (t)Glencoe photo, (r)Art Montes de Oca/FPG; **738** Giradon/AR; **740** S. Brookens/TSM; **742** (l)courtesy Mrs. Bernard Evslin, (r)Museo Gregoriano Etrusco Vaticano/AR; **743** Japack/Corbis Los Angeles; **744** (t)Gianni Dagli Oriti/Corbis, (b)Japack/Corbis Los Angeles; **745** Japack/Corbis Los Angeles; **747** Giradon/AR; **749** (t)courtesy Audrey Wood, (b)Milan Sabatini/courtesy Julius Lester; **750 through 753** Reprinted by permission of Scholastic, Inc.; **755, 756** Private collection/Christian Pierre/SS; **758** ©Walt Disney Productions; **761** Mark Burnett; **765** (br)Mark Burnett, (others)AH; **768** Wally Findlay Galleries, New York/SS; **770** The Cartoon Bank; **772** (l)courtesy Scholastic, Inc., (r)CB; **773** Scott Camazine/PR; **774** Larry West/FPG; **775** C. Allan Morgan/Peter Arnold, Inc.; **776** Free Library, Philadelphia, PA/A.K.G. Berlin/SS; **778** CI; **782** (t)courtesy Joseph Bruchac, (bl)FPG, (br)Jeff Lynch/Mendola, Ltd./TSM; **783** Michael P. Gadomski/PR; **784** Richard Price/FPG; **786** John Cancalosi/Peter Arnold, Inc.; **787** Photofest; **788** (l)FPG, (r)Len Rue/Stock Boston; **789** Keith H. Murakham/Tom Stack & Associates; **790** Stafford Cliff and Suzanne Slesin; **791** Victoria & Albert Museum, London/AR; **792** B.N.S. Deo—TCL/Masterfile; **797** Nigel Dennis/PR; **798** Telegraph Colour Library/FPG; **801** R. Dev/PR; **802** PR; **803** Gunter Ziesler/Peter Arnold, Inc.; **805** (t)Steven Walker/Peter Arnold, Inc., (cl)John Cancalosi/Peter Arnold, Inc., (cr)Jeff Lepore/PR, (bl)Steve Kaufman/Peter Arnold, Inc., (br)Doug Cheeseman/Peter Arnold, Inc.; **806** (l)courtesy Arcade Publishing/photo by Arb, (r)Janet Adams; **807** Jim Strawser from Grant Heilman; **808** C. Blair; **810** Private collection/Sherrie Silverman/SS; **812** David M. Dennis; **813** C. Allan Morgan/Peter Arnold, Inc.; **817** (t)Larry Moore/SIS, (b)John Lund/TSI; **818** (l)courtesy Jane Katz, (r)Gary Rosenquist/Earth Images; **819** Carmona Photography/FPG; **820** Bios (A. Compost)/Peter Arnold, Inc.; **822** (l)FPG, (r)Fred Bruemmer/Peter Arnold, Inc.; **823** Thomas Gilcrease Institute of American History & Art; **824** Jeff & Alexa Henry/Peter Arnold, Inc.; **826** (l)courtesy Alfred A. Knopf/Spencer, (r)reprinted by permission of Houghton Mifflin Company. All rights reserved; **827** Tom Vezo/The Wildlife Collection; **828** Tim Davis/PR; **830** Lynn M. Stone; **834** (l)E.O. Hoppe/Corbis, (r)UPI/CB; **835** CI; **837** Alan & Sandy Carey/PR; **838** Color Box/FPG; **840** (tl)Tenri University/Japan, (tr)Lynn Saville, (bl)courtesy Scribner's, (br)AP Photo/Marilyn Sanders; **841** G. Buttner/Naturbild/OKAPIA/PR; **842** Mark Burnett; **843** Mike Dobel/Masterfile; **844** Hans Pfletschinger/Peter Arnold, Inc.; **847** Fred Bavendam/Peter Arnold, Inc.; **851** (br)Geoff Butler, (others)AH.

Editing/Proofreading Checklist

Use this proofreading checklist to help you check for errors in your writing , and use the proofreading symbols in the chart below to mark places that need corrections.

☑ Have I avoided run-on sentences and sentence fragments and punctuated sentences correctly?

☑ Have I used every word correctly, including plurals, possessives, and frequently confused words?

☑ Do verbs and subjects agree? Are verb tenses correct?

☑ Do pronouns refer clearly to their antecedents and agree with them in person, number, and gender?

☑ Have I used adverb and adjective forms and modifying phrases correctly?

☑ Have I spelled every word correctly, and checked the unfamiliar ones in a dictionary?

Proofreading Symbols

⊙	Lieut. Brown	Insert a period.
∧	No one came to the party.	Insert a letter or a word.
=	I enjoyed paris.	Capitalize a letter.
/	The Class ran a bake sale.	Make a capital letter lowercase.
⌢	The campers are home sick.	Close up a space.
ⵔ	They visited (N.Y.) ⵔ	Spell out.
∧ ;∧	Sue, please come, I need your help.	Insert a comma or a semicolon.
∩	He enjoyed feild day.	Transpose the position of letters or words.
#	alltogether	Insert a space.
ℐ	We went to to Boston.	Delete letters or words.
∨ ∨ ∨	She asked Whos coming?	Insert quotation marks or an apostrophe.
/ = /	mid January	Insert a hyphen.
¶	"Where?" asked Karl. "Over there," said Ray.	Begin a new paragraph.

Proofreading Checklist

- ☑ Have I avoided run-on sentences and sentence fragments?
- ☑ Have I used every word correctly, including frequently confused words and homophones?
- ☑ Have I formed plural and possessive nouns correctly?
- ☑ Do verbs agree with their subjects? Are verb tenses correct? Does verb tense shift correctly to show sequence of events?
- ☑ Do pronouns refer clearly to their antecedents and agree with them in person, number, and gender?
- ☑ Have adjective and adverb forms been used correctly?
- ☑ Have I avoided or corrected dangling participles and misplaced modifiers?
- ☑ Are all words spelled correctly? Has every unfamiliar word been checked in a dictionary?
- ☑ Are all punctuation marks used correctly?

Proofreading Symbols

⊙	Lieut Brown	Insert a period.
∧	No one came to the party.	Insert a letter or a word.
⋏	The bell rang the students left for home.	Insert a semicolon.
≡	I enjoyed paris.	Capitalize a letter.
/	The Class ran a bake sale.	Make a capital letter lowercase.
⌒	The campers are home sick.	Close up a space.
🔴	They visited N.Y.	Spell out.
⋏	Sue please help.	Insert a comma.
∩	He enjoyed feild day.	Transpose the position of letters or words.
#	alltogether	Insert a space.
℘	We went to to Boston.	Delete letters or words.
⌄⌄	She asked Who's coming?	Insert quotation marks.
/=/	mid January	Insert a hyphen.
¶	"Where?" asked Karl. "Over there," said Ray.	Begin a new paragraph.
⌄	She liked Sarah's glasses.	Insert an apostrophe.